Who One Is

PHAENOMENOLOGICA

SERIES FOUNDED BY H.L. VAN BREDA AND PUBLISHED

UNDER THE AUSPICES OF THE HUSSERL-ARCHIVES

190

JAMES G. HART

WHO ONE IS

BOOK 2: EXISTENZ AND TRANSCENDENTAL PHENOMENOLOGY

James G. Hart

Who One Is

Book 2

Existenz and Transcendental Phenomenology

 Springer

J.G. Hart
Indiana University
Department of Religious Studies
230 Sycamore
Bloomington IN 47405
USA

e-ISBN 978-1-4020-9178-0

Printed on acid-free paper

springer.com

Preface

In Book 1 we sketched an ontology of the agency of manifestation that is this side, on the "hither" side, of the displayed world. We said the source of this agency, the transcendental I, can be referred to non-ascriptively, i.e., as without properties. Normally when we confront something about which nothing can be said, e.g., where the subject under consideration is said to have no distinguishing properties, we rightly lose interest. We have not even a triviality, but rather we have nothing to take hold of conceptually, what the Greeks called a *meon*, non-being, not-anything. But in Book 1 we spelled out that what we refer to with "I," i.e., "myself as myself," and what we experience prior to the reflective indexical achievement, i.e., the lived "myself," is just such a propertyless not-anything. The first-person singular pronoun, we proposed, builds on a prior sense of oneself, for which we have used reluctantly the awkward term, the "myself." We said this was evident prior to reflection, and the indexical, "I" is how we bring to light "myself as myself." Both the ineluctable non-reflective self-presence and the referent of "I" are ways in which we are present to ourselves without any assignment of predication or properties. It is a "non-ascriptive" presence in the former case and a non-ascriptive reference in the other. The former case is not properly a case of reference, i.e., there is no intentional act, but it is always a non-ascriptive presence; the clear indexical reference to oneself with "I" is likewise a non-ascriptive self-reference. In each case of the prior "presence" and the referent of "I" we have to do with what is "non-sortal," i.e., we do not ascribe properties to it. With "I" I am aware of myself without being aware of myself as anything but myself, i.e., without needing to know any third-person, token-reflexive free, indexical-free description or characteristic about myself in order to make present or think of or know myself as I myself.

We have presented a "meontology," of the "I" in another sense than that having to do with the referent of "I" being non-sortal or not a property (non-ascriptive reference targets what is "non-sortal," not a sort, not a kind, not a property). The "I" is the "pole of the world," the dative and agent of manifestation of the world, that to which the world is displayed in its agency of displaying the world. What is properly "being," i.e., what is posited or what is the target of an act of belief as something real, what is an entity, an object in the world, etc., is what is intended in an intentional, ascriptive act of displaying something in the world. We see particular things as…, e.g., as trees, as maple trees, as sources of maple syrup, as diseased trees, etc. But the "I" in its agency of manifestation is on the hither side of all such beings and predications. As "this side" of all properly intentional acts, even when it reflectively refers to itself, it is not-anything-in-the-world, a *meon*, a non-being.

We further argued that although the reference of "I" resembles the non-ascriptive reference of other demonstratives, like "this" and "that," our self-reference is not a mere empty place-holder for predication. In spite of being free of properties, it is rich in meaning for each us, even those of us who are very young, amnesiac, or are in danger of being persuaded that we might have a *Doppelgänger*. This richness of meaning that is bereft of properties we have called an "individual essence" or haecceity. The emptiness of the *meon* of the "I" is not a negative nothing, a *nihil negativum*, but rather something uniquely rich and positive, in spite of its being bereft of properties.

For transcendental phenomenology this "I" has a declarative function at least implicitly associated with all the propositions it authors, like "There is a zebra." In all such declarative sentences there is the transcendental pre-fix, "I think that…," "I judge there to be that…" "It seems to me that…" etc. which is tacitly the prefix of, e.g., "There is a zebra." This "agent of manifestation" (Robert Sokolowski) is, as agent of manifestation, not in the world, not a posited being in the world. The agent of manifestation is, as the Greek *me-on* suggests, not a posited being. Again, there is symmetry between this "meontic" feature of the transcendental pre-fix of the agent of manifestation, with the odd non-ascriptive presence of the first-person presence in the natural attitude.

Thinking about the transcendental "I" and the "I" of normal self-reference led us, especially in Chapter IV of Book 1, to think of some of the features of second- and third-person reference, and in what sense these are non-ascriptive. We are also led to distinguish the ineluctable self-presence of the "myself" from our fuller sense of ourselves as agents and as referents of reflection. We introduced the category of the "person" to refer to how the "myself" is in the world in an embodied and inter-subjective way. In this volume we call this its "personification." Nevertheless, the theme of "person," as it emerges in our first-personal, as well as in the second- and third personal, life with Others, reflects the non-ascriptive self-reference and the rich non-propertied referent of "I." Indeed, "person" is properly to be contrasted with sortal categories like "human" and "citizen." Ultimately, i.e., where our reference aims properly when referring to persons, there is not a *kind* of being, even though we never have persons present to us without the cluster of sortal categories like biped, risible, animal, human, rational, etc.

This comes out further in the unique second-person references whereby the other person is present to us as through, but as beyond, the personal properties. Love is especially important as the intentional reference that discloses the Other as transcendent to her properties. We return to a discussion of love in Book 2 when we inquire how one knows who one is supposed to be and what path in life one ought to take.

The consideration in Book 1 that, for transcendental phenomenology, the person is always also a transcendental I, moved us to consider in Book 1, Chapter VI some of the paradoxes of the person when considered from the transcendental standpoint, i.e., paradoxes of the transcendental person. Of especial interest is the problem of the mortality of the transcendental person, whose beginning and ending, nevertheless, are non-presentable for the transcendental I (Book 1, Chapter VII). This led us to a beginning discussion of death, which we resume in this volume. It also led us in (in Book 1, Chapter VIII) to entertain various conceivable versions of the "afterlife" as well as the possibility that the afterlife may well refer to a possibility of the "myself" when it seems not to be applicable to oneself as a determinate identifiable person.

In this Book 2 we study the "I" in some of its guises, the personal I in the natural attitude, the transcendental agent of manifestation as the center of acts, and the founding "primal presencing" with its egological and hyletic moments. The primal presencing undergirds all senses of "I." Following Husserl, Kierkegaard and Jaspers we are moved to study the core of the personal I. With these two latter named thinkers we will call this core or center of the personal I, *Existenz*. Existenz as the center of the person comes to light especially in reflecting on the way death appears as "my death." It also comes to light in reflecting on conscience and duty, and what have been called "limit-situations," as well as the way one's calling surfaces in what Husserl calls "the truth of will." (See below Chapters III–V.)

Death is a pivotal consideration in both volumes (Book 1, Chapters VII–VIII; Book 2, Chapters I–II) in bringing to light central transcendental- and existential phenomenological matters: It plays a role in speculatively thinking about the ultimate destiny of the "myself" and person; it is, as noted, pivotal in bringing to light the core of the person, Existenz.

Existenz is at the heart of the question: What kind of person do I (who, as I myself, am not apprehensible as a kind), want to be? This, we shall propose, is also a question of one's calling. The position in this work can readily acknowledge that in a bureaucratic, positivist, and reductionist-scientist world "to be is to be a collection of properties" and to be "a man without properties" is to be nobody and nothing.[1] This state of affairs can well occasion rebellion and this rebellious reaction might well be an aversion to the very notion that the intrinsic and normative sense of who we are is to be found in a sortal, propertied way of being. In which case, one might hold open the hope for a utopian existence which, bereft of properties, would be without any sense of propriety, i.e., where there would be a liberation from moral and social self-determinations and where action would be tied sheerly to human purposes and we would live in a world without natural kinds with their intrinsic ends, i.e., in a world without ends! (See below Chapter V, §7.) Such a reaction is in part indebted dialectically to a third-person hegemony which portrays the self in terms of a contingent bundle of properties. In contrast our position has been to acknowledge the "myself" as the non-sortal bare substrate of the person. But we have insisted that this is only part of the story, and that each is given to herself to become a certain kind of person laced with properties and one *fails* to be oneself in so far as one misses the mark as revealed by conscience, one's obligations, and, if such there be, one's "calling." (See below Chapters IV–V.)

The theme of being given over to oneself to be a *certain kind of person* returns us to the important matter in Book 1, of who one is and the odd occasional circumstances when one asks "Who am I?" We may here recall the famous exhortation of the ancient Greek poet, Pindar, usually rendered as "Become who you are" (*Genoi hoios essi*; γένου᾽ οἷος ἐσσί).[2]

The context is Pindar's song of praise to a king who is surrounded by courtly sycophants, schemers, and slanderers. He perceives that the King may be tempted not to believe in his own excellence but rather be swayed by the views of others who surround him. Pindar's song is a boost to the king to trust in his better self and his excellence, because that is closest to "who he is."

The translation of Pindar's exhortation as "become who you are" is problematic because *hoios*, means "such as, what sort or manner of nature, kind or temper." It approximates the Latin *qualis*.[3] Thus it would seem to be best rendered as "Become what or the sort of person you are." This raises the central question of this Book 2: Is it proper to say that the answer to "Who am I?" is in terms of "What I am?"

We find the text translated in Nietzsche in what corresponds to the English, "become who you are." In a letter to his friend, Erwin Rohde, Nietzsche thinks of this phrase as appropriate for his friends who had recently gathered together and were "themselves." The very concept of the Pindarian phrase, as Nietzsche understands it, had demonstrated its appropriateness in this memorable gathering with his friends. Nietzsche in this letter uses the phrase to embody his deepest regard and wishes for, and exhortation to, his dear friend, Rohde, and will always look back on a time where he gained a friend who "was himself."

In another letter to Lou von Salomé he comments how "nature" gave to each being different weapons of defense, and, he says, to you, Lou, she (nature) gave a marvelous "openness of will." Nietzsche approves of this and exhorts Lou with Pindar's phrase, "*Become* the one who you *are*." The openness of will here appears to be a necessary condition to such a becoming. Openness of will we may assume contrasts with the obstacles occasioned by a closedness or restriction of will.

In another letter to Lou von Salomé, he comes back to this "old deep, heart-felt request," "*Werden Sie, die Sie sind!*" "Become the one who you are!" He then comments that each must emancipate herself from *chains*, and finally "one must *emancipate* oneself from one's emancipation." Each of us has to labor at this "*chain-sickness*," even after he has smashed the chains. Pindar, we might note, was concerned that the King smash the chains that would inevitably bind him if he allowed himself to measure himself by the sycophants surrounding him. Nietzsche, however, goes further and sees the emancipation itself as a possible determination, therefore a kind of property, from which one must be liberated if one is to be who one is.

Clearly Nietzsche thinks of **who** one is as something beyond one's properties (chains), and yet it is also some *quale* that "nature" gives, i.e., the property of openness of will. It is both who one is and at the same time the deepest distinguishing property or What of the person.[4]

The exhortation to become who one is presupposes that one both is and is not what one is exhorted to be. This could be taken as a matter of discovering some truth about oneself, as when an educator urges students to learn, e.g., Greek, because this language is their cultural roots and because there is a sense that one is inseparable from whence one has derived; unearthing one's roots, whether historical-cultural, racial, linguistic, biological, etc., is discovering who one is. If we want to know ourselves we have to know our roots. In this sense it implies that we remain ignorant at our peril because, e.g., our history and our cultural background is our destiny and as such it exercises influence over us even if we are oblivious to it. We are less free in our agency because the conditioning context of the agency, i.e., the presupposition of one's cultural roots, is hidden. We cannot be free if our will is conditioned by hidden factors. (Cf. our discussion of some of these matters below in Chapter IV, §8.)

The Pindar phrase has also been taken to be less a question about the truth of one's unconscious heritage and destiny but rather as a question about the kind of life we want to live. This itself is a question about the kind of people that there are, i.e., how other people fare based on how they live, and it is about the habits they have which enable them to live well. Because each wants to live well each may well have the capacity to adopt and share in such exemplary self-enriching styles of agency and character. Such an appropriation is in each's potentiality, and therefore, as what one now is potentially, it is who/what each already is as a real possibility. Yet here who one is, is a communicable property or constellation of properties; it is not something unique – unless realizing what sort of person we are "called" to be is, in an important sense, becoming who one is. (See below Chapters IV–V.)

In all such cases the Who of the exhortation, "become who you are," is typically rendered with a more or less complex What. Nietzsche's enthusiastic exhortation to his friends, however, suggests a close tie between the persons whom he loves, and as ones beyond any complex of properties, and the sorts of person they are and can be when they are faithful to themselves as who they are. His view is closer to Fichte's exhortation, which is itself the inspiration for Husserl's "absolute Ought": "Will to be what you ought to be and what you can be – what you indeed want to be."[5]

Of course, I must always answer under all circumstances to the question "Who are you?", "I am myself," and here we meet again the ineluctable "myself." But the question also suggests the obvious question of one's lineage, one's ID or autobiography, as when an official of the state, asks "Who are you?" Here there is an inquiry into the distinguishing properties that will in some way or other identify or legitimate me in the eyes of the one asking the question. But "Who are you?," like "Who am I?" may well be an inquiry that moves beyond what I have accomplished, what address I have, what my salary is, what my marital status is, etc. It may have as its context a crisis in one's life, where all of life all at once is balled up into a tight focal unity. In which case "Who am I?" or "Who are you?" may ask about "What kind of person am I?", "What kind of person are you?" Here we in some respects have to do with what we have done and do in a quite different way than what we have achieved and hope to achieve. The non-ascriptive rich sense of one's unique essence here does not provide an answer to "Who am I?" when the question surfaces in certain crises. Here we are asked or we ask ourselves about what this unique essence has done with the odd gift of being given to oneself. Here we have to do with how we have responded to the fundamental call to shape ourselves and our lives in accord with our lights. Who I am is of necessity always already completed in the "myself." But who I am as the person I become through my agency is the way I complete what otherwise is ontologically incomplete. The ontology of the human being in this sense is a deontology. Thus our position is that the ancient mandate of Pindar, "Become who you are," found an appropriate explication in

Fichte's "Will to be what you ought to be and what you [alone] can be – what indeed you want to be." They are equivalent if we see that who we are is a matter of each, as an I, shaping herself in a certain way according to an ideal that she has or to which she can be awakened, and which she must espouse. If she does appropriate it, it will be because it has come to light, i.e., has been recognized as her true self. Because this shaping of one's life involves typically what appears to all as a matter of excellent qualities, and because this capacity is inherent in each, "Become *what* you are" makes good sense. The *kind* of person we are called to be is in some ways, which we attempt to spell out, inscribed from the start. Yet becoming the sort of person we are supposed to be is itself becoming Who we are, and, in this sense the sortal feature of *what* we become is subordinated to the non-sortal "myself" that informs the becoming. The unique essence each person ineluctably is awaits a normative actuation by herself in the world with Others, and until this occurs the person each is remains incomplete. This norm is not exclusively one that is "the same for us all" or one that is valid if and only if it is universalizable. Nor is it a norm that arises from the responsibilities and claims which are ours by reason of being in second-personal relations. (See Chapter V, §9.) Indeed, as the norm for a unique essence, it lays claim to a unique disclosure and unique binding force. Becoming who one is is not merely becoming a certain kind, it is really realizing the truth about oneself, i.e., who one is in the light of "one's calling."

In this Book 2 we will pursue in detail these issues.

Finally, is there any sense to asking whence comes this norm for this Who? Or does who one is itself have a principle that is not a mere What? It would seem a What-principle threatens to make subjectivity ultimately impossible by reducing who one is to a What. Are we thus in a position to say that, after all, this uniquely binding "calling" is due not to a What but a You that can lay claim authoritatively to determine the ultimate drift of our lives because this You is the transcendent author of our lives and our being? But talking about a "principle" in this sense is beyond the reach of the "I" of transcendental phenomenology, which (who) we have shown cannot, as transcendental phenomenologist, presence its coming to be. For this we need a "likely story" which moves us beyond the standpoint of transcendental phenomenology. Plotinus, and eventually St. Thomas, are our guides to uncovering an eternal incomparably exalted noble sense of our selves because of our lineage "Yonder." We address these matters in the final chapters (VI and VII) on the philosophical theology of the self and vocation.

Notes

1. Robert Musil's monumental, encyclopedic novel, *Der Mann Ohne Eigenschaften*, raises questions which get at the heart of this work: a social world where one's recognizable identity is determined by social categories, positions, perqs, badges; where how and where one lives determines who one is; where who one is is determined by what one has done and what one owns; where "substance" is nothing but the congeries of contingent qualities; where the peeling away of these properties can only result in more impersonal properties or the revelation of "the

subject" as the imaginary meeting place of the properties; where love of oneself and others is therefore not possible but rather where one can only love the qualities; where the encounter with someone who is indifferent to the esteemed qualities is disturbing to all those around her or him, and perhaps even unsettling to himself. If reality is nothing but bundles of qualities, and if one is nevertheless discontent with this, then one might well long for a utopia where other circumstances prevail; where one can properly be "someone" quite apart from these definitions, borders, boundaries, proprieties, etc.; where there is awakened a richness and depth of meaning of the referent of "I" quite apart from and transcendent to the properties; where love creates a universal beauty which not only transforms the surroundings but enables whole-hearted communication unencumbered by proprieties and properties. But conceiving this utopia of selves without defining properties faces the difficult task of avoiding a nightmare of improprieties wherein formless abysses are opened up.

2. Pindar, *Pythian Ode*, 2, 73. English Ed. Steven J. Willet, at <u>www.perseus.tufts.edu</u>. My thanks to my colleague Betty Rose Nagle for this reference. Consider the way our queries into who and what sort of person someone is dovetail when we think about someone we find fascinating, e.g., the puzzling artist and personality, Bob Dylan. "Today – over forty years later! – we are still trying to answer the same questions. If it ain't you, Mister Dylan, then who is it. Or better yet, *what* are you, Mister Dylan? What lies behind the snarl, the shades, the long stretches of silence? What kind of cruel artist destroys his work in order to make his fans beg for more?" Edward P. Comentale, *The Ryder* (Bloomington, IN, October, 2006), 25. We strive to get behind the masks, personae, ruses, modes of expression; we try to get a fix on "what kind of cruel artist," he is, but is the answer we want a What? Is our fascination merely with a motive, a type, a kind, a distinguishing property? Will we rest when we find this "secret?" Or are these not ways which we believe the Who is to be revealed, even though this itself incessantly eludes us?

3. See Liddell and Scott's *Greek-English Lexicon* (New York, 1888).

4. Friederich Nietzsche, *Nietzsche*. Vol. III. Ed. Karl Schlecta (Munich: Karl Hanser, 1965), 984, 1181, and 1187. We will see in Chapter V that Willa Cather has a similar view.

5. J.G. Fichte, *Fichtes Werke*. Ed. I.H. Fichte (Berlin: Walter de Gruyter, 1971), 533.

Acknowledgements

In addition to the list of thinkers to whom we expressed our gratitude in Book 1, for Book 2 we may add Plotinus, St. Thomas Aquinas, I. Kant, J.G. Fichte, Jean Nabert, Erich Frank, Franz Rosenzweig, Paul Ricoeur, Barry Miller, Peter Bieri, and Stephen Darwall.

Thanks again to Michael Koss for the proofreading of the text.

James G. Hart

Bloomington, Indiana and Manitoulin Island, Ontario, Summer, 2008

Contents

Chapter I
Assenting to *My* Death and That of the Other

Remember, friend, as you pass by
As you are now, so once was I.
As I am now, so you must be.
Prepare yourself to follow me.

(Headstone in Brown County, Indiana and
throughout the USA)

We imagine we will die only because we believe we were born.
We don't trust the sense of endlessness, of edgelessness within.

(Stephen Levine,[1] *Who Dies?*, 3)

Death's appearance at first glance might well spell danger. Our word "danger" comes from Old French and Middle English words suggesting the absolute power, e.g., of a lord. What has absolute power over us suggests that what we hold dear, including perhaps our ownmost selves, is in peril. Absolute power suggests the power to deprive us of not only of our dear possessions, but also to deprive us of our capacity to have these things, to turn our ownmostness that cherishes these dear objects into something alien and objective, to estrange not only what we have but also what we are from ourselves. In short, absolute power can annihilate us. It is not merely that what has absolute power, e.g., death, casts everything into a radical new light of vulnerability and ephemerality, and therefore our attachment to these things is perforce loosened. But furthermore, the very experiencing of these things and ourselves is encroached upon; this experiencing is imminently in danger of annihilation.

The word "peril" itself is tied to the Latin word, *periculum*, in which one may glimpse the *periri*, the root of "experience"; it may even perhaps contain the hint that life-*experience* is trial by fire. Because death is "loss of life" and life is the condition for having what we hold dear, death is the utmost danger that one will meet in any of life's adventures, and the stories about the great adventures of life are stories about salvation from such dangers within life and even the danger that threatens to rob the hero of his soul.

Not only is this true of the great adventures, but what we call news is to a great extent about death's ubiquitous presence in life. For example, on any day, the local

J.G. Hart, *Who One Is: Existenz and Transcendental Phenomenology*,
© Springer Science + Business Media B.V. 2009

newspaper will run stories many, if not most, of which deal with death. For example at this writing the local newspaper features: War and hurricane casualties, downed planes, a politician's having an induced coma, hearings about a nominated judge's views on abortion, grief over miners killed in an explosion, animal lovers marching for anticruelty legislation, tsunami centers on alert, brochures for dealing with pandemics, DNA tests on what some believe to be Mozart's skull, etc.

Philosophy and religion to a great extent are about salvation as it is connected with the peril of the ultimate loss, the loss of "the one thing necessary," the loss of which is incommensurate with the riches of the whole world. If there be such a treasure, whatever it might be, it is not a matter of indifference to philosophy and religion, and it is for good reason thought to be not absolutely disconnected from or unrelated to oneself. Thus philosophy and religion raise the question of the possibility of a danger greater than loss of life; they raise the possibility of losing one's soul or one's self while gaining the whole world. Death is a theme of philosophy and religion because it is a phenomenon testifying at least to the loss of one's worldly being, if not to the loss of oneself. For to lose or gain oneself or one's soul, one must still be; death bears witness, in the second- and third- person, to the loss or absence of life and of the soul that bestows life.

If death's unpredictable and latent ubiquitous presence becomes felt in life then any understanding of the meaning or purpose of life as the filling of all desire requires reassessment. We have reviewed considerations that offer a kind of inoculation against the sting of death. Yet the transcendental phenomenological meditation does not equate with some forms of Vedanta that argue that death is a dreadful affair only because of confusing one's self (or the Self) with one's personal life in the world. In this view of Vedanta, the one who is enlightened sees that her true self exists beyond the world and death can never appear to her as a mystery.[2] A strong statement of this view is found in the *Katha Upanishad* where it is taught that both the killer and the killed fail to understand that strictly there is not killing or being killed, if these mean extinction of someone; rather there is only the eternal *atman*, i.e., the self unified with the absolute or Brahman. Yet clearly there is the *phenomenon* of killing and being killed, and it was this, i.e., the phenomenon of death, that led Naciketas to ask Yama, the Lord of Death, "What happens at that great transit?" The revelation that each person is fundamentally *atman* forces us to reinterpret the phenomenon of death. However, this reinterpretation does not destroy the manifest phenomenon of what gets named as "that great transit" and its at least appearing to be "a deep mystery."[3]

For transcendental phenomenology the transcendental perspective on death does not negate either the appearance of death in the natural attitude, nor does it offer a decisive definitive answer to the question of the meaning of the mystery of "that great transit." Transcendental subjectivity, we have seen, is characterized by a unique facticity and this raises the question of the radical contingency of "I myself." Furthermore the transcendental discovery that I cannot presence my ending does not necessarily mean that I might not end without my knowing it. The phenomenological standpoint intensifies the experience of death's puzzling presence because it compels us to witness death as befalling a transcendental person who experiences herself as unbegun and unending. This means that the phenomenological standpoint enables death to appear from the perspectives of both the natural and transcendental attitudes. This standpoint enables the further explication, not resolution, of the phenomenon of death. In what follows we wish to meditate on the transcendental person's death and let both the transcendental and natural attitudes inform the experience, remembering all the while that it is not two different I's or the points of view of two different kinds of persons but rather the experience being studied is that of I myself both in my natural attitude as well as I as agent of manifestation.

§1. *My* Death

Tolstoy's novella, *Ivan Ilych*, brings to light that for most of us most of the time death does not concern us in the first-person, but rather it is "his" or "her" affair. We are all deft in keeping death at the margins of our first-person life, i.e., keeping it where it is a natural, social, political or economic matter. I see everyone as a more or less protracted event. Each has a beginning, middle, and end. Even if I am a "conservationist" and hold that Life does not die, only living things, it is still evident that the living things are ephemeral. What characterizes persons, as all living things in the world, is that they do not continue forever. In the living of my life, I, of course, do not experience myself as merely something living in the world; as living in the first-person, I am that to which the world appears, and not part of the world. It is no wonder that I, in the living of life, think of death as what happens to others. However, there comes a time when each realizes that it is one's own affair, *mea res agitur*, i.e., I cannot any longer keep my ending from myself by considering it primarily as a third-person phenomenon nor can I postpone attending to it. I too am a being in the world and share the properties of a living being in the world. My life in the world too will end; indeed, regardless of who I am, relatively speaking, it will end soon. I have no choice, but I have to face up to it now. Prior to this one could chatter, "everyone has to die" and "each's turn will come." Upon hearing of a neighbor's death, we might chirp, after a few solemn words, "Oh well, life goes on." But now it has to do with me. How it has to do with me is not merely that I see things now as ephemeral but I myself as the agent and dative of manifestation, I myself as the condition for the world's display, am in question. Not only all that I have but my very being as the condition for having and display is menaced by *It*. It confronts me and I cannot turn away from it. It draws all things I live and love into itself. As Tolstoy describes Ivan, he was driven to be alone with *It*: "face to face with *It*. And nothing could be done with *It* except to look at it and shudder."[4] In the middle of a court hearing, Ivan, a judge, while attempting to weigh the pro and contra evidence, reaches the conclusion: "It alone is true."

Of course "It" is made present not by anything in the world but by the conviction, typically pressed upon the one dying by an increasingly conspicuous pain, that It will move inexorably to my annihilation.

And no less disconcerting is that in the presence of others who are close to me I apperceive that they don't want to know it either. They want to keep at a distance what I have realized because they, very much like myself, do not want to hear of it. As Tolstoy reflects on the dying Ivan's perception of his family and friends, "No one felt for him because no one even wanted to grasp his position." Everyone is just like Ivan was prior to his realization. Ivan looks desperately for someone who is not repressing her or his mortality; he wants a comforting that is founded in an honest recognition that the minister of comfort too will die, and that she or he too does not really know what this means.

Of course the sharp distinction between my death and that of others is eroded with the dying and death of a loved one. Tolstoy's story is able to make the sharp distinction because of those around Ivan, i.e., his family, colleagues, and acquaintances, it cannot be said that they love him, or that they truly share a life together. Only a young innocent servant boy is perceived by Ivan to approach sizing up what is happening appropriately, i.e., compassionately and lovingly. His decency and guilelessness enable him to participate in the event as the common lot of humanity. When the other's good is mine and mine his or hers, then our hearts and wills are intertwined forming a higher-order will and a community. Husserl, we may recall, speaks of the "we" as a higher-order "I." The death of the other would, in such a case, approximate my own death. With the death of the beloved, part of me, as this person, JG Hart, in so far *I* am identified with *us* (the whole comprised of JG Hart and the deceased), is extinguished. With the death of a loved one, because of my community with her, my own contingency and that of the whole world press upon me. Through love the other is habitually for me in the second-person, never simply in the third-person. Indeed, she is present in the first-person as constitutive of *us* and *we*, as the subject of "our common life." Perhaps we can say that if the other is simply for me in the third-person, and there is not a habitual love between us that makes him always a *You* and part of *us* with whom I share a life in common, then the distinction Tolstoy makes remains sharp. Further, the neglect of the love relation in the presentation of Tolstoy has the merit of highlighting the essential aloneness and ownness of each ipseity: Love's great power to bind us never confuses us; a genuine "we" is never a merging or dissolution of the unique I's, but rather presupposes the essential individuality; I am never you or you I, nor may the We ignore or "sublate" the I's.[5] Let us return to the more typical, if not always essential, distinction between my death and the death in the third-person captured by Tolstoy's story.

Before the moment of the first-person realization of my death the inevitable is kept at bay. Although I could not have any first-person familiarity with my death and know of death only in the third-, and possibly second-, person, I know it is certain and inescapable. This ineluctable certainty of death for all of us surely frames all of one's life, and determines the sense of one's projects, the care one takes of oneself and one's loved ones, the risks one is willing to undertake, etc. But now with the realization of "my death," something has changed. I knew "All men are mortal"; I knew "JG Hart is a man"; I knew "JG Hart is mortal"; I knew "I am JG Hart"; therefore I knew "I am mortal." It is one of the most certain things one knows. Yet it is able to remain abstract, conceptual, actuarial, third-personal, and seemingly endlessly able to be postponed.

As Jankélévitch loves to repeat, "I know I will die, but I don't believe it." Eventually there may occur a shift from the mere "notional" to "real" assent, to use Newman's terms, and to anticipate our later discussion of Existenz, a *realization* happens. That is, there may be a shift from an empty intention of a concept or from what was or is a real reality for someone else to a filled in-the-flesh presence for me that refuses to go away and demands my attention. A "realization" resembles Plato's recollection or *Anamnesis* in that it is a knowing of what I always knew before. But now it is not an abstract, conceptual knowledge. Nor is it something I may regard as merely objective and in the third-person. Rather now "death comes/ like an iceberg between the shoulder blades" (Mary Oliver).

Such a horror, such a dread, is not occasioned by something that is absolutely unfamiliar and strange. At some level It, whatever "It" is precisely (and we want to dwell on this necessary imprecision), is known, avoided, and repressed. In fact, because I myself am in question, i.e., because the very being of myself is facing apparent annihilation, I cannot regard it as something transcendent and other to me in the sense of "about" me or a property I am acquiring or losing. Rather it is the lived sense of "I myself" which is not merely cognitively ineluctable, like the "realization" that the *cogito* necessarily exists while it is in act. Rather "my death" as the extinction of the "myself" from the world now absorbs and pervades all senses of my will and agency, even though it is not clear what I am to do in as much as what is revealed is my not having a future, at least as a person in the world.

Kierkegaard likewise saw this and called attention to the distinction between how we may relate to things objectively and subjectively. His point is not so much the earlier one discussed in Book 1, where we, following Castañeda, distinguished between, on the one hand, an external reflexive reference to oneself, as when we refer to ourselves as anyone else would, i.e., we make a third-person intersubjective reference, and, on the other hand, the internal reflexive reference where we recognize in our reference that the one we are referring to indeed is ourselves. And here there is the further distinction to be noted in the transition in the former reference to oneself where one refers to oneself but need not recognize that the one referred to is oneself and the realization that indeed that one, who is oneself as the world sees me, is indeed myself. A famous example of this is from Ernst Mach, where I see that the shabby old pedant coming my way is indeed a mirror reflection at the other end of the tram of myself. Kierkegaard's example builds on the Machian one but has a moral or, better, "existential," aspect. Here we find ourselves passionately relating the matter under consideration to ourselves, yet initially not knowing that it is ourselves to which we are referring. The "realization" is not merely epistemic but "existential." The existential difference that Kierkegaard wants to bring out is implied in Tolstoy's distinction between how we refer to our death in the third-person as a feature of humans, i.e., that they are mortal, and the realization of one's own death. In Kierkegaard the matter is captured in the biblical story of King David learning from the prophet Nathaniel of a scoundrel rich man who treacherously takes advantage of his power over his poor defenseless neighbor. David has the external reflexive knowledge of himself transformed into an internal reflexive knowledge when he learns that he is the scoundrel. But it is not merely a reference to himself as himself, but he is revealed to himself at his personal core in regard to what is of unconditional importance. Here the internal reflexive knowledge of oneself is "existential": as we shall say one is gathered to oneself in terms of what is of unconditional importance. Now, as in the case of realizing one's death as one's own death, the person may say I refer not only to myself as my self, but to myself's ownmostness, i.e., Existenz.[6]

Clearly "my death" is not "my loss" in the way the death of another causes bereavement. I envisage the world and my life after the beloved's death as suffering a loss, as missing a crucial dative and agent of manifestation. I can recreate such a loss in my case only by putting myself in the position of others and imagining their experience of my absence. The death of the Other may be the extinguishing of what has been the most important event in my life; this beloved person may be the nodal point of my life-decisions and she may be the actual and tacit interlocutor in all that I experience. With her passing the focal points of my life may vanish. My death, of course, is nothing like this.[7]

As we have indicated, the death of the Other for herself is not an event among other events or, more clearly, it is not an event within her life, as it is doubtless an event or happening in regard to her biography. We may in our composition of the story of the other person's life envisage her death as *part* of her life and not at the boundary of her life. Certainly this is done in the stories of gods and mythic heroes as well as by Christians in the story of Jesus' death. Here death does not have finality and life is not limited to "life on earth." But we may do this also with lesser personages where we see their lives as heading toward their heroic death or martyrdom. Thus we can follow the film and audio clips of Martin Luther King's life until near the end of his life when he singles America out as the most violent nation on earth and where he insists that the civil rights movement must also be part of a movement in opposition to America's imperialism and injustice at home and abroad. And then we may follow him to his final talk to the striking garbage workers in Atlanta, the speech where he seemed to have intimations that he himself would not "enter the Promised Land"; we can feel the tension because of the imminence of what for us and apparently also for him is his inevitable assassination. And in our telling of this story his dream for America as a beloved community and peaceable kingdom continues and the commemoration of his death is always a commemoration of not merely his life as something over and done with but also of his dream and our participation in it. His death is but a moment in "the life of Martin Luther King," i.e., in the life which is not properly his and his alone but which continues in the public appropriation of his life and in the national narrative which is both the story of his life for us and the participation in his dream – and it can even become a formative moment in our lives so that his life's will and dream are inherent ingredients in our lives. Nevertheless we may have reason to doubt whether for such a hero's death is apperceived as a moment within his life.[8]

We may say that the world's generational features, i.e., that actual beings are alive now through the agency of beings who are no longer living, have a validity and certainty that resembles, e.g., gravity and seasonal changes or other various forms of causality in terms of necessity and universality. We find it obvious that all living bodies are mortal and more or less ephemeral events. And because I take myself to be, among other things, a living being in the world, the protentions and expectations I have toward all living beings in regard to their tenure apply also to me. But, for reasons we have given, and for others still to come, we also do not see ourselves as mere ephemeral events in the world. The death that awaits all that I perceive to live, of course, awaits me as a being that I perceive to live. But I am not exhaustively summarized in that which I perceive to live. I protend all living things as mortal on the basis of my retention of the manifest evidence of the finitude of their temporal being; I as a living thing too am protended in this way. But at some time, at the time of *realization* of my death, this protention of myself comes up against the first-person, transcendental sense of myself as not an ephemeral event in the world. I am not merely a passing more or less protracted event: I am a perpetual presencing of all events, a presencing whose presence is not now, nor, a fortiori, no longer or not yet. This awareness, no matter how obscure, confounds the matter of fact attitude toward my obvious ephemerality – yet it in no way has the power to silence it absolutely.

The realization that I, as an ephemeral event, am dying is not a filled intention. It is not as if I have or could have in a perceptual present my death. My death, we have insisted, is not properly conjugated in the first-person singular indicative of "I die." "I die," or "I am dying" always is properly "I will die" or "I am about to die." "Realization" therefore is only a relative filled intention that is facilitated by the work of the imagination in filling out the protended not yet. But here realization is not a mere phenomenological exercise. No longer am I able to postpone filling out that remaining futural space. The inevitable pre-determined sense of my imminent death cannot be dodged or postponed. Yet, of course, I have no idea what this absolute dreadful certainty means.

It is natural to life that my death has been kept at the periphery of my life. All of my life as a life of plans and desires assumes that I will not die. Each step is undertaken for the next, and the next is undertaken for what is to follow that. My being in the world is a given for my life of desire and hope in the world. Because this is so, the typically marginal presence of death is, when it becomes a central theme, a distraction and an interference to living out this life. Yet, it is there, at the periphery, quite early, even for young children. Each year that I get older, I feel its presence more pronouncedly. But even when young, I had an awareness that the sense of my prospects and my possible achievements were contingent on my being alive and well. Of course, dwelling on this seemed "morbid." But one faults being morbid, i.e., dwelling on death, not because its basic beliefs are false but because it is clearly irrelevant to the joys and tasks at hand and it can be a hindrance to living one's life. Thus the aspect of distinctive oddness especially for young children of some religious education which dwells excessively on: *memento mori*.

"Realization" here is thus not knowledge of something new, e.g., a new piece of information. Nor is it properly *understanding* something that we before failed to grasp. Yet there is something like a surprise, even though it is one of the things with which we are most familiar and of which we are most certain. Because what we know we have always known, it clearly is a matter of now knowing it differently. And whereas other forms of knowing may be turned away from and set at the outer margins of one's life, the realization that "I am dying" affects me at the center. And yet this is an odd sense of "knowing" because I really do not fathom or grasp what it means – apart from the obvious third-person sense of a discontinuation of life for something living.

If there is anything of importance, something weighty, something that has to do with me, it is my death, because this is the "importune" matter of the annihilation of the one for whom things have importance. Even though there was a time when everything else took precedence before it, now such a hierarchy is out of the question. Even in sacrificing my life for someone, it is precisely because nothing is more important, nothing weighs more; there is nothing that I can esteem higher that I am in a position to "give." There is nothing that has priority over this way of positioning or disposing of my life. Or, to put the same differently, the nothing of death itself is reduced to nothing for the person who sacrifices her life because she is prepared to give up everything.

Like love, and perhaps some forms of suffering, death presents itself as happening for the first time in history. Ivan exclaims, "It is impossible that all men have been doomed to suffer this awful horror!"[9] As the experience of being-in-love discovers the original springtime of all life, so when one is dying it is uniquely one's own affair. As the lover recites the love formulae as if delivering them for the first time in the history of the world, so the dying person faces death absolutely isolated and alone, and may well have the inclination to think of his ordeal as if no one else had done it before him.[10] Even with the knowledge that others have preceded him, that knowledge is irrelevant. What is at stake is uniquely mine and myself; it is a most explicit ritual of ownmost ipseity. It is inconceivable that someone else should do it for me or that its happening have the same significance for someone else.[11] Thus it resembles the universal token reflexive "I," which is achieved by everyone, but means something essentially different in each case. (See Book 1, Chapter III, §2.) As in the case of "I" one may be tempted to regard this "paradox" as merely formal, empty, or even vacuous; but, of course, this is precisely what it refuses to be.

Yet what is "it" that the knowledge through realization brings about. What is it precisely that I "know" in knowing that I am dying, that I will die. Clearly "it" is not anything that I can comfortably categorize and allocate within the meaning-spaces of the categorical display of the world and history. Rather it resembles my awareness of my unique ipseity. I know "myself" but I cannot say what it is that I know in this knowing. All content, all properties, all categories, are useless. The "myself" as an individual essence is bereft of properties; its ending is first-personally phenomenologically unpresentable; therefore how could "death" be "understood?" What is the property of that which is "not something," i.e., not in principle able to be first-personally witnessed, that "happens" to what is property-less? As Jankelevitch puts it: "I don't know what it is that I know" (*Je ne sais quoi*) when I come to the realization of death or when I am aware of the unique ipseity.

But this, a knowledge that is almost nothing (*presque rien*), is far from a knowledge of "a mere nothing," if this means what, given the present horizon of concerns, is judged to be trivial, insignificant or utterly vacuous, as sometimes the very obvious or tautological can appear, perhaps like the knowledge that the sky is up or things are colored or being in pain is not fun. We shall return to this soon.

§2. Inherent Obstacles to the Real Assent to *My* Mortality

We have said that it is no wonder that in the living of my life, which requires at every level of desire and hope an affirmation of not only the world but also of myself, my continued existence, and my continued powers, I regard death as what happens to others. Further, as we have seen (see, e.g., Book 1, Chapter VII), in the living of my life, I myself, in the temporalizing-presencing of the world and myself, am not myself lived as temporal but as timeless, at least in the sense that I am not lived as something having the modes of time's presentation, i.e., present, past, and not yet. At the heart of the "myself" presencing my stream of consciousness or the ephemeral world there is the non-temporal sense of myself: As the primal presencing I am not among that which elapses, or that which is not yet, or now.

Furthermore, as we have seen, there is the unique necessity of the transcendental I in its presencing of the world's necessities and contingencies. All these unfold within the field of presence that is opened up by the agent of manifestation's being awake. All that has "validity," all that holds with regard to "the whole show" in terms of the ontological modes of being actual, possible, necessary, probable, and contingent, as well as all the epistemic modalities of being apodictically certain, practically certain, doubtful, uncertain, clear, vague, etc., presuppose the field of presence as the stage in which these all come to light. The agent of manifestation, as what sets the stage for these ontological and epistemic modes, is utterly presupposed and, as such, may not be considered as contingent, necessary, certain or uncertain in the same way something in the world may be so characterized. (Cf. Book 1, Chapter VI, §9.)

All these considerations relate to the problem of death as a kind of manifest absence, or phenomenal disappearance, or appearing of extinction. In the third-person and second-person it *seems* clear that with the definitive absence through death of the soul's or self's manifestation to us – which we are moved to take as its absence of its self-manifestation to itself – the soul no longer exists. From these perspectives, it is apparent that if the soul decidedly does not manifest itself to us as self-manifest, it is no longer – unless we are disposed to postulate an eternal unconscious sleep or rest, or no less strange, an "afterlife" that is invisible to us. In the first-person, however, the soul's or self's self-manifestation has a kind of necessity. Its *esse* is *percipi*. As self-aware I cannot not exist. And, further, I cannot perceive, conceive, or imagine my coming to be or passing away. I must be to be aware of my not yet or no longer being. This raises the issue of whether there is a coincidence between the non-manifestness of the self or soul in the second- and third-person with that in the first-person. Even though my coming to be and passing away are not conceivable in the first-person, i.e., are not phenomenologically presentable, and thus even though I cannot imagine my demise, can it be that I become extinct without having the benefit of knowing or perceiving my demise, without my demise being manifest to me? There is no way around this question and no phenomenological access to its answer.

Thinkers such as Schopenhauer, Freud, and Unamuno have had intimations of the theory of the immortality of one's own being and proposed that it is demonstrated in the thought experiment of entertaining our non-being. Unamuno holds that conceiving one's death is simply not possible. When I attempt to envisage myself as not being, e.g., as absolutely not conscious, I bring upon myself a "tormenting dizziness." Freud's view is basically an echo of Schopenhauer's, whose position merits being quoted at length.

> Let a person attempt to present vividly to his mind the time, not in any case very distant, when he will be dead. He then thinks himself away, and allows the world to go on existing; but soon, to his own astonishment, he will discover that nevertheless he still exists. For he imagined he made a mental representation of the world without himself; but the I or ego is in consciousness that which is immediate, by which the world is first brought about, and for which alone the world exists. This centre of all existence, this kernel of all reality, is to be abolished, and yet the world is to be allowed to go on existing; it is an idea that may, of course, be conceived in the abstract, but not realized. The endeavor to achieve this, the attempt to think the secondary without the primary, the conditioned without the condition, the supported without the supporter, fails every time, much in the same way as the attempt fails to conceive an equilateral right-angled triangle, or an arising and passing away of matter, and similar impossibilities.[12]

There are two closely connected issues here. (A) The difficulty of thinking I myself as not being, and (B) The difficulty of my displaying my being dead. In (B) the display of my death bumps up against I myself as the assumed and tacitly affirmed agent of manifestation. (We may here neglect Schopenhauer's claim that the world exists alone for the I and rather interpret his language to point to the agent of manifestation as a necessary but not sufficient condition for the world's display.) As Freud puts it: "Our own death is, indeed, unimaginable, and whenever we make the attempt to imagine it, we can perceive that we really survive as spectators."[13] With (A) there is an attempt to self-displace myself to an objectification of myself where I am no longer "there," no longer I myself. We saw earlier (e.g., Book 1, Chapter VIII, §§6 ff.) that I can only imagine myself as different from how I am now, e.g., as older or younger, tired, sick, having a different body, having a different career, differently gendered, etc.; I cannot imagine or conceive myself to be someone else. Similarly, imagining myself to no longer be, in whatever way I do this, e.g., to be in an absolutely unconscious state, brings up nothing but, as Unamuno put it, a "tormenting dizziness."[14]

Of course one may adopt a naturalistic view and *conceive* that all that exists is the world prior to human consciousness as complete without consciousness. And this person might add: I am not *imagining* this scene and therefore you may not point out that I am implicitly affirmed as the one for whom the imagined scene is. Rather, the world is one without qualities and perspectives and therefore it is the world as conceived by a mathematical physical description. Thus there is a *conceived* world where there is not any implicit standpoint, and it is not a viewpoint but rather is free of points of view; in this sense it is a view from nowhere.

It must be granted that this is a world where neither the theorist is nor I am. However, it is not really conceiving or imagining one's non-existence; it is simply conceiving something else, i.e., the world portrayed by a mathematical and/or physicalist description, and by implication there are no consciousnesses on the scene, unless we have reason, as we well might, to insist that even here the equations, quantifications, summings, etc., involve syntax and other forms of synthesis requiring consciousness. Nevertheless, if this is, indeed, a *conceptualization* and *description* of the world, then we may posit a real mind for whom this description makes sense and at least there is implied a possible living mind, if not some actual individual, for whom this theoretical presentation is. And because such theoretical presencings are by possible or actual persons and not computers or zombies, an individual is implied. No abstract description is conceivable that does not have somewhere indexical reference and the life-world at its foundation. Furthermore, although it is a view from nowhere in the sense that it is a description of a world with the universality and necessity of nature as described by mathematical equations of physics, it is one with "universal validity for us all." This pervasive feature of publicity shows that, after all, minds are implicitly present in the presencing of this world.

Louis Lavelle has his own version of much of what has preceded, and further adds that it is contradictory to require of someone that he imagine his own absence in being. Requiring such a feat only results in his rendering himself a phenomenon capable of appearing and disappearing in an act of experiencing, or in an act of presencing, in which he himself would be the subject making present himself as no longer – or not yet. It is simply not in one's power to perform an operation of negation of a comprehensive sense of being that ineluctably would at the same time require a self-positing. Imagining the world in one's own absence, i.e., imagining that whose every aspect of manifestation cannot be without the thoughtful perceiving of the one imagining, stops the one imagining in his tracks.[15]

Permit us to shift gears slightly here. Alfred Tennyson reports a strange feeling that often came upon him when, in solitude, he continually repeated his own name silently

> till all at once, as it were out of the intensity of the consciousness of individuality, individuality itself seemed to dissolve and fade away into boundless being, and this not as a confused state but the clearest of the surest, utterly beyond words – where death was an almost laughable impossibility – the loss of personality (if so it were) seeming no extinction but the only true life.[16]

Admittedly this text might be taken for an expression of evidence for the Vedantist or even a Buddhist theory of the ultimate extinction of all senses of ipseity. It recalls Simon Weil's claim that contemplative devotion and pure loving attention require the extinction of "I" in favor of "impersonality." But it also may perhaps be a kind of witness to the first-person experience of one's ipseity as not coincident with one's self as an individual personality in the world and whose essence is not individuated by any worldly consideration but is, in some odd sense, boundless, like perhaps the way a genus, essence, or species, e.g., a number, is not bounded by another genus or essence, as a color. It may also testify that this first-person experience does not admit of a sense of cessation. Further, the alleged "loss of personality" emerges out of an intensification of the sense of individuality. Furthermore, we may note Tennyson's hesitation to remove all senses of personality from the experience, where, in regard to the loss of personality he states, "if so it were" – reminding himself that there was, after all, a dative of manifestation here.

Another consideration (see Book 1, Chapter VI, §9) connected to a rich sense of individuality that is not bounded by individuation and death is that the "myself" may be said to be uniquely necessary in the sense the "myself" is a unique essence the presence or manifestation of which requires its existence. The unique *eidos*, the very distinctive ipseity of me myself for myself, is such that it cannot come to light without its existence.

"I myself" is not the sort of *eidos* that can be conceived in the absence of its actual existence, like the essence of Dickens' Uriah Heep, northern lights, a lunar eclipse, a trade union, or a centaur. This sense each has of him- herself as well as the difficulty of envisaging one's non-being accounts in part for the resistance toward thinking of death as happening to oneself. Thus there is the temptation to think of death as what happens to others, and, of course, not without a kind of poking fun at oneself, that perhaps I am a uniquely privileged god among other men.[17]

It has been said that the reason one is not able to imagine or conceive of one's own death is that this consideration is tied to the wish that it not be true. The desire is so strong and the expected pain that this desire not be fulfilled is so great that there is a psychological necessity that one believes in one's continuance. But, in the light of the preceding considerations does it not seem equally if not more likely, as Raymond Smullyan has proposed, that people believe in an afterlife because they cannot conceive of their own non-being? One simply draws a blank in the effort to conjure up, through an imagining or conceiving, oneself as absolutely absent, unconscious, dead, etc. In our context, this would mean that the desire for the afterlife, doubtless a common thread in many religions and philosophies of religion, has a more basic consideration in the way the transcendental phenomenological perspective shines through some creases in the natural attitude. The first-person experience of ourselves in the natural attitude intimates (because it is not yet the disclosure of transcendental phenomenological reflection; see Book 1, Chapters VI–VII) an unbegun, undying, non-temporal, non-spatial individual who is not individuated by being a person in the world. But this is but an intimation and quite easily submerged by the weight of the obviousness of the natural attitude. But the Schopenhauerian thought-experiment nicely works against this submersion. Nevertheless, Plato's claim has merit that because we want to possess the good we want to posses it permanently – and this would be impossible if death is decisive. (We approximate Plato's position below when we argue that intrinsic to the self is its inadequation to its ideal of itself.) Therefore, Plato may be said to argue that everyone necessarily will desire immortality along with the good.[18]

Another inherent obstacle to a real assent to one's mortality comes from a discussion by Thomas Nagel. Nagel holds that there is an element of truth in what he regards as the false view that it is impossible to conceive of one's own death. I take him to mean that it is possible to conceive one's own death in the sense that we suppress the first-person point of view and having done this we take up the point of view of the natural attitude or the objective point of view towards ourselves, e.g., of the conservation optic or the natural scientific account of death. We do this all the time in talking about population problems, fatal illnesses, making wills, taking out insurance policies, etc. He also says "there is no way to eliminate the radical clash of standpoints in relation to death" – perhaps implying that in the first-personal point of view there is a difficulty in conceiving one's own death. Indeed for Nagel, the element of truth in the false belief [that one cannot conceive one's own death] is that the subjective first-person perspective does not allow for its own annihilation "for it does not conceive of its existence as the realization of a possibility" that emerges out of the world we experience. In the world around us something is accounted for both in terms of its existence and non-existence, its possible being and its actual being. There are underlying actualities which account for the possibility of all that we experience in the world. For example, the possible synthesis of chemical compounds has as its underlying basis the actualities of the chemical elements and the laws of chemistry.

But there are possibilities which seem to be basic features of the world and these themselves do not depend on more deep-seated actualities. The example he gives is: The number of possible Euclidean regular solids does not depend on more deep-seated actualities. Nagel proposes that our first-person experience is given to us precisely as such a basic feature that does not depend on a deeper actuality. My world is given to me as soaked with possibilities that depend on my existence. "My existence is the actuality on which all these possibilities depend."[19] As Husserl would put it, the phenomenon of the determinability of the world is tied to my I-can which is inseparable from I myself. In the world from the objective, third-person point of view the possibility of existence of things stands in a correlation with their possible non-existence, both of which, i.e., their possible existence and their possible non-existence, are based on the same actualities. In contrast, the possibilities of my world, e.g., what come to light through protentions and expectations, depend on my existence. But my existence, from the first-person point of view, does not appear as a contingent realization of deeper actualities or possibilities other than I myself. Nothing is related to my existence as the source of my possibilities in the way the existence of the chemical elements is related to the possibility of a chemical compound. Of course, Nagel adds, to explain my existence we have to go outside the subjective point of view and have recourse to the brain and the actualities which account for its possibility. But we face an insurmountable obstacle in making such external conditions an inherent part of the first-person subjective point of view. "In fact we have no idea how they generate our subjective possibilities on any view." They seem to constitute "a domain within which things can occur but which is not itself contingent on anything. The thought of the annihilation of this universe of possibilities [JGH: of the first-person subjective perspective] cannot then be thought of as the realization of yet another possibility already given by an underlying subjective actuality." That is, the subjective point of view presents itself, as Husserl would say, as given to itself and in itself and not in need of another consideration upon which it is dependent; its annihilation would have to be a *datum*, i.e., something *given* to itself, but this would mean that it still exists in witnessing this datum. Thus Nagel concludes that the subjective view cannot conceive of its existence as the realization of a possibility and that is why people think that it is impossible to conceive of one's own death.

But for Nagel the matter must not be left as a standoff. His is not the agnostic position we concluded to in Book 1 (Chapter VI). There we stated that the third-person point of view's evidence essentially clashes with the first-person point of view, and we, in the first-personal point of view, are left in the position of not being able to conceive of our death. But we also claimed that it could be that we die without our knowing it. Rather for Nagel, the third-person point of view ultimately trumps this perspective. Most dramatically this is because Nagel holds: "I am my brain" even though he acknowledges that this brain perspective fails to do justice to the subjective point of view. Further the third-person point of view must learn to accommodate itself to the irreducible clash of perspectives and not pursue an absolute hegemony.[20]

§3. Death as Danger and Destiny

Our use of Tolstoy's account of Ivan's death shows how death may appear as unique *for everyone*, and in this sense an instance of a universal state of affairs, namely that one's own death must appear as the most dreadful of things. Yet we hear professions of disinterest in death or even disdain at the prospect of immortality and often such persons find no reason to think of their death as in any way a misfortune. Others admit being depressed by the prospect of death. However, because of their heroic struggle against a first-person point of view and their conviction that the essential states of affairs of first-person experiences have no legitimacy unless accounted for by empirical physical public intersubjective data, they take consolation in being able to see the self as a corporation or nation. In such a way of taking death they are enabled to be persuaded that the importance of ownness is inflated and that experiences are best thought of as no one's. In such cases these thinkers explicate their own death with such formulae as "what I call my experiences may continue forever in some split-off other consciousness which did not really have these experiences but into whose brain they were 'interjected.'"

Our Book 1 indicates in a variety of ways why we are unconvinced of the merit of such views. Likewise one hears also of an equanimity where one does not dread death as either a thief of one's inalienable dearest possessions and dearest attachments or as a brutal obstacle to one's hopes and ambitions. For such a person there is a contentment with herself and the world because she has accomplished all that she strove to do. She has no longer any outstanding aspirations and rests content in her achievements. In which case, death is greeted with peace of mind. So it is alleged. Perhaps there are such persons, yet like the protagonists of what we called the "conservation optic" (Book 1, Chapter VIII, §5) and those for whom the "insufficiency of life" thesis is mere crypto-theology (see below, Book 2, Chapter IV, §2) we find the placid equanimity neither enviable nor convincing. The chief reasons are that it denies the evidence for unrestrictedness of the horizon of the will and therefore the evidence for the essential insufficiency of our achievements; and it further misses what we are calling the mystery that suffuses both the unique essence of what "I" refers to and the "phenomenon" of death. In what follows in this chapter, we will argue that the dread of death has to do not merely or only with the dread of loss of possessions and the possibility of achievements, but with the dread of non-being.[21]

Unamuno not only was beset with a tormenting dizziness in the effort to imagine his own nonexistence, but was also overcome with horror at the thought of his own nonexistence. But, Smullyan asks, how can he be horrified at something he cannot conceive or *"can't even imagine?... He must have some idea of what it was that was horrifying him."*[22] We may take this as hinting at the peculiar nature of *mystery*, which we will discuss in the next section. A famous consideration that may be brought forth in order to undo the mystery of death in favor of its "meaning nothing" is that of Epicurus. Epicurus acknowledges that most people regard death as "the most frightful of evils." But if one grasps that there is nothing fearful in not living, one will see that there is nothing fearful in living life facing inevitable death. Epicurus holds that because the presence of death cannot be painful it is only the anticipation of it that is painful. In sum, "death is nothing to us, seeing that when we exist death is not present, and when death is present we do not exist."[23]

In so far as fear and terror have to do with evils present to us by way of anticipation of the more or less imminent future, they presuppose that these evils exist as possible. But, argues Epicurus, because the worst evil is that which takes away from us what we cherish most, our lives and ourselves, we dread that which threatens to bring about this loss. The dread implies that the evil is future. However, when we realize that this evil is evil only because we take it to inflict present harm on us by depriving us of what we cherish, then we see it cannot harm us when it is present because its presence means we are not in a position to cherish or lose anything because we are not, i.e., we do not exist. Thus we may steel ourselves against it.

This recalls our earlier discussion (in Book 1, Chapter VII). Whereas Husserl *et alii* proposed that because we cannot presence our non-being without the actual and conscious continued being of ourselves, and thereby without finding ourselves in the paradoxical situation of being witness to our non-being, Epicurus holds that because the presence of death means we are not, and its non-presence means we are, we have no reason to be afraid.

Yet Epicurus' argument is not really a first-person consideration, but one drawn from the third- and second-person. He applies the evidence from the third- and second-person, i.e., the presence of death as the absence of the person, to interpret

the first-person. Indeed, he uses (without phenomenological warrant) the first
person when he says, "if it is, I am not: if I am then it is not." But this can be rendered equally, and with an evidence that most would grant, in the third person: if
Peter's death is, then Peter is not; if Peter is, then Peter's death is not. But Husserl
establishes the evidence in the first-person of the I's unpresentable cessation and, as
a result, problematizes the evidence of the third- and second-person and challenges
what Epicurus puts in the first-person. The third- and second-person evidence
present their own strong evidence of my own cessation in so far as I share the
features of the others' undeniable ephemerality for me. Both Epicurus and Husserl
attempt to throw a bridge over the two points of view and thereby establish a continuity between the two perspectives. Epicurus takes the third-person perspective
as the way we are to understand the first-person; he takes the demise in the third-
person to apply to himself, the one observing the demise of others. Husserl states
that the third-person is not the last word because the first-person perspective cannot
be handled by that in the third-person. He shows that if my last moment is present
as my last moment, then I must live beyond it as a fullment of the protention of
"no more," I must be to experience the end "no more."

Both views seemingly have the power to assuage the one who is terrified.
Epicurus says that the terror is what you manufacture because you do not see that
the (third-person) annihilation is to be applied to your experience of your own
demise. Husserl, while not addressing explicitly the issue of the terror, finds that it
loses its sting if one permits the first-person perspective to be part of our interpretation of what is evident in the third-person. Husserl himself took comfort in knowing that although Edmund Husserl would die, he himself as transcendental I did not
die. Both perspectives, in some way, inure us against the threat to our non-being
that is the root of the terror of death. Even though Husserl himself took comfort
in the consideration that although he himself qua transcendental I could not perish, it remains unclear what significance the transcendental perspective has for
the transcendental person.[24] This absence of clarity is the basis for our meditation
on the problem, paradox, and, eventually, mystery of death for the transcendental
person.

Epicurus, like other Stoics, exhorts us to act within our freedom and not be
concerned with what is beyond our field of agency. If we concern ourselves only
with what we have control over we establish a kind of invulnerability. If I realize
my self is inseparably my possibility for freedom and action, my I-can, which no
one can take from me, I am invulnerable to what others can do to me because this,
I myself as my I-can, i.e., that over which I alone have power, is inalienably me
and mine alone. We are exhorted to withdraw from our vulnerable, contingent, and
especially unnecessary havings to our being; and if we realize or identify ourselves
with this core citadel of "being" rather than "having" and only this, then we may
rest secure and inviolable. If we become basically indifferent to our possessions
and from what can be done by Others to our body, and even what Others can do
to our good name, we establish ourselves in a safe place that inures us against
the surds and brutalities of life. Of course, this view makes love and our attachment to others a liability. The great scandal that the death of Others causes for us

is precisely that I become through love and friendship, within ontological limits, indissolubly one with others, I become part of a "we" and I have permitted Others, in so far as that is ontologically possible (I can never become you or vice-versa), to enter into a sphere of my existence that is tangential with my sphere of ownness and I have thereby established a life in common with the others. (Recall the lovely biblical metaphor: Jonathan was the "other half" of David's soul, and Plato's speculation of lovers making whole what, after birth, was separated and destined to be reunited.) The death of the beloved Other is a scandal and a crisis because everything about one's life, i.e., our life together, has been called into question and endangered.

Whereas the Stoics would inure us from such vulnerability, they would also, at least implicitly, deprive us of the good of love and community. I myself as a personal unity rooted in position-taking acts and my ideal of myself in the world am not a monadic impregnable fortress. There is not personal self-*knowledge* without the struggle to understand one another and there is no community without risk and making oneself vulnerable to the Others and to the loss of Others. Further, even the Epicurean withdrawal from political action and the city, i.e., from a mode of existence that is at the mercy of chance and hostility, is not secure in its retirement to the garden even with the possession of the skills of agriculture and medicine. Rather this life of withdrawal faces the possibility that nature reveal itself not merely as beneficent mother or Venus, but rather as having no face at all, i.e., as utterly indifferent to human kind.[25]

Even if I am courageous in regard to the external dangers, there are, at my very core, essentially fragile points. Consider that the personal-moral self of even the exemplarily virtuous person is constituted in time from out of the primal streaming that itself is laced with facticity. The Stoic view envisages an impregnable core of ourselves that can only be attacked from without; it does not capture the presence of ultimate danger and therefore the kinds of death or annihilation at the core of our very selves, even if we envisage this self as independent of all its vulnerable possessions. The Stoic does not seem to have any resonance with what we today, since Kant, call the problem of "radical evil" – a theme which we postpone in this work. It does not consider the moral *acedia* or the way we, to speak with Karl Jaspers, have the capacity "to fail to show up to ourselves." Each can fail to have the energy, devotion, or voluntary agency that is called for in a particular situation; each can be beset with *acedia*, listlessness, or melancholy and thus impervious to the beauty of the good to be done; each can fail to be moved when she knows that it is appropriate that she be moved; each can fail to do what one would do, whether or not it be a more noble exhortation or an obligation; and each can find herself doing precisely what she despises in others and herself. We are often in a position of being either surprised or embarrassed by ourselves. When Cressida reveals too much of her love to Troilus, she says: "Why have I blabb'd? Who shall be true to us,/When we are so unsecret to ourselves?"[26] Cressida feels consternation at this loss of reserve. Implicitly she affirms that the better policy is guarding the secret of one's innermost, and not acting as if one were all on the surface, as if one's non-objective sense of oneself were not something to cherish.

Euripides gave expression to this disconcerting capacity not to show up to and for ourselves:

> Many a time in night's long empty spaces
> I have pondered on the causes of a life's shipwreck.
> I think that our lives are worse than the mind's quality
> would warrant. There are many who know virtue.
> *We know the good, we apprehend it clearly.*
> *But we can't bring it to achievement.* Some
> are betrayed by their own laziness, and others
> value some other pleasure above virtue.[27]

Five hundred years later St. Paul in *Romans* 7:15 and 7:19 similarly articulated this capacity to fail to show up to and for oneself in observing, "For what I am doing, I do not understand. For what I will to do that I do not practice, but what I hate, that I do" (New King James). Or: "I do not even acknowledge my own actions as mine, for what I do is not what I want to do, but what I detest" (New English Bible). The "fault" or split in what "I" refers to is nicely revealed in these texts by Euripides and St. Paul. This clearly is not merely "cognitive dissonance" but rather it has to do with the center of the I, and how this center bears an ideal of itself which gets drowned out. By what? By oneself in tension with one's ideal of oneself or one's true self. "For the good I will to do, I do not do; but the evil I will not to do, that I practice" (New King James); or: "The good which I want to do, I fail to do; but what I do is the wrong which is against my will" (New English Bible). St. Paul concludes that it is not longer *I* who do it but "sin"; sin is the agent not I. Sometimes "flesh" is used instead of "sin." This displacement of the "I myself" by a personification of the quality of an act must reverberate with Paul's claim that the true center, "the inner man," is never absolutely displaced. We may also recall Paul's willingness to supplant the I myself with Christ in *Galatians* 1:19–21; this new bondage to Christ is not to be understood as a forfeiture or annihilation of oneself. (We will return to these matters in Chapter VI).

We interpret these passages to mean that at the core of what each of us refers to with "I myself" there may surface a danger of, in some sense, losing oneself. (This is the source of the lamentation of Euripides and St. Paul.) There lurks the danger of the center of the I failing to be actual, or the very center of the I being complicit in this failure. Of course, there is the anomalous case of the wanton who is driven by the present impulse and appears to be nothing but this impulse without a center. But more familiar cases are, e.g., the person whose "buttons get pushed," or who "loses it," i.e., who for the moment has no control over herself, or the person who is addicted and for whom, at certain times, the addicted will takes charge over the center of the person. Why we become our own worst enemies, and how this proneness of persons to foster this fracture in their very cores is the question perhaps of Euripides, St. Paul, and Jaspers. (We will return to some of these matters later in this book.) Guilt is the sign of the conditions that we ourselves establish to our self-affirmation. This may take a variety of forms, e.g., of an absolute self-condemnation where one cannot forgive oneself or hope for forgiveness from another, or a resolution to begin again once the Other accepts my apology, etc.[28]

The Stoic quest for a citadel of the self which excludes it from radical ontological contingency and fragility at the heart of the self, poses special problems for this Husserlian phenomenology. Husserl himself sets the scene for the problem when he shows, on the one hand, that the root sense of I myself is inseparable from the primal presencing. This places the facticity of temporalization at the heart of the myself. From the transcendental point of view of the world's display the transcendental I is a necessity; and yet it is not an absolute necessity. I myself in my essence and as transcendental I cannot be made present without positing my existence. (See Book 1, Chapter VI, §9.) Yet this existence itself is not absolutely necessary. I am necessarily being as long as I am self-aware and the agent of manifestation, but it is not necessary that I be, or that I be self-aware and an agent of manifestation. I can moreover, perhaps, cease to be without my knowing/presencing my cessation.

There is another facticity indicated in the consideration that the I myself's primal presence is itself tied to an odd flow. Although the primal presencing's *self*-experience is not of a flow, it does experience the incessant and contingent flux of Nows of its conscious life in the world and the world's passage. This presencing of the duration of the stream of consciousness and the elemental basis of the world is not temporal or a duration. Nevertheless it has a facticity tied to its constituting-displaying of duration. Following Husserl we hold that with each Now there is a posited a "novel" pulse of primal presencing (the "flow"). And with this we are inserted "constantly" into being in the world. There is nothing we can do to bring it about, change it, or slow it down, or accelerate it. As Sokolowski puts it: "It is not within our power. We do not control our origins. It just keeps on fluttering on its own terms. And yet we are identifiable with it; it is 'ours,' as our origin and base."[29] But, as we have urged, it is "our origin and base" in the sense that it is the origin and base of us as persons in the world. It is not the origin and base of the "I myself" whose temporalization it is.

This "facticity," i.e., temporalization of our being, a contingency that may not be compared with any contingency in the displayed world, reveals a non-being at the heart of our personal being. The threat of non-being is not primarily something transcendent as lurking without; rather at the core of our being is the radical contingency of our selves as primal presencings. The primal "motion" of our personal coming into being in the "flow" (see Book 1, Chapter VII for the problematic nature of the "flow"), which is not Now but my ongoing presencing of Now from out of "I know not what," is on the edge between the non-actuality of what lies in between each primal presencing. This "space in between" the being of the primal presencing*s* (please take note: the plural is not evident but postulated as parts of the "flow," nor can its members be counted, only the phases of what it presences can be counted) is the space between being and nothingness.

On both sides, as it were, of the heart of our personal being, the heart of what is most certain and taken for granted, i.e., the "pre-being of the primal presencing of Now," there is the sharp edge of nothingness. As each Now surfaces into actuality from out of the protended Now only to pass into the actuality of the no longer, so the primal presencing of each Now surfaces out of nothing that I know of, only to vanish back into this nothing that I know nothing of. In itself the primal presencing does not have itself but is given to itself as a fact.

Although I do not, in experiencing myself (as transcendental I), experience myself as Now but as timelessly presencing the flow of Nows, and although I cannot make present my ceasing to be, I still experience myself as not the master of my continuing to be a primal presencing-temporalization. This is given to me and no aspect of this is within my power. That there is protending and filling of protentions is a fact, and it is not in my power to begin these, bring them to a halt, or, more obviously, it is not in my power to bring it about that I in the future exist and be able to have filled intentions. Therefore each must give a negative answer to the rhetorical question posed by Descartes: "I must now ask myself whether I possess some power by which I can bring it about that I myself, who now exist, will also exist a little later on."[30]

But Descartes' statement holds not only for my personal being in the world through wakeful temporalization, but also for "the myself" which, as such, is *not* exposed to this facticity, contingency, and nothingness of personal being as rooted in temporalization. Even though we have claimed (in Chapter V) that it is the bare substrate of personal being, we have also left it open whether in any sense it can be said to exist independently of the primal temporalization. Permitting this abstraction and this independence, it can be said that there is nothing I myself posses by which I can bring it about that I myself will "continue" (transtemporally) to exist. I might cease to be without my knowing it; just as I might begin to be without my being aware of it. Likewise there is no power I have which brings it about that I am I myself, this unique essence. Although it is necessarily so that there is no power that can make me be someone else, that I am I myself is not my doing. Again, that I myself "continue" transtemporally to be me myself is not in my power.

My non-being is at the heart of my being and awareness of this can break forth and awaken within me a sense of absolute facticity, absolute vulnerability toward and absolute dependence on "I know not what." This is the most basic consideration for our discussion of the dread of our non-being that death brings. Death, or the event of my non-being as it is manifest in third-person experience, is not therefore, as it is for Epicurus, something that remains apart and extrinsic to one's being, i.e., always a genitive of appearing, whose presence is nothing for me, the dative of appearing, because its presence means I am not, and when I am it is not. Rather at the heart of I myself as that to which and by which everything whatsoever appears, there is a taste of my non-being; in this sense there is a scent of death.

From this angle, the Stoic or Vedanta effort to inure us from the event of our deaths is misguided as a philosophical disclosure about the ultimate state of affairs, even though it might well be useful as a strategy for repression of this state of affairs. Further it is not wrong in counseling us to be courageous in the face of the most dreadful of things and be concerned about what authentically constitutes ourselves and our lives and to distinguish ourselves from our vulnerable havings and attachments. Rather it is mistaken because this refuge of I myself over against my havings itself is not an invulnerable citadel but is itself pervaded by a kind of a radical contingency and "anguish of the instant." This is to say that the self properly is pervaded by a sense that its being is not something absolutely within its own power. Further, as a primal temporalization, i.e., the primal presencing by which it is inserted in the world, there is a constant bridge-making over the abyss of non-being and there is nothing it can do to insure its continuance in being. The "motion" of the presencing of the Now is a motion from the non-actuality of non-being into the actuality of being, back into non-being, back into being, etc. – all within the continuousness of an abidingly present Now through the "flow" of the primal presencing. But both the abidingly present Now and the "flow" rest on the edge of non-being out of which and back into which the Now-moments flow.

Of course, I am I myself, and if I have anything I have the integrity of "myself." Further I *have*, and *am not* absolutely, the irrepressible churning of my primal association, the ongoing "gift" of passive synthesis – always pervaded by my unique I myselfness. And the danger that death unequivocally brings for us in the third- and second-person (because there is no unequivocal manifestation of death in the first-person), is the utterly irretrievable absence and non-being of those whom I love. And these become ciphers of my own possible non-being, both at the core of my being and at the termination of my life.

To this we may relate the consideration of the way death's danger figures into the difference between how our lives are first-personally given to us, how Others are given to us upon their deaths, and how we may apperceive ourselves to be given to Others upon our death. Our non-ascriptive sense of ourselves as ipseities is inseparably bound up with our necessarily ascriptive sense of ourselves as persons perceived by Others. In our global pre-thematic sense of ourselves we are always at the mercy of Others' interpretation of our speech and deeds, and therefore who and what we are for ourselves is at the mercy of how others take us. We hope from our friends and loved ones generous interpretations; from strangers and "the world" we can expect sometimes the worst. In death the matter is exacerbated. Our lives are never given to us in the way Others are given to us upon their deaths. Only perhaps in the case of deceased loved ones does the force of one's love work to sustain the other's ipseity and self-presence against the inevitable reduction of who she was to properties and qualities and narrative strands that describe her. When Others, even friends, die, they and their lives are inevitably present at hand as a result of having been summed up and transformed into consummated wholes for us. Their stories can be told with a beginning, middle, and end, and become, like any event, both subject to the inevitable process of being buried in oblivion under the heavy cascade of ever new emergent ones as well as open to manifold interpretations which more or less render alien the first-person experiencing of a life.

But, as we have urged, the first-person experience of one's beginning is far from evident. Further we experience ourselves in the first-person always as having a Not-Yet, as always ineluctably protending what is still to come, as unconsummated, as still having possibility. My life is always lived as unbegun and still outstanding; the horizon opened by protentions, expectations, and hopes is never absolutely closed, even when, at death, we say "I cannot" and concede, "It must." In this sense we essentially experience ourselves as unfinished and not as complete wholes. In the first-person, any version of ourselves as completed wholes, just as any reification whatsoever which would purport to have absolute finality, would be a destruction of the lived sense of ourselves.

Thus the death of someone as an event in the world provides a kind of evidence for the truth to the post-modernist theory that I myself am nothing but the more or less abstract narratives enacted by more or less connected personae. But such an apperception of myself as, in the defining eyes of "history," a more or less connected finished whole, a story which itself is a bundle of past events or narratives within the ongoing world, is an apperception which suppresses my first-person sense of myself. For someone who cannot help regarding himself in the light of how he is perceived by others – and who is completely exonerated from this? – this apperception typically is unsettling if not dreaded.

(Most people are not remembered for the myth with which they have been surrounded or which they themselves have propagated, as in the case of persons whose identity is "publicity" or the choreographed image of their handlers. It is of interest that some will die rather than permitting a demythologization, i.e., they will go into "the Dark" of death preferring to have sustained a deceitful persona. In which case, they either have a keen sense of their core selves as distinguished from their public persona and perhaps cynically foster the illusion; or they have sold themselves to their images and thus have become alienated from their core selves. They love the lie about themselves rather than themselves. They perhaps act out of the fear that if the public image is shattered they are no one and have been no one at all because the only one they have known, i.e., identified with, is a lie.)

Of course, any form of remembrance is perhaps to be preferred to those faceless millions who are "disappeared" or who die in anonymity in slavery, massive natural disasters, or in the so-called "collateral damage" of wars. While living we live in the first-person the rebuttal to the historical intersubjective defining interpretation and we can protest such summaries of ourselves. However, in the anticipation of our death, when we apperceive ourselves to be, in the eyes of others, an ephemeral event, this apperceived inertness of ourselves seems to legitimate the position that the lived sense of ourselves is a lie. Thus an aspect of the fear of death is the fear of being so eternally denied, violated, misunderstood, and disfigured.

To put all this in another way: This apperception of ourselves, i.e., the anticipated being-perceived by others, as a consummated whole is also, at best, the reduction of ipseity or "I myself" to a narrative confined to my actual achieved personality. The lived experience of myself as more than my constituted personhood and of who I am as exceeding what I am, is permanently discounted, and there is no more to be said or done by me to challenge this version of me. Upon my death, my story, if there is anyone to tell it, will capture who I am in a more or less inadequate narrative; but this cannot, in the best of narratives, represent the unrepresentable "myself." Further it will foreclose my living sense of myself incarnated and "personified." i.e., I myself as still unfinished and "I can."[31] Of course, at the end of my life my I-can gives way to the body's cessation. It gives way to: I cannot any longer and It must. But this characterizes one only at the end of life – which may come "out of season" – it does not characterize one's living one's life. In any case, even with the concession, "It must," there is till the irrepressible emergence of protentions of not yet.

In Chapters III–V we will give reasons why it is proper that we be remembered in stories that tell about "the sort of person" one was. This, *not* the pure "myself," is what can and ought to be commemorated and celebrated, especially in narratives. Of course, we have said the person, although not strictly identical with, is the same as the "myself." We have further argued that the ultimate intentional referent of the person, i.e., the "myself" as an "ontological value," is incommensurate with anything in the world and that it merits celebration. Indeed, this is precisely what love properly does. But how does one commemorate the individual propertyless essence? Love reveres it, but how is the unique ipseity bereft of properties commemorated if commemoration requires recollection of what has been inserted publicly in the world? We will argue that there is a kind of ontological incompleteness to the "myself," and of necessity it *must* with a moral necessity founded in its ontological constitution, fashion itself in the light of its self-ideal, i.e., become a moral person. Eulogies aim to capture in an important sense Who someone is in terms of what sort of person she constituted herself to be in the light of her "true self." Here the "sort of person" is its unique personal *eidos*, its "best look" (Sokolowski), which, as something beautiful, we love to behold, share, and cherish in stories. It is this which is foremost entitled to be commemorated and not allowed to pass into oblivion.

It seems that someone's apperception of how she and her life are apperceived by Others can only be met without dread when the apperception is sustained by love and the hope of a hearing before judges whose magnanimity, mercy, and justice are only surpassed by their capacity for empathy. Traditionally such a judge has been named God and the just person strives to anticipate daily this judgment (*coram deo*). Human judgment in these matters typically is laced with the darkness of ignorance and prejudice.

§4.   The Meaning of the Annihilation of an Individual Essence

For the transcendental phenomenologist, in spite of the evidence that in the first-person death is not presentable, there is not provided a firm handle on the meaning of death. At the core of being of the primal presencing there is a radical, peculiar contingency. Further, that I cannot presence my beginning or my end does not, with absolute necessity, in and of itself, rule out that I have a beginning and end; it could be that I begin and end without being aware of this. If on this most fundamental matter it were so that I would end without my knowing it, phenomenology would fail in its fundamental thesis about the inseparability of being and display. I might die and my death would not be something that I can make present. I might have begun absolutely; I have no first-person evidence that I have or have not so begun even though I cannot possibly present my so having begun. The origin of my originating as a primal presencing remains hidden from me and I likewise remain in the dark about my ultimate destiny.

The person who has died, although perhaps missed, is not, properly speaking, missing; it is not the absence that one can make present, like someone who is lost. It is rather closer to the Latin American term for the agency of state terror, "to disappear." Here what grammatically was an intransitive verb is made transitive in order to describe a statist action where a loved one's being absent or missing turns out to be a case of state kidnapping or murder; her sudden disappearing was an act of secret "liquidation" or "rendition" that makes her incapable of a reappearing to the loved ones. From the start of our being with others we sense a distinctive and fundamental helplessness in the face of the other in so far as she remains absolutely transcendent to us and the most important things in her life reside within the sphere that she refers to with "I can" and what she alone can do. There is no way we can make present her self-presence to herself; there is no way that my actions can substitute for hers or fathom the depths from which hers spring. For all that she reveals, she remains hidden and, in this respect, absent in an essential way. We "appresent" her as one appresenting, as one seeing, without ourselves experiencing her own seeing or interpretating. No matter what she reveals to us we sense the abyss between us, not only because we know how words fall short of lived felt meanings, but because what she refers to with "I" remains by necessity transcendent to me just as what "I" refers to in my case remains uniquely hidden in the sense that no explication in terms of properties displays what is essentially non-sortal.

Now that she is dead the helplessness is magnified: There is no possible appresentation. There, in the body, is no spiritual or psychological depth; the corpse reveals everything about itself as corpse and the revelation of the corpse may tell us much about how she lived and died, but in another sense it is no revelation at all of her. Her unique individual essence, her ipseity as such, leaves no trace. There is no way we can conjure up her presence in this body once (convinced that) she is dead.

The way she refracted the world in her face and action is irreplaceably annihilated. The deceased Mary was perhaps for a few or many a central "you" around which perhaps for long stretches of time their lives revolved because she was a source of consolation, nurture, strength and wisdom. She was perhaps the Other whose unfathomable generosity, creativity, and freedom often amazed, surprised, and delighted. Or she was perhaps one who too casually shared her burdens, dodged her responsibilities, and overly displayed her pains, weaknesses, and despair. Whether inappropriately exuberant, splendidly virtuous, troublingly vicious or puzzlingly passive and inert, we apperceive that she experienced herself as more than these qualities, and occasionally we too perhaps gained a glimpse of this "more." In any case, she was one who had regrets, plans, hopes, and tasks. While alive, her life was present to us as a future pregnant with possibility. And, especially if she died young or even died as a senior full of hope, this future lingers like an important unfinished sentence hanging in the air in our midst. In so far as the surviving friends and family were "involved" in this future, their continued agency may well be a continuation of hers. They continue what she willed, but it is far from evident that her will continues. (We return to these themes in connection with "ghosts" in the next section.)

The person who has died was *Dasein*, and as such not merely a being within the world along with all the others, but she was a *Da*, a "there," that held open the world-space within which everything appeared (*Sein*) and to whom everything appeared. She, that one "there," was the hinge of a unique display of the world, a *Geltungsträger der Welt*, one who was the support of the world articulated in terms of its truths, values, and validities. If we think of the world as a universe, as an integrally unified whole, then its richness is comprised of the totality of *eidé*, i.e., essential disclosures that bind the manifold into unities and all of the *eidé* into a unity. Essences as these essential disclosures are the necessary nodal points of the world. For many, the deceased Mary was essential to their social world. In her death her unique agency and unique display of the world as an integral whole is annihilated. Now this unique perspective on the world and essential sparkle within the world is extinguished. Her death is not absolutely the loss of meaning, but it is the loss of her display of the world and the meaning that uniquely coalesced in her display of the world.

Most basic, however, is that our presentation of Mary includes the apperception of herself as a unique individual essence which, like the pure essentiality or what-ness, is not merely the essence of something, nor merely the *eidos* that would come to light with invariant properties through a free imaginative variation. Rather in her self-experience and our apperception of this as like unto our own, she experiences herself and is experienced by us as a pure unique essence. (See Book 1, Chapters III–V.) And as such, i.e., as long as the essence is experienced it cannot not be (see Book 1, Chapter VI, §9). And now this essence, as far as all the appearances go, has been disappeared; it apparently has been destroyed.

Death casts the long shadow that arises from the query: If this one who bore and disclosed the world can vanish into nothingness, cannot the world itself, the whole realm of meaning as well as being itself, vanish into nothingness? The "second death" of which Jonathan Schell wrote in terms of a nuclear holocaust, i.e., the death not only of all individual persons, but of meaning, is the death of the world's display. In Mary, as an agent of manifestation, we found a necessity that, while she was alive, was presupposed by all the necessities and contingencies of the world. Indeed, we knew one who could conceptually annihilate the being of all that is given as being, but who could not, in so doing, annihilate herself as agent of this thinking. And therefore we had present in our midst one for whom absolute nothingness was inconceivable. In her, we were in the presence of one for whom her beginning and ending were not presentable. But with her death the one who so apperceived herself and who was so appresented by us, i.e., as necessary to the display of the world's necessities and who was not able to make present her ending, herself is annihilated for us.[32]

No less unsettling is the consideration that her unique individual essence, as revealed in her presence, agency, and articulation of the world, *is* no longer and is not able to be substituted for. In empathically presencing her we make present one who, for herself, transcends all sortal determinations, and decisions, and who cannot be replaced by another. From the second- and third-person perspective each unique self is a new beginning, the antecedents of which in the inherited personality traits, etc., do not capture the person's uniqueness for others and, a fortiori, for herself. And when she dies, an "essence," and in this sense, an eternal truth of the world, disappears seemingly forever. Thus each death raises the question of how it is possible that there be the extinction of meaning. And if a unique essence is able to be destroyed, may not the whole display or *eidos* of the world equally face extinction or "be disappeared?" With the annihilation of a unique person, the presence of the individual essence, which is the eternal truth of this unique ipseity, becomes absent. Is not therefore an integral truth of the world thereby annihilated? This much is true: for some who knew her the world is without an essential component. And for anyone who met her, a unique presentation of the world is extinguished, and along with it its unique irreplaceable dative of manifestation.

But how can an "eternal truth" be extinguished? I cannot extinguish the truth of the proposition that "The US invaded Iraq at the beginning of the 21st century" or "$2 \times 2 = 4$"; I cannot eradicate the essence of the number 4 by erasing all its symbolic manifestations in the world, or by eliminating all instantiations of sets of 4. What would a social world be without the eternal essences of intersubjectivity and justice? Here in these aforementioned cases we have not individual essences but essences that are universal. Further, these questions have to do with what is impossible to conceive. Is there not an analogous inconceivability in the death of someone for those who lived lovingly in the presence of this person? The natural world itself is of course intact, but not the social world, the world wherein we lived. Rather there is a gaping hole. But there is also a gaping hole in the *kosmos noetos*, the cosmos of essences.

One might say that her individual essence that now is destroyed can be reduced to the undying validity of propositions about her having been or acted. But whereas this is easy to grasp with respect to an individual existing thing that is now extinct, it seems to be inadequate for an individual essence which was not merely an essence of an individual substance, or an instance of a kind, individuated by the contingencies of time and space. Indeed, if we may think of essences as essential, i.e., necessary, for the world, then they comprise the world as such, and are always true of the world. But how is Mary necessary for the world? Since Plato we have distinguished a hierarchy of essences or forms, even meta-forms that everything else presupposes. We surely cannot envisage a status of the world where sameness and difference are retained only by way of the validity of past states of affairs wherein they at one time held sway. Less clearly evident is a social world where "justice" was able to be absolutely dispensed with or a natural world where final causality was absolutely missing. Yet millions have integral worlds without the essence of Mary, and only a few know the essence which "Mary" is. The individual essence which someone is is clearly irrelevant and accidental to the integrity of the display of the world by most people. Yet this was true also for Socrates, and, as we shall see (in Chapter VI below) Plotinus posited a "form of Socrates" which was inseparable from the world-constituting Mind (*Nous*).

Of course, we may think of Mary's essence after the fashion, e.g. of the "essence" of a platoon sergeant, a stock option, a university vice-president of development, a Nike basketball shoe, a shop steward, or a vice grip. These essences are cultural universals and at one time were not and at another time will cease to be. They contrast with 3 ("threeness") or justice, or time, and (a fortiori) with sameness and difference in so far as it is easy to consider a world in the absence of these cultural universals. But "Mary" is neither a cultural universal or necessary for every actual instance of the world. If "Mary" is a genuine individual essence she would seem to have a status that, like "soul" or "human," defines a region of the world. But whereas "human" or "soul" make up an "ontological" region of the world, we have found reasons to regard Mary's self-awareness as essential in itself. That is, her self-presence is essential not merely as the essence of an individual substance nor merely as the whatness that eidetic variation lifts from out of this individual substance by showing invariant properties. Rather, Mary is, in her self-presence, present to herself as an individual essence even though this is a non-sortal self-presence.

But Mary's individual essence is also essential for the world's display by Mary and perhaps for those who loved Mary, even though it is not essential for every actual display of the world. Only if we say that every display of the world involves the empty apperception of unknown Others' and their displays of the world does Mary's necessity sneak in, as it were, by being necessarily apperceived as a possibility.

Although Mary may be non-eliminable from the natural and social world of the people that know her, her essence could not lay claim to the non-eliminability for any world, as do, e.g., sameness and difference, justice, number, etc. In this sense the individual essence of Mary is accidental and contingent. And there is no doubt about this contingency in the face of her death. Yet, if she is a unique individual essence then how can such an essence simply vanish. Plotinus' establishing Socrates' form in *Nous* was a way of dealing with this matter.

With someone's dying the eternal truth that makes up her unique essence is, for all appearances, forever vanished. Further, her passing is not merely the passing of a part of a whole that continues, like a leaf on the tree, that next year will bear more leaves. Rather she was a microcosm (see Book 1, Chapter VI, §8), a little All, a diminutive universe, and thus a whole unto herself and not able to be simply subordinated to a larger whole, or be understood as a function within a larger whole. The whole, the world, was "contained" in her by reason of her unique display of the world, which itself affected and was incorporated in (and itself an incorporation of) the displays of numerous others. Because she is not a property, accident, instance of a kind, but a unique ipseity and individual essence, her passing cannot be considered a mere ephemeral natural fact, but rather has the aspect, for us who witness her death, of the annihilation of an essence.

In this sense, and quite in contrast with other events in the world, the event of death breaks the continuity of the flow of events where everything is continuous with everything else and every ending is a new beginning. The death of this ipseity is decisive: Mary is; and then Mary is no more at all. The world, of course, persists and holds sway as the frame for all events. But because death is the apparent annihilation of an individual essence, it is not like other events. It is not merely an incidental change within the subsisting whole; death itself is the disappearance and annihilation of a whole that itself is not to be subsumed as a part within the whole of the world. In this sense death is also a cataclysm of the world for those who witness it. Again, death casts the long shadow of the death of display, the death of meaning, and the emergence of nothingness, because with her, a "bearer of the validity of the world," an "eye of the world" is darkened, and there is foreshadowed the possibility of total darkness.

The prospect of obliteration of truths we now experience not only casts a shadow over the present, it seems to turn it into maya or illusion. This becomes evident by reflecting on the temporal sense of what is real and actual. If the death of someone points to the possibility of the extinction of all manifestation, then the death of a single individual essence adumbrates the total darkness of the death of display and meaning, because what happens to one can happen to all, either eventually or all at once. Given the temporal sense of the world, the adumbration of this total darkness affects the sense of the actual present. Of course, the sense of the ephemerality of existence, i.e., the imminent passing away of the present, especially cherished presents, affects our sense of the present. For instance, we may experience sadness in the midst of delighting in something beautiful if we are reminded of its prospective passing away.

But the threat of a possible total darkness has a capacity to unsettle the present experience in an even more profound way. This is because the present actual reality of life has its sense bound up with the future and the past – a future and a past that are inseparable from a presencing of a future and a past. The Now is precisely what before was protended as not yet and the Now is also lived as becoming no longer or what will have been. The Now is thus experienced (constituted) by us as what was future and as what will eventually have been. What is now once was not yet and, at some time it will have been. That at some time it will have been is essential to it being lived as now. As Robert Spaemann, whom we are dependent on here, puts it, "The *futurum exactum* is inseparable from the present." If we say of a present event: "It will at one time not have been," we are equivalently saying that in reality it is not now. "In this sense all that is really actual is eternal."[33]

As long as there is a primal presencing of what is now, there is a presencing of Now as what will have been and there is a retaining of it has having been. If it is true that only what will have been can be said to be now, then necessarily it is true of what is now that it will sometime have been. But if some time there is no agency of manifestation, then there is no retention and no anticipation of the Now as what will have been. The essential connection between Now and that sometime it will have been is destroyed. But then there is also destroyed the very sense of the actual reality of the present. If at some time it is true that it will not have been, then what is now is not actually now. For tense-logic to be sustained there has to be an agent of manifestation for which the syntax of the being-present, being-past, and being-future holds. The death of meaning and display is not just one fact among others because it undoes the very sense of facts as displays or articulations of the world.

This holds no less for the tenselessness or omnitemporality of essential truths. Their transtemporality, i.e., their not having their validity established by being true at sometime, but rather by being true regardless of temporal perspective, still requires the agency of manifestation which brings to light this non-temporal syntax through the transcendence of temporal perspective. This timelessness characterizes essences and the propositions expressing the essential properties of whatever exists. It is also, we have argued, what characterizes the unique individual essences of ipseities. And this is what is vexing about their deaths. Already, however, in any temporal truth, like "The apple tree is now blooming," it is eternally true that the apple tree was at that time blooming. This merely explicates the basic truth that if it is now, at sometime it will have been. But there is also indicated the basic, non-worldly truth of the "transcendental pre-fix" or declarative sense of "I" of the agency of manifestation: ["*I see that* (the apple tree is blooming and of necessity it will have been blooming)"], in as much as the display of the modes of time and tense-logic imply the agency of manifestation. (Cf. our discussion in Book 1, Chapter II.)

The basic feature of the present reality, i.e., that at some time it will have been, is a feature of not only public entities and events, but also of unique and private experiences, judgments, evaluations, etc. All actual present reality, whether immanent to streams of consciousness or enjoying the publicity of events in the world, comes under the cloud of possible non-being in the face of the death of a unique essence or a "myself" in so far as this passing can imply that at some time it will be true that some event happening now will not have been. That is, once again, of necessity it is true that anything actual we experience will sometime have been. And yet this necessity *as a display or articulation of the world* is eliminated along with the death of the agents of manifestation. What happens to the past when there is the ultimate and universal death of primal presencing of the present Now and retaining of what was now? The Now loses its necessary feature that of necessity it will have been if there is no appropriate dative of manifestation for whom this is so and which retains what is no longer. If there is no "space" within which the actuality of events and experiences is retained, then not merely the unique essence that Mary experienced at one time in experiencing herself, but the very talk of the present actuality as what some time will have been, comes undone. In as much as this requires an agent and dative of manifestation for all presents and presencings of Now, it moves beyond the transcendental I with its unique essence and essential self-experiencing itself as the "myself" to an infinite transcendental intersubjectivity. Or given the postulated ephemerality of this infinite transcendental intersubjectivity it moves to what alone would be adequate to the infinite presents, an infinite divine subjectivity.[34] Again, with the death of, e.g., Mary, there is an extinguishing of a unique self-experiencing essence, an "eye of the world," or, rather, of a subjectivity, that is interlaced with the transcendental intersubjectivity that holds open the world as the clearing within which things appear. With her death, the death of a unique essence self-experiencing itself as a primal presencing of the flow of Nows, there appears the possibility that the very sense of the present, the Now, upon which all our perceptions build, is in danger, because it becomes palpably possible that the endless intersubjective community itself be extinguished. That moves us into theological areas that we postpone until Chapters VI–VII.

§5. The Secret of Death

In referring to death we use many images of taking a journey. "She passed on," "She went into the Dark," "She crossed the divide," "He went to the other shore," "He went to meet his maker," "He is gone," etc. Of course these are metaphors. Kant, we may recall, thought of the afterlife as a change in the form of our knowing, where we "then" know the noumenal reality that now is perceived darkly as phenomenal, especially in terms of our noumenal selves. Thus death is not a "passing on" because we, noumenally, are not "anywhere."

But this is all *postulated* by Kant. What we *experience* is the deceased's absence, her disappearance. The metaphor of a journey comforts us to think that her life has not stopped and the absence is not absolute or forever. The absolute stopping that is evident in the corpse stands in flagrant contradiction to the lived life of the deceased, especially if she were still young and energetic. The metaphor helps us to avoid the crushing sense of absolute cessation.

The journey metaphor shows perhaps that we apperceive each to live necessarily with open future. Even the very old person facing imminent death still lives in a future in this respect at least: Protentions are irrepressible and the time of death, although certain, is unknown. It perhaps shows also that we apperceive each to have not found an abiding dwelling here in the sense that the heart's desires are never adequately met.

The deceased is one who, on the one hand, in the first-person experienced herself within the openness of the world and as necessarily having an unending future, and, on the other hand, whom we experienced as You, as *Dasein*, as microcosm, as bearer of the world's validities. Now she is forever gone and what remains of her is there as a lifeless decomposing corpse. She no longer hears, smiles, displays, responds. No entreaties, scenes or rituals can bring her back. There is silence. But the silence is that of the absence of a voice and the absence of a presence. It is not the silence of what was never a voice or a presence. It is the absence of what once was present because in her death we experience her now as of necessity sometime having been.

In this sense the absence and silence of the corpse are a kind of secret. Something is held back that the witness wants to have disclosed. Each of us who grieves experiences the question that the deceased's absence poses for us and that we want to address to her. The question is so massive that it is difficult to formulate in a satisfactory way. In any case we do not really ask her a question nor do we expect an answer. The corpse cannot answer or hear our question. Whether we are mourners or not we experience ourselves on edge not only because we face the irretrievable unfathomable absence of someone about whom we cared, but also because we are confronted with our own non-being, own extinction, and the fragility at the heart of ourselves, perhaps even the fragility of the very agency of display. The vague but irrepressible question of the meaning of being and its relation to non-being is on the edge of our minds. And now, in the presence of the corpse, we know the deceased either knows whether the first-person perspective has ultimate validity for interpreting our third- and second-person perspectives or she does not know because she died without knowing it. In either case we are left in the dark.

Death of a loved one is accompanied by mourning and grieving. This is not merely the sadness of an interruption of a common life where individual lives continue within the life of the world. Rather here not only is the common life interrupted but the other has vanished forever. It is not merely that circumstances have changed and we do not share our lives any longer, but there is no way we can share our lives because one of us is no longer. For all practical purposes she is as nothing; she has to be regarded as annihilated in terms of a life together in the common world. Of course, I can, indeed I may feel that I must (see the next section) remember her, carry out her wishes, help realize her dreams. But it is not at all evident that these wishes and dreams are still actual. Her wishes and dreams were experienced by me as now through her communication and behavior; they were experienced then and now as sometime having been. Now that she is "gone" they are experienced as having been. I do not know whether they still are, even though I retain them as having been. She is plunged into the great darkness of the realm of the dead and the realm of what I know absolutely nothing about even though a short time ago we were busy perhaps talking with and caressing one another.

Death of a loved one is met by grieving. Like any emotion, grief is not merely a disclosure of the world, but, at the same time, it is our coming undone, unhinged. We may keep our composure when we intend the world through sadness. In sadness the world is disclosed as being without something or someone that delights and gives us joy. We experience loss and disappointment. The absence makes us heavy-hearted but we may get on with our living. We may focus on something else and make marginal the loss and disappointment. But in the circumstances that bring about grief the basic capacity to orient ourselves in the world is not at hand. We cannot arrange the world in terms of center and periphery, means and ends, or a hierarchy of preferences. Rather we are riveted to our sorrow and we cannot disregard our loss and disappointment and rearrange our lives with prospects for new joys, etc. Rather in grief we are overcome and delivered over to our loss, sorrow, and pain. We lose control over ourselves and cannot compose ourselves in the face of what causes us to grieve. Sobbing overtakes us. It would be a willful materialist dogmatism to posit this as a sheer blind, biological-physical response to death. Whatever the undeniable biological ingredient in this response is, it does not account for grief as a metaphysical interpretation of the world and my being in the world.

Although we do indeed, as it were, collapse into our lived bodiliness and relinquish the distinctions of spirit, soul, and body, e.g., where "I" act and "have" my sensibility, etc., this collapsing into the body in weeping and grieving (as well as in laughing, as Plessner has shown) is at once a relinquishing of my self as *I* as well as a self-affirmation. I exist not only as *I*, intellect, agent of manifestation, and voluntary acts, etc., but am whole as an incarnate person and this situation is interpreted in such a way that *I* am overcome, *I* cannot manage it, *I* cannot handle it. My weeping or grieving is a way in which I express this interpretation of my impotence through a self-relinquishment whereby I permit myself to collapse into the automatic operations of the body. Grieving is the insightful response to my powerlessness facing death and the inability to integrate death into the whole of life and the basic fragility of our being. Sobbing and weeping are both not merely bodily reactions "triggered" by external circumstances but expressions of interpretations of situations in life that interrupt our everyday orientation in the world where we can manage things, deal with problems, etc. When we sob or weep, in contrast to the more typical emotive stance toward the world with which we can deal, we stand helplessly before a great "I know not what" where our ready categories do not help us and where the world has the gaping hole of her disappearance forever.[35] Grieving and weeping reveal the deep contingency and vulnerability which pervades our ipseity and therefore bring to light a deep stratum of the ontological structure of I myself in the world with others.

The undeniable wisdom of the Stoics, conservationists, and deep ecologists give us only part of the story; and they are not totally convincing because they too cannot handle death's secret. The evidence brought to light by the transcendental phenomenological and Vedanta positions offers a kind of uneasy comfort because they too are not easily integrated into our obligation to "save the appearances" of the second- and third-person display of the world. The theological-religious doctrines and myths similarly tend, in so far as they present an afterlife as more of the same and as an easy assurance, to be inappropriate and not commensurate with the questions that death generates for us. It is not merely that they err in proposing that it is easy to imagine one's immortality (just as people err in proposing that it is easy to imagine one's mortality), as if there were no obstacles to imagining a life pervaded by the seeming required negations of the body as we know it, or of perhaps a life bereft of time and space, of nature, of the social world, etc. (cf. Book 1, Chapter VII). But they appear, in certain presentations, to render banal the deep mystery or question mark with which death confronts us with.

The difficulty with the answers provided by the received traditions is that they often neglect the fact that our experience of the death of our loved ones not only unsettles us but we do not know what questions to ask and what the answers would look like that would adequately answer the questions. (Here we may think of Kant's insistence on the radical difference between our phenomenal and noumenal existence, by which he meant not only participating in the divine archetypal knowledge of the things in themselves, but also the radical transformation of our cognitive state and ability.)

Great saints and heroes have offered their lives and continue to offer themselves as martyrs because of answers that their traditions have provided them with. But these answers are at best expressed in analogous terms that serve only as pointers. If, e.g., "heaven" or "paradise" appear to the believers through intentions that imaginatively fill in what is regarded as absent or deficient in the quest for happiness in this life, those for whom death remains an unfathomable secret may well sense a kind of blasphemy resembling that which monotheists experience in the face of idols or Kantians experience when moral agency gets described in such a way that obligation is subordinated to sensible rewards. Such a filling in through a faith-filled imagination of the absence that death confronts us with might well seem to desecrate death's relation to life.

Further, martyrdom, or the willingness to die for the promised happiness of the afterlife in the name of divine commandments, is not the norm for life but emerges out of situations that reduce life to the limit-situations (see below, Chapter III). Here, because the realm of everyday reality which is laced with matters of conditioned importance is cast into upheaval, a decision of unconditioned significance is called for now, e.g., a decision between one's death and absolute bondage and shame for oneself, one's religion, and one's people. The categorical display of life that would propose that this reduction (of life to limit-situations) is an adequate interpretation of all of life must be by necessity a simplification of the full richness of normal life. If taken as something other than a simplification it is a distortion. (Some forms of monasticism make a similar reduction.) This does not mean that martyrdom or dying for a principle or ideal is reprehensible and that, e.g., participating in the heroic struggle to rid one's country of a hateful oppressive genocidal occupation is to be condemned. It is only that the limit-situation's proper function is to inform and shed light on all the other situations; a distortion occurs when the limit situation reduces all situations and all of life to itself and denies their relevance. Although we may live in an era when even generations of us are involved in a mortal struggle for basic necessities as well as principles, the temptation to see all of life as facing the limit-situations, as in warfare, distorts life because it, of necessity, defers peace to the afterlife. Perhaps we can say that one of the benefits of the democratic ideal is that it enables the limit-situations not to define life and that it permits the acknowledgement that although peace, as something positive (and not the mere absence of war) and as inseparable from social justice, may well be a regulative ideal, and therefore it requires of the virtuous citizenry the habit of struggle, it still permits one to acknowledge a peaceful kind of political struggle that keeps political life from ever being confused with war. Permitting one's life to be taken because one of one's allegiance to a principle higher than one's own continued living, as in an act of resistance to a murderous occupation force that has overwhelming military strength, is not the ordinary but the extraordinary. If it were the ordinary there would be no living of life and no dealing with the abundant life-affirming situations that life calls forth. Indeed the very notion of a limit-situation would make no sense.

§6. Ghosts, Corpses, and Homer on the Secret of Death

In this section we wish briefly to pause to think about how the theme of ghosts reflects a phenomenology of death. It is of some interest to recall that etymologically the sense of "ghost" was less a third-person reference than something very close to a first-person reference or at least an appresentation of such, i.e., what animated or excited what was before us. That is, "ghost" derives probably from the old English, *gast* or Middle English *goste*, which are kin to the modern German, *Geist*, or "spirit." Of course it came to be associated with "apparitions," shadowy semblances, traces, as in "the ghost of a smile," and haunting memories. These are all connected to its well known sense of disembodied spirits of dead persons. In what follows we wish to think of this ancient theme in relation to death.

The essential sense of distance-taking that the presence of the Other requires of us, i.e., the foundations of the feelings by which we give her space and are respectful and deferential, takes such root in us that even when the Other, through death, is no longer there the essential respect extends for an indefinite period.[36] Thus, e.g., we fulfill promises made after someone has died, or tend to include the revered deceased other's point of view in our position-takings and our forming opinions. How often students hesitate even to criticize views that a deceased revered mentor held! And, of course, this awe extends to the corpse as the way the person *was* present with us. Even though respect properly is founded in an empathic perception of an actual other, we "pay our respects" by an intentional act directed at the corpse which itself is held in awe because of who once besouled it or was present to us in this way. Although there are occasions when one might follow the exhortation to "let the dead bury the dead," for good reasons we regard as disrespectful the failure to bury with solemnity the dead or say goodbye to the recently deceased.

Death is unexpected always in the sense that we experience one another as necessarily having futures and the death of a friend is particularly shocking when our futures are bound up with one another. As divorce is disorienting because a couple has built up the habit of seeing the world with one another's eyes – whether the other is present or not – and now each is forced to undo this habit, so death violently, but not necessarily more painfully, eradicates this disposition. All the expected futures that, by force of habit, appear to be awaiting "us" undergo an automatic modalization that may make the present and future appear drab indeed. The habit of seeing something in such a way that one can later relate it to the beloved as part of our life together now is dismantled without *my doing* anything.[37]

The difficulty someone finds in simply mentally terminating the connection with the person's life at the moment of her death may well indicate this person's apperception of the deceased's never having stopped living her life with a necessarily open future and, of course, the remaining still-alive person's living his life with her. Rounding off the span of her life to the point of her death is especially difficult if someone is violently slain. Our apperception of the vector of her life is that it is a straight line that wants to continue, in spite of this punctual termination. This apperception can be a fertile field for the mythic imagination. And it can also be a fertile field for the guilty conscience of the person responsible for her death.

The general incomprehensibility of death, how it is always a kind of surd, the confusion before the fact that the once unique personal presence has disappeared forever from the stage of life, when combined with intense feelings of fear, remorse, regret, guilt, etc., can occasion the creation of substitute forms of presence of the person that are the material of stories that are eerie and terrifying. The ghoulish ghastly menacing specters that seem to haunt, e.g., the places of a person's murder or their former dwellings, can perhaps best be accounted for, by the cautious observer, in terms of imaginative fillings of empty intentions. Such fillings are projecting intentions nurtured by fear and perhaps guilt.

Or, as a member of a culture, I may appropriate the belief that the souls of some of the dead return on specific occasions. The encounter with these ghosts would be the encounter with what or who has experienced the secret of death and perhaps with that which (or who) has the power to destroy one's life and soul. By definition this would be an encounter with what menaces and is to be feared. Also the unbearable pain of guilt, e.g., in regard to my failure of courage, can perhaps have the result that I imaginatively fill in the absence of the other who would not have died had I faced up to my responsibilities. The result could be the projection onto this felt absence that is nurtured by my guilt a vengeful presence of the deceased. Strictly speaking, i.e., for an intersubjective perspective where publicity is the norm, there is nothing "there" to enable the filled intention of someone present in the flesh, in person; but there is present the deceased's absence and perhaps fear because of the survivor's beliefs as well as the pain of the coward's guilt.

Thus the intention of what is absent, as nurtured by one's fear or guilt, is such as to render the absence of the deceased monstrously palpable. We say of such experiences that they can "make my flesh crawl" or cause the hackles on one's back to rise, or they can render one paralyzed with horror. Such reactions reveal the terror of that which threatens us ultimately and can invade our secure personal vaults and spaces. That our flesh can crawl or paralyzing horror beset us from within "the marrow of our bones" indicates the conviction that our selves "at bottom" are not absolutely at our disposal and that the threat is not only from without but also from within our ownmostness. (Cf. the description of grieving earlier.) Thus the experiences of the eerie or uncanny can indicate the sense of my basic contingency where my facticity and contingency is sensed or where I may fail to "show up to myself" or where I may fail to be the one I must be if I am to be able to live with myself.

The sense of the vector of the lived life of the person beyond the present into the future, the apperception by us of him that he does not conceive of himself as dying or about to disappear from the world – perhaps because of his beliefs in his invulnerability or because when he died "he never knew what hit him" – may have supplied some motivation to the pre-Homeric Greek religious belief in a kind of continuity between life and death. In this view death does not mean absolute disappearance, vanishing, and absence; it does not mean an interruption of the continuity of life. Rather even though it was manifestly evident that the deceased was no longer "there" besouling the corpse, there was the *overbelief*[58] that he had departed to another realm. From the third-person point of view, his desires and will are as vanished as his ongoing agency of realizing what he desires and wills. Yet those who remain behind can very well "recognize," i.e., through a memorial appresentation of the deceased person's (first-person) desire and willfulness, that the deceased did not ever give up his willed projects, plans, and desires. In this sense there is a recognition that his will and desires did not die when he died. Such an appresentation would support this sense of continuity between life and death. Finally, the habitualities of those who lived with the deceased, the patterns of living that might have centered around this perhaps fearsome now deceased authority, themselves would continue in spite of his death. He may be absent but we are still set in motion toward realizing his will. Thus Patroclos' death was followed with a ritual funeral pyre where not only sheep and cows, horses and dogs, but also twelve youth were slain and incinerated with him.[39] Thereby, in performing this ritual, there is indicated from the standpoint of the living the continuity between the living and the dead. Likewise there is indicated an apperception that the deceased experiences a continuity between his life among the living and his post-mortem existence.

The function of the sacrifice is to honor the continued powerful presence of the deceased. In death the dead do not completely depart. They do not absolutely vanish for the ancient Greeks, especially the pre-Homeric Greeks. A further motivation for honoring the deceased is that they "hear" the pleas of the living and protect them with their uncanny power. Thus the practice of honoring the dead is bolstered by the belief that if one does not honor the dead and pay respects at their burial site, then bad luck and grisly dangers might well ensue. Thus the deceased still maintain a kind of link with the realm of the living.

Further, even though there is often a pervasive sense of the dead returning to the creative forces of life, to the womb of Gaia, who with her creative abundance overwhelms the power of death,[40] nevertheless, in this early Greek perception, although bereft of a formal concept of the person, the individuality of the deceased is preserved in a shadowy manner. In other words: although there is a conservation optic in play, nevertheless it does not bleach out absolutely the experience of the distinctive individuals, who continue in a shadowy form after death.

This sense of individual extends even to the dark, shadowy forces of the netherworld. Hades is the Lord of the realm of the dead. He is portrayed as having dark majesty that causes chills to the one beholding him. He is the strong one, the unconquerable, the powerful keeper of the gate, who with his many-headed and fiercely growling dog keeps watch there below.[41] Although Lord Hades has properties and functions that could be filled by anyone, one senses throughout the descriptions a dark inscrutable unique ipseity and will that underlies these properties. The same might perhaps be said for the figure of Satan or Lucifer.

A function of incineration was to insure that the dead not tarry around the place of the living from which they departed. Whereas burial meant that the bodies, and perhaps the souls that departed from them, would be present until they decomposed, burning the bodies hastened the departure to the realm of the dead. But there are variations on this theme. For example, the connection between the deceased person and her body is so strong that even if there is a belief in the continuation of the person after death, i.e., that she is departed to the realm of the dead or that she is launched on her journey to this distant realm, the act of caring for the body *now*, even the preserving of it, may be another way of insuring that the person safely reaches the other side, and does not come back to haunt the living here.

In so far as there is a strong belief in the continuity between the living and the dead, the realm of the dead may well be believed to be similar to the realm of the living. On the other hand, if death is taken to be something of a breach with the living, then the afterlife loses its resemblance to life. W.F. Otto believes that Homer introduced a novel insight when he portrayed a chasm between the living and the dead. The tension between the pre-Homeric and Homeric understanding is with us to this day in the popular attitudes toward the dead. For example, some Hollywood comedies present the ghosts as deceased who are indistinguishable from the living except for being invisible to most people; in the horror movies those from the "other side" tend to be continuous only with the deranged forms or nightmares of the living. For Homer the basic distinction to be made was between what is and what has been, between being and having been. This is not to say that Homer could offer a phenomenology in the manner of Jankélévitch for whom death bespeaks absolute discontinuity, an absolute cessation, an absolute disappearance, an absolute annihilation, i.e., an account that we ourselves have proposed in our description of the third- and second-person experiences. Nor is Homer everywhere consistent. Nevertheless after Homer there is a radical difference introduced between the realm of the living and that of the dead.

A scene that brings this home is Odysseus' frightful encounter with his mother in the realm of the shadows.[42] There we meet her as bereft of consciousness, zombie-like until she partakes of the blood offering (see below). The deceased here seem to be portrayed as without first-person awareness and are present to us and to others who meet them only as having been; they have no present or future until they drink the blood.[43] Further, they are not only cut off from the present and the future, and therefore the land of the living, but their mode of being is likened to that of a shadow, breath, or schema. Dido on her deathbed, as portrayed by Virgil who is dependent on Homer, says: "I am at the end of my life. I have finished the course that was allotted to me. Now my great shadow flees from life's wild game to the peace of the grave."[44] Departed souls are a flimsy, insubstantial, faded image of what they once were. When they are able to make their presence felt among the living, they no longer have the power they had previously. Homer names and shows deference to all the powers of the dark deep realm of death, but the "holy ground that is their home, has lost all of its monstrousness."[45]

The encounter with the dead by the living reveals that they are drained of the vital sap that flows through the living. The dead are bloodless shadows bereft of consciousness and genuine personality. And if they are given blood offerings that replenish them, it is only for a very short time that they have this vitality. Their sudden appearance into the lives of the living and their capacity to be other than zombie-like hangs on this blood offering. This faintly resembles how we moderns recover the presence of the deceased in our lives by way of a sudden, perhaps startling, recollection. (One of Odysseus's former companions, Elpenor, asks that he be remembered and properly buried. This seems as important as drinking the blood offering for his present state of soul.[46]) Whereas up until this moment they were consigned to the cold anonymity of oblivion, now they come forth to us with a vitality that makes us wonder how we could have forgotten them. Our recollections which quicken the presence of those who have been utterly forgotten thus resemble the blood offering that is itself the source of the life-blood by which the shades are nurtured back into life, only, in the blinking of the eye, to fall back into the murky dark, when we no longer are mindful of them. Thus they return to the underworld where they, without consciousness, wander through an eternal night. (Husserl's analogy with how past experiences "slumber" in an undifferentiated horizonal mass of retentions, which he calls metaphorically "death," until awakened by the appropriate present association is apt here.)

In Walter Otto's interpretation of Homer, the dead are not capable of an agency on their own in the land of the living but rather their eternal Gestalt is that of having been and what agency they have is only through the life-giving blood (homologous to the recollection) of the living. Upon Odysseus greeting the shade of Achilles with, "We honored you as we did the gods... No man has ever been more blessed than you, and now even in this place you have great authority over the dead," Achilles tells Odysseus: "Never try to console me for dying. I would rather follow the plow as thrall to another man, one with no land allotted to him and not much to live on, than be king over all the perished dead."[47] For the Homeric hero, and this is why Achilles' choice of death is so extraordinary, death "means that life in the light of the sun is over and that with it, everything of value ends."[48]

Rilke, however, reminds us that Homer's view of the dead as vampire-like, requiring to be quickened by the strength of our blood sacrifices and our memory, hardly tells the whole story. Indeed, Homer too appreciates that the memory of the dead can quicken us, the living. The recollection of the departed loved one can strengthen the living and make us appear as if we were the ones who were dead and in need of the departed's life-sap. The resurrected presence of the deceased not only brings before us exemplars of life, but our being mindful of death enables us to clear from our lives what distracts from the essential and enables us to be, if only for the moment, our better selves. Of course, such a resurrection of the dead still depends upon the life-giving act of our recollection. Let us listen to Rilke:

> When, though, you went, there broke upon this scene
> A ribbon of reality
> In the crack through which you disappeared; green
> Of really green, real sunshine, real woods.
> We go on playing our parts. Saying tremulously what was
> Hard to learn, gesturing now and then;
> But your existence and the part you played,
> Now withdrawn from the play we are in,
> Sometimes comes upon us, like an insight sinking in,
> A knowing of that reality,
> So that for a while we are captivated
> And play our part in life, not thinking of applause.[49]

Death, like many phenomena with which religion has to do, appears charged with thick "overbeliefs," i.e., acts of making sense that need to be unpacked or dismantled so that we can distinguish between what appears and the rich interpretation which empowers, but can also obscure, the display proper to the matter at hand. This is not to hold a "myth of the given," i.e., to state that reality consists in raw impressions that we first passively receive and *then* overlay with our interpretations. Rather it is to say that the life-world, although already interpreted, itself has layers of interpretation, overbeliefs, that can be brought to light. Our language says "she is gone," "she has passed on," etc. And yet what we see is the body of the deceased. The use of the past participle of "to go" or any verb suggesting travel is an overbelief. We experience the uncanny absence, disappearance, discontinuity and nihilation, and this demands interpretation. One cannot remain indifferent to the issue of one's own death or that of a beloved. The overbeliefs are not wrong simply because they suffuse what appears with more than what is perceptually evident. Our apperceptive acts always entail an "excess" or surplus in regard to the given. But here in the interpretation of death the surplus of the excess becomes a prominent theme because so much is at stake. Further the excessiveness comes to light not only because of the discrepancies among us (in our overbeliefs, or absence of them) in perceiving death as…, but also because there is no possible filling intention that confirms the apperceiving interpretation or that justifies the refusal to permit any overbelief to hold sway. The wraiths, departed souls, phantoms, spooky drafts, etc., are not clear and strict identities with the former person. They manifest themselves differently and require interpretation. Of course, the excessiveness in, e.g., seeing death as a "passing on" and the implied thesis of a kind of continuity of the dead with the living is motivated, as we have tried to show. But the overbeliefs demand analysis through a dismantling and uncovering of what indeed is "given." When this is accomplished we appreciate them as the interpretative act's exceeding what is given. With excess brought to light its merits may be reflected on in the light of other forms of evidence and other beliefs (other overbeliefs).

Clearly overbeliefs suffuse our modern perception of corpses. Radical dualist doctrines would seem to have the least motivation to show respect to the corpse because the body is easily considered a mere tool or even an encumbrance. Proponents of radical monist materialist doctrines, such as eliminativism, which hold the person to be nothing but the body that now is decomposing, assuming that, in spite of the pressures, they, *mirabile dictu!* are not nihilists, would have reason to reverence the corpse of a loved one, even though the *meaning* of reverence would ultimately have to be profoundly demythologized or put into neurological language. Aristotelianism, we as saw earlier (Book 1, Chapter VIII, §7), also provides reason to reverence the corpse because the body's unique relation to the soul. The modern American preference for the embalmed body in the expensive ornamental casket – not even a sarcophagus wherein the limestone eats the corpse quickly away – in spite of the knowledge that such burials take away scarce space, and that both the embalming and the casket are harmful to the groundwater and the soil, is probably a testimony to a mix of pressures variously distributed among members of the population: The venerable tradition of "paying one's respects" at the showing or the wake, adherence to a kind of literalist understanding of the resurrection, the unreflective everyday confirmation of an unexpressed Aristotelianism, dread of the approximation to annihilation that cremation involves, and the power of the lobby of the funeral industry to shape state and county laws that oblige the survivors to follow the familiar procedures that insure the continuation of this industry.[50]

Notes

1. Stephen Levine, *Who Dies?* (New York: Anchor, 1982), 3.
2. Cf. S. Dasgupta, *Indian Idealism* (Cambridge: Cambridge University Press, 1933), 17–18.
3. See Katha Upanishad, 1, 28–29; *Upanishads*. Trans. Olivelle, 235.
4. Leo Tolstoy, *The Death of Ivan Ilych and Other Stories* (New York: NAL Penguin, 1960), 134.
5. For a Husserlian discussion of how community, and love is a form of community, requires the monadicity of the member I's, see my *The Person and the Common Life*, 255–274.
6. I have benefited in this paragraph from reading Tony Aumann's excellent (2008) IU dissertation, "Kierkegaard and the Need for Indirect Communication." Kierkegaard uses the Nathaniel–David story in *For Self Examination and Judge for Yourself*. Trans. H.V. Hong and E.H. Hong (Princeton, NJ: Princeton University Press, 1876/1990), 38. The discussion by Aumann of self-implicating propositions refers to Bowsma, O.K. "Notes on Kierkegaard's 'the Monstrous Illusion,'" in *Without Proof or Evidence*. Ed. J.L. Craft and R.E. Huswit (Lincoln, NE: University of Nebraska Press, 1984), 74.
7. See the discussion of M.M. Bakhtin, *Art and Answerability*. Ed. M. Holquist and Ed. and Trans. V. Liapunov (Austin, TX: University of Texas, 1990), 105–107.
8. Cf. Robert Nozick, *The Examined Life* (New York: Simon & Schuster, 1989), 23.
9. Tolstoy, *op. cit.*, 130.
10. Jankélévitch, *La Mort*, 8.
11. I am much indebted to Jankélévitch throughout this section and this chapter.
12. Schopenhauer, *The World as Will and Representation*. Vol. II, 486–487.
13. Sigmund Freud, *On Creativity and the Unconscious* (New York: Harper and Row, 1958), 222–223; cited in Raymond Smullyan's excellent *Who Knows? A Study of Religious Consciousness* (Bloomington, IN: Indiana University Press, 2003), 14. Smullyan's sparkling discussion here has encouraged my phenomenological interpretation of these matters.
14. Robert Sokolowski has made a similar point in regard to the difficulty of understanding the "nothing" in the Christian doctrine of creation from nothing. See *God of Faith and Reason* (Washington, DC: The Catholic University Press, 1982/1995), 32.
15. Lavelle, *De l'Âme humaine*, 481.
16. Cited in Rudolf Otto, *Sensus Numinis* (Munich: C.H. Beck'sche Verlagsbuchhandlung, 1932), 276.
17. Lavelle, 482.
18. See *Symposium*, 207a.
19. Thomas Nagel, *The View from Nowhere* (New York and Oxford: Oxford University Press, 1986), 227.
20. On the other hand, Nagel's suspicion "that the proportion of those who think that death is not the end is much higher among partisans of the [thermonuclear] bomb than among its opponents" seems quite correct. For this discussion, see Thomas Nagel, *The View from Nowhere*, 229–231.
21. See again Thomas Nagel's remarkable discussion where he confesses his inability to believe in an afterlife and assumes that "death is nothing, and final." But then Nagel acknowledges his inability to understand those for whom their mortality is not a misfortune. He then proceeds to eloquently wrestle with what this nothingness and finality of death can possibly mean in the first-person. He reaches the paradox that "death is the negation of something [one's first-person experience] the possibility of whose negation seems not to exist in advance" because the self's self-manifestation is not compatible with the sense we have of something being possibly negated, senses drawn from our experience of the world. He further shows that there is no way to accommodate onself to the objective impartial standpoint nor can this standpoint accommodate itself to the "perpetual cataract of catastrophe in which the world comes to an end hundreds of thousands of times a day." From this wonderful poignant analysis the question arises whether Nagel's assumption of death's finality can amount to anything like a philosophical conviction, or whether it is not closer to the agnostic position we urged in Book 1. See *The View From Nowhere*, 224 ff.

22. Smullyan, *op. cit.*, 16–17.
23. Letter to Menoeceus, 124–127, in A.A. Long and D.N. Sedley, *The Hellenistic Philosophers* (Cambridge: Cambridge University Press, 1987), 149–150.
24. See Alfred Schutz' observations in his "Husserl's Importance for the Social Sciences," in *Edmund Husserl: 1859–1959* (The Hague: Nijhoff, 1959), 87.
25. Thomas Prufer, "Notes on Nature," in *Recapitulations* (Washington, DC: Catholic University of America, 1993), 22–25.
26. William Shakespeare, *Troilus and Cressida*, III.ii., ll., 124–125; Riverside edition, 470.
27. See Euripides, *Hippolytus*, in *Greek Tragedies*. Eds. David Grene and Richmond Lattimore (Chicago, IL: University of Chicago Press, 1968), 249–259, lines 375–383. We have italicized the formulation which captures the way we fail to show up for ourselves in David Grene's (1942) translation. Robert Bragg's (1973) translation of this passage runs: "Most people see clearly what is right for them, attracted by it, but we can't make it, we freeze…" See Dennis Duffy's article on a recent translation of some plays of Euripides where he shares with the reader five different translations of this passage. See Toronto's *The Globe and Mail*, Saturday, August 5, 2006, D5 (Book Section).
28. Cf. Paul Tillich, *The Courage to Be* (New Haven, CT: Yale University Press, 1964), 41 ff.
29. Robert Sokolowski, *Introduction to Phenomenology* (Cambridge: Cambridge University Press, 2000), 142. Cf. also my "A Précis of a Husserlian Philosophical Theology," in *Essays in Phenomenological Theology*. Eds. Steven W. Laycock and James G. Hart (Albany: Suny, 1986), 118 ff.
30. R. Descartes, *Meditations*. Trans. Donald A. Cress (Indianapolis, IN: Hackett, 1993), 33.
31. Cf. M.M. Bakhtin, *Art and Answerability*, 107–108. Also J.-P. Sartre, "The Singular Universal," in *Kierkegaard: A Collection of Critical Essays*. Ed. Josiah Thompson (New York: Doubleday/Anchor, 1972), 230 ff.
32. For this meditation on the appearing of death as the apparent annihilation of an essence I am indebted to Jankélévitch, *Philosophie Première*. Chapter IV.
33. Robert Spaemann, *Das unsterbliche Gerücht* (Stuttgart: Klett-Cotta, 2007), 35.
34. Spaemann, ibid., 35 ff. and 50 ff. Spaemann uses the preceding consideration to argue for a divine consciousness or interiority as a "space" in which all events are maintained. The point of departure for us is a transcendental I or agent of manifestation, as the "transcendental pre-fix" for all tense logic, all display of the modes of time. But in as much as we have also claimed that the transcendental I is finite and contingent, even if extended unto an endless transcendental intersubjectivity, Spaemann's conclusion regarding the divine consciousness holds for our position also. We approach this theological perspective in Chapters VI and VII.
35. See Helmuth Plessner, *Lachen und Weinen* (Munich: Sammlung Dalp/Leo Lehnen Verlag, 1950), 185–211.
36. Cf. J.N. Findlay, *Values and Intentions* (London: George Allen & Unwin, 1961), 310.
37. Cf. the phenomenon of the retroactive modalization to which Husserl calls attention in *Husserliana* XI, 30–31 and 41–42.
38. Every act of thoughtful perception involves a giving of meaning that exceeds what, strictly speaking, is "given." The "overbelief" is the excess of meaning bestowed upon data by religious people in the project of interpreting the data. Of course, the data or "given" are never merely atom-like sensa. As a rule religious people draw on their religious beliefs, the sense and referents of which exceed what is constitutive of the perceptual horizon of their experience. Cf. William James, *The Varieties of Religious Experience* (New York: Penguin, 1982), 513 ff.
39. Walter F. Otto, *Die Götter Griechenlands* (Frankfurt am Main: Gerhard Schulte-Bulmke, 1934), 178. The following paragraphs are much indebted to this work, especially 176–199.
40. Otto, 196.
41. Otto, 177.
42. Homer, *Odyssey*. Trans. Richard Lattimore (New York: Harper Coliphon, 1975) 11, 204 ff.; in Otto, 188.
43. Actually this presentation oversimplifies Homer. While the mother of Odysseus appears without self-awareness, others whom Odysseus meets greet him and speak to him, perhaps

languidly. Nevertheless, prior to their drinking the blood, Homer refers to all the dead as "strengthless heads."
44. Vergil, *Aeneid*, 4, 683; in Otto, 186.
45. Otto, 192.
46. See the Lattimore translation, 170.
47. Homer, *Odyssey*, 11, 487; Lattimore translation, 180; in Otto, 180.
48. See Erich Frank, "Religious Origin of Greek Philosophy," in *Wissen, Wollen, Glauben* (Zürich/Stuttgart: Artemis Verlag, 1955), 72.
49. R.M. Rilke, "Tod-Erfahrung." I have modified, but benefited from, the translation of J.B. Leishman in his edition of R.M. Rilke, *New Poems* (New York: New Directions, 1964), 107.
50. See the discussion by Mark Harris, *Grave Matters: A Journey Through the Modern Funeral Industry to a Natural Way of Burial* (New York: Scribner, 2007).

Chapter II
The Transcendental Attitude
and the Mystery of Death

"How shall we bury you?" "As you please," he answered;
"only you must catch me first and not let me escape you." And
he looked at us with a smile and said, "My friends, I cannot
convince Crito that I am the Socrates who has been conversing
with you and arranging his arguments in order. He thinks that
I am the body which he will presently see as a corpse, and he
asks how he is to bury me."

(Plato, *Phaedo*, 115cd)

§1. The Mystery of Death and Ipseity

We wish to bring to light some senses in which death and ipseity may be said
to confront us with a mystery. Before we do this it is good to see the connection
between a mystery and a secret. In even some modern languages the same word is
used, e.g., in German, *Geheimnis*, for both mystery and secret.

We may initially think of a secret as what gets revealed when someone breaks
her silence regarding a matter she knows and that her interlocutors want to know
but do not know. This is a second- or third-person sense of secret. Of course, the
one keeping the secret has, in the first-person, a sense of her knowing something
that she is hiding from others. Another first-person sense of secret, which we will
study in connection with the notion of vocation, is the sense of one's self that each
has and is the referent of "I" and what each apperceives others to have but which
essentially seems to elude any decisive revelation. (See our later discussion of the
Fichte-Husserl position in Chapter V below.) This first-person sense of a secret
resembles another second- and third-person sense where it is clear that the other has
a secret, but we, the onlookers, do not know what is being hidden; we only know
that there is a hiding of something. There is a revelation *that* there is a secret (in
the case of the other ipseity, an unfathomable depth), but not a revelation of what
is held back or secret.

Death surely does not reveal a secret in the sense that what was hidden is now
disclosed. No one carries the secret of death to the grave if this means she knew it

J.G. Hart, *Who One Is: Existenz and Transcendental Phenomenology,*
© Springer Science + Business Media B.V. 2009

while alive and refused to reveal it. No one knows the secret or answer and no one knows for sure how best to formulate the question. Rilke frequently wrestled with the abyss of meaning as well as ignorance that comes to light when we face death. A translation of part of one such wrestle is the following:

> We know nothing of this going hence
> That does not tell us anything. We have no reason
> To greet with admiration and love or hate
> The death whom that mask-mouth of tragic
> Lament disfigures so incredibly.[1]

"We know nothing of this going hence" points to the awareness of our ignorance in confronting death. This abyssal ignorance as well as the disfiguring of the familiar face into an inscrutable sign places the shadow of possible extinction and nothingness around all our established arrangements and categories. They all are transformed by something like scare-quotes and question marks, even though what precisely the question might be is difficult to formulate. It is "a going hence that does not tell us anything." We are not sure whether, when we contemplate the distorted face of the dead person, which for Rilke appears as a tragic lament, we should love or hate or admire death. Obviously we do not know to whom or what to address our question, because all sources of answers are equally affected by the "question" and the scare-quotes; all are equally ignorant of any knowledge.

In Ingmar Bergmann's *The Seventh Seal*, the knight asks his chess opponent, Death, whether he is about to reveal the secret of death. Death answers coldly that he has no secret. And more decisively and chillingly that he, Death Himself, has nothing to tell.

This unique ignorance in the face of the rug being pulled out from underneath us, so that all our familiar categories are made unstable, can well lead to a distinctive kind dizziness or vertigo that is inseparable from the terror at the abyss of nothingness that gapes before us. And Jaspers and Heidegger have pointed out the strong sense of anxiety that besets us in this regard. This is not a normal anxiety that may surface when, e.g., a source of income is shut down, as when we lose our job. These thinkers, with Freud, call this normal case *fear* because it takes an intentional object. Rather this distinctive anxiety is when we are moved to face the prospect of our annihilation and the realization that there might well be nothing rather than something. Or we are anxious in a general way and cannot say what precisely it is even though it pervades everything in our life. Here that about which we are concerned is not, strictly speaking, any thing.

Perhaps for all religions, everything depends on answering the question posed by death. For the Buddhist, the Buddha and the Path answer the question, but the answers are no less mysterious than the questions that generated it. What precisely it means to exist with the negation of all that keeps us from the universal enlightenment and compassion is not a matter for understanding in any familiar sense. The enlightenment in the first-person is self-realization where the entanglements of desire, discrimination, etc. are surmounted. In Buddhist self-realization, which of course involves a dissolution of distorting senses of self, the illusory character of the annihilation of death in the second- and third-person is evident; but this evidence is available only for the one for whom her discipline has resulted in self-realization or release from self. The nature of the understanding of the enlightenment as incomparable bliss, light, freedom, etc., is not intelligible outside of this first-person experience of it because the concepts used to describe it are precisely drawn from first-person experiences of events within life, not life after death. Frequently this enlightenment coincides with death or a kind of death where the enlightened one can only "reveal" her lights by way of dark analogies.

For the Christian, Jesus is precisely the one who came back from death, but not so much as to reveal its secret but rather to take away its sting because he himself is the resurrected Lord over life and death. Christians typically believe Jesus "descended into Hell," i.e., "like all men, he experienced death and in his soul joined others in the realm of the dead… proclaiming the good news to the spirits imprisoned there."[2] Christians are taught that Jesus "was awakened from the sleep of the dead," and appeared to the disciples and promised victory over death's apparent victory if they let themselves be ruled by the life of the Spirit that exists among them. This "answer" does some justice to the second- and third-person perspective: Jesus died truly; he disappeared from the realm of the living; he was not "asleep" in the proper everyday sense. He then appeared, but in ways that raise as many questions as they answer. The narratives surrounding the resurrection appearances, regardless of one's faith, are fraught with difficulties of understanding and seem to be deliberately elusive regarding the bodiliness and bodily presence of Jesus among his friends.

The transcendental and first-person perspective, however, is not done justice to here as it is in, e.g., Vedanta. We find an approximation when we take "sleep" in the manner of our prior transcendental and Vedantan meditations – and this is how we must understand the realm of the dead if they are to be preached to by Jesus (in his "descent into Hell") while they are "dead." (See 1 *Peter* 3:18–19.) Again, much depends on how we are to understand the use of the term "sleep" for "death" in the mind of St. Paul and the other scripture writers.

Further there is the new promise of the gift of the inconceivably rich eternal life that is a participation in the very life of God. This is more than a revelation that removes the sting of death; it is a revelation of another secret, one as incomprehensible as death and the resurrection appearances that served as the "answer" to the beginning question regarding the inscrutable secret of death. It resembles Jesus' calling forth Lazarus from his death/sleep: it reveals something of the power of Jesus, but Lazarus is still mortal, and a few years later, as far as anyone could see, Lazarus was dead and Jesus was crucified. Jesus' reported resurrection was believed in by his followers, but in itself that report and belief do little to remove the mystery of death.

Again, the revelation or disclosure of a secret has two senses. The first sense is when the person who knows the secret speaks out, brings to light what was hidden. Prior to this the others may or may not have known that she was keeping a secret. The second sense is the revelation that, in fact, she is keeping a secret. We do not know what the secret is but we know, e.g., by her behavior or by what she says, that she is keeping a secret. The revelation is of the fact of the hiddenness and reserve that we do not have access to; it is not a revelation of what the secret is about. It is this latter sense of secret that seems closer to what we meet in death. There is a truth, an insight, a disclosure that is undisclosed; but there is "evident" the withholding of the disclosure.

This recalls Kierkegaard's distinction between an "essential secret" and a merely accidental one that we earlier mentioned (Book 1, Chapter V, §2). The latter secret is one which may be made public and it remains a secret depending on the discretion of the one who holds it. The former, which for Kierkegaard is the proper way for thinking about subjectivity, proximate to what we are calling the "myself," is what by its essence cannot be made public, and this remains true of the one who "holds" the secret, i.e., who is this subjectivity.[3] The knowledge of oneself as a subjectivity is, to use our terms, non-sortal and non-reflective, and any making public or revelation of this secret in terms of property ascription is out of the question. There is a necessary and essential withholding of such a display.

Not only ipseity or the "myself" qualifies for being an essential secret. Death too withholds revealing its sense to us. In a secret such as death, there is no place where we might go where the disclosure might happen. In which case it might be that the secret is not being deliberately withheld, but rather the one seeking presently the revelation is burdened with a condition that makes it impossible that there be a revelation, i.e., she is not capable of grasping it, somewhat analogously to a young child's seeking to know what a transcendental I or an irrational number is. The Western Tradition, e.g., in Aquinas and Kant, requires a total transformation, a *lumen gloriae* or an unveiling of the phenomenal so that the noumenal may assert itself, for a human comprehension of the afterlife. Similarly medieval thinkers like Aquinas speculated on how pure spirits could communicate with one another given the absence or transformation of embodiment, i.e., they raised the possibility of there being a state of affairs where the secret of subjectivity itself might no longer be an essential one.

The disclosure in the *Upanishads* that Atman = Brahman appears to be a clear revelation of the secret of death. One is tempted to say that it resembles the position of Kant in so far as the devotees are to regard death's phenomenal definitive absence not as mysterious but as a form of mistaken perception. But this surely oversimplifies the meaning of the *Upanishads* and its Vedantan interpretation. Atman by definition, e.g., as the "witness consciousness" is not something that can be properly "known" and a fortiori Brahman as the all-encompassing and absolute eludes any grasp. The "revelation" in the third- and second person of the proposition, Atman is Brahman (A = B), is a massive empty intention that can hardly be said to result in any cognitive disclosure. If appreciated as indeed a revelation in the third- or second-person, and not in the first-person revelation or mystical intuition brought about by religious discipline like yoga, it requires assent to an empty intention, like the citizen's assent to the report of the use of depleted uranium weapons in Iraq. This assent may well be a centering position-taking which is motivated by what we will call a gathering act wherein there is a massive pre-propositional passive synthesis of one's life. But its propositional status as the doctrine A = B inadequately explicates this pre-propositional gathering act. But this assent is still to what remains impenetrable darkness; the sense of Brahman and Atman and their ultimate unity are but glimpsed.

Analogously, the revelation of Jesus's resurrection is a revelation of a secret but it is not as if that which was hidden has now been made clear. This is a fortiori true of the revelation of the calling to participate in the divine life. One hears the words, one develops a symbolism and theology of sanctifying grace, the indwelling of the Spirit, participation in the divine life, etc., but as much remains concealed as disclosed because no one has a filled intention of what precisely these terms mean. One's "having faith" means there is a loving assent to them; but that does not of itself bring about filled intentions. And all the symbols and doctrines stand behind the blackness of death which faith is commissioned and invited to penetrate.

This seems true of most religious revelations. This is clearly true in Christianity and perhaps the other "Abrahamic religions" in so far as the mediate target of faith is the teaching of the tradition about the transcendent God. Because faith aims properly at the divine or God as revealing, it assents to the content or dogma on the basis of God revealing. And in as much as the latter too is the pre-eminent "mystery" faith's filled intentions are postponed in regard to both in whom one believes and what is believed. A great work of art, e.g., a Greek or Shakespearian tragedy or a symphony by Beethoven or Mahler, can have the effect of being similarly a disclosure of the mystery of life. Its overwhelming power, its sublimity, like that of a huge storm, is a filled intention in the sense that the listener's total life-intentionality is filled with a sense of importance and depth. This "revelation" is less a disclosure of what was hidden from the listener than a disclosure of the intimated unfathomable depths of life's mystery – and this is the basis for the delight it affords. It is less a filling of an intention in the form of an answer to an explicit question which itself may take the form of hypothetical propositions, but rather it is a disclosure that life has depths that before lied more or less dormant and implicit. Again, the revelation is not an answer to a question and certainly it does not lend itself readily to a propositional display. Rather it is a "raid on the inarticulate" but the result of the raid still is relatively inarticulate and dominated by felt, adumbrated meanings that await further conceptualization, syntax, etc. In this sense the great works of art resemble the sense of filled intentions that religious liturgies can evoke. But in both cases (of art and religion) the filled intentions themselves are filled intentions of what themselves are intimations, hints, symbols, and (if literature is involved) mythic narratives. These fillings of intentions, i.e., the rich intuited given symbols and symbol-rich narratives, serve as the basis for the higher-order empty intentions of the elusive encompassing transcendent "signified." These "fleshly" symbols are present in filled intentions which in their very presence are experienced as embodying the transcendent and absent mystery. As Tillich put it, the being of the symbols participate in that which they signify and the reverence that is due the signified is shown to the signifier.

A difference between the religious and artistic symbolic filled presences is that the religious symbols are intended in an attitude of faith, i.e., an assent to the truth of the symbols and what they symbolize and the transcendent mystery, in some sense, at least for the "Abrahamic religions," a Who, that the symbols mediate. Such an allegiance and assent require that the symbolic presences take on the distinctive, even if "mysterious" form of doctrinal propositions. Assent to the truth of the revelation itself involves syntax and that to which the assent is given itself must have minimal syntax and conceptuality. This assent in its purest form, at least in Christianity, is often without the support of aesthetic delights and emotional consolations. The artistic symbols and performances are essentially intended in emotive-evaluative intentionality. Of course, there may be and often are accompanying the artwork deft propositional explications of the momentary massive feeling of depth and mystery; but the telos is in the delight in this rich felt-meaning not in the, e.g., libretto's truth or the critic's explication. Thus there is no epistemic allegiance to the explication of this rich felt-meaning as is the case with the religious symbolic explication, i.e., it is not necessary to believe in a particular articulation of what the artistic work means. (We return to the topic of *dogma* in Chapter VII.)

Thus the religious symbol has guidelines for the explication of the symbols, i.e., the dogma or true teaching in the form of true propositions regarding the mysteries, however emptily intended, mysterious, and dense they themselves are. In this sense religious revelation is more explicit than art, even though its propositions too remain in the realm of mystery and empty intentions.

A believing assent does not itself amount to a filled intention. This is surely true when one receives a report from someone, delivered in the flesh in the first-person, that this person, the speaker, has reached "the other shore" or ultimate transcendence and unity, Nirvana, Heaven, or Brahman, etc. The report might be that this revelation, which occurred through either an anomalous experience, or a practice, or sudden insight, is something that is accessible to all. But for the listener this remains incomprehensible in the sense that the reported reality contradicts the second- or third-person experience because it appears as if it were merely a competing second- or third-person fact. In such a witness, one's experience of death is denied on the basis of our not having the information the speaker has.

But death as one's own death is not simply one fact in our world like others. Its presence informs our understanding of everything. This is hinted at when Ivan Ilych observed, "It alone is true." The odd thing about the denial of its finality by the speaker's report is that it too is merely one more fact to be digested, but one which purports to have the power to get rid of our "mistaken beliefs" about death.

The speaker bearing witness to her first-person experience of the "other shore" is presented in such a way that it can become mine simply by way of believing her report at the cost of contradicting the absolute darkness of the phenomenon of death as it is present in the first-person as well as second- and third-person. Religious faith very often does this. The price that is paid is a transformation of our essential abyssal ignorance into a form of privileged acquired information provided by an otherworld expert. For example, the Christian belief that Jesus has gone ahead to prepare a place for his followers can be interpreted to mean something quite like one's mother departing early to get the summer cottage ready for the family. If the dissimilarities of the analogy do not profoundly challenge the similarities that the language encourages, if the similarities are authorized to eliminate the abyssal ignorance that is ours in the face of the phenomenon of death, the religious message becomes banal and bereft of depth. When one's belief becomes such that the "sting of death" is lost in favor of the report of mansions awaiting one's occupancy, the very sense of the world as the horizon of our experience is undermined as is our understanding of ourselves. Doubtless such an undermining is cultivated by some religious practice, but at the expense of reducing religious teachings to esoteric information about an unseen world continuous with this one – which information renders the experience of death "merely phenomenal" in the sense that it is to play no ultimate significance in our understandings of our world and ourselves.

The reports of the "near death experiences" also make similar remarkable claims. But they leave us with more questions than answers, however reassuring they might be for those who had them. Strange lights, tunnels, a sense of calm, etc., raise new questions and do not do away with the questions death raises. In short, religious and other beliefs about the meaning of death, to the extent that they aim at eliminating the *mystery* of death, deceive us in regard to what is ineluctable about life and ourselves and perhaps even verge toward destroying the mystery that is basic to religion itself.

In Greek the word, *muo* (μύω), has to do with the closing of the lips and eyes and the *mystes* (μύστης) was one initiated in the sacred cultic mysteries of, e.g., Demeter at Eleusis. Our word "mystery" derives from the Latin *mysterium* that translates the Greek μῡστηριόύ. They are both translated with either "mystery" or "secret." In the Letters of St. Paul we find the theme of secret and mystery commingled. In *Romans* 16:25 we even find the phenomenologically rich formulation: "the revelation/uncovering (*apokalypsin*) of the mystery/secret (*mysteriou*) kept silent (or secret) (*sesigemenou*) for long ages but now manifest (*phanerothentos de nun*)." Here we have a disclosure of a secret kept silent; not even the disclosure of the secret as secret. Rather it is a hiddenness that might never have been revealed, perhaps an essential hiddenness, that could never have been found out by humankind unless an initiative, not in the power of humankind, was undertaken. (This consideration recalls our earlier discussion of the utter contingency of the connection between being and display. Perhaps the ultimate sense of being is absolutely transcendent to display – assuming of course that the ultimate sense of being does not involve self-awareness.) But then, according to Paul, a kind of disclosure occurs. Now the secret is manifest. Is the manifestation a revelation of the undisclosedness or is that which the secret itself reveals now no longer held back but completely out in the open?

It would seem that Paul thinks that the former is the case; similarly we have stated that this is the proper understanding in the case of death, at least in so far as its sting is mitigated, as well as in perhaps the case of a religious revelation. Yet the revelation that there is a secret/mystery does not *eo ipso* mean that we have no further questions, or that the disclosure itself is unmysterious, or that there is a total disclosure. Indeed, in as much as a revelation takes forms pervaded by metaphor, analogy, opacity and determinability to that extent endless interpretations are invited. And in as much as the most basic dogma for the "Abrahamic religions" involves a sense of God which is beyond all worldly categories, all of the other teachings are steeped in mystery. (See below, Chapter VII.) Thus, e.g., the stories of Creation, Passover, atonement, the prophetic references to the promised land, the Messiah, the kingdom of God, the narratives of the Resurrection and Ascension of Jesus, etc. are inexhaustible pointers to inexhaustible horizons of meaning. Here understanding these "revelations" as total disclosures of what before was hidden is a contradiction in terms if they themselves are understood to be mysteries/secrets. Here we may recall Kierkegaard's distinction between essential secrets which cannot be made public and accidental ones which may be made public. Subjectivity or the "myself" may be understood as the prime analogue for the essential secret for the proper sense of mystery, even religious mystery. If this be true then the religious revelation of the secret is always at once an unveiling and a concealing as a matter of necessity, not by reason of any divine parsimoniousness, dissemblance, or coyness.

In death we do not have any unveiling of what is behind the veil; other considerations may lead us to the belief that what we have not only in death but in other religious matters as well as aspects of life is the disclosure that there is a veil. In the third- and second-person we face the absolute disappearance or annihilation of what was before present and perhaps loved and revered. We suggested above at §4 of Chapter I that such an annihilation of an essence may, given the considerations we urge, pose a crisis of meaning. In the first-person, I experience my death as an unthinkable experience and have no clue as to what my disappearance from the world means. The testimony to death's meaning in the second- and third-person is less than decisive because of recalcitrance of the first-person witness to conform to their witness. But this witness is less than decisive also because of the epistemic devastation caused by the huge hole in being and the discontinuity in our synthesis of the perspectives and meaning spaces of the world created for us by the seeming annihilation of an ipseity.

However, this way of putting it veers too much toward the "problematical." Here we may take advantage of Gabriel Marcel's famous distinction between "problem" and "mystery."[4] A problem is what is thrown across (*pro-ballein*) our path on life's journey. As a problem it is of the purely cognitive order and we face the task of knowing something that we are presently ignorant of, or making a distinction where before there was a confusion, or of gaining an insight into what before lacked a unifying pattern, or seeing *a* which we know is connected to *c* which we need to know through *b* which we also know, etc. It may be of a purely theoretical nature, and in this sense it resembles a "puzzle" that we can solve or a conundrum that we can eventually think our way through, an unknown that we can deduce from the knowns, an absence we can infer from what is present. But also the problem may be tied to our agency and the cognitive achievement of resolution might stem from the requirements of agency. For example, it might be the case that the proper conceptual issue will not emerge until we begin to act and move in the general direction we need to go. Or, something appears to be a hindrance to our immediate plans and to overcome this we have to think and act in order to move beyond the obstacle. In this sense the hindrance appeals to the sense of ourselves as having the capacity to act and eventually transform the world's real possibilities.

In this latter aspect, it is an obstacle that we can remove, a knot we can untie, an obstruction that can be dismantled, a nuisance from which we can walk away or walk around, a demand that we can temporize, etc.

A problem is what we have to deal with in the sense that it can hold our attention; but, on the other hand, life still will go on more or less if we do not deal with it. It is not at the defining center of our lives but it is something that either is already on the periphery or something that can be marginalized. At this point the contrast with "mystery" begins to emerge. Let us initally use death as our prime analogue. Death is clearly a professional problem for the medical scientist, neural scientist, sociologist, politician, military officer, etc.; for the rest of us who have everyday plans it obviously likewise poses problems but not of a professional nature. All of us develop cognitive and practical strategies in order to solve or avoid it, or at least "factor it in." When I *realize* that what is at issue is *my death*, marginalization or avoidance is essentially out of place. It is not just one consideration or situation among others. I am always taken up with something within the flux of my stream of consciousness, just as I am always in a situation. And as I can turn my attention from one theme to another, so I can move from one situation to another. But with the "limit-situation" (see below for our appropriation of this notion of Karl Jaspers) of death I am not in one situation among many. Rather my death is not really a situation, as what I can move in and out of, any more than, at the moment of realization, it is a theme that I can focus on as one among many. Both for ordinary reflective experience as well as those of extraordinary "realization," death is a defining condition and informs all my situations; I have never left or entered this "situation." And, in an odd respect, I have never not known this "situation." Yet prior to the emergence of the reality, perhaps because of the imminence, of "my death," this limit-situation never limited in the sense of constricted and forced my facing it. My death now appears as my inescapable destiny that I alone can deal with, not in the sense of a problem that can be solved or eliminated, but in the sense that I *must* face it, I must face it alone, and I must take up a position toward it. It is not something out of which I can buy my way, pay for a stand-in, have an alibi, walk away from, circumvent, or supercede by taking another route. Further all themes ultimately may be shown to have death as a horizon, even if by way of its repression. Happiness, birth, life, success, failure, desire, anxiety, etc., are all incomplete themes if one's being-towards-death and the ultimate danger and facticity of I myself are not addressed. Even ideal objects like those of logic and mathematics ultimately derive their ideal, all-temporal or eternal sense from how we understand the contingency and death of the agent of manifestation. (Cf. our discussion of Spaemann's thesis that the reality of Now is that it of necessity will have been. What phenomenology calls ideal trans-temporal objects have their sense precisely as a negation of their ever being Now in this sense.)

What we are calling "mystery" is never bereft of intellectual or cognitive interest. It still correlates with an attitude of inquiry or wonder, if not necessarily a specific question or even direction of query. Further the "mystery" is not commensurate with the purely cognitive interest where a precinct or a specific field of meaning or a conceptual field is delineated. Rather it is encompassing in its scope and it puts everything in its appropriate light – without thereby resolving our questions. The mystery precisely is what we do not understand and in confronting it we are stopped in our motion forward. What is at stake is so momentous that we can well be unsettled when meeting it: If it is indeed capable of shedding light on everything, including myself, it is not completely clear that I am strong enough to bear it. Do I really want to hear the truth of the matter? And yet, of course, one does, at least at some level. And that is why it is not only dreadful but inviting and fascinating. Ultimately we will say the "mystery" is of necessity correlated with what we will call "Existenz," i.e., the very core of the I or self in so far as what is of unconditional importance is at stake.

Obviously the mystery has to do not with something of which I am absolutely ignorant. Just as anything about which I can ask a question or have a query, I emptily intend with a more or less rich conceptual fleshing out of a question. In this respect I know what I am seeking and am invited to pursue the matter on the basis of what I know and what is given. But the mystery, like the secret, is essentially withdrawn. And like the regulative idea the mystery is asymptotic: The more I might be persuaded I am drawing near, the more it is evident that I am still endlessly remote from the sought-for revelation. I can perhaps think I have finally a grasp on the matter, but this typically turns out to be that I have a handle on what turns out to open up into even greater abysses. The "answer" is but a revelation of an even darker abyss and depth of incomprehension.

(This claim for symmetry with the regulative idea has numerous implicit theological assumptions which we will spell out in the final chapter. Here suffice it to say that it does not presume to legislate what a divine revelation must be. That is, no one is in a position to rule out a kind of *lumen gloriae* where all there is to know and love is given all at once. But such a gracious "light of glory" does not make the creature's power of apprehension adequate to the divine essence and there is still the infinite distance between God and the creature. Further the claim aims at the typical religious person who, in the course of her life, admits to having "insights" but then comes to realize that these are just the beginning.)

Thus what is at stake clearly is not merely cognitive because it has to do with what is supremely and unconditionally *important*. And it is important not only as what bears on me uniquely and presumably analogously for everyone else, but it has a measure of urgency in the ancient sense of being the *unum necessarium*, i.e., that which marginalizes or renders insignificant all other issues. Thus it is *the* question, so to speak, even if I cannot formulate it precisely. The sought-for answer is *the key* even if I am not in a position to say what exactly it is the key to.

Rudolf Otto famously linked mystery to the holy. Many, if not each, on occasion have experienced a massively thick rich phenomenon, as in the presence of someone with whom one is in love, or in the presence of someone's death, or during an experience of nature's sublimity, or in witnessing a great political event, or in beholding a great work of art or a religious ceremony, or, of course, in an unusual experience, whether religious or not, of, e.g., gratitude. In these moments there is present a unique, "saturated" intentional "object." Undeniably something is in some way present, something is given in some respect. The magnitude of significance of what is given in experience is such that it far outstrips our categorial and horizontal framing capacity. But in the attempt to articulate what it is, we face the difficulty that not only is there *present* or given a sense of absence that outweighs and even defies what our articulation makes present. Further, if we tried to single out its properties for ourselves upon reflection or to someone who was absent we would find great difficulties.

Nevertheless this X could be evoked by analogous, related, even though inadequate parallels. What is intriguing about such a phenomenon that does not admit of a clear analysis into genus and specific difference is that, for the person who has experienced it, there is no temptation to say, "After all, because I cannot assign any properties to it, it must have been a mere nothing. An object with no or only negative determinations is not anything at all, and therefore it is nothing of importance." Just the opposite, of course, is the case. Consider the famous biblical passage: "Eye hath not seen, nor ear heard, neither have entered into the heart of man, the things which God hath prepared for them that love him." For the believer, and perhaps for others, hearing the list of negations does not leave him with zero or nothingness. Indeed the intentionality that is evoked by the passage is such that the mind does not dwell on the negatives as privations or subtractions from the fullness of being but rather uses these negations as a "way of eminence" and transcending. As a result there is an undeniable positivity in the givenness which surpasses any specific filling of an intentional act. And this givenness is independent of the incapacity to assign properties. It is independent of the negation of properties and the recognition of the inappropriateness of the ascription of properties.[5] Similarly the peculiar transcendence of the phenomenon is such that it is regulative and pervasive and this is quite the opposite of a license to think or react as we please. Like a felt-meaning of what we want to say at the beginning of a sentence, simply any word will not do, even if, at a certain stage we only can say, *Je ne sais quoi*.

As we saw in Book 1 this revelation of what is beyond the properties that suffuse it is most properly the work of love. In important texts in the Christian mystical tradition, love is assigned an essential part in the presencing of "mystery." There it is affirmed that "God" is precisely what we most love and want most to love but what we cannot think or comprehend. But, e.g., the anonymous author of *The Cloud of Unknowing* states his (or her) preference to abandon all that he (or she) can *know* and chooses to love him whom he cannot know or, as another translation has it: "I would leave all those things of which I can think, and choose for my love that thing of which I cannot think." And the explanation is offered that God may be loved but not thought or known. God may be held by means of love but not by means of thought. The real work of the contemplative is to let love set aside even the wonderful properties of God's majesty and kindness and have this love pierce the darkness.[6]

Again, we earlier (in Book 1, Chapter IV, §§14 ff.) saw an analogous role for love in regard to the finite Other. And most of Book 1 argues for a pre-intentional non-ascriptive presencing of the "myself" as non-sortal; this too, of course, is the most basic analogy. In both cases, we have a case for "mystery" as what is presenced beyond all properties. But in the cases of the "myself" and the beloved Other we make present what is beyond the pervasive properties but which is "properly" embodied and propertied; and in the other case faith-filled love makes present or is able to "hold" or pierce through to God who properly is in Godself beyond all properties. In the great works of art there is an analogous evocation of a transcendent exceeding density and depth of meaning the display of which in propositions likewise is inadequate to the excess.

And one's own death too confronts us as a mystery, as "I know not what," bereft of properties. It too is not anything we may encounter. It is not an event or a property of a person or ipseity for the obvious reason that we meet an absolute absence of the ipseity. Of course it is a third-personal event of the body which is the perduring substrate of the biological event of death; but this substrate is not the ipseity which has apparently been annihilated. And how does that which itself is bereft of properties, i.e., the unique essence which we have argued is the substance of the person, enjoy the property of "death?" We may say that death has the tautological property of "nihilability" or "able to annihilateness"? But how does that which is not anything, and which has the property to annihilate what is of necessity without properties, itself be something with a property? It scarcely needs mentioning that thinking of death as in some sense a substance with properties, as in the figures of the Great Reaper, misleads.

Yet what we have before us with the phenomenon of death is not merely a *nihil negativum*, a dismissible negligible "nothing" or irrelevancy. It, of course, is not something we typically are moved to penetrate with love, but it nevertheless confronts us with an unfathomable significance in its blackness which we very much would like to penetrate by whatever means, certainly not excluding the possibility of love. (Cf. the conclusion to Tolstoy's *The Death of Ivan Ilych*.) The Other, the "myself," and one's death thus have affinity with the religious mystery as described by Otto and the contemplative tradition as well as with the saturated givenness of such phenomena as the sublimity of nature as layed out by Kant and Marion. But death has the special function in such "mysteries" because it is both the gateway and the veil which stands between us and them. All of them are shadowed by it in the sense that if it is as impenetrably dark as it seems they too lose their glory; but in so far as they demand to be articulated as precisely penetrating death, having power over it, and removing its sting they are enriched by the blackness of death. Death provides them with an unapproachable otherness and separates them from what is banal and cheap.

Jankélévitch observes how there is a deep need to regard all mysteries as secrets. That is, there is the treacherous tendency to reduce mysteries to a knowledge comparable to scientific unraveling. Oftentimes such a science is in search of a formula or a code which "unlocks the mysteries of life." This is so because, if mystery is a secret, we know that what is hidden will come forth eventually. The guardians of secrets, the weavers of "mystery stories," constantly place obstacles in the way, incessantly lay down new demands as a condition for new revelations that point to "what will make sense of everything." Intellectual excitement is always about the unraveling of new layers of secrets. For science there will always be new revelations; there will always be the vertigo of new, ever more intricate, increasingly tiny keys to the universe or ever new insights that will tie everything together.

For the intellectual eros there is a motion toward complexity while striving at the same time to attain the encompassing "Ah Hah" or simple insight that brings it all together. Even when this is realized, it itself becomes a piece of an ever larger whole, and takes on the sense of the surface of the depth of endless secrets still to be plumbed, deciphered, and interpreted.

This unraveling of the depths of being is *allegorical* in the sense that one mean-ingful thing points to another, just like the deep-sea diver may go to ever further depths. In contrast, the mysteries of ipseity and one's death are not "allegorical," i.e., requiring the *other* level of meaning that the last revelation of secrets pointed to. Rather these mysteries are but "tautegorical": Each does not signify anything other than itself. It is mysterious not because it is a pointer to something else, but rather by its very presence itself and by the fact that it exists. The one for whom the "mysteries" of life are "allegorical," i.e., enigmas, resembles the sorcerer who has forgotten the password or the banker who has forgotten the combination to the vault's lock. He "knows" the answer to the riddle, but right now it doesn't seem to work or he can't gain access to it.

According to Jankélévitch, true mystery, in contrast, as in the instance of one's ipseity or one's death, is not an X that is only unknown for the time being. It is not the tempting conundrum which continuously piques our curiosity and awakens our desire to "get at the bottom of it." It is not the *arcana* of a secret society where only the central authorities and initiates know the deepest secrets. Rather, it is unknown because it is intrinsically unknowable. It is a mystery in itself, esoteric and unknowable for all of us. Thus instead of merely piquing our curiosity it is something calling for deep respect and reverence, if not adoration.[7]

Yet there is a difficulty in holding that the mystery is *absolutely* unknowable in so far as it presumes to hold that the perspective of mortals is absolute and abso-lutely insurmountable for mortals. Further, this position stands in tension with our comparison to the regulative idea. What follows is an attempt to reach an agree-ment between the two interpretations. We must presume the eros to understand and that the proper fulfillment of this eros is in knowing wherein there is syntax, concepts and property ascription. In the case of the tautegorical mystery this eros is brought to a halt with the insight that here we have something else. The allegori-cal sense of mystery, i.e., of moving deeper into something other than the original given, *pace* Jankélévitch, at least in the area of science and the pursuit of regulative ideas, is not a move into what is simply other and different but it is always also an uncovering of what is the same. Thus it is always "nature" or the "cosmos." Further, in the pursuit of what surfaces as a regulative idea there must surface a realization of the asymptotic character of the pursuit: One might seem with certain advances to get to the bottom of the matter, but, upon deeper reflection there is the insight that of necessity one is still infinitely removed from the goal. Both the ones involved in a tautegorical and allegorical mysteries begin with the quest, at least in a general sense, to understand. But in so far as the allegorical quest is indeed of a regulative idea it too finds that it is confronted with what is not comprehensible ultimately. The encounter with mystery, even the purely tautegorical kind, would seem to share with the allegorical at least the semblance of the secret in so far as there was a disclosure of what was absent. But presumably the tautegorical quest eventually sees, if not always at the beginning, that what is to be known *essentially* eludes being grasped. Because it begins with what is present as hiding what is essential, it seeks to read in what is present a meaning commensurate with what is absent. The allegorical quest discovers often enough properties of X, whereas the tautegorical grasps from the start that the discoveries are at best ciphers of what transcends the properties.

This recalls our appropriation (in Book 1, Chapter IV, §17; see also below Chapter VII, *passim*) of Barry Miller's distinction between, on the one hand, the ideal limit which resembles the Kantian infinite regulative ideal that, in turn, occasions an "endless task," what Miller calls the "limit simpliciter," and, on the other hand, the "limit concept" which is, in a special sense the telos of the ideal limit, yet of a completely different order than what orders the endless task. We may think of coming to know a person, especially through love, as an increasing revelation of the person's properties; but the ipseity is beyond the accumulation of properties as the circle is beyond the infinite task of conceiving an infinite-sided polygon and as the point is beyond the infinitely ever smaller divided line. The question we face with Jankélévitch's tautegorical mystery is whether the revelations or secrets may be said to possibly belong to the ordered series analogous to the way the quest for the every greater-sided polygon or ever shorter line belongs to an ordered series. In following Miller we may say that the ordered series aims at the "limit concept" that is not of the same order as the members of the series. That at which they aim is different in kind or heterogeneous to the ordered series even though it is precisely that at which the ordered series heads and what gives it its direction. This is the relation the point has to the series of ever shorter lines or the circle has to the ever more sided polygon.

Whereas this appropriation of Miller's schema sheds some light on the "mystery" of ipseity as being an X present in love but as essentially beyond the cherished personal properties, does it shed light on the mystery of death? (We postpone its applicability to the matter of the mystery of "God" until Chapter VII.) Death confronts us with the X of an ipseity's apparent annihilation (in the second- and third-person). It is utterly inaccessible to us in the first-person. Yet the corpse and the transition from a lived-body to a corpse are present to us. And we may say that the medical and neurological sciences help us to appreciate ever more the biology and physiology of death. The social sciences, psychology, anthropology, and religious studies help us to see it as an intersubjective and deep subjective phenomenon. And in one's own religious and existential encounters with it we learn to use innumerable metaphors and beliefs to deal with its unparalleled challenge. Yet it is doubtful that this knowledge and shifting beliefs form an ordered series pointing precisely to a regulative idea whose telos is an incommensurate limit concept. Nevertheless the Miller's schema is not totally useless here. This is chiefly because it does not reduce the mystery to the allegorical outing of a secret. But again perhaps the mystery of death is not to be thought of as if death were "in itself" something substantial. Its mystery is tied to the mystery of ipseity. It raises self-involving questions for those who witness the effect of death and for those who imagine their own death there seems to be no matter which is more self-involving. And for religious persons its mystery is tied to the quest for the significance of one's personal journey through life as well as to "God," "Transcendence," etc. The divine is precisely that for which death has no power; and death is precisely that which concentrates the question of ipseity's contingency, frailty, and responsibility for itself.

In spite of the dissymmetry it is worthwhile to explore the symmetry between the mystery of death and of ipseity. "Mystery" we have urged, following Marcel, cannot be reduced to an unresolved "problem" of a merely epistemic or cognitive nature. Yet, it would seem that it is only because of an epistemic-cognitive context of searching for answers that we come upon the peculiar "problems" that we call "mysteries." Ancient philosophy claimed for itself a beginning in wonder or amazement. Here one is stopped from being pulled by the exigencies of life's practical demands and moved to attend to something that draws attention to itself and for itself quite apart from how it fit into the realm of praxis. Furthermore, one is not merely stunned and fascinated, but the spirit of inquiry or the cognitive eros is in play. The interrogations regarding why, how, whether, when, etc. open the mind to intimations of answers, but these remain outstanding and not yet given in intentions of what is present. But the thrill of wonder is found precisely in the moment leading to the intimation when the intention was yet unfilled; there was delight in the intimation and even in an accompanying subordinate pleasure in the questioning and inquiring attitude.

Mystery moves beyond this thrill of wonder in so far as the inquirer has come to a stop in the anticipation of a filling an intention because of the realization that what one has to do with eludes the filling of an intention – even though the matter still intrigues and thus is emptily intended. Think of Hobbes' observation, seconded by Jaspers, that the most amazing of appearings is that of appearing itself (cf. Book 1, Chapter I, §1). How could we, as it were, bring to a stop this wonder with an "explanation" that would get behind and not presuppose appearing? Yet properly Hobbes' amazement here does not quite cross the threshold of the problematic in so far as this matter may appear as a kind of mere philosophical conundrum. Although appearing pervades all properly philosophical problems, Marcel rightly emphasizes that mystery has to do with what is more than merely cognitive and theoretical problems. It has to do with what is a matter of supreme importance because its "subject matter" has a way of encroaching on the destiny of the inquirer, a destiny with which the person in her innermost center has to do. Given the position we have put forth in Book 1, the mystery of the "appearing of appearances" is inseparable from the existential concerns: That one is at all, and that one is given to oneself to shape one's eternal destiny are inseparably tied to the appearing of the world and oneself appearing to oneself; yet one need not be and thus there need not be any self-appearing, nor need anything be or any appearing of anything.

There are two aspects to this point. The first is that whereas most problematic matters are those which may be posed adequately in the third-person, death and ipseity bring together the third-, second-, and first-person perspectives. The third-person is the perspective thought to be properly that of rationality with its universal publicity and view from nowhere. The second-person stance is the proper home for transactions of respect, justice, rights, accountability, etc.; but it, along with the first-person plural, is also the basic perspective of love and community. In death and ipseity the third-person "rational" perspective meets ineluctably resistance from the first- and second-personal points of view. From the third-personal "epistemic" perspective, the first- and second-personal perspectives are typically the realm of the irrational or cognitively deficient or irrelevant. Yet the questions surrounding especially one's own death or that of a loved one are essentially questions about what is of utmost importance. If there is an "epistemic" access to the "secret" of these matters it finds its home primarily in the first- and second-personal perspectives; the third-personal, public, intersubjective forum only restates what we already basically know: she is not there; who was there is now a corpse.

Secondly, the question of the "myself" or ipseity and one's own death are not problems in the sense that one can simply solve them or find a way to avoid them, and then get on with "life." In our living they press upon us always and in numerous ways which are often bound up with one another. For example, the questions having to do with *who* one is and how this is tied to what sort of person one is, surface poignantly in facing one's death.

Another point of symmetry in the mystery of ipseity and one's death is that they reveal the fact of a secret, i.e., that knowledge is withheld, not the answer to a secret. As death remains silent before our questions, so ipseity, we have said, is given to us in advance with an excessive super-intelligibility that resists any naming and ascription of properties. Like death it remains not the postulated philosophical whipping boy of Locke's substrate that he called a "I know not what," but rather more like the French *Je ne sais quoi* where there is an intimation of meaning that resists revealing itself. In the former Lockean case nothing is known or perceived or intuited, but merely postulated in an empty intention; in the latter French expression there is intuited a richness which eludes adequate articulation. In this respect with ipseity and death we have to do with what is uniquely known and not merely an absence emptily intended. Of course, the rich intuition in the presence of someone's death is a kind of intention, whereas in the case of the "myself" or ipseity the intention of reflection reveals it as prior to an intention. But in both cases we have the saturated givenness, i.e., a richness which outstrips the empty intention provided by our categorial schemes.

"Mystery" may be associated with what we call "deep" or something having "depth." With "depth" we typically have in mind the spatial image of the bottomless or the bottom or backdrop that is remote from the surface of our perception or grasp, thereby appearing to open up a greater volume, if not an infinite space. What is deep thus extends beyond our grasp – understood kinaethetically, visually-perceptually, cognitively, or all these together – and puts us in a state of both uneasiness and suspense. We then apply this to a realm that is not properly spatial. Thus, famously, St. Augustine: "You seek the deep of the sea, but what is deeper than human consciousness?" "When what is without a ground is the abyss, must we not say that the heart of man is an abyss?… Whose thoughts penetrate what one sees when one looks into the human heart?" "Do not you believe that there is in man a deep so profound as to be hidden even to him in whom it is?"[8]

Death is precisely what eludes our grasp by providing a dense experience which stops our concepts and questions in their tracks. Death pervades life as dying pervades living but the precise metaphysical sense of this pervasiveness eludes us. And as life is a miracle or a chance over which we have little control, so death's ending of life is often as incomprehensible as someone's coming to be. And on top of these third-person speculative matters there is the odd poignancy of "my death" which makes these considerations incomparably "real." At the same time and inseparably it makes out of myself a question: who am I? what sort of person am I? have I lived as I ought to have?

Similarly, like death, our self-experience is curiously of what is archonal and deep: we know of nothing in the world or our experience that can bring oneself, i.e., one's self, about; nor is there any such thing that is the explanation or source of our free agency. If we ineluctably think of ourselves as not having a manifest beginning that is apart from ourselves and if we think of ourselves as the beginning of our agency, it is a beginning that gives us nothing to take hold of. Further, there is the matter that pervades this work: We know ineluctably who we are and yet, at the same time, we have had no say in accounting for this even though we ineluctably know that we are accountable for who and what we make out of this person that has been given to us to form. And in all of this there is the consideration that we are sometimes surprises to ourselves, e.g., we are able unaccountably to be ourselves at our best; but we also fail, much to our eventual dismay, to show up for ourselves, i.e., we fail to be the one we expect ourselves to be and whom Others have a right to expect us to be.

Finally, in each case of ipseity and death we have to do with what occasions awe. We have seen that in empathic perception and foremost in love the presence of the Other awakens an awe for the transcendent self-experiencing "myself" which is beyond all properties. We will have frequent occasion to return to this matter. In death part of the experience is being dumbfounded at the peculiar absence of that which itself is transcendent to our grasp. The vanished ipseity leaves us grief-stricken and at a loss to find the appropriate categories that will make sense of the death. The deceased is intended in her absence as beyond her properties. Yet the bodily fleshly presence which was the vehicle for her presence, a presence laced with distinctive qualities, is now collapsed into a corpse. And because all of our making sense has in great measure to do with her being with us in the world, we have no way of making sense of her as "being" absent from the world.

Death as death of the Other always hints at the absence of the unique ipseity which is beyond all the marks of personality and character; these latter, as stylistic traits, may be still around or come around again (but, of course, not as *her*, the deceased beloved one's signature traits). What is lost, we sense, is precisely what is not able to be duplicated or substituted for. But does death extinguish the radiance of spirit, the *dignitas*, of the person? Clearly there is obliterated the radiance she has which is associated with her actual physical presence. But for those who lovingly recall the deceased, the radiance of spirit is inextinguishably present in the recollection. Yet, of course, this is a remembering and not making her actually present.

§2. The Transcendental Attitude and the Mystery of "My Death"

We, following the lead of Husserl and Jankélévitch, have seen (especially in Book 1, Chapters V–VI, and Book 2, Chapter I) why with death's appearance, as the possible extinction of I myself, everything seems to be at stake. We have urged that this is not a claim on behalf of egocentrism in a moral sense. Even if I believe that there are worse things than death, and even if I am prepared to sacrifice my life, death adumbrates the possibility that that for which I am prepared to die is itself in question. Facing my death in the light of the possible annihilation of everything else means precisely that all of my life along, with all whom I know, along with my and our order of preferences and hierarchy of values, may be extinguished. It means that with the extinction of my individual essence, there is the possibility that all agents of manifestation and, as well, the very of the world itself as the correlate of agents of manifestation can become annihilated.

Further, with someone's extinction as "bearer of the validity of the world," the prospect of the ultimate death of meaning and the annihilation of the very field of manifestation as what holds open the appearing of all that appears is possibly at hand. As such this reflection verges moving away from the "ontological mystery" of one's death where what is at stake implicates the reflecting person's reflection. In order that we may pull the matter back to the "existential" dimension, consider how this openness of the field of manifestation can disclose itself to us vis-à-vis death through a metaphor provided by the sky. There is no strict eidetic necessity here, but there is perhaps a kind of poetic logic. Consider how, in the natural attitude, we find ourselves at night where the sky's blackness renders everything absolutely impenetrably dark. Here, as in Beckett's works, *The Mouth* (or *Not I*) or *Murphy*, a poignant sense of ourselves surfaces as both being alone and even perhaps in this aloneness unique. We as flickering consciousnesses are surrounded by the "real stuff" of dead whirling random particles. Consider how the pitch blackness of the dark might reign above and below and how one could eventually feel oneself to become extinguished by becoming part of the darkness. This is the prospect of death if the third-person perspective reigns. Ingmar Bergmann's Death says, "I have no secret – and I have nothing to tell." Here *I myself* may sense a pull to merge into *It*, the darkness and let the darkness prevail and disburden me of self-awareness. This seems to be the allure of much materialism today.[9] This circumstance is quite in contrast to another one that might occur when one finds oneself under the darkness of the night sky, that is "threaded through with inaccessible brilliance" (Valéry) of the stars. Here too one's sense of being unique and alone surfaces, and yet one also experiences oneself as a part of an awe-inspiring infinity before which we perhaps, and only perhaps, appear. (C.S. Lewis once commented on the horror that filled a modern such as Pascal when he looked up into the post-Galilean sky which was filled with random dead and incandescent bodies. He noted that this contrasted markedly with the pious medieval observer who, upon looking up to the night sky, believed he was privileged to have a peek at a riotous party attended by resplendent rejoicing angels.) Both the daylight sense of our aloneness and individuality that we are co-existing wholes/worlds or parts outside of one another, and the precarious and lonely sense of being oneself in the engulfing absolute darkness might give way to a new sense of an endless field of manifestation. This new sense does not obliterate one's "I myself" as an individual essence and microcosm of this field, but nevertheless this I-ness might well be overwhelmed and subdued and perhaps rendered a matter of only minor importance within this field of "inaccessible brilliance." But minor importance is infinitely more than of no importance.

Only for someone who appropriated completely, *per impossibile*, a materialist-technocratic ideology would his death appear without remainder as a problem requiring a solution. By definition such a one would not appreciate what here is meant by one's own death. One's *ownness* would itself be alienated into what is an interchangeable piece of resource to be manipulated. Of course, a detached, disinterested attitude toward's one death might be what the situation requires. A single mother may well force herself to step back and consider the problem her imminent death will create for her children and those who are remaining. Circumstances might be such that the dying mother alone can attend to her children and make arrangements. She might well take calculated steps to insure that there is as little suffering and inconvenience for the children as possible. But if she does this well her calculation of what her task is would be precisely what anyone would decide upon in her shoes, e.g., a friend or counselor. In this respect her dying would be "everyman's," and quite the opposite of the first-personal sense that one alone can die and dies only alone. Such a detached facing of death might seem to be not yet facing one's own death; it is facing the consequences of a death, which happens to be one's own, for others. Yet what she is doing, what she alone can do, is what she ought to do, presupposing she remains capable and competent, in regard to her children. The only way she may face her own death is not focusing on her death and doing what she can do for her children and this means not having the "luxury" to face her own death.

Here there would not be any conflict between facing one's own death and not taking the time to do this. She would face her own death precisely by attending to the children because her own death's exigency would not override the care of her children. This alone would be the "one thing necessary." Her death would not appear as a technical or theoretical problem or theme but it would necessitate her *acting* with maximum conscientiousness and focusing totally on the task of arranging for the care of her children.

Such a story presupposes that when one's own death as such announces itself it does indeed press upon us the "one thing necessary," the Ought which overrides all other considerations. We will repeatedly return to this. Another connected essential point here is that facing one's own death involves a modification of intentionality, even the intentionality of the transcendental I. In confronting one's own death the cognitive relation that establishes the objectness, the being there and the "over-againstness" that creates a unique unity of the known and the subject in the intentional distance is no longer in play. My death does not affect me or confront me as an object inviting analysis, contextualization, or elaboration. It is not there soliciting further categorial determination and syntactic ties with other meaning-units in the world. This is not merely to say that death is not simply a peculiar theme within the larger horizon of the world. No, death fills the horizon. My death enables the world "to world," i.e., it brings into view and condenses the whole or the full scope of my life, i.e., the empty intentions of being, value, and meaning, in a way that perhaps no other consideration does. In the case of the dying mother her life-world unfolds before her in terms of the required agency with respect to her children's future. Ivan Ilych, even in the last hours, grasps that at least now he must love and forgive and seek forgiveness. Because so much is brought together into a single pregnant felt horizon, speech about its meaning palpably falters. That is the tragic-comedy in Ivan Ilych who, in asking for forgiveness, because of the loss of his speaking ability, manages to get out something that sounds like "I forego."

Mystery, as exemplified in my death, is not merely a meeting with what is *not* an object of a merely epistemic intentional stance, as, e.g., the horizon of the world and one's kinaestheses; but rather it encroaches on the very intending, the very agency of display, and the agent of manifestation as well. By encroaching[10] I mean a kind of encompassing concentration and self-transformation where the ipseity as the agent of manifestation and the absolute "from which" or "whence" of the field of manifestation itself is not merely changed from its position of agent holding cognitive sway over that of which it is aware, but it itself is changed into an analogous being questioned and commanded. And neither the question (nor its answer), nor the command (nor its response) is clear. Yet the question and the command seem ineluctable.

Thus what is here meant by encompassing concentration is not merely something like the self's capacity for reflection on itself or, even less, the cursive capacity of a computer program that monitors "itself," e.g., in checking for illicit commands and irregular procedures. Nor do we have in mind conceptual self-reference or semantic self-inclusion, like the word "word" or "set of all sets" or the sign that reads, "This is a sign." Rather what is at stake is how the typical intentional situation is transformed. Typically, we have noted, the agency and the agent of manifestation occupy an epistemic intentional stance which enables the theme or object to be "there" and the agent of manifestation and its displaying are left out of the picture. They are, we have said, the tacit "transcendental prefixes." Further, the intentional correlation between manifestation and what gets manifested is secured by the basic intentional belief or doxastic allegiance to the being of what gets disclosed.

In contrast, the presence of one's death subverts the typical attitude and weakens the motive for the transcendental attitude because the distancing involved in the positing of both worldly as well as transcendental objects is undermined. As we noted in reference to Ivan Ilych, the very agency of display is affected, and therefore the "declarative I" or transcendental prefix is displaced or decentered in the sense that what is at stake is a more central sense of "I myself" than the transcendental agent of manifestation. But here we do not have in mind the emotional displacement of "I myself" where I myself am momentarily collapsed into the emotional situation, e.g., that of anger. Such a collapse of the I myself can properly be reproached by the detached agent I of manifestation. But what we have in mind is a center that is more basic even than the agent I of manifestation.

As we have seen, for phenomenology there remains, ultimately, a phenomenology of phenomenology, i.e., there is a display of the transcendental I's displaying itself and its constitution of the world and there is the meta-phenomenological "eidetic" analysis of display as such or manifestation as such, and, as we have seen, an analysis of the non-presentability of the beginning and end, as well as the necessity and contingency of the transcendental I that is neither begun nor ending. But this display of the theme of the death and birth of the transcendental I still maintains the intentional distance. Even the focusing on the rock-bottom issue of the primal presencing as self-luminous, and not luminous by reason of an act of reflection, i.e., even the display of the most elemental manifestation that founds all the others, even the display of the *eidos* of display – all these are still theoretical discussions. As a theoretical discussion it does not "encroach" on itself or the agent of manifestation in the way a "mystery" and in particular "my death" does.

Even the display that the "myself" is a unique individual essence in itself and not by reason of some other consideration may be purely theoretical. And it may not be until death and the power of its presence to let the question of one's destiny surface that the mysterious aspect of this theme comes to light. (Cf. the discussion of senses of mystery in Chapter II, §1 above.)

We have said *my death* is not at all "there" simply as something given awaiting the agency of manifestation. Of course, writing about it now is just such a categorical intuition and display. But this is perhaps the ultimate ruse of the temptation to let death be other than *my death*. Writing about death, doing a transcendental phenomenology of the death of the transcendental I, by no means is necessarily an authentic encounter with death, by no means an indication of the honesty and wisdom of the writer in this matter; it might rather be the most desperate dodge.[11]

Even Husserl's reflections on the deathlessness or unending character of the transcendental I (see Book 1, Chapter VI) do not deal with Edmund Husserl's own death. That Edmund Husserl took consolation in the phenomenological evidence for the unending character of the transcendental I reflects Edmund Husserl's confronting his own death with the fruits of his philosophy. Even the language of "the transcendental I," as we have seen, renders the irreducible first-person experience into a third-person term. The same holds for the "whiling," "primal flow," and "process" of the primal streaming as it witnesses the beginning and ending of whatever event. This by no means invalidates the discussion of the impossibility of the primal presencing's presencing its beginning or its ending. It merely is to say that in these analyses "my death" is not present but rather the problem "per se" and "as such" of experiencing death in the first-person. The latter is by no means the *realization* of my death.

§3. "My Death" and the Prospective Retrospection of "My Life"

We have seen that death, as it is present in the third- and second-person perspective, is always final, always an absolute cessation. Yet in the first-person one lives forward and, as we have seen, not only never experiences this absolute cessation but also finds it impossible to envisage it. Thus when the "hour of my death" is there I apply to myself the decisiveness and finality that my appreciation of death has for me in the inescapable second- and third-person perspective. Yet my death always involves the sense of my momentum into the future even though the evidence is now compelling that I am about to be stopped dead in my tracks. Even here I am, as everywhere, always ahead of myself, not merely collapsed into the present. And doubtless of all things inviting repression and inattention because of the "pain and inconvenience," death surely is the outstanding candidate. But death means, for both the transcendental person as well as or the naïve person, as well as for the most efficient repressor of inconvenient truths, always the apperception of one's absolute cessation. Thus one's momentum is derailed from the apperceived future of one's destiny in the second- and third-person. One's time has run out; one knows that it is coming down to the absolute cessation in the world. One is wrenched from the relatively capacious "not yet" that is founded in one's protentions. Yet inveterate self-deception is often no small factor in holding open this space of the future. Now with the realization of one's death, one's momentum toward the future is toward the only "not yet" that remains, the moment of death. It is to here that one is launched, i.e., to a vantage point from which one's life in regard to the future is absolute darkness. Thus the only space in which to look is back to what one has been and done – even though now one still automatically protends and perhaps even has expectations that surface out of sheer habit. At the moment of the realization of death one is aware that one can only grasp one's life in retrospect; plans, hopes, and expectations are irrelevant because nonsensical. (Cf. Ivan Ilych's last days, spent tossing and turning on the couch as the selected memories of the past surface for him.) The realization of one's death, whenever it comes in the course of one's life, i.e., whether it comes early, or in the middle, or at the end, whether it comes once only, recurrently, or rarely, always involves one's self-displacement to that "moment of death," which is one's ultimate and final "not yet," from which one gathers one's life into a kind of present.

The prospect that "my life," the life that was given to me, is coming to this absolute cessation is a demanding and commanding presence. Further, for good reasons which we have discussed, I may dread it. It is only a neutral matter of fact for one who thinks of himself as such a neutral matter of fact. In such a case, an abstract limit-case, the person's moral agency, the agency of manifestation, and the agency of world transformation would be so swallowed up in the world of facts that he cannot differentiate himself from the ephemeral worldly things and events brought to light by experience.[12] For one who is not so lost, death makes present that beside which everything else pales. Some traditions of spirituality refer to this as "The One Thing Necessary." This is inseparable from my facing the fact that I have been given over to myself without any merit or say and that before me there lies my possible non-being, which itself may stand as a cipher for the annihilation of everything.

Facing one's death returns us to the theme of how what is Now, of necessity will have been. Facing one's death can take expression in the future and future perfect tenses: "At that time, I will no longer be but have been." "Then (at the 'moment' of death or after I am dead) I will have been (or will not have been) faithful, will (or will not) have done such and such." In facing my death I face the prospect of being, like the Homeric shade, a creature where life is one of having been. If my having been is meaningful, i.e., there is an encompassing agency of manifestation whose retention keeps and displays my life as having been, then at least I will have the shade-like existence of one of Homer's figures. But even though there is a strict eidetic necessity that I will have been as the condition for my being Now, and even though the displayed sense if my having been requires the retention in something like an eternal all-encompassing consciousness, this requirement is postulated in an empty intention. Death as the extinguishing of unique essences undermines the vigorous allegiance to this postulation. Thus, in death, in spite of the resistance created by the first-personal perspective, one's faith, and other possible considerations, I face my own absolute extinguishing. But in facing the prospect of my absolute annihilation I do not face it merely as a neutral fact but as a call for my being present to myself in a way that I normally avoid.

Normally I attend to myself and my life piecemeal, dealing with distinct responsibilities, tasks, aches, etc. If I displace myself to face my death, or the "moment" of my death, there is strictly speaking nothing "there" to attend to. Yet I place myself before my possible annihilation, before the absolute darkness of non-being. I myself at all levels of "I" as well as "my life" and my life-world stand before the utter blackness of extinction. This self-displacement has the power to congeal what is otherwise scattered and strewn out over time because, with the imminent closing of the irrepressible future horizon, the field of awareness gathers one's past into the present and one presences the whole of one's life as having been. One's life and one's self, normally launched into the future, now rebound off the closed off future to what alone one, "for the moment," has, one's past. When the future that one takes for granted as the field of one's aspirations is closed off the question of the point or sense of not merely this present but all the former presents comes to mind. Not only does it come to mind, but the way one has addressed or suppressed this matter of which one has had intimations in the past also forces its way into one's life. This view of one's life from the vantage point of one's anticipated death we call a *prospective retrospection.*

This situation of at least an impulse toward a prospective retrospection and congealing of one's life seems ineluctable. We may distinguish the way in which our life-world and our surrounding world are habitually for us in a field or intentional horizon of retentions and protentions and where what is of significance or importance for us is not delineated and not "making an impression." This may be because our attention is wholly focused on the matter at hand. Or it may be because we are in a quasi-dormant state, etc. Then we may consider the matters that in this field are of importance and, e.g., we have had to postpone. Then the horizon presses upon us even though we are taken up with the present. Here the horizon has unfinished matters which are not simply neutral but rather are loaded with a kind of validity lying in waiting. Husserl notes that in such cases there are matters of importance, *Wichtigkeiten,* in a deeper sense. And what may be regarded in a general sense the ethical aspect of our lives is when we have an occasion to survey our life in terms of the abiding matters of importance toward which we have and can have an abiding stance. He refers to the "ethical life" as the "movement of these matters of importance" in one's stream of consciousness.[13] As we shall see, both "conscience" and the gathering acts, such as prospective retrospections, are forms of movement of these matters of importance and intrinsic to our ethical life. The *reflection* on these movements, however, is not "ethical" in this sense. We will return to these matters soon.

How life unfolds subsequent to this tremor or impulse to this "movement of matters of importance" is open to various possibilities, none of which is necessary. If this impulse happens early enough in life, and there are usually many opportunities for this to happen, e.g., through a narrow escape from death or in the wake of the death of a loved one, and if I do not suppress this impulse, I can well be moved to displace myself prospectively to a retrospective perspective, a future perfect, that I know I can live with. We occasionally see such rare people in our midst or we learn of them, e.g., people who take life-long vows and devote their lives to a cause, such as aiding those who have no one to aid them. They do this in spite of the discomfort, absence of recognition, remuneration, etc. The *realization* of my death calls me now to live in such a way that I will not, at the "moment" of death, regret my resolve and my fidelity to my resolution. The realization of my death, or the realization that a loved one is dying, especially if I am graced with it early in life, beckons me to displace myself to a future standpoint, i.e., the time of my death, where I will not have regretted having chosen the path I am now on. And the evidence for that choice may be the simple insight that to have acted and lived differently would have been frivolous and a denial of my self, my essential self. (This is a theme to which we will often return.)

When clearly aware that I am at the door of death, I can, if I have been so fortunate, take satisfaction in being aware that I have, for the most part, lived as I wanted; if we are less fortunate, and most of us will be in this position, we may well have numerous regrets. In any case, it seems that there always is possible, even up until the "moment" of death, the prospective retrospective gathering of my past. Even at the moment of death, I may be beckoned to face up to myself by resolving to live or decide now in such a way that I will have had no regrets when death finally "takes me." For the one dying, theoretically there is still time for prospective retrospection, i.e., for a resolve to live in such a way that at death one will not have regretted how one lived. (Again, cf. Tolstoy's Ivan Ilych.) Of course, if one is burdened with guilt and regrets, such a prospective retrospection would make little sense unless one believed in and hoped for forgiveness.

Another good fictional example of a prospective retrospection is given by C. S. Lewis. When one of the protagonists of his novel believes he is about to be put to death, his life comes careening before him in a concentrated way. Obviously not every moment or experience comes into relief, but only those which highlight the moral tenor of his life. He recognizes that his ambition has blinded him to seeing things that he should have seen in the course of his life and which, had he seen them, or if his ambition had not blinded him, he would not now be in the dreadful position he is in.

> He himself did not understand why all this, which was now so clear, had never previously crossed his mind. He was aware that such thoughts had often knocked for entrance, but had

always been excluded for the very good reason that if they were once entertained it involved ripping up the whole web of his life, canceling almost every decision his will had ever made, and really beginning over again as though he were an infant. The indistinct mass of problems which would have to be faced if he admitted such thoughts, the innumerable "somethings" about which "something" would have to be done, had deterred him from ever raising these questions. What had now taken the blinkers off was the fact that nothing *could* be done. They were going to hang him. His story was at an end. There was no harm in ripping up the web now for he was not going to use it any more; there was no bill to be paid (in the shape of arduous decision and reconstruction) for truth. It was a result of the approach of death which [his executioners] the Deputy Director and Professor Frost had possibly not foreseen.[14]

Here Lewis nicely indicates how the hero becomes aware that he kept at bay certain important truths by permitting them to be submerged in an "indistinct mass." He did this by familiar techniques of distance-taking and empty conceptualization ("'something' about which 'something' would have to be done"). He was motivated to dodge these truths because of the painful alternative, i.e., the arduous task of reconstructing the web of his life on the basis of what is true and not on what he wanted to be true. But now the awareness of his impotence in regard to the inevitability of his extinction through his execution enables him to rip up the web of falsehood that was his life; this is easy now because everything is over and there is no price to pay for living the truth. The only price he now has to pay is to die at the hands of enemies of the truth.

In the prospective retrospective future perfect resolve I engage myself now for a future from which I can look back with no or few regrets because I will have been faithful to myself, my "essential ownmostness." I put myself in the position of being able now to say: I then, at the "moment" of death, will have done such or such and, by implication, I will not have done such and such. But at the same time I am awakened to myself by facing my impotence in regard to my possible nothingness and even the possible futility of my life's projects. I am awakened also to my moral weaknesses in regard to my ability to be faithful to myself and my life, as so prospectively envisaged.

This kind of prospective and retrospective self-gathering is regarded today by some as delusional, or based on a belief in a myth (e.g., The Last Judgment) or rooted in the influence of an outdated aspect of Greek philosophy that argued for a strong theory of the unity of the soul. One reason for the skepticism is that self-awareness is conceived in terms of acts of reflection or reference and the knowing that comes from introspection and perceptual identification. If this is true, then not only are the acts of reflection or reference themselves of necessity unconscious (because they are not objects of reflection) but also massive areas of the self remain unknown to itself at any one time, because the mind can only focus on a very finite sphere of things at any given time.

This particular version of the reflection theory of self-awareness is inseparable from the widespread post-modernist belief that the self is not only not a self-aware unity but an irreducible plurality of only contingently related "systems" that function often independently of and unbeknownst to one another, after the fashion of a mechanistic view of the bodily organisms. In this case egological self-awareness is merely one of the systems, and perhaps just a minor one. Examples are certain understandings of Freud's systems of *das Ich, das Id,* and *das Überich* or computer models of mind where independent hardware and software programs function together without a center that brings these into contact with one another. Such a view may perhaps not collapse philosophical reflection completely to the third-person point of view, but it surely assumes that the third-person perspective has priority. Further, it requires the extinction of the notion of the self as a center of awareness and responsibility and it posits as well a renunciation of a first-person account of agency in favor of a third-person template that overrides the phenomenological detail of the first-person account.

But is not the foil to this post-modernist view, such as the view of this book, perhaps a crypto-theology? Why can we not simply acknowledge the fortuitousness of our existence, the essential alienation and accidental unity of the components of the self, the unpredictability of the time of death, and the general dubiousness of there being a meaning to all of one's life? Of course, we can do this and many do. But it happens against the grain of the ongoing passive synthetic unification of our life that is indispensable for our wakefulness. Living as a wanton, or learning to be comfortable with one's blind spots and repressions, is not as easy as it might seem. Not being interested in and concerned about the consistency and kind of lives we live, the choices we make, and persons we are, goes against the very constitutive elements of being awake. Whether we want it or not our lives are given to us pervaded by a nisus and ongoing pressure toward unity and striving for consistency that we may strengthen or weaken, honor or despise. But at death all of one's life comes to a head, willy-nilly; our being launched in life teleologically comes to a stop. We realize that we have no future horizon for our plans and we may suppress the prospective retrospection by reason of our nihilistic or skeptical beliefs. When it comes time to "cash in our chips," "call it quits," "hang up our boots," "kick the bucket," etc., we all face the impenetrable darkness. Obviously the person for whom personal integrity is a matter of importance ineluctably will have a prospective retrospection; but the cultivated wanton, aesthete, or master self-dodger is not without indications of the extent to which she is going against the grain that is her makeup. (Cf. our discussions of conscience in the next chapter.)

We return to the topic of prospective retrospection below when we discuss one's "vocation." But now we wish to turn to it as a unique possibility that may or may not materialize. The prospective retrospection is a kind of necessity, but whether it takes the form of a realization does not seem necessary. In any case it is not a logical necessity, and when it comes, it may appear as a "grace."

§4. "My Death" as a Gathering Experience

Although the presence of my death is doubtless the result of intentional acts that interpret my being in the world, the prospective retrospection can take the form of a realization of my death which is not properly thought of as an act of self-reflection, i.e., whereby I am an object for myself. The realization is a gathering of myself for myself, a prospective retrospection, in which I have all of my life brought together in a distinctive non-objective experience. Of course there is a sense in which "my life" is an object in the sense that the field of awareness is absorbed by this very thick and rich consideration. We may say that it swallows all other considerations in a multi-stranded "polythetic" act[15] that stands in contrast with other objects, even huge ones, like "Operation Iraqi Freedom," because it includes everything of importance for me. There is nothing besides it of importance. Doubtless it presupposes intentional acts that interpret my being in the world, but the experience itself of realization is not an act of reflection; it is not disclosed by intending it in an act of reflection. Rather, in the wake of appropriate intentional acts a massive synthesis occurs that phenomenologists have named a "gathering" act.[16] We wish to develop this.

We have already (e.g., in Book 1, Chapter VII) called attention to how each Now that we experience does not fall off into total oblivion. Absolute forgetting of our former experiences would not only makes remembering impossible, but it would also confine our life to the narrow slice of Now and only Now, the home of the famous "wanton." This of course would free us from the "burden" and "prejudice" of former experiences, but "we" would not be *anyone*, as a person perduring in time with the project of being faithful to our stances or position-takings, because we would only be the one now experiencing Now, and even the experienced Now would be an impoverished experience because there would be no apperception enriching it, no bringing to bear, through associations, the relevant past. This is not to say that there are not anomalies where a Now passes into total oblivion, or that there are no occasions of forgetting, amnesia, dementia, etc. But these would never come to light if the Now were the wanton-like flux for which there is only discrete punctual Nows and no passive synthesis. We wish once again to turn to this matter of passive synthesis.

We have said that the ultimate basement of the I, besides the "myself," is the primal presencing. This ebullient luminosity not only presences the actuality of what it encounters, but this presencing presences at once as parts of the thickness of Now the Just Past and the Not Yet. Thus this presencing is at once an informing of this actuality with the "more" of what was just experienced, what was retained. Indeed it is informing it with the more of this more because retentions are always retentions of retentions. And we said that as retention is the way the Just Past informs the Now, so protention informs the Now with a Not Yet, but about to be, Now. These "acts" are the basic ingredients of wakefulness and the presupposition for our proper act-life. Our fundamental ability to recollect (recall, remember) presupposes that we have retained the former experiences. But, as Husserl teaches, remembering is different from retaining. To remember, I must detach myself from the perceptual Now and displace myself to a former Now. This presentation of the past makes explicit what was merely implicit in retention.

The primal presencing is ongoing and may be thought of as a churning substance spewing out identity syntheses: *d* is present now, but it is present as having followed upon *c, b, a*. We may call this presence of the just past being *co*-present, if we understand that here present does not mean that the past is now, but that it informs the Now, and that it is experienced immediately along with the Now. At *c, b* is co-present as just having preceded. *a* is co-present at *d, c, and b*, not as it originally appeared as Now, but nevertheless "each time" (at each Now) it is co-present as the same, although different, because at each time (each Now) its relation to Now is different. At *d, a* is co-present as having preceded *d, c, and b*; at *b* it is present as having just preceded. But in each case *a* is the same, but seen from a different Now perspective. This is true for the other phases too, of course. Similarly each Now is the same as Now, although filled with a different content, and at each time it is informed differently, e.g., by *a*, then a*b*, then *abc*, then *abcd*, then eventually *a...x*.

Each of the above-italicized letters may stand for any event or any temporal slicing of an event. Thus it may stand for the temporal phases of something experienced, e.g., a race, or an experience, e.g., watching the race; or it may stand for a phase of an individual stream of consciousness, e.g., JG Hart's, which is also busy with other things than races. These italicized letters may also stand for the phases of all of one's life. The point here is that in the course of our life our past adheres to us because we willy-nilly retain it. It, like the protended future, is the inescapable background of what we now experience. All memory and imagination, as the way we attempt to render explicit our retained pasts and protended futures, are possible because of this background.

The I, as primal presencing, ineluctably and irrepressibly churns out these identity syntheses. This is called by Husserl *passive* synthesis because *I* am not actively doing anything. Before I am an active agent of manifestation I am first a passive primal presencing, a dative of manifestation, i.e., a passive agent of manifestation. Yet this is I myself most passively and elementally, and the field that passive synthesis opens up is the field of my life. It is all there even when I am not remembering it, i.e., actively recalling the past Nows as past Nows. Memory, recollection, recalling, etc. are the terms we use to point to our capacity to re-presence in the present the former Nows, not as Now, but as former Nows. The past is always being called forth in the sense that it is constantly informing the present in our perceptual life; this is the achievement of the primal association of simple retention and retention of retentions, but it is also the achievement of the more familiar senses of associations. First there are the patterns of instinctual association that reach back into our hazy impenetrable past. Then there are the patterns of association that make up the habits of perception as in acts of recognition. But this is not properly a calling forth in the sense of an act of remembering, as when something occurs that awakens in us a visitation from the past. In the case of remembering we detach ourselves from what is perceptually present in order to make present a former present. But in order to recognize the thing before us we need not leave the perceptual present. For example, we need not, on the basis of the present thing's similarity to what we earlier experienced, go back in an intentional act to when we first grasped the essence of the device we call the corkscrew, and then consciously relate this known to the present novel thing. This happens quite automatically through "association" and we are doing this all the time. This reminds me of that, where *that* is called forth in such a way as to enable an "apperception" which enriches the present in such a way that the novel experience is able to be recognized or interpreted without my having to leave the perceptual present.

The second familiar sense of association is when, without my doing anything, something from the past is summoned forth into my present, not merely as an association in the service of interpreting and recognizing what is now present, but rather as something to be entertained for itself. Of course, this which is summoned forth is founded in an association, i.e., something in the present reminded me of this, but its appearance is such that I attend it for itself; it is not merely functional for my present interests. For this to happen, I must still hold some affection for and attachment to this part or these parts of my past, even though the memory as well as the attachment perhaps have been "asleep" for many years. Obviously old photos, old songs, and, most famously, scents can "trigger" a cascade of such visitations from the past.

Connected here is the phenomenon of "living memory." This need not be of a mere cognitive or intellectual order, but it may also characterize our affective life. Thus, e.g., when writing a paper, listening to a symphony, reading a novel, watching a movie or play, we have the capacity, if we are awake, interested, and energetic, to hold the relevant past in retention and to keep it alive so that when the right moment is upon us the past comes into the present in a condensed form so as to render the present palpably thick with meaning. This is over and above the halo of retentions and protentions that surround any present or any Now. Rather, with living memory the present is suffused with a richness of sense whereby, e.g., the whole novel is placed in the last paragraph of the last chapter. As Roman Ingarden puts it, we have in the unfolding of living memory in the present "a quality of intuitive content" that to a certain extent "presents a resumé or a synthetic version of that which unfolded in a complete manner in the recent past but which now echoes in this condensed form."[17] Note that "living memory" is more than the mere halo of the past retentions and it surely is not the result of a specific act of remembering. Indeed, through it *I* do not displace myself from the actual present to a former present, as in remembering, but rather *it gives to me* in the actual present a condensed form of the more or less recent past. It resembles what Proust named "involuntary memory" in his account of the distinctive event of nostalgia. Thus involuntary memory contrasts with memory proper, by which we act, i.e., will, to recall a former present. In living memory, like Proust's "involuntary memory," something instigates its coming into play so that it explodes the present, quickening it in a way that is not characteristic of either normal retention or normal memory.[18]

Our thesis is that "the realization of my death" occasions something like a living and involuntary memory. Such a realization clearly is not the result of single acts of remembering. Such would seem to be incapable of bringing one's life together in a prospective retrospective realization that one's destiny is in question. There is, as Husserl shows us, amidst the course of our scattered, disconnected, inconsistent lives, a feeble unity and a feeble general will (which we will discuss later) that binds our whole life together synthetically. But no series of individual acts would conjure up all of one's life as it faces death. Rather, such a thick noema would require a unique kind of synthetic, polythetic act that gathers the multiple strands of the acts of one's life.[19]

Any affective awakening of the past through an association presupposes the prior affective bond, i.e., *this* reminds me of *that* because *that* still is of interest or of importance to me. May we not say that how we have lived our lives is of a fundamental importance? For Husserl "conscience" is precisely the way the life-identity of the personal I, as constituted across time through position-taking acts, is held open and disclosed to oneself. As we shall see, conscience is our awareness of our being true to ourselves or not. An understanding of conscience is essential to an understanding of what we will call Existenz. Indeed, there is a kind of unique revelation of conscience with the realization of one's death. Like conscience, "realization of one's death," in contrast to the realization of "living memory" that might occur in a theoretical, cognitive, or merely aesthetic matter, concerns oneself in one's inmost core. I am at issue for myself.

In all moments of realization, whether a matter of conscience or not, whether a realization of one's death or not, we can say that nothing in particular detail need be present at the moment of this realization. But, as Scheler says, everything is somehow "there" and "operative."

> We are, in these cases, not empty but indeed, "full" and "rich." Here we are truly "present with ourselves." Operative-effective experiences address us from all points of our life. Innumerable soft "appeals" from the past and future sound within us. We "look over" our *total I* in all its manifoldness or we experience it as a whole in *an* act, a deed, or a work.[20]

We do not usually have ourselves together in this way; we are not usually in such possession of ourselves. If we have explicitly in mind the palpable fullness and richness attendant on an act like nostalgia, repentance, the occasional realization of one's death, the recollection of one's life that a great work of art might bring about, etc., then we may aspire to have at will this extraordinary self-possession, but such striving or willing would seem to be ineffectual, because such a self-possession is not something we can typically will. Poets like Wordsworth strove to induce the gathering act by techniques, e.g., of revisiting a place or setting that originally had occasioned it in the past and patiently awaiting the recurrence of the visitation of the nostalgic gathering act. I myself used to listen to Mahler's Fourth Symphony hopeful of just such a visitation. We may strive to have this self-possession, and take steps to bring it about, but it is not something we typically can will. Of course, one can concentrate on the task at hand and in this sense gather oneself together. But such a centering requires sustained effort and is not the "gracious visitation" of what we are calling the gathering act. Further, such concentration is not a concentrated gathering of one's whole life. "Concentrating" is narrowing a horizon within the wider horizon of life. What we have in mind here is a gathering of what one identifies with as the whole of one's life.

Yet because there is always a synthesis of our whole lives in the making, even when we have been wanton, dissolute, inconsistent, etc., our freedom to choose ourselves and the direction of our lives may be posited as possible. (This issue will return frequently, especially in conjunction with "one's calling.") Clearly, in the wake of these special gracious moments, moments of what we (with Jankélévitch) call "realization," we grasp our lives palpably more or less as a whole. "My death" can occasion such a gathering event, an involuntary, living memory that takes in, synthesizes and condenses not just a specified recent past, but the whole of one's life.

§5. Transcendental Reflection on the Realization of the Mystery of "My Death"

We have insisted that the gathering act of realization of one's death is not properly an act by which some object in the world is brought into view or articulated. A condensation of one's whole life is summoned up, but not as one theme among others or as a theoretical theme. It is not the result of an explicit act of reflection. Although the presence of one's death involves ineluctably the prospective retrospection, it is not at all certain whether it inevitably amounts to the grace of the gathering act which achieves a concentration of one's life through an involuntary "living memory." It could be that the ineluctable prospective retrospection is simply a matter of being stopped in one's tracks. One is willy-nilly catapulted into the future, but now there is nothing more or less than the realization that there is no future. The only viable horizon is one's past. But instead of the past opening up in the massive synthesis of the morally salient moments of one's life, the past itself remains an empty intention, that is, its synthesis as a "living memory" does not occur. But even in this case what is brought before the mind's eye is oneself in a massive implicit way, but here it is indicated only emptily. Here perhaps the life-long practice of being estranged from oneself triumphs in the end.

Of course the massive implicit presence of one's life in prospective retrospection contrasts with the way the "myself" is always already and ineluctably self-present without perspectives. This latter is neither an object nor is it capable of perspectival elucidation. Rather, prospective retrospection's massive noema has to do with the "I myself" *as* an incarnate person and temporal agent existing in the world with others. It is necessary that we relate the realized and gathered sense of oneself to "Existenz" and the "myself." But before we do this we wish to return to the relationship of the transcendental attitude to this realization, whether it is presenced in the simple ineluctable prospective retrospection or whether in the gathering act.

The transcendental reduction as including a specific kind of reflection is always of necessity a reflection on what was present prior to reflection. This which is prior to reflection is either what is horizontally or marginally implicit, the pre-reflective, or is the self-awareness of the I and its acts, the non-reflective. Even when I reflect on an act of reflection, the act of reflection, prior to the reflection, was lived but not reflected on. What we typically mean when we refer to our lives is our conscious life. By this we mean life as it is lived or lived through, and not necessarily something perceptually experienced or known, i.e., as a result of intentional acts, and in particular acts of reflection. A fortiori it is not an official or public version of one's life. This lived life, we have argued, is a non-reflective form of self-awareness. In German there is the lovely word *Erleben* that can be used for that straight-forward, non-reflective self-awareness of life, of *Leben*. In English we approximate it (and the German *Durchleben*) in so far as we can say, "She did not merely hear about it or cognize it or reflect on it, but rather lived it" (or: "lived through it"). First-person experience is always properly *Durchleben* and *Erleben*.[21] Reflection, even philosophical and transcendental phenomenological reflection, does not live in that upon which it reflects. As Husserl put it, "[intentional] consciousness and the content of consciousness as object are no longer living consciousness, but rather precisely reflection of the same…"[22] Reflection may be said to actualize *cognitively* lived life. That is to say, if we think of the prior-to-the-reflected-on, whether it be the marginal or the non-reflective self-awareness, they both are, relative to the reflective intentional act, implicit and potentially known or actual. But I cannot enjoy in reflection the actuality of my life in its vitality prior to reflection any more than I can make immediately present the ipseity or non-reflective self-awareness of the Other in my making the other present to me. The act of reflection may bring to light cognitively the lived living of life, but it, the (lived) reflection, is not itself the lived living of life that the lived reflection intends. Of course, there is an evident sameness between oneself as lived prior to reflection and oneself reflecting on that which was prior to reflection, and this kind of unique evidence for sameness is not able to be achieved in my reflection on or intending Others. In intending an Other, Peter, e.g., as the same as whom Paul intended or as the same as Peter intends in his autobiography or detached self-reflection, there is a sameness in regard to what the acts bring to light; in the first-person case, the sameness is between what is lived and an act of reflection on what is lived. Obviously such sameness is not able to be achieved in *my* reflection on the ipseity of Others. An abyss of difference and transcendence reigns between my self-consciousness and the Other's self-consciousness, and this abyss stands in contrast with the sameness that comes to light between the consciousness reflecting and the consciousness reflected on in an act of *self*-reflection. This is lived *as an act of reflection and not empathic perceiving* precisely because the acts are lived as acts of the same stream of consciousness and the reflected on is apperceived to be essentially part of the horizon of the pre-reflected on.

Nevertheless, it must be said that the phenomenologizing I of reflection, which manifests the realization of my death in a gathering experience, is not simply identical (nor does it coincide absolutely) with the I of a gathering experience. The transcendental observing I makes an object of, thematizes, the actuality of herself facing her death, but it does not live, exist, immediately participate in the actual person's facing her death. To anticipate our later terminology, the transcendental I in its achieving does not immediately participate in or awaken to its Existenz. Whereas the I of the gathering experience or the I that gathers and determines itself in the face of its destiny, (let us call this self-gathering, self-determining I *Existenz*), is manifest to itself in a pre-reflective prospective retrospection of its destiny, the transcendental I reflecting on this, as such, is not impacted, gripped immediately, or self-gathered in this way – even though the transcendental reflecting I and the self-gathered I are lived as the same. In *thinking about* or objectifying the self-gathered I or Existenz, I do not *eo ipso* exist in the mode of being self-gathered or in the mode of Existenz. In the mode of philosophical reflection on my life, I am not immediately gripped or affected as that which I am reflecting on, i.e., myself summoned to a prospective retrospection and immediate engagement with my destiny. The transcendental observer in his reflecting objectifies and distances himself from this, his mode of being gripped and gathered, for the purposes of manifestation and articulation, and thus as such is not characterized by the urgency and agitation that pervades such an Existenz as a result of facing its destiny.

Of course, in so far as transcendental phenomenology undertakes a reflection on Existenz, makes a theme of it, articulates what it is, etc., it is "existential phenomenology" or "existential philosophy." But qua existential philosopher or transcendental-existential phenomenologist, the philosophizing I is not pure and simply existing Existenz because it is not existing in the mode of Existenz.

Is therefore "existential knowing" or "existential phenomenology" an oxymoron? Does the mode of realizing one's death or, more generally one's being as Existenz, not exclude a reflective analysis and thematization, such that there is no such thing as a knowing of Existenz? This view has been the temptation of some existentialist philosophers who are tempted to hold that there is no knowing of Existenz precisely because knowing necessarily requires an intentional thematizing act, e.g., an act of reflection, in search of what is essential. And because reflection is always on what has been, we know ourselves as Existenz only through a remembering. In this view we know ourselves in our acts and expressions in so far as they objectify us and we are able to reflect on them or remember them, i.e., bring them before us in an intentional act. In this respect we can describe and determine Existenz. But at the middle of this description there is, as it were, a hollow space or blind spot where what is centrally constitutive of Existenz is supposed to have its place. (This is analogous to the mistaken view that Husserl's primal presencing is a dark spot for itself because it is aware only of what it presences and knows itself only in retention.) Yet it is unlikely that these same thinkers would hold that there is no experience or living through of Existenz. Indeed, if the phenomenon of Existenz is the I's making an appearance of itself to itself in its self-gathered mode, then it would seem that all that appears is the gathered personal I and the dative of manifestation remains unknown, anonymous and ungathered. In which case the transcendental I is not compatible with Existenz, and transcendental phenomenologists are incapable of Existenz. Yet surely any transcendental I can be awakened to Existenz in a gathering experience and, in due course, reflect on itself as Existenz, e.g., in remembering.

But someone might want to hold that Existenz cannot come to light if it is lived essentially non-reflectively. What is lived is unknown and in the dark. All that comes to light is what reflection and memory bring to light and therefore what comes to light are acts and the expressive embodiment of acts. In which case we may know ourselves in an objective and fallible way, but there is no special gnosis of Existenz.

Obviously, here is an expression of a legitimate concern.[23] But what would such a responsible reflection build on, to what would it direct its attention, and what would be the source of the absolute demand that we will assign to Existenz, if it only came to light in, and as a result of, a reflection? Because of this unique coming to light of Existenz apart from and prior to a reflection, Jaspers hesitates to call it a knowing and uses the term *Erhellung*, or the illumination or coming to light, of Existenz. Doubtless eventually Existenz requires another knowing than that with which we are originally confronted in the illumination of Existenz, as in a realization of one's death. Prior to reflection, Existenz, as the self-illumination of the center of the *person*, is both pre- and non-reflexively self-aware. Prior to reflection, personal self-awareness, in contrast to that of the "myself" as the unique essence of the person, is properly pre- rather than non-reflexive. It requires further a responsible reflection, i.e., a self-knowing and action which is a response to an original claim that evolves out of that pre- and non-reflective and reflective self-knowing. But if it is true that there is no sense in which Existenz is immediately known or illuminated, i.e., pre- and non-reflectively self-aware, lived, or experienced, then it in no way is manifest and the very foundation of a philosophy of Existenz is non-existent. Existenz would be the creation of reflection, and its status of being more than a fiction would be impossible to establish.[24]

The reflection-theory of the knowledge of Existenz short-changes the richness of the non-objective sense of oneself, e.g., in facing one's own death, as in the prospective retrospective act or in the gathering act. It is forced to this position of denying that Existenz is in some sense a unique phenomenon (while seeming to practically affirm it) because of its holding to the reflection theory of self-awareness. By holding to this view it must hold that Existenz is absolutely a non-phenomenon even though it holds that Existenz is capable of making a phenomenon of the world or of being in the world in such a way that how things appear correlate to Existenz; but this view must hold that there cannot be any *knowing* of Existenz *in any sense*.

Again, there is a very good reason for wanting to hold this position: We do not have something before us that may serve as a substrate of predication and analysis. Yet this rich non-reflective awareness of oneself as a single individual person with possibility and freedom, even though merely "lived" and not an object of intentional acts, is entitled to being named in an odd, but genuine, sense a "knowing." At the very least each would seem prepared to say that one is not unconscious, e.g., in the realization of one's death. Further, if the knowledge of Existenz and one's ipseity is primarily to be accomplished after the fashion of a reflection, and this is an inward-directed intentional apperception, and this merely results in probabilities and possibilities, then one wonders what it means for proponents of Existenz's primacy to insist upon the priority of its primacy before reflection, and that its unconditioned demands are not such as to be brought to light by mere philosophical reflection.[25]

The philosophical reflection on my death is not living the realization of *my death* but thinking about it; the phenomenological reflection thinks about it in its essential display, but is not gripped by the unconditioned nature of the situation. The earnestness, if not the reverence and piety, to which the realization of one's death beckons, is not identical with the kind of seriousness characteristic of phenomenological reflection.

This realization discloses in an immediate way a sense of ourselves that, upon reflection, is at odds with any naturalist or reified version of ourselves, however much official weight such views might normally have in our lives: ourselves as single individuals, not mere worldly things or events, who are inseparable from our freedom facing our destiny. Such intimations are faint adumbrations of the transcendental person's self-understanding, paralleling those we earlier discussed in Book 1, Chapter VI.

§6. The Question of the Appropriateness of the Transcendental Attitude in the Realization of "My Death"

We have been claiming that as transcendental phenomenologist I live in my *reflecting on* and *thinking about* e.g., my death, not in the realization of my death (or my Existenz).[26] In reflection I actualize a possibility of my being, that of thinking, and it is this in which I live, but in this attitude I do not actually exist or live in that which I am thinking about, e.g., the realization of my death, which has to do with not *a* possibility of my being but the very possibility of my non-being and with the responsibility I bear for how I have been. In the central stance of transcendental phenomenological philosophy where the task is explicitly the display of what is there and the display of the displaying of what is there, there is an explicit practice of a disengagement from one's life in the natural attitude.

In assuming the transcendental phenomenological stance there is presupposed a sense of one's freedom and the availability of the power to extricate oneself from the exigencies of one's involvement with life and the demands of the world. This assumption does not always obtain. And here we wish to dwell briefly on some of the kinds of necessity we all face that interfere with our philosophical freedom to reflect or enter into the transcendental attitude.

In extreme pain, sickness and weariness there is a kind of necessity that hinders theory because the I-can of reflection and focusing is incapacitated. As has been shown by numerous thinkers to whom this work is indebted on many points, there is evidently a sense in which I do not *have* extreme pains, but I *am* them or I exist them; they absorb the typical "distance" that the intentional relation establishes between subject and object, knower and known. I do not have the capacity to distract myself from them and attend to something else. In extreme pain, sickness, or weariness, my sense of my bodily I-can is not fresh or quickened but rather enfeebled because of the pain, the weariness, etc. Even the "distance" between my self and my I-can seems undermined or collapsed to "I cannot" and "It must."

We noted earlier how our emotional life similarly can engulf "I myself" and one's *I can* as one's reflective and transcendental capacity. Thus in extreme fear or anger I find myself identified and involved with the personal situation provoking the fear and anger. My "myself" as transcendent to this identification as this person in the world is occluded. But the occlusion in intense emotions differs from the way *I* recede in extreme pain and weariness. In the former case there is a kind of "moral" necessity that I have constituted, for which I am more or less responsible, and for which I am more or less remiss. I am more than the person so identified and so involved in this emotion-producing situation. In traditional terms we can say, I am not what my capacity for, e.g., courage and temperance, could enable me to be.

Clearly in the lived body's incapacitation through extreme pain and weariness there is an evident sense of more of a "physical," not "moral," necessity – granted that we can imagine cases, as in the cases of saints and other heroes where this distinction is blurred[27] – that hinders assuming the transcendental attitude. But the necessity that pain and weariness impose on me that make nearly or clearly impossible the transcendental attitude is different from the necessity my moral weakness creates for me in intensely emotional situations. Similarly the necessities imposed by pain and weariness differ from the way my death imposes a necessity on me to face it and its exigencies. In the realization of my death, as in situations of intense emotion, there are pressures or motivations that dissuade me from assuming the phenomenological attitude. But in the realization of my death I am required to face the situation with my core and entire self, and to do it directly without explicitly an eye to phenomenological display. In the case of intense emotion it is not at all clear that my core and entire self are in play. Indeed, the attempt at the interjection of the transcendental attitude in the case of fear and anger has clearly the benefit of reminding me that I am more than the personal self with whom I am identified in the emotional situation. The recourse to philosophical reflection, foremost the phenomenological display of the emotional situation, is something to which we may be exhorted because it helps to loosen the grip the situation has on me. In this sense, assuming the phenomenological attitude in this situation is laudable.

The emotional situation thus contrasts with that of extreme illness in so far as in the latter case the impotence, the "I cannot," which I experience with extreme pain or weariness, trumps the "I can" that underlies my life of freedom and wakefulness. In the emotional situation, e.g., of fear and anger, the "I cannot" wins out over the "I can" only because I, in some sense have willed that it be so in that I have so constituted myself with this weakness in identifying myself with this kind of personal being in the world.

When speculating on how it will be when we face death it is not clear whether our facing death will more resemble how we face the emotional situation or that of extreme pain and weariness. The necessity of my facing my death "when it is time" presupposes that my "I can" has not been rendered null, e.g., by my illness or by my fear and cowardice. We cannot therefore count on our ability to face death "when it is time." *Memento mori* is not necessarily morbid advice but rather can well be prudent common sense.

Clearly we have in the lived body's incapacitation through extreme pain and weariness an evident sense of a kind of lived bodily necessity that hinders assuming the transcendental attitude. But the necessity that pain and weariness impose on me that make nearly or clearly impossible the transcendental attitude is different from the way my death imposes a necessity on me to face it and its exigencies. We might imagine a case where the resolve to phenomenologically display the weariness or pain might have salutary results, e.g., warding off the weariness or distracting from the pain. The necessity to face my death is such that I am beckoned to face it directly and without an eye to phenomenological display because the mediacy of the reflection and the display would be inappropriate in the way profane or frivolous behavior is during a solemn or sacred event. In contrast, the impotence, the

"I cannot," which I experience with *extreme* pain or weariness, trumps the "I can" that underlies my life of freedom and wakefulness. The necessity of my facing my death "when it is time" presupposes that my "I can" has not been rendered null, e.g., by illness. Again, to the extent one has finds reason through philosophy or faith to regard this "facing one's death" as a moral duty, then *memento mori* itself becomes in advance of the "time of one's death" an obligation.

Given the essential ignorance about the meaning of death and how beliefs fill in this vacuum, the differences in the kinds of necessity made present by "my death" may draw together and appear to become indistinguishable. The fear of the imminence of the presence of extreme pain may be compared with the dread of I myself being threatened by the engulfing darkness of absolute extinction. The horrifying prospect of remaining conscious forever while collapsed into a pain that swallows me and my being in the world, explains in part the trauma occasioned by doctrines of Hell. Of course this pain need not be that of something physical in origin. Having to live with oneself after one has irreparably betrayed all that one holds dear, knowing that those whom we betrayed know we have betrayed them, is conceivably the worst form of suffering. Death is what makes possible this prospect of an impossible reparation and "Hell," whether one understands this theologically or not. Even if there is no afterlife, it remains true that, e.g., for all eternity I have determined myself as the betrayer of my friends, either because of the finality of my death or that of my friends. Here again we meet the problems connected with the claim that of necessity the Now will have been: Of what is true now it must be said that will have been true.

Beside the necessities occasioned by pain that result in behavior over which I have no control or in the incapacitation of my agency, we may, by way of contrast, consider another kind of necessity. This is the familiar one of the necessity that evidence imposes, i.e., one that is commanded by the matter at hand itself, whether it be a matter of perceptual evidence in a filled intention or the relationship between propositions and concepts evident in empty intentions. Thus there is the necessity of intellectual integrity, as when we say, "One may not hold X if she holds Y, because Y implies the negation of X," or, "This is the way I saw it, I can't say I didn't see it this way."

All of life involves intellectual activity as the work of the categorial display of the world. The properly practical, aesthetic, and evaluative engagement of the world requires an awareness of appropriate categoriality, as well, of course, of identity. Yet clearly not all intellectual activity is theoretical. Further, not all the theoretical activities are always appropriate, and moral and practical necessities dictate that other activities occur or that the intellectual activities be suppressed or postponed. Thus there is the necessity of whole-heartedness or whole-mindedness that may be contrasted with that of forms of intellectual activity, even though the necessities here involved need not contradict. And even the necessities brought forth by phenomenology can be contrasted with other intellectual necessities, and these latter may lay claim, at least pragmatically, to a greater necessity. Thus, for example, it is clear that phenomenological display of one's involvement in a task at hand may be harmful as well as irrelevant to the performance of the task. Removing a splinter or transplanting an organ requires utmost concentration on the matter at hand; a display of the mode of manifestation of this wound or organ and of this concentration and what it enables and reveals of the matter at hand, while concentrating, is harmful to the appropriate performance and achievement of the matter at hand.

But even if reflective display were possible without interfering and without harm to the matter and performance at hand, even if one got good at doing these two things at once, there are times when phenomenological display is improper, irrelevant and irreverent. When phenomenological display is concurrent with, e.g., prayer, love-making and professing one's love, consoling, counseling, grieving, etc., it is degrading of both the matter and agency. It borders on being inappropriate in the same way frivolous or profane behavior is inappropriate at a solemn or sacred event. The reason is that the matter at hand demands whole-heartedness or whole-mindedness. To be otherwise is to have a divided attention when simplicity of mind, in the sense of undividedness and whole-mindedness, is called for. Indeed, transcendental phenomenologists, when practicing their profession at solemn times, may be charged, indeed, must charge themselves, with being at least double-minded, if not duplicitous, narcissitic, and disrespectful. The nature of the matter and task at hand may require a kind of unreflective respect and reverence that forestalls phenomenological reflection; the phenomenologist who does not heed the required postponement contradicts this attitude. Of course, this is not to say that certain matters are out of bounds for phenomenological reflection. The phenomenological reflection that may take place may be in the reliving, recollection, and imaginative conjuring up of the former event and intentional stance. If phenomenological activity takes place during, e.g., the realization of the phenomenologist's death, it destroys or detracts from the realization, just as awareness of one's being humble destroys it, just as benevolence done out of the desire to reap political favors is no longer benevolence; just as reverential demeanor displayed for the good effect is not really reverential, etc. The essential quality of these acts is negated or at least diminished by the concomitant self-reflective agency.

The chief reason for the threat of impropriety of a phenomenology of my death is that it interferes with the realization of and meeting my death. The realization of my death calls me to be absolutely intimate with myself; it does not call me *now* to *display* "for us all" how I myself face my destiny and how my death raises the question of my destiny. It calls me not to display but to face my destiny and to be unconditionally myself. The presence of death's imminence demands that I face it and take a position toward my life in the face of it; it is not the philosophical call to display my facing death.

The secret of my death is inseparable from the secret of me myself. If there is ever a time when I ought not to flee from myself and to avoid "being busy," if there is ever a time for me to be honest with myself and be honestly myself – whatever this may precisely mean, and this depends on who one has become and what else one believes – it is now at the hour of one's death or when the grace of the realization one's own death makes itself present. The reason is that this is indeed, at least metaphorically, a "grace" to be with oneself and one's life "appropriately," i.e., in accord with one's ownmost essence as a mortal whose time has come, i.e. there is at hand the imminent prospect of one's annihilation. As we noted, the ineluctable prospective retrospection need not result in such "gracious" gathering acts.

One's intentional life in the world is centrifugal of necessity, and the opportunities for the intimate examination of and coming to terms with oneself in the light of the mystery of death are unique privileges, if not "graces." "Oneself" as this absolutely unique "I myself" as incarnated, communalized, enworlded, acculturated, and historicized, in short, as individuated as a person over the time of one's life, is stopped in the vectors that propel it to attend to the body, nature, the community, the world, the culture, and history, and instead it is beckoned to be gathered to itself in the moment of the presence of "one's death." To refuse this exhortation is to refuse to be centered with oneself, or to refuse to be with one's core self, or it is an affirmation of oneself as without a center. Doubtless there are times when this refusal to be with oneself might be justified, as in the unhesitating risking of one's life for another. But surely a philosopher must take the time (and who is to say how much time is enough?) to face her death. And then she might well be moved to work out a phenomenology of one's death. But perhaps many such philosophical exercises are precisely the most subtle forms of refusal to come to terms with one's death.

In short, doubtless the display of the presence of one's death is an important philosophical undertaking; but just as in prayer, love-making, and reverent attention to someone in need of one's counsel, the philosophical work should not supplant the present moment's demands on our single-minded and whole-hearted attention. There is a time and a place for philosophical display; philosophical agency in the classical sense, the pursuit of wisdom, is not coincident with phenomenology as what happens within the transcendental attitude.

But have we done justice to the unity of I myself who am at once this person, gathered I, or Existenz, and Transcendental I? After all, I as Existenz might believe myself "called" to be a philosopher. As philosopher of whatever stripe I also face my death. As will become clear later each is Existenz, even if each is not a philosopher. But reflection, including transcendental reflection, is also an exigency, indeed an "existential" one in the sense that as a person I face the necessity of reflection to be honest with myself. The unexamined life is not worth living and display of what and how life is experienced is exemplarily the examined life. Furthermore, are we not, throughout a large part of this book, ultimately talking about the proper and authentic manifestation of "my death" for transcendental phenomenology – especially and precisely when we claim that the transcendental disengagement is inappropriate for permitting its proper presencing?

As Husserl has taught,[28] it is an a priori truth that every practical proposition, (such as the one we are making in this book, i.e., "The realization of my death ought to avoid being at the same time a philosophical-phenomenological analysis") can take a theoretical turn and thereby itself become a theme of philosophical-phenomenological analysis. As Husserl also has taught,[29] transcendental phenomenology creates a habitus that is not simply relinquished when the exigencies of the natural attitude require us to stop our philosophizing. The philosopher is abidingly disposed to return to the transcendental attitude, and the transcendental issues of the display of life and the bracketing of the natural attitude are always on the verge of being reactivated. The possibility of the transcendental person is the possibility of a new kind of Existenz wherein the presentations in the natural attitude are seen over against the backdrop of the remembered transcendental considerations. Thus, in regard to the present issue, *it is ultimately a transcendental phenomenological insight that the transcendental attitude is inappropriate on certain occasions*, like the realization of "my death." This is not an insight that requires a simple return to naivety but rather it is the insight of one for whom the transcendental attitude is a philosophical disposition, but who realizes that there are kinds of necessities to which the transcendental attitude must allow precedence. The transcendental habitus of disengagement must, on occasion, itself be disengaged, and this is a transcendental-phenomenological insight and doctrine.

Further, it must be said that the wonderfully nuanced *displays* of Existenz by, e.g., Kierkegaard, Jaspers, and Heidegger are neither themselves acts of resolve to face one's destiny nor are they necessarily the fruits of such acts of resolve. Rather, they bear witness to the disengagement of a philosophical observer for whom the compelling presence of Existenz's call to be resolved is bracketed in favor of the display of the call to be resolved, and thus it is a bracketing and resolve not itself to now resolve the demands of Existenz but to display the demands of Existenz.

This disengagement need not be indifference to Existenz's demands and may reflect one's own single-minded response to them. In any case the matter of the relationship of phenomenological-philosophical reflection on one's dying and the exigencies of one's death brings out the seriousness of the matter of a philosophy of Existenz as well as the philosophical vocation. The immediate compelling necessity of the "deadly earnestness" of Existenz and the distinguishing properties that distinguish Existenz from "existence" or bodily objects in the world, as well as its distinctiveness from an instantiable "essence," universal theoretic consciousness, etc. – all these distinctions are finely brought to light not merely by Existenz's self-awareness in the wake of the crisis or limit-situations of everydayness that, e.g., the death of the writer poses, but by a kind of transcendental eidetic display of Existenz (Existenz as such!) as it emerges out of this crisis.

Such displays, which find expression in exquisite philosophical books, are not themselves an immediate expression of a shattered bodily being in the world occasioned by a limit-situation such as one's death. Rather they are displays by one who has practiced a kind of reflective disengagement from Existenz and the gripping limit-situation. Such a one appreciates at least implicitly the notion of the transcendental person, i.e., a perspective on our being that reflects both the natural and transcendental attitudes, especially the unique transformation of the natural attitude that adumbrates the transcendental person, i.e., the emergence of Existenz out of limit-situations.

Existential philosophers as a rule shy away from the transcendental attitude and the transcendental I, but one can always ask of them: Is the standpoint of the author of their books on Existenz included in the book, i.e., is the display and articulation of Existenz adequately accounted for by *Existenz*? Or does this book on Existenz (or *Dasein*) not need to have for part of its philosophical content the standpoint and agency which enable the display by which the fundamental features of *Existenz* (or *Dasein*) are brought to light?

§7. Philosophy as Theoretic Analysis and as Preparation for Death

Philosophy in antiquity was regarded as serious *play* because it was thought to be *preparation* for the mystery of death. Ancient philosophy never really believed itself to get to a position where the philosopher *knew* what death means. Thus what was achieved never had the definitiveness of the absolutely valid articulation of what we most wanted to know and what was most worth knowing. For those of us for whom philosophy has not been a preparation for death, for those of us for whom philosophy itself has been something else, e.g., a "career opportunity," death's sudden distinctive realization places demands on us, e.g., a gathering of our life, not a disengagement of our life in favor of how it appears. Some of the issues we have just discussed are implicit in the death of Socrates. When Socrates, for whom philosophy was a life-long preparation for death, faced death, his last oration just prior to his death was an exhortation to his friends to prepare for death properly. Yet Socrates never seemed to stop talking, stop doing philosophy, right up until he took the hemlock.

We are left with several possible interpretations. First, may we not assume that Socrates's final displaying of the third- and second-person phenomenon of death was for the edification of his followers, i.e., an effort to move them so that they too would prepare for death. Because his whole life was philosophizing as a preparation for death, he, at the moment of death, only needed to live as he always had lived, i.e., doing philosophy. Secondly, may we not assume that the display of death was such that it did not permit the second- and third-person perspectives to enjoy a hegemony in the understanding of death? His own life of philosophy had already provided him with just such a preparation and he might have wanted to share this insight. We may recall the text we used as an epigraph for this chapter. Here Socrates explicitly distinguishes the first-eperson sense of himself and his dying from the third- and second-personal view of Crito.

Yet, thirdly, if we interpret Socrates to be involved in dialectic, essence analysis, as well as the display of the phenomenon of death as it appears in the third-person right up until he took the hemlock, i.e., if the "philosophical" preparation for death was simply more philosophical analysis and dialogue right up until the end, and thus e.g., a confirmation and celebration of philosophy as foremost an epistemic stance of learned ignorance and knowing that one is not wise, then we could well be puzzled by calling it a preparation for death. Indeed, then one might wonder whether Socrates ever *realized* that he would die, and whether his final discourse in the *Phaedo* was not a sustained repression of that realization. Of course, his final celebration of philosophy was also one of mind over the forces that appear capable of destroying it. And perhaps it was also an acknowledgement by Socrates that, in spite of the received answers, he best bore witness to the truth by continuing to question and thereby defy death's apparent necessary finality as well as the non-philosophical solutions to the questions death posed.

Doubtless in the face of the mystery of one's death we all may confess to an ignorance, whether learned or not; but the question remains whether the appropriate stance in the face of one's death is primarily a theoretic-cognitive one, or is not something else called for, especially by one who has professed a vocation to pursue wisdom or the knowledge most worth having? Assuming that theoretical knowing detaches us personally from the known, can, on occasion, theoretical knowing deprive us of something else, i.e., a more appropriate, personal knowing? This something else would not be itself display but the agency of facing one's destiny. But what precisely does that mean? What does "facing one's destiny" mean if at best we face what is faceless and mysteriously unknown. Is, after all, the unknowable knowable? Typically the pretentions to knowledge are speculative philosophical theories or there is the essentially different "knowledge" of religious faith. If "facing one's destiny" is an act of self-realization which is more appropriate than philosophical analysis, then there might be something, at least on occasion, more "philosophical" than philosophical analysis. Of course, making evident to others the importance of this subordination of philosophical theory and display is only through philosophical theory and display.

But the "existential" position is not to be merely juxtaposed to the theoretic one. Further, in this matter of one's death there is an angle from which we need not distinguish the theoretic concern that is not transcendentally disengaged from one wherein there is transcendental disengagement. On the one hand, in the natural and transcendental attitude there is the unrestricted desire to understand, which itself has a telos which is infinite intelligibility and the "unconditioned."[30] This infinite unconditioned intelligibility is, of course, presumed and postulated. It is of necessity without foundation in a filled intention. Such a postulated telos doubtless goes against the grain of those ancient and modern thinkers who believe that the universe is laced with surds and *anangke*, and not just randomness and random probability. Yet, modern science and philosophy are, as Husserl would maintain, within a horizon or idea of infinite and unconditioned intelligibility, even if this horizon is apperceived as laced with surds. Cognitive striving in its essence aims at an ideal position-taking which is a definitive Yes or No wherein I am not vulnerable to the embarrassment of modalizations of doubt or uncertainty and wherein I rest in certainty on the basis of evidence.[31] What we genuinely *know* in filled intentions or as conclusions to premises are limited matters whose intelligibility is correspondingly limited; and we know conditioned states of affairs whose conditions happen to be fulfilled; and this filling itself is conditioned by the presumptions tucked into how we have framed the matter in terms of the most recent reliable hypotheses. Knowing important and massive matters like the influence of the emissions of fossil fuels on global warming, whether there is life on Mars, or what the Bush Administration actually did know prior to 9/11 are still very finite matters of intelligibility and our assent to judgments about the truth of any interpretation would have to be a matter of the conditions of the assent being filled.

An integral part of this meditation is the odd fact that some philosophers and theoreticians have a distinctive passion, which seems to lie more or less dormant in most of us. Here is a passion for the infinite intelligibility and "formally unconditioned," i.e., the assent to that which has no conditions whatsoever, e.g., it is not framed by empty intentions which condition its presence in a filled intention. For such thinkers the infinite intelligibility and formally unconditioned are insistently in the horizon of all their undertakings. That is, they are "in love" with theoretical truth, i.e., infinite intelligibility and the formally unconditioned. For such a person facing one's death may well appear distinctively as one's own and not just a neutral possibility or fact, and this may move one to confront one's own self with a prospective retrospection. That is, such a person does not doubt that the unconditioned quest for theoretical truth is not able purely and simply to be equated with what is of unconditional importance here and now for the person. Nevertheless for such a person the drive to understand is the dominant disposition and consequently the distinction between, on the one hand, the illumination of one's gathered self before the mystery, e.g., of one's death, which beckons to a kind of agency, and, on the other hand, the dominant passion to *understand this mystery* becomes blurred. While acknowledging that the mystery of death demands a kind of agency or demeanor rather than understanding, the desire for understanding of the mystery resists subordination. This is perhaps a way to understand Socrates doing philosophy until the very end.

In which case, the theoretic side is in tension with the existential. This is the inherent Faustian ingredient in philosophy. It is perhaps latent in the venerable tendency to single out intellect as the distinguishing excellence and power – even to the degree that it is alleged that it is the principle that accounts for the unique singularity of ipseity. The desire to know and understand what seem to be impenetrable mysteries may claim one's allegiance to such an extent that the thinker is willing to undertake this disclosure no matter what the cost. The cost might well mean the sacrifice of the Ought or the One Thing Necessary.

The tension was keen in Husserl but he ultimately acknowledged the primacy of will and was prepared to defend a version of intellect being a servant of the will.[32] What precisely this means is worth dwelling on. It seems uncontroversial to state that for Husserl the "I myself" has to be regarded as the center of agency. Thus the question of the priority of will or intellect is, it would seem, a question of which power is the seat of the "I myself" or whether "I myself" *am* and do not *have* these powers or whether indeed "I myself" *have* them and neither is to be assigned primacy. The very notion that intellect is a servant of the will suggests that I-ness inhabits will more so than intellect. In Book 1, Chapter V, §3, we proposed that we think of "the myself" as a bare substrate having intellect and will as "tautological properties." Most discussions of this matter seem to us to be on the wrong path if they take a third-person view of the powers contesting with one another, as if the first-personal perspective was an afterthought. In the question of primacy we have often an echo of a mythic struggle between the eternal dark forces of will and the lightsome forces of intellect.

As we shall see, Husserl himself was moved to claim that the center of the I was not foremost an act-center of intellectual acts, but love. But no form of will, foremost love, is a blind force deprived of a displayed object or person, nor is it itself bereft of the capacity to display. In Book 1 we said that empathic perception targets the ipseity of the Other as beyond her properties and that love's disclosure, which builds on the empathic perception, celebrates this transcendent ipseity.

"Will" is inseparable from "I myself' and intellect or reason and there is no willing in the form of wanting or wishing which is not in intentional correlation to what is appreciated or displayed as good, important, or desirable in some respect.

This work holds for the tautological view that some sense of myself as willing is to be given priority over myself as understanding in my dealing with both what is of greatest importance as well as in the position-taking toward what is philosophically ultimate; this is a sense in which it is an existential philosophy. This view is tautological not only in the sense in which it may be said that the true is the good of intellect, but also in regard to what is unconditionally important, i.e., the Good, as what draws or binds the will without conditions, enjoys priority over the True. In these matters will is more intimately "I myself" than is intellect because here we have to do with what is absolutely important and yet what eludes articulation by intellect. As in the case of death and the transcendent ipseity of the Other, what the unconditionally important calls for now is a solemn prospective retrospection or love, and a reflection on or display of these is out of place. What is most important is not primarily a matter of reason and intellect, even though dealing with what is important cannot be done without reason and intellect actively opening up the field of agency by articulating the syntax of the values and disvalues.

Thus philosophy, and here connection may be made with the ancient etymological root of the word, *philein sophia*, is clearly not driven either exclusively or primarily toward knowing what is of unrestricted intelligibility and the formally unconditioned in regard to objects of general validity and universal scope emergent out of our being in the world. Rather, there is an irrepressible aspect of philosophy that has to do with the knowledge having to do with the lived experience of the individual essence facing its destiny, and thus philosophy has to do with the knowledge most worth having. And, as in the matters of death, myself, and love, there is a limit that is intrinsic to the cognitive motion, even though it is not the limit of triviality, nonsense, or banality. We have suggested the (philosophically suspect) term of "mystery" for these matters.

However, this view in no way purports to suggest that such a version of the primacy of will represses or displaces the drive toward unrestricted intelligibility in regard to what comprises the personal life in the world. Indeed, the very sense of will as the source of an action is that the will act is completed in a decision. And the decision itself is the result of the reflection that clarifies and articulates the will's momentum as wishing, desiring, wanting, hoping, etc. If someone would refuse to submit a course of action to reflection, given the opportunity to do so, or if someone were to embark on a willful commitment, refusing thereby to take rational stock of this willing, this person would be acting "irresponsibly," i.e., the person would be faulted for not appropriately responding to what is called for, i.e., what a person is supposed to do in such a situation, i.e., know what one is doing, look before you leap, pay attention to what's ahead, be mindful of how others around you are affected, etc. As is well known, an ontology of persons is implicit in our moral expectations and "reactive attitudes," i.e., those attitudes like resentment, indignation, guilt, etc., where we expect certain modes of comportment from one another.[33] We will return to this matter later.

Further, because the reflection in the face of, e.g., love, the ipseity facing its death, limit-situations, etc. finds nothing there to illuminate in the sense of articulate or analyze into properties, and, at the same time, the situation creates a demand for a response, e.g., reverence and a solemn position-taking, there is nowhere for the drive to understand to go. There is nowhere among the objects in the world to which to turn. Therefore, even though the center of attention of such a reflection is in the service of my habitual life-will and there is an impulse toward clarification, as a prelude to action, there is "nothing" to shed light on and nowhere to go. The reflection which typically illumines the will and enables decision is stopped, and yet one must take a stand, assume a posture, e.g., of joy, love, dread, reverence, etc. The encounter with death, the beloved, limit-situations, etc., suspend the natural attachment to objects in the world and propel us to attend to, or, rather, be awakened to, ourselves at our center, one's Existenz. This creates a space not for a typical action in the world as would a normal reflection and deliberation, but rather it makes room for *acting* or position-taking without reserve and hesitation, i.e., unconditionally, in regard to that which merits this unconditional action and this is not, in the proper sense, something in the world.[34]

Yet the claim of the necessity of such an existential attitude ultimately needs theory and understanding to clarify what precisely it is that merits this action and what this position-taking is. As Husserl says, "willing to know is presupposed by all other willing if willing is to possess the highest form of value."[35] This is evident in the consideration of the necessity of "deliberation" in responsible agency and what "deliberation" is. Clearly deliberation or rational reflection on one's possible options influences, indeed, shapes and transforms our willing. Although the eventual action clearly is an expression of our willing, and willing typically awaits the clarification of deliberation and reflection, yet the prior will (as wanting or wishing) may not at all be justified by the reflection but rather we may come to find our volitional impulse moved to a quite different, perhaps even reversed, action by reason of a new consideration. In this sense one might be tempted to say that rational reflection determines the will and thus becomes its moving principle and in this sense the intellect is the true subject of the self and has primacy over will. And in this sense reason or intellect in the form of rational deliberation is both the necessary and sufficient condition of willing. In such formulations one might be tempted to wonder whether the will were indeed "free" and not in fact impotent in regard to reason or reflection, as some passages in Socrates suggest. Yet, as Peter Bieri has nicely pointed out, I am not distinguished from my reflection and my decision such that they interfere with or dominate my freedom of willing. My freedom of willing is precisely to be found in acting upon reflection's articulation and display of my field of agency. My free act of willing is not my willing bereft of the display of reflection. In wakeful (not blind, "willful" action where I am at the mercy of what lures and beckons, but without any syntax, any distinctions), *I* seek clarity regarding my wants and impulses through reflection. *I* enact my powers of reflection, and therefore *I* act on behalf of what is "truly important" in regard to that to which I am drawn. Thereby I become indeed properly the subject of the agency. In the terminal

moment of action, in deciding, I am most properly myself in arousing my capacity
to reflect and judge to display my situation, articulate its values and disvalues, and
thereby to influence my will both as the power of decision and execution.[36]

Further, consider a situation of "deliberation" and "reflection" where someone is
torn between either staying behind with his compatriots to fight the brutal occupying forces or fleeing this scene with his family in order to bring them to safety. In
meeting his underground compatriots in the resistance, while fleeing with his family,
he must meet their scorn and their doubts about his courage, his commitment to
justice, and perhaps about the genuineness of his gratitude to and veneration of the
all the brutally murdered compatriots who have fallen in the resistance movement.
Here, doubtless, deliberation and reflection shed light and influence the will, but
this illumination is precisely the articulation of what one most truly cherishes and
values, that with which, as we shall say, one most identifies. Surely what is to be
brought to light is not merely what is logically consistent, or what is prudential in
terms of what is most likely to succeed, or even what is morally correct and what
one's obligations are. These ride on the deep loyalties and the depth of one's loves
as well as one's personal essence. The weighing of the matters is not merely bringing to light reasons and arguments but a clarification of what one loves and cherishes
and, in this respect, who one is and what sort of person one is or wants to be. I
myself as willing have no less primacy than I myself as reflecting and displaying
or as intellect, and my intellect is in the service of the clarification of my will and
heart – even if it be the value or good of what is the true.

Assigning intellect (myself as intellect) a primacy does not take account of
several things. It fails to consider that its function typically is to clarify the will and
"reasons of the heart." Further, it neglects that the dynamism of intellect is a desire
to understand that heads toward the intelligible as its fulfillment and even if we call
this fulfillment "theory" we must not neglect that it as *theorein* is a passive gazing
delight in its telos as present and attained – even if the telos is but a way-station
in the opening up of further horizons of understanding. Furthermore, it does not
account for the cases where what intellect has to say must defer to the "reasons of
the heart." We saw this in the case of assuming the appropriate prospective retrospection before death, but it would seem to be a factor in most of life's decisions.
And in these everyday cases too, something like an evaluing act is no less basic
than rational reflection and the latter stands in the service of the former. But again,
talking about these powers as autonomous competing agencies neglects that it is
I who reflect or fail to reflect; it is I myself who face imperatives which by their
very nature appear to me to require the postponement of reflection, etc.

And further, to assign the intellect the status of "I myself" and primacy over
will, and even when this thesis takes form in the claim that deliberation is said to
be both the necessary and sufficient condition of willing, does not do justice to
cases where I fail to show up to myself in spite of my knowing what is right, where
I have judged what the reasonable course would be but choose instead to follow
another path. We will return to such complex matters in the next chapters. Surely
often enough in cases where I act from out of addiction or under the duress of a bad
habit I have failed to so constitute myself that my power to let rational reflection
influence my will has been lost to me. In this sense, there is a clear testimony to

the necessary status of intellectual wakefulness in determining one's action and in being properly oneself. It is unclear whether such cases cover those where there might not be an obscure "reason of the heart," as in the cases of "the sickness unto death" or melancholy or *anxiety*, whereby I fail to act and/or fail not only to follow the path indicated by reflection but fail to embark on the very reflection, which failure for me is at once a matter of shame and astonishment.

The view we are holding is that there properly is neither a clear primacy of oneself as intellect nor as will. Rather we are proposing a primacy of the existential and this is therefore a primacy of "I myself" and this is often, if not always, intellect in the service of will. The coaeval status of intellect and will is indicated in the very notion of the unrestricted *desire* to understand, for this desire or passion is there from the start and self-legitimating and self-perpetuating. This unrestricted desire to understand, as we noted, does indeed find itself in situations where "reason" or "understanding" is called to a halt. This is because there is evident a compelling evaluation that it is more appropriate, e.g., to love, pray, forgive, repent, gather oneself, pay one's respects, etc., rather than to understand. One may, indeed, still have the desire to understand, but now what is before us demands that one find one's center elsewhere than in the agency of manifestation, e.g., in an act of solemn veneration, adoration, celebration, etc. Subsequently one may bracket this, call it into question, analyze it, etc., but now the solemnity emergent from the evaluating stance curtails the philosophical attitude understood as the agency of manifestation.

The interplay of will and understanding and the primacy of will in the pre-intellectual and pre-rational foundations of the desire to understand surface in how one wrestles with the recurrent challenges to and crises of the life of the mind and the institutions of science, technology, and politics. We will spell this out as a conclusion to this chapter.

Philosophy and science of necessity involve the postulate of an intelligibility as the "meant" of the eros to understand. Traditionally in the West the life of the display of this intelligibility, whether conditioned or unconditioned intelligibility, has involved the belief in the special, even blessed status, of the pursuit of this life. But this postulate faces massive challenges by the recurrent surds and irrationalities like mental and physical diseases and natural disasters. These become obstacles not only for the theoretical undertakings but also for the practical applications. Similarly we have the perennial moral disturbances such as ignorance, pride, ambition, lust for power, weakness, and greed among scientists that affect the integrity of the entire enterprise and establishment. Such obstacles to the life of the mind and the conditions of the good life and peaceable kingdom or polis do not have merely local significance but rather may well issue in a nuclear or ecological holocaust that would destroy the entire human adventure. What will the pursuit of science and philosophy mean, i.e., what will it have meant, when the only sentient life form remaining is that of the cockroach? What will the progress of science, culture, and civilization have meant when all rational consciousness is obliterated?

For hundreds of years circumstances have arisen which generate apocalyptic scenarios that compel a prospective retrospection of not merely one's own life but also that of all of humanity. The past one-hundred years, and especially today, provide us reason to be moved toward a collective, species-wide, prospective retrospection.

What, in the face of the "inevitable" obliteration of humanity, does the struggle for the Beloved Community, the advance of science, the celebration of universal dignity in the form of social-political equality, and an earthly approximation of the Kingdom of God mean? Do such considerations make Kantians out of all of us for whom continued progressive consequences were not part of the justification for required action. What do the advances in science and philosophy mean when there is more or less imminent a "second death," i.e., not only the death of each of us, but of the very luminosity and display of the world? If humankind is destroyed, and the astrophysical community teaches unanimously that this is inevitable if humans are confined to this solar system – it is just a matter of a few billion years – what will the record of achievements in data bases, libraries, etc., *mean*, assuming that there is no one there to read or interpret it? What will the thousands of years of collective cooperative scientific-academic work *have meant* – we know, of course, it *is meaningful* in the actual doing of it – when it is all absolutely extinguished? Recall our earlier discussion (Book 2, Chapter I, §4) that the sense of what is now or the present of necessity means that "it will have been." When consciousness and thus all learning are obliterated, what do the eulogies mean, that Professor X, a member of the School of Z, makes or made distinguished contributions to the field of Y if what Professor X now does or did will not have been? Does research not entail that what one displays as true is something that (always) will have been true – or at least the truth that one once held this (which subsequently proved to be erroneous) belief will have been true forever? Is it not intrinsic to what we call "research" and being a scientist, scholar, and academic that there be a sense of contributing to the enduring project, if not the body, of knowledge, and thereby to the well-being of humanity? But if there will be no humanity, no agents of manifestation, no retained knowledge, no remembered body or project of knowing, does not the sense of what is being done change significantly?

Thus there is occasioned a kind of prospective retrospection by the modern apocalyptic ecological, thermal-nuclear, cosmological narratives. For example, for some scientists who think about these matters the obvious and foremost imperative is the need for space exploration and a terra-forming of some planets, in spite of the long shadow of suspicion that the human formation of *terra* is in part the source of the apocalypse.

Yet there is in this same scientific community a deeper and darker pessimism that is connected with the theory of the eventual extermination of our galaxy and our natural surrounding. According to some spokespersons for the official scientific world-view we are counseled against any view of purpose in the scientific description of the world. Officially the view, according to the physicist, Peter Atkins, is that we are "children of chaos." A kind of entropy pervades all the world in which we live "and the deep structure of change is decay. At root, there is only corruption and the unstemmable tide of chaos. Gone is all purpose... This is the bleakness we have to accept as we peer deeply and dispassionately into the heart of the universe."[37]

If human life requires meaning and purpose, it can, in this view, find no support in nature. This means that meaningful life must be found only in the life of ipseity detached from its "existence condition" of being human, or it must acquiesce to the view that the natural kind called human is pointless in the natural scheme of things. The latter seems to be the explicit motivation for the recommendation of some such "philosophical physicists" that we humans must therefore create playful niches of psychological warmth. Within this psychological refuge, which we disengage from any wider cosmological or historical context, we act as if there were meaning and purpose in the narrow confines of our life together knowing full well there is no such meaning or comfort to be found in the historical or natural-historical adventure of the species. Thus in addition to the creeping malaise fostered by the geo-political and ecological prognosis about the human enterprise, there is the pessimistic doctrine of decay and dysteleology of the scientific astrophysical establishment.

Let us leave aside the issue that for phenomenology all of these opinions and claims are forms of empty intentions and do not admit of being given in anything like a filled intention. (Many of life's important matters that have to do with our natural, social, and intersubjective life resist being given in filled intentions.) Let us also neglect the question whether a philosophical resolution of these matters could be rooted in metaphysics or ontology and whether these would have to be compatible with a philosophy of nature that is in sync with contemporary natural science. What is without a doubt evident is that the realm of human meaning as pursued in *die Geisteswissenschaften* is, for this modern official scientific point of view, increasingly strange in so far as the *Humanities*, for essential reasons, cannot give up their moorings in the first-person perspective which itself is pervaded by teleology.[38] Rather, from the scientific view from nowhere, science is "foundational" for any "sane" view of things, and therefore life's lived meaningfulness and purposefulness are increasingly idiosyncratic and mere fictional manufactures. In short, most of these theories see the "explanation of the meaning of life" in terms of efficient physical causes wherein human consciousness is but an epiphenomenon and human purposes and articulations of meaning and finality are fictions.

Yet the science itself is conducted in the first-person activities of the scientist. Thus, e.g., the conditional hypotheses and the modalities of the scientist's judgements, intrinsic parts of the mode of operation of the scientist, have no place in the physical world of "absolute reality" to which the scientist holds allegiance. She herself functions within the idea that is the horizon of the desire to understand. (This too is not to be found in the absolute reality of the physical world.) This desire to understand is the basis of science and philosophy, as well as the horizon of the desire that founds action and the quest for happiness and general well-being. Thought and action cannot thrive in the vacuum created by the view that the universe is one of dysteleology, chance, surds, chaos and decay. ("Chaos theory," for example, offers universal patterns of causal explanation.) There is incessantly required means to keep open this horizon of the desire to understand. Because the motivations to do this are being shut down from the official scientific, and often enough as well from the contemporary geo-political and ecological scene, there is little or no prior evidence to hold open the horizon and thus motivate inquiry and action. This means that in advance of the evidential deliverances of science and the world-political scene the hope and desire that indeed all is not decay, dysteleology,

and chaos must somehow go in advance. It would be a mistake to regard these pronouncements from the scientific community as approaching anything like apodictic
evidence or logical necessity. It seems to me that they even go beyond the limits of
modern science's probabilistic-statistical canons of evidence, even though it is clear
why one might be tempted to such pessimistic possibilities.

Yet, if science, philosophy, and action are to continue, in so far as possible and
in accord with intellectual honesty, there must be postulated believed-in alternative narratives that hold open the horizon of hope and desire that sustain thinking
and action. These, at least from the perspective of the apocalyptic scenario of
the scientific establishment and the geo-political analysts, are of necessity willful "existential" commitments to the necessary non-evidential, and in this sense,
non-rational prior conditions for reason. The belief in the conditions of the eros of
rationality, what Kant called *Vernunftglaube*, is the necessary non-rational basis
for reason, science, and philosophy. Only by this prior hope, faith, and desire can
rationality be sustained. At the heart of the dispassionate, detached, so-called
hard-nosed third-person, non-sentimental account of the world as it is there is the
passionate, engaged, first-person will to believe and will to postulate the conditions of reason and the good life. And when these postulated conditions are not
in harmony with the view from nowhere, then this view from nowhere that leads
nowhere must revise its crypto-metaphysical narrative and not pass itself off as
anything more than it is: the way the scientific establishment's implicit metaphysics
paints the nature and destiny of humanity and the cosmos.

"Irrational," i.e., non-evidentially founded, faith and commitment serve as the
necessary condition and basis for the rational-theoretical and even the ethical life in
so far as it is not purely deontological. Husserl wrestled with this cultural pessimism
fostered by the view from nowhere, and here as elsewhere we may learn from him.

> As long as I have an open practical horizon for which no termination is definitely prede-
> lineated, and so long as I have given to me a recognized realizable value – even if it be
> merely in a vague presumptive mode of givenness – which presumably can lead to new
> practical values in the direction of the best possible or the absolutely binding, I have the
> duty of acting. ... When I believe [in the practical realizability of the *telos* of theory and
> practice] and make myself aware of this belief, when I freely perform this belief out of this
> practical source there is given meaning to the world and my life; there is given also a joyful
> confidence that nothing is in vain and that all is to the good.[39]

Husserl did not appear to believe that a new narrative was needed but he was clear
that a creative self-displacing into a horizon nurturing hope was in order when
faced with the predictions of the end of meaning and the annihilation of the enterprise of spirit.

> I will do best to overestimate the probabilities and to act as if I was certain that fate was
> not essentially hostile to humanity and as if I could be certain that through persevering
> I could ultimately attain something so good that I could be satisfied with my perseverance.
> What is theoretically reprehensible, i.e., the overestimation of probabilities of what is only
> slightly likely at the expense of empirical certainty, is practically good and required in the
> practical situation.[40]

We will return to the problem of the will to believe and fiction in Chapter IV, §5.

Notes

1. R.M. Rilke, "Tod-Erfahrung," in *New Poems*. Trans. J.B, Leishman (New York: New Directions, 1964), 107.
2. See the *Catechism of the Catholic Church* (Liguori, MO: Liguori Publications, 1994), 164.
3. Kierkegaard, *Concluding Unscientific Postscript*. Vol. 1, 79–80; I am indebted to Tony Aumann for this text. See his Indiana University doctoral dissertation (2007), *Kierkegaard on the Need for Indirect Communication*.
4. This distinction appears in many of Gabriel Marcel's writings. For an attempt at a systematic summary, see Roger Troisfontaines, *De l'existence a l'être: La philosophie de Gabriel Marcel*. Vol. 1 (Louvain: Nauwelaerts, 1953), 263 ff.
5. See Rudolf Otto, *The Idea of the Holy*. Trans. John W. Harvey (Oxford: Oxford University Press, 1964), 34. See also Max Scheler's discussion of Otto in his *Vom Ewigen im Menschen* (Bern: Francke, 1968), 166–168. Jean-Luc Marion has nicely developed the theme of "saturated intentions" in his writings. See, e.g., *Being Given*. Trans. Jeffrey L. Kosky (Stanford: Stanford University Press, 2002), 199 ff. In "saturated phenomena" we have to do with a givenness where there is an excess of intuition over intention. We need not agree with all of the author's analyses to acknowledge that he has made us aware of important, very distinctive, modes of givenness. That the "myself," as we have developed it, is a case where "the concept no longer foresees, for intuition fore-comes – comes before and therefore, at least once without it" (226) seems clear; but whether this holds true for all the other cases of "mystery" (and by implication, saturated phenomena) is less clear.
6. *The Cloud of Unknowing*. Ed. and Introduction by William Johnson (New York: Image Doubleday, 1996), Ch. 6, p. 46; also cf. the translation of Ira Progoff cited in Thomas Merton, *The Inner Experience* (New York: HarperSanFrancisco, 2004), 82–83. Merton also cites a text of St. John of the Cross: "Passing beyond all that can be known and understood both spiritually and naturally, *the soul will desire with all desire to come to that* WHICH CANNOT BE KNOWN, NEITHER CAN ENTER INTO ITS HEART. And leaving behind *all that it experiences and feels both temporally and spiritually and all that it is able to experience in this life, IT WILL DESIRE WITH ALL DESIRE TO COME TO THAT WHICH SURPASSES FEELING AND EXPERIENCE*." See Merton, ibid., 97, who cites *Ascent of Mount Carmel*, ii, 3.
7. Vladimir Jankélévitch, *Traité des Vertus* (Paris: Bordas, 1949), 786–788.
8. *An Augustine Synthesis*. Ed. Erich Przywara (New York: Harper Torchbook, 1958). See the texts at 421 ff.
9. In novels of C. S. Lewis and Madeleine L'Engel one finds the theme of the siren call of this black death that consumes first-person awareness and replaces it with the artificially constructed minds. The black death in effect is the materialist scientistic redutionistic metaphysics of our day. Today some forms of "trans-humanism" and the infatuation with robotics are the flowerings of trends these authors foresaw. Ullrich Melle has presented with essential precision the issues raised by the trans-humanists in his "Die Zivilisationskrise als anthropologische Herausforderung. Paul Shephards' neoprimitivistische Anthropologie."
10. Cf. Marcel: "A mystery is a problem which encroaches upon its own data, invading them, as it were, and thereby transcending itself as a simple solution." *The Philosophy of Existentialism* (New York: Citadel Press, 1995), 19.
11. This is a point made by Jankélévitch in his little book, *Penser la mort* (Paris: Édition Liana Levi, 1994).
12. Charles Dickens, in *Hard Times*, wrestles with this when the apostles of "nothing but the facts" face love and limit-situations, foremost death.
13. *Späte Texte über Zeitkonstitution (1929–1934). Die C-Manuskripte*. Ed. Dieter Lohmar. *Husserliana* VIII (Dordrecht: Springer, 2006), 39.
14. C.S. Lewis, *The Hideous Strength* (New York: Simon & Schuster/Scribner, 1996), 246.

15. A polythetic act is one that has a plurality of "theses" or positings or position-takings. It is what presences a higher-order object that may be the foundation for a complex act of veneration, revulsion, or a mix. As an example of a higher-order, polythetic object founding an act predominantly of revulsion, consider the multi-strands of "the Iraqi War" which single object is held in mind by unifying a manifold of these strands, themes, or positings, such as the tyrant Saddam Hussein; the imperial need for oil; the US administration's mendacious claims for unquestionable evidence regarding Saddam's having weapons of mass destruction poised to attack the US; a half-million children killed through a prior boycott after the first attack on Iraq in the 1990s; the evisceration of the Iraqi infrastructure and its continuing incapacitation for at least seven years after the invasion; the appointment of a pro-Consul, Paul Bremmer, who opened up Iraq's wealth to private US and European investors; installation of a corrupt puppet Iraqi government; the outsourcing of rebuilding jobs to cheaper foreign labor, thereby exacerbating the unemployment rate among youth and fueling the insurgency; 160,000 combat troops plus 160,000 private contractors serving as occupying forces, many of which latter earn ten times what the US troops earn, some of whom were kidnapped or enslaved (e.g., by a Kuwaiti contracting group); the use by the US of depleted uranium weapons that have poisoned the Iraqi soil and water and caused severe illnesses for both Iraqis and the occupation forces; 1,200,000 Iraqis dead; over 2,200,000 Iraqi refugees in the country and 2,200,000 in neighboring countries; a US "embassy" almost the size of the Washington, DC. Mall; at least 60,000 seriously wounded US vets; the desecrations at Abu Ghraib prison; the refusal to prosecute military and civilian leaders for what Nuremberg called "war crimes"; the President's use of "signing statements" placing him above the law; 4,400 slain coalition soldiers; 1,000 dead tax-supported mercenaries; over 2,100 suicide attempts by US vets in 2007; thousands of vets finding themselves homeless upon returning to their return homes; as of 2008 the costs of $17 billion per month adding up to $3 trillion overall and bankrupting the public treasury; The gouging of US taxpayers by the corruption of the State Department, especially in its dealing with contractors like Halliburton, Blackwater, *et al.*, etc. Most basically the primal synthesis rooted in the awareness of time makes all of life an elemental form of polysynthetic "acts," wherein, for those in my generation similar "higher-order objects," which include WWII, the Korean War, the Vietnamese War, the Cold War, the terrorist wars by the US in Central America, the bombings of Grenada and Panama, the Kosovo War, the US funding of the Taliban war against the USSR, the Iraq Wars, the ongoing war against the Palestinians financed by the US, etc. punctuate with ugly darkness the entire synthesis of our lives. For polysynthetic acts, see Husserl, *Husserliana* III, §118.

16. The phenomenon of "gathering" at its various levels is a main theme of Husserl's analyses of passive synthesis. We find it reworked in most of the main authors in phenomenology. A particularly good and concise statement is in Max Scheler, *Der Formalismus in der Ethik und die materiale Wertethik* (Bern: Francke, 1966), 417. For what follows and some bibliography, cf. my "Toward a Phenomenology of Nostalgia" *Man and World* 4 (1973), 397–420.

17. Roman Ingarden, *Der Streit um die Existenz der Welt*, II/2 (Tübingen: Niemeyer, 1968), 282.

18. See my "Toward a Phenomenology of Nostalgia."

19. Cf., my essay on M. Bakhtin, "The Acts of our Activity" *In Other Words*, a Festschrift for Vadim Liapunov, *Indiana Slavic Studies* II (2000), 69–76.

20. Max Scheler, *ibid.* Eugene Gendlin has made the same basic claim for the felt-meaning awaiting explication which surfaces in the present within the therapeutic situation.

21. Roman Ingarden in his 1921 essay, "*Über die Gefahr einer petitio principii in der Erkenntnistheorie*," displayed the senses in which the life of consciousness, foremost the life of intentionality, is *erlebt* and *durchlebt* and these latter are a knowing, an intuition, quite apart from any intentional acts. This work originally appeared in Husserl's *Jahrbuch* and more recently is to be found in Roman Ingarden, *Frühe Schriften zur Erkenntnistheorie* in his *Gesammelte Werke*, Vol. 6. Ed. W. Galewicz (Tübingen: Max Niemeyer, 1994). This rich, but relatively unknown, essay is perhaps the first sustained analysis of non-reflective self-awareness as a theme essential to the phenomenological enterprise. For Husserl himself

such self-awareness was an "operative notion" which did not receive the systematic attention
it deserved; Sartre and Henry made it part of modern phenomenological doctrine. see also
the work of Dan Zahavi, especially in *Self-Awarness and Alterity*. (And it is a discussion
with Zahavi to which I am indebted for the discovery of this work of Ingarden.) For our
work, Ingarden's claim that consciousness's *Sich-selbst-Durchleben*, as a knowing of what
is simple and uniquely individual and identical, offers a strong case for what we are calling
the "myself." Nevertheless, the fine-grained analyses of Ingarden do not always agree with
the positions we are carving out. But we will not dwell on the differences here. We already
touched on the difference in the appreciation of the I-pole, as it appears in a later study. See
Book 1, Chapter III, §4.

22. Husserl, *Husserliana* XXV, 89.
23. This is basically the position of Heinrich Barth in his *opus magnum*, *Erkenntnis der Existenz*
(Basel: Schwabe, 1965). See, e.g., 123, 269, and 339.
24. Jaspers himself seems sometimes very Kantian regarding the prospects of a non-phenomenal,
non-reflective "knowing" of oneself. Yet the teaching on "absolute consciousness" seems to
require it; further, there is a fine statement of it to be found in *Von der Wahrheit* (Munich:
Piper, 1947), 170–171. Cf. my "Intentionality, Existenz and Transcendence: Jaspers and
Husserl in Conversation" *Jahrbuch der Österreichischen Karl Jaspers Gesellschaft* 16 (2003),
167–203.
25. Even Kierkegaard seemed inclined to a reflection-theory of self-awareness. See, e.g.,
Philosophical Fragments/Johannes Climacus. Trans. Hong (Princeton, NJ: Princeton
University Press, 1985), 168–169.
26. See Heinrich Barth, 264–265.
27. Because it is blurred in these "anomalous" cases, we may well think that it is not an essential
distinction at all, but rather in some persons the physical and moral necessities interpenetrate
in ways we scarcely fathom. Yogis have taught us this. The account by the brain scientist,
Jill Bolte Taylor of her brain hemorrhage, and her awareness at the time of the increasing
vanishing of all her linguistic, kinaesthetic, and muscular skills as she tried to call for help on
the phone is a vivid example of the power of spirit to transcend and resist the "I cannot." It
is also an example of the power of the scientific, even phenomenological, impulse to prevail
even in the face of one's own dissolution. See her *My Stroke of Insight* (2006/2008). And I am
also reminded of Sartre's example of someone suffering, e.g., torture through electroshock,
where the suffering person states: "I can't endure any more; I am absolutely at my limit." But
then is asked, upon appropriate motivation, whether he could endure 1/1,000 of a volt more.
And most likely the person will say, "Yes, I can endure that little bit." And thereafter, and
perhaps numerous times, is asked the same question, and answers in each case, "Yes, although
I appear to be at my limit, I can endure a tiny bit more." I am indebted to Steven Laycock for
this reference to Sartre which illustrates an intriguing aspect not only of our knowledge of our
capacities but also of the will and its freedom in the face of obstacles.
28. *Husserliana* XXXVII, 20–21.
29. See, e.g., *Husserliana* XIII, 206 ff.; *Husserliana* XXXIV, 43 ff., 462 ff.
30. For the distinction between the formally and virtually unconditioned, see Bernard Lonergan,
S.J., *Insight* (New York: Philosophical Library, 1958), see the index. For parallel discussions
of the cognitive striving after the unconditioned in Husserl, see, e.g., *Husserliana* XI, 83 ff.
and the next endnote.
31. See, e.g., *Husserliana* XI, 49, 53, and 59.
32. For some references and discussion, see my "Wisdom, Knowledge, and Reflective Joy:
Aristotle and Husserl" *The New Yearbook for Phenomenology and Phenomenological
Philosophy* II (2003), 53–72; see also *The Person and the Common Life*, 17–23; please note
the error in the reference on 23 to the fifth of the *Logical Investigations*, which should refer
to "the position reached in the Appendix to §11 and §20..."
33. The term "reactive attitudes" is from Peter Strawson's essay, "Freedom and Resentment," in
his *Studies in the Philosophy of Thought and Action* (London: Oxford University Press, 1968).
I owe this reference to Stephen Darwall's *The Second-Person Standpoint: Morality, Respect,*

and Accountability (London: Oxford University Press, 1968), to which we will return in Chapter V.

34. See Karl Jaspers, *Die geistige Situation der Zeit* (Berlin: de Gruyter, 1932/1999), 149; also *Basic Philosophical Writings*, Trans. and Eds. E. Ehrlich, L.H. Ehrlich and George B. Pepper (New York: Humanities Paperback Library, 1994), 58.

35. *Husserliana* VIII, 201.

36. I have been helped in these paragraphs by reflection on Peter Bieri's excellent work, *Das Handwerk der Freiheit* (Frankfurt am Main: Fischer Taschenbuch, 2007), 54, 74 ff. and 259–264. We return to a discussion of this work in Chapter V.

37. Cited in Adam Phillips, *Going Sane* (New York: Fourth Estate, 2005), 56–58.

38. See my "The Essential Look (*Eidos*) of the Humanities: A Husserlian Phenomenology of the University" *Tjjdjschrift voor Filosofie* (2008).

39. *Husserliana* VIII, Beilage V, 351 and 355.

40. Husserl, *Nachlass*, F I 24, 88b. Cf. for these matters my "The Study of Religion in Husserl," in *Phenomenology and the Cultural Disciplines*. Eds. Mano Daniel and Lester Embree (Dordrecht: Kluwer, 1994), 286–296.

Chapter III
Existenz, Conscience, and the Transcendental I

If circumstances lead me, I will find where truth is hid, though it were hid indeed within the centre.

(Shakespeare, *Hamlet*, Act II, sc. 2, l. 157)

Of all the things which a man has, next to the gods, his soul is the most divine and most truly his own... and in our opinion he ought to honour her as second only to the gods.... We must believe the legislator when he tells us that the soul is in all respects superior to the body, and that, even in life, what makes each one of us to be what we are is only the soul [or what gives each one of us his being].

(Plato, *Laws*, 726–727, 959)

We have been urging that the realization of the mystery of one's own death is such that it takes precedence before not only the understanding of oneself in the natural attitude but also that it can, indeed, on occasion must, take precedence before the transcendental attitude and transcendental I. Of course, as in the case of Ivan Ilych, the presence of one's death may take place solely within the natural attitude. Given the natural attitude's allegiance to oneself as a body in the world with Others, what is more natural than death? What is more natural than feeling one's vulnerability as one moving body in the world among other moving bodies which are beyond one's control, especially given that many if not most of these bodies appear to play out their tenure by random and mindless "behavior." But the sense of oneself that surfaces in facing one's own death, as exemplified in Ivan Ilych, is not simply that of something in the world along with everything else, i.e., a body among bodies, a being among beings. Ivan Ilych, e.g., could not get used to the naturalness of death. One becomes aware of oneself as a single individual facing one's destiny. One's whole self and life, which appear as that which one more or less freely shaped, are called forth. In this chapter we wish to dwell on what "I" refers to in this mode of self-awareness that we are calling Existenz.

§1. Existenz as a Third-Person Term of Reference to First-Person Experience

The word *Existenz* is a Danish and German term that we choose to transpose into English because of the richness of the concept in the historical tradition of existential phenomenological philosophy. *Existenz* is the term we use for the "center" of "I myself" as a person in the world with Others. We have seen some reasons for thinking about the core or center of the personal I, and in this chapter and later ones we will find some more. In this sense Existenz does not stand in opposition to essence but rather refers to what is most essential about oneself, and in this sense refers to the essence of oneself. Earlier (in Book 1) we saw reasons to hold that the "myself" is an individual essence and holds a distinctive, indeed, essential meaning, even though we are at a loss to spell out its properties. This recalls the somewhat popular sense of "essence" as the sought-after, secret hidden core of something, in this case, the core of the person, the revelation of which in appearances is always inadequate and sometimes misleading. We argued (in Book 1, Chapter V, §3) that the "myself" is the pure, bare, substrate of the person. As such a bare particular and radically unique essence, "I myself" informs the person throughout as her entelechy, i.e., providing the person with her inalienable unique essence and her telos, i.e., her ideal self. Existenz is the emphatic, centered way the "myself" comes to light in its decisive moments of centering and integration. With Existenz we have to do with the "myself" as it is the manifest center of the person, and in this sense Existenz is not merely the "secret" of the person but of the "myself." Existenz is the secret of the "myself" in so far as its disclosure is the revelation of the secret of the innermost essence of the person as well her telos. In what follows we hope to show in what sense the "myself" is the "entelechy" of the personal I.

Thus much of what we have to say about the "myself" is an explication of the remark of Paul Valéry's Monsieur Teste[1]: "My most intimate idea is not to be able to be that one who I am. I am not able to recognize myself in a finite figure. And *I MYSELF* always escape my personal essence although designing and imprinting it even in eluding it." The effective "designing" and "imprinting" of one's personal essence is, of course in *I-acts* and *I* am indeed revealed in these acts as their source. But this revelation is first-personal and therefore eludes being found among what is an object in the world. Further, the I MYSELF, we propose, is the form and telos, i.e., entelechy, of the person. As such it is "my most intimate idea," and because it is not only I myself most formally but also, as entelechy, the dynamism for the regulative ideal of the person who I am to be, this most intimate idea of mine, the idea of me myself, is such that I am "able to become that one who I am."

Furthermore there are decisive moments when the person is awakened to herself at her center, i.e., this is an awakening to herself as Existenz. This is an illumination of herself at her core, the coming forth (*ex-sistere*) of the "myself" as her center. Like the "myself" *qua* substrate and entelechy of the person, Existenz *qua* the coming forth of the "myself" as the integrating center of the person is not ourselves as recognizable in a "finite figure" of the world. But by reason of this illumination the sense of the weight of the world is displaced to the basic exigencies of the person, i.e., to her dealing with what appears as of unconditional importance or the *unum necessarium*. As such it provides an opportunity and invitation for one to shape in one's person "that [person] who I am."

However, as is well known, the term Existenz is often juxtaposed to essence. Let us review four reasons for doing this within our context. *First*, essence is often taken to refer to *how* something exists or the "whatness" or "suchness" that informs the actuality or the factual *existence* (the clear cognate of *Existenz*). The "whatness" therefore is the defining consideration or principle for another principle that accounts for the actuality, the existence, of the "whatness." Establishing "what" something is does not imply necessarily "that" it is or exists.

Among things we experience, we never experience existence that is not determined by being a certain kind, i.e., having an essence. Nevertheless we know of kinds of things, e.g., elves, Hobbits, peace without the need for weapons, the next mutation of HIV, etc. which do not exist actually. The "existential" here has a note of actuality that is missing in the merely essential. However, in Book 1, Chapter VI, §9 we discussed how the "I" is an exception. The unique essence expressed with "I" necessitates that it exist in its self-presencing. In this sense the essence of I is to exist, even though what exists is not necessarily I and even though this I is contingent. In the final theological chapter we will wrestle further with the senses in which what I refers to exists of necessity and senses in which what I refers to of necessity is contingent.

Secondly, in the framework of this book, the emphasis on the human person as Existenz stresses that its actuality is of greater significance than any established array of properties presuming to define its essence. This is because the "I myself" exists precisely as a *radical individual*. And it is a radical individual because it is not divisible, nor is it replaceable, nor individuated by nor communicable to what is outside of itself. In this sense it does not need anything else for it to be itself. Therefore, it is exemplarily "subsisting" as what exists for itself and by itself. But the person as the incarnation of the "myself" has communicable properties, e.g., it has the character of being just and courageous, and it is individuated through, in part, its dependence on others as well as on the natural and social situations and surroundings.

"*Existenz*," whose etymological roots are the same as *existence*, is a well-conceived term, the etymology of which itself brings out this basic distinction between the "myself" and the person. The Latin root of "exist," *ex-sistere*, means to come forth, to come to light, to appear. The person is the *Ex-sistere* of "I myself," the coming forth for myself and, indirectly, for others in the world (as Existenz is the coming forth of the "myself" as the center of the person). As a person I am "non-sortal," not because how I, as this person, appear in the world cannot be captured by properties, but because I "myself" am beyond all such characterizations. Yet I myself am properly actual as I come forth for myself and others, and thereby gain the actuality of being in the world with others, only by becoming a person with individuating characteristics.

Thirdly, to exist as a person is inseparable from the first-person non-objective experience of freedom. Freedom may be understood negatively or positively. We will have frequent occasions to attend to its sense in subsequent discussions. But negatively it means at least that the will is free of what constricts personal choice and in this sense what constricts Existenz. Some thinkers have thought that Existenz not only is more basic than essence but the being of Existenz is to be free of any essence as an a priori determination. One was free only if Existenz as the free "myself" bereft of properties was the sole source of all its determinations. (This is the well-known view of Sartre, but cf. our discussion below of Chapter IV, §§5–7 and Chapter V, §7.) Aside from the consideration that this characterization itself would seem to be, in a basic sense, an essential determination, i.e., a matter of essential necessity and not a mere coincidence or accident, it is still hyperbolic because freedom as we know it is human, and being human obviously conditions agency. Further, it assumes that there is no positive sense of freedom wherein Existenz might find fulfillment by freely endorsing or renouncing its prior self-determinations, or submitting to ideal norms, or appropriating exemplary embodiments of what is good. Existenz's awakening to itself is an awakening in which I discover among my wishes and willings, some of which are not only peripheral to what I value most but also some of which alienate me from myself, i.e., are alienated from the willing which is at my center and with which I am most one, the willing with which I most identify. (We will return to this, especially in Chapter IV.)

Fourthly, the standing out or "coming forth" of Existenz is primarily, and often exclusively, *for oneself*. This is not only because the *radical individuality* is evident only in the first-person, but one comes forth for oneself at one's core or center. There is revealed in this coming forth a depth of the wellspring of oneself which often enough seems hidden. With its coming forth one discovers what it is to be "whole-heartedly" alive to oneself. Similarly my "innermostness" and "ownmostness" may be said to be revealed. We will have often occasion to return to this and explicate it.

"Existenz" was perhaps first used by Søren Kierkegaard as a term for the unique referent of first-person experience and reference. It was richly orchestrated by Karl Jaspers and Martin Heidegger almost eighty years ago and over eighty years after Kierkegaard. Since this time there have been other important philosophers for whom the concept, if not the term, is central. It is a third-person term, like "person," that necessarily indicates that the speaker is aware that the entity referred to is "first-personally aware." The third-person pronouns which indicate persons do not necessarily refer to this state of affairs (the person may be in a coma) and in certain contexts the third-person pronoun alone is misleading. In such a case the intensive modifier, e.g., "she herself" can make precise what the speaker means. The *quasi-indexical* is a term (put forth by Castañeda) to nail down this achievement by the speaker. By the quasi-indexical, e.g., "she herself," the writer or speaker refers to another's first-person experiences as precisely first-person self-aware experiences. Thus we may contrast when the speaker says, "The editor of *Nous* believes that she is a millionaire," with when the speaker says "The editor of *Nous* believes that *she herself* is a millionaire." In the latter case, the speaker, through the grammatical device of "she herself," reveals her own knowledge of another's first-person experiences. She does this by using the quasi-indexical which secures for the listener or reader the speaker's beliefs about the editor's own beliefs about herself, in this case, the belief of the editor regarding her own being wealthy. This belief about the self-awareness of the editor would not be secured if the speaker left out the "she herself" and used merely "she." If the quasi-indexical were left out, if the speaker used merely "she," as in the first example, the speaker might well be leading the listener to believe or himself reporting the fact that the editor is referring with "she" to someone other than herself, for example, her publisher, Mary.[2]

The term "Existenz" is not part of our natural language as the quasi-indexical is. It is a convention by philosophers which is intended to do more than they can do with the quasi-indexical. It does not merely provide us with a term in the third-person that enables us to reveal our knowledge of others' self-awareness, or first-person experiences and beliefs. In this case it parallels the way the writer implicitly refers, in the third-person, to himself, as when someone speaks or writes about "the I." "The I" appears grammatically like "the house" where a definite article individuates a general term. But "the house" individuates what is general and "the I" generalizes what is radically individual. "I" properly is not a general term like "house" referring to no one house in particular. In this respect Existenz, although a third-person term, resembles "I" rather than "the I" because it rather refers to the person's awareness of him- or herself as a single, unique individual whose "essence" is available only to him- or herself in the first-person.

As we have seen (in Book 1, Chapters II–IV, especially Chapter III, §2 and Chapter IV, §2), when we use "the I" we make out of the first-person singular a universal term so that the reference to the uniquely unique can become what is common without distinction to all the cases wherein the unique referent is achieved. Its oddness is reflected in a language like German where one can refer to a unique person with the definite article, "Der Ullrich." This is unlike "the house" where the referring of a general term is to an individual. In German the proper name (even though common) is not referring in a general way, and the definite article may be said to intensify for the speaker the individualness of Ullrich rather than making of Ullrich one among many Ullrichs. We get another analogy when a grammarian or philosopher might speak of "the this," where the demonstrative pronoun, "this," which is reserved for indicating a particular in the presence of the speaker, itself becomes a referred-to-concept that displays how this pronoun has a universal kind of reference as a grammatical term. (See our earlier wrestle with these matters in Book 1, Chapters III–IV.) "The I" enables us to prescind from the absolutely unique referent of "I" and talk about what I and the other I's have in common as I's, e.g., as speakers of sentences, as poles of acts and sensa, as agents of manifestation, indeed, as uniquely unique.

Thus there can be an eidetic analysis of "the I" but not of "I" in so far as the indexical achievement refers to oneself as a single individual. But on occasion "I" may not refer to myself in a merely indexical manner; I may prescind from the consideration of its reference to me in my singularity as a unique essence. Thus, e.g., I may be merely singling myself out as the agent of manifestation, where my uniqueness is not explicit, except as the responsible speaker of the sentence, agent of manifestation, doer of a deed, etc. This declarative sense of I, although indicating individual responsibility, contrasts with the term "Existenz" which refers to the core of the unique individual "I" of the person. In this respect "Existenz" resembles how we may use "person" for a non-sortal reference to the other in her unique individuality. Yet "Existenz" stipulates the first-person awareness of this individuality in a way "person" does not. Although the awakening to Existenz by definition is an effective responsible taking a stand toward one's whole life, there does not seem to be any distinctive linguistic expression for Existenz's coming forth. In most cases silence, and perhaps an altering of one's breathing, e.g., a deep breath, are the fitting responses because intersubjectivity is not necessarily involved. (It might well be; cf. our discussion below of the limit-situation of the struggle to communicate and live with Others.) Of course, in the face, e.g., of the realization of one's death one might make an exclamation, followed by something like "OK, I'm ready." In the biblical tradition, it is perhaps captured by, "Here I am, Lord."

Existenz refers to what concerns me "unconditionally." Kierkegaard put it bluntly: The coming to light of Existenz or (here his term is) "subjectivity" is inseparable from the unique revelation of the truth of what he called the "infinite passion." "The infinite passion is the very truth. But the passion of the infinite is precisely subjectivity, and thus subjectivity is truth."[3] We may paraphrase this rather gnomic declaration by saying that what is the knowledge most worth having is not merely knowledge about an objective state of affairs but of necessity it must be related to the question of who and what one is. These latter matters are not known through empty intentions, nor can they be truths grasped from a "view from nowhere," nor can anyone else tell us the answers so that they become true for us because of the trusted expertise of the witness.

They do not have to do with contents of *what* we know but *how* we are and how we affirm, live, profess, and state the contents. *How we are* is summarized in the reference to the "infinite passion." Indeed the knowing and the answers are of necessity of a non-objective sort, if by "objective" we mean matters having to do with our interpretation of the world through intentional acts. And, further, these "subjective truths" are not matters that are commensurate with any other matters of more or less importance. These are matters toward which we as Existenzen or subjectivities have an infinite passion.

Indeed, the lived, non-objective, infinite passion itself reveals oneself to oneself at one's center. The passion is in a distinctive comprehensive sense intentional, i.e., it is about… or aimed at…, but it is also always self-involving, and a self-experiencing. "Infinite passion" here is not commensurate with other accidental passions, enthusiasm, or waves of longing (which, of course, are also intentional and self-involving) because it defines the person constitutively at her core and has for its intentional correlate what is of infinite importance. Further its intentionality encompasses and transforms all of one's life. (Cf. our earlier discussion of gathering acts; also the discussion below in Chapter IV of self-identifying acts; and in Chapter V the discussion of "truths of will.") Kierkegaard also calls this a relating oneself absolutely to one's absolute *telos* which he also names "eternal happiness" or "the highest good." These are matters which call forth not only the sense of the inadequation of ourselves with all that we experience but which also awaken us to ourselves as incommensurate with all that we experience as objects in the world. (See our own version of these matters below in this chapter as well as Chapter V, especially

§2.) This awakening to this deep dimension of oneself may be an occasion of terror for the ethically minded person because it inserts a deadly seriousness and radical upheaval into the quotidian. If the self-relating in the infinite passion toward the absolute *telos* does not "absolutely transform the individual's existence by relating to it, then the individual does not relate himself with existential pathos but with esthetic pathos…. The pathos that corresponds to and is adequate to an eternal happiness is the transformation by which the existing person in existing changes everything in his existence in relation to that highest good." The esthetic relationship, whereby one is outside of oneself "in the ideality of possibility with the correctness of the idea" is precisely the alienation which determines that the person is not "in himself in existence" and where he is "not himself transformed into the actuality of the idea."[4] (Cf. our discussion in Chapter II, §6 of the inappropriateness of the transcendental attitude in the realization of one's own death.)

Existenz is analytically explicated with the infinite passion for eternal happiness and "the truth of the infinite passion," i.e., the lived first-personal, non-objective wakefulness to the infinite passion for one's eternal happiness analytically explicates Existenz. The passion for the infinite is a decisive truth and necessary condition for awakening the person to her center, to herself as Existenz.

Paul Tillich's discussion of what he calls "faith" echoes Kierkegaard and it brings to light an important aspect of what we are calling Existenz: "being seized unconditionally by what matters or by what is unconditionally important," "*das Ergriffensein von dem, was uns unbedingt angeht.*"[5] *Das Ergriffensein* might leave the impression that *I* am in no way active and rather passively at the mercy of something apart from I myself, like a wave of passion or emotion, and as if here there was an experience bereft of any cognitive or epistemic achievement. Yet we may think of this passion for or being seized by what is of unconditional importance as not merely compromising the I's involvement by overwhelming it, but rather as embodying it "whole-heartedly." Whole-heartedly means that no aspect of my self resists allegiance to or conditions this concern. This importance bears upon me (*es geht mir unbedingt an*) wholly and refuses to be deflected and allows me no refuge because I am absolutely at stake, i.e., given to myself to be myself truly and to sustain my integrity. Thus the importance here is unique because strictly there is no object having the value-property of "importance" that affects me, but rather I am aware that I myself am at stake and my proper response to the call is the prior condition for all that is important, even the matters that I cherish absolutely and for which I am prepared to sacrifice everything else, including myself, i.e., my life. Here I engage myself and am moved to be engaged in regard to what is unconditionally important by both letting come forth the core or center of myself as well as participating in this moment and task of centering. Thus Existenz's coming forth, or one's centering of oneself in one's ownmost self, is quite compatible with being, in some respects, coolly dispassionate, as one might well be in meeting death. Thus being resigned, being calmly courageous, etc., are compatible with the infinite pathos or passion for what is unconditionally important or "eternal happiness" or "the highest Good." As Kierkegaard suggested, the I arouses the I to apply the situation at hand, e.g., one's death, one's commitments, one's calling, or whatever is "glorious" in one's situation, to itself "personally," not "objectively."[6]

Perhaps instead of applying the matter at hand to oneself "personally" – which, after all, might have to do with trifling matters of little consequence – we might better say, "being-self-gathered with infinite passion in the face of what appears as unconditionally important." This is not primarily an act of belief or faith (*Glaube*) if we take this as an epistemic act involving assent to empty intentions or even an emotive volition of trust or belief-in. Rather it is an *ex-sistere*, a coming forth to myself, a distinctive self-awareness, in which I am gathered and centered. Tillich's own explication of faith as "the most centered act of the human spirit (*Geist*)" gets at what is basic for us. Yet this centering act is a disclosure not only of me, this person, to myself but of what is of unconditional importance in regard to how I am in the world, and in this respect a disclosure of something about the world.

The discussion of "my death" pointed to the more than theoretical question in regard to both oneself and the world, why something and not nothing at all? We want to dwell further on what this means. In a sense this realization of my death is the ultimate one, and the mystery it makes present encompasses everything else. Yet the analysis can be broadened and enriched even though we neither leave behind nor negate the mystery of one's death.

Finally, when we, in the following, use expressions like, "a person's Existenz," or "the Existenz of the Transcendental I," we do not mean to refer to some arcane part of the object called "self" or "soul" that philosophers or religious people have discovered. Thus there is not meant something other than what the person or the transcendental I refers to with "I." Rather we intend to refer to the I of this person when regarded under the aspects of its being a unique single individual facing, in the first-person, what is of unconditional importance for her. Yet, as we have already noted, there is reason to think of what "I" refers to, i.e., what is most central to the life of a self, as itself meriting a kind of center-periphery, innermost and less innermost, distinction. This presumably is not a distinction unknown to anyone, even though it might well have never become a theme.

In this and the next chapters we will discuss how Existenz refers at once to (a) how I come forth to myself in non-reflexive ways as a singular individual; (b) how I, as a single individual, affirm myself transcendentally as inseparable from my freedom; (c) how this transcendental self-affirmation is at once awakened as well as called into question by the limit-situations, e.g., of death; (d) how I, in living through the limit-situations, am opened to a unique sense of myself in the world, what we name one's "calling"; (e) how my calling is tied to a sense of what is of unconditional importance; and (f) how I cannot be myself and turn away from this appeal and command. We can begin with limit-situations as occasioning our awakening to Existenz.

§2. Limit-Situations and Existenz

Earlier it was said that my death comes to me in a way that may relativize the philosophical (*philosophia* = *philein sophia*) ultimacy of the transcendental attitude as well as the transcendental I. We showed that there was an inappropriateness in assuming the transcendental attitude in the face of one's death because something else is called for than the philosophical display of oneself facing death. Further, we have seen that one's own death can be presenced in a gathering experience, a realization. As such it is not a novel piece of information nor is it something we encounter within the world, even though its proximate occasion can well be something in the world. Of course, as Heidegger has taught us, death itself is at the edge or on the horizon of all experiences; indeed, it frames them in the sense of providing a necessary context for understanding them. My death, we have said, is not one situation among others. It is not the sort of novel state of affairs one finds by a turn of events or by changing places. These are arrangements that will pass or that one can move away from. I never can move away from my death, even though through much of life I can repress or marginalize it so that it is seems irrelevant to the flux of my situations. As we said earlier (Chapter II), my death is a limit-situation.

"Being in a situation" and "being situated" are ways of referring to the spatial-temporal-meaning determinateness of our life. Bringing this to light is inseparable from a phenomenology of perspective (cf. Book 1, Chapter II, §7). Shifts in spatial location and the advance of the time of the day or the time of life are obvious shifts in "situation," i.e., they are changing sites, phases, events, or scenes. But we can remain in the same place where the meaning for us changes, where, e.g., a metaphorical or real storm cloud sets in. And in important senses we cannot go home again. Our ineluctable being in the world is always being in a specific place, time, and meaning-context. Our practical interests dictate what the "situation" is. Thus "being in the woods" is conceivably a different situation for the hiker, highway construction engineer, lumber businessman, lumberjack, lost child, geologist, botanist, biologist, ecologist, ornithologist, etc. And each of these may put on a variety of hats so that, in the course of the week, the same woods will present different situations dependent on the specific interest. And here we say nothing about how the forest is different for the ant, owl, hawk, butterfly, raccoon, turkey, vulture, crow, etc. Thus the "situation" is not the geometrical or mathematical relation of things in the world as determined by a view that is unsituated or "from nowhere." It is not as if the situation was already there fleshed out in all its meaningful detail prior to my entering it, as would be the case if I were to come upon a graph or map. In such a case I might find a natural-scientific and mathematicisable disposition of space and of relationships of things existing within this selected setting. Or we could come upon a quantitative diagram bereft of all individual human perspectives which would list all the "items" in the forest in terms of their chemical composition, their intake of the molecules in the environment as well as their off-gasing, their spatial relationships to one another as well as their patterns of flight and locomotion, their relationships to the boundaries of the graph as well as to the territories of other entities, their rate of growth, their relationship to the sun and the Global Satellite Positioning, to the clock in Greenwich, England, etc.

In contrast, the lived situation's meaningfulness, its sense, is inseparable from my own way of entering and engaging this scene and this may have nothing to do with these measurements, graphs, diagrams or maps. My expectations and manner of viewing disclose the situation to be of a certain kind. Thus situations appear to me in a certain light, and I am always situated in a certain way, on the basis of my fears, desires and knowledge. What comes to light, the situation, is tied to my standpoint or perspective and stance, and each of these has its horizon of interests, knowledge, fears, and desires. At the same time I can, and willy-nilly as a person to a certain extent do, include the perspectives of Others and thus included in my perspective are their situations and how this situation for me is not necessarily the same for them. Thus each human using the woods might well take account of its being also a "situation" for bears. (When we, using the natural setting in accord with our interests, come upon a mother bear protecting her cubs, we then have a "situation" in the way the US corporate media use the term.)

Life may be thought of as continually unfolding from one situation to another, and each situation is apperceived to be connected to or encompassed by other situations, and all of them encompassed by a sense of world – as the same for us all. World, as the same for us all is the total- or all-situation.[7] Each situation has its distinct "province of meaning" within the total-situation of world which a single person may move in and out of in the course of a day, e.g., from work to play, from the importunity of daily pressures to fictional worlds, etc. Each situation with its finite horizon of interests and agency will change through the course of events initiated from without or by the person himself. All of these are ways our life is determined, ways our being in *the* world, the all-situation, is defined and limited by the scope of our agency, interests and concerns. Thus, when we ask regularly one another, "What are you up to?" "What is going on in your life?" "How is it going?" we assume of one another that we are in the one same all-situation of the world. The answers we give might well be a result of a "gut check" or overview of the thick synthesis of one's life that gets summarized. But typically the courteous "How are you?" is offered in such a situation that our interlocutor does not really want any detail. As a result we say "OK," "Not bad," etc. But these answers, as compressed as they typically will be, reveal, if we are honest, how we find ourselves in particular situations in the larger being in the world. Thus if our interlocutor clearly appears to want some detail we might, instead, say: "I am broke," "I am working on a book chapter" or "I am getting a divorce," or "I just learned I have cancer."

Karl Jaspers has shown how boundary- or limit-situations contrast with the typical situations in which we find ourselves that emerge out of the specific horizon of our current interests and that presently delimit and define our lives. Limit situations limit us in a different way. They are not finite situations in and out of which we move. They are not defined by a determinate standpoint, perspective, and horizon of interests. They are not reserved to certain times, places, or specific meaning contexts within life. Rather, like the all-situation of "world," whose deepest sense they pervade, they inform all of the situations of life and lurk on the horizon of each of them. Thus even though I am involved in situations requiring my whole-hearted attention, e.g., doing philosophy or making love, the limit-situation of, e.g., death is never absolutely absent from the situation. Further, limit-situations differ from the all-situation of "world," not merely by defining us as human persons in the world but by awakening us to the center of ourselves, i.e., to ourselves as Existenz. With limit-situations we come alive to ourselves in a way that is dormant in our typical everyday being in the all-situation of the world. Typically the limit-situation is occluded or repressed.

Thus it is a feature of the limit-situations to have the power, on occasion, to "announce themselves" in a forceful, not easily avoidable way. Indeed, they appear to us as being in a distinctive sense "necessary." They are ways in which we have "reality checks" that simply do not permit our evasion. They may well appear initially constricting and may well cause numbness, vertigo, and panic. But this is only because of the intriguing inveterate disposition to live as if the limit-situations did not exist. In this sense at least we can say that the limit-situations bring to light a vague but undeniable truth about ourselves. And this is a truth in itself, having transcendent "objective validity," even though we may have little or no grasp of what it means beyond itself. Reflection on the limit-situation does not permit "the essence of the matter at hand" to yield the universal necessary properties that elucidate for our understanding what our being in the world means in the light of the limit-situations Yet what the limit-situations reveal is of utmost importance – this is analytic to their sense.

Thus what they reveal is not necessarily anything positive or any decisive essential properties that shed light on our quest for intelligibility about our being in the world. Rather they reveal the fragility of the reigning and typical senses assigned to our being in the world, and the questionability of identifying the sense of "I myself" with something existing in the world. In this sense they always inevitably exercise pressure on our willing, i.e., they provide an urgency, indeed an emergency, in regard to clarifying for ourselves what we most properly want – or perhaps what we most properly should have wanted prior to this moment. Such crises may make it clear that how we have been living only seemed to express what we really wanted. Now it becomes evident that this has been a form of alienation or self-deception. In this respect the limit-situations force us to articulate our choices and the direction of our will and to work on uncovering what we really want and the willing with which we can whole-heartedly identify.[8] However, it might be, as with the limit-situation of one's death, that the clarification of the will is not a re-orientation of one's life but rather is a prospective retrospection and a preparation for death. The presence of the limit-situation does not guarantee that we will have the opportunity to clarify our will – they may come upon us "as a thief in the night" – or even that we will have the disposition to undertake such a clarification. But in most cases they would seem to offer such an opportunity and they would seem to have the power to awaken such a disposition.

Limit-situations also reveal the unintelligibility and surds that are at the horizon of all of life. There is thus an encroaching despair about finding any proper meaning of our life as a life among anything in the world. In this sense, with the realization of the limit-situations the rug is pulled out from underneath us in terms of the ready at hand explanations of what it is all about. With this total placing in question of myself and my life in the world I come up against the specter of meaninglessness and nothingness, in so far as I seek and have sought ultimate satisfaction, intelligibility, and meaning in my being with things in the world.[9]

With the notion of the limit-situation, something resembling the classical Greek notion of *anangke* or "Necessity" is introduced into the life-world and our being in the world. Here we meet Necessity in the form of what must be and cannot not be, and yet it is inseparable from fate and chance. Here, in contrast to the sense of "necessity of reason" or "rational Necessity" which provides the highest form of intelligibility by presenting us with a reasonable explanation in terms of cause and purpose, we have rather a meeting of what defies such intelligibility, i.e., what is without cause and purpose.[10] Thus often, if not always, the importunity of the limit-situation has the feature of a chance surd, i.e., without rhyme or reason. And yet it is the encounter with these "necessities" of the limit-situations that define personal being in the world at its core. For a similar reason we may say that tragedy too is a key vehicle for bringing to light the center of our personal being or Existenz.

With this shattering of the prevailing sense of one's self as a being within the world a sharply contrasting sense of oneself emerges. The core of one's person, of one's "I myself" as the center of the person and the willing with which I can wholeheartedly identify, comes to light. It is not merely that every human is called into question, limited, and defined by the limit-situations, it is rather that every person becomes through the limit-situations uniquely self-aware and this awareness is connected with the prospect of losing himself into the abyss of nothingness. As we have seen in the case of death, the danger is not merely or primarily from without: The threat of non-being is no less real from within the most basic constituents of our personal being in the world.

The limit-situations, exemplarily death, do not merely awaken us to our nonreflective self-awareness and unique uniqueness of "I myself" (see Book 1, Chapters II—IV) inextricably enmeshed in the lives of others. Further they awaken us to our ultimate accountability and calling in regard to what is of unconditional importance, for which no alibi is possible.

Because limit-situations awaken us to the ultimate determination of ourselves, a determination that transcends our determinations of being persons in the world through finite situations, we may say that through them we come to ourselves in terms of what is uniquely necessary (cf. the biblical *unum necessarium*, as in *Luke* 10:42). Again, this is also what is of unconditional importance. Limit-situations awaken us to what is uniquely necessary in terms of appealing to us for decisive thought and action in the determination of our lives. Even though we may very well not be in a position to say what precisely "the meaning of it all," "the whole show," etc. are, we become aware that such, whether or not there is an answer, is at stake. Of course, "the all," or "whole show," etc. is the ultimate horizon from our standpoint. It does not actually include all possible standpoints.

Jaspers lists along with death other limit-situations, e.g., guilt, struggle with Others, and suffering. Let us briefly review some aspects of his presentation, with a few additions of our own, without pretending to do justice to these rich matters.

Guilt has to do foremost with the intersubjectivity and the karma of agency. In the limit-situation of guilt one struggles with the complicity that is ineluctable in the way one is necessarily entangled with others. Being awakened to this burden both reveals the ideal of purity and negates the original innocence of the person in spite of the transcendent unique I-ness and original sense of I-can. The limit-situation provides the occasion to emerge as Existenz, as a single individual acting from out of one's center, in spite of this immersion in an ancestral and historical web of determinations and indebtedness.

Each's sense of I-can has for ballast the boon and bane of one's predecessors and milieu. We are who we are as persons in the world with others because of our indebtedness to the often invisible gracious agency of others and the inheritance of the past. Yet our deficiencies, handicaps, baggage, etc. are not all our own doing, and we spend all of our lives wrestling with this heritage. Moreover, we are inextricably entangled in webs of agency and our own actions set off waves of consequences that we are more or less responsible for and some of which come back to haunt and burden us, even though we perhaps never could have foreseen these consequences. By facing the limit-situation of "guilt" we acknowledge the burden of our personal being in the world but we are given the chance to arouse ourselves to be responsible agents and not mere passive fellow travellers, victims, or pawns. (See Chapter IV, especially §7.)

Inseparable from this is the *struggle* that our ineluctable involvement in community and intersubjectivity brings, especially the "loving battle" to communicate and live with others at the level of Existenz, not merely the superficial level of "existence," e.g., chatter, information transfer, entertainment, commerce, economics, etc. as painful as even these interactions can be. The deep and often tragic misunderstandings as well as the lack of virtue and the frailties we bring to our relationships interfere with our being able to really hear and be with one another. Yet without this deeper kind of community we fail to gain the clarity and honesty about ourselves (cf. the tragic-comic exclamation in one of Dickens' novels where one family member cries to another: "How dare you tell me the truth!"). We further can and do nurture self-indulgence and fail to "show up" for ourselves as well as others. Authentic communication defines us for ourselves, reveals our identity by bringing before ourselves an essential and necessary aspect of ourselves, namely, that our being alive to ourselves as *Existenzen* is bound up with our being with and for one another. Without this loving dreadful struggle to be with and for those who matter most for us we may remain forever hidden to ourselves as *Existenzen* and distinct persons, and likewise the richness of the common life that emerges during and from this struggle forever remains absent. (We return to this limit situation below in Chapter V, §4.)

Suffering in the form of pain, like the prelude to our dying, brings us before the essential finitude and solitude of our selves, where not even those who are most dear to us can come to our aid. Suffering calls to a halt our typical being in the world with Others concerned about this because of that. If it looms as permanent it undoes the identity we have created, indeed our personal essence, as the expression of how we are so in the world. In extreme forms we are even removed from our being in the world with others to a strange monotonous life that scarcely permits being remembered when we subsequently are healthy once again in the world with others.

Suffering too is a matter of the lottery of inheritance at every level of our being; it also refers to the fateful contingencies that happen to us in the course of living our life; but it is also most basically both what reveals and what stands in the way of the deep sense of ourselves as freedom, possibility, as I-can. Only when we see our inveterate quest for happiness, always, in a certain respect, a quest for the unconditioned and the infinite, over against the contingency and ephemerality of life does the deep dimension of ourselves and our destiny awaken. (Cf. below, Chapter IV, §2.) As long as happiness lingers as the filled positivity of worldly life, i.e., as possessions, consumable things, successes, fame or something else in the world, we remain on the surface and at the mercy of the discord arising from the essential discrepancy and incommensurability between our actual life in the world and the horizon of happiness. With this torment and flux of discontent and dissatisfaction we also are bereft of the deep joy that the constancy of Existenz awakens in the face of these discrepancies.[11] The limit-situation of "suffering," as an essential determination and condition of personal being in the world, awakens us to an aspect of ourselves and a possibility of life which is not identified with the personal being in the world.

Simone Weil's descriptions of "affliction" (*malheur*) recall the limit-situation of suffering and yet under it she encompasses much more than mere suffering. Indeed, her description of "affliction" especially recalls the Greek theme of *anangke i.e., fate or blind Necessity*. It also surely has the power to reveal to us our core selves, which, as we earlier saw, for her must become bereft of any sense of "I." Affliction occurs whenever Necessity, under no matter what form, is imposed so harshly that the hardness exceeds the capacity for the person to erect defenses that deny Necessity its capacity to call the apparent groundedness of life into question. Affliction then is inseparable from a unique self-revelation.

"Affliction is the uprooting of life, a more or less attenuated equivalent of death, made irresistibly present to the soul by the attack or immediate apprehension of physical pain." This uprooting of life attacks one's life in all its social, psychological, and physical parts, and social degradation or fear of such degradation are essential to it.[12]

Affliction "introduces into the soul... the immensity of force, blind, brutal, and cold." For a while, it is the crucible for the spiritual transformation for those who are to get clear on what is of ultimate unconditional significance. For Weil this means it has to do with our union with God. In it, "the infinite distance separating God from the creature is entirely concentrated into one point to pierce the soul to its center."[13]

Nevertheless, and here her discussion clearly agrees with Jaspers, affliction does not automatically result in transformed souls. It can kill the soul. The destruction of the "I" does not automatically result in the consent to God's grace. Affliction can so destroy the person that the "I" is made a quasi-damned soul in a quasi-infernal state. Human injustice in general produces quasi-damned souls, not saints and martyrs. She sketches a state of the spiritual zombie who is the product of massive social injustice and chaos. There seem to be degrees of such spiritual zombies whose "I" is dormant, inanimate, or dead. For these latter we can do nothing. But if affliction comes when one has already begun the process of destroying the "I" one is in a position to prevent affliction from causing deep spiritual harm, Indeed, it may then bring about redemptive suffering.

Whether Weil is offering a theological version of the limit-situation and *anangke* or whether Jaspers is presenting us with a secular-philosophical version of what

Weil might call the spiritual life need not detain us. It is clear that for both of them suffering and/or affliction, and this is characteristic for Jaspers of all the limit-situations, interrupt the routine flow of life. They unsettle us and compel us to come to grips with the whole of our lives and how we are living life. Further, they raise the question of the depth of our resources for dealing with the "misfortune" that befalls us. They can make or break us, as the saying goes, even though there remains a philosophical disagreement between Weil and this work regarding how best to describe what precisely is made or broken.[14]

We need not take Jaspers to be offering an exhaustive list of limit-situations. This is suggested by Jaspers himself, when he observes that the "basic situation" (also called a "basic limit-situation"), which itself is a mode of limit-situation, i.e., it too is one that defines the human condition, is inescapable and cannot be left behind.[15] Whereas in the elaboration of the particular situations, Jaspers merely verges on a discussion of *the* "basic situation" or *the* "basic limit-situation," later he spells out what he has in mind by these terms. "The ultimate unintelligible limit-situation that includes all others within it is: Being (*Sein*) is only if existence [*Dasein*, i.e., the realm of thingly material objects to which I myself and others also, in part, belong] is; but existence (*Dasein*) as such is not Being."[16] We take this to mean that the honorific term "Being" is to be reserved for what beckons at the horizon of the thingly matters that we know and have to do with in our agency; but this horizon is only held open by what is within the horizon and what we have to do with in our ordinary and natural attitude, i.e., "existence," or the realm of objective things in the world or ourselves as related to these.

We tend to make ourselves at home among things, amidst existence; yet we willy-nilly face contradictions, disappointments when we do this. The limit-situations have a way of pulling the rug out from underneath us and calling everything into question. Husserl himself sketched the limit-situation precisely as one in which, metaphorically, the rug is pulled out from underneath us. This would occur not merely with the fate of a misfortune, untimely death, etc., where something or someone within the world undergoes a calamity, but rather it would occur where what we call normality totally breaks down, i.e., the cohesiveness of the world which holds everything together dissolves, and this breakdown brings me into a situation where I must say: "I do not any longer know up from down and do not see how life can go on, how it can again take a semblance of normality and stability so that there is some point to it." Husserl then asks: Is there not possible a total breakdown for all of humanity where nothing more can be relied on, and where one can no longer even rely on oneself, where the entire world loses its character of a world with goals, etc., and where "we all could land in a limit-situation (*Grenzsituation*)?" This thought experiment that brings to light the radical contingency of the world leads Husserl then to ask in tones reminiscent of Jaspers: "The Being of the world has only the appearance of stability. In truth it is the stability of a structure of normality. But from this there emerges, just when this manner of instability is discovered or becomes palpable, the highest question about the world, i.e., the philosophical questionability of the world as such in its totality. And when this is understood radically it explodes all horizons and calls them into question."[17]

Typically for Husserl (but not always, see Chapter II, §7, and also later in this book), this kind of discussion remains at the level of theoretic consciousness and is an achievement of the disengaged transcendental observer. Or it remains a "thought-experiment" and the Existenz of the transcendental phenomenologist is not an issue, nor is there a thematization of the realization or coming to light of Existenz.

For Jaspers, in contrast, the transcendental observing of Existenz, e.g., the I and achievements of the author of the three-volume 1932 classic in existential philosophy, *Philosophie*, typically remains anonymous. Rather, the focus in the meeting with the limit-situations is *how* we are awakened to our well-spring, with the agency of the manifestation of this *how* remaining anonymous. Jaspers calls this an awakening to "absolute consciousness," which is a non-reflexive awareness of the inmost "I myself" in my origin (*Ursprung*), the innermost core of Existenz. This manifests itself as a kind of movement, a "motion at the origin" or motion within our "well-spring." The first motion in the self-sourcing Jaspers discusses is the coming to light of the unique absolute ignorance we experience in the face of the limit-situation, e.g., of "my death." This serves as a turning point in encountering the well-spring whereby I am moved through a kind of dizziness and horror at the abysses that open before my ignorance and the prospect of my annihilation. This prospect of annihilation spills over into a unique anxiety and a sense of utter emptiness that can find no definitive consolation or assurance through anything existing in the world. Then, Jaspers observes: "If ignorance is the turning point, from out of which the well-spring of all possibility is effective, if dizziness and horror urge us to movement, if anxiety, as the consciousness, in confused freedom, that I might possibly be extinguished, permits me to emerge as a gift to myself, so conscience is the voice at the turning point that demands that there be *distinguishing* and *deciding*."[18]

Of course, conscience may not emerge, nor need love, trust, and faith – other possibilities of Existenz's core that fulfill "absolute consciousness," some of which possibilities we will later study. Indeed the anxiety can result in a crippling vertigo. The magnitude of the No to life as defined by the present typical way of being in the world, a No that the limit-situations occasion and perhaps bring to light, may overwhelm and result in the destruction of hope in reason and incapacitation of will; or it may result in an enthrallment with the spiritual forms of darkness and night that serve as sources of vertigo and negation. Thus suicide can be an expression of someone awakened to Existenz. Existenz here appears as an incommunicable secret of this single individual and what it is of unconditional importance to freely determine in the face of a life that has lost its bearings and holds no meaning.[19] "Unconditional importance," in terms of the "noesis" or intentional act, refers to a willing with which one whole-heartedly identifies, a willing without which one cannot be oneself; in this sense its modality is absolutely and uniquely necessary. The "noema" is what here appears as intrinsically valuable and this without conditions. (We will have occasion to return to this theme in this chapter and the next one.)

If this sense of one's life is determined by the awareness of one's implication in the lives of Others and Others in one's life, suicide can be an expression of a desire for purity and release from that implication and the identity fashioned by it; it may be the act of renunciation of that seemingly inextricable social bond and the desire to maintain or retrieve one's integrity. Here the limit-situation of guilt and the struggle to communicate precipitate the limit-situation of death in the form of suicide.

Existenz as the awakening to the center of the person in the face of limit-situations such as death or guilt is a coming forth of one's unique uniqueness. It is thus a kind of being wrenched from one's proclivity to identify oneself with the world, social conventions and norms, or things in the world. It thus may be thought of as a fundamental motion of pride or even defiance (*Trotz*), as Franz Rosenzweig has suggested. In the face of the worldly and natural determinations with which fate confronts us and which want to subsume the "I myself" into themselves, as the masks and roles of a play may absorb the actor's sense of herself, the "myself" comes forth at the center of the person in a *Trotz*, a "nevertheless," or elemental self-assertion or even defiance. This may be what we revere in some of the tragic heroes of the great tragedies. We will later attend to an elemental self-affirmation which finds expression even where we would expect least to find it, i.e., in the people studied by James Gilligan. These are persons whom we call pathological killers, whose dreadful lives have been informed by early abuse and violations of the sanctuary of their inmost selves while they were infants or children. This *Trotz* is Existenz's coming forth in spite of and in the face of the ineluctable events of determination and individuation handed out by fate. It comes forth as uniquely unique in itself and not so by reason of these events. For Rosenzweig, as we shall see, it comes forth and works its defiance through the "character" it assumes or rather the *Daimon* that serves as the engine for the direction of this unique self.[20]

The limit-situations disclose us to ourselves at our core; they reveal to us our inmost I. "Inmost" and "center" must be taken metaphorically; strictly it is not some isolatable thing that is central and inmost that we would find by arranging our selves according to a spatial center and periphery. In Book 1, Chapter III, we reviewed Husserl's notion of soul as what the I has and what affects the I. The soul is clearly a more voluminous sense of oneself than the transcendental I as pole or source point; it is more voluminous, because soaked with the pre-reflective, pre-thetic, and pre-conceptual, than the "myself" for it extends to the far reaches of ownness in the mind, memory, emotions and body, and it is that which supplies the stuff upon which the I-center acts. Yet there is a certain fluidity in the notion of center and periphery. Think of how the metaphorical sense emerges and, indeed, is in flux in the following example. I might be thinking about something that I regard as of great philosophical importance, e.g., the distinction between the phenomenological and natural attitude. The neighbor might have begun to play his super-bass stereo system. Initially it does not catch my attention; but then after a while, because all the windows are open, I realize I am not only fighting the noise but also the vertigo coming from his source of pleasure. The peripheral invades my center. I, for a brief moment, have the notion that he is disdaining me and my desire for quiet of which I presume he is clearly aware, and the anger begins to consume me; but I realize I can close my window, talk to him, and move to another portion of my house. The feeling is subordinated to a more reasonable center of myself. I return to my reflection when I realize that I have promised my wife to clean the bathrooms. Although the philosophical reflection is where I most want to be and where perhaps I experience myself to be most alive and "centered," I now move to "another center" which has greater claims on me, i.e., that of keeping my promise, and my intellectual center is subordinated to another center. The "center" in all these cases is bodily in the sense of the lived body which encompasses all of my experienced "I can." It is not bodily in the way an organ in the space of my body is or even in the way a felt-meaning like resentment can seem to lodge itself in the stomach or forehead. The "I myself" as a historical person in the world with others includes capacities, skills, and interests that display themselves at any time in terms of a kind of center-periphery arrangement. Different times and situations will determine where *I* will be occupied in this voluminous self. Throughout this voluminous lived sense of myself a sense of my center is "there," ready to announce itself, unless I have built up a wall against its entry.

We may say that awakening to Existenz is awakening to the center of one's person. It is the metaphorical place where one's ownmost self is in question as well as being the place where one's deepest capacity for devotion and ardor are palpable. It is wherein not only one's ownmost self but also one's most ardent ideals and convictions are highlighted or called into question. Yet it is evident that this center may lie dormant and not be what William James once called the habitual centre of one's personal energy. Rather, this habitual center may be on the periphery, i.e., it may be what we are alienated from by reason of our self-deception or habits of self-obfuscation. What is the actual center is what stands in contrast to the peripheral parts of ourselves and our lives, towards which we have a measure of indifference. That we may be indifferent to this more authentic center and keep it displaced to the periphery is not only paradoxical and ironic but it is living in the mode of being perversely ironical. In which case this true center may have a kind of subterranean existence, i.e., these ideas, ideals, and convictions, as well as the ardor for them which is at our center, may remain peripheral and dormant. Nevertheless, the proper arrangement, the proper centering of one's life may slowly, through the "unimaginable touch of time," i.e., passive synthesis, and the elusive creative processes of cogitation, take place first pre-thematically and then explicitly. Typically, to say someone is "converted," at least in a religious sense, is to say that those ideals and convictions that were previously peripheral and pre-conscious or pre-thematic now take a central place and one's prior arrangement of one's self and life suffers an upheaval.[21] This is a gathering experience and an awakening to the center of one's person.

What we refer to when we refer to "conscience" discloses us to ourselves in an exemplary way as having a center. (As we shall see, love and devotion are also exemplary disclosures.) A solemn ecclesiastical opinion of the twentieth century put it this way, "Conscience is the most secret core and sanctuary of a man."[22] In the next sections we wish to attend more explicitly to the senses of the metaphor "inmost," "secret core," "sanctuary," etc. as they reveal themselves especially in relation to the theme "conscience." We want also to determine the sense of the "voice" of conscience and whether the "sanctuary" is the "voice" or the center of the I called to respond to this "voice."

§3. Conscience and Ought

We face "matters of conscience" in many contexts apart from limit-situations. Indeed, Helmut Kuhn's picture of conscience as the compass of life's ever present quivering needle captures the way conscience emerges in the everyday and not merely in the limit-situations.[23] As we shall argue, following Husserl, conscience is never far away, never merely occasional; rather, it pervades all of life. But the awakening of ourselves to ourselves as Existenz is an awakening of conscience or rather, we shall propose, it is the response of Existenz to this awakening. There is a more decisive revelation of ourselves to ourselves in the crisis limit-situations than in the constant but often "softly spoken" revelations of conscience in everyday life. But "limit-situations" and "crises of conscience" themselves bring conscience to light in a thematic way that legitimates the appropriateness of featuring conscience and honoring the familiar metaphor of the "voice of conscience." The often-held view that conscience is the "center" of the person offers a further opportunity to contrast Existenz with the transcendental I.

As phenomenology from its beginnings faced the eliminativist and objectivist temptations of scientism that would reduce consciousness to physical causes and first-person experiences to third-person descriptions, so it has faced the ancient, modern, and post-modernist critique of conscience in the name of the superhumans who have conquered the superego's control of the herd. Here "conscience is but a word that cowards use/Devised at first to keep the strong in awe." Or as in *Hamlet*:

Thus conscience does make cowards of us all;
And thus the native hue of resolution
Is sicklied o'er with the pale cast of thought.
And enterprises of great pith and moment,
With this regard, their currents turn awry,
And lose the name of action.[24]

Our word "conscience" obviously is connected with the word "consciousness." Both derive from the Latin, *conscientia*, that contains two Latin words, *cum* (which became *con*) denoting "with" and *scire*, the infinitive for "to know." Thus *cum-scire* = a knowing-with, or an accompanying knowing. The two-ness hinted at in the word "consciousness" is muted in various English usages, as we exhort someone to be more aware or more conscious, which is equivalent to exhorting them to be more awake and attentive. It is muted also when phenomenology attends to consciousness as the pervasive non-reflexive self-awareness that characterizes human life. The twoness is evident, however, in some earlier and modern English uses, as "she was conscious of her embarrassment," where self-awareness of a certain kind, here, one's embarrassment, is attributed to a self-directed act or an act of reflection on oneself. As we have urged throughout this book, there are numerous reasons not to confine all senses of being-conscious to an act of reflection. But in the cognate "conscience" (in French, *conscience* serves for both what we translate into English as consciousness and conscience) the twoness readily comes to mind. Thus conscience in English and German is often associated with the conflicted self or soul that is torn in incompatible directions. *"Zwei Seelen wohnen, ach!, in meiner Brust! Die eine will ich von der anderen trennen."*[25]

Conscientia reflects the earlier Greek words found in Aristotle, Plotinus, the Stoics, and St. Paul in the New Testament. Aristotle's and Plotinus' *synaisthesis* suggest more the phenomenological "being conscious" whereas *syneidesis* can reflect either being conscious or conscience, a knowing that accompanies knowing, a knowing that one knows or a knowing that knows one knows and which affects us in a moral-emotive way. As in the case of "consciousness" the difficulty is spelling out the nature of the self-awareness or the accompanying knowing of "conscience."

As we have often seen, the temptation of "ontological monism" (Michel Henry's term) to conceive the self-awareness of consciousness exclusively as a reflective intentional act is great. But even though the twoness is more pronounced in *conscience* than in *consciousness*, this temptation to anchor *conscience* in an act of reflection is not as strong as it is in *consciousness*. Conscience clearly involves a passivity where a sense of being "conscious" to which we might be exhorted requires reflection. Reflection generally is an autonomous act one brings about as a result of a motivation, e.g., an exhortation. But one can become reflectively aware of oneself when overtaken by, e.g., an emotion like shame or embarrassment. These examples indicate that the awareness of self, even the self-awareness that is marginal or quasi-objective, need not be the result of an act initiated by the I. My awareness of how you do or might perceive me results in my unwillingly regarding myself in a certain way that we call embarrassment.

Conscience in this sense resembles the non-egoic-initiated forms of self-awareness that characterize some emotions. Whereas emotions, we have said, are self-involving, i.e., the person we have constituted is involved, they are not all equally self-referring. Shame and feeling proud self-refer whereas anger and fear are self-involving. Conscience involves a twoness not evident in the self-referring feelings or emotions; in these latter I feel, e.g., embarrassed, I am not addressed or admonished to feel embarrassed. This latter is closer to conscience. As with emotions in general conscience too does not seem to be the result of the I's explicit agency. We will have to consider in what sense conscience is or is not effected by *me*. In any case, at the start, it is clear that the kind of self-awareness that conscience is happens quite without our willing it in the sense of its being a direct response to our cognitive agency, choice, or volition. In the case of conscience, although the twoness seems evident, there is a kind of receptivity and passivity, or at least an aspect of *me* is "addressed" without, as it were, my leave or initiative. In this respect we can say that consciousness as non-reflective self-awareness perdures throughout all of life, whereas conscience would seem to be occasional. Thus we speak of the voice of conscience making its appearance to us, occasionally bothering, tormenting, reproaching, unsettling, etc. We will soon return to this.

Conscience comes to us most clearly in action rather than in theory, although there is doubtless an ethical aspect to thinking and speaking. We touched upon this at the end of the last chapter when discussing the way philosophy may relate to one's death. More generally, some blunders of thought appear "unconscionable." Thus there is the interesting paradox of the speaker who does not believe in the reality of

conscience presupposing in his listeners a kind of conscientiousness in their listening to what he is saying, if what he has to say is to get a fair hearing. Similarly, he
must presuppose that they apperceive a kind of conscientiousness in him, if he is to
merit a fair hearing. There are also the ethical issues where "the compass needle of
conscience" registers a sensitivity within intellectual life, e.g., in not merely meaning
what we say but saying precisely what we mean, the patient searching for the right
word, the writer's and speaker's struggle with the vagueness of a thought buried and
entangled in a recalcitrant sentence or paragraph, the thinker's sensibility shaped by
the distinction between articulating what is present in an empty and what is present in
a filled intention, etc.[26] Thus in a theoretical stance we typically face the task of rescu-
ing clarity from vagueness, establishing correctness over incorrectness, being attuned
to validity and keeping invalidity at bay, etc. in our articulations or arguments. Our
failure can reflect the quality of our minds, e.g., our being fresh or weary, slow-witted
or dimwitted, lazy or insufficiently fussy. It is a difficult matter to determine to what
extent these flaws *necessarily* reflect on our moral person or character.

The Husserlian position we will here present shows that conscience reflects
primarily the "position-taking acts" by which we constitute our personal moral
essences as well as their correlate, the world. In this case, moral and intellectual
integrity are difficult, in many cases, to separate. Later we will have occasion to
return to the topic of integrity when attempting to locate the "center of the I."

A unique feature of conscience comes out in its German word, *Gewissen*, where
the etymology suggests that it is a certain (*gewiss*) knowing (*Wissen*). It is certainty
tied to its imposing and imperative status. Although the deed may be done in private, yet by reason of its essence as a deed or action it is not hidden from the doer.
A deed for which one is responsible cannot be absolutely unknown to the agent.[27]
Further, there can be a doubt whether what I am doing is right or wrong, but there
can be no doubt that at the moment I am in a unique position to know whether
I believe (or disbelieve) I am right in acting in this way. Kant expressed this in
this way: conscience is a consciousness that is an obligation for itself. It is simply
the (apodictic) awareness of obligation – quite apart from the question of whether
I ultimately am right or wrong in this matter.[28]

Conscience surfaces most emphatically when we are in a situation calling for
action or a practical stance. Further, even in the realm of the theoretical, the syn-
tactical-judgmental activity involves more of the "I myself" than does the merely
intellectual as the work of categorial framing and understanding. The reproach of
someone for bad judgment is a moral judgment in the way our finding fault with
someone's inability to understand or grasp the point is not.[29] Intellectual capacity is
not equal among us and no one is responsible for that. Yet saying one knows when
one might have qualified his remark with "it seems to me" or "it was reported to
me," or saying something *is* the case when one ought to have said that it might be
the case are reprehensible. Further, even in the order of judgment, the carelessness
and lack of rigor and clarity of the speaker and thinker may reflect certain external
pressures, such as a time limit, or it might reflect his or her incapacity to deal with
a complex matter because of weariness. The effects of this occasional or chronic
incapacitation might well be limited to only his or her argument; it need not involve

a betrayal of the self-ideal or the sacrifice of integrity, as in lies, broken promises, or deliberate obfuscation. Further, it need not have harmed anyone else.

The practical-moral situation, i.e., where moral categoriality is formed, is one where the weal or woe of oneself and others is in question, where one's being true to oneself and respectful of others is an explicit issue.[30] This is inseparably, we shall argue, where one determines oneself to be the sort of person one is. Although a strong case may be made that the home base of the realm of moral obligation is in the second-person and first-person plural, nevertheless I believe it is evident in the descriptions in this section that there is a legitimate and important first- and third-personal sense of moral obligation. We return to these matters in Chapter V, §9. In taking up another's good as one's own we respond to requirements on us to be open to what is real and transcendent to ourselves and our own interests, foremost in terms of the reality and dignity of other persons. This is why the realm of conscience is more emphatic here than in the theoretical or cognitive stance, i.e., here more is at stake regarding who we are as what sort of persons we are. The way I am "conscience-stricken" for my failure to be true to my word contrasts with my self-reproach for failing to make a distinction or not getting the point. Of course, I can be embarrassed when this failure in acuity comes to light. But this could be less *conscience* than my shame before others that I was not sufficiently "sharp" or intellectually rigorous and wakeful. Yet doubtless I might have occasion to reproach myself with conceptual slovenliness and that I was not properly intellectually alive or awake. This latter has less to do with the requirements made on my native abilities than my responsibility, my "conscientiousness." In these latter cases intellectual "virtue" has clear moral components.

Thus the theoretical stance may well involve such situations where conscience reproaches severely; and this is especially true for the professional educator and thinker who professes intellectual and theoretical integrity and this is precisely inseparable from his or her true self. But this commingling of intellectual and moral virtue is made less puzzling when we consider that conscience has to do with our personal moral essence and this is inseparable from position-takings by which we have shaped our world. Position-takings are both theoretical and practical. Our being true to ourselves is being true to both the theoretical and practical position-takings. We will return to this soon. But now we turn to conscience's imperative character, how "I must" or "I ought" relates to "I can."

In a most basic sense, i.e., that disclosed by the ultimate phenomenological reduction, I am aware of myself as having possibility ("I can") and aware of myself as able to actualize this being-able: I can think, I can will, I can move or look this way rather than that, etc. Concomitant with this sense of being-able is life's excitement and occasional intrusiveness. Here we have to do with our elemental passivity: I undergo willy-nilly this attraction or repulsion, but that *I* give in to the attraction or repulsion is not a matter of necessity.

We may be tempted to speak of our basic possibility, most elementarily that provided by retention, in the possessive case as "*my* I-can." And we may be tempted to speak of our elemental sense of moral necessity to pursue a good or course of action as "*my* ought" as we do, indeed, speak of "my duty." Yet these "possessions" are inseparable from I myself and we never have "I myself" *as this person* apart from "I-can" and "I-ought."

My I-can pervades my conscious life, but so does my I-ought. I exist always living futurally – even in memory there is an irrepressible protentional horizon of the present act of remembering. I typically exist living futurally pursuing desired objects and facing the exalted heights of ideals, not least of which is the ideal of my true self, which will occupy us in the next section. "Being human is teleological being and an ought-to-be and... this teleology holds sway in each and every activity of an ego."[31] My existing teleologically is not something accidental or separable from my "I myself." Let's dwell on this.

When we think of conscience as tied to action we are compelled to see its various manifestations as tied to the modalities of time's appearing, i.e., past, present, and future. The ineluctable pervasive sense of oneself is actual in the present; we call this being attentive, being wakeful, being conscientious. This sense of ourselves as actually being and being in the present, i.e., this "ontological" sense of self, however, is inseparable from the self as "deontological" (*deon, deontos*: what is binding; *deomai*: ought). I myself am essentially tied to a future good, the sense of which is that it is to be brought about by my agency; my essential determination is to live in a horizon of goods that are to be realized by me. *Bonum faciendum est.* My essential determination is self-determination in as much as I am given over to myself not only as "I am" but also as "I-can," i.e., with my possibility awaiting my actualization; but further I am given to myself as "I-ought," i.e., my actual existing determination requiring my responsibility through action. Prior to this I myself am undeveloped as a personal I; as Husserl says, I have not determined myself as an I. (See our discussion below, Chapter IV, §3.) This is a way of saying that my essential determination is a self-determination through facing the ideal of my true self. Indeed, in as much as this self itself has an intersubjective ideal, this ideal is of an eutopian community requiring communal self-actualization.[32] I am determined not merely a priori and *a tergo* but freely and *a fronte*, i.e., by the way my personal essence is open to ideals as emergent in the present. We will have frequent occasion to return to these themes.

Even if the ideal is interpersonal, obligations can appear as uniquely mine, i.e., they may appear as what must be done in the sense of what *I ought* to do. When I believe that "we ought to conserve natural resources" I believe "I ought to conserve." But when I believe that "someone must aid the people in the Sudan" I do not imply I ought to aid the people in the Sudan because perhaps I am not in a position to help them and am already deluged with responsibilities. But when *I* ought to do something, no one else can do it for me. It may be true in a particular case that *we* ought to do it, but if it is genuinely *our* responsibility your doing it does not relieve me of doing it. Nor is it something that "one" must do, as with perhaps the devastation of the people in Haiti. (In all these matters we touch upon the complex issue of the phenomenological-ontology of "we" and representative democracy. When one, simply by reason of one's being a citizen in the representative democracy, is complicit in the heinous deeds of the nation state to which one professes allegiance and pays taxes, as, e.g., in Iraq and Haiti, the exoneration is less easy.[33]) What appears as "I ought" is what you can never do for me. If a deed appears to me as what you ought to do, e.g., forgive your friend, rather than what someone must do, I cannot do it for you either. But such an appearing, i.e., "You ought…," is always a *videtur quod*, something that I cannot know in the way I know "I ought." This is in part a matter of the difference between first- or second-personal point of view; inseparably it is also a matter of the bearing of the responsibility as inseparable from one's self-awareness. I am not bound in my knowledge of your duties; your duties are not at the center of my self in the way my "I ought" is. I can let my conviction rest about your obligation and do nothing further; not so with my awareness of my "I ought." Even though I hold myself obliged to attend to, e.g., a child left in need by your apparent neglect, this is a response to what I must do; it is not a response to your obligation or even your failure to meet your duties.

Pervading one's personal life-world is an ideal unfolding of life in terms of a unique personal life as well as an intersubjective ideal. The ideal is not a goal within life, e.g., it is not like a career goal or a good to be possessed, but it emerges as the good which informs all of life and which can only be approximated. That all of life is surrounded by such a good is not of our choosing. Nor is it of our choosing that life appears to us to be a unity wherein all the moments aspire to be in harmony with one another. (Similarly I have not chosen who I am or that I must determine what sort of person I am to be.) The basic sense of Ought arises out of the way this ideal of a unique individual and intersubjective life is manifest in the unfolding of this life. Each phase of this life, of course, contributes to the whole context of the personal life-world, but this personal life-world, along with its ideals, informs each phase. The basic Ought of the ideal is inseparable from the whole which is the personal life-world and its ever emergent ideal. The individual actions that are called for, that appear as requirements on me to be fully and properly myself, i.e., which appear as Oughts, are precisely those which have as their palpable horizon the whole of the personal life-world and its emergent ideal. When conscience "speaks" the basic Ought of the ideal of all of my life is disclosed because "all of my life" is precisely the identical personal I constituted by my decisions, promises, position-takings, etc.[34]

In the light of what has been said it is hopefully clear that what is meant by "ideal true self" is not some image, picture, or reverie that may pop into consciousness occasionally. As a regulative ideal it is not anything given at all. Rather it is co-meant and given along with what is given. Just as when we say of something, "That is quite good," there is co-given what is less than this as well as what is better than this in terms of the good quality under consideration. Of course, we might well have in mind something we have explicitly experienced that is better than what we are now experiencing, but even this better, which might be the "best" we have ever experienced, might still be measured by a never-given but co-meant better than this. It might well be the case that there are possible experiences of flawless unsurpassable perfections in some areas of evaluation, e.g., some musical or sports performances, but it is doubtful that this is conceivable in terms of a personal life.

Laws, imperatives, maxims, or even virtue-ethics may appear heteronomous and may "de-individualize" the Ought in favor of universalizability, conventional standards, and official authorities and traditional exemplars. If these do not find integration in one's personal life world and its emergent ideals they can very well alienate and appear as extrinsic hostile forces. Although obligations attached to one's self-ideal must, when integrated into the intersubjective ideal, co-intend the universal moral community, the Ought does not arise merely from a rational principle of universalizability. With Husserl we may say that what we ought to do in any concrete situation, (whether or not a properly moral one, i.e., one that involves my determination of myself as living in accord with my personal essence and self-ideal, or where my taking your good as my own and your evil as my evil), is respond to the obvious imperative to act reasonably and judge rationally. What I must do in concrete cases emerges out of the particular states of affairs at hand and on the bases of content-laden premises and motivations. And we may assume that this would be the same for anyone in our shoes. But to look away from the demands of the concrete context toward a principle of universalizability to account for or justify the obligation seems as absurd in the sphere of willing as it is in judging.[35] In the properly moral case of self-determination, where one determines oneself in accord with one's true self or personal essence, and in this sense as I myself, the act of looking away to a principle of universalizability seems even more askew. This is a far cry from saying that I may act morally without including Others in my point of view. Including Others is not moving to a principle of universalizability, but living in accord with the true sense of oneself as a member of a moral community.

Whereas doubtless there are Oughts which surface in connection with goals and means to ends, etc., the moral Ought does not arise merely from a purpose, or from a clear relation of means to an end. Rather it arises also from *me myself* entwined with a practical state of affairs as regarded within the totality of the personal life-world and its emergent ideals. Properly, the Ought coincides with my lived ideal, and appears as what is necessary if I am to realize my true self. Rational integrity is indeed integrity regarding me, but it can be restricted to my intellectual life or me as an agent of manifestation. I can be rationally true to myself, i.e., consistent, alert, etc., and yet be repressing or avoiding the demands of others and the larger and deeper senses of myself. For example, I can manifest intellectual consistency and integrity in various areas while repressing the realization of my death.

Obligation or the lived "I ought" implies I can, but not every "I can" implies "I ought." I ought implies I can, but this implication only refers to my possibilities which relate to my personal essence as it is evident in my personal being in the life-world with its emergent ideals; they do not refer to just any possibilities I *de facto* have. A present "I ought" indicates the future, not the past, even though, of course it, as *my* ought, is inseparable from all the temporal modes. (Conscience, as we will see, can indicate the past ["I/You should not have…"] and can indeed indicate the future perfect: "I/You [shall] ought to have…" Conscience in regard to the future and the unfolding present coincides simply with the appearance of Ought.) The Ought can only be manifest to me now, who am ineluctably continuous with the one I have been. Even the call to engage in a prospective retrospection, e.g., in facing "my death," is a call to what I have not yet done.

In I-ought, I live toward the future in a pre-determined way. The proximate source of this determination is the horizon of my life, as it has been determined by my past;

the ultimate source of this determination is my personal essence, i.e., the way the "myself" is realized in life's phases as "I myself." In this sense I go in advance of myself and beckon me myself with "I ought." This personal essence is, we shall see, both constituted in the course of life, as well as a priori because tied to one's calling. The "myself," we have claimed, does not as such have properties that are identifiable and which individuate. But as constitutive of the ideal of the personal essence, we are calling it the "entelechy," it creates in the personal essence of the "I myself" the distinctive properties that surround the person's ideals and obligations.

May I say I *am not*, but rather *have*, my obligations? The answer is yes if we add that I do not have these in the way I have things I may renounce or dispose of. "My essential personal determinations or properties," my body, etc., are both what I have and am. I cannot simply dispose of them and still be *me*, i.e., this personal essence which I myself and Others who know me identify as me. My obligations are constitutive of my personal I and simply getting rid of them is getting rid of what I have constituted myself to be. In getting rid of them, of course "I myself" am still "I myself." But as I approach a limit of exonerating myself from allegiance to my position-taking acts, I approach the non-identifiable "identity" of one who is whatever the present momentary impulse dictates. Thus, of course, I can get rid of obligations in a way I cannot get rid of my body. Getting rid of my body robs me absolutely of the necessary condition of being a personal agent in the world. Getting rid of my body is suicide, even though it is conceivable that one believes that she is *only* getting rid of her body. There would have to be thick "overbeliefs" if one were to hold that she *may* and *can* get rid of her body.

I can but *may not* get rid of my obligations. If I do get rid of them I contradict myself. "I *may*" means that I am permitted, i.e., I can without self-censure, i.e., without violating obligations. Thus I can do what I may not do and thereby I violate what I am obliged to do without being released from the obligation to do this. When I so contradict myself I endanger and belie the conditions for my being a personal agent in the world. I meet these conditions by being the same one as I committed myself to be in my past position-takings, e.g., the one who says what he means, who is respectful of distinctions he has made, who keeps his promises, who is faithful to his ideals, who is consistent in his judgments if the evidence continues to warrant this, etc.; and yet in not meeting my obligations I, in fact, exist precisely as the one who does not stick to his past position-takings, etc., yet who is the same "myself" and is identified with the same proper name by himself and those who know me. In this sense JG Hart exists without being the same JG Hart whom he has determined himself to be.

Of course, it can come about that the former validities *must* be relinquished. I discover that they were in fact not valid. Or the conditions of a promise no longer obtain, e.g., I have become deathly ill. Clearly if this is an encompassing and central issue for the person there is a crisis of identity of the personal essence and her life-world. Until it is resolved there will be great instability, if not anxiety. Or it may be a less encompassing matter, e.g., I break the promise because I came to see what was not foreseeable, i.e., that to keep it would involve maintaining circumstances that I am unable to sustain or that would undermine the very purpose of the promise. In such cases I might have to live with the fact that my integrity was blemished because I am too weak or I thoughtlessly committed myself. Or the promise dissolves because the future evolved in ways that undid the very reason for the promise, e.g., I totally misperceived the situation and the other party did not need my help nor did she really want me either to make or fulfill my promise.

I have my obligations in a different way than I have possibilities. I can recognize possibilities, e.g., logical possibilities, without recognizing them as mine. Possibilities are *mine* only when they enter into the sphere of my I-can and my life-world. They then take on the status of becoming not merely logical possibilities or real possibilities, but my real possibilities. As such they become actual only by way of my agency. My real possibilities determine me as real possibilities which may be *uniquely* my real possibilities. But their determination is still real possible determination and not actuality. But emergence of them as real possibilities is nevertheless, even though they are mere possibilities, a decisive determination: In their emergence as real possibilities, a horizon which was indeterminate is transformed (determined) to one which has determinable vectors, from an empty possibility or one that is possible or conceivable to a real possibility of "I can."

All of these can be taken from me, e.g., by chance, or some of them I myself can dispose of. Yet in either case I will still be the same me, the same "myself." It might be true that if I myself dispose of some of my possibilities, I remove from myself the more appropriate realization of my "personal essence" (which we distinguish from the essence of the "myself," see Book 1, especially Chapters III–V and VIII), i.e., who I am called to be. But nothing that is removed from me by chance would seem to be essential to my being "I myself." But this does not rule out a priori the possibility of the tragedy that interferes with my realizing a fuller actualization of my personal essence.

"Ought" determines me in the way my possibilities do not. "I ought" means I am already determined actually in regard to the future; "I can" means I am determined by having these real possibilities, e.g., I have land for a garden and a good supply of manure, but these are not actual determinations until I actualize them by determining myself in a certain way. I am not yet a gardener, i.e., one who gardens with a passion and who has worked on this soil, planted the seeds, watered the plants, etc. I am free to actualize these determinations or not. I am not free, if I wish to remain true to myself, my personal essence, with respect to an "ought."

Yet the "I ought" refers to my unique personal ideal. All of my position-taking acts are taken in the horizon of this ideal. It is not as if the personal moral essence is written in stone after the first couple of acts. It is true that the position-takings, e.g., decisions, are valid "from now on" and in this sense have a kind of trans-temporal validity – until they are revoked. Yet they are achieved from finite perspectives, and acts are undertaken within the horizon of the ideal, and in this sense the essence as it now stands is an approximation of the infinite task of "my true self." Nevertheless, we wish to maintain the distinction between the actual determination of "my I ought" and the merely potential determination of "my I can" because my ideal is *my* unique personal essence's ideal, i.e., it informs my personal essence actually and the Ought is the way this unique ideal essence is revealed. We will more explicitly attend to the revelation of the unique personal moral ideal later in this chapter as well as in the following chapters.

In spite of our not following Kant in opposing teleology and ought, there can be no doubt that the Ought often enough stands in conflict to our inclinations. Our emphasis is rather on the exalted *telos* that beckons us and toward which we can display a chronic lethargy or indifference. In this respect there is little distance between us and Kant. Further we can acknowledge the merit of Kant's praise of the life that corresponds to the Ought, what he calls the "holiness" of will. (See our discussions in Chapter IV, §7 below.) There is indeed a basis for being amazed that our responsiveness to the Ought raises us above all the bonds of dependence by which we are entwined in nature and society.

Kant has offered in this context a helpful phenomenological experiment for the evidence for the unconditioned nature of our freedom as it is manifest in response to the call of the Ought. We may ask ourselves whether we are immediately certain of our capacity to be able to hold fast to a resolution in the face of powerful pressures, e.g., torture. The answer is that each of us would confess: I simply do not know whether I would have the strength to hold to the resolution. Nevertheless if it is true that the obligation is clear to me that I *ought* to hold fast, then I *infer* that I must be *able* to remain firm. This points to an inexhaustibly deep sense of our freedom.[36] This thought-experiment decides nothing about whether we would be faithful to our resolve; but it shows the essential connection between Ought and freedom: If we are aware of the Ought, we are no less aware of the I-can, the freedom, to fulfill it. This theme points to one we shall soon study: How the sense of Ought is so central to I myself that I would rather follow it and be able to live with this sense of myself than to "gain the whole world." Thus the thought experiment does not merely point to a deep sense of freedom; it also points to the formative power of the Ought in determining an important sense we may give to "who we are."

§4. The Problem of the Pure Conscience

When we think of conscience and the Ought in the present we have to do with our being now "conscientious." Here we attend presently to the appropriate realizing of a deed, but its aim and completion are futural, just as its accomplishment is not possible without the retention of the past. In the present I am conscientious in the sense that I am so acting now that I will be able later to take responsibility for this act before others and myself. Being conscientious, being wakeful to my present responsibilities, and thus anticipating having to answer, in a retrospective critique, to myself and others, is weakened in the wake of a habit of not fulfilling one's obligations or in the wake of a life that is thoughtless and irresponsible. For such a one, a "wanton," to live with himself requires dulling his conscience because if the conscience were not dulled he would have to live with one, i.e., himself, who incessantly reproaches him for how he lives.

This sort of person is to be contrasted with someone whose conscience is tender or sensitive and who too may have trouble living with himself because the conscientiousness takes on a pathological from of scrupulosity. Typically we have reason to esteem and honor the person whose conscience is tender; but we can only pity the person suffering from the tyrannical conscience. Indeed, from the Husserlian perspective, this would not be conscience but rather the weakness of the alienation from oneself, the inability to act for oneself, but rather always to let the tyrannical other(s), whom one has permitted to substitute for the "I myself," dictate the source and course of one's agency. This is the pathology of the Freudian superego. But the tyrannical conscience can also be due to the confusion of the ideal of perfection with the believed-in obligation never to make a mistake, suffer a spell of weakness, or have a moment of inadvertence. "Perfectionism" is a form of self-idolatry in so far as one conceives of oneself as obliged to embody completely the ideal, thereby constituting oneself as beyond a finite perspective, insight, vigilance, energy, intelligence, etc.

The clear, pure, or clean conscience refers less to being conscientious than to *having been* conscientious. One is aware not that one *is* good or that one is anchored in a permanent disposition which assures that one will do only what is good. Rather, the clear conscience is the awareness that one is free of guilt in regard to a certain present matter or in regard to the recent past. This is, in part, because conscience announces itself in its most familiar form as a negative and prohibiting "voice" revealing to me that in the prospective deed, I will dishonor myself; in the past deed I was not true to myself; or in the present deed I am not being one with myself. When conscience is positive, I am at one with myself. When I am at one with myself, conscience need not speak but may remain silent because I am I myself and at peace, and even joyful, in being so. In this case my freedom is a necessity; my willing what is called for is something I must do. As a stable disposition it approaches the utopian or heavenly, the "holy will," the *beata necessitas boni*, i.e., the blessed necessity of the Good, which moral theologians have reserved for the saints and the divine. Because this is a limit-case that has rare approximations, we have reason to suspect, at least in our own case, self-deception and the superficiality of one who is a stranger to herself if she thinks or believes that she always joyfully and inevitably wills what she ought to. For mortals, awareness of one's goodness, awareness of oneself as being totally faithful to one's commitments and being essentially disposed to do only the good, is not possible. This position rests on unique essential matters. Let us briefly consider some of them.

Jankélévitch has nicely brought out an aspect of this matter by claiming that no one we know can say "I am pure." The predicate adjective "pure" cannot be applied to someone by him- or herself in the first-person indicative timeless or intemporal present. As we earlier saw, following Jankélévitch, no one can say "I die," i.e., use the verb "to die" in the first-person indicative singular present, so similarly no one can say "I am pure" in the first-person singular indicative. (*A fortiori* no one can say, "We are pure.") It might seem to be the case that I can use the past or future tense. For example, one has doubtless occasion to say in regard to a specific matter, "my conscience is clear in regard to how I acted." Similarly one may say in regard to a specific matter, " I will act conscientiously." But if at no time I can say "I am pure," then how I might say "I was pure" or "I will be pure" is problematic. Let us consider the reasons for holding why no one can say "I am pure."

One decisive reason, and this is not the argument of Jankélévitch, for our inability to say "I am pure" is the hermeneutical moral circle of truth uncovered by Aristotle that to do the right thing we must perceive perspicaciously; but to perceive perspicaciously we must have done the right thing. As adults our agency informs our moral vision even though our moral vision sets the stage for our agency.[37] Although we are responsible for our beginnings, in so far as the beginnings of moral vision by which we perceive something to be good or evil lie in the habitualities derived from our agency, no one has absolute power over his or her beginnings. Our moral beginnings are begun in fortunate or unfortunate circumstances and foremost the circumstance of the exemplars informing our beginning agency as children. But the perception of these circumstances and of these exemplars, the significant adults at our beginnings, themselves were shaped by the ethos and adults that constituted *their* moral climate. Here Jaspers' theme of the limit-situation of guilt is adumbrated in Aristotle. In any case, perfect moral clarity and purity may not be assumed to be givens, even in the best of beginnings. The "brightest and the best" of any class and culture still are burdened by the limitations of their class and culture and the exemplars of their class and culture.

Further, there is the essential "fact" that we incline toward a subtle self-indulgence and narcissism that often, if not always, fosters dishonesty with ourselves: we muddy our conscience, i.e., muddy our selves to ourselves, even in our efforts at selfless devotion. We create a confusion by which we hide from ourselves and by which we enable ourselves not to be true to the Ought, not true to ourselves. Under the best of circumstances we are only more or less faithful, and thereby the very best of us have shaky dispositions with which to greet the future challenges.

But another and essentially connected reason, and here we draw on Jankelévitch, for why "I am pure" is not possible has to do with the relationship of explicit self-awareness and first-person self-reference to one's being virtuous.[38] Think of the purity of the infant or the child: She is pure precisely on condition that she is ignorant of her purity. When a hint of narcissism or self-awareness (e.g., of being cute) surfaces, the original innocence vanishes. Adults cannot easily refrain from or avoid explicit self-awareness, especially in terms of matters of virtue and integrity. Because I am always ineluctably non-reflectively self-aware, I am always on the verge of reflection. Plotinus already seemed inclined to this view in regard to virtue: Virtue is contaminated by (reflexive) self-awareness.[39] Reflexive, intentional self-awareness, on the one hand, and purity and innocence, on the other, are mutually exclusive.

Jankelévitch overstates this when he implies that only "unconsciousness" is compatible with virtue. We would not be agents if we were, strictly speaking, unconscious of our agency. But surely he is correct in claiming that being aware *of* our agency *as* virtuous, praiseworthy, etc., affects the status of the act. Whether it destroys absolutely the virtuous quality, even though it evaporates the innocence, seems, however, doubtful. The chief reason to doubt the claim that moral agency is necessarily unconscious rather than conscious is of course tied to our position (see Book 1, especially Chapter II) that as a matter of necessity one is non-reflectively self-aware and thus always on the verge of reflection in so far as it lies with in one's "I can." But ineluctably and gratefully one is self-aware in one's agency and therefore ineluctably and gratefully there is reason to believe that there are perhaps some forms of self-esteem and pride that are not reflexive and thus do not involve the contaminating narcissism that Jankélévitch wants to highlight.

Whereas I do not become non-existing when I reflect on myself and my act, i.e., the act of reflection does not annihilate my being, reflective self-awareness does destroy the innocence as well as the purity of the act. Jankelévitch goes so far as to say that purity is a moral quality that does not tolerate the I. This is surely correct in so far as "I" is an indexical by which I refer to myself as myself. Yet "I," we have said, is a non-ascriptive reference and therefore what I" I refers to is non-sortal and as such and *per se* it does not tolerate any properties. However, in self-ascribing virtue to me, the person I am, by using the indexical "I" I refer to myself as myself in regard to my virtuous behavior as a person in the world. "I am modest," "I am humble," "I am kind," etc., of necessity affect the purity of the act. But, as we have seen (throughout Book 1, especially Chapter III), there is a sense of egoity or I-ness of the "myself" that is prior to the performance of the indexical "I" which is the condition that the act is a conscious act that belongs to someone's, i.e., my, stream of consciousness and for which I am responsible and which I am capable of recalling. In this respect all virtuous acts are I-acts, even if they are not explicitly self-referential or expressly self-conscious.

It would seem that no one *is* ever pure, in the sense that this property characterizes her life definitively. But not only can one strive to be pure but the striving for purity defines us, i.e., is our calling as a regulative ideal. Further, the effective wanting and striving to be pure itself is a form of purification. Husserl himself said that one can never be good but can only become good, and one can be good only in wanting to be good.[40] We are awake to ourselves when we resolve to answer the call of the Ought. One sense of purity is answering this call unreservedly and without being motivated by applause or reward. The ideal of the Ought beckons us to integrity, honesty, responsibility, in short purity in the sense of a life not contaminated by duplicity and self-estrangement.

The ideal of a pure life is to be able to place the infinite manifold aspects of our life under a unifying perspective and motivation, permitting ourselves to be guided by nothing else. This is the sense of purity of heart as willing one "thing," i.e., some consideration that refracts the full thickness of life and that is able to inform every moment of one's awareness. This ideal of moral purity is the "holiness" which humans are capable of approximating but never actually achieving. (We bracket here the Christian theological issue of grace.) This ideal of purity then animates and holds sway over our striving and over all the endless details of our agency and becomes the measure by which we determine our conscientiousness, i.e., our attunement with the Oughts that surface in the flux of our life.

But clearly we aim not at "purity as such" nor even at conscientiousness. These are not the target of our intentional acts nor are they a purpose or goal of our agency. Rather we aim at doing the particular act because it presents itself as what is worthy or as what ought to be done, and our doing it is a way of being faithful to the person we are and have constituted ourselves to be. This of course will involve in the most proper and juridical senses being faithful to and respectful of Others. The direction or signposts of this way of being through being faithful to oneself is revealed within the horizon of the ideal as it is manifest in each passing phase of life. Each phase of life is more or less punctuated by "Oughts." In the present agency right now, conscience functions in our being "conscientious" about what we are now doing and what we are called upon to do. Formally, we have suggested, this can take the form of the imperative to do the best here and now under the circumstances. We will visit again this theme of purity in Chapter V when we discuss the "calling" as the way the Absolute Ought reveals itself and which becomes the angle under which all of the details of life are refracted. Now we wish to examine whether conscience may be said to be the metaphorical center of the I.

§5. Conscience and the Center of the I

The picture of conscience as a compass for life may be taken in the following way: The wisdom and knowledge of the world is something we may appropriate and master. It provides us with mentors, guideposts and maxims, as well as theories, which serve as aids in life's journey. But conscience provides us with an internal compass that is not identical with this worldly knowledge. Indeed it enjoys an independence from this worldly knowledge – which is not to say that conscience is absolutely independent of the person's interpretation of the world – and has its own independent mode of revelation. It can err occasionally in the sense that by following its judgments as they are commingled with the person's worldly knowledge the person heads in the wrong direction, but like a good compass it aids the person in finding out the basis for her being misled. Thus it gets "unstuck" and finds its way back to the "magnetic pole," the true telos, of life. In this respect, conscience is an "organ" by which the person enjoys a proper moral perception or cognition that has an important independence from our knowledge gained from our perception of the world's authorities. This view is often connected with conceiving conscience as "the voice of God."

> Yet still there whispers the small voice within,
> Heard through Gain's silence, and o'er Glory's din,'
> Whatever creed be taught or land be trod
> Man's conscience is the oracle of God.[41]

This picture conflicts in an interesting way with Husserl's notion of conscience as the way the personal essence with its correlate of the totality of the life-world, as constituted through position-taking acts, is disclosed.[42] For Husserl, the personal essence and its correlate, the world, "speak to us" on the basis of our having constituted them in our position-taking acts. Conscience is this address of the personal essence of ourselves that we have constituted in position-taking acts. In Chapter IV, §3, we will dwell further on these acts. Here suffice it to say that much of our act-life is like the performative act of promising, whereby, with an act that only takes "so long," there is established a state of affairs whose validity makes a claim on us for the unforeseeable future. It makes this claim until it is revoked or repudiated, or, as in the case of a promise, until fulfilled. It is clear that promises and vows have this character, but acts of, e.g., courage and justice, or their opposites, have also similar "policy-establishing" effects. Their enactment is on the basis of doing or not doing *what is right* or *what is called for* in a particular situation. What is right is not primarily following a rule or a law, but of acting in accord with what the situation demands. We act in accord with the kind of person we in fact have become as a result of our position-takings. But we also act in accord with the kind of person we want to be.

The self or personal essence is the synthetic unity of foremost the position-takings that comprise one's life. Moral agency always apperceives, however vaguely, the unity of the self before and after the act, i.e., the self-identification and self-determination that the act involves. It therefore apperceives more or less lucidly suffering or living with the consequences of this self-determination. Of course these acts not only build on massive blocks of more or less connected beliefs (or propositions) we hold and to which we are responding, but they build also on emotions which have implicit beliefs (or propositions) and policies. All of these make up implicit self-defining policies for how we will be in the future. As Aristotle said of the decisiveness and reverberations of actions in the web of intersubjectivity as well as in the matter of self-formation: "Once you have thrown a stone you cannot call it back." (See *Nicomachean Ethics* 1114a 16–19.)

Therefore both our fidelity to our personal essence and our infidelity set precedents. If we act cowardly for a first time we newly define ourselves; this new definition is perhaps painful to accept because it contradicts our self-ideal. Because of this pain we may be inclined to redefine ourselves, hide from and lie to ourselves by, e.g., devising strategies which camouflage what we have done and transform the act from something reprehensible and unjustifiable to an act that is, if not exemplary, at least justifiable. This itself becomes an establishing of policy and the personal essence, along with its ideal, are capable of only an increasingly muted revelation. Because the esteem we have for ourselves in being true to ourselves evaporates and gives place, at least latently, to disdain and shame, the personal essence is torn between protecting itself and hiding itself from itself and others.

We have said that not only do promises and moral acts have this character of policy-setting, but so do the epistemic acts whereby we establish that something is the case. When we establish that P is q, even if were able to be determined that this judgment lasts but one second, it holds "from now own" or until I revoke it. (Recall our discussions of it being eidetically necessary that of Now it must be said that it will have been.) Having made this determination of judgment I, in the foreseeable future, have to think and act accordingly in order to be one with myself. Of course, "the wisdom of the world" might well shout to me here and there, but it is part of my world only through my having made it present and having appropriated and integrated its alleged validities into the unity of my personal life-world as it is founded on my position-taking acts. The person, as we have said, is a unique I myself, called to realize his or her unique essence. But this realization is a matter of the temporal unfolding of position-taking acts *as well as* the fidelity to them.

Conscience is the wakefulness of one's fidelity or infidelity to the one who one has been, and to the one who one has committed oneself to be, and to what encompasses all temporal modes, i.e., the ideal one who one is being "called" to be and has been "called" to be. (We will later spell out this metaphor of "calling.") The greater the infidelity, the more muted is the wakefulness. The only way conscience becomes absolutely mute is for wakeful consciousness to cease, i.e., for the person no longer to live through the medium of position-taking acts, i.e., no longer to distinguish, judge, evaluate, value, decide, resolve, promise, etc.

The world in which one lives, one's life-world, is inseparable but necessarily distinguishable from the person one has constituted oneself to be. I, as this person, live in my life of action and am the abiding subject of the acts. In performing them I recognize them as what I committed myself to, and I recognize myself as identically the same in this fidelity, i.e., I recognize whether I have remained true to myself in them. As the primal presencing presences the total horizon of our past and future presencings, so conscience is the attunement, founded on the primal presencing, to the position-takings by which one has shaped the world and shaped oneself in the face of the infinite idea of one's true self. "I ought" or "I should not have" is tied to the awareness of the universal context of life and the essential person as she has been constituted in the position-takings. When I have been aggressive or impatient, and when I know that these ways of acting defeat what I want to accomplish and who I want to be, I betray myself and my self-ideal, and I vitiate the fundamental ways I articulate my world and myself in the world. How I am now being or just have been is inconsistent with the kind of person I have constituted myself to be and the kind of person I apperceive myself called to be.

Note that we could have put the last sentence this way: "How I am now being or how I just have been is inconsistent with who I have constituted myself to be and who I apperceive myself called to be." The trouble with this formulation became evident earlier in Book 1. There is a sense in which *who* we are, as "myself," is *not* a matter of personal constitution. The "myself" is at the core of the constitution of oneself as a person in the world with others and this personal "I myself" reflects and expresses this ultimate core sense of who we are, but it is not absolutely coincident with this sense. We will return to this soon. Here we can state that the identity, the essence, the moral person I am is constituted as a being in the world with Others, and the position-takings constitutive of it are the basis of my identity and integrity in regard to the world and Others.

For Husserl, conscience is the ongoing revelation and reawakening of my actual and real essential self to me. We might better say it is my being reawakened to myself. But by whom? By what? By the ongoing validity of my position-taking acts as they are functioning in passive synthesis, and this very ongoing validity is the personal essence of me myself that I have constituted. It is I myself at a distance from me myself. What permits me, as I have constituted myself across the totality of my life, to be both implicitly and admonishingly present to me now is passive synthesis. Passive synthesis is the source of my wakefulness to my temporality in its phases as well as in its totality as a life-synthesis. Conscience, in contrast to passive synthesis as primal association of all past presencings, is the association of my major delineations of myself as this person in the world with Others, foremost through what we will call self-identifying acts; it is the association of the Now-circumstance with the punctual moments by which I have constituted me and that hold "from now on." Conscience is the wakefulness of me to my personal essence. Like the passive associations, it happens thankfully whether we want it to happen or not.

But if we grant the power of passive synthesis and association to awaken my former but still valid personal essence, what is the source of the "admonition"? Passive synthesis "permits" the admonition, but as such it does not admonish. What admonishes is I myself as constituted by identifying acts brought before myself. Conscience is the presence of me myself as the still valid personal essence that I have constituted more or less in conformity with the light of my ideal.

Disregarding the visual-optic aspects of the mirror metaphor, conscience's presencing of one's personal essence may be regarded as a mirror. A mirror reflects back without the mediation of position-taking acts – and that is why when we look in the mirror we may reactively tuck in our stomachs or put on our "best face," etc. Of course, conscience is not myself being *seen* but *witnessed to*. But it is not through intentional acts. If we say it is an "ongoing process of affective, perceptual and intellectual self-mediation" or self-mirroring, we run the risk of thinking of conscience as the witnessing or presencing of the essential self as the result of affective, perceptual, and intellectual acts. Rather what is mirrored is the self's personal essence that I, the substrate of this self, have constituted through the salient affective, perceptual and intellectual acts in the light of its self-ideal. These are what have been formative of the essence it has to date.

Again, it is one's constituted personal essence suffused with the ideal of the self that establishes the quality of admonition to this witness. The personal essence is a genitive of appearing or witness. We later will discuss the dative of the witness. The witness, after all is *of* my personal essence *to me*.[43]

Who I am called to be, my true self, is as essential to my being this person, JG Hart, as the unconstituted individual essence of "myself." The actual essential personal self I have constituted has a validity since the beginnings of the personification of the "myself," but the valid identity of the personal essence undergoes changes, sometimes dramatic ones. Conscience bears witness to the self-same self-ideal that provides the horizon for the present personal "I myself" as well as the horizon of the former but still valid personal "I myself." But this self-sameness is not settled in cement. My constitution of my personal essence is as much a discovery as something I author. When it functions as a cage that stunts me, it is not because of still-valid self-identifications and definitions, but it is due to, e.g., "scruples," which are, among other things, a matter of confusing lingering allegiances to former no longer valid commitments with that to which one now is presently insightfully bound. The admonition of conscience thus is not merely myself at a distance – the genitive of witness and the dative of witness – but has the intimacy of I myself actually now and I myself as who I have been and still continue to be through the validity of my commitments. Not being true to the constituted historical sense of myself is a contradiction, but it is also shameful because I self-destruct by denying myself whom I am given to love and cherish. I am ashamed foremost before myself for not loving and esteeming myself whom I have constituted in constituting my world. Thus not being true to myself is not merely a logical contradiction or an invalid move because "my true self" as framing my personal essence claims my allegiance not merely as a matter of propositional consistency, as important as this is, but it claims my allegiance as the condition of responding to the call to hold myself as this identity in being. I may be wrong or make a false implication in the one case, but in the other I am not holding up what is given to me to do in order to be. In both cases there is a matter of consistency but the logical consistency does not involve a struggle toward the higher self-ideal as the responsibility for being oneself.

Tucked into the ideal of my true self are the ideals of unity, harmony, consistency, integrity – all within a wider social ideal. The very dynamism of passive synthesis is pervaded by an interplay of presence and absence informed by the ideals of unity, harmony, consistency and integrity. This is part of its amazing character, the *Wunder* of reason.[44]

Conscience, therefore, is not really a knowing apart from our knowledge of the world: the knowledge of the world is precisely always also a self-constitution. (My learning about the behavior of bodies in space under certain conditions, as in baking pastries or preparing spaghetti, determines my attitude and actions in specific provinces of my life. My learning about the arithmetic and mechanics of spending, saving, and banking money determines the horizon of my agency in the personal and world economy.) Of course, this is not to say that there is an equivalence between the "wisdom of the world" and the person-world correlation as derived from I-me acts, i.e., acts that are targeted at the world but at the same time shape the personal self.[45] As we noted, the "wisdom of the world" may or may not appear to me as wise. In which case I take up a position towards, e.g., the principle of might makes right, the end justifies the means, buy low/sell high, always chose among equivalent commodities those that cost less, democracy is the equivalent of free-market capitalism, nice guys finish last, etc. The way one has shaped her world, with the help of the beginnings of character over which she has no control, may well be such that these "worldly maxims" appear obvious, inevitable, and commonsensical or as harmful, phony, and reprehensible. Thus conscience is not a compass apart from my personal world as constituted by I-me acts which at once I as nominative agent inaugurate but which at the same time constitute my personal essence. This point recalls our earlier observations in the last section about the difficulty of saying, "I am pure."

Conscience in this sense is a species of "gathering act" that we have called also "realization." The gathering act of conscience clearly is different than that of realization in so far as the latter involves a thickening of my first-personal awareness of myself as scattered throughout time. In conscience the twoness in the form of self-awareness is more emphatic: My personal essence as I have constituted it and as I face my ideal of myself bears witness to me. And most typically it bears witness to me where I am not being one with myself. In "my death" the gathering act more likely than not will eventually amount to the witnessing of conscience, but the initial stages of the prospective retrospection, and the initial achievement of the gathering where I am present all at once to myself, need not, or at least need not yet, be the witnessing of conscience. Similarly, the gathering act distinctive of nostalgia is not at all identical with conscience. It condenses our life in the living memory of a former present, and the pain of loss which prevails is not the same as either the reproach of conscience or the call for repentance. There is nothing we can do about the pain of loss that nostalgia reveals. Likewise the gathering acts occasioned by great works of art can condense our lives and worlds, but they need not feature the admonitions of conscience.

What are we to make of the famous metaphor of the voice of conscience and the metaphor of conscience as the core or center of the I or person, as in the Second Vatican Council? Let us first offer reasons for these metaphors, which we may regard as connected. Obviously conscience is intimate to us, uniquely one's own, indeed one's own self, at least in the sense that "it" is not another who speaks to me but I myself. Conscience's persistent insistence makes it appear nearer to me than any other "voice" of others or any means of knowing. From all these, e.g., perceiving, reflecting, remembering, hearing, I can distract myself or shut them down. Conscience is uniquely importunate and even relentless, even if it too may eventually suffer defeat at my hands, a defeat that I pay for profoundly.

Conscience is uniquely I myself in the sense that no one else's conscience may substitute for my own.[46] We thus have to distinguish false guises of conscience, like the superego, understood as the way we passively internalize without authentically appropriating what the conventional "they" think or will think of us, e.g., certain authorities, like parents, religious officials, and teachers, who have been formative of our way of thinking about and experiencing ourselves and the world. These too, if we become mature, are submitted to the deeper sense of the world and ourselves that conscience is, even if the "voices" of these formative authorities accompany us throughout our lives and serve as protagonists in the dialogue formative of the witness of conscience. Conscience is the voice of our essential self as pervaded by our true ideal self, the self we have dedicated ourselves to, to which we are called. Conscience awakens us from our moral holidays, from our immersion in group pressures and forms of bonding, from our flirtation with wantonness; in short, it awakens us from our disavowal of who we really are. In this restricted sense, conscience is "the most secret core and sanctuary of a man."

Yet we think of "the voice of conscience" as what we must listen to whether we want to or not. In this sense "I" am addressed by "It." "It" witnesses *to me*, the dative of the witness. In this regard *It* is not *I*, and *I* am the one who is addressed, must respond, has to change, repent, etc. "It" as what witnesses, accuses, admonishes, etc., is not as such pained or admonished. Rather, this "voice" addressing me awakens the pain in me, the one addressed. The witness of conscience is thus directed to *me* who must deal with this witness. Further, if conscience is to realize what may be cautiously called its "function" I myself as who is addressed by the witness of conscience must not only listen to its reproachful "voice" but I must respond to this address and identify with its "perspective." The "function" or process of conscience is effected or realized by me, I myself to whom conscience bears witness by my agreeing with it, going along with its "directives." Thus my atonement or repentance is called for, and *I myself* must do this. The "I myself"

who is addressed is not merely the bare substrate (the "myself") of who one is or
the unique individual essence (see Book 1, Chapters IV–V), but rather it is who we
are as we have personally constituted ourselves, and which personal I has its motor
or dynamic principle in the bare substrate of the "myself."

We here have, on the one hand, a de-centering of "I myself" in as much as
conscience bears witness to me, i.e., I myself as constituting-constituted person
am born witness to by myself as constituted person. An essential feature of being
authentically me this person lies, in some sense, beyond me. This of course is true
of my true self as a regulative ideal; it calls me; it is *I* who must strive toward it and
answer its call. Similarly with conscience as a kind of gathering act: *I* receive *It* and
its call, I am "graced" with its agency and yet conscience is a grace, a gift, given to
me by myself. Yet it seems also true that *I* have a conscience and am aware *of* it. It
is in some sense peripheral and in respect to its admonitions it is "ground." It is, as
Hans Reiner once put it, "circumground" to the "I-center."[47]

Even though the metaphor of the "voice of conscience" is helpful, nevertheless,
it is not really a transcendent "someone," not an I, addressing me in the second-
person, as it would be if we held the view that all senses of obligation place us in
the second-personal stance either toward Others or toward ourselves. A fortiori it is
not a thing, an "it," as a software program giving me directives. I do not apperceive
a You addressing me as a You – even though I may have religious motivations to
transform the witness of conscience into just such an overbelief.

Nor is my own consciousness inhabited by a plurality of I's, e.g., that of I myself
and that of the I of conscience and the chorus comprising the superego. Thus
although conscience is "within my depths" it is not I myself actually now as I, i.e.,
as subject, dative and agent of manifestation, agent of deeds, etc.; and I myself now,
in this central way of being subject and agent, am not my conscience. Conscience
is "I myself" at a distance, i.e., the I whom I am called to be and whom I have
constituted and who is still valid, addressing me through passive synthesis; it is
who I have constituted myself to be in the ongoing validity of my position-taking
acts "reminding me" of who I have defined myself to be and who I am called to be.
The call derives from me and yet it comes upon me. It is never merely a result of
my direction or my strategy; I am at its mercy. But as deriving from me and mirroring me it is a kind of objectification, an "object" in the way an association as
the basis for a memory is, of the still valid personal essence of I myself; but it is
derived and subordinate to the actual I. (By "actual I" is meant the now functioning
wakeful agent/dative of manifestation and action.) It is derived because the once
actual I took positions and made commitments, and these derived from the former
actual I and still enjoy validity and reveal themselves to the actual I. It is derived
also because its appeal has no sense except as addressing me and being responded
to by me, i.e., the actual I myself.

Again: These position-takings constitutive of my essential person enjoy an
actual validity for the actual I through passive synthesis. They constitute the personal I through their continued validity, but they are not actual positions now being
taken. Thus no one apart from me myself calls me. Conscience as the manifestation
of my currently valid position takings is thus *for* the actual I and awaits the actual

I's appropriation of its revelation for it to fulfill its purpose. Conscience provides a mirror in which I appear to myself in a way that permits an indispensable communication of me with myself for the purpose of being one with myself and faithful to my ideal of myself. Without this witness of me to myself I could not be able to be my essential personal self throughout the flux of time. The personal I has conscience as its necessary condition.

I who am addressed am appealed to, admonished, exhorted, etc. by me myself as my personal essence facing my ideal. Its appearing to me is not a result of my willing it or valuing it. There is no more willing or esteeming or disvaluing in its appearing to me than there is in a retention or protention. Yet my weakness of will, my not following my conscience, my living inconsistently, etc. – all of which are modalizations of will or acts of will – undermine my commitment to my personal essence. In betraying myself I equivalently invalidate what, in a more or less disso-ciated form, I still regard as valid. Because of this the witness, mirroring, or "voice" of conscience can be muted or murky because I am becoming accustomed to being out of touch with myself.

By way of contrast, conscientiousness is the habit of listening to myself and others in regard to my basic stances; it involves routines of recollecting myself and attending to whether I am living the way I really want to live, i.e., in accord with my personal essence. This is a way of taking stock in the present of whether my present squares with my past or whether in the present I have been inattentive to my past and projected future. The past and still valid acts were brought about in the wake of the same ideal of the true self, which must not be confused with a self-image or self-concept, that provides the present horizon of my agency. (See Chapter IV, especially §6.) We are familiar with the phrase, "examination of conscience." This is the act by which I myself make a theme of my fidelity, over a swath of time, to me myself as my constituted personal identity. And as an actual witnessing of conscience can bear witness to my present inconsistencies, so an examination of conscience can bear witness to my repressions of conscience, my past shortcom-ings. And if this having-fallen-short remains valid to this day, it demands either a disavowal of the original position-taking or it requires acts which seek to atone, rebind, make whole my dissolving of myself, Thus there is a demand for regret or repentance of the disavowal or betrayal. To the extent the past unrevoked and unrepented position-takings abide, in spite of myself, I have always an undercur-rent of self-repugnance or self-esteem, depending on my faithfulness and veracity with myself. Again, the idea of the true self frames both the still valid, but formerly constituted, self as well as the actual self to which this prior constituted self bears witness in conscience.

The actual I must not be thought of as an entity frozen immobile in time having within it a chamber called conscience. Conscience is the revelation of the personal I to itself across the time of its personal ideal and essence as this revelation is appro-priate in the flux of situations. "I myself" as a personal-essential I cannot exist as a temporal identity across the differences without conscience. Again, typically the display of conscience, apart from the resolve *to examine one's conscience*, is not something "I myself" actually undertake, but it is undertaken for me by me myself at a distance through passive synthesis. But without the actual I myself there would be no "dative of manifestation," no one *to whom* the revelation would appear. Without the continued validity of my former I myself there would be no witnessing of myself to me. Conscience is not properly an "agent of manifestation" apart from or independent of the "I myself" to whom it is witnessing and who constituted it. I myself am the agent simply by being "conscious," simply by being awake to myself as having constituted myself across the temporal flux of situations calling for position-takings. The conscience is continuously being shaped and modified as is the world and the personal I through the position-taking acts which always are, as Husserl says, I-me acts.

"I" who am the agent, I who reflect, I who act, am the I that announces itself in the emphatic and intensive form, "*I myself.*" "I myself" am the primary I-consciousness, not conscience, which is merely my witness to myself at a distance through passive synthesis and the call of my ideal true self. It is a witness of who I am and have been and who I have committed myself to be and how my present action or purported action is or is not coincident with these. Thus conscience as the witnessing mirror is the I myself decentered; it is not the "center" or inmost sanctuary of the I. Rather, the "sanctuary," what, e.g., the Second Vatican Council wants foremost to accord a sacred inviolable space and freedom is the center of the personal I to which is borne witness. The I constitutes ineluctably its personal essence or personal I and the witness of this to the I discloses the center of the I as both that to which is witnessed and that which is called to respond. Not responding to conscience as the decentered I myself is a kind of self-annihilation by self-denial; responding to this decentered I myself is self-actualization of one's inmost center and core. It is the strongest form of self-affirmation and confirmation of one's self-determination. This sense of the I center as facing the appeal of conscience, which is the revelation of the I of the personal essence, is an exemplary sense of what is meant by Existenz in this volume. Conscience, in this sense of Existenz's responsiveness, is the way I hold myself and my destiny in my own hands to preserve it, guide it, or to let it slip away from me.

This point is captured in an exchange between St. Thomas More and his daughter, Margaret, as portrayed by Robert Bolt in *A Man for All Seasons*. Thomas More, the former Chancellor of England, used every legal argument and ruse he could use in good conscience to avoid open conflict with the King, Henry VIII. But Thomas More's non-support of the King is insufferable for the King and he demands of More an oath of allegiance. Margaret does not want her father to be executed by the King for not supporting his policies. She urges her father to go along with the King's required oath but think otherwise in his heart. Thomas More replies: "What is an oath but words we say to God?" To which Margaret replies that is this is a "neat" reply. Thomas More gets his daughter to admit that "neat" does not mean false. And then he says to her:

> Then it's a poor argument to call it "neat," Meg. When a man takes an oath, Meg, he's holding his own self in his own hands. Like water. (*He cups his hands*) And if he opens his fingers *then* – he needn't hope to find himself again. Some men aren't capable of this, but I'd be loathe to think your father one of them.[48]

The phenomenology of conscience attends to the display of "the voice of conscience" to me, the agent who constituted this voice in the course of his life; thereby phenomenology disengages the actuality of the imperatives of conscience. But the phenomenologist is not always free to disengage the imperatives of conscience because conscience may require that something else be done now rather than phenomenology. Conscience is central to our notion of Existenz because conscience's witness to me regarding myself necessitates that I be serious in a way analogous to the realization of my death. By definition what is important, i.e., what has moral "weight" in my life, what forces itself upon me as decisive for not only the correct living of my life but the possibility of being harmoniously one with myself, is here present. For me as this person everything is at stake here. I am not free, if I am to be true to myself, to turn away from what it reveals, what it demands. This is a basic sense of the being-seized (*Ergriffensein*) of Existenz. It is not properly understood as being flooded with paralyzing emotions. But it does refer to being stopped in one's tracks and facing what one cannot simply walk away from without walking away from what is of unconditional importance, namely one's own will and disposition of oneself and one's life; in short one's being true to oneself. Here clearly what is important is importunate, i.e., urgent and refusing to be denied.

A brief word here about the "objectivity of conscience." It can only be brief because this is a core issue of moral philosophy and its appropriate development would lead us too far afield. Here we may note that if it is true that conscience bears witness to the person and personal life-world we have constituted, and that this constitution is primarily through position-taking acts, then the testimony of conscience as to what it is right to do in a particular situation is fallible. Position-taking acts are always founded on inadequate presentations of the world and of our situation in the world. Thus, e.g., the citizen who follows the dictate of his conscience that he ought not to vote on the basis of his evaluation that his political leaders and representatives are lackeys of corporations, an evaluation stemming from extensive first-hand and second-hand experience, and that voting only legitimates the corrupt practices, is not necessarily correct in his estimation nor is his choice of the path of action necessarily the objectively best one under the circumstances. Nevertheless he might well be true to his conscience.

Further, there is the dependence on the depths of the primal association of passive synthesis which awakens one's past position-takings as bearing on the present. Upon this level of the mind's functioning everything depends. Yet that this functioning occur without hitch, error, glitch, etc., is not absolutely necessary. Even though it is the condition for the possibility for all our ongoing cognitive and moral achievements, surds happen, madness happens, and there may well be more or less satisfactory explanations for this. But these anomalies cannot be the foundational premise for any moral or theoretic epistemology without such theory proposing a theory which makes theory impossible.

Thus the veridicality of the testimony of one's conscience is not precisely the same as that of one's first-person experiences of one's remembering. Let us spell this out. As we have attempted to argue (in Book 1, especially Chapter VIII, §8, in our discussion of Sydney Shoemaker's theory of quasi-memory), it is eidetically, i.e., synthetic a priori, necessary that in remembering a certain perceptual state of affairs, I remember that it was I who had that perceptual experience, and it is not possible that my memories are those of someone else. This is true even though I may have been mistaken in my original perception of the state of affairs. Similarly, in matters of conscience I may be mistaken in how I have interpreted the matter at hand in the framing of my position-taking, but it would seem that typically it is eidetically necessary that the gathering of the position-taking into forming an ingredient of one's personal essence is such that it is evident as a position-taking undertaken by me and it is not possible that it or its antecedents or the personal essence they constitute be that of someone else. In the matters of conscience we have to do with not an isolated experience but with the ongoing synthesis of these experiences and the gathered whole of one's life. The extent of the damage of mental illness and the decline of age on the work of passive synthesis requires that we take account of the enormous gaps and confusions that occur in people. I think the evidence is such as to give reasons to maintain a kind of defense of the veracity of conscience for reasons similar to those we have for maintaining that first-person memory experiences are incapable of erring. Yet because conscience is pervaded by admonitions and painful humiliations, temptations to self-deception and dissociation surface here in a way that is not normally the case with retentions and memory. Therefore the work of the gathering act of passive synthesis toward achieving purity of heart becomes enormously burdened. In which case, given the debilitating forces of mental illness, brain disease, and the aging process, the case for the inerrancy of conscience's witness becomes weakened.

Aside from the personal confusion regularly accompanying my examination of conscience as I approach the end of my life, I am moved to ponder a man who regularly receives messages from God the Father and Jesus, whose virgin bride this man believes himself to be. These messages come with the authority resembling conscience, and seem to summarize this person's way of being in the world with Others: They reveal his life-long struggle with his sexuality and gender, his family, and his religion. It also appears that if he does not heed these "revelations" he betrays his ownmost self. His heeding them, his being his ownmost self, which is inseparable for him from this presumably heteronomous authority, has gotten him in trouble several times with the police. I know of another man, a very bright student, who believed himself to be the recipient of orders from God in the socialist war against the capitalist West. This was a war of cosmic forces and God, who was not omnipotent in his struggle with evil, enlisted his special agents among whom was my student. I, who early in our relationship was an ally, became part of the dark forces when I did not give him money to go to Russia so that he could work for the KGB against the CIA. This ended our relationship, but apparently the cosmic battle became increasingly frightening and hideous. My student, a few months later, hanged himself in his apartment. Perhaps his "conscience" admonished him that he had failed his struggling God and his ownmost self.

Of course, the witness of conscience is initially pre-propositional because it is the work of passive synthesis. But, with reflection, and the ensuing formation of propositions, genuine moral perplexities or dilemmas can arise. These may indeed eventually amount to the tragedy of the conflict of duties or absolute values. This cannot be a priori ruled out. Nevertheless, in spite of all these caveats, there is a sense in which it is true that the conscientious person has her path delineated for her. But this delineation does not dispense with the need for reflection nor is it guaranteed that the path that comes to light as the best might lead to what appear to be dead-ends. Nevertheless the person might well have done what was morally the best under the circumstances.

A final word about conscience and exemplars. If the "myself's" normative personification is in constituting a moral person, and this requires of necessity responding to the witnessing of conscience, then we may come to understand the extraordinary importance of the witness of moral exemplars.[49] Aristotle saw clearly that the early inclination to moral excellence is not derived primarily from argument and teaching. Although each begins and authors her own moral self, here in the matter of primal exemplarity we have the beginnings of one's beginnings which are beyond the individual's control. (Cf. our earlier discussion above in §4 and *Nicomachean Ethics* 1114b 30–1115a 3; all of Chapter 9 of the *Nicomachean Ethics*.) Rather, this early affinity is through the cultivation of the right dispositions, right likes, and the right preferences. Moral exemplars in the most basic sense may be said to be the earliest influences deriving from interaction with persons that cultivate both behavior and the young person's acts of valuation. Here commingled with learning to perceive articulately and learning language is the appropriation of basic values and attitudes. Of course, early on the appropriation of these ways of valuing and dispositions will involve instinct, imitation, play, and make-believe. But this will be part of the burgeoning sense of "doing the right thing" and being at peace with oneself. The activity of the good man is in itself good and pleasant (as Aristotle says, *Nicomachean Ethics*, 1169b 33).

Here moral exemplars inculcate the presuppositions for all of our initial valuations and preferences. We spend a good part of our lives catching up with these and finding a way to critically examine and appreciate them. Subsequent to this hidden primal or basic function of exemplars in shaping the child is the derivative role they play in those to whom we are spontaneously drawn (as a result of the primal functioning of the examplars) because they embody that which we most love in our hierarchy of preferences in terms of the way our ideal life and true self are presently delineating themselves. Again, as Aristotle noted, observing the actions of our friends and neighbors is easier to us than observing our own moral agency and we can learn from their actions in no small measure about our own. We are drawn, in short, to the person who is friendly toward himself and befriends himself in the best possible senses (and it is precisely such a person who makes the best friend because he wishes the same for the friend and is best at being friendly): he does what is best for the best part of himself; he seeks to live in such a way that he may persevere in this good life; he enjoys his own company, he strives to be in harmony with the best part of himself (See *Nicomachean Ethics*, Chapter IV and 1169b 33.)

Aristotle further pointed to a contrast between young people not blessed with these basic cultivating exemplars and those who are. Those who are so blessed respond to example and the reasons offered by the significant Others. Force and intense emotions like fear are not part of the interaction. Someone whose life is guided by intense emotion and violence only will not be able to listen to reasons but will respond only to force and intense emotion. "Therefore there must first be a character [inculcated by the basic exemplarity] that somehow has an affinity for excellence or virtue, a character that loves what is noble and feels disgust at what is base" (*Nicomachean Ethics* 1179b 27–31). What Aristotle calls this affinity for moral excellence that loves what is noble is tied first of all to the experience of "good examples." We learn what courage is and to love it, along with patience, kindness, fairness, etc., in experiencing significant Others live in that fashion. Thereby we first of all have all our own forms of agency predelineated. But with the approach of adulthood, commingled with one's rejoicing in the exemplars, is a deeper insight into the nature of exemplary *agency* behind "the good example" set by the agents. Here there is no question of two distinct perceptions, the outer and the inner, but rather the enriching of the appresentation of agency. Here, the affinity for or love of the *deed* that is noble blends with the love of or affinity for the *integrity* of the person setting the good example. Again, the good example appears as good within the hierarchy of values opened up and embodied by the context set by the basic exemplarity; but now in the young adult there is the further dimension of the appreciative appresentation of the person's integrity. And this is a result of the coming to awareness of the moral dimension of the young person's burgeoning self-understanding as a moral person. The hierarchy of values and types of exemplars to which our culture and tradition introduces us is inseparable from valuing ourselves as persons who are responsive to and at peace with their consciences. This too is evident in the exemplars' agency and not merely in terms of what examples they set.

This is in part the basis for the familiar phenomenon, which of course may be undermined in cultures of death and violence which give rise early to cynicism, of the "idealism of youth." It is also perhaps the basis to the hyper-allergy of youth to what appears as hypocrisy. The values manifest in the exemplars closest to our self-esteem and true love of ourselves are those that embody our sense of the ideal way in which one is awake and responsive to his- or her self-witness in conscience.

Each of us early realizes, even as children, that "doing the right thing" in the sense of appropriately responding to the witness of conscience is, in some often inarticulate sense, more important than whatever else one does or accomplishes. One also realizes that this is both a very difficult as well as an inescapable challenge. Its difficulty is tied to the fact that conscience is invisible and in the intersubjective and public realm motives, as an inherent part of actions, likewise are invisible. The superficially right thing may be done for very wrong reasons. Further, often times what the public realm most rewards and celebrates abstracts, with no little measure of the connivance of individual and collective disingenuousness, from this most important dimension of life. Yet there is early the inkling that one cannot truly live with oneself without being responsive to conscience's witness to oneself. When we appresent Others, we present not only the drama of their public agency and speech but we willy-nilly are drawn to the inner drama (which is not always obviously connected to the public drama) when we appresent them as persons, as subjectivities, borne witness to by themselves, and who live accordingly or not.

Because evidence in such matters is so opaque the exhortation "not to judge" is part of common sense and decency. We might say that a strong motive for habitually thinking poorly of Others surfaces when we are not honest with ourselves and seek to assuage our discomfort with ourselves by assigning a corresponding lack of integrity in the Others.

The thesis here is that if we have the moral luck to be well brought up, and if we have been conscientious we are drawn to people we take, rightly or wrongly, to "have integrity." This is tautological to the extent that being "well brought up" means being drawn to people with integrity. It is less tautological in the claim that being conscientious does not mean being drawn to people who are conscientious. But if being borne witness to by another's conscientiousness is an encouragement to our own call to be responsive to the witness of conscience, then the claim (that we are drawn to people who are conscientious) approaches the obvious quasi-tautology that we take delight in what occasions our delight, we are encouraged by what encourages. Further we early and easily assent to the maxim that "actions speak louder than words," i.e., we give credence to those who "walk the walk" and in this judgment their agency need not be accompanied by any narrative by the agent herself. Typically what we regard as the most important forms of influence derive from I-you or second-personal kinds of communication. We can all acknowledge the power of second-personal forms of address and agency, where the speaker/agent acts toward the Other as addressee in a way such that the addressee understands the nature of the "illocutionary" act or speech. Therapy, giving counsel, consoling, advising, grieving along with, etc. are some examples of second-personal reference that powerfully affects at least one of the parties. Yet it is well-known that persons are often equally profoundly affected by Others acting solely in a first-personal, "monadic" manner, minding their own business, attending to their own responsibilities, without any second-personal or third-personal reference in mind. (Again: sometimes when we are repelled it is precisely because they bear witness to the witness of our own conscience.)

Of course, a parent's or lover's waking hours might be taken up with third-personal actions or even first-personal ones that are acts of love. Thus, e.g., the parent's repairing a doll or even earning a wage may be directed at some thing; yet it is for the sake of the child even though the acts are not directly targeting the loved one. The recipient can say you did this, you intended this, but you did it for my sake. Indirectly you were loving me in your being directed toward that. And clearly what we call loving one's neighbor and perhaps even much of loving God is precisely *not* a matter of a second-personal action. And if one were engaged only in second-personal acts regarding the beloved and refused in principle any third-personal acts of benevolence on behalf of the beloved there might be reason to doubt whether the second-personal acts of love were genuine. On the other hand, if one were engaged in only acts of benevolence and refused in principle to initiate any second-personal acts of love one could likely have doubts about the genuineness of the love.

This phenomenon of "actions speaking more loudly than words" bears witness to the effective witnessing of exemplarity not having for its reference merely the deed as the good example that is set but inseparably the doing of the deed as a response to the witness of the doer's conscience. The encouragement to respond to the witness to conscience through the deeds of Others as responses to the witness of *their* consciences is one of the great blessings we bestow on one another in the pursuit of the good life. It is basic to the dynamics of a social protest movement.

Here there need be no speech acts or narrative by any parties involved. Of course, sometimes, uninformed bystanders will, in order to appreciate the beauty of the agency, require, however, someone's articulation of the agency's meaning in the concrete historical context. Of course, on occasion, the most difficult *action* called for is *speaking* or saying something in response to the situation or to what is said, e.g., speaking "truth to power." The exemplarity of the agency of the speaker/agent is conveyed further in how one speaks, e.g., speaking in a way that is free of narcissism, grandstanding, self-righteousness, and respectful and open to the viewpoints of the others involved, especially the opponents.

If in our most formative years the significant persons who surround us appear to us patently to lack integrity, then the point of our conscience in promoting our own integrity has to seem pointless. This lack itself will appear as "the right thing to do" and "right" here will mean the expected, the universal, the normal, etc., because conscience's power to witness or mirror will be dulled. The great social crimes of slavery, genocide, ecocide, etc. bear witness to this mass, collective dulling of conscience. Today's crazies, subversives and radicals occasionally turn out to be tomorrow's saints, prophets and heroes.

§6. Conscience, Existenz, and the Transcendental I

Again, where is the transcendental I in all this? Clearly it is what the phenomenological attitude discloses as the agent and dative of manifestation of all these poles and distinctions. It has been active in the preceding section as the reader and writer have reflected on this most pressing and precious sphere of intimacy within oneself. It is what brings the "personal-essential I" as such to light, i.e., as what has constituted the content of what gets passively synthesized, as that for which the passive synthesizing, retaining, and associating occurs, as what suffuses this hyletic ebullient realm with I-ness, mineness, and ownness, and as what permits itself to be revealed to itself in this importunate way of conscience. It is not as if the transcendental I were *doing* the revealing of conscience or were the agent of the revelation of "the personal-essential I" to itself as the dative of conscience's revelations. No, the transcendental I is merely the philosophical agent, in the phenomenological attitude by which all these matters come to light, matters that are already there, i.e., what the intellectual and moral agent experiences prior to reflection. It is what shows that the unique agency of this revelation, conscience, itself is "I myself" in a most intimate way, and shows that nevertheless conscience is not the center and most proper sense of "I myself" because it rather is the continued validity of the actual essential personal I, and further, it awaits *my* acknowledging and responding, e.g., in the sense of repentance. The transcendental I thus reveals conscience as I myself at a distance from myself.

As we have seen (see especially Book 1, Chapters I–III and V) the transcendental I is the ultimate pole of all reflection and display. The joke has been made that like the North Pole, it takes a lot of work to get to it, and when you get to it there is nothing there. Of course, as the I-*pole*, it is the supporting substrate of all levels of reflection. Thus, it is this supporting substrate which illuminates the personal I's reflection in the natural attitude in its indexical self-references, in its ethical and theoretical reflections, where the subject-poles of intellectual and moral acts of reflection, conscientious reflection in which Existenz's reflection comes to light, as well as the transcendental reflection which brings all of these to light as well as itself as the ultimate agent of manifestation, as well as how all these are founded in primal sensibility with its pre-egological pole of passive synthesis. And, as Husserl (and before him, Kant) noted, this pole has an emptiness and absence of qualities or properties. As such it seems bereft of anything except its status as an I-pole of the streaming presencing.

For many post-Kantians, the I-pole is associated with the I-think of Kant that can accompany all our acts. As such it is not in any way a unique ipseity, but rather as an I-pole or I-point is a way of talking about theoretic consciousness as such. For Husserlians, this is not quite right. I-ness pervades consciousness even prior to first-person reference and reflection. The transcendental I is always uniquely unique. (See Book 1, Chapter II–V.) But this level of unique uniqueness that we have seen in conjunction with the I-ness that emerges, e.g., out of the thought-experiment of the doubling of oneself, or with the inerrant self-reference of the two-year old who already says "I," or the amnesiac who, after having lost her life as a certain person in the world, still says "I," still may not serve as the center out of which I live and face what is of unconditional importance. This philosophical theme of the transcendental I, which is abstracted for good reason from the personal moral essence and from one's being-in-the-world-with-others, obviously is a founding consideration for the display of all that I call "I myself." However, because it is bereft of identifiable properties, it cannot, as such, provide a basis for moral reflections and conscience. In the next chapter we will further relate the unique uniqueness of I myself qua the transcendental I to the I myself that refers to my personal moral essence. But here it suffices to say that I do not live from out of the abstract sense of the "myself" that is without any recognizable properties nor do I live from out of the "I-pole." These specialized philosophical considerations, that are abstracted from the full concreteness of "I myself," cannot serve as the source of my decisions, my life, my ideals. Rather, this I-pole and the peculiarly abstract sense of the "myself"[50] that emerges in phenomenology are aspects of myself that appear when I prescind from the personal I-center and my personal being in the world and busy myself with the issues of individual uniqueness, and with the founding considerations of the agency of manifestation. We have said (Book 1, especially Chapter VII), following Husserl, that also at the bottom, so to speak, along with the I-ness or the "myself" there is the primal temporalizing that constitutes the temporal unity and difference as the primal having or *hyle* of this I-ness and I-pole.

But, again, this hyletic streaming is not I myself in my concrete fullness facing my destiny nor is it something existing substantially apart from the moment of "I myself" but rather is a coeval moment constitutive of the transcendental "I myself." And the transcendental "I myself" itself is an abstract aspect of the full concretion of my personal being in the world that reflection and the reduction bring to light. The transcendental I is I myself, JG Hart, appearing in this different aspect. And when I myself reflect and disengage the strata of belief-gossamer, I myself appear (merely) under the aspect of I as the uniquely unique I, transcendental I, or the "myself" along with the primal temporalizing.

In an important MS,[51] Husserl explicitly discourages taking the I of transcendental phenomenology primarily as the I-pole of reflection that disengages itself from its elemental strata of constituting and its binding attachments to the world. Of course, at an ultimate level of reflection on the foundations of phenomenology and the phenomenology of phenomenology, the transcendental I is a "pole," a living pole of the primal streaming presencing around which the hyletic affections and acts gather; but at no time may it ever be thought of as an existing empty space, even an empty "point," or as an empty and dead substrate of properties. Nor may it be said that transcendental phenomenology's work has to do properly with this ultimate agency of manifestation that is the I-pole of reflection of manifestation that brings to light what makes all the prior levels of manifestation – as if the of the prior theoretical, personal, ethical-evaluative, and existential modes of manifestation were of lesser account.

As we shall see, when discussing the pertinent sections of this MS later, the pole that is brought to light in this transcendental focus of reflection is able to be brought into an identity synthesis with the I of Existenz and the I of the person; the transcendental I as an I-pole is but a profile of the same I that is actually loving or capable of loving devotion. The transcendental reflection simply brings a different aspect of the I that is a concretion of the person in the world with others to light. The I must be always thought of as the one same I that has an ever deeper center or ever greater depths of unfolding I-ness. (See below, Chapter V.) Of course, one must not only always think of the I as having actually these ever greater depths that conscience or limit-situations or loving devotion reveals. Rather, they may well lie dormant or even repressed. Nevertheless this ever deeper center is always within an individual I that is called to respond to conscience's revelations, to the disclosure of the realizations of limit-situations, and, as we shall see, of loving devotion to the ideal.

In the light of our other considerations it is clear that philosophical reflection that forgets or is unmindful of *this most basic* sense of I as a center with ever deeper centers and dwells in the merely theoretic consciousness or universal consciousness as such has lost Existenz and its ineluctable quest for what is of unconditional importance, and thereby it has lost in an ancient sense its philosophical path. I, qua transcendental I, i.e., in the course of revealing the gossamer of the transcendental realm, can suddenly be interrupted by a memory and struck with remorse, and thereby I can be admonished by I myself at a distance, i.e., by conscience. Or, I can be graced with love, and the emptiness and abstractness that characterize me as uniquely unique I, transcendental I-pole, and disinterested observer, may give way to I myself in the fullest possible sense. Thus I myself, qua transcendental I, may well be drawn into relinquishing the doxastic disengagement. I may be graced with a wave of love or seized by the importunate importance of realization or conscience, and know that what is called for is not their display, but, e.g., a gesture of affection, atonement, apologies, restitution, repentance, etc.

§7. Excursus: "I Myself" and My *Daimonion*

Socrates occasionally referred to his "Guardian Spirit" or "Daimon" (*Daimonion*) as the source of guidance in his making important decisions. The case can be made that Socrates was familiar with our phenomenon of conscience in so far as he had as a major theme the examined life, a life of responsibility and reflection. His view was that the Daimon was the warning voice within his inmost self; whether it is a voice *of* his inmost self is unclear. He does say "the mind itself has a kind of divining power." Socrates referred to this as a "sort of voice which comes to me, and when it comes it always dissuades me from what I am proposing to do, and never urges me on."[52] Here he speaks of it as uniquely his own as if he were singling himself out. Yet on other occasions it assumes a kind of universality, i.e., "the mind itself has a kind of divining power." This finds approximation later in the Stoics and St. Paul where a phenomenon proximate to conscience is referred to as *syneidesis*.[53] For our purposes it is intriguing that this *Daimonion*, on the one hand, seemed not to belong to him but come to him from outside of himself. And yet, on the other hand, it was that to which he gave his allegiance in the most important matters.[54] As Eric Frank says, his true self appeared to him as something foreign; at the same time, this strange "demonic" power was the most exalted and most intimate aspect of himself. The ultimate decision that Socrates himself alone makes is not understood to be simply as his own act, but rather that also of an external authority upon which the decision bases itself. In this sense the true power of *one's own* life, i.e., the life of *psyche* or the soul is the Daimon. It is the scarcely graspable essence behind the surface of one's manifestation in the world.

The otherness of the Daimon we might well trace to *conscientia* as the admonishing voice. We have wrestled with the senses in which conscience is and is not the most intimate sense of I myself. But Erich Frank makes another point worthy of our attention. For the Greeks before Plotinus "I" was not a philosophically relevant concept. What each refers to with "I" (εγώ) is not able to be said, therefore not a matter of reason (*Logos*) or display in the common world with Others. Each can say "I" but in this respect "I" is the most universal of terms. But what is meant by "I" is not among the *Logos* of what is sayable, but it can only be meant as *Doxa* and thereby falls into the darkness, intransparency, and silence of one's own being. What "I" refers to is not merely unsayable but it is also not able to be manifested by speech. (Cf. our version of this in Book 1, Chapter III, §2.) But in the "moral" situation, each then knows in a unique way what "I" refers to and what is not able to be manifested by speech. Daimon is other to myself and other to what is in the world and other to what is able to be manifested by speech. This is so not only because of the otherness to the I myself of the admonishing voice of conscience but also because one's intimacy to oneself is not of the order of *Logos* as what is brought by speech to light in the world. The otherness of *Daimonion* is thus also the otherness to this sense of Logos as the same for us all, and for that reason its "voice" may not be subordinated to the common Logos that speech makes available. It must be uniquely heard because it is the essence of one's self.

Frank does not make this precise point, but he goes on to say that for the ancient Greeks, the *Daimonion* was regarded as the proper metaphysical substance of one's own life, the proper "liver" of one's life, and the *principium individuationis*. As controversial as this is there are passages in Plato which support such an interpretation. We know that for Plato the guardian spirit was indeed the ever present guide without which each would be lost at the many forks and crossroads on life's labyrinth. It is clear that each soul has the capacity to be instructed and to listen to this appointed guide. And at least in one place this guide is described as the "divinity of each one," being that "part which, as we say, dwells at the top of the body," and which raises each from the earthly to "our kindred who are in heaven" (*Timaeus* 90a).

It is a controversial matter whether the ancient Greeks had the modern (originating in trinitarian theology) concept of the person.[55] But in Frank's suggestive interpretation, the Daimon was the core of one's ownmost individuality out of which ultimate ground all of the individual's life, action and thinking flowed. As the proper metaphysical substance of someone, it was inseparable from the widespread view of transmigration of souls and perhaps had connections with the mystery religions which showed the way to immortality and liberation from the cycle of births.

We may thus say that according to Frank, *Daimonion*, like Existenz, becomes a technical third-person term for indicating incommunicable unique first-person experience about what is of unconditional importance. Furthermore, the *Daimonion*, as is witnessed to in the theory of rebirth, was linked to one's destiny and calling from which one cannot flee. Only in heeding one's Daimon does one become aware of one's true self and one's destiny.

In our presentation Existenz is that which heeds conscience, not conscience (the Daimon) itself. Yet Existenz cannot exist without the witness of the oneself at a distance from oneself, i.e., without the witness of the personal essence to the sort of person one has committed oneself to and to which one is called. In this respect no one can live without being guided by the "Guardian Spirit."

We perhaps find another strain of an ontology of the person, indeed of ipseity, when we consider that prior to the human soul's being linked to his Daimon in this life, there is the speculation in the *Republic* of the Myth of Er. Er, a valiant soldier, returns to life after being killed in battle. He relates his encounter with all the souls who have died and who are assigned places in a kind of purgatory and heaven. Many are to be reborn and these hear the proclamation of Lachesis, maiden daughter of Necessity, that they are about to begin a new round of earthly life which will end in death. As a first preparation for this life they will receive their "lots," i.e., they learn that they will receive their allotted destiny, which is tied to their deity or Daimon; but this allotment will be tied to their own choice: "No guardian spirit (*Daimonion*) will cast lots for you, but you shall choose your own *Daimonion*." She exhorts each of these souls to choose a kind of life to which he will be bound of necessity under the tutelage of his Daimon. But it is suggested that the wisest choice is the life of virtue, and each shall have of virtue, i.e., will prosper from the benefits of virtue, to the extent he honors her. "The blame is his who chooses. God is blameless." The myth of Er suggests that there is a primal choice of our lives, as we shall say, a willing-will, that governs all of life and it is in the wake of this will that the rest of our life is determined.[56] This determination of one's Daimon is a self-determination of the most basic sort.

Yet there are deep philosophical puzzles for us here. First we may note the symmetry to our view that the "Guardian Spirit" as guide itself is constituted by the person (soul) herself. The Daimon thus reflects oneself back to oneself. Yet the pre-existent or not yet born souls seem to have an ambiguous status of being now free of character. And in this sense they are merely the "myself" prior to any personal characteristics which they acquire in the course of living their lives. Yet in the further narrative of how various people choose their lots, it is clear that they are "acting in character," i.e., they act in the wake of the karma of their prior lives and make poor choices. Thus we have two problems of the freedom of choice here. (A) There is the matter of how the pure souls or ipseities could choose in the absence of any horizon of interests at all. Would they have to choose from a radically libertarian or indeterminist position? (B) The second problem of how they *choose* their lives under the tutelage of their guardian Daimons if in fact the radical inaugurating choice casts their lot, their destiny, in such a way that all is pre-determined, including the choice of the Daimon. We will wrestle with both aspects of Plato's theory in the next chapter.

In any case it is clear that Frank's reading of the Daimon suggests that in the "phenomenal" life the essential personal self is what must be listened to if one is to be eventually genuinely free of the karma of one's past decisions – even though one might well have chosen a Daimon on the basis of a very burdensome karma, i.e., one that blinds one capacity to choose clearly. Furthermore, it seems that in Plato's Myth of Er the soul is more than the character, more than the personal habitus and personality, and it is more than these qualities and properties, and that it is invested with a capacity of freedom and insight, in the guise of the Daimon, that can be a guide in spite of the burden of the past. Further, there is nothing more important for the soul than its Existenz, i.e., to so center itself as to be able to choose on the basis of what is most important in its determination of its destiny.

In the Chapter IV we will wrestle with some of these issues of freedom and character and in Chapter V we will present a theory of vocation that also holds that only in heeding one's true self does one properly realize one's inmost I-ness, one's Existenz. In the final chapters we will return to an ancient understanding of the self enjoying a puzzling existence prior to its existence in the world. Here we consider Plotinus' theory of the form of oneself. This theory was inspired in great part by

Plato's wrestling with the nature of the soul and its destiny under the tutelage of its *Daimonion*. But we will also consider the religious and theological aspects of this theme in Plotinus.

Franz Rosenzweig's use of Daimon in his philosophical-theological anthropology has many points of contact with Plato's ruminations as well as with our project. Here we will restrict ourselves to how he develops the notion of Daimon in conjunction with our topics of Existenz, the unique individual essence or ipseity, personhood, and character. We earlier appropriated Rosenzweig's view that at the heart of Existenz's emergence in the face of crises there is pride bordering perhaps on rebelliousness or defiance. Rosenzweig distinguishes the "self" (*Selbst*) from the "person" (*Personalität*) in a way that has kinship with this work. The chief difference is that the person essentially is a being in the world with Others. The person's individuality is in virtue of this intersubjective, communal, historical, and natural being. In the terms we used in Book 1, the individual person instantiates types and kinds, and is an individual by reason of these extrinsic relations and determinations. Without them there is no particular person. But most basic to the human is the willing of its *Eigenheit*, its unique ownmostness. This is the root of the *Trotz*, the defiance, in the face of the necessities, surds, and involvements that surround, determine, and individuate the human. "I" is always "I, however"; it is always an illocutionary act through a word of qualification which of necessity is a negation, a "No," wherein opposition is stressed.[57] The self thus is uniquely unique and not an individual by reason of its being related to or individuated by anything else. Yet, so it seems for this reader of Rosenzweig, our position differs in so far as the ontological status is secured apparently only in Rosenzweig's emphasis on the self's being itself by reason of its *not* being individuated by its relationship to others. Thus, the individuation by way of its relations persists in a dialectical manner as a constitutive factor. We have earlier argued that the "myself" is an individuation *per se* and not *per accidens*. Yet Rosenzweig's claim that prior to individuation there is a willing of its ownness suggests that individuation is *per se*; indeed, prior to this willing there is something more basically individual, i.e., what Rosenzweig calls "character," which has an intricate relationship to the Platonic notion of Daimon. We will now turn to this.

The radical, ontological, *Trotz* or defiance at the root of the self is this self-assertion of itself over against what would define it, subsume it into itself, and make it a mere instantiation or particular. *Der Trotz trotzt auf den Charakter* (73), the radical ontological self-assertion through its "character" is an insistence on its unique uniqueness. "Character" here is therefore not to be taken as the abiding habitus which may be thought of in terms of universal moral qualities. Yet character is more than the mere will to being one's unique self. Willy-nilly in the absence of defiance one is one's unique self, i.e., one remains necessarily who one is. But the sheer will to be oneself in the absence of some feature, some character, is a will not to self-affirmation and preservation but to self-destruction because it is a will to being nothing, i.e., a propertyless, characterless self. It is the will to be *Der Mann Ohne Eigenschaften*, to use Robert Musil's phrase. The defiance and self-assertion needs content and it is on the basis of "character" that the will realizes its defiance.

"The 'self' is that which originates in this meta-concept of free willing of its own-mostness, as the *And* of both defiance and character" (73).

We may contrast this rooting of the self in the uniqueness of its character with its rooting itself in the particularity of being a human or a person in the world with Others. In this latter case the one is individuated by finding one's voice in the symphony of humanity. One has the role to play allotted him by fate, society, history, and culture. One lives essentially by sorting oneself from out of the plurality of persons. One is always one among many and of necessity who or what one is as a person is a result of comparison with others. When regarded from a public, third-person perspective, the self is indistinguishable from the person. As such it is an individual determined by place, time, nationality, gender, etc.; it has a natural birth and death.

But sometime or other the self, we may say *Daimon* here, seizes the person or individual human being and robs him all at once of all his possessions, of his identity as a mere person in the world with others. Prior to this the person for himself is part of the world and sees himself primarily as someone in the world from, more or less, a third-person perspective. Awakened to himself as a daimon-self he finds himself totally poor and alone. Now the third-person version of himself falls away and the first-person gains ascendancy. No one knows him and he knows only himself (77).

The self-illumination through the seizure of the person by the self is being overtaken, states Rosenzweig, by a blind and mute self-enclosing *Daimon*. For Rosenzweig, "self," which here approximates somewhat what we are calling Existenz, is awakened by *Anangke*, the necessities which come upon us and undo our identity as a person in the world. (Cf. our discussion of limit-situations.) This visitation by Daimon takes place first under the mask of *eros*, and this accompanies the person throughout his life, until the time when this mask is removed and it reveals itself as *thanatos*, death. Death awakens one unto the self because the person is awakened to ultimate singularity and loneliness. The day the self is born is the day on which the person, the individual instance of the species, dies (77).

But the second birth of the Daimon in death gives to life a dimension beyond that of the species – which very notion of "meaningfulness beyond the species" is something vain and meaningless for the life of the person in the world – and this is to give to the self its most proper rank wherein it no longer has to appropriate what is common to humanity at large. In this case one can say the less there remains of personal individuality the more singular will be the self and the more firm will become the character. For Rosenzweig, this development has an especial significance in old age.

The proper individuality of the self, the proper ownmostness (*Eigenheit*), is its *character*. Again, it is this through which the will or drive to be itself is realized. He also calls this character its *ethos* and its *Daimon*. He quotes Heraclitus: "For the human his ethos is his Daimon" (77). The Daimon-self *is* the character but the Daimon-self is a self because it *has* this definite character. Whereas the atmosphere of the life of the person is the life of the species, the nation, the state, etc., the life of the self is only itself. It is beyond all these, not in the sense that it does not need them, but in the sense that it goes beyond them and their laws are not recognized as binding on itself. For the life of the self these laws are merely presuppositions which belong to him but not necessarily what he must obey. The self is meta-ethical (79). The eternity of the person is satisfied with the eternity of its relations in the world with Others. The self as such does not have relations, cannot enter into any, and remains always itself. As such it is conscious of itself being eternal. Its sense of its immortality is its not being able to die (86).

Clearly Rosenzweig's notion of the Daimon-self has affinities with the classical Greek tragic figure, whose individuality is inseparable from his character and his tragic flaw (cf. 80 and 237). The self, under the sway of its Daimon/ethos/character, is of necessity self-contained, self-enclosed, and self-directed. Rosenzweig speaks of the self in its being possessed by the Daimon as resolved once and for all for its whole life to pursue the direction which is his destiny (238). "His will is determined now to take its course in this once and for all directed orientation; in that he holds to this direction he is directed in the truth of his path. For that which in the human stands under judgment, i.e., the essential will, is fixed already once and for ever in its direction" (238).

There are numerous themes in common with this Husserlian work which will occur to the reader. Because the Husserlian position we are developing claims for the self a unique individuality as an evident ontological matter the theme of *Trotz* and the drive to transcend the immersion in the matrix of human society is less emphasized. On the other hand, because we have been at such pains to make this ontological matter so evident, perhaps closer attention to the *Trotz* would afford another necessary form of evidence.

Further, Rosenzweig's notion of character echoes the Husserlian notion of Existenz that we are proposing, i.e., the shaping of the personal self by the will in terms of a once and for all position-taking that one may pursue without regrets. Thus Existenz is not merely the "myself" bereft of properties but is the center of the person who, unless she self-determines herself ethically, remains ontologically deficient. Here Rosenzweig and Husserl draw near. For Husserl the exemplary and for Rosenzweig the ineluctable determination comes upon one and is not solely a result of the I's agency. For Husserl it takes the form of a calling or direction of will, which, as we shall see, may be named a revelation of "the truth of will." It moves in the direction of our effort to tie together the sortal feature of character and the non-sortal unique ipseity of the person by claiming that the issue of voca-tion, and therefore the matter of utmost importance in one's self-determination, is determining the sort of person one is and an awakening to the deepest depths of one's I. Further, this awakening will effect a resolve which is not rigidly fixed but which must constantly be self-renewing.

For Rosenzweig this comes upon us as a Daimon which awakens us to our sin-gular individuality and our unique destiny. Similar to Husserl's "absolute ought," in Rosenzweig, the self possessed by the Daimon is fixed for ever. In this case defiance and character, hybris and Daimon go inseparably together (186). That is, such is the case until that occurs which alone can interrupt and dissolve the judgment regarding the direction of life: an internal reversal. This happens when the reserve and self-enclosure of the self is overcome; when the self's once and for all resolve is turned into a denial of this self-enclosed self; when the character loses its once and for all fixed direction and, instead, from moment to moment renews itself in a new character not rooted in defiance. All this happens, according to Rosenzweig, when the light of divine revelation breaks forth. This is not the destiny-laden overpowering of the human by the Daimon, but rather comes ever again anew in each moment and in each moment from out of the ownmost interior of the soul with the force of a no less directed will. The self/soul now breaks forth from out of its isolation and reserve and is invested with the power that stems from the divine commandment to love one's neighbor. But God must first turn to the human being before the human being can convert to God's will (238). There is thus possible a new kind of character; Rosenzweig does not here use the pagan term, Daimon. Rather, instead of its being inseparably tied to defiance, there is a new dimension of pride which is at bottom the humility of resting in the security and peace of the creator God (186–188).

In our final theological chapter we will turn to some of these themes opened up by Rosenzweig's theological anthropology. Here we may note that we, with the help of Erich Frank, have found the Platonic notion of Daimon useful for getting clear on what Existenz is. Similarly we find a philosophical kin in Rosenzweig's notion of the self as Daimon which is clearly differentiated from personhood, and yet has an important connection with character as the determination of what sort of person or human one is. However, whereas we have intended our discussion of Existenz, personhood, etc., to be philosophical, Rosenzweig introduces through the association of the self with the Daimon, character, and *Trotz* a theological consideration: defiance is not merely the expression of the ontologically unique self's self-assertion, but it is a matter of being closed off from the creator, creation and the neighbor.

It seems to me that the ontological claim about the non-sortal nature of the "myself" is theologically neutral. Whether it must find expression in the *Trotz* that Rosenzweig highlights itself seems to be a theological judgment. Nor need it be connected to the blindness and imperviousness of the classical tragic hero. Likewise, the "once and for all" determination of one's way in life may or may not be one in which one is blind and closed off from more basic moral, religious, and theological dimensions. Yet, having said this, we acknowledge in this work having neglected any discussion of "radical evil" or "original sin." Furthermore, the struggle for the emergence of the "true self" from out of the various "false selves" with which one identifies, and with which one persists to identify is, so it would seem, both a philosophical and theological theme.

In any case, we have attempted to show that being a person (or personality) precisely, as Rosenzweig describes it, is an essential part of our being human and the individuality that is proper to it, although doubtless pervaded with possibilities of inauthenticity, must reflect the unique uniqueness of the "myself." It is here, as we shall see, where character in a normative sense, and perhaps one closer to what Plato and Aristotle refer to, comes in. This appears to be quite remote from the blind possession by a Daimon who it seems, at first glance, is much less than Socrates' divine guardian spirit.

Yet, as Rosenzweig further teaches, we may not underestimate the new birth which occurs when Daimon befalls the person. Just as even the birth of one's personal being, or personality, in the world with Others is not a pure accident, even though it may so seem to be such for "paganism," but rather is creation, so the rebirth of the self in its being possessed by the Daimon is not sheer fate, as it may seem to be for the "pagan," but rather it is Revelation. We must live from where we find ourselves, for where we find ourselves there the hand of the creator is to be found (436–437). We will return to these same themes in our final Chapters VI and VII.

§8. Excursus: The Illumination of Existenz and the Proustian-Stoic "Cataleptic Impression"

In order to shed further light on *Existenz*, this section draws on a rich essay by Martha Nussbaum and pursues a quibble. The context is her discussion of Proust in connection with the Stoic theory of a unique kind of experience which is compressed within what is translated as an "impression" (*phantasia*). This impression, according to some Stoics, was *kataléptikē*, which literally perhaps is rendered by "firmly grasped." In English we are familiar with the derivation, "cataleptic," as a way of describing an altered state in which a person loses consciousness and in which her muscles become rigid, i.e., when a person "has a seizure." But the Proustian-Stoic sense, as Nussbaum presents it, is less a neurological seizure than what one might call an "existential seizure" (cf. the "prospective retrospection" occasioned by "one's own death") or emotionally powerful experience in which one's prior take and orientation on something is "shaken up," as in he encounter with a limit-situation.

According to Nussbaum, this existential seizure, for the Stoics, is tied to the psychological quality of assent which we call "certainty." But the fuller sense of the cataleptic impression is that the person "has an absolutely indubitable and unshakeable grasp of some part of reality." By its very nature it is self-legitimating and self-validating. Sextus defined it as an impression in the soul "that is imprinted and stamped upon us by reality itself and in accordance with reality, one that could not possibly come from what is not that reality."[58] The issue we wish to pursue with Nussbaum is in what sense we are to understand this "impression" and its claims to be self-legitimating.

In Nussbaum's reading of Proust, there is an application of the cataleptic impression to a less limited range of experience than experiences of, e.g., *quale* or pains. Rather, it is used as a way of explicating Proust's critique of intellectual knowledge in favor of the superior revelatory power of emotions. The setting is where Proust's character, Marcel, is busy in a purely intellectual manner with the question of whether he loves Albertine. Proceeding intellectually, he calculates the pain of staying with her in comparison with the pain of not being able to be with other women he desires; he calculates the pleasure he has with her in comparison with the pleasure he gets and fantasies he will get from other women. He intellectually analyzes his "heart" and believes that he can conclude that he does not love Albertine. But then Marcel hears the announcement, "Mademoiselle Albertine has gone." As Nussbaum summarizes it, "immediately the anguish occasioned by these words cuts away the pseudotruths of the intellect, revealing the truth of his love" (263–264). Marcel himself acknowledges how mistaken he was in thinking that such an intellectual knowledge could reveal his heart. "But this knowledge, which the shrewdest perceptions of the mind would not have given me, had now been brought to me, hard, glittering, strange, like a crystallized salt, by the abrupt reaction of pain" (265).

But the pain here is that accompanying an emotion, "anguish." It is not an impression in the same way pain is an impression as caused by, e.g., a flash of light or a burn or a needle prick. Nussbaum does not sufficiently attend to the possibility of a more massive "impression." Earlier in this and the preceding chapter we discussed how one's death, as well as the experience of other limit-situations, may occasion a realization or gathering or prospective retrospection, wherein one is "seized" with a thick passive synthetic total "impression" of one's life. Proust himself seemed attuned to this sort of experience with his famous account of nostalgia and of "involuntary memory." Similarly, what we call conscience is a kind of "impression" whereby one is "stricken" or "seized" by the revelation by oneself to oneself of the self one has pledged oneself to be. We have said that this witness of conscience is a passive-synthetic congealing in this particular occasion of one personal essence which shows how this essential personal self stands in conflict with this deed of the actual personal self. Nussbaum is clear that these surely are not raw impressions, *hyle*, such as conceived by perhaps the Stoics and certainly by Hume. Marcel's experience of Albertine's departure is an occasion for both a "gathering" experience of his lived life as well as how he, in regard to Albertine, has been shabby.

But in spite of Nussbaum's cautioning the reader against equating Proust's pain with a "raw" impression, apparently like a qualia or pain, she herself is very restrictive in her applying the notion of "impression" to Proust's account of Marcel's experiences. She elucidates this non-raw impression by reminding us that impressions "can be, and frequently are propositional – that is, impressions *that* such-and-such is the case (265, n. 7). She further reminds us that such impressions "require interpretation" (270).

Of course it is true that an emotion like Marcel's experience may be prepropositional, and doubtless in any case it is at least implicitly propositional. Indeed, such an emotion would seem to have folded into itself numerous propositions. After all, Marcel explicates the emotion in terms of how much Albertine meant to him, that her absence will be very painful, that his prior reflections were without merit, etc. But the anguish is already an interpretation of the way he has behaved toward Albertine. It is, among other things, a prospective retrospection in the face of Albertine's having left him; it is also conscience as a testimony of whether he is in accord with himself as he has constituted himself. Like the raw experience of pain such a massive impression does not need an interpretation for it to be painful. It is not as if we have first the datum of pain, and then the interpretation.

The anguish itself, as it impresses itself upon us and overtakes us, is at once an impression, an interpretation, and a revelation. Again, Nussbaum acknowledges that emotions are not mere "raw feelings" and that Proust does not hold this view (269–270), yet the overall effect of her analysis is to treat the emotion not as a rich massive "impression" but as a raw datum needing an interpretation.

Nussbaum's highlighting that the interpretation we might give is not absolutely inerrant and apodictic is important and unobjectionable. Thus what Marcel interprets as his "love" of Albertine might really be a "longing for his grandmother, or some more general desire for comfort and attention." She further faults Proust (through Marcel) for not seeing that love is really a relation of mutuality where certainty and possession and control give way to uncertainty, vulnerability, and trust. I do not wish further to discuss this critique of Proust here, except to say that Nussbaum's frequently stated thesis (in her book), that love is a (reciprocal) relation, seems to neglect the many forms where love is one-sided (cf. our discussions in Book 1, Chapter IV, §§13 ff. and Book 2, Chapter V). Numberless cases of parental love, unrequited love, secret love, saintly love, etc. would be cancelled as forms of love if one took Nussbaum at her word here. My chief point, however, is confined to the observation that her criteriological-epistemological critique of Proust, especially her reading of his anguish as a raw impression (in spite of her caveat against this), overlooks the richness and essential nature of such Proustian "cataleptic" experiences. In such cases there is, as Nussbaum seems to acknowledge, an apparent "depth and importance" (see 264) in comparison with which the merely intellectual analysis could not compete (266). Nussbaum does not contradict this but this dual feature of "depth and importance" of such experiences is itself philosophically interesting. In contrast to the homogenizing work of intellect where Marcel was able to hide behind habit, routine, male-patriarchal convention, etc., the emotional "being seized" is "hard, glittering, strange," "a physical blow… to the heart," "like a thunderbolt," that makes an open wound (266).

In the light of what we have said about ipseity and the depth and breadth of personal life, and given the fact that, as a rule, we live superficially and cut off from the depth of our lived life, it is of great interest when suddenly and without preparation a large swath of our whole life appears before us and we find our current sense of ourselves and our lives derailed. The necessity and importance of *such* "cataleptic impressions" gains intelligibility when we see them as the work of passive synthesis, whether in the form of a gathering act of "living memory" or in nostalgia, or whether the work of conscience or the prospective retrospection of one's life vis-à-vis another who has vanished from one's life, as in the departure of Albertine from Marcel's life. In any case, one's life is summarized in a moment. We always tacitly presuppose and depend on passive synthesis, but for the most part what we are busy with is the tip of the iceberg – except in such gathering experiences.

Granted that the propositions that explicate such passive synthetic total impressions, like Marcel's anguish, might turn out eventually to be wrong, that in fact Marcel is merely longing for his grandmother's comforting presence and he does not really understand what love is and therefore does not really love Albertine, the anguish itself, in its unexplicated pre-propositional form itself is, as Gendlin would say, a felt-meaning and it is "true" as such, i.e., as a felt-, unexplicated meaning. That is, Marcel, and certainly we, cannot deny that he is experiencing such and such a feeling that he (rightfully or wrongly) calls anguish. In as much as it is a felt-meaning it is implicitly propositional, and this subsequent propositional explication is a further aspect of its truth. The power of the anguish's revelation is that there is not only the intensity of the revelation of the undeniable first-person anguish but the power lies also in what the anguish has to reveal about Marcel's relationship with Albertine and how this shapes his general being in the world.

These two revelations come as one, but they must be distinguished. Let us suppose that Marcel, perhaps with the help of his therapist or friend, comes to doubt his original interpretation of his anguish. Disclosing the falsity of one interpretation (or proposition) would mean to let go of it and to revert back to (the undeniable truth of) the felt-meaning of the empty intention (what Husserl calls *ein dunkles Etwas*) he earlier named "anguish" in order to wait, e.g., for the "loss of the grandmother's comforting presence" to come forth as the right explication or interpretation of the felt-meaning. It would not be a matter of getting rid of the experience of the felt-meaning where one experienced oneself as being gripped by anguish, but it might mean that the felt-meaning undergoes a metamorphosis such that it eventually no longer actually is such a seizure that was called "anguish regarding Albertine's departure." There is no other way to establish its ultimate truthfulness except by recourse to this felt sense that seemed at the time to be properly named "anguish about the loss of Albertine."

However, what Marcel labeled "anguish" in regard to Albertine's departure and what catapulted him out of his complacent and self-deceiving intellectual analysis may indeed be a revelation of his love for Albertine. Only subsequent reflection on his "anguish" will enable him to determine whether that is truly so. Such reflection would perhaps reveal that he loves Albertine herself, and not only the grandmotherly properties of comfort and security her presence afford him. It might reveal that Albertine awakens in him depths not only of longing but also of devotion, both of which were hitherto concealed from him. (Cf. our discussion in Book 1, Chapter IV, §§13 ff., and Book 2, Chapter V, §3.) Perhaps these are tucked into the anguish he felt when hearing the announcement that Albertine has left him. If so, then this emotive disclosure is indeed a thunderbolt that shakes him up and reveals his center to himself through his love of Albertine.

Concentrating, as Nussbaum does, on the fallibility of the interpretation distracts and detracts from her excellent essay and what I take to be Proust's basic point which has to do with anguish's capacity to reveal not only Marcel's love of Albertine but also Marcel to himself. Nussbaum's critique hides Proust's point that such experiences not only typically but also with legitimacy become the axial points of both practical as well as theoretical life. Philosophy itself often has its point of departure as well as its recurrent home base in such Proustian cataleptic impressions (assuming some lineage between Proust and the Stoics), because they have a unique power to raise the issue "of the whole show," even though they initially were emotional seizures and mere food for thought, i.e., not yet well-honed concepts, distinctions, and propositions.

A philosophy which is intellectualistic in the sense Proust is opposing "lacks all sense of proportion, of depth and importance…" and is inclined to "reckon everything up in terms of numbers" which render everything commensurate with everything else (264). It is a homogenizing third-person view from nowhere. As a result, it is, of necessity, indifferent to the revelation of the self's deeper center. Existenz is a further articulation of the way the "Proustian cataleptic impressions" have the power to reveal me to myself in terms of what is central and what is peripheral. Whereas there is corrigibility in our interpretation of the massive "Proustian cataleptic impression" or in how best to articulate what the emotion presents as unconditionally important, Existenz's coming forth to itself in the face of this "thunderbolt" enjoys a kind of apodicticity. We may say this even though there is good reason for anyone to step back from the emotion's initial claim to be an epistemic thunderbolt. But neither these reflections nor a transcendental phenomenological reflection will be the source of the emotive revelation but rather will presuppose it. And nothing these reflections reveal can contradict the original sense of Existenz coming forth and being shaken out of one's routine and everyday superficiality, but rather they will bring this to light. As a transcendental phenomenological reflection, it might further provide the scene in which emerge the distinctions between the pre-anguished intellectual Marcel, the initially anguished Marcel, and the subsequent metamorphoses of Marcel as he sorts out what the anguish further reveals. If the original sense maintains its power to disclose Marcel's heart, it is easy to imagine circumstances in which Marcel will renounce his reflective stance and take up the appropriate stances and agency of the penitent lover. If it is true (cf. our discussion below in Chapter V) that in love we actualize the center of ourselves, and if Marcel is free to pursue his love, for Marcel to do otherwise would be to renounce himself at a deeper level. Of course, for Albertine Marcel's coming to his senses may be too late.

Notes

1. Paul Valéry *Cahier B (1910), Oeuvres* II, 572.
2. Castañeda, *The Phenomeno-Logic of the I, passim*, especially Chapters I and II.
3. *Concluding Unscientific Postscript*, 203 and 258–259.
4. Ibid. 387–389.
5. Paul Tillich, *Wesen und Wandel des Glaubens*. Trans. Nina Baring, Renata Albrech, Eberhard Ameling, reworked by Tillich (Ullsteinbuch), 9. The English text, "the state of being ultimately concerned," creates a special task of understanding what "state" means here. See Paul Tillich, *Dynamics of Faith* (New York: Harper Torchbook, 1957), 1.
6. Søren Kierkegaard, *Journals and Papers*. Vol. III. Eds. H.V. Hong and Edna V. Hong (Bloomington, IN: Indiana University Press, 1975), 651, Section 3587. I am indebted to Tony Aumann for this text.
7. See Husserl's *Nachlass* MS, B I 21 V, 137a–b.
8. Peter Bieri, *Das Handwerk der Freiheit* (Franksfurt am Main: Fischer Taschenbuch Verlag, 2007), 387 ff.
9. See Karl Jaspers, *Philosophie*. Vol. II (Berlin: Springer, 1956), 249 ff.
10. See Cornford's Commentary on Plato's *Timaeus* in *Plato's Cosmology*. Trans. and Commentary by Francis MacDonald Cornford (Indianapolis, IN: Bobbs-Merril, n.d.; preface, 1938), 161–177.
11. See Jaspers, *Philosophie*. Vol. II (Berlin: Springer, 1956), 201 ff.

12. Simone Weil, *Waiting for God*. Trans. Emma Craufurd (New York: Harper Colophon, 1967), 118–119; *Simone Weil: An Anthology*. Ed. Siân Miles (New York: Weidenfeld & Nicolson, 1986), 266.
13. Weil, *Waiting for God*, 135.
14. See our discussion of Weil's claim that the "I" must be destroyed in Book 1, Chapter II, §3.
15. Karl Jaspers, *Der Philosophische Glaube angesichts der Offenbarung* (Munich: Piper, 1963), 317 ff.
16. Jaspers, *Philosophie* II, 253.
17. Husserl, *Husserliana* XV, 213–214.
18. Jaspers, *Philosophie* II, 268.
19. See Jaspers' discussion of suicide in connection with the "passion for the night" in *Philosophie* II, 300–313. On Nov. 3, 2006, Malchi Ritscher stood by an off-ramp in downtown Chicago, doused himself with gasoline, and set himself ablaze. He left this note: "Here is the statement I wish to make: If I am required to pay for your barbaric war, I choose not to live in your world. I refuse to finance the mass murder of innocent civilians who did nothing to threaten our country... If one death can atone for anything, in any small way, to say to the world: I apologize for what we have done to you, I am ashamed for the mayhem and turmoil caused by my country." No one was listening. It took five days for the Chicago Cook County medical examiner to identify the corpse which was charred beyond recognition. (This is from an AP release found in *The Herald-Times* of Bloomington, Indiana, Nov. 27, 2006, C3.) Mr. Ritscher's experience of his situation shows how one's life is inextricably tied up with "the megamachine" and how one's authentic ethical agency is compromised constantly by being implicated in corporate and nation-state decisions. Cf. my "'We,' Representation, and War Resistance," in *Phenomenology, Interpretation, and Community*. Eds. Lenore Langsdorf, Stephen H. Watson and E. Marya Bower (Albany, NY: State University of New York, 1996), 127–144. Malachi Ritscher, it would appear, believed he could not be authentically himself by continuing to be complicit in his inevitable support of the war machine and preferred to end his life rather than continue to take part in the slaughter of innocent Iraqis. He wanted his death to be a gesture of apology and atonement. Its not being covered by any news media made this latter aspect of his deed impossible – until it was picked up by the blogs.
20. Franz Rosenzweig, *Der Stern der Erlösung* (Frankfurt am Main: Suhrkamp, 1996).
21. See William James, *Varieties of Religious Experience* (Cambridge, MA: Harvard University Press, 1985), Lecture IX, 162–164.
22. *Gaudium et Spes*, 16, p. 615; cited in 7. Gary Wills, *Why I am a Catholic* (Boston, MA/New York: Houghton Mifflin/Mariner, 2003), 23.
23. In what follows, besides Husserl, I am happy to acknowledge my debt to Helmut Kuhn, *Begegnung mit dem Sein* (Tübingen: J.B.C. Mohr/Paul Siebeck, 1954).
24. *Hamlet*, III, sc. 1, 183.
25. "Two souls, alas! reside within my breast/and each withdraws from and repels its brother." Goethe, *Faust*, I.2. 307. The citations from literature in this section I have found in the listing under "conscience," in *Hoyt's New Cyclopedia of Practical Quotations*. Compiled by Kate Louis Roberts (New York: Funk & Wagnall's, 1922), 130 ff.
26. For the ethics of thinking, besides the writings of Eugene Gendlin, I have in mind Robert Sokolowski's discussions of clarity and confusion and distinctions in, e.g., *Presence and Absence*, as well as his *Pictures, Quotations, and Distinctions* (Notre Dame, IN: University Press of Notre Dame, 1992); also Stanley Cavell's writings are very much about this theme. See, e.g., his *The Senses of Walden* (San Francisco, CA: North Point Press, 1981). Of course, Heidegger's life-time meditation on *Was heisst Denken?*, i.e., what do we do when we think, what beckons us to think, and what do we do when we listen to and answer this beckoning, serve perhaps as a background for all of these thinkers.
27. Cf. Aristotle, *Nichomachean Ethics* 1111a7–8.
28. Kant, *Die Religion* (Hamburg: Meiner, 1956), 209–210.
29. This is a point Bernard Lonergan has insisted upon, see especially his *Insight*.
30. Cf. Robert Sokolowski, *Moral Action* (Bloomington, IN: Indiana University Press, 1985).

31. Husserl, *Husserliana* VI, 275; *The Crisis of European Sciences and Transcendental Phenomenology*, 341.
32. See my *The Person and the Common Life*, Chapters IV and V.
33. Besides *The Person and the Common Life*, Chapters IV–V, see my "We, Representation, and War-Resistance."
34. See Husserl, *Nachlasss* MS, A V 21, 84a–84b.
35. Husserl, *Husserliana* XXXVII, 234–235.
36. See Kant, *Kritik der praktischen Vernunft* (Hamburg: Meiner, 1974), 34–35. We earlier (Book 1, Chapter III, §3), following Conrad-Martius, called this deep unsearchable sense of freedom the "reverse transcendence of retroscendence" and "archonal being."
37. See *Nicomachean Ethics* 1114b.
38. Vladimir Jankélévitch, *Le pur et l'impur* (Paris: Flammarion, 1960), 5 ff.
39. Cf. *Enneads* I.4.10.
40. See his *Nachlass*, E III 1, 4; also cf. my discussion in *The Person and the Common Life*, especially 119–124.
41. Byron, *The Island*, Canto I, st. 6.
42. For more detail, see my *The Person and the Common Life*, Chapters II and IV; here I draw on this work.
43. These paragraphs have benefited from a reading of an earlier version by Claudia Welz; my thanks to her here for the very good questions she raised. I have adopted her use of the mirror metaphor from her excellent essay, "Keeping the Secret of Subjectivity: Kierkegaard and Levinas on Conscience, Love, and the Limits of Self-Understanding," a chapter in a book she is editing, *Despite Oneself: Subjectivity and Its Secret in Kierkegaard and Levinas*.
44. For an interpretation of Husserl's theory of passive synthesis with this theme in mind, see my review essay: "Edmund Husserl: *Analyses Concerning Active Synthesis. Lectures on Transcendental Logic*" *Husserl Studies* 20 (2004), 135–159.
45. See, e.g., *Husserliana* XIV, 370.
46. John Henry Newman, *Grammar of Assent* (London: Longmans Green, 1870/1947), 177 and 296.
47. As we noted earlier, phenomenology, perhaps especially under the influence of Alexander Pfänder, especially in his *Zur Psychologie der Gesinnungen*, found the metaphor of center and periphery useful. It was used by Husserl in his sorting out the source of the I-acts, which he often called *Geist*, from soul. The I is the center of the periphery of soul. Hans Reiner discusses conscience with this in mind and assigns it to the realm of soul which he also calls the "circumground" primarily because it is not subject to our free will and because it is what offers itself to us and obtrudes upon us. Another reason he gives for assigning conscience to the I-circumground (and not the I-center) is that it is the realm where "the nature of the hereditary psychical characters determines (not wholly, but *partly*) the manner in which things present themselves and are obtruded on us." See Hans Reiner, *Duty and Inclination*. Trans. Mark Santos (The Hague: Nijhoff, 1983; 1st edition, 1974), especially §18. As is evident from our earlier discussions in this Book as well as in Book 1, Chapter III, §3, there is much to agree with here. But numerous formulations, like the claim that the I-circumground is the source of creativity upon which the I-center or I-proper is dependent, or the suggestion that conscience, as inseparable from inherited characteristics and instincts, is rooted in this aspect of "soul" or the I-circumground, are very unsatisfactory. Reiner is right in claiming that there is a sense in which the agency of the I-center is "founded" on soul or the I-circumground, because the origin of the will acts and valuations begins in the being affected by what is in the I-circumground; position-takings from the center of the I presuppose this being-affected. But his sense of founding, which he ties to creativity and his celebration of the great unconscious realm of soul or I-circumground, leads him to say that "responsibility should be *founded* in the sphere [of the I-circumground] that is not under the government of one's own free will" (125). In so decentering the I and, at the same time, impoverishing the authority of conscience, we subordinate the I-center or I-proper to the I-circumground and forget the debt of the great swath of the I-circumground (of position-takings holding as valid) to the I-center. In this

regard the realm of passive synthesis and position-taking acts are absent from Reiner's discussion. We also miss the legitimate normative character of conscience in sustaining the moral personal essence which we have been at pains to describe. Doubtless there are illegitimate or inauthentic guises in which conscience may appear in the I-circumground on the basis of past, e.g., traumatic, experiences, but simply locating the various guises of conscience within the I-circumground merely makes conscience into a homogenous stew. For a brief critical overview of Reiner's book which, however, does not do justice to many of its suggestive discussions, see my review in *Husserl Studies* I (1984).

48. Robert Bolt, *A Man for All Seasons* (New York: Vintage International, 1990), 140. Cf. the "Parable of the Prodigal Son" (*Luke* 15: 11–32) where "the Greek word used in the parable for the property that the son dissipates means 'essence' in the vocabulary of Greek philosophy. The prodigal dissipates 'his essence,' himself." Joseph Ratzinger (Pope Benedict XVI), *Jesus of Nazareth*, trans. Adrian Walker (New York: Doubleday, 2007), 204

49. Max Scheler's "Vorbilder und Führer," in *Schriften aus dem Nachlass, Zur Ethik und Erkenntnislehre*. Vol. I (Bern: Francke, 1957), 255–344 is an important meditation on these matters. Among the many achievements here is to sharply distinguish exemplars from leaders, whom we may follow and yet despise. What we today call "role models" gets close to the derivative sense of exemplar we mention in the text. Scheler never developed, as far as I know, his thinking on this matter – which is not to say that this text is not worth serious study. It is *in nuce* a philosophy of culture and history. It offers a typology of exemplars that correlate with the hierarchy of valuations, as Scheler then saw it. Thus there are brief studies of the saint, the noble person, hero, genius, etc.

50. This is peculiarly abstract in the way the demonstrative pronoun "this" is: It too refers to what is superlatively concrete and it too is ineluctably, in a non-objective sense, present. Yet how we are for the most part is pre-philosophical and thus the "myself" as a theme is abstracted from how we are living our lives as persons in the world. But even Existenz can appear peculiarly abstract for the person for whom oneself is a thing in the world and life is understood and lived for the most part as bereft of the gathering acts or realization, of conscience, and the devotion of love. Of course, for the transcendental phenomenologist displaying Existenz's coming to light, not living in the unconditioned of one's own Existenz, "Existenz," as one theme among others, is also "abstract."

51. See Husserl, the 1917–1918 *Nachlass* MS B I 21 III, 53a.

52. *Apology* 31d; also *Phaedrus* 242 b–c.

53. Erich Frank, "Begriff und Bedeutung des Dämonischen," in his *Wissen, Wollen Glauben*. Ed. Ludwig Edelstein (Zürich and Stuttgart: Artemis Verlag, 1955), 56 ff. St. Paul also has a theory of the "inner man" which each must listen to in the war with the "flesh." See *Romans* 7: 15 ff.

54. For a rich historical-thematic discussion of the daimon with a special interest in the alterity of the "voice" within the self, see Jean-Louis Chrétien, *The Call and the Response*. Trans. Anne A. Davenport (New York: Fordham University Press, 2000), Chapter 2.

55. For a case that they did, see C.J. de Vogel, "The Concept of Personality in Greek and Christian Thought," in *Studies in Philosophy and the History of Philosophy*. Ed. John K. Ryan. Vol. 2 (Washington, DC: The Catholic University of America Press, 1963), 20 ff.

56. Plato, *Republic* 617d–621. See also *Phaedo* 107d–108a. See our discussion of the theory of original choice in J.-P. Sartre and Jean Nabert in Chapter IV, §4,

57. Franz Rosenzweig, *Der Stern der Erlösung*, 193. The numbers in brackets in the body of the text will refer to the Suhrkamp edition of *Der Stern*.

58. Martha Nussbaum, *Love's Knowledge* (New York/Oxford: Oxford University Press, 1990), 265. Hereafter, all the pages listed in the text will refer to this volume.

Chapter IV
Ipseity and Teleology

Mon idée la plus intime est de ne pouvoir être celui que je suis. Je ne puis pas me reconnaître dan une figure finie. Et MOI s'enfuit toujour de ma personne, que cependant il dessine ou imprime en la fuyant.

(Paul Valéry, Cahier B (1910) in *Oeuvres*, II, 572)

Once when my lord the Archmage was here with me in the Grove, he said to me he had spent his life learning how to choose to do what he had no choice but to do.

(Ursula LeGuin, *The Other Wind*, 200)

We can never choose evil as evil: only as an apparent good. But when we decide to do something that seems to us to be good when it is not really so, we are doing something that we do not really want to do, and therefore we are not really free.

(Thomas Merton, *New Seeds of Contemplation*, 199)

Existenz comes forth (*ex-sistere*), i.e., I become aware, through conscience and limit-situations, of "I myself" as a single individual facing what is of unconditional importance. In reflecting on one's death we gain a glimpse of how what is of unconditional importance surfaces in our lives. Similarly, in the witness of conscience we face the crossroads of whether to be true to ourselves or not. We pursue these matters further here. We begin first with a sense of what must be done absolutely by recalling the discussion of ought.

§1. Willing as One's Determining Oneself to Do Something as Done by Oneself

We have said that Existenz is the core of my personal "I myself," the center of the personal I. It has primarily to do with what I must do, what I must attend to, if I am to be me myself. Obviously what threatens to annihilate my very existence places me in a situation which initiates this kind of reflection. But there seem to be things

J.G. Hart, *Who One Is: Existenz and Transcendental Phenomenology*,
© Springer Science + Business Media B.V. 2009

161

worse than death, i.e., there are things the doing of which is a betrayal of myself at my core. In such a case I am not merely dead, nor do I cease to be, but I have chosen to live in such a way that I deny and disrespect the essential self I have constituted myself to be and which I have revealed myself to be before Others. Obviously these issues arise not in conjunction with the pure ipseity of the "myself," for this, we have seen is without content and properties and there is no way of not being "myself." Rather it has to do with I myself as in the world with others, i.e., in regard to me as a person. But I am a person both in the sense that I am for myself and Others a propertied person and, as well, I am first-personally for myself. First, this means both I am a *kind* of being and I am *not a kind* of being. I am a human, but as this individual essence I am not merely a human but am apprehended "non-sortally" as a Who beyond all wordly categories. Secondly, my personhood is given to me to create in my interaction with Others and through the intersubjectivity by which I am fulfilled. Who I am is strangely complete from the start, yet my personal being-in-the-world with others is an ongoing task.

The task of creating myself is given over to me, and this is something that I do freely. If I do not undertake this freely through living my life in action I am merely a potential person in the sense that my personal essence in unformed.. In this respect I myself am my power, my I-can. My freedom to make myself is adumbrated in any act. Whereas, like "free will," there is a sense in which "free act" is a pleonasm (assuming that an action is not determined by the causality of nature), nevertheless "free act" is a phrase that is context-dependent. Let us briefly sketch some of the issues.

In as much as it is an act within the stream of consciousness it therefore is not reducible to the physical conditions, and in this sense it is "free from" the physical causality. Thus an act of feeling, attending, perceiving, and scratching is free. But "free act" is also inseparable from one's impulses, longings, and strivings which solicit the I-center. I can go along with these solicitations without deciding from my center. But even then this being so impelled requires a kind of consent, a kind of giving in to these allures. Properly the free act comes from out of the I-center and is to be distinguished from mere wishing, striving, and going along with. In properly willing I am not merely longing for, entertaining, suffering; rather, *I* act. Willing is always self-involving, I-involving. In willing I am self-determining, self-moving. Here Conrad-Martius's terms for the spirit or I being "archonal" and enjoying the "reverse transcendence" of "retroscendence" are especially evident. (Cf. our discussion in Book 1, Chapter III, §3 and Chapter IV, §3; we return to this topic of will as an "unmoved mover" below in this, Chapter IV, §8.)

Willing as acting is always in view of something. It is motivated. But the motivation is not the willing, even if the motivation is a necessary part of the willing. The motivation is never the sufficient condition for the free act, as if we could think of the I-center as a scene wherein competing motives struggled for ascendancy. There are philosophical accounts which portray the motives for the choice struggling with one another and the strongest of these prevailing; this is said to be the choice. But this is a false description. If there were such a struggle going on with regard to me or "within" me which I would suffer, and who can deny that this occasionally happens!, then the so-called choice or action would be of a detached observer or witness who would not herself have done anything. The meaning of choice would amount to my being, as a passive sufferer, the observer of the contesting motives and of the emergence of the strongest propelling one. If I were merely the spatial container for the struggle, no one would be there to observe it, and I would be no more an agent than a thermostat. Even if I am the mere observer, consent by me would be unnecessary and "choice" would be separated from an *I will* or *I consent*, or the *fiat*!

Further, choice is not the dominance of a powerful motive because occasions may surface when I can decide for what is weakest in terms of its affectivity and driving force. Doubtless there is a struggle among motivations where one may come to dominate without its being chosen to dominate. But we do not speak of willing until we have the clarity of "I choose," what Husserl calls the *fiat*, even if it be only a consent. Here the person is not only moved by motives but he stands over them as the "I will that it be so."[1]

Therefore this view contrasts with the Freudian and Klagesian view where will is merely the means of channeling the forces of soul. In such a view, the self's true essence is in these "circumground" powers not in the egoic will itself. In such a view I myself am imposed upon of necessity by these forces and myself as my will limits the power of these forces by negotiation, but what we call choice is what wins out among the forces; I myself do not make any choices nor do I realize myself as a person through my will.

Yet even though there is a strong sense in which *my action* is what *I* will, and therefore there is an intimate connection between my willings and me myself, it does not follow that a willing can never transpire without "I myself" or "the myself' knowing it in advance, as if all willing was co-extensive with the self-awareness of "I myself." The personal self-awareness encompasses far more in its pre-reflexive horizontal self-awareness than does the non-reflexive self-awareness of "myself." If willing would occur only in regard to acts which were encompassed by the non-reflexive self-awareness of the "myself" no willing would ever occur without my knowing it in advance as inherent to my "I myself." In the view we are proposing, "I myself" am in play in all my willing and, of course, it is also true that I can surprise myself as this person in the world with Others and find myself on occasion full of startling, e.g., murderous intentions. But here we must distinguish again what is inseparable in our concrete life, namely, on the one hand, the non-reflective non-ascriptive self-awareness of my unique essence and, on the other hand, the pre-reflective, pre-thematic self-presence of myself as JG Hart. In the former case I am present with full adequation as the unique ipseity; in the latter case I, JG Hart, am of necessity present to myself inadequately and, upon reflection, am present as having such and such properties, as this person in the world with Others. My will in the former case is a "tautological property" of my unique essence; in the latter case it provides the effective and teleological dynamism for the self-realization of the person. Thus it is the vehicle for this unique essence's actuation of itself as a person. Yet it acts through time and through specific willings, what we will call (adopting the terminology of Maurice Blondel) the "willed willing," and as such it may take on habitualities and dispositions through passive synthesis in the "circumground" of the soul which may surprise me, foremost when I myself give into what, upon reflection, I myself profoundly regret. We will (again using the terminology of Blondel) call the underlying will of the "willed willings" which is the basic entelechial principle of "the myself" as it exists in the person, "the willing will."

When we suffer from an addiction, of course we are responsible for acquiring the addiction but when wanting the drug has a hold of us and when, at the same time, we genuinely despise and regret the addiction, it is different than when we act, say, because there is a gun held by a robber to our heads. Here we act, and it is not merely a matter of physical necessity, i.e., we act from out of a hierarchy of motives, and choose freely one option over the other. Yet we would rather not do what we wind up doing. In the case of the addiction we similarly say, "I could not do otherwise." But clearly the meaning is different. In both cases we act "against our will" but the addict does not freely act against her will in the way the person who has the gun to her head acts against her will. The latter person chooses to do what the gunman directs because she chooses to live and turn over her money rather than die. The necessity is in this sense external to her will. But the addict's necessity is internal to her will and her will is external to her self, i.e., the sort of person she wants to be and who she typically constitutes herself as being. She can say: I have struggled with all my will to control my will to take drugs (or gamble, drink, etc.), but I can't help it. I simply do, as St. Paul put it, what I would not do. I am not strong enough to follow my better judgment; I am not strong enough to love myself and be who I want to be.

A key matter here is whether we best describe the powerlessness as one of will or as one of deliberation, i.e., the power to let one's judgment determine one's will. Peter Bieri, upon whom we are here dependent, makes a good case that it is the latter formulation that best hits the mark.[2] But those who run addiction programs where the "12 Steps" are emphasized often suggest that something else could be in play which brings it about that one finally is enabled to let the better judgment be decisive. This could be described as discovery of love by a "higher power" or an empowerment to love oneself in the wake of this higher love. I confess to be uncertain about this matter. But even if this description has merit, and even if it appears to support a case for an enhanced will-power, Bieri's description is not invalidated, i.e., one thereby attains the power to let one's judgment determine one's will. In such a transformation we have a candidate for what we call a "whole-hearted" willing.

All willing is self-actuation in the form of self-willing or willing actions that are emphatically self-involving. This important feature of willing comes out when we consider "intentions." Here we do not mean the generic directedness of consciousness in terms of the variety of intentional acts. Rather, we have in mind the specific intentional act that we refer to when we say, e.g., "I have the intention to…" or "I intend to…" Here "intending" *is an initial motion of the will which finds its completion in a future moment of the action*, e.g., the *fiat*, that results in a future state of affairs. "What are you up to?" "I am going to join the army." Thus intentions are wakeful willings of a future state of affairs not merely what future indicative statements express.

Following Castañeda, we may say an intention is a possible first-person answer to the question, "What shall I/you do?" or "Shall I/you do that?" ("I do not know" is an evasion or postponement of the answer; "No" is a kind of not willing to intend.) The affirmative answer which is the intention will be primarily in the form of future-tense indicative sentences of the form, "I shall [or will] do X." The noema of the intention is not a proposition. "John intends to come" may thus be contrasted with "John believes that he (himself) will come." The latter example shows nicely two important features. The noema (not of the speaker's intentional act, but of John), as the subordinate clause of the epistemic act in the main clause, is a proposition in the future indicative form ("he will come"), and as such it may be true or false. The intention, "to come" is neither true nor false. But this latter example also makes explicit, through the quasi-indexical "he (himself)," that the subject referred to in the noema, i.e., in the subordinate clause, is the same as the subject in the main clause. If we left it out, the speaker could mean that John believes that someone else, not he himself (John), would come. (Cf. our discussion of quasi-indexicals in Book 1, Chapter II, §1.)

Although the noema or target of an intention is not a proposition, highlighting the quasi-indexical signals nevertheless the self-reference of an *intention*, in the sense of "I intend to…" In the intention's noema the self of the agent (not a proposition about the agent) is involved. But this is not disclosed in ordinary English. In an intention, John does not merely intend the action, e.g., of leaving. He intends leaving as *his* action. The action may be thought of as such, as a universal action which anyone might instantiate; but in *intending* the action is intended as done *by him*, this unique essence as inseparably bound up with the embodied personal I. Thus even though ordinary English leaves out the self-involvement, as in "X intends to A" (where X stand for the personal agent and A the action), the quasi-indexical is here appropriate even though linguistically inappropriate. That is, the proper rendering of an intention is, "X intends that he (himself) A." Because intentions are characterized by self-involving actions, we may follow Castañeda and think of the noema of intentions not merely as actions, but as rather as self-involving actions.

Nor are intentions to be assimilated under prescriptions or commands to oneself. Prescriptions or self-commands are fundamentally and necessarily third- and second-person forms of reference. In Castañeda's analysis there are no first-person prescriptions. (We hold that weaker, but important, senses of obligation and duty arise in first-personal experiences and reflections, e.g., in conscience. See our discussion in Chapter V, §9 of the view that all prescriptions and obligations and duty are second-personal.) Even when I command myself, as standing before the mirror, screwing up my courage to do something, and saying "You, Jim, tell George what you think of him," the self-feature of this "self-command" is external to the command. I imaginatively with the help of the mirror displace myself and make myself a You with appropriate authority to command me. In the intention the self-feature of the action is intrinsic to it. That is, I am absolutely one with my willing the action.

Yet because of the complementary nature of the structures of commands and intentions, Castañeda says they have the exact same "intentional copula" that links a subject and an attribute which is an action. Consider the *command*, "John, leave!" and the *intention*, "John intends to leave" or "John intends-to (I = [John] to leave).[3] In the former case someone else imposes her will on John; in the latter case John reflexively "imposes" his will on himself.

Finally, intending resembles deciding in that it too is a first-person form that is a counter-part to mandates or prescriptions. But a decision comes as a result of a deliberation and there are intentions which do not follow upon deliberations, e.g., our immediate agreeing with a friend's proposal that we go to a movie.

There are abundant riches in Castañeda's phenomenology of intending that we here leave out. Our goal here is to link our action or doing to intending and this to willing and willing to self-involved actions.

Willing is a relating to oneself, a self-awareness in which I do not observe myself or perceive myself through an identifying act, but rather in which I actively behave toward myself, i.e., toward me with whom I am ineluctably familiar. In thinking about or practically entertaining an action, "I myself" must be made a kind of referent of the proposed action. Nevertheless, it is misleading to say that the act of willing "refers to one's own ego" as if the target of the act were foremost oneself. Rather *I* act and the act of willing, as precisely what *I* do, does not refer to me this person or the I myself (these are not the targets of the will) but to the action, and not merely just the action as a type or kind, but as done by me, this person, not merely the abstract "myself."[4]

If willing is initiated by intentions, and if intentions intend self-involving actions, and if intending to overcome an addiction intends an action in which the whole self is involved then the intending must involve that with which the person whole-heartedly identifies, even though for the addict there might still be a trace of the pull in another direction. In the case of addiction one intends not to take a drink or shoot up and then when the urge or opportunity arises one succumbs in spite of all the intentions. If one is able to cast off the addiction one must intend this behavior of abstinence as an act that one could not possibly not do if one intended to do it, i.e., one intends it as one where one's very self is at stake and willing it without doing it would be willing not to be oneself. It is a willing behind which one fully stands and which one fully authorizes and with which one fully "identifies."

Kierkegaard used the expression, "sickness unto death" for forms of spiritual and moral sickness. For the addict, as for anyone not serious about moral or "spiritual" growth, the capacity for such self-implicating, self-authorizing, self-identifying acts is what is undermined. But then there are the success stories where one finally decides, seemingly "whole-heartedly," NO.

But Kierkegaard, and perhaps St. Paul, were not talking primarily or exclusively, it seems to me, about addictions, but about a spiritual malaise, where in the face of the undeniably good, better, and best, perhaps even in the face of that which is of unconditional importance, a kind of listlessness, melancholy or acedia surfaces. They are pointing to a deeper illness where we fail to show up to ourselves in the sense that the self that we most want to be, the self with which we most identify ourselves through specific acts, lacks the "strength" to act, i.e., to achieve through one's agency these very self-identifications to which it is invited by that which the agent perceives to be the better course or even a good without conditions. Doubtless there is a parallel with the compulsive will of the addict. But such a case of spiritual malaise only superficially resembles addiction. In both cases the reason for the failure to act seems intrinsic, not extrinsic, to the will. The "I cannot" is not due to an external necessity as in the bank teller's agency in response to the robber. Yet, if it is "selfishness" it is not the obvious kind for the person may appear to be exemplarily disciplined if not virtuous. Yet perhaps there here is inertia because the invitation is to such an exalted version of oneself that the adumbration of the cost of having to become a profoundly different sort of person appears excessive. In which case there is, after all, perhaps a kind of "selfishness."

We can say, in the light of our earlier discussions of the distinction between the "myself" and "I myself" as this person, that whereas in the former there is a propertylessness wherein even will is muted except as a "tautological property," and thus a kind of "absoluteness," the "I myself" as person does not exist in such an absolute way but only in a willing which may be considered a form of incremental self-creation of a fragile self whose "growth curve" indicates typically not a linear upward line but a rather jagged affair.

Here we find an echo of Kierkegaard's well-known view, "the more will the more self" (cf. our discussion below in Chapter VI). Because willing has to do with the constitution and origination of the personal self, it is not to be understood exhaustively as a willing of something; rather, in the willing of something the something that is willed always has a self-feature or is a kind of self-willing. But because what we have to do with is not merely the personal self but also the "myself," there is an ambivalence in all willing. On the one hand, willing something is at once bringing the finite personal essence of the self into appearance and it will be always be tied to a specific intending. On the other hand, the willing will also be the actualization of "the myself." The willing of the person as a personal self-willing through a specific willing is also a willing of "oneself" whose willing, we propose (see §2 below), surpasses any specific intending. Thus no specific act and intention and motivation will be adequate to this self-willing. We return to this in the next section on the essential inadequation of the self.

We get at a related ambivalence and problem of the inadequacy of any motivation when we consider that at my core center, myself as Existenz, I find that I both am reason and have reason. Clearly as agent of manifestation I am a principle of *logos*, I am inseparably grounded in "reason" and the quest of intelligibility. Further, my evaluation of myself is through my not merely having reason but through my self-agency being in principle that of reason: acts of will that do not find clarification in the illumination of reflection are less acts of will than dark impulse. However, the power to be myself is also the power to reject my being reasonable. I can reject my being reasonable both in favor of what is beyond reason, as the loving appreciation of an ipseity is beyond reasons and without properties, or in the realization and prospective retrospection in the face of the mystery of "my death." I also can reject my being reasonable by preferring what is below reason or what detracts from my being reasonable, e.g., my addictions, impulses and passions. I am not identical with my being reasonable or an intellect. I can act against my being so. More basic than my reason is my self-being and its I-can.

Yet, as we discussed in conjunction with the question of the "primacy of intellect or will," these are fundamental ways of *my* being in the world, i.e., intellect is I myself understanding and striving to understand; will is I myself willing and choosing. Further, will's actualization is imperfect in the absence of reason's articulation of it. And intellect's fulfillment is in the insight or theory, which are, at least typically, accompanied by a delight in the filling of that which the desire to understand emptily intended.

Can we say similarly that I both am will and have will? Is not the self-selfing basically will or the I-center primarily I-will? In admitting this we do not say that "will" or "freedom" are able to substitute for "I myself."[5] Will and freedom are always "mine" and pervaded by ownness. Further, in admitting the I-center to be I-will we do not admit that the will may be bereft of motivations, and therefore concede that it may properly be without some sense of *logos* and light. Further, even our capacity to refuse to be an agent, to endlessly postpone acting by inconclusive deliberation, or to enslave ourselves to an addiction, or to fail to will to have a will and a certain kind of future (letting ourselves be wantonly driven by whatever impulse occurs), are forms of self-determination. I *have* will in the sense that it bears in a special way the character of ownness and incommunicability deriving from me myself. Will, we have said, involves intentions which always are self-involving acts.

The I, bereft of will and the *power* to be me, bereft of its being a center of possibility or an I-can, is conceivable if as "myself" I would be present for myself as sufficient absolutely as I am, i.e., as an absolute "myself" where possibility and the actualization of possibility would be superfluities. If will is the condition for what appears to me my possibility and my future, then an "I myself' without will must be in need of nothing beyond its own ipseity; it must be a god. This, of course, is an inconceivable and unimaginable life for a human person. Or if I attempt to conceive a "myself" bereft of any past or future, bereft of any I-can by reason not of absolute sufficiency, but absolute privation, then I clearly am not conceiving or imagining a human person, or I am imagining a human person deprived of essential conditions of being a human person. Furthermore, to reason that because the core of self-reference and self-awareness is the non-propertied "myself" therefore one must envisage will as unconditioned and not indebted to anything one has done or experienced in one's past, not shaped by any motive which has to do with motivations emergent from one's life-world or hierarchy of preferences, would be to substitute the "myself" for the person in the world, making of it a little person, a homunculus, within the person. (See our discussion below in Chapter IV, §8.)

I may well "intend X" or "want X" but my capacities, the weight of my past, my inclinations, capacities, vitiating habits, etc., may hinder me from grasping what is at stake in willing X, or they may not permit me to bring it about to will or intend effectively X. It is of interest here that, in spite of the inefficacy of the act, the very nature of the act, assuming it does not involve the self-deception occasioned by an addiction, bears within it this ideal of a causality that does not know these limitations. In any case, in spite of the weight of the past and one's habitualities, in spite of one's being the personal essence one has become, whether this be a matter involving vitiating habit or addiction or not, the act as my initiative challenges my character and any other contingent inheritance as my fate or destiny.

Through this consideration of the "unconditionality" of willing we once again are pointed towards the distinction between who one is as the propertyless "myself" and the person one is or the sort of person one has constituted oneself as being. This "pointing towards" is hardly any essential or logical entailment. Nevertheless, the sense of the ideal of unconditional agency, would it seems, merit the speculation that the "myself" as trans-propertied and trans-temporal is the dynamism of the person and that it comes especially to light in Existenz as the center of the person wherein the unconditionality of living one's life is at hand. These are speculations to which we will soon return. Again, whether this warrants conceiving the will and its freedom as an absence of all conditions will be discussed in §8 at the end of this chapter.

Conscience, we said, provides us with a call from my essential personal self addressed to me myself, this very same essential personal self, as responsible addressee, to do X; conscience gives voice to me as I have constituted myself in terms of the world and ideals that I have appropriated and it gives to me as responsible addressee the opportunity to appropriate, endorse, and identify with this person I have declared myself to be. If I am to remain who I am, i.e., the sort of person I have constituted myself as having been, I must do X. But I now may be under severe temptation not to do X, e.g., the pain of doing X, or the pleasure of avoiding X, might be such that the self that conscience represents is sacrificed to the importunity of the present pain or pleasure. In which case when I do not do X, I am torn from myself and am in profound disagreement with myself. I must either repair the breech or disengage myself from the claims of this old, still-valid, self – something I cannot do unless I renounce the massive synthesis of validities and loyalties comprising who I have come to be. This temptation, when evident as temptation, reveals the agent's belief in the act as infinite causality, i.e., that it is such that I am never reducible merely to my having been, regardless of my having been ever so consistent and virtuous. Even in the shameful moments when I betray myself, not merely in the moments when I resist pressures of pain or pleasure, I reveal this ideal of my act as infinite and unconditioned. Even in the self-deceiving betrayal of myself there is revealed the ideal of unconditionedness latent in the exercise of my I-can as my freedom. Thus my sense of my initiative as unconditioned can, and this is a paradox, be used to act in such a way that I deny what appears as an unconditional Ought.[6]

We have said that Existenz is precisely the being seized by what is of unconditional importance through an act of realization. This we are calling the absolute Ought. (This sense of Ought jars with the thesis of Darwall that there are absolutely no first-personal prescriptions and self-directed duties; see Chapter V, §9.) As with conscience we are witnessed to and called to act. Existenz is illuminated through being witnessed to and with the realization of what is of unconditional importance. However, if I do not act unconditionally upon this call or this which appears to have unconditional importance I slide into inauthenticity in the sense of *Uneigentlichkeit* or denial of one's personal essence, i.e., I slide away from my ownmost core sense of myself and make myself at home in what is relatively peripheral and superficial. In appropriately responding to the realization and the being witnessed to by conscience I affirm the unconditionedness of that which is important and the unconditionedness of the capacity or I-can to accede to, act upon, or carry out what is revealed under the guise of what is of ultimate importance. We follow Jaspers in holding: "As the unconditionedness of willing in the absolute choice Existenz realizes itself."[7] We take this "unconditionedness of willing" (cf. Kierkegaard's "infinite passion for eternal happiness") to refer to the wholeheartedness of the willing, not to the claim that the willing is absolutely bereft of all conditions. (See our later discussion below in §8.) And we can further agree with Jaspers that this illumination of oneself at one's core through the appropriate action, i.e., the coming forth to oneself that we are calling Existenz, can give the manifold phases of life an unconditioned importance and release them from their being fixed in the narrowness of the homogeneous and more or less axiological neutrality of the everyday and routine.

§2. The Self-Inadequation of the Person

Existenz, as awakening to oneself as a single individual having to do with what is of unconditional importance, is not evident in something objective, e.g., some fact, in the world. One's awakening to oneself as Existenz is an awakening to the truth that in some sense one has moved beyond the realm of things, facts and values in the horizon of the world, i.e., from the realm of thingliness (*Dinglichkeit*) to what is somehow "beyond" this and not conditioned by it (*das Unbedingte*). Awakening to oneself as Existenz is not merely an awareness that one has, as it were, surmounted or transcended the world as the realm of objective things and values; rather, there is the further requirement that one must act in accord with one's awareness of oneself in regard to what is of unconditional importance. This parallels the theoretic awareness that emerges in the phenomenological reduction, i.e., that I myself am not completely to be identified with something in the world. But here with Existenz, we do not have a mere theoretic or cognitive disengagement from one's involvement in the world.

This returns us to what Jaspers has called the "basic situation": the encompassing "limit-situation" that is inevitable and inescapable. That is, we are never not in this situation. In short, this basic situation is that we as persons in the world "can never be adequately true and pure, never completed, and never adequately fulfilled."[8] Thus world and what is within its horizon is always something conditioned, i.e., ephemeral, dependent on external causes, having limited value, etc., and thus can never be the place of ultimate fulfillment and satisfaction. Our lived experiences of striving and willing are always surrounded with an openness to the More and a possible Better, and this inseparably is the fuller axiological sense of our present Now being surrounded necessarily with a Not Yet. Each phase of present experience is present in some axiological guise over against a horizon of not yet fulfilled horizons. If we are fortunate to experience it as good this of necessity is over against a background of what is possibly better. And this is a matter of existential-phenomenological necessity.

If we further assume that of necessity the better, *ceteribus paribus*, is preferable to the good, then we face the claim that by its nature all conative-valuational experience is "insufficient" and "inadequate" to the scope of the person's will. Of necessity what we conatively-valuationally experience is pervaded by this axiological insufficiency. Thus entertaining a presencing of something that is fully adequate and consummating of our conation and willing *within the flow of time* is "a consciousness with which one can do nothing or with which it is impossible to live."[9]

These abstract statements about the tension between the actual present valued moments in life and the apperception of the immense concretion of value of life as a whole might well appear arbitrary. The apparent capriciousness of the thesis lies in the seeming gratuitousness of the claim, i.e., it is question-begging by reason of being a generalization purporting to cover all human action. Here is a more formal version of the claim: Good X promises completion for P. P strives and successfully achieves X. P subsequently realizes that X either seemed to promise more than X could possibly deliver, or that P himself had projected onto X endowments that X did not have. The generalization thus involves the following: (a) We all function a good part of the time like P in our being in the world by way of extravagant and infatu-ated forms of constitution, and (b) a good part of the time the goods we experience resemble X. "A good part of the time" purports to ward off the claim that we never properly size up the goods of life; it also means to suggest that large and important stretches of life involve this distorted value perception.

As to (a): The thesis is not that we never experience the proper finitude of life's goods and always project or laminate on top of them an infinite unconditioned value, but that we have a tendency to do this. What traditionally was called idolatry, i.e., substituting a finite conditioned good for the infinite unconditioned good, is a familiar human tendency. "Falling in love" often times can be described in this way. Plotinus offered the classic religious-philosophical interpretation of these matters when he stated that our being struck by beauty in any of its finite manifes-tations evoked a recognition that we were estranged from our "ontological home" which was elsewhere. Similarly, political movements in history can be analogously described, where the leaders of a nation state or revolutionaries opposed to the extant political order envisage political goals that are endowed with a status that exceeds their proper bounds. Thus the telos of history, like the classless society, is where and when humanity finally reaches its true destiny: *U-topos* and *Eu-topos* – in spite of the apperception that this "end of history" will be within history and, pre-sumably, in spite of the apperception that the moral struggles and conflict of values that give rise to the forms of structural violence such as class and patriarchy will persist with the elimination of a ruling capitalist class. Analogously, career choices in one's youth often involve laminating on top of a certain prospect a magnificent unsustainable aura of importance and contentment. Similarly, scholars "fall in love" with certain theories or authors from which or from whom they expect endless riches, as "the reversal of all values," "the archimedian point," or "the universal theory of all theories." And so on.

In passing we may note that utopianists inspired by biblical prophets tend to be circumspect to the point of holding that the *telos* to be striven for is not ultimately within our grasp; that whereas our agency may bring about a meliorization, the consummate state requires the fulfillment of some other condition that is beyond the achievement of human agency. Indeed, it is shrouded in darkness in as much as it must pass through the mystery of death. Foremost in the Hebrew Bible, the major inspiration of many utopianists, there is a strain where, on the one hand, the ideal of the good life is the enjoyment of finite goods into a ripe old age; part of this ideal is delight in seeing one's offspring possibly doing the same. On the other hand, there is the doctrinal note that death itself is a penalty, and therefore the equanimity toward death as a natural term of life is undermined by an intuition or belief that it is not "natural," that indeed it is a catastrophe that properly should not have been the lot of humans. The point, of course, is not merely that a form of human immortality is conceivable. Equally important is the implication that the utopian and dystopian versions of life without death made possible by science are irrelevant to the theory of history implicit in the prophets. Similarly, there is the pervasive ancient Hebrew sentiment of the restlessness of the human heart that cannot find peace until it rests in God, as Augustine put it. "As a hart longs for flowing streams, so longs my soul for thee, O God." The soul that thirsts for "the living God" is compared to "an abyss calling to an abyss" (Psalm 42). Here the psalmist gives expression to his deepest desire "to dwell in the house of Yahweh all the days of my life." This sentiment of the psalmist would suffer a distortion for most who read the Psalm as a referring to a central aspect of "the spiritual life," if it were taken as a mere desire of the psalmist to be able to worship in a certain place which, because of exile, he presently is hindered from visiting. This "certain place," for which the psalmist might be said to long, would not be axiologically or ontologically commensurate with any other place in which one might find oneself because, after all, that for which he longs is the divine presence. However, even though this presence may not be made equivalent with a piece of real estate, it would be a mistake to underestimate the "sacramental" nature of the historical building and place.[10]

As to (b): The ephemerality and deceitfulness of life's goods and pleasures is the stuff of much poetry and religious literature. Do we not often experience and have presented to us variations of: "Nothing is ever as good when I get it in my hand as when I had it in my head"?[11]

> The flower that smiles to-day
> To-morrow dies;
> All that we wish to stay
> Tempts and then flies.
> What is this world's delight?
> Lightning that mocks the night,
> Brief even as bright.[12]

Shelley's image of the world's delight presents it as real and genuinely delightful, but it stands over against the infinity of the night sky which perdures everlastingly and swallows up the lightning flash. A pressing philosophical question, of course, is whether this backdrop portends eternal black nothingness or, as with the Psalmist, Plotinus and Augustine, an unpenetrable mystery of which the delight and brightness of the world are ciphers.

Ancient forms of wisdom, as "the wisdom literature" in the Hebrew Bible and Stoic, Cynic, and Epicurean writings, contain recommendations to wariness in regard to the seductive and tinsel character of life. For these ancients true wisdom is simplicity in terms of life-style as well as the prioritizing of goods, which are of necessity finite. The point is, are they not right? Is it not possible to get it right and see life comprised exclusively of finite goods that can be hierarchically arranged? And is the therapeutic task not to eradicate and demythologize the futile fluke endowment of an infinite passion (cf. Kierkegaard) or will which generates an endless "neurotic" search for self-adequation?

Our answer is that this is only partially correct. Obviously we can get it right by, e.g., avoiding wantonness and prioritizing the relatively necessary finite goods of life. But is the horizon of life, "happiness" (*eudaimonia* or the blessed life comparable to the indwelling of the guardian spirit of the god), able to be determined as merely the indeterminate "more of the same," as in the Kantian incremental approximation of the infinite ideal, and therefore is not the indeterminate elusive halo or horizon of life, which is ineluctable, itself the source of the illusory overdetermination? Or is it not essentially ambiguous? Is not "happiness" as the elusive background halo of life "a good that is *other* to everything we do, but is also *in* everything we do," "a good that shows up in all the good activities while never being possessed or done purely and simply by itself"?[13] But how are we to think of this being *other* to all we do and in everything we do which is never possessed and attained simply by itself? If we think of this formulation as capturing what Aristotle meant by human happiness, what did he have in mind when he contrasted human happiness with that other absolute or supreme happiness that seemingly beckoned to him as at the edge of the merely human happiness?[14] Was he being wistful in regard to human happiness because life's horizon beckoned to a "more" that he presumed the gods to have? What does each of us "have in mind" when, after chasing the promises of blessedness of the career, glory, status, love, power, and beauty, we find, when in their possession, i.e., in the filled intention, a disillusionment? Is the illusion an illness or is there in that which is *other* to all we do and possess a cipher of something more that merits philosophical examination? Even the wise recommendation to recognize and cherish the occasions when we may be pleased with our lives (as in "wake up and smell the roses") points to the inveterate and pervasive inadequation with ourselves which tends to deprive us of the will to pause and take delight in the blessed moments where contentment is appropriate.

The most comprehensive theory for understanding these matters is the phenomenological consideration that our epistemic and moral agency is lived within an infinite horizon. On this basis Husserl himself argued that it is no accident that we, immersed in the details of life in our sizing it up, planning, striving, deciding, appreciating, etc., *never arrive at a state of satisfaction*. This means no satisfaction is "true and complete." The reason is that satisfaction points ineluctably to the totality of life of the person, to a "unity in the totality of habitual validities which transcends all finitude." The unity of the concrete personality exceeds what is offered in a particular value or validity within the personal life-world; indeed, it exceeds the unity of a "concrete community of persons living in the open historicity of the streaming of time and the world." Thus each patent explicit willing has a "latent 'will-horizon.'" This latent will-horizon becomes patent and explicit in the course of the individual's development not in the sense that the horizon is fleshed out with explicit content but in the sense that the horizon as horizon is palpable – just as we noted how a mystery or a secret, as the withholding of the truth of a matter, is itself manifest without that which is hidden becoming manifest. And this latent will-horizon can become awakened in the community of individuals in the course of its development so that there can emerge a sense that the actuality of this community is surrounded by this potentiality and latency.[15] Further, given both of these considerations as well as the scarcely avoidable learning that derives from what life's flow of experience has to teach, it is irrational to seek one's peace and joy in the adequate fulfillment of one's aspirations. To expect fulfillment of all one's desires, wishes, and plans is unreasonable in as much as the flow of experiences teaches that the meaning of life is laced with irrationality, surds, and disappointments.[16]

Besides, joy is not properly a *telos* of our agency but what accompanies the striving after and the realization of goals. Husserl acknowledges the special joy in the striving and attainment of the goal, but the goal is the appreciated and striven for, not the joy accompanying the appreciating and valuing which often are part of the striving. If I make the joy itself the goal, and this is something I am free to do, we have quite a different matter. But it is not clear that we wind up with what we initially strove for. If I strive for joy, then the joy itself is valued as a telos, and this is different than the joy accompanying the striving and attaining of a goal other than it.[17]

What is eidetically evident is that we live within a cognitive, conative, and volitional horizon where "a More" always beckons. And this cognitive and axiological "More" is inseparably tied to the horizon of the Not Yet that surrounds what is present. This is a basic feature that pervades all of our waking life. At the most basic level of wakeful perception there "is a pretention to accomplish something that, by its very nature, it is not in a position to accomplish."[18] In this very "pretention" we have the fundamental ambiguity of the "basic situation," indeed the ambiguity of the "basic limit-situation." In our perceptual presentation of events, tasks, people, etc., "in the flesh" or "in person," there are always outstanding facets. As Husserl put it:

> No final presentation in the flesh is ever reached in the mode of appearance as if it would present the complete, exhausted Itself of the object. Every appearance implies a *plus ultra* in the empty horizon. And since every perception does indeed pretend to give the object [completely] in the flesh in every appearance, it in fact and by its very nature constantly pretends to accomplish more than it can accomplish.[19]

The life of the "heart" (*das Gemüt*), Husserl's term for the primal presencing as the foundation of the I-center, and as it is prior to the acts of cognition or volition, is the centripetal center (dative of manifestation) that is affected by the distinct allures of the perceptual world. Further, along with being the centripetal center of affections of the allure of the world, it is as well the centripetal center of the ongoing temporal syntheses of the totality of these allures. These past and future allures, called forth by way of association, tug at our attention as more or less relevant frameworks for our thought and agency. Because of this massive horizon provided by the "heart," ordinary perception "is a constant pretention to accomplish something that, by its very nature, it is not in a position to accomplish."

Kant was surely right in calling attention to the regulative character of "the idea" that frames our epistemic, moral, and axiological striving. But he also found it philosophically unacceptable to transform this (for him) *assumed* or *postulated* infinite horizon, however ineluctable it is in the ongoing epistemic and moral life, into some perceptual-phenomenological given. And a fortiori he rejected envisaging it as an ontological surety, e.g., the actuality of an unconditioned being. Similarly, for phenomenology the ineluctable proto-thesis of this endless horizon (which for phenomenology is co-given and not assumed or postulated) cannot amount to the positing of an infinite transcendent *being*. Whether phenomenology could be moved to affirm that there is some transcendent being which founds the co-posited and ineluctably affirmed horizon is a central theme in the philosophical phenomenology of religion. We will touch upon an aspect of this matter later in this section. But in any case the inveterate temptation to this "transcendental illusion," the "pretention" to accomplish in one's striving-presencing more than one can, is at the basis of the ambiguity of this fundamental situation.

At the base of the I-center is the élan or general feeble will of the primal presencing passively-synthetically bringing about a synthesis of one's whole life. This general will surpasses any particular will and any particular willing is inadequate to this general feeble will. We propose that we think of the "myself," in the establishment of its personhood, as a *dynamism* or entelechial principle that inaugurates this general willing of the person. We might call this "empersonation," because, like "incarnation" or "enworlding," there is suggested that the dynamic principle is transcendent as to its origin and yet its fuller life is in the immanent actualization of itself in, e.g., the body and world. "Empersonation," however, suggests "impersonation" and we do *not* want any hint that there is impersonation here by the "myself". It is not at all as if what was occurring was a full integral person, a homunculus, taking on the appearance of another person who she, in fact, was not. But the personal essence is not absolutely stable and there are profound changes in personality and radical alterations of the person and this would be hinted at in "empersonation." We find the term "personification" slightly more appropriate than "empersonation," even though it too is capable of misleading. Here we do not mean to say that a person represents or stands for some universal quality – which latter in fact is the more basic and more real consideration; we do not want to suggest that an abstract communicable ideal entity is instantiated in a person, as when we say "Peter personifies patience." Rather, the "myself," even though an abstract philosophical consideration, is a unique essence individuated *per se*. And as the dynamism of the realization of the person its function is not the instantiation of a universal. Yet "personification," as its etymological root suggests, is the making of the person and this gets close to the heart of the issue.

As such the "myself" is not inert but, as some Scholastics might have put it, it is the *nisus*, *pondus*, and *conatus* of the substance of the person. We have claimed (in Book 1, Chapter V, §3) that "will" might be argued to be one of the "tautological properties" of the "myself." We have also proposed (in the same place) that the "myself" or "I myself" is the bare substrate of the embodied person in the world. The person is this "myself" laden with qualities or properties; the person is this "accidentalized 'myself.'" As so embodied or personified, the "myself" is inseparable from intentional consciousness, the general will, and temporality – even though it can be brought to light in non-ascriptive reference as what is non-sortal. These, the "myself," along with intentional consciousness, the general will, and temporality, are "moments" constitutive of the elemental conditions of personhood. While the "myself" informs both the general will and temporality, there is a certain interpenetrating isomorphism in the moments which comprise the general will and temporality. This is indicated in passive synthesis as not only an interplay of presence and absence, but an ongoing nisus toward consistency, unity, and harmony. In fact, this interpenetration of will-ing and temporality is a rather round-about, but analytical, way of affirming that we best understand intentionality as the personified "myself's" consciousness of having a pervasive tending or tendency and not being merely non-reflexively self-aware.[20] Willing at its basis, we have seen, is "intending"; it is myself moving myself to bring about what is not actual through a deed enacted as done by me. I will what draws me to be realized by me according to my capability. (Cf. our discussion of "intending" in the prior section.) That is, I will now what is not yet through my having been. In my desiring-presencing and willing I extend beyond what is present to me. And this which is beyond moves me or draws me to do, on the basis of what I am and have been, what is of importance to me as I am and have come to be. What is present in my desiring-presencing and willing appears as it does by its being inseparable from my forecasting of what I want to be according to what I am capable of bringing about. As a person determining the world and myself within the open cognitive and axiological horizon I am always present to myself as not yet complete. Indeed, it is inconceiv-able that I be present to myself actually (with no surplus of empty intentions) as all that I can be – and thus with a coincidence between "I am" and "I can" – and thus without an open axiological cognitive horizon, and still be myself as a person in the world with others.

When we claim that the "myself" is a dynamism that "personifies itself" and thus the person is born by the general will inaugurated by the "myself," we make, needless to say, a speculative leap. (We will return to this speculation at the conclusion of this chapter and in the last chapters of this book.) It is a speculation because the "myself," as brought to light in reflection on self-awareness, as well as in our non-ascriptive referring through the indexical "I," as well as in the thought experiments, and in the transcendental reduction, is without any specific striving or willing toward any specific horizon. Here the "myself" is bereft of properties, habituality, and projects. Yet what we know in our proper cognitive acts of knowing is the personification of the "myself" who is laced with properties; we know the "myself" only as an abstract moment in what we are calling its "personification," i.e., the full concretion of what we refer to with "I."

Further, the "myself," apart from the important considerations which permit the "myself" to come to light abstracted from its concrete personhood, is always lived as a person in the world with others. And this life, we propose, is pervaded by a general latent will heading toward an intersubjective ideal.[21] Personhood is thus carried by the "myself" functioning dynamically, expressing itself in the flow of cognitive acts, drives, longings, strivings, etc., but more decisively in discrete acts emergent from the I-center. "Position-taking acts" is a general term for such acts wherein the "myself," functioning dynamically as regulative idea of the person, realizes itself in finite I-acts. Through definite explicit finite I-acts one self-realizes the infinite ideal of oneself.

To shore up our position as at least implicitly Husserlian we may note that Husserl spoke at least once of his own philosophy as a universal voluntarism. For our purposes here of special interest is his view of a basic *will of the I* (*immerzu bin ich Willensich...ein im Ichpol zentriertes Gewebe von Willensmodis... Regierung des ganzen wachen und durch all Wachperioden hindurch synthetisch sich einigen- den ichlichen Daseins unter der Idee eines Willenslebens...*) that pervades all the particular drives, impulses, wishes, wants, and willings which may appear to have nothing to do with one another apart from belonging to the I – and these, therefore, may be said to be modes of will. This universal willing pervades clearly the per- sonal I in its essential identity and gives to all the particular interests the pervasive sameness of the willing of this one same person. All the interests are led by the rule of the wakeful synthesizing unifying egological principle facing an ideal of a unified life-will, "in which all the particular interests are not only, as they always and necessarily are, woven together, but all are subordinated under the unity of a single interest, a life-goal-interest, which has all the particular goals subordinate to itself and giving to them a predelineated form once and forever."[22] This description applies to the personal I, the "myself" personified, as we have put it. Here Husserl clearly distinguished willing as the intentional purposeful striving from this massive willing which holds together, joins and holds sway in a unified connectedness all of the active and passive affections, impressions, etc. Here will is co-extensive with waking life and perhaps with aspects of sleeping life. In any case, it holds what has "fallen asleep" as a sedimented retention in readiness to spring into actuality with the appropriate associated present occasion. In the spirit of Husserl we are propos- ing that we envisage this comprehensive will as the general personal life "instinct" or "drive" that the "myself" bestows in its process of personification. Of course, we have here not to do with the "ontic" drives of hunger, sex, breathing, etc., but these, although clearly "autonomic," nevertheless are under the sway of the general will and its essential function in personification, and in this sense they are modes of it.

The general will may be regarded after the manner of a drive or instinct in as much as it itself is not brought about by a will nor by reason of any prior experi- ence of an object of desire (or objectifying act). Both instincts and the general will derive their conative force from origins which are hidden and which head toward the filling of empty intentions, the horizons of which are in no way or scarcely predelineated. The pervasive teleology of consciousness and the I-life is described by Husserl as having its origin in a "transcendental instinct." This has symmetry with his discussions of the general will. It also may be regarded as quite different from a wish because although a wish might be a necessary condition for the realization of its objects it is not a sufficient condition. Instincts, on the other hand, e.g., breathing and hunger, might be thought of as containing within themselves both the necessary and sufficient power to realize their objects.[23]

Important for us is Husserl's analogy (in the same MS, D 14, 28 ff.) with the vocational or career will/interest which subordinates all the other willings. The general will similarly but in a more fundamental way holds together all of life's interests in the unity of the interest of one's life, just as the career will/interest subordinates and hold together all of the interests, projects, etc., of the career. But, it is clear, that the life-will facing the regulative ideal of personal life-ideal rarely ever reaches the level of explicitness and focus of the vocational ideal and vocational will. These issues, we shall see, are fundamental matters for the constitution of the moral person.

Nevertheless, it is clear that the career is chosen within the horizon of the general will and the general will is not chosen in the light of anything but it is that within which all choices are made.

When we will anything or undertake anything in the pursuit of our career, we will each thing in the light of the career choice and its idea or ideal. In this sense whatever we will in the framework of the career, in the service of the career, we ineluctably will in the light of the apperceived telos of the idea or ideal of the career. The ideal is willed in everything, but it is not, once having chosen the career path, something which itself we will. In the analogy with life everything is willed in subordination to the ideal of the life-will and each thing we will we will with the apperception of willing of the ideal. The ideal is willed in each particular willing but it itself is not something to be willed. The original will to or choice of the career may be renewed and thereby re-energizing the devotion to the manifold individual willings that are entailed in the career, but how can the career itself as the endless open horizon with an infinity of implied will acts be willed? Clearly one may do this by a self-identifying act with a remarkable synthetic, i.e., polythetic, objectifying of one's career as it may be conjured up in a cipher, memory, or ritual. As we shall see, for Husserl it is important to be able to gather the ideal of life into a kind of unifying resolve so that we may gain clarity and focus in its regard.

The general will, like an instinct, is also a kind of desire and longing for an absent good. Of course, as the framework for all our willings and desires it itself can never be desired in one of the specific projects we desire; it cannot be willed as a present good. Typically the ideal of the general will, like the career–goal, is that towards which one moves step by step. Yet, as we have noted, there is in the living of life a propensity to conceive of this open emptily intended ideal as something to be willed or loved in some form of presencing filled intention. This goes under many names: success, bliss, happiness, and the numerous symbols for what is of unconditionally important power. Clearly such interpretations of the emptily intended horizon of the will reveal the ambiguity. It is uncontroversial that the horizon points to an endlessly determinable indeterminacy. And as an idea or ideal there is a sense of an axiological "more." But to name it an unconditioned Good in itself as do the various religious interpretations is surely a speculative leap. Indeed for Kant, Husserl, and Heidegger, in spite of their different categories or concepts, it is a categorial mistake and what cannot be thought without contradiction. In Kant's terms, the "unconditioned is intrinsic to the idea of reason" and is what "drives us necessarily beyond the limit of experience and all appearing," and is that which reason requires, "with necessity and with full legitimacy, to be in things themselves in order to complete the series of conditions."[24] Even though the unconditioned *cannot be thought* without contradiction, that it is ineluctably affirmed is in itself of philosophical interest.

Let us, with Maurice Blondel, call what we are naming the dynamism or general will of the personified "myself" the "willing will"; let us also name the explicit acts in the course of life, displays of "the willed will."[25] This situation of the willing will realizing itself in the willed will can be thought of analogously as the situation of desire and love in an extended sense. In the desire of erotic love, there is a vivid demonstration of the tension between the willing- and willed-will. Nothing that the lover does to express his love is adequate to the love that is in his heart. This is captured in Shakespeare's Troilus' words to Cressida: "This [is] the monstrosity in love, lady, that the will is infinite and the execution confin'd, that the desire is boundless and the act a slave to limit."[26]

The horizon of this original general will has an intertwined twofold aspiration: (1) it aspires to an unconditioned and infinite goodness by way of an adequation with the original will's infinite scope, even though it can only realize finite goods; (2) it strives to realize the ideal true "I myself" through the personal agency of I-acts that bring about this self-adequation. Thus behind all our agency is the dynamism of this latent "willing will" which is tacitly present in more or less explicit wishes, willings, longings, strivings, desires, etc. These forms in which the latent will is present take definitive self-determining form when they serve as motivating forces for a will act, i.e., when they emerge out of the I-center. But even in the forms of desire and striving I am capable of a confusion that permits "myself" as willing will to inflate or magnify selected goods beyond their proper boundaries, and perhaps the most treacherous form this takes is the inflation of a false version of oneself for the ideal true "I myself." Thus, from this "idolatrous" distance certain goods, not least of which are certain versions of oneself, appear to be what we most truly want and need. We all know the perennial candidates: fame, glory, power, wealth, love, etc. Our explicit will-acts that emerge from the I-center are ways we identify ourselves with these goods. These explicit acts reveal also the excess of "myself" as the willing will, in the wake of which the explicit will-acts (acts of the willed-will) take shape, come to light. Through the acts emergent from the I-center, which seeks to be adequate to the "myself's" excess through the willing will, the inadequation of ourselves with ourselves comes to light.

Most of our agency is arranged around choosing particular goods as leading toward those candidates that will provide us with the endless fulfillment we require. Behind all agency there is thus the shadow of a kind of analogous idolatry, which in fact is a form of self-love and an attempt at self-adequation. As Kant urged that the sublimity of nature was a surreptitious projection (a "subreption") of the sublimity of the soul (a provocative thesis whose truth we will not examine here), so we are urging that the willing will is behind the propensity to *infatuation* as a typical way we get lost in the world's projects and certain versions of ourselves. Our modern English word, "infatuation," lets both *fatum*, i.e., fate or destiny, as well as *fatuus*, i.e., inspired, or insane and foolish, be heard. In action infatuation may well seem to be inspiration and one's destiny. In the sober light of day or in the aftermath of the pursuit it can appear to be foolishness or madness. Lovers and philosophers, Plato taught us, were both born of the god and appear to be mad. (From at least the third-person perspective, it seems in the nature of both philosophy and love that the truth of Plato's opinion is plausible even if not able to be made apodictically evident.)

Just as we do not constitute or create our unique ipseities, nor do we create the temporalizing from which the ipseity is inseparable, so we did not constitute or will this willing will. And because this willing will launches us beyond what we can and do possess, must we not say that there is an *essential* self-inadequation? As we are given to ourselves and are not creators of our individual essences, so it is not given to us to find any willed good or any self-determination capable of consummating our conation and willing. Rather, we are forced to will our selves as infinitely inadequate to ourselves, and yet both the individual essence and the willing will are constitutive of our most intimate selves and these are behind, i.e., they are the principles of, everything we will.

Existenz, we may say, exemplarily comes forth in the willing of itself in the face of the essential inadequacy of itself, as willing will, to itself, to its willed will. This recalls Jaspers' ultimate or basic limit-situation, i.e., the permanent lived discrepancy between existence (*Dasein*, i.e., the realm of thingly material objects to which I myself and others also, in part, belong, and with which I have a tendency to identify myself) and Being which is other and transcendent to such existence and which only comes to light when Existenz is illumined. To will "the one thing necessary" in regard to oneself as Existenz is not to will any particular thing about oneself or about the world even though particular things can became means to or ciphers of the *unum neccessarium*. Rather, it is to will what is other than mere existence or the realm of things in the world. What is other than existence from the point of view of existence is nothingness; for this reason willing the one thing necessary in regard to oneself as Existence resembles one's facing one's death, i.e., facing nothingness. Here too everything is at stake in the sense of our imminent absolute loss of being, and yet we face as a "phenomenon" only the nothingness or no-thingness of what is other than or beyond "existence," beyond the impenetrable darkness of death. Of course, this "other than" or "beyond" may find a symbol or cipher in the existence that is present before us.

This "fact" of the essential inadequation of the self with itself is a central theme in the Neo-Platonic tradition where there is claimed an essential restlessness of the human heart, and this is believed to be the basis for moments of melancholy where we "fall into grief like exiles," and where there is found a "short and false sweetness" soon covered by a "long and true bitterness."[27]

But the question thus surfaces whether indeed this restlessness of the heart is not appropriately understood as a kind of pathology born of what Kant regards as the effort to think what is inherently contradictory. The evidence for the essential inadequation is odd, because although someone may find it, in his or her own case, to be evident, with an essential necessity, that one exists in self-inadequation, we know very well that another may deny it and find our claim utterly gratuitous, if not fatuous. Further, this other person may well find cause for resentment if we presume to transpose our experience on top of his. And who can gainsay someone whom we admire when he tells us that he is absolutely content with his life or that life has had no essential inadequation with his horizon of hopes and desires? Are we empowered to say that because of the eidetic necessities regarding the "more" of the epistemic and axiological horizon of the world that he cannot be truthfully assessing his situation? That would surely be received as both boorish and ungracious. Indeed, he might further say that he finds it his good fortune that any such talk of "essential self-inadequation" is always meaningless for him. If "essential inadequation" means "essential disappointment" and that means that that which is achievable in life does not saturate the infinite yearning, our skeptic might find this trivial because that is what any adult believes. Or, he might find it false because he denies such an infinite yearning. Doubtless, he might add, finitude, and surely death, make it impossible to enjoy the meeting of other people and think other thoughts and fight other battles, discover other truths, hear new musical performances, receive loving embraces, etc. But, he will say, one can and ought to recognize and rejoice in one's finitude; that is obviously all there is. Being discontent because one is finite is a kind of pathology founded in a false, if not absurd, position. Besides, there is the simple wonder of the "gift" (without a giver) of having the chance to take this ride. How can life be an "essential disappointment?"

Thus the above description of essential self-inadequation is not de facto universally compelling when it is applied to an essential understanding of the self or the "existential situation." This raises the question of whether what is at stake is an eidetic claim and a kind of necessity lived by Existenz, and not Existenz as such but certain Existenzen. We may ask whether being aware of Existenz in this form is a real possibility for just some persons; whether the privileging of the experience of these other persons for whom life has essential disappointment is not elevating a pathology to a norm.

Surely one for whom the evidence for the essential disappointment is compelling holds it as an essential feature of personal being in the world and his Existenz. It is indeed part of the otherwise scarcely analyzable meaning of a limit-situation. Indeed, for such a person, it is a synthetic a priori feature of the world. Yet there is no logical contradiction in holding its opposite even though this reversal would essentially transform the sense of one's life and world. The horizon may merely beckon to more finite goods, and some of these, but not necessarily all, might well bring a sense of a greater fulfillment to life. Indeed, the claim for phenomenological evidence pro or contra the "essential disappointment" thesis may for the skeptics reveal more about how the particular person is in the world than about how the world and personal being in the world are essentially the same for everyone. But, again, for the Existenz for whom the insufficiency defines being in the world her incapacity for self-adequation gets at the core sense of who she is and what her life is.

Furthermore, it is not merely the crypto-theological tone that observations about the insufficiency of life have (and which some may well find repugnant) which undermine their credibility for some; rather it is the fact that even the one, the Existenz, for whom the evidence is today compelling may, by reason of often a subtle transformation in perspective that settles in like the dissipation of the haze by the burning sun, tomorrow find the opposite view more compelling. The instability of the evidence itself then becomes a crisis at the core of the person – analogous to the way the third-person perspective on death may some days seem to outweigh the first-person transcendental one, or the way this third-person perspective may even in a moment of *acedia* outweigh the awakening to Existenz in confronting one's own death.

However, the eidetic claim necessary for the "essential self inadequation" or "insufficiency of life thesis" gets strengthened when we distinguish what we may call "test cases" for the doctrine of *essential inadequation* from the more familiar and undeniable failures, disappointments, or lived insufficiencies that come upon us in the coursing of our life. This essential inadequation appears in the failures occurring when we, in the pursuit of real possibilities and successes in the course of our struggles, prevail, i.e., when we have attained what we have longed and striven for. Jean Nabert is doubtless right that the fuller more significant sense of life being essentially insufficient, if not disappointing, and pervaded by an essential failure "will appear only when the self [read "person": JGH] no longer has the feeling of having remained inferior to its deepest possibilities." In such a case it is evident that being "I myself this person" is precisely being one with this essential self-inadequation, and *this* sense of "failure" is different from that wherein one finds obstacles to the will's expansion in the world or in aspects of oneself. Essential self-inadequation is manifest most poignantly in the awareness of having actualized one's potentialities and realized through one's own agency one's personal being. One realizes further that one has been, in the course of one's personal life, as successful, fortunate, prosperous, etc. as one could reasonably hoped to have been. It is precisely the "failure" revealed exemplarily in success that reveals this disappointment as an "index of a desire embodied in determined goals but never exhausted by these goals and their success."

It is reported of St. Thomas Aquinas that when near death he valued all of his work to be no more than "straw." And Aristotle, who cannot be accused of a Christian theological bias, displayed an awareness of a "more" to life as we know it in an apperception of a superior form of happiness than what we attain in our lives. He did this when he observed that the (intimated or apperceived) absolutely good in itself cannot be "realized in action or attained by man"; he also distinguished between the *telos* of human life that is final in every respect, a state of being blessed, and the kind of blessedness or bliss that accords with the actual human condition with all its contingencies and surds.[28]

As long as we are immersed in the confrontation with opposition and struggle, as long as we remain removed from one another as *Existenzen*, the sense of failure's proper or deeper meaning remains hidden because we will be tempted to regard it as tied to the contingent complications and conflicts of the world, or dependent on conditions which make success or happiness difficult but not truly impossible. Thus we will regard the failure as a passing and relative experience. When, however, we realize the difference between the essential failure that is manifest in supreme success and contentment and these particular contingent faults, worldly mishaps, and disappointments then we realize that the "I myself" as this person in the world is essentially inadequate to itself and essentially superior or transcendent to the world and nature. This entails a liberating insight that frees from all "fallacious hope as well as from all pessimism."[29]

But we might ask, when does such a "test case" get realized? Who ever is aware of fully actualizing one's talents and of being as successful as she could have been? Is this not proximate to envisaging oneself as all that one could possibly be so that the axiological horizons are collapsed? No, not necessarily. Nabert's point can be taken to be that when by the common standards of being a "success" or even in the case of meeting our own standards of success, there is still abides a sense of inadequacy and incompletion.

Nevertheless such a transcendental philosophical move will probably not be decisive in delivering the evidence, especially for our contented materialist friends. Nevertheless, it is of great philosophical importance that such an important philosophical issue must be decided by each in the first-person, and no one else's solution can replace this. Second- and third-person evidence is not merely inconclusive; it would seem to be irrelevant. It is a unique evidence for a unique Existenz. This is, as Bakhtin would put it, a no-alibi matter: no one else can answer this matter for us. Nevertheless, what can be said is that for the person for whom evidence on behalf of the essential insufficiency prevails, it comes down to affirming something like this: No matter how wide I expand the horizon of my willing, and this expansion itself is not primarily a matter of my choice and willing it, my action explodes the parameters, i.e., they become ever larger. I do not have the power to limit or control this incessant enlargement. In this we may speak of the nothingness of what I will in terms of its insufficiency. I will of necessity something other than what I explicitly will, something in comparison with which what I explicitly will can appear as nothing. Yet without this which is apart or other than what I will, that which I explicitly will would lose much if not all of its allure; and yet it, apart from the manifold goods that I will, would not appear at all.[30] "I will; and, if nothing of what is willed satisfies me, or rather, if I will nothing of what is and of what I am, it is because I will myself, more than all that is and all that I am."[31] There is thus revealed a sense of "I myself" which transcends all that we experience and will, and this sense of "I myself" we will or will to be more than all we experience and will. The essence of "the meaning life" is to will one's true self, whatever that might mean in terms of specifiable goods and projects. Of course the "we" here is only a presumptuous royal or editorial we for the contented materialist friends.

Still, one may ask, could not the infinite will-horizon simply point to "more of the same," i.e., endlessly more finite goods? And, indeed, if it is in some sense knowable and able to be pursued or chosen, it must. Yet we must face the following paradox that seems to be implicit in the position of willing will and the essential inadequacy: I must choose because I ineluctably will what cannot be present as something able to be chosen or possessed. The intimations of and desire for happiness which are inseparable from the axiological horizon of the person, which itself is rooted in the "latent will-horizon," are ineluctable. In this sense they are necessary. But they also seem to be not really possible, i.e., realizable, in the normal course of things. Here we have at least two options: Either the basic situation is absurd or life is surrounded by an impenetrable horizon of mystery – quite like death surrounds life. That is, in the latter case, it is surrounded by a "I do not know what." (See our discussions of death and mystery in Chapter II.)

The first option is the strongest argument by those for whom the case for a latent willing-will is either invalid or for whom it is to be suppressed or eradicated as a pathology. In what follows we will not take the route of ruling in advance what is or is not possible and we will take the evidence for the self-inadequation as established even though we acknowledge the possibility of leaving skeptical friends unpersuaded. In any case we will continue to marshal evidence for it. We will thus assume that there is an excess which informs the basic dynamism of personal consciousness and this accounts for the sense of insufficiency and "failure" that we call, with Blondel and Nabert, self-inadequation. Whether it is merely a hole in being, a useless passion, as Sartre would say, is not yet our preoccupation.

A final consideration is that if the matter must be decided ultimately in one's first-person experience, and if one has persuaded oneself that such is of no account, that one has got oneself right, so to speak, when one knows how to talk about oneself as a machine or a neuro-physiological process, and that values themselves are to be understood in third-person quantifiable terms whose significance is in their correlation with the neuro-physiological processes, the discussions we have just undertaken, as well as all perhaps all the others in both volumes of this work, have no merit whatsoever. Then obviously, given such a meta-theory, any talk of the "essential inadequation" is so much irrelevant gibberish.

§3. Position-Taking Acts as the Medium of Personhood

In the previous section we attended to self-inadequation as launching us beyond the sphere of the goods we choose, but we only mentioned the connection with the willing will of "I myself" problematically moving us toward the constitution of our personhood. In this regard we have three theses to develop: The first and more abstract one is that ipseity as the "myself" is actualized in the world through personhood; in this sense, personhood is the telos of the "myself." But personhood is also the means because the ideal person, which is the telos, is realized through the personification of the "myself," i.e., actual development and metamorphoses of the person. But the "myself" is not discontinuous with the ideal person even though there is not an absolute identity. After all, the unfolding "from start to finish" is of and by me myself and the ideal person as the telos of "myself" aspires to be precisely the most perfect actualization under the circumstances of *me myself.*

Second, just as personhood is the medium of the realization of the "myself," so position-taking acts are the medium of personhood. "Medium" as applied to person here is the means, "that through which"; but the means itself contains the driving force, the dynamism which we will name the "entelechy." In Aristotelian scholasticism and Leibniz "entelechy" refers to what is inseparably both a "formal" and a "final" cause. The "myself" is the formal cause in the special, stipulated sense that the person throughout all its changes in its "Whats" (roles, identities, character, moods, etc.) is pervaded by the same Who, the same *haecceity* or *individual essence.* (See Book 1, Chapters III and V.) This expression "formal cause" is, of course, idiosyncratically used here because in the ancient tradition it referred to a communicable, participable What. Yet we have attempted to show the appropriateness of holding that this Who, this individual essence, is not a What if that requires its being or having manifest essential communicable properties.

This "formal cause," i.e., the Who or "myself" alone, however, is abstract and incomplete. Of course, we only know it as alone and incomplete by way of non-ascriptive reference or non-reflective self-awareness or through thought experiments. Concretely it is the "I myself" of the developing person facing her infinite ideal. That is, we know the "myself" in the living of life as tied to its personification and the person's struggle to realize her *telos*, i.e., the "true self" and "self-ideal." That is, in the living of life we know the "myself" not merely in non-ascriptive reference and experience and thought-experiments but also as "entelechy," as the dynamic principle of personification which is both formal and final cause. "Entelechy" in Aristotle is often translated as "actuality" or the state of being actually complete. But this emphasizes the telos as achieved rather than the process or development toward the telos. In the latter sense, surely also intended by Aristotle, it is what has the end immanently in itself in a way which is not yet complete (*entelos-hecheia*) but which has a drive (or dynamism) toward this completion.[32] The position-taking acts as acts of self-realization ideally reflect that entelechy but they need not do so. In any case, the personal essence is a work in progress because the entelechy opens the person to an infinite ideal of herself.

This brings us to our third thesis: There are whole-hearted or gathering acts that approximate the willing-will in a more concentrated way than do the typical position-taking acts because they are self-identifying. We best make this case by turning once again to the theme of position-taking acts and deepening our appreciation of what they achieve.

We may here recall our earlier remarks on "soul" (see Book 1, Chapter III, §3). We may think of the ongoing flux of the stream of consciousness with its passive flow of innate impulses, repulsions, drives as well as the whole realm of passive syntheses, associations, modalizations, i.e., the "sedimentation of "reason" or position-taking acts, as the realm of "soul," the tug of which contents, in the normal course of things, resides at the periphery of the I-center or "spirit." This realm of "soul" has its primal *logos* or rationality and conation quite apart from *me* or the realm of the agency of the "I myself." Soul's primal *logos* is the automatic, passive-synthetic working out the unity in the plurality and disunity, the sameness in difference, the whole present within the parts of the stream of consciousness. As rooted in time-consciousness its work sets the primal scene of the basic form of "the unity of identity or objectiveness, and then of the forms of connection, of coexistence and succession of all objectivities being given to consciousness."[33]

The passive synthesis of time-consciousness may be said to join *logos* or proto-rationality and will in this elemental striving for this unity, harmony, and consistency throughout the flux. Indeed, its ongoing achieving may be seen to have a general volitional sense. The stream of consciousness, the incessant event of primal presencing, is pervaded by the dialectic of itself being always now but always a different Now. Further, it incessantly elapses into no longer and is always on the verge of not yet. These, the incessant No Longer and Not Yet, are contained in the always Now which is both always different and always the same. It is always the same in its present being inseparable from an always different No Longer and different Not Yet, always the same in its presently having an ever changing retentional and protentional horizon. This streaming has a motion that is always a massive synthesis of all the retentions of retentions and protentions toward a teleological ideal of harmony, unity, and consistency of all the phases of life. Each phase of life that passes or has passed is incessantly integrated into a unity now and there is a pervasive ideal of harmony that occasionally is violated by inadvertence, self-deception, illness, fatigue, etc.

This massive passive flow and general will is in play when I am peacefully merely "watching," e.g., the sea and delighting in its colors and moods. I might well experience a joyous contentment because the roll of the waves and the glistening sunlight bring in cascades of association with my childhood spent at a seaside similar to this one. As I gaze, I see the sea with the sky above; I, without reflection, perhaps intend the sea as limitless and relish the soothing nature of the sea as a metaphor, even though I know in a marginal way that it is not an endless expanse of water (I have seen its boundaries on maps) and that the toxics in the water contradict the redeeming consoling appearance of the water. In spite of the pleasures of the metaphorical reverie, I "know" (i.e., I have appropriated the knowledge of those I believe in a position to know) it is finite and not an infinite boundless abyss, i.e., I "know" it is eighty fathoms at its deepest, even though I do not see the bottom or the remote shores. Apart from the reverie I apperceive what is under the surface of the waters (e.g., the fish afflicted with mercury) even though I see only the surface. I delight in the cloud formations in a similar reverie even though there might surface a note of sadness because I cannot blot out the thought that the cloud-formations bear acid rain and other pollutants coming from the southeast. This spontaneous knowledge of the harm done to the sea, the wildlife, myself, and others thickens my perception and casts a shadow of sadness over the delight in the beauty of the sea's appearing.

This slice of the world is present thus as a categorical, syntactic, conjunctive value-whole that is not a result of *I* actually doing anything, but rather as a result of the ongoing passive synthesis of prior achievements that I incessantly undergo and go along with.

Now consider how the shriek of a bird might penetrate this relatively blissful contemplative trance and *I*, in order to determine the nature of the bird's call, must break the continuity of the passive flow. *I* insert myself in the passive flux, direct my attention, strive to get clear on the matter, and eventually determine whether it is a case of distress or only the petulant antics of a gull. Here I interrupt my passive enjoyment; here is where the realm of spirit or I as act-center may be seen to come into play. Here I may make a categorical determination that requires a kind of active intervention in the smooth passivity of my placid gazing: "That large gull is bullying the smaller one; shoo!"

The I of the person is the central agency that correlates with a life-world it has delineated for its theoretical and practical purposes. This *I* may not be actively "there" but rather may be only "undergoing" this implicitly categorically constituted world. The world appears as a categorical, syntactic and conjunctive whole because of the prior categorical intuitions, associations, and judgments achieved by the *I*. These manifold aspects of the world are there now in my actual gazing through the wonder of passive synthesis.

But my engagement is not merely an arrangement or constitution of the world; it is also world-maintenance. By interpreting, appropriately responding, i.e., acting upon, heeding, obeying, negating, quoting, reformulating, etc., I contribute to the maintenance and reshaping of this world held in common with others. As we have urged, this happens at passive and active synthetic levels. At the passive synthetic level I go along with the ongoing stream of my wakeful life; at the active level I punctuate, interrupt, delineate, revise, and appropriate this stream.

Husserl calls this active articulation of the world *position-taking acts*. They may be cognitive, as in insightfully getting the point, raising a question, making a judgment, withholding judgment, making a distinction, affirming an hypothesis, agreeing with an argument, etc. They may be also moral acts of valuings, deliberations, decisions promisings, etc. Moral acts of valuing participate in the position-takings of cognitive-theoretical acts by building on them. Whether cognitive-theoretical or practical-moral they are acts that not only delineate the world but shape one's personal being in the world with others.

Both the moral and cognitive position-taking acts have the general feature of what today we call "performatives." They are not merely displays but also a doing. They are achievements which, after the exemplary fashion of a promise, bind us in the present in a more or less determinate way to be and act in a certain way in the future. Both the moral and cognitive position-takings are something *I* do and are acts by which I acknowledge my unique display of and participation in the world, and for the achievement of this display and participation I have "no alibi."[34] I must do these and no one can do them for me. And when by force of circumstances or by reason of habit I enunciate views and adopt moral stances that are not really my own in terms of first-hand insight, but rather are those of others who have influenced me, I have the responsibility to myself and to others to take account of my dependency and not mask my own ignorance and passivity by giving the appearance of having knowledge and experience. Otherwise I am portraying myself to myself and others as what I am not and, at least in this respect, living the life of a fake.

Through position-taking acts I leave my unique signature which renders the world always also *my world*. The world which is the world for me, as *my* world, is dependent on my unique ipseity. World eludes an adequate proper articulation of its properties in propositions. This is true because the world itself is a *concretum*, and any propositions, even though of necessity "the same for us all," are founded on this *concretum*. Any propositional articulation of the world brings to light properties and features of the world but the endless concrete whole of the world still eludes these endless propositions. But further, in so far as this world is my world because it reflects the unique "I myself" actualizing itself, it necessarily is not capable of being simply the world as the "same for us all." There is a stamp of uniqueness pervading the personal life-worlds, even though the articulations in propositions necessarily have the feature of being "the same for us all." Nor, and this claim depends on the thesis that personhood is the medium of the "I myself," is my life-world capable of being perfectly duplicated in the science-fictional world of my ontological clone.

This claim stands in tension with our earlier appropriation of Klawonn's analysis that there is the possibility of there being identical properties for the cloned person and her world. (See Book 1, Chapter III, §1.) In this case, the personal life-world would admit of perfect duplication. Yet the personal life-world would itself bear this stamp of singularity in some way. Let us try to spell this out.

Of course, the evidence for the uniqueness of the personal life-world would itself not be a piece of evidence which is "the same for us all" in the way the things in the world or propositions about the world may be said to be evidently "the same for us all." Its being a unique world would be like, and inseparable from, the peculiar evidence for the unique ipseity. The proposition is evidently the same for us all that each is uniquely unique; but the unique uniqueness, i.e., the individual essence, is not a public matter, not a proposition, and in this sense the evidence for the unique essence is not the same for us all, even though the proposition that the "myself" is a unique essence is public; and for those who agree with it, so is the evidence as it emerges in first-person experience, the thought experiments, etc. It is a universal claim about a necessary state of affairs that becomes evident in philosophical reflection. But it is not evident as the same for us all, not a piece of public evidence in the sense that either the roundness of the sun or the properties of the number 3 are. "World" as such is precisely a genitive of appearing, i.e., the manifestation of things in the world and of the world itself as the horizon of these things. As such, "world" is necessarily a matter of common and public properties: For example, it is inhabited and co-constituted by people, there is the lived perceptual-kinaesthetic division of sky above and earth below, and there are living and non-living things.

Where then is there to be found this uniqueness of world? Note that here we are not referring to the uniqueness of one's world *in contrast to* the plurality of common and unique things and in contrast to the plurality of worlds one may be alleged to inhabit. Rather we are referring to how each may live uniquely in the one encompassing unique same world. May we not say that given the necessary relationship between the "myself" and its personal self-expression and self-realization in the world, that the evidence for the uniqueness of the world is to be found in the passive synthetic intuition of the world as the whole or all which incessantly frames every more or less explicit experience? This framing is the achievement of the person as the expression of the "myself" immersed in the world. World in this sense would not be the double or clone which would have a duplication of the same features or properties. Rather it would be the unique encompassing sense or feeling that would, as an ongoing synthesis, pervasively characterize all perceptual experience.

This would be to remind ourselves that the personal life-world is never pure noema, what is intended and a genitive of appearing, but is always also inseparably noesis, the lived presencing and felt-meaning. This felt-meaning obviously would not be a form of evidence "for us all," but especially qualified perceivers like lovers and parents could perhaps have an inkling for the uniqueness of the world. In which case there would be available in other than first-person experience evidence for this uniqueness. Thus they could come to recognize how the loved one or child saw things distinctively, why they singled this out rather than that, why their descriptions or sketches had such and such peculiarities, etc. Of course, because this would approach naming the distinctive properties, this "distinctiveness" would approach that which is in principle able to be cloned.

At the moral-ethical level, I act either according to my lights or not. In these acts, just as in cognitive position-taking acts, I do something, e.g., make a promise, a decision, speak truth to power, mislead, gossip, each of which takes only "so long," e.g., five seconds. With many moral acts, e.g., being patient, resisting a temptation of sensuality or infidelity, etc., there is no explicit constitution of a validity lasting for the indefinite future as there is in cognitive acts like making distinctions and judgments. But there is an implicit judgment of the rightness, the moral validity, of doing this at this time. A promise, of course, does constitute a validity that may last for the indefinite or definite future. There is also the tacit self-approbation of one's appropriately responding to conscience's indications of what sort of person one has professed to be.

All moral acts have a way of empowering or stalling our subsequent agency. They empower because they are reaffirmations of what sort of person one wants to be and therefore they are what we will call self-identifying acts. They further assure that the future, even if difficult, is possible because what it calls for we have already done; in this respect they both set a precedent and facilitate. They stall because a different course in the future must go against the sort of person one has determined one wants to be; this future course goes against the precedent and goes against oneself. And they do so for the indefinite future until we repudiate them and work against the precedent they set. As unrepudiated or unrepented they display the way vice vitiates: They establish both an inertia against change and a momentum to continue in a certain direction. Connected to this inertia and momentum are the inconsistencies or self-betrayals wherein we hide from ourselves either the professed personal essence indicated by conscience, or we hide from ourselves that the present deviation is a deviation. Because we are empowered by these acts or because we find ourselves weakened and diminished by these acts, both the inner tenor (*Befindlichkeit*) of our selves and our self-definition are affected. This is why self-esteem or self-disdain lies close to the center of what "I" refers to. (See below, Chapter V, §8.) The acts that empower us and are in our best interests enable us to esteem ourselves; those that tear us down and work against what we most want put us at odds with ourselves and generate a self-contempt. We noted earlier Aristotle's simile for such "voluntary acts": Once you have thrown a stone you cannot call it back. That is, our actions have a way of "sealing our fate" for better or for worse. Once we act or let ourselves act in this way the acts have not only the tendency to provide the comfortable future path, but a tendency to set up further similar patterns, e.g., those of impatience, cowardice, violence, sensuality, etc., as well those of self-control, patience, courage, compassion, etc.

At the cognitive-theoretical level, position-taking acts are ways I interpret my past and organize my present and future. (We, however, ought not to underestimate the implicit propositions, policy, and theoretical commitments that our moral and emotional acts contain.) Thus these acts, like the moral ones, are not merely world-directed; they too reflexively redound to me. My agency of manifestation is thankfully indebted to the habitualities of my prior acts of manifestation.

Let us consider how this is so. The categorical intuition by which I determine that the rock is volcanic and not a meteor, even if this is the result of believing the testimony of an expert and not a consequence of my own insight, takes only "so long," i.e., usually a brief psychological or worldly time. But its validity lasts "from now on," i.e., indefinitely until revoked. From now on this is the way this sort of rock gets categorically perceived. What I achieve cognitively now makes future demands on me without my having to do explicitly something extra. My judgement that P is q now will, through passive synthesis, surface in my subsequent reflections on both P and q, and to be true to myself I must integrate P is q into the wider fabric of my life. Thus, e.g., the volcanic rock on this beach which is thousands of miles from any known volcanic sites compels me to "see" this geological landscape's temporality; this might further provoke me to an awareness of how global weather produces enormous changes which in turn have enormous power such as to occasion glaciers that could have caused volcanic rock to be found in this place. Or should one reach the determination that the administration that governs one's country acts essentially not with an eye for protecting human rights and dignity or for the purpose of securing the common good, but rather is motivated primarily out of a desire for imperial power and corporate economic self-interest, then one is moved to link many aspects of one's social-political world. At the same time, there is determined not only the sense of the public statements and acts of this government, but inseparably how one will interpret the acts of this government, how one will monitor one's emotions, and how one will act in regard to this government.

The acts that shape the sense and validity of the world and the specifically moral acts that shape how one is in the world originate from the *I* and inform the world and one's being in the world; but they redound to shaping the habits of perception and agency of the agent of manifestation and moral agency. They are, as Husserl has said, "I-me acts."[35] Their intentional target is typically something in the world, but they of necessity shape how I am in the world and my personal habitus. They shape the world categorically and me myself dispositionally. Of course I may explicitly be aiming at shaping or transforming myself, as in programs of drug addiction or other acts of self-discipline, like fasting, resolutions, penance, or even kindness and forgiveness directed at myself.

These acts which determine or constitute *me* and which *I* do cannot simply be contradicted and renounced. It is *I* who do them and it is I and not someone else who stand behind these acts and who persist after these acts. If I renounce or contradict them I undermine myself as this person constituted in their achievement. In the decisiveness of the position-taking act I live out of the well-spring that gives the scatteredness of my life continuity. The decisiveness of the position-takings are born of my willing or general will; they do not merely reveal how I operate in the world and categorically display the world, but rather they are how I constitute my own personal being or my personal essence in a historical continuity.

Thus position-taking acts, whether the cognitive-theoretical or moral ones, exemplify not only the more or less punctual character of the act, exemplarily instanced in the decision or what Husserl calls the *fiat*, but they also display a more extended and pervasive sense of will. Of course, the cognitive act of judgment and the intellectual acts by which we make syntactic ties and distinctions are acts which display the world and not acts of will in the sense of a *fiat* which initiates an action with an aim to bring something about in the world. But these acts of display emanate from the I-center and they determine the personal self. This clearly is characteristic of the intellectual acts of making distinctions when they ripen into firm theoretical judgments by which one habitually delineates and creases the world. They do not determine the person morally in an explicit way, i.e., in making an incorrect judgment I am not *eo ipso* morally corrupt. But having made the distinction or judgment I am "obliged" or "required" to let it function or be integrated into the future displays of the subject matter to which the distinction or judgment is related.

Through these cognitive-theoretical or moral-emotive-evaluative acts I do not determine my being in the world with others in any causal sense. Of course, this display is not wholly my responsibility because much of the display is the result of the inheritance and appropriation of the display already achieved by my intersubjective cultural community. The cognitive-theoretical determination of my being in the world is not one of world-transformation but a determination of how the world appears to me as an independent agent of manifestation as well as an agent of manifestation who ineluctably is indebted to a tradition. The explicit will-acts, of course, emerge from me myself alone, and are ways I change the world as well as ways I explicitly determine the moral kind of person I am. Yet these acts too are typically social or communal acts, where the sense of the act is necessarily tied up with another's initiative or presence. An act of mine having to do with or deriving from in every respect solely me myself is difficult to imagine – in a manner analogous to the difficulty of imagining a private language.

Both the cognitive and moral position-takings ride on the general will. It is this which puts us in the position of always pretending to bring about or make present more than we can. Further, the general willing will provides an infinite horizon for both the cognitive and moral agency which beckons each act to be but an approximation of the infinite ideal of this willing will.

We may think of position-taking acts as reflecting a puzzling idea of absolute causality, bound up with the lived sense of I-can. They have the power (with their explicit determinations as well as implicit ones), to define our future being by being perpetually self-propagating. As a gathering act brings together into a kind of focus or thickness all of our willings and longings of the past, so the position-takings centered in the I prospectively gather us toward the future as determined by these acts. Further, a position-taking act, in so far as it is uniquely *my* act, is the way I define my future being by reason of my *identifying myself* with this sort of agency. (We will spell out this self-identifying below.) These acts do not simply fall out of the present into an oblivious past as soon as they are accomplished. Rather they, whether cognitive-theoretical or moral acts, are ways we inevitably design our future because they design the actual and possible shape of the world as well as how we are to engage the world. Through these acts we establish demands on ourselves in the future course of life, e.g., to maintain this distinction as long as it is evident, to hold to the being-p of S, to keep one's promise to X, etc. In short, such acts are I-me acts and thus ways I define the world, myself in relation to my personal life-world, and ways I maintain or revise my self in the world. They establish the world of the particular person, the life-world, which is an embodiment of the person's life in the world as an intellectual and moral agent.

Each position-taking act mirrors the emergent sense of "I myself" as it takes shape in its life in the world with others. The conscionable sense of the position-taking act is how it fits in this larger scheme, this larger identity I give myself. We wish to distinguish in the following pages the proper constitution of the moral personality, which has to do with the position-taking, by which I emphatically self-determine myself as a moral person, and moral categoriality.

With Sokolowski, we may hold the proper or fuller sense of moral categoriality of acts surfaces when I move beyond the simple enjoyment of something good to appreciating it as good. And "this enormous complication," i.e., of whether it is truly good, inserts the act into a manifold of perspectives. The two chief perspectives are, first, the goodness of the thing for me as the one wanting it, i.e., the one who apperceives himself in the light of who I want to be. The second perspective is the ineluctable presence of relevant Others with whom I am inseparably bound in a common world. Moral categoriality emerges out of the recognition and celebration of this "we" as the ineluctable context for our agency. Moral categoriality surfaces as such in a unique kind of position-taking vis-á-vis Others, i.e., my identifying my good with yours, or your good with mine, or your good with my evil, or your evil with my good or your evil with my evil. Thus, in the constitution of moral categoriality, I include the woe or weal of others, with whom I share a common world, into my own life.

With moral categoriality of "goodness" I create a unique analogous sphere of moral ownness that was not there prior to this unique position-taking. Whereas prior to this position-taking, the actuality of others was beyond my sphere of my own life, even though *we* shared a world in common; subsequent to this position-taking others are related to the sphere of one's unique incommunicable ownness in an explicit way (cf. Chapter III, §1) but which is not identical with the "ours" and "we" of sharing a common world through ideal objects, common goods, and, in general, the realm of the public as the same for us all. This identifying your good with mine, etc, does not create an intersubjective public sphere of ownness as does "we" but it is an acknowledgment that community or the "We" is basic in my determining my sphere of ownness in the world. (In my repudiation of any such analogous sphere I reject the role of "we" in defining my sphere of ownness in the world, and thereby I constitute the category of "evil.") In this volume the intersubjective aspects of moral categoriality take a back seat to "moral self-determination," i.e., my identification with such acts as determine the kind of moral person I ought to be and want to be and my responsiveness to conscience as a form of moral determination.[36] (See also our discussion in Chapter V, §9.) Moral self-determination does not happen in a vacuum utterly bereft of moral categoriality. Yet moral categoriality both presupposes that the agents are such as to be capable of moral self-determination, but at the same time moral-self-determination finds its fuller moral sense, i.e., the sense of responsibility and explicit senses of Ought, in the intersubjective transactions that generate moral categoriality.

Let us return to moral-determination and position-takings. I, having made this judgment, having made this distinction, having made or fulfilled the promise, having arranged this hierarchy of preferences by this act, etc., am now one for whom these views or forms of agency hold as valid and approvable. I am the one who so links and separates these things and aspects, who is determined by these commitments and distinctions, as well as by their theoretical and practical implications. A habituality, a *hexis*, is formed that gives the world these abiding contours, and one that gives me these abiding orientations and dispositions, even when I am not thinking about these things at all or when asleep.

But the whole arrangement of my being a person-in-the-world is fragile. My personal essence, indeed, is always surrounded by dangerous contingencies and surds that could possibly undo it. My position-takings are soaked with presumptuous evidence and empty intentions garnished from the position-takings of Others. These can all be turned upside down. Further, I cannot foresee the implications of all my moral acts in terms of the web of agency it inaugurates, e.g., how my example will be interpreted, how my thoughtlessness will lead to my and/or another's ruin, etc. Nor a fortiori can I foresee all the cognitive implications of any interpretation or judgment that I achieve. What I foresee and what I do not foresee are inseparable from and conditioned by the fate of the personal character I constitute. Yet it remains true that any such act is carried forth with the belief in a limitless freedom of initiative that challenges the dominance of the fate of character. As theoretically difficult as it is to describe and to account for this freedom that spites character, there is a unique kind of evidence for it when there are major reversals and personal revolutions. This means that the present centered act of willed willing can both reach back (exercise a transcendence in reverse or a retroscendence) into the general willing will and unite one's dispersed life into a unity, inspite of the disharmonies, false steps, misdirection, etc. Of course, this extraordinary freedom over one's destiny is tied to the clarification of one's values, hierarchy of preferences, etc., provided by rational reflection.

Further, it is not as if the ongoing passive synthesizing under the sway of the willing will has not been preparing for these shifts. Doubtless it is a murky matter of the affections of the *Gemüt*, the "heart," as the way I myself am extended to the periphery of my passive synthetic associations and am functioning in the formation of an habitual center of energy. It is one of the goals of Husserl's analyses of passive synthesis to bring to light how I myself can indeed be present at a distance in the subtle workings of flowing temporalization, wherein a shaping and ripening of motives transpires which, when they effectively surface, shake the stable senses I and others have had of "what sort of person I am."[37] But focusing on these stable senses can mislead because they may occasion that we overlook the essential inadequation of the self with itself; it forgets that the personal essence is always taking shape and is in a process of self-discovery and self-definition within the parameters set by the entelechy of the "myself"; it could also occlude the essential fragility of the personal essence; it may also lead to a failure to see how the I-center is indeed a center that radiates out to the periphery of the former phases of the willing will and centers all of one's life.

§4. Self-Identifying Acts and the Moral Person

Clearly the notion of the person, as correlated to a personal life-world and which correlation is constituted by position-taking acts, is inseparable from the moral person. The person has integrity in so far as she is attuned to all of herself, i.e., all aspects of body, soul, spirit or mind, and intersubjective involvement. But this integrity is foremost maintained in fidelity to the commitments which the position-taking acts have established in one's world-life with others. There is thus a natural kind of loyalty to one's world, one's land, one's country and one's self. This loyalty is integral to the sense of being somebody identifiable in the world. We have urged that basic to personhood is a loyalty to oneself and one's ideals analogous to one's loyalty in keeping one's promises.

Essential to the persistence of the personal identity is "being true to oneself," i.e., being faithful to one's "I-me acts" by which one's world and oneself have been sculpted. But this form of fidelity is not an absolute and sufficient virtue for the integrity of the person, because the person is also spirit, and this means not only an agent of manifestation but a free agent of self-constitution. And times might call for conversion, revolution, transformation, renunciation, etc., of oneself, one's country, and the major contours of public definition of one's world-life. We may find that our hearts are divided, our loyalties incompatible, our goals at odds, and our friends saying either you are with us or against us. Here "courage" or the strength of heart to make distinctions, not be drowned in clichés, and stand up for what seems to be right becomes the truly cardinal virtue. Here the "courage to be" might require the agony of being in conflict not only with one's loved ones but with oneself in terms of one's public or social identity. It might, because it involves fidelity to the evidence made available in a recent reflection, appear to place one in the dark novelty of one's new understanding rather than in the comforting "light" of one's earlier, no longer valid, beliefs.

One's life is pervaded by these moral and cognitive "position-takings" or "attitudes." These, at once, create stable idealities or features of our world and, as well, dispositions or habitualities. Thus at the same time position-takings shape our world and sculpt our personal identity. Yet, although these attitudes are able to be described in universal terms, e.g., of virtue and vice, the unique ipseity and ownness (see the discussions in Book 1, Chapter III) pervade and go in advance in the unfolding of my life and of all that is objective "for me." This is the a priori necessity that pervades my agency and establishes the unique necessity of my life.[38] This is another aspect of the essential inability to be "adequate to myself" because for essential reasons I myself am always transcendent to my personal being.

This necessity that establishes a most basic sense of the imperative to be true to oneself suggests that ipseity has radiance and dignity prior to the agency. (See Book 1, Chapter IV, §20 and Chapter VI, §7; also below, Chapter V, §§8–9.) It thus casts doubt on the view that personal worth resides merely in the integrity and stature that accrue through responsible agency. "Being true to oneself," like "become what you are," points to a sense of oneself that goes in advance of our having done anything and which is not only our beginning but our *telos*. The notoriously hyberbolic notion of the "worthless" person who has never got anything right or done anything well, who has no value accruing from her agency, and, who, indeed, is guilty of monstrous crimes, still is "she herself" and still has this inviolable dignity which is the basis of all rights. It is also the basis of all her duties. In this sense even what Christian theology refers to as Satan or Judas have the inviolable dignity of the "myself." She, regardless of what she has done, is always "she herself," a unique incommunicable individual essence, an "ontological value"; she further is one for whom the world is, and who is not merely a negotiable something in the world.

Even in the third- and second-person apprehension of the natural attitude, there is a glimmer of this transcendental dimension. In the first person, this means that there is a basis for self-love and esteem that is a pure grace of being oneself quite apart from "works," quite apart from any form of merit. The fundamental imperative, inseparable from a person's unique vocation as this ipseity, rests in this odd kind of complacency and innocence, which, of course, have never existed at any time in absolute purity.[39]

In discussing conscience we had occasion to consider a "call" to be oneself, i.e., "a pull" to be true to one's self-ideal as it emerges out of one's self-constitution, to be the most fundamental imperative and the yardstick for all arrangements of life and its goals, all choices of careers, professions, etc. This duty, like ipseity itself, from which it flows, is common to everyone and yet not commensurate with that of the others because not only is it private or exclusively one's own but it is also the condition for the integrity, consistency and truth of all the other duties. We will return to these matters later.

In order for this sense of one's self to be the yardstick, the unique uniqueness or absolute individuality of the "I" must palpably enter into the *personal* I and there must be "an individual law"[40] that pervades each human person's working out his or her destiny, in spite of the sameness that might pervade the historical human personality along with the genetic and acquired makeup. The articulation of this sense of oneself, of one's essential calling or the calling of one's personal essence, and the establishment of one's life in accord with it is the most central problem of ethics.

As we noted, we can think of the most elemental stratum of life as the primal presencing. This, we also claimed, is to be thought of as pervaded by an analogous sense of will, and the ongoing passive synthesis is itself the expression of this "general will" or "willing will." This will is not itself a decision or the result of a decision but goes in advance of all decisions, commitments, etc. The original willing will provides the horizon of our agency and itself was never willed. Thus it is the dynamism and horizon of all our explicit decisions and position-takings, what Blondel called the acts of the "willed will."[41]

We return here to a speculative theme of this work. We have argued in Book 1 that the "myself" or ipseity is the basic moment of the person. And we have attempted to show that the "myself" is propertyless. Yet we have also found it necessary to recognize the "tautological properties" of the "myself," foremost for our present context, intellect and will as ways in which the "myself" is conscious. But, it would seem, the willing will and willed will, as the way we face the horizon of the infinite ideal, etc., are the result of the personification of the ipseity. We never have ipseity apart from personal being, yet we have insisted on the distinction. (In the final chapter of this work, we will tell "a likely story" that will use this distinction for metaphysical-theological purposes.)

Furthermore, we have proposed that personal being is constituted by the position-taking acts, and that these acts are all within the horizon of the willing will and the ideal of self-adequation or the realization of one's true self. In this respect all of our ongoing epistemic, conative, and emotive acts are self-forming, "I-me" acts by and through which the person is constituted.

Nevertheless, with Husserl, we wish to claim that for the proper constitution of the person as a moral person it is necessary that there be acts of explicit self-determination. This is, of course, not merely what we achieve in the ineluctable indexical self-reference and self-reflection. In such acts there is not achieved the kind of massive self-determination we here have in mind. Nor is it what we achieve through the ordinary position-taking acts by which we articulate the world and give shape to our cognitive and moral being in the world. Rather, it is an explicit emphatic self-determination which makes possible a deepening self-acquaintance. Prior to this, as Husserl observed, we live in an undeveloped naivety and paradisiacal innocence. Prior to this we need not be mere wantons, led by whatever impulse surfaces. But our personal essence is scarcely a theme and even the responses to the indications of conscience do not have this emphatic and explicit mode of self-identifying self-determination. In this emphatic self-determination there is an actualization of myself as an I, indeed a realization of oneself precisely as a unique personal, moral self. "The I wills itself as I and, indeed, from now on, as an I purely willing the Good."[42] This is not merely a matter of a resolve to produce acts of a particular prescriptive sort (or where moral categoriality is in play) or not to be dull to what conscience dictates. Rather, the resolve is such that I will myself to be renewed interiorly and incessantly in a complete manner.

Thus there is here in question a coincidence of the therefold sense of I: the "myself," the personal I, and the moral person or self. Of course, typically in one's personal life the "myself" is of necessity present and so is the more or less stable, more or less fragile personal essence; but we know ourselves also to be merely more or less conscientious, often to be rudderless, without orientation, on a moral holiday, searching for ourselves, and even behaving wantonly – driven from whatever impulse or desire happens to surface, etc. What Husserl has in mind in the emphatic, explicit self-determination of the person is where all parts of the threefold are actual. In the absence of this self-determination I am not yet properly and truly a personal I because only in the self-determination of myself as a moral person do I become properly, i.e., explicitly, committed to being a wakeful personal I throughout my life. Short of this will to self-determination I hover in a shadowy state of inauthenticity, dullness, and incompletion where I live in a merely naïve and/or bogus manner.

Of course the naïve and bogus "I myself" is "myself," not something less than "myself." But this propertyless sense of "I myself" prescinds from one's life as a person in the world facing one's unique idea of oneself and one's life through proper moral self-determination. And the naïve or bogus person is one for whom the issue of self-determination and fidelity to who one has determined oneself to be is dormant. Therefore the personal essence's realization of its ideal is not a concern and that it has a more or less stable identity is not due to any earnestness in regard to it. Her life and self, as given to her to shape, have not yet become a concern. Surely it is not yet something of unconditional importance.

Thus we must say, and this seems to be the position of Husserl himself, that without the explicit self-determination the self, the "myself," is ontologically incomplete as a person or personal I. Not only is the ontological description of the person not able to rest with a third-person account of a nature or a kind, e.g., a human being or a self-referring, self-aware being. Rather it requires the moral "existential" and deontological account which must build on the first-person experience of and response to the call to self-determination. The ontology of the self or person is, in this sense, of necessity deontological. To properly be myself I, and I alone, must explicitly self-determine myself to be the sort of person I want to be and ought to be. This is a "no-alibi" situation: I must do it and no one can do it for me and there are no excuses for my not having done it and my not having done it is itself a disastrous commission by omission. Here we have another Husserlian version of Existenz, or the coming forth of one's center in a matter of unconditional importance, i.e., one's self-determination.

The acts of self-determination are acts by which one posits oneself as a unique person in the world facing one's unique ideal and positing oneself as precisely this self-determining self incessantly renewing oneself facing this infinite idea. This is at once a matter of willing "the good" and willing oneself to will "the good" and willing oneself as the one who wills "the good." Husserl speaks of this also as willing the best possible life, willing one's own best possible, the best possible that one can will.[43]

To the extent "identifying with" implies a valuational affirmation with that with which one identifies, then it seems that of necessity one would "identify with" what appeared as one's best possible life. If there were a path or a commitment which would assure one of attaining one's best possible life then we may say that there is a sense in which one *identifies oneself* with just such acts that determined oneself along this path or commitment. But what do we have in mind with this "identifying with?" When we typically use the term "to identify with" we have in mind a making one out of what is somehow two, a making the same out of what is different. This is different but dependent on our use of "identity" or "finding identical" whereby we claim A = A (and not-C). When we come to claim A = C we assert C as being different in some respect, or as appearing to be different from A, but this difference is not a difference in being but a difference only in aspect or only apparent because of a faulty perspective. In most cases of "identifying" or "finding identical" we know in advance in some way that which is identical in the differences. We know in advance the properties of the one as they get transferred to the others, e.g., in perception we know in advance that the spatial-temporal object admits of a variety of aspects, sides, and moments of duration. In other words, we have a general framework or anticipation of the sort of thing it is. We know that we could not identify the thing in question unless it bore these markers. If it soon proved that it had none of these aspects we would question whether we were dealing with "it" as identically the same.

In many cases of a personal identification we do not have a matter of "identifying with." Thus in determining whether it is truly she from this angle when she looked so different from that angle, with this hair-do or with that hair-do, the one making the identification will have to have a sense of the defining features and how they themselves might be altered or even disguised. In the case of the identifying person identifying herself she similarly will have to have a prior sense of her defining features. Here, of course, we here are talking about the *personal* identification and not the identification of the "myself" which is known in a prior non-ascriptive way. (See Book 1, *passim* for this.)

A common sense of "identifying with" has to do with how one relates to a public personage or celebrity. Here there will indeed be in play an implicit thematization of one's own personality. One will find in the "star" some aspect of oneself or one's eutopian self. Or the "star's" image serves as a handy and welcoming receptacle for projections of one's own personality. Often what is at stake in such cases of personal "identification with" can only be brought to light by a kind of soul-searching or psychotherapy, i.e., we have do here with cases where the implicit horizonal apperceptions, whether traumatic or not, are unlikely to come to explicit awareness, but which, nevertheless, function in one's personal self-apperception and sense of one's personal identity.

Nevertheless, it seems clear that proper senses of "identifying with" presuppose some sense of oneself. If the self is constituted properly by the self-identifying acts we therefore must say that the self is authenticated by the appropriation of the acts, foremost those moral acts of the will, that exist in advance. If we do not hold this, then we must say that the self is brought about by the identifying acts, the acts which one appropriates and authenticates – but which are not anyone's acts. In this case, the person-constituting acts and the acts of authentication or self-identification are achieved by a "subject-less event."[44] This is a necessary position if the subject is considered to be the person as the bearer of the distinctive properties by which it has its distinguishing identity and the person itself is itself brought about in every respect by these "position-taking" acts.

In this case, we could not speak of the authorizing, authenticating acts with which one identifies as "self-identifying acts" and which acts constitute the person because there is no self, no subject, there to do this work. This position is facilitated, indeed it is necessitated, by neglecting to attend to the non-ascriptive, non-identifying senses of oneself, and therefore holding that the only sense of self-awareness is reflective and ascriptive and the only sense of self is sortal. Therefore if the only legitimate sense of self is the identifiable person constituted by determinate acts of willing (and what we are calling position-taking acts), then the person is constituted by a subject-less event and we have the person brought about by self-authenticating acts by a self-less event.

In the course of this work we have claimed that we avoid this self-authenticating, self-identifying by a non-self-event by insisting on the "myself" as pervasive and foundational for the person. We speculated that the person was a "personification" of the "myself." Thus in the case of the identifying with certain acts that determine one's best possible life and/or one's self-ideal of the person we have interjected a speculation: Because the "myself" is the dynamism for personal unfolding and development it functions as the entelechy, i.e., both form and telos of the personification. The self-identifying acts are not simply and purely bereft of a self; rather the unfolding burgeoning moral person self-determines herself under the guidance of the entelechy of the "myself." Indeed, the "myself" as informing the burgeoning person is already at work in the personal essence's indications through conscience of what sort of person it ought to be.

We have further said that the self-ideal is present in the interplay of the willed will and the horizon or backdrop of the willing will. As such it is ineluctably willed. There is here willy-nilly a willing and not properly a personal identification. Yet this willing of what the willing will opens up can only take place in the particular situation of willed-wills. The exemplary act of moral self-determination is an explicit actuation of this a priori implicit situation. In this latter case we have the explicit act of will (the willed-will) willing something against the backdrop of the willing will; what this will wills is a more or less explicit articulation of this backdrop of the willing will, and this Husserl calls "the best possible life." This willing of the best possible life is a willing of a unique difference and sameness because it is a willing by me myself of me myself to will this life. It is a unique position-taking whereby I will myself as I myself and, indeed, from now on I will myself as I myself willing the best possible life in this and every situation.

In such a case the self-ideal, my best possible life or I myself self-identifying with specific acts which are the equivalent of myself willing myself to will the best possible life, is at once a priori and implicit and a posteriori or explicit. The self-ideal is also at once oneself and what is other to oneself by reason of its infinite axiological distance. It is at once one's actual self and yet it awakens the center of one's self. The center of one's self is not properly thought of as different person from oneself, no more than is the nisus toward an adequation of oneself to be conceived as a motion toward what is a different self from oneself, no more than the willing will as the horizon of the willed will is to be envisaged as separated from this explicit act of will or willed will.

We believe in this matter to find a parallel with Kant's own distinction between one's being human and one's becoming a person. He holds that the susceptibility for the respect for the moral law in itself is susceptibility for the respect of oneself as self-determining. That is, there is a respect for oneself as determining one's will by reason, i.e., self-identifying with this aspect of oneself, and not identifying with oneself as mere impulse, drive, caprice, etc. This respect for the incommensurate importance of an appropriate self-determination, a respect for the truer aspect of oneself, is a disposition to *Persönlichkeit*, i.e., to becoming a moral person. He even says that this respect for the appropriate form of self-determination (rooted in respect for the "moral law" which is explicated in one formulation as a regard for the inherent worth, i.e., as an end in itself, of oneself and other persons) is what it means to *be* a moral person.[45] Fichte, we will see, picks up these themes and roots self-respect in the basic ineluctable constitution of respect for what is true in itself, in what we might call the ineradicable condition of "truthfulness" as a feature of persons, i.e., their being agents of manifestation. Being a human person inescapably faces the ineluctable imposition of being reverent for what is true in itself. Self-respect, because it has to do with what is inherently a value in itself, an "end in itself," is an ineluctable veneration for one's own value and one's own being truthful. We take these themes to explicate our interpretation of Husserl here, that this sense of "deontology," or the affixing to the Is an Ought, is a necessary *ontological* completion of the essential account of human persons. There is an incompletion of the human person, of oneself (of the "myself") until she takes upon herself her moral self-determination, her identifying herself with her deepest and truest self. Thus the theme of self-determination, as bound up here with self-respect and self-love, is not a conditioned respect and love based on prior attributes and merits; it has to do with one's ontological value in itself. Thus it is not a self-loving determination of oneself as having the familiar weaknesses, comfort zones, resistances, and self-deceptions; it is a respect and love for one's inherently worthy self, and this, we have suggested, is always evident to us both in terms of conscience and the "true self" which is indicated and opened up for us by the willing will.

As we shall see, Husserl believes that there is an especially powerful manifestation of one's vocation or path to determine oneself in terms of one's true self in what he calls "the truth of will," which is the way the truth of one's life which is the truth in the universal context of one's will, i.e., one's willing will, manifests itself as what one uniquely ought to do in a concrete situation. (See below, Chapter V, §2.)

All these claims are facilitated if we think of the "myself" as being an entelechy for the human person, regardless of the darkness we encounter in any attempt to think of how the "myself" gets personified – which, to be sure, is a special, perhaps insurmountable, problem if we think of it as an independently existing substance, a move which we are hesitant to make. (See our prolonged meditation on this matter in Book 1, Chapters V–VIII.)

Further, the "myself's" personification is the self-realization of a regulative ideal, i.e., through finite position-taking acts, piecemeal and step by step. This position we are proposing is nicely stated in an already cited passage of Paul Valéry: "My most intimate idea of myself is not to be able to be that one who I am. I am not able to recognize myself in any finite figure. And the I MYSELF always eludes my person which, however, it designs or imprints in fleeing it."[46] Here we may appropriate Valéry's *MOI* as the equivalent of the "myself" or "I myself" which is of necessity non-sortal and transcendent to all properties. As such it must elude any shape I give myself in my position-takings even though it functions as the entelechy through effecting "design" and "imprints" in the unfolding, never completed, process of personification.

The psychotherapists Carl Rogers and Eugene Gendlin support our position when they claim that a key to the healing process is the ability of the client to trust her own experience of life and by implication her own self in the process of carrying forward the articulation of one's life out of the "dark somethings" or empty intentions (Husserl) in play in one's "wanting to say." What we can trust is not just the felt sense (which is prior to any mind-body split) and which exceeds any conceptualization;

we do not merely trust the step where there is a bodily shift in reaching a new explication of a felt meaning and the sense of relief that this explication is more right than
the earlier one. We trust the series of steps, the entire process, and ourselves as both
the agents and patients of this process. Rogers likens this process to the likelihood of
an El Greco or Ernest Hemingway saying "good artists do not do this kind of work,
but *I* do." And we are grateful that their esteem and appreciation for this sense of
their unique selves prevailed. (Nevertheless, we have to distinguish between being
true to one's "genius" and being true to this deeper sense of oneself that Rogers here
wants to signal out as the basis for therapy; being faithful to one's genius does not
guarantee the kind of health and wholeness and authenticity that we take Rogers to
be aiming at; see our discussion in Chapter V, §6.) The esteem is not merely for the
abstract "myself" but the "myself" as entelechy working out one's "personification."
For Rogers this is a balance between being and becoming. The ideally functioning person moves toward and through the process she inwardly and actually is and
moves away from being any façade of herself. Such false versions of herself, as
Gendlin would say, cause her to get "stuck" and not be able to carry forward the
process of explication of her felt sense. She does not try to be more than she is in
the sense of what is less true of herself; such acts lead to feelings of "insecurity and
bombastic defensiveness" which of necessity interfere with the process of letting
one's capacities carry one forward. Nor is it a move toward less than she is "with
the attendant feelings of guilt of self-depreciation." Rogers believes that the work
of sorting out and choosing in the course of living to be the sort of person that she
most values being is the truest expression of who she really is.

Rogers uses the phrases interchangeably, "to be what one is" and "to be who
one is." This is here unobjectionable because who she is as the unique essence or
"myself" is functioning as the entelechy of the person in her work of personification. The person is working out what to feel and what to do in particular situations
as the pathway for working out what sort of person she wants to be and ought to be
in the light of the deepest values she holds. Who she is is a constant, but it is also
an entelechy, not a form that creates a rigidity and stasis. What is key is the person
experiencing her unique essence and joyfully sensing the freedom, in spite of the
trepidation, of taking responsibility. Now she may say, "*I* am the one who chooses"
"*I* am the one who determines the value an experience has for me." Here the person
delights in identifying her life with the life *she* constitutes and *she* experiences. The
therapy process awakens her to her self and away from what hid her from herself.
There is thus awakened a disposition to be herself by staying in touch with herself,
i.e., who she is as this expresses itself in her pursuing her life in accord with the
values she cherishes most. (In Chapter V, §8 we discuss senses of what we call
transcendental self-esteem and self-trust.)

Rogers is famously sanguine about how trusting oneself and being true to oneself involves no fixity but rather embraces continued process. Likewise Rogers
holds that "being who/what one is" is not conceding to evil or wanton impulses.
His reasoning is "the more he is able to permit those feelings to flow and to be
in him, the more they take their appropriate place in a total harmony of his feelings." Of course, the process of being in tune with, attending to, and sorting out

the feelings in the light of what one really wants and esteems is itself a remarkable disposition or virtue. It may perhaps be assumed to be a capacity for everyone, but its actual appropriate acquisition requires usually initially guidance. In any case it does not happen without a keen wakefulness and courageous patience, the excellent character of which may not be underestimated. In both Rogers and Gendlin we have this strong affirmation of the fundamental goodness of ourselves if we only put ourselves in a position to listen to ourselves, i.e., to heed the deepest constitutive processes and dimensions of ourselves. Within each of us there are enormous resources for healing, creativity, and goodness.[47] Anyone who has reflected on the latent nisus toward harmony, unity, consistency, and fullness of living in Husserl's analyses of passive synthesis would be moved to agree. Yet, nevertheless, there are the times when we, perhaps inexplicably, fail to show up for ourselves, when *acedia* takes hold, where one does what one would not, etc. Rogers and Gendlin would want us go to the felt-meanings that underlie these allegedly inexplicable moments and find out what they are about. My point is both that one occasionally simply refuses to "go there" or that when one does the process of carrying-forward the felt-meanings only reveals what one already was aware of, e.g., that one failed to show up for oneself, e.g., one was stupidly stubborn. These bumps in the road do not nullify the basic Rogerian-Gendlinian claims and themes, but they complicate and mollify the strong optimism that this reader occasionally overhears.

We believe this basic theme in Rogers and Gendlin is consonant with our notion of the "myself" as the entelechy for the personification of the person. To return to our earlier terminology we may say: The acts of the willed will that are position-taking acts taking root in the center of the I are acts by which I identify myself with this willing and with what this willing wills.[48] This happens more or less with all position-taking acts, but persons need not act whole heartedly. I may act against my will, my heart might not be in doing something, I may do something listlessly, distractedly, etc. In such cases I half-heartedly go along, consent, and languidly involve myself. Further, most cognitive acts of recognition have a great measure of passive association that informs the perception conceptually and in this respect *I* am much less active than when, e.g., I have to make a judgment as to the truth or falsity of a claim. The philosophical temptation to name the agent of manifestation a universal agent intellect or theoretic consciousness, even a universal I, derives not only from the consideration that theoretic consciousness is concerned with what is the same for us all, but also because of the universality of logical and scientific procedure. The uniqueness of "I myself" is irrelevant in this procedure. Further, although *I* am active, e.g., in my distinguishing and weighing evidence, it still might be in this particular case a form of cognitional activity that is removed from the center of my life. Thus, e.g., the distinction between a performative speech act and one that is merely descriptive may have little to do right now with my life. Seeing the distinction, although it has a validity that lasts for an indeterminate time beyond the insight, may not immediately affect my life, as, e.g., the decision to act in a certain way toward my closest friend who has betrayed me. This latter act is one where I bring together my life and my self into this very act. I identify myself with this act and I invest myself in this act in the way I do not invest myself when achieving an insight, e.g., into the illocutionary nature of a speech act. The "willed will" having to do with my friend approximates "the willing will" in a more concentrated way than do most of my everyday voluntary and cognitive position-takings. In the decision regarding my friend *I* at my core invest myself, and thereby my life is stamped with me myself in a way it is not with much of what comprises the stream of consciousness.

A final point for this section regarding the "myself" and the basis of personification in the willing will: We can think of how the self-identifying acts reflect the self-ideal and willing will by thinking of how the general or willing will is analogous to the kind of willing we call a career or vocational choice. We can say that the general, latent will or "willing will" goes in advance and pervades all active achievements analogous to the way the pervasive ongoing willing of the massive life-choices, such as those that launch marriages and careers, pervade and serve as the impetus for the myriad actions that one does in living out these commitments. For example, my decision to be a professor involves explicit and implicit commitments to do research, to teach, to be a responsible citizen within the department and faculty communities, to do my share of administrative work, etc. Each of these explicit and implicit commitments, which follow in the wake of the decision to be a professor, has myriad responsibilities and endless tasks. For example, deciding to be a professor involves decisions about which courses to teach and when. It implies the commitment to meeting with students outside of class, reading papers, holding discussions. Deciding for a particular course requires deciding which books the students should read, what the design of the course is, what the sequence of the lectures will look like; it requires designing each lecture and preparing oneself to deliver the lecture.

Further, to pursue the analogy of the career with the willing will and the matter of self-identifying acts, we can think of explicit moments when my identity with my career is called into question by a crisis, e.g., temptation to violate its basic code of conduct. Or we may think of how a special project of research or teaching brings together in a unique way one's whole life as a professor. In these cases one's identity as a professor is conjured up and we have the opportunity to celebrate it, affirm it, and reconfirm it.

Of course, the general or willing will is more extensive and pervasive than the massive will generated by a career choice because it functions in each temporal phase of all of life in the way no choice possibly could, regardless of how encompassing the career choice is. No one decides to have a general or willing will and be a "passive synthesizer." These both are and constitute me at a most basic level and "I myself" presuppose them in all that I do. I no more decide to have these capacities than I decide to be who I am at the basic level of the haecceity of the "myself." Because the willing will, like the "myself," is given in advance of all constitution by the I, and because the work of personification rides on the willing will, we posit that the willing will is the primal work of the personification of the "myself." And what Husserl calls the self-determination that constitutes the moral person is precisely the actuation of the opportunity to determine ourselves that is given us to sculpt in accord with the entelechy of the "myself." This horizon opens up for us by the "excess" of the willing will and self-ideal that extends beyond our specific willed wills in the form of roles, projects, even careers.

§5. Ipseity and Freedom

We have repeatedly run into the necessity to distinguish the familiar identity that each of us has as a person in the world from the "myself," which we are also calling I-ness and ipseity. We have been at pains to distinguish the personal-essential identity (personal essence) constituted in time through position-takings, and which we can know to a great extent as others know it, from the non-ascriptive unique uniqueness that each is for him- or herself in the first-person. We have said that this latter is expressed and is the frame for the former. We never know single individuals apart from incarnate concrete persons. As such they are all amenable to descriptions that necessarily involve universals, types, generalities, i.e., "sortal terms." Yet we have seen reason to hold that when we use the word "person" we do not refer to some kind, like "Catholic," "Democrat," or "human," and therefore "person" is not a sortal term. We never have before us persons in a filled intention apart from the more or less unique configuration of endless properties (sortal terms), but the person is, we have argued, not reducible to these, and these properties, as well as the relatively unique configurations, are, in principle i.e., conceivably, able to be duplicated.

The first-person awareness of oneself and its capacity to elude being adequately captured in the language that applies to things in the world are basic aspects of Existenz. And *in so far as* all the things in the world are able to be "represented," duplicated, substituted for, and replaced, and in so far as all these things can be captured by universal terms and described by common properties, to that extent Existenz insists on its exceptional status. In Book 1, Chapter V, we raised a classical objection to this ontology of things being individuated by communicable properties, namely the view that whatever actually exists, exists in so far as it is uniquely individual. But even if there is a radical uniqueness or *haecceitas* at the heart of whatever is in so far as it is, this merely highlights the status of the "myself" which experiences its being as a "selving" (G.M. Hopkins) and is aware of its uniqueness. (Whether there are other than human persons or selves need not busy us here.[49]) We have argued that although "I" is a universal token-reflexive expression, what we basically refer to with "I" is not anything common or able to be grasped in the language of objects in so far as these are brought to light through sortal determinations. We, our personal embodied selves that are both lived and "for us" in the world, have this ambiguity of both sharing in what is capable of a sortal description and in not being capable of such a description. Thus, e.g., bodily movements and pains, as ways I am in the world, are both amenable to a third-person general description; but as disclosures of the "I myself," they elude such descriptions. A pain named a "sciatica pain" lends itself to a description in sortal properties; as I myself engulfed in the pain and deworlded, we have almost nothing to describe or disclose – which "almost nothing" reflects, but is not identical with, the rich non-sortal referent of "myself." Further, as we noted, if we think of all objects as things (*Dinge*), and thus in a network of conditions *(Bedingungen)*, then this sense of "I," and "Existenz" as its center, are not things; they are *"unbedingt."* That is, the I, as the agent of manifestation in its exercise of its agency as well as Existenz as the center of the I, enjoys a status of being other than a thing, and in this sense unconditioned, *unbedingt.*

This consideration has at least two implications. First, it means, of course, that the agency of I myself may not be thought of exhaustively as part of the network of the natural world's thingly and causal conditions. (See our discussions in Book 1, Chapter VI.) This is a basic sense to be given the notion of freedom of spirit. Secondly, it means that because we remove senses of "I myself" (as pole of acts, as referent of "I," as subject of non-reflective self-awareness, and as the center of the I or Existenz) from intentional display, we remove it from any proper sense of knowing. (As Kant and Jaspers have insisted, the sense in which we properly *know*, i.e., make present through an intentional act, the basic freedom which sustains the intentional act, is highly problematic.) Indeed, we saw that there is a basic sense of "myself" that is independent of any personal properties we might have. As with the phenomena of mystery and my death we here are *essentially* ignorant, i.e., in the case of the "myself" we are not in a position to say that we *know* who we are if this means identifying what our distinguishing properties are. I cannot say what are the necessary and sufficient conditions that account for my self being myself. I do not and cannot *know* for essential reasons the properties that determine "who I am" or *what* the "I myself" is. This is a matter of necessity because I am as "myself" not a *what* but a *who* and do not have essential properties – apart from the "wiggle ones" that we have called "tautological properties." Yet this is not to say that the first-person non-reflexive self-awareness is utterly bereft of any sense whatsoever of knowing. The ignorance that may be said to characterize this self-awareness, precisely because it is not an intentional knowing and categorical display, may not be characterized as purely a "negative nothing."[50]

A way of resolving this is to propose that the "myself" is, at the beginning of life, absolutely indeterminate, and present to itself as "I (myself) can," i.e., it is awake to itself as sheer potentiality. The indeterminacy is enabled to become determinate by way of the temporalizing at birth (or conception or some stage of conception) and the eventual actualization of potentialities. In this respect freedom of the self could be seen as the principle of individuation of the self, which freedom itself is conditioned by temporality.

There is doubtless merit in this view,[51] yet it needs some precision. The "myself" that emerges in transcendental phenomenological reflection and in the thought-experiments indeed is bereft of worldly determination. Yet this means that no properties actually articulate it because it is a *who*, not a *what*. Further, no determinations through the actuation of the potentialities adequately render the "myself." The "myself" is not merely indeterminate as a *nihil negativum*. It has a "positivity" that does not admit of presentation in terms of any properties.

Further, we have been proposing that *I* come forth, ex-sist, for "myself" in the position-taking, in the exercise of my freedom. The awareness of the actualization of my I-can is an original awakening of me to myself. Apart from the *ex-sistere* of myself as *I* "come forth" to myself in self-identifying, gathering, centering acts, I am not aware of myself as having a center, as being Existenz. This coming forth to myself is inseparable from my will and its freedom. But the unique individuality of the "myself" is not a result of a freedom apart from the "myself." Free will by itself is not a principle of individuation or a condition of individuation of the "myself" apart from the "myself." Freedom, like I-can, is inseparable from I-ness and "myself." Freedom and will are always already my will and my freedom, and the acts are always already someone's, i.e., mine. Freedom cannot account for individuation because freedom already presupposes the unique essence of the "myself." Of course freedom accounts for the individuation of the determination of the unique properties characterizing one's personal being in the world by which we are displayed and by which we display things in the world. But we have insisted that that is not the sole sense of personal individuality. The same holds for temporality. Temporality, the ongoing elemental primal presencing, retaining, and protending, too is always pervaded by I-ness and belonging to an I, a unique I, that reflection brings to light. Having a future and having a past are tied to the primal presencing that is always an I-ness for whom the future and past are.

Thus the position put forth here is that there is reason to hold a sense of I-ness, which is an identity that is not identifiable, if this means by way of properties. And this I-ness is individual in itself apart from the determination by freedom in time. Nevertheless our previous discussion of Existenz as it comes forth in conscience and limit-situations has been dependent on a strong sense of personal identity, as a kind of ideality, which exists freely across time. We can recognize this identity in a quasi-objective way in our emotional life, in making long-term decisions and through the revelations of conscience. Of course this is not a public revelation, it is not of something in the world, as is my identity as a professor or an American, and it does not enjoy the status as the same for us all. Yet there is a measure of intersubjectivity whereby we recognize one another from day to day, and speak of one another as "being the same dear old friend" or as "not having been herself when she committed that horrendous deed." Here we need only mention our prior discussions of ways in which personal identity is inseparable from the world that each, along with one's neighbors and strangers, constitutes, and the great difficulty one has in being oneself if transplanted to another world in time and space. (See Book 1, Chapter VIII.)

The knowledge of other persons and of ourselves as identifiable persons is inevitably a search for the distinguishing properties, propensities, desires, habits, etc., just as we want to reduce mysteries to secrets whose disclosure is inevitable. Yet, at the same time, I myself as well as the Others are apperceived to be not exhausted by these distinctive marks. Indeed, in "explaining" Others or ourselves, as in "psychological explanations," we strive for something that is truly and evidently irreducible and not a mere postulate, that underlies the peculiar characteristics. Mere postulates, like the unconscious or some thing in the world, e.g., "neural fibers" do not give us an account of why, e.g., Peter, as this unique ipseity, acts this way. They give an account of why anyone, given these conditions, would act this way. This irreducible something is inseparable from the unique ipseity and itself not to be explained by something like traumas or hidden drives or dispositions. Rather, all the properties, traits, drives, etc. find their original unity in the total phenomenon of the person as a more or less tight unity of a self and life-world.

Sartre urges us to think of this unity of ourselves and our world-project as a kind of "basic choice" or original project.[52] He believes that this "likely story" enables us to come as close as we can to grasping what is unique about ourselves or others as persons in the world. In so far as we are talking about a "choice" which pervades all other choices, there is a sense in which the unity of our personhood and world is a voluntary matter. Yet, for Sartre, this choice stems from a desire, inseparable from our ipseities, which is a lack and thirst for "being," as something existing unconditionally in itself. This thirst or lack of being is precipitated by a dissatisfaction with myself as a sheer contingent facticity. As such I am propelled by a desire to secure ipseity, which is not any thing in the world, to some thing that provides it with a ground and which also does not turn itself into some thing in the world. This desire, as ipseity's felt lack of its being grounded by itself, does not exist *first*, and then find expressions in the myriad a posteriori position-takings and desires that comprise our world-life; rather ipseity's desire to be and its desire to be grounded and not a contingent facticity, exist and are manifest only in the myriad contingent empirical desires and position-takings. The so-called "basic choice" is in fact an explication of the original *lack* at the heart of ipseity and its original intuition that no thing, entity, or event in the world can satisfy it.

Here we wish to point out that the distinctive person as rooted in a "basic choice" is not for Sartre a "radical voluntarism" in so far as this means absolutely unmotivated. On the contrary, it is motivated by ipseity's desire to be (which, fleshed out, is the desire to be God); this is, in Sartre's "likely story," ipseity's primal impulse out of which all desires and position-takings emerge.

Sartre's position has symmetry with the phenomenon of the general latent willing will which we earlier discussed in conjunction with Husserl, Blondel, and Nabert. There we assigned to ipseity, in so far as it is personified, the willing will as the basis for the sense of self-inadequation that pervades all of life. As a property of ipseity as a person, this burgeoning primal will threatens the propertylessness of ipseity. Yet, like intellect, ownness, and the non-reflective awareness of "myself" as the source of uniqueness, the willing will too is an analytic or tautological property. It is not a distinguishing property of anyone but belongs to the lived tautological essence of I-ness or the "myself." Yet it would seem that this particular tautological property only comes to light when we think of the "myself" as already "personifying," and not merely the referent of the thought experiments, amnesia, etc. (On this ambiguous matter of tautological properties, see Book 1, Chapter V, §3.)

"Basic choice," however, is misleading. It is a postulated "likely story" to account for phenomena that we named the latent will-horizon or willing-will. We too told a "likely story" in comparing the willing or general will with a "basic choice" after the analogy of a career choice. Still Jean Nabert proposes (in a 1924 work) similarly that there is a basic first choice. This choice is specified by one's idea of one's unique personhood and all subsequent acts are successful or unsuccessful efforts to be faithful to this original choice. In Sartre the choice does not seem to be historical at all, but a postulate of a pre-historical determination ("project") of one's unique personhood. For Nabert, when and how this basic choice happens is even less clear. What is clear for all the thinkers, including Husserl and Blondel, is that the free self-formation of oneself and the belief in this freedom takes place within the horizon of an idea of oneself as constituted by oneself. This constitution need not be thought of as a primordial choice but rather we can think of the ideal as emergent out of the horizon that dawns with the developing basic latent willing will of "personification." Each position-taking act mirrors this idea and this idea holds sway over the manifold of acts.

Thus we will not follow the postulate of an original basic choice, whether Platonic (see Chapter III, §7), Nabertian or Sartrian, except in so far as it is a metaphor for the latent willing will whose beginning precedes any choice, and for which there is ample evidence in the insufficiency of the willed will to realize the promise or lure of what the willing will adumbrates. But the now familiar analogy holds: As a massive will act's *fiat*, e.g., to take a vacation, to follow this career, to marry this person, etc., creates an endless temporal-spatial field of activity comprised of acts, and as this *fiat* informs and sustains each and every act, and thus serves as an encompassing project, so the latent willing-will facing the horizon of an idea of one's true self informs and sustains the entirety of position-taking acts comprising one's life, foremost those massive ones that define oneself through, e.g., a choice of career or mate.

Personhood, understood normatively and properly, is precisely the idea of this unified totality that is mirrored in each of the position-taking acts. One's true self is a way of thinking about this ideal of a unified totality. As position-taking acts themselves have a kind of transtemporality in that their validity perdures "from now on" so the person as the unity of the totality of position-taking acts enjoys a kind of transtemporality, what we have called the personal essence, because the person gains an identity which, although steeped in the changing relations to others and the world, nevertheless is an ongoing, if not absolutely stable, synthesized sameness across the flux of the stream of consciousness and across the punctuations of this flux with position-taking acts. Yet each act, of necessity, is inadequate to this transtemporal totality. Even in the gathering and totalizing acts in which the person disposes of her life (we will once again return to this theme below) and in which she expends herself, the person perceives that she is not equal to herself. Such acts are an index of freedom as well as one's self-inadequation. And there is the keen awareness that any effort to consolidate our personification is borne by a surplus that threatens to shake this consolidated framework. And we agree with Nabert who observed, there is no one who has not clearly experienced an astonishment at an act's capacity to rebel at the effort to make, maintain, and defend the consolidated self and its development.[53] Thus the person is never definitively consolidated; the personification is never not a synthesis in the making, a process; the personal essence is never finished once and for all; and the structured whole remains fragile because acts are always possible that could, with the aid of the revolutionary clarification of a reflection, disavow what has preceded. Again, this is a cipher of the distinction between the "myself" as propertyless and transtemporal and the person. (This topic of the relationship between the self's freedom and its character will occupy us in §8 of this chapter.)

It, however, remains true that each act that is conscionable is precisely one which aspires to be in harmony with the drift of the whole of one's personal self. Further, the specific acts have a nisus, of course one that is repressible to a degree, to be equal to the underlying basic willing will that always exceeds and goes in advance. And each act furthermore aspires to sustain the unity and harmony of the whole. For this to happen each conscionable act is one that apperceives the form of the personal self, one's personal essence, to which the person is required to remain true. This is a sense in which a pervading Ought rides on a current of Is. This is the basic moral implication of the feature of position-taking acts that they are valid "from now on." They are ways I freely constitute myself by acts which exercise a kind of hegemony over my future life by permitting the form of "I myself" to be present in each phase of my life.

Because normative personhood is a totality there looms incessantly the prospect of an act that one could achieve that would forever, and without regret, determine oneself in accord with one's unique ipseity. As the limit-situations are not properly particular situations into which one enters and which one may leave behind, so the quest for a position-taking that will bring together the multiplicity of one's life in a fulfilling direction in accord with the best, and wherein one's true unique self, as it stands in the larger scheme of things, especially one's relationship with one's fellows and nature, is ever on the horizon of one's life. In the ongoing project of getting oneself together and finding one's way each faces the great problem of whether there is possible a self-positing, a self-formation, a self-identifying act that would take place in accord with an idea of one's own self that could be so absolute and central to one's inmost self that it could be made irrevocably and without regret for all eternity.[54]

Such a self-constitution clearly is eutopian, i.e., an actualization of what other-wise would appear to be too good to be true. Clearly such a self-determination is what is at the foundation for ancient understandings of "conversion" and religious vows. Yet it may also appear as too good to be true because each effort to gather oneself in the face of the infinite self-ideal is always an inadequate appreciation of what is at stake, what is now required, and whether this path is indeed, as so outlined, the one to which one is to commit oneself forever. How the way appears at any particular time will be dependent on the interpretive powers of the person at that time and these will always be corrigible. Therefore its validity "for all eternity" might well seem to be an impossible demand to be placed on any self-determination. And yet, such a possible resolve, commitment, and fidelity are the substance of the great personages and stories that have edified us throughout history.

The hope for the actualization of the best as a position-taking that was irrevocable and without regret for all eternity seems to contain a desire to leap beyond the human condition of guilt and perhaps sin – at least because the hope promises endless for-giveness and endless renewal. Is not a view, such as the one ascribed to Arthur Miller,

that "maybe all one can do is hope to end up with the right regrets," a more realistic
formulation? But does not Miller's statement reveal a resignation which reflects,
albeit from afar, the awareness of the other absolutely best position-taking and hope
for life – just as Aristotle's remark about a happiness for the gods in contrast with
the properly human form of happiness reflects an apperception of another possible
happiness? It would seem so. For to hope to end with the right regrets presupposes
not only that one will inevitably have regrets, but that one will fall from one's infinite,
only approximatable, ideal of the vocation wherein there are no regrets. After all, the
best for us is the best under the circumstances. And to hope to end up with the "right
regrets" presupposes a hope in their being a genuine knowledge of the ultimate order
of things and that one has not been misled about this, and that one has been able to
follow the right path indicated by this presumptive knowledge.

§6. Summary: Teleology of Personal Being

The position we are developing proposes that the problem of bridging the seemingly incommensurate aspects of oneself, i.e., as the non-ascriptive referent of "I"
and as the property-rich person in the world, is to be resolved in the entelechial
function of the "myself." This has required the further speculation of "will" being
in the former aspect a tautological property which in the latter aspect becomes the
general or willing will. Will as tautological property of the "myself" is manifest in
the personification when we consider the phenomena which we encompass under
the topics of self-inadequation and the willing will. Let us look at the matter from
a more explicitly teleological angle.

   A person's life is laced with desires that give birth to plans. Prior to these desires
the life of perception and passive synthesis are pervaded by a teleology. That is to say,
the flow of life is pervaded by the structure of an interplay of empty and filled intentions arising out of the primal presencing and this presencing itself is laced with an
eros. Husserl even describes the flow of life as being under the sway of an *entelechy*:
the *telos* of one's personal being dwells immanently within in a way which is not
yet complete. This *telos* ought not to be thought of after the fashion of the acorn's
developing into the oak tree, because the personal telos is not a specific concluding
inner-worldly goal, but it is an infinite idea, and yet an idea of my unique true self, not
an idea of a universal self.[55] We have already noted that the most elemental teleological phenomenon is consciousness' eros to fill in its ineluctable empty intentions; and
with the filling of these new horizons of empty intentions there opens, in turn, new
horizons emptily intended which consciousness aspires to fill in. The elemental teleological structure is basically that of presencing what is absent, unconcealing what is
concealed, and the revealing of secrets. This structure pervades the elemental stream
of consciousness upon which conative, volitional, and cognitive life builds. And no
less basic is the presence of transcendental or regulative ideas at the heart of this
elemental stream. An analysis of the essential inadequate presence of any perceptual
thing as presented in the theoretical stance reveals a nisus toward filling the intimated
absences of the other aspects with filled presences.

This structure is analogously ubiquitous in both the practical and theoretic realms. What is scientific verification and confirmation of scientific hypothesis if not the strategy to have filled intentions, even if they are the mediated types provided by advanced technology's microscopes and telescopes? A sheer mathematical-conceptual "necessity," to say nothing of a "probability," is not enough for a natural-scientific "confirmation." In spite of the post-Galilean prejudice, mathematical equations are not the equivalent of "nature" and the theoretical entities remain "merely theoretical entities" until there is a kind of confirmation of these hypotheses in the nature that we experience in the flesh, however highly mediated this experience is through technology, and however true it is that were it not for the mathematical equations we would not know what to look for. This structure of the interplay of presence and absence pervaded by the eros of filling empty intentions has its analogate in the realm of will. Our proposal, following Husserl, of a pervasive general latent will (cf. Blondel's "willing will"), what Husserl on occasion called a doctrine of "universal voluntarism," holds that even at the most elemental level there is an eros that holds sway in the establishing of empty intentions and their being filled in, and their being incessantly related in a unifying synthesis. This consideration serves as the basement for our focus on how "I myself" am inseparable from an ideal of myself, "my true self."

The personal ideal is not separable from this general or willing will, indeed the general will is the ideal's correlate at the most feeble level. Yet the person as constituted by the position-taking acts builds on this general will; each act, taken as a kind of willing, an actuation of I-can, is within the horizon predelineated by passive synthesis. And its ideals of unity and harmony are the general ineluctable frameworks for what emerges for the person as the good life and one's true self. There looms before each a skyline of a better world and oneself as better within this world. Husserl often referred to this dramatically when he referred to the "better" as the enemy of what is "good." "Better" here is to be thought of as including the moral, aesthetic, intellectual, sensuous aspiration.

My agency builds on the position-takings that are founded on empty and filled intentions, but its guiding motive is the world and myself with the horizons of the "more." Every act is determined in the sense of being part of an axiological- and meaning-context. What appears as good, or as worthy of doing, is inseparably tied up with prior experiences, judgments, etc., and what is expected from the present experiences, judgments, etc. Agency is tied up with the meaningfulness of my categorical-perceptual display of the world, just as the latter is often in the wake of the actions I have had to do out of necessity. And the horizons surrounding my thoughtful perceiving and agency themselves are immersed in horizons that I apperceive, some of which are unfathomable. Doubtless they are unfathomable because I could never bring many of them to intuitive givenness. They are entangled in past retentions that are beyond reach of memory and connected to associations that perhaps only several lifetimes of therapy could bring to light. And even then there would remain the essentially elusive presencing of my beginning. (See Book 1, Chapter VII.) Yet these motivational connections are mine in a very distinctive way.

But we have asked whether these motivational connections are unfathomable merely because they point to endlessly more of the same or is it more like the problem of my beginning and ending where I face a "I know not what," i.e., where I come upon a dimension of non-being which is not a *nihil negativum* but where what is to be explained, i.e., the principle of "myself" and the meaning of "my death," does not lend itself readily to the available explanatory categories. (Cf. our discussion of "mystery" in Chapter II above.)

In any case, the motivational connections determine me as my life-horizon, not as oxygen and the gravitational field determine me. They are biographical determinations, not physical, chemical, or biological ones. But am I therefore not free in regard to them? This question can only be answered in the first-person. One's freedom is evident not primarily in an intellectual insight but in one's deed. Its evidence is not an inference from a fact to the transcendental condition of the fact but in the expression of one's being oneself which of necessity involves the awareness of one's possibility to exist, one's "I can," about which one decides.[56] We will soon return to the issue of freedom.

In the wake of the willing will personal life is necessarily a living toward what is good, but the good is always over against a background of the better, and the better contrasts with the background of the best. The teleological drift of the mind is such that we not only prefer joy to what brings sadness, what is clear to what is confused, what is evidently true to what is an error. And it is not merely that there is a natural preference of the better for the merely good; but there is an exhortation or dynamism in our will's life such that the good is the foe of the better and the better the foe of what is the best. (Because this "best" requires "all things considered" it may not be construed as implying an argument for, e.g., an economics of wanton growth.) As the better "absorbs" the good, so the best absorbs the good and the better. There is an essential natural dynamism leading persons to a kind of unregrettable position-taking that enables them, from now on, to live a life aimed at what is the best such that it absorbs all that is good and better and is not capable of being absorbed by anything else.[57]

Here we have a Husserlian version of the Is founding the Ought. The tendency toward the pursuit of the best under the circumstances and the aspiration to a good that cannot be absorbed by anything else gives rise to an overriding absolute Ought that pervades the drift of the stream of life. It may take the form of "Do at each time the best amidst the achievable."[58] This best is always inseparable from how it emerges within the framework of my personal life-world. As we have seen, the lure of the best becomes an "absolute ought" in the form of a moral self-determining of oneself. And this position-taking is in the form of a resolve to live from now on and without hesitation the best life, and to do the best possible, as it is evident in each situation. But ineluctably this best possible involves the apperception of my best possible and best possible for me, "under the circumstances."[59] This, we have said, is a self-identifying act.

Nietzsche's imperative, "Act now in such a way that you would want to live in this way, doing what you are doing, repeatedly forever," may receive a transformation in our context to read: "Ask yourself whether you can will that this your deed is such that it may determine your entire life for better or for worse. There is no question that it does this; but now act knowing that this indeed is its significance."[60] Here the natural teleology of life itself *commands* that we *Be!* by pursuing the Ought of the best, the Is, intimated at the horizon of life. Our best position-takings, which also are our delineations of the adumbrated and indicated, aspire to best shape us and our world "from now on" and, as our *hexis*, follow us like karma and await us as our fate.

This doctrine of the inevitable drift of the human person, by which, of course, we do not mean to suggest an inevitable inescapable propulsion, towards a more rich, more perfect life, a true self, is perhaps compatible with any political ideology regardless of one's place in the class structure or social ladder. The "better" "best" are not only for the well-established; they loom on every horizon. The best under the circumstances appears equally as part of the belief in the need to maintain or reform institutions, to secure or displace power from traditional centers. It not a priori clear what form the pursuit and presencing of a best that could not be absorbed by anything might take. In so far as the person is of necessity interpersonal the various dogmas or myths would seem to find their norm in a communitarian arrangement. Thus however the Best would be articulated, e.g., as a kind of inner-worldly telos like "the classless society" or whether as a non-historical, non-political goal, e.g., "Heaven," or "the kingdom of God," or "Nirvana," somehow the intersubjective, interpersonal, and communitarian aspects would be addressed.

Yet the focus of this Book 2 is the essential teleology of personification, i.e., the entelechial power of ipseity to function as an ideal of one's personal being. We need not address here the social-political-theological aspects of this teleology.[61] Ipseity's (or the "myself's") personification is not only incomplete but essentially missing until the person determines herself to be a moral person. Ipseity, we have said, is not properly and normatively a person until it resolves to realize the true self which is delineated from the start in its personal being in the world with Others. This is, at the same time, a self-identifying act, i.e., I identify myself with the desire and what appears to be the means to realize my true self. Ipseity as such is tautologically will, but it as such is not evidently entelechy and the willing will pervading the willed will until it is personifying. This, of course, is how we know it from the start of our philosophical reflections, i.e., this is how we are for the most part and apart from the abstract considerations and thought experiments which reveal its propertyless character. Its identification of itself with itself is with itself as this person, this I self-determining itself; this is its choosing itself and realizing itself facing an infinite ideal. This we have called the awakening of the center of the I or Existenz. But this self-actualization of itself as a person is an actualization of what is inherently interpersonal and intersubjective. Its self-realization of itself is always of the ideal of a person of a higher order, to use Husserl's terms. Self-determination as identifying oneself with one's unique self-ideal is always also the achievement of the moral self and moral categoriality as the identifying oneself with another's good, or identifying another's evil with one's own good.[62]

It is the actuality of the ideal of ipseity which, from the standpoint of the present struggle, is the person's future possibility. The telos of the person as an ideal is an ideal of what is possible for the present struggling person to be realized step by step unto infinity. This possibility in this sense is both an ideal endlessly remote, and to this extent merely ideal, possibility and also a real possibility of a human person; but clearly the possible ideal as a real ideal is not a merely conceptual possible ideal, just as the "myself" or the ipseity is not itself a mere ideal nor merely possible. Yet, in order for the original "myself" to appear as an ideal, as the telos of personal life, it must be embedded in an ideal framework, one that infuses the existence-condition which is humanity. In order for it to be the dynamism which creates and is borne by the general will there has to be a further speculative consideration with which we are now familiar. Simply as lived ipseity it is *not* the ideal true self, but rather the ineluctable "myself." We are speculatively postulating that it serves as the entelechial base of the ideal true self of the human person. As such it functions as the final and formal cause of the moral life. But to have this status it must be "personified" and embody the latent life-will. It is with the horizon of this willing will that I identity in the desire for a complete and perfect life. As such the ideal is always elusive and given in the horizon of endless empty intentionality.

How can the ipseity function as the entelechy of my life as a person? Our answer has been clear: In order for it to function as the entelechy, the unique essence of the "myself" has to be embedded in an "ideal" axiological context. This context is opened up by the general will. Thus the condition for the possibility that ipseity be the principle the teleological perfection of one's personal existence is that it be embedded in the horizon opened by the willing will. Because the "myself" as abstracted from its personification, and thus as the transcendental I and as the non-ascriptively lived referent of "I," or as what comes to light in the Klawonnian thought experiments, does not admit any teleology it cannot *as such* be the entelechy and principle of perfection of the person. But this is not our first and sustained ineluctable acquaintance with the "myself" because it is always the "myself" as the substrate of what it has personified. In order that the "myself" as the individual essence that I am be not only the bare substrate and ideal unity throughout all my life in all of its metamorphoses but also be the principle of the teleological perfection of my personal being as it is inserted in the web of nature and history, it must reach into ideal axiological frameworks infinitely wider than the "unique essence" of the "myself."

Thus this ideal self as that to which we endlessly aspire and which endlessly eludes our approach cannot be understood simply as "the myself." But neither can it be understood as a mere empty projected ideal of what each aspires to be. Rather it must be the actualization or personification of the "myself," its "truth."

In the final chapter we will reflect on the traditional speculation that this ideal self, the fuller sense of "myself" as an individual essence, is one with the divine essence. From this "point of view," ipseity's truth as the ideal is not merely possible, empty, elusive, and futile, as it is for us in our struggle which is immersed in ignorance and finitude. Rather, it is eternally actual and existing. In any stage of the person's self-realization the divine individual essence is not actual for the person; it is the merely possible and the elusive horizon. Yet ipseity's individual super-essence can be the entelechy precisely because the "home" of this individual essence is the divine essence itself.

Clearly such a move is not one that phenomenology can make. Rather it is a speculation that, given enormous assumptions, i.e., those of faith, or the willing suspension of disbelief in "a likely story," can provide another, perhaps deeper context for reflecting on the relation between the person and the unique essence of the "myself."

Nevertheless, the status of such a "likely story" need not be reduced to a mere fiction that functions as an "As If" which serves to hide from us bitter truths. Let us briefly spell this out.

The ideal true self is a regulative ideal. This properly is not a fiction, even though it may legitimately serve someone as what some regard as a fictional function in so far as it is a source of hope and energy in regard to both the present and the future. As Husserl has said, in times of dire crises we have a duty to nurture the unique presence of the ideal.[63] For phenomenology the ideal is not merely a dynamism of reason, as it is for Kant, but it is something intended or noematic, indeed, something perceived in the way the horizon or what is co-perceived and co-meant may be said to be perceived. Initially the idea is not, as a co-perceived, co-meant, and/or co-given horizon, given as such if this means in a saturated filled intention. It is only when we attempt to present something and we realize that we can only present it inadequately, i.e., that what it is we want to present has an essential excess of meaning that eludes our acts of making it present, that we are aware of the something in question as an idea. The perceptual something, e.g., a barn, a cube, the world, or a person, including oneself as a person, cannot be given all at once but only piecemeal and endlessly. Such, of course, are real or spatial-temporal things, but the phenomenological reflection on the sense of their presence shows that part of the sense of their being present is that they come, as it were, endowed with an ideal version of their presentation. Barns of course have high ceilings and often weather-beaten sides and ideals have no such properties. But a barn or any barn as presented in phenomenological reflection shows its self as being present as an infinite ideal – and although presenting the aspects of the barn is an infinite task this is not to say that the barn or any barn has actually infinite sides.

There are noteworthy differences between the ideal and a fiction; there seems also to be a common root. Fictions need not be and are present through a modification of the spontaneous doxastic allegiance to their actuality. They are present *as if they were actual or real*, as David Copperfield and Doonesbury. But we all know in retrospect, and psychoanalysts remind us should we have forgotten it, that we, in order to protect ourselves, invent stories about the world and ourselves. In such cases, the As-If is transformed into great likelihood and eventual hyper-reality. What is possible becomes the really real. But, of course, such fictional-imaginative positings often turn out to be ruinous for their authors as well as those with whom the person is involved. The jealous man sees everywhere signs of his wife's infidelity; the envious woman sees exceedingly numerous signs of her rival's hostility to her; the psychopath is disposed to see everywhere people who are disdaining him. These defense-mechanisms or projections shape the world in accord with the deep-strata of weaknesses that we do not permit to come to light. Whereas passive synthesis properly would call them forth for us in their relevance for the present, if we are strong and honest enough to handle them, when we are weak we have developed devices to hide these wounds and weaknesses from ourselves. Traumas have the unique phenomenological property of being atemporal.[64] They resist the ongoing interpretation of the past that characterizes typical past events. They thus seem to maintain an ideal sameness. This accounts for the rigidity of the associational response and behavior when they are called forth. Because they resist being re-interpreted they come forth with a force resembling the original experience. The victim relives her part in the re-enactment of the eternal return of the same traumatic formative event. This, of course, at least superficially, resembles mythic cult practices.

Thus there is room for the theme of fiction in regard to the ideal if we consider both some psychogenetic considerations as well as the way the ideal is transformed in the course of one's own evolution towards normative personhood. We may here merely brush up against the surface of the issues.

The self-ideal as it emerges when we are children surely is related to the vulnerability, powerlessness, and smallness of the child. Thus the child may envisage her being a heroic policeman, or soldier, or Kung Fu expert. In this circumstance the self-ideal may well function as a device for overcoming the sense of her vulnerability and inferiority. The self-ideal may thus have a kind of compensatory function. That is, it may be so posited "as if it were able," by effectively guiding the direction of the child's will, to bring her greater security and a more firm orientation and basis on which to take her stand. The self-ideal is a device which provides a compensation in the present by providing a token feeling of security because it enables her to feel superior to the difficulties that she perceives.

In holding that the self-ideal is tied to the essential self-inadequation as this comes to light in the distinction between the willing will and the willed will, we have the foundation not only for the ideas of perfection, the perfect clay vase, utopia, sainthood, etc., but we have of necessity the seeds of the general pathology classically called neurosis. We may say that all the neurotic phenomena like aggression, narcissism, chronic envy, a sense of inferiority, etc., have their foundation in the ineluctable horizon of one's self-ideal as an inadequation with oneself and with one's ideal being in the world. It is not only the child or the abnormal or mentally unhealthy adult who strives to make an end to the uncertainties, difficulties, surds, and fears that incessantly comprise one's life. What determines infantilism and what we come to call pathology and abnormality is how the ideal is permitted to dominate the horizon of one's life, how one lives with doxastic allegiance in the idealization and its fictions, and how traumatic the early experience of vulnerability and helplessness was. Surely the ideal's beckoning the mature adult to the perfection of a self-determining, self-renewing, self-identifying life facing the best under the circumstances contains within it not only the sense of inadequacy but it also edifies and exhorts to overcoming the temptations to paralysis and despair. The agitation and unsettledness before the horizon of perfection can move one to strive for progress and improvement and resolve not only to resist wallowing in a sense of inferiority, but to console oneself that these very temptations are indirect ways of honoring the exalted destiny of oneself. As Alfred Adler has put it, inferiority feelings – and we may substitute: the lived experiences of one's self-inadequation – are not in themselves abnormal, but rightly understood are the causes of all improvements in an individual's life and in that of humankind as well.[65]

But the self-ideal of the person who is mature and honest is not primarily a fictional device that compensates for the fears and sense of inferiority that life's circumstances occasion. Ancient associated motivations need not function, like traumas, atemporally. They may with the proper patient explication of the present felt-meanings they constitute be brought to light for what they actually were. Similarly, the self-ideal of a position-taking of self-determination that I can stand behind for all eternity may gain a luster that is tied to a person's growing love of himself and Others as well as, e.g., a growing love of the life of reason and the pursuit of what is intrinsically beautiful.

In the interpretation that sees the self-ideal as a compensatory fictional device the self-ideal's functioning would resemble what one might call the "hedonistic ruse." The "hedonist" position is that all of life is undertaken for the pleasure deriving from one's actions. The pleasures become the telos of agency and the purported target is not really the goal of the action or even the action but merely a means to the pleasure deriving from the action. Thus one loves one's neighbor, one studies philosophy, one fights for civil rights, etc., because of the "satisfaction" or "pleasure" one derives from these matters, whether it drives from the praise of others, the enhancement of one's self-esteem, or some warm comforting feelings. In this respect all agency is self-referential and self-centered. The transcendence of that which one strives for and the value of the thing in itself are denied in favor of the value of pleasure – which itself has become a transcendent aim for which one strives. Similarly, one might say, the functional-fictional theory of the self-ideal of the unique ideal person I am called to be and which I want to be holds that what one strives for, i.e., this unique person I am called to be, is not worthy in itself of devotion but is of value only because it allays my fears and assuages the wounds of my soul – which, perhaps, has the same vulnerability it had when I was a child.

The Husserlian-Aristotelian position we espouse here is that there is, indeed, a "blessedness" and a satisfaction in pursuing the Good, in particular the ideal of pursuing the best under the circumstances through a self-identifying, self-determining irrevocable act. But this self-ideal emerges out of one's life-horizon as containing a genuine real possibility of approximate realization. In this sense the self-ideal is a transcendent ideal, an ideal essence, a value-essence of my personal self, in itself. It is not merely a device for meeting one's feelings of inferiority or inadequacy, i.e., one's neuroses, however strong such a motivation might have been in earlier parts of one's life. "Blessedness" and "satisfaction" in the living of life occur precisely because I strive for and bring about the good for its own sake; they are never properly the targets of life. If I strive for the good purely and simply for the sake of itself, in this case the good of my ideal self, then I have blessedness in any case. The joy and delight are in the possession and incremental realization of the ideal, but I do not strive after the blessedness, satisfaction, joy and delight. To strive for these is a completely different agency with a completely different intentional object, just as my striving to raise my child in the best possible way for her sake is different from striving for the satisfaction I might get from the striving for what is best for my child.[66]

§7. A Sense in Which Who One Is Equates with What Sort of Person One Is

The (at least conceptual) possibility of there being incomplete persons existing without any or very little self-determination (as in perhaps some forms of handicapped persons or wantons) returns us to the fundamental issue of the distinction between *who* one is and *what* one is. In the self-identifying, self-determining acts by which one acts so as to realize one's unique self-ideal within the social-communitarian framework in which one finds oneself, one determines not absolutely *who* one is but rather, in a special honorific sense, what kind of person one is. In the self-determination of oneself to pursue one's ideal self and the best possible life, one determines oneself to act throughout one's life in accord with the best possible life and in accord with what one wants most in regard to oneself, and in this sense one engages in a self-identifying act and determines oneself to be a certain kind of person, an exemplarily moral person. And this is a determination to constantly renew one's self-determination, and this implies determining what desires and hopes one will have. This obviously has affinity with what in classical thought was named giving oneself *character*.

In giving oneself character, one does not give oneself a moral straightjacket which is extrinsic to oneself; rather, one gives oneself (emphatically) oneself by giving oneself a life in accord with one's deepest desires and ideals. In this sense character is neither an automatism extrinsically determining our will nor is it a standard of excellence other than oneself. Character in the most honorific sense is the moral person, the sort of person personified ipseity has constituted in the light of the ideal. Character in this honorific sense is the result of my doing acts *I* have identified with as piecemeal realizations of my true self.

We acknowledged that we are using "character" honorifically. Clearly its intrinsic nature comes to light equally when we think of it in terms of forms of deficient or harmful self-determinations which we unhesitatingly find blameworthy – providing we are prepared to rule out agency which is not free. Thus we distinguish, e.g., the referents of moral judgments from those regarding mental illness. Of course, we are always mindful of the "sociological factors," i.e., beginnings of the beginning of character over which the agent has no control. These come to light especially in the cases of the extraordinarily good and extraordinarily bad characters. (For this matter of the beginning of the beginning of character, see the next section.)

We repeatedly fuse who one is with one's character in our third-person observations. We observe, perhaps after someone has done something very courageous or vicious: "Now I know who you are." "Now you have revealed who you are." All of these observations could be paraphrased as "Now I know what kind (what sort) of person you are." Or when we want to summarize who someone was, e.g., in giving a euology at his funeral, we give an account of his most splendid virtues. Here *who* one is, is inseparable from *what sort of person* he is. We think of the person in her innermost core in terms of her virtue (or lack thereof) and we celebrate her in terms of this unique kind of excellence. We do not, in eulogizing *who* someone is, e.g., someone who was well known for her professional talents, celebrate her accomplishments, unless we mean thereby to single out some virtues like conviviality, dedication, self-discipline, etc. I recall hearing a prominent philosopher euologizing another distinguished philosopher. "He had the greatest mind I ever knew. You know he worked twelve hours a day!" Here the great quality, even genius, of the deceased colleague was acknowledged, yet this was made inseparable from his extraordinary work ethic. Of course, if this work ethic and philosophical genius were all that could be said in praise of this person, we might have occasion to be saddened.

All this reveals the conviction that the virtuous acts behind character are acts with which the person in her core is identified in the doing of these acts. This is where her center was perhaps in spite of, or amidst, the glitz of fame, or the revulsion, dread, or fear of the situation evoked. Of course, virtue and character can be simulated; one can act "in good form" and to "keep up appearances." Further, the praise can be directed at isolated acts and not the character which underlies them. In any case, the praise aims not merely at the character as manifest in the excellences or strengths the tradition called "virtues" or the isolated contingent acts but foremost at the person who performs the acts and has the character.

Genuine praise does not aim at mere appearances, even though the one giving praise might well be taken in. We eulogize someone's generosity, kindness, patience, etc., because these reflect the core of the person, i.e., they capture that with which she identified and what was central in her life. If someone does "the right thing" in order to "keep up appearances" we may be glad and even rejoice in this because, e.g., the dreaded consequences are avoided, but this is not praising the person. Such a person's center is elsewhere, not in this deed. Similarly we do not praise someone for being lucky. If the acts were mere random or non-self-determining acts that might have been done by, or happened to, anyone under similar circumstances, we would not be moved to single them out as targets of praise. When someone does something praiseworthy on a single occasion which appears to go against his character, we are puzzled and perhaps suspicious because such an act does not reflect what we take to be the center of the person. Of course, it might reflect the person's change of heart, but because this deed is out of character we have reason to be hesitant to praise the person. When we eulogize we praise the person in his core, not incidental aspects of his being.

Praise is always of someone for something. Praise here is contrasted with *admiration* in the sense of being amazed at. This latter may be directed purely and simply at some non-personal thing. An issue of special interest for our present theme is the way we do and do not identify the person or ipseity with her praiseworthy or reprehensible qualities. Although one may indeed scold and/or praise one's car or computer this is not to be understood as perceiving the car or computer as a responsible agent. Thus the praise of the accomplishments of a computer is implicitly directed at the workers behind the manufacturing of the computer. Therefore, praise that targets a "what" must always aim at least indirectly at someone, a Who. Of course one can celebrate, be astonished at a What, e.g., the quality of a sunset, and we can "praise" it in this more general sense, but we obviously are not praising a Who; in a proper sense we are not praising the sun and the sky and the atmosphere for an act for which they are responsible.

Yet clearly there are contexts where appreciation aims at achievements or qualities more or less isolated from the person as the source of the agency. Or better: being taken with the achievement or the quality someone has, e.g., her skill, beauty, or grace, may be such that one postpones or suppresses knowing what she is *really* like, i.e., one has an aesthetic delight in the qualities and defers knowing what sort of person she is. In such a case, the marvelous quality or deed may supervene and define in the admirer's eye the person or agent. In which case, projections and imaginary empty intentions are occasioned whereby the doer or person is replaced by the "image" of the doer or person. Indeed, one might resist an "insider's report" on what she is "really like."

In such cases the praise is directed at the qualities and achievements (or perhaps the exalted office) and the issue of who the achiever is, i.e., what sort of person she is, is of interest only in so far as the achiever has the qualities which enabled the achievement. Here the real character of the person, i.e., the sort of person one is based on the agent's self-identification with her acts and manner of life, recedes in importance. For such an observer, the splendor of the quality of the achievement overwhelms the moral person and reality of the agent. This may result in the seduction that the agent himself, quite in consonance with the public perception, finds his identity exclusively in this quality or achievement. The hero of John Updike's *Rabbit Run* is, even into his middle age, at the mercy of his *having been* in his high school days a sports hero. Indeed, the fans or those bestowing praise create for the achiever an identity that conforms to their past and present delight in the achievement. The mystery behind the "lives of the rich and famous" is sustained not only because of a need for privacy but because the luster of the qualities and/or achievements and the perpetuating of the praise require that the doer of the deed conform to what the fans' imagination creates.

This is related to the consideration that praise is of someone for something. Thus someone's being praised is conditioned by the deed. In the sensational world of media events and its own creation of a mythic consciousness, praise typically is directed at the actual achievements and qualities foremostly and only indirectly and mediately at the character and then even more indirectly and mediately at the ipseity.

Politics and the world of publicity or media construe someone primarily in terms of the public, official-governmental, corporate-media interpretation of the public office or deed. The celebrity is in the familiar sense the "personification" of the esteemed qualities and exalted office. Thus in a funeral eulogy of a public person or celebrity, like that of a normal non-celebrity, praise is directed indeed at the ipseity, but via the qualities as indications of the person's character. Of course, for the general perception much depends on who controls the public display. In any case there will always be at least the few who know the difference between the public or official version and what the truth of the matter is. Whether bogus and contrived or honest and true, the eulogistic praise of a person's core is conditioned by and dependent on these qualities which are taken to reveal at least what sort of person the deceased was.

In contrast we may say that love in the essential distinctive sense we have sketched is directed at the ipseity, but of necessity goes through the qualities. Yet, in its ideal form, it is not dependent on the qualities and, in contrast to the praise directed at the esteemed person, love is not withdrawn when these estimable qualities prove to be bogus or are no longer actual. (See our discussion in Book 1, Chapter IV, especially §16.) The scandals that surround celebrities are often connected with the revelation that the lauded qualities are fake. When these qualities turn out to have been a deception then the interest in the one having the qualities evaporates – except in so far as one may find reason to turn one's anger at the person whom one has surrounded with a comforting mythology commensurate with these super qualities, and whose unmasking is the occasion for the bursting of the bubble of one's own making.

The identification of one's character with oneself is evident in the first-person when one speaks of the necessity of having to act in a certain way. One might say: "If I did not act in this way I could not have lived with myself." And, of course, shame and feelings of guilt reflect that how we have determined ourselves through our action reveals in an intimate sense who we have identified ourselves as being. Or, we similarly ask ourselves, "*who* am I?" perhaps in the wake of a surprising decision we recently made, or in the wake of a trusted friend's daring to share with us his candid perception about some aspect of ourselves.

Here in such contexts clearly *who* one is, the strongest sense of one's (identifiable) identity, is not the mere ipseity, the mere "myself," about which there can be no doubt; nor is it about one's professional identity and the list of one's accomplishments. Rather it refers to "what sort of person I am." And this points to our basic thesis that ipseity and personhood are incomplete until there is moral self-determination.

In this case *who* one is, is not the propertyless "myself" but the radically situated and contextualized, historical, and interpersonal person as she has self-determined herself in her core. The moral person *who* one is, is a result of one's position-taking acts, foremost those with which one self-identifies, and the habitualities one has built as a result of these acts. But this habituality does not prevail after the fashion of a programmed robot or an automaton, and one's self-determination is a will to constant renewal and renewed self-determination. Whereas there is truth in the notion that habit is a second nature, for persons much of even what we regard as original nature or "first nature" must be monitored and is something which in many aspects is not absolutely divorced from freedom and responsibility. For this reason we have "vices" or "addictions" which are precisely disorders of "nature" for which we typically bear a measure of responsibility.

Nevertheless, it remains true that the personal moral identity is tied to the historical context, and character has an abiding sameness over time, even with the relapses and renewals, the shades of modification due to adjustments to ongoing novel circumstances, etc. In extreme cases, as we have noted in Book 1, the question of the identity of the person may become acute, especially if there should intervene pathologies of a physical or mental order. In which case, we may presume, as Book 1 attempted to clarify, the "identity" of ipseity or the "myself" as the basis for the evolution of the person and character. Of course, this is not an identity by way of identifying acts but is the "identity" of the "myself" which all identifying acts presuppose.[67]

Yet this latter "identity" of the "myself" comes to the fore even in the contexts of evaluation of "what sort of person" the person is. Consider how we, in our ungenerous moments, identify the sin with the sinner or the reprehensible act with the person. When we see, e.g., viciousness in others, there may rise up a temptation to deal with them by destroying them as persons, e.g., making sub-persons or demons out of them, i.e., persons who are in the possession of an evil will, character, or spirit. Yet in our own case, should we recognize our sins, weaknesses, viciousness, we give ourselves a wide berth and separate our reprehensible acts from our basic will and our selves. We readily take the attitude that the act was perhaps not really voluntary, but rather a moment of weakness and an anomaly; it did not really represent me because I am so much more than that moment of stupidity, etc.

In any case, we want to believe, and want Others to believe, that it was not a self-identifying act that reveals who I am in my core. "Yet at the same time we are fully aware that others do not make this convenient distinction for us. The acts that have been done by us are, in their eyes, 'our' acts and they hold us fully responsible."[68] Of course such an intersubjective reciprocity of perceptions contains the seeds of acrimony, violence and war.

When we are more generously disposed, e.g., as in giving eulogies of someone who is dying or dead, we will more likely make allowances in others and make a distinction between the achievements, deeds, character, and person. Thus we typically focus as much as possible on the good character of the person more so than on the accomplishments, in so far as these latter reflected the realization of talents that the person was endowed with. Of course, when the talents were actualized for the benefit of the community of the person, there is special reason to eulogize and be grateful. Yet there is clearly the occasion when we might say to a dying loved one: "We, of course, love you for what you have done and accomplished, what sort of person you are, etc., but we also love *you*; we love who you are for your own sake, apart from your achievements." This might seem to be a pleonasm to one for whom who one is, is identified with the person's properties. But for the person being appreciated, who knows of his weaknesses, his failings, how often he failed to show up for himself and his friends and neighbors, and who knows the inadequacy of his actualization of his self-ideal, these might well be the most welcome words. In the first-person there is the "myself," i.e., "unencumbered," "simple," and "naked" self (as the mystics put it) that is other than and more than the person, and if this is not ultimately appreciated and loved, it is not clear that the person himself is truly loved. It is this sense of oneself as the radical principle of ipseity and freedom of which each is aware, and which is keenly aware of the "grace" of being and the fragility of the moral achievement of "the sort of person" one is. Again, although we have reason to approach an equivalence between "who" one is and "what sort of person" one is, the distinction still remains.

Yet it is of interest that even the spiritual writers who insist on the need for the person to be loved for her unencumbered naked self might, because of the unconditioned importance of the task of self-transformation (or normative "personification," to use our earlier term), also say that there is *no special* identity unless persons become, through self-renunciation, the true self they are meant to be. This coincides with the philosophical view discussed in Book 1 that what is foremost required of us by the Good or Beauty is a radical "unselfing" and de-construction of any sense of "I." Here there would seem to be a confusion. We begin with a person who suffers from a false identity and strives above all else to preserve this identity which in fact is, because false, a deleterious, self-destructive one. Unless the person becomes receptive to the contours of her true self (and, as classical Christian spirituality puts it, submits her will to God's will) she cannot undo this identity, and she will lose her true identity. But, after all, as we showed in Book 1, there is the unidentifiable identity of the unique ipseity throughout this biography, whether it leads to healing or destruction. And, as we have proposed, there is a special kind of congruence between the naked self bereft of all properties and the true self.[69] (We will wrestle with this at length in the final chapter in a theological context.)

It is intriguing to note that, over and above the distinct senses of selves as "naked ipseities" and as persons we praise them as individuals in terms of a normative sense of *being human*. Being human is thus not here regarded as a mere ontological or biological category but rather as a moral and perhaps existential one. We rarely say as a compliment in English, "He is a human being." But in German and Yiddish it is common to say "Er ist *ein Mensch!*" "He is a *Mensch!*" But even in English we may ask of someone who has done something reprehensible, "Are you a human being?" "Have you no humanity in you?" Thus there seems to be perfect symmetry between "What sort of person am I?" and "What sort of human am I?" There seems to be a belief here that the guide for being a moral person is outlined in normative humanity. Here the "sort" or kind of human suggests not merely particular instantiations but moral gradations, again, in terms of virtue and vice, good character and bad character. Further, acting in an exemplary fashion suggests that someone merits the praise of being a "human," in part because she embodies all the core excellences of the kind of being we call human. In calling someone in this honorific sense a "human" or *Mensch* we have uttered the highest praise conceivable; anything else is superfluous. The highest praise would be when all the core excellences of all possible humans are embodied in this individual.

Yet it is clear that we do not know what this is in advance. "Human" is a third-person "theory-laden" concept that can well reflect historical and cultural contexts that are divorced from the moral ideal as it arises for a single individual in a concrete circumstance. Jesus and Gandhi, we may assume, would have been poor representatives of "humanity" in both earlier and later cultural settings. Consider how in international hostilities "humanly degrading" is a taboo when applied to one's own country's behavior but is the norm for what the enemy typically does.

In spite of the questions that arise in determining the precise ontological and moral sense of "humanity," the personal ideal that emerges for the unique single individual will always be a human personal ideal. This is because the exemplary form of the person is known by us in the existence-condition of the kind we call human. The telos of personal life will conform to the form of human as the form will reflect the telos. Nevertheless there need not be perfect coincidence in the unique personal ideal and a reigning honorific understanding of "human."[70]

We hope that none of these remarks which discourage an identity between humanity and the "myself" may serve as an excuse to ignore the profound natural-essential solidarity of human persons with one another and the natural, interdependent relation with the natural world. A strong case can be made, we believe, for the "kinship" humans have with all living beings. It is doubtlessly true that high on the list of extraordinary challenges that persons face today is to recognize their human solidarity and the need to address the great dangers to the common earth through, e.g., global warming, pollution, and the catastrophes of a nuclear melt-down or a nuclear holocaust. Only a distorted angelization or spiritualization of the human person would amount to a reason to deny the imperatives of the ecological movement to recognize our solidarity with other humans and other natural species. But having affirmed such important matters, there are still a basic philosophical distinctions between our being human, our being persons, and the basic issue of the "myself." One reason for reminding ourselves of these distinctions is that there is a pull to identify personhood and ipseity with being a member of the contingent random biological species called "human." This too we believe leads to errors that can have very harmful consequences. In any case, let us briefly engage in some reflections which encourage the distinction between being human and being a "myself."

Whereas in the first-person, "who am I?" (understood to be equivalent here to "What sort of person am I?") seems to prescind from a reflection on the biological category human species (as distinct from the ontological category of human kind), it might well be implicit in "what sort of human am I?" In the third-person, the answer to the question, "what sort of human is he?" might be: "He is a snake!" In which case, "snake" refers not to the moral standing of serpents but to how the way the serpentine being in the world can be a metaphor for a deficient human being, perhaps for someone who slithers through the moral categories in a base way and will harm you when you least expect it. A key issue here is: In what sense does being a human in a normative sense override the purposes and intentions of a person? Is being a person, a non-sortal referent, less basic than being the kind of being which is human? In what sense does being or having human nature dictate the ends to which the purposes or intentions of humans must be subordinate? In what sense is the teleology of ipseity a matter of ontology, i.e., a matter of the ends of the ontological form of the kind of being we call human? We will address directly these important questions in Chapter V, §7.

Furthermore, as suggested in Book 1, especially Chapter VIII, we can imagine for ourselves forms of agency which stretch the conditions of our personal identity, including our humanness, but which would not thereby eliminate our moral personhood. Thus, e.g., one might imagine oneself with an utterly "eutopian" or "glorified" body free of the limitations, ailments and burdens that the embodiment of humans entails; or we might imagine ourselves having to deal with persons whose self-presentation differed exceedingly from anything like a human one. And perhaps the imagination was capable of making *oneself* a member of such a non-human community. Angels, demons, elves, and titans are some familiar examples. But this imaginative experiment would not result in my being dispensed from a normative sense of being a person, of being me myself, but the sense in which my being human would be placed under stress. (Ancient and medieval writers on angelology as well as modern authors like C.S. Lewis, J.R.R. Tolkein, and Ursula LeGuin have all given us intimationa of such imaginative variations of what it means to be a person.)

§8. The Sort of Person One Is and Freedom

If the person as an identifiable entity is founded on position-taking acts which are both cognitive-intellectual as well as moral-emotive, it would seem that we must distinguish the person from what sort of person one is, because the latter involves a moral appreciation. The person is the identifiable identity constituted by the position-taking acts. But the sort of person one is, in the special honorific sense of one's moral person, marks the person in the way many position-taking acts do not. Position-taking acts, such as judgments and decisions about states of affairs in many areas of life, like those of house-holding, recreation, and the workplace, may well be achieved without being explicitly, decisively, or emphatically self-determining. (Of course, general or generic judgments and decisions having to do with these very areas may themselves be pregnant with self-determination. For example, one may radically simplify one's householding in terms of living a sub-sistence economy which uses only local and organic products, or one may give up a lucrative job for one more in line with one's basic values.) This emphatic marking of the person, what we are suggesting is the coincidence of the sort of person one is with a special "personified" sense of who one is, involves a centering and whole-heartedness, i.e., a self-identification with the act, that does not characterize much of the flow of our personal lives.

Cognitive-theoretical acts which establish and characterize our perceptual and intellectual, reflective and theoretical life are typically not self-identifying acts. Sizing up a situation, analyzing something, following an argument, being logically consistent, etc. are ways of being cognitively awake. Although they are pervaded by one's unique personal horizon, there is a sense in which anyone in my shoes would pursue the matter or go about solving the issue in this way. I myself in the emphatic sense am not in question. There is not a case of my integrity being on the line; nor is it a case of whether I can live with myself if I do X rather than Y. Of course, getting comfortable with logical inconsistency verges on self-betrayal and self-alienation. On the other hand, rigor in logical consistency need not at all imply moral earnestness.

It is noteworthy that in the acts that reveal one's characteristic behavior, there is a diminishment of one's self-agency in this behavior precisely because it is characteristic. This is obvious in one's following one's tastes and preferences in more or less morally neutral matters, like selecting an item on a menu or the choice of a preferred form of recreation, etc. One usually goes with the drift of one's prior choices or dispositions, or the conventional practices established by one's community and circle of friends. It is also obvious that one's class or upbringing may provide enough economic and emotional security to enable a person to be free of the numerous temptations that afflict her neighbors or fellow citizens who are raised in very poor, violent, and morally sordid environments.

Aristotle, for whom our actions were the beginning of character, hinted that there was a beginning to this beginning of character, i.e., the beginnings of one's moral beginnings, over which the person had no control. This meant for him primarily a beginning where the child is enabled to love what is noble and feel disgust at what is base.[71] Character as one's *habitus* or abiding disposition, as, e.g., integrity in the work place, being honest, courteous, non-aggressive, and kindly with one's colleagues and neighbors, being faithful to one's commitments and friends, etc., reflects the way prior agency has a validity, legitimacy, and staying power throughout one's life until revoked or contradicted. Because one has been prudent, patient and generous, because one has early practiced fraternal charity in the forms of not gossiping or not defaming, because one has long respected the rights of others, etc., one has grown accustomed to comporting oneself these ways and numerous occasions of immorality in the course of the day simply do not arise. For such persons of virtue, there is not even a flutter of a temptation to defame or steal from one's neighbor. In this sense character as the firm disposition to act in a certain way diminishes the freedom of many praiseworthy forms of behavior. What has become one's second nature is not at the present moment an explicit matter of one's freedom because it does not have to be chosen in each instance.

Now, it might well be the case that sobriety, mildness, veracity, etc., which are automatic in one's behavior at the present were won at a cost. That is, one had to act against the drift of one's earlier character and the earlier tendencies and dispositions of one's life. Presently one acts with relative moral effortlessness, but prior to this the *autos*, the self, had to be engaged with great effort to overcome the pull in the other direction. In this respect there is more freedom (from temptations, pitfalls, etc.) and yet less of self-enactment, i.e., less "auto-nomicity" and more "auto-maticity," in the present life of virtue than in the life of someone for whom there are numerous temptations at every level because of the burden of impulse and the weight of the past.

Perhaps the most fundamental consideration here is that the weight of the vitiating past hinders freedom for the good, for that which is appropriate and in one's own true best interests; bad character hinders one from appreciating the good as the good, the noble as the noble. Goodness and decency appear repugnantly as, e.g., for "saps" or "goody-goodies," and do not have the luster they have for one raised in a different social milieu.

But if good character not only provides a clarity of moral perception but also enables us to act from our strengths and in this sense empowers our freedom and makes the good life ours without any or with less a struggle, then is there not a greater moral heroism for the weak person who cannot count on these acquired habitual strengths? (Let us leave aside the question of moral blindness, and assume an "equal moral perceptual field." If only the good person perceives the good, then we would seem to have a problem of every being motivated to be good. We must assume that clarity of moral perception and moral blindness are not absolute.)

Someone who is a recovering addict and who maintained the addiction through robbery and stealing, and who has become adept at numerous deceitful practices, like hiding the addiction from himself and loved ones, faces every hour of the day a moral struggle. It is usually acknowledged to be a moral miracle when such a person realizes that this way of life as a whole has to be rejected; he has finally come to realize that both literally and metaphorically to continue to live this way is to choose death rather than life. We will return to this. Here we wish to highlight that, on the one hand, such a person's success in the moral struggle might appear to the observer to be little, given the frequent failures, but on the other hand, such a person might, in the core of her self, be involved in heroic adventures of the spirit. The advice not to judge applies especially here. (And the power of love to move beyond the qualities of the person to the person herself becomes especially appropriate as a general mode of being with Others, but especially with those who appear repugnant by reason of their weaknesses.)

This raises the question of whether the "sinner" could not be a "saint" or even the exemplary "saint." Certainly in the eyes of most Christian saints they are the greatest of sinners. But could it not also be said that the genuine saint too, and not the person of "good character," as praiseworthy as this person might be, is engaged in struggle, darkness, and a mighty wrestle with temptation, even though this perhaps is much less evident to the outside observer? Is there not a law to the moral-spiritual life of ascent, a law which both Husserl and Whitehead recognized: If one is not ascending one is falling, if one is not struggling for a greater form of moral perfection one is then relapsing.[72] Gandhi is reported to have said that one can never make the institutions of a society so good that people do not have to be good[73] – so similarly one's character, a personal "institution," can never be so good that the good person will not have to struggle with fulfilling her duties and resisting temptations. In both cases we have the implication of an elusive core that the respective "institutions" of society and personal character or habitus do not determinatively reach.

H.D. Lewis, with whom this work has a special kinship on key issues, clearly wants us to avoid thinking of the institutions as having the power and privilege of subsuming this elusive core. Lewis again gives us food for thought on the issues of character and freedom, as well as on the matter of what we are calling Existenz and self-identifying acts. In order to see this kinship we must first address Lewis's view that *only* the acts which we perform in resisting temptation not to do our duty are properly free and therefore properly moral. If we acknowledge that character or the sort of person we have become empowers us, with little or no effort, and therefore without any properly self-identifying intervening emphatic *I-acts*, to move through much of the day with little moral effort, then these acts are more or less automatic and I-less. In this respect they are not properly moral (because *I* am not actively engaged). They are not properly acts which *I* do because they are ineluctable, given the sort of person I have become over time. Of course, we can say that our character traits, i.e., our being disposed to be just, kind, temperate, etc. are themselves praiseworthy. But the acts done in the wake of these traits enjoy a kind of necessity, the necessity of my being trans-temporally this sort of person, and therefore are not free, and therefore the sense in which they are laudable as characteristic acts is diminished. Lewis says that *they are not properly moral acts precisely because they are determined by one's character*. Lewis speaks of the gloominess and "unrelieved inevitability about all that we are and do," in those stretches of our life where "we have no genuine part of our own to play," because we in and of ourselves as purely ourselves do nothing, and the reason for this gloom is that "all the selfhood… we have is itself embodied exhaustively in the propensities that have come together to make us the persons we are."[74]

We might say, Mary's conduct is characterized by her being consistent with and acting out the requirements placed on her by her prior cognitive and moral position-taking acts. And these enable her to enjoy a life with excellent friends, pursue political causes of social justice, have a fine taste and astute critical mind in literature and music as well as a predilection for philosophical and scientific argument, at which she herself is proficient. There is no purely moral effort in her conduct in these matters, and the necessity that pervades her conduct is brought to light if we consider that neither she nor we can easily imagine her behaving differently. This is the freedom of "superior attainment." In so far as there is a kind of automatic functioning in the person of good character such that a person is not drawn to what is puerile, stupid, banal, self-destructive, obviously harmful to others, etc. this person is less free in regard to such matters.

Clearly there here is an enormous "freedom from" what is vicious, in the sense that it does not enter one's horizon of interests. But this is not the freedom which, Lewis says, is *common to the sinner and the saint*, and which they both exercise in the same way and to the same degree. It is only, Lewis claims, when someone, whether sinner or saint, *faces a temptation* to go against what is required of her, i.e., to go against what appears as her duty or obligation, by reason of this drift of her character and/or her other inclinations, that she engages in a properly moral act.

If one were to live perpetually from out of and in the wake of "good character" one would never have to act from out of the core of her being. In such a case there would be the irony that the struggling "sinner" is more free than the "saint." In the struggle with temptation in the face of one's obligations, one is wholly thrown upon oneself, upon one's being and not one's having and all the gifts of nature or fortune, all the rich past experiences, habitualities, and endowments, count for nothing. Here no one has an advantage over others; no one has here an edge in life. Here "we are all equal in the awesome solitariness of our supreme personal agency" (51–52).

By "effort" we mean generally acting against some resistance. Obviously of relevance here is not primarily physical effort, which may or may not have any moral aspect affixed to it. We thus may extend "effort" to following one inclination rather than another one. Thus we have effort in resisting the temptation to break one's fast as well as in the effort to keep climbing, even though tired, so that we can get to the top of the hill (which, of course, might be construed as a conflict between coming to someone's aid and indulging one's tired body). For Lewis, *effort*, in the sense of the struggle to let one motivation or one interest dominate over another one, which characterizes both the course of typical intentionality as well as the effect of character on the course of life, is of a completely different order than *moral effort*. Thus consider where, in confronting a moral perplexity or dilemma, there may come an insight in which one is able to "think outside the box" and see a better course which not only does justice to all the concerns of the contesting parties, but one which in fact is better for each. In such a case we are moved by, e.g., the new Gestalt's evidence, and, being normally intelligent people, we will gladly take this route as a matter of rational-practical necessity. But being so moved, Lewis thinks, is a matter of course precisely because a matter of rational nature or character; it is a matter of necessity and thus it lacks the purity of oneself acting from out of oneself alone. If normally awake and intelligent, it is a matter of necessity that we are not stupid. The truly moral effort "is wholly free, it is against the line of least resistance, it could have been otherwise and the issue thus remains in doubt until it is made. It is the core of our moral existence" (62).

Here too, with the order of purely moral effort, we have the proper foundation for thinking of moral acts as praiseworthy and blameworthy. If *I* alone do them, and if my agency is properly mine, and not a result of my upbringing, my natural intellectual and moral endowments and habitualities, my education, etc., then I am the true author of the acts. I am alone accountable (58).

Lewis answers the criticism that such a view proposes that "any action could come from any man at any time" in several ways. The first is the one we have just seen. He acknowledges character or personal moral identity as something holding sway over our behavior. He admits fully what we have described, following Husserl, as the weight and drift of passive synthesis and position-taking acts. This ongoing achievement, independent of our present actual I-agency of our drives, patterns of perception, hierarchy of preferences, and distinctive styles of conduct, is undeniable. Further, he acknowledges character and virtue as having genuine ethical value: It is good indeed to have the virtues of compassion, courage, etc. Further, we have every reason to admire the person's stability, as someone we can trust in and count on in the future to keep her commitments and to conduct herself in the way she has behaved in the past. Furthermore, Lewis does not wish to deny that having sound moral views and opinions is of great moral importance.

But the key for Lewis is that if, in our self-reference with "I," one refers not to something in the world, not to something I have, not to what is part of the causal network, and not to something that we identify with properties, then when *I* act, and not I as a result of my character, personality or other endowments, then the properly moral act must be *radically free*. Because the "self," which for Lewis is proximate to what we mean by the "myself," knows itself to be other than itself as a particular identifiable person, it knows itself to be other than its constituted identity and its passing states or any patterning of dispositions, and knows its proper agency will transcend these. And although this self is involved necessarily in all these patterns and dispositions, the self's proper choice is an "open choice," i.e., one that is absolutely undetermined, or one that could be different even though everything else remained the same (43, 67). The properly moral choice may well appear to others who observe my conduct to be random and capricious, but it is not random at all. It "is what we ourselves most firmly determine, the supreme exhibition of our unique functioning in the way of what it is to be a person" (42).

We may now relate Lewis's views to this book.

When Lewis here refers to the person he means, I believe, often what he frequently calls "the self" and what this work has referred to as the "myself." That is, he too makes the distinction between the person and the "myself." This is the central point which binds us to Lewis but which also becomes the basis for our criticism. We will return to this shortly.

Lewis does not want to say that in these situations of tension between inclination and duty that the agent's perception of duty is inerrant, and that moral perspicacity is of no importance either in terms of the validity of the moral obligation or the knowledge of the consequences of one's agency in the matter at hand. Both of these are important ethical considerations. But they do not get at the core of the moral act.

A central issue for the perspective of this work is whether there need be this Kantian opposition between duty and desire. Lewis, of course, acknowledges that ideals guide our choices. Integral to his position is the claim that our *personhood*, i.e., *our character*, guides this horizon of values, and acting in the wake of this motivation is simply being the person and sort of person we are. But key for Lewis is that this is not the person in her "purity"; that is, it is not *the self*, or H.D. Lewis's equivalent of what we have called the "myself." Our ideals, indeed, our duties, may shape our inclinations and we might become the sort of person who has an abiding preference for doing our duty. But this inclination to do one's duty, as a natural spontaneous response to do what is fitting and required, however it comes about, e.g., through discipline, or cultivation, or some inherent nobility, "is in no way the same as the resolve to do one's duty when not even the thought of its being one's duty prevails over other inclinations in the shaping our own preferences in relation to each other at the time" (45). The properly "open choice" happens when we move beyond the process by which we are shaped by our preferences and by which we choose on the basis of this horizon of values. For Lewis, the proper moral choice does not flow from anything other than itself. There is no feature in our personal make up, understood as our natural and acquired endowment, our habitualities, however elevated, that matters, "but the supreme and peculiar exercise by the self, solely of itself, of the determination of the course it will set itself, subject of course to conditions by which the choice is set" (45).

It is thus important for us to get clear on what is meant by "being subject to the conditions by which the choice is set." Lewis also speaks of this as the "setting for our moral choices." This setting is our drives, instincts, character, history, our spontaneous likes and dislikes, our hopes and regrets, our hierarchy of preferences, endowment, and circumstance or, the Husserlian would say, life-world as the correlate of our constituted personhood. It is this which determines the degree of freedom from some temptations. Moral choices are made within this setting, but the setting does not provide the power of the moral choice. The only determinant of this is I myself, Lewis's "pure self."

Lewis poses two fundamental issues for our thesis on Existenz and self-identifying acts. The first is the relationship of the setting, especially as a horizon of desires, to the moral choice; the second connected issue is the relationship of the self to the person.

The restriction of moral choice to situations of temptation not to do one's duty would seem to have the absurd implication that "to be free" involves of necessity that I go "against all my wishes." Lewis does not address this explicitly but we can say, from an Husserlian-Aristotelian perspective, which is in conflict with Lewis' Kantian orientation, that this sounds prima facie absurd only if we think of freedom as being able to do whatever we wish or freedom means to be able to follow every impulse. In this respect the thoughtless wanton is the most free of persons – most "free" by not having a will but in being led by the impulse of the moment. But Lewis can ignore this criticism because of his prescription that freedom is tied to the purity of the self's agency, which means that its agency or choice is not determined in the way the agency of the wanton or person driven by impulse is. Further, Lewis thinks that it is undeniable that there are circumstances in which "we are challenged by a claim of duty to which we may or may not respond." In this of course he is right. But in question is whether there is any sense in which the claim of duty itself is or is not correlated with something we desire. Is the (value of the) "Ought" here only in contrast to and the negation of the "Is" of value? Deontology as the Ought in contrast to ontology of being of course presupposes this opposition, but we need not oppose what we ought to do absolutely to what we desire. Lewis does this, as we shall see, because for him any correlation of intentional acts to the Ought is a form of subjectivism. Our view is that the Ought might need to struggle with other desires, but it can do so only because it appears as something especially or overridingly desirable, i.e., worthy of our allegiance, reverence, and homage. Of course, the Ought may surface in second-personal relations wherein there are claims or demands for respect or recognition or where there are commands by authorities, etc.; but this does not exhaust the sense of Ought. With Lewis we affirm first-personal senses of obligation. (Besides earlier discussions in this chapter, see also Chapter III and Chapter V, §9.)

Further, and this point is connected to the prior one, we must account for how what appears as an obligation appears with the unique compelling and necessitating power to move the will. The most basic instance of this is the exemplarily moral context, as especially in its second-person form. Here the correlation of the dignity of the Other, which with Darwall (see Chapter V, §9) we may say is the locus for the authority to demand, and therefore the proper site for the morally obligatory as what binds and for which one is responsible, is respect. For us (not for Darwall) one's respect and responsible recognition of the Other's claims is first of all a recognition of the splendor of the *dignitas* of the Other; this founds the basis for the recognition that the Other makes claims on me and this serves as the basis for what I ought to do. (See Book 1, Chapter IV.) For Lewis, what we ought to do appears sometimes to be opposed to what appeals to us, and at other times it appeals to us but "in no final way" (96). He seems to think that by appealing to us in its splendor and dignity it *eo ipso* conditions us, and therefore our agency is not pure; or the Ought is conditioned by our desires and therefore is contaminated. And as the moving force of our agency the Ought as desire robs the agent of the authorship of the act, and, as correlated to our desires, it loses its objectivity. We see here in Lewis a dread of tying what is displayed to the display, i.e., of value and the Ought to intentionality. This thesis of intentional correlation for Lewis equates with subjectivism.

Furthermore, there is the basic issue of how we can will what in no way elicits the will. We side with Husserl who holds that a willing is inconceivable that does not have as its basis a felt-evaluation. A willing to fulfill an obligation which would be free of all evaluating-appreciating is as incapable of being entertained as a sound without intensity, pitch or timbre.[75] Of course, willing is not coincident with wishing, desiring or wanting. I may will a medical operation as an instrumental good, but there is a clear sense in which I cannot be said to want an operation. But still I do will and want my health or my life to continue. An addict typically wants to return to normal life and health, but this is not to say he wants to be sober and free of drugs. If he wants to be a recovering addict he must will this sobriety, even though he does not want it. But only if he wants to return truly to himself and his life can he will the means. A willing bereft of any connection to wanting or desire and value is a square circle. One can neither decide for what is impossible nor for a deed the result of which would be no realization of value.

But this gets back to the earlier issue of whether, after all, virtue is not at the core of morality, in the sense that one may discipline oneself to have the inclination toward doing one's duty. Virtue, as the scholastics put it, was the habit which enabled one to do good, the doing of which good made one good; it made one excellent in the doing of what was excellent, made one morally strong and beautiful in being morally strong and beautiful. Virtue, according to our embellishment, is doing things with which one identified and which enabled one to be the sort of person one wanted to be, and which one sought to be by reason of the self-ideal.

Lewis adopts Kant's phrase of the "holy will" for someone's will so shaped that all of her characteristic acts are conformed to what is morally required, i.e. to one's duty. He admits that such a will is more likely to be realized in so far as continual resistance to temptation is likely to reduce the force of temptation. The exercise of virtue in this sense, like the practicing of the twelve steps toward recovery by the addict, will bring one closer to closing the gap between inclination and duty. Here Lewis offers the relatively uncontroversial view that it is doubtful that mere mortals ever reach a stage where duty and inclination coincide, where someone's resisting temptation will be a matter of moral necessity or the necessity of character, and where the necessitating factors of character will motivate to an unconditioned love of one's duty (53–55). The prospects for the realization of a "holy will" or coincidence of inclination and duty in the long space of a person's life do indeed seem slim. But this seeming rarity does not in itself nullify the essential question of whether it is an ideal of action; nor does it negate the episodic revelations of the Fichtean-Husserlian "truth of will," to which we will turn in the next chapter. And, more to the point, it points to Lewis' affirmation of the conceptual possibility of a coincidence of freedom and good character or freedom and a holy will, i.e., one informed by the disposition to will only what one ought.

A reason for Lewis's insistence on keeping desire and duty separate is his concern to preserve the transcendence of the validity or truth of that to which we are obliged or of that which we are required to do. For Lewis, like Kant, if we tie duty to "the desiring side of our nature" we "derive" the obligation from the vagaries of our desires and we also rob it of its objectivity. Although the sense of "I ought" implies "I can," Ought, as a command or prescription, does not imply or derive from "I desire" and no content of the obligation is derived from an analysis of any reaction of our own.[76] My basic respect for you does not create the dignity of you in your being you; but is this to say that the respect is not how the dignity is displayed? Is the authoritative claim that your dignity as a person makes on me present to me apart from some disclosure on my part, e.g., my act of respect or reverence? Moral and ideals, he says, "stand over against us; as *demands* they cannot be rooted in our desires."[77] But granted that the desire is not the "causal root" of the demand or dignity, the phenomenological requirement of an intentional correlation of respect may not be understood to be an instance of selfish desire, nor need the correlate respect be without the kind of love or affection that correlates with the good and the beautiful and the true.

It is important to heed Lewis's important point about the claim to objectivity of (what gets displayed or is manifest to us as) duty. The display of something as binding displays what lays claim to being exemplarily true in itself and not merely for us. When we say that "**X ought to do Y**," we are saying something like: There is a certain set of true propositions, **B** (all of which would have to do with, e.g., Peter (**X**), his having made a promise to Mary, she having understood him, etc.), such that it implies or rather occasions by way of a unique value-Gestalt, **X, do Y**, where with "**do Y**," we may understand an obligation, mandate or command addressed to **X**.[78]

In the case of conscience, the scene for the manifestation of one's own obligations, all the relevant particulars are less a "set of true propositions" than the polythetic Gestalt or personal essence made present in a passive synthesis. Here is revealed in the present moment the sort of person I have constituted myself to be. Under pain of my not being one with and true to myself, a particular course of action is required of me by myself. In this sense there is an esteeming of oneself and being oneself that goes in advance. But even the second-personal response to a command done out of pure obedience – in contrast to submitting to fear or might – is done out of the esteem for the authority and perhaps the value of pure obedience.

What is missing in the third-person account of obligation is what is analogous to the transcendental pre-fix, "I think that, I see that, etc. [there is a certain set of true propositions, **B**, such that, etc.]" In the first-person, "**I ought to do Y**" implies there is a certain set of true propositions, **B**, such that there is brought to mind the value-implication, not merely logical implication, to me, **Do Y**. But **Do Y** has not only the belief in **B** as the doxastic basis which presupposes the transcendental pre-fix, "I see that, I think that, etc. [Mary is there, having claims on me subsequent to my promise to her]," but also the transcendental *moral* pre-fix **I ought to [do Y]**. Peter's experiencing **Do Y** makes no sense without the transcendental moral prefix, **I ought to**, by which the obligation/command is displayed. (For the transcendental pre-fix and declarative sense of "I," see Book 1, Chapter II, §4.) The **Do Y** as a self-directed imperative does not exist antecedently to and independently of one's being affected by a perceived felt value and the emergence of **I ought to** as a response to the value perception, e.g., what is required to bring it about, protect it, etc. Clearly what is required is not the emotive-evaluation; the objective requirement is not collapsed into a subjective feeling, but it presupposes this valuing.

Emotions or intentional feelings like desire reveal not merely one's involvement in the emotional situation or desired state of affairs, they do not merely reveal what sort of person one is, they also reveal something about how the world presents itself. Further, whereas it is doubtless true that a valuing-esteeming-feeling is not equivalent to an Ought, an Ought in the absence of any evaluation is impossible. (I respond to your command because of my respectful appresentation of your ontological dignity as a source of claims, demands, agency of manifestation, etc.) One goes against an inclination because of the compelling higher value, e.g., of fidelity or health; one forfeits the much-needed free evening because the meeting which one "ought" to attend is about a worthwhile project that is judged to take precedence over a comfortable relaxing evening, etc.

This transcendental moral pre-fix is not a matter of explicit self-reference replacing either **B** or **Do Y**, but rather it is the anonymous self-presence of the agency of display functioning in the form of a moral valuing/judging (**I ought to**). This self-presence of **I ought to** is inseparably the display of an obligation, duty, or requirement. The display of an obligation or a duty is inseparable from the display of a value that is to be willed, pursued, preferred, protected, celebrated, recognized, etc. This is evident in our account of conscience (in Chapter III) where oneself, as the person one is required to be if one is to be identical with one's personal self, indeed, if one is to affirm and celebrate appropriately oneself, indicates **Do Y**. But this requirement is precisely oneself at a distance and only makes sense in the correlate valuing-presencing **I ought to [do Y]**. That is, the center of the I that is witnessed to values-presences its personal essence, i.e., itself at a distance, and it is this valuing-presencing that enables the personal essence to appear as authoritatively demanding. (For senses of transcendental self-esteem and self-respect, see Chapter V, §8.)

As the phenomena of "courageous," "charming," "elegant," "articulate," do not come to light without an emotive-feeling-appreciation, so the Ought, as the unique necessity laying claims on one's free willing, does not come to light apart from one's appreciating the demands or claims, i.e., being aware of oneself as required or obligated, and having the appropriate willing-response. In the case of the second-personal appresentation of Others, the I-ought is founded in the appreciating recognition and respect of the transcendent *dignitas* of the Other. As we saw, the moral Ought has to do with what uniquely concerns me myself as inseparable from my moral identity and my destiny; it is that by which I am required and exhorted to will and love in a special way. (See above, Chapter III, §§3–6.) All of this is quite removed from reducing the objective necessity of the requirement of the Ought to a subjective whim or desire.

Lewis's efforts to establish the pure acts of freedom in the face of an objective duty have a parallel in another theme: his discussions of how moral attainment and "the good will" have to do both with "the core of our existence" as well as with what is transcendent to the self. The ability to relate to persons for their own sakes, and not as appendages to our own life and as projections of our own needs, the capacity to appreciate the alterity of the Other, is the theme of genuine "realism" and it, along with the recognition of the objective validity of obligation, which in its most explicit form is tied to the recognition of the dignity of the Other, is the core stuff of all that matters in personal life. In genuine moral attainment there is this deference for reality. And therefore there is purity in the agency, i.e., it is not contaminated by self-interest, etc. This, for Lewis, is the purity of the freedom of the self in genuine moral attainment. In such moral attainment there is authentic existence at the core of one's existence correlated to genuine transcendence where "the otherness of the Other" comes fully into its own (102–103).

We can endorse all these propositions of Lewis and remind ourselves of how the limit-situations themselves, which awaken us to the core of our selves, our Existenz, do so precisely because of the way they impose on us truths about our selves and our situation with which we have to deal. Also these propositions of Lewis parallel the correlation of Existenz and transcendence because the truth of one's death, one's guilt, one's struggle for integrity with and through Others, etc., as they appear through (what we have called) realizations have become realities which cannot, at least for the moment, be denied.

The final point of convergence and difference with Lewis is his tendency to fuse the self with the person, and yet, in the discussions of morality to insert a deep chasm. Our position has been that the "myself" is always already "personified," already incarnated as a person in the world and that the unfolding of the "myself" is from the start the unfolding of a person. The "myself" is not a mini-person, a homunculus, having special functions inside the whole person. This means what each refers to with "I" is always already inserted in temporality, nature, intersubjectivity, history, culture, etc. Of course we can pry the "myself" from this rich embedded personal context and see that the personal context must take account of the distinctive features of the "myself." Husserl's theory of position-taking acts, we believe, is a way of talking about the concretion of the agency of the "myself" that does justice to this insertion. Lewis, however, insists on the free act's being wholly undetermined and therefore places the determining forces of what we are calling one's personal being at odds with or extrinsic to the properly moral attainment of what for him must be the unencumbered agency of the self. We have urged that the self-identifying, self-determining acts are precisely the free acts of the "myself" as it coincides with the person in its temporal realization. But this self-identification is of me as "encumbered," i.e., as necessarily immersed in the thick weave of my personal being in the world with Others.

Yet, are we not saying the same as Lewis when he says that the person or character "sets the scene" for the agency of the self? The difference is that Lewis hesitates to acknowledge the incompletion of the "myself" in its embodied personification, how there is required an appropriate fit, in this sense a coincidence, of who one is with what sort of person one is through the self-identifying acts. Lewis does not acknowledge the Husserlian thesis that moral self-determination in the form of the absolute Ought is how the deontological completes the ontology of personal being. He does not see the "myself" as the bare substrate of the full actuality of personal being. He does not see how we are given to ourselves to become who we are by becoming the sort of person we are called to be. For Lewis, it would seem, who one is is always separated by an abyss from what sort of person one is, because the latter detracts from the pure freedom of the pure self of who one is. For this reason H.D. Lewis would not be able to acknowledge the possibility of anything like the "truth of will" wherein one's vocation would be displayed, and where one would be, by the power of the revelation, in a situation, however short-lived, of a holy will. But for similar reasons he has difficulty tying the phenomenon of the obligatory (e.g., the dignity of Others) to the intentionality of the subject (e.g., respect), so that, in his account, obligatory claims are to be divorced from the person's concrete life and rather restricted to a matter of the will of the pure self in its undetermined freedom.

We believe that our account of conscience does justice to the phenomenon of the obligatory as precisely a power to command a response from what is not merely identical with what issues the command, i.e., one's personal character, but from one's core self that is more and other than one's character and personal identity. Indeed, that was precisely the conclusion of our discussion of conscience: the I myself (as Existenz) and not conscience was the core of the self because I myself am called upon by my essential personal self (the call of conscience) to be responsible for and responsive to this very self I have constituted. Yet here the "I myself as Existenz" is "myself" as the center of my personal being. It does not exist independently and apart from this.

In spite of these basic differences, we want to note some puzzling aspects of the matter that may well partially dissipate the differences. Lewis continually insists how I, as the pure self (cf. our "myself") am more than I am as this person or character, because even though my stream of consciousness, my acts, my traits, etc., are pervaded by me myself, I transcend them and am other than them. Whereas these come to light by the displaying properties, I myself am able to be present to myself non-ascriptively. For Lewis this accounts for how we surprise ourselves and how freedom is never exhausted by character and how we can transcend our character. And this we too want to acknowledge, with some qualifications to which we will soon turn. It also means however that on occasion we do not show up to ourselves, as Jaspers would say. In this respect we have the problem of the times when I myself am indeed uncharacteristically me, i.e., when I am other than my person and character, and, in these cases, I either fall short of them or I pleasantly surprise myself and my friends. Then there is the occasion when the person wants to be loved for who she is, quite apart from the issue of her character about which she, in her veracity and humility, may have profound reservations. In the end what separates us from Lewis is not that there is an essential distinction between who one is and what sort of person one is; we both agree on this. Rather it is whether our holding that there is a sameness (not identity) between who one is and what sort of person one is detracts from moral attainment, as Lewis thinks. Our view is that it does not. Without the ongoing self-renewing, self-determining we are not complete as persons and *who* we are, as the personified "myself," of necessity is incomplete. We are not completely who we are called to be even when we are personified but as of yet still undeveloped moral persons. As such we lack the full ontological-deontological status to which the person is called. It is not true that the self is complete as a person apart from the position-takings and foremost those by which it determines itself with self-identifying acts. In this sense, ontology is completed by deontology; and moral excellence, as a way we at least in part are called upon to author our persons, is not an option. As we saw, this view finds some resonance in Lewis's own appreciation of the rare phenomenon of instances of the "holy will." In the next chapter we will look at a version of this in terms of the Fichtean-Husserlian notion of "the truth of will" (Chapter V, §§2 and 5) and what has been called "teleological determinism (in Chapter V, §6).

Peter Bieri offers an eloquent critique of a theory of a radical unconditioned will such as that proposed by H.D. Lewis. A review of his basic positions advances our discussion of the relationship between character and freedom. But along the way it permits a resumé of much of both Books 1 and 2 in regard to the "myself," its "personification," person and character, and the freedom of the person.

What Bieri most fundamentally opposes is to be found in statements by Roderick Chisholm:

> If we are responsible, then we have a prerogative which some would attribute only to God; each of us when we act, is a prime mover unmoved. In doing what we do, we cause certain events to happen, and nothing – or no one – causes us to cause those events to happen.... We cannot say, "It is causally necessary that, given such and such desires and beliefs, and being subject to such and such stimuli, the agent will do so and so." For at times the agent, if he chooses, may rise above his desires and do something else instead.[79]

We have drawn near to this view in adopting Conrad-Martius's position that with "I" one also says "I begin," i.e., that with "I" we have something "archonal" that of necessity is self-initiating and "retroscending" in the sense that its movement or actualization is unmoved self-movement. We have also drawn close to this view when we have appropriated Nabert's claims that I-acts have a way of defying character and in this sense they have inherent in them an idea of an "infinite causality."

In many discussions of these matters there is an ambiguity attached to saying the will is "caused." The Chisholm text intends to include whatever "conditions" or motivates, qualifies, or affects the will. It does not distinguish how the will or consciousness is "conditioned" by physical-natural causality from the way it is conditioned by its historical-social-psychological-phenomenological milieu. Many thinkers, including Bieri, would seem to want to make this distinction. Thus one could hold that the will and other events of consciousness are not caused by the nexus of physical causality and yet hold that they are conditioned by endless other, desirable and undesirable, events of consciousness. But if one extends the freedom from natural causality to mean that human personal willing is unconditioned by any consideration, then we move in the direction of conceiving a "pure unconditioned will of a pure unconditioned self," if not a homunculus inside the person. And even if one does not take this clearly odd position one tends to be suspicious of the theme of the person and character (as developed, e.g., in this volume) which of necessity would seem to compromise the purity of the pure self.

Peter Bieri makes an elegant case for why a theory of an unconditioned will is unintelligible if we mean that our acts of will, i.e., our deliberations, choices, and decisions, have nothing to do with our autobiographies and social milieu. Each act is done over against the backdrop of what one has experienced, what one has done, and what one hopes to come from one's choices, and these horizons determine the framework of one's choices. Bereft of this framework there would be "no one" choosing "anything at all." That is, being persons requires this history of experience, desire, and formation of the will. An unconditioned will would not be mine as this temporal-historical person, but would be a willing by an unidentifiable timeless no one from nowhere. As such I would be unfree because I would be controlled by a will which was not mine, i.e., the willing would not belong to this identifiable historically conditioned person. A will is always determinate and thus determined by conditions; it is always the will of someone who has been determined and individuated by history. An unconditioned will would be a will removed from the world and nothing in the world could be an occasion for soliciting it.

Bieri argues that personal willing is exemplarily free when the person lets rational reflection and deliberation illumine the scene of what is wanted, who one wants to be, what is entailed, whether one really wants this, etc. I am the author of my willing, the prime (if not unmoved) mover, when I let my willing be conditioned by my reflection on my willing. Of course, my reflection itself will be conditioned by the person I am; my reflection on my life cannot be a view by no one from nowhere but has to be the reflection of this person who has these habitualities, etc. But what we mean by unfreedom in the form of wanton, uncontrolled, addicted, hypnotized, obsessive-compulsive, extorted, etc. action is precisely when one is not able, or fails to let, reason and judgment influence one's willing and action. In all of these cases one can say "I could not help doing what I did" even though in each case the person may be said to have done it and in each case the utterance of "I could not help doing what I did" will have different senses, all of which Bieri richly articulates.

When one is appropriately reflective and deliberative about one's agency there is undeniable compatibility between freedom and the conditioned will because freedom is precisely one's exercise of one's will by letting one's desires be illuminated and articulated by reflection. Such reflection gives syntax and names to one's willing (232 ff.). Incidentally, this resonates quite well with Husserl's position that a basic sense of being reasonable is precisely to submit one's impulses and drives to reflection. Such reflection then bestows upon one's being pulled in that direction a *fiat* or a relenting to the tug, or one exercises a veto, inhibition or denial.[80]

Bieri's most basic theme, perhaps, is: To say that one was pre-determined to make the decision one did because one's horizons of reflection and agency conditioned one's will is to insist at all costs on the illusory myth of the unconditioned will. A corollary of this is the following fallacious reasoning or counter-myth: Because of the proposed doctrine that the will is not unconditionally free one believes oneself empowered to create a fatalist pre-determinist myth that regardless of what one does in one's deliberations it is decided in advance what one will do by reason of one's will and one's articulating reflection. But Bieri is eloquent in opposing both of these myths. He argues that it belongs to the logic and meaning of the process of making a decision that I know that in the end I will reach but one decision. That is why I deliberate and entertain other possibilities. Not bringing the reflection to a conclusion is not freedom but the incapacitation of freedom. That my being me (this person) can only result in my making this decision is the sense of the decision being *mine* and done by *me*. My willing is exemplarily free in my letting my reflection, which of necessity is conditioned by the horizons of my experience, influence my agency in illuminating and articulating my will. (See 287 ff.)

Even though the absolutely unconditioned will is a "*fata morgana,*" Bieri acknowledges matters that are central to our discussion: We have the capacity to distance ourselves from ourselves, and foremost in reflection, we can exercise influence over our life-wills in significantly transformative ways, and we have the power to submit to this distance-taking or to go along with it. Philosophically, however, what is at stake is whether we employ the myth of the unconditioned free will to explicate these phenomena. The lived experience of freedom is not best explicated with a concept of unconditioned freedom but with the fact of conditioned freedom. We ought not to say: The idea of the person is inseparably an idea of freedom and freedom is freedom from conditions and thus unconditioned; therefore if it can be shown that freedom is of necessity conditioned we will be shown to be not persons. This assumes the *fata morgana* and leads to disastrous conclusions (244–245).

When we must acknowledge that I and my willing are metaphorically at the center of oneself or one's person, and one's instincts, impulses, emotions, etc. at the periphery, and that one, in one's rational reflection, can take up a standpoint apart from this flux of inclinations, it is not as if one takes up a standpoint outside the flux of one's personal will and life. My deciding and my self-identifying are not something that happen outside the flux but rather I, with my conditioned free will, am this event of the deciding. This is not a decision of a pure self that is transcendent to my person but which, nevertheless, has to do with my person, but rather it is a decision of the whole person identifying with this act. The prime (moved) mover is the whole person not a pure self that is transcendent to the historically entangled person (266).

The taking up a critical distance to oneself in one's reflection, this sense of finding an inner refuge, is not a move to a pure subject. Such a pure subject could not be the one who centered itself in the midst of its thick tangled horizon and chose, e.g., courageously to risk her life for her compatriots. The pure self, as we would say, would be free of properties and thus would not have, as such an example requires, a gender or compatriots. The pure subject is, qua pure, cut off from this thick messy conditionedness of personal life and incapable of such a self-identifying act. All distancing of oneself from oneself is not an absolute distancing or a flight to a pure subject, but rather is oneself as this concrete person identifying with or focusing on certain aspects of oneself rather than others, e.g., by identifying with one's capacity to reflect rather than with one's present impulse to pleasure.

The hidden motive for the irrepressible theme of the distance-taking to an interior refuge typically involves the desire to substitute a homunculus, a pure self, for the actual thick personal self, as if the pure self itself were an identifiable someone with properties, a mini-person, with the capacity to function as a person inside the person, on occasion doing what the entangled historical person cannot do. It is this which is the source of the myth of the unconditioned free will (269 ff.). In this mythic narrative, if it is true that our truly free decisions are the work of the pure self, then the person would stumble along from one decision to the other in as much as each decision would have nothing to do with the others, and have nothing to do with the person's lived continuous history, but rather have to do with the pure prime unmoved mover self's discrete staccato-like sporadic enactments (286).

Bieri's chief claim that the free will is a will conditioned by the person in the world with Others is consonant with the view we have been proposing of the inseparability of the person and life-world as this correlation is constituted by position-taking acts. Where we differ is on the phenomenological ontology of the person. And, given this difference it raises the question that Bieri himself raises. Bieri notes that the data or lived experience of freedom and will is informed by our concepts. The lived experiences go in advance, but how we take this data conceptually will provide a content which will shape our philosophical articulation of the phenomena (368 ff. and 385–396). It seems to this reader that Bieri's own phenomenological ontology of the self is used to clarify the felt, implicit meanings of the lived experiences of freedom and will. If we have an alternative account of the self, in spite of the massive areas of agreement regarding the conditionedness of the personal will, it occurs to us that some of the other phenomena might have a different meaning than his account allows, and then we might retrieve some reason to offer a middle ground between Bieri's rejection of any sense of unconditioned will in favor of the totally conditioned personal will, and the Lewisian suspicion toward the totally conditioned personal will in favor of the totally unconditioned will of the pure self.

Although Bieri is *not* here offering primarily a philosophical discussion of the self, nevertheless there are clear positions on the self enunciated that we want to sketch. The first point to be made is that for Bieri freedom is quite conceivable without any of what he calls the "interiority" of experiencing of the person because Bieri holds that any such experiencing is a matter of reflection, and, as we all know, our free agency can indeed unfold without acts of reflection. (This is how I interpret his discussion especially at 299–300.) Self-awareness in the form of *Erleben* and *Erlebnisse* is through acts of reflection and much of our agency can, indeed must, unfold without such. Therefore the experience of freedom is not a non-reflexive experience but one deriving from reflection. Therefore Bieri can propose the thought experiment (301 ff.) that all of our stream of consciousness is, through some novel technology, utterly transparent "like glass" to Others. This he admits would be a nightmare because of the invasion of intimacy but it would not be loss of freedom. We would, upon overcoming the intrusiveness of being exposed, go on acting freely as before.

But, *we* may ask, how does one's lived experience of one's experiences become "visible"? If it is essentially invisible precisely because non-reflectively self-aware or lived, and because it is pervaded by the first-personal "mineness" by reason of emerging from the "myself" there is something essentially impossible in regard to Bieri's thought experiment. (See our Book 1, especially Chapters II–III.) For Bieri there is no problem here because all lived experience in the realm of interiority is a matter of reflection and what is available through the making visible is simply making visible all that there is "within," because all that is there "within" is a matter of a reflective turning back which is our "interiority." I myself as subject, in my having become visible, become an object for others, just like I am for myself through reflection in the privacy of my "interior refuge." With the elimination of interiority by regarding what is available to me in reflection as what is available to others in observation, I am through and through an object. Here there is no subjectivity whatsoever; first-personal experience is replaceable by second- and third-personal perspectives; and in this sense no sense of one's freedom if we tie freedom to a lived essentially private (uniquely one's own) experience; here there is no originating and depth but all becomes surface. (Cf. 303 ff.).

Thus, for Bieri, there is no connection between freedom and subjectivity such as we have proposed in declaring that the "I" is archonal, an unbegun beginning. For Bieri we need the therapeutic insight that what bothers us is the resistance to seeing ourselves from an external perspective; we wish to think of our willing as coming unconditionally from within us, but that has nothing to do with freedom. The Within is not anything other than what comes up for inspection in reflection – which in principle can become visible to Others. Making our acts objective and visible to all only threatens the sense of intimacy. That we are basically objects (for others and for ourselves) does not affect the sense of the freedom of the act. For Bieri what is key here is to avoid positing a pure non-reflective, non-ascriptive subject, and to attend to the whole person. And the whole person as subject merely is I in my conditioning contexts of agency and this has no depth or surface (cf. 266–277).

Bieri is right in so far as knowing that one is completely visible to the perception of Others would not affect of necessity one's agency by way of manipulation. But there would be an essential difference in the sense of one's agency if he is saying, as he seems to, that there is no lived experience of our acts that is ours; that there is no non-ascriptive experience of a non-sortal "myself" and that what I experience in experiencing myself in principle is an object open and available to everyone just as my experiences are open to me through reflection.

Bieri admits that of course I cannot have your experience, e.g., of being torn in facing a moral dilemma. Only you can have it because it belongs to its identity that it is yours and not mine. (All identity and individuality for Bieri seems to be through the identifiable objective determinations that are in principle public.) I can have the same kind of experience but I cannot have the experience which belongs to your stream of consciousness *as your episode of experience. But* then he adds immediately that I can not share in it in the sense that I live it: *was wir nicht können, ist...Anteil haben in dem Sinne, dass wir sie durchleben* (299). But this, it would seem, opens the door to what undermines the drift of Bieri's theory but what is essential for us, i.e., that there is a non-reflective experiencing that is one's own, and what makes it one's own is not a result of belonging to the identifiable personal Gestalt or essence but belonging to the non-identifiable, non-criterial "myself." But, as far as I can see, this *durchleben* is either a lapse or indicates an unresolved tension in Bieri's thought.

In any case, it seems to me that Bieri does not have any place for a non-ascriptive reference to a non-sortal aspect of oneself, what we have called the "myself." Further, as we have argued, this "myself" is a unique essence individuated *per se* not *per accidens*. But for Bieri, it seems that because the only legitimate sense of self is the "whole person" and because for him the person and the willing of the person are individuated by the limitations and determinations that come from the determinations of her autobiography and biological-social-cultural setting, there is no room for the notion that there is a non-sortal uniquely individual sense inherent in the person. (Cf. 240.)

Thus for Bieri the pure self, what we are calling the "myself" and "I myself," as transcendent to the stream of experiences, is as much an illusion as is the unconditioned will. He rejects any sense of the self as transcendent to the stream of experiences, a dative of manifestation. Rather we *are* the stream. Of course, what he wants to say is that the person is not something apart from the web of agency and stream of consciousness. If it is outside of the stream in any sense we are back to the myth of the unconditioned will. But his focus on the extirpation of the illusion of the unconditioned will makes no room for a phenomenology of the "myself" as that which precisely pervades all experiences and yet is not any one of them. And implicitly the very project of a transcendental reduction would seem likewise to be a chimera or *fata morgana*.

Thus the pure self and the unconditioned will imply one another and it is equally important to be rid of both.

As we earlier saw, a remarkable consequence of Bieri's view is his position on how the self comes to be out of the articulation and understanding of the will. This articulation enables the illumination of one's personal essence, as we would put it, and enables the appropriation or authentication (*Aneignung*) of the direction of one's life and one's willings. This *Aneignung* resembles our self-identification with one's willings. It is not that the antecedent self goes about authenticating its willings; rather, it is through the authentication of willings that a self comes about. "In a certain sense, the authentication itself is a subjectless event" (414). Yet it is interesting how this is spelled out. The evaluation of my willings is such that they take place in *me*, the whole person; it is a question of my evaluation and my reflective understanding of them. But this means that they belong to this person and no another. Now this might mean that somehow I make a comparison and think: "These belong to my stream of consciousness and not yours." But Bieri properly does not say this but rather stays with the experience and, it seems to us, implies a sense of oneself that is not a result of an identification through criteria. Rather, this sense of oneself that is non-ascriptive and non-reflective; it is through a *Durchleben*. But if this is so, then we have a sense of oneself that is quite different from the person with identifiable qualities.

If this is so we get to what this Husserlian work has in mind with the "myself" and what is approximate to Bieri's nemesis, "the pure self." Such a position avoids the necessity to posit that the person comes about through self-identifications by a subjectless event. I have great difficulty grasping how the whole person originates in self-authenticating, self-identifying acts by a subjectless event. How does that which is self-less authenticate and identify itself?

The "myself" that is proposed in this work is not a subterfuge or surreptitious substitute of a mini-person doing the work of the person. We have acknowledged that it is a "moment," albeit the *substantial* one, i.e., it is the bare substrate. And we have proposed that because it is the form of the person one is, i.e., whatever changes in the person, one is always "oneself," it is to be regarded as both a formal and tele-ological principle, the "entelechy," of the person. It is a principle brought to light foremost in the non-ascriptive forms of self-awareness and self-reference, but it also comes to light in the teleological reflections of this chapter. As non-reflectively lived it is not a merely posited principle but one whose fundamental character can be made manifest in ineluctable first-person experiencing. Thus the person has an ideal-normative sense and this is its telos, the fruit of the dynamism of the "myself" as an entelechial principle.

While accepting Bieri's account of conditioned freedom on the basis of the necessary determination of the person, we nevertheless claim that the person has for its principle the transcendent non-sortal "myself. This enables us to give another interpretation to the phenomena of self-distancing that he acknowledges. Obviously for transcendental phenomenology the move to the pure I by way of disengaging one's doxastic attachments to one's life-world and one's personal being in this world is not meant to be a move to a homunculus which makes the personal I redun-dant; on the other hand, it is not a move to what is in every respect ontologically irrelevant in thinking about what it means to be a person. In our view it provides a framework to make sense of Bieri's own view that somehow I am more intimately immanent in the will, and how "the I" is a center of the person which admits of ever deeper depths. It also accounts for how the personal self comes about by self-identifying acts. This means an observation like Chisholm's, that on occasion "the agent may rise above his desires," may mean not a flight to a homunculus but that there is a transcendental/transcendent dimension of the person.

Furthermore, this means that there is always "more" to being a person than what presently one's explicit and one's pre-thematic understanding apprehends. It may mean that, as Nabert claims, in the very exercise of our freedom, we are aware of an "idea" of will which, in spite of the weight of the past, is not merely a result of the past but has a different absolute kind of "causality" that is capable of defying fate. It is a familiar first-personal as well as public experience that one does not know in advance what one is capable of willing, e.g., how well one may perform, how much more one may endure, etc. The boundaries of one's will are not known in advance and it is not evident that they are determined in advance. This is part of Kant's insisting on spirit, i.e., the transcendental I, as existing by essentially facing infinite ideals. The consideration of a transcendent/transcendental dimension to the person may also explain the nature of the addict's complaint where he senses a dimension of himself that is inappropriately enslaved by his habits. One can want and even will impotently that one's decisions be other than what they are and that they not be the burden of one's pre-history (cf. 330), without appealing to an absolutely unconditioned will. After all the content of the addict's will is to overcome *his*, this very addict's, miserable plight of being an addict.

Here the addict might be indicating that even in his bondage he has an inkling of a freedom and personal possibility that transcends that of one's actual personal form, Gestalt, or essence. This is implicit in Bieri's own discussions of the need for the authentication of one's will, i.e., the requirement that one be able to "identify" with one's willing. We have insisted that this is always a matter of a quest for self-adequation with an ideal that eludes us. It is not a matter simply of finding some equivalence or balance between the determinacy which is one's person and the determinacy which is one's willing. For Bieri will is always something determinate and belonging to a determinate person. Yet if the person has inherent essential transcendent-transcendental dimensions, such as the essential inadequation of the will to itself, then what we mean by major shifts in the kind of person one is could be accounted for – or at least given a "likely story." Will is essentially, we have proposed, always facing the endless value-horizon or the Good, and to conceive of authentication and identification as looking for commensurate items among (a) one's person and (b) one's willing distorts the phenomenon of self-inadequation and the "restlessness of the heart."

Or the major shift in a person's life might be accounted for by the odd transcendental determinateness of a unique individual non-sortal essence which is transcendent to the flux of experience and the vicissitudes of being a person – a shift which we considered, e.g., in terms of the thought experiment regarding one's double, or the victim of amnesia, but which we also introduced to wrestle with the problems of immortality, transmigration and metempsychosis, where we have radical "changes in personality."

We may link the principle of the "myself" to a central phenomenon that is singled out in Bieri's excellent book, namely the emergence of an ideal form of personhood. Bieri does not give this emergent ideal the ontological significance we do, i.e., he does not claim that it points to the entelechy of the person; nevertheless it serves as the culmination and conclusion of his book. Bieri states that the ideal of an autonomous will and way of life is to be found in living in accord with a will with which one identifies and which one can, through appropriate reflection, authenticate. This does not mean that one's personal essence or Gestalt is fixed once and for all; rather, the formation of the person is an unending process. (This clearly destabilizes the position we earlier ascribed to Bieri, namely that willing is finding some balance between the determinacy which is one's person and the determinacy which is one's willing; will is always something determinate and belonging to a determinate person. The insertion of a [constitutive] ideal means that there is always an apperception of what is transcendent to the determinateness.) This ideal of a position-taking act with which one whole-heartedly identifies expresses the formal feature (he does not say categorical imperative) regarding the richest and most authentic life we can live. This is to be related to Bieri's notion of "passionate freedom." He says it can be called a "passion" (*Leidenschaft*) when there exists as the substance of one's life a life-determining willing which is not enslaved by a rigidity but which is character-ized by a liberating and identity-forming continuity throughout one's whole life. He singles out what we have called the "calling of someone" who can say of his life that "I cannot do otherwise." But this "cannot" has nothing of the compulsive and heter-onomous necessity or "must" that such a claim has for the obsessive-compulsive, or for an addict, or for someone who acts because a robber is holding a gun to her head. Rather, for such a person, as we would say, she is manifest to herself as Existenz facing the *unum necessarium*. Or as Bieri puts it: "Everything is at stake in being one who sees no alternative to such a willing" (425). For us there is indicated here not only the theme of Existenz, but also the regulative ideal of the personification of the "myself." This in turn points to the considerations of vocation and what Husserl calls "the truth of will." Before we turn to these matters we conclude this chapter with a brief discussion of the self as it is determined by its story.

§9. Who One Is and One's Story

Whereas Peter Bieri is at pains to keep the person from being contaminated with a pure self and an unconditioned will and H.D. Lewis was concerned to keep ipseity from being identified with character, some theories of personal identity contend that who one is the equivalent of one's character and the character is inseparable from the *intersubjective* narrative in which one finds oneself – and such a position would be different from both that of Bieri and Lewis. Neither of these thinkers would displace the individual self or person from the community, nor is there any reason to think that they would propose that we could dispense with narrative and intersubjectivity in the constitution of the person.[81] But narrative and intersubjectiv-ity and the narrative of intersubjectivity are not central themes in the discussions we have just reviewed. Further, the perspective of this book is remote from sug-gesting that intersubjectivity was more basic ontologically or phenomenologically than subjectivity.

In what we are calling the narrative view of the self, one's personal identity is who one finds oneself to be in one's life story. But this story has numerous authors and protagonists who take initiatives, some of which are one's own but many of which are ones to which we respond. Let us assume that our personal identity, i.e., our coming to be who we identifiably are, is a matter of being responsible for our position-takings, actions and our expectations and fore-castings, and as well our being faithful to our life-projects. Granting this, we must also acknowledge that although each one is the chief author of one's self as the central character in one's life story, nevertheless the story has numerous other authors. Biographers and historians become, if they are permitted by readers or listeners, dominant voices which subsume or drown out others in favor of their own. And whereas it is true that who one is as this person gets constituted by one's position-taking acts by which one is inserted in the world with Others, and for which one alone must take responsibility, these acts are not intelligible apart from the historical community because they, in great measure, are responses to position-takings by Others. As our stories constantly undergo revision and edition, so does who one is.

The narrative view of the self, i.e., the person, implies, of course, that the person is constituted by temporality. Persons, ontologically considered, are temporal beings. Of interest is how we make present such temporal beings. Like perceptual spatial objects, and in contrast to non-temporal objects, like idealities such as numbers, temporal objects are strewn out or scattered in time and they cannot be made totally present all at once. Numbers or formal objects like a syllogism are not so strewn out in time, even though it surely takes time to grasp as a unity a number raised to the fiftieth power or to grasp a ten digit number or to follow a formal argument. But once one has taken the time to do this, thereafter one can make it present all at once.

In this respect, the "myself" as the non-sortal referent of a non-ascriptive reference has greater similarity with an ideal object – even though it is the most incommunicable of entities – than it does with a temporal being, e.g., a person. But the "myself," of course cannot be "presented" but merely lived or appresented. Some forms of temporality, as well as perhaps the abstract form of temporality would seem to be able to be made present all at once. Thus Aristotle's definition of time as "the measure of movement with a before and after" captures formally an important feature of experienced time. Similarly the process of water freezing, melting, or boiling, can be given a formal all-at-once presentation by the chemist or physicist. Sports events and many art works, like a novel or drama might, as an objective public, intersubjective event for us all, be summarized or offered in a resumé. "Although he trailed throughout the race, he was able at the last second to beat his opponent at the finish line." We grasp the essential unfolding of the story, but, of course the lived subjective time of the protagonists which we spectators and fans have access to through empathy is missed. Similarly a symphony might be summarized with a description of each of the movements; but such an abstraction misses the work in its essence which is tied to the appropriate experience of the work in its own temporality. If the temporality, with its flow of harmonies, melodies, and dissonances, along with its rhythms, silences, rests, new beginnings, etc. are not lived step-by-step in their own sequence, there is no presentation of the work. The resumé in the concert program resembles the artwork as much as the table of contents of a novel resembles the novel. The performance of the symphony and the reading of the novel are the only ways to make present these art works.

Persons as having ideal trans-temporal personal essences can be made present by listing their distinctive qualities, as in a eulogy. But such an account gives no indication of the unique personality. To do this the eulogist inserts the person's quality in a narrative context that purports to individuate the example. The anecdote illustrates the basic virtue or underlying disposition of this person. A good biography will strive to capture these identifying characteristics and horizons of motivation. It will reveal how the "myself" has been personified and how it has personified itself. If possible the author will be able to share with the reader the moments of gathering acts, where and how the person dealt with limit-situations, and how, in spite of the layers of public personae, she struggled to come forth to herself in her center, i.e., as Existenz. The significant Others in this struggle, how their voices and perspectives commingled with hers, will be brought out. But the "good biography" will always be from the point of view of the author who strives to reach the point of view of her subject matter.

The author will acknowledge the multiplicity of voices, agents, interlocutors, etc., through whom and with whom the subject of the story came to be who she is. In any case, there is no way of re-presenting the personal life as there is in re-presenting the symphony. The symphony's essence, although having in each performance a kind of individuating instantiation, nevertheless is transtemporally the same and is itself presented in each performance. The author may aspire to lead us "step-by-step" through the performance of the person's life. But there is no way of "performing" or recounting the person's experience of the stream without living the stream. Yet in so far as we have been correct in proposing that there is a personal essence, then the project of biography is meaningful. But the "subject matter," as an ipseity who has this personal essence, of necessity transcends the narrative because she transcends her personal essence. Even in our living a life together with spouses, partners, and friends, "making music together" (Alfred Schutz), i.e., constituting a common life-time together, we are separated by the abysses of our ipseities and the absolutely incommunicable streams of consciousness.

The problem of autobiography is essentially the same as biography. One's personification, although accessible by memory, also is a fallible, inadequate theme. It may be that the author of one's biography has better insight into aspects one's life and personal essence than does oneself, the central agent of one's life and author of one's autobiography.

Paul Ricoeur has a version of the narrative theory of the self that wrestles with many of these themes. He makes a distinction between two forms of identity of the self: *idem*-identity and *ipse*-identity. Identity as *sameness* (*idem*) is that which is the unchanging core sameness in the manifold acts of identification. These acts can be acts of memory, perception, imagination, reports, etc. They can be the same acts of identification, e.g., acts of perception, intending the identical same at different times and different places. In these cases the "same thing" or "person" is revealed in a manifold of different profiles. "The same" here is always identically "the identifiable same one" even though it is given in different profiles. Thus it might appear to be similar to what we have called the bare substrate. But here we have to do with not a bare substrate but with one which has *core identifiable properties* as it is evident always and exclusively in the *third-person* perspective. Typically the identically same substrate must be somehow known or recognized, and this means it has to do with the sameness of a core composed of identifiable properties which, although identically and unchangingly the same, is richly textured through its being presented through the difference of the setting, the new acts, new properties, etc.

The other kind of identity is *ipse*-identity. With this identity of ipseity, and not with *idem*-identity, we have the issue of *who one is*. In Ricoeur's view ipseity can never be identified with a permanent unchanging substrate, or a fortiori with the causal links and identity criteria which secure sameness. Nevertheless it has a kind of temporal unity that gains a recognizable durability, namely the patterns and configurations of the actions within the narratives in which it is involved. Ipseity is always what emerges in my evaluation of my life and it has to do with my projects, values and goals. The answer to, Who am I?, is never adequately forthcoming but is the ongoing fruit of the examination of one's life as it unfolds within the narrative of one's story as it is immersed in the stories of others.

What we call "character" is the realm of the limit between sameness and ipseity. Character is the sedimentation of one's past agency as it guides and shapes one's future and it is this "which confers on character the sort of permanence in time that I am interpreting as the overlapping of *ipse* by *idem*.... Character is truly the 'what' of the 'who.'" For Ricoeur, the sameness of character requires the ipseity in order for it to be the sameness of the Who and to be the way this ipseity characteristically is and acts. But if we grant that these are overlapping they must nevertheless be distinguished. Thus, as we have seen earlier in our discussion of position-taking acts, the acts which only take "so long," nevertheless have a validity "from now on," or until explicitly revoked. The promise, we have suggested, illustrates this general nature of position-taking acts, whether they be cognitional or actional, theoretical or practical. Although the claims of validity are "automatic," the *sustaining* or being faithful to the requirements of the "validity" is not automatic; the freedom of ipseity must come into play. Thus, e.g., keeping one's word expresses a constancy and fidelity of the self to itself. As such it cannot be inscribed solely within the dimension of character which is the realm of the typical or general, the habitual, and the repeatable, but rather it must be ascribed to "who" one is. (Here applause would be meted out by H.D. Lewis and perhaps Peter Bieri would begin to be uncomfortable to the extent that freedom is here being conceived as absolutely independent or as the work of a homunculus.) In keeping my promise there is a clear sense in which *I* must be constant, hold fast, be faithful. Nothing substitutes here for me myself.[82]

Indeed, in crises (especially what we have called limit-situations) there arises the strangeness where "*ipse* poses the question of its identity without the aid and support of the *idem*" of character, and presumably of one's narrative context.[83] Again, Lewis would applaud and Bieri would be puzzled. Indeed, this is very puzzling for Ricoeur's position in so far as he ties ipseity to narrative because ipseity must be uniquely aware of itself as the central agent of the narrative. As such ipseity would always be aware of itself through self-identifications and its apperception of Others' identifications of it. Yet, as Dan Zahavi points out, "it takes a self to experience one's life as a story." This means there is a sense of ipseity, of oneself, which experiences the self-narrating and being-narrated which is distinct from what the narrative discloses. This very ipseity authors the narrative and lives the internalization of the narrative of Others and is not itself merely a result of a narrative. This sense of oneself as experiencing or lived ipseity is distinct from the identifying self-awareness and apperceptions essential to experiencing oneself as the center of a narrative. Thus there is a sense of ipseity which is not to be identified with the *idem* which is repeatably the same from a third-person perspective armed with identification-criteria. Zahavi elaborates: "In order to begin a self-narrative, the narrator must be able to differentiate between self and nonself, must be able to self-attribute actions and experience agency, and must be able to refer to him- or herself by means of the first-person pronoun. All of this presupposes that the narrator is in possession of a first-person perspective"[84] which is not reducible to the third-person property-description account. Fundamental for the first-person perspective is the non-ascriptive sense of the "myself" that is not coincident with the identifiable property ascriptions.

Ricoeur, so it seems, would need to recognize this (and overcome his tendency to a reflection theory of self-awareness[85]) in order for him to develop one of his key theses in response to the thought-experiments, such as the teletransportation ones as conducted by Parfit. Parfit thinks of identity primarily in terms of *idem*, and he is able to urge ways in which we may think that our identities dissolve, bifurcate, fuse, etc. Thereby we are forced to think of "ourselves" apart from our properties, our characteristics, which mark how we are inserted in a narrative and where our character overlaps with our ipseity. In our earlier discussions (in Book 1) we found this necessity liberating and occasioning the discovery of the "myself" in contrast to the identifiable personal I. For Parfit it occasions the dissipation of *any* sense of identity for the self, and thus apparently any sense of self. (We found this calling into question the equivalence of the self with identifiable properties to be an occasion for prying off an aspect of the self, the "myself," from the person; for Parfit with the disintegration of the personal identity, founded in identifiable properties, there appears to be a nihilation of the self absolutely and we must come to learn that being a self does not matter. We earlier in Book 1, Chapter II, §3 we discussed what here resonates in Parfit's position, namely some Buddhist themes.) Whereas Parfit reduces all self-identity to *idem*-identity which eventually dissolves the self of I and mineness, so that the very question of whether identity matters seems to be self-dissipating, Ricoeur rightly hesitates:

> I still do not see how the question of 'who' can disappear in the extreme cases in which it remains without an answer. For really, how can we ask ourselves about *what* matters if we could not ask to whom the thing matters or not? Does not the question about what matters or not depend upon self-concern, which indeed seems to be constitutive of selfhood?[86]

Such moments, where *who* we are is called into question because we no longer know what we are and what sort of person we are, in the past were called existential crises. Ricoeur observes that many conversion narratives and ascetical treatises "attest to such nights of personal identity. In these moments of extreme destitution, the empty response to the question 'Who am I?' refers not to nullity but to the nakedness of the question itself."[87]

Such occasions where the self is stripped of familiar identifying properties drew the attention earlier of Gabriel Marcel.[88] Marcel's own example is how one might encounter a bureaucrat in applying for a passport, credit card, state certification, driver's license, identification card, etc. The bureaucrat may interview me or give me a document that requires that I give my gender, age, color of my eyes, height, weight, profession, of whom I am the son, where born, what my occupations is, with whom I am married, where and to what extent I was educated, etc. Here the insertion of who I am in what I am may become pried away. Marcel notes that "a silly feeling" can surface in filling out the questionnaire or answering the questions, as if one were "putting on fancy dress, not to go to a costume ball, but to set about one's daily labours." Now even if this were a game, and not a form of civic necessity and thus important, as is the case with the state's requirements that I fill out the form, even if I were to make up or create an identity, the silly feeling would again surface, and perhaps eventually take the form of a "peculiar, intimate disgust – like some shabby garment, not my own, that I was forced to drag around with me everywhere."[89]

Marcel's point is that the questionnaire or interviewer wants to categorize me as a definite somebody with identifiable properties, yet I sense a resistance to this.

There is thus, or so it seems to me, a sense in which I am not a definite somebody; from the moment when I start to reflect I am bound to appear to myself as a, as it were, non-somebody linked in a profoundly obscure fashion, with a somebody about whom I am being questioned and about whom I am certainly not free to answer just what I like at the moment when I am being questioned.[90]

Ricoeur finds that Parfit's examples point to a self unrecognizable by identifying properties and this suggests Robert Musil's *Mann ohne Eigenschaften*. Here we have a person who, when faced with the dissolution of his identifiable qualities, confronts, in a special way, his nothingness. But this is not "the nothing of which there is nothing to say…The sentence 'I am nothing' must keep its paradoxical form: 'nothing' would mean nothing at all if 'nothing' were not in fact attributed to an 'I.' But who is *I* when the subject says it is nothing? A self deprived of the help of sameness…" This for us points to the "myself" which is a *Je ne sais quoi*, which is quite other than a *nihil negativum*. Yet the fuller sense of that forever eludes us if we look for objective properties. Ricoeur himself states:

> The absolute impossibility of recognizing a person by his or her lasting manner of thinking, feeling, acting, and so on [but still, nevertheless, knowing or "recognizing" him or her: JGH], is perhaps not demonstrable in practice, but it [i.e., the "recognition": JGH] is at least thinkable in principle. What is practicable lies perhaps in acknowledging that all the attempts at identification, which form the substance of those narratives of interpretive value with respect to the retreat of the self, are doomed to failure.[91]

Ricoeur would have been helped by the application of the Parfitian thought experiments by Klawonn, who transposes them from their confinement in the third- and second-person to the first-person. But here there is not properly a question of "recognizing" but of a lived first-person self-experiencing of one's individual essence. Here he could witness "in the flesh" the ineluctable "myself" and *not* the identifiable person. (See Book 1, Chapter III, §1.)

Marcel wrestles with assigning a positive character to this experience of "not being a somebody" or not being a particular identifiable individual. The properties that are mine I recognize as being contingent, and somehow "belonging" to me. But this "me," as the *relatum*, is hidden completely if I attempt to consider it as an object in the world. Rather it is the *I* as an "existential indubitable" that best is thought of as "ex-sisting," i.e., self-manifesting to myself and others with the exclamation of utter novelty and child-like innocence. Here its self-awareness is at once an announcement: "Here I am, What luck!" The bare self is inseparably an "exclamatory awareness" of its existence and this is also an awareness of its poverty, ignorance, and its vulnerability.[92]

Here, with Marcel's wrestle to find a positive expression of "not being somebody in particular" we enter into murky but familiar matters. Our concern is merely to see that the effort to capture the positivity in the third-person of the undeniably rich first-person experience leads to analogous empathic speculations by an adult of a child's awareness breaking in upon us. The child's awareness is the analogate for the bare ipseity that comes to light, e.g., in the crisis situation of the dissolution of one's sense of who one is as tied to what one is. Yet, in the first-person the *nothingness* of the "myself," foremost as it is awakened to itself in, e.g., reflecting on the encounter with the *Double* wherein it is deprived of all its distinguishing qualities, is indeed an awakening to what is undeniably impoverished, vulnerable, and ignorant; yet there is also the unique essence of the "myself," the value of which may not be compared with these privations. We further see that our position and that of Ricoeur draw near because we both can affirm, with Marcel, a very elusive, odd sense of ipseity which may not be confined to character, personality, or narrative, and yet without these the important normal senses of theoretical and moral discourse are missing.

We further draw near when we see that this notion of the self as nobody and nothing is precisely the beginning of the illumination of Existenz as the center of the I because I am called upon from my personal center to come to grips with what is of unconditional importance. These moments coincide with H.D. Lewis' concern in his thesis that the exemplary moments of moral agency are where I, as transcendent to my character, act not in the wake of the momentum of character, but rather in the face of resistance and effort. These moments also coincide with our account of conscience: In the admonitions of conscience, the person we have constituted ourselves to be addresses us to be faithful or change our course. The addressor is the particular someone whom we have constituted and identified with; the addressee is ourselves as not absolutely coincident with this person; it is the center of the person who must respond to its being addressed. If, for some reason, this personal self in its matrix of meaning should dissolve or lose all of its validity and legitimacy, then we face the unique crisis of conscience where we are called to be who we are apart from any sense of an identification of who we are with what sort of person we are. This seems to be the ideal norm for Lewis; but in our theory it is a crisis, as it would surely also be for Bieri.

The "myself," as bereft of properties, is always simply myself and the center-periphery distinction does not hold for it, if we consider it abstractly as the referent of our self-awareness and non-ascriptive self-referring. Yet we typically never know ourselves only as the "myself." (Its coming to light, e.g., in the non-ascriptive indexical "I" or in non-reflective self-awareness, is always an abstract moment within the wider horizon of our pre-thematic full personal self-experiencing.) Further, we have proposed, the "myself" provides the entelechy of the person. Being awakened to the personal core is being awakened to oneself as "myself" *as the center* of the and more than one's properties. When the clear propertied display of the world and myself in the world, usually woven by a more or less consistent narrative, comes undone then I am thrown back on me myself – which is always the "myself" as informing my person – and I am forced to make my way and keep the remnant of my commitments in the face of this nothingness. Following Jaspers, we have said that "limit-situations" may well precipitate this. But here in such crises, we have also suggested, we are faced with a decision in the face of "I know not what," i.e., in the presence of the mystery of the "myself" along with "death," guilt, and the struggle to communicate with the Other. Most fundamentally we are faced with the basic situation of the self's essential inadequation with itself and the task to find Being while having to negotiate with beings.

Again, the "myself" as not anybody in particular is not where we, as Existenz, are to take our bearings in relationship to the world. The "myself," we have proposed, provides our particular personal narrative with a teleological vector propelled by the self-inadequation. We have described this as the incessant pressure of the "one thing necessary" and the willing will in the face of all the contingencies of the willed will. Yet, even though character and the individuation that comes from our story provide an inescapable framework, there is always the pressure of the "myself" to explode these parameters and to provide us with a constitutional discomfort (cf. Marcel's "silly feeling") when faced with the requirement of identifying ourself with a list of defining characteristics and markers. Let us attempt a theory of "vocation" with these considerations in mind.

Notes

1. For discussions of Husserl's theory of will, see Ullrich Melle, "Husserl's Phenomenology of Willing," in *Phenomenology of Values and Valuing*. Eds. James G. Hart and Lester Embree (Dordrecht: Kluwer, 1997), 169–192; also my *The Person and the Common Life*, 81–124; for the immediate discussion I have been helped also by Karl Jaspers, *Philosophie* (Berlin: Springer, 1948), 424 ff.; also *Philosophie*. Vol. II (Berlin: Springer, 1956), 150 ff.
2. Peter Bieri, *Das Handwerk der Freiheit*, 96 ff.
3. Hector-Neri Castañeda, *Thinking and Doing* (Dordrecht: Reidel, 1982), see Chapter 6, but also 41 ff.
4. Cf. Alexander Pfänder, *Phenomenology of Willing and Motivation*. Trans. H. Spiegelberg (Evanston: Northwestern University Press, 1967), 22–23.
5. Cf. our discussion in Book 1, Chapter IV, §3 of the analytic-tautological "properties" of the "myself."
6. I am indebted to Jean Nabert here, but I am not certain whether he would agree with precisely my formulations. See his *L'expérience intérieure de la liberté, et autres essais de philosophie morale* (Paris: Presses Universitaire de France, 1924/1994), 150–151, 174–187. Nabert's position on the surplus or transcendence of the will to character and destiny will be returned to at several junctures. It is especially in §8 of this chapter when we discuss H.D. Lewis and Peter Bieri that the themes become our focus. Similarly, our discussions of Conrad-Martius's theory of a "transcendence in reverse" as well as Thomas Nagel's view that first-person experience does not having any antecedent in worldly conditions touch on these themes in Nabert.
7. *Philosophie*, 433; *Philosophie II*, 160.
8. Karl Jaspers, *Der philosophische Glaube angesichts der Offenbarung*, 317.
9. Bakhtin, *Art and Answerability*, 121.
10. See Bernhard W. Anderson, *Out of the Depths* (Philadelphia, PA: Westminster, 1983), 166–167.
11. The speaker is Starbuck in a play I once came across titled *The Rainmaker*.

12. P.B. Shelley, "Mutability" in *Shelley's Poetical Works* (Oxford: Oxford University Press, 1936), 634.
13. Robert Sokolowski, *Moral Action*, 203–206.
14. *Nichomachean Ethics*, 1101a19–1101a20.
15. *Husserliana* XV, 404–405.
16. See Husserl's *Nachlass* MS, F I 25, 151.
17. See *Husserliana* XXXVII, 70–84.
18. *Husserliana* XI, 3; trans. 39.
19. *Husserliana* XI, 11. Cf. the poem of Emily Dickinson in, *Final Hours: Selections and Introduction*, Thomas H. Johnson (Boston, MA: Little Brown, 1961), 240:

> Perception of an object costs
> Precise the Object's loss –
> Perception in itself a Gain
> Replying to its Price –
> The Object Absolute – is nought –
> Perception sets it fair
> And then upbraids a Perfectness
> That situates so far –

20. Cf. Husserl's note to §65, relevant to p. 324 of the 1962 edition of Heidegger's *Sein und Zeit* (Tübingen: Niemeyer, 1962): "Welche Umständlichkeiten und Unklarheiten nur um Intentionalität nicht zu gebrauchen." *Salva reverentiae*, these analyses not only deepen the understanding of intentionality but, when studied along with Husserl's C-MSS and the other writings on passive synthesis, show how an elemental tending/intentionality or analogous will pervades the primal temporalizing of primal presencing.
21. This is the subject matter of our *The Person and the Common Life*.
22. See the *Nachlass MS D14;* cited in Nam-In Lee, *Edmund Husserls Phänomenologie der Instinkte* (Dordrecht: Kluwer, 1993), 147.
23. Besides Nam-In Lee's book, see also Rudolf Bernet's, "Zur Phänomenologie von Trieb und Lust." Also my review essay, "Genesis, Instinct, and Reconstruction: Nam-In Lee," *Edmund Husserls Phänomenologie der Instinkte* (Dordrecht: Kluwer, 1993), 101–123.
24. Kant, *Kritik der reinen Vernunft* (Hamburg: Meiner, 1956), Preface to the 2nd edition, 22.
25. Maurice Blondel, *Action (1893)* (Notre Dame, IN: University of Notre Dame Press, 1984), *passim*, but see especially, 32, 47, 52–53, 113–114, 134–134, 218, 245–245, 280, 285 ff., 292, 297, 302–303, 309, 395. Cf. my essay, "Blondel and Husserl: A Continuation of a Conversation," in *Tijdschrift voor Filosofie* 58 (1996), 490–518.
26. William Shakespeare, *Troilus and Cressida*, in *The Riverside Shakespeare* (Boston, MA: Houghton Miflflin, 1974), III, ii, ll. 75, 469. The ambiguity and "monstrosity" of love is thematized here in several ways. In response to the words of Troilus cited, Cressida notes: "They say all lovers swear more performance than they are able, and yet reserve an ability that they never perform; vowing more than the perfection of ten, and discharging less than the tenth part of one. They that have the voice of lions and the act of hares, are they not monstrous?" (469–470) Here again the interplay between the willing will and willed will announces itself in the disingenuousness and perhaps self-deception of the lover. Thus here is also the suggestion of what Nabert calls the idea of the unconditioned causality of the act.
27. The central position of self-inadequation as well as its being understood as connected with pathology are found in the fifteenth century Neo-Platonist, Marsilio Ficino. See the discussion in Paul Oskar Kristellar, *The Philosophy of Marsilio Ficino*. Trans. Virginia Conant (Gloucester, MA: Peter Smith, 1964/New York: Columbia University Press, 1943), 208 ff. Readers may well overhear my scholastic roots in this application of these Blondelian-Husserlian themes. Scholasticism distinguishes the formal and material object. The formal object may be said to be the generic framework of a consideration as it is correlated intentionally with the agent of manifestation in terms of a power or capacity (or more typically with the powers or capacities because the whole person engages the objects in the world and does

not typically shut down all of her powers). Thus the presence of anything will have many formal considerations under which it may be considered. What Husserl calls "thematization" presupposes the extant formal generic frameworks. This involves abstracting from the other possible formal considerations that co-exist and are co-given in the fullness of the perception or presencing of something. Thus sight, hearing, smell, understanding, will, emotions (or for the Scholastics, the appetites), etc., all establish a generic framework in which things appear as, e.g., shaped colors, sounds, intelligible forms and properties, good and desirable – and for the emotions they appear as correlates of anger, joy, love, dread, etc., and so they appear as what threatens our well being, or what is delightful, or the beauty of the ipseity, etc. The material object is *the thing* having these aspects, what appears in this light, what is taken in this way. Thus for the material object we may consider the lovely aromatic red rose, the exquisite Beethoven sonata, the elegant logical argument, the dear generous friend, the person who is being contemptuous of me, the person who is the light of my life, the charging bear, etc. All of these present objects may be prescinded from and a formal aspect thematized. Scholastics also distinguish between the adequate and inadequate object. The adequate object is correlated to the intentional power in such a way that it renders it fully present in its full scope. In this sense the adequate object is the material object embodying the full presence of the formal object. The inadequate object is that which precisely is more narrow and only renders present partially what the power is capable of making present. The adequate object of the will is the good as such; or it may be named happiness or beatitude as the possession of the good which satiates the empty intention of the will. But, as Sokolowski has nicely put it, happiness, is "a good that is *other* to everything we do, but is also *in* everything we do"; it is "a good that shows up in all the good activities while never being possessed or done purely and simply by itself." (See above n. 12. This is a lovely example of the good or happiness as the formal object of the will. For St. Thomas and St. Augustine, that which alone can so still and satiate the will, that alone which could be the adequate object, is God. See, e.g., *Summa Theologiae* I–II, q. 2, art. 8. God therefore may be said to be in a certain sense a person's beatitude. In our final chapter we will wrestle with some of the theological aspects of this matter. But our focus will be from the perspective of the "myself's" essential self-inadequation.

28. See Aristotle in the *Nicomachean Ethics*, 1096b34 and 1101a17–1101a21. Cf. my "Wisdom, Knowledge, and Reflective Joy," in *The New Yearbook for Phenomenology and Phenomenological Philosophy*. Vol III (Seattle, WA: Noesis Press, 2003), 68 ff.
29. Jean Nabert, *Elements for an Ethic*. Trans. William J. Petrek (Evanston, IL: Northwestern University Press, 1943/1969), 25–27.
30. Maurice Blondel, *Action (1893)*, 312.
31. Ibid., 311, translation slightly modified.
32. Cf. Hegel: "In nature the concept exists, but not for itself as thought in its freedom, but rather it has flesh and blood, and is burdened through exteriority. This flesh and blood, however, has soul and this is its concept." In our speculative view here, the "myself" or ipseity (here Hegel's "soul") as it is manifest, e.g., in self-awareness and in the thought experiments, is present in a kind of "freedom" from nature; but as person it takes on "flesh and blood." For Hegel's use of Aristotle's notion of "entelechy" see Erich Frank, "Das Problem des Lebens bei Hegel und Aristoteles," *Wissen, Wollen, Glauben*, 214–249. For Husserl's own use of this Aristotelian notion, cf. my "Entelechy in Transcendental Phenomenology: A Sketch of the Foundations of Husserlian Metaphysics," *American Catholic Philosophical Quarterly* LXVI (1992), 189–212.
33. *Husserliana* XI, 128.
34. See M.M. Bakhtin, *Toward a Philosophy of the Act*. Trans. Vadim Liapunov (Austin, TX: University of Texas Press, 1993), 57.
35. See, e.g., *Husserliana* XIV, 370.
36. See Sokolowski, *Moral Action*, 58 ff.; also my *The Person and the Common Life*, 300–309, for a comparison of Sokolowski and Husserl. But in that work I did not undertake to relate Husserl's proper emphatic sense of moral self-determination to moral categoriality as Sokolowski develops it. See our discussions of "moral categoriality" in this Book 2 Chapter IV, §§3, 6, and 9; Chapter V, §9

37. Cf. William James, *Varieties of Religious Experience* (Middelsex, England: Harmondsworth/ Penguin, 1985), 193 ff.
38. Cf.*Husserliana* XIV, 21–22.
39. This is a rich theme in Jankélévitch's writings. See especially *Traité des Vertus* (Paris: Bordas, 1949), especially Chapters XIII–XIV, and especially 786–788.
40. This is a technical term for Georg Simmel, which gives expression to a kind of situation-ethics founded on the thesis that the unique individual is at the basis of all ethical considerations. See my "The Absolute Ought and the Unique Individual," in *Husserl Studies* 22 (2006), 223–340.
41. See n. 19 above.
42. *Husserliana* XXXVII, 162.
43. For these last three paragraphs, see *Husserliana* XXXVII, 161–167; cf. my review of this work in *Husserl Studies* 20 (2004), 143 ff., upon which I have here drawn; also my "The Absolute Ought and the Unique Individual,"
44. This is the position "in a certain sense" of Peter Bieri in *Das Handwerk der Freiheit*, 414; it also is an interpretation of Husserl's *lebendige Gegenwart* which we reject in Book 1. We return to the theme in Bieri below in §8.
45. Kant, *Die Religion innerhalb der Grenzen der bloßen Vernunft* (Berlin: Meiner, 1966), 27.
46. Paul Valéry, *Oeuvres II*, 572; thanks to Gerhart Baumann *Robert Musil* (Bern: A. Francke, 1981), 119, where I first came across this text. The French text is given as an epigraph beginning this chapter. In reading more of Valéry's writings I have become uncertain whether he would approve of my interpretation of his text. My initial impression is that in his assorted writings he seems to have a deep sense of the uniqueness, albeit easily alienatable, of what each of us refers to with "I" or "myself"; but this conviction is side by side with utterances that I am nothing but what Others have made of me, and this conviction stands along side a pervasive skepticism toward any philosophical position, including such as that contained in the text I have cited several times. These of course are all possibly compatible views, if the necessary distinctions are made.
47. Carl Rogers, *On Becoming a Person* (Boston, MA: Houghton Mifflin, 1961), especially Parts III and IV; cf. pages 115–124 and 167–181. I am grateful to Julia Livingston for calling my attention to this discussion in Rogers. The theme of self-trust appears frequently in Gendlin's writings. For a brief early statement, see *Focusing* (Toronto/New York: Bantam, 1981), 165–166.
48. Cf. F.H. Bradley's discussion of volition as the "self-realization of an idea with which the self is identified" in *Collected Essays* (Oxford: Clarendon, 1935/1969), 477. This view is already to be found in T.H. Green, *Prolegomena to Ethics* (New York: Kraus Reprint, 1969 of the 1883 edition of the Oxford University Press edition), see §§102–105, 143–146, *et passim*.
49. See the entire volume, *Animal Others*. Ed. H. Peter Steeves (Albany, NY: SUNY, 1999), including my contribution, "Transcendental Phenomenology and the Eco-community."
50. See the rich formulations of Jaspers, *Von der Wahrheit*, 170–171.
51. Louis Lavelle, *Du temps et de l'éternité* (Paris: Aubier, 1955), 91 ff.
52. Jean-Paul Sartre, *Being and Nothingness*. Trans. Hazel Barnes (New York: Philosophical Library, 1956), 557 ff.
53. Nabert, *l'expérience intérieure de la liberté*, 177
54. Cf. Husserl, *Husserliana* XIV, 19, n. 2.
55. The ideal, as Husserl has proposed, even of one's unique self, is a person of a higher order wherein one's unique self is joined in a universal community. See *The Person and the Common Life*.
56. Cf. Jaspers, *Philosophie II*, 176.
57. Husserl's published early lectures on axiology are to be found in *Husserliana* XXVIII; for a presentation, see Ullrich Melle's Editor's Introduction. Melle has numerous other excellent essays on Husserl's ethics. For an overview, see his "Edmund Husserl: From Reason to Love," in *Phenomenological Approaches to Moral Philosophy*. Eds. John J. Drummond and Lester Embree (Doredrecht: Kluwer, 2002), 229 ff. See also my *The Person and the Common Life*, especially Chapter IV, upon which I have drawn here.

58. See my *The Person and the Common Life*, 297 for a Husserlian discussion of this matter.
59. *Ibid.*, Chapter IV, for a discussion.
60. This formulation is taken from Georg Simmel, *Lebensanschauungen*, 234; it synthesizes what I regard as an Aristotelian-Husserlian position that reflects concerns of Nietzsche. Cf. my "Absolute Ought and the Unique Individual."
61. Cf. my *The Person and the Common Life*.
62. For this Husserlian theme, see my *The Person and the Common Life*, especially Chapter III, ff.
63. *Husserliana* VIII, *Beilage* V.
64. Rudolf Bernet has given an excellent phenomenological analysis of trauma at a past SPEP meeting.
65. I have been helped by Alfred Adler here. See *The Individual Psychology of Alfred Adler: A Systematic Presentation in Selections from his Writings*. Eds. Heinz L. Ansbacher and Rowena R. Ansbacher (New York: Harper Torchbooks, 1956), especially Chapters III and IV.
66. See *Husserliana* XXXVII for an excellent discussion of these matters.
67. T.H. Green has helped me in these last paragraphs. See his *Prolegomena to Ethics*, 117–129.
68. Thomas Merton, *New Seeds of Contemplation* (New York: New Directions, 1972), 112–113.
69. See Merton, *ibid.*, 161.
70. Ullrich Melle has called my attention to the new (twenty-first century) movement which calls itself "post-humanist" or "trans-humanist." See his forthcoming, "Die Zivilisationskrise als anthropologische Herausforderung. Paul Shepards neoprimitivisische Anthropologie." "Human nature" here has typically only the significance of the chance arrangement of a gene population which seems to invite eugenic tinkering. A positive consequence of the discussions emanating from this movement will be a fresh a re-examination of both what a natural kind is and what a utopian, eutopian and dystopian human future will look like. Having these discussions now in advance of the march of the megamachine may deter some nightmares. The reason for this belief is another one: It seems to me that we cannot count on the greater number of human persons making commonsensical good decisions which will forestall disasters when the megamachine of the military-industrial-congressional complex has already set the stage where the best possibilities are lesser cataclysmic disasters.
71. *Nicomachean Ethics*, 1179b, 30.
72. See *The Person and the Common Life*, 316 ff.
73. I am grateful to Bruce Bundy for calling my attention to this remark of Gandhi.
74. Hywel D. Lewis, *Freedom and Alienation* (Edinburgh/London: Scottish Academic Press, 1985), 63. The numbers given in the body of the text refer to the page numbers of this work. The issue that distinguishes the Husserlian position we advocate and the one Lewis urges here continues our discussion of a similar question broached in G. Bachelard's critique of Bergson and our attempt at a Husserlian resolution of the matter. Bachelard's critique of Bergson's "automaticity" in favor of the discontinuous and sporadic acts of spirit has affinities with Lewis's critique of the Aristotelian position on character. See *The Person and the Common Life*, 131–137.
75. F 1 28, 37 ff.; see my *The Person and the Common Life*, 92.
76. H.D. Lewis, *Morals and the New Theology* (New York: Harper, n.d.), 33.
77. Ibid., 22.
78. Cf. Hector-Neri Castañeda, *The Structure of Morality* (Springfield, IL: Charles C. Thomas, 1974), 63 ff.
79. Bieri refers to Chisholm in this regard in *Das Handwerk der Freiheit*, 440–441. Chisholm's full statement from which we have cited is to be most recently found in his *On Metaphysics* (Minneapolis, MN: University of Minnesota Press, 1989), 12. Besides Chisholm, Bieri mentions that the second part of his book is an implicit critique of Peter van Inwagen's view of the unconditioned will. Key for us is Bieri's mentioning also that Sartre's position is a misunderstanding of the interior refuge of the self. The numbers cited in the body of the text refer to the pages in Bieri's book.
80. See *The Person and the Common Life*, especially 91–113; also the remarks of Rudolf Bernet in "Zur Phänomenologie von Trieb und Lust bei Husserl," in *Interdisziplinäre Perspektiven der Phänomenologie*, 40.

81. For our own statement of this perspective, see *The Person and the Common Life*.
82. Paul Ricoeur, *Oneself as Another*. Trans. Katherine Blamey (Chicago, IL: University of Chicago Press, 1992), 121–124.
83. Ricoeur, ibid., 124.
84. Dan Zahavi, *Subjectivity and Selfhood* (Cambridge, MA: MIT Press, 2005), 114.
85. See, e.g., Paul Ricoeur, *Freud and Philosophy*. Trans. Denis Savage (New Haven, CT: Yale University Press, 1970), 42–47, and 377 ff.
86. Ricoeur, *Oneself as Another*, 137.
87. Ricoeur, ibid., 166–167.
88. Gabriel Marcel, *The Mystery of Being*. Vol. I. Trans. G.S. Fraser (Chicago, IL: Henry Regnery, 1950), 85. Ricoeur acknowledges that along with Marcel, also Nabert and Levinas had similar trains of thought.
89. Marcel, ibid., 84.
90. Marcel, ibid., 86.
91. Ricoeur, *Oneself as Another*, 167.
92. Marcel, ibid., 90–91.

Chapter V
The Calling of Existenz

> *It seems to me that every mortal possesses, very nearly at the center of his mechanism, and well placed among the instruments for navigating his life, a tiny apparatus of incredible sensitivity which indicates the state of his self-respect. There we read whether we admire ourselves, adore ourselves, despise ourselves, or should blot ourselves out; and some living pointer, trembling over the secret dial, flickers with terrible nimbleness between the zero of a beast and the maximum of a god.*
>
> (Paul Valéry[1])

> *[In the case of one's vocation] each should do that which purely and simply only he ought to do...he and absolutely no other... the individual does not, as it were, give himself a task, but rather this is given to him at the same time as his being. Of course, the individual gives it to himself eventually* **with consciousness**, *but he can do this only because it is given to him originally without consciousness and through his mere being.*
>
> (J.G. Fichte[2])

§1. The Ideal True Self and the Metaphor of Vocation

"Vocation" or "calling" would seem to be, with the exception of those exemplary cases that we my find in sacred scriptures like the biblical calling of Moses and the prophets – providing we believe ourselves authorized here to assign a literal interpretation – similes or metaphors. That is, we speak metaphorically of a calling where it is assumed that there is no question of an actual second-personal address, a *call*, i.e., an emitted sound of a voice beckoning someone to come towards the one calling. Yet it is uncontroversial to speak of oneself drawn, moved, urged, etc., to follow a general direction in one's life. Writers have made the intriguing point that "beauty" or what is beautiful, *kalon*, itself of necessity calls, *kalein*, to produce beautiful things, *ta kala*. And Jean-Louis Chrétien, to whom we are here indebted, further notes that *kalein* has the same double meaning that words for "to call" have in French (and, we might add, also in some contexts Latin, German, and English): To summon, hail, beckon, on the one hand, and to name, on the other.[3] We will attend to the theological dimensions of this in Chapters VI and VII. Here we prescind from this more precise sense of vocation and attend to the more general and less theological metaphorical meanings of vocation.

The theme of vocation is a metaphor that joins with the numerous other metaphors that grapple with illuminating the thick endlessly complex referents of "one's self" and "one's life." We can note at the outset that all of these metaphors seem to have at least a latent teleological aspect. For example, the darkness of ignorance that surrounds us, interspersed with sudden ephemeral clarifying moments of insight, have motivated the time-honored metaphor of life as a mere dream – of course, implicitly contrasted with something else and more preferable. Or, in Plato's famous allegory in Book VII of *The Republic*, we are prisoners in a cave compelled to interpret reality through the passing shadows of the likenesses of real things. The essential temporality of life with its ineluctable prospective futural bent occasions the metaphor of an adventurous journey, e.g., from out of the cave where we have been imprisoned. The need to make decisions naturally evokes taking paths, being at crossroads or at a dead end. And many of the features of the considerations from which the metaphors are drawn, e.g., the beginning, middle, and end of the journey, the dangers and obstacles on the way, the issue of knowing one's way or getting lost, etc. stand ready to be themselves metaphors and used to interpret life.

The metaphor of a journey presupposes a direction and a goal. This is doubtless true for what happens within life. There are numerous metaphorical and real journeys within life that have beginnings, middles, and ends. But is all of life, or life as a whole, heading toward a goal that itself culminates as an event "at the end of the journey," such that this culminating event would be both within life and its end? Or is life itself a journey toward something beyond life, where the end is not an event within life? Or is there no end and only the "journey"? Or is it only apparently a journey whose temporal duration may no more find a direction in life than the swat experienced by a fly may figure into the direction of the fly's tenure.

If we take life itself as a journey, as many do, we have the analogy with journeys within life where along the way we are beset with darkness amidst the light. As to the light of our vision when underway, we can say with a Native American poet that the occasional clarity we have "is a fragile movement of shadows and silence./A strange little dance through a long dark night."[4] Further, as this same poet urges, the path we take winds like a snake into the future and once we are on it the question surfaces of whether we are taking the path or whether the path is taking us.

At the first level of the analogy, taking the journey might entail listening to cautions in regard to enchanting sirens that beckon us from afar and which reveal the ambivalence of what is beautiful for mortals. Or taking the journey might entail taking the true path by reading the right signs, listening to good advice, being lucky in spite of our mistakes. It also involves the adventure of interpreting the path in the light of the advice and interpreting the advice in the light of the path. We have no choice in life but to embark on the adventure and take certain paths, i.e., we must of necessity make decisions that have consequences.

But taking the right path as a matter of necessity is not at all the same as being called to take a certain path even though making decisions involves conscience and the Ought. When one says one has been "called" there is expressed a sense of this direction being one's own and if one does not follow it one is in some sense lost. Thus there is a sense of self-identifying with this way, this path, this career, this calling, even if it has placed heavy demands on the one who has been "called." Here the call has symmetry with conscience and the Ought. And these too may be thought of as pointing and beckoning. Calling, conscience, and the Ought as factors in one's journey imply that the path we take is not a matter of indifference. In this sense we do not merely take just any path, we are called to take certain paths rather than other ones. And in this sense, being on the right path is not merely a matter of being lucky in spite of ourselves.

Yet, if one's journey may be tied to a "call" through conscience and obligation then the journey is tied to the necessity of one's moral self-constitution. There is an ancient saying alleged of Pythagoras which nicely ties our theme of the necessity of the self-constitution of the person in self-identifying acts with the metaphor of a path or journey: *Quod vitae sectabor iter?* "What way, what road shall I choose for my life?" Ortega, who cites this text, makes our point when he says that "Man is the only reality that does not simply consist in being but must choose its own being" and, by way of implication, the choice of our being, the moral self-constitution, the necessity of a "deontological completion of the ontology," is metaphorically a path.[5]

A revered metaphor for life as a difficult journey is the labyrinth. Ancient peoples even used it as a ritual of initiation into different critical periods of a person's life. Think of the labyrinth as a finite, enclosed space that has numerous confusing but connected passageways with an entrance and an exit – but there is only one way in and one way out. Once one has entered this space one faces the difficulty of getting out or finding the exit. The reason for the difficulty is that the passageways look the same and yet most lead nowhere differently; and even in backtracking, one can become uncertain whether one is coming or going. In short, the labyrinth is an enclosure where the passages are such that it is easy to lose one's way.

This is an objective, third-person view of the labyrinth. To apply it to life is to think analogously and therefore to acknowledge similarities and differences between life and the labyrinth. The similarities are clear especially if we believe that in spite of the confusion, false starts, and losing one's way, ultimately things work out fine; if we believe that at the end of the journey one can look retrospectively at one's life with a contented sense of peace and clarity. In which case we might hear:

> Like distant landmarks you are approaching, cause and effect begin to align themselves, draw closer together. Experiences too indefinite of outline...to be recognized...connect and are identified as a larger shape. And suddenly a light is thrown back, as when your train makes a curve, showing that there has been a mountain of meaning rising behind you on the way you've come, is rising there still proven now through retrospect.[6]

Of course, it must be admitted that such a retrospection is not the good fortune of everyone. Indeed, what we earlier called a prospective retrospection may not at all provide us with such a pleasing optic on our life. Further, in many cases there are often religious beliefs that inform the appropriation of the metaphor. However, it would seem that in the living of life we do not live it *as* a labyrinth for at least the reason that typically we do not live life as having a decisive resolution like the releasing moment of taking the final correct passageway out of the labyrinth. We do not know life as the sort of thing that has absolutely correct paths which will result in our coming decisively out of its darkness and confusion. Of course, great narratives which feature heroes like that of Odysseus, who, in spite of the monstrous odds, pull through to safety and make the final journey home, can be so impressive that we may think of life properly as terminating in a hero's welcome home. But who among us can look upon her life in this way?

Further, this presents us with another distortion because the life of most is not heroic in the classic sense of gaining fame by slaying monsters before which all the world quakes, but rather a life laced with a series of labyrinths comprising the routines of ordinary life, which themselves manage, often enough, to create crushing, responsibilities and sufferings. Further, even the fabled hero, now at home from the wars and other adventures, faces the rest of his life with its own monsters, labyrinths, bodily and mental decline, and death.

Of course, we may well *believe* that there is an ultimate release from all suffering and this release is coincident with a kind of enlightenment. Or we may believe that upon coming into the light at the end of life there is a new kind of journey with new and even more blessed adventures, but ones without the deep anguish, darkness, and doubt of this life. In any case, in play here would be typically faith or religious beliefs. The living of life itself apart from, or having suspended, these beliefs does not provide a perspective which enables us to be outside the labyrinth so that we may experience life *as* a labyrinth; something present that is without an evident entrance and exit is not the presencing of something *as* a labyrinth.

There is the additional consideration that the metaphor of the labyrinth tends to suggest that life is a problem which can be solved by our ingenuity or good fortune. The appropriate skills which enable the good life, the virtues, only go so far. They do not guarantee that life will turn out as we want. More basic is the consideration that there is no assurance that these strengths can make up for the deficiencies in our beginnings. And clearly there are no guarantees that we will be fortunate enough to have the necessary good beginnings in our life which are prior to our own volitional beginnings. These first beginnings enable our own beginnings, i.e., our actions as the source of our character, to launch us with the appropriate strengths and skills that empower us for the good life. The ideal of the virtuous life goes a long way in enabling and encouraging us to do what is in our power to do. But not only is it obvious that how life unfolds is beyond our power, but our capacity to deal with what we of necessity must deal with often enough notoriously exceeds what is in our power. Even those of us fortunate enough to take advantage of our good beginnings can meet afflictions which have the power to crush us quite in spite of our moral and intellectual strengths – except, of course, in the cases of moral heroes, most of whom probably are totally invisible to us.

Our proposal is that, like one's death and ipseity, one's life is more in the category of *mystery*. We simply do not occupy a perspective which discloses to us what its "path," "solution" or "secret" might be any more than we have any light on how it is that *who* each of us is can be accounted for by the salary one has or what preceded our births. Rather, all we know is that *the* "answer" or "meaning," if there is one, is withheld from our thoughtful perception, agency, and reflection, and what is palpable is the excess of this meaning. This leaves us with the attitude of questioning born of an awakening to the center of our selves, our Existenz, rather than merely to our cognitive epistemic curiosity.

Nothing brings this home better than tragedy, where the path of life is shown to involve insurmountable conflicts of values and where the essentially impenetrable limit-situations, which may understandably be associated with kinds of forces (which subordinate even "the gods"), e.g., of fate, chance, destiny, etc., are in full evidence. This meaning-space opened up by tragedy is perhaps not shunned by believers for whom their religious dogmas are taken precisely as the good news which eliminates or illuminates such a dark space; but this comedic attitude remembers the dark place precisely as what faith has overcome and incessantly strives to overcome. In the meaning-space opened up by tragedy the only resolution is in the experience that life has this impenetrable dimension of depth to which we must resign ourselves. Indeed, the cultic function of the presentation of ancient Greek tragedies was precisely to deter humans from dulling their sensibilities and perceptions with the easy, harmonizing, conventionalizing ("hollywoodizing") myths. The catharsis sought was, among other things, the appropriation of the *truth of tragedy* by way of a purification from whatever clouded our perception in regard to the impenetrable *anangke* or blind necessities we face in these limit-situations. In the cultic enactment of the classic tragedies, the viewers were cleansed from whatever had the ability to distract them from the metaphysically perspicacious restlessness. This purification could bring with it the illumination which beckoned to live at a deeper level than most of the conventions inculcated. We have suggested that this deeper level, to which we are called, is oneself as Existenz, i.e., becoming aware of the center of the "I myself," occasioned by the urgency of the limit-situations.[7]

Another ancient metaphor is to see all of life as kind of divine play, *lila*, and thus we are urged not to let either our decisions or the course of events overwhelm us. A version of this is that life, or at least what most concerns us in life, is a joke or a comedy and behind the scenes there is a divine sense of humor which we are exhorted to appreciate, even though the exact "reason" for the humor or point of the joke eludes us. If life is most basically comedy rather than tragedy, then tragedy itself must give way to the deeper affirmation of the good regardless of the seeming power to negate that evil has. Such a conviction might lead one even to attempt to smile or laugh in the face of life's surds and tragedies.

Of course, these metaphors require a perspective that transcends what is given to us. A more immanent cognate position is the one which sees life as something like a prank. This is not the belief in a transcendent divine sense of humor behind the scenes, but rather the dawning conviction that life is pointless or absurd. Here there is acknowledged a former, perhaps irrepressible, desire and hope for meaning and intelligibility. With one's awakening to cynicism, there is acknowledged the

prior ineluctable affirmation of life. Further life may have been credited with seeming to have a sense, not necessarily as a pre-given goal or purpose, but at least as a
drift or direction that might support hope. But now one has reached the conclusion
that this is perhaps the root error. One has discovered that "the joke's on us" in our
presumption of things making sense.

But such a position presumes to know more than what one can know. We get a
clue of this from laughter itself. We earlier (Chapter I, §5, using Plessner) noted
that laughing, like grieving, is a total response to an aspect of life wherein we
find a lack of intelligibility. This is not to say that life's essential absurdity is the
source of laughter, but that in laughing we give expression to the felt-meaning of
our powerlessness to deal with life in so far as our power is tied to intelligibility.
The ready-made categories for interpreting the world do not deal with what we
must deal, and, in the situation occasioning laughter we accept this incapacity of
ourselves as minds to deal with the matter. Thereby we collapse into our whole
bodily selves and respond in this holistic way. This again is a way of opening up
the theme of "mystery."

In Franz Kafka's rich and dense mini-short story, *"Gib's Auf!" ("Give It Up!")*,
we have an allegory whose first level is of someone experiencing that it is late and
wanting to find his way to the train station. He comes to a policeman and asks the
way, and the policeman, says, "What! You want to learn the way from me?" and he
"turned with a sudden jerk like someone who wants to be alone with his laughter."[8]
This has numerous possible directions of interpretation. But one surely is that
finding one's way in regard to what is most important is not to be done primarily
through someone else's directions. Further, the humor might be precisely in the
belief that someone else's expertise could possibly be substituted for one's own task
of finding one's own way, given that what is at stake is the essential ("non-alibi")
task of the mystery of one's own Existenz.

There is a difficulty here with the proposal that "mystery" is essential to the task
of finding one's way or vocation. Not only does "mystery" at least, on the surface,
negate a revelation of a direction, but further we *must act* as if there was a more or
less comprehensive sense, even though what this is, is not evident. This is because
"one's life" and "one's life-world" are experienced more or less as meaning-wholes
which surround the more or less connected perceived segments of one's life. Herein
lies precisely the usefulness of religious-artistic narratives regarding the "labyrinth,"
pilgrimage, *lila*, the seven-fold path, the kingdom of God, etc. because they provide
us with frameworks which overcome the paralysis that emerges in the face of the
lures, dangers, and conflicting imperatives or moral perplexities which we ineluctably face. Yet for these narratives to keep pace with the depth of life, especially its
tragic aspect, they must keep open the rich sense of *je ne sais quoi* and not appear
as univocal unambiguous answers to the original complex questions the tragedies
(and comedies) in life occasion. They must foster living life from out of our center
rather than distracting us from this. Of course, it can well be the case that living
life from out of a religious narrative may well deepen one's sense of the mystery of
Existenz and not be a distraction from it. Our view is that in every case the integrity
of Existenz is the key both to finding one's way and appropriating narratives.

Aside from wholesale applicability of the metaphors or analogies of journey, labyrinth, and vocation, and apart from religious faith, is there anything about the experiences or analogous passageways that might have some way of revealing by intrinsic or immanently evident means that the decision or pathway is the wrong or right one for us? This, of course, is how we interpret the Kafka story and what we claimed for the self-ideal, Ought, and conscience. These, we have urged, are precisely ways we are awakened to our Existenz and directed to act from this center. And these have served initially as a way of indicating our metaphor of the "calling." Yet there is a distinction between being called or admonished to take a certain path by reason of our self-ideal, conscience, and the Ought, and another sense of being called that we wish also to highlight. In the former case it may not at all be inviting, but a burden. Yet we may think of the calling in another familiar setting, where it resembles more an invitation, even a fulfillment. This brings us back to our initial remarks about the "calling" as an expression or address that anticipates a response, indeed it is a gesture to which one may not remain indifferent without being ungracious. In mythical-religious settings this may portend the "one thing necessary," or that without which the hero believes he cannot be complete or truly himself. The ideal and true self, as the best under the circumstances that one's project hopes to realize, clearly has this aspect.

We shall attempt to do justice to the proper second-person sense of "calling" in this and the following chapters. Yet there is in the notion of an ideal true self an analogous first-personal sense of "calling." At first glance it seems absurd to speak of calling oneself. But this is only so if we do not attend to how we are in various respects transcendent to ourselves or inadequate to ourselves or how we now are not yet completely ourselves. Conscience, we have suggested in Chapter III, is ourselves at a distance. We also dwelled on how our basic willing will seems always to exceed our explicit achievements. (Chapter IV, §§2–3.) Further, we are transcendent to or at a distance from ourselves when we think of both our former selves as well as our future possible selves. The ideal true self is a unique future possibility for me that is eminently desirable. Yet as a regulative infinite ideal, it is not a real possibility can be realized, like my becoming proficient in Spanish. What is realizable is a goal and that would put it in time and make it something finite. The ideal true self is constitutive of me, therefore not something finite to be realized in time. If it were merely a fictional creation or a matter of pathological dissociation then the metaphor of being called by one's self-ideal would be troubling and objectionable. But as constitutive of the essential transcendence of oneself to oneself it does not warrant such concerns. One's self-transcending, we have proposed (in Book 1, Chapter I) is, of course, a constituting. But this is not a mere *poesis* or manufacturing of being, but a display of being, and foremost a display of the necessary features of how we are in the world.

The metaphorical call of one's self-ideal is a being pulled by the future as one's unique possibility, as a for-the-sake-of-which or end that is always in advance of us. As an infinite ideal it is an infinite task that always requires of us something new, something more, still to be realized. The call is actual as constitutive, but it is possible as my ideal future possibility. It is actually constitutive yet does not exist on its own but rather exists inseparably from the factuality of my being, both as my factual being is present and open to the future and as the being that I have already given myself. As one's completion it is necessary at least in the sense that being whole and fulfilled is a unique kind of exigency or lived necessity. Yet it is clearly not possible that this essential inadequation be surmounted decisively in the course of our living. And in this sense the call is to what is impossible. We thus may resign ourselves to the endless task. Fulfillment then lies in striving for this approximation. In this sense, the end is present in the means.

A danger of talking about the true self or false self is that one displaces oneself to an alleged finished self that one is not and yet one is called to be. As Thomas Merton once said about the notion of the "true self" and "false self" as he had previously discussed it: "I must manfully face this judgment [that I might have distorted the sense of the "true self" and "false self"] and find my center not in an ideal self which just *is* (fully realized) but in an actual self which does all it can to be honest and to love truly, though it still may fail...."[9] (Yet we will, in the final chapter, have reason to account for this temptation to look for an ideal self in a self which in some sense "just *is*" by way an ontological consideration of the divine exemplarity of the unique essence of the "myself.")

If we think of a calling as an address to us that we follow because of an interest it has awakened, then the horizon of the best may be said to "address us" by way of reaching us from what is beyond us, at the ideal-pole or horizon of our life. It may be said to awaken an interest in our pursuing it, because ineluctably that is what we do as intentional beings, i.e., fill empty intentions. "The calling of the ideal emergent in the horizon" purports to describe what is the same for everyone, even though the basic theme of this work is that the ideal must address the unique, non-communicable ipseity.

The theory of "calling," furthermore, must make allowances for the limitations imposed by circumstances. It presumes that the weighing of the best will employ standards that most, if not everyone, would agree to. Furthermore, "under the circumstances" always means the "absolute" or "categorical" imperative is not absolute or unconditioned but rather is, in fact, conditioned. It means that from the start one recognizes that there are conditions beyond one's will, and therefore one's own will is conditioned in this respect. This again reflects Aristotle's distinction between the properly human happiness (*eudaimonia*) that is the ethically significant horizon of our agency and the intimation of the absolute or supreme happiness that is at the fringes and out of reach of humans.[10] In both cases happiness is never a filled intention in which one rests but rather it is always the meaning-giving horizon of agency. But from the start it is evident that human happiness is always conditioned, partial, vulnerable, and not without the threat of surds.

"Vocation," even more so than the metaphor of "labyrinth," is a term properly greeted with suspicion when it purports to describe a person's life. This is because it appears to provide clarity and certainty to what of necessity is pervaded by opacity and uncertainty. In our formal analysis we highlighted the horizon of the I-can and I-ought along with the teleology of will and the self-ideal. This might well appear to be a sleight of hand for what is intrinsically a muddled state of affairs.

However, we may not forget that in speaking of the horizon we are speaking of what is essentially ambiguous. The horizon is precisely what is not determinate in either its categorial display or its motivation, even though it, of necessity, has certain vectors of determinability. There is the further obfuscating consideration that "vocation" to one's true self is to one's own unique future possibility and yet one is free not to realize it. This is not merely a matter again of the indeterminacy of the ambiguous horizon. The vocation to my true self is my unique future possibility that I am required to realize and what analogously demands to be realized, and yet I am free not to realize it. The call resonates precisely as what I can refuse to listen to. Indeed, we are often at odds with it. And this reveals that "vocation" only makes sense in the context of the often opaque and obscure struggle with oneself and with one's natural and social surroundings. This, my unique possibility, my I-can, is not a freedom without frameworks, conditions, or determinations made possible by my being this person in the world with Others.

I am how I am in the present only as informed by how I have been, and what I can expect on the basis of how I am and have been. What I want and my wanting are dependent on the person I am, what is available, what others also want, and these are dependent on countless conditions and circumstances. My *achieving* what I want similarly is dependent on countless considerations both within me and without. Thus besides the needs, claims, and rights of others, the abundance or scarcity of social goods, and nature's abundance and cooperation, there is my moral disposition, based on how I have lived; there is, as well, my health and the various ingredients of luck, e.g., of my being in the right situation. Overarching all of this is the question of Ought: my desiring what my true self desires or my desiring what I ought to desire, my being awake to the "call" of the best possible under the circumstances.

Thus the ideal of one's true self takes on the flesh of a distinctive calling or career when the individual pursuit of what is best under the circumstances is integrated into a sense of the individual's personal ideal being entwined with that of others and perhaps even the whole human community. Here one's unique essential ipseity, i.e., being an individual *per se* and not merely by reason of incidental determinants of personal individuation, becomes intertwined with these very individuating factors of the person as an interpersonal, intersubjective entity. Here, furthermore, the ideal of the true self has ingredients of impartiality and impersonality in so far as the good will that is called for is a moral good that requires a moral imagination and willingness to self-displace oneself to the points of view of others, to take up their points of view as one's own.[11] If the person takes account of the fact that the constitution of one's personhood or personality is essentially tied to others in myriad bonds of claims and mutual dependence, such that one's weal or woe is bound up with that of others, and that the moral good lies precisely in taking the Other's goodness as one's own, then one sees that, as a matter of ontological and moral necessity, the constituted essential person has essential intersubjective and historical aspects. The personal essential ideal is then also, at the same time, intersubjective because as a person one is essentially a part of a whole, what Husserl called a personality of a higher order. Of course, such considerations never have the weight of making the person a non-subsistent, non-free, part of a more basic whole. It is incompatible with both volumes of this work, and our understanding of Husserl, that the whole, e.g., "society" or "the state" be considered a subsistent whole and the person a contingent, non-subsistent accidental part. Everything we have said works against such a notion.[12]

§2. Truths of Will

But is there any evidence that each has a calling which is uniquely *one's own* and which reflects one's own unique ipseity? What we have just outlined as the absolute Ought or categorical imperative merely describes the formalities of the requirement to seek the good that cannot be absorbed by something higher; we have merely outlined the categorical imperative as best "under the circumstances." This is a universal formulation for anyone whosoever. True, the exhortation to it and its conceivability as our calling and overriding Ought is not founded on its being universalizable. We are not exhorted to it *because* it is universalizable, but rather because it explicates the essential drift of the heart and mind. The Ought emerges out of necessities having to do with what is the case; it is not in opposition to what is or what is not taken to be good. But this is applicable to anyone whatsoever, any agent whatsoever. It reveals nothing of an agency that reflects one's unique ipseity. It indicates nothing of a "calling" that is uniquely mine. Not only is there a universal formula, but even when we apply it to the individual situation of a personal life-world with all of the complexity of its gossamer of motivation there is still the possibility of the process of deliberation from out of this unique constellation being duplicated in so far as what is weighed may be put into comparative and commensurate values. This is the work of a good part of "axiology."

Is there any phenomenon that demands recognition as a unique calling? Is there anything that justifies our paraphrase of Fichte's exhortation: "will to be what you alone ought to be and what you alone can be – what indeed you alone want to be."[13] Is there, as Husserl claims there is, an unconditioned Ought that is addressed to the person in his or her unique ipseity which is for the one experiencing it an "absolute affection" that is not submitted to a rational foundation nor is it dependent on any such connection with such a foundation?

We propose that there is such a unique, albeit philosophically problematic, "address." For Husserl this overriding Ought goes in advance of all rational reflection and deliberation, even when these are possible.[14] The Ought as we discussed it earlier was tied to action in general; and as we just depicted it in the prior section it was tied to reflections that enable weighing whether this is the best thing to do, given these circumstances. But also, in Chapter III, we related it to conscience, which is uniquely one's own. And because all deliberations on action ultimately are decided in the form of conscience, even these universal considerations are directed at me, and in this respect they are my "calling" and to be done because they are my calling and not because they are universalizable.

But it remains true that the sense of the earlier discussions of the categorical imperative or how Ought differs from Is or Can were of a general nature. Clearly not only the Kantian categorical imperative, but also Husserl's axiological-teleological ethics have to do with what is universal. Husserl's axiology involves considerations such as whether one good outweighs another; whether this good is a better means to that good; whether if good A is conjoined necessarily with B, then can I will A without willing B? Whether if A is a greater value than B, and B is a greater value than C, then is not A a greater value than C? And so forth. These axiological deliberations, just like the theoretical ones of formal logic or mathematics, are truths that can take place in a public space and anyone can participate in the deliberations of what "one ought to do." The evidence of the emergent value is always in principle what is evident to everyone. But to claim that this adequately accounts for this ultimate kind of moral deliberation is too simple given our prior consideration of the uniqueness of ipseity and what the evaluating process entails.

Further, as we argued in *The Person and the Common Life*, the absolute Ought involves a kind of impersonality whereby we take up the point of view that everyone "in our shoes" would approve of, and wherein we presumptively take up everyone's point of view. Whereas this effort of benevolence and moral imagination is necessary in the unique common good of a personality of a higher order, it still does not do justice to the issue at hand, of whether there is a unique personal calling tied to one's personal ideal and sense of one's ideal self. It is this unique sense of one's self and calling that one would integrate into the presumptive trans- or impersonalization of perspectives required for the common good of a personality of a higher order.

We have noted that every good appears within the personal life-world of a unique individual. This massive unfathomable background of apperception, as informed by the general latent willing will of the individual, has a unique cumulative value that cannot simply be explicated by the conceptual or logical analysis of the propositions implied in the position-takings. Of course each judgment, each decision, each conviction, each promise, each preference, etc. could be spelled out in a formal-logical way. But even these explications could never capture the unique massive backdrop out of which these position-takings emerge.

There is an analogous individuality at work in thought and speech. Speaking is preceded by the empty intention of the right words. But the right words are chosen from words at hand, at my disposal through my linguistic competence. And these words themselves by their very nature and apart from me have a kind of meaning-tendency or meaning-intention which is actualized by me, the speaker, in using them in my "wanting to say something." This meaning-tendency or meaning-intention is "the same for us all" quite apart from my intentionality. Yet I intend these words in such a way that they say what I now want to say. This "wanting to say something" is through the intending to use the word's meaning-intentions. But this "wanting to say something" is the more fundamental empty intention encompassing and inseparable from the intention of the right words from among the words at hand, words which have their own public or universal meaning-intention quite apart from my intending them as means of my wanting to say something. The achievement of coming up with the right words is an authentic achievement by me, a fulfillment of the empty intention of "wanting to say something." As such it is always a perspective on what *I* want to say (on this matter in this context).[15]

The proposition, as the telos of what I want to say now, of which I have a "felt-meaning" (Gendlin) or an empty intention as an implicit "dark something" (Husserl) out of which definite statements emerge within the determinate context of a conversation, is finite. Yet even the proposition admits numerous if not endless refined sentential versions as in paraphrases and translations. And as this proposition is integrated into the string of sentences that inadequately articulate *a* life-world it becomes inexhaustibly explicable. And as we insert it into not *a* but *someone's* life world, there emerges the phenomena of both the potential conceptual inexhaustibility as well as the unique personal slant and nuance of this proposition which is essentially elusive of efforts to articulate it because the unique person's wanting to say transcends the explications.

This matter reaches a new level of complexity if we consider that our valuing position-takings give expression to and articulate the infinite ideal of ourselves in the world with others. The valuing acts, e.g., initially delighting in the passing parade, then finding it boring, etc., presuppose the articulation or position-taking that manifests the categoriality and syntax that constitute the presence of the object, the parade. Yet both the valuing act and the object-rending position-taking (categoriality and syntax), which has provided enough of a hold for us to value "something," are carried by the general willing will of the person which itself pervades the continuous passive synthesizing and unifying of these specific acts within the context of all of life's other acts. The propositions one articulates are abstractions from the thick tangled web of the endless other objective or evaluative position-takings. This richly textured web is always someone's and why a particular valuing appears at a particular time, like Proust's investment of the smell of the biscuits with such enormous significance, can only be recounted by a narrative that has the logic of the autobiography as revealed by passive synthesis, not the logic of a third-person observer dealing with either biographical truths that point to the logic of the person's life or which hold for everyone who is this sort of person and into whose shoes we can place ourselves. What might appear to be foolish for the understanding by a theoretical observer, oneself or a stranger, in the matter of comparing values and valuings, might appear for oneself in the reality of living one's life, and not in the transcendental or theoretical stance, to be just the opposite, i.e., wise and of utmost importance. Like Proust's biscuits, this simple "worthless" matter might occasion veneration and awe.[16]

Whether this massive horizonal apperception which makes up the appreciating and understanding of a person might be cloned or find a *Doppelgänger* might well be doubted. In Book 1 we wrestled with, and granted, its possibility. But in so far as our thesis is accepted that the "myself" is precisely what cannot be doubled, and in so far as one accepts our "likely story" that it is the "myself" which informs the person as the formal and final cause, there is given a further speculative reason to weaken the possibility of such a metaphysical cloning of a life-world.

Husserl's notion of "the truth of will" purports to illuminate what we are calling "vocation" as the proper path toward realizing one's true self. Sometimes this phrase is used by Husserl merely to refer to how reason is implicit in feeling and will. But it also has the more specific sense of "the truth in the universal context of will of the particular subject of will, what the subject truly ought."[17] Husserl states that here we do not have to do with an act of will regarded in isolation, about which we raise the question of its truth, validity, or appropriateness. Rather we must think of the act of will within the universal context of will of the particular subject of will. "Only in relation to the full individual life can one speak of the truth of a specific willing, therefore we are speaking of what the subject truly ought to will. What I ought is determined by what 'I can,' but this is different from what another can."[18] Thus the "truth" of the "truth of will" has not its proper sense here with Husserl's theory of truth in the Sixth of the *Logical Investigations*. It is more the truth in the (Hegelian!) sense of the whole or the "wider fuller significance," of which the particular will acts are parts and, without this wider context, are mere abstractions. But it is not a third-personal universal perspective from nowhere; it is disclosure of the wider whole of one's life as it is lived a unique filled intention from within a specific act of will.

The appropriate analogy is: As each act, e.g., of the professional, e.g., teacher, reflects the universal willing initiated by the vocational choice, so each particular willing in life reflects this universal context of will, i.e., the accumulated, synthesized, and passively associated life of the will's willing. The sense of each willing needs to be explicated by this wider "truth of will" and there are occasions in life, what we have called "gathering experiences," in which the truth of one's life and will become poignantly palpable in a unique filled intention. The truth of will reveals oneself to oneself as having a deeper center, i.e., as Existenz, and as given to oneself to determine oneself in this particular way.[19] We return to this matter of "the truth of will" below.

In this respect "the truth of will" is a species of what Aquinas called "connatural knowledge," i.e., a mode of knowing that is in accord with the "nature" or habitualities of the person. In all cases of experiencing something as good we find that there is consonance with the inclinations or desires of the person, what we have called the "personal essence." An example is that the virtuous person, e.g., the person for whom justice is a pervasive value in her life, will have a greater sensitivity and accuracy of judgment in regard to unjust situations that will not be found in a more egocentric person. Such a person has an intuitive accurate judgment about the situation because of her susceptibility or affinity with the things about which one is to judge. In this respect Aristotle's view is in play that for the virtuous person what is actually good appears as such to her and what appears good to her is indeed what is actually so. Here there is a truthful knowing brought about by the dispositions and will of the virtuous person and in this sense the basic directedness of the person as an expression of what we are calling the general or willing will brings about intellect's recognizing the truth of the matter.[20]

This consideration may be extended to the "truth of will" and the matter of vocation. The person who honestly is seeking with her whole heart the path which best leads to her realizing her true self similarly will have sensibilities in play when the appropriate path opens up. The disclosure need not be the result of an extended deliberation but rather will be a kind of "connatural" recognition and will enjoy a certainty that deliberation might not be able to deliver.

Nevertheless some considerations may aid us in letting the distinctively Husserlian sense of "the truth" and our capacity to "be truthful" be applicable in the case of "the truth of will." Thereby we can weaken its appearance of being either irrational or a paradox in as much as truth is typically at home in cognitive-intellectual acts. Truth for Husserl is displayed as such in the making present of an empty intention. But it is not merely a making present of what before was intended in its absence. Coming upon my key in a certain drawer is not bringing to light the truth of "the key is in my drawer." Similarly, expecting to find my key in a certain drawer and then finding it does not bring the truth of the matter to light. Rather, the truth of the claim or hypothesis that the key is in that particular drawer comes to light in my finding the key precisely there after the empty intention of propos-ing this view to my self or hearing you propose it to me. I say, "it's true that the key is there" instead of "here is the key." The truth of something comes to light in making present as it was intended in its absence what before was intended in its absence. Making present as it was intended in its absence hearkens back to the distinctive way it was emptily intended, i.e., as a presumptive truth claim that was not yet verified. It is presencing what before was proposed as true, but now there is a confirming, verifying intuition of what before was proposed as it was before proposed. We further must recall that for Husserl emotions and will are not blind but also are ways we display the axiological features of what is within the world and the horizon of the world. Our willing will holds open the space, in an empty intention, of our well-being and our true self. Our willed wills, our explicit *fiats*, decisions, and resolutions move us in the direction of this well-being – or at least move us away from what harms us – by acting upon what is present in the light of how it appears within the willing will's horizon. If we further think of will and the willing will to be the dynamism of passive synthesis massively and continuously synthesizing the retentions of "the heart's desires" and other habitualities, we may think of this massive ongoing synthesis as an empty intention of the unique good of the personified "myself," its true self. Then, on the occasion of the distinctive asso-ciation, there is initiated the unique gathering act that distills one's life in regard to a present path toward one's unique good. This would be a unique quasi-filling of this empty intention of the quest of one's life direction.[21] Of course, it is only upon reflection that it would be seen to be a presencing as it was intended in its absence of what before was emptily intended in its absence. Only upon reflection could one say, "It is true, that this is my calling. I sought in my prior paths what they could not deliver. But now I see that this is what I wanted without ever knowing it clearly. My other paths pointed to this and now I see that this is so."

Following Husserl, we may speak of those truths as "truths of will" that are not continuous with the public states of affairs or determinations reached by theoretic consciousness or an objective weighing of values by some intersubjective standard that requires commensurability. A busy activist parent may choose to spend the evening playing with his child rather than participating in an important action that could possibly eventually lead to a condemned person's being taken off death row. The choice may not make sense outside of the personal life-horizon. Only within this horizon does the "truth of will" of this person emerge in this regard.

Simone Weil's thought on the notion of "vocation" seems to be in remarkable harmony with that of Husserl here. She thought of the vocation precisely as having to do with the acts and events that were strictly personal, such that the one who leaves them on one side never reaches life's proper goal, and dishonoring them is to dishonor oneself. Vocation is of a distinctively different order than that of reason or inclination, even though it may be described as due to a unique impulse that contrasts manifestly and essentially with a code of moral practices common to all as well as with impulse and reason. And "not to follow such an impulse when it made itself felt, even if it demanded impossibilities" appeared to her the greatest of ills. The most beautiful life possible, Simone Weil wrote, "has always seemed to me to be one where everything is determined, either by the pressure of circumstances or by impulses such as I have just mentioned and where there is never any room for choice."[22] The parallels with Husserl's theories of vocation, truth of will, and the "teleological-determinist" position will become more evident in the rest of this chapter.

When Kierkegaard observed that "I can discover my own untruth only by myself, because only when *I* discover it is it discovered, not before, even though the whole world knew it"[23] he is pointing out that the first-person truth about my being true to myself, or the insight that I have been dishonest with myself, does not mean the same thing if it is a proposition known by others. We all are familiar with the common opinion that takes the form of, e.g., "Everyone knew that X was bad for her except she herself"; "everyone but he himself knew that he was self-deceiving himself in regard to her." Others knowing that I have self-deceived myself do not know it in the way it requires to be known, i.e., known in the first-person by the one whose moral deficiency or evil it is, who alone can overcome it, and for whom it is of essential relevance and greatest importance. This is to say that there is a truth to be known by me as a truth of my life-will or a truth of this Existenz. If known by them as a truth about me it is, for them, merely one fact among others. As such it is clearly outside being a truth applying to my Existenz and of what is unconditional importance, just as it is outside being a truth applying to their Existenz or a truth evident within their life-will. Similarly, if known by me in a merely propositional attitude it may not be equivalent to its being a truth having its distinctive evidence within my life-will. Thus our claim here is analytic: As a truth of will it is what only I can know in this way, in my life as an agent self-determining myself; outside of this framework, its sense is different. Furthermore, and this too is analytic, as a truth of will, it is a truth that I alone *must* come to know.

The claim that there is a truth of will revealed in a unique "impulse" (Simone Weil) or "affection" (Husserl) should be less surprising if one is prepared to hold that even the secret implicit workings of the mind's rumination in passive synthesis are already stamped by not merely "laws of association" and an unfathomably subtle implicit pre-propositional logic, but these forms of law-likeness themselves are pervaded by the willing will as the basic dynamism of the personification of the original "myself." This latent willing will aims at constituting a unique focus, i.e., the true self. This latent willing may be thought of as passive-synthetic "mulling things over" in the light of one's emergent unique personal ideal. In the case of the truth of will it is less the unique application of universals to particulars in a massively implicit manner than a matter of the individual taking a particular, i.e., the present indicated path, for absolutely and unconditionally binding for herself.

One facet of this theme of unique good and truths of will is that matters of the highest importance are not always public and intersubjective. Thus not only are there valuable aspects of things, i.e., things that are regarded as beautiful, exquisite, charming, magnificent, sublime, etc., that I will never be able to appreciate, but it is also possible that there are valuable aspects that I alone, or someone else alone, is in a position to appreciate. It could be the case that because a person belongs to a people which has unique dispositions founded in cultural practices, and which also has a unique knowledge of certain truths, that this person enjoys the disclosure of values that are not available to any other persons not belonging to her people. A fortiori someone might be the only one to hear certain exquisite sounds, smell intoxicating scents, or perceive distinct dazzling colors. But this in and of itself would not make it *absolutely necessary* that these sensa or the values that are *de facto* enjoyed by this imagined people be *de jure* or with existential necessity be revealed to these people. *A fortiori* it is not absolutely necessary that these values or sensa be revealed to me. I might very well be fully and authentically me myself as this person without these values, and they need in no way be a matter that reveals my unique calling or what is uniquely mine to do at this time as an ingredient of my truth of will.[24]

Husserl discusses another aspect of this same matter. "I am who I am, and the individual particularity shows itself therein that I, as who I am, love exactly as I love, and that precisely this calls me and not that."[25] Several questions surface here. Is this uniqueness of the act of love and the uniqueness of the object loved to be assigned to any act whatsoever or is it especially true in the case of love? Our answer (given in our earlier discussion in Book 1, Chapter IV) in part is clear: Love targets exemplarily the unique ipseity. Further, all acts take place within the endless strands that comprise the individual person's horizon of experience, and therefore they all will bear the mark of the individual person's unfolding. This personal individuality seems scarcely evident in the carrying out of formal cognitive operations. It is more evident in the imaginative aspects of research, even though the nature of scientific procedure requires suppressing as irrelevant personal individuality. In ethics many of the fundamental imperatives and values have both a simplicity and universality, as in "Do not kill," "Do good avoid evil," "one must tell the truth," etc. Of course, the interpretation of these and their application is often a highly individual matter. But ethics and religion both are matters where, besides the relevance of "the same for us all," and the exhortation not only to place oneself in the perspective of others but to let the others' perspective become part of one's own, there is also in play "truths of will" which are restricted to the single individual. (Consider, e.g., the task of facing one's death and the prospective retrospection it may call forth.) Further, in so far as these acts are pervaded by position-takings where the *I* comes forth in order to give the unique expression of the "myself," it is hard to conceive what a genuine duplication or communalization of these acts might mean.

If we grant this and we also acknowledge that some acts are more I-centered than others, then an even stronger case can be made for the uniqueness of the act of love. The act of love opens us up in an intentional act to the realm of "mystery" where the excessive *Je ne sais quoi* of unfathomable riches is present without the determinacy of properties. Indeed, it is in the region of love and no other act that we reach the *ne plus ultra* of disclosures of the other *spirit* along with the disclosures of the center and depth of the loving I. Indeed, just as it is not evident whether there is a limit to the disclosure of the depth of the other ipseity, so it is not evident that there is a limit to the depth of disclosure of this center of the one loving.

We will return to the extravagant features of love in the next section where we also hope to make evident that the claim that love is at the core or center of "I myself" is a synthetic a priori claim on the basis of the first-person experience of loving and being loved. If this is true then it is also true that not only is the love directed at me unique, but also no one can love as I do (otherwise she or he would be me). Nevertheless, there can be no doubt that the other lover or suitor can love with the same form, essence, or type of love I, the other to the other suitor, do. And, as bitter as it may seem to me, the other suitor could love the same person with the same form of love that I do. In which case, the acts of loving would be not merely numerically distinct but for *each lover* they would be "essentially" unique by reason of the truth of will ("no other can personally value as I do, otherwise he would be I myself"). Thus, not only the form of our acts and the target of our acts could be identically the same; furthermore, this act of loving of the same person by the lovers could be occasion for the self-awareness of the deepest sense of each lover's unique individuality. In addition, the other suitor could stand in relation to the same correlate person or matter by way of what amounts to an essentially or formally the *same* personal necessity or "calling."[26] Whereas all these considerations might be material for comedy or tragedy in the artistic presentation of love triangles, one can imagine that in imaginative-utopian and religious settings that it could have quite a different sense.[27]

Valuing position-takings typically, of course, are directed to matters that are of finite importance. They are directed at what is "merely" good, or at what is more or less good, pleasing, etc. These are always experienced against the horizon of the "more." But this ought not to be construed to advocate the ungracious position that would always demean what is good because it is "the foe of the better." Small things are truly beautiful; everydayness is laced with ordinary but truly good things. To depreciate them because they are finite or to regard them as mere instrumental goods for what is more or higher is a mistake of great consequence, as we can readily see in environmental and economic matters. From an ontological perspective, it might be an error if the case can be made that each entity is an haecceity and thus an expression, a "selving," of a unique and therefore incommensurate value.

Further, it might be that these merely finite goods are ultimate in the sense that when they are gone, there is no possibility of other goods (founded or dependent on them) whether or not better ones. (In which case, these finite goods would have to be appreciated at least as the necessary conditions of the higher ones.)

As we noted earlier, all considerations that we can make present and actually enjoy are finite. Further, without the enjoyment of the good, the better and best are invisible. Once we make present the better and the best, they themselves become what is good over against the horizon of the better and best that lies beyond them. They become conditioned, *bedingt*, over against the horizon of the presumed or imagined unconditioned, the *Unbedingt*. But the quest for the realization of the unconditioned can be perverse when it involves depreciation of the finite and conditioned goods, not only because of the reprehensibility of the disdain for them but also because these goods are clearly what are actual and what we enjoy, whereas the better and the best, vis-à-vis the present good, exist (as enjoyed) only presumptively or imaginatively – and perhaps that is the only claim they will ever have on actual existence. Further, the better and best, upon its being enjoyed "in the flesh," becomes what is "merely" good over against the new axiological horizon with its new promises of what is better and best. "The grass is always greener on the other side of the fence" ought not to be an occasion for denying the good greenness on this side. On the other hand, the fact of the danger of the slippery slope of "the better is the foe of the good" ought not to blind us to the better.

§3. Love and Existenz

Thus in our appreciation of finite things there is the horizon of the skyline of the ideals, the infinite ideas, which provide the horizon of our engagement. The truth of will is the truth of what I appreciate within this horizon as it has become configured within my lifetime. The truth of will is the truth of my duties, hopes and desires, and loves; it is the truth of the loving that I do. It is "the truth of will" in the sense that this willing, this intending, this agency, etc. is a uniquely compelling filled intention of what prior to its presence I seemed to have emptily intended. Earlier (in Book 1, Chapter IV) we saw that love is an emotion whose primary intentional target is another person's ipseity. Here in this section we want to resume the discussion of love in Book 1, Chapter IV, §§ 13 ff. and elaborate on how in loving there is awakened in the core of the I a centering and gathering act. This act has two moments, both one of restful contemplation and the motion of desire and devotion.

Love's target, we claimed, is the ipseity, the "myself," of the Other. We face the immediate problem that the Other is present *as loveable*, indeed as incomparably good. This is the contemplative moment of love. But how do we square our claim that love presents the Other beyond all properties and characteristics with the one which we seem also to be making that the Other has the properties of being loveable and good? The response is that what we mean by goodness here is not present as a property of the person or ipseity. Thus the claim has nothing to do with the obvious assertion that it is easier to love someone who has loveable qualities. Here we may recall our discussion in Book 1 where we appropriated St. Thomas's position that the person *is* the *dignitas* of an individual substance. We took this to mean that the dignity *is* evident in the presence of the person. We thus said, following Von Hildebrand, that here we have to do not with something having a property which we call a value but rather we have to do with something that is itself an "ontological value," i.e., an ipseity is to be identified with this exceptional sense of *dignitas* or "value." For that purpose we proposed an analogy that takes advantage of Barry Miller's distinction of the limit-simpliciter and the limit-case. Similarly here: What love targets is the unique ipseity in its own essential goodness. It is not a general communicable and shareable property; rather the *unique goodness* is coincident with what love targets. Does "goodness" as a universal property get cancelled by "unique"? Yes, in so far as "goodness" requires comparison and communicability. No, in so far as it is equally applicable in other cases of "ontological value," but with "uniquely essential" differences.

It would seem that Jankélévitch had this in mind when he wrote of an "essential," "translapsarian" innocence which was at the "base of the soul" and which was to be contrasted with a pre-lapsarian and post-lapsarian innocence. Simone Weil has a similar theory of the sacred "impersonal" dimension of the soul, just as Buddhism speaks of the trans-personal Buddha-nature in which each is grounded. Dogmas and myths of paradise and of Heaven take their bearings from our immersion in an awareness of our guilt or "fallenness." They have the capacity to permit the mind to intend (emptily) states of Existenz which antedate or surmount our present awareness of our moral frailty. The "essential," "translapsarian" innocence to which we here call attention is the pure non-reflective ipseity living ineluctably the truth of itself *now* perpetually and continuously and *not* aware of itself in terms either of its failings or strengths, ugliness or beauty. As we said in Book 1 in the discussion of indexicals and the "myself": One can be aware of oneself as oneself without being aware of oneself as anything except oneself. Again, there is no third-person special characteristic that one has to think that one possesses in order to think of oneself as I. Thus, if I am aware of myself "without inferring this from anything else that I know about myself, my knowledge that it is myself of whom I am aware has to be independent, at least in some respects of knowing anything else about myself."[28] In the present context, this means that I am present to myself as "beyond good and evil" or in a "translapsarian innocence."

Of course we know persons and ourselves as moral persons primarily in the display through action and therefore as having done something, and therefore at least as having done something which is potentially praiseworthy or blameworthy. Innocence of pure ipseity is withdrawn or abstracted from this context. Ipseity is envisaged in the richness of its non-reflective awareness of its essentially mysterious self-being and thus not unconscious or ignorant. Perhaps we may think of this analogously as a "state of grace" that is fundamentally a disposition to receive and not impose itself on the world around it. This elemental ineluctable being oneself which one can never lose, but which has an analogous exemplarity that one never can attain in one's historical personal existence, perhaps serves as the basis for the mythological projections (e.g., a primal paradisiacal innocence) or the aspirations of a holy will, an absolutely disinterested love, etc. But all these personal versions of innocence have to do with understanding the person in terms of quiddity or qualities and properties, and not the pure that-ness ("quoddity") of the Who or the "myself." Yet it is this translapsarian, essential innocence, or *dignitas*, which is the target of a pure love because it does not appear in the world as providing "reasons" for love. And love affirms, sustains, and creates for the person the possibility of a life in accord with this "innocence" and dignity.[29]

Another way of putting this is to say that love lets shine forth the unique splendor or radiance of the Other. (See Book 1, Chapter VI, §7. What immediately follows supplements our discussions in Book 1.) This radiance is the very presence of the ipseity, it is not some thing belonging to the Other or this presence as a property. Even in perceptions of Others where love is not in play, the Other's presence involves her being herself present without one's attending to her eyes, nose, lips, etc., as the surface of and properties of the body; rather these become diaphanous to this presence. Indeed, we can imagine or recall times when we are at a loss to say how precisely she looked, what kind or color of eyes, what shape the nose and mouth had, etc.

The monk and poet, Thomas Merton, has a beautiful statement of the radiance of ipseity. He reports of an experience he had in the wake of a dream. In the dream a beautiful young girl showed him deep affection and embraced him. He was "moved to the depths of his soul." He learned that the name of this girl was "Proverb" and this was something she was not proud of. A few days later in Louisville, Kentucky (not far from his monastery) at the corner of Fourth and Walnut, he was walking down the street and suddenly everyone there shone with the beauty of "Proverb" and similar to her they were shy of their true names and this was because, like Proverb, they were mocked because of their true names. In another account of the same experience, he reports that in the center of a shopping district,

> I was suddenly overwhelmed with the realization that I loved all those people… that we could not be alien to one another even though we were total strangers. It was like awaking from a dream of separate-ness, of spurious self-isolation in a special world…. There is no way of telling people that they are all walking around shining like the sun… If only everybody could all see themselves as they really *are*. If only we could see each other that way all the time. There would be no more war, no more hatred, no more cruelty, no more greed…. I suppose the big problem would be that we would fall down and worship each other…[30]

This all illustrates Merton's classical theological metaphysics which we will study in a larger context in Chapters VI–VII of this Book. But note that the radiance appears here subsequently as a property like the shining of the sun, when in the experience it is simply the very persons or ipseities present as themselves.

When talking about radiance and splendor, I do not have in mind parapsychological "auras," for the perception of which I myself have no capacity. But perhaps these auras are ways some gifted people are especially attuned to the ipseities. Nor a fortiori do I have in mind some sort of physical light-ray or radiation. I have in mind rather something resembling more "the sparkle" or "intelligence" in someone's eyes, as when they are especially "bright" or even "dancing," which in such cases can even be evident in strangers. The sparkle is not really some intense physical light but rather the "intensity" or "quality" of the presence of the Other as it is evident in subtle cues that emanate from her bodily presence. We notice the "light" in someone's face when the dullness vanishes as she comes out of an illness or a depression, or even in response to a kind word. In none of these cases do we have in mind something related to the way the Other's body surface, in particular the eyes, is affected by the sun or the artificial light in the room. And all of these cases only serve to highlight how the other ipseity is able to become especially vivid for us.

Of course, the person whose eyes are furtive, dull, groggy, vacant, etc., lack the radiance and sparkle that we often delight in. Nevertheless, this very privation of the obvious sense of "radiance" does not negate the foundational radiance of spirit. It rather means that more love, faith, and hope are required for it to become evident. This, of course, is, in some circumstances, by no means easy to achieve. Indeed, we know that the harshness of life's necessities (*anangke*) can turn persons into apparent zombies and/or monsters.

In this regard Simone Weil claims that human injustice produces not martyrs but "quasi-damned souls" whose "I is dead" and for whom we can do nothing. We never know in fact whether the I is dead absolutely. In any case it is only an utterly pure love without the slightest trace of condescension that can reanimate these moral zombies. Weil seems to suggest that the "radiance of spirit" of which she so eloquently speaks can be completely extinguished in terms of its manifestness in both oneself and Others.[31] It is unclear to me whether she holds that people become ontological-moral zombies while still alive.

To grasp initially this dignity and radiance we might also appeal to the odd neurotic projection, or odd quasi-parapsychological presences or fictional evocations of a unique recognized presence in a room where we are in spite there being no physical body there. Here minimally we feel ourselves felt, sense ourselves seen – even though the Other is not present in a normal visible way. In such a case we make present a "presence," and even though indeterminate, we apperceive it rightly or wrongly as the unique presence of a unique presencing of us by another. Presence here is able to be abstracted from the distinct bodily propertied someone. In spite of the inability to determine who this is, this someone "radiates" herself.

The splendor and radiance that we wish to assign to the ipseity may be thought about also in the way grace and graciousness, elegance and charm can suffuse someone's physical presence and in which these can be present in an endless variety of personal physical presences. The elusiveness of these qualities, we suggest, does not detract from their reality, and in this respect they aid in thinking about the unique dignity of the unique essence of the "myself." These qualities, especially as they are tied to "elegance," are bound to a sense of taste and selectivity, which, in turn, may be affixed to one's upbringing and social class. To this extent they are more superficial, i.e., they reveal less of the character and ipseity of the person. Yet in any case we might *want* to think of them as revealing something more profound regarding the person – and not to reduce them to such social advantages. And a clear motivation for this is when we find these qualities in persons who have not had the social advantages. Grace and graciousness are difficult to conceive apart from a person's movement. In a context where perception of bodily motion were impossible the presence of grace and graciousness is much more subtle and elusive. Typically the movement is easy and effortless but there is also a connection with the kindness, generosity, and sympathy of the manner of communication and interaction, which analogously are easy and effortless. In this one finds a spontaneity informed with wisdom and intelligence, freedom and generosity.

Mark Musa's translation of Dante's *Vita Nuova* renders *gentil* and *gentile* not with "gentle" and "gentleness" but with some form of "grace" and "graciousness." John Ciardi notes that the Graeco-Latin root *gen* underlies and ties together many seemingly unrelated English words. Its connection to "kin" and "kind" as the sort of thing something is by virtue of a relation also relates it to having the "manners of our kind," i.e., being kindly, and thus gentle.[32] Graciousness in the absence of a manifest kindness and gentleness is inconceivable. The opposite is someone who is dull, surly, heavy- hearted, begrudging, clumsy, out of control or excessively self-controlling.

These very real eidetic but elusive properties are decisive for the lover in the distinctive presence of the beloved. The Greek word *charis* serves for both what in English are the words for charm and grace.[33] Charm as *Anmut* perhaps more explicitly refers to the effect on the perceiver, whereas grace and graciousness refer to the perceived person's inherent qualities. Liberality and generosity are affixed to grace in a way they need not be tied to charm. In any case we do not have to do with a "natural property" as a color, motion, size, shape, etc. but something that pervades these and transcends these. They resemble the way we are taken with someone's moral beauty, as their humility and integrity, in so far as they tend to vanish when the person becomes evidently aware of her- or himself having these qualities. In contrast, one does not become less clumsy, dull, begrudging, etc. in being aware of these qualities in oneself – although they might shift into a more interesting key because they might appear to be tainted with irony and self-deprecation. But being aware of one's graciousness, like being aware of one's humility, annihilates it. Further, the grace and graciousness of the beloved, even though tied to an effortlessness, is, in the case, e.g., of dancers and athletes, a matter of work, practice, learned self-control. Yet it appears as graceful, indeed it appears as most graceful, when it, like *charis*, is itself purely a grace. The grace and graciousness are itself graces, at least in the sense that merit and responsibility are underplayed and the grace of the gracious person itself seems to be a favor bestowed on her or him. Here the *gen-* root to which Ciardi called attention is once again overheard: grace is "genial" and "genius" where a tutelary spirit of childhood is indicated. And, of course, no less overheard perhaps is the *generosus*, or being of noble birth which itself is attached to not being small or miserly, but to the graciousness characteristic of "generosity," a giving not founded on merit.[34]

Yet these qualities are more or less communicable, partakable eidé, and in this respect only suggest the even more elusive unique splendor, radiance, or *dignitas*, we find in the unique ipseities.

We approximate the *dignitas* when we think of an occasion such as when we meet someone of extraordinary intellectual power and acuity, or when we meet someone who is deeply committed to a cause we admire but whose humility is both evident and genuine. Is it not true that in these cases, where again the person might well be a stranger, the undeniably admirable qualities become transparent to a vivid sense of *who* the person is? (This can be founded in the Husserlian position that the intellectual acts are *I*-acts, and the quasi-Aristotelian one we have proposed, that virtue and character, precisely because they are rooted in *self-identifying acts*, have the power to reveal *who* one is. That is, there is an approximation of the core sense of who one is, the "myself" with the "sort of person" one is.)

Of course we get closer to what I have in mind here when we think of the unique intentional target that comes to light when we think about someone in her absence and how she is present quite apart from the ascription or conjuring up of properties. I can recall you without any conjuring up of physical, moral, and mental properties I associate with you.

My claim here is that love enhances this presence and more, i.e., the "more" of the actual reality and unfathomable depth of ipseity. This intentional target comes forth in its singularity inseparably from a unique "splendor" and "radiance." This splendor or beauty is the correlate of love; what we love we find beautiful. What we mean by beauty is always what is loved by someone and the beauty we find in the world, whether or not through the work of art, "has its origin in the power to make intelligible a love."[35] Thus we have the circular definition: The beauty that is the ipseity or the "myself" of the Other comes to light in the celebration, devotion, and veneration that is love; love is what brings to light by its celebration, devotion, and veneration the beauty of the ipseity.

Beauty here is tied to the act of love, which is a uniquely centering act of the person. It is a centering act of the lover directed to the center or core of the beloved. This core of the person is transcendent to the particular properties and affirms the "ontological value" of the unique Other. And it aims at the Other in her core self-presence, which is non-ascriptively present for both the beloved and lover. For the lover this presence which is at once definite and unpropertied awakens in the lover infinite depths of devotion.

Because love presences the unique beauty, splendor, or radiance – which is the very ipseity – the beloved's goodness is incomparable and no limitation is placed on the lover's response. That is, what is loved is not a kind or an instance of a kind, even though these surely can be the source of amazement and approval.

What I give myself to in the course of my life, what occasions my devotion, is always present to me as embedded in an infinite ideal. In the case of the devotion and dedication of love, the infinite ideal is of what is uniquely unique who herself/himself is an actuality and as such not merely an infinite ideal. The unique essence of the beloved is finite as *a* unique essence which is not identical with existence pure and simple. Nevertheless the unique essence is, as Scheler noted, a value-essence (see below, §8) to which no finite act of devotion is adequate. (Cf. Von Hildebrand's "ontological value.") Further the beloved as person faces an infinite ideal and this also the lover loves). Here the reality of the Other, the reality of the inexhaustible value of her unique essence, and the apperceived reality of her own personal infinite ideal work against any temptation to confuse my self-ideal as it is founded in my self-inadequation with the infinite self-ideal which is the Other.

In love the lover loves the actual ipseity as inseparable from the beloved's infinite unique ideal. Love illuminates not only the actual splendor of the beloved ipseity but love's generosity brings out this ipseity as coincident with its ideal true self. This is to say that love "idealizes" and creates space for the beloved to realize her true self. Of course, the lover cannot apperceive the unique ideal true self of the beloved, but rather can only apperceive the beloved's own apperception of this unique ideal true self. Yet the incomparable goodness is precisely the unique radiance born of this apperceived coincidence of the beloved and her ideal true self. The lover's awareness of love needing to create space for the actualization of the ideal is precisely the awareness that the actual is not identical with the ideal possibility. Of course the "myself" of the other is, we have insisted, complete in its actuality. But what we apperceive in the beloved's apperception is the "myself" of the Other as the entelechy of the person in the world with others; it is this for which the lover creates space. The lover creates space for the coincidence of who the beloved is with the sort of person she or he is called to be. An aspect of this desire and devotion, motivated by the delight in the inherent goodness of the beloved, is a creative making room that the other might flourish.[36]

This is not to say that the person is loved for the sake of his ideal self or possible qualities. Nor is it a claim that there never has been a lover who has been side-tracked from love or a lover who has never failed to promote the well-being of the one he loves. But in these failures we have a conspicuous failure to love. Love requires the initial contemplative "complacency" in the transcendent ontological value, dignity, or splendor of the beloved. Desire for union with the beloved or for her well being follows upon this.

It is evident that we must distinguish our appreciation of persons in contexts calling for comparative evaluation from those in the context of love. The former necessarily involve the appreciation of "good," "better," and "best" by which persons are distinguished, but what love reveals resists such a comparison. Similarly, ipseities as present in love are not present as finite conditioned goods over against conditioning horizons. As individual essences, they do not admit comparison in terms of good, better, best. In love they are revealed as each being endless depths of beauty and goodness and this endlessness is revealed only in further loving and revealing.

In sum: Love's target is the ipseity of the other. The other is present as loveable apart from and beyond properties or characteristics that comprise the beloved as a person in the world with others.

But even though the beloved ipseity as such is not determined by properties, the incomparable goodness of the other is such that there is no limitation that can be placed on the lover's response. What I love, what I give myself to, what occasions my devotion, is always present to me as an infinite ideal. The other ipseity is of course a unique individual essence, and therefore does not encompass all Others; but in and of herself she presents a unique inexhaustible depth of goodness and value. Of course my friends, I myself, my projects, and my secret dreams are present to me and in this respect are finite. Yet those whom I love open endless horizons that I pursue by loving more. This metaphor of opening myself to the horizons can be explicated by saying that I pour myself out to the riches to which they invite me. It may also be explicated by saying that the lover discovers depths or centers yet unfathomed in herself.

It may also be explicated by the familiar theme of the "fertility" of love. Love is fertile in the sense that it gives birth to endless other acts and supplies the life force and energy for these acts. And this is, in part, what we mean by devotion as the self-donation of the lover to the beloved. Love is fertile in that it, as Plato puts it, "gives birth in beauty," i.e., it is tireless in revealing the beauty of the beloved, revering the beloved, and creating a richness of life for the beloved. Or, because of the radiance of the beauty in whose presence love is, the lover is tireless in her creativity, "in body and soul."[37] Love is fertile in the sense that whereas the person without love may find only obstacles and paralyzing difficulties, the same person in love, in the blinking of an eye, can dissolve all the complications, remove the obstacles and perform what seem to be miracles. Thus love is fertile in the sense suggested by St. Paul's hymn (1 *Corinthians* 13): It transforms and energizes the whole person so that it becomes the root and well-spring of all the good qualities of the person. Love is fertile in the sense that it awakens me to ever greater resources within myself, an ever deepening sense of my center. In short, love is the most basic stance of Existenz.

We spoke earlier about the grace in which the beloved appears. This reflects the way the new center of the lover opens up untold depths and bestows upon her not only a novel energy but also an encompassing unifying dimension. All of her life is one of love, even often enough an effortless love. Every act is suffused with love and all that the lovers perceive is in the light of love. She exists as loving and loveableness bathes all that the lover comes upon. There is thus the appearance of love becoming the very substance of the lover.

Here, there is an unusual feature of love as an I-act. In acts of memory, perception, evaluation, willing, etc., we have said the I is present as the source-point of the acts. But with the I-acts of love the I is not merely a source-point but there is a sense of the I deepening and centering itself, i.e., of the I as the source-point. In love the I in its center becomes evermore itself; I become ever more truly and deeply myself. As Husserl himself notes, ever greater depths of "the I" come into play. That is, I myself at my core can be evermore deeply moved, ever more profoundly called to act and achieve. I myself can be ever more devoted, ever more giving of myself.[38] This revelation and realization of ever more of "I myself" is not a revelation apart from the first-person: It is an ever greater self-awareness, in this sense a revelation, of me myself to myself. Again, it is the foremost awakening to Existenz.

Dante was moved to appropriate the ancient Greek theme of love as a god. Love so possesses the lover that it takes on the aspect of something substantial that subsumes and consumes the lover and for which the lover becomes an instrument or a property. In Dante the description is of the positive self-transforming power of this god; the dark demonic and even comical features of such a possession, as portrayed, e.g., in Iris Murdoch's *The Black Prince* are not brought to light.

But Dante turns from the poetic personification to scholastic categories when he describes this love-god as a potentiality that may be actuated by the beauty of the beloved. This actuation of the god is an actuation of the lover to a depth of himself that before was inconceivable. The person realizes that properly love is the king of his heart and the heart is to be love's home. Then Dante critiques any suggestion that love is the substance of the lover; rather it is but an accident.[39] We may take this struggle in Dante's presentation to indicate that love is uniquely capable of awakening the "substance" of the "myself" to itself in its personification. That is, the person is awakened to herself in her deepest core through love.

Love, observes Dante, "drives a killing frost into vile hearts that freezes and destroys what they are thinking" and it changes the person encountering it into "something noble or he dies." Love itself thus can be a limit-situation for the person for whom life's design has been such as to exclude it. But in contrast to the self-identifying act by which I wholeheartedly find myself through investing myself in the target of the act, in love I wholeheartedly find myself, but further invest myself in the act of love in a way in which I uniquely transcend myself. In this sense it is not merely a finding oneself but a finding oneself in transcending oneself. This self-transcending is a deeper self-centering and thus love too may be said to be an uncovering of oneself and thus a kind of self-identifying act. But one is revealed to oneself as ex-centric, i.e., as exposed and indebted to the Other, as a condition for sustaining this centering.

In conscience one has oneself laid bare before oneself. I thereby bear witness to the crack in the interior secret citadels, the false self, I have erected before myself and Others. That is, I am, often perhaps reluctantly and unwillingly, rendered bereft of any refuge or hiding place from myself by conscience's revelation of myself to myself. Here conscience is not "infinitely exterior" but rather a transcendence within the immanence of my person.

In contrast we can say that in love the infinitely exterior of the other ipseity becomes infinitely interior in the guise of myself now existing "for the beloved." But this welcoming of the beloved brings with it a witness both to a melt-down of the hiding places I have constructed as well as to unknown depths which up until now were secret or unknown even to myself. As conscience reveals me to myself, awakens my innermost center, my Existenz, so Existenz is revealed to me in the loving affirmation of the transcendent ipseity's beauty and dignity. And, as Dante has pointed out, the humility that such a grace awakens within one is itself the dismantling of any interior protective refuge and we are rid of the wish to be in hiding or to be seeking a shelter where we are unexposed.

Conscience's witness is not that of the "infinitely exterior". It is exterior, but it is interior to ourself; it is ourself at a distance from our self. Yet, like love, conscience exposes one at one's core and strives to make impossible any hiding from oneself. In both conscience and love one is awakened to a depth of oneself that heretofore was a "secret." But in the presence of the graciousness of the one loved, who indeed is "infinitely exterior," one does not want to hide but rather one welcomes that this infinitely exterior become infinitely interior. This again contrasts with conscience where one often would like to hide and in fact one is tempted often enough to develop strategies for hiding out from oneself. (See Chapter III, §§2 ff.) In love the infinitely exterior is welcomed and this welcoming awakens in the lover the generosity of a "fission of the interior secret" in the sense that one becomes "for the Other" and deepened within oneself.[40]

Love reveals ever greater possibilities of value attainment in the life of the beloved which possibilities are correlated to the depth of the lover's devotion to the beloved's flourishing. This does not mean that the beloved is revealed as impoverished and in need of aid, as in the case of persons calling forth our compassion, sympathy, etc. Rather there is a fullness here, a kind of perfection – we have called it "beauty" – that calls forth acts of devotion which create a greater space for this perfection to become ever more manifest and actual. This devotion may well, however, be accompanied by the awareness that it may be possible that the life of the beloved flourish most if I, the lover, am absent from her life. The fertility occasioned by love may be one that paradoxically creates one's absence and self-limitation. This is an aspect of loving that not only lovers, but parents and teachers must learn to practice. Indeed, "because I never restrained you, I have held on to you tightly." Or:

> We need, in love, to practice only this;
> Letting each other go. For holding on
> Comes easily; we do not need to learn it.[41]

Here again we may note that this may serve as a test for distinguishing eros from other forms of love. What we want to possess or cling to is already, or on the verge of becoming, a quality. Lust and sadism presuppose that the Other has attractive qualities that bring pleasure. But whereas in some cases of lust a robot or mannequin seems to work, that is because the dummy is bestowed with personal qualities, i.e., the dummy is animated with an imagined ipseity. In any case, lust and sadism require the real or imagined apperception of the ipseity. Further this is typically for a narcissistic purpose, i.e., the other is desired for one's own dominant desire to be loved or feared. For this to happen the embodied presence of the other's ipseity has to be manipulatable or subjugated. This requires in the case at least of sadism that intentionality involve a stopgap: It must repress the claims of the dignity of the transcendent ipseity by halting at the qualitative, lust-occasioning, presence which serves as the vehicle for the apperception of the transcendent ipseity, without, however, the repression being absolutely successful.

Whereas sadism represses the dignity of ipseity in favor of the lusting brutal self, classical forms of mysticism suppress the self of the mystic in favor of the divine ipseity. In classical theological reflections on mysticism the question arose whether the soul's love of the divine would not have to be absolutely selfless, to the point of willing one's own ruin or destruction for the sake of the divine ipseity. Sadism is prepared to ruin as far as it can the ipseity of the Other for the sake of its own lust. And yet, for the sadist the brutality would seem, of necessity, to be contained because the ipseity of the Other must remain intact if the lustful deeds are to maintain their piquancy for the sadist. That is the Other's look must be preserved. In this respect, sadism differs from the "psychopath" for whom the extinguishing of the Other's threatening presence is essential to protecting the egg-shell thin wall of defense of his self-respect.[42]

The ancient question of whether the ideal love, the love of the divine, the love aimed at God, that would be absolutely selfless, to the point of willing one's own ruin or destruction for the sake of the divine, echoes the conviction of there being different forms of love besides eros where we always have a form of self-reference on the side of the will and desire.

Love is an act whereby we gather our lives around the beloved person and emphatically believe in *her*. This belief, which is also an act of affection and esteem – we have called it also a celebration – is not conditioned by any of her properties or characteristics. Further, in this centering of our lives around the beloved, others and other values are necessarily rendered peripheral. (We refrain here from attending to the special nature of the love of a community and the exhortation to a universal love.[43]) Because love aspires to be a generous encompassing devotion to the apperceived other, it is solicitous to anticipate the beloved's projects in such a way that the beloved's will draws the lover's will into itself. This initial step toward unity leads to the lover's desire to join his will to that of the beloved's. This is not experienced as a loss but an amazing enrichment of the lover's life.

The respect, otherness, and depth implicit in empathic perception are magnified in love, and the Other in her sheer presence embodies an actual fullness that creates an initial moment of passive delight and a stillness of contemplation. The Other is present as good, complete, and sufficient unto herself. As we have claimed in Book 1, in love the mystery of ipseity is revealed – not in the sense that a secret is "outed," but in the sense that the withheld beauty and depth as a unique ipseity beyond our ascription of properties as such is revealed. Husserl would call this revelation an "affection." But this affection that awakens a moment of complacent delight, in turn, typically provokes an unrest in the form of desire or concern.

Of course, the complacent delight may first be preceded by being drawn to certain attractive attributes of the person. Love may follow upon this desire or eros. Indeed, the thought experiment of "loving someone" who had no lovely or loveable qualities suggests that love always is correlated with some discovered beautiful properties. But the thought experiment points only to love as eros or friendship's affection. It does not deal with what we are calling love in the most proper sense which finds its beauty not in any qualities but in the beauty or *dignitas* we are equating with ipseity. In Book 1 we discussed the remote possibility of whether this could happen totally in the absence of the loveable qualities. But for our present discussion we may state that there is no necessity that desire, which of course is tied to loveable or attractive qualities, ever evolve into pure love, even though it seems to be nurtured by its anticipation of this by reason of its appresentation of the ipseity herself/himself as beyond the qualities. Thus we claim that love has its proper beginning in the moment of complacency or delight in the revealed ipseity. After the initial moment of complacent contemplative delight, there is typically the second moment of a form of desire wherein one discovers the completion of oneself in the devotion to the other.[44] The devotion responds both to the delight in the intrinsic goodness of the beloved as well as to the lover's awareness of his distance from the beloved. The perception of the distance and absence from the beloved who first appears as good in herself and loveable for herself and as beyond all qualities result for the lover in what at once appears to be an exigency for, an invitation to, and a promise of fulfillment. But these latter motions toward the beloved presuppose the complacent delight or love that reveals the ipseity for itself and beyond its qualities.

And these latter motions have their moments of rest in the periodic contemplative moments of complacent delight. Having said this there is still the possibility, if not the likelihood, that the complacency in the beauty which is the ipseity is preceded by not the delight in the ipseity but rather the delight in the qualities the person has. We find it easier to love, i.e., come to love, someone who is loveable – or rather, the person's "loveability" enables us to go through and beyond the loveable and admirable qualities to the ipseity itself. (See Book 1, Chapter IV, Part Two.)

Love in and of itself, as an emotion, is not properly a cognitive position-taking. But its appreciation of the unique splendor of the beloved as beyond all properties gives rise to acts, like avowals and vows, which themselves are exemplary position-takings. In all these aspects of love the willed-will aspires to approximate the willing-will, and its possibilities for "idolatry" are notorious. The sought-for presence of the Other as she is present to herself is unattainable, and the lover apperceives that as a matter of necessity the beloved only becomes present graciously, i.e., on her own terms. And always there is the acknowledgment of the essential absence and distance which is the beloved's own self-presence to herself. Any revelation of the intimate sphere of the beloved is necessarily unmerited. The lover's spontaneous devotion reflects the humility that arises out of the conviction of this unmerited reciprocity and self-revelation by the beloved.

As we noted in Part Two of Chapter IV (Book 1) in love there is the amazement on the side of the beloved that "she loves *me!*" When the love is reciprocal there is this two-fold amazement, devotion, and humility arising from the insight *that* one is loved, that *I* am loved. As we have urged, love is directed to the ipseity or person herself and not in respect of her qualities, and, most amazingly of all, it is directed to the person independent of the qualities.[45] As we noted in Part Two of Chapter IV (Book 1), this occasion for wonder is not only evident for the lover, but equally so for the beloved.

Love, as we use it here, includes what in the West was named *agape, philein,* and *eros.* These various terms, although usually not used with technical precision in the New Testament, suggest differences and acknowledge forms of love other than what we moderns call eros, i.e., desire laced with a sexual interest.[46] In eros love is inseparably tied up with my own lived necessity, if not my own pleasure, in relationship to the beloved. But thereby we do not say that eros, that mighty force that visits us and which is capable of transforming the appearing of the world into a softer and kinder eutopian light, is not directed at the person himself and is merely an egocentric extension or projection. Rather, for eros, the beloved's intrinsic beauty as an ipseity is at leased glimpsed but the beloved's necessity for the lover is posited in a way that is different from other forms of love. In the other forms of love the intrinsic goodness and loveableness of the beloved come to light in such a way that the self-identifying acts are precisely those of selfless devotion and self-giving; these, although also acts which are lived as essential to one's being who one is, are understood to be more appropriate than the erotic acts in which the beloved is believed to be essential for completing the life of the lover. Thus the desire that takes the form of the selfless devotion of the friend or mother is not merely a form of eros.

Again: In contrast to all other acts, love in its various forms is a uniquely centered act wherein the very core of the I, what we are calling *Existenz*, comes forth to itself and reveals itself capable of ever deeper levels of devotion on behalf of another. In love there is an especially unique and incommunicable expression and revelation of the ipseity. In loving, love discloses itself first-personally as the proper ownmost core of one's individual essence.[47] One's ownmost, innermost self (i.e., one's Existenz) and love enjoy an identity in the act of loving. Yet, in spite of this inhabiting the innermost sanctuary of one's ownmost self, love is not something I have absolute charge over, not something I can bring about on my own; it is a problematic, if not mysterious, gift given to us. In this respect however it profoundly resembles the unique "I myself" which too is given to itself and not a result of one's own doing. Although love centers us, and in this sense it is an I-centering act, it is not something I may simply will. Yet when it is present, all the other acts which I can will, often with difficulty, like compassion, patience, insight into the other's own sphere of ownness, etc., become a matter of course and doable with little or no difficulty.

The religious *mandate* to love one another, which is also tied to a doctrine of love as a grace, need not contradict what we have said. (We return here to some themes we touched on in Book 1, Chapter IV, §18.) Let us regard this Great Commandment hypothetically as having some possible philosophical significance. We all know what it means to say I cannot love someone at will, especially when we seem to have reason to dislike the person. We also know that we cannot love anyone at will, especially if what is meant is eros or "being in love" with someone. (We recognize that someone may be addicted to "falling in love" and seek out settings where the conditions for this "fall" may happen again and again. But what one directly wills is putting oneself in the setting, not the being in love.) In any case, we can exercise at will forms of behavior that are, in spite of the repugnance, less hateful or more kindly; indeed, we can will benevolence. We can take steps to be extra patient and develop strategies where, in the one case, we do not give into our repugnance or animosity; and, in the other case, we can will to be patient and compassionate even if we do not feel patient or compassionate. Whether these acts of necessity evolve into love is an open question. In any case, it is clear that like "falling in love," love is not something we bring about by an act of will, however much we may try.

But the command to love one's neighbor, to love even those who hate one, etc., also reflect perhaps the deeper ontological issues and may generate the following hypothetical meditation: Love goes to the ipseity of the beloved. "Even the Gentiles" are kindly to their kith and kin and to those who do them a good turn or who are loveable persons. If one's ipseity is a gift of being given to oneself, and if the love of God is the sustaining source of the gift of each and every ipseity, and if the ipseity is beyond all attractive and repugnant attributes, then the "causal" or occasional motivations which bring love about can be neither the necessary nor sufficient conditions for love. We will never truly and properly love if we only wait to be moved by the attractive qualities. Love of the other in her ipseity requires that we make the effort to surmount and move through and beyond these qualities to what St. Thomas called the *dignitas* or radiance of the ipseity. The evangelical commandment of love gives us a case where the Ought takes precedence over the Is, at least until the love is underway, and then, when the ipseity becomes luminously radiant through the loving intention, the Is might make the Ought superfluous and irrelevant.[48]

This reflection is based on the hypothesis that the biblical "commandment of love" might have some philosophical implications. Furthermore, this positing of the primacy of the Ought adds a new wrinkle to our contention that a contemplative or complacent delight is the first moment in the directedness of love. The primacy of the Ought here, the "commandment of love," might be taken to anticipate that the ipseity of Others tends to be camouflaged. It may mean that the attitudes which foster the suppression of the transcendent ipseity will rarely be demolished if we posit desire, which is drawn to the Other only because of "winning qualities," to be always the prior condition for the transcendence – even though there are occasions when such desire itself undergoes a metamorphosis into love. The attraction of desire as such is a form of motion dominated either by self-reference, or a kind of ontological reductionism of the Other to her pleasing or useful properties, or a mixture that might include an intimation of the intrinsic beauty of the ipseity. The commandment to love may thus serve as an implicit ontological pointer that indicates that the transcendent ipseity is ultimately what is most essential in dealings with one another and our erotic attraction to Others may never suppress this transcendence.

Although we never have the ipseity apart from the way the other "myself" is steeped in the concrete person with his qualities, in love we are drawn not to the qualities as conditions of our interest in the person, as in some forms of friendship and admiration, but rather we are drawn through and beyond these to the person himself in his ipseity. We know that "being in love" overlooks the faults or negative qualities, and the more profound forms of love persist in spite of the loss of the originating attractive qualities. Love then has both the task and the ability to close its eyes to the distracting qualities and loss of qualities and hold them open to the ipseity of the person who is beyond the qualities. But this cannot mean that we forsake the "visible," i.e., the person in his concrete qualitative presence, for the "invisible," i.e., the ipseity that transcend these. The person's ipseity, if not evident in the concrete person, is not evident at all. Of course we are capable of suppressing the concrete person in favor of an imagined version of the person, and thus favor the "invisible" over the "visible." But this is not love of the other but love of our imagined creation or of ourselves. As Kierkegaard has put it, the task of love is not to search among what is absent and invisible for the loveable one, but rather to find loveable the one who is present and to love him and find him loveable in spite of the changes he undergoes. Kierkegaard is speaking of the Christian command to love, but this seems to be what love does and can do when it makes its rare wonderful appearances.[49]

This phenomenon of the presence of the other "myself's" goodness and beauty draws from me devotion, self-dedication, and self-donation, if not veneration. The self-donation and devotion are exemplary moments of the revelation of my unique uniqueness and Existenz. If we think of the phenomenon of "one's calling" as a unique disclosure of what is uniquely one's own way in life, what brings forth oneself to oneself in one's unique individuality, and what enables one to flourish as this individual, then we have here not only an exceptional revelation of the calling, but we also have reason to think of love *as the calling* or of an identity between love and the calling.

Further, the full actualization of ipseity in the center of the person, i.e., Existenz, is through love. As Husserl put it, in love, "the I, as which such a one has his innermost I in giving himself over to the calling, his ownmost calling that beckons this I, has individuality."[50] Again, this may be said to be a Husserlian version of Existenz. It is not as if the person in question here did not have individuality prior to the act of loving devotion. Husserl assigns to the person a unique uniqueness as a transcendental I. We have extended this and sought to show that the "myself" is a unique essence that personifies itself in the world with others, and this too appears to have a uniqueness. But there is a kind of unique self-awareness in the loving devotion that enables a unique display or sense of oneself as a single individual. Thus the I is an individual I in all of its presencings, feelings, valuings, and decidings. But "it still has a deepest center, the center of its love in an especial personal sense, the I that in this love follows a 'call', a vocation, a most inner call which has to do with the deepest interiority, the most interior center of the I itself...."[51] This is to say that the exemplary form of knowing oneself is knowing oneself as Existenz, and this is eminently in discovering one's own calling to love and devotion. All other forms of non-reflective and reflective forms of self-knowledge are relatively deficient and they gain their proper context here.

The depth of the interiority of love, its being the vocation of the I, is what enables it to be distinguished from other emotions. We have already seen how what pleases and displeases can be tied to the personal life-world constituted by the person in the course of her history. Phenomenology has always called attention implicitly to this by noting the intentionality of the acts, and it has always insisted on the I-involvement of all acts. We have already noted differences in the I- or self-involvement of the acts. The cognitive-theoretical acts have the necessary feature that the I is anonymous, as in "The tiger is a dangerous animal" even though such declarative sentences imply the "declarative sense of I" or the "transcendental pre-fix". They exemplarily are I-acts. But the emotional intentionality and I-involvement, as in an experience roughly approximated by "I am terrified of the approaching tiger," is of a quite different order. Emotions are, indeed, intentional or directed toward something. As an act, anger is being angry at...,. Fear is being afraid of..., joy is being delighted with... or taking joy in..., etc. But emotions for Husserl are also acts, and this implies that the I is involved. Emotions are I- or self-involving. Thus in being afraid I am not the impartial spectator or mere dative of manifestation of a tiger approaching and appearing menacingly and of it being me for whom this threat appears. Rather its appearing menacingly to me is equivalent to *me being afraid* and "*I* am afraid." In the emotive intentionality, expressed somewhat feebly by "I am terrified of the approaching tiger," I am immersed in the revealed state of affairs in a way I am not in the cognitive-theoretical display, as in "The approaching tiger is both a dangerous and beautiful animal." "The approaching tiger is dangerous and beautiful" is a display through an I-act of an objective state of affairs. But the emotional intention, "The approaching tiger is dangerous (for me)" means I am not there merely as the dative of manifestation. Nor am I "there" merely as the declarative I, as "I believe that" is the transcendental prefix to: "The approaching tiger is dangerous." In the case of the declarative I or transcendental prefix I am not at all a genitive of manifestation and part of what is displayed; properly this is not at all a manifestation *of* me, even though it is eminently an I-act. But in the emotional act, I am there as part of the genitive of manifestation, i.e., there is a display of the menacing approaching tiger and inseparably myself as terrified; this is the sense of the display approximated in: "I am terrified of the approaching (dreadful) tiger." In emotional intentionality I am inherently part of the displayed scene in a way I am not in cognitive-theoretical intentionality. Further, even though there is self-involvement and the emotion is an act of mine, *I* may be said to undergo my emotional displaying whereas in my cognitive theoretical display, foremost the judgmental expressed in propositions, I am eminently active and responsible for the display.

Thus in the emoting acts there is not the responsible, emphatic, initiating I-enactment that is evident in our cognitive acts as in judging, inquiring, distinguishing, clearing up a muddy state of affairs, etc. Nor do we have emphatic acts I-acts approximating those intentions and of moral self-constitution which we discussed in Chapter IV (of Book 2). Rather, the I is involved by reason of a passive synthesis, and therefore it stands in debt to earlier active and passive acts.

Love also typically has a kind of passive synthetic inauguration but its culmination is in a whole-heartedness and a total self-identification with the act and the target of the act. In love the self-identification is essential whereas in the other emotions the self-identification tends merely to *appear* at the moment to be essential or total. Following Husserl we may say love, as a response to the calling of the unique essence or ipseity of the person, involves a devotion wherein there is a total and essential self-identification. In this respect, the self-identification evident in the typical run of emotions is but a feeble adumbration or reflection. The wholeheartedness of, an emotion, e.g., anger, which may clearly momentarily absorb me and claim absolute legitimacy, may therefore be distinguished from the wholeheartedness of love. In both cases my personal being in the world informs and conditions my identifying myself with the loving of the beloved or being enraged at the insult. This self-identifying is both a passive synthesis and an act with implicit commitments of oneself for the future. Anger and love both imply propositions and future strategies but in the former case these typically are not based on a whole-hearted centered result of a self-identifying act. I say "typically" because we must make room for the kinds of self-identification of the types of the military hero and martyr for whom hatred and anger with the enemy – as expressions of devotion to and love of an ideal – are part of the deep centering of the person.

In anger my response is typically tied to my current identity as this person in the world but it usually is not an identification with my wider reflective self. It does not, upon reflection, express the "truth of my will" and my calling. Indeed in anger typically I am at the mercy of this identification, i.e., I am more or less at the mercy of this emotional state, and often enough upon reflection I recognize this identity and identification as a weakness. Thus in the emotions other than love, the person finds herself in a situation provoking, e.g., anger, desire, delight, fear, dread, jealousy, envy, etc. An aspect of my self or person, as constituted in my inter-personal life-world, is brought into a distinctive high definition. Nevertheless, I have, in the course of the emotion, reason to believe that this highlighting does not do justice, is not an adequate display, of who I am or even the sort of person I am. Further, I can conceive of myself as reacting otherwise as when in an earlier instance I was able to remain calm and collected, or if, e.g., I were of a different character, if I were raised differently, if I had more virtue, if I had had the appropriate exemplars in my youth, etc. Further, I can take steps to work on myself so that I do not "lose the handle" and enable the fury to subside, e.g., by deliberately waiting a few minutes before saying or doing anything; or I can take steps to avoid the debilitating feelings created by the surfacing dread by practicing thinking of something else, etc. In all these cases, as in feelings of pleasure and pain, I can become aware that I am more than the self so configured in the emotive situation just as I am more than the pleasure and pain.

Thus, in the moment of anger, where the "righteous indignation" sets in, where there is a strong conviction of the infallible evidence for the justice of my cause and the unquestionable outrageousness of my antagonist's behavior, I may develop the discipline to step back, make the anger itself the target of my attention, and diffuse the situation. Instead of living in the perverse pseudo-*nunc stans* of rage where the past and future do not pertain, I eventually may even recall the other numerous times when I had this "apodictic" certitude and where the possible remonstrations of the past and the future moments of regret were, to my shame, obliterated, and this may have the effect of convincing me that although I am now impelled wholly to be identified with this moment, I, indeed, am more than the person this moment of anger highlights. Now at this moment I may well be identified with the anger and the imperative to irascibly right the situation, but I can come to be reflective and realize that this is illusory. Further, upon reflection I might come to resolve to be the sort of person for whom such an irritating situation is able to be handled without perturbation.

Something similar holds for my other emotional states and dispositions, e.g., my fearfulness, grief, temptations to cowardice, my proclivities to be wantonly distracted in certain sexually provocative situations, etc. I can come to see that these indeed are "who" I am in the sense of what sort of person I am. That is, when the situations surface I am involved in a certain way through my emotional reactions which reflect who I am as the sort of person I am. The sort of person I am is inseparable from my apperception of my being in the world with Others in the distinctive way that is my constituted personal being. My "identity," i.e., my apperception of myself as this person in the world with others, requires behaving this way on the basis of evaluating the situation in this way. But this identity, for all of its seeming strength and authority, is a contingency and a partial aspect of me.

And I am capable of at least experiencing that I am more than this, as I can see that I am more than the pain and pleasure in which I am immersed.

Emotions as I- or self-involving acts are first-order actuations of myself and revelations of my personal being as the sort of person I am. They are not the kind of identifications which I have in "intentions" where I will self-involving acts, nor are they the equivalent of those acts I whole-heartedly make, but rather they are the way my existing personal being is actuated pre-reflectively. Certain configurations of my being in the world call forth these first-order actuations (e-motions) and thereby reveal my personal being in a congealed way. But the situations and the emotions they call forth may be contrasted with other situations, what Jaspers has called limit-situations, whereby another kind of self-identification is called forth. As we saw (Book 2, Chapters III and IV), in the limit-situations a definitive version of myself is called for because what is of unconditional importance is at stake.

Similarly, in love there is an essentially different self-illumination and commitment and self-identification to what is of unconditional importance. In love there is the revelation not only of the unique essence of the Other but of one's own unique essence and truth of will and calling to devotion and self-dedication. The self-illumination in love may be contrasted with how one is brought to light in an emotion, e.g., anger. In the latter, we said I myself am not only a dative of manifestation but also part of the genitive of manifestation. But in love, even though I am revealed to myself in my center and am maximally self-aware there is little trace of awareness *of* myself. Rather, the beauty of the beloved ipseity for his own sake is what is revealed and what dominates my attention. For this reason love properly is less "self-absorbed" and more pure in the sense of self-empowered and self-actuated than in other emotions of affection. Erotic love, in contrast to sheer lust, is always also taken with the ipseity of the Other as beyond the properties. The case is similar for most forms of friendship and fondness. Pure lust, it would seem, is always merely self-absorbed and suppresses, without complete success, the ipseity of the Other as pervaded by *dignitas* and the radiance of spirit.

As an awakening of the center of one's I the acts of love are pre-eminently I-acts, yet they flow with the energy of the passive synthetic momentum of emotions. Of course, this utopian state does not last forever, and, as we saw, the Is may be transformed to an Ought. In the best of love relationships where the properties of the Other are transcended in favor of the unique ipseity – and precisely because the "loveable qualities" have become invisible either because of, e.g., the decline in the health of the Other, or one's own weakness due to, e.g., of illness and weariness has become pronounced – the life of love can, on occasion, come to resemble the Ought found in the "commandment of love." Here the radiance of spirit gives way to a darkness where pure faith in the other ipseity's unique essence alone remains. Here love of one's dearest can approach the measure of difficulty of love of the stranger or even the enemy. Again we may note here that this basic affirming faith can give rise to a remarkable perspicacity which transforms the Ought to an Is.

This is evident in the testimony of saints and perhaps is the underlying theme in Dostoevsky's *The Idiot*.

§4. Existenz, Love, and Communication

As another aspect of "Love and Existenz," I wish here to discuss the theme of "communication." This enables us to sharpen several claims that we have made. One is the special bond between love and Existenz. The other is that Existenz comes to light especially in the discovery of one's calling, and this, exemplarily, is a calling to love. Another is that love is not only the exemplary way in which the first-person illumination of Existence occurs, but it also is the intentional disclosure that brings the ipseity or unique essence of the Other to light.

Karl Jaspers, who has been both in the background and foreground in much of this work, assigns to what he calls "communication" the major function of bringing Existenz to light. He speaks of it as the origin of the self-being (*Selbstseins*) which we take for a synonym of "Existenz." This means, among other things, that it is not through reason primarily that I am most myself, even though I cannot be my ownmost self without reason.[52] Most communication is pervaded by a sense of insufficiency and dissatisfaction. Thus I can communicate in the very deficient mode whereby I place myself in a position to think of others with whom I speak, even those before me, as things or items to be managed or turned to a profit. Or I can communicate in regard to universal ideal states of affairs with the explicit concern to be "objective" and present the standpoint of the view from nowhere. Or I can be immersed in the everyday chatter that tends to keep at bay what concerns me most. These forms of communication have their value but they also have the capacity to divert communication from realizing its most essential function, i.e., the awakening of those communicating to Existenz.

The insufficiency in communicating may have to do with not only the "subject matter" but also the unwillingness of the Other to communicate. I cannot be opened to myself if the Other does not want to be opened to himself, just as I cannot be free with the Other when the Other is not free to be free with himself and with me. Communication is a dynamic unceasing process, a "loving struggle" (*liebender Kampf*), that requires the courage to be honest and not to play games. It involves the commitment to solidarity where there are no winners and a reciprocity in which the inevitable advantages among different persons do not become weapons to establish superiority. There are many other considerations we might, with the help not only of Jaspers, but also Aristotle, Buber, Marcel, Levinas, Habermas, *et alii*, dwell on for sorting out the conditions for the possibility of an undisturbed and undistorted communicative situation – but that is not necessary for the central matters of this book.

Jaspers orchestrates a point that our discussion has neglected. The relationship of friendship between persons slacks off, becomes shallow, and exhausts itself in the absence of communication. Granted that there is a sense of immediacy in some forms of interaction, especially among youth, as in erotic attraction and playing together, nevertheless without communication there eventually is dissatisfaction. Our discussion of love could lead to the impression that love involves the disclosure of the unique ipseity and could rest in silent contemplation and thereby dispense with communication. Doubtless there are occasional and even prolonged moments when lovers are content merely to be in one another's presence in silent communion, or in what we called the complacent delight. No less evident is the unilateral, unrequited love-relationship where great lovers have been content to hold themselves in reserve and love unconditionally from afar. But although it may be indeed, as Rilke suggests, the highest expression of love, typically this is notoriously unsatisfactory and a "dark night of the soul." The love of such great lovers is sustained not only by a perception of the splendor and dignity of the other but also by the recognition that one might love best by not intruding and by letting go of one's desires precisely because they hinder the intimate and personal space of the beloved.

The life of faith, especially in its arid "dark nights" can be experienced as precisely such a unilateral intending of what is not perceptively-cognitively there. Such a unilateral intending is because of the absence of any perceivable properties that would sustain and nurture the transcendent target of faith and because the target of faith is taught to be beyond all comprehensible properties. Of course faith is richly self-legitimating in this regard precisely because its darkness is taught to be a necessary stage in the perfection of both faith itself and the individual's "spiritual" development. It is sustained further by faith's teaching about itself that the ability to continue to believe and pray is itself a gift and that the divine is precisely that One who is beyond all descriptions and who absolutely is to be adored and loved without any expectation or desire for recompense, because such would reduce the divine to a means for one's own blessedness. (We return to these matters in the final chapter.)

But if love is a relationship between what ultimately are propertyless ipseities, how can there be anything but the silent "communion?" (Consider that the angels of St. Thomas, whom we may regard as pure ipseities, were invested with a kind of a priori knowing of one another and of other non-angelic ipseities; that is, they did not know one another through contingent forms of bodily expression, i.e., "communication.") We must distinguish Existenz from the pure ipseity. Ipseity is the propertyless referent of *who one is*. In the second- and third-person ipseity is not evident apart from the propertied presence, i.e., the incarnate personification of the "myself." Love is directed to the ipseity through the body, foremost the face, as the diaphanous medium of the personified "myself." But love is directed not merely to the ipseity but to the Existenz, the center of personified "myself." Existenz as present in the first-person is a centering of the I that comes forth in the course of personal life, in particular through love and the gathering acts that focus on what is of unconditional importance. Although love may initially arise through a kind of silent intuition and impulse, its deepest and ripest form is not the silent intuition existing between pure disembodied ipseities. Rather, it is what happens between persons. Persons, as essentially in the world, are essentially correlates of the world and one another. That is to say, their being is to have a life together rooted in their manifestation of the world and one another as well as their agency in the world.

The disclosure of themselves as persons is inseparable from their enworldment, i.e., inseparable from their disclosure of and agency in the world and their being with one another. As Jaspers puts it: "Without the contents of the world, existential communication has no medium in which to appear; without communication [of Existenzen], the contents of the world become meaningless and empty."[53] You take me seriously in taking seriously my articulation of the world and my justification of my agency in the world. The person I am, I am through my position-taking acts. But communication, although of necessity about the interpretation of and disposition toward the world, moves through this dimension of being a person in the world; this dimension of one's constituted person, oneself as a more or less unified whole whose salient synthesized parts are the position-taking acts, is the medium, for both parties, of "communication." What is at stake in communication is the loving struggle of each to bring to light each's own as well as the Other's Existenz as what is of absolute importance in one's being in the world. The deep dimension of the person is not merely what she refers to with "I" and her constituted person, but the center of this I. Jaspers rightly maintains that this remains hidden to each apart from the loving struggle to communicate.

Here again room is made for a sense of selflessness and impersonality in the most central I-activity. Attending to the Other, listening to her, following what she has to say and where she is coming from, etc., require profound personal self-displacement. Yet in as much as truth and the common life are at stake the selfless movement is pervaded with one which emanates from and returns to one's center (as an I-me act). The self-displacement is never self-obliteration just as the existential grounding and centering of the self is never an obliteration of the Other. The "we" in communicating encompasses both the I and the You.

We may say that Jaspers' theme of communication enriches Aristotle's classic discussion of friendship. Both communication and the most excellent form of friendship are intrinsically good and may be said to exist for their own sakes. They do not need any purpose beyond themselves. Friendship, of course, as having a life in common, even the sharing of the consciousness of this life, encompasses more than "existential communication," which may be said to be for Jaspers, the heart of the most noble forms of friendship. But we may, following Sokolowski's interpretation, say that for Aristotle, noble friendship "is the culmination of moral virtue; the ability to be a friend in the highest and best way is the moral perfection of human nature." Further, "we become virtuous only through our activity with other people and toward other people, just as we actualize our reason only with other people and toward other people."[54]

In this connection we may note the claim that

> [erotic] lovers are always talking to one another about their love; Friends hardly ever about their Friendship. Lovers are normally face to face, absorbed in each other; friends, side by side, absorbed in some common interest. Above all, Eros (while it lasts) is necessarily between two only. But two, far from being the necessary number for Friendship is not even the best."[55]

The reason C.S. Lewis gives for this position is that true friendship is "the least jealous of loves." He summarizes Charles Lamb here: "if, of three friends (A, B, and C) A should die, then B loses not only A but 'A's part in C', while C loses not only A but 'A's part in B'. In each of my friends there is something that only some other friend can fully bring out." The facets of one another are brought out in a limited way by each of us. Each of us inadequately displays one another. Thus any two friends are bound to be delighted to be joined by a third "if he is qualified to become a real friend" and then these friends will be able to appropriate Dante's saying of the souls of the blessed: "Here comes one who will augment our loves," for with this love "to divide is not to take away."

Yet Lewis's qualification, "if he is qualified to become a real friend" is significant. What qualifies the friend is in part hinted at by Aristotle's noting that we cannot have many friends. How can we share our lives together with an endless number of people? Further, although Lewis seems to be on target in regard to solely erotic love, it is clear that as the love of ipseity for its own sake emerges the face-to-face engagement merges with a side-by-side display and agency with regard to the world. Yet his treatment of erotic lovers "always talking about their love" neglects how this may be the first stage of authentic communication and the emergence of Existenz. Indeed, even the friends of Lewis's Friendship, who share together a passion, e.g., for philosophy, may or may not let this passion turn in the direction of "communication," as we are using this term here. Normally, as a discussion requiring the integrity demanded by the dialogical display of the subject matter, it would lead to "existential" communication. But the possibility of the communication that Jaspers bespeaks and what Sokolowski suggests in his reading of Aristotle cannot take place within the dynamics of a "club" or fraternity such as Lewis suggests, where the Friends are facing their common passion and *not* one another. In the existential communicative context it would seem that to divide the love is to lessen it. And this is not a matter of jealousy or stinginess; it is rather that the finitude of time and energy simply do not admit of this openness to include an indefinite addition of more Friends.

But C.S. Lewis's image of the two friends admitting an indefinite number of more friends, where "we possess each friend not less but more as the number of those with whom we share him increases," is indeed a lovely explication of what classic theology has meant both by Heaven as well as the vision of God.

Earlier, in our discussion with H.D. Lewis on freedom and character, we made a connection between virtue and the enactment of one's personal being in the world from out of the I-center. Here we insisted that if virtue is nothing but "automaticity" then it is hard to see how it is praiseworthy; but we also acknowledged that the wonder of ipseity's "personification" is precisely that agency can become embodied and the I-center be present throughout and subsequent to its inauguration of position-taking acts. Communication illuminates both the excellence as well as the deficiency in the excellence of the persons because it takes place properly when the conversation has to do with the manifestation of the Existenz of each of the partners in the conversation. Perhaps we can say that Aristotle saw that the bonds of the most excellent forms of friendship made possible this illumination and actualization of Existenz in its most laudable forms.

Aristotle does not thematize the center of the self, even though he clearly states that one's ownmost self is the rational dimension, and for this reason the noble forms of friendship with the vicious person are not possible. Because such a person is not in unity with herself she cannot live in unity with another. For Jaspers, and perhaps Husserl, the center of the I, Existenz, it is not primarily the "principle" of what makes me reasonable. It is not through reason alone that I am most myself, even though I cannot be my ownmost self without reason, Still this might be enough to claim for the Aristotelian-Husserlian precisely because being reasonable is being truthful and this is of necessity being responsible for one's agency of manifestation. Further in daily life "practical reason" is a way of being one's ownmost self with and through reason. (Cf. our discussion of reasonability as a condition of willing in Chapter IV, §7.)

Further, as we already noted (Book 1, Chapter IV, §17), Aristotle's noble friendship is not love, which, as we have claimed, targets the unique singularity which is transcendent to the Other's properties. For Aristotle, this noble form of friendship is not only fostered but conditioned by the noble qualities of the Other. This resembles Jaspers' position that existential communication requires the courage which enables a commitment and honesty from both sides, otherwise it will succumb to the pull to play games and hide out. Clearly love has no such requirement even though obviously a reciprocal love-relationship that develops into friendship does.

Jaspers makes another claim that, at least in some of its formulations, followers of Aristotle and Husserl would find difficult to accept. He states that existential communication is the reciprocal creation of the self-being [JGH: or Existenz]. I am first of all myself in my freedom as a single individual when the Other is herself and strives to be herself, I with her and she with me. We miss the significance of communication, he believes, when we hold that the self-being is a firm ontological substance which exists in advance of communication. Jaspers thus claims that only in communication does the self (we take this to mean Existenz) exist for itself. Only in the reciprocal creation with the Other in communication does an Existenz awaken to itself. Because the disclosure of Existence is what is at stake in proper, authentic "communication" it is *not* like a disclosure of what is something already existing in advance, whether in the person or in the world. It is not, as Sokolowski has put it, a matter of an activity "with other people and toward other people," assuming that "people" here would come already endowed with self-being and Existenz. The disclosure of Existenz is not the disclosure of my personality traits, my virtues and vices, my inherited dispositions, etc. It is not a disclosure of something objectifiable which friendship or therapy can bring to light. These, along with my world-beliefs, my personality and character as constituted through position-taking acts are the medium. If I take these as the target of communication, if I take the Other or myself as a solid ontological state of affairs, authentic communication ceases.

Rather, in proper communication a process occurs in which Existenzen, as centers of the I, are brought into being, rather like a coming to be out of nothing.[56] I myself lose myself in order to gain myself. I am, as a unique single individual, neither manifest to myself nor actual; rather, only in the loving struggle of communication do I become actual and manifest to myself as Existenz. Indeed, for Jaspers, love as the groundless, unconditioned, palpable feeling of these unique singularities belonging together itself is the transcendent substance antecedently existing which creates Existenzen in a relationship of love.[57] Somehow, in my addressing you in the "loving battle of communication" you and I are not yet there until the battle has commenced.

We confess to being confused with these claims. Jaspers repeatedly gives other occasions in which Existenz is illuminated, foremost through the limit-situations. Nevertheless, if Jaspers' chief point is that the center of the I comes to light with a deepening of the personal life, a strengthening of friendship, and a facilitating of an authentic life in the kind of ruthlessly honest *liebender Kampf* that he outlines, there can be no objection. We can thus follow him in his claim that communication enables the mutual Existenzen to be "illumined" or brought to light. We find it important to insist that people who find themselves in a communicative situation are possible Existenzen. But the possibility of Existenz or the center of the I coming to light is there from the start as a lived real possibility, and it is not as if communication creates it *ex nihilo*. It is possible that the persons never engage one another as Existenzen, and that they remain in the situation in a way where they regard one another as mere entities ("existences") in the world, as obstacles, as tools, etc., oblivious of this deep dimension of themselves; in such cases they may *behave* in accord with statistical probabilities. But if an absolute love of the other ipseity, the other Existenz, as well as and inseparably a love and concern with one's own Existenz can surface then, indeed, do the Existenzen emerge out of the prior existing love. Thus we may further agree with Jaspers that love is, in this ideal forum of existential communication, typically a necessary condition, but surely it is not a prior existing substance in itself.[58]

Jaspers is surely not saying that consciousness is created by the "loving struggle" of communication even though his view seems to be that the "I myself" as the center of the non-reflective "myself" exists only in the guise of the reciprocal creativity of communication. (He does not make explicit room for what we are calling the "myself"; non-reflective awareness is typically discernible in his discussion of the emergence of Existence in "absolute consciousness.") Nor is he saying that the person is brought about by communication, because what communication deepens and transforms is the person as already existing. Thus the substrate of authentic communication is not Existenz, which presumably is created by the authentic communication of the persons. What this substrate is, i.e., who communicates authentically, remains obscure.

The interpretation that we would find acceptable is that through this ideal communication, the center of the I myself, the center of the person, itself is actualized and illumined in a non-reflective self-awareness, and *in this sense* it is brought into being. (The idea that this is a *creatio ex nihilo* or that there is no ipseity or I-substance there in advance we take as hyperbole.[59]) Communication and friendship thus appear to be indispensable ingredients in the realization and clarification of who one is, foremost in the sense of the core of the sort of person one actually is, i.e., one as Existenz, and the sort of person one ought to be. Therefore they also can be in some cases necessary in the disclosure of the truths of one's will and one's calling.

§5. Evidence for a Unique Calling: Husserl's Example

For Husserl, what serves as an example of the unique manifestation of one's calling, along with the truth of will and one's single individuality, is the phenomenon that founds Fichte's theory of higher morality. Here, in response to the question regarding what kind of decision to make in arranging one's life in a fulfilling and unregrettable way, a dramatic disclosure occurs in the form of an illuminating emotion, what Husserl calls an "absolute affection," that goes in advance of all rational deliberation and fills the heart with love for the pursuit of eternal values.

When this revelation occurs and the heart is filled, the command of duty or Ought can only appear as too late. The battle with distracting tendencies is not an issue and the beautiful and the good are already chosen and done.[60] Freedom is not even an issue here because in the presence of this symbol of the ideal pole-idea of one's unique personal life, one is moved by all the forces of the center of oneself as well as the peripheral habitualities that may be gathered. Thus one experiences the "blessed necessity of the good" and there is no sense of obligation or the need for the agent to exert himself on recalcitrant desires.

Of course, this disclosure or perspective is fallible. Doubtless, in the course of time, it might be seen to have short-sighted aspects, and need to be supplemented by rational reflection. But for those who have had it, it can be the basis for a life-shaping decision which provides an endless source for a power of renewal. As such it serves as the point of departure for the periodic reorientations and rejuvenations of life's direction

Even though it brings a revelation of one's own uniqueness, it cannot be a decision that would disrespect or fail to acknowledge the Existenz of others and the possibility that they too have an absolute calling. My being in the world is not thinkable without the Others as my necessary condition and the condition for the world we have in common. Further, if love is most basically (as we earlier proposed; cf. our earlier discussions in Book 1, Chapter IV, Part Two, §§13 ff.) the affirmation, celebration and pursuit of the well-being of the beloved, and hate the negation of the Other which aims at the undoing and evil of the Other, then we may say that this general sense of love and hate are at the root of moral categoriality. This latter, we have said, following Sokolowski, comes to light in taking the other's good or evil as one's own. But it is a basic love which makes possible the disclosure of the ownness of the Other. And in so far as love in its full expression is coincident with a loving devotion to the ipseity as what is of infinite moral value, hate, as the pursuit of positive harm to others and the negation of the infinite value of ipseity, is unacceptable.

Further, in so far as the personal moral or self-ideal is necessarily social and thus enjoys a measure of publicity and intersubjectivity, it can be shown that there is a tendency for this ideal to implicitly include others within its perspective, i.e., to aspire to a unique perspective that is compatible and coincident with a universal "impersonal" perspective. This trans-individual perspective is not one that suppresses the individual ones but rather one wherein there is an aspiration to an apperception that each would find fulfillment in such a perspective if such a trans-individual perspective were granted them. This, of course, is not to say either that the personal perspective is justified by reason of this possible communalization (and "universalizability" in the sense of an aspired to communalization) or that the unique perspective is able to be substituted for by another perspective, as if the unique perspective could be nullified. In short, what looms as part of the personal ideal of the unique ipseity is the horizon of an ideal communalization of perspectives that does justice to the unique "each" and the universality of "all." But such implications of this ideal need not emerge in the revelation of the unique call as an absolute affection but only in the subsequent reflection on this call.[61]

In the calling it is evident that to have turned away from the life of devotion and commitment as it was manifest analogously in, e.g., the choice of a profession, is to have profoundly betrayed oneself. Again, as Husserl admits, "enthusiasm is not everything." But this call, as evident in the unique experiences of the truth of will, is not a mere rush of feeling and emotion whose significance and validity are only apparent because they are tied to the urgency of the time of the emotion. Just as I cannot say I love you at 5:30 PM on such and such a day, and confine it to this moment, as if the unique ipseity of the Other was something "worth loving" only for this short time or that it belonged to the essence of love of the Other to be momentary, so the time of the devotion to and revelation of the calling is not confined to the highpoint of the enthusiasm, as if one was in love with the enthusiasm and not the Other, or as if the calling had only to do with an occasional deed. It is a call of the I to decisive action that binds it absolutely. It is experienced, in the wake of the enthusiasm, as a call to a deep seriousness requiring an absolute commitment that inaugurates a will that suffuses and empowers the rest of life's willings. In this sense it inaugurates an analogous "willing-will."

Of course, rational reflection may offer necessary insights. But the revelation of the depths of oneself as a single individual through the devoted love of the ideal is of a different order that may well appear to be irrational by most standards, just as it may well appear irrational that one can come up with no compelling objective reasons that found one's love for the other. The self-revelation in the loving devotion is a revelation of what is most originally ownmost to I myself; it is completely personal. As such it is not commensurate to the universal standards that rational reflection would bring. Indeed, the values that can be comparatively weighed, in contrast to the value rooted in the ownmostness of the I as it is revealed in the loving devotion, are as nothing – unless they can be embraced by me as belonging to what awakens this devotion and what this devotion aims at.

Husserl used also the example of "the mother's love for her child" to illustrate the unique calling, and other matters we have just discussed. This example serves to "the truth of will," illustrate (a) how someone can be loved only by one person, or how a valued matter can appear of single importance only to one person and not to another; (b) how we have to do with the core of what is of ethical importance, i.e., how this uniquely appearing "object" awakens an affection that is the source of an absolute ought; (c) how this absolute affection goes in advance of any rational deliberation; (d) how this absolute ought is inseparable from being this person and no one else. Let us attend to each of these.

(a) The example is surely able to conjure up an "affection" that is not "the same for us all" and one that is uniquely poignant for one particular person. Husserl is not saying that every mother embodies what he wishes to single out in the example; nor need he be taken to be saying that a father is not capable of also serving for the example. Surely there would be a special appreciation for the child among many who meet it besides the parents, e.g., that it is beautiful, that it is needing our solicitude, that it completely dependent, that it is exquisitely charming, etc. In this sense, something like "the same for us all" would be approached, i.e., serve as a measure of common shared affection, and these common qualities would be evident to us all. Yet that the child of the mother might appear "radiantly" or in a special value light is also not controversial, however we might disagree in regard to any articulation of what the source of that special affection is. To say it is "instinct" has merit in so far as it may very well appear spontaneous, connatural with her innermost feelings, and not learned for the mother. That it might not appear in some mothers, however, or that the mothers confess to not having any instinctual attraction at the start, but after a period fell absolutely in love with the baby, could weaken this claim. But even if were conceded that it is, in some sense, "instinctual," e.g., that "instinct" is a precipitating occasional causal factor, it does not detract from the uniqueness of the "value" which it brings to light nor does it account for the devotion when that impulse is no longer in play. That it appears as an "absolute Ought" does, however, detract from its status as an instinct, if we think of instinct as necessarily a natural impulse that is not to be identified with an Ought and which carries no responsibility. Further, as an absolute Ought, it generates a general will or commitment in the mother that includes all the endless details of caring for the child, attending to and anticipating what is best for its growth and development. But all of the endless detail rides on the general will (or "willing will") which issues in the absolute Ought.

(b) The mother's love and concern for the child can well appear as an overriding Ought to which everything else is subordinate. Husserl describes this in the following way: The correct designation here is *not*: The weal and woe of the child is *my* weal and woe, but rather: What is at stake is *more than my* weal and woe. Relatively speaking I can neglect my weal and woe, but not that of my child. Thus one's own safety, salvation, or well-being are subordinated to that of the child. The well-being of the child is unconditioned in the sense that there is no other concern to which the mother would give priority. This is a way of stating that love goes beyond all qualities, including one's own weal and woe, to the ipseity itself. It should be obvious that this cannot mean that one may be indifferent to the qualities. The reason for this ability to subordinate one's own (the mother's) weal, as if it were something in addition to or in competition with that of the child, is that the mother could never forgive herself if she acted otherwise. In the basic sense we have been pointing to, the mother recognizes herself in this imperative and recognizes the denial of this fundamental sense of herself if she does not follow it out. The love creates a bond of identification between the lover and beloved. The absolute Ought not only awakens her to herself, but binds her to this child; to give up this call to loving devotion would be to betray her true I, to lose herself.

(c) This "absolute affection" goes in advance, and in almost every instance renders all rational, ethical deliberation of no importance. We say "almost every instance" because we might conjure up cases wherein in fact the "mother" had no child, the child was a delusion, the child upon which she doted was in fact stillborn, etc. The objective values and standards, whether deontological, teleological, consequentialist, pragmatic, etc., that are the same for us all, and that render the values as commensurate and as what can both be weighed with one another and appreciated by us all, count for nothing over against "a value that is absolutely rooted in the I" unless these other objective considerations are evidently encompassed by the absolute Ought and what the loving, valuing I intuits as belonging to its aim, in this case the loving care of this child.[62]

(d) The mother has the conviction that the neglect of the absolute Ought would mean her most profound denial of herself precisely because she is aware of herself as most truly and originally herself, most herself as Existenz, in the loving devotion to the child. She further, as we noted in the other cases, in giving herself over to this calling, gains an unparalleled sense of herself as a unique individual. She becomes aware of her self in her self-ideal's unfolding in the devotion to the child, and she, in this devotion, discovers unfathomable depths in her ownmost I.

It is evident that there is symmetry here between the explication of the revelation of the truth of will in regard to one's calling and our discussion of the coming forth of Existenz in facing one's death. In each case we have to do with what is of unconditional importance, the denial of which would be the profoundest denial of oneself.

Thus the vocation of one's unique self is inseparable from the ideal of one's self, and this can be manifest in a variety of ways. The chief mode of manifestation is when what is present before us is present in such a way that it calls forth our loving devotion. Such matters may well be "truths of will" that make sense only within a personal horizon. Such truths of will may well surface as opportunities to devote oneself unconditionally to a cause, work of art, a career, or a profession. If love is at the heart of the matter, then these latter must, in some sense be tied to beloved ipseities. But this surely is not obvious. If one's vocation is inseparable from love because love is the way the innermost center of the personal I comes to light, or it is the way we are properly revealed to ourselves as Existenz, then clearly the calling typically centers around ipseities. The good work of a career will be within the framework of a devotion to others, either through working with or working for them. However, philosophical eros, devotion to art and science, etc., would seem to be a forms of devotion quite apart from love as the intention of ipseity apart from qualities and properties. In such forms of devotion there is a comparable opening up of endless horizons. However, it seems to me that the eros sustaining these devotions is comparable to the love of ipseity beyond qualities in so far as they target the *je ne sais quoi* of mystery. Without this, it is doubtful that Existenz is awakened to itself, and these careers are properly revealed as vocations. (Cf. our earlier discussions in Book 1, Chapter I on the aesthetic reduction and in Book 2, Chapters II and III on the relationship of Existenz to the disinterested observer.)

The disclosure of one's unique calling through loving devotion requires that we see that the infinite ideal is embodied in a suitable matter, like one's child, beloved, profession, or way of life. This embodiment may not be seen as merely of an instrumental value for the ideal that lies beyond. This would not do justice to the loving devotion to the person herself and the lover's finding unconditional value in what is present at hand. That something undeniably conditioned may appear as having unconditioned aspects is a central theme of a philosophical phenomenology of religion. In the inauthentic cases we have, of course, what Western religions call idolatry; in the authentic cases we have, e.g., love's display of ipseities, or the event of great works of art, or for faith the embodiments of the "holy" and "sacraments," which of their nature, as in Moses's encounter with the burning bush, signal the danger of idolatry. In any case, what is at issue here, as an absolute Ought, is of unconditioned importance and typically involves an infinite task, even though this is realized in endless finite conditioned tasks.

We have urged (in this Book 2, Chapter IV, §§2–4) that we think about the unique calling in terms of the analogy with the career or profession. If we think of the endless tasks of the lover, mother, teacher, homemaker, housebuilder, the spouse, the nurse, the minister, the doctor, etc., we see that all this comes in the wake of an initial position-taking, like the inaugurating decision to build this house, marry this person, or become a high-school teacher, which decision is massive in terms of its implications.

Another aspect of the vocational revelation of the single individual in loving devotion is the presence of a "teleological determinism" where, at least initially, there is a commingling of an absolute moral necessity with freedom. (We resume here a theme we touched upon in Chapter IV, §8.) That is, even though the agent could have done otherwise, yet he acts under the strongest form of moral necessity because he does what he supremely wants to do, and in the face of having chosen not to do which he could not live with himself.[63]

We find a similar theme in Peter Bieri when he writes of "passionate freedom" wherein one finds a "life-determining willing which is not an enslaving rigidity but rather a liberating and identity-forming continuity." Here we do not have something that overpowers the heart but rather a "constellation of wishes which constitute the substance of a life." Here we do not have to do with a work that one likes and believes is valuable. Rather, something much stronger is in play, namely: "He *must* will what he wills." This has nothing to do with the way the addictive or compulsive person must do what he wills. Such a person is run over as if there were an inner avalanche against which he is helpless. Rather, here we have to do with what *carries* or *bears* one. Nor is it like a person who becomes a doctor because of the external pressures of his father wanting him to do it; rather, we have here a case more resembling the person who shares with his father the passion for being a doctor. The former person experiences a kind of necessity of powerlessness or weakness. He cannot choose to follow another willing even though this person is still at a distance from his willing what he wills and he could take up another standpoint which is external to his present will, i.e., external to that of his ownmost wishes and desires. The will of the other doctor who passionately shares his father's passion also has a necessity; he too says: I can not do other than I am doing. "But there is not any tacit distancing [from his will] and therefore there is no powerlessness." Just the opposite: for him it is important, indeed *everything* is at stake, to be the one who sees no alterative to his present willing. This is famously recorded in Luther's "Here I stand, I can do no other." Bieri goes on to say that in these cases of "passionate freedom" the inner center of gravity is not only something that determines the one willing, but rather something of whose determining power he is aware. He is aware of it is as a power that gives contours to himself as a self because it is that with which he whole-heartedly identifies and, as we would say, reveals his innermost core.[64] In passing we may note that here we find a qualification of Bieri's central thesis that willing is properly conditioned by reflective deliberation. As in Aquinas's "connatural knowledge" the willing as informed by the self's life-identification goes in advance. Of course, to deliberately exclude any reflection on this passion or enthusiasm would be reprehensible.

The prima facie absurdity of "become what you are" in the case of passionate willing and the truth of will gives way to a unique experience that is not absurd at all, but rather becomes the standard for one's proper life. Even though one may be, in an important sense, "compelled" and "have no choice" still the agent acknowledges both that she experiences herself maximally free and that in this undertaking she is uniquely herself, self-aware of her single individuality. She may well further acknowledge here a kind of moral necessity, a kind of loss of a freedom of indifference; but at the same time, the agent will testify that there was no question of her being enticed by anything else and, further, this was not some heteronomous demonic possession but rather she was never more herself than during this disclosure and its correlate loving devotion.

For the view we are proposing there is a nisus, a kind of "teleological determinism" of the will to will what is good, to will the better before the good and the best before the better. This is not a matter of indifference for the will, and the will's freedom is not dependent on being indifferent in such matters. This of course is not the determinism of a natural or even instinctual causality, but it has a sense of necessity analogous to logical necessity. Yet whereas there is a strict impossibility in a logical contradiction or strict necessity in say, a logical equivalence, there is a "moral" necessity in matters of the will. One cannot *be* reasonable and violate logical necessity, but one can *be* a moral agent and violate moral necessity.

Thus we here side with Leibniz's view, a position endorsed by Husserl, that at least in the light of the case of "the truth of will," it is an imperfection in the kind of freedom we have that permits us to choose the evil in place of the good, and it is a greater evil to choose a greater evil in place of a lesser evil, and to choose to choose a lesser good in place of a greater one.[65]

The conjoining of the themes of the "truth of will" and "teleological determinism" is a phenomenological way of thinking about what theology has called "predestination." "There is nothing less servile and more befitting the highest degree of freedom than to be always led towards the good, and always by one's own inclination, without any constraint and without any displeasure." For the wise person "what is necessary and what is owing are equivalent things."[66] Leibniz holds that the more wise the person is the more she is bound to choose the best. (Here again we have an echo of the medieval view of "connatural knowing.") This wisdom is the supreme form of blessedness. Whereas for Leibniz "wisdom" was a matter of knowing the principles of everything and having the art or skill of applying them, most of us never can hope to attain such an exalted state. Nevertheless there are moments in which what characterizes the wise person also characterizes most or some of us, i.e., there are blessed moments, and those of "the truth of will" embody them, when of one of us it might be said "the future act stood there, fixed and unaltered as if he had already performed it." The power of choice is set aside and "an inflexible destiny" is substituted for it. Yet, one might also say that the person is liberated from the chatter and rhetoric of his passions and has come into a place of incomparable freedom. In such a moment the agent may well believe that some sense of predestination and freedom were identical. In such a moment the person will not ask, "Why me? Why not someone else?" These questions will not surface because the person knows that in this moment, in this situation calling for her action, her freedom and destiny are identical and both are inseparable from who she is and who she is "supposed" to be.[67] In this sense the truth of will is a "grace" which facilitates the realization of who we are in the direction of being the sort of person we are called to be. (We will return to some of these matters in the next chapter in a discussion of Leibniz and "pre-destination.")

§6. The Calling as Limit-Situation

We have been guided by the Fichtean-Husserlian presentation of the "enthusiastic" revelation of one's calling. Later, of course, when the details of the past commitment surface with often increasingly less luster, when the memory is seldom a "living memory" (see Chapter II, §4), the original revelation may still carry weight, but the enthusiasm may well have diminished or vanished. However, even though the passion of the "passionate freedom" has diminished one's moral identity and self-identification with this willing is the same and therefore the resolve is the same.

Because of the agony of holding together one's life amidst the distractions and scattered temporal phases and meaning-contexts, the issue of the evidence for one's vocation as an analogous profession becomes evidently of importance. The analogy with a profession or a career indicates that there is a position-taking act with massive consequences for huge segments of life. And although one need not explicitly be reminding oneself that "this is what my profession entails," "this is what I committed myself to," etc., nevertheless this act which gathers the general will, this position-taking that informs the whole of the rest of one's life, makes at least implicitly present the sense of the myriad details of one's life.[68] Further, we may note that for Husserl the resolve to the self-determination by which one becomes a moral self, the absolute Ought, is a matter of willing oneself to renew one's resolves regularly. There is thus a recognition of the danger of the ensuing passivity and automaticity which can amount to a misplaced trust in the ability of passive synthesis and character to do the work of the center of the I.

In this context of Existenz, i.e., of I myself being awakened to myself as a single individual facing what is of unconditional importance, the issue of vocation appears as a limit-situation. Even though Husserl's depiction of this experience of calling has an unusual aspect in its enthusiastic appearance, we, nevertheless, regard this depiction as the articulation of the quest each has for the right "path" in life. We wish to spell this out.

Fichte's "higher morality" (cf. the next chapter, §2, E) as well as the revelations of vocation (after the fashion described by Husserl), would seem to occasion enthusiasm and appear dramatic precisely because they disclose, at least for the time being, one's ownmost self in loving devotion to a project that appears as evidently one's "calling," i.e., as what one cannot avoid doing if one wants to be most truly oneself.

One can suspect that the enthusiasm of the loving devotion would eventually wane and thus prove insufficient for sustaining the vocation and the position-taking. Indeed, one may even doubt whether such revelations, in their dramatic forms of Fichte's higher morality, are even a necessary condition. Doubtless more sober, subtle, and gradual disclosures might prove to be the more effective disclosures. Nevertheless, we may think of the Fichtean-Husserlian disclosures as the exemplary form of disclosure of the unique vocation. Even though it is conceivable that the enthusiasm, on occasion, be short-lived, it would seem that in so far as they are genuine they would of necessity have staying power. One is awakened to one's innermost core and a way of life with which one whole-heartedly identifies through a commensurate resolve. However great the sag toward *acedia*, melancholy, and pettiness, the resolve emergent from such awakenings will always be the antidote to this sag. Thus, e.g., typically parents may be dead-tired through caring for their sick babies, but there is no question of their not doing so. Furthermore there is at work another factor that speaks for its relative longevity: Even granting the conceivable short-lived cases of enthusiasm and the resurgent possible sag in self-esteem, there is still the joy of the revelation, the commensurate response to which can only be gratitude and renewed resolve.

Of course, making this staying power depend on genuineness does not mean to suggest that there is a universal standpoint from which to judge these matters. But as in the case of Kierkegaard's presentation of Abraham's suspension of the ethical and the *Bhagavad-Gita's* Arjuna violating his conscience and sense of loyalty to his family in favor of Krishna's injunctions, we observers might have occasion to think the person has lost her mind. But as these classic examples intend to demonstrate, whether or not successfully, the "higher truths," as in the truth of will, by reason of their essence, do not *really* admit of such an "external" critique. In this view the first- and second-person perspective is totally self-legitimating. And in a setting where sense and truth are held to be found only in the third-person, the prejudice against the first-person claim to an unconditioned truth such as the truth of will is massive.

The ideal arrangement of one's life in this maximally unifying fulfilling way resembles the limit-situation. Typically we find ourselves ineluctably more or less lost and more or less "on the way." Thus on the periphery of our life is always the quest for "the way" and a life to which we can commit ourselves without regret and which calls forth our total devotion, i.e., it awakens us to ourselves as single individuals facing what is of unconditioned importance. And because it stands at the margin of life as its ideal arrangement and as the ever sought-for "way," it is always our situation even though, like the other limit-situations of, e.g., one's death, chance, the struggle with others for the awakening of Existenz, it is typically kept at the margins and may not intrude upon us as defining us. The calling is being "situated" within a horizon which one cannot leave and which ever accompanies us even when and after it has been decisively revealed; further it is the definitive disentanglement from an identity dictated by third-person standards towards oneself, i.e., criteria of machines, worldly things, profitability, utility, the crowd's opinion, etc.

If the calling is a limit-situation, then so it would seem are love and happiness. These too are at the horizon of all activity; these too know occasional moments of fulfillment, which, of course, often enough prove to be deceptive and ephemeral. These too can serve as a guide to a fuller life for the long haul where the enthusiasm has diminished or vanished and there is only a sense of joyful resignation and a memory of its former presence.

To conceive the calling, love, and the desire for happiness as limit-situations contradicts the drift characteristic of any metaphysics of shipwreck which an exclusive focus on the unsettling impact of the crisis limit-situations would generate. If we can withdraw from our inauthenticity and awaken to our singular individuality or the center of the I only through the threats of our absolute undoing in death, suffering, struggle, chance, and guilt, then it would seem that the deepest knowing of which we are capable is the tragedy at the heart of being. That is, if for philosophy (apart from faith and revelation) the limit-situations lead us only to turbulence and vertigo, even though these are an effect of the revelation of one's not being something in the world and "archonal," i.e., we discover that we do not have a beginning or principle in the world, then philosophy's proper task is to focus on tragedy at the heart of being. But, clearly, and this is surely the view of Jaspers, the turbulence and unsettledness of the illumination of Existenz need not slide into the pit of despair. The illumination of Existenz, we saw, e.g., in facing one's death, can result in gathering acts where conscience, repentance, and perhaps love become possibilities. Conscience itself is at least a gesture of protest against the ultimacy of absurdity and tragedy and that is why it must be disdained by nihilists and apostles of the absurd. The unconditional imperatives of conscience point to an order, however occluded, that is to be affirmed and respected which is not merely one of our own making.[69] Further, the irrepressible desire for happiness, i.e., the awareness of that good which accompanies but is transcendent to and not to be identified with all the goods we experience in life, points to the incessant inadequation of hopes and dreams with reality; and it can raise the question of a hope that points beyond tragedy.

Our point is that in being awakened to Existenz I am awakened, amidst the unsettling turbulence occasioned by the limit-situation, to the certainty of my self-being and my unconditioned responsibility for determining my being. This is what is of unconditioned importance. I am not awakened to certainties in regard to my life-world but rather I am unhinged from the familiar certainties operative in an identification of myself with being a being in the world along side of other beings. Whatever legitimacy such an identification has, it is only part of the story and the failure to appreciate this lesser significance is at the root of the sense of life as laby-rinthine, a dream, a joke, etc. Neither my shipwreck nor my salvation has its sense in an occurrence that happens to a being among beings in the world. Thus, neither the prospect of shipwreck nor ultimate fulfillment as something that happens in the world is a compelling resolution of the vertigo awakened by the limit-situations. Further, to opt for salvation (on the basis of faith in a revelation), even a purportedly demythologized non-worldly sort, which fosters a suppression of the evidence of the possibility of ultimate shipwreck and tragedy, verges on rendering the saving faith and its salvation shallow. This is because the darkness surrounding death and the mystery of our being is belittled. In our view "salvation" must mean being saved in the face of the mystery of death. In this respect we acknowledge that in the face of the answers provided by faith in adhering to these answers we, at the same time, must confess that we do not know how to formulate adequately the questions to which they are answers. This, of course, is a sense people give to "growing in the darkness of faith." Further, there is a different distortion if "salvation" is understood primarily in terms of "safety" after the fashion of being insured against and liber-ated from the dangers befalling beings in the world.

The limit-situation, as we have presented it, is nevertheless a moment of ship-wreck for the self in so far as she persists in a form of inauthenticity, i.e., in a form of being a stranger to herself. The person is thrown back from out of her prior life and her identification of herself with entities or values of entities, and awakened to herself as a single individual facing what is of unconditional importance. The calling, we have said, is a limit-situation that is just the opposite of the crisis of the self, as a threat of total foundering, in so far as it appears as a fulfillment of the self. Or it appears at least as the right path for the right infinite task of the self in the face of the abyss and mystery of death. The calling, of course, may present itself as a crisis in so far as it makes evident that one's life up until the present must be relinquished. In this sense its revelation might well be painful. The calling as a limit-situation does not suppress the darkness of the abyss of a possible shipwreck, but it mercifully places one on the way in spite of the abyss. It does this, especially when revealed through a "passionate freedom" or "truth of will," by providing a wind at the person's back that enables a unique resolve in the face of the maw of the monster of self-dissolution occasioned by the other limit-situations.

Why the Fichtean and Husserlian disclosures of one's calling seem rare or "precious" beyond belief can be explained in part in terms of today's pervasive framing of selves, goods, and values in terms of what is commensurate to materialist ideology and/or capitalist economics, and, inseparably, the reification, functionalization, mechanization and routinization of life. Modern career and vocational notions are tied foremost to wages and "earning a living" within a corporate-capitalist culture. If waking life is for the most part what is called "earning a living" (a phrase which presumably would be unintelligible to an aborigine) we see that living must be earned and it can only be so merited at the hands of someone else, the employer or wage giver. And if "earning a living" is tied primarily to work undertaken for an acceptable if not good wage or salary, and if this is thought to be the equivalent of meaningful and good work, even though the worker must become indifferent to what she wants to do during the best hours of her waking life, then the normal condition of "earning a living" is living a life that one would prefer not to live; in this sense it is not a good life. And if the fruit of one's labor, i.e., money, is understood as something to be exchanged for an ever more intensive and ever more conspicuous consumer life, then work can be neither good nor meaningful. This is so for the following reasons: Work is meaningful if it is for a desired end for the sake of which the work is undertaken. Work cannot be meaningful if profit and increased production for the sake of increased consumption (and perhaps power) are the ends because these ends are mere means and such means for non-ends are meaningless. Work is a means to a means to an endless series of means. If work is meaningful only because it gives me the means to rest from work so that I can go back to work, then that for which I work is not really an end but a means. If meaningful work is understood teleologically in terms of promoting the true self of the person, much of modern work is without meaning. It is at best wage slavery because the best hours of one's waking life are extracted from one's life for the sake of making money for, typically, a corporation whose reason for existing is to increase the earnings of its shareholders. Mere working for a "good wage" is, as Aristotle noted, a form of slavery precisely because one has not the disposal over her own life, but turns her will and mind over to the wage giver. Earning a living, as being forced or as permitting oneself, i.e., one's stream of consciousness, one's mind, will, and heart, to be turned over to another, is having the best time of one's life, one's best wakeful hours, extracted for the sake of someone's profit enterprise. One does not live one's own life in terms of constituting itself in the world but the life of another. And if one is indifferent to or ignorant of what this enterprise produces, how it produces, and what its impact is on the social and natural surroundings one lives like a zombie for whom there is no question of a good life. And what one does cannot be good work if good work means enhancing the worker's depth of Existenz and developing her spiritual strengths, and if these are connected to her beautifying and improving her natural and social surroundings, and contributing to the material and spiritual well-being of her neighbors.

Inseparable from the reification, etc., of persons in the modern megamachine is the prejudice against first-person perspectives. Along with this everyone contends with the more or less official decree that first-person awareness is not only dispensable but a hindrance to realistic economics and appropriate analysis. Perhaps we can say that the crises occasioned by limit-situations do not easily lead to the discovery of Existenz unless there are outlets in the official society or in the underground of this society. The limit-situation of the vocation can scarcely surface at all in the economic context where each is forced to "earn a living." If it surfaces it must do so outside of this context of economic necessity, as with academics, clergy, teachers, etc. Yet today most of these careers are dominated by economic necessities and here too one "must earn one's living." We thus have not merely a philosophical query but also a pressing question of mental health and social justice: How does one foster one's identity as something other than as an entity or function in the military-industrial-congressional complex? Without exit strategies, outlets, or escapes from the economic necessities of the megamachine persons are led to despair or alienating definitions of themselves as a function within this ever growing "machine," i.e., they are led to a decisive denial of themselves.[70] The super rich are in the curious position of being, to a degree, free of these necessities, and thus free to face the limit-situation of the calling. Yet the only life they tend to know is one which involves total submersion in the megamachine which *eo ipso* threatens the calling's materialization. In any case, for "the middle class" there must be strategies of coping and resistance which enable one to deal with the fact that although one's best hours are extracted from one's life for often objectionable purposes, one is still more than this indentured servant. And one is called to be more than a slave to the economic necessities.

Thus another obvious difficulty with the Fichtean-Husserlian theory of vocation's revelation of truth of will is the fact of class divisions and dire poverty. It is interesting that Husserl's example of the mother as exemplifying the truth of will is indifferent to social-economic matters. But the other examples of both Fichte and Husserl, e.g., of one's career path, reflect class privilege. Throughout most of history there have been persons who have had to struggle moment to moment, day to day, just to stay alive and avoid being crushed, slain, or robbed. Such persons, present as well as past, even though they may not face or have faced the necessity to "earn a living," they, nevertheless, have had to struggle to stay alive. The question surfaces then to what extent the material conditions of living are necessary for the themes of the truth of will and the calling. Surely we can know of or can imagine persons who would seem to have very diminished leisure and freedom for these matters. We can well conceive cases where there is no freedom from the necessities enjoined by poverty, famine, and war which would permit freedom for reflection on the "human calling"; no realistic freedom to think of one's life analogously to a profession or career – as if one had, as an obvious matter of course, "career options." Nor has such a person had other appropriate conditions fulfilled that would permit a reflection on the ideal of an unregrettable position-taking by which she could arrange her life for all eternity. Doubtless we might still believe and hope that in the most dire straits and tormented pain conscience may still make itself heard. No one can speak in these matters for others, but only for oneself. And as we do not know with certainty in our own case how we would act, so more certainly we do not know how others will be.

Here is where some form of religion is at once the opium as well as the life-line of the poor and the afflicted. That is, it provides consolation and hope as well as dulls the pain and distracts from the contingent social arrangements that cause the pain; but religion also points to the basics of the human situation, namely that everyone, at some time or other, faces shipwreck along with engulfing forms of pain and suffering. Here a fortiori is also where ideal political arrangements designed to maximize the flourishing of unique persons comes into play.

In the contemporary "megamachine" as well as in desperate social circumstances people come to be seen as *disposable*. A worse state is that of alienation when persons come to think of themselves in this way. For such persons the theme of "calling," as a serious personal matter, appears to be irrelevant. Persons for whom extreme fear, pain, and need determine their lives, are handicapped in terms of a being-in-the-world that enables the limit-situation of the calling as a personally and socially relevant matter to emerge. Rather the "calling" here has to do with the basic struggle to act and suffer with decency and self-respect when everything in life works against these by reason of the overwhelming degrading forces. Here, again, religion serves most people because it enables them to believe that suffering can have a deep meaning. They, as afflicted persons, although robbed of their life in the world with Others as full-fledged co-agents, nevertheless have an eminent calling and destiny to be realized precisely through their suffering.

If conscience itself is at least muted, if not silenced, as it perforce seems to be when life is nothing but agonizing pain or a desperate struggle for survival, a fortiori, the invitation to quest for one's true path is in peril. The awakening to one's self-being in the limit-situations presupposes a sense of one's I-can; in *extreme* pain it is not clear whether one *has* a sense of oneself as having possibility, as an I-can free to actualize herself, i.e., it is unclear whether the pain does not diminish one's capacity to be anything but the paining. In extreme pain we are, after all, excised from the world and collapsed into the peculiar ownmostness of our privacy. Precisely because we are collapsed into our ownmostness the matter is never clear what resources we have for agency based upon clarity in the field of consciousness. If the field is narrowed to the point of the paining, conscience itself, which is always a way in which we are distant from ourselves, is in jeopardy. To be awakened to the call of conscience *I* must be appealed to by my still-valid position-takings. But in extreme suffering I do not have this distance from my self; I am collapsed to the pain – at least almost collapsed, or so it seems.

If this is so, the calling in the sense we have, following Husserl, attempted to develop seems to be a relevant consideration only when certain conditions of health and social-economic circumstances are fulfilled for the person in question, i.e., circumstances that permit them to be not collapsed into their pain and affliction, but present to themselves in terms of their freedom, along with the call and admonitions of conscience and self-inadequation. It might seem that the person who is starving or wasting away from a disease is too constricted by the suffering to be unhinged by the pressing issues of Existenz as a crisis in one's being in the world. Such a person already lives without respite the limit-situation of suffering. The despair over being oneself in the face of the limit-situations, the despair over one's ability to be true to oneself, would, it might seem, presuppose a kind of minimal health and social-economic reality as its necessary condition.

Yet it belongs to the mystery of ipseity that this cannot be said of oneself in advance and *a fortiori* it may not be said of another. We are such that in the first-person we do not know in advance how we will be when faced with the extremes of pain. We do not know the actual limits of our freedom, even though we know that it is not infinite. As we cannot know precisely what "the hour of death" means or when it is no one knows in advance what one can do when put to such a test as that, e.g., faced by the inmates of Guantanamo Bay. In any case, extreme forms of suffering, hunger, and poverty surely diminish the vivacity of the sense of one's I-can and one's sense of oneself as possible Existenz facing what is of unconditional importance. And it is no small matter that the religious message which permits believers to convert their pain and suffering into a new light, a way of seeing-as, whereby they may take the pain and suffering, e.g., as a privilege, is not done justice to with the dismissive references to "dope," masochism, or self-deception. On occasion, the pain and suffering as suffused with faith are the bases of personal transformation with the end result of not only moral giants and heroes but extraordinarily beautiful human beings.

Another sense of calling that we must here at least mention is that of one's "genius." The property of genius is appropriately made by a competent judge regarding someone's ability on the basis of the extraordinary quality of their expression of their work or performance of a work deemed beautiful and/or of great importance. Often genius is ascribed in the context of works where there is a felicitous untaught, unlearned combination of one's imagination and cognitive powers, as in poetry, science, and philosophy. Thus Kant spoke of genius as the masterful originality of the natural gift of a subject in the free use of his cognitive power (*Kritik der Urteilskraft*, §49). But does this do justice to a painter, a musician, and especially a singer or a dancer? But Kant surely is right when he speaks of there being a gift of nature which the recipient, the subject, freely, especially with the aid of imagination, actuates. And further, he stresses elsewhere the originality and that in the case of genius it is "nature" which prescribes the rules of art and not the other way around: The extant rules of art do not dictate what good art is in the case of genius.

This making room for a power within the person recalls one's Daimon, as a deeper or other self that indicates one's path. But rather than a deeper or higher self genius refers to buried but undeniable talents or abilities, without the actualization of which one might well be destined for a life of discontent. Further, having not actuated these talents one might well have deprived one's fellows of great blessings.

The appreciation of not merely the natural aristocracy of human abilities but how they, on occasion, are so great that they scarcely admit comparison might well lead one to the conclusion that *who* one is this talent; in the case of those possessing ingenious talents, one is who one most properly is, and called to be, through the actualization of this talent. In Willa Cather's *The Song of the Lark*, the heroine, Thea Kronborg, is enabled by her teacher to see that through pursuing a career as a professional singer she will awaken to her true self. Pursuing her other considerable talent as a pianist will not enable this to happen. By becoming a pianist she would be eventually unhappy and her playing will become "warped, eccentric." Cather traces the talent to Nature's beneficence and it becomes like the Daimon in as much as it is identified with one's true self. One may hide it, regard it as one's secret; one may hesitate to give it space. For one who has such a talent or gift there is an urgent drive to find oneself, to emerge *as* oneself by putting all of herself into the cultivation of this talent. She might well be timid before what the gift might demand of her: It will absorb all of her life and devotion. Yet it is her "vocation." Evidence for this gift is compelling first for the expert eyes of her teacher and then for the subject herself: The talent is there independent of work and practice; the beauty is there wanting to break forth. Yet one may hold back from or even hide this *reality* until one is sure that one is ready because of its daunting demands. For: "One can fail one's self, but one must not live to see that fail; better never to reveal it."[71]

Clearly here we have symmetry with what we discussed under the rubrics of "truth of will" and "passionate freedom." More of the story would have to be told. That is, we would have to learn how this talent is joined to what we are calling the general or willing will of the ipseity, i.e., to what extent pursuing this path is "passionate freedom" and is the vehicle of a self-identifying act. Clearly merely as *a talent* which one *has* and which one may develop to one's own benefit and those of others, it is not equivalent to the "I myself" who has the talent and who actuates it. Further, our reservations toward it as being the proper way to talk about one's calling would recall those we expressed in regard to the Fichte-Husserlian view: As not everyone has the privilege to find a vocational path in life because either of one's poverty, suffering, or incapacitation, so here, a fortiori, the rarity of genius or great talent precludes this being a universal criterion of a calling. Yet in Cather's example the gift is not experienced as universalizable; it is wholly personal. This, of course, is what we mean by "genius." Yet we also distinguish geniuses from the "sort of persons" they are, and surely in this work we would distinguish the genius from the "myself" of the person. However admirable the genius of the person might be it is compatible with the person being reprehensible in vast areas of her life. Nevertheless, the awakening of oneself to one's gift, the need to discover oneself in relationship to one's gift and the urgency it imposes on one, resembles the Fichtean-Husserlian truth of will. Again, a talent typically is what one has and it is not who one is. But this is true also of one's path, career, and calling. Being a person is more than these and more than one's talents. Foremost, if a talent is left to the random "graces" of "nature" and the contingencies of one's station in life it cannot be the *unum necessarium* of the person. It cannot be what we must have and do at all costs if, in fact, we have no talent; it cannot be that which is of unconditional importance if we cannot pursue the talent for reasons over which we have no control.

Another sense in which the calling is a limit-situation and a crisis is when there is a conflict of absolute values both with regard to Others as well as within the person. If we may think of the calling as beckoning us to what is of absolute value, it is not clear in advance that this necessarily will be a calling that does not conflict with other values we cherish absolutely. Thus, e.g., wars are generally portrayed, by those who are not pacifists, as one nation state, through its army, defending matters having absolute values which the army of the enemy state assaults or threatens to assault. (For pacifists persons typically *are* "ontological values"; in this respect they are not commensurate with things alleged to have non-negotiable or absolute values.) Here the calling of the opposing sides, i.e., the calling of members of nation-states, is allegedly to defend what has absolute value. This legitimates the slaying of other persons on the other side, whose absolute ontological value or their being ends in themselves has been trumped by the call to war, i.e., the call to preserve what has absolute values. More basic than the enmity between nation states are fundamental disagreements between persons that are irreconcilable and which lead to the dissolution of families and friendships. Two friends may believe themselves "destined for" another person who appears to each of the rivals as the *unum necessarium*. But the situation may be such that it is impossible that they both be the lovers of the beloved and remain friends with one another. Further, lovers (as in Romeo and Juliet) may have destinies that involve their unconditioned love for one another. But this very love might conflict with other matters of apparent infinite and unconditioned value, e.g., the honor of the families of the lovers.

Such conflicts between persons resemble the tragic conflict within a person where an absolute value, e.g., the parents' love for their child, stands in conflict with the apparent unconditioned duties they must fulfill in regard to the tribe, country, or nation state, as when the child must risk his or her life, e.g., in relief efforts of an emergency disaster or in war. In such a case, Husserl speaks of sinning against oneself in so far as, e.g., the parent must do something against herself or what she regards as inseparable from herself for a "higher cause" (e.g., contributing to the nation-state's defense of its international rights through letting one's child be cannon fodder). Such relinquishing nevertheless violates what the parent most loves and what is some integral aspect of her identity and self-ideal – and yet, so it seems, the other value of patriotism to which one has unconditioned allegiance is thought to have a superior claim. Often in life the better and best absorb the good. The features of this object (e.g., Ford car) that are good are also to be found in the better and best goal or object (e.g., the Mercedes). Thus a well-planned eco-city-state would include the undeniable contemporary advantages of advanced technology as well as the wildness, cleanness, and integrity of nature. In the tragedy, an absolute good that must be relinquished or sacrificed is not simply absorbed by the other absolute good. It is not like how notes of dissonance may be absorbed by the final movement of a symphony that elevates them into a higher harmony. Rather, the sacrificed value is irreplaceable and the love of it is never extinguished or cancelled. It is retained as forever at odds with the other value because it appears as not ever able to be harmonized. It keeps its value and there is no manifest evidence for a higher harmonization and one's self is torn in two, as it were.[72] Similarly in the case of Willa Cather's Thea, a tragedy would ensue if she, having discovered her genius and having felt its beauty and power, were called by her duty to aid those suffering from war, illness, or poverty.

This would seem to be the dilemma of the conflict between preserving the integrity of non-human nature and the endless drive towards growth. This latter is sustained by the belief in the legitimate value of endless profits and by the value of endless technological progress propelled by the engine of corporate capitalism.

These are based perhaps on the belief that improved material well-being for humans is an incommensurately superior value to the well-being of non-human nature.

In such conflicts, one may, like Dostoyevsky's Ivan Karamazov, even if there is an invitation to the grand party in Heaven at which the revelation of how the conflict of values is to be harmonized, e.g., through the disclosure of how the divine "permission" that innocent children be tortured and slaughtered served a higher cause, refuse the admission ticket to the heavenly festival. (Of course, for Ivan, "Heaven" does not represent at this time a genuine absolute value; so in fact there is no tragic dilemma, even though it may pain him to give up the faith of his youth.) One refuses because one becomes most oneself, one comes forth as Existenz, in loving devotion to what is of absolute value; this cannot be sacrificed without renouncing oneself. But in the conflict of classical theodicy to which Ivan alludes one must devote oneself to another, not evident believed-in, absolute value that is in irreconcilable conflict with manifest absolute values, the well-being of children, and by which one is awakened to one's ownmost self. The self one is, the deepest I, is torn asunder and there does not appear to be any reconciliation.

When the individual faces a conflict of absolute values, when, in this sense, the person faces a tragic situation, then there is the crisis of the limit-situation: one faces ultimate destruction of the being of one's self. It approximates the wreck of the annihilation of oneself at death and/or universal extinction. It is even closer to the crisis of the "eternal" guilt of betrayal where one cannot be forgiven or forgive oneself. In all these cases of disaster and peril the themes of salvation and transcendence are on the horizon. But these themes are properly made present through philosophy's reflection on religion; on its own, apart from the deliverances of "positive" religion, philosophy would seem to come up empty.

In any case, all these surds with which history is sprinkled offer evidence against a theory of the truth of will that would claim for it the power to manifest one's vocation as an inevitable linear unfolding in a person's life which leads to salvation from life's surds. The proposal that it is helpful to think of the calling as a limit-situation presupposes the other crises-limit-situations and it presupposes also that one has not succumbed to the vertigo, despair, and incapacitation they may occasion. It further assumes that Existenz has come to light at least as a power to love and endure, if not as an actual loving. Like love and happiness, the calling is a limit-situation that always frames life and as such evokes not dread but hope; but its being crushed after having surfaced in all its beauty can be an occasion for all the bitterness and despair of tragedy.

§7. The Ontological End and the Purposes of the Person

In this section we want to address the question, To what extent is the calling of the person a disclosure of the purposes of the person in contrast to the ends of persons as determined by the person having a human nature? We will wrestle with this matter with the help of Francis Slade and Robert Sokolowski who have developed the distinction between ends and purposes.[73] *Purposes* have to do with goals we intend. They correlate to the appetitive, conative, affective, cognitive intentions that persons have. The *ends* of something, in contrast, are the telos or completion of things when they have reached their completion or perfection. Both are goods, both are something we appreciate or value, but they do not belong to the same order and the appreciation requires different perspectives. Purposes arise solely out of our intending them; in the absence of human intentions there are no purposes. Purposes are good as what we desire and strive for. They are our conscious goals and what we want to realize. Ends are not dependent on our desiring, purporting, aiming, etc.

Ends have to do with the nature or essences of things. Natural things, artifacts, institutions all have ends that correlate to their essences. Thus a dandelion, a bicycle, and a profession all have proper ends. Dandelions are plants and find with their blossoms a completion that gives forth seeds as the form of "their own" self-preservation. They also produce nectar for other members of the ecosystem who in turn pollinate and thereby enrich further other members, etc. Perhaps we need to see them as parts of the larger whole which is the earth or soil as the skin of the earth, which, in a state of disturbance, requires these plants for its replenishment. If we include human members of this system we may say they are able to add intelligence, grace, and charm, to the ecosystem for at least some of its members. A bicycle clearly is for transportation and recreation for minimally healthy humans. A profession, like medicine, is for the sake of health and making healthy. Of course, in the latter two cases the essence is a result of human purpose and design; in this sense the telos is not independent of human intentions. Yet once the artifacts and institutions are created they have an essence or specification of kind that exists independently of the human purporting. A medical doctor whose main work is torture and killing clearly violates her profession. A bicycle used as a hammer suffers a distortion of its end. We might make the case that the eradication of dandelions from the grass by weed killers may be in accord with some human purposes but is at cross purposes to the ends of the dandelion and the ends of the soil and in opposition to the purposes or interests of many of the neighboring residents for whom the weed killers are toxic.

Of special interest in our immediate context is the question of the overlapping and separation of purposes and ends. Obviously there is an overlapping of the end and purpose when a medical doctor strives to heal her patients or when a professor purports to impart to students a grasp of the key distinctions in an area of her special competence. Nevertheless there is not a coincidence or equivalence here of end and purpose. The end of being a medical doctor is not dependent on this professional's intending to heal. And, the good that the doctor pursues comes to light in the first-person aiming and doing; the end of the profession gets displayed in the third-person witnessing of the fittingness of the end to the profession and, how, in this case, such fittingness is being instantiated. It is also evident in the doctor's objective self-awareness, (a kind of transformation of the first-person self-awareness into a third-person self-awareness), that what he is doing is in accord with his profession. Thus "the end does not turn into a purpose and the purpose does not become an end."[74]

Francis Slade has nicely made clear that when the world is bereft of ends and all of life is reduced to purposes, that is, when we have a "world without ends," we have a world where purposes cannot be measured by ends, and in so far as purposes are irreducibly private to individuals we have a world where purposes are incommensurate and incongruous with one another. This is a world where people are together in terms of conflicting desires and there is no public background of displayed common natures and ends. Rather, everyone is propelled not by the displayed common world but by the private forces that are at cross-purposes. Thus there is a world of competition, violence and war. It is also a world where guilt is made impossible in so far as guilt requires responsibility for actions and in so far as actions are thought of as acts reflected on and as measured by ends.[75] For Slade and Sokolowski, we have a robust sense of "natural law" when we recognize the ontological priority of ends over purposes. The recognition of the primacy of ends means we recognize the inherent nobility in the displayed natures, essences, and their ends. The manifestness of the "way things are" awakens a fundamental respect for the inherent dignity of things. Our life of passion and choice will be responsible and in accord with "the natural law" if it is guided by this basic respect of the intrinsic nobility of things.[76] Throughout this work, we have had occasion to call attention to the way the presence of the person is inseparable from this intrinsic worth or *dignitas*. Kant put this nicely when he noted that the person does not have for other persons an end beyond itself but is an end in itself. But we have also raised the question of whether a person is a kind of being or a nature.

Obviously the respect for the intrinsic nobility of how things are is not to be reduced to a worship of convention. It would seem that most critiques of an institution, e.g., the state, city, jails, churches, etc., arise from crises in the essence of the institutions, and appeal to what the true, rather than distorted nature of the institution is. What we mean by a radical critique in this context would be one which would propose that the very institution is morally evil and/or a mistake of political theory and practice. This would mean that it would be contrary not only to purposes of persons but more basically to human ends. In any case, Slade and Sokolowski make clear that this position does not reduce natural kinds to institutions nor does it reduce all institutions to conventions and thereby reduce what is *de jure* to what is *de facto*.

Of especial interest for *natural law* is its "legislative" functioning in determining that human agency and human purposes be in conformity with the ends of human nature and its various powers.[77] Yet in the course of this work we have made central the concept of person and not human nature. We have featured the ipseity, person, and Existenz and moved the question of the human nature of the human person into the background. (But see our efforts to imagine the limits of human ipseities in Book 1, Chapter VIII, especially §§6–7.) For what has preceded in this work, the essence of ipseity is not first of all the essence of being human. Thus we sought the end of the person, and in this sense its "vocation," in the disclosures of conscience, obligations, and the "truth of will." Of course, these are vague disclosures in the absence of the respect for the natural kinds and their ends in our surroundings. They also are vague in the absence of recognizing that the ipseity that we are able to bring to light through philosophical reflection is always necessarily a *human* ipseity with its natural ends.

Yet the first-person reflection on the vocation of the person may not be trumped by the ontological prioritization of ends over purposes. The vocation we seek to elucidate is that of the person at her center, i.e., in her Existenz, and this enjoys a kind of priority to the person as an instance of humankind or individual human. One reason for this priority is that the unique essence is revealed not as a What available in the third-person, but rather is properly available in the first-person and through love in the second-person. One sense of this has come to light in the notion that the person is not given to herself as a completed kind. A tree as a kind is complete, and as having an entelechy, does "what comes naturally." Even if we take a Scotist-Hopkinsian position and propose that everyone see this dogwood tree, existing now in this place under these circumstances with this environment and having this biological history, as a unique essence, it would be true that this tree is of necessity itself completely itself and cannot be otherwise that as it is given itself (not *to* itself, strictly speaking) to be. (It does not have "to self" in an appropriate way for it to complete itself.) We have said the human self is given to complete itself to self-determine itself, to establish freely itself in the course of its life. In such a matter we do not know in advance who and precisely what sort of person we are to become, although it is unlikely that anyone doubts it is a sort of human person.[78] *In this sense* who we are to become remains hidden to us, at least at the beginning of the journey. Sorting out this "identity" of who we are to become does not merely have to do with what is available in terms of the defining properties belonging to the kind of being one is. This is one of the senses of holding that "person" is not a sortal term, i.e., being a person is not exhausted by sortal considerations.

Again, such a prioritizing of the non-sortal over the sortal does not mean being indifferent towards the person's human context and human nature in determining its way in the world. Nevertheless, if the disclosure of ends is made possible by the working out of the properties and powers of a kind in regard to its perfection and completion, such a path does not properly show the way to the "myself" and Existenz as such. It is possible that the themes of ipseity and Existenz surface in some form when we take up a third-person ontological perspective and reflect on *human* beings as persons. But distinctive aspects of ipseity and Existenz only come to light when, in the first-person, we wrestle with the person and ipseity as precisely what does not come to light in this objective third-person fashion. To treat the essential subjectivity of the individual essence as an objective essence in the world with distinctive properties and ends is to miss what is essential in the ipseity. This is part of the sense we may ascribe to Kant's dictum that the person is an end in itself, i.e., we may not, in this case, assume an objectifying relationship to the person as an entity so that the person may be inserted into a hierarchy of means and ends and ends which are means based on the relative natures and worth of the entities in question. Of course, the first-person sense of personal destiny must be supplemented by the objective reflection on one's human nature because this nature is the "existence condition" of this ipseity, i.e., that being a self is always also being this (human) kind of ipseity. But, again, the properties of this existence condition cannot substitute for the ipseity's unique essence which is available only in the first-person and implicitly in empathic perception. To consider its end to be exhaustively available by regarding the end of the nature in which it is embedded is to make of the person a sortal term.

In the next chapters we will wrestle with a possible theological perspective on ipseity which transcends that of the first-person analogous to the way ipseity transcends kind or nature. The person can reflect on a nature, including her own, and determine the end of the nature vis-à-vis this nature. In these concluding chapters we will find a speculative sense in which the unique essence may become objectified and correlated to its destiny in a definitive and objective manner, in the manner of an end – but in such a way which does not destroy the essential subjectivity of the unique essence, and in a way that lets the purpose be decisive over the end.

Further, in terms of the basic positions of this book, in an effort to establish the "end" of the unique essence without recourse to a third-person ontological perspective which would reduce the ipseity to a kind correlated to an end, we have sought a first-person disclosure of the proper end that would guide the manifold purposes. In doing this, foremost in our pursuit of the issue of "vocation" and "truths of will," we have not always found it possible to keep distinct the question of ends and "purposes" in our pursuit of the issue of "vocation" and "truths of will." We pursued the theme of "vocation" as not a particular or specific essence of a profession but after the analogy of the human vocation, or better, the personal vocation or unique call of this unique person. We used the analogy of the way a general will establishes the manifold wills that comprise the detailed life of the professional. We assumed the institution of a profession or career as already established and we assumed that choosing it was embracing this instituted essence. Furthermore, in our examination we have seen how the general will is manifest in the particular "willed wills" and how it provides them with their essential sense, as being appropriate to the instituted essence of the profession. In the case of the question of the human or personal calling, we postulated an analogous willing will that accompanied all our agency and on occasion made itself felt in a particularly palpable way.

Can we presume to say that this is a coincidence or identity synthesis of the end of the unique essence with the purpose in the particular instance of the revelation of the truth of will? That surely is the drift of our presentation. We have sought to find a sameness and coincidence of who one is in terms of the "myself" as the entelechy of the person with the "sort of person" which is the result of the proper self-determination by the person. Yet we have already noted both the rarity and the fallibility of such achievements and disclosures. These weaknesses alone provide reason to doubt that we here have an apodictic disclosure of any such coincidence of purpose and end. (A similar uncertainty arises in the Aristotelian context where the agent, on the basis of its practical reasoning, determines how to realize its "end" of happiness in unique complex circumstances. The prudential judgment in the concrete circumstance is always pervaded by inadequate evidence just as is the agent's determination of what "happiness" truly is for her in her concrete situation.)

Because we are dealing first of all with the first-person revelation of ipseity's destiny and vocation any position which has recourse exclusively to the third-person disclosure of human nature leaves out the unique person's "end." This is the vocation of her personal essence at its core, her Existenz. Because there is no other way of getting access to Existenz's end except through the "purposes" of one's willing will and the truth of will, the analysis in this Book has muted the classical ontological approach to *human* ends. But along the way we also pointed to conscience and obligation as standing in need of essences and ends that are not merely coincident with purposes and intentions. Conscience, we saw, emerges out of an "ontological affirmation" of the order of being. For the Husserlian this means it emerges out of the position-takings by which we shape the world in terms of our desires and purposes. But fundamental for these is how we have displayed the world through the position-taking acts by which kinds and ends come to light. It is not as if conscience and duties surface apart from a displayed world of essences and ends or as if our purposes would have any hold, publicity, or possibility of critique apart from this display.

In short, the reflection on vocation and the truth of will, whereby we may under-stand the disclosure of purposes in the form of the intention of goods of utmost importance, can never be a reflection pursued solely within the parameters of a pure ipseity and the existential core of the person or Existenz. Such would veer towards an angelology or spiritualism abstracted from the person's being in the world and nature with Others. We here must to retrieve our notion of soul that we earlier discussed in Book 1, especially Chapter III. This is the realm of sensibility and animation quite apart from I-agency or spirit. In the third-person perspective this animation may be held to account for us as a living human being, like any other ani-mal or plant. Angels, we may speculate, have neither passive synthesis, nor bodies with capacities for sense perception, nor, a fortiori, cardio-vascular and digestive systems. They are pure ipseities, and in this sense pure spirits. They are therefore bereft of souls as animating principles of bodiliness and passivity. By contrast, in the human person the ipseity as principle is inseparable from soul animating a body inserted into the natural cosmos.

In the Western philosophical tradition a dominant position has been that there is one soul which is the source of the spiritual life as well as the bodily. This is the human soul.[79] In this ontology typically the rational principle or reason becomes the principle which accounts for ipseity and personhood. A strong statement of this is that reason "makes us to be persons and not just individuals. Our reason singu-larizes us and makes us subjects as well as members of a species. Because of our reason we share in the form of personal being that is proper to angels and even to God"[80] But could we not say that it is because we are first of all persons or ipseities and have this "form" which is that of being uniquely unique selves that we share in what is proper, e.g., "to angels and even to God?"

If the form of *human* reason accounts for our unique essence as well as our specific difference an ethical-ontological account of the purposes of the person would have to be in terms of the ends of human nature. If reason is conceived as what singularizes and therefore has within it the principle of haecceity then rea-son's functioning is to be seen in relation to the uniqueness of the person and its normative agency will have a component which is not legislated by the specific essence and ends of nature alone. (Again, we might find echoes here of Aristotle's *phronesis*.)

In this work we have been hesitant to follow this subordination of the principle of ipseity to reason and human nature. We have insisted on the primacy of the first-person perspective. The ontological prioritizing of human nature and ends displaces that primacy. We have attempted to show how the first-person revelation of ipseity is more basic than the essence and end of human nature. We have given numerous reasons for this, not least of which is the non-sortal referent of the "myself." We have also (in Book 1) undertaken various thought-experiments which put to the test the total coincidence of oneself with being human. We do not claim any finality and conclusiveness for these discussions. But they do raise some questions about the subordination of ipseity to the nature which is human. Nothing of what we have said would seem to point to the conclusion that a person may be indifferent to her human nature or that the self constitutes arbitrarily human nature. The specific nature which determines the existence condition of an ipseity is not some property that the ipseity may dispense with or neglect to take into account. It is a necessary condition of one's being and a necessary ingredient in one's self-determination. But having said this much we hesitate to say it is what founds ipseity.

Further, the self is self-constituting in the sense that it, as the "myself" which is personified (or "incarnated" as a person), requires that it self-constitute, self-determine itself for its ontological completion. As we have attempted to show, without this self-constitution it, as pure "myself," is ontologically incomplete, i.e., not a proper, moral, person. It is called to determine itself as an I, as an ipseity, throughout its life. It is called to determine, we have said, the *sort of person* it is. This is not simply a matter of acting in accord with the ends of human nature. Rather, it is acting from out of its center, from itself as Existenz, in regard to what is supremely important. This ideally may involve a disclosure of the truth of will, something which is not an "end of nature" that is public and universal for all persons. This is a sense in which we can appropriate the Sartrean "its essence is to exist" and the priority of Existenz to essence. Again, however, there is no question of a license to be heedless of one's nature, let alone giving room to the phantasy that ipseity creates it.

Of course, whether ipseity is to be subordinated to reason or reason to ipseity depends on how we define "reason" and ipseity. In the first Book we discussed the inherent difficulties of the definition of the latter because of the absence of distinguishing properties. Yet there we had to face the seemingly ineliminable "tautological properties" like reason, will, consciousness, etc., that accompany the unpropertied "myself."

Further, if reason is taken in a way that may be regarded as a "tautological property" of ipseity then there is no real tension. Thus to the extent that ipseity requires person and person requires reason as what its agency of manifestation employs in its responsibly achieving the distinctive unique identity synthesis of ideality and publicity and the embodied syntactical-categorial structures of language as carried out in human interactions, then clearly ipseity or "person" are analytically related to reason and the human person. But that does not seem to capture sub-, trans-, and para-human (thought-experimental) ipseities (see Book 1, Chapter VIII). For example, is not there not a form of proto-reason in passive synthesis, reflection, and the perception of Others where there is to be found pre-linguistic identity syntheses – these being a measure of the presence of reason?[81] Does not the establishment of the ideality of language, as in phonemic structures, presuppose more basic kinds of "syntax"? Of interest in these acts is the muted sense in which I may say that they are *my* acts or *I* have achieved them. The realm of soul or passivity is pervaded by a rationality, some of which is a result of I-acts, but the most basic dimension of which, the realm of drives, instincts and passive association, is independent of I-acts. Here at this level of proto-reason clearly *I undergo being reasonable* as the condition of my wakefulness. This makes rationality mine, me myself at a distance, and mine to attend to and appropriate. At this level there is loosened the claim of the strict identity of reason and I-acts.

Reason here is always mine and undergone by me even though it is properly and exemplarily tied to I-acts. And no less basic is the presencing of Others, without which there is no constitution of linguistic idealities. Is not the presencing of other minds, whereby one becomes an Other to the Other, and whereby publicity and language get constituted, a kind of "proto-rationality." Further the subordination of person to reason does not capture all senses of person, e.g., the ipseity of infants and dogs.

Having said this, nevertheless we must heed that which Husserl also makes clear, namely, not only am *I* to be, in a strong sense, identified with *reason*, but *reason* is inseparably *I myself*. Reason in the proper sense, and this is juxtaposed to the latent reason of passive synthesis and the perhaps pre-linguistic rationality to which we just alluded and where *I* undergo reason, is always I-acts, and even the non-intellectual, non-cognitive acts are I-acts and in this sense acts of reason. In this sense to hold that reason "singularizes" us is merely to say that reason is always an I-act and the *I* is always singularized. This goes back to our early discussion of the tautological properties of the "myself" in Book 1, Chapter V.

One's singularity, and thereby one's unique essence or "myself," in being rational is revealed, as Castañeda and Sokolowski have noted (Book 1, Chapter II, §4), in the tacit transcendental pre-fix or declarative use of "I," that may or may not explicitly accompany the agency of manifestation, but which always is implied. Every articulation of the world reveals not only the world but the agent's responsibility for the articulation in the form of the transcendental pre-fix that declares the agent and in what mode her display of the world is made. That is, the agent reveals her responsibility through her signifying the quality or mode of the epistemic achievement. The authentic agent thus pays tribute to being in possession of a strong sense of knowing rather than a weak one. Thus when the achievement is expressed in a declarative statement and uses a strong epistemic formula wherein the agent lays claim to certain evidence upon which others may count she says "I know." Or when the evidence is weaker she indicates it to be less evident yet reliable, as in "I believe," or if it is doubtful or if it is worthy of suspicion because it is only a hunch, she uses the familiar disclaimers that display the mode of her uncertainty: "I've heard," "It could be," "It seems to me," etc.

This declaration of the agent of manifestation's responsibility may well be utterly tacit in the face of the various kinds of logical or mathematical necessity or the necessities of common sense and everyday practice. We may thus be tempted, like Simone Weil, to think of the core of the self as I-less and an impersonality. But even here there is personal freedom and responsibility because even logical and mathematical necessity require that we consent to the necessities, consent to be reasonable, logical, rational, etc.

This freedom of the person in the face of logical necessities comes further to light when we question the premises of arguments that before were unquestioned. Or this freedom comes to light when we examine the foundations of logic and mathematical evidence. Questioning may betray ignorance regarding the subject matter, as when the child persists in asking, "What does the earth rest on?," after asking about what all the things in her world rested on. But to say that she may not properly ask this question (i.e., she would not ask the question if she grasped what "resting on" means) cuts short the fertility of her question, even if it contains a confusion. It assumes that the necessities of nature or logic work on minds in the manner of a kind of efficient causality or that the mind works in the way the computer program design functions in response to the wiring of the electronic circuits of a logic machine. The question raises precisely basic questions about "resting on," gravity, and the relationship between freedom, meaning, and the nature of questioning. If her question is a logical "limit-question," i.e., one which may not be properly asked because all the other questions cannot properly happen without presupposing the state affairs this question raises, i.e., they presuppose the gravitational relationship of bodies in space to earth, then a whole host of basic issues in both physics and philosophy would never get discussed. If reason revels in and pays homage to the necessity of the way what is different may be brought together under the same, it also revels in and honors the freedom to see the same differently and raise questions about the sameness of the same.

In this inquiry into the primacy of "reason" over ipseity, and the question of whether human nature as constituted by reason enjoys a priority over or constitutes the singularity of the unique essence of the person, we open up a nest of difficulties to which we make no pretense of having done justice.[82]

§8. The Calling and the Analogous Love of the Self's Essence

Existenz, as one's ownmost self facing what is unconditionally important, is most basically manifest in love. Love, as the most centering, unifying, and comprehensive act, the position-taking that in and of itself is unconditioned and does not know of its possible termination or invalidation, is inseparable from one's most proper essence and reveals the bottomless ground and innermost center of I-ness of both the beloved and lover. There is thus revealed in love an infinity not only in terms of the unfathomable depth of the other ipseity but also in terms of the lover's capacity for dedication.

Here we wish to return to the theme of Existenz and love in connection with a topic opened by Husserl in a working manuscript. Here he refers to "a value that

is absolutely rooted in the I and original in the I out of its love (as absolute love)."
Such a love, Husserl goes on to say, renders null "objective value." On another
occasion he spoke of the truth of one's vocation as the truth of one's will, as "the
demand of one's own absolute value."[83]

What can be said of this "demand of one's own absolute value" that is rooted in
the I in an original way and comes to light in love and the truth of one's will? We
already came across something similar when we reflected on Kierkegaard's claim
that subjectivity as awakened by infinite passion is truth; it also surfaced in our
thinking about the peculiar subjectivity awakened by the non-objective revelation
of the "truth of will." We also uncovered it when we reflected on how the discovery
of being loved (in the typical youthful experience of one's being in love) is precious
because one is awakened to another's appreciation to some of the beauty which one
is aware of in oneself quite apart from one's properties, achievements, etc. We said
that then we see in the eyes of the one we believe to truly love us not only a won-
drous love that is not for the sake of anything else than ourselves, but also we see
something of the beauty of our true selves which even we manage to keep hidden
from us, but of which presumably we have an inkling.

But what is this "value" that is "absolutely rooted in the I" beside which objective value is as nothing? Recall that the context is (a) the teleological aspect of
our being in the world, our living our lives within a horizon of the best under the
circumstances and (b) the question of whether there is such a thing as the unique
person's unique path. The first consideration uses the metaphor of the "call" in so
far as we are beckoned by the ideal "more" to life. I am drawn to what the call beckons. Because I live futurally and in the Not Yet of my projects within the horizon of
my ineluctable self-inadequation and constitution of regulative ideals, I may, *with
a measure of caution*, be said to beckon to myself. (The caution is because of the
danger of regarding the horizon opened up by the empty intention or apperception
as a mere imagined projection and not a disclosure to myself of genuine possibility
transcendent to myself.)

The second consideration uses the metaphor further to signify a call that is recognized as addressed to me. It is not merely what I am drawn to but I recognize
that it is addressed uniquely to me and that it would be ungracious, if not unfor-
givable, if I were to spurn it. Metaphorically, I hear my name being called. Or, in
so far as analogy advances us beyond metaphor as providing a *ratio* or measured
proportion of concepts to one another: As the familiar sense of a call from someone
to me specifically awakens me to myself and draws me to the person addressing
me, so the truth of will awakens me to myself uniquely and beckons me to pursue
some agency. And, to play out the analogy, as in hearing myself addressed by my
name, I therefore must know my name, know the one being addressed by this
name, and esteem at some level me myself as being called in this way because
this call bespeaks my self-realization, of which I am now aware as incomplete or
unfulfilled.

Max Scheler had this in mind when he faulted Georg Simmel for failing to see
that the experience of the absolute ought presupposes the loving-valuing experience of one's unique "value-essence." It is this latter which founds the Ought of the

unique truth of one's calling more basically than the value of that to which one is beckoned. Because of the unique "value" I "place" on my unique essence, the call of the Ought has a uniquely compelling power over me. The scare-quotes here indicate precisely the problem of this section: Understanding a prior self-esteem that is inseparable from one's being oneself.

We can extend this thought by considering how the "call" might be understood to be analogous to an invitation to share in an exalted life or calling, e.g., to be not merely an heir to an extraordinary legacy but a call to be one who herself is to enrich and further the legacy. (Surely some forms of genius, some children born into famous distinguished families, some of the major professional careers, etc., can be so understood.) Such a call addressed to a zombie-like wanton person; or to one who is utterly estranged from herself because she is disposed to be the sort of person that powerful persons in her surroundings want her to be; or who thinks of herself as an objective physical thing accessible only in the third-person discourse about physical things; i.e., a call addressed to persons who are almost bereft of a sense of their own dignity, could very possibly not be heard, or be overlooked and disregarded. But a call addressed to one who is attuned to her own unique dignity and sense of her own agency would not miss the mark. Thus Scheler's point serves here: As the lived "value-essence," i.e. the sense of one's own unique dignity may be said to found the Ought, so in the metaphor of the call, the person who has this prior sense of her dignity, when she is called by name to a higher station or work, will already be open and ready for this invitation, and, indeed, find something fitting, even if surprising, in the call.

Scheler further wished to argue that one's unique value-essence, the uniqueness by which I am myself, is an absolute good in itself, even though it is also what is necessarily *good for me*. It is this good in itself, i.e., it is the essential, in this sense objective, value of my unique ipseity, which is independent of my intentional knowing and yet inseparably and necessarily lovingly lived by me as a good that founds the call. (Here again we approach the theme of the subjective side of ipseity as an "ontological value" which we earlier discussed (Book 1, Chapter IV, §20). This, in turn, founds the Ought which may well have to do with something existing in itself and transcendent to me. In this case the call would be free from capricious subjectivism. And, *pace* Kant, the self's unique value-essence is objective in itself, and thus in no way requires that it have universal validity or be a universal good for everyone.

The only quibble we have with Scheler in this matter is how the self-evaluing, or the original disclosure of the unique "value-essence," is a positing or thetic act like any objective valuation. Of course, if it truly is only in an act of valuing, it must be a position-taking founded on an objectifying act. But it seems to me that this original revelation of one's own value-essence is not, as Scheler has it, exclusively through a proper intentional love of oneself or through a being loved by another. Our position is that these both presuppose the prior non-intentional, non-reflective "love" for oneself, even though doubtless this latter "love" is but a feeble analogous, if not equivocal, form that is surely enriched by the intentional forms, whether from another, or from oneself.[84] In the following discussion we will be at pains to do justice to this feeble form of self-love, i.e., to appreciate how the transcendental dimension is presupposed in everything else we display and value; at the same time, we will show that, although it is to be presupposed in all proper senses of self-love in important senses it is ineffective in the absence of one's being the recipient of more proper senses of love.

It is thus clear why Scheler would want to claim that the unique value-essence was what was loved in some legitimate sense. The value-essence, or as we put it, the unique individual essence of the "myself," is manifestly an "ontological value" as it is personified in the world. The ontological value is evident to oneself in reflection and present to Others in the second- and third-person. And the way the unique essence's proper self-love takes form in the time of one's life must involve intentional acts. We here merely want to insist that these occasions of acts of proper self-love presuppose the prior non-intentional self-"love." The transcendental analogous self-love is a self-revelation of the unique "myself" in itself in its ongoing functioning. Yet it appears as properly good in itself only with the revelation of the truth of will or when one is awakened to oneself by the love of another. These revelations are what enable the realization that it is called to actualize oneself as a unique sort of person in the community of other unique ipseities. Thus the personification of "myself" as a dynamism toward what is intrinsically good in itself also appears under the aegis of the call, and thus also appear as good for me. Thus in awakening to one's call, even if it does not have the full drama of the disclosure of "the truth of will," there is a coincidence of a delight in that to which one is called as good in itself, and which at the same time is good for me; and at the same time it is an original non-intentional self-"love" which founds one's awakening to oneself as Existenz.

Our thesis in this section is: Of necessity there is an a priori transcendental constitutive self-esteeming sense of oneself. Here "self" refers to the "myself" in its personification with a center and periphery. The fuller transcendental self-love regards the voluminous self, i.e., takes in the periphery. The thinner, more merely formal, self-love affects the center, approaching the bare "myself." This latter is "formal," and merely as such may find no proper effective expression in the person's life. Yet we are also claiming that the proper self-determination of the person qua moral person requires an effective, material, not merely formal self-esteeming and self-respect. But this may be ineffective by reason of a personal-social history wherein one has never been enabled to come forth to oneself as having absolute value; or one has never come forth for oneself as demanding one's own absolute value; or for whatever reason, one has never responded to this exigency of one's own absolute value. As we shall see, especially when we discuss extreme forms of shame deriving from violation of the self, accompanied by the absence of any love of the person by Others, the original non-intentional self-love is sometimes merely formal and transcendental and thus impotent to secure the palpable self-esteem which provides for the self a robust integrity. Thus we will entertain instances where there will be a self-affecting/self-love that is without any real self-feeling and therefore incapable of feeling what Others feel. Someone who has lived a life without experiencing the intentional love by Others of herself, as this unique person in the world, has, we will claim, a kind of formal-transcendental self-love, but it is ineffective in her life. In such a severe "pathological" case the self is numbed. This is to say that without the actual intentional self-love mediated by being loved by Others, the non-reflexive transcendental self-love is ineffective in hindering the "death of the self" to which therapists or psychiatrists dealing with the "criminally insane" are all too often witness. (See our discussion below at §8, D.) For this reason, Scheler's position of the necessity for a reflective love of oneself or a being loved by the Other is never simply trumped by our claim for a transcendental non-reflective form of self-"love."

The position we here advocate of a non-reflective self-love seems prima facie absurd if we regard the self-love not in a loose or analogous sense but rather in the familiar sense of a distinctive act. Thus we may put our position in the form of the question: Is there not a kind of transcendental self-love of our own unique individual essence that has to be taken account of if we are to account for the teleological drift of our personal being as it becomes evident in the revelation of oneself as Existenz and in the inmost I revealed in loving devotion, friendship, and existential communication? Prescinding from the target of devotion, and attending merely abstractly to the I myself revealed in another's devotion to me or in my devotion to another, there is a disclosure of myself through a self-affection, a "love," not directed intentionally by me at myself as other to myself and as beyond all qualities, but rather an "affection for" myself beyond all qualities.

This, in its most formal and ineffective functioning, is the elemental non-ascriptive self-awareness that adumbrates and is the condition for the indexical non-ascriptive, non-identifying self-awareness. (See Book 1.) Here we call it "love" because of the way it keeps, preserves, and sustains the "myself's" primal presencing. But there are other forms of an "affection for oneself as beyond all qualities," as in the way one comes to light in the truth of will or being loved. These are not the familiar forms of love of oneself, e.g., egotism or egocentrism, which describe not only the infant, but many of us most of the time. Nor would it be the philosophical hedonist, or rationally self-enlightened, or philosophical solipsist who places everything as a means to himself or places himself above everything else. Nor would it be the widely-disseminated injunction to use love of oneself as the measure of the love of one's neighbor, nor is it a rational self-love, recommended by both Aristotle and Kant, by which one appropriately attends to one's needs and interests. Instead, here we have in mind nothing like an intentional act, whether cognitive or emotional. Rather what we have in mind in the following sub-sections is a complex weave of forms of pre-intentional self-"love." Although we here discuss the most elemental form of self-"love" of the "myself's" primal presencing and temporalizing which is foundational for all intentionality and therefore all forms of love, we also shall consider the self-love of the center of the personal I, one's Existenz, which coincides with the minimalist transcendental self-love of I-ness in the constitution of and responsiveness to the personal essence that the "myself" personifies. Even this self-love is prior to our reflective love of ourselves as an embodied person in the world with others. We undertake this study of a multi-stranded transcendental self-"love" because we regard self-love and self-respect, however analogous, as the condition for being wakeful to any robust sense of a calling. This study has several strands: (A) self-"affection," self-"awareness," and the "flesh"; (B) original self-"love" as self-"trust"; (C) self-"love" and the love of living; (D) Kant and Fichte on self-respect; (E) self-"love" as a condition of dread of one's annihilation; (F) self-"love" as the basis for self-constitution and self-preservation; (G) Original self-"valuing" and shame.

A. Self-"Affection," Self-"Awareness," and the "Flesh"

As we have said, in its most transcendental and formal functioning, the kind of self-love we are proposing here is so elemental that the term "love" can be used only in a loose analogy. This becomes clearer when we see that this original "affection" may be extended to include the non-reflexive presence of oneself to oneself. We can take our cue here from Husserl, even though it is Michel Henry who has brought this to the fore in phenomenology. Husserl once called this original affection "first-belief" so as to distinguish it from the doxastic positing or thetic, position-taking intentional stances by which we greet and display the world and the things in the world with syntax.[85] The "myself's" primal presencing, the "primal impression's" very essence, is to have this so-called first-belief in its being present to itself in its presencing of the Now of the stream of consciousness and the elemental flow of time. It is by this that the "myself's" self-luminosity is thickly self-manifest with the body and the world and it is this which by its nature can never be modalized or invalidated. We see here how odd the expression "belief" is here (to say nothing of the oddness of "love") in as much as there is no positing in the sense of predicating and no valuing intentionality. There is only the self-luminous, self-shining self-affection. It is clearly an affirmation or basic belief whose actuality and certainty cannot be invalidated, doubted, or mentally eliminated because it is the presupposition for all actualities, validities, and considerations that may be mentally eliminated (*wegdenkbar*). (We discussed some of these issues of the awareness of "inner time" in Book 1, Chapter VII.)

Normally, and there is good reason for this, phenomenologists want this primal self-presence to be *sui generis*, i.e., to be a form of "knowing" that is without any parallel in intentional life because without its ongoing actuality there would be no intentional life whatsoever. It is simply self-"luminosity" of the "myself" in its self-affecting through the primal streaming as the condition for all intentionality by which intentional life is "lived" and "alive" to itself and not unconsciousness; it has no content over and above being intentionality's and the I's self-presence in its primal streaming. Therefore one is at pains to make sure that it is bereft of any descriptions that surreptitiously sneak in "the reflection-theory of self-awareness." (See Book 1, Chapter II, especially §6.) Therefore there is the caveat that this is not to be equated with any kind of intentionality. Yet we see that already this maxim appears to be violated by the terms "self-affection" and "primal belief." Because the self is the origin of all valuing, and because of its own upsurging into self-presence in the world, values in the proper sense come to be. Because the upsurging is inseparably a primal affecting, and because all other senses of the love of the self presuppose an elemental love in this self-affecting, we claim for this original self-presence analogous senses of valuing, affection, and love.

Both Husserl and, in a magnificently orchestrated way, Michel Henry, echo Aristotle and call this self-manifestation and primal affection "life." Henry proposes that we use the word "flesh" to be synonymous with this sense of life.[86] (We discussed the "flesh" in connection with erotic love in Book 1, Chapter IV, §15.) The "myself" in its personification is immersed in bodiliness, nature, time, and intersubjectivity; all these are modes of "flesh" as self-affecting/self-othering, i.e., they all are forms of self-awareness in their awareness of the alterity within time's passing, the body's externality, and the presence of the Other. All of my life is pervaded by this self-feeling, and this self-feeling/ self-affirming that goes in advance is presupposed by my I-me or position-taking acts. All action is pervaded by the feeling of the actuality of the original self-affecting of I-can, which is itself an experience of "the flesh." This transcendental self-affection that goes in advance of all properly conceived affections (as specific pleasures or pains), emotions, desires, satisfactions of desires, etc. is the self-"affection," self-"affirmation," self-"delight," self-"valuing," etc., of first-person life in itself.

B. Original Self-"Love" as Self-"Trust"

The primal presencing is not merely an original, albeit improper and merely analogous, self-"affection," self-"delight," and self-"belief," it is a primal self-"trust." We may think of this self-trust most basically in terms of the I-can, as the original self-affecting and being given to ourselves, the original gift of our possibility to ourselves. I am able to act, to move, to reflect, etc., because I am given to myself. The original basis for this is the "myself's" self-aware primal presencing. This presencing is always also my keeping or saving the original presencing and being given to myself. Each primal presencing is always a keeping that is also an integrating, i.e., it is always also a passive synthesis, an original association. This means it is a saving of what was just presenced. But this keeping and gathering-integrating of what it has kept is also and, "at the same time," a gathering into itself of that not-yet which it is about to presence, and "at the same time" both of these are gathered as the retentions and protentions of the myself's primal presencing that is always also a primal self-presencing. The original *extasis* or centrifugality of temporality as retention and protention is always also an original gathering, a centripetal motion.

We have said that the "myself's" primal presencing is a "happening" upon which all display as the display of an agent of manifestation depends. We have also said that this presencing is irrepressible and also is a "first-belief" and primal "self-affection" which has elemental durations as their correlate. For these durations to be established and secured as the sort of entities that I may orient myself towards, the "myself's" primal presencing must "possess itself" and "count on itself," count on its original keeping-preserving-integrating. In ordinary language we speak of "having time" or "taking time" and measure this often by, e.g., looking at a clock. But when I use a clock to tell the time, I am making an inquiry as to how much time I have left, or how much time I may "take." Yet, as Heidegger has claimed, "if I am to *take* time then I must have it somewhere or other. In a certain sense we always have time. If often or for the most part we have no time that is merely a privative mode of our *original having of time*."[87] This original having of time is the original self-having, self-preserving. It is the taking time of primal presencing and its primal retaining, primal synthesizing and integrating. All of our agency, all our possibility (one's I-can), and all our passivity rests on this original having of time. This means not only that all of my doings take time, but that my taking of time to do whatever I do builds on the irrepressible "temporizing" of the "myself's" primal presencing and presupposes the original having of time. Further, this taking time is a most elemental trust even more basic than the trust in my I-can as founded on my lived bodily kinaestheses. This is because these latter have a duration that presupposes the "temporizing" which constitutes the elemental having of power or capacity. Because it is a trusting in the primal presencing and its passive synthesizing that founds my free intentional agency it is a transcendental self-trust. Further, in order for anything to appear or disappear primal presencing must be able to take the "times" it has taken and is about to take. Without the original taking and having of time and trust in this, there are no intentional acts, no achievings/achievements, no appearing of what appears.

Indeed, without this primal passive synthesis or primal self-trust there is nothing present whatsoever. This self-affecting self-trust is that without which there is no sameness and/or difference, no duration, no discrimination. Although it is what I supremely "count on" in the sense that all powers, capacities, and resources which I have and am presuppose it, here there is not a proper trusting, not an act of believing-*in*, not an active rallying around and taking a position with regard to a trusted-in source of power. Rather all such acts presuppose this self-trust. They of necessity implicitly trust in this self-trust. Further the self-trust "is counted on" (the passive voice seems less inappropriate) by my simply "being there," "awake," and doing nothing besides simply "taking my time."

We take the liberty of stretching this transcendental "trust," which is also a self-"affecting" and self-"believing," to be also a self-"love" and self-"esteeming." And it is precisely this that is menaced by the presence of death and the other negative crisis limit-situations. The danger of death is the danger to the continuation of myself as an incessant being given to myself by and through which I affirm, esteem, and count on myself as the basis for my life in the world. And with the prospect of the annihilation of me myself there is the accompanying prospect of the annihilation of all there is. It is fitting that the presence of death is unsettling because its third-person presence threatens the unique individual essential self-presence of the "myself" and its irrepressible self-"belief," self-"esteem," and self-"trust." (See Book I, chapter VIII.)

We experience an essential danger whenever we experience either the threat of annihilation of our essential self or when we face a choice by which we establish ourselves in opposition to ourselves even though we continue to be given to ourselves and continue to affirm, esteem, and trust ourselves in this transcendental elemental way. The limit-situation of calling, in contrast, is a promise of salvation, a promise of a path wherein one's essential being is made secure. But even here, as we have seen, there is a possibility of tragedy and the shipwreck of the self. And the specter of error, self-deception, and the failure to show up for oneself – a failure which itself would depend on the elemental self trust – can never be absolutely ruled out.

C. Self-"Love" and Love of Living

What we here are calling attention to is a more basic kind of self-"affection," self-"delight," or self-"enjoyment" of what each refers to by "myself" that perhaps Aristotle had in mind when he waxed eloquently on the unique delight each of us takes in his life and which seems to be at the basis of all other delights.[88] "Life" here then is not so much a biological term as what we mean in "the living of life" or "living through" an event or an experience. It is the non-intentional self-awareness that makes the intentional life a conscious life. This life is incessantly self-affirmed and analogously "delighted in" throughout the course of life, regardless of the turns life takes! The oddness of the self-love is evident when one considers that even the person who cannot live with himself because of his failure to do his duty presupposes this original "love" of himself for himself that accompanied his agency before and after his crime. The person who radically renounces or betrays her life still "loves" herself, still "self-affects," and this is the cause of her misery: She has betrayed herself, the sense of which is both in the betrayed self and in the betraying self; it is in the non-reflective self-affection, as well as in the act that turned from this sense of self. But this misery is in reference to a person on the verge of regret and repentance. It does not reflect the imagined person who we earlier described as "damned," i.e., who is aware of her being at odds with her original dignity through committing herself forever to being the sort of person she is. Perhaps we can even say that the person committing suicide ineluctably affirms and esteems his singular individuality and the essential aloneness of his essence and by "taking his life with his own hands" he is loving himself in spite of the cards life has dealt him. In his self-destruction he is affirming himself as above this mess in which he has become immersed.

D. Kant and Fichte on Self-Respect

Kant pointed to the position for which we wish to argue without taking the step we find necessary. We also here disregard the consideration that on this point Kant seems to be arguing for the respect for the *idea* of personality and humanity as these ideas reside or are instantiated in me; in such a case the respect would not be for me myself as a unique individual, but for me as an instance of humanity. Yet matters are not quite so simple because Kant distinguishes, at least on occasion, the person (*Persönlichkeit*) from humanity. On one occasion the latter is what is a phenomenon, the former has to do essentially with one's freedom, and is not a mere phenomenon but belongs in the noumenal dimension. The person is defined as a susceptibility for respect (*Achtung*) for the moral law. Such a susceptibility for respect is a susceptibility for self-respect in the sense that respect for law is respect for oneself as a unique will freely determining itself according to its rational lights, i.e., according to its basic deference for itself as reasonable rather than a wanton. He then adds that the moral law, which is inseparably tied up with one's respect for oneself as inherently of worth and reasonable, is not properly called a predisposition for the person, but rather it is the personality itself. Respect for one's inherent dignity in itself and reasonableness is what it means to be a person. By "person" (*Persönlichkeit*) he says he means humanity regarded "purely intellectually," i.e., apart from sense intuition. How for Kant we *know* anything (noumenally) apart from sense intuition, especially ourselves as free, is a difficult matter. (See Book 1, Chapter V, §5.) Here we would say that what Kant has in mind approximates both what in one's own case is first-personal non-reflective self-awareness, and in the second- and third-person case – even though it would be a tough case to make – a mode of apperception which targets the non-sortal ipseity as in and through but beyond the human or personified being.[89]

Kant notes how "the honest man" avoids even small misdeeds so that he does not have to be disdainful subsequently of himself. He also points out the consolation such a person takes in knowing that, at the time of his greatest misery and misfortune, which he could have avoided if he failed to do his duty, he in fact was faithful to his duty and did not have to be ashamed of himself. He notes that this consolation is not "happiness" nor is it connected with a future threat or reward. No one wants to land in such miserable circumstances, but nevertheless such an upright person chooses to live with himself and does not have to tolerate living unworthily in his own eyes.[90]

Kant here points to a sense of ourselves of which we are aware in a most intimate way that is prior to and independent of our agency. Likewise it is prior to and independent of a self-esteem dependent on our being esteemed by Others or by ourselves by reason of some properties we have displayed. He put this on one occasion in this way: "A human being regarded as a person, that is as the subject of a morally practical reason,... possesses a dignity...by which he exacts *respect* for himself from all other rational beings in the world."[91] Here "person" is not identified with "human being" but rather with the "subject of a morally practical reason." As such the person possesses a "dignity." This dignity clearly has a form of manifest evidence, evident foremost, (as Stephen Darwall would put it), in the second-person situation whereby the person manifestly has the authority to make claims and manifestly the competence to recognize claims. Furthermore, presumably for Kant, this dignity is not unknown to the subject herself. This sense of herself as having the power to exact respect serves as the basis for a basic self-esteem and sense of having "rights."

As we saw in our discussions of conscience, we wish to cherish, i.e., preserve, protect and honor this basic sense of ourselves that has dignity and worth in itself and to which we have given our allegiance. We have said that we are addressed by this constituted essential personal self to which we have given our allegiance (and respect). We have also said that here in conscience this is ourselves at a distance from ourselves and it is oneself at one's center and core, one's Existenz as the center of the personified "myself," that is addressed and called to respond. Not responding appropriately degrades one's personal essence as well as one's core. We may not say that whereas the former has contingent properties, the latter is who we are inescapably at our non-sortal core. We may not say that in this latter case we have to do with the pure propertyless transcendental "myself." Rather we have to do with Existenz as the center of the "myself" personified. The "myself" as the unique essence, form, and bare substrate of the person is not to be identified with the propertied essential self, nor is it simply to be identified with Existenz. However, in Existenz, it comes forth as core and center of the personal self. In this moment of emphatic "personification" it thus takes on the property of being the center of the person. It is here where it may take on the forms of self-approbation or reproach. Thus in failing to respond appropriately to the dictates of conscience I find reason to contemn inseparably myself as Existenz or center of my propertied essence, as well as myself as constituted propertied personal essence with the distinctive qualities. I "know" in the distinctive essential way that is constitutive of being a person that if I honor this sense of myself, "myself" personified as the sort of person I am and want to be, I will be honorable and at peace with myself; if I neglect or fail it, I will be ashamed and disdainful of myself. This sense of ourselves accompanies all our agency. (Cf. our discussions of conscience above in Chapter III, §§3–6.)

Yet it remains true that the "myself" as who I am as this unpropertied unique essence and substrate of my personal being as such enjoys an "innocence" and transcendence to such self-ascriptions of praise and blame. Here, in this transcendental dimension abstracted from its personification, there is not ever the coincidence of who one is with what sort of person one is. Here in this transcendental agency of the nominative, genitive, and dative of self-manifestation of conscience's bearing witness to oneself as Existenz, coming to expression in the self-attunement (*Befindlichkeit*) of being OK with oneself or profoundly disdainful of oneself the "I myself" is not itself blamed or praised. My remorse with myself bears witness to the fact of the basic esteem of myself; my impulses to remedy the situation bear witness to my not being coincident with my despicable self.

In this transcendental self-esteeming and self-affecting as the very condition for the self-display of conscience there obviously is not properly a *love* or *respect for* ourselves rooted in intentionality's bringing to light and valuing endearing and praiseworthy qualities. This we may say is evident in Kant's notion that the person *is* the respect for itself as of inherent worth and as will self-determining itself through its self-illumination. Such intentional acts of love and respect for myself, just like those that bring to light the ipseity of the Other beyond all properties, would, we suggest, presuppose the original self-esteem as constitutive of the myself's primal presencing. However we characterize what this sense of ourselves is (in terms of self-"love," self-"respect," etc.), it is surely not a reflective and intentional presence of the personal essence and its core to itself. And if love and respect are the way we characterize this original self-esteem, and if these are properly intentional acts, then the sense of original love and respect at issue here is at best only analogous.

But can we be said to love or esteem ourselves in any meaningful, however analogous, way when we have been despicable? Is it no less difficult or impossible in our own case as in that of loving Others? We have earlier (Book 1, Chapter IV) addressed the difficulty in regard to Others of transcending the character in favor of the transcendent ipseity. The answer in regard to our self-esteem is similarly that the self-reproach that surfaces in our failure to live up to our basic sense of our dignity and self-ideal does not ever obliterate the original ontological value or dignity of the "myself." Indeed, one's self-reproach assumes the original sense of oneself as more than and superior to the reprehensible action or habit with which I have burdened myself. Yet it is evident that for one stepped in shame and guilt, being awakened to the original *dignitas* might appear as a "grace" or require the blindness of trusting faith that is required of us in loving Others who have lost their loveable qualities. Nevertheless, our position is that we can, with appropriate reflection, pry loose the "myself" with its inherent dignity from the reprehensible actions with which it becomes burdened in its personification. This self-respect or self-love is constitutive of ourselves as the elemental affection or disposition to constitute our wills sheerly on the basis of ourselves as rational and capable of enlightened self-determination and not be driven by mere caprice, need, etc. Here Sokolowski's major theme that the person is most basically an agent (and servant) of truth resurfaces.

In Fichte we find similar themes and worries. Fichte rightly places respect and self-respect at the center of all ethics and morality. Respect is named an *affect* and thus not the fruit of an act of understanding. (For us, its earliest appearance in regard to the Other is in empathic presencing; see Book 1, Chapter IV; for Fichte it burgeons here also, but it also has to do with the basic ineradicable reverence (respect) for the truth and objectivity – even in arguing for a solipsistic position.) Although it can lie dormant it cannot be extinguished. In being concerned about a world in which things can be respected and in being engaged in respecting Others there is developed at the same time in us a drive to self-respect. And this drive likewise is ineliminable or extinguishable. For Fichte a thought-experiment here is decisive: To be coldly contemptuous of oneself, to regard oneself detachedly as worthless, is not possible for anyone.[92]

Yet Fichte also says that it is not possible to respect oneself when one behaves contemptuously. This is uncontroversial and does not contradict the impossibility of being coolly disdainful of oneself. When one is so disdainful because of what one has done it is not a matter of detachment and being cool toward oneself, but of a sharp pain and regret in regard to that about which one is supremely concerned. Further, Fichte also holds that the drive for self-respect is not extinguishable. May we not take this drive for self-respect as a kind of affirmation of the worth of oneself and of the effort to restore one's unity with oneself and one's respectability? This seems to be Fichte's position. When one finds that one has lost one's own self-respect, the self-disdain is so painful that the person either attempts to flee from himself or distract himself from himself, perhaps seeking an external basis for self-respect. He may attempt to rationalize and come up with new standards upon which to base a new sense of self-respect. But one cannot be reconciled to oneself in one's center or heart unless the bases for the self-respect are met.

But does it not seem that to undertake this reconciliation there would have to be even here a measure of self-love and self-respect already in play? Can we not make the case for a basic ineradicable self-respect and self-love that is at the heart of the anguish over one's having betrayed oneself? One cannot be pained, or the pain will be considerably less, at having offended or betrayed someone about whom one does not at all care about. (Of course, there can and should be pain in regard to oneself for having done this.) Is there not something analogous in regard to the sufferings one experiences in one's having betrayed oneself and one's allegiances? If one cares little about oneself (about "one's soul") there will be less pain perhaps for one's "dead" soul, no or little pain in betraying oneself. Of course, if self-respect is taken to mean an intentional attitude based on the worth manifest in positive qualities, then, of course, a transcendental self-respect is ruled out. But so are all our other terms such as love, esteem, etc. Because we have to do here with what is a priori and transcendental, we have claimed that there here is only an analogy.

Fichte says, when a person is so dragged down by shame and guilt that he approaches despair we may attempt to show the person that he is not without some goodness and we may point out that there is in him a hidden ineradicable goodness. Fichte says the good principle in every person that cannot be eradicated is the condition for the possibility of being able to regard something disinterestedly and respect something – without any regard for self-interest. (How this is an "affection" and not the very nature of intellect as the agency of manifestation is not clear to this reader.) Fichte's chief argument on behalf of this is that if anyone argues for the exclusively self-interested position he does so presumably because it is true in itself, and not because he gets something out of it. But inseparable from this possibility to appreciate disinterestedly something is the drive to want to respect oneself and the impossibility that anyone can sink so low that he could disdain himself in an unperturbed cool way. This for Fichte is convincing because the thought experiment imagining the contrary itself brings the evidence.

Fichte does not entertain a case of dissociation, which itself might have been precipitated by such a crisis in conscience and self-disdain, where one might indeed coolly and placidly harm or disdain one's reprehensible personal self. Admittedly that would be a form of illness and the normal person's involving herself in the thought experiment would be sufficient proof of the position. Nevertheless, even in the case of dissociation the observing dissociating "myself" would still have a transcendental self-affecting that constitutes the dissociated personal essence from which it is estranged and detached. Even if *I* dissociate myself from my personal essence; even if I am not any longer JG Hart, I am still myself and as such the primal presencing of the dissociated JG Hart. Further, presumably in this case JG Hart would be part of my ownness and thus would be more me than John Doe, whom I might also despise; it is precisely because I am aware of JG Hart as part of my ownness that I especially despise JG Hart. (These were central themes in Book 1.) But this primal presencing itself, we have suggested, is pervaded by an analogous self-esteem and self-affection. Our central point here is that this ineradicable "drive for self-respect" supports our claim for a kind of self-respect and self-affection that has nothing to do with the merits of our agency. It as a drive is an affirmation (or pre-affirmation) of what I ineluctably treasure and in this sense "respect" or "love" and am always in danger of losing. As such it has to do with an original sense of oneself as a trans-propertied "myself." (Cf. especially §§8, A, B above and §8, G below.)

E. Self-"Love" as the Condition for the Dread of One's Annihilation

May we not say similarly that there is a unique kind of "love" of our ownmost essence in play in the dread of annihilation occasioned by the realization of my death? The "negative" limit-situations, i.e., those apart from love, calling, and happiness, are crisis situations precisely because they endanger the fundamental analogous self-affirmation, self-valuing or self-esteem that anonymously accompanies us throughout life. Yet these situations, because they have to do with what endangers the essential I myself, endanger this elemental self-affirmation or love of our essence. We have already seen how death presents us with the prospect of our annihilation. This nullifying of myself is not merely a possible fact but it is the ultimate danger. Of course, if it is true that when death is I am not, then it is true that there is no danger for me. Yet, as we saw, this hypothetical truth, even if internally cogent, is not decisive because even if the third-person apprehension of ourselves as absolutely ephemeral is taken to be true, nevertheless this epistemic stance does not eliminate the first-person sense of ourselves. And this first-person sense of ourselves is one wherein there is an ongoing self-presencing and self-esteeming. Further, this self-esteeming has to do not only with who I am but also is an ongoing esteeming of my ideal self and my power to live in accord with this ideal.

Because I cannot conceive my non-being in the first-person I cannot help but think of my death as my loss of what, in a special odd sense, is most dear. That is, I cannot help but think of myself, at the moment of death, as still being (alive) while I lose my life as a person in the world. (See our discussions in Book 2, Chapter I; also Book 1, Chapter VI and the beginning of Chapter VII.) In the utterly non-reflective first-person sense of myself I am not identified with any thing I have or my being a person in the world. If this is so, then what do I dread? What can I lose? And yet this loss is the loss of what is most important at least in the respect that it is the condition for having or losing anything or everything. But there is also the compelling evidence of the third-person perspective: When she dies she is absolutely absent, gone, annihilated. Therefore the irrepressible suspicion: With death I myself am annihilated.

I myself as the lived pre-condition which loses the condition for its pursuit or enjoyment of what is most important, i.e., its proper constitution of its personal being, is itself what is also the most important in the sense that with our being awakened to Existenz we are awakened both to what is most cherished as well as what does the cherishing, and to that for which we alone are uniquely responsible. The other limit-situations of guilt, suffering, and struggle, likewise confront us with this question of possible ultimate loss. They also highlight the loss as the danger of losing oneself by way of being permanently alienated from oneself. This danger can happen by reason of one's being an agent and co-agent in the world. Here one takes initiatives and initiatives are undertaken by one's co-agents over which one loses control. Thus one finds oneself implicated in and identified inextricably with what is alien to the sort of person one wants to be. Further and no less constantly one is inveterately not transparent to oneself and finds that, at decisive moments, one has the capacity to fail to show up for oneself. In each limit-situation there is the sense of being given to ourselves at once as the masters of our fate and, at the same time, imperiled by the fate that is not merely external but also internal. This sense of ourselves as fault-lined masters of ourselves goes beyond all that over which we have mastery.

There is symmetry in the way we ineluctably are, on the one hand, self-affirming, self-delighting, and self-enjoying and yet buffeted, bruised, and demeaned by our inadequacies as well as by the blows of fate and, on the other hand, the sense of being given to ourselves as masters of our fate who of necessity are forced to live a life laced with dangers to our essential being. In the self-affirming as well as in the self-mastery there is a distinctive self-affection amidst the challenges of chance and fate. This is one way of accounting for the emergence of the quest for our vocation. We seek a path which we may tread where we will ensure not losing ourselves as well as fulfilling ourselves.

F. Self-"Love" as the Basis for Self-Constitution and Self-Preservation

Recall that one's personal essence is constituted as having a transtemporal validity by position-taking acts. I constitute myself as a personal essence with acts whose validity is "from now on." Even here there is an expression of a "basic" love of oneself because one establishes oneself as transtemporal, i.e., as not completely at the mercy of time and existing irrelatively to the passage of moments subsequent to the position-taking acts. Through our position-takings we overcome the ravages of the flux of our life in the world and our stream of consciousness by establishing idealities and identities that transcend the temporal flux. These idealities and identities have corresponding transtemporal habits and dispositions. In this sense our ineluctable position-taking acts may be said to reveal a desire for "eternity" or at least for what enjoys a measure of permanence that is beyond the ravages of time; they are ways in which we ineluctably give a transtemporal sense to ourselves and our lives. This, of course, can turn into something perverse and something that the no-self or no-ownership metaphysics and soteriologies of the self rightly worry about: a clinging to an idol that is inimical to self-transformation and that conceals what is most important and essential. Our point here is that it is ineluctable. We have seen how this transtemporal shape bestowed on my world and myself is brought about by an ideal that emerges in the course of life. The love of the self-ideal is not a love of something other than oneself. This ideal is inseparable from our unique ipseity; indeed, we have regarded it as its "call." But this self-shaping and self-affirming of what is transcendent to the "myself" presupposes a prior self-affirming of the "myself" for the sake of which this self-affirming, self-shaping is done.

The derived self-affirming is of me myself as a person in the world. Further, this constitution of me as this person in the world is within the call of the horizon of the ideal of the "best under the circumstances." But when this call is heard as mine, there is the ideal of bringing my personal self under the sway of this call, of giving to my whole life the direction which is in tune with this sense of I myself.

My position-taking as a pursuit of permanence and transtemporality is an affirmation and actualization of my unique "I myself" as a presence in the world. Yet I am more than this actualization. Again, this is where we may honor some of the concerns of the no-ownership theory of the self. Yet the self that is awakened and called in the loving devotion to what embodies the infinite ideal is not unknown to us prior to the distinctive call of the vocation. It is known throughout our life, and more explicitly in conscience and the Ought.

The entire theme of the ideal of one's true self presupposes an odd kind of love of oneself, not merely as one actually is but more properly as one essentially is, i.e., as an essentially personified individual essence or "myself." And when we think of the massive changes of which one is capable, as in a conversion, do we not recognize a kind of love of one's self beyond all the qualities which accrued to it by one's agency, i.e., a love of that one who I was, who also was the one who wanted to change, at least at some level, and also a love of that sort of one into whom I wanted to change and into whom I was called to change? In my radical change I do not ever wish to annihilate myself in order that another take my place. Rather, I want to be that one who my conscience and self-ideal bear witness to, who also is me as both whom I have constituted and by whom I am constituted or determined by way of the "voice" and the "call."[93]

From the perspective of this work we can say that the state of being ultimately "doomed" or "damned" would obtain when one becomes aware that the sort of person one has established himself as being, and for whose perpetuity he is prepared to sacrifice everything, is essentially at odds with and opposed to who one is in one's "myself" and who one is in his original dignity, self-love and calling. Again, the real possibility for this is a matter that can not be decided "for us all" in the third-person, but, if at all, only in the first-person. Obviously it assumes that it is meaningful to assign to the propertyless "myself" the (tautological?) property of a calling that could be in essential conflict with the actual constituted personal essence. This would require perhaps an elaborate "likely story" – one which we will soon undertake to tell.

G. Original Self-"Valuing" and Shame

We are proposing that the self-presence in play in the Ought and conscience and the calling always involve a kind of self-affirmation and self-love. The witness of myself to myself in conscience and the call as well as the authentic response to these witnesses are both a kind of self-affirmation and self-love. This self-affirmation and self-love is basic and perduring because it is inseparable from I myself.

If we think of what one esteems or loves as always transcendent in some respect, if we think of what appears as the loveable or valuable requiring the loving or valu-ing "myself" for its display or sustained phenomenality then, in the case of the original self-affection that we attach to the very agency of manifestation, there is, at bottom, a self-esteem, love, and value that are "in some sense" coincident with the *myself*. (See A. above.) In the original upsurge, self-affection, or self-presencing of myself in the primal presencing of the hyletic streaming, there is not yet the proper sense of esteem nor is value posited; yet the self-"affection," self-"esteem," and primal presencing, and myself here are all coincident with one another in the original upsurging.

In this view, it is not quite correct to hold that the "myself" as the principle at the root of the display of values in the world, and as the principle objectified in my personal being in the world, itself is not a value as something estimable. Recall our introductory remarks to §8 where we cited Husserl's reference to "a value that is absolutely rooted in the I and original in the I out of its love (as absolute love)…" This we tied into the truth of one's vocation, as the truth of one's will, as "the demand of one's own absolute value."[94] Of course, the I myself is not a value in the sense that I, *as* the principle of valuing, and of values, as the display of the goods of the world, am not myself able to be the target of a value perception or predication. As the principle of valuing, I am not the object of a position-taking (*wertnehmen*, value-perceiving) act. In the case of the truth of will and my coming forth to myself as Existenz there is "a demand of my own absolute value." This sense of oneself as demanding one's own absolute value is to be distinguished from the "valuing" one may ascribe to oneself as the agent of manifestation of value, where there is not a question of the truth of will. In the latter case of the truth of will there is doubtless a kind of value ascribed to one's personal essence at its core. But in the case of the "value" ascribed to the agent of manifestation there is no such lived evaluation or ascription of a distinguishable property belonging to me. Rather, the value surfaces in our reflecting on this agency in its formal feature as a self-affecting. But as the self-aware principle of value I "appreciate" myself in a distinctive way, namely as precisely the self-aware, self-affecting principle to whom and for whom values come to light and are appreciated. Because I am the principle who is inseparable from value and valuing, the "self-valuing" here cannot possibly be understood to stand in competition with other values, as does egotism or self-esteem in the proper intentional sense.[95]

Thus the original albeit analogous self-love and self-affirming of I myself is more basic and perduring than that kind which is the more or less explicit taking delight in oneself as this constituted person in the world; it is more basic than the rich awareness of the absolute demand for one's value that arises in the truth of will; it is more basic than the tenor and mood of self-esteem that accrues through accomplishing what one sets out to do and, perhaps also as a bonus, receiving recognition for one's efforts. All of life, as we have seen, may be thought of as an uninterrupted project of empty intentions seeking fulfillment. A life in which there is seamless continuity of the filling of empty intentions in terms of uninterrupted satisfaction, "the happy life" or joy-filled life, is not, as Husserl himself has said, to be regarded as a reasonable goal, even if it is not essentially or logically contradictory. It perhaps is a blessed or a divine life, but it is not what we know either as the actual pattern or as the drift of life. (This is not to say that this odd fleeting presence of moments of "happiness" is irrelevant and unimportant for thinking about "transcendence.") Nevertheless there can be a kind of "reflective joy" and self-esteem that emerges out of life, in spite of the failures, surds, and calamities that befall us. And as there is conceivable the ideal of a life lived with this even keel of equanimity, self-esteem and self-trust, so then there is in this proper, pre-reflective or reflective self-esteem a most fundamental kind of moral excellence that facilitates or makes possible other virtues, inseparable from the ideal of one's moral personality.[96] But again, as we said above, this self-esteem and self-respect derives from the more basic sense of self-"love."

We can get at this basic self-love, self-esteem, or self-respect – we use these terms interchangeably here because they depend on a feeble analogy – also by considering shame. Shame, like all the emotions, bears witness to how we have constituted ourselves as beings in the world with Others. Shame is symbolically expressed in the biblical account in *Genesis*, Chapter 3, of discovering one's nakedness before one another and the need to cover up the nakedness. It is of interest that nakedness as in nudity displays what we have in common with very small variations and what does *not* distinguish us. It is our clothing that better expresses to the world the individuality of our interpersonal public persons. The case of being ashamed of one's nakedness as in *Genesis* Chapter 3, perhaps expresses awareness of one's inmost unique interiority (the "bare" substrate) before the gaze of God, and one seeks in vain to hide that betrayal of the original innocence, with which they just identified, with clothing. Our English word, "shame," comes from an old Germanic word whose roots mean to cover up or clothe oneself. In some languages, the same words are used for shame and the genitals, e.g., *Schamteile, pudenda.*[97]

Clearly not all shame has to do with sexuality and bodiliness, but this feeling of oneself exposed at one's core and the bodily comportment of fearfully protecting or hiding what is exposed seems to cover the various kinds of shame. James Gilligan, upon whom we are here dependent, cites Darwin: "an ashamed person can hardly endure to meet the gaze of those present…" And Gilligan quotes also Eric Erickson: "he who is ashamed would like to force the world not to look at him, not to notice his exposure. He would like to destroy the eyes of the world."[98]

Shame is a famous datum for comparative anthropology. Most of us have at least anecdotal information showing that what shames members of a particular culture does not cause shame for persons of another culture. What is shameful in one culture might well be prudishness in another. Fig leafs over the genitalia, after all, are "less modest" than bikinis.[99]

In our framework the theme of shame hearkens back to our discussion of "conscience" in Chapter III. Shame, like conscience, is a way in which we are borne witness to by the person or self we have constituted. The one borne witness to thus is not perfectly coincident with the one bearing witness. We have proposed that the self to which is borne witness is Existenz, i.e., oneself called into question in regard to what is of unconditional importance. Shame only rarely has this appeal to Existenz, to our core selves, even though at the moment it may seem so, as in the case of appearing naked; oneself is not typically in question but rather it is only an aspect of ourselves of which we are ashamed and seek to hide. In the case of naked-ness, through ancient and intensely taboo-laden beliefs and valuations, we have accustomed ourselves to believe in the grave importance to keep "private" what, in the case of the person made ashamed, has become exposed. Nevertheless, as we shall see, because of circumstances beyond one's control, one might make a strong connection between one's core self and this aspect of oneself. In such cases, which we might sometimes regard as "socio-pathic," one's very basic sense of oneself, indeed one's Existenz, is made vulnerable. Shame reveals that the situation at hand poses this threat. In this case shame becomes "existential," because there is no other sense of oneself in question than the one being threatened through the shaming.

In cases of shame this is not always or even typically the case, even though at the moment one might admit to being "mortified," i.e., there is something of the threat of death or even of wanting to die in such situations. Reflection, conversations with friends, etc., can shed light on the fact that that of which we are ashamed does not exhaust the sense of ourselves. We will return to this.

Typically in being ashamed, e.g., of one's behavior, one faces the coming to light before Others of a displeasing aspect of oneself that one would prefer to have kept hidden. But it is not merely a matter of being found out before Others, it is not merely that the sort of person one wants to appear as is not the sort of person one really is, but this shame can also be an instance of being ashamed of oneself in the presence of oneself: Not only has one shamed oneself by violating oneself as identified with the ideal of being other than the sort of person one has been, but the sort of person who one has been, the person with whom one has identified in this moment of, e.g., anger, shames who one now is.

Shame is not the equivalent of having an aspect of ourselves revealed that we want to keep secret. For example, the found-out spy has massive aspects of himself that he wished to keep secret. In no way does shame necessarily ensue with the rev-elation of this secret part of himself. Indeed, the spy might be proud of this aspect being out in the open. It is when there is revealed that aspect of himself with which he has identified and which identification he wishes to remain secret, perhaps both to Others and himself, that he is ashamed. In such a case shame can reveal us as more than and as transcendent to the hidden shamed aspect of ourselves which has been revealed. This concealing of an identification which one wants to conceal cov-ers many but not all instances of shame.

As in conscience, shame is always ourselves at a distance from ourselves, even though the extent of the identification of oneself with the shameful aspect may make such a distance for the moment invisible and negligible. In this respect shame is always being ashamed of oneself. (We will look below at how language mirrors this.) Shame thus always involves being ashamed before oneself in the presence of which one is ashamed. Yet clearly there is a distinction between being ashamed of oneself, which may be metaphorically described as the witness of the reproach of the constituted personal essence, i.e., conscience, and the case of being ashamed (in the presence of oneself) for something for which one is not responsible and for which one cannot reproach oneself. Thus we may be ashamed that something about us, not necessarily something reprehensible, indeed, perhaps something praiseworthy in a different context, has been made public, e.g., by a friend, that we wanted not to have been revealed. Thus, e.g., a modest self-effacing person keen on a low-keyed status among a circle of cherished friends might have revealed to these very friends by another friend that he once did some heroic deed that saved the lives of the relatives of these friends.

But how are we here ashamed *of ourselves* of the revelation of an aspect of ourselves with which we have identified? In the case of the revelation by the friend, he is displayed to others and before himself as once having identified with a certain kind of action or behavior. This revelation at the present time is awkward, "embarrassing," and better concealed. In the case of a stranger coming upon us while we are naked preparing to bathe, we are comporting ourselves as alone with our bodies; we are comfortable in our first-personal lived bodily privacy; we are not naked persons intending to display ourselves to the public. The third- or second-person perspective, especially by strangers, intrudes on and asserts the perspective of others into one's unique lived bodily experience. Thus one is made to appear to oneself and Others as an exemplification of male or female sexual private parts. Strictly here we are not ashamed of either our bodily being alone, our nudity, or our bodily parts, but of the transformation of ourselves into an unwanted spectacle. Again *embarrassment* better captures the event.

Why it is important to keep the private parts private is cursorily explained as a taboo. Do taboos have any other possible significance than their status of being the refuse of the unconscious repressions occasioned by extraordinary social pressures? Could it be that the concern to keep the private parts private is a deep intuition which has pervaded the body, in part through the clues of cultural-intersubjective behavior, that each is constituted most profoundly by an essential secret of the "myself," i.e., a secret, as Kierkegaard says, that cannot be communicated directly and which is distorted profoundly when it is so communicated? The private parts symbolize to oneself and to the world the essential secret of oneself. That the secret has to do with the organs of procreation perhaps indicates an intimation of the mystery of our origins.

Perhaps here in the phenomenon of nakedness is also the shame of being reminded of the illusion of "spiritism" one might nurture, i.e., the temptation to see oneself almost exclusively from a first-person perspective and to suppress that one's being also involves the objective third-person bodily perspective. Perhaps it is this self-deception that is unmasked and is what one wants to have kept hidden, even from oneself. Finally, here there might also be in play the recollection of times when one has identified oneself with being a body as it is for others, and it is this which one wants to keep hidden.

In terms of a general theory of shame we perhaps can say the following: Prior to any shame is the essential secret of oneself that may not properly be displayed.

There are personal and collective artifices aimed to protect this essential reserve. Yet there are assaults and betrayals of this essential secret which shame reveals. Torture and rape are strategies to destroy one's protection of the essential secret. Further the betrayal of ourselves by ourselves when we act more or less whole-heartedly in ways which themselves degrade the essential *dignitas* of our ipseities is a secret akin to the essential secret; it is a secret about who we are, i.e., the sort of person we are. Such self-betrayals we may well want to keep secret and towards that end we erect devices like disguises to prop up this secret. When these are dis-mantled there is a revelation of that with which we have identified. Shame is the futile effort to seek refuge from the gaze of Others and ourselves.

We are helped to grasp shame if we contrast it with shamelessness. The latter is the at least momentary desire to be identified with an aspect of ourselves, per-haps to exhibit ourselves as totally identified with this aspect, as if this were our ownmost selves. Such a person is shameless not primarily because he does not conceal what the spectator thinks he ought to, but because for the moment at least he identifies himself with merely this aspect of himself and behaves as if there were nothing essentially in reserve, invisible, and secret, i.e., transcendental, about him. He, as we say in American English, "lets it all hang out."

The reason sexual intimacy between lover and beloved, i.e., where there is the display of one's genitalia or private parts, does not involve shame, is because sexual intimacy, as we have earlier suggested, is a unique bodily commingling and com-munication of incarnate persons as ipseities. (See Book 1, Chapter IV, §16) That is, there is not the alienation from one's being alone with one's lived bodiliness that occurs when one is surprisingly come upon by the stranger, whether or not his gaze is lewd. Sexual intimacy, when pervaded by love and not mere lust, still aims at the ipseity even though the Other's sexual aspects are, through caresses, the vehicle of this love. Here lovers intend lovingly the naked beloved as a unique individual and the disclosure of the "private parts" is part of the ritual of the revelation of love of incarnate ipseity.

In this regard Scheler calls attention to settings where there is a shift from the absence of shame to the onset of shame. For example, a model can pose for a painter, or a patient can disrobe for a doctor, and there need not be a trace of shame. What is at stake is this person's bodily appearance as an artistic subject or as a patient, or medical case or instance of the human body. She does not identify here with her bodily self but allows her bodiliness to be made present by the painter or doctor according to the aesthetic or medical framework of the profession. She is present not as this individual person freely opening herself to the sexual love or lustful gaze of these strangers. But if she feels that the gaze of the artist or doctor is directed at her as an individual person whose presence is being construed as compliant with the observer's sexual interest then there sets in the turning back on herself which is shame. She becomes aware of having an aspect of herself revealed which under such circumstances she would otherwise conceal. We may also think of the setting where the spouse or lover feels herself in her nudity to be intended by her lover or partner, but then realizes that he is regarding her *merely* as sexually attractive and indifferent to herself, or intending her merely in comparison with other sexually attractive women; then it might well be the case that the turning back on herself of shame occurs. Or it might be the case that someone who is very shy and easily shamed might become lost in the loving gaze of the lover and let fall away the normal bodily shyness and reserve. But should love's ardor as directed at her ownmost self relent and be displaced to her bodiliness apart from herself, the feeling of shame might kick in. The point we make here depends on one we earlier insisted on, namely that love, even erotic love in so far as it is not merely lust, intends the ipseity through the passionate enjoyment of the incarnate person but does not stop at the arousing sexy qualities of the other.[100]

Scheler has noted that shame is a self-reflexive feeling. This is clear in German because the verb for "to be ashamed" is reflexive, *sich schämen*. "She was ashamed when she saw you" is "*Sie schämt sich vor Dir.*" "Shame on you" is reflexive: *Schäm dich!* In English, as in German (*beschämen*), we may use the verb transitively and non-reflexively, as when we say that "He shamed the boy," but often it is used in English passively, as "The boy was made to feel ashamed through the scolding" or "He was ashamed." The passive verbal-predicative use gets closer to the German reflexive use and provides evidence for Scheler's claim that shame is always a self-reflexive feeling in which one turns back or is turned back upon oneself.[101] Shame, furthermore, is being ashamed about something, and this being ashamed is always a way in which one is ashamed about oneself (and before oneself) in some respect.

In shame, and here we find another point of contact with conscience, there is a self-retraction approaching "mortification." This English expression in the active voice expresses the practice of self-denial, e.g., in acts of penance. In the passive voice, as "I was mortified," it does not refer to either a penance or lethal or death-bringing situations, but rather situations that are only metaphorically such and where there is therefore a hyperbole. Yet the metaphoric hyperbole is of interest because even though it does not refer to any physical threat, the situation is painful enough to suggest both the danger to our sense of ourselves as well as the urge to hide and retrench from the onslaught. It is a move toward protection in regard to one's self. In English, when there is no or little hyperbole, we say the shaming occasion is "mortifying," i.e., it deals an onset of deathlike numbing of the self.

A massive shaming assault can threaten the core of the self and this can lead the assaulted mortified person to self-protection and aggression. For this reason the accusations by oneself to oneself in conscience, if they are informed by appropriated inner (heteronomous) voices that shame us, may not result in the appropriate response, e.g., of acknowledgment and repentance, but of self-protection and repression, even defiance, of what shames. Of course, they may, if the heteronomous voices appear to have authority, result in suicide.

Shame thus is a self-retraction of oneself before others in regard to an aspect of oneself that one desires to remain hidden but which is revealed. In being ashamed before others one is ashamed of (an aspect of) oneself that one does not want exposed. Yet one may be ashamed of oneself before oneself because one has acted shamefully. The person who has his disfigurement revealed to someone of whom he is fond and from whom he has kept the disfigurement a secret is "ashamed of himself" in a way that differs from the one who, on the morning after a debauchery in a public place, recalls his drunken disgraceful behavior. This is a different case from where the person realizes that his weakness jeopardized the good fortune of a friend, a weakness which the friend will never discover – perhaps because there are no witnesses or because the friend has died. This latter case is the clearest case among the three that could be construed to be one where the shame is *not* in having a hidden aspect of ourselves revealed to *Others*, but where the shame derives from one's being ashamed of oneself before oneself.

We have had occasion to note that one reason for the delight in being loved, especially for the first time by someone who is not a family member, is because one sees in the eyes of the lover some beauty of oneself which before was hidden from others and even to a degree from oneself. (On-going parental love may not awaken it because the child has blessedly learned to take it for granted; it has become like gravity and the air she breathes; if the parents die in the child's youth, then their love and the child's sense of herself as loved become present.) Love, we have proposed, aims at what is most hidden and secret about oneself, one's unique ipseity. The unique ipseity, what is most hidden to the gaze of others and even oneself (as an appreciable thematic consideration) precisely because it is one's ownmostness, is reached by love. But love is not a prying into what this ipseity wants to conceal. Love alone can lay bare what is most precious and uniquely oneself and what is beyond all that with respect to which one might be either proud or ashamed. Love intends what is transcendent to what one has, what one has or has not done, what one wants to hide or is ashamed of. In the presence of the one loving, one is unconditionally affirmed in spite of one's power to hide and set conditions. Love is uniquely powerful because it affirms the beloved ipseity regardless, and thus affirms the beloved not only in what the beloved most wants to reveal, but in its own I-can, even in its power to reject love.

Apart from the formal transcendental self-love or self-affection, which is love only in a loose analogy or equivocation, any such genuinely analogous love for oneself would seem to be dependent on Others having first loved us and awakened us to ourselves. In such gracious moments we may come to appreciate palpably in intentional acts our "ontological value," *dignitas*, and beauty beyond all our properties. Love in its infallible targeting of the beauty of the unique ipseity has the capacity to awaken in the beloved the self-respect and self-love that the unique individual essence demands. The beloved sees in the loving eyes of the lover what she has perhaps never before observed in anyone else's gaze, but this something which she sees is something of which she has ever been non-reflexively aware but never intended and never gave expression to.

Shame has a similar capacity. In reflecting on the various ways in which one is ashamed of oneself and felt exposed one can come to appreciate that these dark aspects of oneself are not who one is and that one is transcendent to these. But for this to happen one must be able not to be totally collapsed into the shameful aspect. And yet such a transcendence to the submersion or collapsing of oneself into the aspect is part of the sense of shame: I am always ashamed (in my own presence) before others about something. "I am ashamed" means that "in your presence my shameful aspect appears painfully to me" and "there is something about me that shames me before you." The passive use of *I* suggests that I am witness to the shaming; it happens to me. The "to me" is a dative of manifestation that is not coincident with or collapsed into the shame. There is a sense of me which remains in tact that I cherish and which this shameful aspect is not ultimately able to detract from or violate.

Shame presupposes an esteemed sense of oneself that is beyond the constituted person in the world. Nevertheless there are cases, which we will call pathological, where this distinction seems endangered. Unless one has experienced a reflexive self-love mediated by the love of another person, one's own value never becomes a felt or palpable consideration. But even in such "pathological" cases we are proposing that this sense of oneself, as before whom one is ashamed, is oneself as ineluctably esteemed and loved by oneself – but transcendentally. In this sense one is always self-affirming oneself as transcendent to one's properties (in the senses sketched earlier), even in the shameful foibles of identifying oneself or losing oneself in an aspect of oneself. But in the pathological cases the transcendental non-intentional self-valuing might appear to be totally ineffective. In these cases we are dealing with the numbed soul who not only has never been witness to someone loving him or her beyond her qualities, but who moreover has been violated when he or she was without any capacity for self-defense.

Typically we may say that, in contrast to love, shame does not awaken us to our transcendental ipseities but rather at least for the moment pulls in the direction of "mortification," i.e., a state where one desires one's extinction, or the extinction of the gaze of those before whom one is embarrassed. The one who witnesses her being shamed, the one who is ashamed, is temporarily identified with the shameful aspect. Yet the mortifying pain of shame moves one to erect devices and strategies for defense of the self who has identified with the shameful aspect. This defensive hardening of the self in being shamed is a firming up not only of the self's defenses of its identification with particular contingent constellations of its personal being in the world, but more basically it is a self-affirmation of the self who is worthy of being defended. If the person has never been loved, if the person has been surrounded by contemptuous violent disregard, she may not be capable of avowing that she experiences herself as more than those aspects valued by these surroundings. The defense she sets up thereby can mute, but not eradicate the original self-love and self-esteem of the self for itself as what is worthy of the defense and transcendent to these identifications – because this has never had a chance to reveal itself. But love has a famous power to melt the defenses, and no one is in a position to make pronouncements on who is spiritually dead or a lost cause. The occasional miraculous power of love makes it evident that the transcendent ipseity of even such allegedly spiritually dead pathological cases is not ever intrinsically shameful and can be awakened to their intrinsic *dignitas*.

If this is so, then perhaps we can say that shame thus always presupposes this original self-love and self-esteem which the shaming circumstance threatens. What occasions shame does this by revealing the self's identification with an aspect of itself and by removing what has served as its defense against the revelation of this identification. The psychiatrist, James Gilligan, holds the thesis that shame brings about the "mortification" of the self through humiliation. Gilligan makes a good case that the "self," which refers at least to what we are calling the personal essence, has its internal integrity and cohesiveness sustained by self esteem.

But Gilligan further notes that self-esteem is not only that which gives to the fiber and texture of the self its tensile strength, it, furthermore, is the necessary condition for the possibility of the life of the person with Others because it is this elemental sense of oneself in self-esteem that enables empathy and love. This is a psychiatric gloss on our earlier Husserlian point that empathy is the presencing of the Other through a self-displacing of one's self-experiencing "here" to "there," to another "here." This is the formal epistemic achievement for the presencing of Others as such. Gilligan is adding that the "identity synthesis" which enables the Other to be present as an Other soliciting our sympathy, empathy, and love requires that the agent of manifestation have self-esteem and that this too be an ingredient in the analogous apperception. I am drawn to venture towards your being you if I am already joyed at my being me myself here because I can look forward to doubling my joy through you and your joy and doubling your joy through me.

The death of the self or personal essence as a first-personal phenomenological reality happens when this basic self-esteem is radically undermined. Without a degree of palpable self-love and self-esteem there is a sense in which it may be said that the soul or self "dies." "Death" here however is not the absolute absence or destruction of the personal self; Gilligan appears not to rule out the possibility, at least on occasion, of a healing resurrection. He compares shame to cold: as cold is the absence of heat, so shame effects the absence of love. Initially both shame and cold start out as a feeling which eventually results in numbness. But eventually in extreme cold and in the severest damage of shame numbness approaches unfeelingness and death. The death of the soul or self is an inability to feel. Gilligan notes the accuracy of Dante's observation that "the lowest corner of hell was a region not of flames, but of ice – absolute coldness."[102] Extreme shaming thus results in this absence of self-love, i.e., this numbness and incapacity to feel for oneself; and without self-feeling, empathy and the capacity to feel for Others is dead.

Gilligan has assembled considerable evidence for his thesis that the most violent crimes, those we affix to the "criminally insane" and "psychopathic killers," have been the deeds of those who have been deeply shamed by way of being violated in their childhood. Yet, in spite of these horrendous beginnings, as adults they wrest from within themselves an instable reservoir of self-esteem and erect a thin wall of protection for it. It is with what serves as the protective wall that they identify. This protective device is very easily affronted and has a highly sensitive "warning system," and when there is an appearance of an assault on this feeble self-esteem, a murderous rage is triggered in these persons. This is occasioned very often by a mis-perception in which a casual, perhaps meaningless, gesture is taken as a "dis'ing" or gesture of shaming or disrespect. Thus even an innocent gesture might be taken as an assault on the feebly constructed citadel protecting the sanctuary of the self. The violent reaction is precisely to remove the source of shame, often enough the look of the Other, as what threatens to tear down the thin wall protecting the feeble self held together by its feeble self-esteem. Shame most profoundly threatens the self because it tends to destroy the self-esteem which gives it its capacity for cohesion and integrity, what in our terms is an esteem and love of one's ownness.

Among some psychoanalysts this is called a "narcissistic injury." The self will do all it can to ward off whatever threatens this feeble tissue of self-esteem, and this we may believe is the root of much, if not all, violence. Both Aristotle (*Rhetoric* 1378–1380) and Aquinas (*Summa Theolgiae* I-II, q. 47; II-II, q. 41) say that the cause of the desire for violence was the perception that one was slighted. We may also call attention here to the fact that the etymological connections reveal conceptual ones. Thus indignation is tied to a suffered indignity and to the failure to recognize the inseparability between the person and her *dignitas*, a theme we have developed earlier in this work. In Latin the fact that one word can be used for both injustice and injury brings this out: The perception of an injustice (*iniuria*) itself has the effect of an injury (*inuria*).[103]

Gilligan interprets the biblical "first murder" by Cain of Abel as a result of Cain's sensing himself "dis'd" by God. At *Genesis* 4:5, we read that although God respected Abel and his offering, God "did not respect Cain and his offering." Cain knew that Abel was aware of God's disrespecting him and saw himself humiliated in God's eyes perhaps through Abel's eyes. His "mortification" could only be stopped by slaying Abel, whose presence was a constant source of his despair to be someone respected. (In Gilligan's interpretation there is no motivation assigned to Cain to see himself infinitely blessed and loved by the creator God; there is only a motive for an enraging invidious comparison with his brother.)

Thus Gilligan's theory that shame threatens to destroy the self by destroying self-love and its wall of defense supports the thesis we are proposing that shame can reveal a transcendental self-love. We have already qualified our thesis by admitting that the transcendental self-love might well be ineffective in the cases in which Gilligan is most interested. But there are some more intriguing wrinkles in Gilligan's thesis which we wish to address.

We have attempted to show that shame often occurs when an aspect of ourselves with which we have at some time identified, but which we do not want to have brought to light, is indeed brought to light. To the extent we have identified with this aspect, to that extent is our self-respect and self-love, in the sense of what holds together our personal being, in jeopardy; and to the extent the shaming destroys this, to that extent is the personal self "mortified." Further, to the extent such a mortified, numbed, and enfeebled self is still moved to construct the feeble fragile defense that is easily menaced by perceived gestures of disrespect, Gilligan's own theory suggests an amazing resilience that the self has to this mortification process rooted in a latent self-love. Finally, this resilience and latent self-love is suggested in Gilligan's own thesis that typical of all the murderers he has studied is an

> unusually strong wish to be loved and taken care of, and unusually strong feelings of being inadequate and unloveable. And when these wishes and feelings are intensified, then the feelings of shame that they provoke are also intensified; as are the feelings of rage and hate, and the impulses of violence that shame stimulates.[104]

Yet feelings of wanting to be loved presuppose one's sense of one's self as loveable. It is the rejection that leads to the belief that one is unloveable and which flies in the face of one's desire to be loved and one's deep sense of one's elemental loveability. Clearly this sense of one's self as loveable does not amount to an effective robust self-love. On the contrary, in the persons Gilligan deals with, the self-love is sometimes only formal. Yet in so far as this wanting to be loved is irrepressible, to that extent is one's sense of oneself as loveable irrepressible, and this approximates but is not an adequate substitute for an irrepressible self-love. When the other person refuses to answer to this need to be loved, or, more likely, acts in a way that confirms the belief that one is unloveable or despicable, there is shame. The deep truth about oneself that one foremost wants to be kept from the light of day is brought to light: I, who have found myself disdained by all from whom I sought spiritual nourishment, can scarcely hold myself together by my feeble self-love; and now I see confirmed in your eyes and behavior that I am not loveable and that very perception is a frontal assault on me. The shame gives rise to rage and impulses of violence as gestures which overcome the mortification brought on by the shame. (Gilligan notes that the extinguishing of the Others' eyes is a telling expression of the shame.) The rage and violence reveal and enact a basic defiant affirmation of one's self, one's loveability, and a sense of one's own dignity. (This recalls Fichte's claim of an ineradicable drive to self-respect.) This can only be sustained if the source of the shame is destroyed. Thus, even the most mortifying shaming experiences are not merely death threats to the feeble self. But even these reveal a kind of self-love in the feeble ravaged self. They do this because the shaming threatens and provokes the self to dreadfully violent death-defying self-protective responses which are forms of self-love, that persist in spite of the horrible fact that the self, in a fundamental respect, is dead. That is, self-feeling and self-esteem are so numbed that there is no capacity to have empathy with Others, and thus those who are perceived to have "dis'd" them are often viciously slain.

If this narrative has validity, even the worst social pathologies reveal the transcendental self-love. Gilligan is right in our view that without self-love there is the death of the self in the sense of the numbing of the self and the incapacity for empathy. But even examples of dead souls, dead because of their inability to feel themselves, feel with others, and feel the enormity of their crimes, reveal persons who can still be "dis'd" and thus who have a sense of self-esteem that feebly sustains the fragile vulnerable self. Gilligan continually observed of such persons who risked everything, and did the unspeakable, that they all said in so many words, "if you ain't got pride you got nothin'." They clearly apperceived that at the most basic level there is no self without self-esteem. But because they perhaps have never had awakened in them a love of themselves through the love by another, they may have reached the pathological stage of not being able to effectively feel themselves and thus they are unable to feel-with or feel what other persons feel. In this sense they were dead and without self-"love" and self-"esteem." Yet their very defiance and capacity for shame reveals an underlying struggle for self-affirmation and self-respect.

In sum, the "myself" that is non-reflectively manifest and at the basement of all temporalizing presencing of our personal life in the world enjoys a unique diaphanous self-presence that we may describe in terms of an analogous sense of self-trust, self-esteem and self-love. We have urged that this is an important topic in thinking about the metaphor of a calling. In being called one is addressed by name, or one is beckoned as this unique individual, to a "higher calling," to be active in this higher life, and this call matches the deepest desire of one's heart for it is a call to be one's true self. For an interest to be awakened in this prospect we have said that one's "ontological value" must be already be lived. This ontological value or transcendental self-affection, we have said, is lived in any case as a formal-transcendental necessity. Yet this lived sense of oneself can be a matter of keen sensibility to one's unique dignity, but it can also be *merely* formal-transcendental and scarcely effective and utterly feeble in the formation of one's personal self. In the concluding chapters we will return to considerations which give other possible "reasons" for assigning this self-love and self-respect an eminent place, but they will involve our telling a "likely story" that moves beyond phenomenological philosophy. Before we do that let us attempt to ties some strings together.

§9. Summary and Conclusion: The Claim that "Person" Is a "Forensick Term"

We conclude this transcendental-existential phenomenology with a discussion of the pre-eminence of the second-person perspective in the determination of the proper sense of Ought, and implicitly, in any discussion of vocation. We do this primarily by reflecting on a book by Stephen Darwall.[105] This work, likewise indebted to Kant and Fichte, also places the person, respect, and human dignity at the center of its philosophical concerns. Further, Darwall's featuring the second-personal stance, his subordination of the first-personal perspective to the second-personal, and his elevation of the forensic realm of rights and duties over the ontological realm echo recent discussions surrounding Levinas' thought within the phenomenological tradition. By doing justice to his concern to root the proper sense of the Ought or moral obligation in the second-person he forces this work to greater clarity on some basic issues. Thereby a discussion of Darwall's key theses occasions a summary of what we have been up to. At the same time discussing Darwall's themes provides a transition from our more properly phenomenological-philosophical discussions of calling to the philosophical-theological ones.

From Darwall's angle it might well appear that there is a serious error in our presentation of the Ought (as fundamental to moral categoriality) in as much as the statements about how I am are alleged to be capable of revealing how I ought to be. (Cf. our discussions above in Chapter IV, §§3, 6, and 8.) The project of founding the Ought on the Is, it may be said, neglects the essential difference of practical and theoretical reason. It neglects that when one says who and what one is, one might very well say nothing at all about what one ought to be. Similarly expressing what it would be good for one to be or what one foremost desires to be or believes oneself called to be likewise does not say anything about whether one ought to be this. Our procedure of making declarative statements about how things are, e.g., my constituted personal essence, along with descriptions of its ideal self, serve as premises for how I ought to be. But is there a warrant for this? In what follows we address this matter especially as it ties to Darwall's restriction of the morally obligatory to second-personal interactions.

We have claimed that the Ought or the deontological aspect of personal agency is inseparable from the ontological. We have argued that the being of a person is such that it is given to itself to complete itself in an ideal-normative way, that the personal essence is constituted by position-taking acts. As one achieves these in facing one's ideal, one binds oneself for the definite and indefinite future. Being a person, therefore not merely a "myself," is being in relation to oneself as one has committed oneself to be in the future. The fact of one's historical personal essence is pervaded by Ought in so far as living in the world is a self-binding and self-obliging affair. The syntactical activity is not merely apophantic but morally obligatory in an extended sense. Often enough the Ought emerges out of our interpersonal, second-personal, reciprocal relations with Others. But it emerges also in our analysis in our first-personal experience and surfaces also in the third-personal presencing of Others. We have claimed in Book 1, Chapter IV that the sheer presencing of Others, i.e., other ipseities, reveals in at least a burgeoning way the dignity or "ontological value" of the person.

Philosophers have wanted to distinguish the realm of practical reason and obligation from the realm of theory and the agency of manifestation by saying the former of necessity involve "agent-relative" actions or performances whereas the latter are "agent-neutral." Thus in describing a state of affairs, as what is happening during a ball game, I am not involving myself in what is intended in the sense that the field of reference does not include a self-referring or a thematic self-determination. But in a properly morally obliging situation as making promises, keeping promises, obeying commands, fulfilling responsibilities, etc., I am always self-referring and myself is part of the target of intentionality, part of what is acted upon.

There is nothing to object to in regard to the claim that in the clear morally obliging second-personal situation one's agency in regard to the Other, e.g., fulfilling one's promise, is self-referential or agent-relative. In such an agency I do what I have promised or I make myself do what the Other has the right to demand of me. But we have also said that cognitive-theoretical position-taking acts by which we display the world are always both I-world acts and I-me acts, and in this sense what these philosophers call agent-neutral acts have a tacit agent-relative or I-me aspect or kind of agent constitution. Even the most theoretical acts are not absolutely agent-neutral in so far as I am shaping myself with this conviction; with this judgment I am determining and informing my future style of living, etc. And furthermore behind every declarative theoretical statement there is the tacit "transcendental pre-fix" or declarative sense of the "I" with its "illocutionary" force (as we saw in Book 1, Chapter II). The agency of manifestation not only displays the world, as in "The tree is diseased," but says at least tacitly to the listener, ("I think that) the tree is diseased" or ("I know that) the tree is diseased." In my propositional display of the world, e.g., in declarative sentences, I am also witnessing to my authority in such a way that you can count of me because I am in a position to provide you with evidence for my claim. Or I may dissuade you, e.g., by saying explicitly "I have a hunch that..." or "A stranger told me that...."

Thus although it is doubtless true that a declarative, third-personal, statement refers to the world and carves up the world with its disjunctives and quantifiers and binds features of the world with its syntactic ties and therefore what it means does not have to do explicitly with the person-constitution of the I-me acts, and therefore it does not explicitly bind the person in its binding the world, still this agency of manifestation is an articulation which binds the agent to the world in the way she is delineating and binding the world: P is q holds from now on and sets up a binding delineation of my future agency and thought, until I have reason to revise it. And the transcendental pre-fix testifies to this.

Our account of the notion of the person is primarily an ontological one – which is not to say that we disregard the moral or deontological aspects. The person is inseparable from the dignity of its "ontological value." This is rooted in its being an ipseity, "another I," who is a unique essence and self-experiencing. The second-person is essentially a second first-person. Empathic perception discloses another self-awareness, unique essence, etc. The sense of one's being under an obligation is not restricted to the claims Others have on me. It is not restricted to Others having power or authority over me; nor is it restricted to my relationship to them. Obligation is grounded in me myself as having the capacity to act freely and bind myself and let myself be bound. This, of course, is typically inseparable from my appresentation of Others likewise being ipseities, unique essences, with their capacity to bind themselves and let themselves be bound by my and Others' demands.

Darwall himself holds that "the second-person stance is a version of the first-person standpoint (whether singular or plural)." I assume this stance in addressing another I in regard to practical thought or speech or in acknowledging an address from another ("I" or "we").[106] Further, he rightfully holds that although the second-personal perspective is always a version of the first-personal he insists that it is never merely first-personal. (For our discussion of personal perspectives, see Book 1, Chapter II, §7.) But our problem is that he excludes from the first-personal perspective, which, as he admits, need not be also second personal, any moral dimension. Not until I am engaged with You do I enter the realm of moral categoriality.

With Kant we hold that we recognize that "I am under obligations to others only insofar as I at the same time put myself under obligation."[107] In contrast to Kant and perhaps Darwall we maintain that the dignity is inherent in one's ontological status. (Kant, we saw, appeared to make ontological statements regarding the dignity of persons, but his phenomenalism forbids his doing this.) One possesses this dignity in oneself of necessity and not through the interaction with Others or a fortiori through the largesse of Others. It is this dignity which one has, we have also said *is*, by which, we may say, again with Kant, one "exacts respect for himself from all other rational beings in the world."[108]

The respect the Others show in calling me to account for my actions is due to the dignity I myself *am* and have in myself, and which they recognize in their expectation that I act responsibly. It comes to explicit light in my taking them as

persons so taking me; but this is not the source of the dignity. The ontological dignity of Others comes to light in a burgeoning way in empathic perception and then
in the fuller forms of engagement that are second-personal engagements typical of
"illocutionary acts." These acts are founded in the recognition that the person is a
"self-originating source of valid claims" (John Rawls). (We have also maintained
that this dignity comes to light "radiantly" in love.) This is the basis for the moral
dignity where we hold Others accountable and where we assign to her the authority
to claim respectful behavior from us. We hold in contrast to Darwall that the dignity is implicit ineluctably in ourselves and in the empathic perception of Others,
whether in the third- or second-person. (We have just discussed in §8 above how it
is implicit in ourselves.)

Stephen Darwall stresses that the ontological or teleological, even the supremely
desirable as that on account of which all else is undertaken, is not normative in the
sense of being part of the sphere of moral obligation. Moral obligation cannot, for
Darwall, be tied, as it is for us to conscience. For us conscience is one's responding
to one's moral essence as one has constituted oneself. Nor for Darwall can it be tied
to the process of being who one is drawn to be and called to be through realization of the ideal emergent out of one's life horizon. This is because moral obligation is tied to that for which one is accountable and for which one is responsible
to Others. What is desirable, even what is eminently desirable and the best under
the circumstances, even that which appears as the *unum necessarium* and "truth of
will," etc., do not have to do with what one has an obligation to do. The reason is
that, for Darwall, the obligatory, the morally demanding, has to do with normative
relations between persons. And foremost it has to do with the normative relations
between persons as they stand to one another in second-personal exchanges. These
exemplarily are forensic exchanges of promises, claims, commands, oaths, etc.,
i.e., what since Austin we have called the "illocutionary acts." Thus the way the
Other's third-personal, to say nothing of the second-personal, presence "obliges"
us to appresent the world with her epistemic and conative perspectives in mind is
not, for Darwall, a proper sense of obligation, as we have maintained (in Book 1,
Chapter VI, §7). Nor would the unique necessities of conscience or even the limit-
situations such as death by which we are "required" to get our lives in order be
called permissibly "morally obligatory." In contrast, our position holds that they,
along with "the truth of will," as what I alone must do and the not doing of which
is the deepest self-betrayal possible, are quite apart from what Others may expect
or demand of me. They are that for which I am accountable foremost to me and to
myself alone. As such, in Darwall's view, they are bereft of the moral dimension
because they have no aspect of accountability to any Others in second-personal
relations. Here in these "existential" dimensions the moral community of which
one is a part is not in evidence.

Thus an extended sense of Ought, as in saying to oneself or Others: "I ought to
do this otherwise I will never be able to live with myself," or "I ought to respond
to the lure of the better over the good or the best over the better," with its correlate regret: "I should have pursued the better or the best," have no proper moral
sense. Moral obligation has to do with that for which we may be held accountable

to Others, and in such examples we are accountable only to ourselves. If we are accountable to God, God must be in some sense a You for us and we a You for God, and God must be present second-personally requiring absolutely these Oughts.

Darwall throughout his book nicely uses the simple example of your stepping on my toe or my stepping on your toe. I might provide myself with reasons for why I should remove my foot from your toe, e.g., the world would have less suffering, or by getting off your foot I would have contributed to the world being a better place. Or one might even say that it is an intrinsically good thing not to be an occasion of suffering for another, and what we ought to do is always something that is intrinsically good, i.e., good for its own sake. We might offer a Gandhian argument, (to which Darwall would not seem to be tempted for he assumes coercion to be an acceptable way to secure rights and thus respect): *Ahimsa*, or non-harming, non-*in-juria*, is analytic or intrinsically-essentially-conceptually linked with the dignity that second-personal presencing brings to light, and therefore no sentient being, including the one under my foot, should be so harmed. But for Darwall such consequentialist or axiological, typically third-personal, senses of moral reflection do not get at moral obligation as one's being accountable to another by reason of the just demands Others may place on us. They are "reasons of the wrong kind to warrant the attitudes and actions in which holding someone responsible consists in their own terms."[109] Only when I realize that in facing you second-personally as an "originating source of claims" by reason of your inherent dignity which I am bound to respect, i.e., in recognizing you as having the authority to say, "Get off my foot!," is there the proper morally obligatory situation.

Darwall's work clearly is near to a central thesis of this work that the presencing of persons is inseparably a presencing of their "dignity." We saw this in Aquinas, and at various junctures have attempted to explicate this. (See, e.g., Book 1, Chapter IV, §21 and Chapter VI, §7.) But Darwall's version of this thesis finds its concise formulation in the claim of John Locke that "person" is a "forensick term," i.e., one "essentially connected to imputing legal or moral responsibility."[110] It means that for Darwall, like Kant, the person's having "dignity" is the subject of practical reason, foremost the subject giving to Others and receiving from them reasons for acting in a particular way. This means that because the intentional correlate of dignity is respect, and the person is presenced with dignity only in the second-personal respectful engagement, and the second-personal engagement or perspective is what "you and I take up when we make and acknowledge claims on one another's conduct and will,"[111] *person* is a term that surfaces only in the second-personal assertion and litigation between those having the competence to make claims, recognize claims, and dispute claims. Foundational is the second-personal presencing of that kind of being that we recognize as capable of making and acknowledging claims.

The person's "dignity" is conceptually-essentially tied to this forensic situation. Dignity is present in the presence of what we accord a standing to make claims and to recognize our claims. This is exclusively present in the presence of "irreducible second-personal authority," of You, to make claims and the power to acknowledge claims. Dignity is the recognized authority of Others to make demands on us and their demands presuppose that we are capable not only of meeting these demands but of making demands on ourselves, and this requires that we take up a second-personal relation to ourselves. One brings one's own dignity to light in the "reactive attitudes" (Strawson) like indignation, resentment, guilt, blame, etc. Not only are dignity and the dignity of the person second-personal phenomena but *the very concept of person is itself a second-personal concept*[112] as framed by this juridical-forensic setting.

I think our discussions in Book 1, Chapter IV make clear that presencing the You foremost brings out the dignity of the Other. But as discussions in Book 1, Chapters IV and VI also attempted to show, this dignity and personhood press themselves upon us in empathic perception which need not be second-personal. (In §8 above we even attempted to show a kind of first-personal dignity.) We have highlighted the connection of the basic dignity as being neither eliminable nor merited and have proposed that the correlate respect is inherent in the presencing of the person, even in the egregious forms of disrespect. Darwall himself nicely distinguishes "recognition respect" and "appraisal respect."[113] The latter is the form of respect tied to "esteem" and it can be merited, earned, won or lost. It has to do with the laudable properties someone has as a moral agent. The former "recognition respect" is not based on one's merit and its targeted "dignity" is not an intentional correlate of any act of esteem. "Recognition respect," Darwall insists, can be "mandated" and one may demand it. Darwall holds that this latter respect is tied to the irreducible second-personal fitting response to what the second-personal stance brings to light. And he ties this fittingness to the "second-personal authority of an equal," to the presence of another equal free and rational agent.[114] Dignity as brought to light by respect is thus the bringing to light another as equally free and rational (even if not, presumably, equally rational). Here there is no effort to unpack further rational agent and freedom in terms of a phenomenology of subjectivity and what kind of intentionality is in play in such a presencing.

Darwall does not pursue, as we do, how this "equal" might reflect back first-personal non-ascriptive self-experiencing and the non-sortal ipseity or "myself." He does not pursue what the dignity is that is not merited, how it comes to light, and in what sense the forensic situation presupposes it. Clearly he has touched upon an essential point in holding that the dignity can be mandated. But what are the prior conditions of the mandate in terms of the recognition? Is this close to holding that there is some estimable property that merits an esteem that founds the respect? Darwall would not say this because dignity would then become a matter of merit. Yet, it seems to this reader, that his distinguishing of respect tied to merit and esteem from "recognition respect" that is not so bound points to an essential ontological and not forensic display of dignity that is manifest even in the typical forms of disdain or contempt. In other words, the dignity which evokes respect is an ontological recognition, an "is." The ought of the mandate, the "ought," of respect builds upon this "fact". There is nothing prior to the recognition of the ontological dignity of the person and it is this which founds and makes possible the forensic situation.

For our work the second-person is in important respects the second first-person. This is to say that the key lived first-personal data of self-awareness, unique essence, I-source, etc. are not first of all second-personal notions. I as the "self-originating source of claims" am first of all self-originating I-source and this is not reducible to a second-personal notion. The point here is not our fundamental distinction between the "I" or "myself" as non-ascriptive, non-sortal referent and the "person" as property-laden – although the distinction between "recognition respect and "appraisal respect" verges on that issue. (Darwall seems to reduce the person to what has the properties of making and recognizing claims. But is there anything to be said about what has these properties? And what if the animal or human one before me does not have these properties?[115]) Rather, for Darwall the essence of the person is precisely tied to the strictly forensic-moral dimension of that entity who, by reason of her inherent forensic-juristic dignity is the source of the authority to make claims, etc. And this comes to light, is displayed, in the ongoing process of second-personal transactions. Persons, as it were, are functions of these second-personal forensic transactions. "Respect for inherent dignity" is the equivalent of "recognition of their authority or competence to make demands." No further ontological issues need be raised about what this "authority" or "competence" mean and what sort of being has these properties.[116] All deliberations about whether I am a person or whether that being over there with whom now I cannot enter into a second-personal relation, can only be decided, according to Darwall, on the basis of whether the beings in question can enter into forensic relations. Prior to this all that might be determined about truthfulness, the transcendental pre-fix or declarative sense of the "I," self-consciousness, self-reference, freedom, responsibility for oneself, etc., would not only be insufficient. Only in so far as they would play into the analytic or conceptual or eidetic conditions for the second-personal forensic relations would they be necessary; it is the second-personal forensic relations that are the necessary and sufficient conditions of personhood.

According to Darwall to be genuinely morally responsible and accountable we must be responsible and accountable to another present second personally. We hold Others responsible when we, from our position of authority that emerges out of our status as persons intrinsically worthy of a respect, i.e., inherently capable of making and acknowledging demands, and not because of our social or moral standing or achievements, demand of them that they be accountable for their agency, e.g., "cease standing on my foot." We thus assume of them that they are present to themselves or experience themselves as accountable to themselves. It seems to me that the first-personal dimensions of this assumption are not adequately attended to by Darwall. Again, as Kant stated: "I am accountable to others only in so far as I at the same time put myself under obligation."[117] Indeed, if I did not appresent the Other as capable of being morally responsible to himself by himself, the very sense of her being an Other or a You would be threatened. But for Darwall such being responsible and holding myself responsible can only occur if I can take a second-personal perspective on myself, i.e., become a You for me, a You that issues authoritative demands to Me.[118] The I is morally significant if it transforms itself into a You for itself. But this does not seem to reflect what we may most properly call conscience. (See above, Chapter III, especially §§3–6.) Nor does it do justice to how such self-directed, self-reflective forms of responsible knowing and agency are first of all first-personal. In most of these cases, their sense is distorted if they are thought of as second-personal. Indeed, their sense as self-determinations requires precisely that they not be second- or third-personal.

Darwall's desire to be in agreement with Kant on the theme of autonomy is undermined with his claim that morality is irreducibly second-personal. That is, it is hard for him to avoid the criticism of heteronomy with his urging the hegemony of the second-person perspective. Indeed, when I take up your good and your perspective as my own, or take up the moral community's perspective as my own, and therefore when I become "one of us" I do not become a You for me, but precisely a founding member of a "many-headed" (Husserl) quasi-person of a higher order. Perhaps my chief objection here is that "we" is a person of a higher-order, and in this sense a "higher-order I." I can join with Others in having a common agency and common goods and common goals. But I hesitate to bridge the abyss of authority and respect which Darwall nicely builds around the second-personal perspective and say that "we" likewise is a higher-order You, giving to the "we," with or without my permission, this authority and respect. The "we" is never simply a You for me, and I, in putting "myself under obligation," do not forfeit my first-personal awareness and agency. *Pace* Darwall, the first-person plural point of view of the moral community is not second-personal: our addressing demands to each of us in forming a higher-order will is not a second-personal standpoint. At best it is an analogous, quasi-personal address; but by "us." Of course, as an analogous quasi-person embodying all of us it is as a "many-headed I." But is this many-headed I a quasi-"You?" As far as I can see Darwall wants the moral community's obligation to be that of a You in the stricter sense than is permissible. I grant that "we" has a "serious second-personal aspect,"[119] i.e., it is founded on such, but we are not a You, and the speaker of "we" who purports to include me achieves this performative only on condition of my permission to include my will and or judgment in the We referred to by the speaker. Only this justifies Darwall's claim that "what the moral community demands… is as much one's own as it is any one else's."[120] But this community's demand does not, *pace* Darwall, amount to the second-personal perspective of a member of the moral community. Whereas it makes sense to think of I myself entirely included in a communitarian We, precisely because the You is the locus of a heteronomous authority founded in the abyssal Other, it does not make sense to think of I myself or we as a You. If, e.g., there was a communal censure of JG Hart, its condition would be my censuring myself and then giving to a representative of the community the right to censure me by saying "we." If I were to address this body it would be more appropriate to say "we are censuring me" than "you are censuring me." The statist We, in the absence of such consent, is presumptive, and I would have no hesitation in addressing its representatives as "you" and not "we." (Indeed, in the case of the state, "we" typically would be an unacceptable form of address.) But as having merely presumptive power, the state would not, so it seems to me, have the moral authority that Darwall nicely founds in the second-personal perspective. With a communitarian censuring of me, we and I censure me, but that censuring of me by me and us still is not any You, even a higher-order one, censuring me.[121] In the final chapter we will return to some theological considerations which might be said to enable We to become You; but in any case, even if this were so, the presuppositions for such a position would be quite different from the ones Darwall would permit.

We have acknowledged (following Sokolowski) throughout that moral categoriality properly surfaces when my agency takes up the Other's good as my own or when I take up the Other's evil as my good. This surely need not be a second-personal transaction. Indeed, a good part of one's daily moral interaction with Others would be this third-person moral categoriality. Darwall is right in seeing the essential-analytic connections between the morality, responsibility, accountability, and intersubjectivity. Darwall's book is especially valuable for his analyses of how the presence of the person (in second-personal transactions) points to the foundations of the proper, fuller, more explicit sense of moral obligation: The person is present as having intrinsic dignity and this is the ultimate foundation of all proper, explicit, senses of moral authority and all notions of responsibility and accountability. We acknowledge that the extended senses of the Ought and moral obligation that we feature in this book do not make an essential connection with accountability. When we attended to the absolute Ought in connection with one's unique vocation and "the truth of will" we noted how the absence of accountability endangers these notions and opens the door to self-deception. But for us that points to their inherent ambiguity rather than to their disqualification as serious moral matters.

Our final concluding chapters on vocation move in the direction Darwall insists on in so far as the proper binding sense of one's unique calling must imply a You who calls and before Whom one is responsible. But this is not a philosophical insight but rather it is the legacy of the theological tradition. Thus we ultimately find ourselves in agreement with Darwall's emphasis that the explicit and fullest sense of moral obligation has to do with "the moral community" and a first-person plural authority must reflect actual transactions in the second-personal perspective, a position we argued for in *The Person and the Common Life*. But we also find agreement on matters that culminate in the last two chapters of this Book 2, namely that the most fundamental dimension of one's unique vocation or calling as more than a mere metaphor and nevertheless as an absolute Ought requires a second-personal transaction.

In sum: The *sensus plenior* of moral obligation is inseparable from the fuller sense of respect and therefore is of necessity tied to accountability, and this implies the presencing of You, or one's presence to the Other as You, in such a way that You, through your (first of all) ontological dignity, require respect and have the authority to make claims, and I through my (first of all) ontological dignity, my "ontological value" (see Book 1, Chapter IV, §21), am entitled to respect and have the authority to make claims that insure that respect. Similarly, there are a variety of claims in these last chapters that can only attain their full status as having accountability and being morally binding by being inserted into the second-personal situation. Thus we have claimed that each person has an ineradicable dignity and that each is called to realize this dignity in becoming the unique person she wants, perhaps in spite of herself, to be. We have claimed that Who one is is not only the finished matter of one's non-sortal being oneself, i.e., each being a "myself," but as persons it is imperative that each self-actualize or self-realize the true self each is called to be in the wider setting a person of a higher-order, a We – and the failure to strive to realize this is a failure to be in an important, "existential," sense oneself. This calling, we said, may announce itself in a variety of ways, the most dramatic of which is the "truth of will" where we are awakened to a unique moral necessity to take a certain path. And if we fail to do this we may well be burdened with the conviction that we have neglected the centermost aspect of ourselves, and that we have missed the opportunity to be who we are called to be. We have missed the opportunity to be in a most proper sense ourselves with a unique richness of life within the larger community of persons.

We have presented all this as having a binding moral force, albeit one tied to teleological and ontological considerations. Yet if the metaphor of calling is to have some genuine analogical value, and if the vocation is to have full and explicit moral force, this calling to this exalted way of being oneself is indeed the calling of "someone." As Fichte put it, each is *aufgefordert*, and Darwall makes good use of this matter as exemplarily the moral point of view. The presence of someone, by reason of her inherent dignity, is inseparable from a basic attitude of respect. The someone in question here must be one whom we may regard second-personally as having the authority not merely to make claims founded in her intrinsic dignity and demand that we comport ourselves respectfully, but someone who calls us as the one determinative of our eternal identity and destiny. *Auffordering* is a rich word that Darwall rightly wants to be translated as "claim" or "summons" because, after all, it appears in Fichte's *Foundations of Natural Right*. But overheard in the word is also an "invitation" and, as Darwall nicely puts it, like any second-personal address of reasons (as an invitation, claim, demand, summons, or command) it comes with an RSVP.[122] A calling which is an "invitation" has a more gracious RSVP than does the forensic-juridical calling which is a (court-) summons or demand. These latter are coercive. *Repondez s'il vous plait*, if not a merely formal convention, appeals to my freedom, my pleasure, my inclination, my desire – i.e., it need not carry the note of reprisals or sanction if I fail to respond or if I fail to respond as the one addressing me wants me to respond. But here we move clearly beyond our phenomenological philosophical concerns and enter the terrain of theology.

Notes

1. Paul Valéry, *The Selected Writings* (Binghamton, NY: New Directions, 1950), 245.
2. *Fichtes Werke, Die Tatsachen des Bewusstseins*. Vol. II. Ed. I. H. Fichte (Berlin: Walter de Gruyter, 1971), 664.
3. Jean-Louis Chrétien, *The Call and the Response, op. cit.*, 6 ff.
4. Michael Robinson, *A Bird Within a Ring of Fire* (Keene, ON: Martin House, 1998), 39.
5. José Ortega Y. Gasset, *Man and People*. Trans. Willard R. Trask (New York: W.W. Norton, 1957), 44.
6. Eudora Welty, cited as an epigraph in Andrew M. Greeley, *Confessions of a Parish Priest: An Autobiograpy* (New York: Simon & Schuster, 1987).
7. We merely touch on these matters of the phenomenology of religion and the tragic which is a central theme in the thought of Karl Jaspers. See, besides the "limit-situations" in his *Philosophie* II, e.g., his *Von der Wahrheit*, 919–923.

8. This can be found in numerous places. See, e.g., *The Basic Kafka*. Introduction by Eric Heller (New York: Washington Square, 1971), 157.

9. Thomas Merton wrote this in a journal. See Michael Mott, *The Seven Mountains of Thomas Merton* (New York: Harcourt Brace, 1993), 453.

10. Aristotle, *Nichomachean Ethics*, 1101a 19–20.

11. See especially Chapter IV of *The Person and the Common Life*.

12. For a Husserlian development of these themes, see my *The Person and the Common Life*.

13. See J.G. Fichte, *Fichtes Werke*. Vol. V (Berlin: Walter de Gruyter, 1971), 533.

14. Husserl, Nachlass MS, B I 21 III, 61a.

15. See Husserl, *Husserliana XX/1*, 85 ff. Also *Husserliana XX/2*, 152 ff. For the intricacies see Ullrich Melle, "Das Rätsel des Aurdrucks: Husserls Zeichen- und Austruckslehre in den Manuskripten für die Neufassung der VI. Logischen Untersuchungen," in *Meaning and Language: Phenomenological Perspectives*. Ed. Filip Mattens (Dordrecht: Springer, 2007), 3–26.

16. See Husserl's Nachlass MS, A V 21, 122a/b.

17. *Husserliana XXXVII*, 252.

18. *Idem.*

19. *Idem.* Cf. my review of this work in *Husserl Studies* 20 (2004), 135–159, upon which I have drawn here.

20. See, e.g., *Summa Theologiae*, I, q. 1, a. 6, ad 3; II-II, q. 45, a. 2, c. For a discussion with numerous texts, see John Naus, S.J. *The Nature of the Practical Intellect According to Saint Thomas Aquinas* (Rome: Gregorian University, 1959), 142–150.

21. In *Husserliana XI* Husserl speaks of the heart (*das Gemüt*) as the living present thickened with the affections of life as they are centered in the primal presencing/living present and its passive synthesis. The heart's affections or allegiances have their own epistemic achievements wherein there is a believing before knowing remembers and where the heart "Believes longer than recollects, longer than knowing even wonders" – to quote William Faulkner. As Husserl himself put it: "It is all the same whether we conceive empty presentations (empty intentions) that are still living as being awakened or ones that are already fast asleep. The motives must lie in the living present where perhaps the most efficacious of such motives were such that we were not in a position [at the time] to take into consideration, i.e., "interests" in the broad, customary sense, original or already acquired valuations of the heart, instinctive or even higher drives, etc." *Husserliana XI*, 178. See *Analyses Concerning Passive and Active Synthesis. Lectures on Transcendental Logic.* Trans. Anthony Steinbock (Dordrecht: Kluwer, 2001), 227–228; cf. my review of this work in *Husserl Studies* 20 (2004), especially 139–145.

22. Simone Weil, *Waiting for God* (New York: Perennial Library/Harper and Row, 1973), 63.

23. S. Kierkegaard, *Philosophical Fragments/Johannes Climacus*. Trans. Hong and Hong (Princeton, NJ: Princeton University Press, 1985), 14.

24. Husserl Nachlass MS, B I 21 III, 65a.

25. *Ibid.*, 60a

26. Husserl, Nachlass MS, B I 21 III, 57a.

27. One theme in Mircea Eliade's great novel, *The Forbidden Forest*, is precisely the eutopian mythic setting where a kind of eutopian community, only intimated in life, could be realized. The hero, Stephan, wants to share his life with two women, whom he loves equally and differently. But pulling this off in this life leads only to tragedy. See *Forêt Interdite* (Paris: Gallimard, 1955). This is also a theme in Robert Musil's *Der Mann Ohne Eigenschaften*, where a conception of utopian love challenges the barriers of an incestuous relationship. Similarly, through the years communitarian experiments in so-called "free love" have sought to realize in multiple hetero- and homosexual relationships what typical historical humans sought to realize in one relationship.

28. Anthony Brook, "Kant, Self-Awareness and Self-Reference," http://www.carleton.ca/-abrook/kant-self.htm, p. 2. See our discussions in Book 1, Chapters II, III, and V.

29. Vladimir Jankélévitch, *Traité des Vertus* (Paris: Bordas, 1949), especially 629–640. We do not claim to have done exact justice to Jankélévitch's own position here. Rather we have appropriated from him what seems to agree with the position we are espousing. As we shall

see mystical writers as St. John of the Cross and Thomas Merton speak of the center of our being as "untouched by sin and illusion" (Merton).

30. These are passages from Merton's letter to Boris Pasternak as well as from his book, *Conjectures of a Guilty Bystander* (New York: Doubleday Image, 1968), 156–158. I first came across the text in the chapter devoted to Thomas Merton by M. Basil Pennington, *True Self/False Self* (New York: Crossroad, 2000), 82–85. We will return to Merton's conceptual explication of this wakeful experience which itself appears to have been an explication of a dream.

31. *Simone Weil: An Anthology.* Ed. Sian Miles (New York: Weidenfeld & Nicolson, 1986), 83–84. For "radiance of spirit" see 61 and 63.

32. See John Ciardi, *A Browser's Dictionary* (New York: Harper & Row, 1980), 140. See Mark Musa's translation of Dante, *Vita Nuova* (Bloomington, IN: Indiana University, 1973), e.g., 35 and 38.

33. I take this from Thomas Prufer. For a remarkable aesthetic and theological meditation on charm and grace in the context of Evelyn Waugh's *Brideshead Revisited*, see his "The Death of Charm and the Advent of Grace" in his *Recapitulations*, 90–102.

34. Of course the theological notion of "grace" is here not far off. We will turn to the topic of grace, especially in the form of an unparalleled generosity that in no way interferes with the grace and graciousness we experience, but which perhaps provides a hint of a reason for why we experience this grace itself as a grace. See Chapter VII below.

35. See Robert Musil, *Mann Ohne Eigenschaften* (Hamburg: Rowolt, 1952), 1204 (from the third and fourth part of the *Nachlass* text of the novel).

36. This is a point Scheler has eloquently argued in *Wesen und Formen der Sympathie*, 176 ff. as a creative motion from lower to higher values in regard to the loved object.

37. In Plato's *Symposium*, "birth in beauty" as "the purpose of love" (206b) is famously ambiguous. But one sense of the "in" in *tokos in kaloi* is "in the presence of." The interpretative note by the translators in *Symposium*. Trans. Alexander Nehamas and Paul Woodruff (Indianapolis, IN: Hackett, 1989) does not take account of how being in the presence of beauty itself might be a source of creativity.

38. Husserl, Nachlass, B 1 21, III, 54a.

39. Dante, *Vita Nuova.* Trans. Mark Musa, ibid. For the clarification see Chapter XXV; for the personification of love as a god, see Chapters XII–XXIV, 17–53.

40. This paragraph and the two preceding ones are an appropriation and rethinking of a description by Levinas of his understanding of the ultimate ethical subjectivity: "The infinitely exterior becomes infinitely interior, in the guise of my voice bearing witness to the fission of the interior secret..." E. Levinas, *God, Death, and Time* (Stanford, CA: Stanford University Press, 2000), 197. I am grateful to Claudia Welz for calling my attention to this passage.

41. R.M. Rilke, *The Selected Poetry of Rainer Maria Rilke.* Ed. and Trans. Stephen Mitchell (New York: Vintage, 1984), 85.

42. James Gilligan's *On Violence* (New York: Vintage, 1997) shows that these "psychopaths", because violently robbed of their personal space and self-respect in their youth, are not capable of tolerating any appearance of disrespect. We return to this in §8, G. below.

43. These are by no means minor topics. We have touched on some of them earlier in Book 1 and in *The Person and the Common Life*, especially Chapter IV. If the exhortation to a universal love is to be both a mandate and desirable it must include the ipseity of the Others and not bleach out their uniqueness and difference.

44. This thematization of the twofold moment of love was first made, I believe, by F.E. Crowe, S.J, "Complacency and Concern in the Thought of St. Thomas" *Theological Studies* 20 (1959), 1–29, 198–230, 343–396.

45. Earlier in Book 1, Chapter IV we outlined and endorsed this position put forth early in the twentieth century by Scheler and McTaggart.

46. See Raymond Brown's discussion of these Greek terms for what gets translated as "love" in *The Gospel According to John, I–XII.* Trans., Introduction, and Commentary by Raymond Brown (New York: Doubleday, 1966), Appendix I, 497–499.

47. See Jaspers, *Von der Wahrheit*, 988 ff.

48. Kierkegaard has insisted that without the command to love, and depending only on the lovers' love sustaining itself, there is a fundamental poetic self-deception. Only when love has undergone

the transformation wrought by the eternal by which it becomes duty does it have the prospects of survival. See *Works of Love*. Trans. H. Hong and E. Hong (New York: Harper Torchbooks, 1962), 46–47. But can this be interpreted to mean that the love required to sustain the radiance of the other's ipseity is never genuine delight in the other ipseity but rather either selfish eros or obedience? No, if we take the eternal to refer to the trans-temporal ipseity itself and the "command" to merely explicate the necessity of a position-taking that is consonant with the eternal.

49. Works of Love, 152–162.

50. Husserl, Nachlass MS., B I 21 III., 55a.

51. *Ibid.*, 54a–55a.

52. Jaspers, *Philosophie*, 340; Vol. II, 53.

53. Jaspers, *Philosophie*, 354; Vol. II, 69.

54. Sokolowski, Christian Faith and Understanding, 206.

55. C.S. Lewis, *The Four Loves* (London/Glasgow: Collins Fontana, 1965), 58 ff.

56. Jaspers, *Philosophie*, 345 and 350; Vol. II, 58 and 64.

57. *Ibid.*, 356; Vol. II, 70–71.

58. I have been helped here by Jaspers' friend, Ernst Mayer, who offers a gloss on Jaspers's theory of communication. See his excellent *Dialektik des Nichtwissens* (Basel: Verlag für Recht und Gesellschaft, 1950), 318 ff.

59. Cf. our n. 79 on Francis Jacques' thought at the end of Book I, Chapter IV, where we find another hyperbolic statement about love which has affinities with Jaspers in this matter. On the problem of the I-substance, cf. Book 1, Chapter V.

60. Cf. my *The Person and the Common Life*, 325 ff.

61. See our efforts to integrate a Husserlian perspective on the ideal communalization of perspectives with that of some other modern writers in *The Person and the Common Life*, 330–357. Whereas the discussion in that volume attempts to do justice to the "we" the presentation of the unique ipseity does not receive adequate attention.

62. Husserl, Nachlass MS, B I 21 III, 53ab.

63. One finds this view in Augustine, Aquinas, and some idealists like T.H. Green and Brand Blanshard. For a clear statement, see Lavelle *De l'ame humaine*, 453 ff., especially 474. For a good general discussion of kinds of freedom, with its own version of "teleological determinism" under the rubric of "natural freedom," see Benjamin Gibbs, *Freedom and Liberation* (New York: St. Martin's Press, 1976).

64. Peter Bieri, *Das Handwerk der Freiheit*, 424–425.

65. Leibniz, *Theodicy* (Lasalle, IL: Open Court, 1985), 319. Cf. our discussion of "Teleological Determinism" *The Person and the Common Life*, 96–98, 138, 321–330, 384.

66. Leibniz, *ibid.*, 386–387.

67. C.S. Lewis, *Perelandra* (New York: Scribner, 1996), 149–150.

68. It seems that the addict's general will as holding sway over the myriad details of life subsequent to a resolution has less power than in the non-addict. The addict must incessantly renew the resolution and develop the discipline to live in the moment and be mindful of the resolve in the way the non-addict need not. In this sense, the addict *must* become a saint in the way the non-addict need not.

69. This theme runs throughout Helmut Kuhn's *Begegnung mit dem Sein*.

70. The term, "megamachine," is a rich metaphor orchestrated first by Lewis Mumford, and more recently by Rudolf Bahro; it is feebly hinted at by Dwight Eisenhower's "military-industrial-congressional complex."

71. Willa Cather, *The Song of the Lark* (Mineola, NY: Dover, 2004/1915), 138; see 135–139. I am grateful to Julia Livingston for having called my attention to these passages.

72. Husserl, Nachlass MS, A V 21, 80b–82b; B I 21 III, 56b.

73. Francis Slade, "On the Ontological Priority of Ends and Its Relevance to the Narrative Arts," in *Beauty, Art, and the Polis*. Ed. Alice Ramos (Washington, DC: Catholic University of America Press, 2000), 58–69; and "Ends and Purposes," in *Final Causality in Nature and Human Affairs*. Ed. Richard Hassing (Washington, DC: Catholic University of America Press, 1997), 83–85; Robert Sokolowski, "What is Natural Law?" in his *Christan Faith and Human Understanding*, 214–233. We have benefited from Sokolowski's summary of Slade's points on these matters.

74. Sokolowski, *ibid.*, 220.

75. Slade, "On the Ontological Priority of Ends," 67–68; cf. Sokolowski, ibid., 222.

76. Sokolowski, *ibid.*, 226 ff.

77. Sokolowski, *ibid.*, 226–227.

78. See the rich spiritual-theological Chapter 5 on these matters in Thomas Merton, *New Seeds of Contemplation* (New York: New Directions, 1961); we will return explicitly to the theological context in Chapter VI.

79. See Sokolowski, *ibid.*, 154–155.

80. See Sokolowski, *ibid.*, 202.

81. This point has been argued by Iso Kern in his *Idee und Methode der Philosophie* (Berlin: de Gruyter, 1976). See also my "The Rationality of Culture and the Culture of Rationality: Some Husserlian Proposals" *Philosophy East & West* XLII (1992), 643–664.

82. Robert Sokolowski, whose ideas have generated these paragraphs, has just completed another *opus magnum, Phenomenology of the Human Person* (Cambridge: Cambridge University Press, 2008), where some of these issues are in play.

83. Husserl, *Husserliana* XXVII, 121. Here again the caveat is registered that for the Husserlian perspective of this volume, the intersubjective context is inseparable from these reflections, and all that one finds in regard to oneself holds *ceteris paribus* in regard to the others in our surroundings. Our reflections here, however, prescind from this context because of the focus that gravitates around the distinctions between the transcendental I and Existenz. Cf. my *The Person and the Common Life*, 330.

84. Scheler, *Formalismus*, 481–485, 489–494. My interest in this theme was first awakend by Jeffmey Fry's fine doctoral dissertation at Indiana University

85. *Husserliana* XXIII, 338.

86. The best description of these matters from a Husserlian perspective is to be found in Dan Zahavi, *Self-Awareness and Alterity, op. cit.*

87. Heidegger, *Basic Problems in Phenomenology* (Bloomington, IN: Indiana University Press, 1982), §19.

88. See my "Wisdom, Knowledge, and Reflective Joy: Aristotle and Husserl," 68–77.

89. Kant, *Die Religion* (Berlin: Meiner, 1956), 21–23, 28.

90. Kant, *Kritik der praktischen Vernunft* (Hamburg: Meiner, 1974), 102. In Kant's transcendental-noumenal metaphysics we learn: "The human being who is virtuous is in heaven, only he does not intuit it, but he can infer it through reason. The human being who always finds causes to despise himself and find fault is already in hell here. Thus the transition from the sensible world into the other is merely the intuition of oneself. According to content it is always the same, but according to form it is different. *Lectures on Metaphysics*. Trans. and Eds. Karl Ameriks and Steve Naragon (New York: Cambridge University Press, 1997), 352; *Akadamie Ausgabe* 28, 592. I am indebted to Seungpil Im for this text in his Indiana University doctoral dissertation in *Dreams of a Sight-seer*. The "content" presumably is I myself. The form is I myself now bereft of the restricting encumbrances of sensibility.

91. Kant, Metaphysical First Principles of the Doctrine of Virtue; cited in Stephen Darwall, *op. cit.*, 119.

92. See J.G. Fichte, *Werke, Zur Rechts- und Sittenlehre II*. Vol. IV (Berlin: Walter de Gruyter, 1971), 317–322.

93. Cf. Lavelle, *De l'âme humaine*, 462.

94. Husserl, *Husserliana* XXVII, 121. Here again the caveat is registered that for the Husserlian perspective of this volume, the intersubjective context is inseparable from these reflections, and all that one finds in regard to oneself holds *ceteris paribus* in regard to the others in our surroundings. Our reflections here, however, prescind from this context because of the focus that gravitates around the distinctions between the transcendental I and Existenz. Cf. my *The Person and the Common Life*, 330.

95. Cf. J.-P. Sartre, *Being and Nothingness*, Part Two, Chapter One, 124–125; Jean Nabert, *Elements for an Ethic*, Chapter V.

96. See Husserl, Nachlass MS, F I 24, 151 ff.; my *The Person and the Common Life*, 286–288; and my "Wisdom, Knowledge, and Reflective Joy: Aristotle and Husserl" op. cit., 77–84.

97. I am indebted here to James Gilligan's rich work, Violence: Reflections on a National Epidemic, op. cit. for thinking about the problem of a basic sense of self-esteem when the self is most under siege. Gilligan is a psychiatrist who directed the Center for the Study of Violence at Harvard Medical School; he was also director of mental health for the Massachusetts prison system; and former medical director of the Bridgewater State Hospital for the criminally insane. Gilligan's work is not only a phenomenology of shame, but a fundamental text for our times, especially in the area of peace studies and criminal justice. For some etymological discussion, see 83. I am grateful to Hal Pepinski for calling my attention to Gilligan's work.

98. Gilligan, Violence, 64–65.

99. See Max Scheler, in his famous (1913) discussion, "Über Scham und Schamgefühle," in *Schriften aus dem Nachlass, Zur Ethik und Erkenntnislehre*. Vol. I (Bern: Francke, 1957), 88–89. Scheler distinguishes being ashamed and being embarrassed primarily because the former has to do with concealment and is founded in a valuation whereas the latter has nothing to do with either of these matters. Embarrassment is brought to light in the way the one who is embarrassed is hindered from doing routine matters because his attention is forced back upon himself and he takes up the attitude of the ones observing him, and thereby loses the necessary concentration on his own matter at hand and thus, e.g., fumbles, stutters, stumbles, etc. Perhaps we can add that this embarrassment is because he wants to be alone at this time and the gaze of the others overpowers his ability to stay focused. The "choking" by athletes, as well as public speakers, is a good example of being embarrassed. Of course, the embarrassment may lead to behavior that eventually causes one to be ashamed.

100. See Scheler, *ibid.*, 79–80.

101. Scheler, *ibid.*, 78.

102. Gilligan, *Violence*, 48.

103. I am indebted to James Gilligan's fine second work on these matters, *Preventing Violence* (London: Thames & Hudson, 2001), 31–33, for these references.

104. Gilligan, *Violence*, 129–130.

105. Stephen Darwall, *The Second-Person Standpoint: Morality, Respect, and Accountability* (Cambridge, MA: Harvard University Press, 2006. I came upon this excellent work (as I was preparing this Book 2 for press) through references in a lecture by Richard Moran at Indiana University in the Spring of 2008.

106. Darwall, 9–10.

107. I take this Kant text from Darwall, 23; he here cites *Groundwork of the Metaphysics of Morals*; in the *Akademie* edition of Kant's *Gesammelte Schriften*. Vol. VI. (Berlin: Walter de Gruyter, n.d.), 417.

108. Again, I take this Kant reference from Darwall, 119; he cites *Metaphysical First Principles of the Doctrine o f Virtue*.

109. Darwall, 15.

110. Darwall, 80.

111. Darwall, 3.

112. Darwall, 80.

113. Darwall, 120 ff.

114. Darwall, 121.

115. Darwall, 43, and 47–48, along with Adam Smith, removes animals from proper second-personal relations because they are not capable of entering into forensic relations. Yet he seems to resonate to Smith's fellow feeling, and implicitly respect, for animals. If this is a recognition respect outside the forensic situation and is granted to animals why would it not a fortiori be granted to human persons outside the forensic situation?

116. In as much as "person" is a term with a long theological lineage it is perhaps worth noting that for Darwall imagined person-like beings existing in a utopian paradisical setting where their being-with-one-another was able to dispense with the authority and competence to demand by reason of the infusion of their lives with love would not really be persons. They

would, in our terms, have an ontological dignity with its correlate respect, but this would be
bereft of forensics. Similarly, the essentially solitary divine ipseity, whose solitariness refers
to the perfection of its "being" and not to a privation of "Others" would not be a person.
The solitary divine ipseity of Aristotle's *noesis noeseous*, who exists transcendentally-
transcendently contemplating these themes would not be a person. Such would be a "mind"
but not a person. The "persons" of the Holy Trinity who exist in one another in an essentially
non-juridical and non-forensic relationship, where claims and demands make no sense,
would similarly not be persons.
117. See Darwall, 78; Kant, *Schriften*. Vol. VI, 417–418.
118. Darwall, 78.
119. See Darwall, 201.
120. Darwall, 35. That which necessarily presupposes my compliance and first-person perpective
     cannot, so it would seem, become the (authoritative) sense of "you". And to the extent it
     approaches the first-person witness of conscience, it still falls short for Darwall of being the
     proper source of moral authority. Yet, having said all this, we approach Darwall's position
     with the following consideration: In as much as the ideal communal perpective is encom-
     passing of present Others who remain essentially hidden as well as absent unknown Others,
     the striving to assume just such a perspective aims at a "godly perspective of a person of a
     higher-order" where "each would envisage him- or herself as uniquely called and uniquely
     envisaged regardless of position." Nicolas of Cusa portrayed this as the iconic (divine)
     gaze, the look of a Thou, which follows the onlooker's gaze "wherever he or she might be
     or move." See *The person and the Common Life*, 341. But as an ideal it is a first-person
     achievement; to become a second-personal perspective, as for Nicolas of Cusa, it requires a
     theological faith-perspective, to which we will soon turn.
121. See Darwall, 35 and 114, n. 44. Cf. my *The Person and the Common Life*, Chapters III ff.
     Obviously our work is not opposed to even feeble analogies but Darwall's thesis seems to
     require that the you of community be understood univocally. It is this which enables it to be
     the originating source of moral claims. That which necessarily presupposes my compliance
     and first-person perspective cannot, so it would seem, become the (authoritative) sense of
     "you." And to the extent it approaches the first-person witness of conscience, it still falls
     short for Darwall of being the proper source of moral authority. Yet, having said all this, we
     approach Darwall's position with the following consideration: In as much as the ideal com-
     munal perspective is encompassing of present Others who remain essentially hidden as well
     as absent unknown Others, the striving to assume just such a perspective aims at a "godly
     perspective of a person of a higher-order" where "each would envisage him- or herself as
     uniquely called and uniquely envisaged regardless of position." Nicolas of Cusa portrayed
     this as the iconic (divine) gaze, the look of a Thou, which follows the onlooker's gaze "wherever
     he or she might be or move." See *The Person and the Common Life*, 341. But as an ideal it is
     a first-person achievement; to become a second-personal perspective, as for Nicolas of Cusa,
     it requires a theological faith-perspective, to which we will soon turn.
122. Darwall, 256 and 21–22. Darwall refers to Fichte, *Foundations of Natural Right*. Ed. Frederick
     Neuhouser. Trans. Michael Bauer (Cambridge: Cambridge University Press, 2000).

Chapter VI
Aspects of a Philosophical Theology of Vocation

Part One: Historical Setting

"There is a cleavage between phenomenal and noumenal, between man insofar as he can show himself and be seen in the world by others and by himself and man as abyss, who is as being known by God, man who is whatever God knows him to be.

(Thomas Prufer on St. Augustine, in *Recapitulations*, 30)

[The pagan] would not consider himself as having been chosen to be, he would not consider his being as having been bestowed, in the way that a Christian would...The fact that we are is the outcome of a personal transaction, not the outcome of chance or necessity, and it calls for a personal reaction on our part.

(Robert Sokolowski, *Christian Faith & Human Understanding*, 44)

Since they do not any more see their father or themselves, they despise themselves through ignorance of their birth and honour other things, admiring everything rather than themselves...for what pursues and admires something else admits at the same time its own inferiority... [To reverse this one must remind such a soul] how high its birth and value are...and when it is clarified [it becomes obvious] how contemptible are the things now honoured by the soul.

(Plotinus, *Enneads* V.1.1)

We have repeatedly faced the twofold aspect of the person in terms of the relationship between, on the one hand, the propertyless "myself" (or ipseity) that establishes each of us in an irreplaceable, incommunicable uniqueness, and, on the other hand, the person in the world who is the "personification" of this "myself," and who, although likewise typically displaying uniqueness, nevertheless in principle is describable in terms of properties that each more or less shares, and which, even though constituted by unique constellations, can, at least in a thought-experiment, be found to admit (in the second- and third-person) a double. The concept of a unique vocation has the prospect of bridging and synthesizing the two aspects of what is referred to with "person" in so far as the embodied concrete human is the way the propertyless I-ness realizes its life in the world in a suitable, i.e., unique way. The "myself" or I-ness, personhood, and vocation are inseparable from one another. The most recent foray into the analogous senses of self-love, self-esteem, self-respect, etc., bring this out in so far as they point to the ineluctable earnestness of even passive senses of self-constitution because without eventually robust senses of self-valuation and respect for oneself, i.e., the awareness of one's inherent essential dignity, the possibility of understanding one's life as pervaded by a mandate, or a call, or a right way seems both gratuitous and irrelevant. In the absence of this sense of one's own dignity there is a vacuum left for reified, materialistic, degraded senses of oneself where even the possibility of self-disdain is effaced.

Thus, inseparable from such phenomenological-conceptual analysis there is the consideration that the "myself" or lived ipseity and one's destiny are lived as more than conceptual puzzles. That is, they point to the mystery and limit-situation that are the background for all of our theoretical and practical life. Religion and theology thrive primarily in this latter background atmosphere. They typically offer resolutions to the questions that arise out of the struggle of Existenz to come to terms with the mystery of ipseity and limit-situations. The resolutions come, for the major religious voices and founders, as first- and second-person experiences. For most followers they are, first of all, third-person claims that may become second- and first-person forms of reference. In these two concluding chapters we will deal with what come down to us for the most part as third-person theological and religious-philosophical claims to do justice to both the propertied and propertyless aspects of the person without conflating them. A pre-eminent project is to offer a traditional "likely story" that purports to shed light on the transcendent and transcendental sense of the intrinsic dignity of one's ipseity and personhood.

The voices heard in this Chapter VI, apart from those of the sacred literature of the tradition, i.e., the Bible, are those of some thinkers, there are doubtless others whom we have neglected either unwillingly or unwittingly, whose own ideas provide inspiration and support for the key ideas of the final chapter. In the systematic theological concluding Chapter VII there is attempted a philosophical theology of vocation of the person and the unique "myself" through the theological speculation on divine exemplarity and divine knowledge of ipseity.

In general these discussions are "speculative" in as much as the fuller perspective is reached by assuming a vantage point which is empowered by resources not permitted to phenomenological philosophy. Because they aspire to offer considerations that are founded in empty intentions, the quasi-filled character of which is provided by faith, they have the advantage for the phenomenological philosopher of offering considerations, albeit ones not available to the phenomenologist as such, that present the possible as actual and which more or less close some gaps opened by phenomenological reflection. This, of course need not say anything about the ultimate truth of these perspectives. For the philosopher these chapters offer trans-rational hypotheses which purport to continue the exploration of the relation between the "myself" and the destiny of the person.

Doubtless the shift of these final chapters into a philosophical-theological context would better accommodate the backgrounds of the philosophical reader if the core issue, i.e., the divine knowledge and exemplarity of what first-person reference refers to, were addressed by purely philosophical-phenomenological analyses. But this is not possible, primarily because with the exception of Plotinus the theme of divine knowledge and exemplarity of first-person reference is motivated by what believers regard as the revealed dogma of God the Creator and what Robert Sokolowski has called "The Christian Distinction between God and the world," but which we take the liberty of naming "The Theological Distinction." For transcendental phenomenology the world, as it is correlated with the transcendental I, provides the most comprehensive field for raising the themes of any phenomenology of religion. With the term "the world" we have a way of referring to the ultimate cognitive and axiological horizon of the mind. This cleared space has served for some fruitful philosophical-phenomenologies of religion. The transcendental I likewise has its philosophical forebearers and versions of it also have generated rich philosophies of religion. But neither of these poles, i.e., of the world or the transcendental I, even with praiseworthy philosophical elucidations, do justice to the dogma of God the Creator whose sense, the tradition teaches, is precisely to be beyond the world opened by reason, therefore beyond the ultimate horizon of intentionality as well as beyond the transcendence in immanence of the transcendental I.

What immediately follows in this Chapter VI is a discussion of some thinkers in the Western tradition whose theological imaginations and philosophical insight help along the philosophical eros we hope we have generated in regard to the issues of this work. In all this, we have featured Plotinus not only because of his extraordinary influence in conceptualizing the matters I regard as central but also because many of the themes we have discussed in this work are adumbrated in Plotinus, especially if we use as our perspective what might be called his theory of vocation. We, in fact, began the discussion of core themes of this chapter above in Chapter III, §7 where we looked at Plato's theology in regard to the *Daimonion* of Socrates. Here the theme, of interest to Plotinus, of the pre-existence of the self to the actual person's world-involvement was alluded to. Plotinus is of interest also of course because his is a pre-Christian philosophical account. This partially legitimates this chapter as a *philosophical*-theological undertaking. Particularly important is Plotinus's theory of divine knowledge of the unique ipseity and the perhaps pathbreaking role first-person reference plays in his philosophy. The topic of the divine knowing of first-person experience we take to be intrinsic to the dogma of God the Creator as an explication of The Theological Distinction.

The case could be made that in a philosophical work these concluding chapters which focus on divine knowledge and exemplarity in regard to first-person reference ought not to restrict themselves to what for the non-Christian reader might well appear as the narrow confines of the dogma of the Christian tradition regarding God the Creator. Such a conclusion to a purported philosophical work would, it might be argued, be more persuasive, and perhaps less gratuitous, if it sought to find parallels and illuminations in traditions outside of the Christian tradition. I wish to apologize for any appearance of indifference to these matters, but here is not the place to work out the tangle of methodological issues having to do with the philosophy of religion and a theology of religions.[1] (Some of our philosophical-theological allegiances in these matters will become clear in the course this chapter and the concluding Chapter VII.) Suffice it here to say that, in my view, the dogma of the creator God is a core teaching in Jewish thought and many of the other doctrines we touch on, such as vocation and messianism, are found, of course, with important differences, already in Judaism. Thus we find not only the obvious and important parallels, e.g., in Rosenzweig and Levinas, but even in the Jewish thinkers influenced by Neo-Platonism. Further, the dogma of the creator God is also at the core of Islamic faith – or at least Islam can be often construed in this light. We suspect also that there are some enlightening parallels in Hindu and Buddhist thought, at least in regard to the task of relating the divine and the individual self. Nevertheless, we have neglected the temptation to extend ourselves even further beyond our competence. However, we did not resist (e.g., in Book 1) briefly discussing possible Buddhist connections and the speculative theory of reincarnation, especially in its Vedanta form, that posits a sense of the Self that is at once transcendent to and yet the same as the incarnated person in the world. We will return to Vedanta in the Chapter VII, §9 in conjunction with The Theological Distinction. And we have entered into a brief discussion (at §3 below) of parallels within Islamic theology as it takes form in Sufi thought, which bears a similar ancestry to Christianity.

§1. Plotinus: The Form of "Socrates" and the True Self

Plotinus' philosophy adumbrates in several respects a transcendental phenomeno-logical meontology. For example, his philosophy has numerous claims that suggest that although human beings have a position *towards the world*, they are not most basically to be thought as having a position *in the world*. Thus in Plotinus' phi-losophy there is a twofold thematization: It regards that which is an object in the world and takes its bearing from something thing-like, and it studies that which is not something thingly in the world but which is lived and takes a position toward the world. This latter, when inwardly experienced in its capacity of ascent or tran-scendence, can call all of external or worldly being into question and provide a new measure for taking stock of what is most important.[2]

Thus in the *Enneads* I.9.6 (hereafter only the numerical reference to the Ennead book, chapter, and section of the chapter will be given[3]) the reader learns that he most truly is a self transcendent to all worldly properties. He discovers further that he has an intrinsic beauty and worth incommensurate with anything in the universe. With the appropriate moral life and discipline one discovers what it is to be "wholly yourself," i.e., "nothing but true light, not measured by dimensions, or bounded by shape into littleness, or expanded to size by unboundedness, but everywhere unmeasured, because greater than all measure and superior to all qual-ity." And in III.1.8 the individual soul is said to be a principle as a cause-initiating activity. Considered in itself and apart from the body, that is, like Kant's noumenal-intelligible and not empirical self, it is supreme in itself and outside the causation of the physical universe.

Thus this intelligible or "inner self" transcends the world. Plotinus offers a distinction between the Living All, which in certain respects may be thought of as the ultimate horizon of what is perceptually given, and the parts that are within it. And he makes a further distinction between, on the one hand, the soul in so far as it is a body which, to the extent it is this, makes it, as such, part of the Living All, and, on the other hand, those things that participate in the All-soul animating the Living All, and in this respect are not altogether parts of the Living All (IV.4.32).

When discussing the wide-spread view that the stars exercise influences on the soul's affections and shape its temperament, Plotinus asks, "What is left which is 'we.'?" Here (II.3.9) as in many places, Plotinus introduces a first-person perspective, most often in the plural form. This would seem to be his way of saying that although each is capable of being described in the third-person as a material thing in the world, this is not what is manifest in the first-person. Further, by employing the first-person plural he appeals to the evidence for the first-person singular as uniquely intersubjectively valid. Thus his answer to the question of what is left is, "Surely just that which we really are, we to whom nature gave power to master our passions." He notes, in another place, if everything happens according to causes, "we are not ourselves, nor is there any act which is our own" (III.1.4). And those who think of themselves exclusively as body-things, and thus absolutely at the mercy of external causes, are, indeed, as in a self-fulfilling prophesy, inextricably immersed in the external forces of destiny (IV.4.32).

In II.3.9, Plotinus reveals his form of dualism when he speaks of everyone being a double. "One has a compound [of body] and one of him is himself (*autos*)." The soul-principle is *how* (or, in some sense, the means by which – see below) what we refer to in the first-person brings about its agency. The first-person singular is what, in this passage, the intensive or emphatic pronoun refers to and what is self-present in the first-person. The soul-principle is not simply identified with what is referred to in the first-person. (See the text we give in the next paragraph.) Although Plotinus thinks of self-*knowing* as a form of reference to oneself as other, he still seems to have an inkling of a non-reflexive self-awareness. Thus although there is in the One no self-reflection, *sunaesthesis*, as J.M. Rist observes, we must not jump to the conclusion that the One is *anaistheton*, i.e., unconscious.[4]

In Plotinus' use of "we" we find many claims for which the original evidence is to be had only in the first-person singular, even though equally often he uses the first-person plural. The first-person plural is founded on and has the condition for its possibility in the first-person singular – if it is not an improper royal, editorial, i.e., presumptive usage. When we reason it is really "we" who reason (I.1.7); and "what is it that has carried out this investigation? Is it 'we' or the soul? It is 'we' but by the soul. And what do we mean 'by the soul'? Did 'we' investigate by having soul? No, but in so far as we *are soul*" (I.1.13). It is not clear to me whether Plotinus' position approaches that of Aristotle that it is the intellectual form as soul-principle that establishes what we refer to in the first-person. The emphatic use of the first-person as a principle, perhaps substance, works against such an interpretation. In any case, there seems to be a hesitation to separate soul and "I" too cleanly, and thus a self/soul and self/body dualism are and are not affirmed. Consider: " 'We ourselves' refers to the dominant and essential part of us; the body is in a different way ours, but ours all the same." And: "So 'we' is used in two senses, either including the beast [i.e., body] or referring to that which even in our present life transcends it" (I.1.10).

Here we approach our topic of vocation. Plotinus' inner soul is also the higher soul or self. Already Plato had called attention to the *daimonion*, and Aristotle urged us to love our better self (*Nicomachean Ethics* 1166a–b, 1169a 1–37). Plato's *daimonion* returns in Plotinus as a "tutelary spirit" that guides the present life. Further, following hints of Plato, we learn that we get the kind of "guardian angel" that we have chosen implicitly by the kind of life we have previously lived. "By our life we elect our own loftier." That is, the self-ideal that habitually guides us itself reflects the kind of life we live (III.4.3). This view suggests that the true ideal self is both eternal and transcendent to the embodied self, but also that the ideal emerges within the context of our moral habitualities. As Aristotle said, if we are responsible for our actions we are responsible for what appears to us as good (*Nicomachean Ethics* 1114b).

Plotinus' true higher self is both what is ontologically prior and the ideal true self. This introduces the theme of "exemplarism" which is central for much of the theology of the "Abrahamic religions."[5] It is also central to the philosophical theology of Chapter VII. The true higher self is ontologically prior because for Plotinus, the actual individual souls are rooted in their eternal forms which themselves subsist as constitutive of *Nous* or the Intellectual Principle. Plotinus seems to hold a general position that everything individual is something in which an essentiality can be detected. Although such an essentiality for the philosophical tradition is usually thought to be a communicable universal form, "Socrates" as a unique ipseity has just such an essence, and yet this essence is incommunicably rooted in the eternal form of the individual.[6] "If I ($\varepsilon\gamma\omega$) and each one of us have a way of ascent and return to the intelligible, the principle of each of us is there" (V.7.1). The argument here is not only: If Socrates always exists, there will be an absolute Socrates (a Socrates itself = *autosokrates*); but it further runs: Given such a rich and evident essence, "Socrates," how could there not be the eternal "myself" of Socrates. The "myself", e.g., of Socrates, always exists in the intelligible world. This is the way we understand the following argument: If there is no such permanent abiding "Socrates" and what was Socrates becomes another, e.g., Pythagoras, the individual "Socrates" has no existence "there" in that divine intelligible world.

We might think of this as a *reductio ad absurdum* position: Of course, Socrates whose rich unique essence has been revealed to us has undeniably existed; therefore Socrates' incommunicable and irreplaceable essence (the "myself" that is *Socratesness*) exists 'yonder,' and cannot have "become Pythagoras," i.e., have become the unique "myself" that is *Pythagorasness*, here below.

Plotinus (at VI.3.15) makes the analogy: The true ideal form of Socrates stands to the embodied Socrates as Socrates of our experience stands to a portrait of him.

We call each "Socrates." We even refer to the portrait as "Socrates." But the true referent in each case is the ideal form of Socrates; the others are guises whose sense points to the true referent.

Perhaps we can say that for Plotinus the true referent must be what Socrates himself refers to with "I" and the sense of what *we* second- and third-personally experience as Socrates, i.e., the embodied guise, does not absolutely coincide with what Socrates refers to with "I," where there is no distinction between sense and referent. And, a fortiori, what Socrates refers to with "I" cannot be the true form of what Pythagoras refers to with "I."[7]

When W.I. Inge claims that "the question whether it is *my* self that has its distant place 'yonder' is simply meaningless,"[8] he is elaborating his view that Plotinus does not have a doctrine of personality as something one clings to above everything else. Inge also holds that all senses of "I" that are not also objective are foreign to Plotinus. Thus Plotinus, like Inge, is, in this view, without a non-reflexive sense of "I myself." Yet Inge also says, basing himself on V.8.11, that there is a "kind of unconsciousness in the highest experiences of the Soul, though we can no more doubt them than our own existence."[9] In this passage of Inge we may indeed have evidence for Plotinus' wrestling with the soul's experience of itself at a higher level of achievement, and thus the soul is bereft, in regard to itself, of objective perceptions. Such an achievement, although impoverished in terms of intentional objects (a "kind of unconsciousness"), cannot be disbelieved, for "to disbelieve would be to disbelieve in his own existence."

Similarly, when A.H. Armstrong, in his commenting on the same problem in Plotinus, holds that self-awareness, as in "*I* am doing something," or "Something is happening to *me*," is an "epiphenomenon, a secondary, and not particularly desirable, effect of our proper activity that, as a form of self-reflective observation, interferes with the quality of our moral and intellectual agency," he is confining self-awareness to reflective self-awareness.[10] Doubtless the achievement of the indexical is an achievement of myself as myself that may well detract from the quality of our agency. But this reflective form of self-awareness does not capture all forms of self-awareness. Further, even the explicit use of *I* to call attention to explicit egoic achievements does not of necessity imply a form of reflective self-awareness. (Cf. our discussions in Book 1, Chapters II–IV.) But presumably Armstrong would be unhappy with the implication of his view, namely, that because we are not self-aware we therefore are *anaistheton*, unconscious. Self-awareness need not involve the actual use of the first-person singular – even if we need to use this form to explicate some kinds of self-awareness; it need not actually involve a reference to oneself as one*self*. But if there were not some sense of "I-ness" in the non-referential, non-reflexive self-awareness what would the first-person singular indexical reference be explicating and would there not be a doubt as to whose experience it was? As we already suggested, Plotinus' refusal to ascribe *anaistheton* to the One, as well as his numerous other references to the first-person singular and plural might very well indicate a sense of the first-person that is non-reflective.

Each of us, because we are minds, i.e., capable of being intentionally all things, is an "intelligible world." As such we are interstices between the higher and lower world. (III.4.3; cf. also our Book 1, Chapter VI, §§6–8.) In actuality, even though what we refer to in the first-person has its exemplar in the intelligible realm which is inseparable from the Intellectual Principle itself (*Nous*), I am not the Intellectual Principle itself. Rather intellect is *mine*, even though it transcends me and is that by which I am illuminated and made intelligible to myself. "For this reason we [both] use *Nous* and do not use it." (This probably reflects the wrestle with Aristotle's passage in *de Anima* III.5.)

Plotinus, at V.3–5, has passages of a mystical quality where the "the I" seems indeed one with *Nous* itself and where seer and seen are one; here each person gives way to the Intellectual Principle itself as each is one with the eternal form which is one's true self. Here, it might be said, one enjoys a view from nowhere of everything in its formal reality. In this respect each is subordinated to a pure "consciousness as such," identical with the purely formal exemplar of oneself.

But is Socrates bereft of all self-awareness of Socrates in this blissful philosophical heaven? Probably not. Two considerations are relevant here: (a) If as a matter of necessity the essence of Socrates is self-aware and self-knowing then the exemplary Socrates that is also the true self of the earthly Socrates, like all the forms encompassed in *Nous*, shares in the feature that here it is both a known form and the knowing. In this case the knowing is a self-knowing. This position is one which we will propose in a theological context but is only at best implicit in Plotinus. (b) When at IV.4.2 Plotinus says that in that highest state of being one with one's true self, "it will not even have the remembrance of itself, or that it is the man himself, Socrates for instance, who is contemplating, or that it is intellect or soul," we find him in fact arguing not for an absence of identity between the incarnate person or "endowed soul" and the higher self. We find rather an argument for the necessary anonymity of oneself as a theme when one is absorbed in the contemplated object or theme. Consider that when absorbed in something "one does not turn to oneself in the act of intelligence, but one possesses oneself." One's attention is not directed toward oneself, but at the same time the act is one's own ("possesses oneself") and one has a concurrent (non-reflexive) awareness of oneself, "as having become one and the same thing with its intelligible object." In such moments of contemplation I am not aware of myself but the myself is most aware.

Each of us is on the way to an ascent to the ideal true self which exists eternally in *Nous*. This is the standard for each soul endowed with a body (or person), and it provides the measure for the ideals one strives to realize in life. The ascent is also a "turn within" away from the empirical embodied soul to the principle of "I myself" as it is evident in all my intellectual and moral agency. The ascent, and inseparably the turn within, is also a return. But as Gerson says "the idea is of a return to what we are, not a return to what we were." Consider how one might, in the first naivety, understand Adam. After the Fall Adam is in a state of decline and might well desire to return to where he was before. "From Plotinus' perspective, however, that pre-fallen state would be just the state of another endowed self," i.e., another incarnation.

Again, following Gerson, the return to the One, from which all of being stems, which return is inseparably a return to one's true ideal self, is not of the same order as paths of repeated incarnations.[11] Plotinus seemed to have believed in reincarnation as a failure to achieve the ideal and perhaps as a self-imposed punishment. The individual self, after death, as the momentarily newly disincarnate agent, for whom the true and ideal self has been rejected and disdained in the prior life, has as his only choice to throw himself "back into the only milieu in which he finds comfort and satisfaction."[12] In the soul's pursuit of what is alien to its true self, it will never arrive at "absolute nonexistence" on its downward path. That is, it can never absolutely self-destruct.

But if it runs in the opposite way, i.e., toward its true destiny, it will arrive, not at something else but at itself, and in this way since it is not in something else it will not be in nothing, but in itself; but when it is in itself alone and not in substantial worldly being, it is in That; for one becomes by this conversion, not substance, but "beyond substance." That is, one is beyond the categoriality of worldly being. If then one sees that oneself has become This, one has oneself as a likeness of That, and if one goes on from oneself, as image to original, one has reached "the end of the journey" (VI.9.11).

The ideal true self is the actuality I recognize as my own and as having a distinctive fittingness to my life. In our prior presentation, the closest we have come to the Plotinian moment of enlightenment is the Husserlian (and Fichtean) discovery of one's call through the "truth of will." But, as we have urged, this contrasts with the more typical state of darkness and groping where the ideal true self is present only in the dim horizon of an obscure regulative ideal. In neither the typical case nor that of the case of the revelations of "the truth of will" is the agent permitted to claim that her present being is one with its ideal exemplar (or the Plotinian divine principle of *nous*). In each case for the agent the ideal is a possibility and one's present state is at best an aspiring to approximate the ideal. For Plotinus, as for Fichte and Husserl, this recognition of a distinct fittingness of the ideal is equivalent to coming to desire a certain way of life, the contours of which are shaped by the desire to be wholly identified with the ideal and the aspiration to overcome all self-inadequation.

It is not as if one were launched toward an ideal that was absolutely other than oneself – as if my fulfillment were in becoming someone else altogether. Even for the person who does not respond to the ideal the ideal is a version of oneself that one represses and flees. All such living in fact is a form of self-dishonoring, just as it is an excessive honoring of that to which one gives one's allegiance. The true path, indeed the true religion, has a twofold epistemic power: First, it shows "how contemptible are the things now honored by the soul" and, secondly," it reminds the soul "how high its birth and value are, and this is prior to the other" aspect of the true path (V.1.1). (Recall our effort in Chapter V, §8 to bring to light a transcendental sense of "self-honoring.")

Life is pervaded by a mix of necessity and freedom. Each soul descends into the body and temperament which best suit it according to its prior life (IV.3.12–13). Life is this intermingling of the noumenal ideal of oneself and the embodied situated self. The former frames our life always and takes form according to our projects; but these have the form they have as a result of our decisions and our actual character. The determinism that weighs on us is not merely that of the ideal that we more or less repress, but it is what we also impose on ourselves. What I am

now doing is not especially because of a synthesis of past events, or prior lives
I have chosen to live. Rather, it is because, in the present, I give myself the eternal
guise that only this act is able, at this moment, to manifest. My present is not only
a result of my past, but rather past, present and future are commanded by a *superior present*. It is not time which constitutes destiny nor is salvation conquered *by*
time. Rather, salvation from time into eternity is in time, since the indivisible ideal
eternal self is immanent in the unfolding of conscious life.[13]

The injunctions to honor oneself and dishonor that which lures away from this
self-honoring provide more or less objective ethical and aesthetic criteria, but ultimately the evidence for this ideal is its "connaturality" with the soul's own a priori
inkling of its divine kinship and beauty. Plotinus uses another poignant analogy:
"A child, certainly, who is outside himself in madness will not know his father; but
he who has learnt to know himself will know from whence he comes" (VI.9.7).
Here Plotinus uses an example of a posteriori knowledge, i.e., how illness can cause
us not to recognize the most familiar things we have come to know. The lesson of
the example appears to be that the ontological illness of our alienation from our true
selves can cause us temporarily to misperceive what in fact is a priori, i.e., one's
ontological home.

The external arrangements of the world, e.g., the way the parts of one's life
get organized into parts and wholes, provide conditions of, or the schema for, this
recognition in the course of life. The inward longing for the Good is at once a longing for the true self as well as for what transcends it (See I.6). The soul loves the
Good because it has been moved by Him, the One, to love Him from the beginning
(VI.3.31). The purest form of the love is becoming one's true self in unity with pure
Intellect. In which case one has given oneself up to what is within. And then one is
not merely an agent of manifestation and self-determination, but realizes that one
is seen through *Nous'* contemplative gaze. Being given up to the higher self within
oneself one becomes "instead of one who sees, an object of vision to another who
contemplates him shining out with thoughts of the kind which come from that
world... If he sees it as something different, he is not yet in beauty, but is in it most
perfectly when he becomes it" (V.8.11). Here love remains desire until its telos is
reached. And this love only appears to be always Self-love, love of one's higher truer
Self. Rather, ultimately it is love of the One which is absolutely beyond all qualities.
(Cf. VI.9.8.) Freedom properly and fully is moving without hindrance through the
ideal self in the Intellectual Principle towards the Good (VI.8.7). Normative freedom
is being teleologically determined by the Good as manifest in one's true self ideal.

As is well known, Plotinus used the center-periphery image to describe the self
in relation to the world and the self in relation to the One (VI.8.18; VI.9.8). Each
"I myself" is an inviolable unique self-aware source and principle of thought and
agency which is not commensurate with or simply a part of the natural causality
of the Living All. Each center is alone for itself a center of the world. In gathering
one's life out of the dispersion to the periphery one naturally moves toward the
center from which the circle of the world takes its bearings. The fundamental task,
according to this metaphor, is "to join ourselves at our own centers to something
like the center of all things." And this is to move beyond our being one with the

ideal true self in Intellect to the One which is beyond all intellection. We are always around this center but do not always attend to it (VI.9.8).

Each "I myself" is essentially alone, i.e., enjoys an essential solitude. Yet each can and must say "we." But in doing so each recognizes that "we" is constituted of a plurality of essential solitudes or monadic centers. The unity with the One is a coincidence and contact with the center of all centers. Each "I myself" is centered in the supremely ineffable center which is supremely alone. Plotinus on several occasions speaks of the ascent to the One as an awareness of the alone being with the alone. On occasion, he uses the emphatic "oneself" (*autos*) with *monos*: "one sees with oneself alone That alone" (I.6.7). The ascetical task as a response to the call of the One is to be purely oneself in the solitude of one's ownness, one's true self, free of all burdens and distracting attachments, in order solely to be oneself with the pure Alone (VI.9.11). Prayer itself is a stretching of "I myself" in my unique solitude to the absolute Solitude, to the absolutely transcendent Ipseity (V.1.6).

We will return to Plotinus when we discuss the differences between Neo-Platonism and Christianity.

§2. Christianity

A. *The Bible*

We find, *ceteris paribus*, hints of similar themes in aspects of Christianity and its historical parent, Judaism. But before we turn to these themes a word is necessary about our use of gender here. The tradition uses predominantly the masculine pronoun in referring to God. We will not always follow this practice. The reasons for deviating from this practice today are obvious and we take further delight in acknowledging the precedent of other writers who have found encouragement in the likes of Julian of Norwich and Anselm of Canterbury in ascribing to Jesus the attribute of Mother, and a fortiori motherhood, and the female gender to God.[14] Yet the preference of one gender over the other, even granting the importance of "affirmative action," must not obscure the fact that, in any case, at best we have to deal with analogy (see Chapter VII) and the dissimilarities are no less important than the similarities.

The theme of the divine calling of ipseity is perhaps hinted at in the Jewish scriptures (in *Genesis*) where we read that God created Adam by breathing into him from the interiority of God's own life, i.e., his own breath. He becomes a living being by way of the divine breath, divine inspiration. For Adam, proper life would mean "being inspired," i.e., "to see things as God saw them, to love them as God loved them, to be moved in all things ecstatically by the spirit of God.... In Paradise ecstasy is normal."[15]

This passage, where Adam in his core originates in the intimate recesses of the life of God and is the effect of the (invisible) breath of God, reflects the earlier passage where man, drawn from the earth, Adam, appears both as a single individual, male and female, and a concrete universal, is to be made "in our image, after our likeness." But Yahweh is precisely the One after whom there cannot and ought not to be any image and likeness. Breath is not a likeness of the breather and the breathed-in soul is a likeness of that which has no likeness. There is nothing in the world which captures the likeness of either God or man, nor anything which serves as a likeness for the "breathing in" which effects the presence of the living "person."

Through the confusion and perversity resulting from "The Fall" the noble lineage and identity of the descendents of Adam are lost sight of. It is the office of the chosen people, Israel, to exemplify this origin and be a reminder of this exalted lineage. This she does by being faithful to the covenant she makes with God and through keeping God's commandments. Israel is entrusted with the mysteries of this divine lineage as well as with a promise of great mysteries to come regarding her and humankind's exalted destiny. Foremost an era will be ushered in by the suffering servant anointed by God's Spirit. Through this Annointed One or Christ good tidings to the poor and broken-hearted will be brought and all those in bondage will be liberated. Through this anointed one, the Messiah or Christ, God will make a New Heaven and New Earth. (See *Isaiah*, especially 61 and 65.)

In Christianity the "image of God" theme moves in two different but connected directions. It explicates the "image of God" in Jesus the Messiah or Christ as the image of the Father and it points out that the basic task of life is the "spiritual" life, which is living in such a way that the person takes her bearing from her ontological status of being indeed the image of God, and this has the bonus that the person, in so faithfully living, is thereby transformed, indeed, deified as far as a creature can be. Here there is claimed an answer to the question whether who one is ultimately is what one is, or whether what one is ultimately is who one is. The "image of God" doctrine teaches not merely that all creation is in some sense a likeness of the unrepresentable inconceivable God, i.e., it teaches exemplarism as a necessary consequence of the doctrine of creation from nothing, but it teaches further that in a special way individual persons are "images" or "likenesses" of the trans-intelligible, incommensurate creator. In Christianity there is the further specification that the New Adam, the "Son of God," Jesus of Nazareth is the exemplary "likeness" of this God and that all are called to participate in this likeness of the "Son" and be a "child of God."

That there is nothing in the conceptual display of the world which captures God, or even perhaps God's image, is most starkly stated in the passage of *Exodus* 3:14, where Moses requests of God that He reveal his name. The immediate context is Moses being called by name from out of the burning bush in which a message or perhaps an angel of the Lord appeared. In response to hearing his name called, Moses answered "Here I am." Here Moses learns in fear and trembling that the God of his fathers, Abraham, Isaac, and Jacob, is present. Moses is told not to come closer, and here, as Martin Buber rightly states, with the restriction on the "approach" to divinity a basic feature of biblical religion is indicated. After hearing what the God of his fathers had to say, Moses asks, "Who am I that I should go to Pharaoh and lead the Israelites out of Egypt?" He hears, "I will be with you." Moses persists: But when I go to the Israelites and say to them, 'The god of your fathers has sent me to you,' if they ask me, 'What is his name?' what am I to tell them?"

Asking for a proper name, we have noted (Book 1, Chapter IV, §3) is not typically asking for a property description. The famous answer given to Moses may be interpreted in the context of the ancient Semite conviction that the knowing of someone's proper name not only established greater familiarity but also power over the being whose name it was because the true name revealed the essence of the person in such a way that the one knowing it had power over the person. The mysterious answer of "Yahweh," frequently translated as "I am who I am," might be a refusal on God's part to reveal his name to man. This would be a way of stating not merely God's transcendence to any property but God's transcendence to any name. This consideration, and perhaps the basic sense of "I am who I am," points to the consideration that God is not only something different or even endlessly more than what is grasped in any name or property ascription, but that the divine is precisely what presents us with the impossibility of definition, description, or intelligibility. And the great mystery is not a *nihil negativum*; that about which there is nothing to say is precisely the "I do not know what" that, rather than appearing without interest or significance, is trans-intelligible and beyond what is good. But the divine mystery is not merely that of the ipseity with which we are "familiar," even if not comprehending, in our everyday experience. Nevertheless the ipseity with which we are familiar is the "image" of that utterly inconceivable and unimaginable mystery.

Two leading candidates for an appropriate translation of "Yahweh" get at the central theme of both volumes of this work, namely how best to think of "who one is." "I am who I am" suggests pure ipseity. The pure Who is bereft of properties; the "I am" is qualified by the tautologous qualifying relative clause, "who I am." This "qualification" is rooted in the "I" and the freedom of the Who to be who one is; in this sense there is no qualification as a specification or delineation by reference to something outside the "I." This leads us to think that the "name" of God as beyond properties refers to the pure ipseity. God's revelation is of the pure ipseity which in no way is a sortal term, in no way a predication as a qualification of a subject but rather the pure subjectivity resisting all such qualification. God, by being pure ipseity, is to be thought of as absolute subject which in no way can either be a predicate or be qualified by a property.

Another candidate for the translation "Yahweh," indeed the one which the biblical Hebrew is said to mean, according to the *Jerome Biblical Commentary*, is "I am what I am."[16] Here the "I am" is qualified by "what I am." The "I" and "I am" are qualified by the relative clause of "what I am." This could be taken to say the essence, the What, determines the existence, the Who, whereas the first translation might be said to resist any such essential determination. Yet if the divine essence cannot be determined by anything apart from itself, therefore "what I am" merely reflects the power and freedom of "I am," it could be taken as a statement not only of a *per se* individuation but also of the identity of essence and existence. Of course, St. Thomas understood (the Vulgate translation of the Hebrew) *ego sum qui sum* to mean something along these lines. God, as *ipsum esse subsistens*, or the pure subsisting To Be, is not limited by anything and it is God's essence to be, and not to be in a certain way, i.e., limited by an essence of form. (We will have ample occasion to return to this topic later in Chapter VII.)

The first-person form of the translation suggests that only God can say who God is or what God's name is, because the report regarding Yahweh, or using Yahweh as a name, and not an evocation, is to put Yahweh's response in the third-person as "and then Yahweh did this." But this is precisely the proposal favored by *The Jerome Biblical Commentary*. In this view, "Yahweh" is a causative form and as such requires the third-person. The upshot is the very Thomist proposal that Yahweh means "He Causes to be what Comes into Existence." God as pure To Be alone is the causal source of what exists, i.e., of any finite *kind* of being or any limited being. Even though this view does not find the first-person form significant, it does not contradict the "I am who I am" as pure ipseity, but appears to say that only a pure trans-conceptual ipseity can cause existence which is necessarily limited and pervaded by kinds.

Martin Buber is skeptical of any such abstract ontological interpretations.[17] He thinks the most appropriate context for understanding this passage is through a contrast with the superstition and magic of Egypt. Here the God is made present by magical practice. In contrast, Yahweh emphasizes: It is superfluous, indeed, impossible, to invoke me or conjure me with your practices. I will be present when I will be present, just as I will be merciful to whom I will be merciful, and gracious to whom I will be gracious (as in *Exodus* 33:19). "You cannot presume to give me a character and thereby chain me to this designation." It is in accord with my character that I will befriend those I befriend and will stand by them. Thus, Buber proposes, "I am that/who/what I am" is not a deliberate withholding of information; nor is it a name which gives those possessing the name some power over the named. The God cannot be so named. Rather it is simply the revelation that "I am 'He Who Is Here,'" "I shall be present," "I am always with you," i.e., to my faithful people.

In spite of the difficulty of finding a definitive and decisive conclusion to the problem of the meaning *Exodus* 3:14, all the serious commentaries suggest (a) God's hiddenness and transcendence; and (b) that God's reality is personal in the sense that there is a trans-propertied ipseity and an inscrutable will; and (c) although this reality is "good news" for the people of God, any presumptuous familiarity with this reality or presence is perilous beyond measure. This presence is expressed by the phrase "my face." The Lord used to speak with Moses face to face (*Exodus* 23:11); yet shortly thereafter we learn that "My face you cannot see, for no man sees me and still lives" (*Exodus* 23:20). Here, perhaps echoing the warning not to get close to the burning bush (*Exodus* 3:5), Moses is instructed by the Lord to let the Lord cover him with his hand until He passes by, and then he can see the Lord's back; "but my face is not to be seen."

We now move to the remarkable emergence of the doctrine of calling and salvation as a piece of the doctrine of creation. Indeed, the core of the theology of the ancient Hebrew faith is to be found not only in the revelation to and covenant with the historical people of Israel but in Israel's prayer life and spirituality. In *Psalm* 139 we have a statement of the incomprehensible immanence and transcendence of God. "You have searched me and known me…" God knows our thoughts as soon as they are formed. "Where can I go from your Spirit? Or where can I flee from your presence. If I ascend into heaven, You are there. If I make my bed in hell, behold, You are there.…" And there is a mysterious divine comprehension of us not only in our conscious waking life but prior to this, prior to our births, God fashions each of us "in secret." "Your eyes saw my substance being yet unformed…" and one's whole life is written in God's book prior to our even having lived. (See verses 15–17.) *Psalm* 32:15 refers to "He who fashions the heart of each individual," or "He who fashions the hearts of them all." In *Isaiah* 43:1 we find the Lord saying he created you, Jacob, and you, Israel, and "I have called you by your name, you are mine."

In the Christian Scripture, St. Paul claims that perhaps he was set apart before he was born and called through God's grace (*Galatians* 1:15). At *Ephesians* 1:4, one finds "He chose us in him before the foundation of the world…" This means those who have been chosen are who they are prior to the world's creation and world's individuating agencies, prior perhaps to space and time.

One of the most important texts supporting a Christian "exemplarism" that encompasses especially the unique ipseities is in the New Testament *Letter to the Romans* 8:29–30. The Revised King James translation reads: "For whom He foreknew He also predestined to be conformed to the image of His Son that he might be the firstborn among many brethren. Moreover whom He predestined these He also called; whom He called He also justified." The *New English Bible* has a more startling rendition: "For God knew his own before they even were, and also ordained that they should be shaped to the likeness of his Son, that he might be the eldest among a large family of brothers. And those whom he called he has justified, and to those whom he has justified he has also given his splendor."

Joseph Fitzmyer claims that Paul does not have in mind the predestination of individuals but rather he has "a corporate point of view" in mind. He suggests that these are mutually exclusive because of the focus, after Augustine, on the issue of "predestination." But it is not at all evident that the "corporate" point of view must exclude that of a doctrine of a call addressed to individuals.[18] Clearly the calling is corporate; it is the Christian reworking of the calling of Israel, understood as a people set apart. But it is also a calling of each individual, i.e., of Moses, Abraham, Isaiah, Mary, Elizabeth, John, Peter, Paul, etc.

The early Christian ("patristic") interpretation echoes this tension between the individual and a people or all of humanity. Gregory of Nyssa fused together the "image of God," "the whole of human nature," and the Christ as the Image of the Father. As we shall see, St. Paul heightened this tension between the individual and the corporate sense of the image of God by claiming each Christian must give way to his old self and let Christ be his true self. This led John Ruusbroec to say that the "image of God" as God's eternal wisdom "is to be found essentially and personally in all men; each one possesses it whole and entire and undivided, and all together have no more than one." This concept of humanity as a whole person is not merely a Husserlian "person of a higher-order" historically built up from below but is a complex corporate person "in Christ" having an ideal existence from before the foundation of the world. Sin is understood to be the division of the corporate "person" that encompasses all humans into divisive and antagonistic factions and individuals. With the event of the Incarnation, states Cyril of Alexandria, "the common personality of man is brought back to life."[19]

Inseparable from this corporatization or personalization of humanity is the sense of the Hebrew "Quhal" which the Septuagint translated as *ekklesia*. We translate this most often as "church" but originally its sense seems to have been tied not merely to actual "gatherings" or communities or congregations, but to these as constituted in response to the universal summons of humanity. De Lubac believes that "*ecclesia* is in logical sequence to the *kletoi*," the *congregation* ensues upon the *convocation* or universal calling.[20] The tension between the uniqueness of the calling and its universality is especially stressed in the second vision of the Shepherd of Hermas who beholds an aged woman who is identified eventually as "the Church" and whose age is explained "because she was created first, before all else; that is why she is aged. It was for her that the world was made."[21] Here reverberates the Judaic concept of salvation and religion as profoundly social, if not communitarian. But "social" and "communitarian," even supposing their eternal exemplarity through "the Church," in no way obliterates the uniqueness of the individuals. This is because the *ecclesia*, whatever else it would be in terms of a social, even authoritative, hierarchical organization, is always also a "person of a higher-order,"[22] where there is an exemplary sense of "we" emergent out of all the "I's." Membership in her in no way extinguishes the uniqueness of the individual and the uniqueness of her calling. Paul's theme in his letters about the Body of Christ having many irreplaccable members is the most obvious support for this view. We shall repeatedly return to this.

How is there someone "there" to be so known, chosen, and called before they were born or before they entered the network of time and history? What does it mean for God to "foreknow?" How is this "knowing" also a "predestining" to be conformed or shaped to the likeness of his son? Most basically, what does it mean to know someone before she is (created) and a community of I's forming "we" before the I's exist?

The traditional theological position, of which we have found some intimations in this work, is that there is a cleavage "between man insofar as he can show himself and be seen in the world by others and by himself and man as abyss." This designation of the self or soul as an abyss (cf. *Psalm* 42:7) that stands in correlation with the abyss which is God is thematized in Augustine. In this work we have called attention to the invisible unpropertied individual essence (the "myself") as the core and entelechy of the exceedingly complex individual person. But in Augustine, formalized in Thomas Prufer's interpretation, each of us is an abyss "who is as being known by God" and each is "whatever God knows him to be." This sense of the abyss, a sense of which the philosophical part of this work has no inkling, is that for selves to be "is for them to be, without remainder or reserve, chosen by and manifest to another," i.e., God. The philosophical sense of being, foremost the being of ipseity, is to be manifest as the same to all. This position is sustained in one aspect of our analysis, namely that the self's unique essence as essence appears to the second- and third-person observer as precisely the same for all in each case. Yet we have insisted that this formal sameness, tokened by the universal term "I," is not merely formal and empty but rather that in the first-person it is inaccessible to Others and enjoys a unique fullness precisely in being uniquely. (See Book 1,

Chapter III, §2.) But the theological sense of the being of ipseity goes beyond the position that the unique essential sense of oneself is available only in the first-person, and that this is true in each case for all and evident to all. It permits a further step which holds that the sense of the unique self "hidden in the hidden God," the sense of which is known only by the creator God, is hidden not only from others but even from oneself.[23] The Christian thus cannot look upon other persons as simply a result of an amazing chance coincidence of this sperm and this egg; nor as a result of the astonishing evolution on this tiny planet of this mammal taking precisely this shape after hundreds of thousands of years of fluctuation of the genetic pool finally arriving at a more or less stable present Gestalt and reproducing itself on this occasion under these circumstances. As Sokolowski has put it, whereas the pagan might think of human persons to be a result of chance or necessity, the Christian must think of persons as the outcome of a choice, a personal transaction,[24] even though what it would mean to choose or call what does not exist remains lost in mystery – a mystery to which this chapter and the next are devoted.

Fitzmyer proposes understanding the Pauline "foreknowledge" (*proginoskein*) as a knowing "with affection, predilection" and not as a purely speculative knowledge. And this is an eternal loving-foreknowledge the evidence for which is one's loving God. "If one loves God, one is known by him" (1 *Corinthians* 8:3). Fitzmyer calls attention to texts from the Dead Sea Scrolls: "Before you created them, you knew all their deeds forever, [for without you no] thing is made and apart from your will no(thing) is known...before they were fashioned he knew their deeds."[25]

Apart from our discussion of Leibniz below, we will not attempt to do justice to the intricacies of "predestination." However, we wish to mention that here we have remarkable claims which defy reason but which may find a kind of dogmatic-theological logic as well as a logic of faith and thus a measure of meaning and intelligibility. This logic is to be found within the parameters set forth by what Robert Sokolowski has named "The Christian Distinction" and we will repeatedly return to it. The God of this distinction is precisely the "one" who knows us before we are, and this "one's" knowing us is inseparable from the Father's knowing his Son and Himself.

No one whom we might imagine or conceive could call or choose "me" prior to my actual existence or enworldment. My parents could not even have wanted *me*; they might have wanted "a boy" or "a girl" or "a healthy baby with two arms, ten fingers, two legs, ten toes, blond hair and blue eyes"; but there is no sense to their having wanted *me*. Thus a sense of God emerges as precisely the One capable of "choosing" or "calling" me prior to my actual existence in the world. This suggests there is a sense of "us," and therefore a sense of each "myself," prior to one's being a person in the world with others. This sense of "myself" is first of all present in God, even prior to God's calling or choosing us. What could this sense of us possibly mean if I "myself" am me only through the individuation process of nature and history? Clearly this latter sense of individual is insufficient. Rather, here in the Bible and tradition is a sense of the single individual that is independent of the conditions of individuation, e.g., space, time, worldly causality, natural process, culture, community, and history.

In the rabbinic tradition we find the theme that the divine desires us to be authentic selves. This may or may not mean that there is an exemplary a priori divine version of us. For example, a story is told of Rabbi Zuscha who, on his deathbed, was asked what he thought the kingdom of God would be like. After thinking for a long time the Rabbi replied: "I don't really know. But one thing I do know: When I get there, I am not going to be asked, 'Why weren't you Moses?' or 'Why weren't you David?' I am going to be asked, 'Why weren't you Zuscha?'"[26] This, perhaps, has affinity with the Plotinian notion of an essential "true self" which is not only what the creature is called upon to realize but perhaps also is one with the divine nature; it could also, of course, be simply a way to talk about being honest with oneself and realizing one's own "talents" and finite contingent potentialities. Although it does not repudiate at least occasionally taking one's bearings from someone else, it discourages any effort to imitate or be oneself by trying to be someone else. In any case, being one's self has a normative component and this weighs more than any internalization of an external ideal. That is, God wants us to be a true version of ourselves which means both not deceiving ourselves and not taking our cues from someone else but pursuing our own path. "Why weren't you Zuscha?" might refer to a sense of Zuscha that was prior to the contingent temporal unfolding of the person; or it might refer to what in any case is necessary, i.e., this person's ongoing struggle to be honest with himself in his self-awareness and self-appraisal.

The theme of the single individual not individuated by worldly conditions is somewhat echoed in the teaching of the Catholic Church that every "spiritual soul" is immediately created by God, not merely "produced" by the parents.[27] But there is an echo only if "soul" is not understood as a metaphysical form that is universally the same in each individual. Often in the tradition, the text of *Ephesians* 1:4, as in St. Thomas, assumed the identity of the unique ipseity as existing prior to the "individuation" of the world. (Usually the significance of the text was discussed in conjunction with the problem of predestination; cf. our discussion of especially Leibniz below.)[28]

The ancient Israelite, later Jewish, and Christian views of creation, as they merge with salvation history, and messianism appear as a call to a unique individual and corporate relationship with Yahweh, a call, at least in some Jewish and later Christian contexts, from all eternity. This makes poignant sin as the rejection by creatures of the gift of being and the eternal call. Sin is in fact an implicit rejection of the gift of life and eternal life; it is indeed the creaturely creation of death. Sin, as precisely this rejection of existing on God's terms and the spurning of God's invitation to the unique relationship, is portrayed as a uniquely individual act, even though, in the case of Adam and Eve, the responsibility for the deed is unacknowledged and pushed off onto someone else. It is also seen as having corporate dimensions with unforeseeable generational consequences. The most bitter consequence of sin as the refusal to be the one whom one is called to be is death, i.e., the losing of life as well as the prospect of eternal life. Cain's murder of his brother and every subsequent murder rehearse the creation of death and the most fundamental rejection of God's invitation to friendship and eternal life. Death as the termination of one who was called from all eternity and who was called to be for all eternity reduces the soul back to mere dirt from which it was evoked and into which divine life was breathed in creation. Death swallows up all living spirits and defeats the

longing of spirit for eternal life as a unique individual. Death is at the heart of all
human misery. Yet death's finality remains somewhat obscure, and in the messianic
prophesies and Christianity the finality of death is challenged.

The poignancy of sin as the rejection of redemption and the eternal calling is not
yet evident in *Genesis* 3:22 where the Lord God expresses *concern* that humans eat
of the tree of life and live forever, and thereby "become like one of us." Whereas such
envy might well be appropriate to gods and titans, it is appears unseemly of Yahweh.
Further, of course, this is precisely the theme of creation and redemption as a call, i.e.,
to be not only like God, in whose image persons are created, but to share not only in
the friendship of God but to be children of God: "To all who did receive him, who
have yielded him their allegiance, he gave the right to become children of God, not
born of any human stock or by the fleshly desire of a human father, but the offspring
of God himself (*John* 1:12–14). Indeed, the Son of God "did not count equality with
God a thing to be clung to but emptied himself, taking the form of a servant, being
born in the likeness of men" in order to raise all persons, indeed all creation, to participate in the eternal Sonship of God (*Philipians* 2:6–8; *Colossians* 2–3). In I *Peter*
1:3–4 this call to share in the Sonship is described as a new birth to a hope in an
"inheritance that is imperishable, undefiled, unfading, kept in Heavea for you."

Early Christians believed that this exalted calling that is inseparable from the
overcoming of death is adumbrated in the message of the messianic prophesies.
St. Paul cites *Isaiah* (25:8) that God "will swallow up death forever" and also
Hosea (13:14) where we find Yahweh promising to ransom his people "from the
power of the grave, and I will redeem them from death. O Death, I will be your
plague! O Grave, I will be your destruction." As St. Paul puts it, borrowing from
these prophetic sources: "Death is swallowed up in victory [of Jesus]. O Death,
where is your sting? O Hades [the shadowy place of departed souls], where is your
victory." He then adds, "The sting of death is sin," thereby indicating both that sin's
sting is precisely the pain of the loss of eternal life which is our proper destiny as
well as that somehow sin is the quasi-personal agent behind the scenes of death,
thereby echoing *Genesis* and *Romans* 7:13 ff. He goes on then to teach that it is in
our efforts to secure salvation through the means of being faithful to the Law that
we experience the strength of sin (1 *Corinthians* 15:54–56). Now with the new covenant we realize that it is only through the grace of the spirit of Christ in us, and not
our own diligent observation of the Law, that sin and death lose their hold on us.

For Christianity, the single individuality, the unique ipseity, of each is founded
in the unique ontological status of Jesus, the Annointed One, the Christ. The pre-
existence of the unique exemplary essence prior to its enworldment has its own
exemplar in the New Testament teaching of Jesus' pre-existing with the Father prior
to his "coming into the world." "Before even Abraham came into existence, *I am*,"
said Jesus to the scandal of the Jews who would have heard an echo of *Exodus* 3:14.
(See *John* 8:58.[29]) Each is chosen in the one who speaks of himself as did the God
of Israel, i.e. that He *is* purely and simply (*Exodus* 3:14).

The Christ as the *Logos*, the wisdom, mystery, and word of God the Father,
encompasses all the exemplarity of creation (*Colossians* 1:15–16) and therefore
encompasses what God calls into being, including what God calls or chooses before

the foundation of the world. In early Christian writings, there is not only a reference to a pre-existing sense of oneself, i.e., as chosen or called before the world's
creation, but to a "new name" given to the one who "conquers." This is a name
"which no one knows except him who receives it" (*Revelations* 2:17).

In all this we see the truth of Franz Rosenzweig's claim that salvation and revelation are as old as creation. The "new name" refers not merely to one's being called
by being given a name before the foundation of the world; rather over and above
or perhaps coincident with this timeless agency a new identity is given that seems
to be contingent upon one's "conquering." This eternal calling can be construed as
somehow coincident not only with one's creation as the realization of the calling,
but further as a kind of "predestination" where the mystery of one's freedom and
cooperation with God's grace are implied.

The nineteenth century religious writer and theologian, George MacDonald,
thinks of this conquering as the realization or approximation of the ideal self as it
exists in "the bosom of the Father – God's *him* realized in him through the Father's
love in the Elder Brother's devotion." This new name is the secret God has with
each person. "In every man there is a loneliness, an inner chamber of peculiar life
into which God only can enter." And accordingly "there is a chamber also... in God
Himself, into which none can enter but the one, the individual, the peculiar man –
out of which chamber that man has to bring revelation and strength for his brethren.
This is that for which he was made – to reveal the secret things of the Father." Thus
each person is an idea of God and this idea is not only the best of each but a calling
to "that which I like best; for my own name must be what I would have it, seeing it
is myself." What God wants to give each through this "name" is a secret between
God and the individual "because only He can know your deepest individuality, and
not the one best loved in the world can come near to know really what that name
is – the name that tells what you are – what God meant you to be when He thought
about you first." (Here we have a clear case of investing in the proper name a blend-
ing of *who* one is with *what* one is; both of these blended together is a matter of
how one is before God.)

A consequence of this is not isolation from all others but rather profoundest
community. Each learns to apperceive the neighbor in terms of his deepest godly
"chamber," feeling "the sacredness and awe of his neighbor's dark and silent speech
with his God."[30] This recalls the Quaker recommendation to address others with
that which is of God within oneself and to strive to meet others in regard to that
which is of God in them. Further, each is exhorted to believe that one's most proper
name is inseparably bound up with each of the Others, both in the divine beginning
as well as in the project of a divine "we" or person of a higher order.

For St. Paul the first-person singular surfaces emphatically in his wrestle (in
Romans 7:13 ff.) with what he calls "my flesh...which dwells within me." Here
the sovereignty of I myself over my life is claimed to be displaced by "sin" and
"the flesh." To both of these are ascribed a quasi-personal agency that threatens
the integrity of the individual person – to such an extent that Paul is provoked to
say that because "I do what I do not want, it is no longer I that do it, but sin which
dwells within me." This seeming exoneration from responsibility for one's agency

is muted by another consideration. This he calls the "law of my mind" and "the inner man" (*kata ton eso anthropon*: sometimes translated as "the inmost self"). This interior dimension seems to be at battle with sin and on its own capable of an a priori delight in God's law, even though it verges constantly on losing the battle. Perhaps it reflects his view of *syneideseos* or conscience by which people have a capacity to be a genuine and honorable law unto themselves and "which is written on their hearts" (*Romans* 2:14–16). It is perhaps this or some other sense of "I" which serves as the observer of this conflict. In any case he proclaims that through (*dia*) Christ "I myself" (*autos ego*) am able to serve the law of God with my mind (*Romans* 7:25).

In *Galatians* 1:19–21 this theme is revisited. Here Paul speaks of himself again in the first-person: "I" who before was under the sway of the domination of the agency of "sin" now through faith in Christ and his passion "have been crucified with Christ." This means that Paul no longer lives according to the Mosaic Law but rather is dead to the Law in so far as its observance is regarded as the sufficient condition of salvation. Furthermore, Paul is dead to the order of this world as defined by the world's powers and principalities. This creates a new vital, even ontological, principle of agency by which one henceforth "lives unto God." Paul may now say: "It is no longer I who live, but Christ who lives in me; and the life I now live in the flesh I live by faith in the Son of God..." This sense in which Christ here is Me or is the I whom I permit, or whom I, by grace, am enabled to permit, to supercede me is a mystery tied to what we will call The Theological Distinction. Obviously it is the resurrected Lord who becomes an energizing, "vivifying Spirit," who is the common principle of all the faithful. Less clear is how this principle remains at the same time a principle of the individual identity of each believer within the Body of Christ. (Again, clarification of such seeming competition between the "being" of Christ and that of the individual is the point of our discussion of "The Theological Distinction" below.) But if each is chosen in Christ before the foundation of the world, and if Christ-pre-exists the world, then the individual ipseities retain integrity when Christ becomes the actual principle of their life in the world.

In the exemplary Christian life, each lives in accord with the ipseity she is in Christ before the foundation of the world. Jesus as "the Lord" is ontologically unique in that his being contains that of all his followers, such that he really, ontologically, both encompasses and is the center of their ipseity, but he does not replace them. This is achieved in such a way that whatever each suffers *he*, Jesus, suffers and the good done to each is done to him (*Matthew* 25:31 ff.) Whatever happens in their lives touches him most intimately. Each "I" refers at once to oneself as well as "the Lord." Each "you" and "he" and "she" refers to the Other as well as to the Lord.

When each Christian refers to himself with "I" there is indissolubly a reference to himself as well as to the Christ, as the true self and "head of the mystical body of Christ." The first-person reference in, "when I was hungry you gave me something to eat," refers equally to Jesus as to those in need. How each exists in Christ, who is the condition for existing at all, before being born in the world and how each exists in Christ, should he or she refuse Christ, are difficult matters for Christian theology. It is the purpose of what we will call The Theological Distinction to offer some clarity. But it is already evident that God the Creator's relating to distinct ipseities is most fundamentally God's relating to the "eternal word made flesh," the new Adam, the itinerant preacher and carpenter from Nazareth, the son of Mary and Joseph. This same Jesus, as the Eternal Word, encompasses and unites all the ipseities, and they find the fuller sense of their uniqueness in him.

Clearly, the Christian notion of "vocation" has its exemplary case in Jesus of Nazareth who, although both human and divine, had the task of discerning in all of life's details the will of his Father. This was his "vocation." Although eternally one in the "Godhead" with the Father and himself the Eternal *Logos* of God and the exemplar of all creation, nevertheless he did not cling to what from our perspective is the "status of God," but "emptied himself," and took on the humble form of a poor, relatively ignorant (by standards of the Empire) Palestinian Jew. The site of Jesus' life was a backwater outpost of the empire which was occupied by the Roman troops who had established a kind of Vichy government. Many of his typical companions were would-be insurgents and revolutionaries (*zelotes*) eager to overthrow the Roman occupation. They were in great measure working-class people many of whom were probably illiterate, and many of whom official society disdained and marginalized. He was regarded at least on one occasion as crazy by some members of his family and they wanted to confine him. It must be believed that this situation framed the horizon of Jesus' perception and understanding of what he was supposed to do. We may assume considerable darkness in his discernment of his path and the biblical texts bear witness to dread at the prospect that the path he had to take would lead to a horrible clash with the Jewish and Roman authorities. Yet we may also assume, and this is the teaching of the tradition, that in spite of at least one moment of near despair, he always remained unwavering in following his calling by centering in his life in unity with his Father, i.e., not only was he never a dissociated or schizophrenic personality but his ipseity was exemplarily one "person" in spite of the two "natures." This state of being centered enabled his discernment of his path.

The prayer he taught his followers, "the Lord's Prayer," was not a prayer merely for them but it was his own life-long prayer to "our" Father in Heaven, whose name, or the ways we use to refer to what was beyond all names, was always to be regarded with the deepest reverence. Every aspect of this prayer was as much his own devout desire as he hoped it would be that of his followers. In saying this prayer Christians not only place themselves in the appropriate attitude of "followers of Christ" but inseparably they place themselves in the very most basic attitude of Jesus toward life and toward his Father in Heaven. The only "non-spiritual" petition in The Lord's Prayer was for "our daily bread," i.e., that the contingencies and surds of nature and history not hinder us from having the basic necessities we need to live to pursue our calling to realize the Kingdom. Yet Jesus himself prayed that he might be spared what he dreaded most for himself and what he feared most for his friends, if it be the Father's will.

Chief among the "spiritual" requests was the delineation of the calling in terms of the work of preparation for the coming of what the symbols of "the Father's Kingdom" or "the reign of God" represented, and this request was not merely the wish for but also the resolve to actively participate in its realization. What proximately and most fundamentally this meant is indicated in the prayer verse that we would strive to do the Father's will during our lives, i.e., the request that the Father's will would be alive in us just as it, with a special necessity, quickens Heaven. Nonviolent forgiving relationships with one another are further explications of this most basic allegiance to the desire that the Kingdom come. Finally, Christians remind themselves with Jesus before the Father that this all may happen only by cooperation with the grace of the Father, i.e., by staying centered in the Spirit of the Father and Jesus. They will surely founder and disaster awaits them if they cut loose from this center and presume to be sufficient to themselves to withstand the seductions of the "world, the flesh, and the devil."

We now move from the Bible to a selection of views within later Christianity that cast further light on problems in the philosophical theology of vocation and which offer us the opportunity also to summarize much of what we have already discussed in the prior chapters of both volumes of this work.

B. St. Thomas Aquinas

Although St. Thomas Aquinas' thought will guide us throughout Chapter VII, we here in this section will briefly consider his development of the Christian theme of the exemplarity of the Eternal Word of God. In this matter he is mindful of aspects of the classical Greek, especially Neo-Platonic, tradition, especially how the *eidé* that ground the necessities of the experience of the world are themselves founded in a divine transcendent intellectual principle. The necessities we experience in the world, when thought about theologically, would seem either to limit the divine omnipotence or the divine omnipotence would seem to render the necessities non-necessary and a matter of divine arbitrariness. Aquinas argued that we can preserve both the experienced necessities and the divine omnipotence by considering the necessities as evidence of how the creation we experience participates in the divine being. Creation happens through the divine mind and will. The divine mind, as the source of all intelligibility, may be thought of as comprised of the forms or ideas which serve as the exemplars of the created things. Those necessities of creation that are metaphysically necessary, i.e., those without which the world cannot be thought at all, enjoy an essential intimacy with the divine intellect which is inseparably one with the divine essence. The ideas do not refer to the divine essence as such which is indivisibly one, but rather they refer to the divine essence as the model (*ratio*) of the plurality of creatures.

A question arises here from the side of transcendental phenomenology: is not the "I myself" as the unique agent of manifestation of the world precisely just one such essence without which the world cannot be conceived? And what of those Others without whom the world could not be what it is for me? In other words, may we include within these metaphysical essences of the world not merely the world "in itself," e.g., "from God's perspective," but also those essences which are necessary for the constitution of the occasional worlds of contingent agents of manifestation? In any case the unique essence of oneself, although doubtless contingent as an actual existent ipseity is nevertheless a genuine essence, the source of whose essential possibility can only be found in the actual divine essence. (See our discussions above in Chapter I, §4 and below in Chapter VII.) As we will spell out, in knowing himself God knows his essence as imitable and as able to be participated in by a creature; God knows himself in the ideas constitutive of his essence but under the aspect of the particular model (*ratio*) of the creature; he knows himself as the intellectual and voluntary originating principle of whatever thing.[31]

In Thomas' view, the archetypal creative thought of God cannot be known "formally" by us, i.e., the proper intelligibility of this form is not given to our thoughtful experience. What is given to us is its exemplification, whether we have in mind particular things in the world, the natural kinds as existence-conditions of the things in the world, or ourselves. Just as one's ipseity is given to us in first-person lived experience and in our experience of the self-ideal to which we are called, the "archetypal creative thought" has its original intelligibility in God's own self-experience, which is impossible for any created person to experience. For Thomas, the ultimate theological "truth" of things made present by created spirit or mind is not a form inherent in things and immediately available to a created mind but rather it is the posited not-immediately given ground through which or by which something is, that is, it is its uncreated exemplary form. As a basis for the evidence for this claim there is an oblique reference to first-person reference when Thomas claims that it is through this exemplary uncreated form and by this same uncreated form that the created spirit knows and experiences itself but this exemplary uncreated form itself is not immediately known.[32] And there is a similar oblique, albeit speculative reference to first-person evidence to illustrate this when Thomas says that angels knows themselves and know their power to know by an immanent self-comprehension (*eam comprehendendo*); but even with this capacity for self-knowledge they are hindered from relating immediately this self-comprehension to the eternal exemplar for this would mean that they could comprehend what they cannot comprehend, i.e., the eternal exemplar.[33] (Cf. our discussion of Eckhart in the next section as well as the systematic exposition in the next chapter.)

Thus one's essential ipseity as it is one with the divine essence remains forever an incomprehensible matter, a mystery, even though, as we saw (in Book 1, Chapter III, §2), there is an immediate non-reflexive presence of oneself to oneself. "The creature is in God the creative essence."[34] "Every existing thing possesses the truth of its nature to the degree in which it imitates the knowledge of God." "What is real is called true in so far as it realizes that toward which it is ordained by the mind of God." "The truth of every individual thing is the special character of its Being that has been given to it as its abiding possession."[35]

Of course, each knows her "myself," and we may know things and people and know them essentially as they fit into our display of the world. But behind the intelligibility we display in our engagement of the world there is the originating impenetrable creative intelligibility of the divine essence of which they are created expressions. "The actuality of things is itself their light," but their light is ultimately received from the divine self-present self-luminosity. But in so far as their origin is their unity with the divine essence they remain unknown. This essence is the hidden unmeasured and immeasurable measure of the creaturely things which are the measure of our true knowing. Josef Pieper calls this the theological truth of things. The human truth is the "adequation" of the mind with things. The theological truth is the adequation of things with the divine creative archetype. "I myself" in my essence, like the divine essence from which it is inseparable, remains an essential mystery to me presumably also in the next life in so far as my individual essence is an expression of the divine essence. Because we cannot know what God is in his essence but what he is not, St. Thomas maintains that "the essential grounds of things are unknown to us.[36] Pieper summarizes: "Not only God himself but things have an 'eternal name' that man is unable to utter."[37] A fortiori this holds for the unique essence which each person is.

In Aquinas' philosophical anthropology there is a tension with this theological view: Form is the principle of perfection, and forms are universal and common. The individuation of something is extrinsic to the principle of perfection; it is assigned to the principle of "matter." In this view the single individual, the unique "I myself," would not enjoy the perfection of form, but would be accounted for by the "accident" of quantity. "I" would refer to this instantiation of the perfection of humanity. The notion of a unique individual "person" as itself a perfection, and not as an instance of a perfection that does not embody the full infinite possible perfection of the form of "humanity," evaporates if the source of the single individual is traced to matter as a source of limitation extrinsic to form. Human persons, as individuals, may be thus compared to things which are the same but individually different. As humans they are identically the same; what makes them different is that they are bigger or smaller, witty or dim-witted, to the left or right of one another, earlier or later than one another, etc. "Accidents" make for the differences. Clearly this discussion is carried out almost completely in the third person.[38] (But Aquinas once said, *anima mea non est ego*; cf. our discussion in Book 1, Chapter VII, §7.) Thus although Aquinas' analysis of reflection and self-awareness point to awareness of the "unique essence" that is ineluctably displayed in the first-person non-reflexive sense of "I myself" (see our discussion in Book 1, Chapter III, §2) and that further seems to be intimated in the discussion of angels as separate species, it gets lost in the philosophical anthropology tied to form and matter. Intelligibility is tied to universal forms; individuals become particulars by the material conditions which are more or less opaque.

Yet in the important question, "whether singulars are ideas in God," Aquinas notes that in the case of "Socrates," the answer is Yes. He distinguishes his position from Plato for whom he says there are only ideas of species. But in the case of Socrates, we have not only the idea of the species, man, but also the genus animal along with the idea of the individual, Socrates.[39] He does not dwell on what the idea of Socrates is, apart from its being an individual of the species man.

Further, if we reflect on the texts cited from Pieper above on the individual existences as having an eternal hidden name in God, and we introduce the most distinctive Thomist theme of *esse* as the perfection of all perfections, we find another, most basic, source of the individual in Aquinas. Much of scholasticism sought to find the perfection of the unique person in the order of "quiddity" or whatness, and it was from this that an *esse proprium* or the unique being of a person would result. But if *esse* is the highest ultimate actuality, then the notion of the person is not able to be realized in the non-ultimate principle of quiddity but through *esse*, indeed the *esse proprium*. According to Joseph Owens, the real cause of individuality is existence (*esse*). Existence or the "supposit" is what "most of all makes a thing a unity in itself and marks it off as distinct from all others."[40]

Owens further holds that in purely spiritual creatures form was "the essential cause of the individuality of the substance, in so far as just by itself it was the potentiality that determined the existential actuality of the thing." Owens here seems to be implying that what we are calling ipseity, the "myselfness" prior to its existential actuation, provided "not only specific but also individual determination to the existence." Here we approach in a third-person speculation Husserl's claim that the eidos of "I" requires existence (see Book 1, Chapter VI, §9). This goes against the typical Thomist consideration that the quiddity of something can be separated from its actual existence – otherwise this whatness, this treeness, would be the basis of its own existence and would of necessity have to be by reason of its being a tree. But *esse* inhabits things with essences; they are not *esse* but "have" *esse*.

In any case, if *esse* is decisive, and if *esse* is most properly a theological concept conceived to work out the metaphysics of the theological dogma of creation from nothing,[41] it cannot help us with purely transcendental phenomenological matters. It would take us too far afield to pursue this scholastic debate on the ultimate source of the constitution of the unique ipseity. Suffice it to say that it would seem that our transcendental phenomenological position is closer to the Scotists, for whom "haecceity" is an ultimate principle of "individual essence." Yet the Thomist doctrine of *esse proprium* itself seems to join with the Scotists in this matter in so far as whatever exists requires its own act of existence, its *esse proprium*, and this serves to account for the unique uniqueness of at least persons, if not everything else.

C. Meister Eckhart, John Ruusbroec, and St. John of the Cross

We find themes of both Plotinus and the Christian tradition echoed in Meister Eckhart.[42] Eckhart is of special interest for us because he frequently makes use of the distinctive kind of evidence that involves the first-person singular.

As in Plotinus and Aquinas, there is "an eidetic pre-existence of the soul in God." That is, the individual ipseity's essence pre-exists in the divine principle and it exists also in the received embodied created existence in the world.[43] Everything depends on acknowledging both the sameness and difference of the individual essence in these two considerations. This position reflects Eckhart's most basic distinction between the *Esse Absolutum*, God's proper absolute existence or To Be, which echoes Aquinas' *Ipsum Esse Subsistens*, and the doctrine of the *esse formaliter inherens*. This latter refers to how creaturely existence is distinct from the divine and how the divine existence does not as such inhere in creatures. It also refers to how the ideas, forms, or perfections we know in creatures do not inform God and are not in God *formaliter*, i.e., in God they do not exist as the forms of creatures, but only *virtute*, i.e., these forms of creatures exist in God in a virtual potential way.[44]

Everything depends on acknowledging both the sameness and difference of the individual essence in these two considerations. In each case the individual essence of "I myself" is the same; yet in one case the "substance" is the divine absolute being, *esse absolutum*; this is "I myself" apart from me myself (the creature) because absolutely one with the divine essence. In the other case, this individual essence is "I myself" and yet not, for Eckhart, another *esse* apart from God, otherwise "I myself" would be nothing. Rather, the divine *esse* is immediately constitutive of me, the creature, and the unique essence and perfection of "I myself" is a result of a "formal causality" that God exercises on what is not in every respect himself. Yet in this case "I myself" am not *esse formaliter inherens*; I do not formally inform God's essence but only "virtually."

A study of the notion of "*der Seelengrund*" in Eckhart can suggest to a phenomenologically disposed reader a third-person account of a transcendental sense of "I." A preferred ontological synonym for the "ground of the soul" was *Wesenheit* by which Eckhart wishes to point to something undifferentiated, pure, nameless, modeless, "naked" or bereft of properties and any description, which is the source of all agency, powers and capacities, and therefore in itself beyond these. Likewise this ground of the soul which is without qualities in itself nevertheless is numerically one, simple, or one with itself and knows no otherness within itself. It is this individual "essentiality" which has such intimate kinship with the divine that it is of necessity and inseparably one with God without being identical with God and has nothing in common with any other being. This is at once most interior to the soul as well as its highest aspect.[45]

Thus I interpret Eckhart to be saying that as the propertyless ground of the soul, analogous to what we have called the "myself," is transcendent to and immanent within and formally pervasive of all its powers, acts and properties, so the propertyless divine *esse* pervades and penetrates, and yet is transcendent to the creaturely *esse*.

It is here in conjunction with the ground of the soul as individual essentiality which, by way of exemplarity, is one with God's essence where Eckhart does occasionally use first-person descriptions and here offers encouragement to the phenomenological interpretation. (Cf. our discussion of St. John of the Cross below where we find symmetry between Eckhart's metaphor of "ground" and John's "center.")

Thus Eckhart distinguishes a sense of "I myself" before creation and "I myself" after creation. Before creation "I myself" am essentially identical with the divine essence; after creation there is a sense in which "I myself" am united with the divine essence but not identical with it – without this creaturely sense negating the sense in which "I myself" am identical with the divine essence. "God's existence must be my existence and God's is-ness is my is-ness." The absolute identity and equality are not nonsense if we distinguish, as Eckhart does not always help us to do, the way each "I myself" as an *eidos* exists eternally in the principle, and the way it exists as a creature. "I myself" is a multivalent referent: as what "I," the creature, JG Hart, refers to, and as the eternal pre-existing form which is identical with the divine essence. Because of this ambivalence both take part in the inner life of the Trinity, but in radically different ways. The actual creaturely individual essence does not formally inhere and constitute the Divine; yet the formal essential perfection of "I myself" does.

Only as the eternal existing form of "myself" as one with the divine essence can it properly be said: "The Father gives birth not only to me, his Son, but he gives birth to me as himself and himself as me and to me as his being and nature."[46] "I myself" as identical with the divine essence do not need "God" nor was there "God" for "I myself." As identically one with the divine essence there is no dependence on a transcendent creative principle. "God" comes into being with creatures. God essentially in himself and for himself is not "God," i.e., *what* creatures refer to when they intend God. Eckhart holds that as a creature one's task is to devote oneself to be free of "God" and to return to "where I was established, where I wanted what I was and was what I wanted."

The basic spiritual calling is to be faithful to this original sense of oneself. The fundamental sense of the evangelical exhortation to be "poor in spirit" is to be bereft of one's own will, indeed to be free of God's will, i.e., to be as I was when I was not (yet created) and willed nothing. "For in the same being of God where God is above being and above distinction, there I myself was, there I willed myself and committed myself to create this man... Therefore I am unborn, and in the manner in which I am unborn I can never die. In my unborn manner I have been eternally, and am now, and shall eternally remain."[47]

In the same German sermon he does not merely hold that the original self as it existed in God is the ideal and vocation to which we are called. He speaks here and elsewhere of the task of an ontological self-impoverishment, of the annihilation of the self, the will, the consciousness of self, etc. He calls this "breaking through" where "God and I are one. Then I am what I was, and then I neither diminish nor increase, for I am then an immovable cause that moves all things." The audacious formulations regarding ontological self-annihilation as the condition of break-through to one's divinity not surprisingly occasioned scandal. In a text doubtless bearing Eckhart's influence "Sister Catherine" announces that she is permanently in the pure Godhead in which there never was form or image: "I am where I was before I was created; that [place] is purely God." The sister then gives expression to the Eckhartian teaching that "no one may come into the naked Godhead except the one who is as naked as he was when he flowed out of God."[48]

What becomes confusing in Eckhart is the sense of the soul's "proper being." As a created being it has a kind of substantial being in itself, it is a *suppositum* or supposit. "I" refers to this proper being. But this is also what must be overcome. "As soon as the interior man escapes spiritually to his proper being, being a solitary ground with the Ground, then the exterior man ought to be despoiled of his proper supposit and to receive totally the supposit of the eternal personal being which is the same personal being."[49]

Indeed, for Eckhart, "I" is only properly said of that divine one who says "I am who I am" and who is "more intimate to things than they are to themselves." "I" is the unfathomable and inscrutable interiority of being which has neither exterior nor interior. "I" properly is that toward which each soul ought to progress, but by despoiling itself of all senses of self and ownness, and becoming "I" only in To Be Itself (*Ipsum Esse*). Such a man "is freed from all otherness and all createdness: God does not come into this man – He is essentially within him."[50] "You should wholly sink away from your youness and dissolve into His Hisness, and your 'yours' and His 'His' should become so completely one 'Mine' that with Him you understand his unbecome Isness and His nameless Nothingness" [i.e., transcendence to all that is positable by us].[51]

Eckhart's meditations seem at once to open the door to our discussion of essential ipseity by giving it both a divine foundation and a wordly reality and then to close it by making impossible this tension of sameness and otherness in favor of the divine sameness.

The referent of "I myself" as exemplary constituent essence comprising God's essence is absolutely necessary but this is only sheer possibility until created and as such only "virtually" the form of creatures. When created the essential "myself" is actual, not possible, but non-necessary and contingent.

Blessed John Ruusbroec (1293–1381) probably knew of the work of Meister Eckhart and was close to him theologically, especially in regard to the themes of this chapter.[52] Although Ruusbroec makes a theme of the soul in its ground and "bare essential being of *our* [emphasis added] spirit"[53] he does not carry out his analyses explicitly with an eye to the distinction of first- and third-person analyses. In his *The Spiritual Espousals*, he echoes the basic Plotinus-inspired "exemplarist" theology where all things are in God in their "intelligible natures" which in God are the same as the divine essence. The eternal procession of the Eternal Son, the Eternal Word, from the Father is itself the eternal birth of all creatures "before their creation in time. God has thus seen and known them in himself – as distinct in his living ideas and as different from himself, though not different in every respect, for all that is in God is God."[54] Ruusbroec uses an expression which gets translated as "apart from ourselves" to refer to "ourselves" as we are inseparable from the Eternal Word's procession or going forth from the Father. Thus the profound paradox of a sense of ourselves apart from ourselves – which the Augustinian thesis already formulated as God being more intimate to me than I am to myself. We saw Eckhart willing to take this literally, i.e., we ought to despoil ourself of all "ownness." For Ruusbroec, as for Eckhart, the eternal procession of the Eternal Word is the ultimate cause of our created being in time, even though this does not happen in time. "Our created being depends upon this eternal being and is one with it in its essential subsistence. This eternal being and life which we have and are in God's eternal wisdom is like God, for it both abides eternally and without distinction in the divine essence and, through the birth of the Son, flows forth eternally as a distinct entity, its distinctness being in accordance with God's eternal idea of it."[55]

God knows himself in this objectified reflection of himself, this image or likeness that God eternally expresses in the eternal process as well as in the exemplification of this procession in temporal creation. This generating, processing, expressing, and imaging is also God's seeing of Himself. "In this divine image all creatures have an eternal life *apart from themselves* [emphasis added], as in their eternal Exemplar."

As in Eckhart, our created temporal being is thus tilted toward this eternal image; it is our eternal vocation to "go out from ourselves into this divine light, supernaturally pursuing this image which is our own life..." This eternal image of ourselves that is our "ground," i.e., the basic "formal" principle of the creation of our selves, "constantly abides in a state of darkness devoid of particular form." Yet this "darkness devoid of *particular* form [i.e., devoid of the individuation that marks the creature]" is at the same time a resplendence that "reveals and manifests the hidden mystery of God in particular forms." The unique essence of each "myself" as it belongs to the divine essence is *quoad nos* darkness devoid of particular form; *quoad se* it is the hidden mystery of Godself. The fulfillment of human persons is the "supernatural" fulfillment by which persons, through divine grace, are "raised above their creaturely state into the contemplative life," and thereby they become "one with this divine resplendence" and are indistinguishable from this divine resplendence.[56]

Although Ruusbroec's asceticism culminates in the life of contemplation that requires mortification or moral self-abnegation, his formulations of self-abnegation do not amount to the ontological self-negation we find in Eckhart. Yet, even though Ruusbroec often criticizes as absurd the claims that some drew from the Eckhartian theology of divine image and exemplarity, such as that I, JG Hart, am God, that there is no distinction between (what we in this work call) the "myself" and God, that the just Christian performs whatever acts God performs, e.g., creates heaven and earth, saves souls, etc.,[57] nevertheless, the ambiguities in any theological formulation of *who one is* and therefore *who is the source of the agency* remain. Unless the speaker/author makes clear that the "I" or person referred to is the creative exemplar or the created exemplified there are bound to be confusions and absurdities. Because what is at stake is the very ground of the soul or of the person which is claimed to be, as an eternal unique essence (what we are calling the "myself"), one with the divine essence, this clarification is not definitive unless "myself" is marked by the qualifiers of "exemplar" or "exemplified."[58]

When someone, i.e., a person, in the world, says or is heard to say, "I existed before the creation of the world," etc. the listener has reason to believe the person is deluded. For example, many of Jesus' Jewish listeners were understandably scandalized when he announced, "Before Abraham even came into existence, I AM."[59] *Prima facie*, such a statement appears absurd because the listener must take the person to be someone who is undeniably mortal and contingent, and yet this person is assigning to himself quite different properties. To say truly, "Before Abraham even came into existence, I am," the speaker must be referring to himself in a way that is hidden to the listener. Of course, of necessity, the "myself" as the referent is hidden to the listener. But here the referent is assigned properties that negate the properties proper to an embodied person in the world speaking to us. The referent, of course, is always also the propertyless supposit of the "myself." But to assign to the supposit of the "myself" the features which mark the uncreated rather than the created person in the world invites confusion, if not scandal. All who are present to us are present as contingent and mortal. Even though we may appreciate that the speaker's first-person self-presence is, in important respects, necessarily bereft of an awareness of her contingent mortality (see Book 1, Chapters VI–VII), her assigning to herself properties such as eternal and creator of heaven and earth must strike us as absurd.

The tradition of Eckhart (Ruusbroec, Tauler, Seuse, Marguerite Porete, and other, more or less, "Friends of God") speculates that the ground of the soul, as what "I" refers to, has its exemplar in the divine essence (uniquely present for Christians in the case of the referent of what the Palestinian Jew, Jesus of Nazareth, refers to with "I"). It further speculates that those who are "just" are confirmed in this divine essential life that is the eternal exemplar of each's essence. These propositions lead some representatives of this tradition to often hold an equivalence of the creaturely self-reference and the divine self-reference. But everything depends on what the speaker is referring to in the self-reference. If the person in the world or if the "I myself" as the supposit of this person in the world is taken as the referent of divine self-ascriptions, or at least our ascriptions to the divine, there can only be absurdity.

In Chapter VII we will make both phenomenological and theological attempts to sort these matters out. As part of our historical preliminary sketch we wish to turn briefly to St. John of the Cross. This gives us an opportunity to dwell further on the transcendental philosophical psychological parallels between the mystical tradition and some themes of this work.

There are discussions parallel to our phenomenological reflections on Existenz as the center of the "I" in St. John of the Cross (1542–1591), who lived some two-hundred years after Eckhart. As far as I know, John of the Cross did not see in the use of the first-person pronoun any philosophical advantage. Thus he used the traditional word, which we translate as "soul" (or "spirit" as the interior or higher part of the "soul"), as the focus of his often very precise descriptions. Of great importance for him was the metaphor of the "deepest center" of the soul. "Center" here parallels Eckhart's *Grund* but, of course, the different metaphors highlight different matters. In John of the Cross the function of the metaphors "ground" and "center" merge. "Center" is not to be understood after the fashion of a body with parts. Rather, because it refers to "spirit" we are not referring to something which can be high or low, deeper or less deep in spatial senses. In terms of a general ontological statement that encompasses material objects and spirit, John of the Cross says: "The deepest center of an object we take to signify the farthest point attainable by that object's being and power and force of operation and movement." He gives an example of a rock or fire which have a natural power and motion to reach their center but they cannot pass beyond it. After a rock has reached a certain depth beyond which it cannot go because of an impediment, we may say it has reached its ground or center, but it has not yet reached its deepest center, the middle of the earth. In this life the soul may find itself opened to various ever deeper centers. When in this life it reaches, with all the "capacity of its being and operation and inclination" its deepest center, it reaches in an obscure manner God who is its center. Thus Edith Stein, in her commentary on John of the Cross, noted that the soul as spirit with a deepest center resting in God, is essentially a mystery and can only be understood from God's consideration of it and a thoughtful consideration of God. When the soul strives and reaches in this life with all its capacity for what is the "highest point of its being and operation and inclination," it, even though it is in its center, "still has movement and strength for advancing further and is not satisfied." This is because in this life it is "not yet in its deepest center, for it can go deeper in God." John seems to be saying that in life we experience our core as having ever deeper centers, but there is a deepest center beyond which we cannot go on our own. But because its center is in God and the depths of God are not fathomable, there is restlessness even when the soul has reached its own deepest center. If this be so there is no analogical equivalent for the soul in relation to God as a body in relation to the middle of the earth which is a center *ne plus ultra.*

We may assume the "center of the soul" here refers to what is originally a lived first-person reference because it is said to be the "substance of the soul" and the "pure and intimate substance." These observations of St. John of the Cross confirm the view here proposed that foremost in love and devotion the center of the I is revealed to itself as having ever greater depths. In this work we have argued that the pure bare substrate of the "myself" is also the entelechy of the person. We have also said that foremost in the self-identifying acts of love and the devotion awakened by the "truth of will," this "myself" expresses and actualizes itself in the innermost center of the I's coming forth or in its Existenz. As such this is not the position of faith and mystical grace from which and of which John of the Cross speaks. Nevertheless it is of interest that he refers to an original inviolable innocence of the soul in this, the "deepest and most intimate part of one's being." That is, he claims that here "neither the center of the senses nor the devil can reach." "The more interior it is, the purer it is" and the more substantial it is. It is myself inalienably, and in spite of my sinfulness, there is here an essential purity. This innocence of each "myself" is possible here because, for St. John of the Cross, one reaches sensibly or consciously this deepest and innermost center (this level of Existenz we would say) only through God's grace. Here, for the soul who is in touch with this deepest center and receptive of God's grace, her primary life is one of receptivity to the workings of God, "who alone can move the soul and do his work in its depths." For such a soul, "all the movements of this soul are divine." Although these movements are indeed one's own ("they belong to it") they belong to it because God "works them in it and with it, for it wills and consents to them." (Here we need The Theological Distinction for the proper understanding of this mystery.)

John of the Cross goes on to confirm our (Chapter V) correlation of Existenz and love by establishing an essential connection between the center of the soul and love: "Love is the inclination, strength, and power for the soul in making its way to God... The more degrees of love it has, the more deeply it enters into God and centers itself in him." Love is by its nature for the soul to be in its center; the greater the love the deeper the centering. When it has attained a final degree "God's love has arrived at wounding the soul in its ultimate and deepest center, which is to illuminate and transform it in its whole being, power, and strength, and according to its capacity, until it appears to be God." In so far as John's deepest center approximates our earlier discussions we may say that for John Existenz in its deepest purest form is a theological category.

Love here is not confined to explicit love of God, for all love is in some way the way the soul makes its way to God. Yet self-love, impure love, or the love which resists God's will, while a familiar possibility, helps us by way of contrast to see that the purest love is that which precisely transcends self-indulgence, which at the same time is an alienation from one's true center. Thus the paradox that runs through John's writings: "Deny your desires and you will find what your heart longs for." Thus the theme of love in St. John of the Cross is essentially connected to the theme of the purity of love. Love moves of necessity beyond pleasant properties to what transcends these. Thinking of love without its nisus or pressure to a transcendent pure form is to miss what is essential about it. (Cf. our discussion in the second part of Chapter IV of Book 1; also in Book 2, Chapter V, §3.)

God's calling from the beginning is at once the beckoning of this center as well as the soul's dissatisfaction with its loves. The divine calling is experienced at least in part as the soul's longing to find the proper object of its love which is inseparable from finding its deepest center. When one reaches the more perfect form of love and one's deepest center all that one does is love. Such a centered soul is love and all her actions are love.[60]

Again, these passages on the "substance of the soul," its inmost center, with love as its correlate agency, have parallels with themes in this work. It, like what we have called the bare substrate of "myself," remains intact and "pure" even in the case of the sinner. In the next chapter we will say that this, as the exemplification of God's own essence, is inseparable from God. As this substrate comes to light in the centering of the "myself"'s personification it is Existenz; but as opened "from the other side" by God's grace this deepest center is deepened beyond measure to be one with the divine center. All this reflects the Eckhartian themes we discussed earlier and how our ipseity, thought of as inseparable from the divine essence and the divine exemplar of our being, remains "pure" in spite of what we have done with our personal lives. This is merely to say that the "center" remains in tact just as does the "myself." At issue here is a kind of ontological innocence or purity. God's "image," to use biblical language, is ineffaceable. But this is not to say that I only seem to be a sinner or that I am, underneath it all, God or, as a person, necessarily and essentially one with God's essence. (See the next chapter.) Nor does it say that I myself am in a position to open my center "from the other side" to be one with the God. See our discussions below in §4.

D. Leibniz

Although Lebniz was a modern in his assigning to reason and rationality a power and scope that would have surprised not only late medieval thinkers but also surprised many of his contemporaries and, indeed, continues to surprises readers to day, he also bridges the medieval and modern eras by acknowledging a privileged status to divine revelation and transcendence. This confidence in reason echoes Plato when Leibniz reduces evil to intellectual confusion and lack of clarity, both of which are tied to egotistical impulses. Humans are burdened with the imperfection of finite perspectives on the universe and the divine. Further, this limitation of perspective is inseparable from an inevitable measure of confusion and lack of sufficient rational wakefulness to the adequate encompassing intuitive grasp of the All. For mostly this reason humans are not impelled always to act with the best possible in view. Nevertheless, as we shall see, the finitude of perspective is also a positive perfection: It is inseparably an expression of the unique individuality of the person.

In Leibniz's reflections there is little sense of the darkness of self-destructive impulses or one's own inexplicable failure to show up to and for oneself, to be consistent, or to do what one knows one should do. What to some appear as dysteleological events, disvalues, or surds in the course of life are, according to Leibniz, the result of our finite perspective which fails to see these matters for what they are. These events resemble apparent thoughtless smudges on a painted canvas which become strokes of artistic genius when we occupy the appropriate position or perspective. This perspective is typically only a promise disclosed through the teachings of faith. It is, in our life, an invitation to a festive higher harmony. Dostoevsky's Ivan rejected such an invitation to such a higher harmony in the name of being true to humanity's ineluctable finite perspective, and out of respect for the dignity of all the innocents who have died through wanton violence. He rejected concomitantly the view that "dysteleological surds" (to use Edgar Brightman's term for what appears to us to make no sense and for which there appears to be no justification in terms of a teleological-theological perspective) were merely a result of the finite perspective.[61]

In contrast, for Leibniz, in spite of this limited perspective, and in spite of the details of "the great future" being reserved for revelation, reason shows that "things are arranged in a way that surpasses our desires." Furthermore, physical nature is not destroyed or dislocated by the perfect state God has in mind, but rather this nature leads to grace and grace perfects or completes nature in making use of it.[62]

Leibniz's philosophical theology of grace is a theology of vocation. The key issue is how divine wisdom and omnipotence predestine individual persons to eternal life or death. For Leibniz, the doctrine of predestination, rightly understood, is necessary to safeguard God's omniscience and omnipotence, as well as the gratuitousness of the grace of salvation. Our freedom to follow the divine calling is a freedom tied to events which constitute our individuality and which "flow from the law of our nature." These events, inseparable from our individuality and from this law of our being, are "rooted in the perfect logical necessity of God's plan – our individual law through the principle of the best possible and our particular perceptions through the functional relations by which they represent the universe."[63] Our vocation is inseparably tied to God's providence or government of the world, and this means that God should have not only foreseen everything but also "that he should have provided for everything beforehand with proper remedies."[64]

In some oblique passages in Leibniz's dialogue, *New Essays Concerning Human Understanding*, the distinction we make in this work between the "myself" and the person is hinted at. For example, Philalethes states that at the heart of one's identity there is a feeling (*sentiment*), otherwise called an intuition and immediate apperception. It is said to accompany all our sensations and present perceptions "and it is this that each one is to himself what he calls *himself* and by which he is distinguished from every other thinking being; it is also in this alone that personal identity consists, or that which makes a rational being always to be the same." It extends as far as the person's past extends and "the *self* is at present the same as it was then." This self-presence is uniquely evident in as much as it is "incapable of being proved and having no need of proof."[65] He uses the formulation, which purports to elaborate *sentiment*: "*la conscience* (consciousness *ou conscienciosité*)" of oneself that pervades all of our acts. This is the ultimate basis of all personal identity and is extended over time such that this self is at present the same as it was at earlier phases of its life.

Theophilus replies by saying: "I am also of this opinion that *consciosité ou la sentiment* of myself (*moi*) proves a moral or personal identity." There then follows a discussion wherein this sense of oneself is tied to reflective acts, and the personal continuity a matter of memory. The original *sentiment du moi* becomes a matter of conscious, i.e., intentional, acts and reflection. Self-identity now, for Theophilus, seems to be tied to acts of which one is able to be reflectively conscious and able to recall. Instead of what seemed to be a pre- or non-reflective original feeling of the *moi* pervading all of the stream of consciousness all self-awareness seems turned over to "apperceptions" as reflexive quasi-perceptions of oneself. This disposition in Leibniz to regard self-awareness as a form of reflection shows itself in other passages, to which we will now turn.

Leibniz does not distinguish between the divine idea of what in this work we call the "myself" and the divine idea of the concrete person. Rather the idea or concept of "myself" is essentially ascriptive. For Leibniz there is no non-reflexive, non-ascriptive self-experiencing of one's individual essence as Plilalathes proposed. Indeed "myself" as known by God is not something known or chosen before the foundation of the world, but rather the person is as God's foreknowledge reveals this person to have already exercised freedom in time, history, and nature. That is, each is creatively chosen as integral to the world's unfolding in the course of nature and history. "I myself" am absolutely nothing without this worldly unfolding. What God creatively knows in the individual idea or concept of Peter is all the predicates that accrue or adhere to Peter as the substance of these predicates.[66] That is to say that Peter is one possibility out of all the possible individuals within the matrix of all the other possible worlds that integrate all the other possible individuals. The idea of Peter "contains the entire sequence of grace, ordinary and extraordinary, along with all the other events and their circumstances, and... it has pleased God to choose this one person for actual existence among an infinity of other equally possible persons."[67]

Thus when God timelessly creates "me myself," there is created the person, JG Hart, who has lived this life and performed these position-taking acts constitutive of him and which determine his eternal life or death. But JG Hart is inseparable from the actual or possible world which the divine also conceives in conceiving JG Hart. The essence of the monad, JG Hart, is actualized in his reflective self-awareness and moral agency in a certain kind of world. Descartes is faulted for thinking of the self as merely a substance who thinks. In fact we are "I's" who perceive and strive. Yet Leibniz here again acknowledges a distinction between our (mere) substance and our person which for this reader echoes the earlier distinction between the *sentiment du moi* and the person. Again, the latter is how we are for ourselves in ascriptive knowing (i.e., predicative knowing wherein properties are assigned), as in memory of and reflection on one's life. The former, i.e., mere substance, is a merely substantial sense of "oneself" bereft of reflection and memory. This is hinted at when we are unconscious as in sleep or when we faint. Here "one" exists or lives but without any sense of I-ness or person. But this does not get at precisely what we have in mind in this work when we refer to "myself," because this has to do with self-awareness of an individual essence or "unique pitch," as Hopkins has put it.

Yet there are indications of temptations to other positions in Leibniz's reflections. Of special interest in this regard is the attempt to establish the individuality quite apart from our living out our lives in the world by the simple consideration of the essence of the individual monad. Leibniz holds that each I is a priori a unique mirroring of God and the world, quite apart from any cognitive or moral achievement. Each individual substance, whether human or not, involves the whole universe in its perfect conception by God. Each is an individual in the sense that the All, the world and God, is mirrored differently. It is not as if the All or universe is one, but rather there are as many worlds as there are monads. Yet the All is itself not divided in this plurality because the All is present in each monad completely. The All is not numerically one, but according to its idea or concept one. Therefore by reason of the plurality of monadic perspectives, it does not cease to be an absolute unity.[68] In and of itself, by the sheer fact of its existing, the monad is an individual by being a unique mirroring or expression of the universe. Humans are, over and above this mirroring of the All, an "omniscient but confused"[69] mirroring and an expression of the divine essence. "Within our self-being (*Selbstwesen*) there lies an infinity, a footprint or reflection of the omniscience and omnipresence of God." And God "belongs to me more intimately than my body." Therefore each I-monad is an idea of the divine essence which, in the plurality of mirrorings of the divine essence, does not dissolve this unity but rather the transcendent unity of the divine essence is actual in the one idea or concept of the divine essence.

But, according to Leibniz, unless humans achieve the reflective "I," which is the source of self-ascriptions, they are not aware of this unique mirroring as an individual essence. Thus the mirroring of the All by each monad, and each human, varies in the perfection of its mirroring, just as some perspectives on a city are richer than others, even though each is unique. Thus persons, even the permanently unconscious or amnesiac ones, enjoy a uniqueness rooted in their being substances uniquely mirroring God and the world. From the point of view of this work this seems to require the paradoxical notion that God know acriptively what has no ascriptive self-knowing.

Leibniz's theory of the self or person is tied to his preference for a reflective theory of self-awareness and therefore a preference for a theory that confines all sense of knowing to propositional truth; and this, in turn, is linked of necessity with his theory of divine knowing and predestination. What God knows in knowing someone timelessly is the complete concept of the substance or person, i.e., the person with all of her properties. Both that which is known by the concept as well as the concept are timeless because they seize the person as a completed life. "The complete or perfect concept of an individual substance involves all its predicates, past, present and future."[70] Our own inadequate understanding of ourselves and Others strives to approximate this divine knowing. What this seems to mean in practice is that if we grasp someone with some degree of depth of perception, we will be able to deduce from our concept of the person the significant predicates that determine the individual.

Quite in contrast to central themes of this book, for Leibniz, apart from his flirtations with a theory of non-reflective self-awareness, the I myself is necessarily propertied and ascriptively referred to. Leibniz's notion of the individual person as an individual essence covers every circumstance in an individual's history "so that none could be thought different without substituting another individual for the one in question." Part of our discussion of ipseity, however legitimate Leibniz's property-laden notion of the individual *person* within world-history may be, frames "a notion of an individual which permits us to imagine him or it differently qualified, placed in differing situations and reacting differently to them, perhaps faced by the free choice of others and reacting freely to them."[71]

For Leibniz, in knowing someone God knows simply the complex proposition which the person is for God. Thus each person is grasped analogously to a super-human physicist's grasping $E = MC^2$, with full awareness of the numerous complex propositions that are implied in it. That is, God knows timelessly all the properties that accrue over time to this person through her stream of consciousness and agency.

Although Leibniz was perhaps the first to thematize the realm of the non-thematic and horizonal aspects of knowing, he seems committed to the view that all true and proper knowing is propositional, and propositional knowing is knowing of identity, as when the predicate is seen to be contained in the concept of the subject. If the predicate is not manifestly and explicitly contained in the subject, and if this is a true attribute, then it is contained implicitly or virtually. An *accident* is not a true essential attribute, but rather is a being whose concept does not include what can be attributed to the subject covered by this concept.[72] Thus for Leibniz all predication is intrinsic and there is no "extrinsic denomination," because the concept of the subject involves of necessity the concepts of the predicates.[73]

In this work, quite in contrast to Leibniz, we have posited that the "I myself" refers to an individual essence, a non-sortal referent. In knowing this one knows the core-substrate of the person and this is not known through knowing properties. This contrasts with knowing someone, including oneself, as a *person*, as e.g., knowing her character or knowing her full story as this person in the world. Here she is known as "propertied, i.e., as having necessary properties as well as endless accidental ones. When the person is "myself" there is a propositional knowing of the "myself" personified, and thus as propertied. We have further said that knowledge of Others, especially through love, is knowing of them through but as beyond their properties.

We have argued (in Book 1) that the more deeply we presence the Other through a loving apprehension the more individual, non-substitutable, and non-transferable does this person become for us. We see beyond the common, communicable, and replaceable features that which transcends these and is unique. And in the course of this loving apprehension we do not proceed primarily by inference but by an ongoing synthesis which makes for a total intention of a concrete whole. Of course, in the midst of this stream of experiences we might well form hypotheses about certain features of the person's character and these will or will not be verified in the course of time. But such confirmation of our hypotheses always takes place as progress in our knowledge of the unique individual. Thus, we may have occasion to ask, is he acting this way because of the situation, or because of an inhibition, or because of a momentary distraction? Whatever the answer that emerges in the course of time, it will reveal, we believe, a feature of the one, same, unique person. Thus it is not as if we compile the features and make an individual out of these; rather, these features, most of which have their counterparts in many others, become manifestly ways in which we make present the typicality of the form of human persons. But as they are present in each case of persons we lovingly apprehend they become the more or less transparent vehicles by which we know the unique person who, we have insisted, is not simply a particular or instantiation of a human being.

This surely is the case in the first-person unfolding of the life of the "myself" and the transformations occurring in one's personal development. And therefore we anticipate this to be the case in our presencing of Others. The individual features or properties unfold only as more or less decisive moments within the "myself." The self-awareness of the "myself" is not something subsequent and inferred; it is not a result of a synthesis of these "constitutive parts." Rather in one's own case from the start there is an immediate self-awareness, and in that of the awareness of Others, at the basis of all the manifold features, there is a kind of intuition of a Gestalt of the unique whole. And the further one advances in the loving knowledge of the Other the more the uniqueness of who it is who has these properties becomes evident.[74] But in one's own case the "myself" is given all at once. It is only in the knowledge of ourselves as persons that there is the parallel of an initial intuition of a whole that subsequently gets delineated.

This is analogous to our knowledge of what is essential and the knowledge of essences: The essence analysis and the searching out of what is essential is preceded by a pre-propositional grasp of the parameters of the matter at hand. Noetically what is at hand is a "felt-meaning" (Gendlin) or an empty intention of a "dark something" (Husserl). This provides the noematic meaning horizon which is to be analyzed in terms of what is necessary and invariant. Analogously with the "individual essence" of, e.g., Peter. (Cf. our discussions in Chapter VIII of Book 1.)

What God knows "when" creating would seem, as a matter of necessity, to be the individual essence of "myself," but whether God knows with equal necessity and in the same way, as Leibniz claims, the quasi-necessary properties defining my personal identity, e.g., that I at T_n reject or accept the grace determining my eternal destiny, depends on numerous ontological and theological propositions that cannot be given a just treatment in this work. In this chapter we propose that God knows in a necessary way the "myself" first as an ingredient of God's own essence and then as the exemplar of the creature. This latter requires God's knowing not only Him-Herself as able to be participated in, but also knowing JG Hart as this person develops in the course of time as well, and if JG Hart is immortal, then there cannot be closure to God's knowing JG Hart as a person. There might be good metaphysical reasons for saying that God's knowing is timeless, but what is clear, we hope, is that what is known in knowing JG Hart is not something timeless and that knowing the individual essence constituting "myself" is not absolutely identical with knowing me as JG Hart. Leibniz denies this distinction because he claims all self-knowing is sortal, i.e., a knowing of a kind or a knowing of properties, and even the implicit or tacit knowing, that of necessity goes into knowing a person, would be knowing of potential sortals or potential propositions.

For Leibniz, it seems, all are chosen and conceptually framed timelessly, and the sense of being called, or having a vocation, is subordinated in almost all of his writing to being timelessly chosen in the timeless frame of the personal essence. Leibniz's highlighting the timelessness of the divine knowing and choice makes the distinctions and drama of the personal adventure as well as the distinctions and drama of creation, revelation, and redemption unintelligible. The divine creative choice chooses the essence or concept of the person whose substance is the form or entelechy that includes all the predicates of one's life. "Who one is" is exhausted by one's personal life as it is present to God as always already having been lived. Is this not an objectivist knowing by God of a person which implies that God is ignorant of how a person experiences herself in the first-person? For Leibniz, who one is for God is the unified a priori analytic concept containing all the attributes or qualities acquired over time by the particular person, but which for this person in the first person is experienced synthetically and in an a posteriori manner. In this analysis, essentially non-objective first-person experience must give way to the divine objective third-person propositional perspective.

And yet, in Leibniz's own spiritual life and writings, the first-person perspective wins out over the theory of the divine propositional objective perspective. He adopts the Augustinian and Quaker image of the Inner Light. This "light" may be awakened by external teaching, yet without the functioning of this "light" no teaching or teacher, no matter how great, is of any avail. The inner light seems to be the equivalent of one's *Selbstwesen* and may be interpreted to mean the wakefulness to the law of one's own unique individuality, and thus one's own unique calling. This light which is of God within us is at once the easiest and hardest being to know. If we are lost in the shadows, whereby we identify being with sense perception, it is the hardest to know; but if we are in touch with the entelechy or inner law of our unique being, it is the easiest to know. Whereas this light may fill us with clarity and assurances, it provides no images, and no "vain motions." Clearly for Leibniz, its *telos* is in propositional knowledge, but it seems to have a dynamism or efficacy that is pre-propositional or non-propositional. His philosophical position seems to require that it be known only in reflection and propositions, yet its pre-propositional workings upon which salvation depends would seem to be presupposed by reflection.[75]

This interpretation that non-reflective and pre-reflective first-person experience is essentially different from third-person objective and propositional knowing is important for thinking about predestination. If the unique essence of the "myself" is known in non-reflective self-awareness, and if one's personal ideal is known in the apperception of the ideal as it emerges in the horizon of experience, both of which are basic theses of this work, then God's knowing oneself as a complex proposition or concept which comprehends all past, present, and future predicates does not exhaust knowing who one is. The theory that God's knowing of persons is a knowing of a complex proposition serves the traditional view of omniscience which usually posits that God's knowing is outside of time. Often there seems to be a fusion of this timeless act of knowing with the thesis that what God knows itself is timeless.

Such a view also serves a theory of "predestination" which aspires to assign to the divine a capacity to preordain the saved on the basis not only of God's free choice but also on the basis of God's knowledge of the particular person's free rejection of God's grace in the course of her life. For one version of this view, God knows tenselessly temporal things. But it is not at all clear that it follows that the temporal things themselves become tenseless. There are good reasons for orthodox theology to remove from the divine an immersion in temporality where there is an incessant loss and deprivation, i.e., the loss of the present one has had and an openness to perfections one does not yet have. A solution to the problem is to say that God knows things as in an encompassing eternal Now all at once together. This serves then as the base for the tenseless divine agency wherein, all at once, persons in the historical world are created, wooed, and saved or damned. But of course the difficulty is that for the "eternist" tradition God does not know the past and future or even the present as such. In this formulation, not only would the Father not know the temporal life of Jesus as temporal but, as we shall see, it seems the divine would be deprived of the knowledge of all finite perspectives, all of which are pervaded by temporality.

It is out of the question that we pursue these matters in depth here. But it is worth pointing out that Husserl's view of the awareness of "inner time" or the stream of consciousness requires that there be a tenseless self-awareness at the basis of the awareness of time. (See Book 1, Chapter VII, §3.) More to the theological point of predestination, we restate our view, which will hopefully more clearly emerge in what follows, that all the problems connected with "predestination" are already contained in the dogma or mystery of God the Creator. And although what we are calling The Theological Distinction between God and the world, which sets forth the parameters for the understanding of this dogma, does not supply the answer to such questions, its delineation of the contours of the basic mystery discourages the formulation of the issues in such a way that leads to either absurdities or scandals, e.g., the view that if God tenselessly chose to create persons, God would know them as non-temporal, and in creating them God would create those whom he would "pre-know" would be damned, and therefore God would be sadistic.

Of course, from the side of the anxious believer, there is the good advice to consider that regardless of God's knowledge of the future as future and future possibles, etc., since God does not, according to the dogma, exist "in the future," i.e., God does not come to be in what is future for us, but rather, as eternal, is now and always now; *now is the only place God is to be met, and now is the focus of our faithfulness.* And how can the believer in the infinitely good God concern herself about a future that the infinitely good God, she believes, will hold sway over, and how can she fret about a future ("perdition") the infinitely good God does not want for her?[76]

Does not the knowledge of a person only and exclusively as a finished story that may be grasped in a concept which itself distills a series of complex propositions, have the deficiency of not knowing what the person "knows" in her non-reflective first-person experience and in her pre-thematic experience of herself as a person facing her future?

Of special interest here is the way the theme of one's vocation within the contexts of "the truth of will" and "teleological determinism" call attention to decisive moments in which persons experience the unity of freedom and destiny. (See above, Book 2, Chapter V, §4.) Such moments provide a kind of existential sense to the word, "predestination," which, in its typical theological sense, is precisely something which by definition escapes any experiential confirmation. Regardless of the rarity, inconclusiveness, and corrigibility of such experiences, Leibniz's objectivistic account of predestination could not take advantage of them as possibly shedding light on the topic of predestination, even though the thesis of teleological determinism would itself be recognized by him as his own. (Cf. our discussion in this Book 2, Chapter IV, §8 and Chapter V, §5.)

Further, if the divine is to continue to know the persons in the "afterlife" does it not mean that God must know them as having been and without a future, i.e., know them as patently clear objects and not as subjects? Is there not eliminated any chance, however analogous, of a "personal relationship" with God either in the present or the future? The answer surely is Yes if God is conceived to be a being in relationship to other beings. The answer is both a Yes and No if what we are calling The Theological Distinction is entertained as a possibility. But this answer provides us with no light for reason; it forms the parameters for faith's assent.

Again: If God is necessitated to know persons only as Leibniz describes this knowledge, is not God's omniscience in danger? In this view God would never know what I live and first-personally know as me in the course of my life. It would appear that such a view fears that God would have to be me and cease being God to have the knowledge indexed by my use of "I." (Cf. our discussion below in Chapter VII, §3.)

If there are creatures, then they are not only truly self-existing beings that are not God and whose being is in some difficult sense "external" to God's being. But this being external to God is not that of the being of a great machine made by a great artist-engineer, as in some forms of theism and deism. Rather, according to The Theological Distinction God is more interior to them than they are to themselves. The problem of freedom does not add anything new to the mystery of creation. That "omnipotence" can permit the free will to will what omnipotence does not will is no more odd than the original admission that creatures truly are even though absolutely and incessantly dependent on being created. The infinity and absoluteness of God enables there to be real finite relative beings; the divine infinity faces

the otherness and subsistence of finite creatures and yet is creatively present in the
very finite being of creatures.

If God's "omniscience" and "eternity" are understood to be necessary attributes
which explicate the God of The Theological Distinction, then their seeming incompatibility with first-person temporal perspectives is not a challenge to the notion of
God, but rather they merely are further aspects of the problem inherent in the very
notion of the God of the Christian or Theological Distinction. We will soon return
to these matters.

E. Fichte

Fichte may be included here as an exemplary form of post-Enlightenment liberal
Protestant Christianity where the ancient tradition is granted authority if and only
if it manifests its compatibility with a certain understanding of reason. In Fichte
we have, in many respects, "Plotinus *redivivus*," and at the same time we find a
direct encounter with Christian themes. This latter amounts to a rejection of orthodox Christianity in favor of commitments that are proximate to those of Plotinus.
Fichte's views are of further special interest to us because they provided the inspiration for some aspects of Husserl's own transcendental philosophy, even in regard to
the doctrine of vocation.[77]

In Fichte we find a wrestle with a theory of an absolute divine principle for
which a plurality of free, self-aware I's are, in some sense, essential. On the one
hand God exists absolutely through himself and only God *is* absolutely. Therefore
the ancient term "Being" (*Sein*) is appropriate for "God." But we must understand
Being not as something substantial and dead but as "life." Indeed, echoing Aquinas,
and adumbrating Heidegger, *Sein* is to be understood "*verbaliter*" and thus "To Be"
is "To Live" and the life of "To Be" is God's externalization and revelation, and this
is said to be necessarily through God's inner and absolute Essence.[78] Furthermore,
the sense of "life" and "being" here are eminently understood as lived and being-
experienced while living, i.e., we best appreciate their sense not in the third-person
but in the first-person.

The term for this essential living of *Sein*, its eternal "is" which can only be an
"immanent creation," is *Dasein*, i.e. the "there" of To Be. A basic philosophical-
theological tension in Fichte is the claim that, on the one hand, God is absolutely
self-contained and absolute, and absolute freedom as being through itself. On the
other hand, God is life and of necessity *Dasein*. We will return to this.

Human beings as self-aware are *Da-Sein*, the "there" (*da*) of eternal Life or
Being (*Sein*). Dasein, as the "there" of eternal *Sein*, is the Being-for-Itself of the
Divine Being; it is the divine being effectively othered in finite self-conscious
substance. In spite of persisting obfuscations Fichte saw early that all explicit acts
of consciousness, including acts of reflection, presupposed the fundamental non-
reflexive self-awareness that Husserl and phenomenology have also emphasized.[79]
For Fichte this self-consciousness is non-ascriptive and beyond all conceptuality.

A reason why self-awareness is non-ascriptive, propertyless, and trans-conceptual is that it is the *Da* of *Sein*, i.e., the "there" or revelation of God himself. Although Dasein is a third-person term (like ipseity and Existenz), its proper sense is grasped only in the first-person non-reflective self-awareness. (Whether Heidegger was familiar with this distinctive use of *Dasein* by Fichte is not clear.) Besides God's own internal being, *Sein*, which is to be "understood" phenomenologically as the absolute non-objectifiable *Whence* of all reflection, there is the eternal othering or "there" of Being, *Dasein*. Dasein is the spontaneous expression of God, of pure *Sein* or being. In some formulations it appears that the Dasein of God is as original and underived as the Being of God.

The consciousness of Dasein is always first of all the non-reflective self-awareness and then secondarily, building on this, the reflective awareness. In the latter case "I myself" is the appropriate form of reference. Both of these require what is essentially hidden and beyond Dasein's power to make present, i.e., the *Whence* of this awareness, the *Sein* of Dasein.

Fichte proclaims that Dasein is the equivalent of the Christian Word of God as it appears in the Gospel of John. This Word was eternally with God. The traditional doctrine of creation as a creation out of God of something that is not in God himself and that has not been eternally and necessarily in God, an emanation by way of an absolute arbitrary power in which finite being is not necessarily and eternally in God himself but forsaken and expelled from his eternal being is "the essentially fundamental error of all metaphysics and religion." The true understanding of "creation" requires seeing what is other than God as the refraction into a plurality of forms of self-consciousness or forms of Dasein in the world, not in eternity.

Yet God does not collapse or coincide with the finite beings of Dasein; rather these, in the face of the To Be of God, are as non-being because God alone truly *is*. Here Fichte faces the basic difficulty of a phenomenological philosophical theology which does not want to be dualistic: In the serious quest for unity one faces the dilemma that either I myself as this autonomous agent and consciousness am annihilated or God is. On the one hand, I do not want not to be and, on the other hand, God cannot be annihilated.[80] But then how are we to understand that in God Dasein and the internal essence of God are identical? How is it that there appears to be two different modes of being of God? Fichte's answer is richly complicated. Sometimes he holds that it is only the limitations that we have as finite Dasein that posits the distinction between the inner essence of the absolute and his external Dasein.[81] Clearly for Fichte what we have non-reflectively as Dasein (as the "there" of God) is a propertyless, colorless, conceptually impoverished realm. As soon as we reflect and conceptually inform our self-awareness it breaks up into an infinity of forms. A fortiori that holds for the Whence of Dasein as the whence of all reflection.[82] The philosopher cannot establish the genesis of Dasein in its primal ground, but only establish the inconceivability and the infinity of its own effort to grasp reflectively its genesis.[83]

We saw earlier Fichte's dogmatic disdain for the dogma of creation from nothing as he understood it. Fichte did not appear to have studied the intricacies of Thomistic metaphysics; nor did he appreciate how exemplarity in this tradition aspires to do justice to his chief concern with the identity and difference of divine and creaturely being. For our later discussion it is of interest that Fichte, on the one hand, seems to deny the basic dogma or faith-claim of The Christian (or Theological) Distinction, i.e., that although it is contrary to fact, the world need not be and God need not have created it. In some formulations of Fichte that is tantamount to saying that God could also not be or that at one time God was not, and God created Godself through a free act.[84] This would appear to be the doctrine of the world or creation as a necessary correlate of God. (See Chapter VII, §9.) Yet the matter in Fichte is far from clear. Fichte's focus here is on the view of creation that involves the popular understanding that to create means that "at one time" something was not and then "at another time" it was. Creation is "in time" and thus one posits a time in which God did not appear and another in which God does appear. Echoing Plotinus (and Augustine), the othering or externalization of *Sein* in *Dasein* is not something temporal. The world, as what *we* constitute and which mediates *our* knowledge of Being, is in time.

Yet, on another occasion, Fichte says that the Absolute only permits itself to be thought in relation to Dasein (or *Ex-sistence*) which makes it present. But he also says that it is only a matter of fact that this Ex-sistence in the act of thinking of the Absolute cannot be annihilated; as a matter of conceptual possibility, of course it can be eliminated. In which case, we then would have pure *Sein* alone without any relationship to Dasein or Ex-sistence. (On this point, it would appear that Husserl would defend more staunchly an idealist position on behalf of the transcendental I. See Book 1, Chapter VI, §9.) Dasein clearly exists only in relationship to Being and is what it is only in opposition to Being in Itself which it itself is not. Thus it is the opposition of Dasein to Sein that is the bearer of Dasein. In these considerations we move closer to The Theological Distinction that God does not need Dasein in the way Dasein needs *Sein*.[85]

For Fichte's strong idealist position, what we call world and nature are only through our constitution; they exist only as thought. (Whether this is the purely Berkeleyan position with its disdain for an integral nature is doubtful.[86]) Only I's or spirits truly exist, i.e., have Dasein. And the task of constitution by spirits is an endless task. But this task is the field in which we respond to the call of duty to realize endlessly ourselves as Dasein, as the representation, image (*Bild*) of *Sein* or God. Thus the creator of the world is spirit as the source of the conceptual frame of the world.

Fichte, as far as I can see, does not have an explicit theory of exemplarity. Yet he, like Aquinas, seeks a way of placing otherness within the absolute Being of God. Dasein as the appearing, representation, or *Bild* of Being, i.e., as the externalization in a likeness or concept, is the divine Being's being outside itself. But this is an othering or externalization in which the divine Being is completely, while nevertheless remaining Itself in this very "othering."[87] Here it is only implicit that the source of the unique ipseity is the divine essence; but clearly the theme of exemplar or likeness or concept functions as the means of sameness and difference within the divine. It also, as we shall see, has the power of establishing the unique identity and calling of the individual. (Clearly for the creationist tradition and The Theological Distinction the being of creatures is, however, not appreciated if we regard their being as that of mere representations or *Bilder*; see our discussions in Chapter VII.)

Although, for Fichte, finite Dasein is projected, refracted, or objectified eternal Being and thereby distinct from eternal Being, it, as such, can never perish.

Yet there is a problem in sorting out in what the individuality of Dasein consists, even though, as we shall see, there can be no doubt that Fichte assigns the highest importance to one's personal unique essence. Self-awareness or consciousness (or *Wissen*) is always I-consciousness, but Fichte points out that this, as a form, is everywhere the same. Thus Fichte, in guiding the reader through his analyses refers often to "we." This means that each reader who refers to herself with "I" is assumed to see for herself the evidence that Fichte is displaying for the reader. This evidence is "for us all." But this "we" is, as a pure non-reflective self-awareness of the evidence, also said to be characterized as immediate lived actual life or living and not something that belongs to any one in particular. And we may think of this absolute living as coincident with *Sein* and as a completely self-contained I. Here To Be is I and I is To Be "which *I* we may name, with regard to a division within it, We."[88] This leads him to say on occasion that the individual thinking I is merely the scene of a unified universal I and its universal thinking.[89]

Fichte clearly sees that "seeing the point" and gaining evidence is a matter of a kind of freedom and he sees that freedom and autonomy belong to the being of the I and that self-awareness is characterized by an "immediate awareness of one's own freedom." He even posits that freedom goes in advance of the self-awareness that characterizes the We or I.[90] But he also says that this absolute life of self-awareness in its freedom is grounded in the absolute life, and this absolute life is said to be God. But instead of juxtaposing a dualism to a monism or a monism to a dualism he surprisingly approaches what we are calling the faith-claim or dogma of The Theological Distinction, something he denied in regard to creation: "The ground of the autonomy and freedom of consciousness is to be found of course in God; but therefore and because of this the autonomy and freedom is truly there and not at all an empty appearance. Through his own Dasein and as a result of his own inner essence God pushes in part, i.e., in so far as it becomes self-consciousness, his Dasein from out of himself and places it there as truly autonomous and free."[91]

The individual Dasein is the way the divine Being's essence is able to become manifold and involved in an infinite progressive development in time. Each individual Dasein, and here personal human being is primarily meant, has its own free choice that cannot be taken from it, even by the divinity itself. Thus although the divine is to be thought more as a principle of Dasein, and in this sense the principle of "I myself," Fichte is also concerned, at least in some instances, that it not be thought of as an absolute "I" that annihilates the unique ipseity of Dasein. The essence of the divine remains essentially occluded for us and should not readily be thought of as a providential personal being or, as in some forms of Panentheism (e.g., see our discussion of Scheler below in Chapter VII, §9), a finite struggling fellow traveler. Providence for Fichte is precisely the life of Dasein living out and being receptive to the divine informing of Dasein, foremost through its pursuit of the Ought and obedience to the moral law. It is living out the absolute Ought and one's unique calling. The absolute is in time and history through our striving in our action to be what we are, Dasein, the reflection or image of God, as we realize this in our spiritual and moral life.

Up to this point Fichte claims there is perfect harmony between his metaphysics and the Gospel of John (of the Christian New Testament). Where the historical enters is the claim by Christianity that the Eternal Word, the absolute and immediate Dasein of God, manifested itself perceptually in the world, without any admixture of impurity or darkness, "or any merely individual limitation," in Jesus of Nazareth. Fichte holds the position that Jesus had the metaphysical insight into the absolute unity of human Dasein with the divine and that this is the profoundest knowledge that can be attained. It would seem that for Fichte it is a contingent fact that it was the unique individual essence who was the historical person of Jesus that had this knowledge. However, Fichte does not believe such knowledge existed before Jesus; further, it existed only very rarely after him. But human blessedness is due to metaphysical, not historical and contingent, knowledge. Thus Jesus has the function of a special embodiment of wisdom that can lead others to approximate the metaphysical knowledge enjoyed by Jesus (and, of course, Fichte himself). Jesus teaches that the essential divine nature is essentially hidden from us; and this itself is manifest in the unique insight of transcendental metaphysical reflection. Jesus leads first through faith in his teachings. But this is preliminary to the metaphysical gnosis wherein each sees with apodictic evidence that he or she is the divine Dasein, the Eternal Word.[92]

For Fichte, Kant's theme of a supersensuous noumenal intelligible realm echoes in his own teaching that the truly religious and moral person already shares in the present moment in eternal life – even though he regards most teachings of the afterlife as philosophically and morally bankrupt. But nature which is "there" for the sake of the I cannot be regarded as capable of annihilating the I. The individual Dasein finds its share in the supersensuous Being by means of immediate self-knowledge and discovers this by annihilating its own will and personal goals. Only one who uproots himself from sensuous worldly existence and rests in his eternal principle of Dasein can be certain of immortality and eternal freedom. Thus the wisdom required is not purely theoretical.

We now come to themes that might well have been a source of inspiration for Kierkegaard. This unique share in the divine life cannot be known by mere thought alone; it cannot be deduced by way of inference from any other truths, nor can it be gained through acquaintance with another individual since this unique portion cannot be known to any other individual. Rather he can attain it only by an immediate personal knowledge. One cannot properly describe this vocation in general terms; rather each can comprehend it only for himself. What we are now doing is using general terms for "the unique vocation." But what we are talking about is distinctive in the sense that it is precisely what only the individual experiences as his or her calling. But, generally, one may further say that continuous revelation is coincidental with the total surrender to it and the annihilation of one's personal will. If this happens one is penetrated with unspeakable love. Finally, the desire and effort to be other than that to which one is called is the greatest immorality. For Fichte, this calling is given with each's unique being. Denying the calling is denying one's ownmost core sense of oneself. The essence of the matter is: I am to strive to be what I ought to be, what I can be, and what at bottom I really want to be.[93]

The individual vocation amidst the plurality of vocations is ineluctably a striving for what is beyond the existing self, and is therefore dependent on contingent factors that are beyond the self's agency. The way to move to a standpoint where the blessedness of the individual is not at the mercy of contingencies and surds, a standpoint of true religion, is the way of love. *Dasein* of necessity strives back and forwards to *Sein*, to the divine. But it is love that makes God and human Dasein one. Love is the original creator of our abstract concept of pure Being or of God. It leads us beyond all knowable and determinate existence and beyond the entire realm of reflection, conceptuality, and empty intention to a filled presencing. Concepts define and fashion our understanding and the sense of the target of love, but conceptuality remains abstract, empty and not filled. Only love goes beyond all this to the Absolute Itself, leaving nothing within it but the negation of all that has to do with conceiving that which is eternally beloved.[94]

Earlier we discussed the basic lines of Fichte's position on vocation, apart from his metaphysical moorings of this theory, in conjunction with our discussion of Husserl's theory of vocation (Chapter V, §5). Fichte's philosophy is one of the very few that has a theory of vocation at its core.

F. Kierkegaard

For Kierkegaard the theme of calling is rooted in obedience to the revelation of the biblical tradition. Its signature formulation rests in the conviction that philosophy (exemplarily that of the Hegel school) could not do justice to the centrality of faith as the center of Existenz. Kierkegaard's "theory of vocation" is subordinated to an interpretation of Christianity that makes central what we are calling The Theological Distinction. This enables his view of vocation to appear as a reworking of the classical *intinerarium mentis in deum*, the journey of the mind into its most inward secret and truest center.

Kierkegaard celebrates Socrates as the forerunner of the teaching of Existenz. This is also a doctrine that "truth is inwardness – or subjectivity." What this means, in part, is a kind of phenomenological explication of the evangelical teaching that "what profits it a man to gain the whole world and suffer the loss of his own soul." For Kierkegaard Socrates taught that unless one really saw and understood for oneself what was most worth knowing, and unless what was known was able to be related "personally" to oneself and one's destiny – and not just parroted, adopted, or consumed as so many pieces of information, one did not live interiorly. For Socrates the truths of eternal validity and eternal importance were within oneself and with the help of an interlocutor functioning analogously as a midwife the person herself in her self-activity could become aware of these truths and live by them from her center. For Kierkegaard's Socrates true learning, truly becoming inward, is the gathering of oneself in one's eternal center or foundation. It is not the mere epistemic or cognitive appropriation of or familiarity with eternal universal and objective truths. But the truths most worth knowing are not able to be taught directly; they are not properly pieces of information about the world communicable by an expert who transfers the information or by one's own empirical inspection of one's surroundings. This is because, as we shall see, they have to do with the unique truth of one's own subjectivity. The Socratic midwife is only a "facilitator" and any appropriation of these truths through direct communication or because of devotion to the teacher is a failure in the process as well as in the bringing to light the truth of subjectivity.

Thus with this reading of Plato Kierkegaard can maintain that Socrates made us aware of "subjectivity/inwardness is truth." But Socrates failed to appreciate how, because subjectivity is actually untruth, there is a barrier to being in the truth, and how the truth of subjectivity requires a greater and deeper inwardness for it to surmount this barrier. This is Kierkegaard's explication of the Christian teaching on sin. The pagan theory of "subjectivity is truth" does not have an inkling either of the obstacles to the thesis of "subjectivity is truth" or the depths of subjectivity to which we must aspire to uncover the truth of subjectivity.

Here Kierkegaard touches on our theme of exemplarity. To say that the subject is in untruth does not mean that the subject is in untruth eternally or that the subject is eternally in sin. Rather, the subject exists in untruth or sin in time. Who one is in one's eternal validity does not exist in sin but one is born into sin and untruth. One discovers this deeper subjectivity not by going merely "back to eternity" or inward to one's ownmost center. For Kierkegaard one discovers the eternal essential truth oddly, paradoxically, even "absurdly," in the reality of the perceivable, historical, essential eternal truth who is Jesus.[95] This encounter, as indirect and odd as it is, is the effect of faith and enables one to exist before God. Here one discovers the truth of one's deepest self as the truth of one's sinfulness before God; but, at the same time, this is a joyful resting in, of all things, one's lowliness, one's necessary humility, because this is the truth of each before God.

The idea that God is precisely the being that could want or call us prior to our being actually enworlded (as in *Ephesians* 1:4, Thomas, and Eckhart) resembles Kierkegaard's notion of God as precisely the One who could create what is free and independent of divine omnipotence without losing that omnipotence.[96] Echoing what we saw in Fichte, Kierkegaard can say that God is precisely the one who could create me, i.e., I myself as this free ipseity, without diminishing any of His/Her power. God would not be God if this were not the case. Similarly God would not be God if God were to directly communicate the deepest truth of my subjectivity. Only in the extraordinary creativity of the indirect communication that fosters maximally my freedom and agency is the power of God manifest.

God is present in all of creation but what God achieves through Jesus and God's teachers is not a direct relation to God. God cannot be directly related to because this places God in the world. For the pagan, God is directly related to as something remarkable in the world. Jesus and his true teachers/followers reflect God's cunning which is such that God's presence is precisely not something amazing and remarkable in the world. God is omnipresent but invisible and thus not present perceptually, directly, anywhere. God's becoming visibly present would annul God's invisibility.

Although God is omnipresent in all of natural creation there is only a relationship with God in the created spirit. And God relates Godself to the human spirit of necessity indirectly because the spirit comes to the eternal truth only inwardly.

Here this means through the free agency of the self in regard to itself. Revelation is of necessity first of all a direct communication of an unknown truth; but such a communication has only a temporary validity and eventually must be appropriated interiorly. In this regard God is more sly and maiutic than the greatest Socratic teacher in bringing about the truth of subjectivity. And those who are called to be Christ for one another must emulate such slyness.[97]

Because the disappearance of religiousness is precisely the disappearance of one's awareness of one's nothingness before God (*coram Deo*), both religiosity and its disappearance are a hair's breadth from the comic. The comic is supremely manifest in idolatry but also in thinking that going about on one's knees should mean anything before God.[98] As with Thomas Aquinas and Eckhart, so it is for Kierkegaard: Because God is the absolute creator and incommensurate with any creature, God does not stand in competition with anything or anyone in the world; when the appearance of competition occurs we face the comic or absurd. (In all these themes what we are calling The Theological Distinction is overheard.)

For Kierkegaard love heads through the visible toward what is invisible and intrinsically of value apart from any qualities or change of properties. This propertyless transcendent target of intentionality ultimately is God but not as if God competed with what we love. The reason is that God is not a part of existence in such a way that he demands his share for himself. God demands everything from us but nothing for himself in such a way that one's giving all to God does not detract from loving creatures as one should.[99]

On one occasion Kierkegaard proposed thinking of creation as the production of meaningful sentences, wherein "individuality is the true period in the development of creation." The period is written down when a meaning is completed, and looking backwards, from the period one finds the meaning, i.e., the full completed meaning, "there" at the period. Not until individuality is given is the meaning of creation completed or is there meaning in creation. We could understand this to mean that in personal awareness and self-awareness is there meaning and display in nature, and in this sense the cosmos gains a kind of perfection it did not have. But we can also take it to mean that with the creation of persons, for whom their awakening to themselves as Existenzen is a possibility, the significance of creation as an articulation of The Theological Distinction comes to light. Each interpretation offers a differing perspective on the same thing and thus they need not be incompatible.

For Kierkegaard the stress on individuality is foremost a way of understanding that "subjectivity is truth," i.e., there is a uniquely necessary truth about oneself that can only be grasped and lived in the first-person. With subjectivity there becomes the elevation of what is inward and what is secret and what is uniquely individual. The general, the universal, even the universality of ethics are ways of concealing the singularity of the single individual. But subjectivity is tied to the norm of faith, tied to the kind of self-presence that comes by placing oneself in the presence of God and becoming aware of one's sinfulness. One is constantly under pressure to hide from oneself, especially by flight to the third-person and the universal – this to a great extent is the work of both culture and society, and even the Church in so far as it takes on aspects of these. We are afraid of others who exist as single individuals, and this in part is because we realize that so living is the most terrible thing of all from which the universal and the crowd cannot protect us. There is no alibi acceptable for the demand on us that we be only for ourselves truthful and responsible; only in absolute isolation can we be in this way and meet the demands placed on us. And what is required of us in being this way is in some sense the defining secret of who we are, a secret whose ultimate rhyme and meaning eludes us even in our pledging ourselves to keep it.[100]

But does Kierkegaard here mean that the "oneself" is not an individual prior to being authentic? Does he imply that there are many persons who are neither individuals nor authentic? (He often writes of the zombie-like existence of which we are capable.) What is a non-individual person? Is she a universal or less than a person by way of being lost in a collective "they?" The "individual" is a theological notion and the concerns we had in Book 1 are marginal for Kierkegaard to the theological sense of the individual as existing *coram Deo*. "Who one is" as the abstract "myself" takes backseat to the coming forth to oneself as Existenz, i.e., to the "myself" actualizing itself at the center of the person as she faces her destiny and determines herself to be the sort of person she is called to be.

We move toward a coincidence of who one is with what sort of person one is called to be and one's divine exemplar when Kierkegaard says "I become conscious simultaneously in my eternal validity, in so to speak, my divine necessity, and in my accidental finitude…" This latter, "accidental finitude," refers to one's being a particular person in the world conditioned by all that this involves. This latter is not to be "overlooked or rejected." Yet these are two and not one. Rather "the true life of the individual is its apotheosis." What precisely this means is surely not the literal sense that man becomes God but rather that the highest life, the "most glorious" life of which a human is capable, is the true authentic life of the single individual, i.e., the ipseity with its eternal validity and necessity as appropriately embodied in the world as a person with others. Kierkegaard elaborates: "the true life of the individual is its apotheosis, which does not mean that this empty, contentless I steals, as it were, out of this finitude, in order to become volatilized and diffused in its heavenward emigration, but rather that the divine inhabits and tolerates the finite." The person, through the work of divine grace, is transformed into the likeness of its eternally valid exemplar. Again, what we shall call "The Theological Distinction" is in play: The divine is precisely the "sort of being" or "the one" that does not compete with sorts of being or with beings in being one with them.

For our context, where the theme of exemplarity of the "myself" is an underlying theme, it is intriguing that Kierkegaard here recognizes the "empty, contentless I" as belonging to "my eternal validity" and as distinct from the temporal and historical. It, of course, is also important for us that he sees the historical and the eternal as inseparable and that the proper individual historical life is recognized to be of eternal significance. And because every aspect of this life has an eternal significance our task is to regard each aspect as a window on eternity both in terms of our agency as well as in terms of our faithful interpretation of it.[101] To the extent that we may regard conscience as the seat of the single individual and Existenz, i.e., where each is aware of himself as Existenz (cf. our earlier discussion in Book 2,

Chapter III), then we may say that through conscience there is "consciousness of being an individual" and this "is the primary consciousness in a man which is his eternal consciousness," the place where one establishes forever for oneself either a lonely prison or a blessed chamber of salvation.[102]

Kierkegaard's theory of vocation is inseparable from his discovery of subjectivity, the single individual, or Existenz. One gets to what is of unconditional importance only in the first-personal wrestle with one's destiny. For Kierkegaard, philosophy is a black hole in so far as it snares us in third-personal conceptual displays or reports which depend for their validity on merely their internal conceptual coherence. We must be wary of cultural or scientific contexts where we are asked to be not ourselves as single individuals but rather to be recorders of information about universal states of affairs or particulars, displayed by authoritative others or by our own prideful ingenuity.

For Kierkegaard, the self may be seen over a teleological continuum of achievements of selfhood. The more consciousness, in the sense of gathered reflective self-awareness, the more, in a qualitatively normative sense, self there is. The more consciousness the more will. The more will the more self. The greater the *Gudes Forestilling*, the presentation of God, the more self there is; the more self, the greater the presentation of God.[103] This continuum extends from the self who is ignorant of herself and might even want to be, or takes herself for, in some sense, someone else, to the self who is a true and honest agent, to the self who is faithful by living before God and resting transparently in God as the source of herself. Prior to this last possibility there is an essential deficiency.

Prior to existing before God one cannot be aware of oneself as a sinner, and it is this awareness wherein resides the most proper sense of being a single individual. In other words, persons are deficient as persons in so far as they are not single individuals, i.e., in so far as they lack that radical individuality that comes with the awareness of oneself as having God as the measure of every moment and aspect of one's life. My awareness of God's awareness of my ownness as it relates to the honesty of how I live is the framework for this talk of "sin." "Sin" thus is not properly a philosophical category but rather derives from one's faithful allegiance to an understanding of God and God's relation to oneself and the world. In holding oneself up to the divine light one becomes aware of one's lowliness. But this humility is ontologically appropriate because the greater the self-emptying, the greater the awareness of one's status as creature.

Being a single individual is being a single individual across time; the measure of being a single individual is normally taken from one's social-intersubjective circumstances. If one lives primarily among beasts then one's life is mirrored back to oneself from this context. If one's life is measured primarily by politics and/or society, then one's self is measured by the success or standing this norm requires. In general, for the person without faith, the world provides the measure of the self. The full and proper single individual takes his or her measure from God – not God as policeman and external to life, but God conceived as necessarily what can never be a third-party, but rather a subject, "and hence only for subjectivity in inward life" in an infinite passion.[104] As such, "God" is the most intimate norm of one's authentic

Existenz. It would seem that "God" in Kierkegaard is no *Ding an sich*, never properly something able to be referred to in the third-person, even though doubtless *an sich*; but often "God" is also to be understood as the correlate to the infinite passion for authentic truth and for the absolutely worshipful by the single individual.

Before God, authentic Existenz may be seen, from one side, as the reaching of true individuality because one exists in the despair to be oneself before God by oneself. One ineluctably exists in a heightened self-reflective state and is thoughtful to an elevated degree about one's choices when one lives in the presence of God. Kierkegaard here echoes Kant's view that prayer is a kind of self-recollection by which I work upon myself by means of the "idea of God." Imaginatively placing myself before God "as if God were actual" enables a quickening of my disposition to act always and everywhere with integrity.[105] Of course, for Kierkegaard the *Gudes Forstelling* is not a mere concept of God, as the Hong translation would have it, but rather is akin to the German *Vorstellung* and thus is really the presentation of God, and this means presencing God *as real* or really presencing God. Yet the "reality" here is of necessity not perceptual. Likewise it is not delusional because it is self-consciously a matter of the grace of faith. If faith could be shown to be fundamentally an error, then, of course, it could be shown to be a delusion. We argue in the next chapter that such a demonstration is not possible. A presentation of God might, of course, take the form of a mere concept or idea. But regardless how rich in texture this concept is it is still an empty intention and, at best, feeble in terms of what faith can accomplish and weak in its power to inform the self's reality. As a mere conception, it does not, as faith does, make worshipfully and adoringly present what of necessity is absent to perception and transcendent to conception. Further, to use our earlier Husserlian terms, it is not a centering position-taking I-me act that shapes one's personal being in the world in an attitude of devotion and worship. The more (appropriate and real) the presentation of God, i.e., the more it corresponds to the divine in Itself, the more the self is transformed and measured by the infinite holiness of God.

Existing transparently before God is inescapably existing with the ontologically appropriate attitude, i.e., humility. This is an attitude accompanied by shame of the awareness of one's own unworthiness, inadequacy and sinfulness. This awareness of *one's own* sinful agency and the sinfulness of *one's own* dispositions is for Kierkegaard the core sense of the awareness of one's individuality, and indeed an awareness of oneself at one's core and center, i.e., as a single individual. But as an aspect of faith, at the same time, it is the self willing to be itself by resting transparently in God, i.e., in the struggle to be itself by synthesizing all its constitutive elements it rests in the creative power that establishes it and it exists precisely as the struggling synthesizing agent. It is important to keep in mind *both* that for Kierkegaard Existenz brings the I into its ownmost by enabling it to *rest* transparently in God[106] *and* that this being in the presence of God is awareness of one's sinfulness as measured by God's holiness. To take these statements as pure philosophical ones, and pessimistic ones at that, is to miss the essential.

It seems that it would be incorrect to make equivalent the self's "resting transparently in the power that established it" and the identity given to one by God. This resting in God is the fullest awakening of each subjectivity to itself as Existenz; it is not an identity in the sense that there are distinguishing personal markers or vocational indicators which one may adopt. Rather, it would be the framework for any effort to discern who and what sort of person one was called to be. It would be one's Existenz or one's core and that around which all identities that one assumes in one's being in the world would take their bearings.

Such authentic Existenz marks the coming into being of the "theological self," the intelligibility of which is inseparable from what we are calling The Theological Distinction. (Cf. our discussion of Von Balthasar below.) This self requires the faithful resting transparently in God and before God, and takes its cues from the "objective uncertainty" of the historical Jesus as he is made present in the scriptures, disciples, the church, etc. Calling or vocation for Kierkegaard has to do primarily with "finding the truth which is true for me" and about which I have an "infinitite passion"; the truth which, even if the whole world knows it, is not true unless I discover it. This "truth" is the equivalent of both my destiny and what God wants from me, something for which I am willing to live and die.[107] Living out this destiny in terms of the individual's insertion in natural history, society and history is not an explicit theme, especially perhaps because of the fear of the individual's being degraded into a thing or lost in the crowd. Vocation, as we have been sketching it, is inseparable from existential truth, the truth of one's "true self," of oneself in one's most secret core. Personhood, as our identifiable historical being in the world with others, is the way the unique ipseity realizes itself in the world with others. Kierkegaard only implicitly makes distinctions urged in this work between ipseity, person, and Existenz. But he pioneered the phenomenological insight that Existenz or the secret depth of oneself to which one arouses oneself when one acts as a single individual is the center of personhood.

We will return to some themes in Kierkegaard in the next chapter when we discuss the paradoxical or absurd nature of faith.

G. Gerard Manley Hopkins

We have had occasion to refer to some ideas of the nineteenth century Jesuit priest-poet, Gerard Manley Hopkins, throughout this work, and here we wish to make contact again in regard to the theology of vocation. This theological theory is one which is thoroughly Christocentric. This is set off by some rich distinctions in regard to the self. We saw how he conceived of first-person experience to be an awareness of one's unique self, analogous to the pitch of a sound and more distinctive than the taste of ale or the smell of camphor. This life of the unique self may be thought of verbally as "selving" because the unique uniqueness is evident in every aspect and act of the self and it is toward the fullest self-expression and self-realization that each self strives. All being, i.e., all of nature, history, and life, is soaked with these individual essences or "haecceities," these selves selving, but the human selves are more keenly pitched in their unique self-awareness and "selving."

For Hopkins this is both a universal aesthetics as well as a theology of nature. It is also a theology of vocation. As Hopkins has put it, the fundamental vocation is to be "more Christ. .../ New self and nobler me…" With the resurrection "I am all at once what Christ is, since he is what I am…" and therefore although "This Jack" is "joke, poor potsherd," it nevertheless is "immortal diamond." Thus one is called to be totally pervaded by this true-self/self-ideal in Christ. Here is a synopsis:

> Each mortal thing does one and the same:
> Deals out that being indoors each one dwells;
> Selves – goes its self; *myself* it speaks and spells,
> Crying, *What I do is me: for that I came.*
> I say more: the just man justices;
> Keeps grace; that keeps all his goings graces;
> Acts in God's eye what in God's eye he is –
> Christ – for Christ plays in ten thousand places,
> Lovely in limbs, lovely in eyes not his
> To the Father through the features of men's faces.[108]

Hopkins gives an analogy for how each, in the obscurity of life, acts out Christ's acting through him and thereby acts "in God's eye what in God's eye he is." This is, first of all, the work of faith. And faith may be understood precisely as "God in man knowing his (God's) own truth." The life of faith, as precisely this living out of the life of Christ and acting in God's eye what one is, is not a matter of clear evidence but rather ignorance and obscurity. And prayer to the Father who is beyond all understanding is what we do in and through life in Christ. Consider how a young child of a great nobleman could be taught by his father and mother to pay to the nobleman's father a compliment of welcome upon the grandfather's visit to them. Of course the young child would not understand the words which he was taught but would only say the welcome by rote. The child "does not know their meaning, yet what they mean it means. The parents understand what they do not say, the child says what it does not understand, but both child and parents mean the welcome."[109]

The person of faith, in regard to the great mysteries, does not know what the words he speaks mean as Christ knows what they mean, but the child even without understanding can mean the meaning, just as he can mean the welcome without grasping the words meant but not said by the parents. The darkness carries over into action and one's calling. At the level of action one can mean to mean what Christ means even though one does not properly grasp, e.g., how Christ is present "in the least of these" (*Matthew* 25:31 ff.).

Let us pursue further this darkness in one's calling. Hopkins' metaphor of the self as a pitch makes a distinction between something proximate to what we have called the pure unique individual essence of the "myself" which we hold to be the "bare substrate" of the person. (Cf. Book 1, Chapter V, §§2–3.) He calls this "a bare self" and conceives of it as possible being apart from its actual being. As such this bare self is not yet inserted into the actual world or nature. "Now a bare self, to which no nature has yet been added, which is not yet clothed or overlaid with a nature, is indeed nothing, a zero, in the score or account of existence; but as possible it is positive, like a positive infinitesimal, and intrinsically different from every other self."[110] Here we take Hopkins to be wrestling with what we discussed earlier as "the myself" (in Book 1, e.g., Chapter III, §2): There is a tension, on the one hand, between the universal formal sameness of the reference of "I" and the unique essence to which is being referred.

The self as bare self is prior to nature but not prior to pitch. Prior to nature it is of necessity pitch but merely possible and not yet properly a personal self. There is nothing prior to being a pitched self because Hopkins thinks of the pitch as the original ontological referent of the persons by God. Prior to their actuality the pitch is possibility, a mere idea. (Cf. our later discussion of the "exemplar" of the "myself.") With their actuality "in nature" pitched persons are to be conceived as properly existing when in attunement with God, foremost through the definite moral state of the self as it is in tune with God's will and grace. The metaphor of the self as pitch is conceived by Hopkins such that each self is at any time in a certain "pitch of itself." That is, it is more or less in accord with itself, with its proper pitch/true self. He draws a thin line between the taste of oneself which is the unique essence and the moral-theological pitch because we always find ourselves, our ownness, in this attunement or non-attunement with God's will; we always find ourselves (our pitch) in a certain "pitch of itself."

> I am gall, I am heartburn. God's most deep decree
> Bitter would have me taste: my taste was me...[111]

Thus any ipseity, although in the first-person present to itself as a uniquely unique pitch, is capable of endless nuances. This unique pitch that each myself is, is capable of an infinite spectrum of shades of distinctions within the one pitch, and each shading is entitled to be called a pitch of the one pitch. "There is a scale or range of pitch which is also infinite and terminated upwards in the directness or uprightness of the 'stem' of the godhead and the procession of the divine persons."[112] There is presumably no limit in the other direction of ungodly pitch. Within this infinite moral spectrum (pitch) one is always oneself, the same "myself," always experiencing oneself in the manner of a "pitch of itself."

All of life is envisaged as an avowal and consent or repudiation or refusal of God's will. From the perspective subsequent to the Fall and Christ's redemption we have a new moral "plane" introduced. The will, apart from this perspective, may be thought of as surrounded by objects of desire as the needle is surrounded by the points of the compass. It is able to move freely to, e.g., point A or point B. As a will, it, like the compass needle, is drawn by affection in endless directions and it has the capacity to choose one over the others. Subsequent to the Fall, there is profound disorder especially in the human heart and Hopkins' poetry is deft in covering this terrain. Not least of the disorders is how our hearts grate on themselves: "Selfyeast of spirit a dull dough sours." Subsequent to the event of Jesus a new dimension is opened up for faith that was not available on the prior compass. The will or the pitched self was not capable of this new direction and dimension on its own. Only God's grace (a new sweetening transcendent yeast of spirit) can bring this about. God's will here is aimed at shifting the self into a higher, better pitch of itself, one that reaches into the Godhead. These pressures or strains of God's will, as "superadded" to nature, take place in a "'cleave' of being which each of his creatures shews to God's eyes alone". These pressures or strains may be very far away from the actual pitch of the self at the moment but they may begin to open actual possibilities that it could otherwise not have. When one begins to be aware of one's own metamorphosis in Christ someone may say: "That is Christ at play at me and me playing at Christ, only that is no play but truth: That is Christ *being me* and me being Christ."

The creature's deed or correspondence to this work of God is initially perhaps the mere wish or sigh to correspond, the wish to say Yes to this shift of itself to a higher better pitch (of itself). Grace takes the form of quickening towards the good as well as correcting and turning the will away from a harmful direction. Finally grace elevates "from one cleave of being to another and to a vital act in Christ: this is truly God's finger touching the very vein of personality, which nothing else can reach and man can respond to by no play whatever, by bare acknowledgment only, the counter stress which God alone can feel..., the aspiration in answer to his inspiration."[113]

Hopkins' rich use of the metaphor of pitch and the pitch of pitch is important for us because it highlights the sense in which *who* one is, is (an albeit legitimate) abstraction from the moral person and yet there is good reason to think of *who* one is as "what sort of person" one is. Nevertheless, it is the form given to and by the "myself," i.e., it is a "pitch of itself." For Hopkins and Kierkegaard this is *how* one is "before God." Being someone, a Who, is completed only by a being-such, a position we found already in Husserl. Yet the fullness of this self-realization is, in the perspective of Hopkins' faith, in contrast to the perspective Husserl can offer as a phenomenologist, a matter of God's work, not our own.

Further, in Hopkins we have a theological version of the individual essences or ipseities existing before the foundation of the world (as bare selves, as possible pitches) enjoying an intimacy with the divine nature prior to creation. The stress of grace is the way this call, which originated before creation, is felt. Intertwined with this we have also a theological version of "the truth of will" and vocation which posits a sense of "myself" which is independent both of nature and personal moral development. But the calling of the "myself" or pitched self as it becomes a person is a calling to what is essentially beyond even the moral self, even though that to which it is called is still a "pitch of itself." But it would seem that even here the calling and its answer do not dispense with darkness and risk. With faith the believer aspires, like the child of the nobleman, ever to mean what Christ in God means, even though when he says or does what Christ would have him say or do he does not know what is meant by the words of the mysteries nor always fathom the wisdom of the action.

But it is not only faith that can provide some measure of light and hope to dispel the obscurity. For Hopkins the darkness of faith and the burdens of the heart are rescued incessantly by permitting desire to be kindled. One is empowered to wish "for all," especially the beauty of other selves. Then there is another moment, one of *Aufhebung*, where, instead of giving in to this beauty unconditionally (for that would be disordered), we rather forego and leave the beauty toward which the heart is launched. Instead, without denying this beauty or ceasing to cherish it, we are exhorted to channel the desire and wish in the direction of the grace of "beauty's self and beauty's giver" and "Heaven" where "the thing we freely forfeit is kept with fonder a care,/Fonder a care kept than we could have kept it, kept/Far with fonder a care (and we, we should have lost it) finer, fonder/A care kept. – Where kept? Do but tell us where kept, where. –/Yonder…"[114]

This "Yonder" of which we are exhorted to be always mindful is the home of all the things we cherish. Everywhere we meet the ubiquitous ciphers of infinite beauty and goodness in the palpable selving of nature, foremost in the "world's loveliest – men's selves" which universal selving is the "fathering forth" of that Beauty which is past change. Here Hopkins echoes Plotinus and, as we shall see, this Yonder which is the home of all cherished things is a recurrent theme in some forms of Christian spirituality. In the next chapter we will envisage this Yonder as the divine essence which, as the creative exemplar and the true self of each self, is the deepest inwardness of each selving.

H. Hans urs Von Balthasar

In this discussion of a slice of a great theologian's work, I find the ambivalent circumstance of both rejoicing in many of the distinctions he draws and being surprised and disappointed by some others. If my criticisms reveal my ignorance of the greater reaches of his thought, I apologize in advance.

Vocation, we have suggested, rests on listening to oneself as in some sense "other to oneself" in regard to the living out of the ideal life of one's ideal self. This would seem presumably to apply *ceteris paribus* to Jesus of Nazareth. Hans urs Von Balthasar offers at once a classical as well as contemporary theory of the vocation of Jesus as well as every other human person. He speaks classically of the "mission" not the calling or vocation of Jesus. A mission is a being sent, and thus is a *vis a tergo*; its energy is in the force, so to speak, at one's back or one's initiating will that rests in a conviction of a higher will. But, of course a human mission, as when we say "a person with a mission," may be preceded by the "call" which is a *vis a fronte*, a beckoning from what lies before. They need not be utterly exclusive and incompatible. In any case, if one is defined by one's own possibility of actualizing ideals, then one's being called is basic; but if one is defined by continuing to realize the actuality of what already exists, then mission is more basic. Von Balthasar ties the earthly *mission* (*ad extra* to historical humanity and creation) of Christ to his eternal *procession* (*ad intra*) from the Father; and in so far as human beings are united with Christ, their mission, and thus their calling, is tied to this procession. As Christ eternally proceeds from the Father as a matter of necessity, so Christ's being on earth was essentially to be sent by the Father. Being sent, having a mission, as is the case with a calling, of course, may be thought of metaphorically. But in this theological context the human mission in its unity with Christ is not metaphorical.

Christ did not have to be called or chosen at a certain time. The mission, i.e., being sent by the Father, admits no doubt, whereas the call may be dubious and require interpretation. But, of course, what the mission may mean in a particular circumstance might well require interpretation. But Christ's self-consciousness from the start is an awareness of himself being sent by the Father; this is an essential determination of the unique essence as the only begotten Son/Word become flesh. Whereas the appropriate response to the call is listening, perhaps even contemplating, and then deciding to follow with a sense of risk, the appropriate response to being sent, the response to the mission, is obedience.

Von Balthasar makes a philosophical distinction between subjectivity (*Geistsubjekt*) and person.[115] Subjectivity has symmetry to what we are calling ipseity. Individual human beings have unique incommunicable existence for themselves, *Je-für-sich*, i.e., a non-instantiable self-awareness. Von Balthasar makes two claims: We have this incommunicable ipseity available to us only in the form of the species-concept of humanity. The species-concept of our humanity cannot be abstracted from this incommunicable ipseity of the individuals which realize this species. (He does not, as far as I can see, address explicitly the question which preoccupied us in Book 1, namely whether it is conceivable that the ipseity can have a different existence-condition than that of the species concept of humanity.) Further, given the species-concept, we cannot deduce the number of individuals realizing the species nor can we deduce the distinguishing characteristics that these individual subjectivities will have. The ever-present mineness, *Jemeinigkeit*, of consciousness refers to the paradox that every being of the species has this feature of mineness, namely the feature of uniqueness and incommunicability of its individuality – a topic which preoccupied us in Book 1, Chapter III, especially §2. This means that for Von Balthasar there is granted a primacy to first-personal perspectives or first-personal appresentations of first-personal perspectives for determining the essence of subjectivity.

Von Balthasar claims that subjectivity or ipseity knows *that* it is such, i.e., that it is, in a unique and incommunicable way, a manner of being human. But it does not know *who* it is. It knows that it is numerically distinct from all the other individual humans, but it does not know how it is different from these others. We have argued throughout both volumes of this work that ipseity is a "knowledge" of "myself" and in this sense it is a knowledge of *who* I am. We have claimed that it is a genuine and unique sense of "knowing" although it is non-ascriptive and immediate. It is more than a knowledge of mere numerical identity. Indeed, if numerical identity requires that it make sense to say I am not two, then we do not have here a case of numerical identity. Knowing the individuality of *who* one is in this non-ascriptive sense is not dependent on one's knowing any third-person characteristic of oneself, indeed, it is not dependent on knowing anything else about oneself. One can be aware of oneself as oneself without being aware of oneself as anything else except oneself. Indeed, in the cases of extreme memory loss I do not know "who in the world I am," i.e., I have no identifying knowledge of myself in terms of definite descriptions, but I still inerrantly use "I" and refer to myself as myself. In this sense, we have argued, one cannot not know who one is. However, we have also maintained that not "knowing who in the world one is," in a sense rather different from that of the amnesiac, is everyone's predicament because it is precisely the task of being a person, i.e., finding one's vocation. We have also argued in this Book 2 that the ipseity finds a completion in moral self-determination. In this sense we find an equivalence between *who* one is and *what sort of person* one is. In this respect, although ipseity is ineluctably the self-presence of a *who*, and it is more than a mere numerical "that" bereft of *who*, nevertheless this *who* is empty of personal determination and resembles the empty "this" or "that" of the demonstrative pronoun where there is no ascriptive or perceptual content. But "who" or the non-ascriptive self-referent of "I" is not a mere "this" and the sense of the "haecceity" is richly different in each case, even if in each case one is not in a position to fill it in with any content. In this sense we draw near to Von Balthasar when he notes that the subjectivity can *ascribe* to itself this *haecceitas* but it cannot positively *describe* what this is.

Von Balthasar goes on to describe how the subjectivity approaches becoming "who," i.e., an identifiable someone, in an individuation process by which one is individuated according to the situations of place of birth, where one lives one's life, the relations into which one is born and which one acquires, the lineage of the family, the name one receives, the education one has, etc. These acquisitions and inheritances are contingent and there is nothing which cannot in principle be the determination of someone else.

Von Balthasar singles out another way of individuation by which a subjectivity or ipseity realizes itself. This is through the self-awareness brought about by significant others in the course of one's life, where others regard one as a single individual and create a nurturing environment in which one may become aware of one's unique ipseity. Regardless of whether this is done by parents, friends, or lovers, the question for Von Balthasar is whether this is a sufficient basis, because all of these attitudes or loyalties, even though they might at the time profess unconditionality, are in fact contingent and conditioned. They can be rescinded. Von Balthsar asks, Are they really enough to form an abiding consciousness of one's qualitative individuality? Is any such commitment or profession by another anything else but a profession of who the ipseity is for the friend, lover, parent? Therefore, Von Balthsar argues, because there is here no such secure ascertainment of the qualitative identity of the ipseity, there can be no categorical determination of this ipseity's vocation in the world, no categorical determination of meaning for its being-in-the-world.[116]

Given the unsecured establishment (not of the *that* but) of *who* the subjectivity is, if all we have are the two typical kinds of individuation just mentioned, then, claims Von Balthasar, there is no basis for introducing personhood into such a subjectivity's life. Being a person is a rare and at best unstable volatile phenomenon.

Only from the encounter with the divine Thou can the subjectivity become a personal I. (Cf. our discussion of Kierkegaard above.) Only the absolute subject, God, who discloses to the subjectivity who this subjectivity is for Him, the eternal, abiding faithful God, and why or for what reason this subject exists, i.e., what this subject's mission is, can say that this subject is a person. From the second- and third-personal perspective this means that only if the person professes to have faith in God can there be before us the strong possibility of an individual person.

As it stands, we might assume that we would have a kind of normative theology of types of cultures and religions: Where space is made for the belief in and revelation of such a divine Thou who deigns to order one's life, we find fulfillment of the necessary condition for this special normative sense of personhood. Yet that is not Von Balthasar's position. Rather, in this theological context we hear the prescription that one becomes a person if and only if one is sent or commissioned with a particular role within the Christian community. In this sense "who we are depends on what we are meant or called or sent to be."[117] Only when linked within the universal community and mission of Christ by the one who alone can claim to know with utter certainty the subject's name "before the foundation of the world" in Christ, is the subjectivity properly named a person.

We too gave special weight to the notion of the exemplary disclosure of one's calling in "the truth of will." And we claimed that this disclosure made possible the coincidence of who one is with the sort of person one ought to be. Yet Von Balthasar stipulates that "person" applies only to one who has the equivalent of such a revelation through faith and her awakening of what this means within the Christian community.

Ultimately Von Balthasar agrees with Kierkegaard that only does the human become truly aware of herself when she meets God. Von Balthasar's notion of "person" seems to have symmetry with Kierkegaard's "theological self." This latter is most stringently actualized in the Kierkegaardian view that one is a single individual (thus a person in an exemplary sense) when one recognizes oneself as a sinner before God. Being a person, a "theological self," is not possible apart from Christianity. The learning of and obedience to one's mission as a disciple of Christ amounts to both an increase in personal determination as well as an increase in universality through the ecclesial community.[118] It also amounts for the ontological elevation into personhood.

The claim by Von Balthasar that there is a difference between the non-Christian and Christian, because the latter is a person or theological self and the former is not capable of becoming a person or theological self because not sent by God, would seem to be chiefly a matter of a stipulated definition. To this reader it sounds, *salva reverentiae*, strangely uncharitable. If it is a phenomenological-ontological claim, which, of course, it is not, it is not convincing. Because it seems to define person in connection with a determination of a specific character a person acquires which is facilitated by the historical believing community, it is not clear how it would address the parallel appearance of such a determination in other non-Christian cultures and communities. Surely many cultures provide through a variety of beliefs a definition of life's path or one's station in life. The question of whether this indeed happens through the equivalent faith *coram Deo* could only be decided by deep acquaintance with the culture and perhaps the individuals comprising the culture. For example, Hinduism, for better or worse, provides an elaborate theory of vocation and station, and it provides a theological-philosophical background with its teachings on the transcendence and immanence of Brahman but also on liberation, karma, and reincarnation. Prima facie it seems rash to exclude billions of people from the status of "person," even from the status of "theological self," on the basis of the specific requirements that one is explicitly Christian.

Further, an inquiry needs to be made as to how Jesus's prayer that all be one in the Father is to be reconciled with the theological exclusivist impulses found in many later disciples. If the issue is the absence of an explicit belief in Christ, then there has to be at least mentioned the ancient themes of implicit faith, baptism of desire, etc. And if one could be a theological self through implicit faith, how would one ever be in a position to say which individuals one came to know were (normative) persons or theological selves? What would be the decisive first- and second- and third-person criterion for being a person? If it is obedience to (what is regarded with certainty as) God's will, surely we will find in the second- and third-person perspective both beautiful and ugly candidates, unless one would naively stipulate that *eo ipso* obedience involves an inerrant grasp of what God's will truly is. Similarly, if the criterion is their "fruits" in their love, a love which embraces all and foremost those in one's life who stand in need, and a love which has died to the old self, then we have the odd state of affairs where there appear to be very few persons/theological selves and of these a good number are not Christian.

The drift of this work, nevertheless, is in great sympathy with what I take to be the basic thesis of von Balthsar, namely, that we are most properly our true selves *coram deo*. The monk M. Basil Pennington put this point in a way congenial, I believe, to both the work of Von Balthasar as well as our work: If we only truly see ourselves as persons in the world when we see ourselves reflected back to us "from the eyes of one who truly loves us," then "the only one who can reflect back to us the fullness of our beauty is God." Thus the importance of contemplative prayer for uncovering one's true self and the realization of who one is as the sort of person one is called to be. (Cf. §4 below.) But no one will claim to have reached a definitive accomplished capacity for this prayer and thus the definitive revelation of oneself before God.[119]

Furthermore, the sense in which it is proper to assign to God the status of Thou or a person is a difficult one. Persons, we have claimed, are property-laced. And "you" is a fallible indexical reference by which someone is temporarily singled out from among a background of other third-person presences. The Jewish and Christian traditions at least have hesitated to claim that God ever is able to be relegated to a third-person status. Further, love, we have claimed, moves through and beyond the properties to the very beloved ipseity in itself and for itself. Only the work (and grace) of a prayer life can become clear on what this means in the reference to God. And it is not at all a priori clear that Christians have *eo ipso* a more perfect path for this referring and therefore to that presence that (faith claims) regards us in return.

We may recall here that thinkers such as Kierkegaard and Hopkins admit that there is a continuum between the pagan and the theological self. If this be true not only is there a universal sense of living *coram Deo*, but further, within the Christian community's ranks, the sense of vocation will admit of endless differences of definition.

If one roots personal identity in the harmony and fidelity to position-taking acts (as we have done in this work), one might ask whether there might not be greater personhood in the non-believer's heroic dealing with uncertainty and an insecure reservoir of doubt that pervades the beliefs implicit in the position-takings by which one's way in life is navigated. In Von Balthasar's sense there are people of great integrity, even "holiness," if this is taken to mean the total obedience in carrying out one's mission, who are not persons. Extraordinary individuals, as Socrates, Buddha, and Gandhi, are not mere "ipseities," but, because they are embodied and encultured, they are individuals that we want to call "persons." But, according to Von Balthasar, it would seem that because they have not received (publicly-officially) the Father's unconditional affirmation through fellowship with Jesus, they are not truly persons. As it stands this is not a helpful use of the term "person" or we need a supplementary discussion of "anonymous" persons and Christians.

It would seem that the mission of Christ is one of obedience in a teleologically determined way. (Cf. our discussion Chapter V, §6.) This means that here there is a determinism compatible with freedom even though, at the same time, not doing the Father's will is not a genuine option. This has symmetry with the evidence for the unique vocation we discussed in the previous chapter. Like the mother's pursuing her vocation (in the example of Husserl), there is a case of *beata necessitas boni*: Freedom is in doing the one thing necessary that defines one's Existenz. Obedience to one's mission or conscientiously following one's vocation, for most of us much of the time – this would seem to hold true of believers too – is never such a clear case of "the one thing necessary." This is to say that it is not something that one always clearly sees and it is not what one alone wants to do at the cost of being alienated from one's essence. In the first-person we rarely have the Fichtean-Husserlian, and *a fortiori* Pauline, sense of being called to be what we are; rather we have darkness, uncertainty, and risk. (That is why Fichte urges love as a higher standpoint – without, however, being able to offer means to acquire this "grace.") If this is so, in Von Balthasar's terms, personhood is always transcendent to subjectivity, or subjectivity is often on the verge of personhood.

But, as we have attempted to show earlier, ipseity or subjectivity as we know it is necessarily wrestling with the ideal of its true personhood. Even a divinely revealed determination of one's eternal essence, as the revelation of one's mission in the life of Christ's mystical body, is itself fraught with interpretation, risk, and with the struggle to be obedient to the not always clear dictates of conscience. For Christian theology, it would seem, all human persons apart from Jesus find a tension in the imperatives of obedience to legitimate authority, on the one hand, and thoughtfulness and conscience, on the other. Certainly, the thoughtful, faithful, and not merely obedient, person, even the theological self of Von Balthasar, would seem to know no path that did not have its dark perilous parts. Often enough it would appear to be an endless task of discernment. Do Christians receive from God an assurance that their tensions and periods of darkness can never be such as to impair their being theological selves, whereas "the others" are by definition bereft of such a status? From whatever perspective we judge who participates in God's life, especially in the case of Others, the Gospels teach us not to judge. In one's own case, as in every case, we are counseled to hope.

Finally we may find in Von Balthasar's discussion an intention which is directed at matters which are of a quite different nature. It seems true that there is a massive difference between the religious view he proposes and the pervasive contemporary one where understanding anything, and *a fortiori* a person, requires bringing this something into a causal relation with a physical thing. Likewise there is a major difference in the appreciation of what it means to be a person from the religious perspective Von Balthasar espouses. This is an understanding that being a self is not a result of chance or blind necessity; that being a person is not exhausted by whatever brain science has to tell us about neurophysiology, etc. When the dominating framework for understanding what it means to be a human person is reductionist science and materialist culture, then there is no room for a person to "consider himself as having been chosen to be"; in such a culture one does "not consider his being as having been bestowed." Even though such a materialist culture is pervasive, the person of faith must choose to live in accord with his having been chosen, and in this respect "sent."[120] This belief, tied doubtless to the teachings of the religions of "the Abrahamic tradition," can effect a radically different understanding of persons in regard to themselves, one another, and perhaps to nature as well. In as much as this is part of Von Balthasar's intention in defining a normative sense of person based on faith, we can agree with it wholeheartedly.

§3. Excursus: The Spiral of Spiritual Ascent in Sufism

What follows is a distillation of some themes in the Sufi tradition that are akin to our project of a philosophical-theology of vocation. As will become evident, the dominant Plotinian theme of the eternal form of Socrates in the divine mind is central. This tradition is not homogenous and uniform, although it was united in its developing forms of mysticism within Islam and in its apperception of itself as often being suspect to orthodox Islam. Because it was often suspect to orthodox Islam it came to regard itself as an esoteric tradition, even though some of its adherents "went public" and drew great attention to themselves. In the Qu'ran, as in the Torah, one finds repeated insistence on the transcendence of God and the incomparability of God with anything. Any teaching of a possible union, to say nothing of equality, of a creature with God was likely to occasion scandal and provoke anathema.

There is a saying, "the Sufi is not created," which derives from a meaning attached to the word "Sufi," i.e., one who is identified with the divine act. Titus Burkhardt takes "Sufi" to mean "that being who is thus reintegrated into the Divine Reality [and] recognizes himself in it 'such as he was' from all eternity according to his 'principle possibility, immutable in its state of non-manifestation." This principle hidden possibility is the reason for one's personal uniqueness, even though it in no way entails positing a multiplicity in the divine.[121]

Sufism's theory of vocation is a theory of the journey to the discovery of the unique soul's destiny – which coincides with its origin in the divine essence. A central theme of this chapter and the next, exemplarism, is believed by a father of Sufism, Junayd, to have a basis in the Qur'an 7.171. In this passage, we find the *Mithaq*, the covenant, by which all human souls swore fealty to God before God created their bodies. "[Recall] when thy Lord took from the children of Adam, from their loins, their posterity and made them testify as to themselves: 'Am I not your Lord? And they said: 'Yea, we testify' – lest ye should say on the day of resurrection: 'Of this we have been neglectful.'" This "Yea" is not only assent to the Lordship of the Lord and each's being eternally present to herself as always before the Lord, but it is also an assent to her own "testing" and "suffering" as a means of restoring herself to the original unity with God.[122] Although the passage tells us little more than that souls pre-exist their bodies, in Junayd's interpretation it refers to the eternal existence of human souls as ideas in the divine mind and the Sufi doctrine that "all that individual man has of reality is reduced to this primordial confrontation of his essence, which is still a simple divine idea, with the divine essence itself."

Junayd sees this covenant text as God addressing the human souls "when they did not [yet] exist except in so far as he 'existed' [in a transitive verbal sense] them; for he was [eternally] 'existing' his creation in a manner that was different from his 'existing' individual souls, in a manner that he alone knows." Junayd goes on to say:

> He was 'existing' them, encompassing them, witnessing them in the beginning when they were no thing apart from their eternal being [in which] state they were from all pre-eternity – and this is the divine existence and divine awareness which is proper to him alone. Therefore did we say that when he 'existed' man, causing his will to flow over him as he wished, [endowing him] with his most exalted attribute in which none can share, this [form of] existence was without doubt the most perfect and efficacious.[123]

R.C. Zaehner interprets this to mean that "in his timeless eternity God contemplates or witnesses, 'mentions' or thinks, encompasses or comprehends all human souls (*arwah* not *anfus*) in one single existential act of witnessing, thought, and comprehension: in this single act he 'exists' them." Zaehner thinks what he translates here as "exists" (as a transitive verb) "denotes the logical priority of God over all souls, but [also] a community of substance, and the 'substance' in this case is eternal extra-temporal being." The creation in time is called "their annihilation out of or after their eternal being," i.e., their entry into time. This existence of the soul is the most perfect existence and is devoid of humanity in the sense we typically understand it, i.e., as a species in nature and the world. The relationship between God and the immortal souls "must therefore always remain unknown to any but God... and any individual soul which God deigns to raise up to him"; for "sincerity is a secret between God and his servant which no angel may know that he should record it, nor devil that he should defile it, nor desire that it should divert it."[124]

In the earthly spiritual life of the soul there is added to it something beyond the original happiness it had enjoyed when it "was not," i.e., when it was only an idea in God's mind. Now it has the "joy-in-agony" of loving and being loved by God.[125]

For the human being there is only "one essential tendency, that which brings him back to his own eternal Essence; all other tendencies are merely the expression of creaturely ignorance and will moreover be cut off and judged."[126] All essences and all possibilities exist in the divine essence; there is no "being" assigned to the realm of the merely possible. There is no being in opposition to the being of God.

Creation is divine self-manifestation. "God said, 'I loved to be known, so I created the world.'" Creatures are possibilities of outward manifestation inherent within the divine essence as it is known by God and as it is beyond being. God's desire to become known "outwardly" brings these essential properties of Himself into manifestation. There are five forms of outward manifestation which account for what we call Heaven and Earth, but each presence derives its being from the Presence beyond itself. Thus bodies are reflections of image-exemplars beyond themselves, which themselves are reflections or shadows of spirits, which themselves are reflections or shadows of immutable uncreated essences or ideas.

The name of "Allah" is a form of Presence and reality or "entification" of the absolutely transcendent Unnameable. Allah who is supremely One creates with a single act aiming at a single object: Allah creates Adam whom he taught all the names, i.e., in whom there were all the essences of things. Adam or the Perfect Man is the "archetypal entity" of mankind and each existing thing displays certain perfections of Allah's reality and each individual human being taken together reflects the whole of this divine reality. In this regard the divine manifestation of Allah in the world is called the Perfect Man. Man is a little universe and the universe is a big man.[127] (Doubtless there are parallels with the Pauline theology of the Whole and Cosmic Christ here.)

Rumi, the great Sufi poet, in addressing the Perfect Man says:

> Thou art not a single thou, but a hundred thousand men hidden in one man; a sun hidden in a mote; the sky and a deep sea which is drowning place of a hundred thou's; a hundred thousand stacks in a handful; a hundred thousand Gabriels in the earthly frame of man, comprehending all realities, unifying all contraries.[128]

The vocation of man is back toward the center of the Perfect Man. But there exists an ambivalence in the human being's individuality. As a Name of God he gravitates toward the center of the Perfect Man; as a particular name he becomes isolated from the center and moves away from this centrality and is distracted from what is essential. His spiritual task is an ascent to the True Perfect Man and his essential self. This requires an uprooting of himself from what distracts and derails him from this center. Rumi once put it this way:

> You were born from the rays of God's Majesty
>   When the stars were in their perfect place.
> How long will you suffer from the blows
>   of a nonexistent hand?
> So come, return to the root of the root
>   of your own soul....
> Soul of all souls, life of all life – you are That.
> Seen and unseen, moving and unmoving – you are That.
> The road that leads to the City is endless;
> Go without head or feet
>   And you'll already be there.
> What else could you be? – you are That.[129]

As the outward manifestation of man's form depends upon God's total attentiveness toward him at the time of bringing him into existence, so his return to the Center depends on God's showing him his "specific face." The "specific face," which approximates what we are calling the divine idea of the individual essence, is inseparably one with the "divine mystery," which is God's theophany or self-manifestation. Its revelation is at once a disclosure of the "divine mystery" as well as the self's archetypal being, the most excellent aspect of the person. This revelation reveals the true self stripped of all that is other than God. Man's "specific face" is the self in its eternal origin. If the persons are lucky, i.e., if they are blessed, they receive special graces, i.e., they are permitted to observe a beauty "manifesting itself to them from behind the gate of the Specific Face, the gate that has been opened for them between themselves and their creator..."[130]

At the bottom of the Sufi debates on mysticism is what we are calling The Theological Distinction between God and the World. But also in question is the nature of the unique essence of ipseity and whether in love, especially divine love, there is a union which annihilates the twoness of the ipseities. Junayd's master once said that "love between two [persons] is not sound until the one can say to the other, 'O thou I.'"[131] Perhaps most notorious were some of the utterances of an earlier mystic, Abu Yazid (roughly contemporary with Shankara, circa 800 CE). "I sloughed off my self as a snake sloughs off its skin, and I looked into my essence (or self) and lo, I was He."[132] In another passage, there is recounted Abu Yazid's odyssey or "ascension" to reach God Himself.

> I plunged into the oceans of *malakut* (the realm of pure ideas) and the veils of deity (*lahut*) until I reached the throne, and lo, it was empty; so I cast myself upon it and said, "Master, where shall I seek thee?" And the veils were lifted up, and I saw that I am I, yea, I am I. I turned back to what I sought, and it was I, no other, into which I was going."[133]

Abu Yazid's formulations, of course, caused consternation, but in time he became universally accepted as a Sufi saint. And the theological-metaphysical issues are intriguing for the purposes of this work in the same way Meister Eckhart's are. They are, as well, quite complicated. Consider the famous text of Abu Yazid's "ascension" (*mi'raj*) with the commentaries in the Sufi tradition. Here Abu Yazid says that he looked upon God with the "eye of certainty." After this God turned him away from all that was not he and showed him "marvels from his secret being, and he showed me his 'he-ness'. And through his He-ness I looked on mine 'I-ness', and it vanished away."[134] The remainder of the ascent wrestles with how God transmutes "mine I-ness into his He-ness" and "caused me to cease from my selfhood in his He-ness." Yet the emphasis is that one's "being God" is through God. Further, there is a subtle development where the divine partner in the dialogue answers Abu Yazid's question: "What have I to do with thee?" with, "I am thine through thee; there is no God but thee." Here begins a labyrinth of tests for Abu Yazid. He immediately recognizes this and responds: "Do not beguile me with myself: I will not be content with myself apart from thee and without thee..." Here the Christian reader may overhear the Fenelon-Bossuet debate of whether it is possible to love God purely and simply for the sake of God alone. For example, God says he thanks Abu Yazid for keeping his commandments and he loves him for what he eschewed of his prohibitions. And Abu Yazid replies: "If thou thankest, bestow the thanks for it upon thyself," which a commentator takes to mean, "it is better that thou should thank thyself rather than a slave."

Again, the basic point of tension is that the unity which "deifies" the soul is through God's grace; and one is oneself and God is God and God alone is God. But even here, Abu Yazid smells danger precisely in the implication of "I am I myself through thee," or that "I see myselfhood in thyselfhood." For God answers, "if thou art through me, then I am thou and thou art I." To which Abu answers: "Do not beguile me with thyself apart from thyself." It becomes rather clear at the conclusion that upon being elevated (in a manner reminiscent of what Christians call *lumen gloriae*) to a condition wherein the unique ipseity is manifest in the divine essence after the annihilation of all that separates the self from God, the language of identity of essence appears to Abu Yazid as appropriate because it is postulated that he returns to the original state of his essence before creation. (Cf. our discussion of Eckhart above.) Thus, e.g., God speaks to him. " 'O thou.' And I said to him: 'O I.' And he said to me: 'thou art the alone.' I said: 'I am the alone.' He said to me: 'Thou art thou.' I said: 'I am I, but if I were I as an ego, I would not have said 'I', but since I never was an ego, then be thou thou, yea thou.' He said: 'I am I.' My speaking of him as 'I' is like my speaking of him as 'he' – denoting unity."[135]

Here Zaehner interprets "if I were I as an ego" to refer to the historical sinful self. Abu says he was "never an ego," i.e., he, as the quintessential Abu in the divine essence to which he has now returned after the divine purgation, was never a mere historical person.

Zaehner enlists Martin Buber to clarify this matter. Buber himself acknowledges mystical experiences whereby he attained something resembling what others might call a union with the primal being or godhead. Buber's own view is "I reached an undifferentiable unity of myself without form or content." This *seems* to resemble our notion of the "myself." What he adds supports this false impression: "I may call this an original pre-biographical unity and presuppose that it is hidden unchanged beneath all biographical change, all development and complication of the soul." Further, he states that this might well be the "ground" of the spirit, and indeed beyond the reach of the multiplicity which accrued to one in living life with all its forms and contents. It is not beyond individuation but, on the contrary, "existing but once, single, unique, irreducible," and not at all the "soul of All."[136]

Buber is thus inclined to deny anything like a mystical union and he would *appear* to interpret what seemed initially to be a mystical experience as proximate to what we are calling the non-ascriptive, non-reflective self-experiencing of the self, i.e., the "myself." It is clear that from what has preceded in both volumes of this work that we do not wish to underestimate the philosophical importance of the "myself." But in our view any experience of union, especially that of love, will properly presuppose this self-awareness (of the "myself") of the lover in his apperception of the beloved, which itself is an appresentation of the "myself" of the beloved.

And this eventually emerges precisely as Buber's point. What he is referring to as "pre-biographical" is not the non-ascriptive "myself," which for us is always an anonymous I-awareness, but some elemental form of consciousness that is "beneath the creaturely [human] situation" of being in a dialogical relationship as an I with the Divine Thou. For Buber the "I" of the dialogical relation is a "subjectivity" awakened by the Thou, not a reflective having of oneself as oneself. Even granting the possible agreement on the non-reflective self-awareness of the "myself" as not merely a lower sub-human self-awareness, it would seem that there are special problems in the "mystical relationship." That is, the issue would seem to require modification in the mystical or theological context. In this framework the "other" is, indeed, absolutely transcendent, and eventually perhaps, through revelation and faith, a Thou. Yet this is the One who at the same time is "more interior to me than I am to myself," as St. Augustine once said. This is a basic claim of The Theological Distinction and perhaps it is also implicit in some of struggles of the Sufi mystics in their use of the first-person singular. We have maintained that another can never refer to me with "I" nor I to another with "I." But the rules change oddly in mysticism and theology. It is not that contradictions are permissible, but the entire framework of what is reasonable is placed in another context. (See the next chapter, especially §§ 1–6 and 8 below.) The Sufi tradition builds on a notion of God that hints at The Theological Distinction, but does not make a theme of it.

§4. Some More Differences Between Neo-Platonism and Christianity

Along with Philo, Origen, Plotinus and St. Augustine, perhaps it was the writings of "Dionysius the Areopagite" (the Syrian monk of the seventh century) that played the greatest role in extending Neo-Platonic thought into the heart of Christian theology. In Plotinus there is not properly an exemplarism attributable to the ultimate divine principle, the One, but exemplarism's home is in *Nous*. But in Philo, Origen, Augustine and Dionysius the forms are placed in the God of Israel and/or Christianity and not left in the subordinate divine principle of *Nous*. In Dionysius, and in his Christian interpreters and readers, the exemplars were at once "pre-ordinations" as well as divine "beneficent volitions" which both create and invite created things to come into their ownmost proper essence or form. For the Christian commentators exemplarism was inseparable from the theme of the grace not only of creation but also of redemption, and therefore it was tied to the dark mystery of "predestination."

Before we turn to the comparison in the doctrines of salvation, a brief anticipatory word about "emanationism", or how what is other than the One comes into being, is called for. It is perhaps no longer advisable simply to contrast Plotinus and "the Abrahamic tradition," in terms of a clear opposition of the theory of "emanationism" and the theory of creation *ex nihilo*. Indeed, one may ask whether, aspects of what Robert Sokolowski has called "The Christian Distinction" (between God and the world) are not already in Plotinus. In the next chapter we will look explicitly at "The Christian Distinction," which we call here "The Theological Distinction" because of the hypothesis that it is a distinction not only proper to the "Abrahamic traditions" but perhaps also to other traditions. Here we may note, by way of anticipation, that The Theological Distinction has as its basic formulation: God plus the world is not greater than God alone, and God minus the world does not involve any depreciation of God. There are indications that Plotinus would be at home with this formulation. For both Plotinus and Aquinas, who is probably the most powerful theoretician of the concepts that generate The Christian or Theological Distinction, hold that God (or the One) is absolute, needs nothing beyond or outside Itself, and is not "really related" to anything outside of Itself, is not a thing or a being, is essentially beyond our capacity to know, and is the source of absolutely everything. The world and the One/God are not two as two beings such that God plus the world or any being increases the richness of being (*esse*) or the perfection of God.[137] For both thinkers our very existence is a kind of continuing incessant "first grace,"[138] even though the One is not amenable to an analogous personalization to the degree the God of the Abrahamic traditions is.

Having said that there are some reasons to think that The Theological Distinction is implicit in strains of Plotinian thought, there are some other strains that complicate the matter and thus cause doubts about this first claim. First of all, the Plotinian universe as it proceeds under the guidance of the world-soul is a devolution to a realm of purely material beings; at the outermost realm we seem to have a kind of opacity to the informing principle of *Nous*. This would seem to reflect poorly on the excellence of the One as the source of all. Or do we have here something feebly existing which nevertheless exists outside the perfection of the divine?

This brings us to the "Fall" in Plotinus. Although the processions from the One of Mind and Soul are not thought of as having any chronological or historical sense, and although all of creation is analogous to an artist's expression, nevertheless there is another, more melancholy, note in Plotinus. The separation of *Nous*, the divine intellectual principle, from the One, and, by implication, the separation as well of the *Psyche*, divine soul-principle, from the divine intellectual principle, and, in turn, by way of further complication, "I myself," as a person in the world, from my true "myself," are mysteriously understood as a kind of illegitimate self-assertion or will to separate existence.[139] Plotinus once exclaimed: "How much better it would have been for it [the divine principle of Intellect] not to have wanted it [this separate existence]" (III.8.8). But to call this an original *sin* as a rebellion against the personal creator "God" says too much. It is a wistful expression of regret rather than an accusation of a heinous deed. The very fact of "creation," or there being beings and principles apart from the One, is deplored and regretted. In this sense the world as a creation is not affirmed as profoundly good. Nor is "creation" (emanation) properly a free personal act of creating.

We have said that a key proposition of The Theological Distinction is: God plus the world is not greater than God alone. In Plotinus, and also in Simone Weil, it would seem that God (or the One) plus all the creatures (all that derives from the One) are less than God alone. For Simone Weil this is because God accepts this self-diminution in creating creatures capable of evil. The existence of evil does not demonstrate the non-existence of God, but rather it reveals God's great power that he is capable of self-renunciation, restraint, even an emptying of "a part of his being from himself."[140]

Further, salvation is not something that depends on a deed, rather it is already done. According to Plotinus, salvation is "waking up to what we already are, getting back to our true and higher selves by a process of purification."[141] For Plotinus, our true selves are already complete; there is no question of our making ourselves or actualizing our potencies, with the help of God's grace. Rather, we have to wake up to the fact that we have our beatitude and salvation already. Plotinus, Sufis, and Christians can say:

"to search for God as an other than oneself is to place oneself outside of him"; or "if he wants to see [God] by being different he puts himself outside" (V.8.11). Yet, for the Christians, Jews, and Muslims, the holiness of God is essentially different from being an authentic self. Further, the personal center of an ipseity, Existenz, the *abditum mentis*, etc. of ancient Christian theologians, does not have the eternal onto-logical stability and inalienability that the true self of Plotinus has. Whereas the true self of Christians, as one with the divine essence and as the metaphysical principle of the created "myself", is eternally secure, nevertheless, as the achievable true self of the individual personified ipseity which is called from all eternity, its possession is vulnerable and fraught with danger. In terms of our earlier terminology, *Existenz* is never in a permanently secure and tranquil state. As we might put it, paraphrasing Armstrong: What Plotinus has to say about the true self in terms of its eternal same-ness and perfection is not, for the Christian, about something that "I myself" *am* but rather about the actuality of the Eternal Word of God who contains the perfection of "I myself." The Christian view is that I am called to participate, through God's grace, in the actuality of the perfection of my pre-existing eidetic Christ-centered "I myself." But this participation is not a "done deal"; it is something that *I* have to do through cooperation with divine grace working through one's life in the mystical Christ.

"Become what/who thou art" is different in each of the three core theoretical-historical contexts of these final two chapters, i.e., this Husserlian transcendental-existential phenomenology, Plotinus, and Christianity. In the former, the indicative of what and who one is is founded in the unique essence, the "myself," as an entelechy constituting an infinite regulative ideal of the ideal true self which shapes our real possibility and founds the absolute Ought. In Plotinus, "become who/what thou art" refers to our temporal-historical existence being a deficient form of our actual true essential selves from which we have strayed by a mysterious contingency and to which we are exhorted to return. The divine selfhood is ourselves of necessity and any alienation or revocation is accidental and temporary. Because one's eternal true self indicates the path one ought to follow, there can be no question about whether one can. For our interpretation of Christianity "become who/what thou art" proclaims that the indicative "is" is the foundation of one's mandate to become what/who we are, i.e., holy and godlike as befits members of Christ We can note three aspects of this: a) One's unique essence has a divine exemplar in the eternal divine essence which eternally expresses itself through the Word who is Christ; b) one is actually heir to the divine life by reason of being a member of Christ through the grace of faith and its constant renewal in love. c) this inheritance which the Christian owes to herself and the creator to claim, however, is only within her I-can if and only if each is joined in faith and love to Christ who is the way, the end, and the means. Both the Plotinian and the Christian are addressed with the calling: Conduct yourself in accord with the noble divine lineage which is yours by an ontological birthright. But the Christian must always at the same time remind herself: Who/what I am as the basis for who/what I am to become is not a sheer given but is through being creatively called into existence and sustained by grace on this journey. This is a *calling* to me not merely as a result of the givenness of my unique essence as an entelechy shaping and beckoning me but by a person and it requires a response of a personal kind. One's being, unique essence, and agency are not starters or presuppositions for appropriately appraising this calling but they themselves are gifts because there is nothing that one has not received. (See Chapter VII.) This divine noble inheritance, itself a gift, is neither an infinite ideal, a limit simpliciter, nor is it a transcendent ontological birthright, where Ought implies Can and where Can is an essential property of the historical person. Rather, the destiny, as a participation in God's own essential inner ("Trinitarian") life and thus a new creation, is best envisaged as a limit concept, i.e., as what is pointed to teleologically by the will's aspirations but which is essentially of a different order than its infinite teleological horizon. (See Chapter VII.) The effective achievement of one's new being in Christ, where the I-ought is realized by the gift of a love-informed I-can, is the "miracle" of one's personification which itself is the working out of one's calling and "anointing," i.e., one's Christification. In this "becoming a member of the body of Christ" each's center is in Christ and from out of this center one's life is ordered by one's love of one's "neighbor" but especially of "the least of these."

For both Plotinus and the Christian, the exemplary, the true self of each is an actuality; but for Plotinus it is my proper actuality; for the Christian, it is God's actuality "in Christ" to which I am called or invited to participate and which is not mine to achieve merely "on my own." The Plotinian finds the central questions to be: Who am I and What sort of person am I? The Christian finds these questions central too, but eventually connected to these questions for her are the questions, Who is Jesus of Nazareth? And, What is the Christ? This is because these latter questions determine in whom one must believe and trust for one's salvation. The target of "salvation" for the Christian as well as Plotinus is the unique irreplaceable incommunicable personified "myself." Yet for the Christians it is not a matter of getting it right philosophically and acting rightly ethically but of making room for God to make of them what they are called to be: children of God, members of one another, and sisters and brothers of Jesus. And because salvation is not simply in one's own hands, there is the constant task of trusting in the divine grace, which, however, for The Theological Distinction, is inseparable from trusting in the gift of one's own powers.

Plotinus' position is more likely to generate the self-affirming great-souled person of Aristotle or the Trans-human of Nietzsche; Christianity's position, like the Sufi's, tends to generate an ontological humility before, and gratitude to, God. Its distinctive, but not exclusive, heroes are not independent and self-reliant, whether yeoman or prince, but Francis of Assisi, Damien of Molokai, Dorothy Day, Gandhi,[142] Martin Luther King, Mother Theresa, *et alii*, for whom the love of, and solidarity with, the most vulnerable of the human community reveal the exemplary path.

Nevertheless, the doctrine of one's impotence for salvation apart from grace along with its correlate doctrine, the theme of humility as the deepest truth, have meant for some Christians that salvation remains a nagging doubt and worry. If, indeed, God "knew his own before they were," and chose those whom he foreknew, then the question presses upon the believer whether she is one of "his own." This can be a question less of whether one has been faithful but whether one indeed is one of the "elect" and "predestined." We thus have the famous quests for "signs" of one's elect status which will assuage one's anxiety. (See our earlier discussions of these matters above at §2, D, under *Leibniz*.)

Exemplarism in Christianity, and not in Plotinus, in so far as it becomes inextricably bound up with a doctrine of salvation through grace alone, is inseparable from the unsettling issue in Christianity of predestination. (For the perspective proposed here this is due in great part because of the failure to situate the matter within the framework of The Theological Distinction.) To the extent this is so it has often led to nightmarish anguish. A chief reason for this aberration is perhaps a deep heresy, i.e., to think of one's life hedonistically, i.e., to see all of life in terms of whether it functions toward one attaining heaven or whether it leads to one's being consigned to eternal damnation. Here there is not possible any room for either pure forms of love or duty (or the good) for its own sake.

The distinctive faith and hope of Origen and Julian of Norwich involved a critique of the theologies which assigned wrath and vengeance as pre-eminent properties of God. In such an atmosphere their own belief that in the end "all will be well" is suffocated. Of course, there is merit in the caution that the robust hope to which Christians are exhorted may not forestall, circumscribe, or pre-determine God's infinite wisdom and judgment.[143] Nor does it seem appropriate that this hope ever resembles a chummy optimism where the infinite distance from God is shrunk to a casual familiarity, and the infinite and incomparable generosity of God is belittled by the creature's presumptuous claims on God.

Perhaps the appropriate approach to this theme is to see the doctrine of "damnation" as a position that surfaces in order to protect and respect human dignity and freedom and as a way to highlight the hideousness of sin. In which case the doctrine of Hell may be understood as a doctrine which ratifies the ipseity and Existenz of the person and underlines both one's own solitary will and the possibility of lying to oneself permanently and willing forever to be apart from oneself as well as the call of grace.[144] In which case "damnation" would be most basically "to abuse" and "kill" God in one's person as far as the person is in a position to do so. Given the incomparable love and generosity of God the Creator, eternal damnation would be a kind of ongoing deicide in one's ownmost center. Or, to put it in terms most fitting to this work, " 'Hell' can be described as a perpetual alienation from our true being, our true self, which is in God."[145] If we may take this "false self" to be a sense of I-ness (not the ineluctable "ownness" and "myself-ness" which we have discussed in Book 1) of which we are called upon to rid ourselves, then "expiatory suffering" and self-abnegation are ways the true, God-rooted self may be affirmed. Hell would be the permanent refusal of this invitation to self-abnegation accompanied by the necessary inescapable, not-freely endured everlasting dismantling of this false I-ness by one's own irrepressible respect for oneself as "truthful."[146]

Even assuming that this is intelligible – and it can only have the intelligibility provided by the "logical space" opened by the *mystery* of The Theological Distinction – no one knows whether this is more than a conceptual possibility. Given The Theological Distinction, with God's immanence, incomparable generosity, wisdom, love, etc., given especially the faith in the power of redemptive grace, the consideration of the transcendental esteem and love for oneself, and given a host of other conceptual difficulties which we my, here pass by,[147] we may say that as a conceptual possibility it is one of the most difficult. But granting all this, no one, including the ardent believer in Hell, knows whether anyone is or has been "damned" nor does it seem to me is there any doctrinal basis requiring that one must believe that anyone has actually been damned.

But who can deny that often the fear of and preoccupation with damnation have eliminated any capacity to live life for the sake of its own beauties? Who can deny that fear of Hell occasions that pious persons become bereft of the power to love another, to say nothing of loving God, intrinsically, i.e., for God's own sake. All of life is reduced to an anticipation of being judged worthy or not of the eternal mansions or eternal flames. Such a deep stance of fear easily tips over into a stance of aggression and envy. And perhaps this is why this stance is often connected with strong beliefs in eternal damnation for all but the select few adherents of the Armageddon theology. This frame of mind seethes with resentment and hatred toward those perceived as libertine pagans or liberal Christians. In such an interpretation of obscure highly symbolical passages in the New Testament one sees present history as pointing to the imminent time when Jesus will come as an avenging warrior and when one's present political enemies along with non-believers, who appear blithely to ignore the threat of damnation (that has so plagued and made miserable the believers), will perish at the hands of the wrathful God. At this prospect these Christians seem to "smack their lips with unspeakable pleasure. Perhaps this is because they derive a deep subconscious comfort from the thought that many other people will fall into hell which they themselves are going to escape… This feeling of complacency is what they refer to as 'faith,' and it constitutes a kind of conviction that they are 'saved.'"[148] One becomes the exemplary Christian by participating in what fosters this ultimate cataclysm, e.g., ignoring the "secular humanist" warnings of global warming or destroying Palestinians for the sake of the return of the glory of the Jewish nation as a prelude to Jesus's return.

Whereas Plotinus has no doubt about the exalted state of the heavenly Self, the resources for realizing one's destiny are within oneself, and one's self is essentially anchored in eternal Beauty. Not properly loving oneself, along with stupidity, are what one should be most concerned about, but this concern is not anything like fear or dread. Morbid preoccupation with salvation is foreign to Plotinus. Such a view for the plotinian has everything wrong: It does not esteem the transcendent beauty and goodness of the One; it fails to see our moral failings and stupidities as the root evil; and it dishonors the exalted dignity of one's transcendent/transcendental self by the blasphemous presumption that this could be ever eternally alienated from the divine eternity.

Another focal point in the comparison with the different forms of exemplarism is that in classical Neo-Platonism the move toward transcendence is toward what is beyond all things earthly. Not only is there properly no sacramentalism, i.e., a belief in the presence of the infinitely transcendent God in the physical-historical aspects of creation, but there is no space for the notion that there might be a sacramental, soteriological, and eschatological dimension to history. For Neo-Platonism the world's natural forms are eternally the same, and furthermore there is no room for the idea that nature might be tilted toward a divinizing transformation by "super-nature" or grace, and that worldly nature and history could culminate in a New Heaven and New Earth. Neo-Platonism would find it odd that one would pray and act for God's

Kingdom to be realized on earth as it is in Heaven, and that one's agency toward the "least of these" would be one of the central forms of this "theurgy."

Inseparable from this is another contrast. Plotinus' notion of ascent and "salvation" could make little sense of the Incarnation and Resurrection. This dissonance is anticipated in the Athenian philosophers' (Stoics and Epicureans) reaction to Paul's speech to them in the agora (*Acts* 17:16–34). For some ancient and most modern Christians, earth, flesh, and bodiliness are not only sacred by reason of their preparatory work in the coming to be of personal spirit-selves over billions of years, but also and foremost by reason of God becoming part of this earthly fleshly process in the event of Jesus. In Plotinus the earth, and all that dwells in it, is fashioned by the divine world-soul, and thus enjoys a measure of sacredness. But in spite of the deference for material being as external limit of informed nature, for Plotinus matter is an impediment to spirit and thus evil for beings destined to existence in pure Intellect (*Nous*).[149] Thus material nature in Plotinus does not merit the deference it is entitled to as being the developing material matrix of the body of God in Christ. Furthermore personal spirit-selves themselves are called to become deified partakers of the divine incarnate life precisely through a "glorified" fleshly body. Clearly here the divine "calling" is not addressed purely to the haecceitas of Socrateity but to the person, i.e., the historical-intersubjective-embodied "myself," whose true and fuller sense is in union with "the perfect Man," "the image of the invisible God, the first-born of all creation," wherein all things in heaven and on earth are united. Whatever this might mean in terms of the appropriate conceptual analysis, it is not an indifference towards and devaluation of materiality but a profound valorization of the cosmos, nature, the earth, dirt, and flesh.

The ancient position of Plotinus that one's destiny and salvation are in some respects a "return home" has not only its echo throughout the world's religions (cf., e.g., our discussion of Sufism) but finds expression at the heart of Christian spiritual and mystical life. The nature of the alienation from one's being at home with the father is part of the story of the "fall" (*tolma*, in Plotinus), one's forgetting one's "Father," and becoming lost in the pursuit of what is dishonorable rather than what is honorable (V.1.1). In the "Abrahamic religions" there is the story of the Fall of Adam and the banishment from the "garden" or "paradise" (*paradeisos*). In 2 *Corinthians* 12:1–5 St. Paul reveals that he was taken up to "the third Heaven" and transported into paradise. And "the good thief," also dying on the cross with Jesus, learns that he will be with Jesus this day in paradise (*Luke* 23:42 ff.). A good case can be made that much of the spiritual and mystical life is steeped in this theme of a return to the home, *patria*, that is paradise, and this is inseparable from discovering oneself and the depth of one's soul as made "in the image of God."[150] Yet the sense in which this is properly a "return" as a cyclical process, whereby one goes back to the "identically same" unique essence, is precisely the ontological question that underlies this chapter and the next.

These ancient Plotinian themes which associate the "return home" to the "Father" with the awakening to one's "true self" find a pronounced echo today in some areas of Christian, especially Catholic, spiritual life. Let us consider some statements of the Trappist monk, Thomas Merton. Merton describes the constant temptation in meditation to be taken up with an objective viewpoint and therefore the likely failure to "find our heart" in contemplative prayer, which he describes as sinking "into a deep awareness of the ground of our identity before God and in God." This is the same as "recovering... awareness of our inmost identity" and consenting to be the self we are in the very essence of God. We are to think of our ownmost selves as a word spoken by God and this is inseparably the meaning of one's life. We are called and given to ourselves to "*create from within,* with him [God: JGH], with his grace, a meaning which reflects his truth and makes me his 'word' spoken freely in my personal situation." This calling is awakened in something like what we earlier called, following Husserl, the "truth of will" and is fundamentally a use of one's freedom to *love* "the personal reality of my brother" and to embrace God's will in its "naked, often unpenetrable mystery."[151]

This always is also an unmasking of the fabrication of the "everyday self." This latter is not "our true self." The true self "is hidden in obscurity and 'nothingness' at the center where we are in direct dependence on God."[152] Merton also describes this reality of centering prayer or contemplation as the coming to light of reality as "subjective" and not so much "my subjectivity" whereby I would be, in some measure, external to or objective for myself, but rather the "'myself' in existential mystery" which "opens into the mystery of God."[153] "Our inmost 'I' exists in God and God dwells in it." Yet we must "distinguish between the experience of one's own inmost being and the awareness that God has revealed Himself to us in and through the inner self. We must know that the mirror is distinct from the image reflected in it. The difference rests on theological *faith.*"[154]

Nevertheless, in this prayer we are exhorted to overcome the "familiar subject-object relationship" which characterizes ordinary knowing and in faith to know God as knowing us. As Gregory the Great put it, it is "rejoicing in one's everlasting incorruption in the sight of God." "We know him in so far as we become aware of ourselves as known through and by him. We 'possess' him in proportion as we realize ourselves to be possessed by him in the inmost depths of our being.... Our knowledge of God is paradoxically a knowledge not of him as the object of our scrutiny but of ourselves as utterly dependent on his saving and merciful knowledge of us." Thus contemplative prayer is about deepening the awareness of one's being created – and a sinner being redeemed.[155]

These themes are richly developed in the writings on Centering Prayer by the Cistercian monks, Basil Pennington and Thomas Keating for whom the fourteenth century text, *The Cloud of Unknowing,* as well as the writings of St. John of the Cross, play a special role. It is probably also true that these monks, like Merton, have learned from some Buddhist and Hindu teachers. For Keating, the false self is a constellation of pre-rational reactions and self-serving and self-protecting habits that "have been interwoven into our personality from the time we were conceived.... Our basic core of goodness is our true Self. Its center of gravity is God.... God and our true Self are not separate. Though we are not God, God and our true self are the same thing."[156]

We hope in the next chapter to provide some clarity to this claim for sameness. As we shall argue, the true self is, first of all, one's unique essence as it is one with the divine essence, and then as it serves as the exemplar, and then ultimately the entelechy of the historical person's lived ideal of herself as this emerges in her life-situations.

For the believing Christian who is favorably disposed to the main thesis of this book, centering prayer is primarily a way to "*go back* to" one's true self in the first sense, i.e., as one is a "word" of God or inseparable from the divine essence. Whereas this volume has attempted to shed light on "*becoming* who one is" by going "forwards," tracing the connection through agency between the essential ipseity and the person, "*What I do is me, for that I came*" (Hopkins), centering prayer for the believer is the time set aside to "*be* who one is," i.e., to rest and be one's true self by being through faith in the presence of God and with oneself as one is one with God. A good part of this set-aside time typically turns out to be time discovering how dominant the false self is and how reluctant one is to devote twenty minutes to affirming through faith one's true self as it rests in and before God. In accord with the teaching of St. John of the Cross, and doubtless to the delight of Feuerbachians, all this is happens in and through the darkness of faith. Indirectly this centering time of self-retrieval enables as well that one "moves towards" the true self, because one's "myself," as the form and telos of the person one is, is the entelechy of one's personhood. And yet, as Keating insists, there is nothing here to get a hold of: the pure faith and pure love enable a Presence of ultimate mystery wherein one *believes* oneself to "know that one is known."

But even this awareness of mystery through faith and love cannot be forced. "It is like coming home to a place I should never have left, to an awareness that [is] somehow always there but which I did not recognize. I cannot force this awareness... A door opens within me, but from the other side."[157] Thus it contrasts with some disciplines of meditation where one is exhorted to think of nothing, stop thinking, and make one's mind a total blank. This in and of itself is impossible. In centering prayer the believer is exhorted to place herself in the presence of what is perceptually absent but which faith teaches is uniquely "present," even if beyond all concepts and categories. This is not a matter of thinking of this which is nothing or "pure being" but rather believing in what is transcendent to all concepts and properties, even those of subject and object, as a friend spontaneously does when in the presence of a dear friend, whom we make lovingly present through his or her personal propertied present but still as beyond all properties. But this trans-categorial presence is believed in and the darkness is thick, and thus the mind of the believer is often enough deluged with its habitual preoccupations which in fact are its "false self" separating it from its true self which comes forth only in the darkness of faith. The technique of the meditation is to gently let go of these and return to one's center or true self which comes forth in its opening itself to this transcendent and immanent mystery.

The metaphysics of the true self will be the focus of the next chapter, whose central theme is "exemplarism," where we will see that the dogma of The Theological Distinction is clearly in play. This dogma is especially of importance in grasping the claim that what must be opened up is I myself from an inside that for me is still the other side. In this ultimate theological sense of "I myself," I cannot do the opening alone by myself. This most archonal dimension of myself, i.e., as I am a word spoken by the creator, can only be opened up from within my deepest self. But, as faith teaches, I cannot do this on my own. But because God is "more interior to me than I am to myself" an opening from the other, divine, side can happen, an opening which does not violate but rather actuates my true archonal self. Apart from this opening to my creative "archon" I am locked into myself and, indeed, therefore closed to myself. But this self-enclosure is not yet my true Existenz but rather a deprivation of it that is a form of self-deprivation. As Kierkegaard would put it, I do not exist properly in the truth but only in untruth. I am opened to myself, to my truth and true subjectivity, if and only if I am unlocked "from the other, most interior, side." (This too finds its parallel in Sufism.)

Plotinus would be disappointed with this position in so far as it is founded in faith. And, in its dependence on grace, it would deprive the person of the capacity to redeem herself. For Plotinus, it would appear to rob her of being the agent of her return home, what he calls, like the medieval Christian theologians, the fatherland, *patria*. Yet for Plotinus one is always present with the divine *nous*, and the spiritual life is the task of removing this otherness that we insert, by force of our stupidity and distraction, so that the Center of all centers, i.e., the One, and the center that is one's ownself come into an ineffable contact.

Finally there is the issue of Plotinus' own mystical experience of the One. Porphyry reported that it occurred four times. If we take this into account we face the question of how this seemingly "gracious" and ephemeral experience is to be integrated into his clear directions of discipline as the seemingly necessary and sufficient condition for preparation for return to one's true self and union with the One. Perhaps we must distinguish the discipline of the return and the anomalous mystical visitation. If it is true that for Plotinus mysticism is much less the sheer "ability of man to raise himself in a somewhat mechanical fashion" in order that he might return home Yonder, than a matter of "the unaccountable 'presence' of the One,"[158] then the question is raised whether this gracious presence is a necessary condition for the journey Yonder, a condition for the aspiration to discipline oneself to return home Yonder. Perhaps the gracious haunting presence of the beauty of the One/Good and one's own sense of one's inadequation to one's true self were the sufficient conditions for the desire to undertake the journey home and the Ought rides more or less comfortably on the Is.

Notes

1. The theology of religions is one of the most controversial of matters precisely because it is dependent on basic positions regarding theology, philosophy, hermeneutics, the historicity of religious matters – as well as the philosophy and theology of history. This complexity recently emerged for me when Professor Peter Phan of Georgetown University (UCTV lecture, UC Santa Barbara, Feb. 2007, "Is Christianity a Western Religion?") questioned the claim of Pope Benedict XVI that Christianity's becoming Hellenized and Europeanized were decisive for the essence of Christianity. Phan pointed out that the earliest forms, centers, and thinkers of Christianity were Palestinian, Syrian, Iraqian, and African, and that the view that

everything centered in and around Rome was pure propaganda. His basic claim is that no culture and no categorical scheme is to be given a privileged status in the explication of the Christian revelation. (The fact that only one fifth of all Christians will be Caucasian or white in 2050 was part of the motivation for Phan's talk. Requiring, e.g., that Africans, Chinese, and Indiana Hoosiers be "Hellenized" in order to be Christian seems prima facie absurd.) The very "Greek" (Plotinian-Dionysian-Thomist) framework in these two concluding chapters of this work does not pretend to decide the question of the theological status of Greek thought in Christian theology. We use it because it appears to give the best theological-categorial elucidation and conclusion to the philosophical conclusions we have reached in the prior two volumes. Presumably the truth of the categories, regardless of their historical-cultural context, plays the decisive role in their adaptation by theologians and the churches. It is not merely the matter, as important as this is, of the universality or catholicity of the revelation and the ubiquitous presence of the Holy Spirit in preparing for this message, but of no less importance also is the appreciation of "dogma" and the hard philosophical-theological work of its appropriate explication. This latter is quite a different matter than appealing to authority and repeating formulae. In what ensues we, following upon the work of Robert Sokolowski, have made the illiberal claim that "The Theological Distinction" between God and the world is the dogma of all dogmas, and in this sense the core doctrine of revelation. It is hoped, in opposition to fears such a seemingly illiberal claim makes, that the presentation is such that the deep compassionate basis of "ecumenical," "liberal," and "catholic" concerns is strengthened. Of course, if one holds that the fundamental truth is that all philosophical-theological distinctions and claims are to be relativized by, e.g., a cultural-historical contextualization, which itself is rooted in caprice or a will to power, then the entire project must appear to be futile.

2. Paul Oskar Kristeller, *Der Begriff der Seele in der Ethik des Plotin* (Tübingen: J.C.B. Mohr/ Paul Siebeck, 1929), 5–6, 11.

3. I have usually followed the translation of A.H. Armstrong in the Loeb series, *Plotinus* (Cambridge, MA: Harvard University Press, 1966).

4. J.M. Rist, *Plotinus: The Road to Reality* (Cambridge: Cambridge University Press, 1967/1980), 41.

5. In a UC Santa Barbara (UCTV, 2007, UC Santa Barbara) lecture on "The Conversion of Abraham," Jon D. Levenson of Harvard made me aware of how problematic the term "Abrahamic religions" is. Historical-textual research leaves us with only a hint as to what the religion of Abraham really was. "Abrahamic religion" properly is the referent of the three religions which derive from this pre-Mosaic personage, each of which intend the referent through three typically different senses: Abraham was true to the Torah, to the doctrine of faith not works, to absolute submission to the divine. Yet on occasion these senses also commingle or cut across the traditions. Whether The Theological Distinction is able to find genuine historical moorings in "Abrahamic religions" is a good question beyond the scope of this work and my competence. It is doubtless true that the doctrine of "creation from nothing" was not unambiguously present or explicit in early Judaism. Similarly, the creator God of The Theological Distinction is at best implicit in the Christian scriptures. For St. Paul, Abraham is interpreted as being exemplary for both Jews and Christians – and for all of whom he eventually came to be regarded as "Father" – for his faith, not his works. He is Father of both the circumcised and uncircumcised, whoever they may be, providing they have faith. Faith in What? In Whom? We know that in Israel and Christianity the answer to these questions evolved, as did the act of faith. For Paul, what is common in this evolution is faith in God when there is little basis for hope, faith in God "who makes the dead live and summons things that are not yet in existence as if they already were" See *Romans* 4:17. For Paul, the God of ineffable mystery and incomparable generosity, the major term of what we are calling The Theological Distinction, is intrinsic to the "Abrahamic religions." In the body of the text we have put expressions such as "Abrahamic religions" in scare-quotes and mean thereby to postulate the hypothesis that The Theological Distinction is a core of the three religions, assuming we understand "core" as something typically only implicitly affirmed and hinted at, and a doctrine that slowly evolved. All the while I recognize that, after all, it is not even

a dogma which finds universal resonance among orthodox or mainstream Christians. The least that can be said, it would seem, is that for interfaith dialogues, especially among "the Abrahamic religions," The Theological Distinction offers a framework for theological clarity. In this work, the author, a Roman Catholic, gives The Theological Distinction a privileged status which doubtless seems gratuitous to others; but the minimal hope is that it provides the grounds for clarification of differences, even if it be the case for some readers that it does not provide a common ground. Cf. n. 1 above. In any case, the motivation here is the conviction that it provides a unique "logic" in which to view some of the major theological questions connected with the main philosophical positions of this work.

6. See Lloyd P. Gerson, *Plotinus* (London/New York: Routledge, 1994), 72–78; and A.H. Armstrong, "Form, Individual and Person in Plotinus," in his *Plotinian and Christian Studies* (London: Variorum, 1979), Chapter XX.

7. Richard Sorabji, *Self: Ancient and Modern Insights about Individuality, Life, and Death* (Chicago, IL: University of Chicago Press, 2006), 122 ff. and 302 ff., holds that the view offered here (which is close to what he calls a "consensus" view such as that of A.H. Armstrong and Lloyd Gerson), the view that Plotinus held there to be a form of (the soul of) Socrates, does not permit us to distinguish individuals in the intelligible world because Plotinus believed in reincarnation. In the key passage of V.7.1, he takes Plotinus to say that Socrates may be the reincarnation of Pythagoras. Our interpretation emphasizes the form of Socrates, not the form of the soul of Socrates. Sorabji is surely correct in placing the weight of the discussion on the form of the soul of Socrates. What I take to be a *reductio ad absurdum* argument by Plotinus (at V.7.1), i.e., because it is evident that the impressive essence, Socrates, cannot become (the impressive essence of) Pythagoras, we may posit there "yonder" the form of *Socrateitas*, is followed in Plotinus text with a discussion of the hypothesis, "if the soul of each individual possesses the rational forming principles of all the individuals which it animates in succession...," then we can speculate that this could very well mean that the form of the soul of Socrates could contain the capacity to animate subsequent individuals. In which case, (the soul of) Socrates could become someone else, e.g., Pythagoras or Aristotle. But he seems to be repelled by this theory which suggests that "one man" would serve "as model...for all men, just as souls limited in number produce an infinity of men." Then Plotinus adds what I take to be his position, i.e., my position, that the form of the soul of Socrates or the form of Socrates is a unique essence. "No, there cannot be the same forming principle for different individuals, and one man will not serve as a model for several men differing from each other not only by reason of their matter but with a vast number of special differences of form." Then he goes on to state, "Men are not related to their form as portraits of Socrates are to their original, but their different structures must result from different forming principles." See the entire passage at V.7.(18), 1–25. Admittedly the texts do not support my view unequivocally, but my sense is that Plotinus is struck by the phenomenon of the "unique essence" of Socrates, and wishes to anchor that peculiar intelligibility "yonder" in the world of forms in *Nous*. In these texts I think it is important to recall that Plotinus on occasion elucidated what we meant by the soul, or perhaps even the form of the soul, with first-person reference. Sorabji (304) perhaps tips his hand here when he states his belief that the *Bhagavadgita* is further along than the tradition of Locke because it makes reincarnation possible by appealing to what "is more central to a person than the ordinary intentions and memories" (which may not only be forgotten but duplicated), i.e., "aspirations, talents, habits, and virtues." Yet surely these too are repeatable properties that are passed down in the reincarnations; as such they do not get at the non-sortal incommunicable foundation of the person, even though they doubtless become configured in ways which, as expressions of the personified "myself," approach a corresponding uniqueness.

8. W.I. Inge, *The Philosophy of Plotinus*. Vol. I (London: Longmans Green, 1923), 246.

9. Inge, *ibid.*, 238.

10. A.H. Armstrong, "Plotinus," in *The Cambridge History of Later Greek and Early Medieval Philosophy* (Cambridge: Cambridge University Press, 1967), 227.

11. Gerson, 209 and 205.

12. Gerson, 209.

13. Jean Trouillard, *La Purfication Plotinienne* (Paris: PUF, 1955), 18.
14. See the introduction by the editor, A.C. Spearing, to Julian of Norwich, *Revelations of Divine Love*. Trans. Elizabeth Spearing (London: Penguin, 1998), xvi ff. I am indebted to Mary Jo Weaver for this reference to Julian of Norwich.
15. Thomas Merton, *The New Man* (New York: Farrar, Straus and Giroux, 1961), 53.
16. *The Jerome Biblical Commentary*. Eds. Raymond E. Brown, Joseph A. Fitzmeyer and Roland E. Murphy (Englewood Cliffs, NJ: Prentice-Hall, 1968), 50.
17. Martin Buber, *Moses* (New York: Harper Torchbooks, 1958), especially 48–55.
18. Joseph Fitzmyer, *Romans: A New Translation with Introduction and Commentary*, Anchor Bible. Vol. 33 (New York: Doubleday, 1992), 522.
19. See the texts assembled by Henri de Lubac and his discussion in his *Catholicism: Church and Society*. Trans. Lancelot C. Sheppard (New York: Omega-Mentor, 1964), 17–27.
20. De Lubac, *ibid.*, 38. He also cites here the definition of Isidore of Seville: "*Ecclesia vocatur proprie, propter quod omnes ad se vocat, et in unum congreget.*"
21. De Lubac, ibid., 40–41.
22. For a discussion of the Husserlian notion of a "person of a higher order," see my *The Person and the Common Life*.
23. See Thomas Prufer, "A Reading of *Confessions*, Book X," *Recapitulations*, 27–31.
24. Sokolowski, *Christian Faith and Human Understanding* (Washington, DC: The Catholic University of America Press, 2006), 42.
25. Fitzmyer, *Romans*, 525; see 521 ff.
26. Cited in M. Basil Pennington, OCSO, *Centering Prayer* (Garden City, NY: Image, 1982), 101–102.
27. *Catechism of the Catholic Church* (Liguori, MO: Liguori Publications, 1994), par. 366.
28. See, for example, St. Thomas, *Summa Theologiae* 1, Questions 23–24.
29. See Raymond E. Brown, *The Gospel According to John, I-XII* (Garden City, NY: Doubleday, 1966), Appendix IV, "Ego Eimi – I am," 533 ff., on the "absolute use" of "I am."
30. See the volume, *The Heart of George MacDonald*. Ed. Rolland Hein (Vancouver, British Columbia: Regent College, 1994), 413–414. Also George MacDonald, *Proving the Unseen* (New York: Ballantine, 1989), 62.
31. *Summa Theologiae* I, q. 15; see also Robert Sokolowski, *The God of Faith and Reason* (Washington, DC: The Catholic University of America Press, 1995), 44–45. St. Thomas discusses this matter also in his commentary on Denys the Areopagite, *On the Divine Names*, especially towards the end of Chapter V.
32. Gustav Siewerth, *Thomismus als Identitätssystem* (Frankfurt am Main: G. Schulte-Bulmke, 1961), 202.
33. *De Veritate* q. VIII, a. VI, ad 1.
34. *Commentaria in Evangelium S. Joannis, cap. 1, lect. 7*; cited in Josef Pieper, *The Silence of St. Thomas* (Chicago, IL: Henry Regnery), 51. I am indebted to Pieper for this discussion of St. Thomas.
35. *Commentaria in Epistolam S. Pauli Apostoli ad Colossenses*, cap. 2. lect. 1; cited in Pieper 62.
36. *Summa Contra Gentes*, II, 3.
37. Pieper, 65.
38. Edith Stein has an original phenomenological critique of the Thomistic position i.e., the view that places all individuality of persons in matter as a principle of individuation. See especially *Endliches und Ewiges Sein* (Louvain: Nauwelaerts, 1950) and *Potenz und Akt* (Freiburg: Herder, 1999). Cf. my "Contingency of Temporality and Eternal Being: A Study of Aspects of Edith Stein's Phenomenological Theology As It Appears Primarily in *Endliches und Ewiges Sein*," in *The Philosophy of Edith Stein* (Pittsburgh, PA: Simon Silverman Phenomenology Center/Duquesne University, 2001), 34–68. For a Thomist response see n. 40 below and our discussion in the body of the text.
39. *De Veritate*, Q. III, art. IV, esp. ad 2.
40. See Joseph Owens, chapter on "Thomas Aquinas," in *Individuation in Scholasticism: The Later Middle Ages and the Counter-Reformation, 1150–1650*. Ed. Jorge J.E. Gracia (Albany, NY: SUNY, 1994), 173–194. See N.-J.-J. Balthasar, *Mon moi dans L'Être* (Louvain: Institut

Supérieure de Philosophie, 1946), 172–193; and Louis de Raeymaker, *The Philosophy of Being* (St. Louis: Herder, 1961), 240–250l cf. also Jacques Maritain, *Existence and the Existent*, Chapter III, where he relates our concern in Book 1 with Existenz and ipseity to Aquinas' theory of *esse* as "suppositum" and what has an essence.

41. See Robert Sokolowski, *The God of Faith and Reason* (Washington, DC: The Catholic University of America Press, 1995), Chapter 5.

42. Through Eckhart, themes and comparisons, the pursuit of which would take us too far afield, in Hinduism and Buddhism are opened up. Cf. our discussion of Sufism below. We have good reason to believe that Eckhart was under the influence of Proclus, a disciple of Plotinus, as well as the Jewish Neo-Platonist, Avencebrol. As a Dominican, the writings of St. Thomas would of course also have been familiar to him.

43. Karl Kertz, cited in *Meister Eckhart: Essential Sermons, Commentaries, Treatises, and Defense*. Trans. and Eds. Edmund College and Bernard McGinn (Mahwah, NJ: Paulist Press, 1981), 52.

44. See College and McGinn, *op. cit.* 33; also Bernard J. Muller-Thym, *The Establishment of the University of Being in the Doctrine of Meister Echart of Hochheim* (New York: Sheed & Ward, 1939), 84–86.

45. See Bernard Dietsche, "Der Seelengrund nach den deutschen und lateinischen Predigten," in *Meister Eckhart der Prediger*. Eds. Udo M. Nix and Raphael Oechslin (Freiburg: Herder, 1960) 200–258.

46. College and McGinn, *op. cit.*, 187.

47. College and McGinn, *op. cit.*, 187 and 200–203.

48. The text in question is the "The 'Sister Catherine' Treatise," which, although falsely ascribed to Eckhart, probably reflects his influence. See *Meister Eckhart: Teacher and Preacher* (New York: Paulist Press, 1986), 361.

49. Cited as taken from Sermon (*Pr.*) 67, in the French edition of J. Ancelet-Hustache, *Sermons 60–86* (Paris: Éditions du Seuil, 1979), 50–51 and to be found in DW II, pp. 134, in Alain de Libera, *Introduction á la mystique rhenane: d' Albert le Grand à Maître Eckhart* (Paris: O.E.I.L., 1984), 257.

50. This text is taken from Sermon 83 in the Pfeiffer edition. Cited in *Meister Eckhart: Sermons and Treatises*. Vol. II. Trans. and Ed. M. O'C Walshe (Longmead/Shaftsbury/Dorset: Element Books, 1987), Sermon 66, 142.

51. Meister Eckhart, see Walshe, 333–334.

52. See *John Ruusbroec*. Trans. James Wiseman (New York: Paulist Press, 1985); I have been helped by James Wiseman's introduction.

53. Ibid., 110.

54. Ibid., 149.

55. Idem.

56. Ibid., 150.

57. See the Translator's Introduction, 26 ff.

58. Cf. the claims of the late thirteenth century Beguine, Marguerite Porete, in *Marguerite Porete: The Mirror of Simple Souls*. Trans. Ellen L. Babinsky (New York: Paulist Press, 1993), 116: "Well, since He will never love, that is, eternally, anything without me, I say therefore that it follows that he never loved anything without me. In addition, since He will be in me through love forever, therefore I have been loved by Him without beginning....if I am loved without end by the three Persons of the Trinity, I have also been loved by them without beginning. For as He will love me without end through his goodness, thus have I been the knowledge of His wisdom so that I must be created by the work of His divine power. Thus, as long as God is, who is without beginning, I have been in the divine knowing, that I might be without end, since He loved from that time...in his goodness the work which He would do in me by His divine power."

59. As noted earlier, in the Gospel of *John* 8:58 we have this famous declaration of Jesus of the *ego eimi* echoing Exodus III:14 where "God's name" is revealed. Jewish listeners to Jesus would have known that if the divine name were used by anyone else it would be a blasphemy

(*Leviticus* XXIV:16). His listeners were understandably scandalized and Jesus hides himself from their ire by slipping out of the temple precincts. Raymond E. Brown finds four more such "absolutist" uses of *eimi* in *John* 8:24, 8:28, and 12:19. It is implied at 6:20 and perhaps also at 18:5. See his commentary, *The Gospel According to John*. Vol. I–XII. translation, introduction, and commentary, 533 ff.

60. See *The Collected Works of St. John of the Cross*. Trans. Kieran Kavanaugh, O.C.C. and Otilio Rodriguez, O.C.D. (Washington, DC: Institute of Carmleite Studies, 1991), 583. Our discussions of John's philosophical psychology are drawn from the pages of *The Living Flame of Love* 644–645 and 709. The reference to the typical paradox is Number 15 of "Sayings of Light and Love," page 86. See also the commentary of Edith Stein, *Kreuzwissenschaft: Studien über Johannes a Cruce* (Louvain: Nauwelaerts, 1954), 135–161.

61. See Leibniz, *Philosophical Papers and Letters*. Ed. Leroy E. Loemker (Dordrecht: Brill, 1969), 489–490. This is from the essay "On the Radical Origination of Things" (1697). For Dostoevsky see the chapter, "The Rebellion" in the *Brothers Karamazov*. See also Edgar Brightman, *A Philosophy of Religion*, the chapter on good and evil.

62. See Loemker, 640–641, from "The Principles of Nature and Graced, Based on Reason" (1714).

63. Loemker, 28.

64. Loemker, 679.

65. Leibniz, *New Essays on Human Understanding* (La Salle, IL: Open Court, 1949), 245, 498–499.

66. Husserl's use of the term "monad," which intends to include the total concretion of the I as a person in the world, reflects this terminological stipulation of Leibniz.

67. Loemker, 323; from Section 31 of "Discourse on Metaphysics."

68. See Schelling, quoted in Manfred Frank, *Die Unhintergehbarkeit von Individualität* (Frankfurt am Main: Suhrkamp, 1986), 109. I wish to express my indebtedness to Manfred Frank's thematic and historical analyses, especially in this case in regard to Leibniz. See also his *Selbstgefühl* (Frankfurt am Main: Suhrkamp, 2002), especially, 104 ff. and 221 ff.

69. Loemker, 18.

70. Loemker, 268.

71. John Findlay, *The Transcendence of the Cave* (London: George Allen & Unwin, 1967), 146.

72. Perhaps the best pages for this are Loemker, 307–312, paragraphs 8–14 of "Discourse on Metaphysics."

73. Loemker, 268.

74. See Max Scheler, *Wesen und Formen der Sympathie* (Bonn: Friedrich Cohen, 1931/1913), 144–146; cf. also our discussion in Book 1, Chapter IV.

75. See the text "On the True *Theologia Mystica*" for the textual basis for this paragraph, in Loemker, 367–369.

76. Cf. the remarks of the monk, Thomas Keating, O.C.S.O., in *Intimacy with God: An Introduction to Centering Prayer* (New York: Crossroad, 2005), 28.

77. See my "Husserl and Fichte: With Special Regard to Husserl's lectures on 'Fichte's Ideal of Humanity'" *Husserl Studies* 12 (1995), 135–163.

78. J.G. Fichte, *Werke: Auswahl in sechs Bänden*. Ed. Fritz Medicus (Leipzig: Meiner, n.d.), IV, 295; text cited in Wihelm Weischedel, *Der Gott der Philosophen* (Munich: Deutscher Taschenbuch Verlag, 1979), 233.

79. This point was made by Dieter Henrich originally in his "Fichte's Original Insight." See the translation in *Contemporary German Philosophy*. Vol. 1. Ed. Darryl Christensen (1988), 15–53.

80. I was helped here by Adolf Lasson, *J.G. Fichte in Verhälnis zu Kirche und Staat* (Aalen: Scientia Verlag, 1968/Berlin: Cotta'chen Verlag, 1863), 86.

81. *Fichtes Werke V*, 510. Fichte's philosophical theology, although dispersed throughout his works, finds its primary expression in *Anweisungen zum seligen Leben, oder auch die Religionslehre* in *Fichtes Werke* V (Berlin: Walter de Gruyter, 1971); hereafter cited as *Fichtes Werke*. The Third Lecture is the most important for Fichte's phenomenological theology. This work of Fichte has been well translated by William Smith as *The Way Towards the Blessed Life, or The Doctrine of Religion* and most recently appears in *Significant Contributions to*

the *History of Psychology*. Ed. Daniel Robinson (Washington DC: University Publications of America, 1970), 290 ff. Note that William Smith interestingly translated in 1889 *Dasein* as ex-sistence, thereby also adumbrating Heideggerian themes.

82. Cf. *Fichtes Werke V*, 457–460.
83. *Fichtes Werke VII*, 131.
84. *Fichtes Werke VII*, 130.
85. See Fichte, *Wissenschaftslehre (1805)* (Hamburg: Meiner, 1984), 15–16.
86. Reinhard Lauth, *Die Transzendentale Naturlehre Fichtes nach den Principien der Wissinschaftslehre* (Hamburg: Meiner, 1984) presents the fuller picture of Fichte's philosophy of "nature." Cf. my remarks at n. 42 of "Husserl and Fichte," 162.
87. This theme appears in numerous places; see, e.g., Fichte, *Die Wissenschaftslehre in ihrem allgemeinem Umriss (1810)* (Frankfurt am Main: Klostermann, 1976), §1, 26.
88. J.G. Fichte, *Die Wissenschaftslehre, Zweiter Vortrag in Jahre 1804* (Hamburg: Meiner, 1975), 152–153.
89. See Weischedel, *op. cit.*, 236 for text references.
90. *Werke*. IV, 111, Medicus ed.; cited in Weischedel, 237.
91. *Fichtes Werke V*, 455 See also, e.g., V, 518 for more claims that seem to reveal allegiance to the faith dogma of "The Theological Distinction" under the guise of philosophical description.
92. In *Anweisungen*, the Sixth Lecture, Fichte deals explicitly with dogma and his interpretation of the Gospel of John.
93. For the theory of the unique individual vocation, see Lecture Nine.
94. For "love," see Lecture Ten.
95. *Concluding Unscientific Postscript*. Vol. I. Trans. Hong and Hong (Princeton, NJ: Princeton University Press, 1992), 461.
96. *Papers and Jounals*. Ed. Alastair Hannay (London: Penguin, 1996), 234–235.
97. *Concluding Unscientific Postscript*. Vol. I, 234. I have been helped by Tony Aumann's dissertation on indirect communication in Kierkegaard in formulating my thoughts on these matters.
98. *Concluding Unscientific Postscript*. Vol. I, 205–210.
99. Cf. *Works of Love*, 159.
100. See Kierkegaard, *Fear and Trembling/Repetition* (Princeton, NJ: Princeton University Press, 1983), 75–81. See the lovely pages of Jacques Derrida on Kierkegaard in *The Gift of Death*. Trans. David Wills (Chicago, IL: University of Chicago Press, 1995), especially 53–69.
101. For the immediately preceding paragraphs I am indebted to Gregor Malantschuk, *Kierkegaard's Thought* (Princeton, NJ: Princeton University Press, 1971), 12, 88, and 98.
102. Kierkegaard, *Purity of Heart*, 193.
103. Kierkegaard, *Sickness unto Death*. Trans. Hong and Hong (Princeton, NJ: Princeton University Press, 1980), 79–80.
104. Kierkegaard, *Concluding Unscientific Postscript*. Vol. I, 66 and 200.
105. Kant, *Die Religion*, 221.
106. Kierkegaard, *Sickness Unto Death*, 14.
107. Kierkegaard, *Philosophical Fragments/Johannes Climacus*, 14; *Papers and Journals*, 32.
108. Gerard Manley Hopkins, "That Nature is a Heraclitean Fire and of the Comfort of the Resurrection," and "As Kingfishers Catch Fire, Dragon Flies Draw Flame," in *A Hopkins Reader*. Ed. John Pick (New York: Doubleday/Image, 1966), 81 and 67. Also in *Gerard Manley Hopkins: The Major Works*. Ed. Catherine Phillips (Oxford: Oxford University Press, 1986), 180.
109. *The Major Works*, 286.
110. *The Sermons and Devotional Writings of Gerard Manley Hopkins*. Ed. Christopher Devlin, S.J. (London: Oxford University Press, 1959), 146; cf. also *Major Works*, 283.
111. *The Major Works*, 166; *A Hopkins Reader*, 77; from the poem beginning, "I wake and feel the fell of dark, not day."
112. *Major Works*, 283–284.
113. *Major Works*, 286–287.

114. *Major Works*, 156.
115. Hans Urs Von Balthasar, *Theodramatik*. Vol. 2. Part 2 (Einsiedeln: Johanes Verlag, 1978), 186 ff.
116. Ibid., 189–190.
117. Robert Sokolowski, *Eucharistic Presence* (Washington, DC: The Catholic University of America Press, 1993), 148. I am indebted to Robert Sokolowski for introducing Von Balthasar's discussion to me.
118. Von Balthasar, 190–191.
119. M. Basil Pennington, *True Self/False Self* (New York: Crossroad, 2000), 46.
120. See Robert Sokolowski, *Christian Faith and Human Understanding*, 44 and Thomas Prufer, *Recapitulations*, 32–33.
121. Titus Burckhardt, *Introduction to Sufi Doctrine*. Trans. D.M. Matheson (Jakarta, Indonesia: Dar al-ilm, n.d.), 21.
122. R.C. Zaehner, *Hindu and Muslim Mysticism* (Oxford: One World, 1994), 139 and 144; Zaehner acknowledges his dependence on L. Massignon, *Al Hallaj, Martyr, mystique de l'Islam*.
123. Zaehner, 147; see also the Appendix, 219.
124. Zaehner, 148.
125. Zaehner, 153.
126. Burkhardt, 53.
127. Burkhardt, 92.
128. Cited in Khosola, *The Sufism of Rumi* (Longmead, England: Element Books, 1987), 101.
129. *Rumi: In the Arms of the Beloved*. Trans. Jonathan Star (New York: Jeremy P. Tarcher/ Putnam, 2006), 4–6.
130. William C. Chittick, "The Circle of Spiritual Ascent According to Al-Qunawi," in *Neopolatonism and Islamic Thought*. Ed. Parviz Morewedge (New York: SUNY, 1992), 188 ff.
131. Zaehner, 210.
132. Zaehner, 113.
133. Idem.
134. Zaehner, 198; here at 198 ff. Zaehner provides the full text with commentaries.
135. Zaehner, 209–210.
136. Martin Buber, *Between Man and Man* (Boston, MA: Beacon, 1955), 24–25, cited in Zaehner, 18.
137. For "The Christian Distinction," see Robert Sokolowski, *The God of Faith and Reason*; see also the important Chapter 5 in *Eucharistic Presence*; cf. also Thomas Prufer, *Recapitulatons* (Washington, DC: The Catholic University of America Press, 1993), Chapters 5–7, 27–42. For perhaps the best place to begin a discussion of The Theological Distinction in Plotinus, see Gerson, *Plotinus*, 17–41, 293 n. 50, 236 n. 43. I outline a comparison with Shankara in Chapter VII, §10.
138. A.H. Armstrong, *Plotinian and Christian Studies*, Chapter VI, "Salvation, Plotinian and Christian," 128–130.
139. See Armstrong's discussion in *Cambridge History of Later Greek and Early Medieval Philosophy* (Cambridge: Cambridge University Press, 1967), 242 ff.
140. Simone Weil, *Waiting for God* (New York: Harper Colophon, 1973), 145. We return to this theme in Chapter VII.
141. See Armstrong, Chapter VI, 132 in *Plotinian and Christian Studies*.
142. Gandhi is a "Christian" hero and saint for many Christians, e.g., members of the Catholic Worker Movement. And to the extent that there is appreciation of Gandhi as other than a heathen, he is an exemplary Quaker and Anabaptist. His exemplary status not only in the Catholic Workers but also in many Protestant Christian congregations is as high as any Christian saint, especially of living memory. This, of course, raises interesting issues in regard to "the theology of religions."
143. Hans Urs Von Balthsar, *Origen*. Trans. Rowan A. Greer (New York: Paulist Press, 1979), xiv.
144. Maurice Blondel, *Action (1893)* (Notre Dame, IN: University of Notre Dame Press, 1984), 342–343; 371 of the French original.

145. Thomas Merton, *New Seeds of Contemplation* (New York: New Directions, 1961), 7. My friend, Mary Jo Weaver, has shared with me Dorothy Sayers adaptation of Boethius: "Hell is the full and perfect possession of one's own will forever."

146. Cf. *Simone Weil: An Anthology*, 79–81.

147. A good critique of the concept of Hell and the doctrine of eternal damnation is to be found in Raymond Smullyan, *Who Knows?* (Bloomington, IN: Indiana University Press, 2003), Part II, "Through Dark Clouds," 47–96.

148. Thomas Merton, *New Seeds of Contemplation*, 92.

149. See the discussion of matter in Plotinus in Lloyd P. Gerson, *Plotinus, op. cit.*, 108–114.

150. See Anselm Stolz, O.S.B., *Theologie der Mystik* (Regensburg: Friedrich Pustet, 1936). The great historian and philosopher of religions, Mircea Eliade, was fond of this book because it showed the prominence of the theme of the eternal return, i.e., the return to paradise, in Christian spirituality and mysticism.

151. Thomas Merton, *Contemplative Prayer* (New York: Doubleday/Image, 1996), 68.

152. M. Basil Pennington, OCSO, *Centering Prayer* (Garden City, NY: Image/Doubleday, 1980), 92, 96–97.

153. Thomas Merton, *New Seeds of Contemplation*, 7.

154. Thomas Merton, *The Inner Experience* (New York: HarperCollins/HarperSanFrancisco, 2004), 12.

155. Thomas Merton, *Contemplative Prayer*, 83.

156. Thomas Keating, *The Foundations of Centering Prayer and the Christian Contemplative Life* (New York: Continuum, 2002), 108–109.

157. Keating, 114.

158. J.M. Rist, *Plotinus: The Road to Reality* (Cambridge: Cambridge University Press, 1967), 192.

Chapter VII
Philosophical Theology of Vocation

Part Two: Systematic-Theological Synthesis

> *For me to be a saint means to be myself. Therefore the problem of sanctity and salvation is in fact the problem of finding out who I am and of discovering my true self.... To put it better, we are even called to share with God the work of **creating** the truth of our identity.... We do not know clearly beforehand what the result of this work will be. The secret of my full identity is hidden in Him.... Every one of us is shadowed by an illusory person: a false self. This is the man that I want myself to be but who cannot exist, because God does not know anything about him. And to be unknown of God is altogether too much privacy.*
>
> (Thomas Merton[1])

> *... but for everyone without exception, there is nevertheless the possibility of this Super-sensuous Being remaining concealed, should he fail to renounce his Sensuous Being and its objective independence. Every one without exception, I say, receives that portion in the Super-sensuous Being which is exclusively his own, and which belongs in the same manner to no other Individual whatever but himself; which portion now develops itself in him in all Eternity, – manifesting itself as a continuous course of action, – in such a form as it can assume in absolutely no other Individual; – and this, in short, may be called the individual character of his Higher Vocation.*
>
> (J.G. Fichte[2])

§1. Analogy, Exemplarism, and the Dogma of God the Creator

We will now begin our systematic-theological discussion with an analysis of "exemplarism." This notion, which we have already seen in the historical setting, Part One, starting with Plotinus, but also in other subsequent theological thinkers, is a key notion for grasping the metaphysics of the unity of the heavenly and earthly self. It also is a notion behind much of mysticism and is a central implication of the dogma of God the Creator. This huge topic will have for its central concern to shed light on the nature of the true self and its vocation. Nevertheless, we must at least mention the background of these matters in terms of the themes of creation and salvation. Although we briefly discussed aspects of St. Thomas Aquinas' thought on these matters in Part One (Chapter VI), in what follows in Part Two, in our systematic presentation, he will again be our primary guide.

First there must be a brief discussion of *analogy* within the sphere of mystery. Analogy has to do with a relationship of likeness or sameness between two or more objects or states of affairs that we experience. In Husserl's phenomenology it is the ineluctable achievement of what he calls "apperception." Apperception is the excess of intention that enables us to see *this* ("core") which is immediately and intuitively given, e.g., the silhouetted and countenanced figure, as a person standing next me in the store also doing Christmas shopping in Marshall Fields; or the flashing light ahead of me as a squad car at an accident site in Chicago. Here an immediate sense datum is richly filled in with a rich categoriality that extends to one's world as the apperceived horizon of horizons. (We prescind here from whether this view requires a theory of a pure hyle or stuff bereft of all categoriality. For our purposes, it is evident that we see things *as*..., and this seeing-as need not be actually universal, i.e., a valid conceptual framing of something as the same for us all, but typically it presumes to be so. Further it is only relatively stable because experience requires its constant modification.

Experience's development is the development of apperception, i.e., the constant flux of core objects become surrounded by the excess of intentionality called forth by the cores. Apperception is this excess of intentionality, which itself is incessantly being synthesized, called forth by the core objects of perception. Of course, the apperceptions are fallible, e.g., the "person" standing next to me may turn out to be a mannequin; the flashing light may turn out to be an ambulance and not a squad car; or it may turn out to be a reflection from a puddle of a nightclub's flashing neon sign. Apperceptions lead us to anticipate possible filled intentions, but they may disappoint.

What makes analogy so fundamental for the phenomenology of perception is that in all apperceptions and in the genesis of apperceptions there is a coincidence of similars with similars. What is given is always related to what is similar, whether it be in regard to objects, relations, contexts, etc.[3] All perception is analogical in a rudimentary way.

It is a good question whether we get at the most basic ground of human analogizing when we focus merely on conceptual or perceptual similarities that happen to exist in the world. We might ask about the transcendental conditions for this drive to make what we experience to be similar or this impulse toward "similarizing" or "assimilation." Is there in play here, after all, a quasi-metaphysical or theological theme, namely the teleology of spirit? May we think of spirit as a dynamism propelled toward the unification of all the plurality of beings in its unifying center and source? The transcendental agency of passive synthesis clearly is one of harmonizing and unifying within a teleology. Such a transcendental phenomenological perspective supports, but is not the equivalent of, Blondel's view that analogies are founded not only on conceptual or perceptual similarities but also on an interior dynamism or impulse which amounts to a an *intentio ad assimilationem*.[4]

Our recognition of Others in empathic perception is one of the most elemental achievements of apperceptive analogizing. In the wake of Levinas' persuasive analyses, phenomenologists have been cautioned about the imperialist and hegemonic temptations here. Analogy has to do with what is different as much as what is similar. But meaningful perception and thought can do nothing with what is *ganz anders*. (That "God" as the core-meant of faith presents us with what is *ganz anders* and therefore nothing for perception and for proper senses of philosophical or scientific thought will preoccupy us throughout this chapter. But we already acknowledged this in our discussion of ipseity as beyond properties.) Thus, e.g., persons have similar properties but as other ipseities are, in spite of their having or not having similar properties, still radically unique and transcendent. Thus when we try to understand another's strange behavior, we appeal to examples in our lives and those others we know well. We can hardly be said to know another person as such or her behavior if we dispense absolutely with analogies. "It is like when..." as a preface to an analogical comparison is the way we get clear on one another, and even how we get clear about ourselves. But what we get clear on is not merely the analogical properties but on who has these.

In the last centuries we have been counseled by the Enlightenment to "disenchant" nature by avoiding the pull to the analogizing of empathic perception in our understanding of nature. Thus, e.g., we might, in naïve moments, be inclined to see the attraction and repulsion of iron filings around a magnet as if the magnet were a sentient subject attracting or repelling the little pieces. Or we, similarly, are tempted to see the unfolding of cells in the development of a seed after the fashion of the way we arrange our lives with purposes.

Following Husserl we may distinguish how analogy functions in a most elementary way in passive synthesis, as when in the repeated occurrence of something similar in similar circumstances we are led to the habitual disposition to regard such a matter in its ever novel appearances as similar and as having similar contexts and settings. When we implicitly compare we have an implicit passive synthetic achievement and not an explicit comparing of objects or states of affairs in terms of an analogy. In this latter case of explicit comparison we have an interpretive apprehension of the matter at hand as an analogy. And we may distinguish this case from the further more explicit and conceptually clean one where we set about to understand something by way of using likenesses and propose that one think about the matter at hand after an analogy by using explicit symbols like pictures and examples.

In the explicit comparison the proper sense of analogy begins to emerge, as when we have two different objects or states of affairs but we see that they both have the same property. Thus we may have a clothes line, air, copper, and water as all capable of being the medium for the propagation of something, e.g., motion, heat, or electricity, through their each being a medium of "waves." In each case we have a substrate through which something moves by way of the pulsation or wave motion. And the use of the clothes line "wave" has the capacity to shed light on the indeterminate apperceived horizons. For example, one may wonder how the lake can now still have such huge waves coming from the south even though there has been no south wind for hours. Then one might appeal to the time lapse between the snap of a clothes line and the time it takes the wave to reach the other end. The initial force (wind) has ceased for some time, but the original impulse is still "traveling" through the medium of the water.

Clearly the analogizing can shed light, but also it obviously can be misleading. When the apperceptive excesses contain aspects or ingredients which contradict the sense of the experience and when they are such that they can never be brought to filled intuitive confirmations we have reason to have our doubts about the merits of the analogies. And because most analogies have terms or relations that can never be brought to such intuitive givenness they always fall short of the transcendental phenomenological ideal of knowing. But that does not mean to say that in forms of knowing apart from the strictly scientific region of transcendental phenomenology they are dispensable. Obviously the essentially inadequate knowledge of the world of empirical science is pervaded by apperceptions which can only be illumined by analogy. Indeed, the language of phenomenology itself is problematic and this is borne witness to by the consideration that it too makes us of analogies, like stream, ray, act, horizon, point, bracket, etc.

Merely following the tugging allure of the analogizing of passive synthesis and its associative tying of likeness to likeness is not authentic thinking. One exercises one's free agency of manifestation in the bringing to intuitive givenness, in so far as possible, what the likenesses are. The mere formal affixation on the symbolical, its syntax and quantification can similarly be a way of avoiding what is at stake, i.e., authentic philosophical thinking, because it can be merely the playing out of the mechanical-technological operations without any insight. What is crucial for all this is analogy's power to bring to light the dark empty horizon that is apperceived. The explicit analogies do their work when they do this. This dark hidden "something" which the apperception emptily intends may be contrasted with the empty intention of the merely routine parroting of a proposition or the empty intention in play in the merely formal working out the implications of a formalized proposition.[5]

The phenomenon of what we have called mystery is pervaded by apperceptions of determinable obscure horizons which resist being illuminated. The mystery of ipseity confronts us, as we have seen, with a phenomenon of exceeding apperception but it is one which, because the intended is bereft of properties and uniquely unique, discourages analogizing. Nevertheless, love poetry's lives off the wrestle with likenesses for depicting the unique beauty of the unique presence/absence of the beloved. Here the analogies prevail in the use of similes and metaphors because the unique beloved, for all she is like, is unlike all of these with which she is being compared. Similarly, religious teachings are plentiful in purporting to offer light on the mystery of ipseity. Thus, persons are "images of God," "children of God," "sparks of divinity," "members of the Body of Christ," "temples of the Holy Spirit," etc. Similarly the phenomenon of the mystery of one's death comes almost automatically with more or less poetic and religious analogies. Thus death is a Grim Reaper, a passing on, a coming like "an iceberg between the shoulder blades" (Mary Oliver), a falling asleep, a meeting of one's Maker, etc. We all know some revelatory gestures, performances, or events within the unwieldy wholes of "the world," "life," "this person," etc. which have the power to be ciphers of these wholes and point to the essentially elusive background, i.e., the mystery of these wholes. What perhaps is meant in part by *homo religious* is this natural desire to apprehend in a saturating intention this infinite dark horizon and mystery of the whole of the world or one's life. (Cf. our discussion of "mystery" in Chapter II.)

Robert Sokolowski makes the important point that the "mysteries" connected to the revelation of The Theological Distinction are not merely a matter of ciphers pointing to transcendence or mystery in the sense we just mentioned.[6] Rather, the dogmas that are connected to these revelations purport to convey "at least a glimpse of an understanding." Analogy in the light of the framework set up by The Theological Distinction is the way this understanding happens. Yet the "glimpse of understanding" provided by analogy is of necessity itself pervaded by mystery.

We will be mentioning "The Theological Distinction" throughout this chapter and will offer an explicit delineation of it below in §§6–8. This is a distinction between God and the world. We call it the most basic dogma or the dogma founding all dogmas. By dogma we mean what is believed by the Church, as the community of believers, to be a revealed teaching which may be expressed in propositions. If prior to this partially cognitive act of assenting faith there is the divine gracious initiative enabling someone to love God unconditionally (and this claim itself is part of The Theological Distinction), then the work of dogma is shedding light on this initial basic moment which of necessity is soaked in obscurity. The most basic dogma will be the most fundamental teaching which illuminates by way of a glimpse of intelligibility this event of grace, the implicit sense of God, and God's relation to the world. It will be this dogma which is presupposed by all other dogmas or teachings. It will presuppose no other dogma and all dogmas will require it for their proper sense.[7]

Analogy is always a straining of the ideal knowing that is realized through intuitive givenness. In religion and faith the matters are strained even further than they are in science and art. But even if we appreciate the elucidation that analogy is capable of providing we must remember that we have to do with the essential mystery, which in English we refer to with "God," which "by definition" is beyond all understanding, all conceptualization and all properties. In The Theological Distinction "God" is reached by way of transcending the natural setting for the criteria of meaning and intelligibility, i.e., the setting of the world. This transcending involves the problematic simultaneous negation and affirmation of "God" as what and who is beyond the world. "God the Creator," as tied to The Theological Distinction and the work of analogy, on the one hand, indeed sheds a glimpse of understanding, but, on the other hand, it exemplarily illustrates the phenomenological sense of mystery where we have a "glimpse" of what is densely meaningful, as in the cases of one's death and ipseity, where all properties and conceptual grasp elude us. The understanding is not such as to render intelligible the central referents of "God" or "creation" but rather is attached to how the intention of faith is directed both away from the mind's home base of intelligibility, i.e., the world, and yet directed at the world's deepest sense, its essence. That is, what we are directed to is beyond the world, and in this sense outside of ourselves, but, at the same time, we are directed to what is more interior to the world than is the world to itself. Similarly we, as ipseities and agents of manifestation, may say that we have to do with what is more interior to ourselves than we are to ourselves. In this sense we are not merely "centered" in faith but properly ex-centric in our being centered. But what we are directed to is not anything we can grasp and array within what we find meaningful, i.e., within the world as the horizon of horizons. The Theological Distinction never amounts to anything resembling a philosophical position or conceptual intelligibility based on the categories in play in our conceptualization of the world. Having said this, let us briefly recall the work of analogy in the traditional framework.

We can begin with the distinction between the analogy of proportionality and the analogy of attribution.[8] The *analogy of proportionality* is the identity or likeness not of concepts or properties but of two proportions or ratios: A is to B as C is to D: Fur is to mammals as feathers are to birds; God is to the world as a parent is to the children; God is to the world as the master builder/architect is to his work.

The *analogy of attribution* has not to do with proportions or ratios but with the way a multiplicity of terms or properties, like "healthy" as in exercise, medicine, complexion, and food, are able to share in this common property by reason of their being related to a focal sense of "health" or "healthy," namely the organism. Food, complexion, medicine, exercise are all causes or symptoms of the healthy organism and for this reason they also may be, by extension, called "healthy."

In what follows in this chapter we will indulge in many analogies of attribution and proportion. The chief analogy of proportionality or ratio is between the architect/master builder and his artifact and God and the world. The Theological Distinction both encourages and discourages the analogy. It encourages the analogy of proportionality because the revelation of the tradition empowers us to use the terms that denote a causal relation between God and the world, e.g., "father," "maker," or "creator," even though the procreating/making/creating in question is unlike anything we know. We further assume the analogies of human mind and divine mind, human agency and divine agency, human intentionality and divine intentionality. These again are terms believers in the tradition are empowered to use, with the caveat that the dissimilarities are greater than any speculated similarities. Thus the chief analogy of proportionality or ratio will employ analogies of attribution. Not only do we posit that God is to the world as the architect is to his work, but we posit that God is wise in a way resembling the wisdom of the good architect. The analogy of attribution requires that we find a focal term which founds, justifies or legitimates the other non-focal ones, and in this case it can only be the human analogate. We know or have unique familiarity with the human mind; the divine mind and agency is what we seek to illuminate.

Again, in the context of The Theological Distinction the analogy of attribution makes the claim that these terms are neither identical in meaning nor are they utterly equivocal, in as much as we have to do with not mere ciphers but with a revealed teaching. Yet in so far as the attributes are genuinely proper in the divine case they are eminently true. If they are eminently true the focal sense is the divine case which we do not know, not the human case which we know. The peripheral one then is in fact the human one which we do know and which purports to shed light "in a glass darkly" on the divine focal case. This seems to put us in an (analogous) position of accounting for the "healthiness" of food and medicine without knowing what the (human) organism is. But this is misleading. The divine exemplary case in itself (*quoad se*) is not manifestly exemplary for us (*quoad nos*). Only our case is manifestly exemplary in itself; but this means that it functions at best heuristically in the work of illuminating the divine analogue. But in the course of developing the analogy we come to see that even our methodologically exemplary case comes to be changed in its sense in so far as we gain a glimpse of the divine exemplary case in itself. Thus, e.g., the sense of the world begins as the ultimate horizon of meaning, and then, to accommodate itself to The Theological Distinction, this ultimacy is relativized.

Perhaps we may want to say that what is in itself the exemplar is for us a regulative ideal. God the Creator as articulated by The Theological Distinction does not have horizons of empty intentions which may be filled in. Thus what for us requires to be raised to an infinitely eminent degree, as in, e.g., the regulative ideal of "goodness" or "holiness," is not so for "God the Creator" who exemplarily embodies these perfections in total actuality. We experience through our emotive-valuating life in the world the value-predicates of, e.g., "living," "just" and "merciful." Because of the teachings of the tradition, foremost that embodied in the dogma of God the Creator as explicated by The Theological Distinction, we know that, although it would be unseemly not to apply these predicates to God, there is a sense in which we do and do not know what they mean in God's case. Aquinas and others thus taught us the way to "name" God properly was the "way of eminence" (*via eminentiae*). Believers are empowered and exhorted to apply such "appropriate" properties to God "dialectically," i.e., we say Yes to the attribution, then No, then Yes again. The first Yes affirms a connection between the goodness we experience and the goodness of God; the same word applies in both cases. But with the reflection on the evident limitation of the finite forms of goodness a No surfaces, whereby we deny this limitation on goodness to God. But having cancelled these limitations, this negation itself is negated or subsumed in so far as the mind gives release to the nisus of its love of the infinite goodness of God.

For example, the "mercifulness" we know is always a mercy that is finite, temporal, and in a certain respect; and "living" or "vitality" is always tied to the finite organic beings we know which are immersed in webs of necessary physical conditions; or it is tied to the persons we know, and when we celebrate them as "full of life" this too is most often only in a certain respect and in any case short-lived. Clearly we may *not* apply these terms univocally to God, and therefore we must cancel their first-order sense. God is not living or merciful in the way we know these, i.e., in the way these appear in the world. But then, mindful of the first-order sense which we affirm, i.e., how we use the term in the ordinary context of our life in the world, and the subsequent caveat, i.e., that God is not, e.g., merciful or living in the familiar senses we know, we, in a third moment, may and do say, Yes God is merciful, God lives, but in a way that infinitely surpasses the way these properties or activities appear in the world.

We are exhorted to such a "dialectic" both because of the revealed dogma of God the Creator (as specified in The Theological Distinction) and also because it is congenial to the infinite dynamism of the spirit which, in arranging and placing all of its intelligible objects within the world, apperceives the infinite horizon of value, meaning, and intelligibility of the world. Furthermore, and inseparable from the believed-in revelation, the believer, whose fundamental gift is the unconditioned love of God, is moved by this love and faith beyond the realm of the finite and unconditioned. As Scotus put it, in spite of infinity being precisely what is beyond our grasp in excess of any assignable measure, it is not repugnant to intellect but "it seems to be the most perfect thing we can know."[9] *Ceteris paribus* the same may be said for the will and heart which are "restless until they rest in Thee." Transcendental phenomenology has its own version of this when it says of the spirit that it aspires to infinite satisfaction in the form of filled intentions. (Cf. our discussion in Chapter IV, §2.) In this respect these divine attributes *quoad nos* are regulative ideas, even though the believer may well believe that they find a "saturated intention" in the perfection of the divine essence and not in the course of spirit's conscious experience; thus the exemplars in the divine essence are the target of the dynamism of the spirit's infinite intentionality of the *via eminentiae*.

But does this infinitizing of spirit do justice to the view that God is absolutely transcendent and beyond the categoriality of the world? In the dynamism of infinitizing, as in regulative ideas which have an unrealizable telos of a "saturated intention," we have an important ambiguity. We are always on a journey of moving beyond the more and better to the most and best. Is the maximum merely continuous with our version of what is good, better, and best or is it something else altogether? If God's wisdom is the supreme case of what we mean by wisdom, then there must be within what we mean by "wisdom" something of the same in our case and that of God's. If so, is not God and the excellence of God to be thought of as part of a continuum of the human spirit and thus to be thought of "anthropomorphically?" Is God thus not thought of as "the greatest being" (which we are capable of imagining and conceiving)? But, if so, does this not reduce God's infinite essence to the limits of our understanding and imagination?

And is there not good reason backed by traditional authority to think of God as beyond, and, indeed, standing in judgment on, the infinitizing powers of reason? And is not God as "the greatest being" conceivable itself a form of anthropomorphizing, i.e., reducing God to human proportions, however greatly enhanced?

Yet the view that God is nothing like what we know, and absolutely discontinuous in every respect with what we admire, poses the problem of how God could be worshipped, how we could in any sense be said to "know" that *God* is absolutely transcendent. There have been many solutions offered to this impasse between God as the greatest being and the God of negative theology, i.e., the view that we only know what God is not, or that human wisdom bears no resemblance to the wisdom of God. In such a "negative-theological" view, we might have recourse to something like religious language as ciphers of transcendence, and the language of revelation and tradition would be pointers to what is beyond human comprehension. All we know is that the theme of God calls forth an attitude of absolute devotion and self-abnegation; but this tells us nothing about what God is in Godself.

Barry Miller has proposed an excellent analogy for theological analogies.[10] His view does justice both to the infinitizing of spirit which propels it to posit God as a limit or telos of spirit and the negative theology which posits that this limit or telos is not of same order but is absolutely transcendent to this order. He makes the distinction between a "limit simpliciter" and a "limit concept." The "limit simpliciter" differs only in degree from that of which it is a limit. Thus the gods of much philosophy and myth are superlatives, greatest beings, and have admirable endowments in a maximal case. As The Theological Distinction would put it, they are the highest, most inner, and most excellent aspects or parts of the world. Similarly we may think of the "shortest line" or the "most-sided polygon" as limits. They may be posited as limits, even though in fact they may very well resemble regulative ideas in being asymptotic: They provide us with an infinite journey and endless tasks and although we may make endless progress along the way (especially if we look backwards to where we have been), and although at some point we may stop and say "pragmatically" that is "shortest" enough or "most-sided" enough, as we may think of the gods as the greatest beings, e.g., "maximally powerful and excellent," because we can't think of anything better, theoretically we can still go further in advancing towards that ideal of the maximum.

The *limit case*, unlike the *limit simpliciter*, does not differ merely in degree from that which it is a limit. Rather, it differs absolutely. How? Barry Miller helps us with some clear simple examples. Think of the theory that the speed of light is the limit of the speed of moving bodies. But if we move in the reverse direction and seek the lower limit of speed of a body we do not find a lowest limit in 0 km/second but rather a limit case. 0 km/second is not as such a "lower limit simpliciter." It is not a speed at all. Not going at any speed at all is not part of the endless series of going slower. The obvious difference between the upper limit simpliciter of 300,000 km/second and the lower limit is that the former is indeed a speed, but the lower limit of 0 km/second is not a speed at all.

Similarly, in regard to ever shortening lines we may go *ad infinitum* towards the "limit-simpliciter"; but yet this continuum points to, but perhaps does not aim consciously at, the "limit case" of a *point*. The point may be thought of as that toward which the members of a series of ever shorter lines heads. But the point is not a limit simpliciter because it differs in kind from the ever shorter lines. Similarly, if we think of an ordered series of every more sided polygons we find no upper limit; but we may think of the *circle* as that toward which the ordered series of polygons points, even though the circle is not a polygon.

As Barry Miller puts it, in the cases of the slowest speed, the shorter lines, and the maximum sided polygon each member is ordered according to variations in a defining characteristic. Each member will vary in terms of the degree of the defining characteristic, e.g., of shorter line, slower speed, more-sided polygon, etc. That defining characteristic according to which each member varies in degree we may call F-ness. Thus the members are ordered according to degrees of F-ness; each member has F-ness in some degree, and in this respect all are equally F. "In no case, however, can the limit case be a member of that series, for it is not an *F* at all."[11] In each of the different examples the limit case is "that in which a defining characteristic of the members has been varied to the point of extinction." The limit case "will no more be an instance of *F* than a rocking horse is a horse."[12]

In Book 1 (Chapter IV, §16) we already used Miller's distinction to illustrate the basic thesis of this work. There we proposed that we may think of the revelation through love of the Other to involve the endless ideal limit of the personal revelation through an ever-deepening revelation through his properties. This "limit-simpliciter" and all the ordered members of this series, i.e., the attractive qualities, take their bearing not merely from the infinite ideal, but rather these head toward what is beyond the ideal limit of the series of ever-more attractive properties, i.e., to what is not of the same order as the properties, no matter how advanced they are, but what gives the flow of disclosure of the properties, as an endless unfolding love-nurturing revelation, their direction. This, the ipseity or "the myself" of the person transcends the series in an incommensurable way and is not of the same order as the properties, i.e., it is no more a property than a rocking horse is a horse or an artificial flower a flower. And the ontological value (Von Hildebrand) or value-essence (Scheler) of the ipseity incommensurately surpasses any value properties the person may have.

But, as we earlier noted, the limitations of Miller's analogy is that in the "limit-case" of the other ipseity, especially as known through love, we are not dealing with a concept but the trans-conceptual ipseity, so in the case of the divine as the analogous "limit case," faith and love do not head toward a concept but what is a trans-conceptual mystery that is analogously an "ipseity" or "personal." Nevertheless when focused on the matter of the divine attributes we obviously are dealing with concepts that are "limit cases." Only if we think of God as kind or a property, which is prohibited in both the instances of ipseity and the Biblical notion of God, may we think of God as either a limit simpliciter or limit concept. Why God may not be thought of as a kind will be discussed later.

However, God's wisdom is to be thought of as a limit case, and although our infinitizations of "wisdom" are pointers to the limit case of God's wisdom, God's wisdom is not the maximum of our infinitization. Here we do justice to Scotus's notion of "infinity" as precisely what exceeds being commensurate with any of our measures. Our measures in the process of infinitization are always commensurate because they all share the defining characteristic. Not so the limit case of God's wisdom. But it does justice also to Scotus's view that the mind does indeed find in infinity not what is repugnant but what most delights the mind by being its most perfect object. Here infinity is not the "bad infinity" of the endless task of the regulative idea, but rather that of perfection beyond all measure.

The notion of the limit case is consonant with The Theological Distinction which places God as essentially transcendent to the world and whose being is to be considered excellent quite apart from the world. The excellence of the world, although perhaps requiring "God" (or a "god") as the limit simpliciter of the perfections that it has, does not *quoad nos* require for its intelligibility the God of The Theological Distinction, as, e.g., the world's limit concept of excellence. Nevertheless this excellence of the world is a pointer to the limit case of divine "excellence" which, as such, is not the consummating part of the continuum of the world's excellence in so far as it is not part of the F-ness that pervades the continuum. These are all claims that both presuppose The Theological Distinction and elucidate it.

We have recognized the way the excellence of the world we experience may be said to point to the divine through the dialectic of a *via eminentiae*. But this infinitization of the world's excellences was qualified with the distinction of the limit concept and limit simpliciter. The former shows in what way God is not simply encompassed by the infinitization of the world's excellences. Rather the divine excellence as the limit concept is incommensurate with them. This is where Miller's position and that of The Theological Distinction sides with the *via negativa*. Yet it provides the excellences with their *raison d'être*; there is a sense in which grasping the limit concept does provide closure to the sense of the excellences of the world. But this status of God as an analogous limit concept utterly transcendent status the world's excellences is not an evident immanent development of rational philosophical reflection on the world's excellences, even though doubtless there are ingenious efforts in this direction. At least for us in this final chapter that there is a limit concept to the world's excellences is not evident *quoad nos* but is the result of the revelation that The Theological Distinction articulates. This reconciliation of the *via eminentiae* and the *via negativa* will guide us in our thinking of God the Creator and the issue of the divine exemplarity of the unique individual essence.

§2. Analogy, Exemplarism, and the Divine Master Builder

We have said that in our context the analogy of attribution, e.g., the wisdom of God, is subordinate to the analogy of ratio: God is to the world as the wise architect/master builder is to her artifact. Yet this ratio or proportionality is exceedingly anomalous. The chief reason is that the essential sense of God is properly not to stand in relation to anything and grasping this basic thesis of The Theological Distinction is key to understanding the analogy with the architect as well as understanding the ratio between the world and the artifact as well as understanding why "naming" God requires the mind extending itself beyond the infinite unsaturated limit simpliciter. But this beyond, this limit case, is not known by this infinitizing intention. This is the most fundamental and problematic matter of what we are calling The Theological Distinction. And whereas philosophically we use analogy to illuminate the hidden apperceived horizons of the world, in The Theological Distinction we learn that the world need not be and in the absence of the world the richness of all apperceived horizons would not be diminished. And whereas normally philosophy uses analogies to illuminate its apperceived horizons and mysteries, The Theological Distinction provides a basic dogma, that of God the Creator, which transforms the sense of the world as it is illumined by intentionality and its apperceptions. The basic dogma provided by The Theological Distinction also provides a metaphysics which undermines any temptation to think of the divine master builder in any terms other than a loose analogy. This metaphysics, as we shall be often at pains to describe, states that God is not a being or kind of being at all, but sheer subsisting To Be, and thus when we propose thinking of the divine as an exemplar after the fashion of the master builder, we must remember the differences in the analogy are at least as important as the similarities. These difficult themes will be returned to often in the remainder of this chapter.

Let us now turn to exemplarism as a key concept in the analogy of proportion of God is to the world as the architect is to her artifact.

Exemplarism within what we are calling the dogma of God the Creator has a nice introductory formulation in this statement, ascribed to Ruusbroec, that clearly echoes Neo-Platonism, and especially Dionysius:

> Through the eternal birth all creatures [in the generation of the Eternal Word] have come forth in eternity before they were created in time. So God has seen and known them in Himself... in living ideas; and in an otherness from Himself, but not as something other in all ways, for all that is in God is God.[13]

The doctrine of the ideas or forms as the source of the patterns and essences of experience has its origins in Plato. But it is in Plotinus that we have a clear doctrine that a divine mind is the home of the forms. The Judaeo-Christian-Muslim move of placing the ideas or forms of the world (or creation) in God before creation, and claiming that this pre-existence of form in the divine serves as the model for creation, is the beginning of the theory of theological exemplarism.

Exemplarism has perhaps its first motivation in the recognition of the abiding patterns of things that exist by nature rather than by art, chance, defect, etc. This by no means is intended to suggest that the patterns that emerge out of contingent factors are of no importance. Further everything, even the contingent or merely factual that we experience, may be taken in a way so as to exhibit an ideal status, e.g., show "characteristics" in the broadest sense, even if it is no more than it belongs to a class of unexemplified events, or an "event" that does not fit into the known larger scheme. These "patterns" of not fitting may or may not fit into patterns of not fitting. In any case, their "patterns" become peripheral and "adventitious" to what we take to be "essential" in our inquiry. (Cf. Book 1, Chapter I.)

Patterns, especially those that prove to be of essences or essential are by necessity what hold our attention and prevail over the particulars of the flux of experience. They lay claim to an enduring invariant status beyond the non-enduring instantiations or anomalies. Much of theory, after Plato, seeks to establish the status of these patterns or forms. We saw that in Plotinus they became inseparable from the principle of the divine mind. Similarly, in medieval philosophy and theology at least some of the patterns or forms found a home in the divine mind. This was in part because of the consideration that excellences and necessities in things would of necessity reflect the excellence and necessity of God. The precise nature of this reflection was thought to depend on the degree of excellence and the nature of the necessity. This, of course, had motivation in the Biblical teaching of the human person being considered an "image [likeness, form, pattern] of God."

There was in play the other motivation that the world is pervaded by necessities that must be regarded as absolute if there is to be a world at all. Thus whereas the natural necessities, e.g., of the temperature of water freezing or boiling, are only contingently necessary, there are reasons to speculate that there are some necessities that would hold in any world whatsoever. Thus there are mathematical and logical necessities. Further, there are the more transcendental necessities (already adumbrated in Plato and Plotinus), like those of the interplay of identity and difference, sameness and otherness, rest and motion, whole and part, or the merontological and axiological necessities. The classical metaphysical question is: Are these so necessary that the divine will itself cannot but acknowledge or heed them in its agency? Or are they, indeed, not external to the divine will or mind but rather constitutive of the divine mind or essence as super-forms or the forms of forms?

But what of the "essences" or "kinds" which perhaps exist only in one world, and need not exist in others, or indeed will soon cease to exist in all worlds e.g., polar bears and monarch butterflies? Is there not reason to speculate that any real essence or unique kind, even though its instantiation is contingent and ephemeral, has a claim on a kind of eternity simply because of its unique and intrinsic dignity, intricacy, and beauty? And perhaps no less important, what of those uninstantiable unique essences or haecceities of persons who are the centers of a unique phenomenological world which itself is not able to be duplicated or substituted for precisely because of the uniqueness of the haecceity of the constituting I? May we not speculate that there is here a form so worthy of our esteem and veneration that we may believe that it too has an eternal a priori exemplarity in the divine mind? This, at any rate, is the postulate of this chapter, and we find its antecedent in Plotinian metaphysics and theology. Before we turn to divine exemplarity let us first briefly reflect on how we are acquainted with "exemplars" in a non-metaphysical and non-theological context.

We may distinguish between examples and exemplars. We use the word "example" in a variety of contexts. In all cases it is meant to shed light on some focal consideration, most often by way of a particular experience. Thus when hearing an explanation of an unfamiliar concept in abstract terms, like a "performative" or "illocutionary act," we may request an example. And someone may say "I command…" or "I promise…" Or, if we are learning a language like Latin, and we want to learn to conjugate a verb whose ending in the infinitive is *are*, we are introduced to a paradigm, e.g., *amare*, wherein not all conjugations of Latin -*are* verbs appear but one that stands for or represents the rest. Thus, e.g., the conjugation of *amare* may be used to stand for the conjugation of *negare*, *explicare*, *sonare*, etc. Here the paradigm is an example by way of showing one conjugation but in regard to its verb endings it reveals the endings of all of the countless other verbs which have an -*are* ending in the infinitive.

Or, if we are learning to solve problems in algebra, we are introduced to a procedure that, although proper to this particular equation, applies to endless other equations. Casuistry in law and ethics provides similar examples where a single instance can shed light on endless particular cases. Thus the "principle of double-effect" as applied to violence and war may be given an abstract formulation of its conditions, but the classic example illustrates the point of willing directly something good, but it shows that this willing can involve an indirect, unwanted consequence of bringing about something evil or unwanted: Someone suffering shipwreck is taking on water and decides to sustain buoyancy and keep the boat afloat by pitching the precious but heavy cargo. Here the example is made by supplying an analogous situation to warding off what is harmful or defending oneself, and this situation of warding off or defending is held to be analogous to war. One is not doing anything directly evil but rather directly one does something good, e.g., warding off the dangerous intake of water. But indirectly one does something harmful, e.g., gets rid of one's treasures. Analogously, one does not will to kill or harm the aggressor, but only to protect oneself and ward off what is harmful. But the necessary proportionate means required to secure the good of one's well-being might require killing the aggressor.

Worth noting is that the beginner using the paradigm or example intends the example or paradigm and not what it illuminates or exemplifies. She studies it, masters it, memorizes it, etc. In the course of mastering the subject matter the paradigm or example no longer becomes *that which* the student intends but it becomes a power and skill *through and by which* she negotiates the subject matter and perceives the field.

In all these cases the "example" or "exemplar" is not ontologically different from what is exemplified. It is also an instantiation of what it exemplifies and does not have distinctive ontological features – as is posited, e.g., by Platonists and theologians, of the form or eidos of "justice" in regard to instances of justice. Thus our interest in the exemplar is not primarily about patterns, examples, and paradigms in so far as these have the same ontological features as what they exemplify. Rather our interest is in what most patterns, examples, and paradigms are not, i.e., we are interested in essences as the ineluctable kinds and meaning frames of the world and all that we know and not as something (also) within the world.

We may distinguish the exemplification of essences from the exemplification of examples. As we say, examples are of the same nature as that which they exemplify. But for metaphysics essences are usually regarded as quite different from their exemplifications. Indeed, for metaphysics a core issue is working out what "exemplification" is. For most philosophers it is undeniable that there is "attribute agreement" in what we experience, i.e., we see many things being round, red, doglike, just, etc. ("Analogy" initially suggests a fuzzy kind of attribute agreement, i.e., one where the "sameness" or agreement of the attributes is imperfect and needing further reflection.) The question arises of whether this merely begins the conversation or whether we here have to do with such a basic phenomenon that no more basic account is called for. Yet for many this merely begins the conversation. They, following in the footsteps of Plato and Aristotle, puzzle how there could be this phenomenon of things being at the same time both many and one, different and the same. Since Aristotle many philosophers have found it difficult to posit a noetic heaven of subsisting Forms, and modern thought has found difficult the postulation of a universal *Nous* which is the essential correlate of forms. But given the phenomenon of attribute agreement one seems to be saying "a is F" where "F" is a universal property being exemplified by "a." But what is "exemplification?" Is exemplification a relationship between an entity and its properties? What kind of relationship, and how does it come about in some cases and not in others? There are numerous kinds of relationships evident in "exemplification," e.g., relations where the particulars "exemplify," "instantiate," or "exhibit" one by one the "form," e.g., of being just or cowardly or green. Or there are exemplifications of universals by several particulars in relationship to one another, as "being a mile apart." Here there is no need for us to follow the thicket of issues; besides, it has been done "exemplarily" elsewhere.[14]

As is well known, Husserlian phenomenology did not participate in precisely the metaphysical debates of exemplarism or exemplification in so far as these required postulating of either a noetic heaven that could be participated in by particulars or that required relating the ideal object-thing, called "essence," to the particular physical object-thing or to a universal mind that housed the essences from all eternity. But it was of the utmost importance for Husserl to bring out the ideality and normativity of the essential idea. That is, what phenomenological essence-analysis pursues is the invariant Whatness in its purity that serves as the governing meaning frame for the experience of the essence in the particular at hand. (Cf. Book 1, Chapter I.) In this sense, for Husserl, metaphysical debates on the *kind of relation* that holds between an essence and its exemplification and exemplarity were marginalized.

In any case "exemplification" is a theme that involves always an intention of something in the third-person. Even, "I am a human being" requires that I regard myself in the third person as a member of a species. That is, we experience something as having agreement with something else in regard to properties or essences. And we may be drawn to working out the machinery of how essences, which have properties proper to ideal objects, can relate to their exemplifications, which have the quite different properties typical of non-ideal objects or particular perceptual objects which exist in space and time. In any case, the intentionality is always in the third-person. With theological exemplarism, by contrast, we have a species of exemplification where the first-person is introduced because the philosopher's intention (in thinking about "exemplarity") is directed to an Other's (the divine or human "creative artist's") first-person intention of the world and Others in the world. We move away from metaphysical speculation on the complex machinery of the relation of the form to its exemplification to a strangely complex, yet profoundly "minded" or "personalized" universe. Behind the things of the universe, at least in terms of their essential forms, there is posited an analogous mind or person. Whereas in perception the person is never given simply in the way an aspect of a thing is given, but rather is analogously given, i.e., co-given, by way of an apperception, the sense of the divine person or mind itself is a matter of faith, and so is this "minded" or personal sense of the universe.

In the theological case as developed by The Theological Distinction, this minded or personalized universe not only permits but celebrates the random, chance, shaping of, and deviation from natural kinds; it permits nature to be thoroughly natural, i.e., self-sufficient, in its intrinsic causality and anomalies; it discourages any immediation of secondary causality by a divine primary causality and thus a bleaching out of the vagaries of nature along with her intrinsic dense necessity and causality. Nevertheless, all the undeniable self-sufficiency, necessity, and contingencies, while affirmed with all the evidence that science and philosophy muster and require, are subordinated to a believed-in and inscrutable necessity and self-sufficiency which both affirms and grounds the nature and necessity of our experience. (We will return to this theme often.)

Further, "exemplarism," as a first-person "architectural" kind of self-exemplification through self-expresssion, introduces the further aspect of the ideal being of the essence-exemplar. Patterns, examples, and paradigms may all be exemplars in the sense of capable of being endlessly embodied and illustrating endless cases. But, depending on the pattern or example, they may or may not admit the infinite horizon of a regulative ideal or limit simpliciter. They may simply be finite examples where the example is no more perfect than what it exemplifies. Thus the paradigm of *amare* is not more perfect than any of the other first-conjugation (*-are*) Latin verbs. Similarly we might say that God's concept of the square root is ideal *quoad nos*, and my concept, as an amateur mathematician, is not. They are both "ideal" in the sense of being endlessly repeatable. Yet the square root may be contrasted with a matter like love or justice where the ideal exemplar is *always inadequately* exemplified or instantiated. Whereas $\sqrt{144} = 12$ no less and no more than $\sqrt{9} = 3$, is adequately presenced. This presumably holds for the divine mind as well as for anyone's. (But in the divine mind there would not be the *inauthentic*, i.e., rote, presencing of these complex matters that characterizes the likes of me). Yet my idea of justice or love must always fall short of the divine idea of justice and love. We saw this in our discussion of the distinction between the "myself," which is always itself, and the person one is, which is always inadequately grasped, always an infinite regulative ideal. The former examples from arithmetic are what they are and always so; the latter are essentially open-ended ideals. Yet, we also suggested, in so far as the "myself' is personified it too becomes an infinite entelechy or ideal for the person – in contrast to the "myself" which is always who/what it is.

But there is the further matter that the divine idea, even of the square root, but a fortiori of the "myself," may be thought to be eminently superior precisely because it has as its *home context* the divine mind (as conceived by The Theological Distinction). Because all essences or paradigms or patterns have their home in the divine mind they find there the infinitely rich contextualization of the divine mind. And thus even "square root" will admit of an unfathomable depth of meaning and comprehension. What is at stake here is the way "understanding" may be thought of as having a "limit simpliciter" which points to the divine limit case. The "limit simpliciter" is hinted at in the most cursory reflection on what is conceptually involved in any matter, e.g., the square root. Let us dwell briefly on this.

First, of all, the square root is a number and thus as such it is not something real which is counted. In counting numbers I am not counting real things like dogs. A number as what can be counted is also able to be thought of as a set or a class or a member of a set or a class. Yet it is a unit and whole, e.g., 6. As such it is constituted by an act of constituting a manifold of units, 1 and 1 and 1 and 1 and 1 and 1. But the acts of counting are not mere discrete demonstrative acts but here a kind of synthesis of "summing" or "addition." But what is this basic operation of summing or adding? The adding together of units is not like the adding of apples. Adding 2, 3, and 5, in the sense of adding unit-entities like apples, would not result in 10 but in 3. We may pause over what we do when we add because each number remains itself. 1 can never be 6 or any other number. The sum is not a collection where each unit remains itself. Thus statements such as $7 + 5 = 8 + 4 = 9 + 3$ are clearly wrong if addition is a collection of self-contained units. Addition must be the uniting of the units in, e.g., 7, with those in 5. That is, we must join the seven units with the five units.

In basic arithmetic the concept of unit requires that of whole and part. And further, the unique part which a "fraction" is comes to light when entertaining the numerous ways the whole can be regarded in its parts: 2 + 4, 1 + 5, 3 + 3. Further, in the square root there is comprehended the unique kind of summing or adding which is "multiplication" where we do not merely sum the units but we repeat the multiplied unit, e.g., 3, by the number of the multiplying unit, e.g., 3. Thus we do not merely add the units of 3 and 3 together into a sum (6) but we "three" (understood verbally) 3 (in English we say "3 times 3") and get "the product" 9. But to get 9 we do not have three threes in an absolute sense (this gives us but 3 number 3's) but three threes which are to be joined in the manner of addition. The square root is thus inseparable from the "operation" of multiplying. It has to do with the "root" of an original unit. This root is one of whose parts, which, when multiplied by itself, equals the original unit. A "square" is a term for the operation of a number being multiplied by itself. The square root of a number is the number which when multiplied by itself gives that original number – of which the square root is the square.

Our point here, of course, is merely to show that "the square root" may be grasped with a relatively languid empty intention, which most of us have by having learned by rote the multiplication tables, and that just a little reflection reveals that its "idea" or its "essence" may have greater depths (a "limit simpliciter") than the empty languid intention has an inkling of. The superficiality of what we have pointed to as "greater depths" of understanding is evident if one were compare what we have just said to what a philosophical mathematician, such as Husserl, brings to light precisely on the topics of number, addition, multiplication, and division.[15] This does not mean that we can say a priori that the exemplary grasp of what, e.g., the square root is, is a regulative ideal. But it suggests that the *contexts* of analysis themselves extend into ever more far-reaching considerations, and it is only when one attempts to unpack any issue whatsoever that this becomes evident. As, e.g., Euclid, Newton, Descartes, Leibniz, Husserl, *et alii* understand endlessly more about numbers than someone like myself, so we may postulate that the divine grasps not only endlessly more than the great mathematicians, but furthermore the divine grasp is superior in an essentially different way. This difference, "the limit case," has to do with the infinity of the divine mind. By "infinity" here we mean what Scotus means "in a popular definition." "The infinite is that which exceeds the finite, not exactly by reason of any finite measure, but in excess of any measure that could be assigned."[16]

But there is also the further consideration that all ideas, even humble ones, like the square root, have their radical *origin* in the divine mind. Here a new dimension of depth is provided by the divine mind itself as the source of all essences, including all geometrical and mathematical notions. Two points may be made here. First, this consideration of the depth of the divine mind could be of no account. It could be that it would add nothing to the richness of what is known. God's knowing the concept of "strike three" in baseball, just as knowing how it emerged in the inventor of baseball's mind, might add nothing to what the average baseball fan knows. But our assumption is that at least in some cases knowing how something originated in an author's or thinker's mind often enriches by shedding light on the matter at hand as well as on the author or thinker. But it still could be the case that we might know something perfectly yet not know the idea of it as it exists in the mind of its creator.

Secondly, locating all essences and necessities in a divine mind may tempt us into thinking that we must ultimately give up the distinction between nature and artifact. If we are to think of all essences and meanings as the product of a divine idea, then must we deny the distinction between nature and artifact or convention? Has all nature become convention and/or artifact? And if nature itself is the work of an all-wise, all-good, all-powerful God, then dare we change anything natural? Would we not thereby harm the work of the most high and most holy through our technology which directs created things to human purposes or ends rather than to their own "natural" ends?[17]

In terms of the dogma of God the Creator, in regard to the elimination of the distinction between nature and artifact just the opposite is the case. It is only with The Theological Distinction between God and the world that we can have a nature that is the solid base for autonomous things and scientific truths in themselves. This distinction permits a distinction between worldly and divine senses of necessity and self-sufficiency where the divine self-sufficiency and necessity may be affirmed as the best possible ground for the necessity and self-sufficiency of nature. And it is only such a ground which is a deterrent to the modernist and post-modernist reduction of the knowing of nature to a mere convention or artifice and nature to unstable random configurations haunted by ineluctable forces that lead to its self-destruction.

As to technological intervention: It is only because we have a robust distinction between nature and artifact that we can find objectionable the subordination of natural beings to human purposes. We will often mention these matters. But here we may refer the readers to fundamental discussions elsewhere.[18]

Even in terms of the distinctions within the world of artifact and nature, it is not evident that when we know something is an artifact that we know the creative idea that gave birth to the thing. A fortiori, in knowing well something natural we obviously do not know the creative idea. In knowing well something natural, but knowing it only naturalistically, there might be a hindrance to knowing it in other important aspects, e.g., its essence and, if there is one, its inner life. If we did not know these we would not know the creative idea of the matter at hand.

Consider how in knowing in intimate detail something, e.g., the plant "St. John's Wort," we know not merely that as a matter of necessity it is produced by one of its own kind, but we further know how this very kind came to be by way of a contingent series of geological and botanical events. Further, we may well know what its curative properties are and its history in homeopathic medicine in knowing all the contingent antecedents, the DNA and other genetic-molecular constituent materials that bring about and shape this plant. But it might well be the case that in spite of knowing all this we might well be ignorant of the organism's intricate form and life. Thus, we might never have been moved to ponder whether there is something over and above knowing all these properties in knowing a plant. We may never have felt or grasped its "inscape" because we were convinced, after all, it is a mere plant: It has no self, no center, does not have the having of itself, is without feeling. In sentient organisms we have an inkling that there is more, and this is expressed in Nagel's well-known philosophical question, What is it like to be a bat? But is there anything analogous in organisms like plants, where we, in contemplating what it is for this "sleeping" organism to have complex physiological processes of growth, cell repair and cell manufacture, etc., might ask, but what is it like for it to be (essentially) asleep – as if the sleep were a modification of waking consciousness? Is it equally asleep when dormant as a seed as when it is a sprout, and then blossoming with its flowers? The scientistic, third-person account prohibits such a reflection because for this perspective sleep and waking are not properly modifications of first-person awareness.

But even if we knew its intricate form and its own life, whether that of a waking or sleeping monad, even if we knew the inborn dynamic form or Gestalt or entelechy and even if we had a glimmer through empathy of its distinctive life as much as possible, we would not know its creative idea. At least in the case, e.g., of the bat's own life, the subjectivity of the bat, its Who, would seem to be precisely something that could not have a "creative idea." That is, unless it could be decisively proven that it was equivalently a robot or zombie, i.e., that it had no "interiority" or self-awareness, it would, as a subjectivity, not be the "sort of thing" which would admit to such an apprehension, even though all the properties of the bat would be precisely something of which we could have an idea.

But furthermore, what could it mean to have ex novo a creative idea of St. John's Wort or a bat if the defining context is that of the modern one that eo ipso tends to exclude empathic perception's power in appreciating nature but a fortiori excludes the theological contexts? That is, in the zoological-evolutionary context things are not made but emerge out of the contingencies of blind "nature's" processes of selection. And these things in their specific form are best envisaged as way-stations, not permanent forms, like "the eternal form of St. John's Wort." As such contingent forms they may be either extinguished or undergo an elaboration or modification fitted to the environment in which they find themselves in the next ten thousand years. Further, and this is the most basic point, we do not know the creative idea because nature as *physis*, even as created *physis*, itself gives birth to its more or less random forms quite apart from any creative mind.

Perhaps with Conrad-Martius, echoing Plotinus and St. Augustine, we might say that the creative generic species-entelechies are the trans-physical self-subsisting expressions of the creative ideas. But even if this very un-modern proposal was accepted, we still would not know the creative idea itself. A fortiori, we would not know what it might mean to know the creative idea of, e.g., Peter.

Further, we do not know the creative idea merely by knowing something artificial or natural because for this creative idea to come to light we must know the matter at hand as derived from some practice or activity beyond the known thing itself, and it is not at all clear that we have access to this.[19] In the creative practice the produced thing, which has its origin in the mind of the creator or maker, finds expression in the world. Even knowing the produced thing as produced does not permit the being-known in the first-person of the creative idea by the creator. This remains hidden or exterior to us who know only its expression.

The basic analogy of creation to the master builder/architect builds on familiarity with the notion of human creation. Exemplarism makes use of the notion of the idea of the product or created thing as having a kind of birth in the mind of the creator, and this prior mental existence informs its incarnation in the world. In this sense, exemplarism resembles aspects of the familiar phenomenon of expression – in so far as expression permits the distinction between an expressed meaning and an unexpressed or inchoate one.

Expression is a term comprehending numerous human activities. For example, we may distinguish within the creative expression the inkling or idea revealed by being brought into being and how one's expressiveness or behavior might reveal something about the author or agent. In the case of action and behavior the character or personality is revealed. An example of the latter is what we call "projection." Here we typically refer to how our weakness provokes us to defend ourselves against a threat to our self-esteem. The threat may take the form of a revelation to ourselves by ourselves of an unacceptable truth about ourselves. We may tacitly acknowledge its reprehensibility, as any person of integrity must, by warding off its painful revelation to ourselves and displacing or "projecting" on to another this very despicable weakness. Projection is a complex self-expression. It's being "there" and appropriately despised by me enables me to do what conscience bids, i.e., contemn it, and at the same time forestall facing the music. When the projection is revealed as a feature of someone's behavior it both reveals something about the agent and how this self-expression transforms (distorts) a pre-existing reality.

Creative expression may well be a way we transform a pre-existing reality by way of something that is first of all dawning within us in the form of a burgeoning idea, but its transformation of a pre-existent reality can have a variety of functions. It may be completely playful and potentially of interest for its own sake or it may, whether intentionally or not, bring about something new which is capable of being revelatory of what is already actual, i.e., it may, by shedding new light, be a vehicle of truth. What we mean by great works of art is precisely that they have this property.

In the theological context the form of human creativity we find most useful as an analogy for thinking about creation "from nothing" is where the artist has an emergent notion of what is to find the light of day through her creative agency. This emergent notion needing to find the light of day we may call an "idea." Once the idea finds expression in an independently existing medium it becomes "objective spirit" or an "ideal object" which enjoys a measure of independence publicity, and communicability.

Of course, the "plan" or "blueprint" of, e.g., Frank Gehry's Guggenheim Museum in Bilboa, Spain is not the creative idea as what gave birth to the actual building, nor is a sketch of a work of Leonardo or Rembrandt the creative idea of one of their masterpieces. Analogous to the divine creative idea, the creative idea of the artist is initially the obscure empty intention of the "dark something" (cf. Husserl and Gendlin) that is in the process of taking shape. In the case of the artist we may find "the unconscious," inklings, agony, tumult, accidents, and chance at work in the formation of the idea; but the creative originating "ideating" or "mentating" is not yet the formed idea. The creative originating idea is inserted into the wide context of the pre-existent ideas and motives for the creation of the work, e.g., the depth of the artist's prior life-experiences and acquaintance with other similar projects.

This depth and non-objective process of artistic creativity may be contrasted with the "context" of the infinite divine essence. Of this in itself we can say nothing because it is infinite as beyond our measuring. It is a *limit case* and not a mere ideal-limit, a limit simpliciter. Therefore it, of necessity, is inaccessible to infinitizing. Nevertheless we can say it is that wherein absolutely all perfections are actual and "functioning" (and therefore which for itself knows no "context" as a determinable horizon or framework beyond itself) and where there is no prior existing source apart from the actual divine essence.

We may think of human creative activity as heading toward a limit simpliciter in so far as there is a maximalization or perfection of both the expressed and the expressing as they stand in relation to the creator and her ideals. Procreation has served as the analogue for divine creativity because it gives birth to what is of utmost dignity, beauty, and complexity within the world. In this case it gives birth to what is of the same kind as the one begetting, and to what can exist on its own after the work of begetting and procreating, indeed to what can eventually beget and procreate on its own. Yet because the parents' responsible agency and creative intention are not necessary in bringing about the work, we hesitate to think of procreation as the exemplar of human creativity. This hesitation persists even when we acknowledge that raising offspring and shaping them spiritually entails a "work of art" in the "spiritual formation," i.e., in the parenting of the offspring. The doubt continues even when we acknowledge the possible symmetry between "unconscious" inspirational sources of the creative idea and product in the artist and the character of the instinctual attraction and ardor of the parents, i.e., that these too might well seem to "come out of nowhere" and be the agency behind the human agents. Nevertheless the parents are not conscious creators and fashioners of the child as what they give birth to, even though they are precisely that in terms of the "raising" of the child, the fuller sense of parenting, which extends beyond "begetting" or procreating. Rather, they have to perform the necessary kind of agency that itself occasions that Nature herself do the fashioning. The parents' procreating is doing "what comes naturally."

Nature's most basic work of *naturans* and *nascendi* or begetting is bringing forth "natures" or kinds by kinds. Thus begetting begets one's kind or kin, and thus a likeness, and if there is not the likeness there is the trauma of the monstrous. Further, it was evident until fairly recently that one cannot make what one begets. This was, in part, because the control over the physical processes, e.g., acquisition and fertilization of eggs and sperms, were not within human capabilities. But more fundamentally, even with the technological intervention which makes possible acquisition of the sperm and eggs, the creative processes themselves were always *natura naturans*, i.e., nature's own. Most decisively, the reason why one doubted that one could make what one begets, even assuming that the basic ingredients of the sperm and egg themselves were totally manufactured, is that what one could procreate far exceeded in excellence what the maker could make. Further, what was procreated was not merely of exceeding excellence, and not only could it come to stand on its own, like any made product, but it can come to have all the excellences of the procreator: A unique trans-propertied ipseity with mind and will. Yet as we will see, in some respects emulating what is begotten is the secret aspiration of any finite creative agent.

Procreating is something the parent does and does not do. Clearly the parent undertakes certain forms of agency, but, as we have noted, these forms of agency do not require any ingenuity, freedom, creativity, thoughtfulness, in regard to the begotten. Clearly there is no artistic exemplarity in procreation in the way it might be envisaged in the creation of an artwork. The begotten is effected by this proper sexual-fleshly agency whether or not the distinctive capacities of creativity of human agents are in play. Again, the novelty of the begotten far surpasses any novelty of which a maker or creator is capable. The novelty of the begotten is foremost that of the unique essence of Who someone is, and this is of a different order than the novel arrangement of pre-existent patterns or Whats. As we claimed in Book 1, Chapter VI, not only the parents but "Nature herself," no matter how we understand what the concept of Nature refers to, is not capable of creating the ipseity of the child, i.e., *who* the child is. Here begetting begets a novelty, an unprecedented novel beginning.

In everyday language regarding procreation we say that the child is "begotten not made." And this formula (of the Nicene Creed) itself points out a necessity and affinity of the begetter and begotten. The Creed wishes to emphasize that the begetting and begotten are eternal and the begotten is of the same "kind" as the begetter. This latter emphasizes that it is to be distinguished from the "creation" where there is an infinite distance. The eternal begetting also suggests that the begotten is not only co-equal but coaeval with and internally related to (as parent and child or lover and beloved) the one begetting. As such it also suggests that strictly speaking a Who (in this case, the eternal begotten Son) is not caused or procreated, but is in an eternal "personal" and love relationship, a "procession," with the begetter; it is not a matter of begetting an ipseity by any causal activity, and surely not bringing about a Who out of some pre-existent materials with their distinctive properties. Thus it suggests that in so far as the begetting is "personal" it is free; but in so far as it belongs to the "nature of the Godhead" it is necessary. In which case, it is best thought of as a unique kind of "teleological determinism" where freedom and necessity are not only not incompatible but of the highest order of perfection.

But we speak also in regard to procreation of "making babies." Here there is noted the possibility of freedom, purpose, and planning. While there is a causal agency of the woman and man cooperating in bringing about the ejaculation of the sperm and the fertilization of the egg, the "making babies" resembles more the work of horticulture where the gardener may be said to make, e.g., tomatoes or apples. Whereas the parents, like the gardener, want "the fruit of their labors and love," e.g., "a baby," they do not intend to "make" Peter or Mary nor could they want Peter or Mary. There is, again, no question of their bringing Mary about out of the pre-existent materials of sperm and egg, even though they do intend to bring about "a baby."[20] And parents often enough wonder during the child's infancy and youth, who this person before them is, i.e., who, we would say, will become personified, all the while loving *them* in spite of their not yet having the signature properties.

This in no way contradicts the obviousness of nature's *naturans*, i.e., its own amazing creative powers and the relevance of human sexual activity in bringing human persons about. Nor does it merely refer to the ancient question of how lower forms of organization can be antecedent to and in this sense causal with regard to the emergent higher ones.[21] Depending on the kind of cause one has in mind the effect must be adequate or proportionate to the cause. The motion of a billiard ball can cause the distinctive motion of another billiard ball, but it cannot be said to cause, in the same way, the insight into the relationship of inertia, momentum, and bodies in motion that might accompany the observation of the impact of the billiard ball. Many things may be said to be necessary conditions for the bringing about of a human person, but we have offered reasons for doubting that the physical causes or conditions are the sufficient reason or cause of the unique ipseity. Our chief concern is how a Who can be brought about by a series of physical causes, given that what we refer to by Who is non-sortal, and given that a causal explanation must have recourses to kinds of causes.

Among proper forms of human creativity we can make distinctions. In the making or fashioning by, e.g., the carpenter or the hack computer graphic artist, the worker typically carries out consciously the idea expressed by another, e.g., the architect or artist, and thus is a mere instrumental cause in the creative process. The master builder/architect/potter finds *herself* inspired and realizes the idea that she has given birth to by the transforming of the materials, even the received ideas, at hand. (An architect/master builder of course needs myriads of instrumental agents doing the bidding of the architect/master builder; she is not the exclusive or immediate agent that transforms the material.) Here artistic creativity involves the incarnation and materialization of the artist's spirit. This spirit may be objectified, as in the character of a novel who takes on an insistent life of her own demanding realization in the as-if reality of the artwork. The artist acts from out of her I-can, her power, that she pre-reflectively lives. Of course, this power itself can appear to have an initiative in the objectified spirit of the fictional character and the artist may learn that she must cooperate with *it*. She must subordinate her I-can to this upsurging and be at its behest. Even so, the inspired idea as such is capable of many realizations and the material of realization, e.g., the flow of sentences, the accessibility of the colors, her bodily strength and dexterity, are always less than perfectly docile and transparent to the expression. And that which she creates may well exist independently for a long time, especially if it is cared for, but, on the other hand, it may not even outlive the moment of its completion.

Thus the work embodies the mind, body, and soul of the artist which themselves are informed by "objective spirit," i.e., the soul, mind, and body of the artist are shaped by the work of other artists, thinkers, etc. Further, the material which is worked upon and worked with is typically pervaded by the design conceived by the artist; it is not merely "raw material" but some of the material itself is made, even made by artists. (Thus we have canvases, brushes, charcoal crayons, computers, computer programs, etc.) The artist's design may well be hidden initially from the artist herself, but eventually the material takes on the contours that become the design. Subsequently, with some intentional distance-taking or reflection on the guiding notion, the design or style as such emerges. And this design or style may set the pattern for many subsequent imitations that reproduce aspects of the original idea. Here there has emerged a sense of "exemplar."

But the produced work itself is not an agent or source of design or of production and self-recreation, and it is fated to be at the mercy of outside forces, e.g., the vagaries of the interpretation of others. It cannot protect itself and cannot talk back. Thus an artist might strive to produce a work which is a Who i.e., is an Other, maximally creative artist, another creative spirit, another source of thought, moral agency, and art which or who is capable not only of beatifying the world and expressing, reproducing, and maintaining and recreating itself, but also forestalling false interpretations or applications of itself. As Sokolowski has put it, the aim here would be that of an artificial intelligence that was not artificial in the way an artificial flower is, but rather in the way artificial light is light.[22]

By extension the great problem then becomes whether there can be an artificial person. Of course, we might say that artistic creation can bring about not only a *what* but a *who*, namely the *who* of a fictional person. But this is "only" a fictional person who "exists" in her fictional as-if world, not in the real actual world. "Mr. Darcy" of Jane Austen's *Pride and Prejudice* is palpably real and I apperceive him to have a quasi-real self-awareness. But nevertheless I do not apperceive an actual "for himself," an actual other "myself," aware of his unique essence. I apperceive a quasi-"for himself" and in this sense my apperceiving or appresenting is only a quasi-appresenting. Our view is that the real unique Who can never be produced by the configuration of Whats, no matter how rich and complicated they become. "Mr. Darcy," "Elizabeth," etc. are evoked for me as quasi-real self-subsisting ipseities by my living through their personal properties. Yet these "What's" are of another ontological order than the Who; the artist creates a fictional *who* through a unique constellation of *whats*, and I might well be taken in as when I am deceived by a robot. But in the case of the robot my appresentation is real, but erroneous; in the case of Mr. Darcy it is a quasi-appresentation. My belief is an as-if-it-were-so.

As Conrad-Martius has put it, the ipseity is *archonal* and therefore there is no beginning principle in the world beyond itself. Philosophically speaking, the origin of *who* one is, is a mystery both in the sense that it is a problem that encroaches on the questioner and it eludes our ready categorial analysis. Furthermore, as we earlier noted, there would not be possible any reproduction of the Who of the artist into his double in the sense that what the artist refers to with "I" is the same as what is referred to by the fictional or artificial person or robot, should these be able to "fictionally" achieve indexical achievements or simulate indexical achievements.

With the project of creating an autonomous Other we must ask whether we have to do with a limit case or whether we draw near to a limit simpliciter where the creative artist strives to make out of her creative idea, and all that it implies, an autonomous, individual, effective, substantial foundation of her work so that this idea, now become autonomous, is able to paint the picture, compose the symphony, construct the building, and be partner to a dialogue. In such a case the artist could not complain that what she envisaged in her mind would be only imperfectly realized in her work. Nor need she fear inordinately for the work's ability to preserve and perpetuate itself. In this respect the telos or limit simpliciter of creative artistic agency would somewhat paradoxically resemble what ancients and some moderns have thought nature was.[23] Creative artistic agency would be thus striving to emulate procreation; but it would not be mere begetting because exemplarity would intervene. In which case, creative artistic agency would strive to emulate the theological notion of creation.

Yet from the standpoint of The Theological Distinction and Miller's notion of the limit case it would seem that the ideal of the artist creating an autonomous work of art would indeed only be the limit simpliciter, i.e., it could be endlessly approximated. But if this ideal is seen over against the creation of another ipseity, a Who, it would seem to be essentially beyond the infinite ideal limit, i.e., it would be a limit case. In so far as artificial intelligence, as in the sense of artificial light and not artificial flowers, is inseparably an ipseity, an archonal being, it moves beyond the *autonomous* artwork to the *autos*; as such it cannot be *made* because as such it is not comprised of natural-physical or artificial components. As a Who, as a "myself," it cannot be derived from objective stuff determined by Whats, i.e., the material fashioned by the artist.

§3. Beginning Reflections on the Metaphysics of the Divine Exemplarity of "Myself"

More basically, for The Theological Distinction, divine creation is a limit case and not an ideal limit of what we mean by creation precisely because the divine does not actuate any potentiality and does not act *on* anything. Creation is not to be understood after the fashion of a "limit simpliciter" of human creative activity. All of these activities are exercised *on* something and make a difference in the creative agent.[24] Let us develop this.

In my transforming this clay into a pot, in my making out of this collection of materials a building, in my writing this essay, etc., there is not only my relationship to the clay, materials, the ideas and writing materials, but furthermore these materials and ideas are related to me, indeed the idea or inspiration may possess me, and the creative activity may well change me.

Yet one might think, that although I indeed am related to the clay, the building materials, and the writing paper, they are not *really related* to me. We might say, they are unconscious, and thereby disregard any panpsychist interpretation of these material things. Similarly, my observing you is a real relationship to you, but your being observed by me is not a real relationship of you to me unless you are conscious of me observing you. This kind of asymmetry between things being related in one direction and not in another Aquinas calls the difference between a "relation of reason" and "a real relation." The unconscious observed entity or the entity not aware of its being observed is not "really related" to the observer or observing. Miller, following Peter Geach, names the property of being related, e.g., observing, in one direction and of not being related in the other direction, a "Cambridge property." Creation, in the sense of The Theological Distinction, and following Aquinas, is a real relation of the world to God but not a real relation of God to the world. Creation and being a creator are "Cambridge properties" in God. The problem of artificial persons, whereby ipseities are the work of human hands, has its deeper level in the dogma of creation where something, rather than nothing, exists, truly exists in itself as a result of the divine creative *fiat*. This is part of the meaning of saying that the being of the creature is a Cambridge property in God.

The notion of the Cambridge property provides us with the possibility of making distinctions between *essential* properties with which the essence of God is identical, and God's non-essential properties which have to do with Cambridge properties and relations. God's being the creator of the universe and the caller of Abraham do not make any real difference to him in the sense that God in creating and calling does not act *on* anything transcendent to Godself nor is God moved by some absent potential excellence to act.

On the other hand, we are claiming that the unique individual essence to which the person Abraham refers when he says "I" is inseparable from the divine essence and is not a Cambridge property. In this respect the calling of Abraham is inseparable from God addressing Godself. Or better, the ultimate foundation for Abraham's calling is the eternal awareness of the eternal divine essence. In the next section we hope to make the necessary distinctions that will make this clear.

Creation does not involve something pre-existing that God relates to and acts upon nor does it involve the soliciting of God by outstanding not-yet realized perfections within the world or possible worlds; in this sense God is not "really related" to the world and the *person* Abraham. Similarly, God's creative agency is not an expression in the sense of actuating a perfection within Godself that prior to creation was only potential. The divine essence does not become more perfect or more excellent by creatively realizing possibilities. The Theological Distinction elaborates this point by holding that the excellence of the world does not add to God's excellence and the diminishment of the world does not detract from the excellence of God.

Human creative agency points to an ideal form of creative agency where the agent is fully receptive to the inspirational hidden sources within and without herself and where the artist is in full mastery of herself in the process of creativity, and where what is created not only fully expresses what the creator wants to express, but the creator is able to give to the created not only the imagined dignity and beauty but also a kind of substantial individuality such that the work now exists independently and embodies all the excellence of autonomous artistic creativity of this unique artist. Yet this limit simpliciter toward which the various forms of creativity point "in itself" has, in the theological case of The Theological Distinction, a totally new dimension which is not evident *quoad nos* in our infinitization: God the Creator does not actuate any potentiality and does not act upon anything and does not receive any inspiration. Because God in creating is not motivated by what is unfulfilled or missing in Godself there is no self-expression as a self-actuation.

Because, in creating, God does not act upon anything there is no resistance to or frustration of God's will. In this sense God's creative agency is, of necessity, as we shall say, a limit case of generosity. Further, divine agency in creating is *ex nihilo*, i.e., it cannot presuppose something existing independently and transcendent to the divine essence. Thus although we see how human creativity tilts toward a divine limit simpliciter, the dogma of The Theological Distinction refers to a divine creativity which is not commensurate with the continuum of the idealizing infinitization of creativity pointing to the "limit simpliciter."[25]

We must now begin to develop our thesis that exemplarity is a theory intrinsic to the dogma of "God the Creator" as this emerges in The Theological Distinction. We wish to claim that exemplarity is a way of explicating the divine "causality" of "creation" in regard not only to essences and kinds, and instantiations of these, but also unique haecceities whose only instantiation is themselves.

The first consideration is the one we have already claimed: God's creation is the limit case of "creation" in as much as *ex nihilo* and without any real relation to what is created, created beings exist and exist truly in themselves. Creatures existing in themselves are *not* God. As not God and having nothing of their own that is not from God, they nevertheless have that by which they are other than God, and this cannot be anything existing in itself prior to and apart from God's generosity. Yet in their being other and different from God and having nothing in themselves they exist truly in themselves. In this respect, although they are separated from God by an infinite abyss, the abyss between what has Being necessarily and essentially and what may lay claim, on "its own apart from God," only to nothingness, the foundation of their reality, what St. Thomas called the perfection and actuality of their *esse*, must be "similar" to the divine Ground.

How are we to understand this "similarity?" This is the theological appropriation of the otherwise dubious ancient formula, *omne agens agit sibi simili*, every cause effecting something effects something similar to itself. (Another allied thesis is that *nemo dat quod non habet*, "nothing can give what it does not have" and the perfection of the effect must pre-exist in the perfection of the cause.) The "similarity" that is here intended is not limited to a matter of appearing or looking similar (as in geometric figures) but applies to more formal considerations, as in "sameness" of form or species. Thus a famous example is the similarity of procreation or begetting where the begotten is of the same "nature" or kind as the one begetting. When the cause and effect are of different kinds, as the sun and what the sun's power generates, the "likeness" might be confined merely to the generic considerations of the cause and effect both being in some sense "material," in space-time, etc. Thus "causality" refers to all that might serve what is to be taken into account in bringing something about and here we would have to do with numerous matters that were of different kinds and species. Causality would thus cover both extrinsic and intrinsic factors, conditions, etc. It thus does not merely refer to natural events but actions. Here obviously there need be little or no similarity between brain lesions and anomalous thought patterns, between lack of sunlight and feeling emotionally depressed, between means and ends, between artistic or philosophical conceptions and the nutrients the artist or thinker consumes, etc.

In the theological limit case of creation we indeed have to do with the bringing about of something, but here we cannot find a similarity of discernible "properties," which is ruled out by God being beyond properties. Indeed, God is beyond all beings, properties, natural or essential kinds, and genera. Here the biblical injunction to avoid images is affirmed. Yet The Theological Distinction, which in this matter finds its metaphysical moorings in the teachings of Aquinas, holds for an analogical likeness of *esse* which is common to God and creatures. It is worth noting, however, that even on the creaturely side, *esse* as the perfection of all perfections likewise transcends all properties. (As Kant famously said, "existence is not a predicate.")

For The Theological Distinction nothing is, there is no "world," if things do not have *esse* and this likeness to God. For the Distinction, it could be, but it is contrary to fact, that God is all there is. Nothing can exist unless it comes forth from God, and it does not come forth from God unless it has *esse* and if it does not in this special sense reflect or resemble God, and in this sense is "similar" to the divine. The sense in which everything is similar to God, who is *Ipsum Esse Subsistens*, pure subsisting To Be, is that it has *esse*, it has the actuality of being. Whereas God's essence is To Be (*esse*), God bestows being (*esse*) on what is essentially not God. What is essentially not God has an essence for which being, *esse*, is not necessary. For such a contingent "kind of being" to be it must be created or receive from God the act of being or *esse*. It is through the actual being, *esse*, of created being that each actual being enjoys the highest and purest likeness of God.[26] Indeed, through *esse* there is such a great measure of "likeness" that Aquinas claims that the To Be (*esse*) of beings is that which is "formal with respect to every thing which actually is." This means of all the considerations that we might make about anything, typically its "property" or its "form," by which we grasp what it is that makes it to be what it is, in regard to the actuality of things it is the *esse* which is most formal, most essential. Further, he says *esse* is most interior to them and what is most deeply present in them: *esse autem est illud quod magis intimum cuilibet, et quod profundius omnibus inest. Esse* inheres in things because they are not *esse*, but only have it.[27]

This formal analytic or tautological reflection that emerges out of The Theological Distinction secures the claim that creatures are of necessity likenesses of the divine but it does not, as such, secure the form of causality that is "exemplarity." Exemplarity as a form of causality surfaces when we transpose this formal third-person reflection on the metaphysics of creation onto a conception of what divine first-person knowledge of creatures must be before, during, and after their creation – assuming that these tenses are not absolutely meaningless in the divine case. The tenses are necessary *quoad nos* because creatures are not coaeval or co-eternal and co-equal with God. They "come into being" even if it is true that in their coming into being time, as "the measure of motion with a before and after," also "comes into being."

Exemplarity is necessary because divine knowledge is at once simple and absolute. As absolute, divine knowledge cannot be an enrichment through the awareness of a form of another extrinsic to the divine. As absolutely simple (without parts), divine knowledge cannot be determined by the plurality of beings of creation or the plural-

ity of possible beings. Rather, divine knowing is of necessity always a knowing of
the divine essence itself which is the absolute source of all the perfections or forms
that comprise the divine knowing. God's absolute knowing is a knowing of Godself
and in this knowing there is not a distinction between self-knowing, self-awareness,
act of knowing, and what is known.

Exemplarity enters with the consideration that God knows and creates what is
other than God. If creatures were begotten they would be God of God. There is no
exemplarity in intra-trinitarian begetting because begetting involves necessity and
sameness of "kind." (The scare-quotes point to the difficulty of thinking of God or
the divine persons as having a "nature" or "kind" as if God, or the Holy Spirit, were
a kind of being – and not To Be Itself.) If creatures were *made* and not created God
would be a cosmic artist or demiurge depending on or essentially correlated with
what is external to God, and and creatures would be comprised of what is of God
and what is not of God.

Because for the dogma of God the Creator there is no question whether God
knows what is other than Godself, the question arises of how to understand God's
creative knowledge of creatures or the knowledge that brings about what is other to
God. Even though the world is created and not made, because the world does not
happen by chance or by divine necessity but through God's gracious generosity –
here in all of these descriptions the analogy of attribution must tilt toward
equivocation – the analogy of the divine architect/master builder is introduced.

In "Abrahamic religion" very often the exemplarity of the divine essence is
in play in the creation of the world. In Christian theology, the exemplarity of the
eternal Son is not in play in the begetting of the eternal Son because the Son is not
subordinate to the Father. However, in the creating of the world, not only is the
exemplarity of the divine essence in play, but the eternal Son is conceived to be
the unifying exemplar of the creation of the world. (Cf. e.g., *Colossians* 1:15–16;
Hebrews 11:3.)

We may note here that for Aquinas the heavenly Church, the community of
glory, is both the exemplar and the *telos*, "our mother, to which we tend; upon it
our earthly church is modeled (*exemplata*)." "The heavenly church" or "Kingdom
of God," like a mustard seed, is, with the urgings and workings of the Spirit of God,
the entelechy, the exemplary form and telos of the human community. It exists in
advance, before the foundation of the world, and it is the *patria*, the homeland, of
the pilgrim church of wayfarers.[28]

As we just suggested, the finite created creative architect is envisaged as having
"in herself" as an "idea" what subsequently exists "outside herself" and independently on its own. The idea as exemplar is not the concept *through which* (*principium
quo*) the architect knows the artifact or the world; it is not the conceptual scheme
or frame for perceiving the thing or world, nor is it that aspect under which the
architect knows the artifact in the world but which itself is not known; nor is it the
burgeoning idea or inkling which guides the creative process in human artists.
Rather, it is the result or fruit of the burgeoning felt-meaning which, having
emerged and upon reflection, is precisely the exemplary idea. The idea as exemplar
is precisely *that which* (*principium quod*) is known by the creator and which serves

as the initial basis of separation for what comes to exist apart from the architect's mind. It is that on the basis of which and from which the architect/master builder understands what is to be done.[29] It is that in reference to which what is brought about is measured. In this respect what is the exemplar is what is imitated or mirrored in forms that shape the actual concrete beings. But how these forms that become manifest are originally contained in the architect's own knowledge of herself is hidden to the onlooker.[30] In the human case we know that often enough they are hidden not only to the onlooker but even from the artist or architect in the process of creating.

Exemplarity emerges for the dogma of God the Creator because of the necessary thesis internal to the dogma that created being (*esse*) of necessity is a likeness of God, and this likeness must be known by God. Again, this is not a perceptual or property/intelligible sense of "likeness" but a rather strange ontological sense that is mindful of the distinction between limit case and limit simpliciter. As an explication of the thesis of the dogma of God the Creator that God is "absolute," i.e., pure To Be Itself, God's knowledge of creation cannot be a knowing strictly speaking of what is strictly other than God. That is, God must know creatures in Godself and must know Godself in creatures and yet God knows creatures as other than Godself. In looking upon creation God sees Godself, but God also sees what is other than Godself. The analogy of a divine architect/master builder, who has ideas of the world which ultimately are constitutive of the divine essence and therefore which are not "learned," "inspired," or "borrowed," goes some way in helping to articulate the dogma.

This doctrine of the One or God beyond all attributes and properties and even "being" is a major source of the *via negativa* in the "Abrahamic traditions." Of course, the primary text is *Exodus* 3:14 where "I am who I am" points to what is beyond all names. In Dionysius the Areopagite, God is referred to as beyond being (*huperousios*), sometimes translated as "super-essential," because a Greek word for being, *ousios*, could also be translated with "essence" or "substance." As beyond being it is non-being or meontic (*to me on*). As in Plotinus, with Dionysius there is a hesitation even to ascribe to this One oneness or unity, let alone "being." The One of Plotinus might be better thought of what precedes the number 1, i.e., it is best thought of as 0 because 1 is limit and has a form and a begun beginning. The One, in contrast, is limitless, formless, and unbegun. But this zero or formlessness is not a *nihil negativum*.

As we have noted, Dionysius and the Christian thinkers coming after him merge *Nous* and the One with God and thus can claim that all essences and particulars are exemplarily contained within the Godhead. And St. Thomas believes his concept of *Ipsum Esse Subsistens* gives a sense of "being" which meets all the objections of the "meontologists." Not only do all essences as the essential attributes of the divine presuppose "The Very To Be Itself," *ipsum esse subsistens*, but this Itself is not a being and is infinitely beyond all finite beings or entities; it is even beyond essence if essence is a determination and therefore limitation of being. Yet, although endlessly transcendent to all forms and beings and thus not being these forms and things as they exist in the world, the Godhead contains them eternally "prior" (a priori) to their actual being. Again, the Godhead contains them less as limits simpliciter than as limit concepts. And in so far as these essences are perfections manifest in the world, i.e., Cambridge properties, they may be considered as not absolutely identical with God's essence.

Exemplarism evolves in "Abrahamic theologies" in order to answer the problem of how God who is infinite perfection can have an other that does not limit Godself and does not introduce into the "absolute" something alien. As Aquinas put it, the exemplar has to do with what becomes other (cf. the *principium quod*) and the divine essence as the exemplar opens the possibility for the divine essence to be imitated and thus "othered."[31]

Again, the basic principle of exemplarity is founded in *esse* as the "likeness of God": God "is" (exists) by reason of his essence, but every other being "is" (exists) by reason of participation in being (*esse*) deriving from God.[32] The "essence of God" is an analogous reference to what "essence" means in anything we experience or conceive. It has to do with the What or kind. As we saw in Book 1, Chapter VI, §9, only in the case of the essence of the referent of "I," or prior to this, the non-reflective "myself," does the presentation of the *eidos* require positing its existence. In The Theological Distinction all qualifications that apply to the transcendental phenomenological case are removed: God's essence requires absolutely God's being, just as any being and essence requires God's being and essence.

In our experience the essence delimits something over against the backdrop of other kinds; all essences occupy a meaning-space in the endless meaning-spaces of actual and possible essences, properties, meanings, etc. Yet the bulk of this work has attempted to show that the third-person understanding of "essence" is not adequate. Below we shall make a case for understanding "the essence of God" in a first-person way.

This perhaps has some encouragement in the dogma of God the creator which may always be connected with *Exodus* 3:14. Here in question would appear to be the proper name or the distinguishing essence of God. The text may be construed as saying that God's name is tied to God's essence and both "God" and the "essence of God" are least violated in their sense if they are taken as proper names. Thus we best grasp "God" if we think of it as resembling the referent of proper names which is the ipseity beyond properties. And even though "the essence of God" refers to a What of a Who, it too, in this respect, resembles the referent of proper names which is beyond the properties. (Cf. Book 1, Chapter IV, §3.) Thus it is not to be taken to refer to what we often think of in terms of "naming" or establishing an ideal entity repeatedly identifiable across the flux of experience. Nor is the "I am Who/What I am" a handle for a God among Gods. Nor is it the naming as a limitation or specification of a kind. As we saw, it is as much a Who as a What, and the "I am" qualifying the prior "I am" does not limit its "am'ing" or its To Be. Its essence does not restrict its To Be and the "I am" or Who cannot be reduced to a kind. Its essence is To Be and its To Be is its essence, and the first-person singular reference is determinative of the sense we give here to both essence and existence, as well as what the proper name refers to. Neither in Its being or being-Who is It countable; Yahweh is not *a* god or an instance of a kind.

But in faith and through the parameters of the dogma of God the Creator, the believer apprehends the divine absolutely unique and simple To Be through a variety of forms of intentionality. Prescinding from the more concrete faith referents, e.g., of Jesus, the Father, the Spirit, the Eucharist, the *Ekklesia*, etc., the cognitive aiming at the intelligible What ("What is God?") is different than the conative-loving aim at the good or God as the Good, as redeemer, etc. and this means that God appears *quoad nos* as having a plurality of aspects. But the tradition has also wanted to say that the divine essence *is* goodness and goodness is not one property next to other properties of the divine. Not only is goodness not accidental but necessary, i.e., goodness is the essence of the divine as much as is To Be. Goodness is not, like God's being the Father of the Palestinian Jewish carpenter, Jesus of Nazareth, a Cambridge property. This means that as "after" creation there is no more To Be (*esse*) than "before" creation, so neither is there any more goodness, value, or excellence after creation than before creation.[33] God and creatures do not make for two in the way two finite beings are two; similarly, the goodness of God plus that of creatures does not make for more goodness. God contains the total value or excellence of To Be, and with the addition of creatures there is not something better. Thus this participation, imitation, and instantiation and, in general, the additional excellences or goods that derive from creation add nothing to the excellence or goodness which is original with the divine essence and goodness. In Aquinas' language all created value or goodness is good and of worth by sharing in the divine goodness.[34] Created goodness is good by sharing in the infinite goodness of God, in whom all created goodness is found not merely in an infinitely eminent way, but rather as a limit case, i.e., as absolutely transcendent to the mind's eros toward the goodness and beauty apperceived on the horizon of experience.

We earlier referred to Simone Weil's view that with creation there is less goodness than prior to creation. The motivation for Weil's proposal is clear: In order that the Other's space of freedom be given full play, I must diminish mine, and therefore my being. Therefore by analogy, God must diminish Godself in order that creatures, foremost spiritual ones with freedom, exist. Yet even if restraint is a proper way to describe analogously God, in the human case it is not an impoverishment but an enrichment of virtue. Further, this view of creatures, whether free ones or not, as being necessarily in competition with the "being" of God, deviates fundamentally from The Theological Distinction. Here we may recall that Kierkegaard pointed to God as a limit case in this matter of freedom and interaction: God is God precisely because God is that One who could create free Others without in any way diminishing God's power. We will return to this basic aspect of The Theological Distinction below.

Of course, for this work "exemplarism" is of special interest in its efforts to show how even the unique essence of ipseity, the "myself," has its "idea" or exemplar in God or the One. The introduction by Plotinus of *Socrates* as "among the primary furnishings of the ideal world," i.e., as an essence or ideal pattern which Socrates alone instantiates and which no other can instantiate,[35] is, for this work, an important speculative innovation in philosophy. Exemplarism in Plotinus strives to show how Socrates is uniquely one in spite of the pull of the many. Socrates is on the verge of being many by being constituted by genus, species, and innumerable other communicable properties; he is also one who is scattered in time and dispersed in space; and, in his own life, he is distracted through the manifold perceptions and ideas pervading his life. Yet, for Plotinus, in spite of this ontological and psychological dispersion, Socrates may find a perfect unified version of himself outside of time and space which serves as his guide for being truly himself.

In The Theological Distinction, as we are construing it in this work, this "heavenly form" of Socrates is a constitutive part of the divine essence and this relation to Socrates is not a Cambridge relation nor is the divine essence's existing "Socratically" or having the property of Socrateity a Cambridge property. God is Godself, God's own being and not my being. I am not *my being* with the same right that God is God's being because I am a creature and God has given me my being. However, as we have claimed, it is an inherent part of The Theological Distinction that God is identical with the perfection of all being. God is infinite, unconditioned, independent To Be/Being. Thus Augustine and Thomas have insisted that God of necessity is more myself than I am myself because he gives to me my being myself. As N. Balthasar once put it: "He is me by excess; he is by excess the perfection of all finite being. He is supra-myself [*hyper-moi*; JGH: both eminently myself and beyond myself] and it is in this sense that he is not myself; God is supra-everything because pure, unique To Be…. It is by default that I am not another being than myself; it is by the excess of the perfection of God that God is only Godself."[36]

In the ordinary context it seems puzzling to say that Socrates could not have come to exist unless, prior to existing, it was *possible* that *he* exist or unless Socrates in his unique essence existed as a possibility. How can we refer to *him*, who does not yet exist? Do we mean that the unique essence "Socrates" exists as a prior possible existence such that prior to his becoming actual there was (is) "he himself," but not yet actual, i.e., there was (is) Socrates who was (is) able to become actual?

Further, does any prior existence of "Socrateity" not presuppose the individual essence as revealed in first-person experience (see Book 1, Chapters II–IV), so that when we refer to "Socrates" or (quasi-indexically) "he himself" we refer to him as necessarily self-aware, and yet believe also that he is not yet actual? Can one whom we refer to as self-aware (and therefore affirming himself with an *Urdoxa*), not be an actual being? Because Socrates was not before he was actual, he didn't exist nor was he self-aware before he existed. But then how can we say that it was possible that *he*, the unique haecceity, have existed? Can we carry out this discussion exclusively in the third-person, leaving aside our considerations that what we refer to as Socrates of necessity requires first-person self-experiencing?

We might say that like Socrates Hamlet and Lear, whom we know as having clearly first-person self-awareness and who for us are present in the third-person quasi-indexically as unique essences or haecceities, and in all cases "as if they were real," do not actually exist but they are so real as imagined persons that they very well could exist. They are present as intrinsically rich haecceities with, of necessity, intricate self-awareness, but they are not actual and not exemplified in the actual world.

The clear and legitimate worry here is that the essence, "Socrates," or "Socrateity," would *exist* as a unique self-aware essence but it might not have become actual.[37] The concern is with setting up a possible world with its own kind of potential existence that parallels the actual world. (Cf. our brief skirmishes with "possible-world theory" in Book 1, Chapter I, especially §2; also Book 1, Chapter VIII, §8, D.)

Exemplarism of the creator God does not permit the free floating ontological realm of such existing essential possibilities, as in "existing" possible worlds. However, it asserts that essences, in so far as they may be said to have the perfection of form or essence, enjoy, even if they do not actually exist as concrete (created) beings, i.e., are mere possibilities, the actuality of being, in some sense, constitutive of the divine essence. Such an existence, we will suggest, can accommodate the essential first-person awareness of Socrates as well as the third-person senses of haecceity.

Doubtless there are great areas of metaphysical obscurity in terms of determining whether all instances of what we are prepared to call essences or natural kinds themselves have eternal ideal exemplars. Are real properties, not Cambridge ones, what alone matter to God's essence? Similarly we can ask: Does every hair of every head, every leaf of every tree, every tooth of every mouth, every deer tick, every virus, etc., have an eternal exemplar? Is the selving of which Hopkins speaks, i.e., that of the haecceity or and individual essence, spread everywhere in the world – and thus must these "inscapes" not themselves have eternal exemplars? Although I presently do not think myself competent to make a clear pronouncement on this matter, it seems clear to me that what each refers to in first-person reference has an intrinsic individuality in the way a ball of dust or a pile of stones or even a particular stone does not.

We will not attempt to answer these questions here. We simply note that we find compelling Aquinas' view that God knows all singularities *through* knowing Godself's own essence. Whether holding this view commits one to the view that the singularities which are supposits or substances are not only haecceities but of necessity also "selves" in a panpsychist sense we leave unanswered. That did not seem to be Aquinas' own view. Further, the "inscapes" which Hopkins brought to light may be said to be often typically "merely intentional objects" which have no substantial being in themselves and for themselves.

An obvious problem for the position holding that all the forms are exemplarily in the divine is not merely conceiving in what sense the divine is or is not that of which it is the exemplary cause, but in conceiving in what sense the divine and the exemplary causes or "ideas" are one and the same. In general everything is "somehow" contained unifiedly in the Godhead's self-presence, and therefore enjoying a measure of both distinctness and indistinctness. Let us spell this out.

§4. Three Aspects Under Which an Eternal Essence or Idea Can Be Made Present

It would appear that the essence, foremost for this work, the unique "myself," can be made present to our speculative theological consideration in three aspects. This threefold would, however, seem to be of necessity not only available to the philosophical theologian but also to God. In so far as these three aspects are aspects of the same we have to do with the unity; in so far as this sameness is not a strict identity but rather a sameness (admitting differences), we approach a matter in which the essence of the "myself" appears to have the plurality of three distinct modes of being.

One aspect is its being indistinguishable and inseparable from the divine essence; this of course is a purely speculated and postulated presentation for philosophy but is a theological commonplace of the creationist theology of The Theological Distinction. We will later dwell on what might be the mode of "presence" of the haecceity or unique essence "for" the divine in this case. Here we may note with Aquinas that the divine act of "simple apprehension" of God's essence apprehends "more than" the divine knowledge of "vision" which is a knowing of all that God has created through God's knowing of his essence. God's simple apprehension wherein God knows Godself through knowing the divine ideas is a knowing of God as imitable and able to be participated in. It is a knowing of "more" because it apprehends the possible and not merely the actual creation. This is not merely to say that the divine knowledge of the infinite possibilities of creation that lie in the divine essence exceed what God knows in knowing creation (through the "knowledge of vision") but also that "simple apprehension" in contrast to "vision" indicates a different mode of knowing of the divine essence.[38]

The second aspect is also a speculated mode of presence *for* the divine. This aspect assumes the thesis of The Theological Distinction, i.e., there need not be exemplifications and that creation need not be, but whatever excellence (or perfection or "form") creation has is pre-contained in the divine essence. The unique individual essence of first-person self-awareness, i.e., how we are for ourselves in a way that we can be for no one else, thus is necessarily a result of the creature being known by God because each is who she is by being known and being known by God through God's knowing Godself's essence, and in this second mode, God's essence *as able to be communicated.* Each is *whatever* God knows her to be, and this *whatever* in this case is the same as *whomever.* In so far as the former, i.e., *whatever,* refers to the *sort* of person one ideally is, it is not *identical* with the knowledge of the *whomever* as the "myself." It of course will be knowledge of the *same,* but it is not strictly speaking knowledge of what is identical. In the second mode God knows the "myself" as part of the divine essence as imitable and communicable, and therefore of necessity knows the "myself" in its perfect form, i.e., God knows, in knowing God's essence as imitable, "myself" as "supra-myself," i.e., knows "myself" both eminently in regard to myself (as the created myself of JG Hart) and beyond this created myself, because it is God's own essence as imitable. *Quoad nos* this is the "myself" in its true self, the Who one is coincident with the ideal *sort* of person one is called to be. The "truth of this identity" is, as Thomas Merton has put it, the work we are called to share in creating with God.

Thus the second aspect has not the absolute necessity of the first aspect or mode, i.e., in the first mode the unique essence of "myself" is inseparably one with the divine essence. In this second aspect the essence is envisaged as a model or exemplar of creation. *Quoad nos,* it is a task we are called to do. With the model or exemplar we have to do with not merely the divine in its essential absolute unity and simplicity but we have otherness introduced because in the second mode the divine's self-awareness is not of absolute identity: Because in this second mode God is now present *to* Godself, God is now present to Godself as "othered" or God is present as other to Godself. Because of the shift from the first mode of absolute unity and simplicity to the otherness of God in God's being present *to* Godself we shall urge thinking of God's self-presence in the second mode as intentionally-reflectively present to Godself.

This otherness is already present in Aquinas's view that in knowing God's essence through God's "ideas" God not only knows Godself but knows Godself as able to be participated in by what is other than Godself. In this theme of exemplarity the divine self-awareness has "introduced" to Godself and God's self-awareness what is not identical with the divine. In this sense what is other to or other than the divine has been introduced. (See our discussion in the next sections.)

The third aspect or mode is the one that we have dealt with in the earlier chapters of Book 1 of this work, i.e., it is the essence of the manifest actual (created) being, foremost for our interests, the "myself." This creaturely being is the strongest sense of what is other to and other than the divine.

In terms of our discussion of vocation and the true self, we may say that the second aspect or mode is for Godself the divine the exemplary form to which each created "myself" is invited; for each self this telos is the home of the true self and is its vocation. To say that the first aspect is the telos would be to suggest that the creaturely "myself" is cable of becoming identical with God or that the "myself" as divine is capable of a having an ideal form or telos. It seems to us that some of Meister Eckhart's formulations leaned in the former direction, i.e., they seem to suggest both that the third aspect is identical with the first and that the third aspect was called to be identical with the first. We saw also that this was a central problem in some figures in Sufism.

Assuming that all three aspects are aspects of the same, but not therefore identical, which aspect does God know in knowing and choosing me "before the foundation of the world" (cf. *Ephesians* 1:4)? It cannot be the third, because I do not yet exist. It cannot be the first, because in this case God does not know me but Godself. It would seem to have to be the second aspect, i.e., God's knowing Himself as able to be participated in. This view is rejected by Barry Miller as impossible because although God

> might conceive of a description that would be satisfied by exactly one individual, he could not conceive of the precise individual who would satisfy it. It might be satisfied by Peter, but equally it might be satisfied by any clone of Peter. In other words, God could conceive of there being exactly one individual that would satisfy the description, but could not conceive of exactly *which* one it would be.[39]

Such a view, of course, runs contrary to the basic thesis of both volumes of this work, i.e., it holds that a person, Peter, in his unique individual essence, is able to be grasped by an identifying description, and therefore is able to be cloned. But the view we propose is that God's pre-knowing of each of us is not merely a general knowledge expressed by, "*Whoever* has such and such properties is Peter;" but rather God will have *singular* knowledge of the unique essence that is the "myself" of the person Peter.

Knowing this essence in the first mode must be distinguished from God's knowing this same "myself" as exemplar and as created incarnate person. In knowing
the latter God is not knowing merely Godself, but Godself as reflected in the person
and his life. And in as much as the classical theology requires both simplicity and
omniscience of God, there is the further implication that in knowing the unique
haecceity there is the foreknowing of the person whose individual essence it is –
and if there are many incarnations of the haecceity, God will foreknow the variety
of personalities. In which case God would not merely have a general knowledge,
e.g., of "*Whoever* is the sole person to be [i.e., to have the distinguishing properties
or descriptions] F, G, H will deny Christ when challenged by a serving girl." But
further he has the *singular* knowledge expressed by "*Peter* will deny Christ when
challenged at T_n by the serving girl, Rima."[40] It is of interest here that the philosopher's reconstruction of God's foreknowledge must assign to God a knowing in the
third-person. It cannot be expressed in the second-person, e.g., to Peter, for the obvious reason that the addressee does not exist. Nor can it be expressed in an analogous
divine first-person because in this mode or aspect we do not have to do with Peter
and his life but with the "myself" of Peter as an ingredient of the divine essence. In
the "calling forth" of Peter from the exemplar emergent out of the divine essence
Peter is called in his unique singularity as an individual essence – and the tradition,
as articulated in the dogma of the divine eternity and in the most basic dogma of
The Theological Distinction, draws the philosophically problematic implication
that the full concretion of the historical Peter is foreknown in this calling.

The knowledge of the "myself" of Peter is not identical with the knowledge of
Peter the person and his personal life. The former, we are maintaining, is, in the first
aspect, one with the divine essence and one with Godself's self-knowledge; this is
not true of the divine knowledge of the unique essence as able to be participated in,
nor is it true of what is known of the contingencies that go to make up the "myself"
personified in the creature, Peter. Given an adequate theory of the relation between
time and eternity (an aspect of the relationship between God and the world), we
may be permitted to entertain divine foreknowledge of the historical personhood as
a theological possibility, if not dogma; but wrestling with this would take us too far
afield to do justice to its complexities. (Cf. our discussion of some of these issues
in connection with Leibniz above in Chapter VI, §2, D and the proposals regarding
"eternity" in Book 1, Chapter VII, §3.) The necessity or possibility of this dogma of
foreknowledge is tied to the position that divine knowledge of contingent historical
events is a Cambridge relation and not a "real one," i.e., it is not one without which
the divine essence could not be or one which is constitutive of the divine essence.
Therefore the ontological status of divine foreknowledge is not such that it transforms the divine essence, e.g., its eternity into temporality.

The absolute transcendence of God is secured in a teaching such as that of
St. Thomas, one very much tied to The Theological Distinction, that with the
creation of creatures by God the divine essence itself cannot be communicated to
creatures or participated in.[41] Clearly some sense of God is able to be participated
in – this is the whole point of exemplarism. Yet the dogma of God the Creator
wishes to maintain an "essential" distinction between God and creatures, between

God's *own* essence and "life" and that of creatures. We propose that it is analogous to the distinction we make between sharing our life and the impossibility of sharing our ipseity. I can share my ideas, dreams, possessions, projects, etc. but there remains the untraversible abyss of my remaining me and you. In some forms of pantheism, panentheism, and process theology this teaching about the incommunicability of the divine essence is contradicted. (Cf. our discussion especially in §§8–9 below.) But here we have also been arguing that whereas God's essence is incommunicable, what each ipseity refers to as "myself" is not absolutely other to the divine subjectivity. That is, there is a sense in which the unbridgeable abyss of my remaining me is not only traversable by intentionality but the absence of such an abyss is precisely what is meant by God's being the creator of me.

When we say God is *hyper-moi* there is a sense in which we are saying that God is "myself" both eminently and as a limit case. But we clearly have difficulties with such claims. Is it not perverse to say I know the "myself," which is complete in itself, through a *via eminentiae* or infinitization or limit-simpliciter? Our answer has been that even though the "myself" is always of necessity itself and as the non-sortal referent of a non-ascriptive reference does not admit being a regulative idea we may posit it as the entelechy of the person, as what constitutes the infinite ideal of the true self of the person. As such, we may speculate, it reflects the way the unique essence exists in the essence of God. In knowing empathically the perfections which are the unique essences we, by the *via eminentiae*, i.e., in apperceiving them through the infinitizing dialectic of the *via eminentiae*, know a glimmer ("similitude") of the divine essence in which these perfections are found as a limit case. And the notion that the "myself" which is inseparably one with God's essence and as the limit case for any infinitizations of, e.g., the myself as the personification of JG Hart, we do not wish to suggest that the divine essential "myself" is as different from the created "myself" as a horse from a rocking horse. The crucial consideration is that each "myself" is "given" by its being known by the divine essence's knowing itself in the three different modes. I myself cannot know myself as I am known in the divine's self-knowing nor as I am given to the divine as communicable. Nor can I know myself as God knows me in creating me. Here is a sense in which the "myself" as part of the divine essence is improperly a limit case. All knowledge of "myself" – even though "I myself" am not a regulative idea as myself personified is – presupposes this limit case of my being first of all known by God in God's self-knowing. This is the presupposed unfathamable limit case at which all knowing, even the "myself" of itself, aims.

Thus the exemplary home of the unique essence of the "myself" in the divine essential self-consciousness is absolutely transcendent and not able to be participated in. Only with the *ratio* or exemplar is the possibility created for the communication of the unique essence of "I myself" outside of the divine essence, and by implication of my created "I myself" in the divine essence.

"Outside the divine essence" is not a pre-existing sphere in which God posits things. Rather it signifies the realm of being of the created as such, i.e., as effected by the act of creation. Therefore it signifies what is outside of or transcendent to the divine act and essence,[42] i.e., it signifies the realm of the "Cambridge relations."

It also negates the view of some competing theologies that the divine essence itself can be communicated and participated in, so that for these there is *no sense* in which we may speak of an "outside the divine essence."

According to the dogma of The Theological Distinction, with the creation of the "myself" according to the exemplar, God bestows *esse*, and along with it a *sameness* or *likeness* to the divine essence; but I myself do not share in or become one or identical with the transcendent divine essence. The ancient teaching applies here: As one does not properly say "I resemble my likeness in the mirror," but rather "The likeness resembles me," so the divine essence (encompassing the uncreated essence of the "myself") does not resemble the created "myself" but it is the other way around. The "myself" personified in JG Hart is a Cambridge relation for God; but for JG Hart the exemplary "myself" is a real relation; God's essence as the source of the being of JG Hart is a Cambridge property of God; God's essence as containing the "myself" which JG Hart embodies or personifies is a real relation for JG Hart. But God's essence *qua* the foundation of the exemplar of the "myself" of JG Hart is not a Cambridge property for Godself but a proper divine name or "attribute," i.e., an ingredient of the absolutely simple and unified divine essence.

The various aspects under which God appears to us because of the finite and shifting perspectives we bring to what we intend under "God" are traditionally called the "names" or "attributes" of God. These properties, e.g., compassion, love, justice, mercy, etc., derive, of course, from our experience within the world. But the dogma of The Theological Distinction empowers us to posit not only that God is the ultimate source of these but that God has some such perfections analogously not only as the limit-simpliciter in a *via eminentiae* or infinitization of excellences but as limit cases, and that therefore these properties belong intrinsically to God's essence and not merely as Cambridge properties which are God's as a result of God's "ad extra" or creative agency in regard to the world.

The basic dogma of the creator God teaches that God of necessity actually possesses all possible perfection. A perfection is understood classically as the actuation of a potential "form," i.e., a quality, excellence, property, or essence. Because there is no perfection that the divine does not have actually, the theological sense of perfection here alters the classical sense, i.e., in what is referred to by the perfection of God there is no actuation of potential perfections. The perfections or "forms" which the divine essence contains includes not only the perfections of this actual world, and all possible worlds, but all the possible perfections that are beyond the reach of what we mean by "world." But, again, the source of the actual perfections is not some eternal realm of "the possibles" that pre-exists as awaiting actuation nor is the divine capable of a "self-actualization" through creative expressivity. For The Theological Distinction, the source of actual perfections is the actuality of the divine essence – no where else. As transcendental phenomenology does not permit possible world theory to displace the actual transcendental I and govern philosophical analysis, so the dogma of the creator God does not permit the elevation of possibility or possible being to the status of the source of all perfection in place of the actual essence of God.

Now let us dwell on this matter of the sense in which these distinct perfections, forms, essences, or qualities may be predicated of God. We can only cautiously say that the first mode, i.e., the "myself" as the foundation of the exemplar for JG Hart, can be predicated of God because, according to the core of the tradition which we are following, especially the Thomist tradition, the constitutive proper names of God are not properly predicates but identical with the divine essence. Because the divine subject is not different from the divine essence and the constitutive essences are one with the divine essence it is somewhat misleading to say the essences are able to be predicated of God.

Yet we may say that the first mode is able to be predicated of God *in so far as* it, as an essence, enjoys a sameness relation with the other modes or aspects of the essence. With "sameness" we have difference introduced; not so with strict identity. And these other (two) modes, i.e., the exemplary eidos "myself" and the "myself" personified in the creature JG Hart, although aspects of the same "myself," are not perfectly identical with the first mode and therefore not identical with the divine essence. The exemplar or *ratio* of "myself" can be communicated in a way the divine essence is not communicated. The divine essence, analogous to an existing "myself," cannot be, properly speaking, communicated or shared with another. And although the unique essence of "myself" can be creatively communicated to the creature JG Hart from God's essence, it, by reason of being the unique essence of the person, JG Hart, cannot be communicated to another created person. Such essences are haecceities, unique essences, not mere forms.

Obviously the third mode cannot be predicated of God without eliminating the distinction between God and creatures as defined by The Theological Distinction. (Again, this Distinction and its parameters we will discuss below in §§6–8.) If such a predication were possible we would become "modes of God" or Godlets. But each of us in the second mode, which designates the unified divine essence in so far as it can become the manifold *rationes* or exemplars of all creation, may be regarded as a predicate of God (God *has* God's own "ideas" or exemplars). If this mode is confused with the first mode and regarded as part of the divine essence it jeopardizes the divine unity. Further, as there are some divine names or properties, usually negative ones like infinity, eternity, omnipotence, etc., that can be predicated only of God vis-á-vis the created world (as Cambridge properties) there are some inherently creaturely or deficient ones that cannot be even analogously predicated of God, as irascible, weary, polluted, drunk, furious, etc.

As for the analogous appropriate (non-Cambridge) predicates that nevertheless are mirrored by creatures in the world, as "just," "living," and "merciful," we have modified, with Miller's help, the famous answer of Aquinas, i.e., the "way of eminence" (*via eminentiae*). The predicates may be said to point beyond the infinite ideal limit simpliciter to the limit case which essentially transcends the infinitization.

Yet if God is not merely just, merciful, living, etc., by way of creating what we know of these but by being these exemplarily in the sense of the limit case, what of the unique excellences (unique essences) which are Socrates, Xanthippe, Peter, Paul, and Mary? These individual essences present perfections that God created and exemplarily contains and exemplarily *is*. *God is hyper-moi.*

Yet this may not be stated in a way that fails to distinguish the three aspects of "the myself" as modes in which the unique essence may exist. Not only is the unique essence of what each experiences as "myself," and what we experience in lovingly intending the other ipseity, not God but created ipseities, created ipseities cannot be predicated of other substances. Furthermore, they are "singularities" and as such are not communicable or countable in the precise sense that a "myself" cannot be two. (See Book 1, Chapter V, §4.)

In my referring to myself in the use of the indexical "I" as well as in the ineluctable non-intentional self-awareness there is a simplicity of reference. In God's self-reference to Godself in regard to the unique "myself" which is the creature JG Hart there is a synthetic reference because it involves the three modes: First, the "myself" as identical with the divine essence; secondly, the exemplary form of the "myself" which is the ideal of the creature, JG Hart; and, thirdly, the created "myself" of JG Hart who is more or less faithful to the ideal. Our position here is that unless the reference of the *via eminentiae* or "dynamic dialectic," i.e., reference to the limit simpliciter, as itself pointing to the divine limit case, is informed by the distinction of the aspects and modes, especially as these are shaped by The Theological Distinction, to which we will soon turn, absurdities soon surface regarding the theology of the unique essence of the "myself."

In this position the divine essence as the "ground" of the "myself" is a limit case, and in this respect a property or predicable of God. When we consider the unique essence of the "myself"as an actual created ipseity (a Thomist "supposit"), we have to do with what is not properly predicable of any other substance.

In what sense is the "ground" of the unique essence of the "myself" in God a constitutive principle or essence or What? Are the divine exemplars as "essential possibilities," as "What's," the source of the "Who's" each of us is? To assume that the eternal What's are the exemplars of the Who's raises the Sartrean question of whether that does not *eo ipso* destroy the Who's. But more basic is whether the eternal What's must not, in the case of the individual essences, be essential "Who's" to whom it belongs to be eternally uniquely essential self-aware ipseities. But if we posit this do we not threaten the unity of the Godhead with a plurality of existing ipseities constitutive of the divine subjectivity?

Our response is: We threaten the unity only if we posit that the eternal ipseities, which we claim are constitutive of the divine essence, are actually subsistent. Let us attempt to spell this out.

Our view has been that in the case of the "myself" we have a unique essence which is more than a mindless form or unconscious concept, bereft of self-awareness. Rather, we have held that here we have an essence which of necessity has the tautological property of being self-aware of itself as a unique essence. As there is no pain without the awareness of pain, so there is no unique essence which is not self-aware. Its essential being is in its self-awareness. Yet I can *think of* your sciatica pain and it need not exist, and I can *think of* (which is different from *experience*) my sciatica pain and it need not exist. Further, I can intend or think of the "myself" of Peter (through conjuring up his image and his properties) and he need not exist or I be mistaken. But I cannot intend or think of, *on the basis of lived experience*, the "myself" of JG Hart and he/I not exist. (See our discussions in Book 1, Chapters III–VI, especially Chapter VI, §9.)

Yet even though it is necessary that unique ipseities be self-aware, and in this sense it is of their essence to be and be self-aware, this does not mean that they are essences that cannot not be independently in themselves. Rather, their most fundamental essential being and their self-awareness have their home in the divine essence. Even though it belongs to the essence of a "myself" to be self-aware, this distinctive self-awareness in the first mode of the divine essential self-presence can be conceived to be a way of thinking of the infinite richness of the divine self-awareness. The Leibnizian analogy of the endless *petits perceptions* making up the sound of the rush of the waves is perhaps suggestive for the unity of divine self-awareness, but it fails because it gives us a unity that confuses or dissolves the plurality of the individual essences. Further, awareness of waves is an apperception, and what we need here is a non-reflexive self-awareness. See the next section. We will continue to wrestle with the analogies in what follows.

Whereas in the created world an essential self-awareness of a unique essence means of necessity a subsisting existence, a "supposit," an essential self-awareness of a unique essence in the divine essence is not the equivalent of an independent subsisting apart from the divine essence, where the sense of one's self-awareness is absolutely I am me and not you. A finite ipseity's distinctive dignity and glory is precisely its incommunicable essence. But in the first mode, the ipseity's unique essence is immersed in the divine essence "organically." By this we mean it is analogous to the way a pleasure or pain in a bodily member, e.g., a finger, is the pleasure or pain of the whole organ although it is the pleasure or pain in the individual member. I say that "my finger hurts" but also at the same time I may equally say, "I am in pain." (See our discussion of Hopkins' analogy in the next section.)

But here the analogy misleads if it suggests that the unique essence or "myself" already is having experiences beyond its essential self-experience, i.e., is already a person in the world with a history. No, all we have here is the richness of the unique essence as one with and constituting the divine essence.

The life of the essence in what Christians call the life "in the Word" or "in Christ," or the life of what the Sufis call The Perfect Man, i.e., the divine life of the ipseities in the third mode, is not yet a theme. This Christian life has an organic unity wherein the fullness of the experience of the multiple individual essences or ipseities finds a central unity "in Christ."

However, here we may illuminate the first mode by another analogy from the third mode: Whereas the finite mind of a created ipseity may be measured by the richness with which a finite number of ideas or essences inform this mind, the infinite ipseity is measured by Its unique essence that encompasses and surpasses all the essences, whether unique and incommunicable or not. And further the infinite mind of this unique divine essence is a richness measured not only by the way the infinity of ideas or essences inform this mind but also by the way the self-aware essences which are among this infinity inform the divine mind or essence, again, analogous to the richness in the third mode of the life "in Christ." Of course, here we may speak with equal justice of the unique divine ipseity or mind measuring the infinity of essences, and this being the ground of *their* richness.

The divine "myself" is to be thought of as encompassing the unique essence of the innumerable unique essences or ipseities. In contrast, the self-awareness of the created "myself" of whatever person does not encompass any other essence – and that is its singular glory and dignity. As N. Baltasar has put it: It is by default that I am not able to be another than myself. In contrast, it is by excess of God's perfection that God is only Godself, and thereby leaves nothing out.

But the unique essence of any "myself" which is constitutive of the divine essence, which of necessity is a self-awareness of the haecceity of the "myself," cannot be posited as being an autonomous self-awareness or a subsisting person existing independently of the divine essence and apart from the infinite encompassing self-awareness by God of Godself. Rather, the unique essences and self-awareness are precisely the contribution of this haecceity to the richness of God's essence. Further, as constitutive individual essences of the Godhead, albeit as unique Who's, they are necessary with the necessity of what cannot not be. But this is not true of the third mode of the unique essence which by definition is a created, i.e., contingent, subsisting being. This confusion, we have said, is Eckhart's occasional temptation. We return to an essential aspect of this difficult matter in the next section. Ultimately its "resolution" is in the terms of what we are calling The Theological Distinction.

(We may note here that in the Christian tradition created persons are not actual subsistences constitutive of the divine essence, even though their unique essences are constitutive of the divine essence. Only the uncreated persons of the Trinity are subsistent Persons constitutive of the divine essence. Perhaps we can say that this totally interpersonal Godhead makes difficult any talk of any "its" or "whats" constitutive of the interpersonal "Godhead.")

§5. Divine Awareness of the Unique Ipseity

We have claimed that The Theological Distinction illuminates by way of providing a conceptual scheme for thinking about the metaphysics involved in the theology of vocation. Along the way we have looked at the focal speculative theological issue of "exemplarism" of the "myself." We studied three aspects under which an eternal essence such as the "myself" may be presented. As important as it is to keep these aspects distinct, it is no less important to recognize the sameness, albeit not the identity, of these aspects. Because these aspects are non-identical aspects of the same we said they may be thought of as modes of being of the unique individual essence, "myself": First and most originally, as inseparably one with the divine self-awareness and essence; secondly, as the exemplar for one's creation; thirdly as one's created unique essence. To further prepare for our discussion of The Theological Distinction's utility in these matters we wish to enter into a more detailed consideration of how each essential ipseity can be sustained in its unique status, e.g., in its non-reflexive *self*-awareness and ownmostness as well as in its unique perspective on the world, while being known by a divine creator and absolute omniscient knower. Because, again, this is essentially a philosophical-*theological* problem, nothing we have discussed prior to Chapters VI and VII necessitates such a reflection. Yet already it is adumbrated in Plotinus in so far as *Nous* is able to be thought of as an independent conscious mind knowing the plurality of essences constituting the cosmos as well as the individual essences that make up the true selves of the historical persons and, in addition all of which as knowings and known comprise *Nous* itself. We thus begin a meditation on this venerable issue within the context of especially Christian philosophical theology.

If one could entertain the assumption that one's essential unique ipseity is indeed an individual essence of *eternal* validity and therefore known by God in God's knowledge of Godself, then the claim that this is not God's knowledge of one's own creaturely self but God's knowledge of Godself would seem plausible. But, is not such a knowledge of God of Godself still an ignorance of me as created by and other than God? How does God therefore know me as an independent free being if I am of necessity exemplarily inseparable from the divine essence? If I, as the "myself" who I am, am of necessity inseparable from the divine essence then am "I myself," i.e., what we earlier referred to as the "myself" in the third mode, not swallowed up in the divine subjectivity?[43] Again: If God is "posited" as the absolute subject who can never become an object, and if God is posited as a subject for whom everything that is other than God is necessarily posited as an object, and this objectness, of me myself in particular, is posited by definition as more real than my subjectivity,[44] then I exist in an essentially alienated way, i.e., "my true self" is posited as an object of Another, and I must learn from an infinitely inaccessible Outside of me what I must be in order to be me and what I am supposed to be.

According to such formulations, when we grant validity to ipseity we undermine divinity, and when we grant validity to divinity we undermine ipseity.

One way of thinking about this matter is to think of the divine or absolute consciousness as the whole and the finite consciousnesses as the parts. To use a metaphor current at the time of William James, "we are but syllables in the mouth of Allah."[45] As the proposition, the *Logos*, might be thought to come first in the order of being, so what is first is *the entire sentence*, preceding all the clauses, words, syllables, phonemes, etc.[46] The entire sentence is "the whole show," "the universe," or "the absolute." We, according to the power of our rank as thinkers, take in a clause, word, syllable, or letter of the sentence. What we are or exist as is to be as the absolute knows us to be, along with everything else the absolute knows.

Of course, this view acknowledges that we have an apparent existence to ourselves, i.e., enclosed in our separate, isolated, ownness, and essentially without, or external to, most other things and actually directly related to only a few. But for this position, ownness, unique ipseity, solitude, self-awareness, and essential privacy are nothing but ignorance and an incapacity to be united in will and understanding with the absolute and an inability to include the divine comprehensiveness in our point of view. Each of us is the metaphorical word, syllable, or letter of the absolute's cosmic *Logos* or proposition. The absolute knows the same as we do in so far as the absolute knows us, the letters or syllabi; but the absolute knows also something novel, i.e., the whole *Logos*, or proposition, which is the universe. The absolute knows what we know, and more; it knows all the "each's" and the whole sentence as whole.

This theory may seem to propose that the divine absolute consciousness consti-tutes all the each's, but it can also be conceived in such a way as to be constituted by them. This would be so, even if one maintains that what it knows is not merely what they know but a novel higher-order unity. If it knows through their know-ing and in this sense knows what they know, it is constituted by them as well as constituting them.

Husserl himself entertained such a view and faced similar problems. He put it this way: If we think of God as an "all-consciousness" which has the capacity to peer into the consciousness of other finite subjectivities *by a means other than empathy* (which of necessity keeps intact the otherness of the other) "the being of God" would have to "hold in itself all other absolute being" of the other subjec-tivities. But for Husserl each subjectivity may lay claim to being "absolute being" because of the incommunicability of first-person experience. Thus for Husserl, in contrast to the position sketched above which we borrowed from William James, the "each's" too are absolute subjectivities in the transcendental phenomenological sense, but are not the absolute all-consciousness. (This in fact is a view closer to the metaphysical pluralism James himself advocated.) But Husserl is not sure whether it is conceivable that the divine all-consciousness contain the plurality of absolute subjectivities in its own being.[47] This, we maintain, requires a move of faith toward The Theological Distinction, and Husserl rightly saw that transcendental phenom-enology as such did not have anything to do with such a dogma. Further, this matter of inclusion is precisely the problem of knowing the ipseities as eternal essences constitutive of the divine as well as knowing these as other, as creatures, having their own created being.

Husserl's way of puzzling out the matter stands in tension with the position of Kant's *archetypus intellectus*, because such a view required that the divine know creatures with the intimacy of the divine stream of consciousness.[48] In one medita-tion (in *Ideas* I) Husserl wonders how absolute subjectivities, which are essentially unique ipseities with inviolable spheres of "ownness" could be held within the sphere of ownness of the absolute divine all-consciousness without being parts of the divine all-consciousness.

Without reaching any philosophical resolution to this fundamental issue, i.e., by his not resolving the problem of how the ownnesses are sustained in a divine all-consciousness, a resolution whose intelligibility eludes the philosopher, Husserl turns his attention to the problem of a divine all-consciousness of what these absolute consciousnesses know. He proposes that we consider the divine all-consciousness as a coordinator of the fields of perception of absolute I's, where God sees something from one side, e.g., with my absolute consciousness, and "at the same time" from the other side with the consciousness of the other absolute consciousness, e.g., yours. Of course, this contrasts with my absolute consciousness which would know perceptu-ally only what is in my field, and I would not have a perception based on another absolute consciousness' field of perception. I can, of course, in empathy apperceive what you perceive, or intend emptily what you perceive on the basis of what you tell me, or, given my earlier and/or anticipated experiences, perceive the thing as having not only my perspective, but, sequentially also I can experience your perspective or I can remember my no longer actual one and/or my expected imagined one, or I can apperceive your remembered one and your expected imagined one.

In the Husserlian hypothesis God sees the thing with all of our consciousnesses, yours and mine, and all the others. God constitutes the manifold of such perceptions as a unity in the divine all-consciousness and establishes as an apperception that of which these perceptions are as one same thing and within the one same world. (Other "worlds" would still be within World as the ultimate horizon of each and the horizon of the divine all-consciousness – if we presume the all-consciousness would also have a synthesized horizon comprised of the horizons of each.) But the all-consciousness would not enjoy the monads' absolute version of the world in a sequential flow but altogether, somewhat like how I can see the thing and its mirror image at once, not sequentially – even though neither my perception nor the other's is a mirror image.

But then Husserl asks, what if one I judges **A** and the other I judges **not A**? My judging **A** does not exclude that the you judge **not A**. Does the all-consciousness both believe **A** and **not A**? At the same time? Sequentially? Does the all-consciousness itself not judge (i.e., does it "bracket" its judgment) where it finds "within it" a judging by a finite absolute consciousness? Does it exercise a kind of epoché?

In this unpublished meditation, Husserl offers no real solution here except to posit that the unifying all-consciousness "must not in any case be absorbed in the individual monads. It encompasses them, but at the same time it is still an excess of consciousness which produces the unity of consciousness between the separated ones." Husserl further posits that the all-consciousness is an "I of all the I's" and thus an absolute willing that impels all the finite absolute consciousnesses to transcend what is given and pursue the "beautiful and the good." He further suggests that all the finite consciousnesses are mere objectifications of the unfolding divine activity.[49]

For Husserl, the divine strives through the monads for a unifying synthesis, a kind of "omniprofile" or "field of fields" that reflects the actual achievements of the All of monads, and thus is confronted with contradictions, discrepancies, dissonances, etc. But the divine also is more than the all of monads and thus is not absorbed in any or all of them. Therefore it not only produces a less than actual ideal synthesis but protends a higher ideal synthesis and urges each of the monads beyond the actual achievements toward a deeper unity and harmony.[50]

Again, this hypothesis sketched by Husserl does not deal with the most basic issue: How can God know the absolute monads in their first-person ownmostness? Perhaps because this seems unresolvable he slides in the direction of a more finite God very much resembling that of the late Scheler (See §11 below.) To be the infinite creator God which knows the monads in their ownness the divine being would have to "hold in itself" all the monadic being, but whether this is intelligible is questioned by Husserl. And in his panentheistic sketch they become part of the life of the "divine entelechy"; they become the means and "objectifications" of this divine life.

In what sense do they become objectifications, while also being within the divine being? Frege raised the same basic question here which Husserl himself raised in §43 of *Ideas*: If my presentations or the entire content of my consciousness were at the same time the content of a more comprehensive divine consciousness, would that not mean that I myself would be part of the divine being; and if so, would they be truly and really *my presencings*? Would I still be their substrate, pole, and bearer?[51] These are questions we already raised in conjunction with Plotinus and Christianity and to which we now return.

Basic objections to the absolute consciousness deal with how the absolute or universal self, to use Hopkins' words, "can taste this taste of self as I taste it." In the framework of the dogma of God the Creator, things and selves are not merely "there" as thoughts *for* the creative mind, they have a real *esse* and subsistence in themselves. Further, if these subsistents or supposits exist each in themselves and *for themselves*, i.e., if these are truly selves experiencing their unique selfhood and ownness, then the sense of privacy is not pejorative, e.g., it is not the mere privation of ignorance of the whole, deficiency of attention, and selfishness of will. Ipseity as self-presence manifests in the first-person an individual essence. This haecceitas has a real being which is its being experienced by and for itself. Regardless of what the absolute mind might think the ipseity or monad ought to be, its reality is surely in part in its self-appearing: The reality of egoic self-conscious beings is in their being experienced by themselves, in their own *percipi*. Each monad's phenomenality is its being and the phenomenon is first-person ownness and irreducible first-person awareness – and vice-versa: Its being is in its lived experiencing of itself in its uniqueness in the first-person. (Cf. our discussions in Book 1, Chapters II–V.)

Further, if we grant that the absolute knows the whole, it is also true that the each's are each also a whole as an individual essence. In this sense there is a kind of perfection in the each's over and above their being parts of a whole.

Further, the absolute's *consciousness* of the "whole" is not simply reducible to the "each-consciousness," understood as the parts of the content of the whole of which the absolute consciousness is conscious. The metaphor of being a "sentence in the mouth of Allah" does indeed suggest that absolute universal consciousness also knows the novel whole which the "each's" cannot know. But over and above this the absolute too is an ipseity, a self-awareness, an analogous "I myself" that none of the "each's" can be aware of except perhaps in the second- or third-person.

The absolute consciousness or self might be analogously compared with how *I* suffer when my finger is in pain. While the finger is in pain from, e.g., the burning of a candle flame, I am in pain. Now suppose that we think of the finger as being analogously a self or personal being without ceasing to be *my* finger. Thus I could still use it and feel it. (This seems to be implicitly the direction of Husserl's thought, and G.M. Hopkins attempts to flesh it out.[52]) If I hold the finger to the flame, there is clearly the difference that the "whole self" of the finger will be scorched, but "to me the scorching only of one finger." If we take this in a moral direction and imagine that *I* put my finger in the flame, then *I* am guilty of self-mutilation but the finger is innocent; if the finger takes the initiative *I* suffer the mutilation and loss of the finger, but "to my finger itself it is selfmurder." Or if we think of it in terms of an act of self-sacrifice, then the finger's deed is nobler, because it is a holocaust, but for me "it was the consuming of a part only." Hopkins concludes from this analogy: "Though then I most intimately share my finger's feeling of pain, for indeed it is to me and to it one and the same, I do not share its feeling of self at all and share little, if I share any, of its guilt or merit, fortune and fate." This being so, "then the universal mind is outside of my inmost self and not within it; nor does it share my state, my moral standing, or my fate."[53] This being "outside" we may take to be a deficiency in the capacity of this analogy to accommodate the position Hopkins wishes to advocate, both in regard to the first mode or aspect of the "myself" but especially for the third mode.

Further, as each self as an existing person (in the third mode) is inseparable from its world, i.e., each ownness is inseparable from what it displays, desires, and hopes for, so in this kind of theistic view the absolute itself would have its ownness and its field. And thus the universal absolute self would have a self and a relation different from all the "each's" and the "each's" would have selves and worlds different from everything else, including the universal absolute self or consciousness. This means not only that there is the numerical difference but the universal absolute self "exists outside" the "each's" and does not truly indwell the interior self of any of the "each's," and therefore there is not really a universal absolute self which would be "selved" in every other self. Hopkins gives voice then to Sartre's dilemma: If there be such a universal self, it alone is the true self and the "each's" selfless, or if they are truly selves the universal is selfless.[54]

The upshot of such a dilemma might result in a theism wherein God is in certain respects finite, i.e., is deficient in the knowledge of the first-person perspective of the "each's" or created persons. Basic to the God's knowledge of others would be an analogous kind of empathy (or presencing of the Other in her otherness). The finite "each's" or monads or centers of consciousness and ownness would be essentially transcendent to the all-consciousness or the trans-consciousness. Before we look at Hopkins' conclusion on this matter let us attend to another perspective which helps us see the motivation for the position Hopkins wishes to maintain.

Recently, in place of empathy (*Einfühlung*, as this is understood in transcendental phenomenology; see Book 1, Chapter IV), the theme of the knowledge of other minds has found fertile insights by featuring indirect discourse and quasi-indexicals, which, of course, for the Husserlian always presuppose the work of empathic perception. Whereas indexical reference is a result of our first-person experience, and whereas we cannot know the indexical first-person experience of others, we gain knowledge of their sphere of ownness through their bodily expressiveness, not least of which is the use of language, and we signal to others our understanding of other persons' first-person indexical reference by the use of quasi-indexicals. Let us remind ourselves of this distinction. (For indexicals see Book 1, Chapter II.)

The proposition, "The Distinguished Professor believed that he himself did not adequately prepare his lecture" is to be distinguished from "The Distinguished Professor believed that he did not adequately prepare his lecture." In the second case, the sentence is such that it might mean, e.g., that the speaker believes that the Distinguished Professor believed that not he himself, but "he," i.e., someone else, did not adequately prepare his lecture. With the *quasi-indexical*, "he himself," in the first rendition the speaker rehearses or impersonates an other's own indexical reference, in this case, the distinguished professor in question who might have said or thought, e.g., "I sure gave a bad lecture today and I did not take enough time before class to get it ready," etc. We do not have access to the direct discourse and first-person experience of the other. When we overhear the other's first-person direct discourse, we still do not enjoy it in the first person, and must express it in second- or third-person indirect discourse by quoting what we heard by using the first-person or indirect discourse, as: "He said, 'I did not give a good lecture.'" Nevertheless, we do have, through empathic perception (which is prior to the quasi-indexical achievement) the establishment of the possibility of indirect discourse; and through the achievement of quasi-indexicals, we have a form of indirect discourse which provides us with a way of capturing and expressing another's own confrontation with his first-person experience.

In the theism or panentheism we have been describing, God cannot know other selves in their own *oratio recta*, first-person experience. God can know other creatures' first-person indexical referential propositions only in *oratio obliqua* by means of quasi-indexical propositions. As no one can refer to another by a genuine first-person singular reference, or to another's experience in the other's direct discourse, so God would know other selves only through an analogous empathy and refer to other selves only in analogous second- and third-person references and to their own experience in an analogous indirect discourse and through the analogous use of quasi-indexicals. As we refer to the Distinguished Professor's first-person state of mind with "The Distinguished Professor believed that he himself did not adequately prepare his lecture," so God would know of the Distinguished Professor's inner life through an analogous appresentation and analogous quasi-indexical reference that would take the expression in the form of indirect discourse.[55]

R.M. Adams interprets this, the position of H.-N. Castañeda, to not really be a serious challenge to divine omniscience, and his reasoning is interesting. Adams takes this position to mean that "it is no more reasonable to insist that an omniscient being must know all such indexical truths than to insist that an omnipotent being must be able to do the logically impossible." He believes that "in an important sense" God knows all the facts in knowing (also) all the quasi-indexical propositions. "Since he is not me, it is no limitation on his cognitive powers that he cannot know that he is me. If exclusively indexical propositions are among the objects of knowledge, nothing that it makes sense to think of someone distinct from me as possibly knowing could be precisely the same thing that I know in knowing who I am."[56]

I interpret Adams here to be saying that God's not being able to know that he is me is the same as not knowing what I know in being and knowing me, and both of these are the same as God's not being able to contradict himself. Not being able to know who I am as the condition of my being me (and not being anyone else) is not something we can expect from God under pain of contradiction.

For Adams there seem to be two equivalences: First there is an equivalence between (a) what I know "in knowing who I am" and (b) my being me. And secondly there is an equivalence between (a) because God cannot be me he cannot know that he is me and (b) because he cannot be me he cannot know what I know "in knowing who I am."

For various reasons throughout this work, but especially in Book 1, we have found reason for accepting the first equivalence. The second equivalence is worrisome. Is Adams right in saying that there is no limitation on God's knowing if God cannot know whom or what someone knows in knowing himself in the first-person? Much of what has preceded in this work has attempted to show that the "nothingness" of first-person reference is not a *nihil negativum*, but rather a richness that proper descriptions cannot grasp. If simply being other than God did not involve the self's ineluctable non-reflexive "taste" of its ipseity, i.e., "knowing who I am as this unique essence," e.g., if it involved merely a contentless empty experience of "here" rather than "there," "now" rather than "not yet," then God's not knowing what I first-personally know in knowing me being me but still nevertheless knowing me would entail the limitation of, e.g., a disembodied spirit. This divine spirit, although Herself having first-personal perspectives, would not have the spatial-temporal perspectives affixed to embodiment. Such a spirit would perhaps grasp conceptually what indexicality-soaked knowledge entailed, but God's not knowing my first-person experience would not be an ignorance of my unique essence because, in this view, there would not be such. All there would be to grasp of my indexicality would be the spatial-temporal location which the divine spirit would know conceptually. God's not being me, and therefore not knowing what I know in my first-personally knowing me, would not entail not knowing who I am and would not entail any ignorance at all on God's side because who I am as an indexical referent would be not a unique essence but the empty indication (like any demonstrative pronoun) of a spatial-temporal location that the all-knowing spirit could conceptually grasp from its universal standpoint ("nowhere") – analogous to my locating a spot on a map. If my knowing me in the first person were merely a *nihil negativum*, i.e., the non-ascriptive reference to what was non-sortal was in fact a reference to "nothing," then God's not being me and not having my first-personal experience would not entail God's not knowing something essential, i.e., it would not entail not knowing who I am in my first-personal being for myself as a unique essence because such would be a chimera, and thus there would not be any ignorance on God's side.

God, in our interpretation of the ancient Christian tradition, must of necessity know the individual essence as a unique essence, and this, we have argued, is known first-personally in non-reflective and reflective self-awareness. But the question is whether when this individual essence is "othered," i.e., when it is *created* and exists as *my* ownness, and if God would not know this, he would not know something "essential." Likewise, when he would know this individual essence as his own and not as my own, would he not be ignorant of something essential?

To say that there is an equivalence between God being other than me and God not knowing whom or what I know in my first-person experience either states that God completely knows me in knowing himself, i.e., there is no difference between God's ownness and mine, or that God is ignorant of me in my first-person experience. For The Theological Distinction the first option is objectionable as pantheistic because it eliminates creation and thus any distinction between God's self-knowledge and knowledge of a creature. The second option, assuming the validity of the early chapters of Book 1, is objectionable in so far as it makes God's knowledge finite in some essential matters.

Here a basic ontological question surfaces for any theological creation theory which aspires to do justice to the divine transcendence and immanence. But in particular it raises the question of how the divine can be more interior to me than I am to myself and not know me as I know myself. The question then is, can God know what I know in my first-person experience without violating first-person experience as what is incommunicably, irreducibly, and non-objectively mine? Similarly: If my self-experience is fundamentally God's experience of Godself, then my experience of me is most basically, in the ultimate scheme of things, God's experience of me as an other or object for God, and it is not God's knowing of me myself in my non-objectifiable ipseity.

G.M. Hopkins, after wrestling unsuccessfully with an analogy aimed at conceiving a universal all consciousness which is "pitched" or "selved" in every other self and which is able to maintain its ownness and the ownness of the "each's," and wherein there is no doubt that the "each's" maintain their ownness in spite of the universal all-consciousness, then offers as a conclusion to his meditation a confessional claim wherein the God, of his Christian, Roman Catholic, tradition, is distinguished from the universal all-consciousness of his unsuccessful analogy. In this brief statement he quotes Augustine to the effect that God is higher than my highest and more interior than my most intimate, *eras superior summon meo et interior intimo meo.* He then adds: "I mean a being so intimately present as God is to other things would be identified with them were it not for God's infinity or were it not for God's infinity he would not be so intimately present to things."[57]

Here God's *interior intimo meo* is an identity with creatures "were it not for God's infinity" which infinity is precisely what enables this extraordinary intimacy. "God's infinity" here probably refers to a Scotist position. The infinite exceeds the finite, "not exactly by reason of any finite measure, but in excess of any measure that could be assigned."[58] God's infinity in this context gives rise to thinking of the divine as not merely beyond the categories of reason and the world but also as supra-personal. But what is it to "think" of the divine as beyond thought, beyond reason, beyond the categories by which we know anything? It is not thought proper if thought is not motivated by thought or what thought makes present. The thought in question here, the thinking of the "divine," is motivated by faith. But this moving beyond what is properly thought and motivated by thought does not make it utterly irrational or necessarily absurd and absolutely unthinkable. We will attempt to say why this is so in connection with the discussion below of The Theological Distinction.

As we have seen, first-person reference, even in its most vulnerable challenge of facing its "double," refers to a unique individual essence. Even facing my *Doppelgänger* I want to say "I am I myself and not you" – whoever you are and whoever I am. In this respect my being a unique individual places me as one unique individual among others, even though what it would mean to count ipseities or persons in the way we can count the number of humans or soldiers is problematic. We can count when we find numerically different instances of a kind or genus. We can count what is meaningfully two or more than one. What we cannot count is the sort of thing of which it is meaningful to say that it cannot be two. Ipseities are uncountable precisely because they are inconceivably two. (See Book 1, Chapter V, §4.) But God is an uncountable individual in a more radical sense because God is not at all of necessity in opposition to another individual ipseity. The transcendental I in its self-reference refers to what is uniquely unique and in this sense there is only one transcendental I. I can not say this I and that I, etc., that is, of I it is first-personally meaningless to think there could be two. Nevertheless I am lived as in relationship to Others whom one addresses as You and who address me as You. As we have insisted, following Husserl, other persons are appresented as saying I to themselves – which is a far cry from saying that the Other is I, that I is conceivably two, or there is properly in first-person experience a plurality of I's. "I" therefore maintains its non-countability in the first-person but becomes present analogously with Others, and therefore countable in its personal being in the world with Others, e.g., as a human, as a musician, as a citizen, etc.

In regard to God, no one can say absolutely and without qualification "I am I myself and not You." And at the same time God's being "I am who I am" in no way involves a reference to me or you nor does it require of necessity distinguishing "Godself" from me or you. We will return to this theme soon. Here we may note that Hopkins' reference to "God's infinity" serves as a cipher to a theological resolution within which a distinctive understanding of God and God's relation to the world is implied. This resolution involves The Theological Distinction. The Theological Distinction establishes a decisive sense of transcendence that guarantees the immanence of Augustine's "You were interior to my inmostness, *interior intimo meo*."[59] This position restates the basic dogma of God the creator which for believers has the status ultimately of mystery because by definition is has to do with "infinity" whose measure is beyond reason. The reflections we have been conducting in this chapter on the possibility of a divine awareness of ipseity merely motivate the possibility of entertaining philosophically The Theological Distinction as a response of faith. They provide no philosophical conclusions. Even though phenomenological-philosophical analogies may help the speculative understanding, one may doubt that there is any strictly phenomenological resolution to this question of the divine awareness of the unique ipseity as this question is raised in, especially, the Christian traditional understanding of God the Creator. We now turn to a brief discussion of "The Theological Distinction" and its application to the issue of the presence of created essences, foremost the individual essence of the "myself," in God.

§6. The Theological Distinction Between God and the World

"The Christian Distinction" between God and the world, as proposed by Robert Sokolowski, is a rich elaboration of certain facets of ancient Christian metaphysics.[60] We have taken the liberty of calling it "The Theological Distinction" between

God and the world. The reason for this name change is the hypothesis that although it seems evident that the distinction is in play in Christian sources, foremost in Aquinas, and it is within this context that Sokolowski magnificently orchestrates it, The Distinction is not utterly alien to the "Abrahamic traditions." Further, it might have some adumbration or approximation in Neo-Platonism, Vedanta, and Buddhism.

The Theological Distinction enables therefore a distinction of "the God of faith" and "the God of reason." The God of faith is God the Creator. This is the fundamental dogma, the dogma of all dogmas, the teaching at the heart of all teachings, the mystery of all mysteries, of The Theological Distinction between God and the world. Perhaps this dogma of God the Creator as the basis for The Theological Distinction is as well the miracle of all miracles, as St. Augustine seemed to think.[61] All the elaborations of The Theological Distinction are tied to this central dogma and mystery. With it properly articulated all other beliefs find their proper sense. In the absence of this articulation all other revealed dogmas may well find a distorted sense. Here "mystery" refers less directly to the phenomenological sense of mystery discussed earlier in this book than to what is revealed by the Church and her traditions, and revealed as beyond reason's capabilities.

It is of interest, however, to note that Kant, in wrestling with the notion of God the Creator as he interpreted what was handed on to him by the Christian tradition, foremost God as the being (*Wesen*) which is absolute and unconditioned necessity, found the very notion itself to evoke in us an experience proximate to that of the holy. It is for human reason a "veritable abyss. Eternity itself, in all its terrible sublimity…is far from making the same overwhelming impression on the mind; for it only *measures* the duration of things, it does not *support* them" (KrV B641). It thus approaches being a "mystery" in the sense that he found it to be both unsatisfactory and unsettling. As to its being intellectually unsatisfactory he notes that we have to seek out a concept which would be such that it would require its necessary existence, or, given the received concept of God, to find some thing that would be absolutely and unconditionally necessary. Actual things, which are the target of genuine knowledge, are things necessarily framed by other things and thus the conditions of the world. They therefore repudiate unconditioned necessity. And a concept which has attached the property of being unconditionedly necessary would seem to refuse the actuality of being something presentable and genuinely knowable, if such is always presentable within the framework of other things and the world and thus in some respect contingent and conditioned, i.e., it would be necessarily presented as unnecessary. As Kant says, both of these projects elude all our efforts to understand the matter.

He then further notes of this unconditioned necessity which is the "true abyss of human reason" that we "cannot put aside nor can we endure the thought that a being which we envisage as the highest of all possible beings, says, as it were to himself: 'I am from eternity to eternity and outside me there is nothing save what is through my will, *but whence then am I?*'"[62] Kant's puzzle is puzzling because he has already given us reason to be bothered by the notion of the project of making present to the mind a being whose existence is absolutely necessary and absolutely unconditioned. This very feat seems impossible if the act of presencing (*Vorstellen*) is capable of rendering only something contingent and conditioned. But then Kant finds especially puzzling the apparently irrepressible question the necessary being asks of itself, "Whence then am I?" That is, "What is My (i.e., God's) condition?"

The reason Kant must stay on this track of the infinite regress of reasons or conditions is not merely because the project of making present, i.e., cognitively placing within what conditions, the absolutely unconditioned being is inherently puzzling and unsatisfactory, but because he is convinced that this absolutely unconditioned being is merely an idea of reason – and this is why we have the inherent and unsatisfactory puzzle. For Kant the best that can be said for the absolutely unconditioned being is that it be something like hidden forces of nature that stand behind all appearings but which themselves elude all observation. The matter (*Sache*) itself might be said to be "given" (through its effects) but we have no way of gaining insight into it. Our problem is solved, however when we regard it as an ideal of reason. In this case we know that it cannot be given in any sense as an object; further, it cannot be said to be inscrutable in so far as we can study it in the way reason unfolds as the dynamism of the mind's inquiry (KrV, B642).

What Kant says here of the notion of the "unconditioned necessity... as the ultimate bearer of all things," is something of special interest for The Theological Distinction: "All support fails us; and the *greatest* perfection, no less than the *least* perfection, hovers without a hold before this project of speculative reason [JGH: of conceiving God], for which it costs nothing to let the one or the other vanish without the slightest hindrance." Here Kant, in reference to the greatest and least perfection which hovers without a hold before this project of speculative reason to make present intelligibly "God," and which perfections may vanish effortlessly without the slightest hindrance, approaches the sense of "world" as the other term of The Theological Distinction. This other term is uniquely necessary and, as Kant suggests, uniquely unnecessary to the divine term of The Theological Distinction (see below).

"Speculative reason," reason propelled by the ideal of reason – and perhaps propelled as well by the theological tradition – is asked to render present to itself what by definition is beyond the framework of reason because God, as unconditioned and absolutely necessary, is beyond the world. And the result is we can neither shove this thought aside nor can we endure it.

For the theological tradition, of course, whether or not the matter is cognitively ineluctable, we can or might shove this thought aside "existentially" because its incomparable importance, or its being precisely "Incomparable Importance Itself," is a matter of a gracious revelation and we are free to accept this grace – even though no one is in a position to say what precisely this acceptance or rejection amounts to in God's eyes.

For Kant, such a necessary unconditioned being is an idea toward which the dynamism of reason is launched. The dynamism of reason has for its correlates the infinite ideas which open reason upon an infinite horizon; as such (the idea of) God cannot be put aside. For Kant, furthermore, we cannot endure it, because to present something before us as actual is to present it as some thing, and therefore as within the wider framework, "the world," as the conditioning framework. This means we cannot make present the absolutely unconditioned necessary being. This places us before an abyss of reason in the face of which one's heart gets dizzy (*macht den schwindlichen Eindruck auf das Gemüt*). Kant is close to acknowledging here that the most basic matter of philosophy opens up the phenomenon of "mystery" not merely as an intellectual conundrum but also as what encroaches on the very foundation of inquiring reason.

For the believer in the biblical tradition the presencing of God *in faith* is not delivered over to the vertigo of speculative reason, even if there is often enough the *mysterium tremendum et fascinans*. By its essence, i.e., *as faith* it cannot be put in this bind of speculative reason. Faith *as faith* does not have to do with what is incoherent and impossible for speculative reason even if it does not shed light in the obvious sense of bringing something to light. That is, the absolutely necessary and unconditioned "illumined" by faith is not present to us as something in the world, and it is the mandate of faith to work against collapsing God to something in the world or within the world's categorial scheme.

Kant is helpful here because he shows "the limits of reason" in making present the creator God. The task resembles the phenomenological one of making the ultimate horizon of the world a perceptual theme or a perceptual object: It of necessity resists and eludes such a project even while remaining the elusive ultimate horizon in all efforts to bring it into view. Similarly, we may hear and grasp the terms used in the explication of The Theological Distinction, but the basic matter at hand essentially fights against our understanding because as Sokolowski says, in his own way echoing Kant and phenomenology as well as the tradition, the fundamental term transcends the framework of understanding, i.e., the world.

Enough of this Kantian interlude on mystery and back to The Theological Distinction and the sense in which it, on its own terms, may be said to be a mystery. (We will return to the interlacing themes in Kant of world, reason, and God soon.)

For a revelation to occur something to which one can assent has to be presented. Thus there is an implicit proposition. But, as we have suggested earlier in this chapter, most of the areas of phenomenological mystery we have touched on, like that of the self being gifted to itself, death's unnamable presence, Existenz's coming to light in limit-situations, what love presences beyond the qualities of the Other, etc., all have to do with an affirmation of what is immanently present as it is rooted in and eclipsed by what is in some respect absent and transcendent. This much is the common ground of the phenomenological and theological senses of mystery. We will have occasion to return to some affinities between the theological and phenomenological senses of mystery later. Here, however, we may note that these distinctions between faith and reason, mystery and evidence, etc., of course have their proper sense as they are used in Christianity, and this consideration weakens the justification of our taking liberties in calling it "The Theological (not merely Christian) Distinction."

We have given enough fiduciary notes and introductions. We want now to offer a distillation of the essence of The Theological Distinction. At bottom The Theological Distinction is a formulation for determining how God is and how the world is and how these are and are not two or one. The basic formulae for The

Distinction run: God plus the world is not greater than God alone; God minus the world involves no diminution of God; the increase in beings (*entia*) in no way is an increase in either the pure *esse* of God or even in *esse* as the theological metaphysical notion which encompasses both the being of God and that of the world; with creation there is not any increase in excellence or goodness (*bonitas*). (We shall return to this last consideration at the end of this section.)

For phenomenology world is the horizon of horizons, the ultimate context or setting which frames all the things that come to light through thoughtful intentionality. Although all distinctions, as the fundamental work of thoughtful intentionality, emerge within the ultimate setting of the world, the work and gift of faith permits another very odd distinction to emerge, the Theological Distinction between God and the world, which is *not* a distinction within the world.

We may distinguish the dogmatic theological-conceptual invitation of faith to entertain the Theological Distinction from the act of faith itself. The former permits us to go outside the ultimate setting of our intentionality, the world, within which are the beings with which we have to do, and to entertain as proposed that this ultimate setting, which itself is the necessary and encompassing matrix for all our thoughtful intentions, is itself not ultimate or necessary, but rather is created. We may entertain, contrary to fact, that "Being" (not a being) as the horizon of the world need not be and, instead, there "is" nothing. We earlier discussed some difficulties in conceiving nothingness, foremost the nothingness of the transcendental I or in the transcendental I knowing its own nothingness. (See Book 1, Chapter VI, §9; also Book 1, Chapter VII, §5; cf. also this Book 2, Chapter I, §§2–4.)

The substantive move toward The Theological Distinction is made when the thinker recognizes that this move is thinkable, i.e., possible, and meaningful.[63] The meaningfulness derives from distinctive "intelligibility" of the dogma or doctrine of God as the basis for The Theological Distinction. This is the thinkability of "infinity" whose measure cannot be measured, but which ventilation of the infinite dynamism of spirit does not destroy thought but invites it to take the wings offered by faith, an offering of light, but also of a darkness which the believer likewise is urged to embrace.

Faith offers to reason an intelligibility "than which nothing greater can be conceived," but this intelligibility is unlike any quiddity, essence, even the unique essence of the "myself." Put most generally, this intelligibility is unlike any Gestalt within the context of reason or the world because it is infinitely beyond these, i.e., it is infinitely intelligible and the absolute source and limit case of all intelligibility. But the intelligibility is not intrinsically evident to us (*quoad nos*), because what is evident has to do with what is within the perceptual world. Or it is within the realm of ideal-formal objects that find a kind of originating base in the world or it is within the sphere of transcendental self-reflection. (These latter two realms of evidence may be taken to be, in an extended theological, but not phenomenological, sense "in the world" as the other term of The Theological Distinction.) Thus its being thinkable means not that it is thinkable in terms of the categories brought forth by reason in its display of the world, but rather it is thinkable that these categories themselves are not the last word and that there is a sense in which they may be transcended in a way that does not destroy them, indeed, in a way that deepens them because it founds them in what is infinitely richer than they are. Thus "thinkable" does not mean that it is either probable, likely, or intelligible *quoad nos*. But its not being intelligible for us does not mean strictly speaking that it is absurd for the believer. Rather, it means we do not have in a filled intention what faith proposes; nor is there insight into the essence of what faith proposes as the divine term of The Theological Distinction.

Even though it would be a mistake that leads to absurdities to confuse the senses of necessity and sufficiency that characterize God with those that characterize the world, it is not clear that for the philosopher it is a mistake leading to absurdity to entertain the possibility that those senses of necessity and sufficiency that characterize the world are not absolutely ultimate and that they themselves are created, and in this sense contingent. And, as we have said earlier, this project of entertaining the proposal that the ultimate senses of necessity characterizing the world are not absolutely necessary does not mean that the necessity we know in the world is abrogated, or to be seen as a fiction, or as "contingent" in the way we, of necessity, recognize contingency in our experience. On the contrary, The Theological Distinction permits an ultimate founding of the density of what we call to intelligibility and necessity of nature and the world. It likewise permits to surface a new sense as well of the contingency of the being of the world; and this latter must be strictly distinguished from the contingency we know in the world.[64]

Inherent in The Theological Distinction is the position that the world or creation, although created, truly is "in itself." It is not a mere idea; its being is not an illusion; its causality is not a chimera; it is not an aspect of God's being. Creation is creation if and only if creation establishes beings that exist self-subsistingly in their own right and have their own being. It exists "by itself" and "in itself." It has in this sense self-sufficiency, subsistence and substantiality. It is in and through itself that it regenerates, propagates, and transforms itself through endless processes and forms of causality. In so far as evolutionary theory offers compelling evidence that nature is self-transforming, that the natural kinds are more or less temporary *Gestalten* of a constantly changing cosmic landscape, then this is part of the sense of the natural created world.

The Theological Distinction, at the same time that it teaches the real substantial subsisting being of the world or creation, holds that the being of the world does not exist with the necessity and subsistence of God's being but that it is created, and "created from nothing." There was nothing of what was other than God "prior" to creation. Creatures are not godlets whereby the foundation of their being would not be in themselves but in the being of God; nor are they a transformation of a primal uncreated eternal stuff, for then their being would be both of a coaeval status to the divine and yet eternally estranged from the divine. And they would not be "created from nothing" but rather from the uncreated eternal stuff.

Thus the created world, although existing truly in itself and of itself, has a being which must be appreciated over against sheer nothingness. It is to be contrasted with this nothingness as well as the being of God which is absolutely necessary, i.e., God's being cannot not be, cannot be nothing; it cannot be reduced to or disintegrate into nothing, or deduced from another ground, and a fortiori it cannot be deduced from nothing. The nothingness out of which creatures are created is not something (some "thing") standing in relationship to God and God's subsisting being, but rather it is only something in relationship to creatures as defining creaturely being, the being of which originates out of nothingness. Nothingness here is essential to understanding the being of creatures because the true substantial being of creatures does not belong to them by reason of their essence or natures, i.e., they are not God, but being comes to them by way of the gift of creation. Only God's "essence" or "nature" is such that being or existence belongs necessarily to It. Yet, it is precisely because creaturely being is grounded in the necessary divine being that it may be believed to have a substantiality and self-generation endlessly more dense and substantial than the manifest dense substantiality that is evident to us apart from The Theological Distinction.[65]

Yet, in spite of the manifest contingency of individual substantial being, foremost oneself – and perhaps even that of the entire "universe" – this *foundation* of the world's density is not perceptually or intellectually evident, but rather believed in. The factual givenness of the beings of experience does not of necessity justify positing a giver of what is given, i.e., the absolutely necessary self-subsisting creator, "God." When this belief is an expression of the revelation of The Theological Distinction, it opens up, as Sokolowski has put it, a kind of novel "logical space" of theological mystery. This is not a novel space within the world's essences and syntax or within the logic of possible worlds. Further, seen from within this "logical space" faith is not opposed to or against the logic of reason but rather is beyond it. In this new space reason sees itself as not standing in opposition to and a rival to faith, but as given a dimension in which it can move on the basis of faith.[66] Here in faith reason may be said to function in the larger context of the center of the person or Existenz, where what is at stake is one's eternal destiny. Thus here, e.g., for the Christian, the mysteries of the Incarnation, Trinity, and Sacraments find a kind of intelligibility that they lack apart from this new dimension or novel logical space.

Therefore the basic mystery of God the Creator, as well as the mysteries for which this mystery and The Theological Distinction provide the context, may be thought to be not impossible because we have, in faith, let go of the world as the absolute criterion of what is possible and impossible. These mysteries may be said to be not impossible and not contradictory because we, through faith and the exigencies of graced Existenz, open up a "logical space" that permits what is, from the standpoint of the world, not possible and contradictory. This "permission," once again, is not guaranteed or justified by the logic of the world; rather, it is made possible by assenting to its being conceivable that the world as the ultimate frame of rationality itself is a "first grace" and has its norms in a higher context which remains essentially hidden to us.[67]

Further, faithful reason can see with a kind of insight, i.e., the insight occasioned by The Theological Distinction opened up by faith, the (theological) context of the world which is beyond reason. Here faith-filled reason grasps what its limits are and what it means to transcend itself, i.e., to be borne by faith and not by itself alone. This sense of the world is not available through reason alone. And faith-filled reason can see that this new dimension of self-transcendence into the theological mystery opens up not new pieces of information or categories which we have by virtue of being thoughtful agents of manifestation of the world, but rather by virtue of an entirely new mode of presentation or display by which a new sense of the whole is disclosed.

Of course, The Theological Distinction and God as the main term of this Distinction are superfluous to the "natural attitude" apart from faith because what we mean exemplarily by intelligibility and self-subsistence we reserve for nature or the world as disclosed by reason. Yet throughout the history of the "Abrahamic traditions," The Theological Distinction has provided a context for reigning interpretations of the world and/or nature. Thus, e.g., the faith of ancient Israel developed an understanding of Yahweh in relation to the world in contrast to the local versions of the divinities' relationship to the world as it was layed out in the Babylonian myth of Tiamat and Marduk, i.e., Israel came to propound a God who was not *a* God and who was radically transcendent to the inherently ambivalent natural (divinely initiated) processes as portrayed by the struggle between the upstart, Marduk, the agent of order with his mother, the amorphous recalcitrant original water deity, Tiamat, and his father Apsu (the Abyss). Yahweh's greatness was appreciated in contrast to the incontestable greatness of the divinity resident in nature's power represented by the struggle between Tiamat/Apsu and Marduk, and this appreciation provided for dealing with the occasional deep pessimism in regard to spirit's impotence in the face of the dense unpredictable, and occasionally capricious and violent whims of nature ("acts of God," as American legalese still has it). Here there is no question of repressing an equivalent of what Nietzsche was later to call the "Dionysian" nor of offering an Israelite version of the Babylonian god of empire and the megamachine. Rather Yahweh is beyond the chaotic vital-erotic forces of nature as Yahweh is beyond the principle of ordering of chaos.

For antiquity, foremost pre-Christian Greek and Roman thought, the deep pessimism one might find resulting from the sense of powerlessness over capricious forces beyond one's control was always mixed with a sense of veneration for divine powers within the world and nature because the world was "full of gods." Even a student of biology like Aristotle could look at the most insignificant living thing with awe and find that even here "gods were present." And for many of his contemporaries even the event of unharmonizable surds or natural devastating destruction was seen as the work of the divine Nemesis, or numinous *Fates* or *Moira* or *Anangke*.

Today's pessimism is of a different order because it is uniquely atheistic. In order for this modern atheism to occur the world had first to be disenchanted and "de-godded" by philosophy and then by the Judaeo-Christian theologies. Greek philosophy was considered atheistic because it transformed the gods, e.g., of Homer, i.e., the gods sanctioned by the state and popular religion, into rational principles that informed and sustained the world. For these philosophers, the world was still godly because these principles as inherent principles of the world merited being named divine. When the Jewish-Christian God was proclaimed as absolutely beyond the world, there was another kind of a disenchantment of the world, i.e., a purging of the conviction that the divine resides in the natural powers and forces of the world. This purgation itself was reason enough to motivate some ancients to call early Christians atheistic because the proper sense of divinity was removed by Christians from indwelling in the world as part of the world.

This early step in the direction of The Theological Distinction prepared the way for modern atheism and the modern pessimism. Only when it is believed that God is essentially *apart* from the world does the atheist view that the world is all there is mean an absolute denial of the divine and a total disenchantment or de-godding of the world.[68] (This has to be said while holding at the same time that it is only when God is absolutely transcendent to the world that God can be immanent to the world without destroying the autonomy of the world; this too is a fundamental assertion of The Theological Distinction.)

At the beginning of the twenty-first century we find in reflections based on some modern extrapolations of physics and certainly in some strains of contemporary philosophy a narrative of the world that is completely free of the presence of divine powers. Furthermore, for this narrative, in keeping with its ancient and modern "Enlightenment" forebearers, theological assertions are thought to be not only irrelevant but also ridiculously childish, and worst pernicious and harmful. Yet in spite of its passion to be rid of superstition in order to permit nature in itself to be our guide, this narrative casts a specter over the very density and intelligibility of nature as *physis*, i.e., as self-subsistent and self-regenerating, and therefore over the significance of spirit's historical achievements, and the substantival density of spirit itself. This narrative tells us that the world is a matter of sheer randomness and chance and that there is no need to have recourse to any notion of spirit. (The narrative is astonishingly oblivious of and indifferent to the agent of truth who tells this narrative.) Further, it goes on to predict the eventual total annihilation of the world by its own processes of entropy and mechanisms of decline. It thus casts a pallor of meaninglessness over the sweep of natural, cultural, and human life and history in so far as all these attainments are both pointless and destined to extinction and oblivion. Nature as *physis*, i.e., as the self-generation, self-creation, of what is in itself the self-generating and self-creating of a *kosmos*, or ordered, intelligible whole, albeit one riddled with chance and surds, is called into question to the extent that contemporary physics and philosophy describe the natural world (with an alleged view from nowhere) as a contingent random ephemeral moment in the quakings of the dysteleological chaos of the "universe."

But perhaps the philosophical musings of the physicists, when meditating on the echo of the Big Bang (via the application the Doppler Effect to CMB or cosmic microwave background), nature's chaos, random probability, black holes, dark energy ("the dispersing of everything in the cosmos into a cold, ever-expanding void"), entropy or the Second Law of Thermodynamics, etc. sometimes reflect less a sober philosophical cosmology than a pessimism born of their materialist ontological bias.

In any case both religion and transcendental, especially phenomenological, philosophies of the spirit counteract this pessimism. Robert Spaemann gives a nice example of this when he writes: "Religion is the hope that the Second Law of

Thermodynamics is not the last word about reality." He sees this happening primarily through forgiveness as a power that works against entropy. If we acknowledge that our agency immerses us in unforeseeable webs of relations and guilt, there is a legitimacy to the teaching of a universal karma, as in Hinduism, or, as Anaximander taught, there is reason to expect a demand for a kind of righting or retribution for everything after its demise, whereby everything pays for the injustice it has of necessity perpetrated on other things. But we cannot possibly properly take responsibility for all the waves of consequences set off by our agency because of the finitude of our purview and our other inherent weaknesses. But at least some forms of religion offer the hope and power to believe that through forgiveness there is a power of a fresh beginning and a retrieval of meaningfulness in our agency without the crushing burden of the past.[69] If this is true of a religious doctrine such as forgiveness it is no less true for the transcendental phenomenological understanding of spirit's primacy to all that science names nature.[70] It is difficult to see how spirit, the anonymous agent of truth behind the scientific narrative, is commensurate with the pessimistic results of the narrative. (See Book 1, Chapter VI.)

In any case, the frequently heard dire cosmological predictions which are based on aspects of modern physics, *even if accurate displays* of the true essence and destiny of nature, and thereby even if such disclosures of nature show it as increasingly losing its capacity to be *physis*, i.e., self-subsisting, self-regenerating, and self-creative of a cosmos, have no effect on the basic sense of the terms of The Theological Distinction. As the story of modern cosmogonies of the world or "nature" generating itself out of an obscure state of affairs of "singularities" that eventuated in The Big Bang and then the cosmos as we know it do not effect the terms of The Theological Distinction, so neither do the narratives of the world's entropy and decline.

Thus it is important to grasp that in The Theological Distinction one makes the distinction between the necessity and self-sufficiency of God and the necessity and self-sufficiency of the world. If the world is the absolute and the best, there is no room for the divine necessity and self-sufficiency; if God is, in the fashion of a monism or absolute one-ism, and *in this sense* "absolute," the necessity and self-sufficiency of the world is reduced to an illusion. But if God and the world (or "nature" or created being) are countable as two or make for two beings, then we have no proper theology of creation and no proper appreciation of God's immanence and transcendence as well as the subsistence and dignity of the world. Similarly, if God has a nature and is a kind of being, then we have two beings and there is incessant competition between the two cases of necessity and self-sufficiency, i.e., that of God and the world.

In The Theological Distinction, we must distinguish the non-necessity or contingency in God (God's "Cambridge properties and relations," e.g., God being the creator and God's creation of the world), from the contingency or the non-necessity within the world. Much of modern religious thought and popular piety confuse and blend these (consider the folk and juridic notion of "the act of God" that refers to natural disasters and accidents). Thus nature is robbed of chance and surds, and all such phenomena are ascribed directly and immediately to God's will. The wonderful property of the "sublime" that Kant saw, albeit surreptitiously, in nature's unpredictable and magnificent power is made impossible. In this kind of religious view any modern physical descriptions of randomness become not the workings of nature but of the divine will. Such a confusion obliterates aspects of nature which The Theological Distinction not only permits to remain in tact, but celebrates.[71] Nature's inherent randomness is kept intact, but so also is its being a creation rooted in God's will.

When The Theological Distinction is appreciated as not inherently contradictory, even though not intrinsically intelligible in the sense that it provides us with filled intentions of the matter in question, then the basic theological move can be made. When this move has been made then this encompassing and necessary matrix that is the world is able to be entertained as neither absolutely necessary nor encompassing, but rather as contingent in a sense uniquely tied to The Theological Distinction and not to the inner-worldly senses of contingencies, and thus subordinate and derived. God, the other term of the distinction, is now posited as more basic than both the world and The Theological Distinction itself. Now the contingency of the world and the necessity of God are seen to be distinct from the necessity and contingency proper to what is within the world.

Thereby does the Theological Distinction respond to the atheist claim that if God encompasses all the perfection there is, then the world is superfluous and if the world encompasses all the perfection there is then God is superfluous.[72] "All there is" or "all the perfection there is" is profoundly transformed by faith; there is now introduced an exalted sense of the being of the world. The world is posited as not necessary in and of itself but is de facto necessary with the necessity of God's choice, a necessity that surpasses any necessity knowable in the world – given the assumption that it is God's choice that creates these necessities.

Similarly, "all there is" or "all the perfection there is" introduces a sense of the divine which, because it founds and is not commensurate with the rationally exhaustible sense of the necessities and contingencies, cannot stand in competition with the rationally exhaustible sense of being, i.e., the world.[73] The goodness and beauty of the world are seen to be real and not negated by reason of their finitude and ephemerality precisely because the divine beauty and goodness are posited to be both incommensurate with that of the world and as well the ultimate creative exemplar of that of the world.

This recalls the already mentioned basic "axiological" thesis of The Theological Distinction, namely, God plus the world is not greater than God alone. Thomas V. Morris discusses in this regard the "dilemma of created goodness," (which dilemma he ultimately argues is bogus).[74] God, *as the most perfect possible being*, manifests a certain, even infinite, positive value n and it would seem that of necessity, i.e., because of the intrinsic goodness of the world ("God saw that it was good," as *Genesis* puts it), the world would manifest at least some measure of value. Thus God + the World = $n + 1$ = God + the World > God (alone). But because it is impossible that anything be greater than God, so it is impossible that the world have any positive value. But if the world has no positive value, it is at best superfluous, and there is no reason to create it.

Morris holds that a way around this seeming dilemma is to hold that we must distinguish between a *being* or entity and a *state of affairs*. God is a being, so am I, so is my pen. There is the state of affairs of my existing or the world's existing (or the pen's being empty of ink). God may be thought of as the greatest possible *being* and this can be true without the proposition being true (about the state of affairs) that God's existing alone is the greatest possible state of affairs. Indeed we can say that God may be thought of as the greatest possible being but the state of affairs of God's sharing existence with the created universe is a "greater state of affairs than God's existing in pristine isolation or solitude."

Thus Morris's own view is not (1) that God plus the World is greater than God (alone), but rather (2) the state of affairs of God's being alone is less good than God's sharing existence with creatures.

It seems to me that (2) is false for The Theological Distinction. But first let us note that Morris rejects (1) for some classical reasons: There is no natural principle of unity that permits there to be any larger object, God + the World, because there is no natural principle of unity joining the parts. He adds another: For "perfect Being theology" it is "conceptually precluded that God ever be considered a part of a larger and more valuable whole, an entity distinct from but partially composed by God."

But this position is based on his holding that God plus the world are not greater than God alone (G + W = not > G) has as a consequence that the universe has no "positive value." And the reason for this is that "God" is thought of as a *being*, albeit the supremely perfect being, juxtaposed to the being of the world. And even though there are problems for Morris of uniting and composing God with other beings (which we will address from the perspective of The Theological Distinction in the next section), his objections do not stem from the basic thesis of The Theological Distinction, namely, that God is not a being but rather sheer To Be. Connected to this is perhaps an ambiguity in holding that creation has "no positive value." If this means that it holds no value in itself apart from what is given it in creation and by participating in the goodness of God, this is true for The Theological Distinction. But to say that in itself the world has no value is for the classical tradition to blaspheme and deny the very sense of creation. But it would also be a violation of the tradition to say that this goodness in itself is *absolutely* independent of creation.

For The Theological Distinction it is essential that the distinction between God as *ipsum esse subsistens* and God as *ens*, God as pure subsisting To Be Itself and God as a being, be maintained because it is this which accounts both for the impossibility of saying that God is the greatest possible being (*ens*) and, as well, for the senses in which God may or may not be united, related, and combined with the world.

Esse is a novel *theological* discovery by Aquinas that emerges out of the distinctive issues raised by the dogma of God the Creator as articulated in The Theological Distinction: Whereas "entity" or "a being" (*ens*) applies to existing things within the world, and "being" (as a gerund or infinitive) as in the "being (or To Be) of entities or beings" is properly applied to the whole or last horizon of the world and what is the reach of reason, *esse* is the term introduced by Aquinas to deal with the new "whole" of God and the world.[75] Because God is not a being in competition with the world and because the excellence of God absolutely contains all possible excellence, the excellence of the world can be positively affirmed both as intrinsic to the world and as not adding to the excellence of the (contrary to fact) state of affairs wherein God alone would exist. Most basic for The Theological Distinction is the Biblical view that there is "nothing that we have not received" (1 *Corinthians* 4:7) or, as Aquinas puts it, "the To Be (*esse*) of whatever created thing is participated To Be."[76] This means both that after creation there are more beings (*entia*) but not more To Be and with creation there is an increase in good beings but not an increase in goodness (*bonitas*). And this is what accounts for the incomparable liberality of creation, i.e., that God is not moved by the goodness of creation nor does God benefit from creatures.[77] This thesis holds regardless for both "beings" and states of affairs, even though this distinction itself is transformed in substituting *esse* for *ens*. This would seem to be the difference between the claim of The Theological Distinction and that of Morris.

But The Theological Distinction has to do not with the *philosophical* conception of a certain kind of being, the most perfect one possible, but with the *key mystery of theology*. Yet it is a philosophical claim within the "logical space" opened by faith to say, with Aquinas, that *ipsum esse subsistens*, pure absolute subsisting To Be, is not an *ens*, i.e., it is not an entity or a being. The Theological Distinction and the dogma of the creator God requires holding this in a way that perfect being theology does not. But this means that the philosophical discussion of this matter is subordinate to the lead of faith.

§7. The Wholes and Parts of the Theological Distinction

We have said that the Theological Distinction establishes a new whole that is not available to the mind apart from faith, i.e., the whole of God and the World. Let us think about this in the light of some famous Husserlian distinctions regarding wholes and parts. Note that what we are doing here is phenomenologically odd. This is because whereas *moments* that are *parts* are properly *eidetically evident* and *seen* as necessarily *non-independent* in the mind's intending them, here in faith the necessities are not properly seen but rather *believed* or entertained as proposed and their evidence rests on the assumptions faith establishes. The whole of the member terms of The Theological Distinction is not made up of *independent parts* ("pieces") such that all the parts can be regarded as subsisting independently of the whole and can be presented to the mind apart from the whole. Indeed, one of the parts, God, can be regarded as independent of the whole and through faith be entertained as apart from the whole, but not so the part which is the world. Of course, from the point of view of rational reflection, especially *pagan* or pre-Christian Greek and Roman thought, the world appears as the ultimate whole which includes everything else, including the divine. Not so from the vantage point of the kind of thoughtful faith which we are privileging here and for which The Theological Distinction is central.

Nor is the whole comprised of the terms of The Theological Distinction made up of moments each of which is dependent on the whole and on one another and not able to be made present apart from the whole and the other members. Husserl's famous example of such a whole is a sound with its "moments" of pitch and timbre. From the vantage point of rational reflection, especially "pagan" reflection, God might well seem to be a moment of the whole which is the world. Not so from the perspective of faithful reason for which only the world is a moment, i.e., non-independent part. The world here is a moment that cannot be entertained to exist independently from the whole of The Theological Distinction.

We may think of reason as the mind's motion from the more or less known and familiar to what initially is the less known and less familiar and then transforming this increasingly to the more known and familiar. Thus this motion of reason is from the same to what is different and back to the sameness of the different and then back to the enriched difference, which is now a difference within the same. It is a motion from the implicit to the explicit, from empty intentions to filled intentions, from hypotheses to more or less filled intuited confirmations, from wholes to parts and parts to wholes, etc. If this is so, then the issue of how reason may come upon God arises. The God displayed by reason is, by way of an analytical definition, i.e., a tautology, because as that than which nothing greater can be conceived or displayed, it is the highest reason is capable of and, in this sense, what reason "mandates." In this regard we can affirm a synthesis of Kant and Scotus that God, although the essentially elusive "Infinite," is the sublimest of considerations that makes the mind dizzy (Kant) and it is that to which the mind is most drawn (Scotus). Yet "God" as the reach of reason is the reach of the world and the God of The Theological Distinction, proximate to the Infinity of Scotus, is not measurable by anything, and therein lies the tension with Kant. Recall that for Scotus, the "infinite" is "that which exceeds the finite, not exactly by reason of any finite measure, but in excess of any measure that could be assigned."[78] The aspiration to a philosophical or rational or "natural" theology is inevitable and healthy, just as seeing is preferable to the empty intention of believing. Yet to the extent that faithful thinking is tempted by the idolatry latent in "rational theologies," where God is fashioned in the image and likeness of reason or one's false self, such persons, as Karl Barth once urged, must pass through the atheistic fiery stream (aka Ludwig *Feuerbach*) wherein God is thought of as nothing but the reach of reason and a projection of human concerns. If such critics of religion as Feuerbach are encountered from the center of one's self, from one's Existenz, they may permit both the correction of faith-filled reason and the healing insight that the God of The Theological Distinction is in many respects a No to the reach of reason.

Typically reason may be said of necessity to make God a part of the reach of reason and, in this sense, a part of the world. In this respect one might say that God is the highest, most excellent aspect or part of the world. God as the ultimate reach of reason may well be in many respects transcendent to total human comprehension, but here God's basic sense is precisely to be tied to the world necessarily as being its ground, soul, center, heart, or telos, and the world ultimately makes sense because of "God" so displayed by reason. This was exemplarily the case in Plato,

Aristotle, and Plotinus, even though we have suggested that perhaps at least in the latter case something like The Theological Distinction is adumbrated. In modern times the philosophical theologies of the process theological tradition similarly make God the ground, soul, and telos of the world. In both ancient and modern times philosophers have argued, often with great eloquence and persuasion, that the sense of the world needs God and the sense of God is tied to the world. To use Miller's terms again, for these philosophers very often the divine is the limit simpliciter (not limit case) of the excellences of the world.

Yet there are "proofs" for the existence of God that do not point to God as a limit-simpliciter but rather more as an absolute limit, thus resembling more a limit case. One can here think of Kant and many philosophers influenced by him, such as Blondel and the Marechalian Neo-Thomists, who argue well that the very sense of meaning, inquiry, judgment, willing, etc. implies a kind of proto- or pre-affirmation of God as limit simpliciter of the world's excellences. They further argue, however, that the affirmation cannot be merely the affirmation of a mere regulative ideal as an idea because such as infinite idea does not support an affirmation of the being toward which the mind's intentionality in cognition, willing, and valuing aims. Rather the sense of the affirmation is an unconditioned ground of meaning and value, which itself is not part of the conditioned innerworldly meanings, beings, goods, etc. This tradition for The Theological Distinction may very well point to what is *not* a limit simpliciter, and therefore what is not on a continuum with the goods and meanings we experience. But nevertheless the very sense of this sense of the divine is that it is the ground of the world, i.e., of all that we experience and cherish; God is of necessity the correlate of a transcendental subjectivity. In this sense God is inseparable from the world and *quoad nos* has no meaning apart from the world as experienced. To this extent the sense of God is inseparable from the world and God is "part" of the world, i.e., its "unconditioned condition" or ground. Yet this may be due to the consideration that a first-person phenomenological account of the divine cannot offer an account of God except as one's own ground or as the correlate of an intentionality; it need not stand in conflict with The Distinction's claim that God is not necessarily related to what God grounds. We will soon return to this.

The Theological Distinction between God and the world proposed by Robert Sokolowski and which we are here endorsing and applying makes this precise claim that God is not "really" related to the world, even though it has no brief to make against the *philosophical* claim that the world may indeed have *in some sense* a divine part. The Distinction's version of the world partly depends on the phenomenological account. But the "world" for phenomenology is the world as displayed through the transcendental reduction or epoché. This is the world as it is for the transcendental I. Yet world here in the context of The Distinction is also what is displayed prior to the transcendental reduction, i.e., what counts for the world in the "natural attitude" is also relevant not only for phenomenology but also for The Distinction. The world for The Theological Distinction is not only the horizon of experience but it is also what the natural attitude refers to as "the universe." Therefore, first of all "world" is what the agency of manifestation, one's own and the community of thoughtful minds, says it is, whether in the phenomenological attitude or not. The world is the world as displayed, whether or not the display itself is a theme of interest. The world of The Theological Distinction encompasses nature because the social-historical-scientific contexts of meaning which enable everything, including nature, to appear are founded on the natural substrates. But the sense of world for The Theological Distinction is a net cast so wide that it includes in the world what perhaps would most adamantly resist it, i.e., it is not only what the agency of manifestation displays but also what phenomenological reason refers to as the agency of manifestation or transcendental I and which is not part of the phenomenological world. Further, "the world" of The Theological Distinction is a *cosmos*, i.e., an encompassing whole that exists in itself with integrity, a whole including created manifesting minds.

This theological sense of world for The Theological Distinction is reasonable "for the most part" for both human reflection and agency. This is not primarily an endorsement of science's use of "probability" and statistical analysis to establish laws, patterns, and forms. Rather, this qualification bears witness to the fact proclaimed since antiquity that the world has a measure of opacity to the theoretical articulation by philosophy and science. The world as the horizon of experience encompassing both the social-cultural world and nature, is often fraught with anomalies, and it is pervaded by surds that come to light in efforts at rational agency as well as in theoretical undertakings as well.

But for The Theological Distinction, which has no quarrel with this view of the seemingly ineradicable presence of surds in the world, it is a matter of indifference whether or not the world is articulated as having inherently a divine ground, center, or telos. What is more basic is that the world's self-sufficiency and integrity are acknowledged. Thus The Distinction is equally at home with versions of the world that are to be found in, e.g., evolutionary atheistic naturalism, ancient Greek pagan thought, and aboriginal "natural" religions. That is, it is not dependent on any world view, even though historic world-views condition its genesis.

The sense of world in The Theological Distinction does not coincide with the New Testament sense of the "world" as the realm of "the flesh," "principalities," and "powers," etc. This latter is a further theological determination of the "world" dependent on what The Theological Distinction brings to light and may be abstracted from in the present context. This is not to say that the New Testament's views on the Flesh, Powers, and Principalities have no theological relevance or truth value. Indeed, their chief relevance is that they pose obstacles to faith by pervading the world with a deceptive atmosphere as to what is possible and true. Foremost they exude the conviction that death, violence, and cynicism are more real than life, love, and hope.

For The Theological Distinction neither the whole of the world nor that of God and the world is the first and last whole, as the whole which of necessity remains intact, regardless of what happens to the world or to the whole of God and the world. Rather, God is the first and last whole and God is not complemented or completed by anything else. Thus we must contrast this divine self-sufficiency$_1$ and necessity$_1$ from that of the world's self-sufficiency$_2$ and necessity$_2$. The former transcend or exceed the whole whose parts are pervaded by the latter senses of sufficiency and necessity. The former may be regarded as the limit case for what may serve as a continuum of forms of sufficiency and necessity extending to a limit simpliciter. God is as interior or intimate to the contingency of the world as God is to the sufficiency and necessity proper to the world; and the whole which is God is infinitely better than the better part of the world, signified by the world's sufficiency and necessity. "Necessity$_1$, not part of the whole [of the world], is freedom of indifference to necessity$_2$, the higher part of the whole, and necessity$_1$ establishes contingency, the lower part of the whole [of the world], in its very contingency."[79] This establishing of contingency, self-sufficiency, and necessity in the world is not a lessening of what we mean by these in our scientific, logical, and philosophical analysis; but The Theological Distinction points to other senses transcendent to these senses which we may believe in as grounding what we experience in the world, but which transcend the intelligibility these have in our experience of the world.

In any case, the God of The Distinction is not evident from within the world; reason has no purchase on it, even as a limit simpliciter. Of course, this need not rule out absolutely or a priori that the various senses or guises of God in the various philosophies and historical religions might all have a common referent, which from the faith perspective is the God of The Theological Distinction. It may well be that each of these guises, as different as they are, have the same referent, as do the Morning Star and the Evening Star. But, on the other hand, and this depends on the particulars, they may point to limits simpliciter toward which the God of The Theological Distinction would be the limit case. In such a case they would not have the same senses or be the same guises having the same referent but would be as different as a rocking horse from a horse. The point for The Theological Distinction is not arrogant elevation of one's faith tradition over others but rather the faith-assertion that the God of The Distinction is not only not a necessary aspect of the world but there is nothing in worldly rational experience which provides evidence for this God precisely because this God is not a necessary implication of the world and the world is not necessary at all for this God. And for the Theological Distinction such a claim does not detract from but rather elevates the ontolgical dignity of both God and the world.

What is further important for our present context is that the issues of theology relevant to the theme of vocation, like the relationship of God to creatures, or omnipotence to freedom, or grace to free will, are typically conceived in theological frameworks for which The Theological Distinction is not central. As a result the setting for these matters is the categorial display of the world by reason. This need not pull God into the world as a supreme or greatest being or god, but the ineluctable use of analogies, as part of one's irrepressible and justifiable desire to understand, not only come up short but come up often enough with insurmountable contradictions, as in the problem with omniscience and indexicality, predestination and free will, etc.

The introduction of The Theological Distinction as a kind of defining parameter has a not surprising and very traditional result, namely the onset of a "cloud of unknowing." This cloud is different for the non-believer for whom it might well appear so obscure that belief in it can only be absurd; for the believer it has the obscure character of mystery. The Theological Distinction does not pretend to create a framework for the believer wherein the cloud lifts, but it provides a new "optic" which sheds light on the basic terms of The Distinction as well as other mysteries of faith, given the basic belief in the dogma of God the Creator. Analogizing continues but it is governed by The Theological Distinction, not by anything else thought to be more basic than this.

"God" is not knowable "in Godself." For The Theological Distinction, we have an interpretation of the world which we know in relation to God (whom we do not know). This interpretation establishes a unique distinction between God and the world and a unique whole made up of the unique parts of this distinction. It is within this framework that we propose that we wrestle with all theological matters.

Furthermore, this whole is not strictly speaking a sum of the parts, so that what we have in adding "God" and the world has more ontological density and dignity than prior to the joining of the two parts. A *fortiori* it is not a whole which surpasses the mere summing of the parts, as one might say is the case in a particular combination such as a unique community, jazz combo, string quartet, or a sports team. Such a whole, often called an organic whole (G.E. Moore) or value-whole (Husserl), is more than the sum of its parts. In such a whole, even though some of the members are not stellar in quality, when they get together in this combination the whole shines far brighter than any other combination.[80] The whole which is God and the world can never be a sum or greater than the sum of the parts because one of the parts contains all possible perfection and the other adds nothing to this perfection. To put it another way, pure absolute subsisting To Be cannot be summed with beings or entities; these are not commensurate with It.

§8. The Absurd, Paradox, and the Theological Distinction

We earlier (Book 1, Chapter VI) discussed some senses of "paradox" in philosophy, and in transcendental phenomenology in particular. We said that facing a paradox can mean being confronted with believing an invalid proposition whose validity is immediately or without reflection believed; or it is being faced with believing a valid proposition whose invalidity immediately or without reflection is believed. The Theological Distinction is not for the believer a paradox in either of these senses. Whereas in both the familiar philosophical sense as well as The Theological Distinction the single referent, which is "the paradox," of necessity requires a polythetic act, i.e., an act with multiple belief strands, in The Theological Distinction there is not the claim that one set of beliefs is invalid (cf. our earlier discussion of paradox in the transcendental and natural attitudes). Faith does not involve believing an invalid proposition whose validity is immediately believed nor a valid proposition whose invalidity is immediately believed. For the non-believer or skeptic, it may well assume the status of an apparent paradox, but the evidence for the validity or non-validity which would clinch its status as a paradox does not seem ever to be decisively in one's reach, *pace* militant atheists. But for them to admit this they would have to admit the terms of The Theological Distinction. The questionable proposition to which the believer adheres is not one that can be disproved in such a way that what the believer believes is able to be shown to be inherently contradictory or in every respect inconceivable – even if what is being affirmed, i.e., that the world as the limit of intelligibility itself is created and is measured by another higher intelligibility, is not intrinsically intelligible in the sense that one grasps what this higher intelligibility means. Yet one can entertain it as a possibility. Of course, the non-believer may martial strong arguments against the plausibility of such a view. Thus the agnostic and believing atheist do not strictly face or resolve the paradox.

But do we not here contradict our earlier discussion (see Book 1, Chapter VIII, §8, C and D.) in regard to the temptation of possible world theorists for whom the essential necessities of our (this worldly) experience are nullified in the consideration of other possible worlds? Our answer is, No. It is of the essence of The Theological Distinction that the fundamental term, God, and the posited relation of God to the world, named creation, (giving thereby to God the "Cambridge property" of "creator") not be one which destroys or undermines the necessities that belong to the experienced world.

Something similar seems to be the case with the suspicion that The Theological Distinction has "absurd" clements. We earlier, in Chapter VI, §2, F, discussed general aspects of Kierkegaard's thought as it related to our discussions of Existenz and vocation. Here our proposal is that a meditation on Kierkegaard's notion of theological paradox and the absurd may shed light on The Theological Distinction and vice-versa. The theme of the "absurd" has some therapeutic aspects if it is rightly understood: Given the ultimacy of meaning and intelligibility of the world it is not an easy step or leap to what is beyond the world and the creator of the world. Kierkegaard's characterization of this leap as absurd can be helpful for undoing any facile understanding of the allegiance of faith and any temptation to see it as continuous with reason. As we have already insisted, this is quite different from saying that faith is "absurd" in the way believing in what is contradicted by evidence is.

We can begin with the major term of The Theological Distinction as it appears to Kierkegaard. The Distinction has to do with the creator God who is omnipotent and the world that God creates. This means not only that God can create things which subsist in themselves, but further God is capable of creating free independent beings or selves. Creation from nothing is divine infinite power's expression of the ability to make subsistent beings who exist in themselves and which independence is manifested, in the case of at least human persons, in their freedom vis-á-vis Itself. What is conceptually odd here is that creation from nothing, a radical dependence, is the condition for the radical independence; this is at the heart of the Christian understanding and The Theological Distinction. All finite power and giving make the recipient in some way dependent; only the divine omnipotence can create from nothing that which has subsistence, continuity in itself, and freedom. Without going as far as Simone Weil (cf. §7 above) for whom God plus the world is less than God alone, we can nevertheless say: In such an act of creation the divine omnipotence may be said to continually, *as it were*, "retract" itself. This was also Kierkegaard's view, which makes clear that the "as it were" is in no way an ontological diminishment: "Omnipotence does not stay in a relation to the other, for there is no other to which it is related – no, it can give without giving up the least of its power, i.e. it can make independent." God is the one over against which, if I had the slightest independence, I would not be free. If a person had the slightest independent existence over against God, God could not make him free because God would not be omnipotent and the creator of selves from nothing. "For goodness is to give oneself completely but in such a way that by omnipotently retracting oneself one makes the recipient independent... If in creating God lost a little of his power, then making man independent is just what God could not do." Kierkegaard adds, we don't really understand this. But it is clear that whereas omnipotence seems to be such a heavy hand laid on the world, actually it is so light that it brings into being a being with the radical independence of freedom. The classic metaphysics of The Theological Distinction echoes here because the divine is portrayed as not standing in a relation to an other; there is no other to which it is related in its infinite absolute being.[81]

For Christian thinkers this ontological situation has had a moral-spiritual equivalent: To assume an attitude that corresponds to the realization that one's ipseity and actuality are gifts. Kierkegaard reflected the great contemplative-mystical tradition in this matter when he said that the key to religion is to understand that "a person is nothing before God." Or rather, the task is "to be nothing at all, and thereby to be before God," or to continually insist upon oneself as fundamentally impotent and without power in regard to one's being, knowing that the disappearance of this would mean the disappearance of religiousness.[82] The "pagan" existence without God in the world becomes for the Christian the will not to be oneself before God, or the despair to will to be oneself by the standard of the world, thereby failing to grasp it can only be before God and through God. To exist apart from despair, in faith, is to consent to one's creaturehood and this consent rests one in the root of oneself because God is the power that makes possible the self as a self-relation, self-reference, self-reflection.[83]

We have called attention to the issue of the conceivability of holding at once (a) the world is the horizon of all proper senses of conceivability and (b) that there is a consideration which makes the world's necessities, contingencies, and logic contingent in the sense of created. If the criteria of this thinkability and intelligibility are determined by the whole which is the world, then thinking of a ground of the world from within this criteria is not strictly speaking possible. Therefore the move beyond the world to the other term of The Theological Distinction which enables us to think of the world as "created" must acknowledge the strangeness, if not the "absurdity," of the move. It is only conceivable if one entertains the possibility that the criteria of conceivability, meaningfulness, etc. as they emerge out of the world and the transcendental I's display of the world are not ultimate. That one is disposed to accept, indeed, to affirm this, is, according to classic Christian theology, the work of "grace." Thus there is doubtless a sense in which from the non-faith standpoint the move of faith is absurd.

Kierkegaard claimed that the "absurd is the negative criterion of that which is higher than human understanding and human knowledge."[84] This is not the famous position of Tertullian, *credo quia absurdum*, where it is precisely the absurdity of doctrine which motivates belief or where, indeed, absurdity becomes a criterion and motive of credibility. Rather, it points to the essentially transcendent and mysterious nature of The Theological Distinction. It echoes Scotus that the Infinite "exceeds the finite in excess of any measure that could be assigned." This Distinction, the relation of the "being" of the world to the "being" of God, does not make sense within the world. By definition, it is only available through faith which is believed to be higher than human understanding, not in terms of its understanding, but in terms of the truth that is believed. The reason why faith "breathes soundly and blessedly in the absurd"[85] is because its basic belief is in the incommensurability of God and the World. Faith does not have to do with belief-that or even belief-in – if this latter has to do with a univocal understanding of trusting something. Belief-that is tied to what is more or less evident and even what is probable. Faith as some analogous sense of belief-in is not tied to what is evident or probable. On the contrary it is to what is improbable and incommensurate with anything we regard as having evidence.

The notion that the Infinite, and by implication its epistemic correlate, faith, exceed any measure that could be assigned, therefore any reason that would emerge out of our reflection on the world, can find a restatement in Kierkegaard's wrestle with the God as the "unconditioned" and faith. In each case we have to do with what cannot be supported by reasons or what cannot be comprehended by reasons. The best we can hope for is in something like the dogma of The Theological Distinction, i.e. "reasons can be given for the impossibility of giving reasons."[86] In another place Kierkegaard cited Hugh of St Victor: "Faith is really not supported by the things that go beyond reason, by any reason, because reason does not comprehend what faith believes; but nevertheless there is something here by which reason becomes determined or is conditioned to honor the faith that it still does not perfectly succeed in grasping."[87] This honoring of faith by reason may take a variety of forms. Most obviously it could mean the acknowledgment of "mystery" as more than a mere problem and as having to do with what perhaps we really most want and, in some sense, need to understand. Or it could refer to what Sokolowski called the new logical space opened by the dogma of The Distinction where reason and philosophy may function but with an utterly transformed landscape. It could also refer to the recognition that it is not inherently contradictory, i.e., the acknowledgement that it is conceivable to hold that the world is created and not the ultimate framework of all meaning and intelligibility. Here reason honors faith by recognizing that it has not power to dissolve it into nonsense. Simply because I cannot understand it, and cannot solve it, and it remains beyond my comprehension, does not thereby render it nonsense. But, of course, if faith is discarded or abolished, then the whole sphere (of faith and the whole of God and the world) collapses and "reason becomes conceited and perhaps concludes that, ergo, the paradox is nonsense."[88]

Consider how we earlier said that there is a natural tendency to think of the divine as the limit simpliciter, the regulative ideal, the most eminent case of positive values we experience. But, in accord with The Theological Distinction, we may also think of the divine as a limit case which infinitely transcends the limit simpliciter, as, e.g., a point may exceed an ever diminishing line. The advantage of this example from Barry Miller, we have said, is that, in a sense, the limit case is that to which the members of the limit simpliciter aspire even though it is incommensurate with them. That works for many of the properties of God, but it does not work smoothly for The Theological Distinction and the major dogmas connected to it and elucidated by it. In so far as the teleological dynamism of the spirit points to a perfection of this world, even granting that the world is endless in every respect (e.g., in regard to space, time, meaning, value, etc.), the primary term of The Theological Distinction is absolutely incommensurate to the world. God is not utopia or eutopia. In what immediately follows we want first of all briefly to dwell on some of the intricacies of faith as it is a light unto one's path as well as an élan to life and secondly as a move into what is called "the absurd" in a stronger theological sense. Before we return to this famous Kierkegaardian theme let us look at the act of faith itself both as lived from within in the first-person and as described by The Theological Distinction.

The Theological Distinction, which pivots around the dogma of God as the absolutely necessary and sufficient term of the Distinction and as what exists even if the other term does not exist, can offer a theory to account for the teaching that faith is a result of God's (the Holy Spirit's) revelation to the person in her Existenz. Perhaps we can say that in St. Thomas we have an effort to offer a first-person account (although given in the third-person) of the beginnings of the act of faith which meets the dogmatic requirements of The Theological Distinction. God here appears as "the First Truth" to which one is to commit oneself. "The First Truth" we take here not merely to mean a special case of the non-reflexively lived, intuitively known, analogous presupposition for all other truths and premises, i.e., a unique instance of the light of immediate self-awareness upon which all other lights depend. We take it also to mean the Truth that has to do with Existenz's self-understanding and the awareness that what is of unconditional importance is at stake as this is effected by God's gracious initiative. (See above Chapter III for our discussion of "Existenz.") In this respect, "the First Truth" is what founds the faith that centers and sustains Existenz's centered life. Although it is occasioned by the presence in the life-world of preaching, sacred texts, loving and holy people within and without one's community, etc., these occasions pose for the individuals the decisive matter of Existenz, i.e., what is of ultimate unconditional importance is at stake and one cannot ignore this without denying oneself in a most fundamental way. And yet this awakening to the *unum necessarium* is an awakening of one's center as love, as being drawn to love that which the witnesses in the world inadequately articulate and exemplify.

Clearly for The Theological Distinction faith is not merely an awakening to the conditions for the possibility of one's Existenz and the embracing of these. It is awakening to being a "new creation," a new form of Existenz not commensurate with the old. Yet it would be odd to suggest that the third-person interpretation of faith would substitute for the first-person lived experience of oneself and one's freedom in believing or that the theological interpretation would nullify the lived awakening to the innermost center of oneself and would deny that what was at stake was the possibility of embracing a greater depth within oneself. The believer may for a variety of reasons grant precedence to the interpretation of The Theological Distinction as being most in conformity with one's lived experience of this transcending of the invitation and life-long task of faith; but the theological interpretation would raise to a new key, "sublate," (*hebt auf*), not merely negate, the sense that what was at stake was of unconditional importance to oneself as Existenz and that the refusal of faith was a refusal of one's ownmostness.

St. Thomas uses analogically the term "instinct" for this basic first motion of faith toward the "First Truth": It is not learned or experienced as something in the world, it is not a matter of deliberation; yet I myself in my ownmostness, i.e., in my will, am drawn to love It and assent to It as the Truth *for its own sake*. (Cf. above our discussion of Fichte's proposal that respect for Others and oneself is to be tied to the love of truth for its own sake; see Chapter V, §8, D.) In this special sense the revelation of the First Truth is its own guarantee and it is inseparable from spirit's essential respect for truth, objectivity, evidence, etc. This is perhaps the sense in which the "formal object" of faith is the very condition of the possibility of truth (the "First Truth"), i.e., faith is awakening to the original allegiance and respect for what is evident in one's self-awareness and to the unconditional importance of one's Existenz. Faith is a gracious opportunity to be awakened to this First Truth as what is to be loved and believed in. And it is experienced as interior to my innermost center as this is connected with what appears "kerygmatically" in the world through, e.g., the love of family and friends and Church teachings.[89] Thus in regard to the First Truth I am not directed foremost outwards to what is in the world but Within, i.e., my ownmost center as this itself is drawn to and moved by the "kerygma" or teaching without. (Husserl echoes this when he says that the intentionality of prayer is comparable to an instinct and is directed "'within' to the inkling of the interiority of God, as a transendence in immanence."[90])

The propositional explication of the First Truth in terms of The Theological Distinction teaches that this awakening to one's Existenz is through the workings of God within, the gracious presence and urging of the Holy Spirit (experienced, claims St. Thomas, as the First Truth), which is a transcendence in the immanence of the human spirit. I, as Existenz, at the core of my personal being, am moved by the Spirit, but, at the same time, I, from out of this very core of Existenz, move myself to love and assent.

Faith may be said to be first of all the effect of love and thus to be an act from out of Existenz or the personal center. Thus faith, as a motion of Existenz in which the center of the I is engaged, is not merely an actuation of the cognitive capacities; it is not merely an intellectual assent nor a mere belief-that. It has to do with one's life at its center and as it is illuminated or called into question in regard to what is of unconditional importance. What is of unconditional importance is this gracious urging to love and believe-in. That in which one believes and to which one is drawn in love is decisively but inadequately indicated by the witness (here clearly the Christian witness is meant, but perhaps we may find sufficient parallels within at least the "Abrahamic tradition") within one's life-world. The nature of the authority of such a disclosure is perhaps hinted at in what we in the last chapter referred to as "the truth of will." Yet clearly, if the "truth of will" is all faith is, then it cannot evidently be equated with the First Truth in which is inscribed, according to the tradition, divine authority. But, at the same time, it is not a priori clear that such authority is to be excluded from the relatively rare instances of the "truth of will."

When asked about it, or when confronted by the non-believer, one may well become alienated from this center and transform one's faith into merely an epistemic position-taking. One may be thus impelled to regard one's act of faith as an opinion or belief in propositions, and not as an act that centers and upholds one's Existenz. In this regard, Marcel spoke of a "disturbing dualism" that might well occur within oneself. When I describe it to myself from the point of view of the Other who does not believe or does not live this truth, the belief "becomes external to me – and, to that degree, I cease to understand myself."[91] The gathering and centering function of faith is evident in occasions where one has occasion to attest to or disavow that in which one believes. Whereas when one "attests" to one's belief, even though the present propositional form might well seem to someone awkward or strange, as in the ritual of "saying the creed" – because it looks like one is achieving a merely cognitive doxastic act of believing-that and not more basically an "existential" resolve or believing-in – one is really stating "that I should be going back on myself, and – yes –even annulling myself were I to deny... this reality of which I have been the witness."[92] The first-person lived sense of oneself as this person in the world is here manifestly tied to faith as a centering and upholding attitude that takes form in certain propositions. We see here that in a religious community Existenz can attest to itself in formulae that are "the same for us all," i.e., all the believers; yet the prior analyses in this work give reason for thinking that even these common creedal formulations would, in so far as they reflect centering acts of faith by distinct persons, also have unique senses for the different believers.

Faith clearly is tied to "vocation" as the way Existenz finds to realize what is of utmost importance. Here in this present context, of course, faith and vocation become more explicitly *theological* themes. Traditional theology can be used to explicate this phenomenological sense of faith in accord with the parameters of The Theological Distinction. Such a theological sense would be: "If I refuse to believe and to affirm by, e.g., repudiating the exterior creedal witness, my eternal destiny, which is inseparable from my true self, is in peril." In this respect faith appears in the first-person as a duty that one cannot neglect without self-betrayal.[93] Later we will have occasion to spell out the metaphysical sense in which this is a betrayal of oneself.

In question here is the *authority* of what faith makes present as the First Truth. Faith presences a unique kind of evidence, importance, and veracity before which familiar forms of veracity, importance, and evidence pale and without which they can have no hold. (Cf. the analogous matter found in our earlier discussions of the prospective retrospection of one's death and the coming forth of Existenz.) The teaching or *Kerygma* is that to which faith assents mediately; it is The First Truth which is that to which faith assents immediately in the sense that it is inseparable from one's center. Dogmatically considered, this is the work of the Godself, the Holy Spirit. The Kerygma as an epistemic target of one's assent is more or less credible; the witness or creaturely source of the teaching (the Church, one's parents) are more or less trustworthy. As such neither of these equate with the wonder of faith as a loving movement toward and assent to the First Truth. Yet because there is always the inadequation between the immediate presence of the First Truth and the epistemic intention, i.e., this latter is always unfilled, needing more light, new interpretive schemes, etc., faith is always "seeing darkly" and never without the possibility of doubting that to which one mediately assents. Similarly separating faith as it is wrapped in one's acculturation as a child from faith as the center of one's Existenz is also always a matter of a journey into a unique light out of darkness which of necessity must also appear as journey into darkness out of light. And even though there may seem to be external resemblances, it would be a mistake to take the sense of the necessity of the affirmation of The First Truth (as mediated by the assent to the creed) as an obsessive-compulsive and superstitious practice or "hang over" from childhood. The difference is in the first-personal sense of the necessity to be oneself and to love the First Truth from one's center. The obsessive compulsive behavior is a form of alienation and torment, and not an expression of Existenz and the Truth of Will. (This, of course, is not to say that within the sphere of faith's practice there are not pathological instances of obsessive-compulsive behavior.) Clearly the adjudication of this complex matter is not that of a third-personal perspective that a priori trumps the first-personal.

Thus St. Thomas' first-person phenomenology of the act of faith (even though he gives a third-person description of it) purports to harmonize with the third-person dogma of The Theological Distinction. He holds that the will is moved to embrace the motion of this divine transcendence in immanence precisely because there is an implicit awareness that it is eminently good "to give himself in this way to the truth of faith."[94] In our earlier terms, one's Existenz is at stake in regard to what is of unconditional importance. St. Thomas tended to link the interior instinct-like assent of faith to the First Truth to the doctrine in the *Epistle to the Hebrews*, i.e., that faith is assent to "the substance of things hoped for," which he translated as the promise of eternal life. "Eternal life" must be taken in both in the first-person lived sense of (the at least limit-simpliciter case of) living as well as the third-person objective (at least limit-simpliciter) condition, what tradition has called "the community of saints" and "heaven." Thus the will or "heart" is moved by the desire of eternal life, but the formal motive is the authority of That One as the Truth "for its own Sake" who reveals to us this very eternal life and who reveals us to ourselves in terms of our eternal calling.[95] Thus the criticism of Kant of a kind of sensualism is avoided, i.e., one is not acting merely out of fear of loss of the *unum necessarium*. Of course, this motion of the heart under the divine impulse is not unmediated. And for us this is a way of saying it is Existenz as the center of the personal I centering its life in terms of what is of unconditional importance in regard to its life in the world. This is to say that the divine motion of the heart described by theology is felt always in connection with the manifold experiences of ciphers in one's life, along with the formative education and edification of one's family, the loving struggle to communicate with friends and teachers, the witness and teaching of the one's Church and religious community, etc. Here Karl Jaspers' religious-phenomenological (not explicitly theological) descriptions have merit: Existenz's illumination and motion toward salvation are always in connection with the disclosure of a transcendence correlated with Existenz's transcending and this transcendence is always in connection with the presence of ciphers.

Yet, as we shall continue to propose, such faith, religiosity, and motion toward "transcendence" may not be simply equated with the transcendence of The Theological Distinction. Nevertheless, it seems of necessity to be connected with the dynamism of spirit and its infinitizations in ideals and limits simpliciter. Or, like the limit to which Kant, Blondel, and their followers point as ineluctably posited in the affirmation of the world (the unconditioned condition), these ciphers of transcendence may be senses of the common referent explicated by The Theological Distinction. In any case, in the first-person lived experience of faith as an assent to the "First Truth" there can be no question of a sense of God absolutely separated from one's Existenz and the experience of one's being in the world. Thus this connectedness to Existenz and enworldment, as well as the various guises and senses of the ciphers in the world, in no ways detracts from the depth of either faith or the authenticity of the piety. Nevertheless, The Theological Distinction explicates this faith experience as a revelation from a transcendent perspective and teaches that the divine source of the faith is precisely the God of The Theological Distinction who invites us to Godself as what is beyond the world and beyond infinitization; indeed, we are invited to a self-transcending to God in Godself.

This first-person awareness of what is of unconditional importance has been called by Blondel an awareness of the "undetermined supernatural." It is "supernatural" because it involves the recognition by Existenz that the world is not the place of one's fulfillment, and that either we are endowed with a futile desire for transcendence or the adequation of the will is not within out grasp. (Cf. Chapter IV, §2.) This undetermined supernatural is at once necessary for Existenz and, at the same time, impossible for Existenz to bring about.[96] What is called the gift or grace of faith is precisely a way out of this dilemma. But, again, this does not mean that what is given in faith is merely the completion of the heart's desire; it does not mean that the ineluctable affirmation of the divine as the ground of meaning and value requires the explication that God is a part of the world, i.e., its ground. The Theological Distinction reveals a gift that, of course, is the heart's desire – and then infinitely more, i.e., a gift that is incommensurate with the heart's desire, a limit case which elevates the eros toward the limit simpliciter to a new "dimension." ("Eye hath not seen, nor ear heard, nor has it entered into the heart of man...," etc.)

In terms of The Theological Distinction we may say that the grace of the Spirit awakens in the person an awareness of the connection between Existenz as inseparable from her willing will and the teaching of the Scriptures and Tradition. And yet, unless this willing will is "elevated" to what is beyond the horizon of the world, we have reason to think of this religious stance as "merely" natural religion, as holy and as edifying as it might well be. That is, it is a stance in regard to the infinite

ideals latent in the world opened up by the willing will's dynamism. As such it is a
stance in regard to the limit simpliciter, and does not move beyond the infinitization
and the ultimate horizon of the world to the limit case (as Barry Miller would put
it). But again, is this so readily discernible in one's first-person awakening to faith
and its "formal object?"

The inadequation of the will may find in the ciphers of religion, philosophy, art,
and nature, referents to mysteries which are essentially beyond objectification and
beautiful beyond words. They may well appear as the numinous ground of life and
the world. They surely are motives of any form of religiosity and faith, and they
might well be part of being human. This is to say it is doubtful whether there is
religiosity absolutely separated from the mystery pointed to by the dense objects of
ciphers such as myths and sacramentals. It approaches inconceivability that there
is religion apart from the space opened up by the infinitization of spirit, for in this
case transcendence would be displayed as the uniquely presenced absence apart
from the absolute position-taking and reverence that one reserves for the divine. It
is hard to think that a form of faith which is bereft of the *tremendum fascinans* of
the holy as the presence in every-day surroundings of what is transcendent to and
incommensurate with all that we cherish and which is bereft of the position-taking
toward what is of unconditional importance could be sustained as an act either of
"natural" or "supernatural" religion. Nevertheless it must be said that even though
natural religiosity's forms are necessary motivating factors in bringing about the
devotion and reverence which characterizes the religious position-taking and faith
as a centering act, and even though they provide a meaning-framework for religion
which provides senses for concepts like God and transcendence, they may well not
be revelations of the God of The Theological Distinction precisely because they
are "merely" expressions of infinitizations of spirit and divinizations that belong
to spirit as correlated with the world. (Indeed, one may as an outsider be moved to
make this judgment if the religious persons themselves articulate their faith in such
a way that, e.g., God is held to be dependent on the world – but such a judgment
has nothing to do with a judgment on the authenticity of the faith of the person, but
only with the content of her faith.) These forms of religiosity may well be aspects of
the intelligibility of the world and one's being in the world. Yet no religion makes
much sense if it does not involve the limits simpliciter that the dynamism of spirit
intends; but such religion might not articulate the transcendent "limit concept" as
such which is incommensurate with this infinitization. This latter absolute transcendence we are ascribing to, at least, "the Abrahamic traditions."

For The Theological Distinction, revelation at the core of Existenz is explicable
as a dogma, and thus the Spirit eventually reveals Itself and Its workings in a proposition. Thus the will's illumination is such that it is moved by the divine transcendence in immanence to transcend its own infinitization and agency of manifestation
in favor of, i.e., in obedience to, "the First Truth." This First Truth reveals itself as
the source of the revealed truth of the tradition, Church, etc., and as the source of
the revealing agency by which it discloses whatever it discloses and as the transcendence beyond the infinitizing transcendence which is the essential inadequation to the
world. This transcendence in immanence is neither double-talk, nor a usurpation,

nor suppression by the divine of the creaturely agency. Nevertheless even this dismissal of the charge of double talk and of suppression is not something that can be properly understood apart from the space opened up by faith and its articulation in The Theological Distinction.

And yet the lived experience of the act of faith is what founds the classic description, e.g., that "no one comes to the Father unless drawn and urged by the Spirit." But in spite of the lived experience being the foundation of the description, as lived experience it is not in a position, apart from the dogma explicated by The Theological Distinction, to sort out the natural from the gracious, perhaps special, "supernatural" motion of Existenz. That is to say, from the first-person living out of faith, as it may be described by such concepts as Existenz, the inadequation of the will, the insufficiency of the world, the truth of will, and the power of the "evidence" of the believed-in "revelation," etc., there is no perspective which sorts out what is natural or supernatural.[97] By definition divine revelation cannot be merely the disclosure of one's "ownness" for one is not God. There must be a standpoint, voice, perspective, etc., beyond my own to which I defer as authoritative even for interpreting my ownmostness, i.e., myself as Existenz. This is the function of dogma as an articulation of this revelation. It is only the dogma of The Theological Distinction, for which the utter incommensurability of the divine and the world is central, that makes considerations such as the "grace" which "nature" receives, perhaps longs for, but cannot demand, important and necessary. And it is this aspect of incommensurability and infinity that bring us back to Kierkegaard's notion of the "absurd."

First, it must be said that the first-person lived experience of the transcending of the world in faith is not lived as "absurd," but rather, in spite of the darkness, a unique form of light. Secondly, the "absurd" typically surfaces when one attempts to adjust one's faith to the intersubjective public criteria of the world and its legitimate claim to set the limits of reason.

Thus Kierkegaard's notion of the "absurd" can be related to the question of the "thinkability" of The Theological Distinction. This exercise in thinkability is not the thinkability within a particular context, e.g., foreign policy, plane geometry, chess, accounting, merontology, baseball, etc. *Widersinn*, a translation of "absurd," is properly a disappointment or failure of an intention within a particular context brought on by the present filled intention contradicting the particular empty one. In this sense "paradox" is the tension in the referent, a tension based on the interplay of a believed-in proposition and a filled intention, and the absurd is the coming to light of the incompatibility of the believed-in proposition and a filled intention. (For example, within the context set up by "circles" – and therefore involving curves, radii, a center – I am required to think of "a square circle," i.e., I am required to think of something excluded by the context; or in the context of a description of someone's appearances I hear that "her long black crew-cut spewed forth invisible denunciations of praise.")

"Thinkability" in the framework of The Theological Distinction refers to the possibility of thinking about the necessities that obtain in the world or in the necessary features or conditions of the possibility of something being thought, e.g., the necessary ingredients of a "conceptual scheme" like gravity, atomic weight, a meal,

a face, foreign policy, etc. "Thinkability" here asks whether these necessities could
be *not* absolutely necessary, i.e., whether they could be created and in an odd sense
"contingent." This is not to hold that all the necessities which we know in the display of the world or in the display of displaying are to be regarded as eliminated in
the most basic believed-in or hypothetical context. The necessity, e.g., of maintaining the foundations of propositional logic in transcendental logic, the inseparability
of intelligibility, display, and acts of understanding, or the necessity of maintaining
as a condition for the intelligibility the existence and interplay of meta-ideas or
forms as sameness and difference and unity and multiplicity might seem to be such
that they are of an "uncreated" nature. That is, they appear to be the conditions of
any sense of intelligibility and meaning that we can bring to mind. If this is true
they would appear to be essential to the divine term of The Theological Distinction,
and in this sense intrinsic to the divine essence.

Such a determination of the absolutely necessary ideas or meaning frameworks
must past the test of what is conceivable for us. But that is precisely the problem
in this case. We are holding open the possibility that reason as confined to humans
may be not only de facto created but even its ultimate principles might be capable
of finding another context which relativizes much of what is basic for it. Thinking
about the de facto necessities of nature as being possibly not necessary is an easier
task than thinking about the de jure necessities or a priori conditions of intelligibility themselves possibly not being necessary. But the Theological Distinction
proposes we entertain this possibility, without knowing absolutely and comprehen-
sively in advance whether, e.g., such meta-themes as the interplay of sameness and
difference, and the ultimacy of the correlation of intelligibility with display and acts
of understanding, etc. are exceptions.

Strictly speaking it is not self-contradictory nor is it "absurd" if one concedes
that the necessary frameworks of the world, apart from those which seem not to
admit of being created (otherwise there would be a loss of the possibility of intelligibility), are not absolutely necessary. If one insists that all the necessities of the
world, the natural contingent ones and the a priori ones, are absolutely necessary
then The Theological Distinction is unthinkable. But surely as we can conceive that
the empirical necessities of nature could be otherwise, so we can speculate that or
posit the hypothesis that even also many of the a priori necessities might be created.
This "thinkability" is an empty intention but it is not inherently contradictory. If the
claims for the absolute necessity and unthinkability are themselves "default" positions in our display of the world, is it not thinkable that there be a measure beyond
the world, even if we cannot conceive what the measure would be? Notice once
more that, for the proponent of The Distinction, there is not the claim to know or
have access to evidence for the more ultimate standpoint, or to understand what it
would mean to know or have access to it or to posit possible worlds which nullify
the a priori necessities of this world. (See our discussions in Book 1, Chapters I and
VIII.) The objectionable possible-world theory posits that our experienced necessities in the world as well as the conceptual necessities may be rendered not necessary because of the posited possible world wherein these necessities do not hold.
The Theological Distinction's positing God does not render unnecessary the

experiential and conceptual necessities emergent out of the world, but God is posited as a more fundamental necessity that creates these worldly necessities.

To say that The Theological Distinction is "thinkable" for the person in the natural non-faith attitude is merely to say that the world's status as the ultimate criterion is able to be entertained as possibly penultimate. But the believer goes much further than the thinker in the natural attitude. For the believer faith is precisely this gift, most basically a gift of love, to move beyond the world and all that is valuable in the world and to affirm God as the absolute source of the world. Religious faith, over and above the faith of the centering act and the act which sustains Existenz's centering, is the power to be moved toward an excellence that is not commensurate with all that we esteem.

Kierkegaard makes this point when he says that "God's love is incommensurable with the whole of actuality"[98] (Cf. our discussion above §§6–7 that God plus the world is not more excellent than God alone.) He makes it also when he seems to distinguish between believing on the strength of or in virtue of the absurd, which is the passion of faith, and believing the absurd. The latter is nonsense; the former, he claims, is normative for Christians. "On the strength of the absurd," means that understanding involves seeing the "absurd" not within the general context of the world, e.g., where a believed-in proposition that, e.g., America is free of problems of race, class, or poverty, is contradicted by a filled in-the-flesh experiences of spending time in a major city; but rather seeing it within the context of faith and, we may insert, within the context of The Theological Distinction. This interpretation is supported in Kierkegaard's statement: "The absurd does not belong to the differences that lie within the proper domain of understanding. It is not identical with the improbable, the unexpected, the unforeseen."[99] Clearly for Kierkegaard we are to recognize "the impossibility as such"; but faith empowers us, and this is what is absurd from the ultimate human perspective, to not let the impossibility as defined by the horizon of the world be decisive. Faith has reasons which reason, as rooted in the ultimate framework of the world, does not know. Faith as the centering act of Existenz opened to The Theological Distinction is always at once both an act for which the being launched into the darkness of infinity is borne by a grace and an awareness that it leaves behind what is the solid ground of the world as the ultimate publicly verifiable realm of meaning, intelligibility, and evidence.

Among the necessities that pervade the world and that condition the very meaning of the human person and Existenz, but which are now believed through faith to be no longer absolutely necessary, are those dimensions of what Plato called *anangke* that we tied to the awakening to Existenz from out of the encounter with life's boundary- or limit-situations. These "situations" are our ever-present necessary conditions by which we frame our lives as persons in the world and which on occasion intrude in such a way that they insist on our giving them our whole-hearted attention and thereby they awaken us to our centers. (See above Chapter III, §2.) But with faith these fundamental ultimate situations which give the contours to the world as the setting of our life appear as not having necessarily to be. They are but need not have been our defining situations. Death, guilt, suffering, the struggle to communicate, and chance as determinative of that which shapes how we define the realities and values within our lives are now "seen" through the eyes of faith as not being necessary at all. To these we may add what is not so much a limit-situation but rather a feature that is both interior to one's own subjectivity as well as pervading the intersubjective world one experiences: wickedness. This clearly is not to say that because faith invites us to believe that these need not be or have been, we may treat wickedness and the limit-situations as actually not defining necessary conditions of our life in the world – any more than we may treat the laws of physics and biology, which we now believe to be created, to be no longer operative. Yet to appreciate these as not ultimately necessary, just as appreciating oneself as "chosen" and not merely a matter of chance, transforms the contours of the world's landscape. But if someone were to presume that the faith-claim that the limit-situations need not be or need not have been grants to the believer a permission to say "I will not die," or "my relations with my friends always are free of struggle and my efforts at communication completely transparent," or "my agency is without guilt," or "pain and chance have no place in my life," etc. – and thereby deny the necessity of these situations as essentially defining and conditioning every aspect of her personal being in the world, there is of necessity awakened for the typical listener a comic situation. These statements appear absurd because they fly in the face of the most stubborn and familiar forms of evidence of what is necessary.

Kierkegaard, on occasion, indulges in "thought-experiments" which approximate our attempt to soften the sense of the absurd. They move the religious dimension away from the theme of the absurd as something to celebrate for its own sake (cf. Tertullian's "I believe because it is absurd") in favor of a meditation on kinds of necessity. They have to do with the "thinkability" that the pervasive necessities that obtain in life may either vanish or be transformed. "If it happened once in the world that the human condition was essentially different from what it otherwise always is, what assurance is there that it cannot be repeated, what assurance that that was not the true and what ordinarily occurs is the untrue?"[100] Yet, it must be said, such conceivability is still within the confines of worldly eutopian possibilities that are commensurate with the world or are limits simpliciter of our reason and understanding in the sense that there is no logical contradiction. The Theological Distinction places us beyond this commensurability because we are thinking beyond the limits of the world and the distinctions within the world.

Clearly we are thinking beyond the parameters of the stock premise of empirical science of empirical science and the conditions for action in the world, and we further think beyond what is a theory of ethics based on being a human person apart from faith.[101] In this respect, God or the supernatural is not something likely or probable; nor is it possible in terms of meliorist or eutopian version of the world. Rather, it is, as the object of faith, incommensurate with the world, and in this sense "absurd."

As to our often repeated question of whether The Theological Distinction moves beyond the foundations of formal logic and propositional logic, the answer is: On the one hand, there is no answer if we intend to establish in advance which necessities of reason and the world are created. Whereas we may get clear on what are the necessary conditions for thinking about, or the display of, anything whatsoever, it is not obvious that these conditions themselves might not be created. On the other hand, the answer is No if this "move beyond" is the philosophical theologian's thoughtful reflection that moves within the new space opened up by faith and The Theological Distinction; here tautologously "thinking" is in play and the principles of transcendental and formal logic hold. Thinking about and within The Theological Distinction does not renounce the fundamental principles of transcendental phenomenology, i.e., the agent of manifestation, nor does it renounce the basic interplay of identity and difference, and the basic relations between propositions of non-contradiction and identity or excluded middle. Nevertheless, it must be said that because God is not an identifiable being, and God's relation to the world is not a relationship of one entity to another entity, and because the other dogmas build on the peculiarity of God not being a being in competition with other beings, the application of the basic principles of formal logic, especially the application of non-contradiction and excluded middle, undergo a strain, if not a transformation. God's not being a being enables creatures to be and God to be more intimate to each creature than the creature is to itself. God plus Peter does not make for two beings. In this sense the identity of the creature with itself and it not being another is strained, because in this case the other is God. The creature is not God, but it is not God in a way that is different from its being different from any other being.

The focal consideration for Kierkegaard's doctrine of the absurd is that the infinite eternal God has come into an "aesthetic relationship" with us, i.e., becomes the referent of a perceptual reality in time, i.e., God appears in the perceptual presence of Jesus of Nazareth. In this historical perceivable being there is a sameness in being God and being an individual human being. It is the contention of this chapter that this theme is continuous with that of omnipotence creating free independent selves; that is, it is no less mysterious or absurd than the more basic dogma that God who is pure To Be, creates creatures that have genuine being or existence in themselves. Neither in the case of God's transcendence in immanence in creation nor in that of the incarnation does God stand in competition with a finite being. God is not a being or a nature and therefore God's presence in the world, and the doctrine of the incarnation of God being present in an individual historical human being or being present sacramentally in the mystery of the Eucharist, are not doctrines having to do with the complex unity of a divine being and a creaturely being; God is not a being that can be negated by other beings or who negates the substantiality of other beings. God has no other to which God is essentially related. But what this means is "absurd" in terms of the categories of the world where each being is what it is by being distinguished from being something else.

Strictly speaking it cannot be that the person of faith "sees" or "understands" from the "perspective" which renders the necessities of the world created. But she grasps that the necessities of the world are, from the faith perspective, not necessary. This grasping precludes understanding and seeing which *eo ipso* are tied to the work of mind within the world. When Kierkegaard says, "He had faith by virtue of the absurd, for human calculation was out of the question…" and "the movement of faith must continually be made by virtue of the absurd but in such a way, please note, that one does not lose the finite but gains it whole and intact"[102] we find confirmation that The Theological Distinction is in play. Kierkegaard can say this, and regard it as part of the *eu angelion* or Good News, because although

"God" is inveterately conceived as within the world, somehow as part of the scene of everything that there is – just as the self inveterately regards itself as existing apart from the presence of God – "God" is nothing like this and our relation to God is very different from our relation to things or persons within the world, even though Christians are called to have also with God "an aesthetic relationship," i.e., acknowledge that the unconditioned God appears as an historical person in the conditionedness of the world.

The movement of faith may be said to have the aspect of the "absurd" because the world is the ineluctable horizon of meaning, and faith moves us "away" from the world – again understood as the ineluctable ultimate encompassing scene of our wakeful, thoughtful life. We are moved from the world to the source of the world and our inwardness, our subjectivity – and then again back to the world. Religiosity is not the religiosity of immanence and inwardness alone. This religiosity has to be reconciled with the "aesthetic relation" to God in the world.[103] But, we are moved away from the world as the ultimate encompassing meaning-framework – and this move away is not a loss but is impelled by the promise of life. Thus absurd here is always "absurd," i.e., the scare quotes are necessary; without the scare quotes it suggests that the "absurdity" of faith is of the same order of the absurdity of a foiled intentionality or contradiction of an empty intention in the world.

In the realm of any rational agency occurring in the absence of faith, faith is a move to the absurd because the rational self necessarily understands itself as at best "the Knight of Infinite Resignation" facing infinite ideals and consoled by his eternal validation of doing what is right in spite of the finitude, surds, and disappointments of life. In contrast, the Knight of Faith, who, like the contemplative, lives from out of a "naked faith" (St. John of the Cross), goes further. Faith does not merely renounce a "happy" existence or morally authentic existence within the world but redefines existence in terms other than that of authentic and rational agency. Its move of resting transparently in God is a move toward resting in the God of The Theological Distinction. In which case, one has faith "that I will get her," i.e., one will get what is the desire of the heart in spite of it being evident now that all is lost, in the sense that God is so incommensurately good that God plus the world is not greater than God alone. "By my own strength I can give up the princess, but by my own strength I cannot get her back again." The Good News is that in faith one has the princess, the world AGAIN, but not as "in addition" to God. This is perhaps a sense to be given Kierkegaard's doctrine of "repetition." Through faith, the believer gets back again the world that has been renounced; this is a repetition. In this life of faith in time this is an imperfect repetition but in eternity it is perfect.[104] (Cf. our discussion of Hopkins where "the thing we freely forfeit is kept with a fonder care...Yonder.") The "young girl" (in *Fear and Trembling*[105]) who remains convinced, in spite of everything, that her wish will still be fulfilled may be thought of as envisaging God as within the world or as something desirable along with the world. She does not recognize "the impossibility"; she does not recognize that God cannot be summed and that God is not measured by the possibilities of the world. Her desire or wishful thinking remains a petition; it is not the faith-informed having of the same again; it is not a repetition.

Finally, a few remarks about faith's "absurdity" in the "aesthetic relation." Because "God" is not a being and therefore not in competition with the world or anything in the world "revelation" as something conspicuous in the world either is or verges on being a form of deception. "If the god wants to reveal himself in human form and is in the least conspicuous, he deceives, and the relationship does not become one of inwardness, which is truth. But if he looks just like this individual human being then he deceives only those who think that getting to see the god has something in common with going to Tivoli."[106] Paganism is to exist in the world without God[107]; this is compatible with the understanding of Paganism as holding that God is part of the world. For Paganism, in this technical understanding, God is not beyond the world, and God is not an absolute transcendence in immanence to be reached only by faithful inwardness and faith in "the absurd." Rather, Paganism relates God "directly to a human being, as the remarkably striking to the amazed." Thus one looks for God as something remarkable in the world, e.g., "a rare, enormously large green bird, with a red beak, that perched in a tree on the embankment and perhaps even whistled in an unprecedented manner."[108] But the authentic relation to God in truth is one of inwardness and the pure faith that involves the insight that with God and Christ there is nothing remarkable to see and if God has something remarkable about him then he is not God.[109] And as a direct communication of inwardness is always involved in a miscommunication, so a fortiori a direct communication of the meaning of the inwardness and purity of faith in the language of the world is a miscommunication.[110]

Miracles pose a special problem because here God appears in the world as "remarkably striking." Here God's agency seems at once to interrupt and yet at the same time be linked to the natural-historical course of events. In other words, the integrity of the world appears to be violated in order that God may appear remarkably within the world. Such an appearance is valid for the pagan standpoint, but for the eyes of faith anchored in The Theological Distinction the miracle, whatever else it may be and whatever shape it assumes, is always also a reminder of the basic miracle of creation: something subsists in itself which has nothing that it has not received, something is free, autonomous, and responsible and yet is absolutely dependent, etc. God's power manifested in the world in the "wonder" is not an abrogation of the world's necessities *quoad se* but only *quoad nos*: In themselves these necessities are rooted in and held in being by the creative will which sustains them; but this perspective is hidden from us and is part of the empty intention of faith. What is evident is the apparent interruption of the causality of nature and history as we know it and the inclination to posit God's agency as part of or parallel to the natural-historical process, just as we find evident, e.g., a person with free will, and yet posit that her change of heart is due to God's working through or parallel with psychological-historical events. In short, we cannot help but be inclined to think that God plus the world are two, and God minus the world is less than God. But God's creating is not incidentally a "conserving." Nor is the fundamental mystery of creating which is inseparably a conserving a limit simpliciter of "cooperation," but rather the limit case of "cooperative agency." If there is a genuine miraculous event, then its proper sense would be that of a sign indicating to the believer the basic miracle of creation, or, for the Christian believer, who and what Jesus was in relationship to the creator; it is not primarily a magic-like suspension of the laws of nature calling attention to itself as a fantastic event within the world. Jesus appears to call attention to this relationship (in *Luke* 5: 17–26) when prior to the physical miracle and subsequent to the spiritual one, he asks, "Which is easier to say, 'Your sins are forgiven you,' or to say 'Get up and walk.'"

§9. Excursus on the Intentionality of Prayer and the Stance of Faith

As we miss something essential about ourselves if we think of ourselves primarily in the third person or in universal categories, so we miss something essential about God if we think about God in the third-person or universal categories. We thus side with Kierkegaard that God is precisely the one who, given an ontology of indexical perspectives, cannot become a third-party[111] or thought about in the third-person; this is the secret of religiousness proper to The Theological Distinction. And God is *uniquely* You, just as God is *uniquely* I. These personal pronominal references border on being equivocal. God is not You merely because God eternally calls us into being, as important as this is for this work. But, further, from the metaphysical and faith-perspective of The Theological Distinction, God is never able to become a she or he or it from whom we are absent although clearly she, he, or it are of necessity only occasionally present to us. And God as You is, in contrast to Others, not singled out from among others known in the third-person, as is our use of "you." (Cf. our discussion of the second-person in Book 1, Chapter IV, Part One.) When I faithfully think of God of necessity God does not remain a third-person but uniquely second-person. God's being You contrasts with all You's who are one among many. God the Creator, who has called me into being and is who is more intimately and eminently me than I myself am, is a You from whom I am never absent according to the metaphysics of The Theological Distinction but from whom I can and do absent myself in mind and will, i.e., intentionally. Yet in this case I absent myself from One for whom of necessity I am always incomparably present. Every You of my experience is ephemeral, i.e., an occasional indexical "you"; the indexical "you" is contingently affixed to everyone in the world with whom I come in contact. Yet, of necessity, according to The Theological Distinction, I am always and of necessity "you" for God not occasionally, but everlastingly, so. In so far as we may envisage our true selves as appropriately responding to this call, then for our true selves God would be never an occasional You but the everlasting You.

As a You God is transcendent in the sense of an ipseity and therefore a limit case; but God is not simply transcendent because God "now" is the author of my freedom and my self-hood and the source of what I refer to with "I." Therefore God is immanent in the sense of a limit case of immanence. God is not something external "in the sense that a policeman is"[112] nor something we could intend directly "like a rare enormously large green bird." God is therefore not merely a

You, but also an "I", a "subject," and a subject that is present for subjectivity only in inwardness. Not in all eternity can God be intended merely objectively, i.e., as some transcendent thing in the world.[113] (Thus the oddness of the intentionality for Christians in the "aesthetic relation" and the intention of Jesus of Nazareth. See our discussion of "centering prayer", in Chapter VI, § 4.)

Apprehending "God" in faith cannot be merely an intentional directedness to what is within the world. If all intentionality is of something within the world, faith is not an intentional act. (Recall Aquinas' claim that faith is loving assent to the First Truth and Kierkegaard's notion of faith as "resting transparently in God".) God is not something, not an *ens*, nor is God within the world. Yet the Christian intends an individual historical human being as God. The intentionality of faith must accommodate itself to this oddness or "absurdity"; we shall return to this. Here is another sense in which faith must continually be made by virtue of the "absurd."

Consider also this statement by Kierkegaard of the intentionality of prayer: "Prayer expresses the highest pathos of the infinite, and yet it is comical, precisely because it is, in its inwardness, incommensurable for every external expression..."[114] At its foundations prayer, like faith, is a suffering (*pathein*) or receiving grace and resting in the infinite God. As such, prayer is constitutive of inwardness. Yet, seen in the third-person, there is no possible appropriate expression that does justice to this attitude. Therefore it borders always on being comical.

Something similar is evident in the bearing of Kierkegaard's "Knight of Faith" in contrast to the bearing of the "Knight of Infinite Resignation" (wherein one can perhaps overhear a reference not only to Kant but to Aristotle's "high-minded man").[115] The "virtue" of the Knight of Faith, just as "God's" incarnation, does not compete with or transform creation (the divine "nature" is not a nature, not a kind of being) but is able to embrace nature in such a way that both its inherent richness as well as its transcendent infinite moorings are manifest to the Knight. "He has felt the pain of renouncing everything, the most precious thing in the world, and yet the finite tastes just as good to him as to one who never knew anything higher..."[116] Whereas to the onlooker there is nothing extraordinary, e.g., the Knight of Faith "looks just like a tax collector" or a capitalist, and his smile does not betray the incommensurability of the infinite with the finite, nor even that of the genius with the ordinary person.[117]

Part and parcel of this is the insight that only eternity can give an eternal certainty whereas faithful existence has to be satisfied with a struggling certainty "which is gained not as the battle becomes easier or more illusory but only as it becomes harder. The absurd, the paradoxical, the incommensurability remain." But one might ask, (a) if grace, if creation, if the forgiveness of sin are like this, then who can believe it? To which Kierkegaard answers with a sense of "belief" that is different from the sense found in the question: (b) If they are not anything like that, "how then can one believe them at all?"[118] That is, "belief" in (a) is used in the one sense as intelligible within the parameters of intelligibility of the world; in the other case of (b) that Kierkegaard proposes, belief is Existenz's leap borne by grace to what is beyond the encompassing parameters of the world to the strange whole that makes The Theological Distinction possible.

Everything is new and yet nothing is changed in as much as everything is embraced (seen-as...) and lived in the light of The Theological Distinction: "...the whole earthly figure [the Knight of Faith] presents is a new creation by virtue of the absurd. He resigned everything infinitely, and then he grasped everything again by virtue of the absurd. He is continually making the movement of infinity, but he does it with such precision and assurance that he continually gets finitude out of it."[119]

Because of the absolute priority of one of the terms or parts of The Theological Distinction, i.e., God, there is a basic ontological and axiological incommensurability in the parts. As we noted, in attending to the world or one of its parts, i.e., any being, e.g., Peter, and in intending God, I strictly speaking am not intending two units capable of being summed. God plus Peter does not make two. Thus it seems ontologically straightforward that I cannot count God among the things or beings that there are. In counting all the things/beings there are and in leaving God out, I am behaving ontologically correctly and am not guilty of atheism. Similarly, in counting on God or praying to God I am not able, at the same time, because I count on you and my family, to say without danger of being misleading ontologically, that I am counting on God, on you, and my family. The familiar refrain often uttered by successful Americans, i.e., "I want to thank my friends, my family, and especially God" has a seeming liberality but it tends toward violating the biblical injunction against worhipping idols in so far as this has to do with positing God as commensurate with anything.[120] This is the way we may understand Meister Eckhart saying:

> If anyone should think that to gain a thousand worlds plus God were any more than to gain God alone, he would not know God or have the slightest idea of God and would be a boor. Therefore a man should heed nothing but God. Whoever seeks for anything *with* God... does not know what he is looking for.[121]

For Eckhart, of course, this seeking God alone is not to exclude creation. The proper or "blessed" intending of God enables knowing "less with Him and outside of Him" and thereby the thousand worlds *in* Him. But God and the 1,000 worlds are there in the true "referent" of prayer to God. This referent is not to the mere 1,000, nor with God is the referent 1,001, "for things are one in God and there is nothing in God but essence."[122] (We here have an echo of our earlier discussion with Morris; but we also have a hint of monism that we hope to dispel at §11 below.)

In short, the intentionality of faith or of prayer cannot be ever merely an intentionality of a being among beings in the world. To say, because the faith-filled intention of God cannot be an intention of a being, it therefore is a consciousness of nothing, is not helpful, even if we capitalize and think Nothing or think no-thing. God is indeed no-thing, i.e., not a being in the world, but the sense in which that which is not anything can be intended or made present in faith is not illuminated by this gambit. Nor when we refer to God are we referring to nothing in the absolute sense as the contrary of being in any sense whatsoever. But, of course, this gambit is motivated by the awareness that the reference is odd. But that is true also of many philosophical terms which, although "objects of consideration," are not simply objects or what we refer to but rather also may be thought to include the referring and the one referring, e.g., the world, the transcendental I, and "being."

Given the world's encompassing anonymous presence as the setting for all thought and action, it is natural to think of the intending of God as merely intending the absent and posited cause of the world. In which case, we perhaps should think of God as the creator or cause of the world who is absent from any kind of worldly perceptual intentionality but whose posited, but perceptually-absent being, through faith, enables us to regard or experience the world *as created*. For example, why not think of our intention of God in relation to the world analogous to the way we may intend or co-intend the hidden energy source (cf. the "life force") of many worldly phenomena, e.g., machines and appliances? In experiencing such things we emptily intend the energy source. Appliances are experienced as propelled by energy even though the energy source is not perceptually present among what we intend when we use or think about our appliances. In fact there is an essential hiddenness or invisibility in our perception of energy. And in so far as the energy is understood to mean *potentiality* for work, for transformation, etc., there is also an imprecision and elusiveness in our conceptualization of it.

A chief reason for not regarding God as made present through an empty intention analogous to the reference to the hidden sources of energy is that specific empty intentions (e.g., of kinetic, electrical, or solar energy) which contrast with the abiding horizonal empty intention of the world are always of things within the horizon of the world. (The intention is not of any thing or any being within the world.) Intending the world-soul, "life-force," or even the extra-cosmic or extra-terrestrial super-natural invisible Artisan of the world, pulls us toward intending God as a being within the horizon of world because the causal relationship, even though conceived as the non-thingly causality of a form or besouling as in an entelechy, or as radically heterogeneous causal relation, e.g., as a chemical causing an hallucination, still enjoys a worldly homogeneity with its effects, i.e., its meaning still involves the nexus of the things in the world. Therefore, to the extent that the sense of cause and effect is at home in the world its transposition to The Theological Distinction misconstrues it by taking the worldly part as legislative for the sense of the chief part as well as the whole.

Yet to intend God in faith and prayer typically, i.e., apart from the mystical graces of sensible presence, seems to be a distinctive empty intention or an intention of what is absent to perception and elusive of conceptualization (as in "that than which nothing greater can be thought") even though believed to be present and believed to be that to which *we* are *necessarily present*. But this intending of what is absent is not an intending of a possible perceptual presence; the absence of God is not like the absence of something or someone in the world that may or may not exist, or even a memory of what was formerly present.

Thus, as we noted, God addressed as "you" is unlike any other "you" who typically is first present in the third-person or who can revert to a third-person status, and then who is selected out of this third-person presence. God's absence cannot be the absence of someone or something, nor can God's presence be the presence of someone from whom I can be absent and therefore something that is "really" absent from me. Even though God is not "really related" to the world and creatures of necessity are really related (through absolute dependence) to God, God's absence from me is never God's doing but my own – and this is never an ontological absence but always an "intentional absence," i.e., one tied to spirit's intentional consciousness.

It might be proposed that God's presence/absence is like the presence/absence of the horizon of the world. We earlier in this Book (Chapter IV, §2) pointed to the value-inadequation of anything, including all objective versions of ourselves with our willing will's intention. The deep intentionality of will, i.e., what we, following Blondel, called the willing-will, adumbrates a horizon that accompanies all our agency and thought. Each being, no matter how rich in goodness and beauty, is surrounded by an infinite "more" and, as Husserl himself holds, there is a deep will for a unity with and satisfaction in regard to the totality of life which is a constant co-presence as the life-horizon. Faith's intention of what is beyond the world finds a "natural" launching pad in the horizon of the world as the horizon of the spirit's desire to understand and find fulfillment. This horizon opens up the world to an indeterminacy and adumbration perhaps of determinable indeterminacy, if not mystery. But this, we have suggested, opens us up to a regulative ideal or limit simpliciter. But in The Theological Distinction we have to do with what is elusive in a different way because it is essentially different, i.e., it is the limit case to which the horizon points but to which it never properly draws near. But this infinite remoteness is *precisely what faith makes present* – obviously not in a filled intention of a perception or after the fashion of filled intention of an insight into an intelligible pattern that before was missing and eluded one's grasp; rather, this infinite remoteness or immeasurable Infinity is present through an unconditional allegiance and devotion, a position-taking that never surmounts darkness and obscurity, and thus it is an allegiance that is never absolutely free of having for an edge a possible doubt.

The dogma of God the Creator who is the other term of The Theological Distinction may be said to foster for faith a virtue of "ontological humility." But this "ontological humility" that emerges out of The Theological Distinction is a richly complicated optic and practice. First of all, The Theological Distinction explicates the very act by which one makes present the infinite darkness and silence of God the Creator as a gift. The odd incomparable move from the world to beyond the world to God as the Creator is not a move of which the natural or transcendental attitude is capable. It is a capacity that derives from a wholly different source and is properly named a gift or a grace. As such, as a gift, and therefore something (believed to be) bestowed by an act of freedom and generosity, it prompts from the receiver the free acknowledgment and stance of gratitude. Gratitude in what sense and for what? For the gift of one's being and the capacity to be grateful for the gift of one's faith and one's being

Thus faith provides a new sense of one's own being: My existing as uniquely myself and my being responsible for my self-determination themselves become gifts of God. Because there is nothing that I have not received (1 *Corinthians* 4: 7), my most basic self-esteem and validation of myself that I have for myself before myself and God now appears most fundamentally as itself a gift. And this very awareness of myself and my validation as a gift of God itself is a gift of God. I thus come to see that I myself, whether I live or die, no longer belong to myself in the way I thought I did prior to this recognition, but "to the Lord." Yet this very awareness of belonging "to the Lord" and not to myself bestows upon *me myself* a magnificence and freedom appropriate only to one who is exalted to participating in God's own life and liberated from the conditions of this world. (See 1 *Corinthians* 3: 21–23 and cf. Rudolf Bultmann's *Theology of the New Testament*, Book 1, especially 331.) The gift of faith of necessity has as its bonus a gift of joy and gratitude.

Without faith the gift of one's self and the world are only matters of contingency, "facts," for which one may (or may not!) be grateful in the sense that one rejoices in one's being rather than one's non-being. But there is nowhere to direct one's joy and gratitude without faith. And without faith one lives with the scarcely noted *fact* of one's being. This fact is greeted with the shrug of the shoulders, acknowledging "chance," or it might take the form of an agnostic being grateful *for* without being grateful *to*. We will return to this soon.

The believer must be foremost grateful and humble because even her faith, gratitude, and humility are themselves, according to The Theological Distinction, also and inseparably the Divine Spirit's caressing her will. Being judgmental and supercilious toward non-believers offends the very essence of faith in God's gracious relation to the unfathomable unique essence of all persons as well as to the mystery of the essential graciousness of one's own power to believe.

This direction of one's joy and gratitude in faith is not the simple matter it appeared to be in one's childhood naivety. Consider that the Whole which is God, oneself, and the world receives from the believer a complex assent. The world's excellences, necessities, and self-sufficiency are the woof and warf of the world and our life. Assent to and appreciation of these is the condition for the possibility for making sense out of whatever we make sense out of and take delight in. The world's intrinsic excellence, self-sufficiency, and necessity are the measure of our thoughtful and responsible display of matters, even the matters that are believed to be revealed. Yet the belief in the dogma of God the Creator oddly measures this measure of the world and resists being measured by this measure. Intending God and the world in faith is not intending two things. We wish here to return to this aspect of the intentionality of faith.

There is a different kind of assent in faith to the two members of the whole of The Theological Distinction. One does not affirm the world's self-sufficiency and necessities in faith – because these enjoy a first-hand evidence apart from faith – yet in faith one affirms differently the world in regard to its excellences, self-sufficiency, and necessities. In faith in God the Creator as the other term of The Theological Distinction one does not deny or supplant the original assent to the world, but neither does this original assent stand as independent and in competition with the affirmation of God. The original assent to the world's excellences, self-sufficiency, and necessities is not restricted to a matter of belief as faith in... or trust, nor is it in many, if not most respects, a matter of belief that..., as if we were dealing only with an impoverished form of evidence requiring that we be content with mere empty intentions. But with faith in the dogma as revealed, the world's basis, its excellences, self-sufficiency, and necessities, are now given moorings "elsewhere." They are not denied or deflated, but their basis is displaced to the other term of The

Theological Distinction. The world in its self-sufficiency, excellence, and necessity is appreciated as conceivably not having been, and although this non-existence is contrary to fact, the world is present over against its negation, i.e., its non-being, and the possibility that the other term, God, alone might be.[123] As the presence of "my death" casts my life into a fresh perspective, one which may render it exquisitely poignant or, in contrast, pallid, so faith in God the Creator presences all of "being" with an edge of nothingness. This sense of contingency is not necessarily experienced or felt but it is believed in. (Various philosophers, whether or not under the influence of The Theological Distinction, have claimed that it is not *how* things are that is amazing, even mystical, but *that* they are.) This means that the faith in this other term is given a different kind of weight than the belief or evidence that greets the world's self-sufficiency and necessities. But this different assent not only does not weaken or diminish the prior "natural" assent and evidence, but deepens the self-sufficiency, excellence, and necessities in the assent to that which (one believes) absolutely cannot not be. We do not assent to the world as what absolutely cannot not be nor do we regard it as that than which nothing greater can be conceived.

Thus the celebration of the genuine excellence, self-sufficiency, and necessity of what is disclosed within the horizon of the world can never be an occasion to detract from the excellence, self-sufficiency, and necessity of God. Indeed, detracting from what the agency of manifestation, in our own case as well as that of the cultural community at large, discloses as undeniable excellence, self-sufficiency, and necessity within the world, is, so at least Aquinas taught, a form of disrespect if not blasphemy toward the creator.[124]

Faith's drawing the believer to the one thing necessary, the unconditionally important, and the absolutely affirmable has for its consequence a fundamental stance, rather like an existential (not merely doxastic) epoché of the world: Of necessity (as Bultmann has taught us) faith's stance is a de-worlding (*Entweltlichung*) or desecularization. (See his *Theology of the New Testament*, 76–78.) As we have stated, the world is no longer the absolute measure of what is and what is important. Faith is a detachment from the idolatrous pull of the world, but the believer is not left with merely the absence of something, bereft of anything commensurate with her will and desire, nor is she we catapulted out of the world, nor does she find some ecstatic fulfillment that is a non-worldly, non-objective Ersatz for the natural attachment to the world. Rather she remains *in the world*, i.e., lives a life that does justice to the inherent dignity and beauty as well as the true necessities of the world, foremost that dignity and unique moral necessity that accompanies the presence of Others. But one is not *of the world* with its rule of death, hatred, and violence (*John* 17: 11, 14–16). Through trust, hope and anticipation it is an overcoming of death and a passing to life eternal, and the chief evidence that the believing Christians have passed from death to life, from the world to the Transcendence that creates, preserves, and saves the world, is the fact that they love one another (1 *John* 3: 14 ff.). This life of love is foremost what does justice to the inherent dignity, beauty, and necessities of the world. It also reflects the humility stemming from the insight born of faith that we exist and love because we were first loved.

The key source of ontological humility is the gratitude for existence, "that there is nothing that one has not received." G.K. Chesterton brings this home in his lively meditation on St. Francis. Francis, upon looking at his home town of Assisi, sees the large masonry of its walls and the massive foundations of its watch towers and its high citadel. All this gives the impression of what is safe, permanent, splendid, self-sufficient, independent, etc. But the dogma of faith in the creator God uniquely reverses this perception. The Latin root for the word for "dependence" suggests what "hangs." "If St. Francis had seen, in one of his strange dreams, the town of Assisi upside down, it need not have differed in a single detail from itself except in being entirely the other way round." That is, he would see all that he loved and appreciated about the town in all its detail, he would cherish it as much or per- haps more than before, "but the nature of the love would be altered even in being increased." He would see everything from bird to citadel "in a new divine light of eternal danger and dependence." Instead of being merely proud of his strong city because of its glorious solidity and its exalted towers, his perception would be suf- fused with a wonder and gratitude that Assisi, and even the whole cosmos, "had not been dropped like a vast crystal to be shattered into falling stars."[125]

For the post-Enlightenment religious person and the non-religious person there are serious obstacles for this gratitude for existence that the religious person such as Chesterton professes. How, it might be asked, can one be grateful for that which is the insurpassible Presupposition for all that for which he might be grateful? And how can one be grateful if one is so unfortunate as to think of one's life as a burden from which one wants, before everything else, to be liberated? As to the first ques- tion, both the believer in creation and the "existence mystic" would reply: But that is precisely the wonder of this unique gift and the unique thanks that one's gift of faith is! As to the second question, there is here no question of being grateful for such a person's misery or insisting that such a person be grateful.

Yet the two questions can draw near when one considers that as one may wonder *that* something is, rather than nothing, even the person cast into despair and about to commit suicide might still wonder that she is so "thrown into being" when she need not have existed at all, and that there are so many other sentient and non-sentient beings who do not exist in such misery, etc. This deliberation need not serve as a deterrent to the act of self-destruction, but it calls attention to the distinction between *that* one exists and *how* one exists. That from the dreadful state of one's own existence one infers that all existence of necessity, in its *how*, is dreadful is poor reasoning, even if such a thinker's lamentable circumstances might merit our deepest sympathy.

Gratitude is both an emotional attitude and a communicative speech act. It is one of those emotions that finds a completion in expression. That is, being grateful prop- erly is tied both to expressing one's gratitude and acting gratefully. Saying "thanks" or expressing one's gratitude in the pre-designated intersubjective-communal ritu- als forms the culture provides is inherent in the meaning of being thankful. If one received a favor, e.g., a gift without which one could not pursue the dream of one's life, yet said nothing to the benefactor and acted boorishly and rudely toward her, we would have reason to doubt that the person was grateful and our opinion of the person's character would sink. Thus *saying* "thanks" for the gift to the giver of the gift is part of being thankful. "Thanks" is an illocutionary act, a "performative," that does not merely describe, e.g., an interior attitude, but effects the ritual of "being grateful" and acknowledging one's standing in debt to the benefactor. As the gift is unexacted and gracious, so the beneficiary undertakes graciously, i.e., freely, the appropriate ritual of expressing her gratitude as a grace in response to a grace. As the gift is not what is strictly owed in justice, so the thanks is not a repayment, but itself the beneficiary's free willing expression of gratitude. Of course, one might imagine a circumstance in which saying publicly "thanks" would be inappropriate, or where acting boorishly was precisely the right thing to do. Thus, e.g., by not showing one's thanks and acting boorishly the beneficiary would in fact protect the benefactor from her enemy's reprisals.

Today we can hear, often from agnostic quarters, of the importance of acknowledging an attitude of gratitude *for*, e.g., one's existence, or the gift of one's life, e.g., in terms of the overall successes and good fortunes that have occurred to one as well as one's being able to occasion some good for others. It would seem that there is something boorish and ungracious if one is not grateful for one's good fortune, that one has been able to do other people some good, etc., even if this is not gratitude for the fact of one's being – for this, after all, could have turned out to have issued in a long series of misfortunes instead of these occasional fortunate things.

It is suggested that in this case of wanting not to be boorish or ungrateful for one's good fortune, there is an important form of gratitude *for* without there necessarily being any gratitude *to* any one. The claim is that one is not merely appreciative, that one takes delight in and feels that one has been fortunate or lucky, but that one is profoundly and genuinely *grateful*, but grateful *for* without being grateful *to anyone*.

Such a view tends to uproot the attitude of thanks from the communicative speech-act situation. For example, here there is no "saying 'Thanks.'" One rather merely feels grateful and assumes a basic attitude of being grateful. There, of course, is still a connection of the felt attitude with one's expression of "gratitude-for" in one's behavior. If one snarled, constantly complained, was surly, etc. at all aspects of one's life, it is hard to believe that such a one had this grateful attitude.

Another example of such being grateful-for without being grateful-to is being grateful for someone being in one's life. In such a case, such a gratitude could not find expression in terms of someone to whom one would address one's gratitude *for*, e.g., the friend. If I am grateful for you (being in my life), what I might well have in mind is the very good fortune that we met and how grateful I am for our having met and for our friendship. And I might want to honor you by telling you how important you are for me and how I am grateful for you being in my life. Yet I am not properly being grateful *to* you for this good fortune. If I am grateful to you, e.g., to you for your friendship, that is a different matter than being grateful for the accident that you are in my life. You, as the one for whom I am grateful, are not the one to whom my expression of gratitude would be addressed if it were able to find expression in the communicative situation.

It thus seems that "being grateful for" requires less the performance of an illocutionary act; indeed if it is expressed it is locutionary, i.e., descriptive of the inner attitude. I may want to share that with others, but it is not an inherent part of being thankful-for, as it is of being thankful-to, that one expresses one's gratitude. Gratitude-for is a basic attitude which remains essentially foreign to the communicative speech-act situation which is the home of proper senses of gratitude, i.e., being grateful-to. Of course, I presumably have reason to be grateful *to* my friend, but, again, this is not being grateful in the same respect as my being grateful that she is in my life.

My own sense of this claim on behalf of a non-theistic thanks-for is that it is made by persons for whom theology's personal God, for whatever reason, has become a burden. This doctrine might well be understandably unsatisfactory because of its theological articulation. Nevertheless, for such a person the disposition and desire to be thankful persist. This is far from saying that this is bogus "thanks" even though it seems to me that "appreciating" or "feeling lucky" might often do just as well to capture what such a person calls "gratitude."

Yet such substitutions clearly will not work in some cases. Indeed, in the case of one proponent of this view, the attitude of "thanks" (along with perhaps "appreciating" or "feeling lucky") pervades this person's life as a meta-virtue informing all of his life. And he traces all of his moral failings to a lapse in not letting the attitude of "thanks" be present at the moment of the conflict or temptation.

I myself remember a deep sense of being grateful for rain after a long drought. "It is raining." But how can I be grateful to "It" and the raining rain? The impersonal verbs in various languages display natural events which are the boon and bane of human life. A believer may well be inclined to be grateful to God for rain, but she might just as well believe in nature's created autonomous realm of causality and be grateful for the raining without being grateful to any kind of "rain god." Ultimately, of course, there is a sense of being grateful *to* but this cannot be a choosing of God out of a plurality of possible targets for one's thanks. My sense of being grateful-for the rain was complete in itself, not because I believe that there is *no* sense whatsoever for being grateful-*to* nor because I believe that the being grateful *to* is unnecessary, but because in this matter the mere being grateful-*for* encompassed the being grateful-*to*. It seems here we have with these impersonal verbs a way of referring to nature's naturing and our thanks may be a being grateful-for without needing a being grateful-to.

The basic issue is that for people for whom being grateful-*for* is sufficient and being grateful-*to* unnecessary and inappropriate, the ultimate category, e.g., "Nature," the "world," the "absolute," "transcendence," "Being," etc., is there as "the way things are" of necessity and being grateful *to* the "universe" inserts a person and graciousness where there need not be such. "Being," "Nature," "the universe," etc. as "ultimate reality" are precisely the setting for everything and cannot be handled by typical theistic notions of a God as a being within or in competition with this ultimate setting. Such notions of God can be derived from stories about God as portrayed in the Bible, or any thoughts about "the greatest being," or any conceptions of God as a super-person. All these appear as stunting and incommensurate to that for which those persons are grateful.

I am thus tempted to say that the claim for a "gratitude for" without a "gratitude to" is based on an opposition to certain theological categories – which are deficient from the perspective of this chapter. For such an anti-theistic view being grateful-*to* undermines the depth and breadth of being grateful-*for*. But it would seem that the person of faith, for whom The Theological Distinction is in play, can rest in being grateful-*for* without the additional explicit being grateful-*to* precisely because the gratitude has to do with the fact of there being anything at all. If we are moved to be grateful *that* we are, what we are grateful for, being itself, is not easily made commensurate with someone, a being among beings, to whom we are grateful. Analogously, being grateful that "it rains" cannot be being grateful to "it" which rains, and yet there is a sense of the additional being grateful to God as a person controlling nature suggests that "it" didn't rain, or that the weather front blowing in had nothing to do with the rain. Here for the person of faith for whom The Distinction is in play it is not a matter of denying absolutely any sense of being grateful-*to*; one simply does not want the *to* to be inadequate to that for which one is grateful. This hesitation highlights the difficulties of saying God is a "person."

In order for God to be an analogous person it is necessary to consider that God addressed as "you" is unlike any other "you" who is first present in the third-person or who can revert to a third-person status, and then who is selected out of this third-person presence to be addressed. God is not a subjectivity whom we may or may not single out from out of the world and out of the intersubjective community and thereby permit to be present. As we have stated above: God's absence cannot be the absence of someone or something, nor can God's presence be the presence of someone from whom I can be absent and therefore who can "really" be absent from me.

Further, in the case of anyone one knows, one cannot say "I" and refer to this person. Yet in the case of God, when I say "I" I cannot not also refer to God, at least as the creator and exemplar of me myself. When this teaching is added to the doctrine that my actual being is precisely as the "image" or exemplification of a unique aspect of God through God's creative call and love – when I might not have existed actually at all – then a motive for being grateful-to surfaces that does some justice to the demands of "the absolute."

Typically for the persons for whom meaningful gratitude for life or existence is a non-theistic thanks-for and not thanks-to, a God who is a person cannot be God as the ultimate consideration. This is because the ultimate consideration, e.g., the "absolute" or "the world," is so encompassing and so penetrating that it does not tolerate the essential distance, otherness, and absence that a personal relationship requires. At the same time, the personal God, as a super-entity or Greatest Being, appears not only to crowd out the space of freedom persons require to actualize themselves in the world, more basically it suffocates the depth of one's own lived subjectivity. As we have seen, subjectivity has, properly speaking, no worldly causal basis and in this sense a ground. The metaphysical absolute would precisely be that which grounds subjectivity.

The agnostic argument might run: If "the absolute" is taken to be a ground of subjectivity, it cannot be a person. The ground of persons, the absolute principle behind the Who, a principle which, as absolute ground, does not have distance from my subjectivity, cannot itself be a person. A principle, a What, is not a Who. Every

Who is essentially distant from my subjectivity. Further, a person cannot give rise to another person, however indispensable the procreative agency of other persons is. Giving thanks *to* can only aim at another person who, by reason of our experience, is another subjectivity over against our own. This is precisely what "the absolute" is not. If I must be thankful for my good fortune, it is not *to* the absolute. Rather I must be content with being grateful-for, without being grateful-to.

In our interpretation, The Theological Distinction is aware of these challenges and purports explicitly to resolve such an opposition between the absolute and God as the One to whom one addresses all one's occasions of being thankful-for. But it does not do this primarily through philosophical insight into the nature of God or the absolute or the person. The philosophical concepts which are employed are faith-based. And what they articulate as an expression of faith is not oblivious of the serious challenges raised by reason and philosophy but rather in part motivated by these. Further, it is only with the divine term of The Theological Distinction that one can be grateful *to* while being no less appreciative of and grateful *to* all the Others to whom one is indebted for all that one is grateful *for*. And further, the believer in The Distinction must believe that someone's being grateful *for,* bereft of the capacity of being grateful *to,* finds unfailingly its address at the One to whom she, the believer, is always and everywhere grateful.[126]

The ciphers of the great reversal in the display of the world through faith, poetically captured in Chesterton's account of St. Francis standing on his head, have direct bearing on how one lives and acts. In the New Testament, The Theological Distinction's reversal of the way of acting in the world with others traditionally is phrased in the context of the symbols of "the Kingdom of God." It is precisely because one believes that there is nothing that one has not received that the presence of the Kingdom of God in history causes an upheaval in the reigning notions of status, power, privilege, and hierarchy. Because of the primacy of ontological humility awakened by the dogma of God the Creator, the first or greatest personages are placed last and the last first. To live appropriately in the world one must die to the reigning "worldly" version of life. To enjoy life's proper riches one must unburden oneself of a reigning version of wealth and poverty. To be the one who one is called to be one must dismantle false versions of oneself to which one clings because of both of one's biographical setting as well as one's lack of faith and love. To those to whom so much has been given, so much more of ontological humility and gratitude and perhaps generosity are to be expected. Of course, this has nothing to do with an institutionalization of a "kingdom" or state; these are not matters to be legislated or codified, so that, e.g., sin is criminalized and piety legislated.

Prayers of petition are given an appropriate setting within The Theological Distinction. The scriptures and tradition of course sanction that we express before God our concerns and needs, always with the condition that it be God's will. Of course, the believers believe that God knows better than they what they want and need, but it is part of the ontological humility that they express their needs. Gratitude for one's being is also an appreciation for one's being well and being at one's best and being with others at their best. But the prayer of petition ought not to be construed as merely our acknowledging our needs and indebtedness; and it is more than an act of alignment of our will with God's. Rather, with The Theological Distinction we affirm through faith that the direction of history is placed under a mysterious "providence" that sustains nature and history. Or as we put it earlier necessity$_1$ and self-subsistence$_1$ sustain or undergird (create) necessity$_2$ and self-subsistence$_2$. Through a prayer of petition rooted in faith's ontological humility the absolute difference of God's will and the wills and desires of creatures of good will are believed to meet in a holy "eschatological" unity and resolution that surpasses understanding. "Providence" is a way faith refers to the essential mystery of the personal aspect of the transcendent sufficiency and necessity that underlie the proper and alone intelligible kind of sufficiency and necessity/contingency with which we are familiar in the horizon of our experience.

Each has been given to herself the ontological dignity of her unique essence. Here is the root of ontological humility as gratitude that one is. This means that there further is not only gratitude for what one has and what one can be and do, but for who one is. (Cf. 1 *Corinthians* 4:7.) The victim of despair over what one is, is unable to appreciate who she is in her unique value-essence. This is a grace we owe ourselves and one another. This of course touches upon a focal theme of this book. The pursuit of justice is founded on "the radiance of spirit," or the inherent dignity of persons. As the giving to each what is her due through our transactions, justice builds upon that respect which each is foremost due her inherent dignity as a person This, of course, is a rich *philosophical-phenomenological* theme which we have touched on earlier (e.g., in Book 1, Chapter IV, §20 and Chapter VI, §7, and Book 2, Chapter V, §8). But in the context of The Theological Distinction the unique essence and dignity of the person, evident foremost in love, is founded in the divine essence. This philosophical-theological claim translates that of the Bible: each is created as an "image of God" and "eternally called" by God; in the traditional philosophical-theological language, each finds her exemplary "idea" in the divine essence. The pursuit of justice can never be anything but the realization of what is due a person based on the recognition and celebration of the intrinsic dignity of the person. When "justice" is pursued by means which disregard this intrinsic dignity, e.g., by torture, there is eliminated any sense of giving to the Other what is foremost due her, i.e., a non-eliminable respect. For The Theological Distinction, there is the further consideration: The respect verges on veneration because each is an exemplification of God's own essence. Each is a child of God, "offspring of God Godself."

The presence of the Kingdom of God completely reverses and makes topsy-turvy the "realism" of *Realpolitik*. Even though the believer still acknowledges wickedness as a necessity pervasive of the world we experience, faith does not submit to its power or reality. It does not accept its view that self-preservation and self-aggrandizement are ends justifying any means. It undoes the allegiance of individual believing citizens to the protocols of nation-states in their domestic policies toward "criminals" as well as in foreign policy toward other nation-states. These policies aim at self-preservation, and often self-aggrandizement, as the supreme end in itself. For the believing person, who is also a citizen of a nation state, there is no need of "legions of angels," to say nothing of intrinsically evil means, whether they be WMD's or Guantanamo Bays, to secure her well-being as a believer.

In the faithful witness to the Kingdom of God "among us" there is no need to suppress evangelical means to realistic ends of security and safety; a postponement of evangelical practice to the "end times" would seem to reflect rather a faithless cynicism regarding the Kingdom of God than prudence and "realism." What the Kingdom of God, as an elaboration of The Theological Distinction, requires is not naivety and being "nice" in the face of the reality of wickedness, violence, cynicism, and the undeniably overwhelming social problems. Rather, it calls for the courage of the radical reversal rooted in ontological humility and courageous-loving evangelical witness with all of its ramifications for being in the world.

Evangelical realism would seem to require recognition that demonization (as the suppression of the transcendent dignity of the person in favor of a guise of a sub- or non-human embodiment of all one's fears) is a failure of imagination. It would require instead creative imagination suffused with patience, non-violence, love, and forgiveness, even of one's enemies, and especially in regard to those who seem "beyond redemption" precisely because of the savagery of their acts or their hostility to reason and kindness. The counsel to be as wise as serpents in the face of the principalities and powers of the world, i.e., the counsel not to be stupid, would not seem to equate with *Realpolitik* or a policy that the end of security justifies whatever means. Further, that faith has so little affected these familiar necessities of the world points to the inherent ineradicable difficulty of ontological humility and the inherently impossible task of any creaturely weaving of the relationship of the parts of The Theological Distinction into a whole where the primary term is transparent in the derived created term. This is another way of referring to what traditionally has been regarded as the staying power of sin; it is also the acknowledgment that faith does not *eo ipso* eliminate wickedness as a pervasive feature of the world.

§10. The Analogy of Divine Self-Awareness and Intentionality

Let us return to our speculation on the terms of The Theological Distinction.

We have proposed that we think of actual beings or entities as identifiable referents within the world. Thus the "being" of the world differs from that of actual beings. But a fortiori the reference to the "being" of God requires major adjustment in our typical manner of reference and categoriality. The device of scare quotes can help with the realignment of our thinking. This traditional determination of God which The Theological Distinction articulates is often referred to as absolute self-subsistence or self-sufficiency, i.e., the divine is not essentially related to anything outside Godself. This is to say that the "being" of the divine, as *ipsum esse subsistens*, is a "being" whose own actuality does not stand in relation to anything transcendent to or other than Itself. Therefore its actuality as one of absolute self-subsistence and sufficiency, i.e., one actualized without reference to something transcendent to itself, may be thought of as a perfection (limit case) of absolute interiority, immanence, and solitude. The Theological Distinction enables us to consider Divine "Being" in itself, as absolute self-subsistence and absolute immanence, outside of which there is nothing which can add or detract from this "being" and outside of which there is nothing which can account for the being of creatures. This permits us to say that in a sense which The Theological Distinction explicates there is nothing exterior to the divine "being" and that it is in some sense innermost to all that is, and therefore each being's innermost core and secret lies outside itself.

Another way of saying this is that what is external to God is only a determination of the interiority of God. Aquinas can say "God knows not only the To Be that all creatures have in God in so far as they are one with him, but also God knows the To Be that is outside himself." And this being-outside Itself is a distinction in regard to God's own being, i.e., it is that wherein the divine essence knows itself as imitated or exemplified. This means that it knows what is other than Godself, i.e., what is other than absolute To Be. Thus God knows Godself conjoined with what is not Godself and wills Godself as so cojoined.[127]

As we have noted, the eternal ideas or exemplars are creative and productive of what is other than the divine essence in so far as these creative ideas have not come into being external to the divine "being." They are not to be thought of as functioning, as it were, autonomously as pre-existing forms or entelechies generating the finite beings in nature. Rather, precisely as divine exemplars, or the way the divine envisages Godself's own essence as able to be "othered" in creation and participated in by beings apart from Godself's own essence, they are creative. That is, in themselves (*quoad se*) or in regard to the divine knowing, they are productive by rendering the perfection that is internal to the divine essence exterior to It. But *quoad nos*, i.e., from our perspective, they are exemplary because through them we posit that the perfection that is exterior to the divine essence is interior to It. As the divine idea able to be "othered," the exemplar mediates or bridges what is interior to and what is exterior to the divine essence; it is not simply the divine essence nor is it the created exemplification.

In regard to our particular focal theme in this chapter, the *exemplar* is *not* the eternal unique essence of the "myself" of JG Hart which is one with the divine self-awareness of its essence; nor is it the unique essence of the "myself" that I, the creature, JG Hart, properly refer to, whether or not amnesiac or *sui compos*. Rather it is what the divine knows in knowing the unique essence of "myself" as this aspect of Godself to be othered in me, JG Hart. The ideal exemplar is distinguished from the actual created thing in so far as it bears in itself in an absolute way the being within and being without the divine essence or To Be. In contrast, the "myself" which JG Hart properly refers to, does not bear in itself (i.e., I do not bear within myself) this being within the divine essence. The being which is exterior to the divine essence, e.g., the created "myself" that JG Hart refers to, is not anything apart from and independent of its ideal exemplar, and this ideal exemplarity is "in some way" its very reality. "In some way" means: There is no perfection which I have which is not endlessly more eminent in the divine essence and self-awareness. Indeed, following Barry Miller's distinction we must say more: the divine perfections are not merely infinite limits but are limit cases vis-á-vis my perfections. Thus the created thing exterior to the divine essence shares something of the infinite measure of the eternal exemplar without thereby overcoming, or we being placed in a position to deny, the reality of its finitude as existing outside the divine essence.[128] (Yet, as we have insisted and will have further occasion to insist, the unique essence of "myself" may not properly have either a limit simpliciter or limit case.)

For The Theological Distinction, the divine act of creation is the act by which anything which exists *is*. Therefore it is innermost to all that is.[129] This means, of course, that the divine "being" may not be thought of primarily as a transcendent object apprehended in the third-person. Rather, because the divine being is absolutely self-subsistent and its life is one of infinite interiority we may therefore think of the divine as exemplarily a subject. Indeed, God in God's essence is not even an object for Godself in so far as this would imply a transcendence beyond God's own life and an intentional relation between a subject and object that establishes a distance between the knower and known or an inadequate presence of the transcendent with regard to the immanent. That pure self-inwardness which is exclusive of anything transcendent cannot be determined by a transcendent object or being whose very nature is to be exterior and transcendent to the act positing it as an object.[130] Rather its "inwardness" can only be that of a pure act whose actuality is self-contained or immanent to itself and within which is contained the actuality of all possible perfective achievements. Thus The Theological Distinction moves us to think of the divine being "in itself" as the exemplary absolute self and as immanently manifest to itself in the pure act which is itself.

Therefore its self-presence is exemplarily non-reflexive, non-intentional self-manifestation. Its self-possession does not require the distinction or otherness of itself from itself that intentionality requires. This "self-possession" would be "exemplary" in the sense that the divine essence would not merely be "lived," i.e., non-reflectively self- present, but such that any analogous divine "act of reflection" brings no additional or specifying light. In contrast to the human case where intentionality and self-reference are necessary to complete the life of the ipseity or the "myself," in the divine case there is no such need of intentional self-reference. This was seen in antiquity, as in Dionysius the Areopagite, when it was claimed that in the Godhead there is an undifferentiation without confusion within the transcendent unity. Recall also Aquinas' distinction of God's "simple apprehension" from God's "vision."

Difference, sameness, unity, and negation are implied in this "undifferentiation without confusion" in so far as the divine essence may be articulated in terms of a manifold of essences, relations, properties, etc. In the plurality of essences, relations, etc., each is not the other and each remains different from the other. But Dionysius and Aquinas emphasize the unity and simplicity which do not lose the richness of the many. We may think of the feeble analogy in our *intentional* (not non-reflective) life where a mother can refer lovingly to her several children in one "polythetic" act which encompasses all of them without any loss of the distinctive love for each.[131] Dionysius and Aquinas claim this undifferentiation without confusion for the divine self-presence which we interpret to be not a "polythetic act" but rather the essential presence prior to any analogous intentional acts of self-awareness, i.e., acts of self-reflection.

But this difference and negation within the unity of self-awareness prior to any intentional act is not the otherness that we seek here to account for, namely that of the radical otherness to the divine of created subsistent beings. Yet finding *within the divine* a form of self-othering, i.e., where the divine is other to *Itself*, helps us on the way to thinking about creation. For this we raise the possibility of introducing intentionality within the divine life.

In each person's non-reflective awareness we recognize that there is a self-manifestation (non-ascriptively) of the non-sortal individual essence. So, similarly, we might speculate, in the divine case, divine self-presence is a pure simple self-manifestation. And, as in our case, the non-ascriptive self-manifestation supercedes the personal properties that reflection brings explicitly to light (in so far as they can never nullify, be the equivalent of, or substitute for this), so in the divine case the divine self-presence transcends any of the properties or essences that may illuminate the divine. If we may think of intentionality as an act which "others" (understood verbally) and enables participation in or unity with the disclosed otherness, the divine then may be thought of as essential pure unothered act, the faded image of which in us is the non-reflexive self-awareness characterizing our wakefulness and pervading our intentional life.[132]

Thus whereas for the consciousness that we know, intentionality, including reflection, enriches knowledge of the person by way of making manifest through a proper knowing or articulation, by contrast, in God's knowing of the world, through a kind of self-othering reflection and intentionality, the original unsurpassable richness of the non-intentional self-awareness remains the norm or measure that cannot be superseded. All that is known is known through this non-intentional knowledge of God's own essence. There is no enrichment by going beyond this non-intentional, unothered act. Again, our knowing only hints at this in the non-ascriptive and non-intentional nature of self-awareness. Yet because it is a genuine although anomalous sense of knowing it may be said to be analogous to the divine self-presence.

Whereas in the divine case there is in the unothered act a self-presence of the infinitely rich divine essence in an undifferentiated yet unconfused manner, analogous to the polythetic act where the mother enjoys all her children in the immediacy of a filled intuitive intention, in the case of human personal non-reflective self-awareness there is the unothered act wherein there is the immediacy of the self-presence of one's unique essence. In each case there is a presence of one's ownmostness and unique essence; in each case it is bereft of any articulation of *eidé* or ascription of properties. But in the divine case what is present without ascription is, within the divine essence the infinite manifold essentialities in all their unity and richness. In the human case there is only the unique presence of one's own unique essence. Further, in the human case the intentional act of self-reflection is necessary to illuminate the knowledge of oneself; being the "myself" does not exhaust the fullness of who one is as a person in the world. In the divine case, assuming the validity of positing such an analogous act of reflection, the divine perfection requires that there is no increase in knowledge.

The actuality and perfection of the divine, in contrast to the human, is not of necessity Dasein or ex-sistence requiring the self-transcending of intentionality, but rather God is the pure interiority of pure To-Be Itself. We propose that in creation

God ex-sists through the incomparable generosity of the creative fiat of what God knows exemplarily in God's Self-reflecting or Self-reference. Let us spell this out.

We can think of creation as inseparable from the moment in which otherness would be introduced into divine consciousness, i.e., in which the unothered act would be othered and make present to itself the other as other. But the otherness here is problematic in so far as strictly speaking there *is* no form, no otherness, no perfection, apart from God, and God's knowing of what is other would not be restricted to a union with the *eidos*/look of the transcendent other. This is because God's being more immanent to things than they are to themselves is a deeper unity than the unity of intentionality as the unity of intentional presence, i.e., the unity of the presented transcendent being through its articulations/looks with the presencing mind.

Thus in an effort to find an analogy for the divine knowing of creatures we can distinguish, on the one hand, the kind of otherness which obtains in the intentional knowing of a being that is transcendent to the knowing stream of consciousness and, on the other hand, the reflective intentionality in which the known belongs to the same stream of consciousness as the knower.[133] In this latter case, the known "other" (oneself as other to oneself) that belongs to the same stream as the knowing consciousness is made present at a distance from the original streaming non-intentional, non-reflexive self-awareness.

Is there not reason to speculate that the divine knowledge of the world or of created being is an analogous form of intentional-reflective self-knowing? The motivating reason for the speculation would be that in the divine's knowing itself it would be not knowing simply what is transcendent to the divine but would also be knowing itself as othered. The divine would enjoy itself as the same from a different or other perspective. In which case, a form of otherness to the divine as pure immanence would be introduced. Thus, this reflection and othering would not be motivated by a retention/affection of an ongoing or prior intentionality, as is the human reflection. Further, this reflection would not be motivated by any inadequacy or imperfection of the divine pure non-reflexive self-manifestation, e.g., its being restricted to the ownness and unique essence, as if it would need intentionality to make up for this lack. There is no reason for the divine in its infinite pure act of self-awareness to intend itself or reflect on itself. This is not to give any privileged status to naivety but to celebrate the divine self-sufficiency and the nature of the divine wisdom.

This echoes the classical theological position that there is no reason or explanation for creation in the sense of a motive that would actualize God's potentiality or make present a perfection that prior to creation was missing. It is also a way of saying that there is no actuation of a potency that was not already present, albeit in a different way, in the divine self-presence.

We anticipated this speculative move when we earlier saw the necessity to introduce otherness into the divine self-knowing with the topic of exemplarity. The exemplar is precisely the divine knowing of Godself as capable of being participated in. Ancient theology also recognized a kind of divine self-knowledge or self-awareness where there was at once undifferentiatedness without confusion and without loss of either unity or essential richness. Indeed, this divine non-differentiated self-awareness of the unique essence of, e.g., the "myself" of JG Hart, even prior to its being an exemplar and prior to its being the actual created unique "myself" of JG Hart, is, as Dionysius says, "more powerful" and has a pre-eminent status even after the existence of the "myself" of JG Hart, even though, I, JG Hart, might eventually be "deified" by the Godhead. "For in the divine things the undifferenced Unities are of more might than the Differentiations and hold the foremost place even after the One has, without departing from Its oneness entered into Differentiation." St. Thomas takes Dionysius here to mean that in spite of the procession of the many from the divine there is no diminution of the divine unity because the divine essential unity goes in advance and is the origin of the manifold.[134] But Dionysius is also celebrating the excellence of the first mode over the third mode of the essence of the "myself" because the former is inseparably one with the divine essence. The third mode, by definition, is not part of the divine essence.

Dionysius's claim that the exemplar of "myself" is more powerful than the actual being of me, JG Hart, found an echo in N. Baltasar's claim that God's infinite being is more me myself than I am myself; God is myself by excess; God is *hyper-moi*, transcendently myself. In the first mode God is more the essential myself of me than I, JG Hart, am. In this mode God is more the essential myself than to whom I, JG Hart, contingently refer, not by way of an infinitizing limit simpliciter nor by way of the limit concept of "myself" because "myself" is always myself; but, rather, because here the, "myself" is inseparably one with God's own essence. (Only in a loose sense may this be said to be the limit concept of "myself."). Thus in the third mode God may be said "still" to be transcendently myself and more me myself than I, the existing JG Hart, am simply by reason of the myself's being me with God's essence as the creative origin of "myself" but in the third mode God's being is not the being of the "myself" nor is myself God's being. God's being transcendently myself makes him not me in the third-mode and makes me not him. It is by default that I am not able to be another being than myself, but it is by an excess of perfection that God is only Godself. But God's being Godself is Very To Be Simpliciter, i.e., God's Being is absolute, i.e., related to nothing, and contains the perfections of all that is; whereas any other creature upon whom *esse* is bestowed is itself and itself alone; I am not you nor a fortiori God. As Walter Hilton once put it: "He is thy being, thou are not his being."

The claim that the infinity of essences is pre-existent or "pre-had" in the divine essence in an absolutely simple unity and not a composite way, in an "undif-ferentiation" without confusion, which repels all plurality (St. Thomas: *omnem pluralitatem refutans*)[135] within the divine, is feebly suggested by the analogy of non-reflective self-awareness of the individual essence (i.e., of "the myself") which goes in advance of and accompanies the endless accumulation of properties which can be ascribed to the person in the course of life – and which endless proper-ties can only be known by reflection or intentional self-reference. These latter, of course, enrich the knowledge and display of the person to herself, even though the "myself" maintains its "super-essential" sameness and fullness. That is, it enjoys a status of limit case in relation to the series of acts of intentional knowing directed toward the limit of a filled intention.

The feeble analogy of a divine self-knowing distinct from the divine non-reflective, non-intentional self-awareness, i.e., a divine self-knowing through a self-othering
in a reflective intentional act, introduces a move away from the absolute unity of
undifferentiation without confusion and plurality to an otherness, plurality, and differentiation in the divine self-knowledge. When the divine knows itself as other to
itself it may also choose to know itself as able to be "othered" by way of participation, communication, and exemplification. This is the classic function of the "exemplars." Already ancient theology introduced a shift in the divine self-knowing with
the introduction of the exemplars: the divine does not merely know itself in absolute
simplicity, i.e., in "undifferentiation without confusion," but it knows itself as able to
be communicated and participated in by what is other than the divine essence.

In sum: With the analogous divine reflection and self-knowledge through knowing itself as an exemplar this transcendent "undifferenced" unity becomes differ-
entiating in terms of the knowledge of the manifold exemplars and the exemplary
form of all exemplars. We are proposing that this be thought of as an immanent
move within the divine mind/essence from an analogous non-reflexive to an analogous reflexive form of self-awareness, wherein the divine is aware of itself as other,
i.e., there is an analogous intentional distance that an analogous divine reflection or
self-reference would provide. A decisive further analogous form of self-awareness
of Godself as other to Godself is knowing Godself as able to be participated in, i.e.,
in knowing one's essence as an exemplar.

And finally we must distinguish a further creative "self-othering" when *this*
other, which is one's unique essence othered as an exemplar (and, of course,
ordered within "the eternal Word" as the exemplar of all exemplars) is itself "othered" by way of the *fiat* resulting in the created "myself" as the exemplification of
the divine exemplar.

The theological move into the differentiation of exemplarism occurs in the New
Testament teaching that all creation has its exemplar and center in the eternal *Logos*
who is also Jesus of Nazareth. In this teaching, all persons are chosen or called from
before the foundation of the world. This being called and chosen before creation
actually exists, and even "before the foundation," we take to mean that the divine
essential self-presence in some way is highlighted as eternal ideas taking the form
of exemplars. This means that God knows not only each ipseity as God knows
Godself but God also, as an ingredient in this knowing, knows each unique essence
along with all the countless other ipseities (unique essences) in their radical first-
person essential self-presence. This is infinitely removed from any human-personal
self-knowledge, because we do not know first-personally Others nor do we know
in the first-person ourselves along with Others. Further, God knows them as united
in the unique exemplar-ipseity, the eternal *Logos*, which/who, for Christians, is
Jesus of Nazareth. This latter is the focal exemplar, the exemplary form of all the
exemplars. This unique kind of knowing would seem to involve a unique kind of
intentionality and a divine "motion" beyond the absolute self-sufficiency of the
divine non-intentional, non-reflective self-knowledge or self-awareness.

Another comment on the three modes or aspects under which an essence, e.g.,
the "myself," may be presented to the theologian and God. The first mode is the

undifferentiated non-reflective divine self-awareness wherein the "myself" is inseparable from the divine essence. The second is the divine self-awareness of itself
as the exemplary unique essence ("myself") that may be participated in uniquely;
this, we have suggested, is made possible by an analogous divine intentionality or
self-reflection by which the divine regards itself "objectively" and thereby enjoys
itself as other to itself. This analogous intention of itself is the basis for the divine
presencing itself as exemplar.

The third mode is the created "myself" as it actually concretely exists and as
it is other to the divine essence and To Be. Although this is known by the divine
"through the divine essence" in the sense that in knowing me myself the divine also
knows Its divine essence, nevertheless in knowing me myself the divine knows a
created exemplification of the divine essence and thus not Godself as exemplar or
Godself as pure essential self-presence. In the case of creation God knows in the
strongest sense what is other to Godself, other to absolute To Be.[136]

The Theological Distinction permits this difference within the "absolute" to not
become either a mere dialectical philosophy of identity or a monism. As to dialectical identity, consider: When we hear that "my discovery of my identity begins and is
perfected in these [divine *ad intra*] missions, because it is in them that God Himself,
bearing in Himself the secret of who I am, begins to live in me not only as my
Creator but as my other and true self"[137] we *might* find ourselves pulled to a monist
or a panentheist interpretation that God is completed in my discovery of my divine
vocation. That is, we might think of ourselves as necessary dialectical and surmount-
able "moments" in God's coming to self-awareness. But The Theological Distinction
works against this. The basic reason is its fundamental assertion that God is already
perfectly complete and creation means that the creature really is and exists "in its
own right." It also asserts that God's creation of the world neither adds to the divine
excellence nor does the excellence of the world stand in competition with the divine
excellence. The eternal source of the exemplar of JG Hart's "myself" is eternally one
with the essence of God; the exemplar as such is also what is known by God alone;
and JG Hart is known both as an exemplification of the divine essence as well as a
(created) other who may love God in return but who in any event is loved by God.

By way of a resumé, consider the following analogy: In the first mode the unique
essential "myself" of the created person Mary Magdalene is present to God in an
analogous first-personal way, and thus inseparable from God's own self and mind.
In the second mode the "myself" is present to the divine as one who, although
originally an aspect of God's own essence, now is present as one who can be called
to "personify" the "myself" that is at home in the first-mode, i.e. one who can be
called to become the sort of person who fittingly personifies the essential Who-ness
or the "myself" in the first mode. In this second mode the "myself" is present in
an analogous second-personal way, but emptily, as a midwife or parent may call
the child coming forth from the womb by its name and thereby intend the ipseity
as beyond the person which she is not yet able to presence. In the third mode, the
"myself" is more properly addressed with You, i.e., in the second person, of course
analogously and *ceteris paribus*, because the "myself" is a created self-referring
capable of responding with "You." Here God's presencing is an analogous

appresentation of the "myself" that God knows already in the other two modes and yet now knows as a created Other, i.e., God knows the "myself" as one who may address God in return. Clearly the first-personal sense of the "myself" of the creature Mary is not identical with the first-personal sense of "myself" of the creator, nor is the first-personal sense of the Mary's "myself" identical with the second mode of the exemplar where God presences the "myself" as a possible creature and possible exemplification of Godself. And clearly God's self-reference with "I" is not identical with the creaturely referent of "I" of Mary and God's non-reflective self-experiencing of Godself, which is a self-experiencing of the "myself" within Godself, is not identical with Mary's self-experiencing of herself – even though this "myself" (herself) as an exemplification of a unique essence integral to Godself's self-experiencing is essentially the *same but not identical* "myself."

The Theological Distinction compels us to conceive a theism that does justice to the absoluteness of Sheer Subsisting To Be and the reality of creatures without being committed to the dualism of deism and some forms of theism. Creatures are not God, not godlets and therefore The Distinction strives to avoid the monism or one-ism of pantheism, as well as the correlational thesis and interdependence theory of some forms of panentheism. (See our discussion of concrete examples later in this Chapter.) Pantheism asserts an identity when it explicates God and the world and God's relation to the world. The "Abrahamic" forms of theism have most often sought a form of sameness theory or sameness relation as, e.g., all creation is a likeness or reflection of God, in order to avoid the dualism or monism. Sameness is always the same with a difference in some respect. We have found reason (in Book 1) to avoid thinking of identity as sameness in every respect when we attended to the possibility of metaphysical clones, i.e., where the non-sortal myselves are not identical but in their personifications are the same in every respect, i.e., every property. Sameness is always "identity" mixed with or bound up with difference; identity is always strictly itself without admixture of difference. Husserlian profilings or "identity syntheses" are examples of sameness, e.g., of "the barn" through the manifold of different perceptions of the different sides and angles, or, e.g., the same referent rendered through different acts, e.g., memory, perception, imagination, etc., or, e.g., the ideal propositional meaning rendered through different sentences, paraphrases, and translations. Identity is sheer "sameness" without these differences, as in I (am) I myself. In the case of the difference between the non-reflective sense of "myself" and the self-reference of "I" there is perhaps a middle case between sameness and identity which we might call the "identically same." This differs from the stronger differences we find in a person as presented first- and second- and third-personally through various moods, lapses, appearances, periods of life, etc., where we have always the same person, me myself (in the first-personal presentation), or you yourself or she herself in the second- and third- presentations, but often the same person is hardly recognized. (Cf. Book 1, Chapter VIII.) We are proposing in our theory of the three modes that we conceive a form of sameness which places a wedge between sheer identity, on the one hand, and the otherness of dualism, on the other. But we also wish to claim that the sameness of an abstract entity or ideality that joins the different presentations does not capture the sameness of the unique essence of "myself" which, we have argued is not a mere ideality. Therefore it would seem that the sameness of the "myself" in the three modes is in between what we have called an "identical sameness" and an identity synthesis of self-presentations through discrete acts.

Clearly none of these analogies do the job satisfactorily. The chief reason perhaps is that although we have claimed that the theme of the three modes is common to both God and the theologian, clearly the differences in the display of the three modes is significant. It would seem that only the divine perspective (as envisaged by The Theological Distinction) on the three modes can do justice to our earlier claim in Book 1 (Chapters II, III, and V) that "I" (or "myself") is not properly a numerical identity and never properly "the I" or "the myself." But such lapses are what inevitably happens for the philosophical theologian. Only in the postulated divine perspective as envisaged by The Theological Distinction is there avoided the presencing of "the myself" in its three modes as an ideal sameness which bleaches out the unique "myself" and transforms it into a mere ideal object or ideal sameness. However The Distinction opens up "the logical space" in which it may be believed or postulated that the "myself" in the three modes does not become a mere ideal sameness but rather is enabled to be and appear in its proper non-reflective, non-objective, first-personal, unique essential light. The Distinction is such that there is not a two-ness and competition between the being of God and that of creatures as there is in the philosophical theologian's speculation on the creaturely referent "myself," the divine referent of "myself" as essential to God's essence, and the "myself" as God's essence objectified or reflected on as exemplar for the creaturely "myself." But this "logical space" opened by The Distinction is not one the theologian sees into and understands but rather it is an empty intention of faith that, inspite of the non-twoness and non-competition between the creaturely and divine, justice is done to the unique essence of the "myself" as it is present in the three necessary theological modes. Here we return to the basic mystery of creation as well as God's knowing of creaturely indexicality. We will return to this when we discuss the monist interpretation of mystic experience below.

These speculative analogies of the non-reflective, the reflective-exemplary, and the intention of the transcendent exemplified may be made more precise in the following summary considerations.

A. *Essential Divine Life Not Necessarily Dependent on Intentionality*

In the pure non-reflexive, non-intentional self-awareness there is necessarily a case of *esse est percipi*, i.e., the being of that which is known is inseparable from the awareness of it and has the same necessity as the awareness. (There are no intentional acts which are not lived; there are no pains without feeling them; if they are experienced they must be, if they are they must be experienced.) In which case, in the analogical speculation, in both the divine and human personal cases the existence is necessary if there is self-awareness. But in the divine case the being is absolutely necessary and so is the self-awareness; in the finite personal case the being is necessary if there is self-awareness, but both the being and self-awareness need not be. Further, the human self-awareness is inseparable from a life of intentionality, whereas the divine self-awareness in its essence is independent of such an analogous life of intentionality. Further, whereas the human personal non-intentional self-awareness is not the proper realm of *knowledge* but must be mediated by the othering intentional acts, the proper realm of divine knowledge is its non-intentional, non-othering self-awareness of its own essence and the intentional is always a gracious elaboration of this. This is an extension of The Theological Distinction that the divine's "self-othering" in either the second or third mode is not necessary.

B. All Eidé Pre-exist in Divine Essence

The phenomenological entertainment of the essence of any being (except one) does not entail positing its existence, i.e., I can bring to light the necessary features of a promise, a centaur, artificial intelligence, a crystal, etc., without thereby necessarily positing the actual existence of such an *eidos*. Here we may compare Aquinas' response to Anselm's conceiving God as "that than which nothing greater can be conceived": this concept does not require positing the actuality of what is conceived. Even assenting to the implication that as "that than which nothing greater" it must be greater existing outside the mind rather than in the mind is not in and of itself a positing of the actuality of what is conceived. As Husserl puts it: "The being of an *eidos*, i.e., the being of eidetic possibilities and the being of the universe of eidetic possibilities, is free of the being or non-being of any actualization of such possibilities; it is ontologically independent of all corresponding actuality."[138] There is, however, an exception: "But the *eidos* transcendental I is unthinkable without the transcendental I as factual." The transcendental I must be posited as actually existing in the displaying of its own unique essence. This is the one case where the essence requires its existence and where there could not be the establishment of the essence without the positing of existence. Or, the *eidos* of my I-ness can only be present on the condition of the actuality of my I-ness. (See Book 1, Chapter V, §7.)

In the divine case, as unfolded within The Theological Distinction, it is a different matter. The divine envisagement of any *eidos* as a perfection presupposes the *eidos'* actuality in the divine being. And whereas the transcendental I exists necessarily in the presencing of its *eidos* its existence is only factual. Whereas it must exist in the face of its *eidos*, that the *eidos* be presented is not necessary nor is it absolutely necessary that the presenting I exist. But in the case of the divine, God must exist absolutely in the face of its essence along with every *eidos*, and God cannot be unaware of its essence or any *eidos* because of its essential interiority, i.e., its unreflective undifferentiated self-presence that, however, no perfection eludes; it does not need a reflective act to render intelligible to itself its own essence (its "self") or any essence.

C. Contingency and Necessity of Creatures Known by God

Furthermore, in our intentionality of the world the being of the things in the world is manifestly contingent and the being of the world itself is contingent in a different way highlighted by both phenomenology and The Theological Distinction. The divine intentionality of the world requires that creatures necessarily be if God intends them as being; but of course the being of creatures does not enjoy the absolute necessity of the being of that of which the divine is self-aware in God's knowing creatures.

In the creaturely reflective act on original finite, creaturely, self-awareness there is *given* a coincidence of the reflective act and the reflected-on and, as we noted, there is evident the *necessity* of the being of what is given (not obviously an absolute necessity, but a necessity having to do with the nature of reflection; it is an essential or "logical" necessity) because of the inseparability or non-independence of what is given in reflection from what is immediately pre-given or non-intentionally lived prior to and during the reflection. (See our discussion in Book 1, Chapter VIII, §8, C.) In which case, in the analogical speculation, if God's knowledge of the world were thought of as tied to an act of reflection, that which is present in reflection, i.e., "the world," would seem to have the same necessity as God. But what God knows in the analogical reflection is first of all not "the world," but Godself and then Godself as "otherable" in a creature, i.e., what God knows in reflection first of all is Godself's own essence and then Godself's own essence *as* an exemplar. Further, if we see that reflection is a free act, a contingency in a sense quite different from that of the contingency of the world,[139] then we may think of there being another kind of self-presence than that of pure non-reflective undifferentiated self-presence of self-awareness, i.e., we may think of the divine's reflective self-being/self-presence as analogous to the presence of the human person through an act of reflection: Reflection enables God to be present through a different presentation of the divine, one which is contingent in the way the non-reflexive self-awareness is not contingent, and one which is contingent in a way that is essentially different from the contingency of and in the world. Further, what is made present in the divine self-reflection in the form of knowing Godself as an exemplar is present as inseparably one with the divine; but now sheer To Be Itself is present to itself as othered to itself. Reflection, after all, is this making two of what is one without shattering the unity, i.e., it is the splitting of the I into being to and for itself.

The presence of the exemplars is contingent only in the sense that there is a free act of self-reflection. God is freely present to Godself as able to be participated in; from the side of what is made present there is the same necessity as what is non-reflectively present prior to reflection. Whereas God's being the creator and savior of the contingent world are relations of the world with respect to God of fundamental importance, for God with respect to the world there here are not real properties but only "Cambridge properties." But God's having acts of reflection or God's being present to Godself exemplarily is a "Cambridge property" only in relationship to what is other than God. It is a real relation of God to Godself. That is, if God as agent of reflection makes present Godself, Godself is made present to God.

D. Problem of the Motivation for the Divine's Being Other to Itself

Although my act of reflection is free it is also "motivated." For example, I am now able to reflect on my perception of the geese because I am "affected" by the just-past perceiving. Although the one perceiving might well have been absorbed in the geese and not in the perceiving of the geese, the retention now of the earlier perceiving of the geese provides a tug, a motive, for a return to one's self and one's act of reflection. In the analogical speculation on divine reflection there is no such parallel for reflection because the divine immanence is self-sufficient and cannot be moved to be at a distance from itself in the way reflection is motivated to overcome the distance from oneself that absorption in the intentional object typically is. Divine reflection is an adumbration of the incomparable generosity of creation because it is an incomparable freedom. Although in both the human-creaturely and divine cases there is an original non-reflective self-presence, human-creaturely reflection typically is a motivated return to oneself wherein one recognizes oneself as other to oneself and enriches the display of what was there before; the divine reflection, on the other hand, is an unmotivated distancing of Godself from Godself that does not enrich the original essential self-presence. Yet we may say that there is symmetry in the divine and human-creaturely cases in so far as the reflection does not add to one's knowledge of one's unique essence, i.e., *who* one is in the sense of the "myself." But in the human-creaturely case, reflection enriches one's knowledge of one's personal being in the world, e.g., it is indispensable for shedding light on *who* one is as the "sort of person" one is. Further, the divine's being other to Godself in the intentional self-reflection that is the condition for creation requires an incomparable freedom that knows no such "motive" because such a "motive" implies an intentional distance from oneself. An elemental version of such a distance is the fundamental function of the proto-intentions of retention and protention.[140]

Nevertheless, and in spite of our prior claim that in God there is no self-actuation of potentiality, the divine self-directedness, just as the act of creation, may be seen to be analogously actualizations of divine possibility or the divine I-can, but what is actualized in the case of God is a Cambridge property, not a real one, because if they were real there would be the implication that there were outstanding or unactualized perfections to which God was related. Although the divine unothered act is self-present in full actuality and without potentiality, the pure simple divine self-awareness becomes different and other through being self-reflective and creative. Otherness and difference are freely adopted modes of the divine oneness and sameness which in no way actuate or complete the divine essence, but they are modifications of it. What is other is still an other of the same divine essence in so far as it originates in an actuality of the divine essence. The other modes, e.g., of the divine self-presence in the form of exemplars as well as in the creative *fiat* that brings about the actual existing created excellence of this other, are nothing else than possibilities of the same infinitely actual divine essence.[141] And from the side of the divine these are all Cambridge relations that add nothing to the divine perfection which is not actuated or completed by introducing these modes of otherness and difference.

E. Again: The Problem of the Transcendent Otherness of Creation to the Divine

That which is given in our intentionality of the world is always of a transcendent, contingent, non-necessary, presumptive nature; it is always an inadequate presencing of something transcendent and exterior to our stream of consciousness. *Pace* Husserl (see *Husserliana* III, §43; see also our discussions above at §5 and below at §11), according to The Theological Distinction, the divine intention of the world, however, cannot be properly a perception wherein there is an inadequate intention of what is absolutely different and transcendent. When God knows creation, God knows what is both the same as Godself and different from Godself. The divine knows Godself as participated in by way of Godself's own free act. Thus we may perhaps say: The divine intention of the world would have to be mediated by the divine's self-reflective intentionality by which the divine is present to itself in a way involving sameness and difference along with proximity and distance. This would be the condition for the divine's self-presence as participatable or as exemplar and the "original" sense of what is bestowed on what is other than the divine. The divine's free "contingent" act of self-reflection, which is a bringing about of intentionality within the divine life, would be the necessary condition for the creation of the world and the participated *esse* of creatures. Of course, the divine's self-reflective intentionality, its presencing itself exemplarily in its "ideas," and its presencing of the created world are always necessarily a knowing "through Godself's own essence," and this knowledge of the divine essence, we have suggested is an analogous divine, non-intentional, non-reflective self-awareness.

F. What It Means to Say that the Divine Knows Itself as "Othered"

We have said that the divine intention of the world would have to be mediated by the divine's self-reflective intentionality. But in order for the world to be "there" as a creation there has to be more than merely the divine's self-reflective knowing of itself as other and at a distance to itself. There has to be the further possibility that the divine essence, in so far as this is possible, be present as able to be communicated and shared in. This we have suggested was in part the work of the "transformation" of the divine essential self-awareness. Because none of this is eternally necessary, we seem to have here a kind of divine freedom and, in this sense, contingency as well as temporality. The divine essential self-awareness not only becomes self-reflective or intends itself but also envisages itself as communicable or able to be shared in. Representatives of the "Abrahamic theological tradition" have held this is the work of the divine's self-presence in the form of exemplars or divine *rationes*. But further, creation is not merely the divine self-presence othered to itself in intentionality and in the self-presence through the objectification of itself as exemplar. Beyond this, and presupposing this, creation is the mystery of the *fiat* by which something other than the divine truly exists in itself. Aside from this being a distinctive act bringing about particular beings, and therefore permitting eternity to be involved in time and time to emerge out of eternity and out of the temporality within the "transformation" of the divine self-awareness, there is inseparably the further mystery: This is an "othering" of necessity surpassing the divine othering of itself in reflection and in its objectification of itself in the *rationes*. And the knowing of this other is not merely that of self-reflection and knowing itself as able to be shared in, but a knowing of what is, in some mysterious respect, not the divine self. We said above it was an extension of the divine life to what is external to it. But this is not a pre-existing external dimension pre-existing within which God creates beings but is the space created by the created beings themselves in their being created.[142]

Clearly the divine knowing of creatures is not a knowing of what is absolutely other to the divine, nor is it a knowledge of what exists absolutely independently of the divine self. As St. Thomas says, God does not know things by displaying or taking (intentionally) from them their features but rather gives to the things known those features that they are able to know of themselves and that others are able to know of them.[143] This is to say, God's knowledge of them is not a conformity or an "adequation" to their prior existent intelligibility, but their very intrinsic intelligibility, which is displayed in a creaturely knowledge of them, itself is bestowed on them by God. Thomas also says that the mode of cognition follows the principle or originating source of cognition, and God, the absolute originating source of everything, does not receive from things intentional acquaintance with their features through knowing them, nor is knowledge a matter of receiving through an agency of manifestation the intelligibility of creatures. Therefore it follows that God does not know the existence of things because of the mode of existence of things, but rather he knows the mode of existence of things through the knowledge which is proper to Himself. He can only know them through knowing himself and as likenesses of his own essential being.[144] Whereas our knowledge of things, even though a constitution of the display of things, is measured by things, the divine knowledge of things is not properly a constitution of the display of things but is, in a sense that has no applicability to the displays of science and philosophy, the measure of the things and thus of their truthful display.

But, one might object, does this not make of nature and its processes a non-nature, i.e., does it rob nature of its self-actualization from out of itself, and render it a mere artifact, because, after all, the measure here of what is known is what is made and what the maker makes it to be? The answer of The Theological Distinction is No: That *God* is the "architect" or "author" of the intelligibility of nature means precisely that nature's intelligibility and self-actualization are truly its own doing. Consider the analogous limit-ideal of the perfect author who can create subjects who create their own stories. In this case, the perfect creator can make self-creating creators. According to The Theological Distinction one must assert, on the one hand, that it is essential to nature that it be the source of its own processes and forms, but on the other hand, there must also be asserted that these very forms and this very creativity have their exemplarity in Godself. Whatever intelligibility, necessity, self-subsistence, self-causation, and essentiality nature has and permits to emerge reflects the divine self-awareness of its own essence.

Thus in God's knowing creatures God knows Godself as "othered." The scare quotes here are important. In the context of the orthodox notion of creation and what we are calling The Theological Distinction, "othering" is misinterpreted if "othering" means that God no longer is God, or if God becomes something different, or if God is conceived to succumb to or be modified by something that contradicts, negates, or opposes God, or if God is conceived to bifurcate or become plural. What is "other" to the divine fullness of being can only be nothing. The Theological Distinction implies that in God's knowing of creatures, God, in contrast to knowing Godself, knows the creatures as having as their other constitutive principle, a "principle of nothingness."

Creatio ex nihilo expresses, on the one hand, that creation is not procreation, generation, or emanation; it is not *creatio ab sive ex deo*, as if all creatures were begotten godlets; on the other hand, it surely does not contradict the view that nothing comes from nothing, *ex nihilo nihil fit*. Rather it wishes to express the conviction of the dogma of creation as outlined by The Theological Distinction, i.e., that there is a genuine other to the divine *ipsum esse subsistens* who stands in no "real relation" to this very creation. Creation is not acting *on* anything. Further, the creator does not "lose or contradict Himself in the being of creatures or in letting be the being of creatures. Because creatures are other than God, it does not follow that they are God othering Himself."[145] They can truly be precisely because the God of the Theological Distinction enables what is other than God to be without God being either diminished or enhanced in this transaction.

G. Creation as "First Grace"

Likewise, the analogy with gift-giving, as in "creation is the first grace," limps precisely because the gift of creation is a *first* grace which undoes all familiar worldly senses of grace and gift. Gift-giving is "gracious" by reason of it being the free giving something of value to someone who would appreciate it. In contrast, the gift of creation is one which brings about the receiver of the gift and which is not given "to" the recipient precisely because the recipient does not (yet) exist. If gift-giving requires the reception by someone of the gift, and such reception of course presumes the receiver already exists to receive the gift, creation is only a gift by a feeble analogy. While it is alone true of God that God could call me before I existed and there is a sense in which God intended to give the gift of creation to me before I existed, strictly speaking the unique essence of I myself was only Godself in God's undivided unified essence. God's eternal calling of *me* as other than Godself requires that I exist in the differentiated divine self-awareness as a *ratio*, i.e., the unique essence of the "myself" had to exist not merely as identical with the divine self-awareness but it had to exist as the intentional object which is an exemplar. In this respect "I myself" exist as the divine unique essence as able to be participated in. Prior to this I myself did not have any distinctness whatsoever from God's essence.

For The Theological Distinction as The *Christian* Distinction the exemplarity of Jesus the Christ must be highlighted. As a *ratio* or exemplar, "myself" is conjoined with the universal exemplar of the *Logos* or wisdom of God as the center and exemplar of all creation for all time, i.e., conjoined with that central essence or meaning in which everything is created. It is this which God knows "before the foundation of the world." As uncreated exemplar, the "myself" is merely a possible creature; as an ingredient of God's essence the "myself" exists necessarily and in its most eminent manner. Within the parameters of The Theological Distinction God's knowing this *ratio* before I am created is a knowing of the unique essence of me myself, and God's being self-aware is more intimate to me than I am to myself; it is not merely knowing a purely possible unique individual essence, but this is a knowing of the most exalted eminent sense of "myself."

In willing my actuality God wills that I conform to this divine knowing of me. Yet in knowing me as actual, weak, blasphemous, and sinful, God knows me no less intimately than I know myself. For The Theological Distinction, God does not just know Godself from all eternity and me as a mere possible exemplification; in knowing Godself God also knows from all eternity the "myself" better than I know myself. And this includes knowing the created "myself," who is JG Hart, immersed in the webs of nature, intersubjectivity, culture, the megamachine, and the gossamer of temporality and history. The Theological Distinction does not shed any light on what this might mean in terms of pre-knowing or pre-destination. It merely highlights that the conceptual problems these issues pose are already at hand in the dogma of God the Creator.

In this regard it is helpful not to be misled by the temptation to think of God's (Cambridge-propertied) relation to the world in terms of the seeming incompatible dimensions of eternity and time. The Theological Distinction compels us to think of eternity as the gracious source and condition of temporality rather than to think of eternity merely as the negation of time. The chief reason God is not thought of as temporal is the obvious one that a temporal being does not have itself but is incessantly losing itself to the no longer, just as it is incessantly acquiring itself from what is not yet. This remains true regardless of the power of its memory or the strength of its imagination, both of which are empty intentions of its prior or future life. Temporal beings are ceaselessly losing their actuality and ceaselessly being actualized. In so far as there are perfections that we may want unconditionally to ascribe to God that are made possible only by being temporal, e.g., creativity, mercy, compassion, growth, etc., God must be thought of as having these in a way which does not involve the vulnerability and finitude of temporality. That is, God must be thought of as having these both as limit concepts and as non-Cambridge properties.

If we think of eternity and time as ontological states of affairs which, because they are conceived to be incompatible and incommensurate, create conceptual conundrums, we are moved to think of creation as a fall from eternity into time and salvation as a deliverance from time to eternity. Eternity thus is thought of as a realm of the static, frozen, and immobile and deprived of all communication with time and creativity.

In this view, as Louis Lavelle has pointed out, time itself then is thought of at once as the destroyer, conserver, and creator of all there is. Yet, he notes, it is the destroyer only in so far as it is identified with a becoming which is forever, even if forever perishing. It is the conserver only in so far as it is able to preserve in itself the perpetual duration of Now in which everything is retained. It is the creative in so far as its novel present does not cease to be actualized by what itself is not temporal. In short, eternity is hinted at in this very notion of the temporal.

T.S. Eliot spoke of "the still-point of the turning world" as where "the dance is." Eternity is thus thought of as an indivisible point from which creation never ceases to flow. If we think, as we ought to, according to The Theological Distinction, of time unfolding as a gracious act of God it is misguided to think of God's creative act merely as non-temporal, i.e., as outside of time and excluding time. Here we may be reminded of Husserl's position on the transcendental I: It is both an atemporal I-moment as well as a temporizing, hyletic moment. The relation of eternity to time then is analogous to our awareness of inner time; it is the perpetual Whiling which itself does not while. As our awareness or presencing of the primal streaming is not now, is not itself something coming to be and passing away, so the eternity of God is not "in time" but the trans-temporal sourcing of time. In our transcendental awareness of the flow we perhaps are permitted to have a dim appreciation of the sense in which eternity is beyond time, not in the sense that it excludes or disowns it but rather in the sense that it is its genesis and it does not cease to nurture it.

If time and creation are seen in this way, we of course do not suddenly "understand" the great problems of salvation, predestination, etc., but we are moved to view them in the proper context of creation as inseparably the creation of time. Eternity as the source-point of time, as the form and foundation of creation, makes no sense without temporality, just as being a creator makes no sense without creation. Eternity thus becomes a "Cambridge property" like "creator." Of course, we still face the dark matter of what divine life or "being" is that is not correlated with creation or time. Consider our earlier analogy of the flow presenced by the creative whiling/presencing. If temporality is necessary for God's life (eternal life or eternity) then the flow, along with creation, has to be. This problem of whether a flow is necessary for transcendental consciousness, as we saw in Book 1, is one of the key ambiguities surrounding a transcendental phenomenological notion of immortality. Time's roots are in eternity, i.e., God's incessant grace of the Now which grace itself is not the ephemeral Now or the standing perduring Now, which latter itself is the abiding synthesis of the ephemeral Nows. Rather the root of time in eternity is to be found in the Now of the gracious While understood as the creative awareness of the passing of time, which While, properly understood is not Now as part of the stream nor is it the abiding Now as the constituted synthesis of the Nows of the stream. (Cf. our discussions in Book 1, Chapter VII, §3.) Thus, for a creature to enter into eternity and eternal life is not at all to enter into a realm of immobility and an escape from temporality. Rather it is to adhere to that which, at least from the standpoint of faith, cannot fail to uphold us and all we cherish. The creaturely participation in eternity might well be for us to enter a realm eternal *life* where we meet unimaginable reservoirs of endless novel ever enriching possibility. (It is hard to conceive of this as "adventure" if there is always the threat of destruction by the novel unknown necessary for adventure.) And if we have reason to believe that we are rooted in the creative exemplary essence which never fails us, i.e., we are one with that to which we have been called to be, then in this "eternal life" there is not merely an undergoing of events but unimaginable exercise of freedom in establishing them. Here, in this act "at the stillpoint of the turning world," there is no loss in succession but superpowers of retention and recall.

But this speculated prospect of eternal life says nothing about the God's own "life." wherein we have reason to conceive it *not* as an actuation of potentiality, not a perfection through process, where the divine I-can does not mean "I am not yet" and where the actuality of Now knows no enrichment by not yet and I can, where fullness of life does not mean repetition, and possession of all perfection does not mean surfeit. When Eliot (along with philosophers, such as Conrad-Martius, Jankélévitch, and Lavelle) say that "there" (at the still-point of the turning world) is "where the dance is," the reference is both to what we know, i.e., the incessant actuation of the magnificence of creation, and also to what we do not know and what we cannot conceive, i.e., what is, as it were on the "other non-Cambridge side" of the point, the infinitely greater magnificence of the hidden divine life, which is not infinitely greater by way of being an ideal concept but by way of being Infinity, i.e. what for us is a heterogeneous and incommensurate limit concept.

To the objection that this does not allow for a creation of *physis* as what exists in and by itself, but rather denies to nature its self-subsistence, the following may be said: The substantial in itselfness of nature and the world is rooted in time and time is the incessant coming to be of the Now. Even if this is rooted in transphysical singularities of hyper-space-time, these too would in some "singular" sense participate in temporality and be informed by it. Creation's inseparable foundation and frame is time. To say that this assigns to God the burden of a busyness beyond comprehension, namely that of creating and retaining each Now, as it emerges in each monad, is not to say it is conceptually nonsensical. It surely says that God's infinity is beyond our comprehension; but to deny this capacity to God would seem to threaten the basic thesis of creation being a gracious act. Of course, God's act of creating time as the foundation and frame of the world need not be thought of as a punctual or staccato agency, where God would be busy making each Now, yet in such a way that it is a "moment" of a continuum. We may rather think of the analogy of the way a will act of a general resolve, e.g., to assume a career, is the source of literally endless specific acts, many of which for us do not ever come to explicit awareness. Position-taking acts set up dispositions for acts which themselves set up dispositions for acts, etc.

Such a proposal clearly does not satisfactorily deal with the issues of predestination, foreknowledge, etc., which begin with the view that eternity and time are incompatibles and mutually exclusive conceptual spheres. The circle of problems connected with these famous theological mysteries, e.g., those having to do with the attributes of omnipotence, omniscience, etc., feed the sense of incompatible conceptual spheres, as does this sense of incompatibility feed the conundrums posed by these famous attributes. Perhaps if we keep in view the first-grace of creation and time as the primal creative act which frames and founds the creation of natural things and processes we can rethink these classical problems. The first step would be to conceive temporality as emanating from the eternal analogously to the way the flow of time is constituted by the non-temporal awareness of this flow. Here we see that there cannot be opposition and incommensurability of regions but mutuality of sense even if fundamental dependence.

The Theological Distinction holds that God is more intimate to whatever thing than this is to itself. This must be said also of the created pulses and continua of temporality and the novelty or "freedom" and creativity of these Nows. They are more intimately present to God than they are to themselves; or they are more intimately present to God than are the modes of the being of which they are modes. This hearkens back to our basic analogy of the intimacy of the awareness of the flow of time to the flow of time: It is both the self-shining and what illuminates what shines. Similarly, in the divine creation of what is temporal God does not eject something "out there" which is "time" but, as Lavelle always insists, "time unfolds in the interior of eternity." This is because time is the flow of Nows of whatever is creatively made present by the eternal Now's creative fiat. As this flow of Nows, time is the most elemental feature and form of the created world. And where else can this take place if not within or at the interior of the infinity of the creator God, i.e., the interior of eternity?[146] Let us move away from the problem of the creation of time and return to that of beings, whether temporal or not.

The first grace of creation is not something given to me, the beneficiary, as the "myself" who is JG Hart, this person in the world, because the grace in fact brings about this very beneficiary. Rather, it is "first" given to the divine *ratio* of the unique essence, i.e., the aspect of the divine essence of the eternal individual essence of "myself" as able to be participated in, and to whom I, upon creation, come to refer with "I," even though I as this person, JG Hart, fall always short of the ideal self to which this *ratio* beckons me in my incarnate being in the world with others.

This grace brings about the relationship, but strictly speaking, as classical theology has put it, there is no "real relation" from God's side. Whereas the beneficiary is absolutely dependent upon, and thus related to, the giver, the giver is not related to the beneficiary. This is because the beneficiary is not "there" to be related to except through the giving of the gift. This is the dense ontological sense of the mere "Cambridge relation" or "Cambridge property." It is not that the creature is not "really" *there* but rather that the "thereness" itself is a gift. Thus the classical thesis that God is not "really related to the world" is a theological-*ontological* statement, not a psychological or, a fortiori, a moral one, as Sokolowski has pointed out.[147] It is not to be taken as a statement about God's psychological inability to be related to the world, as is the wont of, e.g., Charles Hartshorne's interpretation of the classical Thomist view. Admittedly St. Thomas' analogy, that God is to the world as a stone is to a sentient being, puts God in the weak light of insentiency or unconsciousness. But Hartshorne is distracted by the psychological aspects of this admittedly infelicitous example, and lets this efface the ontological thesis. There are enough statements and arguments in the "classic" theology to suggest that it is by reason of ontological deficiency that I am not able to be another than myself whereas it is by an excess of perfection that God is only Godself and is more the "myself" of any being than that being itself is.

However, from the standpoint of The Theological Distinction the mystery of creation and calling of free persons to be offspring of God would be equally slandered by denying God's own real loving redemptive agency as it would be by demoting God to being the supreme and most excellent being of the all of the world. The Distinction not only discourages our conceiving God as a being in competition with other beings it encourages an analogous understanding of creation involving an analogous personal relationship between the created persons and the uncreated Creator of heaven and earth. The ontological position that God is absolutely self-sufficient and not really related to the world sets the stage for the analogous thinking or optic in which there is encouraged our believing in God as desiring and seeking the love of creatures as much as the bridegroom desires the bride. As an explication of "the Abrahamic tradition" it teaches that we think of God longing for us to turn to Godself and away from our false selves. It preaches that in Christ God gladly suffers torment and death that we might live as offspring of God. We are permitted to analogously believe, i.e., to have a glimpse of understanding, the claim that in the framework of our redemption God can do nothing without us and that the greatest hindrance in the universe to God's will and one that is capable of withstanding God is the perverted will, etc. Yet such teachings must be understood in the light of the "logical space" of The Distinction. They must be understood in the light of the mystery of God the Creator who brings into being not only real subsistent beings but beings endowed with a freedom to obey the "Great Commandments" and be grateful to God – which exercise of freedom believers believe is what God wants more than anything else in the world. The "communication of idioms" made possible by (at least in Christianity) The Distinction, does not modify the ultimate ontological situation as layed out by The Distinction. *Pace* Hegel, "God suffered" is not a description of the nature of God the Creator. Its sense is tied to the mystery that God can take on a creaturely form without obliterating the creature or without ceasing to be God. That the eternal Son of God died on the cross is not a negation of the classic ontological thesis that God is not really related to the world. It is a statement about the mystery of the incarnation where God and the human individual, Jesus of Nazareth, were so united that what happened to the human individual happened to the divine person and analogously could be said of God – all the while keeping intact the distinct "natures" of the divine and human. (We return to "process theology" in our discussion of Scheler below.)

If the condition for God to be related to the world, e.g., through compassion and love, is that God be really related to the world, and not therefore have a mere

"Cambridge relation," in the sense that the creatures or some principle of creature-hood ("the irrational given," "creativity," "the receptacle," "prime matter," etc.) pre-exist God's creation or are theologically-ontologically independent of the creator, then we have moved outside the parameters of The Theological Distinction and established a different theology (and perhaps faith), because we have a radically different understanding of the distinction between God and the world. One might want to do this for good philosophical reasons. Yet the sense of these "reasons" being truly legitimate critical reasons in regard to the Theological Distinction is, as we have suggested, a priori questionable. (That is, they would have to be drawn from the ultimate framework of meaning and reason, i.e., the world, and they would be providing a [conditioned] reason for the unconditioned.) Further, if the world or creation is necessary for God to be God, we have made infinitely less amazing and gracious the act of creation. We have perhaps rationalized the mystery of creation and made it more conceptually clear and clean by either getting rid of analogies or using less ambiguous ones, but it is not at all clear that it has done better justice to the *eu angelion*, or that it has better unfolded the logic of the "good news" (evangel-logic), or that it captures all the richness of the original tradition.[148]

What creation or this giving of "being" is remains essentially hidden to us and it is the aspiration of The Theological Distinction to spell out parameters in which this gift-giving is to be taken, without thereby presuming to dispel the mystery: There is no increase in perfection in Being; there is no diminution in the perfec-tion in Being with either the creation of creatures or the annihilation of creatures; and there is no competition or conflict between the divine "nature" and human nature precisely because the divine or God is not a nature, not a kind, not a being among beings, not even the greatest being or kind of being conceivable: God can be present in me, indeed, more present in me than I am to myself, without infring-ing on my self-presence or freedom. Indeed, what is meant by God is precisely the "One" who, in a most fundamental sense, knows me before I exist and who can create me to be free and autonomous, even before God the Creator. And, in terms of exemplarity, God is precisely the "being" who in knowing God's own essence knows me more profoundly than I can know myself, and in knowing what I refer to with "I" knows (an aspect of) himself. Further, God is the one whom I, in refer-ring to myself, also refer to. All this is possible "because" of The Theological Distinction. But this "because" is not an "explanation." There is no true "reason" except this particular understanding of what is meant by faith in God the Creator of Heaven and Earth.

§11. Three Alternatives Avoided: Correlationism, Monism, and Process Theology

Before concluding we will sketch three prominent views that The Theological Distinction rejects: the correlationist, monist, and process-theological views. (1) The correlationist or di-polar view will be taken to be represented by Franz

Brentano, (2) the monist view will be that of Shankara, (3) the process theological view will be that of Max Scheler. Each of these representatives is chosen because of proximity to and yet distance from both transcendental phenomenology and The Theological Distinction.

A. *The Correlationist Position of Franz Brentano*

For Franz Brentano intentionality seems to be essential to the being of God or it is at least a necessary enhancement. For this reason we may speculate he is led to deny The Theological Distinction. He faces the question: If the creator plus the creation would be better than the creator alone, then would the creator be God? For God is that than which nothing greater can be conceived. Brentano's answer is: This would be to take the creator and the world together as the *Pan*, the all. But this is wrong. God and the world are not a being but a plurality. God is indeed that than which no greater being (*Wesen*) can be thought and the world is of infinitely less value than God regardless of how great the world may come to be. But we must, holds Brentano, deny that God, taken together with the world, is no greater than God alone. The reason is that this would make the value of the world the equivalent of zero. (Cf. our discussion of Morris earlier at the end of §8.) But this would mean, Brentano continues, that a preference of its being to its non-being could not take place. In God being, willing, and essence are always one and God therefore of necessity always chooses the best possible. Therefore we may assume that although prior to creation God's being without the world was the best possible, after creation the best possible is not God alone but God with the world that is subordinate to him.[149] This argument of Brentano reflects Leibniz's position, but whether it is truly that of Leibniz is questionable.[150]

Thus perhaps we can say that for Brentano the being and essence of God require intentionality as a perfection there from the start, and therefore the divine is essentially characterized by intentionality. (I mean by this primarily the intentionality of transcendent objects or the world. Even though Brentano does not introduce the intentionality of reflection into his philosophical theology, if my interpretation is correct, it would also seem to be included.) If an analogous intentionality essentially belongs to God's being, and if we may think of intentionality both as having the *eidos*/look of the other as another as well as the self-transcendence of being conscious of…, then it is natural to hold with Brentano that God separated from the world is an artificial abstraction, i.e., such a separation is not merely to be conceived as something possible but contrary to fact, but rather God and the world are to be thought of as inseparable from one another because they are essential correlatives, and that God apart from the actual world is an artificial abstraction – even though he adds, "God is in Himself necessary, but the world in terms of how it is, was and will be, is necessary through the necessity of God Himself."[151] This seems to say *that* the world is, is necessary, but *how* it is depends on God.

But is this the correct way to understand this last admission? Clearly it moves toward the direction of The Theological Distinction in so far as the necessity of

God is taken as absolute and that of the world totally dependent on the necessity of God. In a dense endnote Brentano expresses dissatisfaction with the theory of correlation. We risk the following paraphrase: It is clear that there is a correlation between the one effecting the world and the world effected by Him, and vice-versa. But even though correlatives are of necessity logically dependent on one another, it is not the case in this matter that one is so tied to the other precisely as correlatives are tied to one another. In any case, granting a correlation between two matters does not provide a basis for drawing a conclusion from the one about the other in terms of the essential fullness of what is involved in the correlatives.[152]

If the text to which the note is added were construed as holding that the world is not necessary at all for God's being (and it is *not* to be taken as holding that God of necessity must create the world) it would seem to undermine the claim that God and the world stand in a polar relation or are essential correlatives. Therefore we might think of Brentano more in the company of The Theological Distinction. Such an interpretation is reinforced by Brentano's answer to a criticism of classical theology that implies The Theological Distinction. This criticism states that if we ascribe all reality and perfection to God, and we assume that outside of God there is no reality and perfection, then there is no room for any perfection and all finite perfection and finite being must vanish in the infinite being of God.

Now, of course, The Theological Distinction would be uncomfortable about the claim that all reality and perfection are alone in God, because that is the very heart of the matter of creation of *esse*. But listen to Brentano's response: "This is not correct that there would not be any room for any other perfection. Rather it is not thinkable that there would be any room for an increase in God's perfection."[153]

Now this position suggests that the essence of God enjoys an infinite insurpassible perfection. But, at the same time, Brentano wants to say that the perfection of creatures adds to the perfection of "being" as the whole made up of the two, God and the world. This whole, with its new perfection, is greater than the perfection of God alone. Here is where the difference lies with The Theological Distinction.

The correlationist view may be compared to what Sokolowski refers to as the pagan view where God is part of the world or where the understanding of God is tied essentially to the understanding of the world. Aristotle's God, as the final cause of the world, stands in correlation with the world, but surely not through an intentional relationship because Aristotle's God cares nothing for the world and is absorbed only in knowledge of Himself. Plato's demiurge or architect (in the *Timaeus*) stands essentially in an intentional relationship to the world, but is not immanently part of the world. Nevertheless this divine architect is to be thought of as belonging essentially to the world because his main function is to be its organizing mind and will. A position closer to the pagan view that God is essentially part of the world can be found in some very modern process theologies. (As we shall see, Max Scheler is, with a few qualifications, a good example.) If the world is necessary as a correlate to the agency of a divine architect, then the theme of exemplarity becomes less important if not totally irrelevant. The essence, e.g., of JG Hart, can be part of the essential or accidental furniture of the actual world, but it need not have its exemplar in the divine essence. Rather the unique essence would be part of the world as presently shaped by God's pervasive purposeful agency. It would be essentially transcendent to the divine essence and life.

But Brentano's own view, as we have seen, has strains that keep God decisively transcendent with hints of a life and being apart from the world, and at the same time the world appears to be wholly derived from God's will. (The theme of exemplarity is reduced to an alleged similarity of caused to cause and finds little or no room in Brentano.) Yet the correlation between God and the world, where neither can be conceived in the absence of the other, moves him slightly in the direction of a process theology. With God and the world being greater than God alone, and with the prospect of God of necessity always creating what is best, there is the prospect of an ever greater increase in perfection. Indeed, God may be thought of as the infinitely perfect artist and as such is one who creates ever more perfect artwork. An actually infinite perfect work is inconceivable. What is conceivable is the advance to ever greater perfection of the artwork.

Brentano once composed this dialogue:

One man will say, this world must be the best possible,
For, in creating, the best must choose the best.
Another man says, No; for if it were,
It would present the measure of God's power.
Oh, listen to me, you two disputants!
Can we say the world is?
No; *becoming*, it oversteps all measures of good,
And strives endlessly, from likeness unto likeness,
Towards the supreme and unattainable image of the Lord.[154]

Although God is as perfect from eternity as God possibly can be, and although all creation can but endlessly approximate the perfection of God, nevertheless there is a kind of change in God in God's knowing this increase in perfection in the world, and the divine essence itself shares in this process of an advance in perfection.[155]

As to the ultimate destiny of humans, Brentano argues in a classical way for the immortality of the soul, or the subject of conscious experiences. The brain is best thought of as an organ of consciousness, but the subject of consciousness cannot be located in any part of the brain. And any analysis of this subject of consciousness as well as study of the brain points to the conclusion that the subject of consciousness is not something material but spirit. The soul as spirit is such that it cannot be annihilated. What its continuation after death might mean is beyond our experience.[156]

Of special interest in thinking about human destiny and that of the world as the correlation of God's will is his critique of pessimism. The critics of religion often espouse the view that there is evil in the world of such a magnitude that any subsequent atonement or higher harmony cannot make things right. Dostoevski's Ivan (in *Brothers Karamazov*), the distinguished American philosopher of religion Edgar Brightman, and thinkers attempting to think of these matters "after Auschwitz" or after Hiroshima, Nagasake, Dresden, Guantanamo Bay, etc., may be considered representative. To use Brightman's language, there are "dysteleological surds" that neither rhyme nor reason can make a means to a higher good or where a perspective might be entertained in which these evils find a legitimate place.[157] These are evils which remain eternally there and no amount of good agency can ever make of them something good or something insignificant in their evilness.

For Brentano such a view is paradoxical. Every evil, however enormous and horrendous it is, is always, in spite of our seemingly endless indignation and outrage, finite. Every finite goodness or greatness is itself only relatively great and compared with something greater it is small; indeed, it is a billionfold smaller and reaches to a vanishing point in comparison with something a billionfold greater or something that reaches into what is infinitely greater. And yet this pessimistic view holds that the evil that is relatively small, no matter how great an evil it may be thought to be, is to be considered of such a nature that it never could be compensated for or diminished by no matter how great an accumulation of goods.[158]

I think that this view of Brentano offers consolation if by a leap of faith, perhaps a leap into the "absurd" in the permissible sense we have sketched, one may take up this third-person point of view of a divine power for goodness. If, however, like Doestoevski's Ivan, we believe that by taking this faith perspective and accepting the invitation to the party of the heavenly Higher Harmony we would thereby sacrifice our human perspective, and then renounce all capacity for moral and axiological judgment, then the argument can offer no consolation. But is it so clear that what I or we declare as the human perspective in such a matter is entitled to such ultimacy? This is the basic question of The Theological Distinction, and at least on the matter of ultimate good and evil, we are offered no other knowledge than this: Our human personal perspective, given that it is often inadequate and fallible, is not the last word. Surely the faith perspective, given the depth of its doctrines of sin and atonement, is neither a whitewash of the evils nor a diminishment of their magnitude – even though it holds that there is a perspective that is incommensurate with ours, and a power for goodness beyond our capacity to comprehend, that may offer an emptily intended consolation in the face of the filled intention of what surely appear to be "dysteleological surds."

A rejection of the deep optimism of Brentano would seem to be reinforced by his own view that the world as the expression of the infinitely great artisan stands essentially in correlation to God's own life, and therefore it offers the parameters of intelligibility for thinking about these matters, e.g., by providing limits simpliciter. In which case, the divine "perspective" is not properly incommensurate with the world and is therefore not a limit concept, as in The Distinction's position that God plus the world is not greater than God alone. For Brentano God is that being, *Wesen*, than which nothing greater can be conceived. But with the world we have more than just that *Wesen*, we have God plus the world, and God would not have created were it not better than not having created. And, as God is of necessity moved to do what is best, the world is in this respect necessary for God. And with creation there is more goodness than there was before, even granting that God alone is that being than which nothing greater can be conceived. Brentano's thinking of God as the greatest being hinders him from appreciating the metaphysics of *esse* and the view that God as Pure To Be Itself is not the greatest being. The greatest being conceivable, to the extent that Its "life" is tied to that of the fate of the world, would seem to be capable of not only endess advance in perfection but also endless decline.

B. Shankara's Monist Theology

The second view The Theological Distinction excludes is the pantheist or monist view. Yet it must be said that the monist principle, "God is all there is," although false because contrary to fact, is meaningful for The Theological Distinction. That is, there is a sense within the framework of The Theological Distinction in which the term, "God," is the alone absolutely necessary term and the one which contains all the excellence and intelligibility of the whole. Yet it is *de facto* false that this term alone *is* or *exists*. This means not merely that creation is not a mere product of the imagination or an illusion, but that it is no less true for the dogma of God the Creator that creation is a "real reality" or a fact. This is said even though creation itself, which is freely enacted and out of nothing, has nothing of its own apart from God. Further, that God is all there is, is false because within the context of The Theological Distinction, creatures are chosen by God "as the alternative to there being only God."[159] The Theological Distinction holds that creatures truly are and that God is the sole source of creatures. It affirms that "it is the same to say that God created all things for the sake of Himself and that He created creatures for the sake of their To Be (*esse*)."[160] That is, the absolute being of God does not stand in competition with the autonomous being of creatures.

We have sought to speculate on this matter in terms of God's being both pure interiority or pure non-intentional self-manifestation and a form of intentional self-awareness in conjunction with a creative act in which finite participations in the divine essence come to be. The view proposed here of God being most fundamentally pure interiority or pure non-intentional self-manifestation finds a parallel in the ninth century Advaita-Vedanta philosopher Shankara. The meaning of advaita, non-duality, is that the creature does not add anything to Brahman or the absolute; therefore it does not make two with Him. For Shankara, the divine or Brahman is pure non-reflexive self-luminosity. But for Shankara, seemingly, intentionality was not necessary for the divine; indeed, it appears not to have been a proper capacity of the divine. For that reason the world could only be envisaged by the adept as an illusion in regard to the world's claim to hold ultimate significance. The task for the adept was to overcome intentional life as being-in-the-world. In so far as one's intentional life in the world lays claims to ultimate meaning the adept must see it as an illusion, and through dis-cipline retrieve Brahman in one's own non-intentional self-awareness.

For Shankara, God plus the world is not greater than God alone; the world can neither add nor detract from the perfection of Brahman.[161] Therefore the task is how to envisage that which is other than Brahman. What is other than the infinite perfection of pure non-reflexive self-awareness is not nothing because, after all, the manifold comprising the world is not nothing.

We can recall that in classical Christian theology the divine creative ("transitive," *ad extra*) activity differed from the sheerly immanent activity in the divine of the internal, *ad intra* ("Trinitarian") processions. Yet, at the same time creation is not a transitive activity relating to something existing apart from the divine or that upon which God acts. God as Creator is not really related to the world in the sense that creation is an acting upon something or in the sense that creation is of a reciprocal correlative dependence of cause and effect.[162] A mystic formulation of this is, "He is thy being, thou are not his being" (Walter Hilton). That is, as we have repeatedly stated in our discussion of the modes of the unique essence of the "myself," my creaturely being is not constitutive of God's being but God's uncreated being is constitutive of mine. Furthermore, as Thomas says, God's creative (we add: "intentional") activity is not properly transcendent, because God's willing creatures for the sake of their own being is the same as willing them for Godself and for God's own goodness. Again: "It is the same to say that God made [created] all things for the sake of Himself and that He made [created] creatures for the sake of their To Be (*esse*)."[163]

Shankara says at least this much. But it would seem that Shankara fears that holding the position that the act of creation, as an analogous intentional act by which there is unity with the other as other, renders the being of creatures into a second absolute next to the absolute. In such a view the doctrine of creation of beings from nothing places the beings in competition with Brahman. And by way of extension, intentionality, in both the divine and human cases, would posit a second absolute and thereby would destroy the absolute fullness of the utter non-intentional, non-reflective, immanent awareness of Brahman. And because Brahman as absolute non-intentional consciousness brooks absolutely no otherness, the realm of the world as what appears to the intentional creaturely being-in-the-world is one of nescience, an ignorance generating maya or illusion. Maya as such is a category of awakened consciousness. Prior to this awakened consciousness what is truly maya would be taken for reality in itself. This is ignorance.

The being of the world, of maya, is neither being nor non-being; neither other than being nor identical to it. But this otherness to being and nothingness is not the perspective of Brahman but of the not yet liberated consciousnesses that intend the world. This means that although maya reveals the infinite riches of Brahman to the adept, it cannot be as such known to Brahman, for this would require the intentionality at least of imagination, i.e., the intending of something as if it were real. Obviously the wealth of maya is known nevertheless *eminenter* in Brahman's pure non-reflexive self-awareness.

For the Theological Distinction, although it is true that God's being alone and without the world is possible but contrary to fact or *de facto* false, it is essential that we understand the being of the world as real and not an illusion, even though we are to understand the "being" of God precisely as that to which the world adds nothing in the order of ontological dignity or value.

Further, the Theological Distinction, we propose, requires that the divine not be restricted to merely non-intentional immediate self-awareness but that the divine be capable of intentionality as a genuine form of the having or presencing of the other as other. How intentionality as self-transcendence breaks forth within the absolute immanence of the divine being as pure unothered act is, as we have suggested, a difficult issue. How otherness to *Ipsum Esse Subsistens* arises within the divine, how the essential divine being, which admits ontologically of nothing beside Itself and in knowing Itself not only knows non-intentionally Godself, but also Godself as imitable and participatable by what is not the divine, remains therefore a key speculative issue for thinking about creation.[164] The term Sokolowski uses to designate this mystery is "incomparable generosity"[165] – a theme to which we will soon turn.

We may consider a final motivation for a monist view. The writings of mystics often incline toward images and concepts which suggest the dissolution of the barriers, boundaries, or walls separating the finite self from the Infinite Self. Often metaphors of fusion, drowning, commingling, melting, etc. are used. And if the mystic intuits, or if the philosopher of mysticism grasps, that the self indeed has a non-ascriptive referent by which it is other than and more than its stream of consciousness and personal properties, that an aspect of the self does not have a describable nature, indeed that it is bereft of properties, then the temptation lies at hand to say that here, in the mystic moment, Reality is precisely one lacking any determination. Everything is united in the undifferentiated All. Now finally the self is released into its true nature of absolute indetermination and is indistinguishably one with the ultimate trans-propertied ground of being, God.

This is more easy to follow if one takes the third-person point of view and holds that what we know about the Other is really a contingent wrapping ("personification") for what is without any delimiting, distinguishing properties. If we thus posit a circumstance in which all the apparent distinguishing properties are torn away, then the true, i.e., bare, self surfaces as bereft of a describable, propertied nature and, as such, the self is without any identifiable features. If the distinguishing properties and boundaries which are obvious in the third- and second-person are posited to have been extinguished, each self therefore may be posited to melt into the infinite transcendence of the absolute One who is exemplarily beyond all properties and descriptions.

But if we think of the self properly, and do not lose how we are for ourselves in the first-person and how others are for us, foremost in love, the temptation to such a dissolution would find considerable resistance. In the first-person we are uniquely and undeniably ourselves and not others, regardless of the sameness of properties or the absence of the sameness of properties in our personal self-presentations, and this is precisely the nature of our being as a "myself," bereft of describable properties.[166] Each is essentially and uniquely oneself and not another or not others, even though our manner of distinguishing ourselves and others as ipseities who are the subject or substance of the personal presentations is *not* merely a matter of identifiable properties, which means of necessity one is finite. I am a uniquely unique essence, an haecceity, and not merely this person or this human being. Qua transcendental "I" I am not an I or this I, and in this sense there are no Others besides myself. The sense of the first-person singular is that the referent is uniquely unique; there is not a plurality of "I's." (See our discussion in Book 1, Chapter V, especially §4.)

Of course, this is remote from saying that I am *ipse ipsissimus* encompassing all unique essences, including in myself all the essentiality of the "myself" as manifest in the infinity of haecceities. I myself exist with the existence-condition of human kind which I share with endless others and the perfection I have of being a human person only reflects in a very finite partial way the infinite fullness of being a human person. Even though I exhaust the individual essence which is the reference of the "I" who is JG Hart in a way analogous to how the angel Michael exhausts Michaelness, I belong to human kind and Michael does not have such an existence condition that limits his personal being to belonging to a natural kind such that he does not embody all the perfections of this kind. Further, because and, as well, in spite of my being I myself, I experience myself to be surrounded by ipseities, by Others, whom I apperceive to refer similarly to themselves with the same token reflexive "I" and who thereby experience themselves as uniquely "myself" or unique unparalleled I-essences. (The archangel Michael must also say this of the numerous Others comprising the choirs of "angelic" persons as well as human and perhaps sub-human persons.) Thus my being I myself uniquely and in my being "myself" and thus being beyond descriptions and properties is not the transcendence of the infinite divine essence who is *ipse ipsissimus*; rather it is but a feeble likeness.

Further, as H.D. Lewis has noted, the elimination of the selfhood of oneself seems more plausible and acceptable "when it seems to be a matter of being taken up into something which we seem to be already."[167] If in "union with God" we ultimately become what we, in some sense, "already are," then there is possibly not a sense of loss but rather a unique joy. But we have already noted, especially in the tradition dependent in various degrees on Plotinus, senses in which the becoming who one is, is both a loss of oneself, i.e., a dying or denying of the old, false self, and a fulfillment of who one is meant to be. Furthermore, we have argued that we do not become one with our eternal exemplary essence as it is essentially one with the divine essence. This is a metaphysical impossibility. Even though the "myself" of JG Hart has its eternal exemplar in the eternal divine essence, the "myself" that I, JG Hart, refers to, although a "mode" of the *same* essence that is exemplary in God's essence, is not *identical* with the divine essence. This latter claim at least should require no further argument.

Moreover, with the heightened actuation of ourselves, which we may presume to be the case in any beatifying vision or union with God, it is doubtless true that any thematic sense of ourselves falls away. This is manifestly true when we are involved in the most exciting, demanding, thrilling, enthralling, etc. activities. Here we may say that we are less conscious *of* ourselves, and therefore we are not conscious of what has distinguishing identifying features which stand in contrast with other identifiable matters of which one is conscious. (See Book 1, Chapters II–III and V for this.) Rather, in the heightened actuation of ourselves, no matter what we are doing, we are less aware *of* ourselves even though we ourselves are more conscious, more wakeful. Thus we may distinguish between ordinary (thus reflective) senses of self-awareness and "myself aware." Here there seems to be an inverse proportion between awareness *of* oneself or self-awareness, in the sense of having oneself as an implicit or explicit theme of knowing or emotion, and the intensity of consciousness of "myself aware."[168] In the latter case, increased self-awareness is not an increased awareness *of* ourselves, even though there is an increased self-wakefulness and intensity or actuation on the side of "I myself." A self which is maximally aware and "self-actualizing" is not at all a self which is aware *of* itself. And such an actuated self is not less itself, not less pervaded by ownness, but rather fully actuated, fully its unique very own self in act.

It appears that Shankara's claim that Brahman, as pure non-reflective self-awareness that is of necessity one and absolute, fails to appreciate this distinction. The difficulty is that it is not easy to determine whether such an analysis accurately explicates the first-person accounts of mystics in their writings. This is primarily because of the extraordinary nature of the experienced union as well. Our point is that in each case it presumably is an *experienced* union and therefore someone's. That is, it seems fair to ask any mystic: "Who" was being so blessed and ecstatically enraptured? "Whose soul" did the Holy Spirit enter? "To whom" were these visions bestowed? "Who" was being loved and uplifted?, etc. The monist interpretations would be such as to leave the mystic in the position of not being able to say they were her own experiences and rather she was absorbed, like a drop in the ocean so that the use of the personal indexical is either inappropriate, irrelevant, or interchangeable. (Cf. our discussion of Sufism in Chapter VI, §3.)

The Theological Distinction would seem to explicate the Thomist teaching of a gracious "light of glory" (*lumen gloriae*) for the blessed "in Heaven" in such a way that it favors neither the monist nor the monadic understanding of ultimate union. This teaching has to do with the essential "mysticism" of the blessed, which we may presume the mystic experience feebly anticipates. Here the created spirit *shares in* the divine intellect's own self-understanding and this is made possible by "the very essence of God" becoming "the intelligible form of the [finite] intellect."[169] Note that here there remains in tact the finite intellect or person, but now its power of understanding is raised to that of the very self-understanding of the essence of God. After such a profound transformation of the "myself" the typical clear state of certitude that the "experience" was one's own might well be altered. Nevertheless, apart from the problems of the interpretation of the first-person accounts of the mystics, it would seem that The Theological Distinction would claim that the evidence for the creaturely "ownness" would not be obliterated even if the person's enhanced power to understand were keenly present as a grace received. Again, the enhancement of "myself aware" is compatible with the anonymity of awareness of myself.

The Pauline view that we "know even as we are known" (*epignosomai kathos kai epegnosathen*, 1 *Corinthians* 13:8) might well refer both to the ontological humility of a self unselfishly aware of itself before God, as well as an awareness of ourselves as unable to know our beginnings as they are to be found in God's knowing and loving us, and thus not knowing ourselves as God knows and loves us. But we could perhaps be said to know ourselves as unique haecceities called from all eternity. This is to say that we would know ourselves as exemplifications of the divine idea, but it would not be to know ourselves precisely in the first and second modes in which the "myself" is actual because this would be to be God.

In any case, for The Theological Distinction there is nothing new in the circle of problems raised by the monist utterances of mysticism and advaita metaphysics. Already in the doctrine of creation we have the basic problem of how there can be anything other than God, and a fortiori, how can the unique ipseity that JG Hart refers to also refer to the divine essence.

C. The Process Theology of Max Scheler

The other, for our purposes, third and final, position The Theological Distinction avoids is that of an explicit process theology which posits a God who is finite in certain respects and who develops through the evolution of the processes of the natural and cultural world and human subjectivities. Husserl and Max Scheler both sketched philosophical theologies that were close to the "process theological" camp. For process theology the classical theology tends to make God unacceptably transcendent in both an ontological and psychological manner. At the same time, some strains of process theology criticized classical theology because its doctrine of radical immanence suffocated the dignity of human freedom. For both Husserl and Scheler the "absolute sphere" of subjectivity was not easily reconcilable with a theism which constituted or created absolutely this subjectivity. As we earlier saw (§7 above), for Husserl it was conceptually problematic how the "being of God" would be able "to hold in itself all other absolute being," a basic thesis of The Theological Distinction. We also saw how Husserl conceived the absolute sphere of finite subjectivities to be the means of God's knowing and acting in the world. Because we have discussed Husserl's views elsewhere,[170] and because Scheler's views are a more explicit and less tentative version of this foil, we will sketch Scheler's philosophical theology as the third alternative that The Theological Distinction avoids. But the following critical exposition must be prefaced with the caution that the sources for this elaborate philosophical theology are themselves unfinished notes that Scheler was working on before death took him.

Scheler throughout his life argued for the uniqueness of the person. He too held persons to be unique substances which possess a genuine individual essence. It was out of this *intrinsically individuated being-such* that the distinctiveness of their actual existence flowed. This determination of radical individuality reached even more deeply than that of "being human" in determining one's destiny, i.e., it reached deeper than the various levels of existence, e.g., the vital, historical, and the mechanical, into which the person was inserted. Scheler, furthermore, early held the classical view that we have here presented in this chapter: Because every true essence must have its place in the realm of essences, which itself had for its subject the divine personal ground of the world, each personal spirit displays its essence in accord with an eternal idea of God. This is in no way a mere imitation of, i.e., an extrinsic likeness to, the divine subjectivity's idea but rather the unique personal essence inheres ontologically in God's very essence, as analogously a formal essential property inheres in the essence of which it is a property. This is not to say that the finite person in her actual existence enjoys experientially this unity of essence with the divine essence, but rather the unique essence of the person rests or finds its existential home base eternally in God. This ontological setting provides the framework for one's life-orientation. Scheler further cautions that one must not confuse the pre-existence of the essence of the person with the pre-existence of the factual existence of the person.[171]

Scheler notes in this early (1913) writing that what he here proposes is not a pantheistic position which would posit a fusion of the person with the divine, e.g., as a mode of the divine, or as a function of the divine spirit, or as a result of a subsequent "mystical" unifying knowing of the divine. Rather here there is posited an identity of the being-such or unique essence of the personal spirit and the idea in God. But, again, this is not an essential identity of the actual individual person with God, but only an essential identity of the personal spirit *in so far as* the essence of this created person and her world finds exemplarity in the realm of divine ideas. The unique individual essence is thus part of the realm of divine ideas, which includes countless other unique individual essences, and these make up for part of the realm of possible ideas which reflect the infinite richness of the divine as the subject of all essences.[172]

Scheler's late philosophical theology contrasts rather sharply with this just-sketched position, even though I am not aware of any discussion where there is an extensive repudiation by him of the earlier more classical position. Yet the rejection of his earlier position is clearly implied in the subsequent one. His later thought bears the mark of a more modernist temper, i.e., one where the presuppositions of what preceded modernity in both Greek and medieval philosophy are occluded by being either forgotten or repressed, but function as both as foils or as encouragements to the new preferred alternative. Thus, e.g., the "communication of idioms" or the permissibility to say, through the Chalcedonian doctrine of the Incarnation, e.g., that God suffered and died, provided a perspective on divinity that philosophers believed to be accessible to philosophy without needing to acknowledge how faith traditionally functioned in permitting such propositions. Scheler's process philosophical theology, like other nineteenth and twentieth century ones, found the classical description of the absolute transcendent God to be morally and psychologically reprehensible in a way the struggling and suffering God was not. Scheler's late panentheistic God, indebted to inspiration from both Bergson and Nietzsche, takes risks, is involved, and even hopes and has faith in Its divine struggle to realize Itself in the world-process.

Scheler holds, without (to my knowledge) working out his position, that we are in a position to know God as the "world-ground." Because God is ground of the world, the sense of God as ground makes God to be part of the world, to use Sokolowski's terms. Yet Scheler also says that the Godhead in Itself is, in Its own life "absolutely unknowable." "There is no revelation of the inner being and life of the Godhead." He further claims to know that being the "ground" of the world does not exhaust the being and life of the Godhead.[173] All these claims remove Scheler's

God from the "pagan" camp and echo the classical tradition of The Theological Distinction. Yet throughout we find Scheler's clear allegiance to the panentheistic theory of a struggling God.

These latter bold and ambitious, if seemingly peripheral, theoretical claims are not given extensive justification. Nevertheless, his statements about God as the world-ground serve as a clear foil for The Theological Distinction. Scheler's work is a phenomenological philosophical theology in that the core of his positions builds on a phenomenology of the human person, whose existential struggles are then postulated to embody or contain the formal metaphysical and cosmological principles ruling all of being.

In this late development of his thought he sketched a position where the unique individual persons, even though intrinsic values, are functions of the deity's self-realization. He claims that a "person" as a spiritual act-center with a unique essence is a "self-concentration" of the divine spirit itself.[174] Apparently the divine agency is realized by its "othering" or pluralizing itself in the manifold personal act-centers. The divine's life and its self-awareness are lived through the finite persons or spiritual act-centers. In the person's act-life the divine ground of the world comes to self-understanding and self-knowledge. Further, in the act-life the divine begins to redeem itself from the demonic divine wildness and exuberance of that with which the divine spirit must creatively wrestle. This struggle is through a process of "ideation" or informing with ideas the divine demonic impulsiveness (*Drang*) of life-forces. This *Drang* is the eternal divine correlative principle of spirit and the stuff of spirit's creative wrestle. The creativity of spirit is its non-inhibition, its non-suppression, its *non non fiat*, to the life-forces by way of channeling and informing them with direction and intelligibility.[175] Here Scheler's "likely story" has affinities with Plato's view that the world is "reasonable for the most part" and that the divine architect must wrestle with the recalcitrancy, "wandering causes," and *anangke* of the primal hyle.[176] (For Plato, however, this "receptacle" was not itself divine, even though equally primordial.)

Thus the human person is not one who, in her agency, reflects or emulates the perfection of the realm of ideas as it existed before the creation of the world but she is co-creator, co-founder of the world process and its organizing ideas, and she is the unique place where God realizes and makes holy His essence. The human person is the flag bearer of deity which first of all realizes Itself through the agency of persons.[177] The realm of ideas thus does not pre-exist the creativity of human persons but rather persons, as vehicles of the divine spirit, constitute ideas, and thus shape and differentiate the world. Thus ideas here seem not to be eidetic displays or disclosures of the nature of the world, but more pragmatic and heuristic devices for organizing one's experience in the service of the vital forces. The constitution of ideas is the encounter of spirit with the force of history and vital processes. The classical doctrine of a God existing in Himself as the subject of an eternal realm of ideas, along with its notion of *ideae ante res*, divine foreknowledge, etc. fails to understand that there are no ideas prior to actual existing things, no world-plan prior to and independent of the world-process or the history which the world is. The ideas which human persons produce under the sway of the urgings of the cosmic spirit do not reflect any prior realm of essences or meanings but rather are thoroughly motivated through the interests of impulse and needs occasioned in the temporal situation, and they function as ways in which the world process is led and directed. Always and everywhere spirit is allured and solicited by the contingencies of the elemental cosmic-historical impulse.[178]

We may say that Scheler, echoing Gustav Theodor Fechner and anticipating Charles Hartshorne, holds that the world is the body of God. (Recall our earlier discussion of Hopkins above, §5.) God does not continuously create the world but permits and orders the world out of the material that emerges in the fanciful formations and creativity of the divine principle of impulse.[179] Prior to persons the divine spirit wrestles and orders the world-process and world-creativity (*Drang*). But the divine itself does not advance in *Its own life* until the creation of persons. (This reader does not know how to harmonize this view with the one we noted earlier that we know nothing of the inner being and life of the Godhead.) The divine may be said to grow and learn in and through the growth and learning of the human person. The only idea that is *ante res* is the idea the deity has of itself in its concrete becoming; otherwise it must be said that there are no eternal forms or categories. The divine ipseity is the only eternal essence. What is "eternal" is the divine process realizing itself through what it has fashioned, and this happens in regard to divine progress in self-realization with self-awareness in persons, which is both the awareness of individual persons as well as the divine self-awareness.[180] (Cf. our discussion of Husserl above at §5.)

Scheler holds that the divine substance does not need the world in order for It to be. (Again, how this is known, especially given the claim that we know nothing of God's own life, is unclear.) There is an eternal becoming in the Godhead independent of the becoming of the world. Yet, given other statements that criticize any theology of God's absolute self-sufficiency, we must assume that the eternal becoming of the Godhead apart from the becoming of the world is itself a necessary preparation for this cosmogony. With the world's happening through the non-inhibition of the divine will, the world becomes pervaded by a teleological process of God's self-realization in the world. Although God is not the "Lord" of the world in the classical theological sense, nevertheless, the human person, as God's flag-bearer and holy essence in the world, is the Lord and King of creation; and both God and the human person are comrades in the suffering and the struggle with fate – and it is unclear whether they will triumph. But God believes in the course of the world-process and in the victory of his idea and love of Himself; he believes in His conquest, though he does not know what the conclusion will be. Scheler adds that although evil can pose obstacles it can never decisively prevent the victory of the good work of spirit.[181] But, in any case, we are assured that this God is more blessed in the struggle than is the perfect God in his peace and rest in heaven.

For Scheler, the perfect God of "theism," who is thought to be all good and omnipotent with regard to its other, the world, is, in truth, the goal of the world-process, not its beginning. The world is intrinsic to God as world-ground, and God is the most exalted and excellent part of the world, i.e., its ground and *telos*. *Drang* or the counter co-primordial divine principle to spirit is the principle of worldly creativity and impulse. Spirit's creativity is precisely the non-inhibition of the principle of impulse. Spirit cajoles the ebullient creativity of impulse (*Drang*) with form and ideas. This principle of impulse accounts for the "drag" or "surds" in the universe and life. Scheler believes that anyone who witnesses the horrors, e.g., of war and natural catastrophes, will find the doctrine of an all good and all powerful God a ridiculous notion. Further, such a concept of God, which implies a theory of foreknowledge, is incompatible with the freedom of the person.[182]

For Scheler, theism is persistently tempted to posit a supreme being who is a supreme thing, an object, a being among beings which stands in competition with or juxtaposition to "creatures." Creation *ex nihilo* has no possible appreciation for the creativity, suffering, and tragedy of the world-process; it has no insight into divine evolution and the earnestness of the moral struggle. For Scheler, dogmatically speaking, creation is God's suffering, death and resurrection. Scheler's God, as Husserl's, is no more an object than is another person. Further, as in Fichte and occasionally Husserl, God is only made present in one's moral engagement and one's self-identification with the moral ideals as they are present in one's historical context.

The modernity of a position such as Scheler's rests in part on the conviction that the classical God is, as another critic of religion has put it, "a robber behind the clouds." In this view, Christianity, and perhaps as well, Judaism and Islam, devaluate nature as the self-bearing, self-grounding, self-sourcing of all there is. In Scheler's version of Christianity, the manifest "nature," as the self-subsisting source of natural kinds becomes "contingent" in the sense that an arbitrary inscrutable divine will ultimately is the source of all the apparent necessities, and all causality becomes "secondary" and thus merely apparent in favor of the inscrutable Necessity of the divine will. Christianity is thus the enemy of any robust sense of nature and the source of the flight from the "one, true, earth." The "elevation" of God to absolute self-sufficiency, for whom the world is absolutely unnecessary and for whom the being of the world cannot mean a diminishment of God, is incompatible with the pre-Christian, ancient, but relatively exalted view of a self-subsisting self-creating nature or creation. By implication, for the modern or post-modern such a Christian God and such a religion are incompatible with the intrinsic dignity of persons. Therefore religion has of necessity the double-aspect of vampirism and dope. It sucks the energy of proper agency from its true tasks while providing a delusional comfort. This latter has the effect of laming the will of proper agency and channeling it to pie in the sky.

Thus in Scheler's view of the classical distinction between God and the world, which betrays, surprisingly, an ignorance of the classical metaphysics of creation, all glory bestowed on creation is a diminishment of such a (classical theory of) God and a maximalization of God's self-sufficiency is of necessity a depreciation of the world. The classical view of God as absolutely self-sufficient and transcendent to the world, as not "really related" to the world, and therefore as ontologically "impassive," is taken by process philosophers like Scheler not to be at all *eu angelion*. Rather, it is seen as a curse and a recipe for the degradation of the world and a prescription for the violation of the dignity of the human person.[183]

Thus process philosophical theology holds that it is proper to God's essence to suffer, evolve, and struggle by being immersed in the natural-historical world-process. Again, the ontological-statements about God's relation to the world in classical theology and in what we are calling The Theological Distinction, e.g., that God is not related to the world, that God is pure actuality and no way capable of being enhanced by the world, are regarded as moral-psychological descriptions, indeed ones highlighting the moral-psychological pathology of the classical God. The incarnation and suffering of God in Christ are not graces but metaphysical necessities. They are not mysteries of faith but philosophical positions.

For such a process critique of classical theology, it is not until the human person is recognized as a co-creator, and not until God is enhanced and exalted (or, depending on one's perspective, diminished and demoted) to an essential co-sufferer whose being is laced with contingency, not until nature's process itself and history as well are seen to be a theogonic process, that there is made possible the proper appreciation of the divine and the human.[184] In this modern Schelerian theory which clearly appropriates themes of classical theology even in its disowning it, and quite in contrast to pagan understandings of nature, it is not until nature is *deprived* of natural kinds and finds its "forms" in the divine-human creativity that justice is done to the transcendence of persons to nature. Not until forms of nature are the result of creative human agency is justice done to the freedom and creativity of God and human persons. Thus this modern anti-theological theology, like much of modern physics and metaphysics, is compelled to eliminate from nature any self-subsistence and natural kinds.

The Theological Distinction here is not explicitly disavowed but is opposed because the basic dogma of this distinction, implied in the teaching of *creatio ex nihilo*, comes to light only under the disguise of a foil and this foil is a feeble version of traditional theism. In this view, if God is not finite in terms of at least God's omnipotence, then the infinity of God removes God from the world or it smothers the intrinsic dignity of the world. Further, apart from the few remarks by Scheler about the mystery of God's own life and God's being apart from the world, there seems to be resentment toward the notion that God's plenitude and the plenitude of goodness would not be diminished if creatures were not, if all there was was God alone, the extreme of solitude. It is as if Scheler would prefer to say: It would be better that we quasi-divine human persons alone were and there were not the self-sufficient God than that it be true, but contrary to fact, that God alone would be.

Such an opposition to The Theological Distinction reaches the highest level of paradox because it is precisely the contingency at the heart of personal existence which the modern existentialist, of which movement the late Scheler was perhaps a forerunner, brings to light. Yet the modern, such as Scheler himself, expresses indignation at the notion that his being is not necessary for the essential goodness of being. Thus to secure this transcendent dignity and necessity, the person is established as a necessary function of God who is in many respects finite, if not contingent.

Whereas The Theological Distinction may acknowledge reasons brought forth to posit parts of the world as "godly" and of an intrinsically higher order than others (in this sense there is no need a priori to deny the status of god to, e.g., a Gaia principle, if evidence for it were strong and if it were to become absolutely

indispensable to cosmological theory), the God of The Theological Distinction is
not such a part. (We may recall that Plotinus' One admitted exalted divine principles as intrinsic parts of the world, e.g., the world-soul.) It neither enhanced nor
detracted from by the excellence or fate of the world. But this does not mean that
nature has no inherent integrity or excellence. Nor does it mean that the divine has
a kind of being or nature that removes it from and renders it indifferent to the workings or inner being of the world or that it is incapable of caring for or loving the
world. For The Theological Distinction, God is not a kind of being nor does God
have a nature. God's not being "really related" to the world is not a psychological
but an ontological description.

Whereas Scheler maintains the central phenomenological notion of intentionality or the act-life, it is displaced from God's own life except in so far as God's own
life is realized in and by the act-life of persons. Further, although there is a concern
with the classical view because it is alleged to obliterate the autonomy of freedom,
in Scheler's view the individual person's freedom is precisely the freedom of God
as concentrated or incarnated in the world. The difference between God's own life
apart from God as world-ground and that of historical persons is not spelled out.
Clearly God's life as world-ground and the life of persons comprise the same life
even though they are not identical. It is not clear that such a view, although motivated in part by the desire to secure the radical autonomy and dignity of the person,
does not depreciate and undermine it.

Scheler further strives to provide persons with an ontological ground by making of them "concentrations" of the divinity in history. Yet it would seem that their
unique individuality is threatened because (the late) Scheler denies that there is
any such essence prior to history beyond the essence of the divine struggle for its
becoming. According to Scheler's late metaphysics, the unique person as a unique
essence or "idea" is no more than a conceptual tool or function aimed at dealing
with the *ad hoc* urgency and importunities of history as it is shaped by impulse.
The historical person's own essence is a function of the struggling divinity's self-
realization. If this reading is correct, it would seem that the late Scheler here holds
a view that opposes much if not all he worked for in his earlier rich theory of per-
sonalism and value-theory.

If the world is without transcendent essences, and perhaps even some natural
kinds, no matter if they are relatively unstable or have evolved, if all essences are
heuristic and pragmatic ideas, and these, as such, are tied to the goals of successful action for an individual, and all action is related to the purposes of the unique
concentrations of deity as they cajole and cultivate the divine impulse, what kind
of common world and common goods do we have? (We presume that for Scheler
the "essence" of the human person, precisely as a unique concentration of the deity,
does not enjoy the unstable reality of other essences – even though functionalized
by the exigencies of the deity.) In a world where there are no essences and absolutely no natural kinds there are no ends and where there are no ends there are only
human-personal purposes. As Francis Slade says, here we have "a world without
ends" wherein the manifold and doubtlessly often conflicting purposes cannot
be measured or adjudicated by any ends. Indeed, if all we have are purposes as

intentions of unique individuals then we have purposes that are at odds and perhaps incommensurate with one another. In which case we have *bellum omnium contra omnes* and violence reigns because there is no natural way for things to move and interact and for human persons to find public, communicable norms and values in order to negotiate their being with one another in terms of the common world and common goods. Slade also notes that this is a world of *fiasco* "in which guilt is impossible, because guilt requires responsibility for actions, and there are actions only if purposes are measured by ends." That is, as one cannot be responsible for a raw impulse, so in a world where there are no proper descriptions or properties of things, agency in accord with such propriety is excluded. Slade's use of "fiasco" here builds on the rich etymological sense of this Italian word. According to John Ciardi, *fiasco* is not just any bottle (flask) but one that cannot stand on its own and one that will surely fall over. Thus by extension it means a project (of end-less purposes) that will surely fail because it lacks support (ends and essences and natures with ends).[185]

Such considerations, not at all foreign to early Scheler, by themselves do not decide the merits of any position on the ontological status of essences, but it does serve to question the rejection of a world with essences if it is proposed because of the determination that essences threaten to devalue human persons.

Thus Scheler's view contrasts with The Theological Distinction by maintaining: God and the world are greater than God alone; the enhancement in the value of the world and persons enhances God, and the diminishment of the value in the world and persons diminishes God. Further, God's own life (as ground of the world), as it develops through the evolution of persons, is juxtaposed to the life of persons for only in this way is their freedom left intact. At the same time, the life of persons is identified with that of God for only in this way are persons elevated to their proper dignity.

For Scheler, when I refer to me myself I must of necessity exclude God's knowing me as the creator of my being for such a knowing would destroy the essential personhood and freedom of my being I myself. Yet this divine ground somehow generates or posits the life of persons as vehicles for Its self-actualization. For late Scheler, it would seem, God cannot know what I refer to when I say "I" even though when I say "I" God is referred to, because I am an embodiment and vehicle of God's self-realization.

The necessary condition for Scheler's modern and post-modern panentheism is that it envisages as its foil a feeble version of the classical God which is bereft of what I take to be the strengths and clarifications of these mysteries by The Theological Distinction. The weak foil Scheler imagines may doubtless be found in some theistic formulations which denigrate the substantiality of nature and undermine the freedom and dignity of the person. It seems to us that Scheler's efforts to restore their proper status by way of his novel anti-theistic philosophical theology unfortunately undermine the "naturalness of nature." Furthermore, (and this is most surprising, given that it is, after all, *Scheler*, the great personalist), the freedom and dignity of the person is less protected than one might expect in these later writings. That is, the person becomes a vehicle for a finite God whose wisdom and goodness are conditioned by the state of the struggle for Its self-realization.

That is, the person is a vehicle for a struggling god whose proper divinity is the goal of its struggling.

Some final comments on the God of The Theological Distinction and some of the concerns of process theology. In the light of the modern post-Darwinian and post-Einsteinian views of nature The Theological Distinction's defense of exemplarity cannot present itself as resting on the eternity of the forms, natural kinds, or species of the natural world. Indeed, The Theological Distinction's position on how God is and how the world is in relation to God, and how God is the exemplary cause of all there is, must, so it would seem, give to the categories or essences of randomness and creativity a greater place in our understanding of God. But there is nothing new here at all. God's creating free persons is, as it were, a greater challenge for the intelligibility of The Theological Distinction than God's creating a randomly self-creating natural realm. The more basic mystery for the tradition is the creation of anything whatsoever, i.e., that God create what has self-subsistence and is genuinely other to the divine being. But especially mysterious is the creation of another source of freedom, i.e., the person. That God is the creator of an unfinished self-composing narrative called the natural universe is no more mysterious than the creation of a finite person who by definition is an unfinished narrative and whose freedom in no way diminishes divine omnipotence.

Some of the modern theological anguish over an evolving universe, like the ancient problems of predestination, assumes that God has to create according to finished plans. But this in fact is to say God cannot create what is free and creative or that God cannot create a *physis*. The motivation for the view that God has to create only according to completed plans is also often tied to the view that God has to know the future as completed. But this view, like the problem of divine knowledge of our indexical reference, seems to require that God's being and knowing be such that God cannot know what it is to be a creature. In our view, The Theological Distinction holds both that God knows the future and that God is not thereby ignorant of what it means to be a finite vulnerable being facing the future, nor does God cease to be God with such knowing or through knowing the referents of indexicality. Needless to say, this is also what the doctrine of the Incarnation teaches.

The weak presentations of the classical theological metaphysics in terms of conceiving God as the greatest being along with the process-theological finitization of God in the face of the surds, creativity, and historical humanity's perversity both are understandable expressions of resistance to the mystery of The Theological Distinction. But this mystery is tied not merely to the theological mystery of the person's creation as indicated in The Distinction. There is also, as we insisted at the start of this Book, a philosophical sense of mystery connected with the person. If the person must be made sense of in the light of the framework of the world, and increasingly a framework dictated by the natural and behavioral sciences, then a reductionist understanding of persons is inevitable. "God," as understood in the indications of The Theological Distinction in the "Abrahamic traditions," suffers an analogous "rationalization." At best God is made the "greatest being" or "finitized"; or more likely than not "God" becomes a social-psychological "function" or/and a delusion. (This, of course, is quite the opposite of Scheler's functionalization of persons for the finite God's divine struggle.)

The *theological* sense of "world" as it emerges in The Theological Distinction differs from both the scientific-cosmological senses of the world as well as the phenomenological sense of "world" even though it takes advantage of phenomenology's clarifications. The theological sense differs from the natural scientific sense of world as displayed through its scientific theories as much as this latter differs from the phenomenological and everyday senses. For the theological sense of world as articulated in The Theological Distinction there is neutrality regarding the genuinely scientific-cosmological accounts of the world regarding theories of the origin, expansion, evolution, devolution, and termination of the natural universe. It is as much a mistake to think that a self-generating world infringes on the majesty of God as to think that somewhere in the scientific cosmological narrative there must be found room for the biblical or theological narrative. Dialogues between theology and science are misplaced in so far as the theologian wants to tame or bend the scientist's science in the direction of, e.g., the biblical narrative or even attempt to see "creation from nothing" in the scientific narrative. The basic philosophical mistake is to permit a description of the world to be dominated by the natural-scientific lens and thereby to be complacent in the subordination or marginalization of the phenomenological-philosophical sense of the world. When theologians accept this state of affairs as normative, then they must enter the discussion by interjecting theological doctrine and the Bible into the scientific –philosophical description of the world.

The natural scientific sense of the world is what the natural sciences legitimately have to say about it. But this sense of the world has to be integrated into the phenomenological-philosophical sense which is foundational as the point of departure and point of return of the scientific account. Yet the philosophical-phenomenological sense is penultimate as far as The Theological Distinction is concerned; but this is not a philosophical proposition.

The consideration that the classical theology requires that God exemplarily and necessarily knows the unique essence of Peter in knowing Godself, along with the universal essences such as freedom and creativity, would seem to be a way of dealing with the evolutionary framework in a way that deepens the reverence for created nature. The contingent essence of the evolved natural kinds can be conceived to be dependent on the necessary essences of spirit, bodiliness, animality, culture, community, morphogenesis, development, materiality, freedom, love, randomness, responsibility, creativity, perception, memory, judgment, imagination, retention, protention, etc. These latter would be part of the divine's essential self-awareness. And in this respect, the divine exemplary idea of "creation" or "the cosmos" would resemble more a regulative infinite idea than a finished blueprint. In which case, God's idea of the world's self-formation of itself might be thought of as an awareness of the felt-meaning of the empty intention searching for the right words, the full propositional sense of which is unknown in the human case until it takes expression in more or less finished utterances; in the divine case, perhaps we may say, it is always known implicitly and is able to be known explicitly through God's self-articulation and self-reflection. This would be in accord with the classical theological claim of there being an undifferentiated but not confused self-awareness of Godself's infinite essences, foremost the unique individual essences of persons. But the consideration that among the essences God knows in knowing Godself were those of freedom, creativity, randomness, etc., can introduce into the divine self-awareness of the exemplars of the world a measure of contingency that would account for the unstable, temporal unsteady nature of the cosmos and its natural biological kinds. Such an understanding of God's self-awareness would open up speculations on the meaning of nature and its relation to history. But these scant remarks do not purport to do justice to this notoriously obscure terrain.

From what we earlier said, such speculation on God knowing Godself in terms of the essences of randomness, freedom, creativity, etc., is consonant with the divine awareness of the unfolding of a person's becoming the sort of person she is called to be, but it would not affect the divine awareness of the unique individual essence of this person. This would be part of the essential divine self-awareness from all eternity. We would therefore have to distinguish God's knowing of the "essential essences" of Godself from all eternity, and those having to do with what we call the third mode, i.e., those like "the actual world," and the person "JG Hart," which essentially are self-creations in the making pervaded by freedom, temporality, and randomness. These latter essences would not be essential to God's knowing of Godself in the first mode, but rather they are what God knows of Godself in knowing Godself in creation.

§12. The Calling of the Creature

Throughout the tradition of "the Abrahamic religions" the positing of God as eternal has had for its consequence the recognition that the conceptual distinctiveness of the moments in "divine economy," i.e. of creation, revelation, calling, and salvation, must be upheld. Yet the priority we assign to creation, although as the beginning it is necessarily what precedes everything else in this economy and from which everything else flows, must be rethought in terms of the possible logical-conceptual priority other moments have, as well possibly in terms of the temporality or sequentiality of these distinctive moments. From God's revealed point of view it is perhaps true to say that revelation, calling, and salvation "are as old" as creation and that it is misleading to think that we must or can conceive creation apart from, e.g., prior to, these other concepts. This comes home clearly in the basic prayer book of the Psalter where the primary sense of God is the one who liberates from a no-exit situation those whom God as created, called, and chosen. Typically this is often enough not only what we have called an existential limit-situation but one of political oppression, which, of course, itself may be the occasion for the other limit-situations.[186] Of course, these limit- or no-exit situations may be understood allegorically or "spiritually." In the Psalms the creator God is inseparably the providential God of history and the One who liberates those whom Godself has called from the forces of darkness and oppression. In this work for the most part we prescinded from this fuller sense of God (but cf. our discussion of process theology above at §11) and focused our thoughts on God the Creator who calls from before the foundation of the world. Here we wish to return explicitly to the theme of vocation.

We have already noted Jean-Louis Chrétien's gathering of ancient texts that dwell on the how Divine Goodness and Beauty, *kallos* and *kalos*, are related to "I call," *kalo*, and God may be said to call unto Godself all being just as goodness and beauty call forth desire. St. Paul, echoing the calling of Moses, Abraham, and prophets, says that God "calls into being what is not" (*Romans* 4:17) and that God chooses us "before the creation of the world" (*Ephesians* 1:4). Thus creation as analogous making must be rethought in terms of the other basic dogmas, i.e., revelation, calling, and redemption. Levinas has insisted, "the word creation designates a signification older than the context woven about this name," i.e., the later context provided by ontological thought. Thus the relationship of God to creation is to be conceived not primarily in terms of a unique causal relation named "creation" as an analogous "making," but also in other analogous relations such as parenting, procreation, and the variety of forms of a relationship of love, foremost the call of the lover. In this respect, the biblical love poem called *The Song of Songs* along with texts, e.g., of Isaiah and the Psalmist, should be as much food for thought for the philosophical reflection on "creation" as the texts in *Genesis*.

When philosophical theologians have taken this into account they have transposed the conceptualization of creation from the categories of causality into different registers such as "calling" or "love." Especially the notion of "first-cause" is transformed into the priority of God's love and God's calling. God's love and God's call are the origin of the beginning created person. But how are we to understand this? Or how does God's beauty as the eminently desirable call forth what is not yet a consciousness capable of desiring? How does God love or call what is not yet an "I" but which, when already existing, is for itself "I"? What is this creature prior to its being able to say "Here I am" before the creator God? Is the created "I," in its most primordial ontological feature as the recipient of a call, best conceived, as Levinas would seem to be saying, as an *It*, a "passivity more passive than any receptivity" to God's creative love and calling? Let us listen to Levinas:

> But in creation, what is called to being answers to a call that could not have reached it since, brought out of nothingness, it obeyed before hearing the order. Thus in the concept of creation *ex nihilo*, if it is not a pure nonsense, there is the concept of a passivity that does not revert into an assumption. The self as a creature is conceived in a passivity more passive still than the passivity of matter, that is, prior to the virtual coinciding of a term with itself. The oneself has to be conceived outside of all substantial coinciding of self with self.[187]

In the exemplary calling by God addressed, e.g., to Moses and Isaiah, the creature responds to the call by saying "Here I am." The addressee is already an I and there is a coincidence of the self with itself and the response of "here I am" testifies to this. In his using these callings as the context for understanding "creation" (and not assuming that "calling" is to presuppose an understanding of creation as an analogous fabrication) Levinas reads this differently. As he puts it, in Western philosophical thought there is a unity of subjectivity and substantiality. The creative call brings about one who is not yet a subject or a being, a substance, but rather a mere passivity not yet coincident with itself. Is this to say, that because one is a sheer passivity prior to any substantial self-awareness, before one may say, "here I am," the I must be the It of the He-it of creation? Does this mean that God's precedent, prevenient love is aimed at an "it" which is a passivity more passive than any material receptivity? Is this a "personal prime matter?" What is this pre-existent passivity which is the target of the divine loving call that results in the actual person?

We need not decide whether it is this theological consideration that determines Levinas's theory of the self or whether Levinas's chief concern is to found the metaphysics of his ethical self and this determines his theology. In either case what is decisive is his view that the "myself" is most fundamentally a dative; not a *dative of manifestation*, but a being responsive *to* and responsible *for* another, as if the latter *datives of responsibility* could dispense with the primacy or equiprimordiality of the former. Instead of its being most basically a self-awareness of a substantial being, and in this sense having self-reference, the doctrine of creation as a call shows that prior to and more basic than having self-reference, "the recurrence to oneself cannot stop at oneself, but goes to the hither side of oneself... to the hither side of its point of departure." We take this to mean that the basic motion of the self is not to itself in terms of a self-awareness but to what is Other and transcendent to Itself. This we are told is not alienating because it is "the point of departure" of itself in the creator God. In its being in the world with others, it is first of all being "for the Others." This ethical dative, this being-for Others in one's midst, is founded in the divine Other calling creatively. And this divine Other is mediately present in one's neighbors even though Itself is the transcendent divine point of departure of oneself as being-for. This means for Levinas, there persists "a gnawing away at itself" in remorse for its recurrent attempt to slide into being for itself when its foundational being is not a resting in itself but a non-alienating "substitution" of Others for oneself in the sense of not asserting one's own needs before those of Others. It is also a substitution of oneself for others in the sense of taking upon oneself their burdens as one's own.

We earlier (Book 1, Chapter II, §2) acknowledged the legitimacy and importance of Levinas's claim that there is an original *phenomenological* passivity that is foundational for the active life of the self and the proper sense of self-reference. But Levinas here appears to be talking about the ontological foundation that is prior to consciousness and any phenomenological passivity. But aside from the ontology of the self whereby self-awareness and "I myselfness" are made to derive from an original passivity and substituting of others for oneself, we must ask whether Levinas's view of the self being a creature more passive than matter and prior to the coinciding with itself has to do with the philosophical-theological notion of "creation." If this means nothing more than his ontology of the self, then the questions have to do with precisely that, and we have earlier touched on some of those matters. But clearly his thought does not confine itself to this theme. That is, it also has to do with the doctrine of creation *ex nihilo*, "if it is not pure nonsense," and therefore we have to do with the quite different metaphysical-theological issue, albeit one connected with the ontology of the self. In this regard we learn from Levinas that there is posited something existing, a unique passivity, which "obeyed before hearing the order" of the call that creates it. Levinas' exegesis of the biblical "here I am" is questionable. He takes this not to be an indexical self-reference presupposing a substantive non-reflective self-awareness, but rather "the word *I* means *here I am*, answering for everything and for everyone." And this "answering for everything" itself is called obeying before hearing the command to obey.[188] Aside from perhaps our being confounded as to what this obedience that is bereft of a hearing the command might mean, we still are left in the dark regarding the matter of what this passivity is that God acts upon, and more basically whether creation indeed is God's acting upon anything at all. Levinas seems to imply that creation is precisely just such an acting *on* when he refers to a unique passivity more passive than the passivity of matter (where we may presume perhaps to hear an echo of both the ambiguity in the Hebrew regarding the primordiality of the primal waters [whether they are there from the start] of *Genesis* 1:1–2 as well as Plato's receptacle and the scholastic's prime matter).

Regardless of Levinas's ontology of the self, we have discouraged the notion that creation involves God's acting on any prior passive pre-existing matter or principle, no matter how it may be construed. But such a position surely could not appear to be novel for Levinas. Although we must honor the circle of questions Levinas raises which generate his "solution," merely postulating a primal passivity does not shed light on the question of "Abrahamic theology" of how we might think of creation as a loving call, given that the one called does not yet exist.

Let us return to our earlier efforts in this matter. If the creation is understood to be inseparable from the analogy with a call and the call is understood to be inseparably "bestowing being on" or "creation of," e.g., JG Hart, then another appropriate analogy is an illocutionary act, like naming, wherein the speech act is both performative and creative, not merely descriptive. "I hereby name you 'James,'" and therewith it is effected that the person is so named. But in the case of creation/calling, the calling is not merely bestowing a name but a creation from nothing. JG Hart, the "myself" in what we have called *the third mode* is the result, the effect, of the creative calling. But because the creative calling requires both that this "myself" pre-exist and be called into being, the same "myself" of JG Hart is distinguished as the addressee or the exemplary "myself" who "hears" from out of the depths of God's own essence and who by virtue of this "hearing" (before I myself, as the created JG Hart, am) I am called into being.

"I am called before the foundation of the world" requires that "I myself" be and be addressed both before and after I, JG Hart, am. In this sense there was never a first moment of response but I, JG Hart, from the start of my being, am both the called and response, but that which is called, the unique essence "myself," pre-exists me, JG Hart.

Levinas and Chrétien both emphasize that the response is "immemorial" in the sense that the "myself" that says "Here I am" cannot for essential reasons remember the beginning of the call: To remember one's being called into existence one would have to have been before one was.

(Recall our discussion in Book 1, Chapter VII. Here we discussed Husserl's wrestle with the awareness of our coming-to-be. This transcendental-phenomenological reflection adumbrates the theological immemorial state of affairs: To presence our beginning we would have to presence the nothing before we got started along with the start or beginning that follows "nothing prior." But to presence the "nothing prior" or the non-being that preceded our commencement we would have to be before and while we began.)

The unique essence, "myself," enjoys a sameness in the difference of the three modes. The exemplary essence "myself" is the same but not identical with and therefore different from the "myself" of the created JG Hart. Obviously the exemplary essence "myself" has an immemorial character for Godself that is different from the way it is "immemorial" for JG Hart, the "myself" that is created. Godself's essence which embraces the unique essence that is personified and embodied in the creature, JG Hart, is eternally present, and "immemorial" merely means that this unique essence is present from all eternity and there is no time when this essence was not. In contrast, I, JG Hart, cannot remember the unique essence of the "myself" as it exists (and pre-existed) in Godself's essence for the obvious reason that it exists before I was created, assuming that I was created in time. Further, I cannot remember the calling of "myself," who I, JG Hart, refer to, because this calling, as authorizing and creating my being, preceded my being. As Levinas nicely puts it, the call reaches to the "hither side of oneself."

We have proposed in the earlier sections that a way of thinking of what "receives" the call prior to the existence of the one called to respond, what Levinas names the passivity or the It which has a "prior existence," is the divine exemplar of "I myself." This sense of "It" in which the "myself" is regarded in the third-person by God and the theologian does not demean the ipseity and avoids the difficulties which would inevitably be associated with regarding the It, as the individual essence, either as it is one with the divine essence or as it is identical with the "myself" of the subsisting creature, e.g., Abraham. The former is oneself from "time immemorial" and, as we have noted, it is this to which we are called "back." But of course one cannot ever return to this mode of "myself" because not only is it left behind in what cannot be remembered, and in this sense I can never be contemporary with it, but what I am called to is to shape myself in the light of this eternal exemplar; it is always also my future.

In the texts Chrétien shares with us from Paul Claudel we find another rich meditation on this same theme. There we learn that one cannot appropriate this exemplary version of "myself" in its origin. It remains with strict metaphysical necessity both "reserved" and "inspiring" the "part that is prior to myself," "the idea of myself that was before I was." As Chrétien puts it, it is "that which was 'us' before us in order for us to be other than us, even though it is the promise of our identity."[189] Each of us is the woman (conceived by W.B. Yeats in his poem "Before The World Was Made") striving to paint the face that was hers before the creation of the world. That is, I must be other than the sheer "myself" "before the world was made," even though this sheer "myself," as a divine exemplar of the created "myself," is the promise and surety of both my personal as well as my eternal ontological being.

Perhaps the reader may recall Thomas Merton's experience in the wake of the dream about the girl whose name was "Proverb." (See above Chapter V, §3.) He also offered a more conceptual explication of the experience, which itself explicated the dream. Our proposal that we think of the unique individual essence of "myself" in its threefold modes, i.e., as intrinsic to God's essence, as the divine exemplar, and as the created person who personifies and embodies this essence, helps us think about Merton's dense conceptual explication of the experience at the corner of Fourth and Walnut in Louisville, Kentucky.

> At the center of our being is a point of nothingness which is untouched by sin and by illusion, a point of pure truth, a point or spark which belongs entirely to God, which is never at our disposal, from which God disposes of our lives, which is inaccessible to the fantasies of our own mind or the brutalities of our own will. This little point of *nothingness* and of *absolute poverty* is the pure glory of God in us. It is so to speak His name written in us, as our poverty, as our indigence, as our dependence, as our sonship. It is like a pure diamond, blazing with the invisible light of heaven. It is in everybody, and if we could see it we would see these billions of points of light coming together in the face and blaze of a sun that would make all the darkness and cruelty of life vanish completely.[190]

The references to "us" and "our" refer here first of all to the unique essence in the third mode, i.e., ourselves as created persons. But at the center of our being there is a center deeper than what we have called the center of the "I" or Existenz. This is a center that faith intends. Of this center contemplatives and saints perhaps have an inkling through their faithful prayer and love. In such prayer and love this center is apperceived in the darkness of faith as "nothingness" and our "absolute poverty," but also our "sonship." This is the "theological self" or the theological dimension of ourselves. This is the same as oneself even in spite of the differences which keep it from being identical with oneself. This belongs to God and is totally at God's disposal because it is the "myself" both as God's own essence and as the eternal exemplar of ourselves. In spite of our brutalities, distorting fantasies, etc., we here are untouched by sin and illusion. But again, this too is (the same as) our essential unique self; indeed it is oneself eminently, the *hyper-moi* (Balthasar). But for one to be truly oneself, to be who we are eternally called to be, and to take the divine form intended for us, i.e., to be the sort of person we ought to be, we must let the diamond who we truly are shine forth. That is, we must, through faith, retrieve an absolute poverty and disburden ourselves of the baggage of our false, fantasized, tormented, brutal selves. This is the work of the Calling in much of "the Abrahamic traditions." For Merton, no small ingredient of this calling is acting on and retaining the faith that lets shine the "diamond in the rough" (G.M. Hopkins) of each of those with whom we come into contact. For Merton, this is not a new dope-like fantasy but the truth of Christ which requires of believers the cross. It surely does not deny the pervasive lie and brutality of *Realpolitik*. But what it precisely means for our agency is not always clear. Merton said at the conclusion of the cited text: "I have no program for this seeing. It is only given. But the gate of Heaven is everywhere."

Merton thus emphasizes that whatever the program, the "seeing" of this universality of the "diamonds in the rough" is a grace which we may strive and pray for; it's being in some measure present and "given" is the necessary condition for the appropriate social agency of the believer.

We may single out three fundamental aspects in the response to the calling of the creature to become who one is called to be as this calling may be delineated within the parameters of The Theological Distinction. The first is to be attuned to the "myself" as precisely the entelechy of my personal being in the world. It is always "what is unheard-of in my voice," that which I have listened to before I begin to speak and act. Although it transcends any voice or persona, it is what gives us a voice, a persona, and a calling, and this giving to us transforms us from the sheer "myself" to our self-creation in the light of that which has given us this voice and calling. This unique voice knows itself as a person and therefore of necessity inter-personal and intersubjective. Therefore the unique voice is always one that knows that it can sing its unique song only in singing with and to and in response to all the other apperceived voices – which is not to say that it is merely the transparent organ for all the other voices or as if it could be substituted for by the chorus of voices.

The original entelechial "myself" guides me as both the most ancient as well as newest guise of myself. That is, it is both the abiding form of the variety of shapes of my "personification" and it is the ideal true self of this "personification." To see the beauty of the ideal true self is to see what is not totally unfamiliar to us, and in this sense it is to see it again. Yet it is not known by moving away from oneself to another self that one is not, but it is known only by the wrestle with the unfolding personification and the hints of the calling as they are intimated in the present struggle and challenges. As we noted earlier one must find one's center, one's Existenz, in an actual self that is constituted in response to the ideals, e.g., as they are manifest in one's straining to be honest and loving in the present. This center is not in an ideal self which is already fully realized. The center is the actual deepest I as it struggles with its personification, which of necessity is predelineated in the ideal true self. Of course, as we have noted, its surfacing is occasional and may lie dormant for both legitimate and illegitimate reasons. The very sense of the true self or self-ideal is precisely evident in the struggle to realize what is the best in terms of honesty, courage, love, patience, etc., under the present circumstances; and this ideal, we have also claimed, may be taken to be the work of the entelechy of the "myself" which itself has its ontological home in the divine exemplar of one's unique essential "myself." To think of the ancient home of the "myself" in accord with the Bible and leading voices of the "Abrahamic traditions" is to think of the center of the "I" as having a depth that reaches into God's own essence and it is this "theological dimension" which constitutes the deepest stratum of the entelechy's work.

The second fundamental aspect in becoming who I am called to be as it may be understood in the light of The Theological Distinction is what we have called "ontological humility." The response to my being called, my "Here I am!" is most fundamentally the affirmation of myself in the form of "thanks." Each is given to herself; there is nothing one has not received; there is nothing we can give back that

God does not already have except the grateful acknowledgment of our being ben-eficiaries. This of course is more than the occasional, performative ritual of "*deo gratias*," but must be lived from out of our Existenz. And even the "thanks" itself is merely the proper expression of the gift of freedom at work under the pressure of grace and not anything of the order of meeting an obligation to God or meet-ing God's needs. Yet The Theological Distinction, wherein there is permitted the "communication of idioms" along with the ontological claim for God's absolute self-sufficiency, does not render null the language and concepts which describe God as redeemer, lover, etc.

This leads to the third aspect which builds on the other two. We have said that the calling to the beauty of the ideal true self is both familiar and unfamiliar; its call is both to what lies beyond where we most want to be as well as a recalling of ourselves to ourselves. We have said, in our discussions of "the truth of will" and the gathering experience of love, that there is an exemplary instance of this self-recall or self-recollection in love. (See Chapter V, §§2–6.) The tradition of The Theological Distinction has taught that God's love, which we may also call an "incomparable generosity," goes in advance of everything, and that behind all our loves there is the love of God – even when we do our utmost to hide this from ourselves.

This antecedent and underlying *love of God* which we hide from ourselves is both an objective and subjective genitive. God's own love as incomparable generos-ity toward us (subjective genitive) is what founds all there is and is inseparably the act of creation and call. At the same time it is the underlying gracious principle of what we may call the objective genitive: Our response is a love of/for God. The love directed toward God is the objective genitive that is undergirded by God's first hav-ing loved us (subjective genitive) and by God's graciously loving us into a response of love of God in return. With Kierkegaard we can celebrate God's cunning in being the greatest of all midwives in eliciting from us the response of love in his loving us into the Existenz each of us is. God is the unacknowledged telos, of all our inten-tionality and in this sense the love of God is the fulfillment of intentionality.

We have the propensity to hide from ourselves the love of God in the perspec-tives of both the subjective and objective genitive. The problem of hiding God's love for us (subjective genitive) is the problem proper to the believer as such. The believer is one who by definition has been blessed with the revelation that she, along with the whole world, has been chosen to be and to share in God's creativity and generosity; and yet the believer's great temptation is to unbelief, i.e., to live as if she were not chosen to be.

The occlusion of the objective genitive is not known as such apart from faith. However, we find an adumbration of the objective genitive and its occlusion in the theory that the basic dynamism of subjectivity is the general or willing will, in regard to which all of our explicit acts of will are inadequate. (See Chapter IV, especially §2.) Nevertheless there is the propensity to take what is within the hori-zon opened by the willing will as an adequate object of the willing will. There is the disposition to invest in what is a proper object of will, i.e., the object of the willed will, more promise and lure than it can ever possibly deliver. In the biblical language, there is a basic propensity toward idolatry, i.e., to substitute finite conditioned goods for the infinite unconditioned good. This may be summarily described by familiar observations, such as that we tend to be inveterate liars, frauds, and self-deceivers – and to hide this very tendency from ourselves. Thus the path that we lay out or have laid out before us is treacherous because false paths and selves incessantly assert themselves.

The habitus of ontological humility as it is informed by the pervasive attitude of gratitude may monitor such dispositions. Such monitoring may result in the resolve to rejoice only in one's being free of whatever attaches us to or promotes self-deception. The monitoring may effect the intention to be exalted only in who one is given to be and who one is called to be and what one has received in one's core. This monitoring also effects a resolve to delight in those whom it is one's charge to care for and those to whom it is given to love. These attitudes serve as the fundamental pillars that deter the false selves from gaining mastery and taking us down the wrong path. Yet these are means and subordinate to the calling to love God with one's whole heart, soul, and all one's strength.

The love of oneself before Others or the love of Others for oneself is shattered in uncovering the transcendent creaturely ipseity whose beauty beckons us beyond even all of her admirable qualities. (Cf. Book 1, Chapter IV.) But can we really love Others properly, i.e., for their own sakes, without recognizing that love for this unique transcendent beauty is sustained only by appreciating it as framed by and a refraction of an incommensurately more beautiful transcendence that traditionally has been called "God?" Such a view would seem to be that of the "Abrahamic tradition." But it also clearly finds resonance in the philosophical tradition that reflects on these themes in the wake of the work of Platonic and Neo-Platonic predecessors. In this tradition, even the present Other in her *dignitas*, whose depth and splendor cannot be exhausted, is for the greatest lovers ultimately but a "sacrament" of a transcendent beauty that might well go unnamed. This is revealed in the various tropes of love's story. For example, where the Don Juan or the female counterpart, aspires time and time again to the consummate relationship wherein the heart's desire will be finally sated. Or where, in spite of the depth of the love for the beloved in her unique essence, a sadness or melancholy appears when one knows that by any known measure one should be serenely happy; or when, in spite of a beautiful loving relationship that one appreciates as a miraculous gift, there nevertheless surfaces a fascination with other unique essences and the siren of the possibility of being simultaneously in love with another unique ipseity; or where there is the sense of inadequation of the heart's desire even though one continues to grow in love for the beloved, etc. Further such a "sacramentalism" is evident where one's worship of the absolutely unconditioned transcendent is felt only in the loving service to finite Others – as in the recognizing of God "in the least of these." Clearly such a theory of the penultimate splendor of the Other does not at all claim that the beloved is a mere instrument or means, i.e., that Other's transcendent dignity and radiance are bogus compared to the "More" which adumbrates the divine transcendent splendor. Rather it merely reiterates the ancient point that one does not exalt God by detracting from creatures, nor does one properly appreciate creatures by fearing that they will detract from God, nor can one properly appreciate the glory of God unless one does justice to the glory of creatures.

The contemplative tradition has rightfully pointed out that the highest form of response to one's calling is not merely love of the Other because the Other is good for and to me. Rather the higher form is loving her for her own sake. As noble and exalted as the love which loves God for God's goodness to me, over and above this there is a higher form of loving which is loving God for God's own sake and not merely because God is good for and to oneself. Futher in all this love there is the I-center awakened within the person as Existenz and as the source of the loving acts and as what is called by and delighted with the transcendent beauty and goodness of God. There is inseparably the ineluctable transcendental self-love that is enacted in one's loving God intrinsically and not as a means to one's own stunted version of oneself. (Cf. our discussion in Chapter V, §8.)

And yet may we, following St. Bernard of Clairvaux, say that loving God for God's own sake may be seen as not yet the highest and most exalted response to one's calling? May we say that there is still, at least for the "pilgrims *in via*," the higher degree of love, a love that is higher than loving God for God's own sake? This for Bernard is the love of oneself for the sake of God, where one "no longer loves himself except for God."[191] Here all traces of idolatry, fraudulence, self-deception, and self-love have vanished because two things have happened at once. One now actualizes the original ontological humility and gratitude, i.e., one lives from out of the conviction that of oneself apart from God one is nothing. But also one acknowledges that all that one is, who one is in one's core, is due to what is on the "hither side" of oneself. Now one sees that in loving properly oneself one can only love the divine essence, *ipse ipsissimus*, wherein one exemplarily is at home and whence one comes. Loving oneself for any other reason than Godself is not to love oneself but to love an illusion. Given what we have said, this is infinitely remote from the self-alienation and self-hate that certain critics of religion, often with justice, find in some religious practices and beliefs.

Of course loving oneself for the sake of God does not cancel the exalted nature of loving God for Godself; but it acknowledges that the agent loving is self-exalted in this loving and exults in this love of God for Godself. Thus there is always the trace of the awareness *of* oneself in oneself being self-aware. In Bernard's proposal, the highest degree of love, the most exalted response to one's calling, i.e., loving oneself for the sake of God, is what finally sets this aright. The drag or fault that is at the heart of all creaturely evils, the inordinate love of self, is here definitively surmounted because one no longer loves oneself except for God's sake. One loves oneself on account of God and on account of one's love for God and this is the necessary condition for truly loving oneself, i.e., one's true self – what one always wanted to do but could not. God here is no vampire, no bloodsucker of the true reality of oneself. Rather one finally loves oneself truly, one's true self, as it is hidden in the mystery of God and wherein alone its true identity is revealed.

Yet St. Bernard's highest degree would appear to be only the highest *in via*, i.e., the highest we earthly creatures are capable of. The love of God for God's own sake can take on a new perfection if the love of oneself for God's sake is actualized and brought to completion. Here is what the mystics seem to have in mind with the maxi-mization of "myself aware" with a minimalization or elimination of any awareness *of* myself. It is the love of God for God's own sake even if it meant one's own annihila-tion or that oneself never existed. It is in this exalted love that the mystic refrain of Bernard, "to lose yourself, as if you no longer existed, to cease completely to experi-ence yourself, to reduce yourself to nothing" has its legitimacy. But its condition is not one's annihilation but what St. Bernard calls a "deifying experience."[192] It is still myself experiencing love, i.e., celebrating and rejoicing in the unfathomable beauty of God. It is not merely rejoicing and thanking God for God's unfathomable generos-ity in permitting me myself and all of creation to be an Other to God. Rather, perhaps we may say proleptically, i.e., when we have finally done with the profoundly distort-ing self-love that marks the human persons (as "the children of Eve and Adam"), one is freed of even this self-reference, and love is directed to God for Godself's own sake in such a way that loving oneself for God's sake is of necessity penultimate.

Here we seem to reach the limit case of love toward which all ideals of love, e.g., that of the parent, the lover, the saint, are limits simpliciter. The traditions of spir-ituality and the contemplation have suggested that "in this life" this ultimate degree of love is not to be expected. Because the ideal dimly points in this direction of the absolute love of the transcendent other for her own sake which is even beyond loving onself for her own sake because in the limit case or concept there is no trace whatsoever of self-reference we have a opened up the possibility for the massive skepticism and cynicism that recurs in regard toward love, love literature, romantic love, being in love, etc. All the love of which we are familiar has a glimmer of the limit concept to the limit simpliciter, and the verdict is that it is not possible in spite of the lovers' endless protestations.

For this writer these claims of the tradition of spirituality occasion a deep resonance but they are in no way for him a matter of experienced filled intentions. Yet, according to the contemplative tradition, these claims need not remain empty intentions, but through the practice of prayer and love there might be kinds of filled intentions which serve as the foundation of these claims. Mystics speak of such filled intentions as gracious foretastes of the presence of God. Further, the doctrines of "heaven," the "beatific vision," the *lumen gloriae*, and the communion of saints declare that such a consummate form of Existenz in perfect love is the ultimate truth of personal life.

§13. Conclusion

Chapter VI began with Neo-Platonic "exemplarism" and the question of the foun-dations of a "divine vocation." We traced this theme through a variety of repre-sentative thinkers who, with a few exceptions, we singled out from the Christian tradition. The speculations of all these thinkers, inspired by both Neo-Platonism and the Scriptures themselves, led us in this Chapter VII to the hypothesis that the divine vocation had its origins in the divine self-awareness which exemplarily contains all forms and even the unique individual essences of persons. The problem then became how we understand God's awareness of Godself to be an awareness of what persons refer to with "I." Three important underlying, if not equally addressed, questions were: (1) How there could be a divine awareness of a unique ipseity, given the consideration that a person's first-person experience, by definition, is what cannot be had by any other besides herself? (2) How could exemplarism's seeming speculative power be rescued from placing a What as the principle of Who one is? and (3), How could this same speculative concept of exemplarity in God be rescued from what seems to be the potentially morally scandalous view of predestination?

Our "answer" to all questions has been basically the same, i.e., the dogma of God the Creator points to a The Theological Distinction between God and the world; but obviously this positing of a dogma which defines itself as a mystery of faith is not a philosophical or a rational clarification or explanation. (Indeed, in many quarters within the "Abrahamic religions," and even within Christianity itself, the claim that The Distinction is *the basic dogma* will likely be questioned.)

The God of The Theological Distinction is precisely specified in terms of being the creator who cannot be limited by creation even though creation is "absolutely real." God is "defined" by being able precisely to create free and autonomous beings without the divine "omnipotence" being diminished. God is "defined" by creating time and indwelling time without thereby "Godself" becoming temporal and ephemeral. God is "defined" by knowing ipseities more intimately than they know themselves without thereby either excluding from Godself's omniscience and eternity the indexicality of creaturely personal experience, foremost first-person awareness, or having God be absorbed in indexicality or first-person awareness. Finally, God is "defined" by lovingly calling all of creation to participate in God's divine life by foreknowing it "from all eternity" in God's non-reflexive self-awareness as well as the reflexive self-awareness in Godself's self-presencing through *rationes,* and this pre-knowing and predestining in no way interferes with the reality of freedom, time, and grace.

The Theological Distinction between God and the world is precisely an articulation of that to which faith is invited to move, i.e., it is beckoned to move beyond the parameters of reason and the world and entertain God as a term of a distinction. The world is defined precisely as what everydayness, common sense, science, and philosophy can categorially display. God as that beyond the world to which the faith-full mind is beckoned is precisely what cannot be handled by the categorial display of the world, whether by science or philosophy, even the philosophy that is concerned about display itself and about the display of the agent of manifestation doing the displaying. Religious faith invites the consideration that there is a kind of contingency to the necessity and rationality revealed by the world and reason, indeed, a contingency in the self-manifestation of the agent of manifestation and a contingency in what it reveals.

Here the suggestion is not being made that we are free to suspend the necessity and rationality of the world, but rather it is offered to us in our freedom of thought to consider the possibility that the world along with its necessity and rationality are created by the other term of The Theological Distinction, "God." The new whole, of God *and* the world, as we earlier indicated, is a unique whole. Yet for all the imbalance and peculiarities of this whole, it is a genuine whole. This is the basic belief and move of The Theological Distinction. And with this move there must be acknowledged that all the tensions of immanence and transcendence, freedom and divine determinism, first-person-awareness and divine omniscience, eternal omniscience and indexicality, etc., are already contained in the notion of God "the Maker of Heaven and Earth." They are contained in this notion which itself is a belief in their reconciliation, even though faith does not know or understand in filled intentions precisely what the "reconciliation" might mean because understanding in filled intentions is proper to the display of what we are generally calling the world.

Thus belief in "God the Creator" is already, in the "Abrahamic" and perhaps some other traditions, a commitment to The Theological Distinction. This whole sets the parameters of all classical and modern theological conundrums and provides a kind of "elucidation," "logical space" (Sokolowski), or focus for faith without providing any proper rational explanation or illumination.

The "incomparable generosity" of which Prufer and Sokolowski speak in elucidating creation nicely summarizes The Theological Distinction. For Aquinas, the universal mentor in this matter, creation is not for the purpose of communicating goodness, as if to fill in a lack in being. Rather, the ultimate end is the divine goodness Itself "out of love of which God wills to communicate that goodness [to others by creating]; for God does not act for the sake of His goodness as desiring to gain what He does not have, but as willing to communicate what He has, because He acts not out of desire for the end [not possessed] but out of love of the end [already enjoyed]."[193]

Here we can hear an echo of the Neo-Platonic *bonum est diffisum sui*, yet rooted in divine freedom and bereft of any sense of need or necessity or the unfortunate lapse or *tolma*. Creation is rooted in the divine love sheerly loving and enjoying (loving) Godself's loving in such a way (or to the extent) that God wills to share Godself's being. Thus the creation, e.g., of the unique essence each person is, is first and foremost an act of God's loving this unique essence which is Godself. And this love is so ardent that God wills that it be shared, i.e., be communicated to and actual in an Other, e.g., the "myself" that I, JG Hart, refers to. The first mode of presencing of the unique essence of the "myself" of JG Hart, identical with God's essence and Godself's non-reflective self-awareness, is the principle of the presencing of the second mode, the unique essence as exemplar, and a fortiori of the third mode of presencing the unique essence of the creature, JG Hart. Only God's love of Godself in the aspect of the eternal unique essence of the creature, JG Hart, accounts for the gift of creation, i.e., JG Hart's essence in the third mode.

Creation is incomparably generous because it involves a giving which is absolutely "selfless" in the sense that the "self" in question is absolutely self-sufficient and cannot give for an "ulterior motive." Only a "being" with absolute self-sufficiency can give with this kind of generosity, i.e., one who neither gains nor can gain anything for Itself and is in no way enhanced by the giving; only such a One gives with absolute freedom and liberality and with no hint of necessity. In such a giving not only is there not any deserving quality, property, or merit on the side of the beneficiary which places a kind of moral necessity on the giver, but antecedently to the giver's giving there is nothing there whatsoever to receive the gift. Here we have a giver who is undiminished by the giving, who would remain perfectly intact without ever giving the gift, who gives Godself in giving the gift of creation – without losing or contradicting Godself – and yet who presupposes no antecedent recipient of the gift but who creates the recipient in the giving of the gift, and who elevates the created recipient to share in the very life of the giver, indeed, who enables the recipient to become the giver of gifts to the divine giver and others. Such "incomparable generosity" may well be utterly removed from anything we know, but it is not impossible by reason of its being inherently absurd or self-contradictory.

Surely this incomparable generosity counts as even a "limit-concept" of generosity for which the forms we are familiar with and strive for are within the ideal order of "limits simpliciter." It does not count as the limit concept of what we know of as love where another unique essence is presupposed and where reciprocity is of the essence of the relationship. Perhaps we find in the doctrine of the Trinity the love relations which serve as the limit concept of love for which all the forms of love to which we aspire are within the ideal of a limit simpliciter.

The actuality of such incomparable generosity, of course, is not a matter of philosophical evidence or reason but it is intrinsic to the notion of God as the major term of The Theological Distinction. Yet it provides a possible context to our earlier discussion, which aspired to be philosophical, of the true self of the person and perhaps a fuller sense of what we have named the calling of Existenz and the mystery of ipseity. For example: We do not give ourselves to ourselves, and our being is being given to ourselves to fashion freely for ourselves. In this sense, what is given, i.e., ourselves to ourselves, is nothing prior to the fact of the gift-giving or being-given. That is, as pure beginnings, ipseities bereft of properties, characteristics, etc., for which each is responsible, there is nothing pre-given. And if the only consideration is that there is nothing prior to this being-given, then any notion of a divine architect or theory of exemplarity is out of place because such a theory presupposes that of necessity there is something pre-given, namely the exemplary eidos of what comes to be. But the position that there is nothing pre-given to the gift of being-given to ourselves may not overlook that this being given to ourselves is the pre-givenness of one's unique essence. That we from the start are who we are is also given to ourselves and the shape we give ourselves presupposes ourselves as who is shaped. We have insisted throughout that in our being given to ourselves we are given to ourselves to constitute our personhood, character, and personality. However, the unique ipseity or individual essence to whom it is given to constitute personhood is a "given" that we in no way can account for by our own agency and certainly not by any agency that we come upon in the world or nature. And yet, in Book 2, Chapters IV and V, we attempted to show that who and what we are called to be is not tautologically who we ourselves are. This is because, we have proposed, what and who we are called to be is what and who we, in some sense, already are, in so far as the "calling" is always the calling addressed to us, to the center of the I of each, to Existenz. In this sense the unique essence of who we are is more basic than the nothingness of our freedom and the nothingness with which we commence to be. It would also seem to be, *pace* Levinas, more basic than any passivity prior to self-awareness of who one is.

Thus, we have found reason to posit that this unique essence indicates a normative way in which it is to be shaped in the world with Others; and although this shaping is our doing, the norms themselves, which are not merely the immanent ones of our ideal selves, conscience, and obligations, but also those of the essences and natures in the world along with their ends, are what we must listen to and heed precisely as what are not a result of our caprice. Further, in the midst of our personification and struggle to uncover our way, the essential ineluctable self-inadequation of ourselves with our selves, our "willing will" with our "willed will," forces us to think of ourselves either as endowed with futile passion or on a trajectory that is "not of this world."

Further, our most basic capacity of our "I-can" itself is not something we have given to ourselves, even though it is the capacity which makes all other powers possible. As Henry says, we "suffer and live it" but the freedom it provides is not a result of our freedom.[194]

And furthermore, our freedom reaches into a beginning which we do not begin and which can cause us vertigo when we contemplate the unbegun beginnings of ourselves, the "hitherside of ourselves," and "our point of departure." No less vertiginous are both the positive ways in which we surprise ourselves as well as the ways in which we fail to show up for ourselves.

Finally, our ongoing presencing of the present is something that happens graciously and inexorably; and yet we cannot guarantee that it will be given to us in the next moment. Further this ongoing presencing is a retaining, protending, and synthesizing which makes up our wakefulness. At the same time it is an ineluctable constitution of being; even in our willful self-deception and chaos, there is presupposed the ineluctable pervasive teleology and constitution of being and world. Over this we have no control but are "condemned to meaning" or, rather, it is gratefully beyond our doing and is given to us with our being given to our selves.[195]

But this richly textured way in which we are incessantly "being given to ourselves," this undergoing the "gift" of our unique essence and possibility, does not warrant a direct explication in terms of a theory of divine exemplarity at the heart of the calling. Such an articulation is the work of the dogma of God the Creator as explicated by The Theological Distinction. The phenomenon of "being given to ourselves" and "being called to shape ourselves in accord with our true selves" no more reveals this mystery than the famous proofs of the existence of God lead to the God of The Theological Distinction. Whereas these philosophical reflections on and questions about ipseity's origination or the absence of self-transparency in terms of ipseity's origins point to each being a mystery and an abyss to herself, they remain puzzles or perhaps mysteries that philosophy by itself may not relate to the dogma of The Theological Distinction.

Similarly, our discussions of the teleology of personal life and the metaphor of "vocation" or "call" remain remote from the deep stratum of meaning provided by The Theological Distinction's understanding that each is called "before the foundation of the world," and that this call amounts to the revelation that one has been gratuitously chosen to be, and that one is exhaustively manifest to God in one's being, and that one is called to choose to manifest oneself "to the creator and to one another both as chosen and choosing and as manifest and manifesting."[196]

Notes

1. *New Seeds of Contemplation, op. cit.*, 31–34.
2. Fichtes *Werke, Die Anweisung zum seligen Leben oder die Religionslehre* Vol. V. Ed. I.H. Fichte (Berlin: Walter de Gruyter, 1971), 531. With only a small modification I have followed the excellent translation by William Smith of 1889.
3. See for all this Husserl's *Nachlass Manuscript*, B I 21 I, 13–28 of the transcription.
4. Maurice Blondel, *L'Être et les êtres* (Paris: Presses Universitaire de France, 1963), 225–226.
5. Husserl, *Nachlass Manuscript*, B I 21 I, 21 of the transcription.
6. Sokolowski, *Christian Faith and Human Understanding* (Washington, DC: Catholic University Press, 2006), 62.
7. For a very good discussion of the philosophical issues surrounding the meaning of dogma, especially as they surface in "modernist" thought and the reaction to it, see Guy Mansini, O.S.B. *"What Is Dogma?" The Meaning and Truth of Dogma in Edouard Le Roy and His Scholastic Opponents* (Rome: Gregorian Pontifical University, 1985); for this immediate formulation I am indebted to his remarks on Bernard Lonergan in his conclusion, 372. See Bernard Lonergan, *Method in Theology* (New York: Seabury Press, 1973), 106–107, 115, 122–124.
8. For a rich discussion of analogy and theological understanding, see Sokolowski, *Christian Faith and Human Understanding*, especially Chapter 4.
9. John Duns Scotus, *Philosophical Writings*. Ed. Allen Wolter (Indianapolis, IN: Bobbs Merrill, 1962), 76.
10. Barry Miller, *A Most Unlikely God* (Notre Dame, IN: University of Notre Dame Press, 1996), 6 ff. *et passim*.
11. *Ibid.*, 9.
12. *Ibid.*, 10.
13. This is a text attributed to John Ruusbroec, cited in K. Khosla, *The Sufism of Rumi* (Dorset, England: Longmead Shaftesbury, 1987), 248. For themes in Sufism that run parallel to this chapter, see 38–39, 53 ff., 64, 101, 222 ff.
14. See Michael Loux, *Metaphysics: A Contemporary Introduction* (London: Routledge, 2002), Chapter 1.
15. Husserl, *Philosophie der Arithmetik, Husserliana* XII (The Hague: Nijhoff, 1970), especially 181 ff.
16. Duns Scotus, *Philosophical Writings*, 76.
17. These are questions Max Scheler aimed at classical theism; cf. our discussion in §11 below.
18. See Thomas Prufer, *Recapitulations*, especially Chapter 7, and Robert Sokolowski, *Eucharistic Presence*, Chapter 5.
19. Cf. John of St. Thomas, *Cursus Theologici*. Vol. II (Paris: Desclée, 1934), Part I, Q. XV, par. 13., 538.
20. This phenomenological point is found in discussions in Catholic catechetical texts; see *Catechism of the Catholic Church* (Liguori, MO: Liguouri Press, 1994), 366. The "Dutch Catechism," *A New Catechism* (New York: Seabury Press, 1969), 382 and 518–519 has in this

regard important passages. It strives to do justice to creation of the person as the unity of the creation of the soul, body, and all of natural being. Creation is what causes reality to be and to grow at each moment. In the beginning of a new human life there is a sacred moment in which creative power is especially evident. "After all, my parents could not have wanted 'me.' At best, they wanted 'a boy' or 'a girl.' Only God wanted 'me.'" The text goes on at 382 to say, "An 'I' which could say 'You' to God, have a direct personal relationship with him, is called into being through human heredity, and hence by the hand of God. These two things form together one action." This text as it stands leans in the direction of Conrad-Martius' position (which I discuss in an essay, "Archaeology of Spirit and the Unique Self," from which this note is taken) in so far as it makes the individuality of each to be sufficiently determined through the contingencies of human heredity, even though, of course, this is itself "by the hand of God." In the Roman Curial Supplement we find what appears to be corrections with which the basic theses of this paper are in agreement. Here the excellent philosophical point of The Dutch Catechism that only God could have wanted 'me' is not permitted to be subsumed by the contingencies of heredity. It states "the existence of each human person follows from the transmission by the parents of a body which is ready for the soul and demands the existence of a soul. For the rest, the existence of the soul goes back only to God. The complete and direct transmission of the body by the parents extends indirectly in a certain sense to the soul itself, insofar namely as the body is for the soul and calls for it" (519). Although the Supplement concedes that the parents are "the parents of the whole person," it insists that the mode of cooperation with God differs as regards body and soul. The claim that "the parents transmit human nature to their children" must be balanced with the claim that "the existence of the soul goes back only to God."

21. In my view the various theories of emergence, even with the extraordinary advancement in the knowledge of genes, genetic pool, and random variation, have not advanced our understanding in terms of the ancient philosophical questions of morphogenesis or how lower-order forms or non-forms can sufficiently account for the emergence of higher-order ones.

22. Robert Sokolowski, "Natural and Artificial Intelligence" *Daedalus* 117 (1988), 45–64.

23. See Hedwig Conrad-Martius, *Der Selbstaufbau der Natur: Entelechien und Energien* (Munich: Kösel Verlag, 1961), 81.

24. Barry Miller, *op. cit.*, 164.

25. Cf. Miller, *op. cit.*, 164–165.

26. I have been helped here by Gustav Siewerth, *Das Sein Als Gleichnis Gottes* (Heidelberg: Kerle, 1958), 43–46. He cites St. Thomas that *ipsum esse est similitudo bonitatis divinae* (*De Veritate* XXII, 2, ad 2).

27. St. Thomas Aquinas, *Summa Theologiae* I. q. 8., a.1.c; *De Potentia* q. 7, art. 2, ad 7.

28. See Avery Dulles, "The Church According to Thomas Aquinas," in his *A Church to Believe* (New York: Crossroad, 1982), 151.

29. St. Thomas, *De Veritate* Q. III, art. II.

30. St. Thomas, *Summa Contra Gentes* (Turin/Rome: Marietti, 1934), I, Chapter 35.

31. St. Thomas, *In Librum beati Dionysi De divinis nominibus*. Ed. Ceslai Pera, O.P. (Turin/Rome: Marietti, 1950), 667, 250.

32. St. Thomas, *Summa Theologiae* I, q. 4, art. 3, ad 3.

33. Cf. Thomas Prufer, *Sein und Wort Nach Thomas von Aquin* (Dissertation, University of Munich, 1959), 37–38. See Sokolowski, *The God of Faith and Reason*, 41–48. See Aquinas, *In I Sent.*, dist. 24, q. 2, a.1, ad 4; cited in R. Arnou, *Theologia naturalis* (Rome: Gregorian University, 1960), 169.

34. "Created good added to the uncreated good does not make for something greater, because if two participant goods are joined there is able to be increased in them the goodness in which they participate; but if the participant [good] is added to that which is such by its essence it does not make for anything greater… Since therefore God is through his essence goodness, and all other goods are good through participation in the goodness of God, God does not become more good by any addition of good because the goodness of whatever other thing is contained in Him." St. Thomas, cited in R. Arnou, *Theologia naturalis*, 168; Arnou gives the

reference of *De Malo* q. 5, art. 4, ad 1 as does Thomas Prufer in *Sein und Wort*, 38. The basic idea may be found also in *Summa Theologiae* I–II, q. 34, art. 3, ad 2.

35. John Findlay, *The Transcendence of the Cave*, 146.
36. N.-J.-J. Balthasar, *Mon Moi dans l'Être*, 116.
37. See Barry Miller, *A Most Unlikely God.* From Book 1, it is clear that we do not share all of Miller's concern with Plantinga's position on haecceities. For Miller, the "haecceities have been saddled with a condition which it is impossible to satisfy, for they are required to be exemplifiable in no individual but the one, if any, in which they do happen to be exemplified. The claim is that, even before Socrates existed, there was an abstract entity (Socrateity) which could not be exemplified in any individual but Socrates. On the contrary, however, it would be an enormous fluke for Socrateity to be exemplified in any *human* individual at all, let alone in Socrates. As I have argued, it could equally have been exemplified in a grain of sand, or a rhinoceros, or even a poached egg." Miller, 32. Miller wants haecceities to be saddled with formal propertied existence conditions. In this sense Socrateity could very well for Miller be cloned, and there appears to be an equivalence between haecceities and definite descriptions. In our view, by way of contrast, the individual essence is, as such, bereft of any properties and is absolutely unique. That is why the possibilities of reincarnation and metamorphosis are not absolutely to be ruled out. But I admit to being uncomfortable with prospect of the reincarnation as a grain of sand or a poached egg. The arguments against these possibilities would require showing in what sense first-person experience of one's ipseity is importantly but contingently human or animal. If the "tautological properties" (see Book 1, Chapter IV; further, see Book 1, Chapter VI for a wrestle with some of the problems of reincarnation) of the unique essence, like spirit, intellect, will, and consciousness, have themselves tautological or essential properties, we may ask whether first-person self-awareness is incompatible with some forms of non-humanness, e.g., what appears as the existence of a grain of sand or poached egg. Surely the quasi-ubiquity of the lived body in first-person experience would be undermined in one's ipseity being saddled with the existence condition associated with being the grain of sand or poached egg in the way it would not be in being saddled with the existence condition of being the rhinoceros. But similarly the quasi-ubiquity of language in first-person experience would suggest that one would be seriously handicapped if not undermined in being the rhinoceros. But none of this means that therefore being who one is, is equivalent to being an individual human being.
38. St. Thomas Aquinas, *De Veritate* 20, 4, ad 1; cited in Prufer, *Sein und Wort*, 20.
39. See Miller, *ibid.*, 126–127. According to Miller, the view we are holding is a species of what he calls "Molinism." For more on our difference with Miller on this matter, see the endnote prior to the previous one.
40. See Miller, *idem.*
41. In *Librum beati Dionysi De divinis nominibus*, 158, 51.
42. See Gustav Siewerth, *Der Thomismus als Identitätssystem*, 68.
43. Cf. J.-P. Sartre, *Being and Nothingness*, lviii.
44. *Ibid.*, 290.
45. William James, *A Pluralistic Universe* (Cambridge, MA: Harvard University Press, 1977), see especially "The Compounding of Consciousness."
46. Actually, this itself is a problem. As Husserl and Gendlin have taught, a felt a meaning to say, a unique empty intention that characterizes speaking, goes first in the order of genesis. Of course, its "sense" is inseparable from and informed by the learned actual language and the conditions for the "deep grammar."
47. Husserl, *Husserliana* XIII, 8 ff.
48. In Husserl's *Ideas I*, §43, he discusses this "basic error" of Kant.
49. See the MS Nachlass, B II 2 (1907–1908), 26b–27b.
50. I owe this term "omni-profile" to Steven Laycock. Later he used the term "field of fields" in *Foundations for a Phenomenological Theology* (Lewiston, NY: Edwin Mellen Press, 1988), see 212 ff.
51. G. Frege, "Der Gedanke," in *Logische Untersuchungen*. Ed. Patzig, 41.

52. See Hopkins, *op. cit.*, 400–401. Cf. also Charles Hartshorne, *Man's Vision of God* (Hamden, CT: Archon reprint, 1964 of 1941 original), Chapter V.

53. Hopkins, 401.

54. Hopkins, 403.

55. See the discussion in H.N. Castañeda, *Thinking, Language, and Experience*, 142–143.

56. See Adams' discussion in Castañeda, *Thinking, Language, Experience*, 155.

57. Hopkins, 403.

58. The authority for my claim that this is a reference to a Scotist position is Christopher Devlin, S.J., *The Sermons and Devotional Writings of Gerard Manley Hopkins*, 286. See also his Appendix II, "Scotus and Hopkins," 338 ff. For this "popular definition" of infinity, see Duns Scotus, *Philosophical Writings*, 76.

59. See St. Augustine, *Confessions*, Book III, Chapter 6, Section 11: "*Tu autem eras interior intimo meo et superior summo meo*" which is often cited and paraphrased by Aquinas.

60. In support of substituting for "the Christian Distinction" the phrase "The Theological Distinction," cf. David Burrell's proposal that we consider the distinction as common to the Abrahamic traditions. See his "The Christian Distinction Celebrated and Expanded," in *The Truthful and the Good: Essays in Honor of Robert Sokolowski*. Eds. John J. Drummond and James G. Hart (Dordrecht: Kluwer, 1996), 191–206. I have suggested that The Distinction is not utterly foreign to neo-platonic and Sufi thought and will propose later that it is not completely alien to some aspects of Vedanta thought. The basic texts for The Christian Distinction or The Theological Distinction are found in Robert Sokolowski, *The God of Faith and Reason* (Washington, DC: Catholic University of America Press, 1983 and 1995) and Thomas Prufer, *Recapitulations*. See also Sokolowski's *Eucharistic Presence* (Washington, DC: The Catholic University of America Press, 1993), Chapter 5, and *Christian Faith & Human Understanding* (Washington, DC, The Catholic University of America Press, 2006), Part I. Some parts of this concluding Chapter VII of our work appeared in an earlier form in the second Sokolowski, *Festschrift, Ethics and Theological Disclosures*. Eds. Guy Mansini, O.S.B., and James G. Hart (Washington, DC: Catholic University of America Press, 2003). In that volume other contributors also discuss The Distinction.

61. Erich Frank, in his *Philosophical Understanding and Religious Faith* (London: Oxford University, 1949), 59, finds this to be the sense of Augustine's *Confessions* at XI, 3, 5; and at XI, 5, 7, 9, and 11. Cf. St. Thomas, *Summa Theologiae* I, q. 46, a. 3.

62. See *Kritik der reinen Vernunft*, B641. I have been helped by Karl Jaspers' commentary on this passage in *Der philosophische Glaube angesichts der Offenbarung*, 406–407.

63. Sokolowski, *The God of Faith and Reason*, 113.

64. See Robert Sokolowski, *Eucharistic Presence*, Chapter 5; and Thomas Prufer, *Recapitulations*, Chapter 7.

65. For an impressive wrestle with these matters, see Hedwig Conrad-Martius, "Die fundamentale Bedeutung eines substantiallen Seinsbegriffs für eine theistische Metaphysik," in her *Schriften zur Philosophie* (Munich: Kösel, 1963), 257–267.

66. Sokolowski, *Christian Faith and Human Understanding*, 4, 18–19, 23, 35, 38–39, 50.

67. Cf. Sokolowski, ibid., 44.

68. I am indebted here to Sokolowski's *The God of Faith and Reason*. For these last paragraphs I am indebted also to Eric Frank, *Philosophical Understanding and Religious Truth* (Oxford: Oxford University Press, 1949), 32 ff. For a lovely support of the thesis of Sokolowski and Frank that for the pre-Socratic philosophers and much of antiquity gods were an inherent part of nature and the world, see the discussions of Alain Besançon, *The Forbidden Image: An Intellectual History of Iconoclasm*. Trans. Jane Marie Todd (Chicago, IL/London: University of Chicago Press, 2000), especially 16–25; especially for the pre-Socratics, the divine is situated in this world. "Gods were engendered by the primordial generating force that is part of the world's structure: Eros." The ancient poets allegorized cosmic forces, envisaging them as gods so that there were equivalences of gods and natural forces. I am indebted to Bob Sokolowski for calling my attention to this work.

69. Spaemann, *Personen*, 109–110. Spaemann here is perhaps echoing Arendt who claimed that Jesus' teaching on forgiveness entitled him to a distinguished place in the history of political philosophy.
70. See Husserl's powerful homily, "The Vienna Lecture," in The Crisis of European Sciences and Transcendental Phenomenology (*Husserliana* VI, 314 ff.).
71. See Sokolowski, *Eucharistic Presence*, 42 ff.; and Prufer, *Recapitulations*, Chapter 7. One may recall that Dante sought to save the appearances of "chance" in the world and not have it obliterated by a belief in God's omnipotence. To this end he envisaged God creating an angel whose special mission was to be responsible for chance.
72. "One has often said that the world is inexplicable without God, but also the contrary is true: If there is a God the existence of the world is inexplicable because it is perfectly superfluous. From a God nothing else follows; everything else outside of him is superfluous. How is it possible that I want to deduce him from the world, to found it on him? But the inverse conclusion is also valid… If there is a world, if this world is a truth, God is only a dream, a being imagined by a man who only exists in man's imagination." Ludwig Feuerbach, *Das Wesen der Religion*, Lecture 16 (Leipzig: Kroner), 1965; cited in Joseph de Finance, *Existence et Liberté* (Paris: Vitte, 1955), 158. De Finance's book is a rich Neo-Thomist version of the position of ontological interiority that I am proposing here.
73. See Sokolowski, *Eucharistic Presence*, Chapter 5; Prufer, *Recapitulations*, Chapter 7.
74. Thomas V. Morris, *Our Idea of God* (Notre Dame, IN: University of Notre Dame Press, 1991), 142–143.
75. See Sokolowski, *The God of Faith and Reason*, 33, 41, and 112–113.
76. St. Thomas Aquinas, *Summa Contra Gentes* III, 65.
77. St. Thomas Aquinas, *De Malo*, 5, 4, ad 1; and *De Potentia*, 7, 10; cited in Prufer, *Sein und Wort*, 21.
78. Duns Scotus, *Philosophical Writings*, 76.
79. Prufer, *Recapitulations*, 40.
80. Cf. my "The *Summum Bonum* and Value Wholes: Aspects of a Husserlian Axiology and Theology," in *Phenomenology of Values and Valuing*. Eds. James G. Hart and Lester Embree (Dordrecht: Kluwer, 1997), 193 ff.
81. See Kierkegaard, *Papers and Journals: A Selection*, 234–235.
82. Kierkegaard, *Concluding Unscientific Postscript*, 461.
83. This is a theme in much of *Sickness Unto Death*, especially 82.
84. *Papers and Journals*, 460.
85. *Papers and Journals*, 460.
86. Kierkegaard, *Journals and Papers*. Vol. 4, 4896 and 4895. My thanks to Tony Aumann for making me aware of this text in his Indiana University doctoral dissertation (2008), *Kierkegaard on the Need for Indirect Communication*.
87. Cited in Kierkegaard, *Concluding Unscientific Postscript*, II, 99.
88. *Ibid.*, 100.
89. See especially Juan Alfaro, "Supernaturalitas fidei iuxta S. Thomam," *Gregorianum*. Vol. 44 (1963), 2–4, 501–542, 732–787; here see 751–752.
90. Husserl, *Nachlass MSS*, E III 9, 30.
91. Gabriel Marcel, *Creative Fidelity*, 121–122.
92. Marcel, *Being and Having*, 210–211.
93. See the discussion of Roger Aubert, Le Probléme de l'act de foi (Louvain: E. Warny, 1958), 611–612, where he discusses especially the work of L. Malevez. Karl Barth's position implicitly appreciates Aquinas' theory that faith is opened by the revelation of the First Truth when he writes of this revelation as "authority, that is to say a truth which owes its trueness to no veracity, not even the most profound and truthful; a truth, on the contrary, on which all conceivable veracity depends with ever-renewed dependence; it is then the truth without whose recognition the most profound and truthful veracity can only lie and deceive." Cited and discussed in L. Malevez, *The Christian Message and Myth: The Theology of Rudolf Bultmann*, trans. Olive Wyon and Bernard Noble (Westminster, Maryland, The Newman Press, 1958), 206.

94. St. Thomas Aquinas, *De Divinis Nominibus*, Chapter 7, lecture 5; cited in E. Schillebeeckx, O.P., "The Non-conceptual Intellectual Element in the Act of Faith: A Reaction," in *Revelation and Theology*. Trans. N.D. Smith. Vol. II (New York: Sheed & Ward, 1968), 56. For what follows, besides Schillebeeckx, see also Juan Alfaro, S.J., "Supernaturalitas Fidei iuxta S. Thomam," *op. cit.* See also Alfaro's "Fides in Terminologica Biblica" *Gregorianum* 42 (1961), 463–505. Maurice Blondel stands in the background of some of these discussions. See the fine theological discussion of Blondel in Roger Aubert, *Le Probléme de l'Acte de Foi* (Louvain: E. Warny, 1958), 277ff. Blondel, we might say, wants to offer a phenomenology of the act of faith, i.e., the movement towards faith as it is lived. Theologically speaking, this is of necessity a commingling of what from a theological perspective is the workings of the experience of grace and nature. In the lived "existential" motion of faith there can be no sorting out the ingredients. Thus Karl Rahner's theory of the "supernatural existential." Yet Sokolowski's position is valid: The act of faith, precisely because it launches us beyond the world and nature, cannot be an act of "natural religion" or an act of piety vis-á-vis the world's depth and center, as perhaps in Plotinus. See his *Christian Faith & Human Understanding*, the essays in Part 1. But it is not clear that the adherence to The Theological Distinction in terms of its propositional explication, i.e., the content of the act of faith, may alone suffice to determine whether it is indeed such a world-transcending act. In the first-person the relation and connection between that One to whom one transcends and what is transcended is not at all clear. This is demonstrated by the consideration that many, if not most, orthodox Jews, Muslims, and Christians would not get passing grades in explicating propositionally the dogma of God the Creator and The Theological Distinction. Yet who would presume to impugn their faith for this reason?

95. *Summa Theologiae* II–II, q. 5, a. 1; see the discussion of Roger Aubert, *op. cit.*, 57ff.

96. See Maurice Blondel, *L'action (1893)*, 357; 378 of English translation.

97. This, of course, was in part the purpose of Karl Rahner's concept of "the supernatural existential."

98. *Fear and Trembling/Repetition*. Ed. and Trans. Hong and Hong (Princeton, NJ: Princeton University Press, 1983), 34.

99. *Fear and Trembling*, 46; see also 40–59 for this distinction between believing in virtue of the absurd and believing the absurd.

100. See, e.g., *Either/Or*, II. Ed. and Trans. Hong (Princeton, NJ: Princeton University Press, 1987), Ultimatum, 343.

101. This is a famous theme in Kierkegaard. It becomes notorious with the "suspension of the ethical" in *Fear and Trembling*. In Sokolowski there is a similar radical, if not so startling, change in ethics because the setting for human action is radically transformed: The world's "steady anonymity" as the setting for action is now seen as "the effect of a choice, and the unforced generosity behind that choice is seen as what most truly exists." The basic context that creation provides for agency results in the insight that "a person's being his own is itself seen as a gift," and the domain of action of ultimate importance is permitting the grace of God in Christ to be operative in one. The obvious reality of "wickedness" is seen as something that need not have been and cannot be understood simply as "part of the way things have to be." Now the believer "is supposed to act in a setting not limited by the necessities of the world." The source of good agency is less acquisition by performance than the grace. This is because the fundamental dispositions for this agency are totally foreign to the world, namely the gifts of faith, hope, and charity. But the evidence for these "virtues" is not verified in the way moral virtue is. "Natural moral virtue is thus made to shift from being the best in man, to being the best in a derived sense, to being, apparently, only a false 'best.'" See *The God of Faith and Reason*, Chapter 7.

102. *Fear and Trembling*, Preliminary Expectoration, 35 and 37 of Ed. Hong.

103. Kierkegaard esteemed the religion of inwardness and immanence, which he called "religiousness A." But this religion did not encompass the central Christian doctrine of The Theological Distinction which involves an "aesthetic relation" to the divine in the world. The Christian "does not find edification by finding the God-relationship within himself, but relates himself to something outside himself to find edification. The paradox consists in

the fact that this apparently aesthetic relationship (the individual being related to something outside himself) is nevertheless the right relationship; for in immanence God is neither a something (He being all and infinite all), nor is he outside the individual, since edification consists precisely in the fact that He is in the individual. The paradoxical edification corresponds therefore to the determination of God in time as the individual man; for if such be the case, the individual is related to something outside himself. The fact that it is not possible to think this, is precisely the paradox. It is another question whether the individual will not be repelled by it – that is his affair." *Concluding Unscientific Postscript*, 561.

104. *Fear and Trembling*, 221.
105. *Fear and Trembling*, 47.
106. *Philosophical Fragments*. Ed. Hong, 219.
107. *Sickness Unto Death*, 81.
108. *Concluding Unscientific Postscript*, 245.
109. *Ibid.*, 245–246.
110. See, e.g., *Conclusing Unscientific Postscript*, 249. This theme of "indirect communication" has received a rigorous analysis in Tony Aumann's doctoral dissertation at Indiana University, 2008, *Kierkegaard and the Need for Indirect Communication*.
111. *Concluding Unscientific Postscript*, 66.
112. *Sickness Unto Death*, 80.
113. *Concluding Unscientific Postscript*, 199–200.
114. *Concluding Unscientific Postscript*, 83. Compare Husserl's discussion of prayer as a turn within in the *Nachlass* text of E III 9, 22a–22b, and my remarks on this in the second Sokolowski, *Festschrift, Ethics and Theological Disclosures*. Eds. Guy Mansini and James G. Hart, 99–100.
115. In *Nicomachean Ethics*, 1125a13.
116. *Fear and Trembling*, 40, cf. again in this regard Robert Sokolowski's discussion of the theological virtues vis-á-vis the natural ones, in *The God of Faith and Reason*.
117. *Fear and Trembling*, 38–41.
118. *Concluding Unscientific Postscript*, 226.
119. *Fear and Trembling*, 40.
120. For a lively Wittgenstein-inspired discussion of these matters which also elaborates aspects of The Theological Distinction and complements nicely Sokolowski's *The God of Faith and Reason*, see Gareth Moore, O.P., *Believing in God: A Philosophical Essay* (Edinburgh: T & T Clark, 1988).
121. Meister Eckhart, *Sermons and Treatises*. Trans. and Ed. M.O'C. Walshe. Vol. II (Sermon Forty Three), 4.
122. Meister Eckhart, *ibid.*, Sermon Forty-Six, 23–24.
123. See Sokolowski, *God of Faith and Reason*, 32. Perhaps it must be said that the condition for the possibility of God's knowing creatures, knowing us in our actual creaturely ipseity and not as inseparable from the divine essence, is God knowing "nothing"; only nothing "is" in its being known by God, and only "nothing" is what truly is not Godself. See Thomas Prufer, *Sein und Wort nach Thomas von Aquin*, 11. This knowing of nothing as ingredient to the knowing of creatures gives to the divine knowing of the self-subsistence of creation both its radical otherness and dependence, which the otherness of divine reflection does not yet provide. (See the discussion that follows in the text.) At the same time faith can only make present the other term of The Christian Distinction by entertaining "nothing," i.e., the possibility that the world not be – and that God alone exists is possible but counterfactual. Cf. n. 127 below.
124. St. Thomas, *Summa Contra Gentiles* Book III, Chapter 69.
125. G.K. Chesterton, *St. Francis of Assisi* (New York: Image Doubleday, 1990/1924), 74–75.
126. I am grateful for and to Rev. Hal Taylor for a wonderful discussion of the possibility of being grateful-for without being grateful-to. For a deep and far-reaching discussion of this matter, see Dieter Henrich's essay, "*Gedanken zur Dankbarkeit*," in his *Bewußtes Leben* (Stuttgart: Phillipp Reclam, June 1999), 154–193. My remarks do not presume to address all of Henrich's concerns.

127. St. Thomas, *De Veritate* Q. 2. art. 3., ad 2; See Siewerth, *op. cit.*, 68. As young Thomas Prufer, helped by Siewerth here, proposed in his doctoral dissertation, in knowing creatures as what is other than absolute subsisting To Be, God must know nothingness: It is alone what is absolutely other than God; "nothing" *is* in the only way it can be, i.e., in being known. In knowing creatures God must know Godself *and* what is other than Godself, know absolute To Be and Its other. Rather than place this in "essence" as a principle of nothingness, which is the proposal of Siewerth and early Prufer, in this work we propose to found otherness to the divine in the divine's self-knowledge in reflection. But the self-knowledge in the intentional "othering" still does not provide creatures with the self-subsistence the doctrine of creation requires. For this, the third mode, there must be the creative act, the creating *fiat*, over and above the reflective act wherein the second mode resides. Here with the third mode we arrive at the situation that Siewerth and early Prufer pondered, namely that in knowing creatures God must know at once Godself and the nothingness or otherness to Godself as pure To Be. But the root of the otherness is not in (or not merely in) essence as what limits *esse* but in God's self-reflection. What enables the essences to appear as communicable or "otherable" is God's being other to Godself in reflection. Cf. n. 145.

128. I am dependent here on Siewerth, 60.

129. "Esse autem est illud quod magis intimum cuilibet." St. Thomas Aquinas, *Summa Theologiae* I. q. 8., a.1.c.

130. Cf. Louis Lavelle, *Introduction á l'ontologie* (Paris: PUF, 1947), 18.

131. *Ideas* I, §121.

132. I owe the drift of this thinking and the term "unothered act" to Thomas Prufer.

133. See Husserl, *Ideas* I, §38. Cf. our discussion above in Book 1, Chapter II.

134. Dionysius the Areopagite, *On the Divine Names and the Mystical Theology*. Trans. C.E. Rolt (London: Macmillan, 1957), 80. See St. Thomas, *De divinis nominibus*, Chapter II, Lectio VI, 69, par. 220. At par. 218 St. Thomas has already stated: "And since God exists in all things he remains indivisible in the divisible things to which He communicates *esse*; and God is united in Godself and is not commingled with the multitude nor multiplied in regard to Godself (*et non multiplicatur secuundum quod in se consideratur*)." These themes of the creator's simplicity and unity are just further amplifications of the basic themes of The Theological Distinction.

135. St. Thomas, *De divinis nominibus*, Chapter V, 1, Lectio III, 250, par. 669; Trans. Rolt, 140ff.

136. This is, as Thomas Prufer once proposed (see our discussion in nn. 121 and 125 above), knowing what is a mix of nothingness (as what alone can be other than sheer To Be and what can "be" not by truly being but only as thought by God) and Godself. See his *Sein und Wort nach Thomas von Aquin*, *passim*, but especially p. 11. This speculation we take to be the beginning of what Prufer later worked out, with Robert Sokolowski, as The Christian Distinction, in particular how God cannot stand in competition with creatures, how God cannot be counted with creatures, how God does not stand in a real relation to creatures, etc.

137. Thomas Merton, *New Seeds of Contemplation*, 40–41.

138. Edmund Husserl, *Zur Phänomenologie der Intersubjektivität* III. Ed. I. Kern (The Hague: Nijhoff, 1973), 385.

139. See Sokolowski, *Eucharistic Presence*, Chapter 5; and Prufer, *Recapitulations*, Chapter 7.

140. This is the best I can presently do to address a critical comment of John Drummond.

141. Cf. Siewerth, 116–117.

142. Siewerth, 146.

143. St. Thomas, *De divinis nominibus*, Chapter VII, 1, Lectio III, 271, Section 724.

144. St. Thomas, idem.

145. Prufer, *Recapitulations*, 68. This is the theme of Siewerth's book, *Thomismus als Identitätsystem*, and is also a theme in Prufer's doctoral dissertation, *Sein und Wort Nach Thomas von Aquin* (Munich: 1959). For a rich commentary, see John F. Wippel, "Early Prufer on Aquinas on Being," in *Commemorating Thomas Prufer*, Kurt Pritzl, ed. (Catholic University of America, School of Philosophy Commemoration, Mar 21–22, 2003).

146. I am indebted here to Louis Lavelle, especially *Du Temps et de l'éternité* (Paris: Aubier, 1945), especially 410–424; *De L'Acte* (Paris: Aubier, 1946), 19 ff. Jankélévitch's *Philosophie Prémiere* touches on similar themes as does Hedwig Conrad-Martius' (1927–1928) article "Die Zeit" in *Schriften zur Philosophie*. Vol. I (Munich: Kösel, 1963), and her book *Die Zeit* (Munich: Kösel, 1954) and Edith Stein, *Endliches und ewiges Sein, op. cit.*

147. Sokolowski, *The God of Faith and Reason*, 34.

148. Cf. my discussion of Sallie McFague's *Models of God*, in "*Models of God*: Evangel-logic," *Religion and Intellectual Life*. Vol. V. 1988, 29–37. This entire volume, edited by Mary Jo Weaver, is dedicated to McFague's book which is a kind of process theology where creation is envisaged as God's body. In my essay I wrestle with the problem of revelation as "Gospel," *eu angelion*, and its logic, its "evangel-logic." This is a matter of thinking of revelation as a matter of being a good correlated to the question and hopes of Existenz. It also experiments with a hermeneutical framework of revelation as something being too good not to be true and its opposite, i.e., it is too good to be true. In contrast to this work, in that essay I leave open the question about the merits of the dogma of God the Creator as enunciated in The Theological Distinction and as it contrasts with process theology. The issues cannot be pursued here, except to say that if there is revelation there would seem of necessity to be dogma, and how dogma is *eu angelion* entails a more complicated "evangel-logic" than I conceived it to be in that essay.

Except for occasional passages and the discussion of Scheler's process theology in §11 below we scarcely touch on process theology in this work. Here we cannot adjudicate either the motivations or proposals of process theology in terms of its philosophical and theological merits. As I have already indicated, however, my impression is that the understanding of the philosophical distinctions that are in play in the articulation of the mystery of creation as laid out in The Theological Distinction have never been understood by process thinkers, and thus have never been met head on. In fact, because God and creation are both from the start taken as mysteries, the basic insights of The Distinction never quite surface and are replaced with more rational and univocal similes and analogies which typically do justice to the requirements of "the greatest being." Thus Sokolowski nicely points out that process philosophy takes the classical ontological claims about God's being in relation to the world (i.e., God not being in a "real relation" to the world) for psychological-moral ones. The misunderstanding also is, in part perhaps, because of process philosophy's modernist reading of the classical traditional doctrine, i.e., it is a reading which introduces elements of the faith-tradition as if they were pure philosophical positions. Such a modernist move will appropriate faith positions, e.g., that God is in history, that God in Christ suffered; or it will assume that the dogma of God the Creator was a philosophical position that needed refuting as such. The modernist reading also assumes that the teachings of the religious theological tradition did not have an a priori context in its understanding of antiquity, i.e., the modernist fails to grasp that the tradition's assertions and questions emerged out of the ancient belief-horizon. This failure to be attuned to what questions the classical theological positions were answers to, and the failure to grasp that the answers were suffused by what was taken to be divine revelation, leads to understanding the classical positions as part of a pure philosophical conversation. But this distorts the sense of classical theology in so far as it was theology founded in faith in the mysteries using philosophy and it clouds the modernist's own conceptual framework which appropriates these discussions as if faith and revelation played no role in determining the basic concepts of the discussion. The modernist reading thus forgets its own philosophical antecedents in both Greek and medieval philosophy; it forgets the context of the ancient tradition as understood by classical theology as the horizon for its own questions, a horizon soaked with a faith tradition which itself was in response to an ancient religious-philosophical "pagan" tradition. Such a modernist reading thereby establishes the philosophical setting by borrowing from these antecedents as if they were all part of a purely "philosophical" heritage. Thus we have a borrowing by modernity without taking account of the proper hermeneutical sense of what it is borrowing, and thus without acknowledging the conditions of its own questions and proposed answers. See the references to Sokolowski and Prufer for discussions of "modernism." Barry Miller's *An Unlikely God* is a recent impressive critique of process theology from a more classical, Thomist-inspired, position that prescinds from this hermeneutical matter of the problem of modernity. Whether this implies a naivety characteristic of a modern I am not prepared to say given my own ignorance of the rest of Miller's thought. Having said this, it seems to me that Thomism and scholasticism in general have been occasionally modernist in approaching their understandings of God the Creator as if the basic theses were purely philosophical.

149. Franz Brentano, *Religion und Philosophie*. Eds. A. Kastil and Franziska Mayer Hillebrand (Bern: Francke Verlag, 1954), 112–113, 118, 176–177, 260, n. 15.
150. Although Brentano's position would seem to find support in numerous passages of Leibniz, it seems to me there are other discussions by Leibniz which pose a problem for this reading. Because Leibniz held a teleological determinist position, that God must will the best, his opponents, echoed in Brentano, argued that the world was necessary, otherwise God would have acted for less than the best. Further, if the motive for creation requires the metaphor that God wills the world because of his "glory," then the world is necessary for God. Leibniz, particularly in response to Bayle, argues that even though God always wills the best the world is not a matter of necessity, and a fortiori, God does not of necessity will the world for the sake of his glory. Whatever God chooses "creates no impossibility in that which is distinct from the best; it causes no implication of contradiction in that which God refrains from doing. There is therefore in God a freedom that is exempt not only from constraint but also from necessity." I take this to repeat the traditional position that God is essentially good and God loves in the strongest sense of metaphysical necessity Godself, but his glory as well as the world are not so loved or willed. (This approaches what we are calling The Theological Distinction.) When we say that God exercises the highest degree of freedom in always being led towards the good by God's own inclination, we cannot mean that God of necessity wills what is external to God; rather it is only Godself that is of necessity loved. It is therefore not a violation of the principle that God of necessity wills what is best if God, contrary to fact, did not will the world. It is, however, for Leibniz, a violation of this principle if God, having chosen to create or will the world, chose not to will the best possible world. Having freely chosen a world God's wisdom determines that he choose the best possible world and the most appropriate means in realizing the best possible world. To call this a "need" of God is to stretch unhelpfully the use of this term. (See Leibniz, *Theodicy*, 270–271, 386.) The intrinsic goodness of God, and the necessity that God will only what is best, does not require that God wills what is other than God. God is the "reason" for the existence of the world; but for Leibniz the world does not provide God with a "reason" for creation, as it does for Brentano.
151. *Religion und Philosophie*, 113; this passage still leaves open the question of whether the world is contingent and the sense in which it is so. Again, the distinction between how the world is and that it is, is perhaps relevant.
152. *Religion und Philosophie*, 260.
153. Brentano, *Das Dasein Gottes* (Hamburg: Meiner, 1980), 61.
154. Brentano, *The Foundation and Construction of Ethics*. Ed. Franziska Mayer-Hillebrand. Trans. Elizabeth Hughes Schneewind (New York: Humanities, 1973), 213. See also *Das Dasein Gottes*, 64.
155. *Religion und Philosophie*, 112–120.
156. *Religion und Philosophie*, especially 221–233.
157. Edgar Brightman, *A Philosophy of Religion* (New York: Greenwood, 1969/New York: Prentice-Hall, 1940), Chapter VIII.
158. *Religion und Philosophie*, 158 ff.
159. Prufer, *Recapitulations*, 28, 32–34.
160. St. Thomas, *De Potentia* V, 4.
161. My reading of Shankara in this section is indebted to Olivier Lacombe, *L'Absolu selon le Védânta* (Paris: Librairie Orientaliste Paul Geunther, 1966), 65 ff.
162. Cf. Sokolowski, *The God of Faith and Reason*, 34.
163. St. Thomas, *De potentia dei* V 4; from Thomas Prufer, *Recapitulations*, 38.

164. Besides the otherness of reflection, perhaps the radical otherness of persons within the Trinity can provide some clue to the conditions for the possibility for this generation of the otherness and transcendence of intentionality and therefore of creation. If within the Godhead each Divine Person as an I encounters the Other within a We which is as always already having been, then there is a co-presencing of other persons (not streams of consciousness). Each is transcendent to the Other although always internally and essentially related. In this view the persons could only be related to one another through an analogous "intentionality" that would not violate either the absolute interiority of each of the persons in their non-intentional self-manifestation or the absolute and eternal community and union that surpasses all forms of union realized by instinct and love. At the same time this essential relatedness and plurality of divine persons would preserve the absolute interiority and unity of the Godhead's being for itself, or its ontological solitude and hiddenness. The persons would be "communally" within one another not in a community constituted from below by individual persons but in the a priori unity of the same divine "nature" or "being" – with the *caveat* that the divine does not have a nature that presupposes other natures for its contrast and completion and that "nature" would not be a natural necessity which would supplant the *beata necessitas* of the love of one another.

165. *The God of Faith and Reason*, 34.

166. I am helped here by H.D. Lewis's discussion of W.T. Stace's temptation to offer a monist theory of mystical experience. See H.D. Lewis, *The Elusive Mind* (London: George Allen & Unwin, 1969), 307 ff.

167. H.D. Lewis, *The Self and Immortality* (London: Macmillan, 1973), 189.

168. I am indebted here to Sebastian Moore, O.S.B. See his "God Suffered," in *Downside Review*, LXXVII (1959), 136 ff.

169. St. Thomas Aquinas, *Summa Theologiae*, q. 12, a. 5; *Summa Contra Gentes* III, 53 and 54.
    In St. Paul's teaching on faith, e.g., 1 *Corinthians* 2: 10 ff. we have a similar problem. Here we are told that only God's own Spirit knows God and what God is. But this is a Spirit we have received and that by which we know/believe what God has revealed. This Spirit of God is also called the mind of Christ. When Paul asks, who knows the mind of the Lord? his answer is: Each of us does who has the mind of Christ. But we take this to mean not a fusion or confusion where the individual selves become indistinguishably Christ, the mind of Christ, or the Spirit of God, but rather the created distinctiveness which is articulated in The Theological Distinction. We find in Tennyson a lovely statement against the "fusion."

That each, who seems a separate whole,
Should move his rounds, and fusing all
The skirts of self again, should fall
Re-merging in the general Soul,
Is faith as vague as all unsweet:
Eternal form shall still divide
The eternal soul from all beside;
And I shall know him when we meet.

Yet, at the conclusion of this very stanza Tennyson suggests nearly the opposite because the love, by which each is enabled to be in a condition of "enjoying each the other's good," shall ultimately give way to a state of affairs wherein the "spirits fade away," and then each will be placed in a position to say, 'Farewell! We lose ourselves in light." Much here depends on the sense which is given to the spirits fading away and the loss of the self occasioned by the divine light. If the earlier claims are not negated that the "separate wholes" of selves re-emerge as unique and distinct ("still divided") and knowable as such in the general Soul then there is not necessarily a contradiction. See *In Memoriam* (LXVII), Alfred Tennyson. *The Poetical Works of Tennyson*, Cambridge Edition (Boston, MA: Houghton Mifflin, 1974), 174. Plato at *Timaeus*, 41, has the great creator of the universe address all his works, all that he has called into being: You are all not inherently eternal or indissoluble. "All that is bound may be dissolved, but only an evil being would wish to dissolve that which is harmonious and happy. In my will ye have a greater and mightier bond than that which bound you at the time of creation." I am indebted for the reference of these texts from Tennyson and Plato to A. Seth Pringle-Pattison, *The Idea of Immortality* (Oxford: Clarendon Press, 1922), 164–165. The Theological Distinction again may be appealed to offer a logic or optic which moves beyond the alternatives of fusion and division in the ultimate union affirmed by mystics and believers.

170. See especially, "A Précis of a Husserlian Philosophical Theology," in *Essays in Phenomenological Theology*. Eds. Steven W. Laycock and James G. Hart (Albany, NY: SUNY, 1986), 89–168; also "The Study of Religion in Husserl's Writings," in *Phenomenology and the Cultural Disciplines*. Eds. Mano Daniel and Lester Embree (Dordrecht: Kluwer, 1994), 265–296.

171. Max Scheler, *Wesen und Formen der Sympathie* (Bonn: Friedrich Cohen, 1931/1913), 143–148.

172. Idem.

173. *Schriften aus dem Nachlass,* Band II, *Erkenntnislehre und Metaphysik* (Franke: Bern and Munich, 1979), 204.

174. *Schriften aus dem Nachlass*, Band II, 156, 262–263.

175. Scheler, *Schriften aus dem Nachlass*, Band II, 190 ff. and *Philosophische Weltanschauung* (Bern and Munich: Franke, Dalp Taschenbuecher, 1968), 27.

176. See Francis MacDonald Cornford's commentary on the *Timaeus* 47e–48e, *Plato's Cosmology* (Indianapolis, IN: Bobbs-Merrill, n.d.), 160 ff. This theme of the wrestle of mind, reason, or form with the recalcitrant *hyle* recurs in Whitehead's juxtaposition of the divine lure and the eternal ideas, on the one hand, with the principle of creativity, on the other; it also finds clear echoes in Edgar Brightman's portrayal of the divine wrestle with the surds of the irrational "given" in his *Philosophy of Religion*. In Scheler, the principle of *Drang* is also, along with *Geist*, a divine principle. In Scheler's case this schema for the basic metaphysical principles perhaps reveals less the influence of Plato than that of both Nietzsche and Bergson.

177. Scheler, *Philosophische Weltanschauung*, 14–15.

178. Scheler, *Schriften aus dem Nachlass*, Band II, 260.

179. Scheler, ibid., 201.

180. *Ibid.*, 261.

181. *Ibid.*, 206–207 and *Philosophische Weltanshauung*, 108.

182. *Schriften aus dem Nachlass*, Band II, 155. On *ibid.*, 206, Scheler wrestles with his version of the modern "problem of evil": Primal divine impulse is unconscious, unresponsible, and innocent in regard to the value-indifference of its chaotic force. But the divine spirit foreknows the power of the divine impulse and the possibility of suffering. He embraced this, wept over it, and echoing perhaps Nietzsche's Zarathustra, experienced Itself as profoundly blessed that he reached the agonizing decision to let the world-process be by non-inhibition of the divine cosmic impetuosity.

183. Cf. Thomas Prufer, *Recapitulations*, 103–104.

184. Note that both of these concerns, which have their theological equivalents in the theology of grace and redemption, have become *philosophical* positions without any acknowledgment of such a lineage. Of course, one could respond that such views might reach back to more ancient sources, where humans were posited as having kinship with the divine and the divine itself was finite. Doubtless this is possible, but Scheler's debt to Nietzsche suggests a more Christian theological lineage for these views.

185. See Francis Slade, "On the Ontological Priority of Ends and Its Relevance to the Narrative Arts," 58–69; and "Ends and Purposes," 83–85. See also John Ciardi, *A Browser's Dictionary*, 130–131. Cf. our discussion in Chapter V, §7.

186. Bernhard W. Anderson, *Out of the Depths: The Psalms Speak for Us Today*, 46 ff.

187. *Otherwise Than Being*. Trans. Alphonso Lingis (Pittsburgh: Duquesne University Press, 2002), 113–114 See also Richard A. Cohen: *Elevations: The Height of the Good in Rosenzweig and Levinas* (Chicago, IL: University of Chicago Press, 1994), 105–106.

188. Levinas, *ibid.*, 114. For a good case for obeying prior to receiving the command to obey which is founded on the concious recognition of and respect for the other, see Stephen Darwall, *op. cit.*, and our discussion in Chapter V, § 9.

189. Jean-Louis Chrétien, *The Call and the Response*, 25.

190. Thomas Merton, *Conjectures of a Guilty Bystander*, 158.

191. Bernard of Clairvaux, *Treatises II: The Steps of Humility and Pride/The Book on Loving God* (Kalamazoo, MI: Cistercian Fathers, 1973), 118ff.

192. St. Bernard, *ibid.*, 120.

193. St. Thomas Aquinas, *De Potentia* III, 15, ad 4; cited in Prufer, *Recapitulations*, 38.

194. Cf. Michel Henry, *Incarnation* (Paris: Seuil, 2000), 268–269.

195. See "A Précis of a Husserlian Philosophical Theology," especially 118ff.

196. Prufer, *Recapitulations*, 33.

Bibliography

Adler, Alfred. *The Individual Psychology of Alfred Adler: A Systematic Presentation in Selections from His Writings*. Eds. Heinz L. Ansbacher and Rowena R. Ansbacher. New York: Harper Torchbooks, 1956.

Alfaro, Juan. "Fides in Terminologica Biblica." *Gregorianum* 42 (1961), 463–505.

Alfaro, Juan. "Supernaturalitas fidei iuxta S. Thomam." *Gregorianum* 44 (1963), 2–4, 501–542, 732–787.

Anderson, Bernhard W. *Out of the Depths*. Philadelphia, PA: Westminster, 1983.

Aquinas, St. Thomas. *Summa Contra Gentes*. Turin/Rome: Marietti, 1934.

Aquinas, St. Thomas. *De Veritate. Quaestiones Disputatae*. Turin/Rome: Marietti, 1942.

Aquinas, St. Thomas. *Summa Theologiae*. Turin/Rome: Marietti, 1950.

Aquinas, St. Thomas. *De Potentia*. Turin/Rome: Marietti, 1950.

Aquinas, St. Thomas. *In Librum beati Dionysi De divinis nominibus*. Ed. Ceslai Pera, O.P. Turin/Rome: Marietti, 1950.

Aristotle, *Nicomachean Ethics*. Trans. Martin Ostwald. Indianapolis, IN: Bobbs-Merrill, 1962.

Armstrong, A.H. "Plotinus." *The Cambridge History of Later Greek and Early Medieval Philosophy*. Cambridge, 1967.

Armstrong, A.H. *Plotinian and Christian Studies*. London: Variorum, 1979.

Arnou, R. *Theologia Naturalis*. Rome: Gregorian University, 1960.

Aubert, Roger. *Le Probléme de l'act de foi*. Louvain: E. Warny, 1958.

Augustine, St. *Confessions*. New York: Barnes & Noble, 2003.

Augustine, St. *An Augustine Synthesis*. Ed. Erich Przywara. New York: Harper Torchbook, 1958.

Aumann, Tony. *Kierkegaard and the Need for Indirect Communication*. Dissertation, Indiana University, Bloomington, IN, 2008.

Bakhtin, M.M. *Art and Answerability*. Ed. M. Holquist and Ed. and Trans. V. Liapunov. Austin, TX: University of Texas, 1990.

Bakhtin, M.M. *Toward a Philosophy of the Act*. Trans. Vadim Liapunov. Austin, TX: University of Texas Press, 1993.

Balthasar, N.-J.-J. *Mon moi dans L'Être*. Louvain: Institut Supérieure de Philosophie, 1946.

Barth, Heinrich. *Erkenntnis der Existenz*. Basel: Schwabe, 1965.

Baumann, Gerhart. *Robert Musil*. Bern: A. Francke, 1981.

Bernard of Clairvaux, St. *Treatises II: The Steps of Humility and Pride/The Book on Loving God*. Kalamazoo, MI: Cistercian Fathers, 1973.

Bernet, Rudolf. "Zur Phänomenologie von Trieb und Lust." *Interdisziplinäre Perspektiven der Phänomenologie*. "*Phaenomenologica*" series. Ed.D. Lohmar and D. Fonfara. Dordrecht: Springer, 2006, 38–53.

Besançon, Alain. *The Forbidden Image: An Intellectual History of Iconoclasm*. Trans. Jane Marie Todd. Chicago, IL/London: University of Chicago Press, 2000.

Bieri, Peter. *Das Handwerk der* Freiheit. Frankfurt am Main: Fischer Taschenbuch, 2007.

Blondel, Maurice. *L'Être et les êtres*. Paris: Presses Universitaire de France, 1963.

Blondel, Maurice. *Action (1893)*. Notre Dame, IN: University of Notre Dame Press, 1984.

Bolt, Robert. *A Man for All Seasons*. New York: Vintage International, 1990.

Bowsma, O.K. "Notes on Kierkegaard's 'the Monstrous Illusion.'" *Without Proof or Evidence*. Eds. J.L. Craft and R.E. Huswit. Lincoln, NE: University of Nebraska Press, 1984.

Bradley, F.H. *Collected Essays*. Oxford: Clarendon Press, 1935/1969.

Bragg, David. Review of Recent Translations of Euripides in Toronto's *The Globe and Mail*, Saturday, August 5, 2006, D5 (Book Section).

Brentano, Franz. *Religion und Philosophie*. Eds. A. Kastil and Franziska Mayer Hillebrand. Bern: Francke Verlag, 1954.

Brentano, Franz. *The Foundation and Construction of Ethics*. Ed. Franziska Mayer-Hillebrand. Trans. Elizabeth Hughes Schneewind. New York: Humanities, 1973.

Brentano, Franz. *Das Dasein Gottes*. Hamburg: Meiner, 1980.

Brightman, Edgar. *A Philosophy of Religion*. New York: Greenwood, 1969/New York: Prentice-Hall, 1940.

Brook, Anthony. "Kant, Self-Awareness and Self-Reference." http://www.carleton.ca/-abrook/kant-self.htm

Brown, Raymond E. "Introduction, and Commentary." *The Gospel According to John, I-XII*. New York: Doubleday, 1966. Appendix I, 497–499.

Brown, Raymond E., Fitzmeyer, Joseph A., and Murphy, Roland, E., Eds. *The Jerome Biblical Commentary*. Englewood Cliffs, NJ: Prentice-Hall.

Buber, Martin. *Man and Man*. Boston, MA: Beacon, 1955.

Buber, Martin. *Moses*. New York: Harper Torchbooks, 1958.

Burckhardt, Titus. *Introduction to Sufi Doctrine*. Trans. D.M. Matheson. Jakarta, Indonesia: Dar al-ilm, n.d.

Burrell, David. "The Christian Distinction Celebrated and Expanded." *The Truthful and the Good: Essays in Honor of Robert Sokolowski*. Eds. John J. Drummond and James G. Hart. Dordrecht: Kluwer, 1996.

Castañeda, Hector-Neri. *The Structure of Morality*. Springfield, IL: Charles C. Thomas, 1974.

Castañeda, Hector-Neri. *Thinking and Doing*. Dordrecht: Reidel, 1982.

Castañeda, Hector-Neri. *Thinking, Language, and Experience*. Minneapolis, MN: University of Minnesota Press, 1989.

Castañeda, Hector-Neri. *The Phenomeno-Logic of the I*. Eds. James G. Hart and Tomis Kapitan. Bloomington, IN: Indiana University Press, 1999.

Catechism of the Catholic Church. Liguori, MO: Liguori Publications, 1994.

Cather, Willa. *The Song of the Lark*. Mineola, NY: Dover, 2004/1915.

Cavell, Stanley. *The Senses of Walden*. San Francisco, CA: North Point Press, 1981.

Chesterton, G.K. *St. Francis of Assisi*. New York: Image Doubleday, 1990/1924.

Chittick, William C. "The Circle of Spiritual Ascent According to Al-Qunawi." *Neopolatonism and Islamic Thought*. Ed. Parviz Morewedge. New York: SUNY, 1992.

Chrétien, Jean-Louis. *The Call and the Response*. Trans. Anne A. Davenport. New York: Fordham University Press, 2000.

Ciardi, John. *A Browser's Dictionary*. New York: Harper & Row, 1980.

Cohen, Richard A. *Elevations: The Height of the Good in Rosenzweig and Levinas*. Chicago, IL: University of Chicago Press, 1994.

Comentale, Edward P. *The Ryder*. Bloomington, IN: Indiana, October 2006.

Conrad-Martius, Hedwig. *Die Zeit*. Munich: Kösel, 1954.

Conrad-Martius, Hedwig. *Der Selbstaufbau der Natur: Entelechien und Energien*. Munich: Kösel Verlag, 1961.

Conrad-Martius, Hedwig. "Die Zeit" (1927–1928). *Schriften zur Philosophie*. Vol. I. Munich: Kösel, 1963.

Conrad-Martius, Hedwig. "Die fundamentale Bedeutung eines substantiallen Seinsbegriffs für eine theistische Metaphysik." *Schriften zur Philosophie*. Munich: Kösel, 1963.

Crowe, S.J., F.E. "Complacency and Concern in the Thought of St. Thomas." *Theological Studies* 20 (1959), 1–29, 198–230, 343–396.

Dante. *Vita Nuova.* Trans. Mark Musa. Bloomington, IN: Indiana University Press, 1973.

Darwall, Stephen. *The Second-Person Standpoint: Morality, Respect, and Accountability.* London: Oxford University Press, 1968.

Dasgupta, S. *Indian Idealism.* Cambridge: Cambridge University Press, 1933.

De Finance, Joseph. *Existence et Liberté.* Paris: Vitte, 1955.

De Libera, Alain. *Introduction á la mystique rhenane: d'Albert le Grand à Maître Eckhart.* Paris: O.E.I.L., 1984.

De Lubac, Henri. *Catholicism: Church and Society.* Trans. Lancelot C. Sheppard. New York: Omega-Mentor, 1964.

De Raeymaker, Louis. *The Philosophy of Being.* St. Louis, MO: Herder, 1961.

Derrida, Jacques. *The Gift of Death.* Trans. David Wills. Chicago, IL: University of Chicago Press, 1995.

Descartes. *Meditations.* Trans. Donald A. Cress. Indianapolis, IN: Hackett, 1993.

de Vogel, C.J. "The Concept of Personality in Greek and Christian Thought." *Studies in Philosophy and the History of Philosophy.* Vol. 2. Ed. John K. Ryan. Washington, DC: The Catholic University of America Press, 1963.

Dickinson, Emily and Johnson, Thomas H. *Final Hours: Selections and Introduction.* Boston, MA: Little Brown, 1961.

Dietsche, Bernard. "Der Seelengrund nach den deutschen und lateinischen Predigten." *Meister Eckhart der Prediger.* Eds. Udo M. Nix and Raphael Oechslin. Freiburg: Herder, 1960, 200–258.

Dionysius the Areopagite. *On the Divine Names and the Mystical Theology.* Trans. C.E. Rolt. London: Macmillan, 1957.

Dulles, Avery. "The Church According to Thomas Aquinas." *A Church to Believe.* New York: Crossroad, 1982.

Eliade, Mircea. *Forêt Interdite.* Paris: Gallimard, 1955.

Euripides, Hippolytus. *Greek Tragedies.* Eds. David Grene and Richmond Lattimore. Chicago, IL: University of Chicago Press, 1968.

Feuerbach, Ludwig. *Das Wesen der Religion.* Lecture 16. Leipzig: Kroner, 1965.

Fichte, J.G. *The Way Towards the Blessed Life, or the Doctrine of Religion* (1889 trans. of *Die Anweisungen* by William Smith). *Significant Contributions to the History of Psychology.* Ed. Daniel Robinson. Washington, DC: University Publications of America, 1970.

Fichte, J.G. *Anweisungen zum seligen Leben. Fichtes Werke.* Vol. V. Ed. I.H. Fichte. Berlin: Walter de Gruyter, 1971.

Fichte, J.G. *Tatsachen des Bewusstseins. Fichtes Werke.* Vol. II: *Die Tatsachen des Bewusstseins.* Ed. I.H. Fichte. Berlin: Walter de Gruyter, 1971.

Fichte, J.G. *Zur Rechts- und Sittenlehre II. Fichtes Werke.* Vol. IV. Ed. I.H. Fichte. Berlin: Walter de Gruyter, 1971.

Fichte, J.G. *Die Wissenschaftslehre, Zweiter Vortrag in Jahre 1804.* Hamburg: Meiner, 1975.

Fichte, J.G. *Die Wissenschaftslehre in ihrem allgemeinem Umriss (1810).* Frankfurt am Main: Klostermann, 1976.

Fichte, J.G. *Wissenschaftslehre (1805).* Hamburg: Meiner, 1984.

Fichte, J.G. *Foundations of Natural Right.* Ed. Frederick Neuhouser. Trans. Michael Bauer. Cambridge: Cambridge University Press, 2000.

Findlay, J.N. *Values and Intentions.* London: George Allen & Unwin, 1961.

Findlay, J.N. *The Transcendence of the Cave.* London: George Allen & Unwin, 1967.

Fitzmyer, Joseph A. *Romans: A New Translation with Introduction and Commentary, Anchor Bible, Vol. 33.* New York: Doubleday, 1992.

Frank, Erich. *Philosophical Understanding and Religious Truth.* Oxford: Oxford University Press, 1949.

Frank, Erich. "Religious Origin of Greek Philosophy." *Wissen, Wollen, Glauben.* Zürich/Stuttgart: Artemis Verlag, 1955.

Frank, Erich. "Begriff und Bedeutung des Dämonischen." *Wissen, Wollen, Glauben.* Zürich/Stuttgart: Artemis Verlag, 1955.

Frank, Erich. "Das Problem des Lebens bei Hegel und Aristoteles." *Wissen, Wollen, Glauben.* Zürich/Stuttgart: Artemis Verlag, 1955.

Frank, Manfred. *Die Unhintergehbarkeit von Individualität.* Frankfurt am Main: Suhrkamp, 1986.

Frank, Manfred. *Selbstgefühl.* Frankfurt am Main: Suhrkamp, 2002.

Frege, G. *Logische Untersuchungen.* Göttingen: Vanderhoeck & Ruprecht, 1966.

Freud, Sigmund. *On Creativity and the Unconscious.* New York: Harper & Row, 1958.

Gendlin, Eugene. *Focusing.* Toronto/New York: Bantam, 1981.

Gerson, Lloyd P. *Plotinus.* London/New York: Routledge, 1994.

Gibbs, Benjamin. *Freedom and Liberation.* New York: St. Martin's Press, 1976.

Gilligan, James. *Violence: Reflections on a National Epidemic.* New York: Vintage, 1997.

Gilligan, James. *Preventing Violence.* London: Thames & Hudson, 2001.

Greeley, Andrew M. *Confessions of a Parish Priest: An Autobiography.* New York: Simon Schuster Pocketbook, 1987.

Green, T.H. *Prolegomena to Ethics.* New York: Kraus, 1969 of the 1883 edition of the Oxford University Press edition.

Harris, Mark. *Grave Matters: A Journey Through the Modern Funeral Industry to a Natural Way of Burial.* New York: Scribner, 2007.

Hart, James G. "Toward a Phenomenology of Nostalgia." *Man and World* 4 (1973), 397–420.

Hart, James G. "A Précis of a Husserlian Philosophical Theology." *Essays in Phenomenological Theology.* Eds. Steven W. Laycock and James G. Hart. Albany, NY: SUNY, 1986.

Hart, James G. "*Models of God*: Evangel-Logic." Comments on Sallie McFague's *Models of God. Religion and Intellectual Life.* Vol. V. Ed. Mary Jo Weaver, 1988, 29–37.

Hart, James G. "Entelechy in Transcendental Phenomenology: A Sketch of the Foundations of Husserlian Metaphysics." *American Catholic Philosophical Quarterly* LXVI (1992), 189–212.

Hart, James G. "The Rationality of Culture and the Culture of Rationality: Some Husserlian Proposals." *Philosophy East & West* XLII (1992), 643–664.

Hart, James G. *The Person and the Common Life.* Dordrecht: Kluwer, 1992.

Hart, James G. "Genesis, Instinct, and Reconstruction: Nam-In Lee." *Edmund Husserls Phänomenologie der Instinkte.* Dordrecht: Kluwer, 1993, 101–123.

Hart, James G. "The Study of Religion in Husserl." *Phenomenology and the Cultural Disciplines.* Eds. Mano Daniel and Lester Embree. Dordrecht: Kluwer, 1994, 286–296.

Hart, James G. "Husserl and Fichte: With Special Regard to Husserl's Lectures on 'Fichte's Ideal of Humanity.'" *Husserl Studies* 12 (1995), 135–163.

Hart, James G. "'We,' Representation, and War Resistance." *Phenomenology, Interpretation, and Community.* Eds. Lenore Langsdorf, Stephen H. Watson and E. Marya Bower. Albany, NY: State University of New York, 1996, 127–144.

Hart, James G. "Blondel and Husserl: A Continuation of a Conversation." *Tijdschrift voor Filosofie.* 58 (1996), 490–518.

Hart, James G. "The *Summum Bonum* and Value Wholes: Aspects of a Husserlian Axiology and Theology." *Phenomenology of Values and Valuing.* Eds. James G. Hart and Lester Embree. Dordrecht: Kluwer, 1997, 193–230.

Hart, James G. "Transcendental Phenomenology and the Eco-Community." *In Animal Others.* Ed. H. Peter Steeves. Albany, NY: SUNY, 1999.

Hart, James G. "The Acts of Our Activity." *In Other Words,* a Festschrift for Vadim Liapunov. *Indiana Slavic Studies* II (2000), 69–76.

Hart, James G. "Contingency of Temporality and Eternal Being: A Study of Aspects of Edith Stein's Phenomenological Theology as It Appears Primarily in *Endliches und Ewiges Sein.*" *The Philosophy of Edith Stein.* Pittsburgh: Simon Silverman Phenomenology Center, Duquesne University, 2001, 34–68.

Hart, James G. "Intentionality, Existenz and Transcendence: Jaspers and Husserl in Conversation." *Jahrbuch der Österreichischen Karl Jaspers Gesellschaft* 16 (2003), 167–203.

Hart, James G. "Wisdom, Knowledge, and Reflective Joy: Aristotle and Husserl." *The New Yearbook for Phenomenology and Phenomenological Philosophy* II (2003), 53–72.

Hart, James G. Review Essay: "Edmund Husserl: Analyses Concerning Active Synthesis. Lectures on Transcendental Logic." *Husserl Studies* 20 (2004), 135–159.

Hart, James G. "The Absolute Ought and the Unique Individual." *Husserl Studies* 22 (2006), 223–340.

Hart, James G. "The Essential Look (*Eidos*) of the Humanities: A Husserlian Phenomenology of the University." *Tijdschrift voor Filosofie* (2008), 109–139.

Hartshorne, Charles. *Man's Vision of God*. Hamden, CT: Archon, 1964 of 1941 original.

Heidegger, Martin. *Sein und Zeit*. Tübingen: Niemeyer, 1962.

Heidegger, Martin. *Basic Problems in Phenomenology*. Bloomington, IN: Indiana University Press, 1982.

Henrich, Dieter. "Fichte's Original Insight." *Contemporary German Philosophy*. Ed. Darryl Christensen 1 (1988), 15–53.

Henrich, Dieter. "*Gedanken zur Dankbarkeit*." *Bewußtes Leben*. Stuttgart: Phillipp Reclam, June 1999.

Henry, Michel. *Incarnation*. Paris: Seuil, 2000.

Homer. *Odyssey*. Trans. Richard Lattimore. New York: Harper Coliphon, 1975.

Hopkins, S.J., Gerard Manley. *The Sermons and Devotional Writings of Gerard Manley Hopkins*. Ed. Christopher Devlin, S.J. London: Oxford University Press, 1959.

Hopkins, S.J., Gerard Manley. *A Hopkins Reader*. Ed. John Pick. New York: Doubleday/Image, 1966.

Hopkins, S.J., Gerard Manley. *Gerard Manley Hopkins: The Major Works*. Ed. Catherine Phillips. Oxford: Oxford University Press, 1986.

Hoyt's New Cyclopedia of Practical Quotations. Compiled by Kate Louis Roberts. New York: Funk & Wagnall's, 1922.

Husserl, Edmund. *Ideen zu einer reinen phänomenologischen Philosophie*. Vol. I. Ed. Walter Biemel. *Husserliana* III. The Hague: Martinus Nijhoff, 1950.

Husserl, Edmund. *Erste Philosophie (1923–1923)*. Part I. Ed. Rudolf Boehm. *Husserliana* VIII. The Hague: Martinus Nijhoff, 1956.

Husserl, Edmund. *Die Krisis der europäischen Wissenschaften und die transzendentale Phänomenologie*. Ed. Walter Biemerl. *Husserliana* VI. The Hague: Martinus Nijhoff, 1962.

Husserl, Edmund. *Analysen zur passiven Synthesis*. Ed. Margot Fleischer. *Husserliana* XI. The Hague: Martinus Nijhoff, 1966.

Husserl, Edmund. *Philosophie der Arithmetik*. Ed. Lothar Eley. *Husserliana* XII. The Hague: Martinus Nijhoff, 1970.

Husserl, Edmund. *Zur Phänomenologie der Intersubjektivität*. Vol. I. Ed. Iso Kern. *Husserliana* XIII. The Hague: Martinus Nijhoff, 1973.

Husserl, Edmund. *Zur Phänomenologie der Intersubjektivität*. Vol. II. Ed. Iso Kern. *Husserliana* XIV. The Hague: Martinus Nijhoff, 1973.

Husserl, Edmund. *Zur Phänomenologie der Intersubjektivität*. Vol. III. Ed. Iso Kern. *Husserliana* XV. The Hague: Martinus Nijhoff, 1973.

Husserl, Edmund. *Phantasie, Bildbewußtsein, Erinnerung*. Ed. Eduard Marbach. *Husserliana* XXIII. Dordrecht: Kluwer, 1980.

Husserl, Edmund. *Ausätze und Vorträge*. Eds. Thomas Nenon and Hans Rainer Sepp. *Husserliana* XXVII. Dordrecht: Kluwer, 1989.

Husserl, Edmund. *Analyses Concerning Passive and Active Synthesis. Lectures on Transcendental Logic*. Trans. Anthony Steinbock. Dordrecht: Kluwer, 2001.

Husserl, Edmund. *Logische Untersuchungen. Ergänzungsband*. Erster Teil. Ed. Ullrich Melle. *Husserliana* XX/1. Dordrecht: Springer, 2002.

Husserl, Edmund. *Zur phänomenolgischen Reduktion*. Ed. Sebastian Luft. *Husserliana* XXXIV. Dordrecht: Kluwer, 2003.

Husserl, Edmund. *Einleitung in die Ethik*. Ed. H. Peucker. *Husserliana* XXXVII. Dordrecht: Kluwer, 2004.

Husserl, Edmund. *Logische Untersuchungen. Ergänzungsband*. Zweiter Teil. Ed. Ullrich Melle. *Husserliana* XX/2. Dordrecht: Springer, 2005.

Husserl, Edmund. *Späte Texte über Zeitkonstitution (1929–1934). Die C-Manuskripte*. Ed. Dieter Lohmar. *Husserliana Materialien* VIII. Dordrecht: Springer, 2006.
Husserl, Edmund. *Nachlass* MS A V 21.
Husserl, Edmund. *Nachlass* MS B I 21 III.
Husserl, Edmund. *Nachlass* MS B I 21 V.
Husserl, Edmund. *Nachlass* MS D 14.
Husserl, Edmund. *Nachlass* MS B II 2.
Husserl, Edmund. *Nachlass* MS E III 1.
Husserl, Edmund. *Nachlass* MS E III 9.
Husserl, Edmund. *Nachlass* MS F I 24.
Husserl, Edmund. *Nachlass* MS F I 25.
Im, Seungpil. *Dreams of a Sight-Seer*. Dissertation, Indiana University, Bloomington, IN, 2008.
Ingarden, Roman. *Der Streit um die Existenz der Welt*, II/2. Tübingen: Niemeyer, 1968.
Ingarden, Roman. *Über die Gefahr einer petitio principii in der Erkenntnistheorie. Frühe Schriften zur Erkenntnistheorie* in his *Gesammelte Werke*. Vol. 6. Ed. W. Galewicz. Tübingen: Max Niemeyer, 1994.
Inge, W.I. *The Philosophy of Plotinus*. Vol. I. London: Longmans Green, 1923.
James, William. *A Pluralistic Universe*. Cambridge, MA: Harvard University Press, 1977.
James, William. *Varieties of Religious Experience*. Cambridge, MA: Harvard University Press, 1985.
Jankélévitch, Vladimir. *Traité des Vertus*. Paris: Bordas, 1949.
Jankélévitch, Vladimir. *Philosophie Première*. Paris: Presses Universitaire de France, 1953.
Jankélévitch, Vladimir. *Le pur et l'impur*. Paris: Flammarion, 1960.
Jankélévitch, Vladimir. *La Mort*. Paris: Flammarion, 1966.
Jaspers, Karl. *Die geistige Situation der Zeit*. Berlin: de Gruyter, 1932/1999, 149.
Jaspers, Karl. *Von der Wahrheit*. Munich: Piper, 1947, 170–171.
Jaspers, Karl. *Philosophie*. Vol. II. Berlin: Springer, 1956.
Jaspers, Karl. *Der Philosophische Glaube angesichts der Offenbarung*. Munich: Piper, 1963.
Jaspers, Karl. *Basic Philosophical Writings*. Trans. and Eds. E. Ehrlich, L.H. Ehrlich and George B. Pepper. New York: Humanities Paperback Library, 1994.
John of St. Thomas. *Cursus Theologici*. Vol. II. Paris: Desclée, 1934.
John of the Cross, St. (Juan de Yepes). *The Collected Works of St. John of the Cross*. Trans. Kieran Kavanaugh, O.C.C. and Otilio Rodriguez, O.C.D. Washington, DC: Institute of Carmleite Studies, 1991.
Johnson, William, Ed. and Intro. *The Cloud of Unknowing*. New York: Image Doubleday, 1996.
Julian of Norwich, *Revelations of Divine Love*. Trans. Elizabeth Spearing. London: Penguin, 1998.
Kafka, Franz. *The Basic Kafka*. Intro. Eric Heller. New York: Washington Square, 1971.
Kant, I. Kant. *Groundwork of the Metaphysics of Morals*. In the *Akademie* edition of Kant's *Gesammelte Schriften*. Vol. VI. Berlin: Walter de Gruyter, n.d.
Kant, I. Kant. *Kritik der reinen Vernunft*. Hamburg: Meiner, 1956.
Kant, I. Kant. *Kritik der Urteilskraft*. Hamburg: Meiner, 1956.
Kant, I. Kant. *Die Religion innerhalb der Grenzen der bloßen Vernunft*. Hamburg: Meiner, 1956.
Kant, I. Kant. *Kritik der praktischen Vernunft*. Hamburg: Meiner, 1974.
Kant, I. Kant. *Lectures on Metaphysics*. Trans. and Eds. Karl Ameriks and Steve Naragon. New York: Cambridge University Press, 1997.
Keating, O.C.S.O., Thomas. *The Foundations of Centering Prayer and the Christian Contemplative Life*. New York: Continuum, 2002.
Keating, O.C.S.O., Thomas. *Intimacy with God: An Introduction to Centering Prayer*. New York: Crossroad, 2005.
Kern, Iso. *Idee und Methode der Philosophie*. Berlin: de Gruyter, 1976.
Khosla, K. *The Sufism of Rumi*. Dorset, England: Longmead Shaftesbury, 1987.
Kierkegaard, Søren. *For Self Examination and Judge for Yourself*. Trans. H.V. Hong and E.H. Hong. Princeton, NJ: Princeton University Press, 1876/1990.
Kierkegaard, Søren. *Works of Love*. Trans. H. Hong and E. Hong. New York: Harper Torchbooks, 1962.

Kierkegaard, Søren. *Journals and Papers.* Vol. III. Eds. H.V. Hong and Edna V. Hong. Bloomington, IN: Indiana University Press, 1975.

Kierkegaard, Søren. *Sickness unto Death.* Trans. H. Hong and E. Hong. Princeton, NJ: Princeton University Press, 1980.

Kierkegaard, Søren. *Fear and Trembling/Repetition.* Trans. H. Hong and E. Hong. Princeton, NJ: Princeton University Press, 1983.

Kierkegaard, Søren. *Philosophical Fragments/Johannes Climacus.* Trans. H.V. Hong and E.H. Hong. Princeton, NJ: Princeton University Press, 1985.

Kierkegaard, Søren. *Either/Or,* I-II. Eds. and Trans. H. Hong and E. Hong. Princeton, NJ: Princeton University Press, 1987.

Kierkegaard, Søren. *Concluding Unscientific Postscript to* **Philosophical Fragments.** Trans. H.V. Hong and E.H. Hong. Princeton, NJ: Princeton University Press, 1992.

Kierkegaard, Søren. *Papers and Jounals.* Ed. Alastair Hannay. London: Penguin, 1996, 234–235.

Kristellar, Paul Oskar. *Der Begriff der Seele in der Ethik des Plotin.* Tübingen: J.C.B. Mohr/Paul Siebeck, 1929.

Kristellar, Paul Oskar. *The Philosophy of Marsilio Ficino.* Trans. Virginia Conant. Gloucester, MA: Peter Smith, 1964/New York: Columbia University Press, 1943.

Kuhn, Helmut. *Begegnung mit dem Sein.* Tübingen: J.B.C. Mohr/Paul Siebeck, 1954.

Lacombe, Olivier. *L'Absolu selon le Védânta.* Paris: Librairie Orientaliste Paul Geunther, 1966.

Lasson, Adolf. *J.G. Fichte in Verhälnis zu Kirche und Staat.* Aalen: Scientia Verlag, 1968/Berlin: Cotta'chen Verlag, 1863.

Lauth, Reinhard. *Die Transzendentale Naturlehre Fichtes nach den Principien der Wissinschaftslehre.* Hamburg: Meiner, 1984.

Lavelle, Louis. *De l'Acte.* Paris: Aubier, 1946.

Lavelle, Louis. *Introduction á l'ontologie.* Paris: PUF, 1947.

Lavelle, Louis. *De l'Âme humaine.* Paris: Aubier, 1951.

Lavelle, Louis. *Du temps et de l'éternité.* Paris: Aubier, 1955.

Laycock, Steven. *Foundations for a Phenomenological Theology.* Lewiston, NY: Edwin Mellen Press, 1988.

Lee, Nam-In. *Edmund Husserls Phänomenologie der Instinkte.* Dordrecht: Kluwer, 1993.

Leibniz, Gottfried. *New Essays on Human Understanding.* La Salle, IL: Open Court, 1949.

Leibniz, Gottfried. *Philosophical Papers and Letters.* Ed. Leroy E. Loemker. Dordrecht: Brill, 1969.

Leibniz, Gottfried. *Theodicy.* Lasalle, IL: Open Court, 1985.

Levenson, Jon D. "The Conversion of Abraham." UC Santa Barbara lecture, UCTV, 2007.

Levinas, E. *God, Death, and Time.* Stanford: Stanford University Press, 2000.

Levinas, E. *Otherwise Than Being.* Trans. Alphonso Lingis. Pittsburgh: Duquesne University Press, 2002.

Levine, Stephen. *Who Dies?* New York: Anchor, 1982.

Lewis, Hywel D. *Morals and the New Theology.* New York: Harper, n.d.

Lewis, C.S. *The Four Loves.* London and Glasgow: Collins Fontana, 1965.

Lewis, C.S. *The Hideous Strength.* New York: Simon & Schuster, Scribner, 1996.

Lewis, C.S. *Perelandra.* New York: Scribner, 1996.

Lewis, Hywel D. *The Elusive Mind.* London: George Allen & Unwin, 1969.

Lewis, Hywel D. *The Self and Immortality.* London: Macmillan, 1973.

Lewis, Hywel D. *Freedom and Alienation.* Edinburgh/London: Scottish Academic Press, 1985.

Liddell and Scott. *Greek-English Lexicon.* New York: American Book Co., 1888.

Lonergan, S.J., Bernard. *Insight.* New York: Philosophical Library, 1958.

Lonergan, S.J., Bernard. *Method in Theology.* New York: Seabury Press, 1973.

Long, A.A. and Sedley, D.N. *The Hellenistic Philosophers.* Cambridge: Cambridge University Press, 1987.

Loux, Michael. *Metaphysics: A Contemporary Introduction.* London: Routledge, 2002.

MacDonald, George. *Proving the Unseen.* New York: Ballantine, 1989.

MacDonald, George. *The Heart of George MacDonald*. Ed. Rolland Hein. Vancouver, British Columbia: Regent College Publishing, 1994.

Malantschuk, Gregor. *Kierkegaard's Thought*. Princeton, NJ: Princeton University Press, 1971.

Mansini, O.S.B., Guy. *"What Is Dogma?" The Meaning and Truth of Dogma in Edouard Le Roy and His Scholastic Opponents*. Rome: Gregorian Pontifical University, 1985.

Mansini, O.S.B., Guy with James G. Hart, Eds. *Ethics and Theological Disclosures*. Washington, DC: Catholic University of America Press, 2003.

Marcel, Gabriel. *The Mystery of Being*. Vol. I. Trans. G.S. Fraser. Chicago, IL: Henry Regnery, 1950.

Marcel, Gabriel. *The Philosophy of Existentialism*. New York: Citadel Press, 1995.

Marion, Jean-Luc. *Being Given*. Trans. Jeffrey L. Kosky. Stanford: Stanford University Press, 2002.

Maritain, Jacques. *Existence and the Existent*. New York: Image, 1957.

Mayer, Ernst. *Dialektik des Nichtwissens*. Basel: Verlag für Recht und Gesellschaft, 1950.

Meister, Eckhart. *Meister Eckhart: Essential Sermons, Commentaries, Treatises, and Defense*. Trans. and Eds. Edmund College and Bernard McGinn. Mahwah, NJ: Paulist Press, 1981.

Meister, Eckhart. *Meister Eckhart: Teacher and Preacher*. Trans. and Eds. Edmund College and Bernard McGinn. New York: Paulist Press, 1986.

Meister, Eckhart. *Meister Eckhart: Sermons and Treatise*. Vol. II. Trans. and Ed. M. O'C Walshe. Longmead/Shaftsbury/Dorset: Element Books, 1987.

Melle, Ullrich. "Husserl's Phenomenology of Willing." *Phenomenology of Values and Valuingi*. Eds. James G. Hart and Lester Embree. Dordrecht: Kluwer, 1997, 169–192.

Melle, Ullrich. "Edmund Husserl: From Reason to Love." *Phenomenological Approaches to Moral Philosophy*. Eds. John J. Drummond and Lester Embree. Dordrecht: Kluwer, 2002.

Melle, Ullrich. "Das Rätsel des Aurdrucks: Husserls Zeichen- und Austruckslehre in den Manuskripten für die Neufassung der VI. Logischen Untersuchungen." *Meaning and Language: Phenomenological Perspectives*. Ed. Filip Mattens. Dordrecht: Springer, 2007, 3–26.

Melle, Ullrich. "Die Zivilisationskrise als anthropologische Herausforderung. Paul Shephards' neoprimitivistische Anthropologie." Forthcoming.

Merton, Thomas. *The New Man*. New York: Farrar, Straus & Giroux, 1961.

Merton, Thomas. *Conjectures of a Guilty Bystander*. New York: Doubleday Image, 1968.

Merton, Thomas. *New Seeds of Contemplation*. New York: New Directions, 1972.

Merton, Thomas. *Contemplative Prayer*. New York: Doubleday Image, 1996, 68.

Merton, Thomas. *The Inner Experience*. New York: HarperSanFrancisco, 2004.

Miller, Barry. *A Most Unlikely God*. Notre Dame, IN: University of Notre Dame Press, 1996.

Moore, O.P., Gareth. *Believing in God: A Philosophical Essay*. Edinburgh: T & T Clark, 1988.

Moore, O.S.B., Sebastian. "God Suffered." *Downside Review* LXXVII (1959), 136 ff.

Morris, Thomas V. *Our Idea of God*. Notre Dame, IN: University of Notre Dame Press, 1991.

Mott, Michael. *The Seven Mountains of Thomas Merton*. New York: Harcourt Brace, 1993.

Muller-Thym, Bernard J. *The Establishment of the University of Being in the Doctrine of Meister Echart of Hochheim*. New York: Sheed & Ward, 1939.

Musil, Robert. *Mann Ohne Eigenschaften*. Hamburg: Rowolt, 1952.

Nabert, Jean. *L'expérience intérieure de la liberté, et autres essais de philosophie morale*. Paris: Presses Universitaire de France, 1924/1994.

Nabert, Jean. *Elements for an Ethic*. Trans. William J. Petrek. Evanston, IL: Northwestern University Press, 1943/1969.

Nagel, Thomas. *The View from Nowhere*. New York/Oxford: Oxford University Press, 1986.

Naus, S.J., John. *The Nature of the Practical Intellect According to Saint Thomas Aquinas*. Rome: Gregorian University, 1959.

A New Catechism. New York: Seabury Press, 1969 ("Dutch Catechism").

Newman, John Henry. *Grammar of Assent*. London: Longmans Green, 1870/1947.

Nietzsche, Friederich. *Nietzsche*. Vol. III. Ed. Karl Schlecta. Munich: Karl Hanser, 1965.

Nozick, Robert. *The Examined Life*. New York: Simon & Schuster, 1989.

Nussbaum, Martha. *Love's Knowledge*. New York/Oxford: Oxford University Press, 1990.

Ortega Y Gasset, José. *Man and People*. Trans. Willard R. Trask. New York: W.W. Norton, 1957.

Otto, Rudolf. *Sensus Numinis*. Munich: C.H. Beck'sche Verlagsbuchhandlung, 1932.

Otto, Rudolf. *The Idea of the Holy*. Trans. John W. Harvey. Oxford: Oxford University Press, 1964.

Otto, Walter F. *Die Götter Griechenlands*. Frankfurt am Main: Gerhard Schulte-Bulmke, 1934.

Owens, Joseph. "Thomas Aquinas." *Individuation in Scholasticism: The Later Middle Ages and the Counter-Reformation, 1150–1650*. Ed. Jorge J.E. Gracia. Albany, NY: SUNY, 1994, 173–194.

Pennington, O.C.S.O., and M. Basil. *Centering Prayer*. Garden City, NY: Image, 1982.

Pennington, O.C.S.O. and M. Basil. *True Self/False Self*. New York: Crossroad, 2000.

Pfänder, Alexander. *Phenomenology of Willing and Motivation*. Trans. H. Spiegelberg. Evanston, IL: Northwestern University Press, 1967.

Phan, Peter. "Is Christianity a Western Religion?" UCTV lecture, UC Santa Barbara, February 2007.

Phillips, Adam. *Going Sane*. New York: Fourth Estate, 2005.

Pieper, Josef. *The Silence of St. Thomas*. Chicago, IL: Henry Regnery.

Pindar. *Pythian Odes*. English Ed. Steven J. Willet. www.perseus.tufts.edu.

Plato. *Timaeus in Plato's Cosmology*. Trans. and Commentary Francis MacDonald Cornford. Indianapolis, IN: Bobbs-Merrill, n.d.; preface, 1938.

Plato. *The Dialogues of Plato*. Princeton, NJ: Princeton University Press, 1961.

Plato. *Symposium*. Trans. Alexander Nehamas and Paul Woodruff. Indianapolis, IN: Hackett, 1989.

Plessner, Helmut. *Lachen und Weinen*. Munich: Sammlung Dalp/Leo Lehnen Verlag, 1950.

Plotinus. *Enneads*. Trans. A.H. Armstrong. Cambridge, MA: Harvard University Press, 1984.

Porete, Marguerite. *Marguerite Porete: The Mirror of Simple Souls*. Trans. Ellen L. Babinsky. New York: Paulist Press, 1993.

Pringle-Pattison, A. Seth. *The Idea of Immortality*. Oxford: Clarendon Press, 1922.

Prufer, Thomas. *Sein und Wort Nach Thomas von Aquin*. Dissertation, University of Munich, 1959.

Prufer, Thomas. *Recapitulations*. Washington, DC: Catholic University of America, 1993.

Reiner, Hans. *Duty and Inclination*. Trans. Mark Santos. The Hague: Nijhoff, 1983; first edition, 1974.

Ricoeur, Paul. *Freud and Philosophy*. Trans. Denis Savage. New Haven, CT: Yale University Press, 1970.

Ricoeur, Paul. *Oneself as Another*. Trans. Katherine Blamey. Chicago, IL: University of Chicago Press, 1992.

Rilke, R.M. *New Poems*. Trans. J.B. Leishman. New York: New Directions, 1964.

Rilke, R.M. *The Selected Poetry of Rainer Maria Rilke*. Ed. and Trans. Stephen Mitchell. New York: Vintage, 1984.

Rist, J.M. *Plotinus: The Road to Reality*. Cambridge: Cambridge University Press, 1967/1980.

Robinson, Michael. *A Bird Within a Ring of Fire*. Keene, Ontario: Martin House, 1998.

Rogers, Carl. *On Becoming a Person*. Boston, MA: Houghton Mifflin, 1961.

Rosenzweig, Franz. *Der Stern der Erlösung*. Frankfurt am Main: Suhrkamp, 1996.

Rumi. *In the Arms of the Beloved*. Trans. Jonathan Star. New York: Jeremy P. Tarcher/Putnam, 2000.

Ruusbroec, John. *John Ruusbroec*. Trans. and Intro. James Wiseman. New York: Paulist, 1985.

Sartre, J.-P. *Being and Nothingness*. Trans. Hazel Barnes. New York: Philosophical Library, 1956.

Sartre, J.-P. "The Singular Universal." *Kierkegaard: A Collection of Critical Essays*. Ed. Josiah Thompson. New York: Doubleday/Anchor, 1972.

Scheler, Max. *Wesen und Formen der Sympathie*. Bonn: Friedrich Cohn, 1926/1913.

Scheler, Max. "Vorbilder und Führer," in *Schriften aus dem Nachlass*. Vol. I.: *Zur Ethik und Erkenntnislehre*. Bern: Francke, 1957.

Scheler, Max. "Über Scham und Schamgefühle," in *Schriften aus dem Nachlass*. Vol. I: *Zur Ethik und Erkenntnislehre*. Bern: Francke, 1957.

Scheler, Max. *Der Formalismus in der Ethik und die materiale Wertethik*. Bern: Francke, 1966.

Scheler, Max. *Vom Ewigen im Menschen*. Bern: Francke, 1968.

Scheler, Max. *Philosophische Weltanschauung*. Bern/Munich: Franke, Dalp Taschenbuecher, 1968.

Scheler, Max. *Schriften aus dem Nachlass*. Band II. *Erkenntnislehre und Metaphysik*. Franke: Bern/Munich, 1979.

Schillebeeckx, O.P., Edward. "The Non-conceptual Intellectual Element in the Act of Faith: A Reaction." *Revelation and Theology*. Vol. II. Trans. N.D. Smith. New York: Sheed & Ward, 1968.

Schopenhauer, Arthur. *The World as Will and Representation*. Vol. I–II. Trans. E.F.J. Payne. Indian Hills, CO: Falcon Hills Press, 1958.

Schutz, Alfred. "Husserl's Importance for the Social Sciences." *Edmund Husserl: 1859–1959*. The Hague: Nijhoff, 1959.

Scotus, John Duns. *Philosophical Writings*. Ed. Allen Wolter. Indianapolis, IN: Bobbs-Merrill, 1962.

Shakespeare, William. *Hamlet, Troilus and Cressida. The Riverside Shakespeare*. Boston, MA: Houghton Mifflin, 1974.

Shelley, P.B. "Mutability." *Shelley's Poetical Works*. Oxford: Oxford University Press, 1936.

Siewerth, Gustav. *Das Sein Als Gleichnis Gottes*. Heidelberg: Kerle, 1958.

Siewerth, Gustav. *Thomismus als Identitätssystem*. Frankfurt am Main: G. Schulte-Bulmke, 1961.

Simmel, Georg. *Lebensanschauung: Vier metaphysiche Kapitel*. Munich/Leipzig: Dunker & Humboldt, 1922.

Slade, Francis. "Ends and Purposes." *Final Causality in Nature and Human Affairs*. Ed. Richard Hassing. Washington, DC: Catholic University of America Press, 1997, 83–85.

Slade, Francis. "On the Ontological Priority of Ends and Its Relevance to the Narrative Arts." *Beauty, Art, and the Polis*. Ed. Alice Ramos. Washington, DC: Catholic University of America Press, 2000, 58–69.

Smullyan, Raymond. *Who Knows? A Study of Religious Consciousness*. Bloomington, IN: Indiana University Press, 2003.

Sokolowski, Robert. *Presence and Absence*. Bloomington, IN: Indiana University Press, 1978.

Sokolowski, Robert. *God of Faith and Reason*. Washington, DC: The Catholic University Press, 1982/1995.

Sokolowski, Robert. *Moral Action*. Bloomington, IN: Indiana University Press, 1985.

Sokolowski, Robert. "Natural and Artificial Intelligence." *Daedalus* 117 (1988), 45–64.

Sokolowski, Robert. *Pictures, Quotations, and Distinctions*. Notre Dame, IN: Notre Dame University Press, 1992.

Sokolowski, Robert. *Eucharistic Presence*. Washington, DC: The Catholic University Press, 1993.

Sokolowski, Robert. *Introduction to Phenomenology*. Cambridge: Cambridge University Press, 2000.

Sokolowski, Robert. *Christian Faith and Human Understanding*. Washington, DC: The Catholic University of America, 2006.

Sokolowski, Robert. *Phenomenology of the Human Person*. Cambridge: Cambridge University Press, 2008.

Sorabji, Richard. *Self: Ancient and Modern Insights About Individuality, Life, and Death*. Chicago, IL: University of Chicago Press, 2006.

Spaemann, Robert. *Personen*. Stuttgart: Klett-Cotta, 1996.

Spaemann, Robert. *Das unsterbliche Gerücht*. Stuttgart: Klett-Cotta, 2007.

Steeves, H. Peter, Ed. *Animal Others*. Albany, NY: SUNY, 1999, including my contribution, "Transcendental Phenomenology and the Eco-Community".

Stein, Edith. *Endliches und Ewiges Sein*. Louvain: Nauwelaerts, 1950.

Stein, Edith. *Kreuzwissenschaft: Studien über Johannes a Cruce*. Louvain: Nauwelaerts, 1954.

Stein, Edith. *Potenz und Akt*. Freiburg: Herder, 1999.

Stolz, O.S.B. Anselm. *Theologie der Mystik*. Regensburg: Friedrich Pustet, 1936.

Strawson, Peter. "Freedom and Resentment." *Studies in the Philosophy of Thought and Action*. London: Oxford University Press, 1968.

Taylor, Jill. *My Stroke of Insight*. New York: Viking, 2008.

Tennyson, Alfred. *The Poetical Works of Tennyson*. Cambridge edition. Boston, MA: Houghton Mifflin, 1974.

Tillich, Paul. *Wesen und Wandel des Glaubens*. Trans. Nina Baring, Renata Albrech and Eberhard Ameling, reworking of *Dynamics of Faith* (Ullsteinbuch).

Tillich, Paul. *Dynamics of Faith*. New York: Harper Torchbook, 1957.

Tillich, Paul. *The Courage To Be*. New Haven, CT: Yale University Press, 1964.

Tolstoy, Leo. *The Death of Ivan Ilych and Other Stories*. New York: NAL Penguin, 1960.

Troisfontaines, Roger. *De l'existence a l'être: La philosophie de Gabriel Marcel*. Vol. 1–2. Louvain: Nauwelaerts, 1953.

Trouillard, Jean. *La Purfication Plotinienne*. Paris: PUF, 1955.

Upanishads. Trans. Patrick Olivelle. Oxford: Oxford University Press, 1996.

Valéry, Paul. *The Selected Writings*. Binghamton, NY: New Directions, 1950.

Valéry, Paul. *Cahier B (1910), Oeuvres*. Vol. II. Paris: Bibliotheque de la Pleiade, 572.

Von Balthasar, Hans Urs. *Theodramatik*. Vol. 2. Part 2. Einsiedeln: Johanes Verlag, 1978.

Von Balthasar, Hans Urs. *Introduction to Origen*. Trans. Rowan A. Greer. New York: Paulist Press, 1979.

Weil, Simone. *Waiting for God*. Trans. Emma Craufurd. New York: Harper Colophon, 1967.

Weil, Simone. *Simone Weil: An Anthology*. Ed. D. Siân Miles. New York: Weidenfeld & Nicolson, 1986.

Weischedel, Wilhelm. *Der Gott der Philosophen*. Munich: Deutscher Taschenbuch Verlag, 1979.

Welz, Claudia. "Keeping the Secret of Subjectivity: Kierkegaard and Levinas on Conscience, Love, and the Limits of Self-Understanding." *Despite Oneself: Subjectivity and Its Secret in Kierkegaard and Levinas*. Ed. Claudia Welz. Forthcoming.

Wills, Gary. *Why I Am a Catholic*. Boston, MA/New York: Houghton Mifflin/Mariner, 2003.

Wippel, John F. "Early Prufer on Aquinas and Being." *Commemorating Thomas Prufer*. Ed. Kurt Pritzl, O.P. Washington, D.C. Catholic University of America, School of Philosophy Commemoration. 2003.

Zaehner, R.C. *Hindu and Muslim Mysticism*. Oxford: One World, 1994.

Zahavi, Dan. *Self-Awareness and Alterity*. Evanston, IL: Northwestern University Press, 1999.

Zahavi, Dan. *Subjectivity and Selfhood*. Cambridge, MA: MIT Press, 2005.

Index

A

Abraham, 307, 378, 381, 385, 478, 593

"Abrahamic religions/traditions," 47, 48, 49, 372, 429, 434, 435, 440, *444–445*, 481, 482, 483, 505, 511, 527, 530, 559, 565, 571, 591, 592, 595, 597, 598, 600, 603, 604, *610*

    vide The Theological Distinction

absolute ought, 169, 212, 236, 244, 266, 268, 269, 302, 303, 304, 359, 360

    in the form of truth of will, 266 ff.

    and teleological determinism, 304 ff., 363, 407

    and prior absolute affection, 302, 325

    always a willing to self-renewal (Husserl), 307

    and second-person, 359

Abu Yazid, 432, 433

Adams, R. M., 501, 502, 610

addict (addicted person), 18, 88, 164, 166–168, 190, 221, 227, 232, 238, 243, 244, 245, 304, 363

Adler, Alfred, 216, 256

agent of manifestation/display,

    vide transcendental I,

    vide dative of manifestation 3, 6, 9, 10, 19, 25, 28, 31, 41, 51, 62, 63, 70, 101, 121, 134, 135, 143, 167, 190, 191, 194, 202, 205, 203, 253, 230, 340, 348, 376, 389, 535, 603, 604

    truthfulness as ineradicable feature of, 200

Alfaro, S.J., Juan, 611, 612

analogy, analogizing

    implicit in apperception, 454–455

    and explicit conceptual comparisons, 455

    and dogma, 457

    and mystery, 456–458

    of proportionality and attribution, 458–459

    and exemplarism, 464 ff.

Anangke (blind Necessity, fate, nemesis), 84, 107, 110, 149, 263, 279, 511, 519, 583, 584

Anderson, Bernard W., 252, 618

Arnou, R., 609

attitude, (*Stellungnahme, Einstellung,* stance)

    vide position-taking

    transcendental, 61–62

Aquinas, St. Thomas, X, 182, 254, 286, 278, 295, 362, 379, 384, 389–392, 446, 447, 454, 479, 482, 489, 525, 526, 528, 556, 565, 571, 608, 609, 610, 611, 612, 613, 614, 616, 617, 619

Aristotle, 95, 115, 125, 126, 129, 139, 140, 151, 157, 173, 182, 185, 189, 210, 226, 246, 254, 266, 271, 294, 296–298, 310, 321, 328, 330, 332, 349, 361, 366, 371, 372, 374, 437, 466, 511, 518, 539, 574

Armstrong, A.H., 444, 445, 450

Augustine, St., 58, 93, 172, 154, 363. 367, 381, 382, 410, 434, 471, 485, 503, 504, 505, 610

Aubert, Roger, 611–612

Aumann, Anthony, 93, 156, 449, 611, 613

authority,

    vide obligation

    dignity ("authority") *of* Other present or presentable in second-person, proper site of authority *over,* 231, 233, 354–357

    conscience and first-personal, 117–142, 354–357

    and ontological value of person, *vide* dignity

    of declarative "I" as speaking agent of manifestation, 352–353

    problem of taking "we" as source of, 358 ff.

LaVergne, TN USA
12 February 2011
216265LV00002B/1/P

9 781402 091841